W9-CJF-673

MUSIC

THE DEFINITIVE VISUAL HISTORY

THE DEFINITIVE VISUAL HISTORY

SECOND EDITION

DORLING KINDERSLEY

US Editors Jennette Elnaggar, Heather Wilcox
Senior Jacket Designer Suhita Dharamjit
Production Editors Rakesh Kumar, Mrinmoy Mazumdar, Kavita Verma
Managing Editor Angeles Gavira
Art Director Karen Self
Senior Jackets Coordinator Priyanka Sharma Saddi
Production Controller Laura Andrews
Managing Art Editor Michael Duffy
Associate Publishing Director Liz Wheeler
Publishing Director Jonathan Metcalf

TOUCAN BOOKS LTD

Senior Editor Julie Brooke
Consultant Nathan Holder
Assistant Editor Benji Hartnell-Booth
Senior Art Editor Lee Riches
Picture Research Sharon Southren
Indexer Marie Lorimer

FIRST EDITION

DORLING KINDERSLEY

Editorial Team Megha Gupta, Ruth O'Rourke-Jones, Vineetha Mokkil, Suefa Lee, Kaiya Shang, David Summers, Jill Hamilton, Margaret Parrish, Rebecca Warren
Jacket Editor Manisha Majithia
Pre-Production Producer Adam Stoneham
Managing Editors Angeles Gavira, Rohan Sinha
Design Team Parul Gambhir, Anna Hall, Konica Juneja, Kanika Mittal, Divya P.R., Anuj Sharma, Shreya Anand Virmani
Managing Art Editors Sudakshina Basu, Michelle Baxter
DTP Designers Nand Kishor Acharya, Neeraj Bhatia, Nityanand Kumar, Mrinmoy Mazumdar, Bimlesh Tiwari, Mohammed Usman

TOUCAN BOOKS LTD

Senior Editor Dorothy Stannard
Editors John Andrews, Camilla Hallinan, Constance Novis
Assistant Editor David Hatt, Sophie Lewisohn
Senior Art Editor Thomas Keenes
Picture Research Sarah Smithies, Roland Smithies (Luped)
Indexer Marie Lorimer

SMITHSONIAN ENTERPRISES

Senior Vice President Carol LeBlanc
Director of Licensing Brigid Ferraro
Licensing Manager Ellen Nanney
Project Development Manager Kealy Wilson

New Photography
Gary Ombler, Richard Leeney

This American Edition, 2022
First American Edition, 2013
Published in the United States by DK Publishing
1450 Broadway, Suite 801, New York, NY 10018

Copyright © 2013, 2022 Dorling Kindersley Limited
DK, a Division of Penguin Random House LLC
22 23 24 25 26 10 9 8 7 6 5 4 3 2 1
001–328732–July/2022

All rights reserved.
Without limiting the rights under the copyright reserved above, no part of this publication may be reproduced, stored in or introduced into a retrieval system, or transmitted, in any form, or by any means (electronic, mechanical, photocopying, recording, or otherwise), without the prior written permission of the copyright owner.
Published in Great Britain by Dorling Kindersley Limited

A catalog record for this book is available from the Library of Congress.
ISBN 978-0-7440-5834-5

DK books are available at special discounts when purchased in bulk for sales promotions, premiums, fund-raising, or educational use. For details, contact: DK Publishing Special Markets, 1450 Broadway, Suite 801, New York, NY 10018
SpecialSales@dk.com

Printed and bound in China

For the curious

www.dk.com

This book was made with Forest Stewardship Council™ certified paper – one small step in DK's commitment to a sustainable future. For more information go to www.dk.com/our-green-pledge

CONTENTS

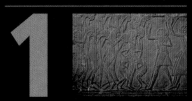

4

THE BAROQUE SPIRIT

5

THE CLASSICAL AGE

6

NATIONALISM AND ROMANCE

CONSULTANT

Robert Ziegler conducts symphony orchestras throughout the UK, the United States, and the Far East as well as original soundtracks including There Will Be Blood, The Hobbit, and Sense and Sensibility. He has written Great Musicians for DK and is an award-winning broadcaster on BBC Television and Radio.

AUTHORS

Ian Blenkinsop
Kiku Day
Reg Grant
Malcolm Hayes
Keith Howard
Chris Ingham
Tiffany Jackson
Damascus Kafumbe
Nick Kimberley
Tess Knighton (ICREA)
Alex de Lacey
Karl Lutchmayer
Jenny McCallum
Matt Milton
Chris Moss
Christina Reitz
Joe Staines
Susan Sturrock
Oliver Tims
Greg Ward

Foreword

Music is an ancient and powerful language: from the prehistoric calls that imitated the animals we hunted and the lullabies that sent our children to sleep, to the stirring beats that rallied our troops to battle and the harsh fanfares that terrified our enemies. It is a short step from the sacred hymns that rose in the immense cathedrals built to glorify God to the pop music thundering in stadiums commanded by rock stars.

Tracing a long and fascinating history, *Music: The Definitive Visual History* illuminates the dramatic stories of the composers and performers who shaped these sounds and guides us, with striking illustrations and photographs, through the many wonderful instruments that we beat, scrape, and blow. As each musical subject is presented in a concise and engaging two-page spread, it is easy to travel between musical worlds that are continents and centuries apart over the space of just a few chapters. And it's not just the notes and sounds themselves that are examined but also the compelling stories behind them.

Music was an essential element of ancient mythology, medieval poetry, and religious life. Later, the 16th-century Reformation shook the Catholic Church to its foundations and set the stage for the great works of J.S. Bach. From the invention of the printing press, through the creation of the phonograph and electric guitar, to the advent of the Internet, technology has consistently transformed the way we make and listen to music.

It is often said that music is a universal language, and that is reflected in the international scope of this book. It would be easy to confine ourselves to the great achievements of Western music, but *Music: The Definitive Visual History* journeys throughout the world to sample the ancient music of China, the frenzied pop of Japan, the tribal music of the African plains, and the passionate rhythms of South American dance halls.

In Ancient Greece, Plato wrote that "Music gives a soul to the universe, wings to the mind, flight to the imagination, and life to everything." Centuries later, the great composer and bandleader Duke Ellington (pictured here with his band) added, "Music is the oldest entity. The scope of music is immense and infinite. What is music to you? What would you be without music?" *Music: The Definitive Visual History* will help you answer that question.

ROBERT ZIEGLER

SG

1

EARLY BEGINNINGS

60,000 BCE–500 CE

The earliest musical instrument is one still used today—the human body. The drum, bone flute, and harp were the earliest musical tools fashioned by humans. Whether in the form of singing, clapping, or rhythmic pounding, music has always been used to celebrate, praise, express sorrow and joy, to rally the troops or terrify the enemy.

EARLY BEGINNINGS
60,000 BCE–500 CE

60,000 BCE

c.60,000 BCE
Early humans start to produce cave paintings, make jewelry, and probably make music, too.

Stone-Age dance in a rock painting from Tanzania, East Africa

c.35,000 BCE
Stone-Age humans in the Hohe Fels cave, Germany, make flutes by boring holes in vultures' wing bones. Early instruments are also made from sticks and shells.

Bone flute from Hohe Fels, Germany

Primitive trumpet made from a conch shell

c.13,000 BCE
Groups of Siberian hunters cross into the Americas, bringing with them the music and rituals of the shamanic tradition.

c.13,000 BCE
A wall painting in the Trois Frères cave in southwestern France seems to show a shaman with a musical instrument. If so, it is the earliest known image of a musician.

10,000 BCE

c.10,000 BCE
The first settlements arise in the eastern Mediterranean, which will lead over thousands of years to the creation of towns, palaces, and temples—all centers of musical activity.

c.6000 BCE
The smelting of metals, especially copper and bronze, begins in Turkey. By 3000 BCE, these metals will be used to make new instruments.

c.8000 BCE
The world's oldest continuously inhabited city, Jericho in the Jordan Valley is founded. In the Bible, the trumpet blasts of the Israelite army demolish the city walls.

c.5000 BCE
In Mesopotamia, Egypt, and the Indus Valley, the first complex societies begin to form, based on irrigated agriculture. Priests and rulers use music for rites and ceremonies.

c.6000 BCE
In China, bone flutes are made from the hollow bones of the red-crowned crane.

c.2700 BCE
On the Cycladic islands in the Aegean, small statues show figures playing the lyre or harp and the *aulos* (double flute).

2500 BCE

c.2500 BCE
Musicians in the Sumerian city-state of Ur, Mesopotamia, play lyres, harps, lutes, wooden flutes, reed pipes, and percussion. Clay tablets preserve instructions for performance.

2040 BCE
Mentuhotep II unites Upper and Lower Egypt. Under the pharaohs, music plays a key role in palace ceremonies, religious rituals, and everyday life.

c.2500–1900 BCE
The civilization that flourishes in the Indus Valley initiates musical traditions that are continued by some of India's performers today.

c.2000 BCE
Central America's first civilizations begin to develop. Ancient instruments include the *ocarina*, a clay flute made in the shape of an animal.

A Minoan aulos (double flute) player

c.1900 BCE
The thriving Minoan civilization of Crete in the Mediterranean develops a rich musical culture.

Egyptian musicians in a fresco from Nahkt's tomb, c.1350 BCE

c.2100 BCE
In Ireland, musicians are playing sets of six wooden pipes. Made from yew, these are the oldest known wooden pipes in the world.

c.1600 BCE
In Ancient India, Vedas (sacred texts) are recited in songs and chants.

1500 BCE

1550–1069 BCE
Under the New Kingdom dynasties, Egypt exerts a major musical influence on other civilizations, including Ancient Greece.

c.1000 BCE
China's distinctive musical tradition begins. Instruments include bells and chime stones, the *qin* (a stringed instrument like a zither), and the *sheng* (mouth organ).

Chinese *sheng* with bamboo pipes

Ivory clappers from Ancient Egypt, 1430 BCE

Music evolved with human societies as they developed over thousands of years from small groups of hunter-gatherers to large-scale states with cities, armies, and temples. In the civilizations of Ancient Mesopotamia, China, Greece, and Rome, musical theories arose alongside musical practice; music was seen as having a moral influence on character as well as a relationship to the fundamental structure of the universe. But it was primarily an integral part of everyday life, an accompaniment to work and leisure, religious ritual, and popular festivities. Written music remained a rarity, with skills and knowledge transmitted from master to pupil in an oral tradition.

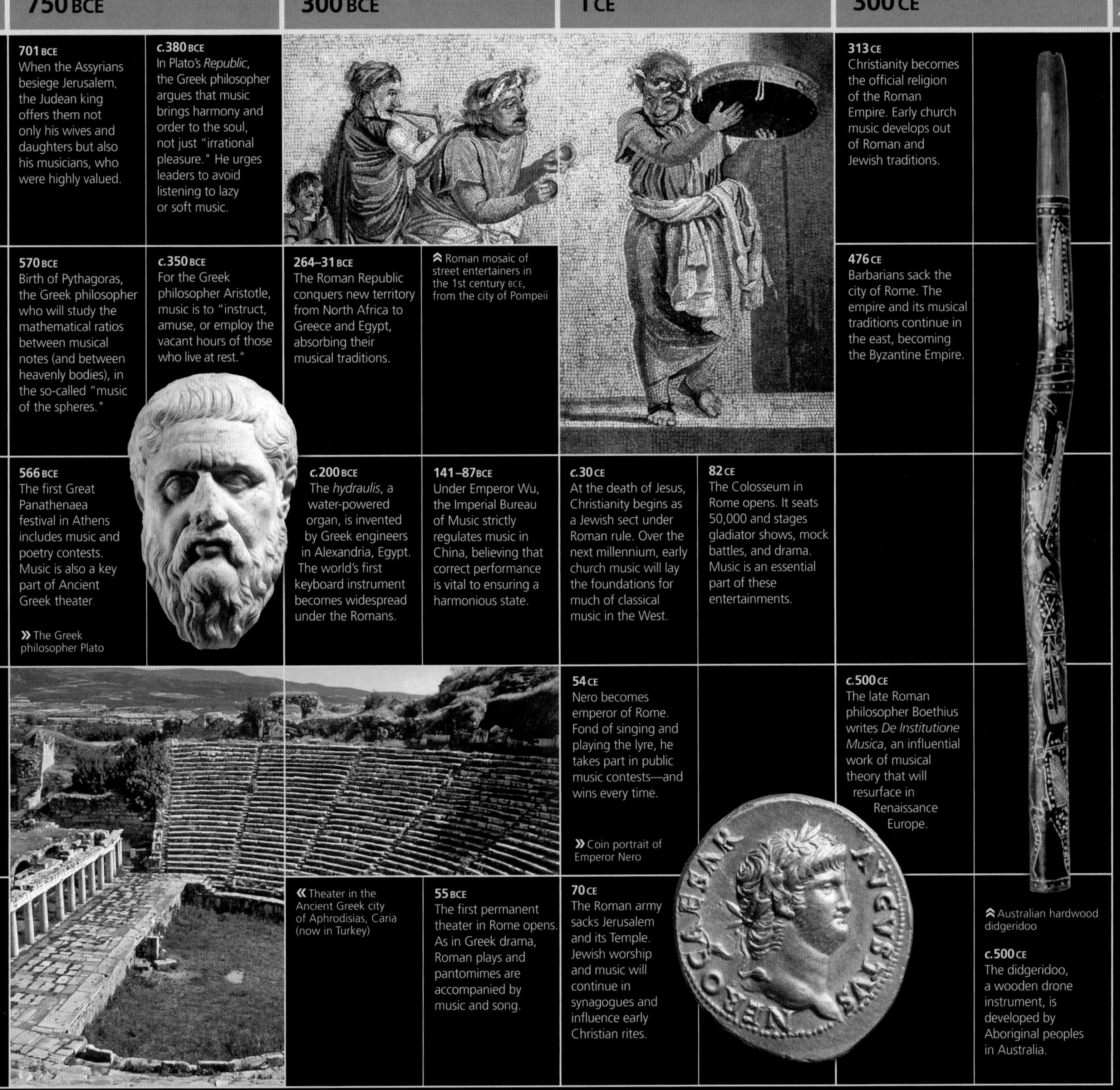

750 BCE

701 BCE
When the Assyrians besiege Jerusalem, the Judean king offers them not only his wives and daughters but also his musicians, who were highly valued.

570 BCE
Birth of Pythagoras, the Greek philosopher who will study the mathematical ratios between musical notes (and between heavenly bodies), in the so-called "music of the spheres."

566 BCE
The first Great Panathenaea festival in Athens includes music and poetry contests. Music is also a key part of Ancient Greek theater.

» The Greek philosopher Plato

c.380 BCE
In Plato's *Republic*, the Greek philosopher argues that music brings harmony and order to the soul, not just "irrational pleasure." He urges leaders to avoid listening to lazy or soft music.

c.350 BCE
For the Greek philosopher Aristotle, music is to "instruct, amuse, or employ the vacant hours of those who live at rest."

« Theater in the Ancient Greek city of Aphrodisias, Caria (now in Turkey)

300 BCE

« Roman mosaic of street entertainers in the 1st century BCE, from the city of Pompeii

264–31 BCE
The Roman Republic conquers new territory from North Africa to Greece and Egypt, absorbing their musical traditions.

c.200 BCE
The *hydraulis*, a water-powered organ, is invented by Greek engineers in Alexandria, Egypt. The world's first keyboard instrument becomes widespread under the Romans.

141–87 BCE
Under Emperor Wu, the Imperial Bureau of Music strictly regulates music in China, believing that correct performance is vital to ensuring a harmonious state.

55 BCE
The first permanent theater in Rome opens. As in Greek drama, Roman plays and pantomimes are accompanied by music and song.

1 CE

c.30 CE
At the death of Jesus, Christianity begins as a Jewish sect under Roman rule. Over the next millennium, early church music will lay the foundations for much of classical music in the West.

82 CE
The Colosseum in Rome opens. It seats 50,000 and stages gladiator shows, mock battles, and drama. Music is an essential part of these entertainments.

54 CE
Nero becomes emperor of Rome. Fond of singing and playing the lyre, he takes part in public music contests—and wins every time.

» Coin portrait of Emperor Nero

70 CE
The Roman army sacks Jerusalem and its Temple. Jewish worship and music will continue in synagogues and influence early Christian rites.

300 CE »

313 CE
Christianity becomes the official religion of the Roman Empire. Early church music develops out of Roman and Jewish traditions.

476 CE
Barbarians sack the city of Rome. The empire and its musical traditions continue in the east, becoming the Byzantine Empire.

c.500 CE
The late Roman philosopher Boethius writes *De Institutione Musica*, an influential work of musical theory that will resurface in Renaissance Europe.

« Australian hardwood didgeridoo

c.500 CE
The didgeridoo, a wooden drone instrument, is developed by Aboriginal peoples in Australia.

BEFORE

Around 60,000 years ago, humans made a cultural leap forward and began producing cave paintings and making jewelry. At the same time, they probably also started to make music.

SURVIVAL AND SEXUAL SELECTION
Various theories have been put forward about the **origins of music** and its evolutionary purpose. It may, for example, have initially evolved from early humans' imitation of animal cries, and even served the same purpose as the **mating calls** and displays of animals.

DEVELOPED FROM SPEECH
Modern researchers have noted how close music is to speech, especially in the **"tonal" languages** of Africa and Asia, in which pitch is used to distinguish words, not just emotion or emphasis. It is thought that music and speech may have evolved together.

Man, the Music Maker

Humans have made music since prehistoric times, when it played a vital role in social life, from healing and ritual to hunting and warfare. Traces of prehistoric musical practice survive in folk and traditional music in many parts of the world.

The first source of music was undoubtedly the human voice. It is thought that as soon as speech evolved, humans began augmenting words with tonal pitch, as well as other vocal tricks such as clicks, whistles, and humming. The only accompaniment to the voice would have been rhythmic clapping and stamping. The human body provided the earliest musical resources.

The first instruments

Humans found their first musical instruments in their natural environment, identifying objects—pieces of wood, stone, horn, or bone—that would make a sound when beaten or blown. Eventually, such objects were shaped and elaborated to develop their musical potential. Around 35,000 years ago, for example, Stone Age humans living in the Hohle Fels cave in what is now southern Germany made finger holes in a vulture's wing bone to create a kind of flute. This and two ivory flutes in nearby caves were among items discovered by archaeologists working in the cave in 2008.

> "**Musical notes**… were first acquired… for the sake of **charming** the opposite **sex.**"
>
> CHARLES DARWIN, NATURALIST, "THE DESCENT OF MAN," 1871

Cave paintings provide other evidence for the existence of early musical instruments. A hunting scene painted on the wall of a cave in the

Spirit man
A shaman in Tuva, Siberia, beats a drum as part of his ritual performance. Shamans attempt to contact the spirit world by entering a trance, induced through song, dance, and rhythmic beating.

Dordogne, France, dating from around 10,000 years ago, shows a man playing a musical bow—one end of the bow is held in the mouth while the string is plucked to make the notes. A similar instrument is still played by cattle herders in western central Africa and southern Africa.

"Idiophones"—instruments made from solid resonant materials that vibrate to produce sound—played a large role in prehistoric music. They include: slit drums, made by hollowing out a split tree trunk; a primitive xylophone; rattles made by filling gourds with seeds and stones; scrapers, such as a rough stick rasped against bones or shells; and plucked instruments such as the Jew's harp, a simple string instrument held in the mouth. Many types of drum were made by stretching animal skins over bowls, hollow gourds, or wooden frames. A range of eerie sounds could be generated by swinging a piece of shaped wood on the end of a cord—creating the bull-roarer, an instrument favored by indigenous Australians.

Aboriginal instrument
The didgeridoo is a hardwood wind instrument developed by the indigenous peoples of Australia. It is made from a naturally occurring hollow tree trunk or branch, which is then shaped and decorated.

Wind instruments were made from conch shells, hollow bones, bamboo, reeds, and parts of trees, and were blown with the mouth or the nose. Finger holes could be stopped or unstopped to vary the pitch, although these early instruments had no significant melodic potential.

Common heritage

Study of the musical traditions of tribal peoples living in Africa, Asia, the Americas, Polynesia, and Australasia in modern times is the best guide we have to the nature of prehistoric music. Although such musical traditions are immensely varied across the globe, they share many characteristics. In general, the music has complex rhythms that are tightly linked to dance and ritual gestures. It is also flexible in melody, following closely the patterns of speech, and is rarely made up of complex harmonies.

Spiritual role

For primitive humans, music was an essential element in rituals and ceremonies that bound a society to its dead ancestors and its totemic animals or plants. It was used as a means of communicating with the benign or malevolent spirits that controlled the fate of a society or individual.

In many societies, the shaman was (and is) someone who acted as an intermediary between the spirit and the human worlds. An individual with the special power to enter ecstatic states through trance, he performed rituals in which words, melody, gestures, and dance were inseparable, his voice accompanied by the beats of a drum. The shaman was a musical specialist, in that his "song" could only be performed by him. The powers of the shaman might be called upon for healing or to summon rain.

Music as history

Another function of music was to record and channel traditional knowledge, legend, history, and myth through the generations. Thus the famous "songlines" of indigenous Australians were sacred paths across the vast landscape transmitted through songs, stories, and dance.

In West Africa, the tradition of the "griot" singer and storyteller has survived into the modern day. The griot's tales preserved a detailed record of local events and celebrations such as births, marriages, wars, and hunting expeditions, as well as a wider repository of legend. It was also the griot's function to invent praise songs honoring the local ruler.

The tradition of songs preserving legends and historical events is also still maintained among Native American tribal societies. The famous Navajo song "Shi Naasha", for example, commemorates an event during the 19th-century Indian wars against the United States.

The pleasure of song

Music in Stone Age societies was by no means limited to specialists. Although only a shaman could perform shamanic rituals, there were many other occasions in which the wider society could participate in music as individuals or collectively. There were songs of greeting, songs of love, praise songs, war songs, and satirical songs. Unison group singing and rhythmic clapping would often accompany the performance of an individual soloist. Native American music distinguished songs to be sung by special individuals from songs that were suitable for general public performance.

Social attribute

In some societies musical improvisation was considered a necessary social skill. An individual was expected to invent impromptu songs in much the same way we might expect a person to engage in witty repartee today. Music formed an essential part of the everyday texture of life.

Tribal harmony
In Papua New Guinea, tribes perform *singsing*, an ancient form of communal singing and dancing to accompany traditional rites and celebrations.

AFTER

The evolution of music went hand in hand with wider developments in human society and culture. Metalworking and the invention of early forms of writing were particularly important to music.

NEW MATERIALS
The beginning of the **Bronze Age**, usually dated to around 5,000 years ago, saw the use of copper and bronze (a copper alloy) to make implements ranging from weaponry and agricultural tools to musical instruments. The latter include the curved **bronze horns** known as "lurs" that have been found in Denmark and northern Germany. **Stringed instruments** became more important, especially the lyre and the harp.

THE RISE OF THE MUSICIAN
When **literate civilizations** **16–17 »** emerged in **Mesopotamia**, the **Indus Valley**, **Egypt**, and **China**, they developed distinctive musical traditions, with musicians in the service of emperors and kings. The first known piece of **written music** is a fragment from around 4,000 years ago found in Sumer, in modern-day Iraq. **Ancient Greece and Rome** **20–25 »** continued and expanded the musical tradition of Mesopotamia and Pharaonic Egypt.

BEFORE

A series of changes in human life between 10,000 and 3000 BCE gave rise to the first complex civilizations, with states ruled by kings and emperors.

A LEAP FORWARD

The development of **settled agricultural societies** in different places around the world led to an increase in population density and the founding of towns and cities. **Metal tools**—bronze and then iron—began to replace stone. In **Mesopotamia, the Indus Valley, Egypt, and China**, hierarchical states dominated by secular rulers and priests emerged. These societies developed various forms of **writing.**

Music's Cradle

Over thousands of years, the world's oldest civilizations, in Mesopotamia, Egypt, northern India, and China, developed musical traditions. Although the sound of their music has been lost, surviving artifacts show the vigor of music-making in these ancient societies.

Around 4,500 years ago, hundreds of musicians worked in the service of the priests and secular rulers of the Sumerian city-state of Ur, in southern Mesopotamia (modern-day Iraq). Singing played a key role in religious rituals, and court musicians provided accompaniment for state ceremonies and banquets. The Standard of Ur, a Sumerian artifact now in the British Museum, shows a lyre player and a singer entertaining the king at a feast.

A few beautifully made Sumerian lyres have survived into the present day—they are the oldest existing stringed instruments. The Sumerians also played harps and lutes, plus varieties of wooden flutes and reed pipes. Percussion included drums, tambourines, clappers, and a kind of metal shaker known as a sistrum. Instructions for performance have been found on Sumerian clay tablets.

Rousing the people

Succeeding civilizations in Mesopotamia and its surrounding area continued and expanded this musical tradition. The Assyrian kings, dominant in the area from 2000 to 700 BCE, maintained a court orchestra and choir that sometimes gave public performances "to gladden the hearts of the people," according to court records of the time. Musicians also accompanied the Assyrian army on its many campaigns, with drums and trumpets used to signal simple orders and messages.

However, music was not restricted to courts and temples. Shepherds played pipes while minding their flocks, and singing and drumming accompanied heavy work in the fields. There must have been a wide range of musical expression because of the variety of purposes for which music was considered appropriate—from celebrating a victory at war to helping induce sleep.

Valued role

Professional musicians were trained at music schools and probably organized into guilds. The value placed upon musical skills is well attested. When the Assyrians besieged Jerusalem in 701 BCE,

Musicians in Egypt
A fresco decorating the tomb of Nakht, a scribe in Ancient Egypt, shows a group of female musicians performing. Their instruments are an arched harp, a long-necked lute, and a double-reed pipe.

Fertile crescent
The area from Mesopotamia (Iraq) to Egypt has often been called the "cradle of civilization." The earliest evidence for music making in a complex society comes from Ur in southern Mesopotamia.

the Judean king tried to buy them off by offering to hand over not only his wives and daughters, but also his male and female musicians.

Music of the gods

Music permeated the myths of the Egyptian gods. Osiris, the god of the afterlife, was known as the "lord of the sistrum" because of his association with the instrument (a kind of rattle). Bes, the god who presided over childbirth, was often represented with a harp or lyre. Egyptian priests and priestesses intoned hymns to the gods as part of their daily duties, as well as at special festivals. At court, the chief musicians had high status and formal rank. Many of the court performers were women, who also danced.

Egyptian instruments were similar to those of the Mesopotamian states, but the harp was more developed, with 6 ft (2 m) high instruments by 1200 BCE (see pp.22–23). The music of Ancient Egypt changed little over the centuries, with tradition upheld by the academies that trained musicians. There must have been a freer popular tradition, however, for Egyptian paintings show peasants dancing to pipes and drums.

Royal orchestra
A relief from the palace of the Assyrian kings at Nineveh, dating from the 7th century BCE, shows musicians in a court orchestra playing angled harps, reed-pipes, and a dulcimer.

Chinese lutenist
A terra-cotta figurine found in a tomb from the Tang dynasty era (907–618 BCE) depicts a female lute player. The *pipa*, or Chinese lute, is still a popular instrument today.

Indian traditions

The distinctive musical tradition of India must have had its origins in the Indus Valley civilization that flourished from 2600 to 1900 BCE, but little is known about this period. From around 1500 BCE, the sacred Hindu texts known as the Vedas emerge. Some of these were recited, but others were chanted or sung. Specific instruments are mentioned in ancient Indian texts. King Ravana—a follower of the deity Shiva in the Hindu epic the *Ramayana*—is credited with the invention of the *ravanatha*, a bowed string instrument made out of a coconut shell and bamboo. Another Indian instrument that has survived from antiquity is the ***mridangam***, a double-sided drum, which, in Hindu mythology, is said to have been played by the bull-god Nandi.

A range of plucked stringed instruments, the *veena*, are believed to date back to the times of the Vedas. Many of the instruments prominent in Indian classical music today, including the sitar and the tabla (see pp.342–343), are of medieval origin.

Bells, chimes, and silence

China has a continuous musical tradition stretching back over 3,000 years. From the earliest times, its mix of instruments was distinctive, including the prominent role assigned to bells and chime stones—slabs of stone hung from a wooden frame and struck with a padded mallet.

The *sheng*, a form of mouth organ with bamboo pipes, and varieties of zither have remained central to Chinese music through its history (see p.45), as have flutes and drums. The Chinese also developed a distinctive aesthetic, in particular exploiting the effect of sounds fading into silence.

Harmony of the state

Music was seen by Ancient Chinese philosophers as reflecting the fundamental order of the universe. China's imperial rulers were convinced that the correct performance of ritual music was essential to upholding the harmony of the state. From the 1st century BCE, court and military music were strictly directed and regulated by the Imperial Bureau of Music (see p.45).

However, most music escaped official control. The Chinese opera (see pp.198–199) developed from the 3rd century BCE, and from the period of the Tang dynasty (618–907 CE) a popular music scene flourished in Chinese cities.

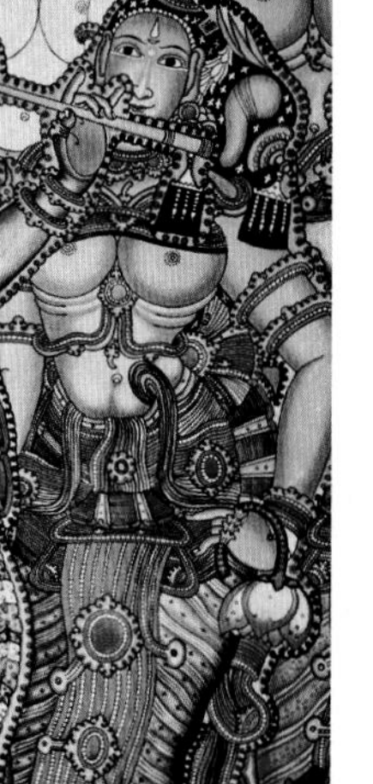

Hindu flautist
The Indian Hindu deity Krishna, portrayed surrounded by *gopis* (female cow herds) in this 16th-century wall painting, is often represented as a herdsman performing on a bamboo flute.

AFTER »

The music of Mesopotamia and Ancient Egypt was inherited by the Minoan civilization on the island of Crete, and then by Ancient Greece and the Roman Empire, the source of European musical tradition.

CRETE PICKS UP THE BATON
Egyptian influence probably provided the basis for the court and religious music of **Minoan Crete**, a major Mediterranean civilization that flourished in the second millennium BCE. From Crete, the torch was passed on to the state of **Mycenae** on the Greek mainland, which declined around 1100 BCE.

ANCIENT TO MODERN
The Classical era of **Ancient Greece** **20–21 »**, began in the 8th century BCE. Greek thinkers broadly accepted their country's musical debt to the Egyptians—whose musical practices they much admired—and to Mesopotamia. Greece provided much of the input for the music of the **Roman Empire** **24–25»** which, through **Christian church music** **30–31 »**, founded the modern European tradition.

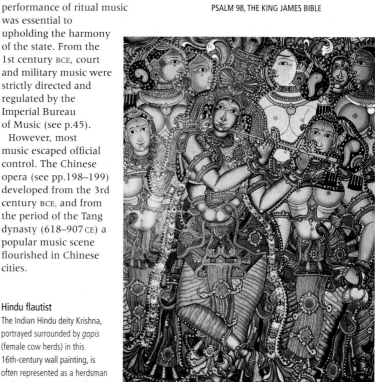

> "**Sing** unto the Lord with a harp and the **voice of a psalm."**
>
> PSALM 98, THE KING JAMES BIBLE

« BEFORE

The Ancient Greeks inherited a musical tradition founded in early Mesopotamia and Pharaonic Egypt.

IDEAS AND INSTRUMENTS

Many of the musical instruments and forms developed in **Ancient Egypt** « 16–17 reached the Greeks via the Minoan civilization, which flourished during the second millennium BCE on the island of Crete and had an offshoot on the Greek mainland at Mycenae. Musical ideas also filtered in through Asia Minor.

WRITTEN MUSIC

Other cultures developed their own unique forms of written music. There is evidence of the use of **musical notation** in China from the 5th century BCE.

MINOAN DOUBLE-FLUTE PLAYER

A Philosophical View

Ancient Greek philosophers, including Pythagoras, Plato, and Aristotle, believed that studying music was central to gaining an understanding of the nature of the universe. For this reason, they gave music a prominent role in education.

Pythagoras of Samos, who lived from around 570 to 493 BCE, is generally believed to have been the first Greek philosopher to develop a theory around music and its importance in the universe.

Legend has it that Pythagoras was intrigued by the higher and lower sounds that he heard produced by hammers of different sizes in a blacksmith's workshop. Experimenting with a monochord—a stringed instrument—he studied the relationship between the pitch of a note and the length of the string that produced it. He then figured out numerical ratios between the notes and theorized about how they affected the musical harmony. He later made a leap of the imagination from his theories about the mathematics of music to a possible mathematical relationship between heavenly bodies.

Heavenly music

In Greek cosmology, the universe was believed to consist of a series of spheres with the Earth at their center. There was a sphere for the moon, the sun, each of the planets, and for the fixed stars. Pythagoras believed that there was a numerical relationship between these spheres that corresponded to musical harmony. Their movements generated what he described as a "music of the spheres." He believed that this music was imperceptible to

Stern philosopher
The Greek philosopher Plato (*c.*427–348 BCE) argued that music must incite people to a "courageous and harmonious life." He rejected musical innovation as a threat to the stability of the state.

Hymn to the Sun
Russian artist Fyodor Bronnikov (1827–1902) painted this romanticized image of followers of Pythagoras performing a hymn to celebrate the rising of the sun. For some Ancient Greek philosophers, music had a close connection with astronomy.

the human ear but that it was nevertheless a sign of the fundamental harmony of the universe.

Music and society

Music and astronomy remained linked throughout the era of Ancient Greek civilization. Plato (423–348 BCE) and Aristotle (384–322 BCE), the leading Greek philosophers in the 4th century BCE, were more concerned with the effect of music on society and on the character of the listener. Plato believed that formal musical performance was essential to the stability of the state. He described any musical innovations as "unsettling the most fundamental political and social conventions." He was deeply critical of the idea of judging a performance by how much pleasure it gave and believed the purpose of music was not to give "irrational pleasure" but to introduce harmony and order into the soul. Furthermore, Plato felt that an elite must uphold musical tradition against "men of native genius ... ignorant of what is right and legitimate." He said that those being educated to become governors of the ideal state must not listen to soft or lazy music, but music that encouraged bravery and restraint.

Aristotle agreed that good music would improve human morals and bad music would corrupt them, but he was more sympathetic to the joyous aspect of performing music. He maintained that the purpose of music was "to instruct, to amuse, or to employ the vacant hours of those who live at rest."

Aristotle also discussed the psychological impacts of the musical modes, or scales, used by the Greeks, such as the Dorian, Phrygian, and Lydian modes (named after different areas of Ancient Greece), and their effect on emotions and character.

Aristoxenus, a pupil of Aristotle, wrote a systematic theoretical description of music in his treatise *Elements of Harmony*. He was more in touch than his predecessors with the practice of playing music and had a different view of musical intervals, harmony, and rhythm. Aristoxenus felt that the only way to gain knowledge of music was to listen to it and memorize it, basing his understanding of music on the truth of the ear.

Ptolemy of Alexandria

The last major Greek contribution to musical theory was made by Ptolemy, an important thinker who lived in the Mediterranean port of Alexandria in the 2nd century CE. In his treatise *Harmonics*, he tried to reconcile Pythagoras's study of music, based on mathematics, with Aristoxenus's theories, founded on musical experience. He expanded Pythagoras's "music of the spheres" into a system of connections between musical harmony, astronomy, and astrology.

UNDERSTANDING MUSIC

EARLY NOTATION

The oldest surviving written music is marked on a clay tablet found at Sumer, in Mesopotamia, and dates from around 2000 BCE. The marks probably gave only a rough idea of pitch.

Evidence of true musical notation—giving both the pitch and length of notes—comes from Ancient Greece on inscribed stone fragments. Known as the Delphic Hymns, they show melodies, written to be sung in Athens in 138 and 128 BCE. The oldest complete notated composition to have survived is thought to be the Seikilos Epitaph, which has the words and melody of a song. Carved on a tombstone found in Turkey, near the Ancient Greek city of Ephesus, it is likely to date from the 1st century BCE.

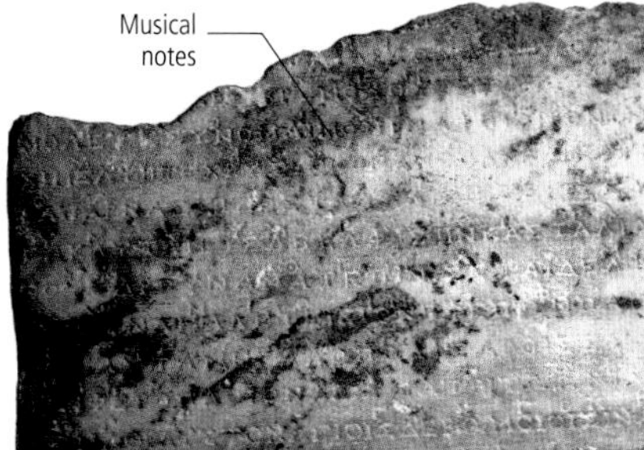

CARVING FROM DELPHI

4,000 YEARS The age of the oldest surviving example of written music.

AFTER

Ancient Greek musical philosophies influenced European musical attitudes all the way to the Renaissance.

TRANSMITTING ANCIENT IDEAS

The early Christian philosopher Boethius (480–525 CE) wrote a work entitled *De institutione musica* that **divided music into three types**: the music of the universe, or cosmic music (*musica mundana*); the music of human beings (*musica humana*); and instrumental music (*musica instrumentalis*).

PRESERVING EARLY WORKS

Muslim scholars 40–41 ›› in the Middle Ages and then European thinkers from around the 15th century, including the Italian Renaissance philosopher Marsilio Ficino (1433–1499), preserved the works of Pythagoras, Plato, and Aristotle. Johannes Kepler (1571–1630), one of the founders of modern astronomy, still believed in a fundamental harmony of the universe as revealed in music and blended musical theory with his calculations of planetary motion.

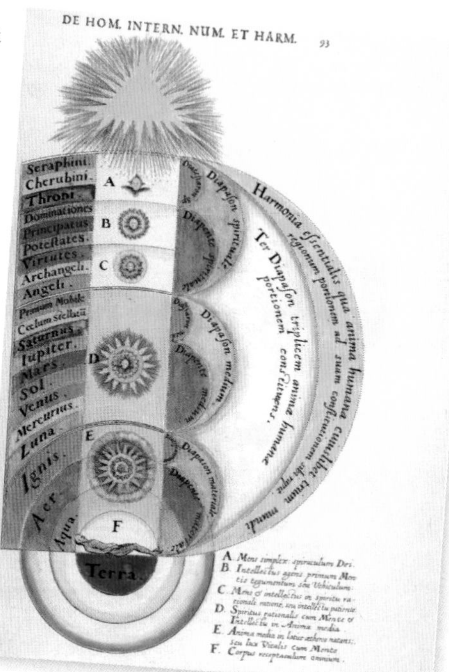

The "music of the spheres"
Pythagoras linked the study of music to the study of astronomy. He believed the sun, moon, and planets, traveling in spherical orbits around the Earth, caused the universe to vibrate, creating music and signifying the fundamental harmony of the universe.

> "**Rhythm** and **harmony** find their way into the inner places of the **soul.**"
>
> PLATO, "THE REPUBLIC," c.380 BCE

BEFORE

Before its full flowering from the 5th century BCE, Ancient Greek music had a long history, reaching back more than 2,000 years into an obscure past.

MUSICAL STATUE

The earliest evidence of Greek musical performance is a **marble statuette** of a harp player from the Cyclades—a group of islands between Greece and Asia Minor—dating from 2700 BCE. The **Mycenaean civilization** that flourished in Greece around 1600–1100 BCE probably imported its musical tradition from **Minoan Crete**.

PHILOSOPHY OF MUSIC

From the 7th to 6th centuries BCE, a **Greek cultural renaissance** associated with city-states such as Athens and Sparta generated the classic musical culture referred to in the **works of philosophers** such as Pythagoras, Plato, and Aristotle « 18–19.

Myth and Tragedy

Music played an essential part in Ancient Greek culture, from religious rituals and theatrical tragedies to everyday work and leisure. It was celebrated in the myths of the gods and its finest practitioners won fame and fortune.

In Greek mythology, the lyre-player Orpheus was identified as the "father of songs." It was said that no living thing could resist the spell of his music, which could tame wild animals and even move stones.

The lyre (see pp.16, 23) was also the chosen instrument of the god of music, Apollo, who was, in addition, the god of healing, poetry, and the sun. In a famous myth, the satyr Marsyas challenged Apollo to a music competition, pitting his own *aulos* (a twin-piped wind instrument) against the god's lyre. The lyre triumphed over the *aulos*, the god over the satyr, and Marsyas paid for his presumption by being skinned alive.

Behind the mask
Masks worn by actors were an essential element in Ancient Greek theater, denoting character and also helping actors' voices to project into the amphitheater.

Lyre or *aulos*?

Such myths represented fundamental Greek attitudes to their musical tradition. The lyre was regarded as the quintessential Greek instrument—at least by the elite. It existed in several forms, from the simple, two-stringed lyre to the *phorminx* (up to seven strings) to the sophisticated seven-string *kithara*, which was strummed with a plectrum. The *aulos*, in contrast, was denounced by Athenian intellectuals as an Asiatic, rustic instrument suitable only for use by the lower orders. They took the same dismissive attitude toward the *syrinx*, or panpipes (see pp.22–23). However, in the martial city-state of Sparta, Athens's great rival, the *aulos* was the favored instrument.

The elevating songs written in honor of Apollo, known as paeans, were inevitably accompanied by the lyre. The spirit of Apollo—serene and orderly—came to be contrasted with that of Dionysus, the god of drunkenness and wild ecstasy. Dionysus was celebrated with hymns known as dithyrambs, designed to excite strong emotion. These were typically sung by a chorus accompanied by the *aulos*.

Open-air theater
The Ancient Greek city of Aphrodisias, now in Turkey, was relatively small, but it still had an *oideion*, or concert hall, where musical competitions were held as well as poetry recitals and other performances.

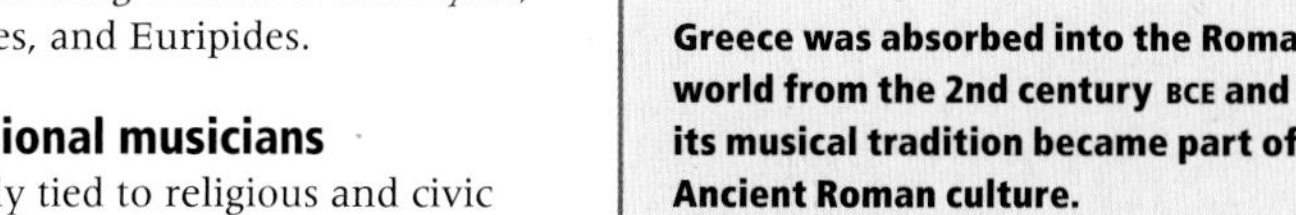

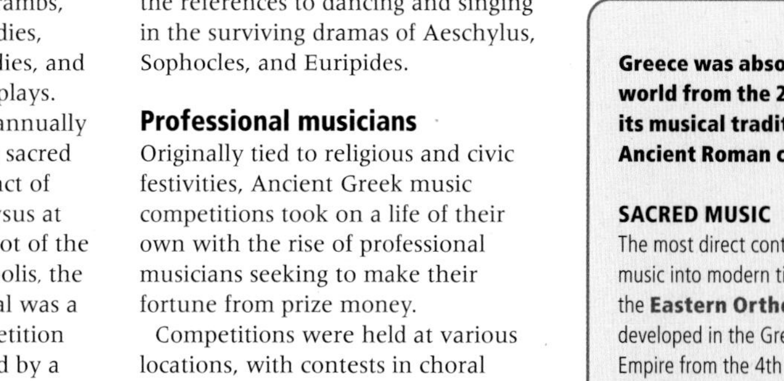

The Greek chorus
An important part of any Greek drama was the chorus, a group of players who collectively commented on the action, usually in song form. This modern chorus performs the Theban plays of Sophocles.

Sung verse

Music was seen as an important part of an elite education, and members of the ruling class in Athens were expected to play the lyre and sing. In singing may lie the origin of tragedy itself: the word *tragoidia* translates as "goat song" (*tragos* means goat, while *ode* is song). Scholars have yet to find a satisfying explanation for the goat, although a link with satyr plays—tragicomedies in which the goatlike companions of the gods Pan and Dionysus feature—is plausible.

> "They found **Achilles** delighting in the clear-toned **lyre ...** singing of the deeds of ... **warriors.**"
>
> HOMER, "THE ILIAD," BOOK IX

The founding of Greek lyric poetry—verses written to be sung while playing the lyre—is traditionally attributed to Terpander, who lived on the island of Lesbos in the 7th century BCE. Other lyric poets who attained fame included Alcaeus and Sappho from Lesbos, Alcman of Sparta, and Pindar of Thebes. Only the words of their musical creations have survived. Although written music existed, most musicians played or sang melodies learned by ear, and performances involved a large element of improvisation.

Music and drama competitions

Festivals involving music and drama competitions were an important part of Ancient Greek life. The annual Carnea festival in Sparta included a music competition, while the Great Dionysia festival in Athens involved the performance of dithyrambs, comedies, tragedies, and satyr plays. Held annually at the sacred precinct of Dionysus at the foot of the Acropolis, the festival was a competition judged by a panel of ordinary citizens. It was funded by the *choregoi*, wealthy Athenian citizens who bore the major costs incurred by the extensive training and preparation of the choruses, musicians, costumes, props, and scenery.

In addition to writing the words, a playwright was responsible for creating the music, choreographing the dances, and directing the chorus for each performance. A group of robed and masked singers and dancers, the chorus occasionally took an active role in the drama, reacting to events onstage and contributing their own brand of worldly generalizing wisdom. Their music was first and foremost vocal, with melody following closely the stress and rhythms of their lyrics—helping audience members in the farthest rows to hear the words. The only instrumental accompaniment was traditionally provided by a single *aulos*.

It is notoriously difficult to reconstruct the music and dance in Greek tragedy, although this has not stopped scholars through the ages from attempting it. During the Renaissance period (1400–1580 CE), Classical scholars imagined that all the acting parts would have been sung; today, however, there is some consensus that the actors spoke their lines while the chorus interjected in song.

Reimagining the movements and sounds made by the actors and chorus mostly relies on archeological remains, images found on Greek pottery, and the references to dancing and singing in the surviving dramas of Aeschylus, Sophocles, and Euripides.

Professional musicians

Originally tied to religious and civic festivities, Ancient Greek music competitions took on a life of their own with the rise of professional musicians seeking to make their fortune from prize money.

Competitions were held at various locations, with contests in choral singing, dancing, and playing the *kithara* and the *aulos*. Increasingly, music became a form of elaborate virtuoso display put on for admiring audiences. Roofed concert halls, such as the Odeon in Athens, were built to supplement open-air amphitheaters.

Tradition-worshiping intellectuals, notably the philosopher Plato, deplored the professionalization of music-making and the cult of virtuosi. Plato described these crowd-pleasers as guilty of "promiscuous cleverness and a spirit of lawbreaking," because of their musical innovations. But surviving Greek inscriptions attest to the fame of the leading performers.

Not only the top stars made a living from music, however. Everywhere in Greek society musicians were in demand, to provide solemn melodies for processions and religious rituals, entertainment at weddings, festivals, and banquets, or the dirges and lamentations for funeral rites. In the working world, rhythmic music encouraged laborers in the fields and kept oarsmen pulling in unison.

AFTER

Greece was absorbed into the Roman world from the 2nd century BCE and its musical tradition became part of Ancient Roman culture.

SACRED MUSIC
The most direct continuation of Ancient Greek music into modern times lies in the music of the **Eastern Orthodox Church**, which developed in the Greek-speaking Byzantine Empire from the 4th century CE.

NEW MODES
In early medieval Western Europe, a system of "modes" was adopted for religious chants. Although they used the names of the Ancient Greek scales, these **Gregorian modes** **30–31 ››** were musically completely different from their Ancient Greek predecessors.

CONTEMPORARY CHORUS
The nearest modern-day equivalent to the Greek chorus might be the **opera chorus**—or the **church choir**, which contributes musical interludes to the words of a service.

Ancient sounds

Considerable efforts have been made in modern times to establish what Ancient Greek music may have sounded like. The survival of a small amount of written music and of theoretical writings, as well as evidence of the nature of musical instruments, provide at least a basis for educated speculation on this subject. Most music appears to have consisted of a single melodic line based on musical scales known as modes. These modes, which bear no direct relation to the scales known as modes in modern Western music (see pp.30–31), were deemed to have different moral and emotional qualities. For example, the Phrygian mode, named after the ancient kingdom of Phrygia in Anatolia (in modern-day Turkey), was "sensual," while the Dorian mode, named after the Dorian Greeks, was "harsh." They included smaller tonal divisions than the semitones familiar in the modern Western tradition—quarter tones and even smaller intervals—which would probably have created a sound alien to our ears.

Ancient evidence
A Greek vase from the 5th century BCE shows the winner of a music contest crowned with laurel and surrounded by mythological figures. The musician is playing a *kithara*, a form of lyre.

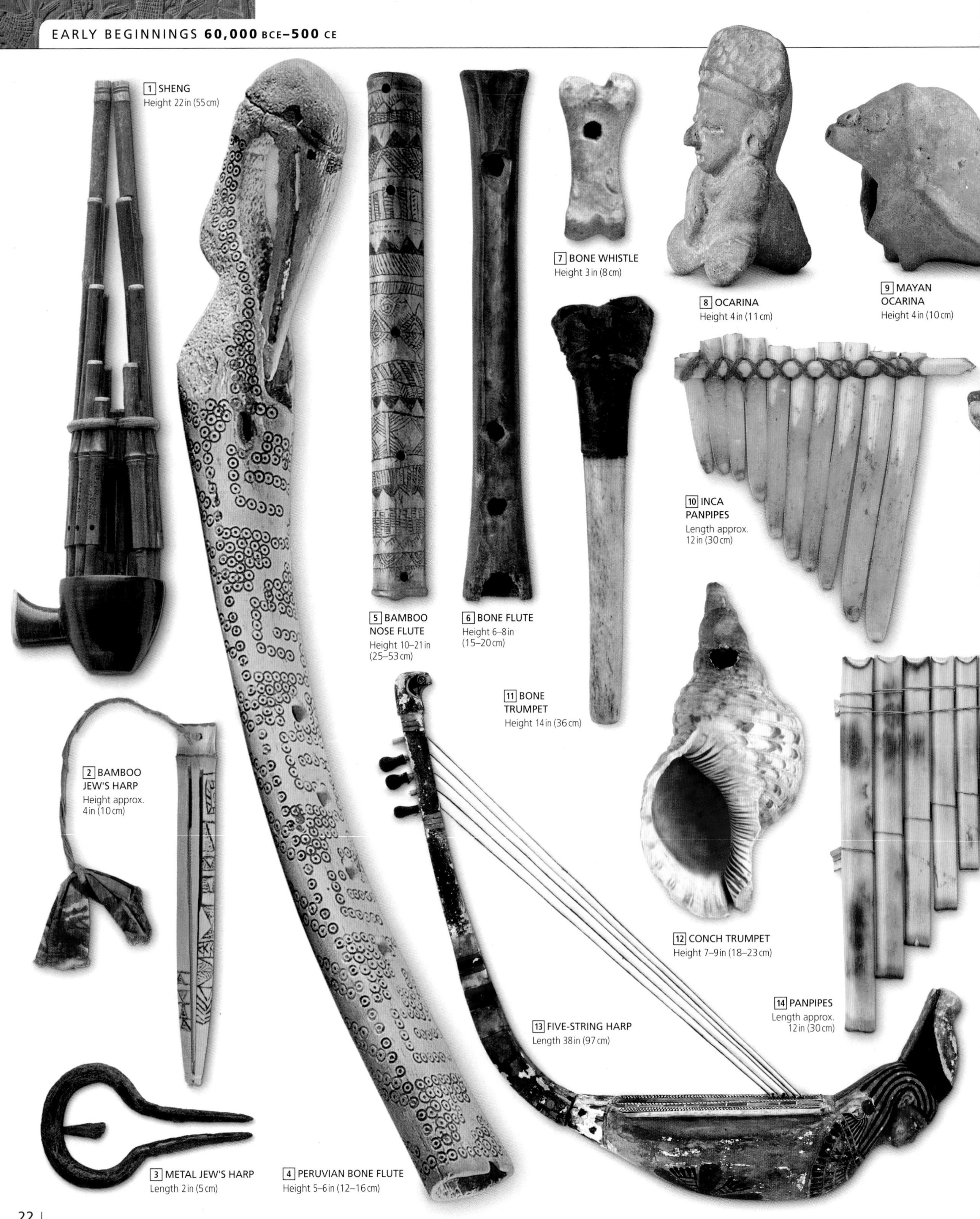
1 SHENG
Height 22 in (55 cm)
7 BONE WHISTLE
Height 3 in (8 cm)
8 OCARINA
Height 4 in (11 cm)
9 MAYAN OCARINA
Height 4 in (10 cm)
10 INCA PANPIPES
Length approx. 12 in (30 cm)
5 BAMBOO NOSE FLUTE
Height 10–21 in (25–53 cm)
6 BONE FLUTE
Height 6–8 in (15–20 cm)
11 BONE TRUMPET
Height 14 in (36 cm)
2 BAMBOO JEW'S HARP
Height approx. 4 in (10 cm)
12 CONCH TRUMPET
Height 7–9 in (18–23 cm)
14 PANPIPES
Length approx. 12 in (30 cm)
13 FIVE-STRING HARP
Length 38 in (97 cm)
3 METAL JEW'S HARP
Length 2 in (5 cm)
4 PERUVIAN BONE FLUTE
Height 5–6 in (12–16 cm)

15 THUMB PIANO
Height 12 in (30 cm)

16 AZTEC CLAY TRUMPET
Length 16 in (40 cm)

17 MESOPOTAMIAN LYRE
Height 3 ft 7 in (1.1 m)

18 BRONZE SISTRUM
Height 9 in (23 cm)

19 EGYPTIAN IVORY CLAPPERS
Length approx. 12 in (30 cm)

20 EGYPTIAN WOOD AND LEATHER DRUM
Diameter 10 in (25 cm)

21 CHINESE PELLET DRUM
Diameter approx. 3 in (8 cm)

Ancient Instruments

The first musical instruments were shaped from bone, pieces of wood, bamboo, or seashells. Metal and stringed instruments evolved around 4,000–5,000 years ago. They were sounded by blowing, beating, shaking, or plucking.

1 **Sheng** Played in China since ancient times, the sheng is a wind instrument with vertical bamboo pipes. 2 **Bamboo Jew's harp** One of the most ancient instruments, this has a flexible "tongue" that is held in the mouth and plucked. This example is from Asia. 3 **Metal Jew's harp** This is a metal version of a Jew's harp. Such instruments have many names in different countries; the word "Jew" may simply be a corruption of "jaw." 4 **Peruvian bone flute** Made by the Chimu people of northwest Peru, this flute is decorated with a carving of a bird's head. 5 **Bamboo nose flute** Bamboo flutes, blown with one nostril instead of the mouth, were common in Polynesian cultures. 6 **Bone flute** This instrument from Scandinavia provided music for Viking voyagers. It has three finger holes for altering the pitch. 7 **Bone whistle** Made from the toe bone of a caribou, this north European whistle dates from around 40,000 BCE. 8 **Ocarina** A type of flute, this was made from pit-fired earthenware clay. Ocarinas were common in Mayan, Aztec, and Incan cultures around 12,000 years ago. 9 **Mayan Ocarina** This early wind instrument is shaped like a bird. 10 **Incan Panpipes** In Pre-Columbian Peru, the Incas made Panpipes from clay, cane, or quills. 11 **Bone trumpet** Made from a human thigh bone, this was used in Buddhist rituals. 12 **Conch trumpet** Common from western Asia to the Pacific, this trumpet was made by opening a blow hole in a conch shell. 13 **Five-string harp** This instrument was played in Ancient Egypt more than 3,000 years ago. 14 **Panpipes** Made of bamboo in five or more lengths, such pipes were popular in Ancient Greece where they were associated with the god Pan. 15 **Thumb piano** Enslaved Africans brought this plucked instrument to Latin America. 16 **Aztec clay trumpet** This clay trumpet was made by Aztec peoples of Pre-Columbian Mexico. 17 **Mesopotamian lyre** The lyre is one of the world's oldest stringed instruments. This one is from Ur. 18 **Bronze sistrum** A handheld metal rattle, the sistrum was introduced to Ancient Rome from Egypt. 19 **Egyptian ivory clappers** This percussion instrument carved from ivory dates from around 1430 BCE. 20 **Egyptian wood and leather drum** This drum, one of many types of drum used in Ancient Egypt, dates from the 4th century BCE. 21 **Chinese pellet drum** The pellets strike the drum when the handle is twisted.

Sound the **Trumpet**

In Ancient Rome, audiences enjoyed music at the theater, at banquets, in the arena during gladiatorial combat, and in the street. Music added dignity and solemnity to rituals and ceremonies, and musicians accompanied the Roman legions to war.

The Romans were not great innovators in music, but across their empire a fresh synthesis of musical traditions was achieved. Although musical notation existed by the Roman period, Roman musical culture was largely aural, with professional music teachers directly passing on their knowledge to their pupils, who learned to play their instruments by ear.

Range of instruments

Among the musical instruments in use in the Roman world were several forms of lyre, including the seven-stringed *kithara* (the name of which is believed to be the root of the word guitar), varieties of harp, and pipes. The Greeks are credited with inventing the first keyboard instrument, the water-powered organ called a *hydraulis*, but it was the Romans who took to this instrument with enthusiasm. They also developed an organ powered by bellows, which over centuries gradually supplanted the water-driven machine. Brass instruments were a prominent part of the Roman musical scene. They included the *tuba*—a long, thin wind instrument that we would now call a trumpet—and various types of horns, such as the *cornu* and the *bucina*.

Cymbals and tambourines were less prestigious instruments. Initially associated with the cult of the Asian goddess Cybele, they became prominent in the popular music played by the buskers who performed alongside jugglers and acrobats on the Roman streets.

Music for war and worship

In the Roman army, musicians had a well defined status and function. The trumpet player ranked highest, with the *cornu* player below him and the

Street musicians
A mosaic found at the Villa of Cicero in Pompeii in southern Italy depicts Roman entertainers playing a tambourine, cymbals, and the double-pipe known to the Greeks as an *aulos* and to Romans as a *tibia*.

BEFORE

The rise of Rome to imperial power was accompanied by the absorption of the musical cultures of conquered countries. These exotic traditions were blended into a unique synthesis.

ETRUSCAN INFLUENCES
The music of Ancient Rome was inherited from the **Etruscan civilization** that flourished in Italy from the 8th century BCE. The Etruscans eventually fell under Roman control, as did the rest of Italy.

EGYPTIAN TOMB PAINTING

EASTERN MEDITERRANEAN
In the 2nd and 1st centuries BCE, the Romans conquered **Greece, Syria, and Egypt**, all of which had sophisticated musical cultures. Most of the **musical instruments** used by the Romans had evolved around the eastern Mediterranean. **Greek influence** was dominant « **18–19**, but the input from Egypt and Asia was also significant.

bucina player of lowest standing. Clearly audible in the heat of battle, the trumpet was used to sound the attack and the retreat. The *cornu* player was always positioned near the legion's standards during a battle, but the *bucina* was exclusively employed to give signals in camp.

In civilian life, the trumpet was also the instrument played at funerals, and "send for the trumpeters" became a phrase synonymous with "prepare for a death."

Religious sacrifices, on the other hand, were always accompanied by a piper playing the *tibia*. Imperial triumphs (religious ceremonies to celebrate military achievement) called for larger-scale musical performances with groups of musicians and choirs. These ceremonies were designed to display the power of Rome.

Music for pleasure

Despite these various formal and official functions, music was seen by the Romans as, first and foremost, a source of entertainment. Skilled musicians from Greece, Syria, and Egypt flocked to Rome in search of lucrative engagements in the private homes of wealthy Romans.

The host of a house party in a Roman villa would employ musicians to enliven the atmosphere. In the novel *Satyricon*, written by the Roman courtier Petronius in the 1st century CE, the vulgar millionaire Trimalchio has a trumpet blaring out music at his feast. The *kithara* or *tibia*, on the other hand, were considered more tasteful instruments to accompany a meal.

Music for the theater

In theaters, frivolous music was played in the interludes of comedies, a practice denounced by moralists such as the philosopher Seneca and the historian Tacitus, who regarded such performances as a foreign corruption of the Roman tradition. However, such criticisms of a backward-looking cultured elite had little effect on Roman taste for musical theater.

By the 1st century CE, the pantomime, another import from Greece, was all the rage. A Roman pantomime involved the enactment of a story from myth or legend by a single performer using dance and mime, with musical accompaniment provided by a singer and a range of instruments, including pan pipes (see pp.22–23) and lyres. The beat of the music was maintained by a percussion instrument known to the Greeks as a *kroupeza* and to the Romans as a *scabellum*—a pair of sandals with cymbals attached to the soles.

The starting trumpet

The lavish gladiatorial games, mounted in vast arenas such as the Colosseum in Rome, were always occasions for music. Such events would open with a procession led by trumpeters and horns. The trumpet gave the signal to start events, which were then accorded a musical accompaniment by a musical ensemble, shown on one mosaic as including a *hydraulis* and a *cornu*.

In the later stages of the empire, games sometimes became occasions for mass musical performances. One series of games held during the 3rd century apparently involved 100 trumpeters, 100 cornu players, and 200 assorted performers on *tibia* and other pipes. This was exceptional enough to have excited much comment at the time.

Wealth and status

The demand for musicians enabled them to achieve prosperity and social status. They were organized into trade guilds, which represented their interests and were respected by the Roman authorities. Outstanding virtuosos were sometimes paid fabulous sums for public performances, and substantial cash prizes were also awarded to the winners of music competitions.

Among the social elite, performing music was considered a valuable accomplishment; Emperor Hadrian, for example, was proud of his ability as a singer and *kithara* player. Emperor Severus Alexander (222–235 CE) is said to have played a number of musical instruments, including the trumpet and *hydraulis*.

Horn player
The *cornu* was a bronze horn with a crossbar that allowed it to be supported by the player's shoulder. It was chiefly used in military bands and to accompany gladiatorial contests.

EMPEROR (37–68 CE)

NERO

The Roman Emperor Nero, who reigned from 54 to 68 CE, was an enthusiastic musical performer. He employed Terpnus, a well-known singer and *kithara* player, as his music teacher.

Nero gave his first public performance at his palace in Rome in 59 CE. He later appeared in the theater of Pompey, in front of an audience that was paid to applaud at the right moments.

In 66 CE, Nero embarked upon a professional tour of Greece, competing in a number of music contests. He invariably won, since no judge would dare vote against the emperor. However, the well-known story that Nero "fiddled while Rome burned" is a myth.

> "In time of action the **trumpets and the horns** play together."
>
> VEGETIUS, "DE RE MILITARI," 5TH CENTURY CE

AFTER

During the 4th century CE, Christianity became the official religion of the Roman Empire. The music of the Christian Church first developed in the empire's declining years.

EARLY CHURCH MUSIC
To what extent the religious **plainsong of the medieval Church** **30–31 >>** in Western Europe, including the Gregorian chant, reflected the musical practices of Ancient Rome is much disputed. The **organ** **96–97 >>**, descendant of the *hydraulis*, is said to have been adopted as a church instrument from the 7th century.

PHILOSOPHICAL INSPIRATION
The writings on music by the late **Roman philosopher Boethius** (*c.*480–525 CE) were an important source of theoretical inspiration to musicians in medieval and Renaissance Europe.

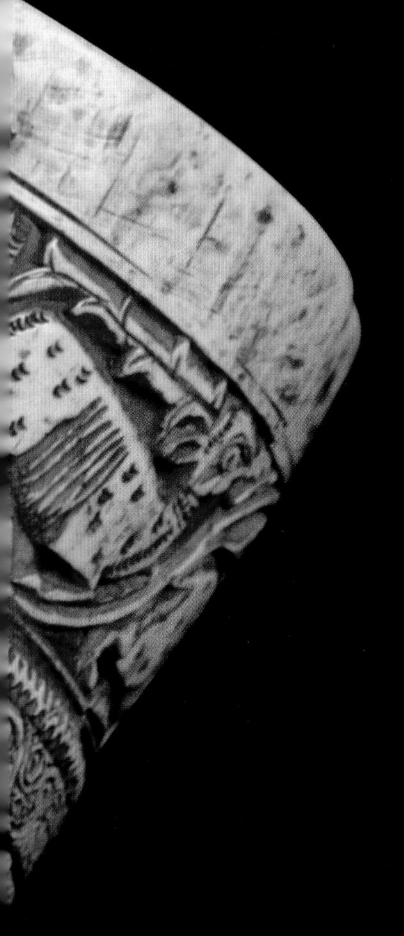

2

MUSIC IN THE MIDDLE AGES

500–1400

The Catholic Church was the single greatest promoter of music in history. Music was in its exclusive domain and used to spread the word of God throughout the world. Secular music began to travel more widely with wandering minstrels and poets, called troubadours. From its humblest to its most glorious forms, the Middle Ages saw an explosion of music.

« Medieval olifant—a hunting horn made from an elephant's tusk.

MUSIC IN THE MIDDLE AGES
500–1400

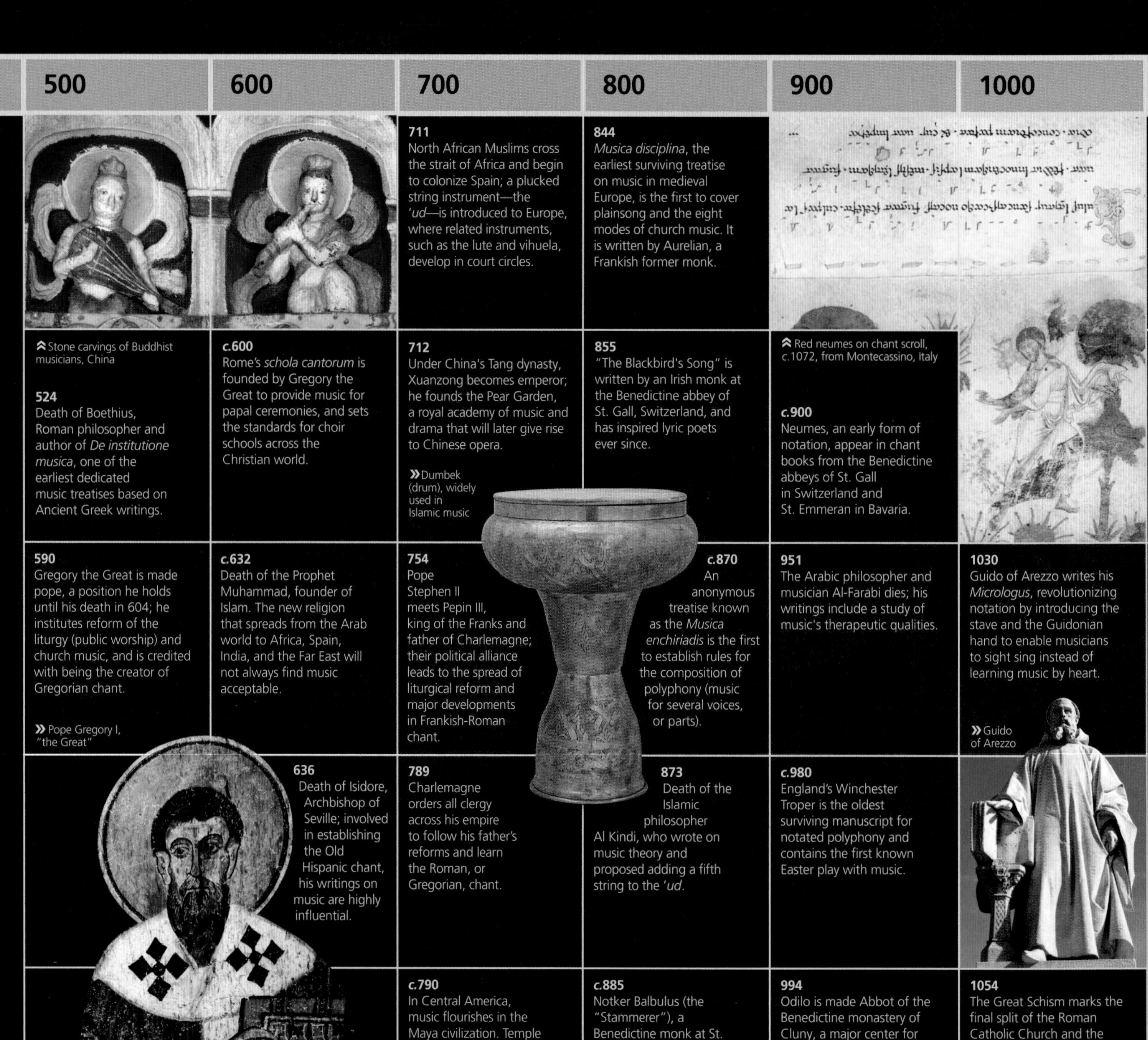

500 | 600 | 700 | 800 | 900 | 1000

Stone carvings of Buddhist musicians, China

524
Death of Boethius, Roman philosopher and author of *De institutione musica*, one of the earliest dedicated music treatises based on Ancient Greek writings.

590
Gregory the Great is made pope, a position he holds until his death in 604; he institutes reform of the liturgy (public worship) and church music, and is credited with being the creator of Gregorian chant.

Pope Gregory I, "the Great"

c.600
Rome's *schola cantorum* is founded by Gregory the Great to provide music for papal ceremonies, and sets the standards for choir schools across the Christian world.

c.632
Death of the Prophet Muhammad, founder of Islam. The new religion that spreads from the Arab world to Africa, Spain, India, and the Far East will not always find music acceptable.

636
Death of Isidore, Archbishop of Seville; involved in establishing the Old Hispanic chant, his writings on music are highly influential.

711
North African Muslims cross the strait of Africa and begin to colonize Spain; a plucked string instrument—the *'ud*—is introduced to Europe, where related instruments, such as the lute and vihuela, develop in court circles.

712
Under China's Tang dynasty, Xuanzong becomes emperor; he founds the Pear Garden, a royal academy of music and drama that will later give rise to Chinese opera.

Dumbek (drum), widely used in Islamic music

754
Pope Stephen II meets Pepin III, king of the Franks and father of Charlemagne; their political alliance leads to the spread of liturgical reform and major developments in Frankish-Roman chant.

789
Charlemagne orders all clergy across his empire to follow his father's reforms and learn the Roman, or Gregorian, chant.

c.790
In Central America, music flourishes in the Maya civilization. Temple murals at Bonampak in Mexico show Maya musicians celebrating a military victory on trumpets, whistles, maracas, and drums.

844
Musica disciplina, the earliest surviving treatise on music in medieval Europe, is the first to cover plainsong and the eight modes of church music. It is written by Aurelian, a Frankish former monk.

855
"The Blackbird's Song" is written by an Irish monk at the Benedictine abbey of St. Gall, Switzerland, and has inspired lyric poets ever since.

c.870
An anonymous treatise known as the *Musica enchiriadis* is the first to establish rules for the composition of polyphony (music for several voices, or parts).

873
Death of the Islamic philosopher Al Kindi, who wrote on music theory and proposed adding a fifth string to the *'ud*.

c.885
Notker Balbulus (the "Stammerer"), a Benedictine monk at St. Gall, Switzerland, writes a book of "hymns" (*Liber hymnorum*) or sequences to be sung on feast days, between the Alleluia and the Gospel in the Mass.

Red neumes on chant scroll, c.1072, from Montecassino, Italy

c.900
Neumes, an early form of notation, appear in chant books from the Benedictine abbeys of St. Gall in Switzerland and St. Emmeran in Bavaria.

951
The Arabic philosopher and musician Al-Farabi dies; his writings include a study of music's therapeutic qualities.

c.980
England's Winchester Troper is the oldest surviving manuscript for notated polyphony and contains the first known Easter play with music.

994
Odilo is made Abbot of the Benedictine monastery of Cluny, a major center for scribes copying music manuscripts; he undertakes monastic reforms that influence developments in sacred music in France.

1030
Guido of Arezzo writes his *Micrologus*, revolutionizing notation by introducing the stave and the Guidonian hand to enable musicians to sight sing instead of learning music by heart.

Guido of Arezzo

1054
The Great Schism marks the final split of the Roman Catholic Church and the Eastern Orthodox Church, each with its distinctive liturgy and musical tradition.

1071
Birth of William IX, Duke of Aquitane and the earliest troubadour known by name.

The Middle Ages was a period of major musical change as music began to be written down with increasing degrees of accuracy—from marks roughly indicating melodic shape, to the invention of a four-line stave that allowed for accurate pitch, and finally the use of different note shapes to indicate duration and rhythm. These advances in notation lay behind the rise of polyphony—music with more than one voice part—that is unique to the Western musical tradition. Writing music down enabled performers to read music without having to memorize melodies, and helped standardize the music of the early Church, allowing repertoires to be preserved for posterity.

1100

c.1100
Aquitanian polyphony develops in the monastery of St. Martial, Limoges, with a substantial and highly influential repertory.

» The dulcimer often appears in medieval depictions of angelic musicians

c.1140
The *Codex Calixtinus* is compiled; the manuscript contains a wide range of polyphonic pieces for two and three voices, and is preserved in the Cathedral of Santiago de Compostela in Spain.

« 12th-century manuscript for the "Gloria," with text and musical notation

c.1140
Birth of Beatriz de Dia, the most famous of the tobairitz—a group of female troubadours in Provence, France.

1150

1160
Birth of Pérotin, French composer of the Notre Dame School and among the first to compose polyphony.

1175
Falconlied (Falcon Song) is composed by Austrian noble Der Kurenberger, one of the first *minnesingers* (poet-singers) whose name is known.

1179
Death of Hildegarde of Bingen, the German abbess, scholar, and prolific composer of sacred music.

c.1190
The School of Notre Dame in Paris flourishes, with polyphonic works (known as *organa*) by Léonin and Pérotin being copied into the *Magnus liber organi* (Great Book of Organum).

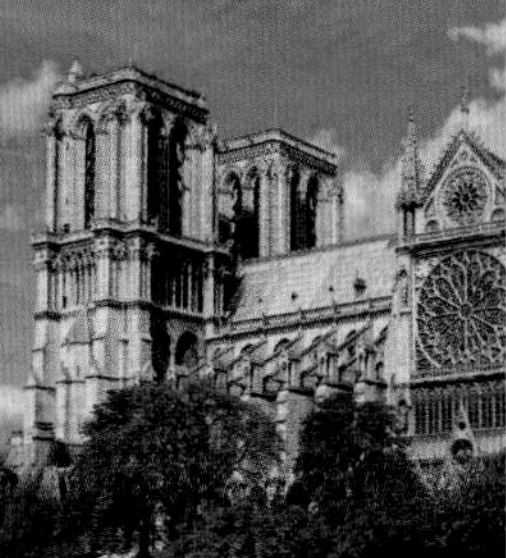

» Notre Dame Cathedral, home to a new polyphony c.1150–1250

1200

c.1207
Spain's epic *Poem of the Cid* is recited by *juglares* (minstrels).

c.1221
Chinese poet-composer Jiang Kui dies; some of his songs are still popular today.

1230
The *Carmina Burana* manuscript contains 254 goliard songs; 24 will be set to music by Carl Orff in 1936.

1236
One of the most famous and prolific *minnesingers*, Niedhart von Reuenthal, dies; his songs are often comic or satirical.

c.1240
An anonymous treatise, *De mensurabili musici* (On Measured Music), is the first to propose a system for notating rhythm, through six rhythmic modes.

1250

1250
In his *Ars cantus mensurabilis* (*The Art of Measured Song*), German theorist Franco of Cologne describes a new method for indicating the duration of a note by its shape, which allows the accurate notation of rhythmic values.

» Troubadours in the beautifully illuminated *Codex Manesse*

1253
Death of Thibaut, count of Champagne and king of Navarre, one of the most important of the *trouvères* of northern France.

c.1260
The English song "Sumer is icumen in" (Summer has come) is the oldest surviving six-part polyphony.

1270
Death of Tannhauser, German *minnesinger* and legendary hero of Richard Wagner's 1845 opera *Tannhauser*.

c.1284
King Alfonso X the Wise commissions the *Cantigas de Santa Maria*, a collection of Galician-Portuguese songs to the Virgin Mary.

1289
The Church bans jongleurs, goliards, and buffoons (jesters) from practicing as clergy.

1300

c.1300
Parisian music theorist Johannes de Grocheio writes *De musica*, one of the first treatises to deal with instrumental music.

1304
Compiled in Zurich, the *Codex Manesse* contains love songs by 137 *minnesingers*.

c.1320
Johannis de Muris sets out a new form of notation in *Ars nove musice* (*The New Art of Music*) with rhythmic modes that allow the rapid development of complex polyphonic works. Philippe de Vitry's *Ars nova notandi* (*The New Art of Notating Music*) follows in 1322.

1349
German cleric Hugh of Reutlingen compiles *Geisserlieder*—songs of wandering flagellants – during the Black Death, a plague that kills around one-quarter of Europe's population.

1350

c.1350
French composer Guillaume de Machaut begins to collect his life's work for his wealthy patrons; his *rondeaux, ballades,* and *virelais* are among the earliest surviving polyphonic *chansons* (songs in French).

1361
A permanent organ is installed at Halberstadt, Germany, with 20 bellows operated by ten men.

1365
Francesco Landini, leading composer of Italy's *trecento* style of polyphony, is organist at San Lorenzo in Florence.

1376
In England, the York Mystery Plays are first documented—a cycle of 48 biblical dramas, each performed by a different guild and accompanied by pipes and tabors (drums).

» Monastic scribe working on a manuscript

Sacred Chant

Music and religion have always been closely associated, and singing formed part of the rituals of the early Christian Church. For more than 1,000 years, the monasteries and cathedrals that towered over the medieval landscape and society were flourishing centers of music.

As the power of the Roman Empire waned, the Church became increasingly dominant in medieval society. The monastic and cathedral communities became centers not only of worship but also of learning. The clergy were almost the only members of society who could read and write, and almost all formally trained musicians were priests. The chanted melodies integral to the celebration of the liturgy (the official form of public worship) were, therefore, performed by men and by choirboys being trained for priesthood. Some nuns also received a musical education and participated in singing the services celebrated daily in convents.

From speech to song

Outside these religious communities and the private chapels of the nobility, most of the population—especially laborers and the less well educated—never heard this music. It was unaccompanied, in Latin (the universal language of the Church), and sung from memory rather than written down. Singers performed in unison, both as an exercise in contemplation and to assert the message of the Church. Early chant probably grew out of the accentuation patterns of spoken Latin, and the natural rise and fall of the voice in reading aloud. Recited on a single tone or with increasingly complex melodic curves, chant was a useful tool for meditation.

Two types of liturgy were developed in the early Church: the reenactment of the Last Supper, which became the Sunday Mass, and meetings to read from the scriptures and sing psalms, which became the Office, or daily cycle, of prayer. As liturgical worship became more ceremonial, music became an important part of the clergy's training, and choir schools were set up to train choirboys to memorize the melodies. Rome's *schola cantorum*, situated close to the Roman papacy that ruled the Church, formed the core of this tradition. The school was founded around 600 CE by Pope Gregory I (Gregory the Great), who was credited with composing plainchant that would come to dominate liturgical music.

150 **The number of psalms in the Bible, sung in a weekly cycle.**

9 **The hours (services) of Daily Office, beginning at sunset.**

Early chant traditions

In the 4th century CE, the split of the Roman Empire and of the Church into Latin West and Greek East (centered on Rome and on Constantinople, or Byzantium, respectively) gave rise to separate liturgies, each with regional variations. St. Ambrose (*c.*340–397 CE) in Milan, northern Italy, favored antiphony, with two choirs singing alternate sections of the chant—a Byzantine practice that was adopted by the Roman Church. He also gave greater prominence to hymns, many of which he is thought to have composed himself.

Other chant traditions in Italy included the florid Beneventan chant melodies, which continued to be sung until the 11th century, when they were supplanted by the increasingly ubiquitous Roman, or "Gregorian," chant as it spread across Europe.

In Spain, the Hispanic, or Mozarabic, rite was observed by the Christians living under Muslim rule. In 1085, following the reconquest of Toledo, King Alfonso VI repressed the Hispanic rite in favor of the Roman tradition, yet its legacy was strong, and the Mozarabic Mass can still be heard in Toledo Cathedral.

The spread of Gregorian chant

In the Western Church, two main liturgies had evolved: Roman and Gallican (in Gaul). The Roman liturgy was spread across Western Europe by the monastic orders. In 595 CE, for example, Gregory the Great sent St. Augustine and 40 other Benedictine monks to England to convert the Anglo-Saxons to Christianity. The teachings of music theorists, such as Isidore of Seville (*c.*560–636 CE), also helped to consolidate the use of chant in the liturgy. As the chant repertory became more extensive, and in order to help the clergy remember the standardized versions of the chant melodies, a simple system of neumes (signs)—initially a sequence of dots, strokes, and dashes added above or below the text—was developed to indicate reciting patterns. By the 11th century, a system of notation had been developed to mark notes and pitch accurately (see pp.36–37).

A key moment in the progress toward a single, all-prevailing chant tradition occurred in the mid-8th century, when Pope Stephen II traveled north from Rome to meet Pepin, the Frankish king of Gaul, to seek an alliance against the king of the Lombards. The Pope was accompanied on his journey by some of his singers, and later popes sent members of Rome's *schola cantorum* to teach the clergy in Rouen Cathedral and elsewhere. These early exchanges eventually led to a fusion of the Frankish and Roman plainchant traditions into what is now called Gregorian chant, which is still performed today.

POPE AND COMPOSER (*c.*560–640 CE)

GREGORY THE GREAT

Born into a wealthy Roman family, Gregory initially followed a political career. In 578 CE, he was ordained a deacon and later became papal ambassador to Constantinople. On his return, he became abbot of the Benedictine monastery he had founded on the Caelian Hill in Rome. Elected pope in 590 CE, Gregory I became known as the Father of Christian worship, because of his efforts to unify liturgical practice. Gregory also helped to establish Rome as the center of Christianity.

Hagia Sophia
The 6th-century basilica of Hagia Sophia ("Holy Wisdom") in Constantinople (now Istanbul, Turkey) was the seat of the Eastern Church, in which the Byzantine chant tradition flourished.

« BEFORE

Christianity became the officially recognized religion of the Roman Empire under Constantine, but the role of music in the Church was a subject of debate.

EMPEROR CONSTANTINE

JEWISH LEGACY
Psalm-singing had formed a regular part of **Jewish worship** and quickly became central to the earliest Christian rites. Biblical references to the singing of angels in heaven and to King David, his psalms, and his musicians were often invoked to justify music's inclusion in Christian worship, but not everyone approved.

THE ROLE OF MUSIC
Christianity became the dominant religion of the **Roman Empire** **« 24–25** under Constantine I (272–337 CE). In his *Confessions* (397–398 CE), St. Augustine of Hippo admitted the **sensual allure of music**, wishing he could banish from his ears "the whole melody which is used for David's Psalter." But he also recognized music's role in inspiring devotion.

Eleventh-century notation
This detail from a scroll from the Abbey of Montecassino, Italy, shows part of the "Exultet" (the hymn of praise sung at Easter). It illustrates the appearance of Christ after his resurrection.

Text appears backward and upside down to the congregation as the singer unfolds the scroll over the lectern

Notation marked in red above each line of text

UNDERSTANDING MUSIC

CHURCH MODES

Around the 10th century, a system of eight church modes (groupings or "scales" of notes) was developed, borrowing from Byzantine modes that were thought to have been invented in Ancient Greece by the mathematician Pythagoras (*c.* 570–495 BCE). The church modes took the Greek names—Dorian, Hypodorian, Phrygian, Hypophrygian, Lydian, Hypolydian, Mixolydian, and Hypomixolydian—but gave them to different scales. Chant melodies were generally characterized according to one or other of these modes, which helped singers when memorizing the huge repertory of several thousand chants. Modes can be played using only the white notes on a piano. The Dorian mode (below) begins on D and uses each white key until D an octave higher.

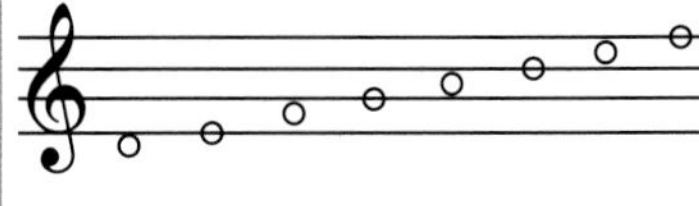

DORIAN MODE

AFTER

Despite the best efforts of popes and emperors, different chant traditions persisted. They were standardized only after the birth of the stave.

NEW NOTATION, NEW VOICES

The most important advance in the attempt to establish a single, standardized chant tradition was the invention of the stave (the horizontal lines on which notes are positioned). Attributed to the Benedictine monk Guido of Arezzo (*c.* 991–1033 CE), it allowed the **notation of melodic pitch** with far greater accuracy **36–37 ››**. It also played a key role in **early polyphony,** in which other voices were added to plainchant **46–47 ››**.

RADICAL REFORMS

In the 16th century, the **Reformation and Counter-Reformation** **58–59 ››** would bring even greater changes to church music.

Minstrels and **Troubadours**

Songs and dances accompanied many aspects of daily life in medieval Europe, enlivening special occasions such as royal visits and religious festivals, as well as entertaining market crowds. Performers ranged from noble troubadours at court to buskers in the streets.

BEFORE

No music survives from before the time of the first troubadours in the late 11th century, because wandering minstrels did not write down their songs.

EPIC POEMS

One genre that flourished widely is the **narrative epic poem**, or *chanson de geste*. These poems were sung to the accompaniment of a **plucked string instrument** such as a harp, with the musician drawing on a number of melodic formulae and improvised instrumental interludes to help convey the verse structure, heighten the more dramatic moments, and generally retain the listeners' interest. Among the best-known examples are the *Chanson de Roland* (The Song of Roland), the *Cantar del mio Cid* (The Poem of the Cid), and the Anglo-Saxon *Beowulf*, which was brilliantly **brought back to musical life** by the 20th-century performer of early music Benjamin Bagby.

3,182 The number of lines in the epic poem *Beowulf*, composed by anonymous Anglo-Saxon poets between the 8th and 11th centuries.

Musical entertainment formed a fundamental part of cultural life at all levels of medieval society. There were different types of music for every audience, from popular tunes played on the bagpipe in crowded taverns to elegant ballads sung to harp accompaniment at court.

Street entertainers

The traveling musicians known as *jongleurs* offered street entertainment featuring storytelling with dance and music, juggling, acrobatics, as well as singing and playing instruments. Minstrels were strictly musicians, initially employed by the nobility, but later performing on street corners or in taverns and inns. Their popularity with the poorer sections of society meant they did not generally have a good reputation. Thomas Chobham, an English theologian writing in the 13th century, was not impressed by the way minstrels seemed to encourage people to sin: "Some go to drinking places and wanton gatherings so that they may sing wanton songs there to move people to lustfulness, and these are damnable just like the rest."

Nevertheless, these wandering minstrels played an important part in transmitting song repertories and dances far and wide in an age when music was rarely written down.

Street music
This detail of an 11th-century manuscript depicts the *jongleur*'s skills. The smaller figure is juggling, while the musician plays a *shawm*, a loud reed instrument well suited to street entertainment.

Itinerant goliards

Clerics and the better educated sections of society listened to sing songs in Latin, the language of high culture throughout Europe, and these songs covered all topics, from love to biting political satire. The songs were performed by goliards, men who had begun a clerical training but, having dropped out of ecclesiastical life, earned their living as traveling songsters, visiting different cities and courts. The famous collection of more than one hundred song melodies, known as the *Carmina Burana*, includes love songs as well as moralistic, satirical, and religious verse. Originally compiled in the late 13th century, in the monastery of Benediktbauern, Germany, the *Carmina Burana* has become well-known today through the colorful symphonic versions of some of the songs made by the German composer Carl Orff in the 1930s.

Minstrels' gallery
For their music to be heard over the noise of the activity below, minstrels often played from raised galleries. This gallery is in the Great Hall at Penshurst Place, a house dating from 1341 in southern England.

Troubadours and trouvères

While the identities of medieval jongleurs and goliards have been lost in the mists of time, from the late 11th century a new type of professional musician emerged—the troubadour. Essentially, he was a poet-composer, who usually performed his own works and either sang his verse as an unaccompanied melody or played a harp or lute as well.

The first known troubadour was William IX, Duke of Aquitaine (1071–1176), who set to music the verse he wrote in Occitan, or *langue d'oc*, a language of southern France and adjacent areas in Spain and Italy. Not all troubadours were of noble descent, but all worked in courtly circles and valued their elevated status. The troubadour song was an aristocratic genre and focused on social conventions and the emotional vicissitudes of courtly love.

More than 40 known troubadours achieved fame and fortune, and many had biographies written about them. One troubadour, Raimon Vidal, described their lives: "You would hear, as I did, the troubadours tell and relate how they lived by traveling and making the rounds of lands and places; and you would see their tasseled saddles and much other costly equipage, and gilded bridles and palfreys." It is clear that these musicians held a valued place in southern French society.

In the north of France, the court of Champagne was the center of activity for the *trouvères*, who also enjoyed an aristocratic pedigree or patronage.

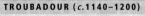

> "I am a man inclined to the profession of **minstrelsy** of **singing,** and I know how to tell … **good stories.**"
>
> THE TROUBADOUR RAIMON VIDAL, "ABRIL ISSIA," *c.*1210

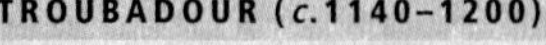

TROUBADOUR (*c.*1140–1200)

BERNART DE VENTADORN

Bernart de Ventadorn led a typical troubadour's life. The son of a servant at the castle of the Count of Ventadorn in southern France, he was famous for composing the classical form of the courtly love song. Bernart learned to compose while in the service of his patron, Eble III of Ventadorn, and he dedicated his first songs to the count's wife, Marguerite. He seems to have fallen under the spell of his own verse, because he was forced to flee Ventadorn after becoming enamored of the countess. Later, Bernart traveled through France before visiting England in the retinue of Eleanor of Aquitaine. Some 45 of his poems have survived, with melodies for almost half of them.

Among the first *trouvères* was Thibault, Count of Champagne, later King of Navarre, and the wealthy landowner Gace Brulé. Later *trouvères* included members of the clergy and the wealthier middle classes who formed brotherhoods known as *puys*. The *trouvères* composed their verse in the *langue d'oïl*, a dialect of northern France, and held contests to choose the best songs.

Elsewhere in Europe

A number of other aristocratic song traditions flourished in Europe. The *Minnesingers* in Germany were influenced by the troubadours and *trouvères*, and developed their own song forms and styles from their local language and verse forms. In Spain, King Alfonso X "the Wise" (1252–1284) commissioned the *Cantigas de Santa María*, a collection of hundreds of songs to be copied into illuminated anthologies. They were composed in Galician-Portuguese, with lyrics about the miracles of the Virgin.

Dance music

Dancing was popular at all levels of medieval society. The steps and musical accompaniment varied with the social context, ranging from the formal, choreographed steps of court dance to the acrobatic leaps of the *jongleurs*. Dancing could also be a spontaneous pastime. A chronicler of the 12th century described a call for dancing between the jousts of a tournament: "Let us dance a carole while we wait here, that way we shall not be so bored." The carole was a sung dance performed in a circle, often with dancers holding hands.

Dance songs enlivened both court culture and more popular festivities. Though many were improvised, some songs survive in the *Robertsbridge Codex*, a 14th-century manuscript of *estampies*—dance music with repeated sections.

Music and dance
Minnesingers at the court of the Holy Roman Emperor enjoyed a high social status. This image is from the 14th-century *Codex Manesse*, which contains about 6,000 songs from 140 poets.

KEY WORKS

Bernart de Ventadorn "Quan vei la lauzeta mover" (When I See the Skylark Move)

Gace Brulé "A la douceur de la belle seson" (To the Sweetness of Summer)

Niedhart von Reuenthal "Meienzît" (May Time)

Alfonso X Cantiga No. 10, "Rosa das rosas" (Rose of Roses)

AFTER

The courtly monophonic song, with a single line of melody, cultivated by the troubadours and *trouvères*, gradually gave way to the polyphonic song for two or three voices.

SONGS FOR MANY VOICES

Adam de la Halle (*c.*1250–1288), one of the last *trouvères* and a prolific song composer, began to write **polyphonic rondels** **46–47 ››**, songs for a few people to sing together. Although monophonic songs were still composed and performed throughout the Middle Ages, polyphonic settings became more widely appreciated during the 14th century, especially in wealthier courts and cities. By the 1350s, the poet-composer **Guillaume de Machaut** **47 ››** had transformed dance songs into sophisticated polyphonic compositions.

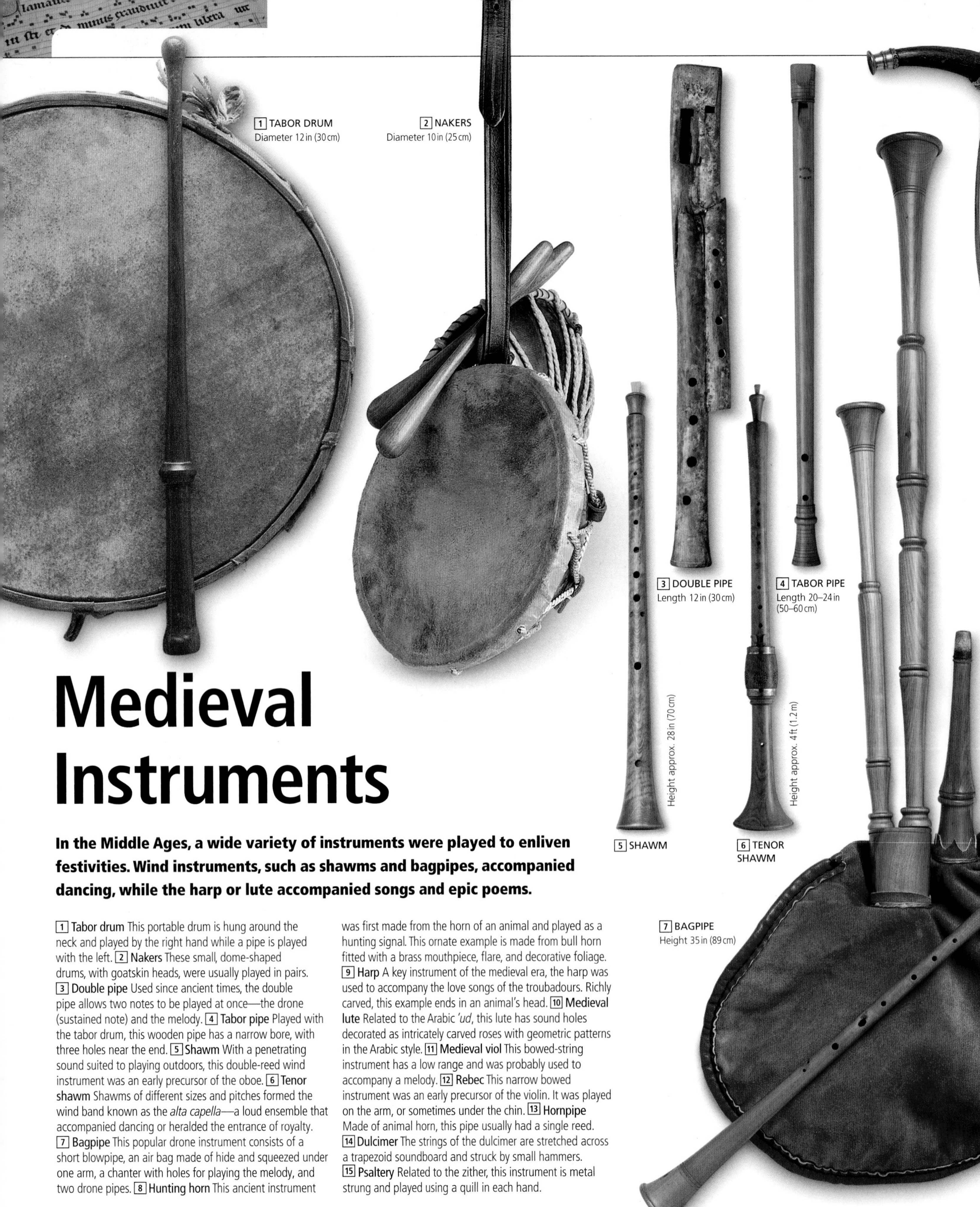

Medieval Instruments

In the Middle Ages, a wide variety of instruments were played to enliven festivities. Wind instruments, such as shawms and bagpipes, accompanied dancing, while the harp or lute accompanied songs and epic poems.

1 **Tabor drum** This portable drum is hung around the neck and played by the right hand while a pipe is played with the left. 2 **Nakers** These small, dome-shaped drums, with goatskin heads, were usually played in pairs. 3 **Double pipe** Used since ancient times, the double pipe allows two notes to be played at once—the drone (sustained note) and the melody. 4 **Tabor pipe** Played with the tabor drum, this wooden pipe has a narrow bore, with three holes near the end. 5 **Shawm** With a penetrating sound suited to playing outdoors, this double-reed wind instrument was an early precursor of the oboe. 6 **Tenor shawm** Shawms of different sizes and pitches formed the wind band known as the *alta capella*—a loud ensemble that accompanied dancing or heralded the entrance of royalty. 7 **Bagpipe** This popular drone instrument consists of a short blowpipe, an air bag made of hide and squeezed under one arm, a chanter with holes for playing the melody, and two drone pipes. 8 **Hunting horn** This ancient instrument was first made from the horn of an animal and played as a hunting signal. This ornate example is made from bull horn fitted with a brass mouthpiece, flare, and decorative foliage. 9 **Harp** A key instrument of the medieval era, the harp was used to accompany the love songs of the troubadours. Richly carved, this example ends in an animal's head. 10 **Medieval lute** Related to the Arabic *'ud*, this lute has sound holes decorated as intricately carved roses with geometric patterns in the Arabic style. 11 **Medieval viol** This bowed-string instrument has a low range and was probably used to accompany a melody. 12 **Rebec** This narrow bowed instrument was an early precursor of the violin. It was played on the arm, or sometimes under the chin. 13 **Hornpipe** Made of animal horn, this pipe usually had a single reed. 14 **Dulcimer** The strings of the dulcimer are stretched across a trapezoid soundboard and struck by small hammers. 15 **Psaltery** Related to the zither, this instrument is metal strung and played using a quill in each hand.

8 HUNTING HORN
Length approx. 20 in (50 cm)

9 HARP
Height approx. 26 in (66 cm)

10 MEDIEVAL LUTE
Height 25 in (70 cm)

11 MEDIEVAL VIOL
Height 24 in (62 cm)

12 REBEC
Height 22 in (55 cm)

13 HORNPIPE
Length approx. 16 in (40 cm)

14 DULCIMER
Length up to 28 in (70 cm)

15 PSALTERY
Length of longest side approx. 18 in (46 cm)

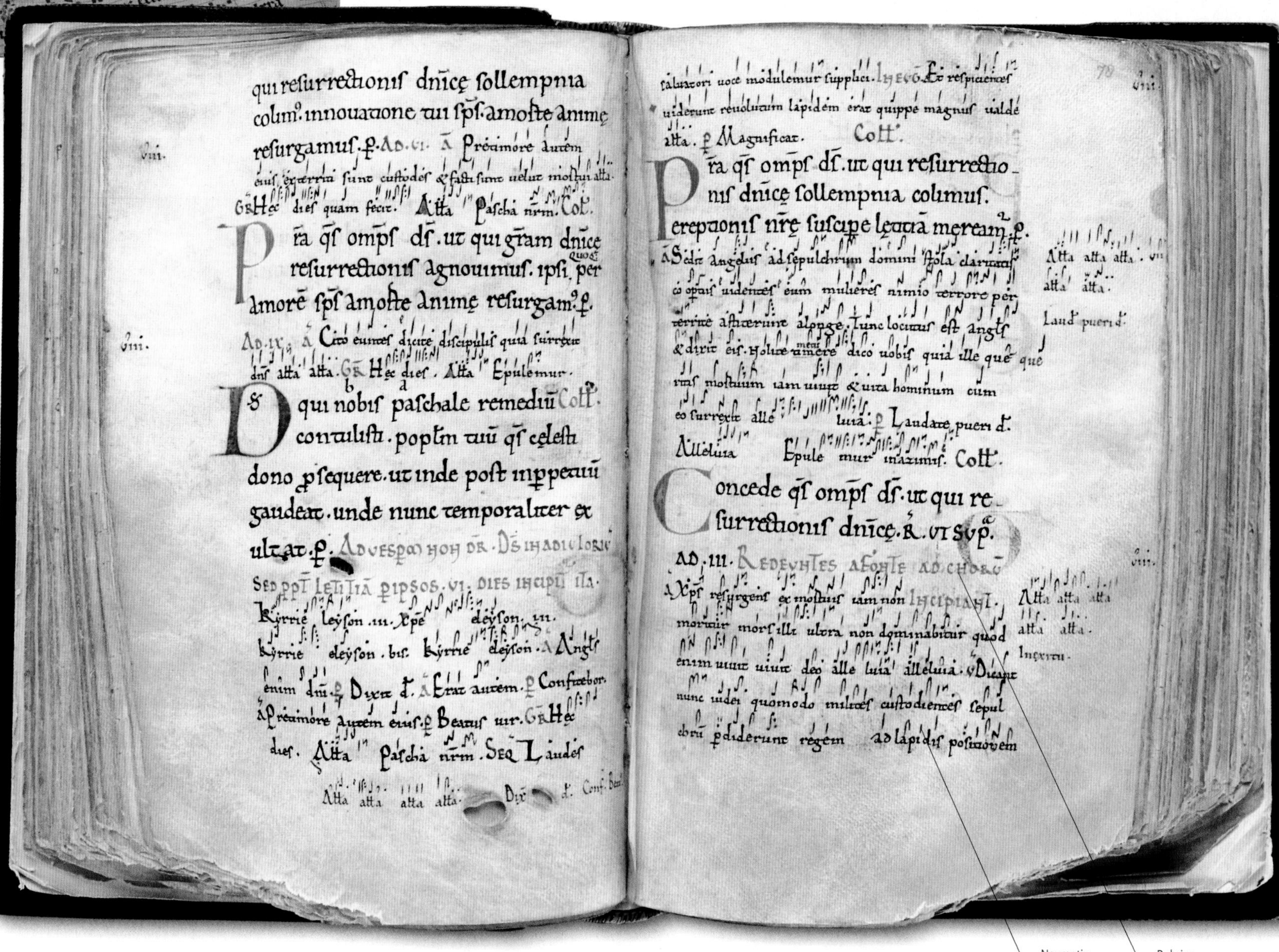

Chant notation
This musical manuscript appears in a book of liturgy and shows the notation of chant melodies. A variety of dots, lines, and squiggles above the lines of text suggested the general shape of the melody.

Writing Melody

Before musical notation, melodies were memorized or improvised. Manuscripts of early liturgical chants or lyric verse give only the texts, but gradually signs began to be added above the words and a means of notating music was developed.

BEFORE

Before the development of musical notation, music was passed on orally or improvised on the spot.

LEARNING LITURGIES
Songsters and minstrels « 32–33 learned their repertories by way of contractual apprenticeships, while those destined for a Church career began to learn and memorize liturgical chants at the choir schools attached to monasteries and cathedrals.

ROOM FOR INVENTION
Improvisatory skills remained important in all spheres. Dance music was improvised over simple **chord sequences** or melodic patterns. In sacred music, additional vocal lines were improvised over chant melodies.

In the early medieval Church, the clergy responsible for music in divine worship were faced with the problem of memorizing an ever-growing repertory of chant melodies that needed to be consistent throughout the monasteries of a specific order or the churches in a particular diocese.

Learning by heart

Studies have shown that the capacity for memorization in the Middle Ages was vast. Widespread illiteracy, and the fact that the production of manuscripts was confined to monasteries, meant that oral transmission of music was the norm. The task was daunting, as Odo (*c.*788–942), second Abbot of the Benedictine monastery of Cluny in France, explained: "No amount of time is enough to reach such perfection of study that we can learn even the smallest antiphon [response] without the labor of a master, and if we happen to forget it, there is no way in which we can recover our memory of it."

A series of signs (neumes), placed above the text, was developed to serve as a memory aid for the choirmasters and singers. Initially, these neumes were essentially inflective marks, a graphic representation of syllabic stress and the rise and fall of the voice, but gradually they became more sophisticated and could indicate quite complex groupings of notes.

The basic forms of the neumes were the dot (*punctum*), a vertical or oblique line (*virga*), and squiggles of diverse forms in which several pitches were bound together (ligatures). Different

> "They could sing **at first sight ...** and **without any mistake ...**"
>
> ANONYMOUS WRITER OF THE 11TH CENTURY, ON THE ADVANTAGES OF NOTATION

neumatic systems were developed in the various chant regions, but all increasingly tended to represent pitch through the height of the neumes.

The revolutionary stave

The use of heightened neumes to indicate relative pitch between one note and the next quite soon attracted the scribal device of a horizontal line, initially imagined in the copyist's eye and then represented by an inked line on the page.

In Italy, Guido of Arezzo had experienced firsthand in his monastery the difficulties faced by monks and clergy in memorizing the chant repertory. He devised a stave of four horizontal lines, an invention that proved to be a distinctive feature of the Western musical tradition and a huge leap for musical composition.

In addition to the accurate notation of pitch, the stave allowed for the clear alignment of simultaneously sounding pitches, which made it an important graphic tool for the notation of early polyphony. Guido claimed, justifiably, that his new system of musical notation would reduce the lifetime of study needed to learn the chant repertory to just two years, so that monks would have more time for prayer and other duties. Notation also meant that the chant melodies would remain "pure," since they could be clearly encoded through the use of the stave and correctly transmitted in written form, together with the corresponding liturgical texts.

POLYPHONY Two or more musical voices playing or singing independently of each other.

Guido also developed a teaching method in which he mapped pitches onto the human hand. His system of seven interlocking six-note scales (hexachords) described the entire gamut of the vocal range, with each note marked on a different part of the hand, starting with the bottom note on the thumb. When coaching musicians, Guido could point to the relevant joint to indicate the note to be sung.

Monastic manuscripts

The scriptoria of medieval monasteries, with their teams of highly trained scribes, were ideally placed to record chant melodies through notation. A particularly important center for the production of chant books using heightened neumes was the Benedictine abbey of St. Gall in Switzerland, founded in the first half of the 8th century. There the scribe and teacher Notker the Stammerer (*c.*840–912 CE), who was responsible for the copying of the liturgical books, compiled a large anthology of sequences (chants or hymns sung during the liturgy).

Another major center of scribal activity was the Benedictine abbey of Cluny in central France, founded in 909 by William of Aquitaine. The community at Cluny grew substantially during the 11th century, partly due to sizable donations from the kings of Leon and Castile in Spain. Cluniac foundations and influence stretched throughout Western Europe, from the Isle of Lewis in Scotland to northern Spain, and its manuscripts were distributed to other Cluniac houses.

A Cluny codex

The illuminated manuscript known as the *Codex Calixtinus*, preserved at the cathedral of Santiago de Compostela in northwest Spain, was probably copied in Cluny. Dating from the mid-12th century, the *Codex* was an anthology of sermons and liturgical texts for pilgrims. It contains monophonic melodies copied on a four-line stave, which is elegantly drawn in red ink, as well as early examples of two-voice polyphony notated on two vertically aligned staves.

Scribe at work
Monasteries were important centers of scribal production. Biblical and liturgical texts were made for use in the daily activities of the monastery and for distribution along the Order's network.

An illuminated initial G begins the "Gloria" of the Mass

Four-line stave in red ink

Decorated manuscript
This text and musical notation of the "Gloria" hymn, with a decorated initial "G," was produced by a professional scribe for St. Alban's abbey in England in the 12th century.

AFTER

Accurate musical notation paved the way for more complex compositions and musical innovation.

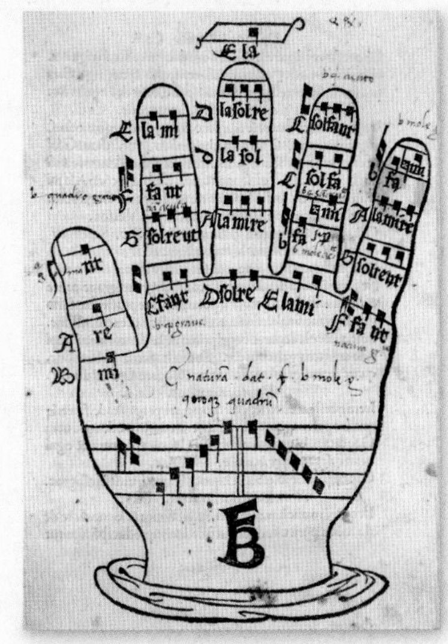

GUIDONIAN HAND IN A MUSICAL TREATISE (c.1500)

DOE A DEER
The six notes of Guido's scales were named after the **initial syllables** of the first verse of the hymn "Ut queant laxis": ut-re-mi-fa-so-la. "Ut" later changed to "do," and an extra note was added, now called "ti." Known as solmization (or **solfa**), the system is still widely used and features in the song "Do(e) a Deer" from the movie *The Sound of Music*.

GREATER COMPLEXITY
Toward the end of the 13th century, a system of **notating rhythm 46–47 ››** was developed by music theorists such as **Franco of Cologne** that enabled the composition of **more complex music.**

MUSICAL THEORIST (991–AFTER 1033)

GUIDO OF AREZZO

Guido of Arezzo is regarded as the inventor of modern notation through his use of a four-line stave, and of the hexachord system taught through the Guidonian Hand (see above right). He became a monk of the Benedictine order at the monastery of Pomposa near Ferrara. His reputation as a teacher was rapidly established, but the hostility this fame aroused in his fellow monks caused Guido to move to Arezzo, where he wrote his highly influential treatise on music entitled *Micrologus* in about 1025. His teaching method attracted the attention of Pope John XIX. It is thought Guido went to Rome at the Pope's invitation in 1028, but returned to Arezzo because of poor health. Nothing is known of him after 1033.

« **BEFORE**

Two key figures from mythology and the Bible achieved lasting fame for their musical prowess and were widely portrayed in the Middle Ages.

THE POWER OF MUSIC

In **Greek mythology « 20–21**, Orpheus and his lyre charmed wild beasts and conquered hell, showing music's power to move the heart of man. Singing to a plucked stringed instrument remained one of the most widespread forms of musical performance.

ORPHEUS IN A ROMAN MOSAIC

In the **Bible**, David soothed King Saul and praised God with psalms accompanied, in medieval depictions, by a host of angelic musicians playing all kinds of instruments.

Zither and **Lyre, Sackbut** and **Shawm**

Illuminated manuscripts, paintings, and carvings show that instrumental accompaniment for songs and dances was an integral part of the medieval sound world. Yet no one is certain exactly what combinations of instruments and voices were heard, or in which kinds of music.

Wandering minstrels and troubadours were expected to play a wide range of instruments (see pp.32–35), as is clear from an anonymous 13th-century poem: "I'll tell you what I can do: I'm a minstrel of the vielle [violin]; I can play the bagpipe and the flute and harp, symphonie [hurdy-gurdy] and fiddle; and on the psaltery and the rote [zither and lyre] I can sing a melody right well."

There seems little doubt that medieval instrumentalists prided themselves on their versatility, but it is difficult to reconstruct what kind of repertories were played on which instruments. Certain instrumental groupings were associated with specific functions or settings: *haut* (loud) instruments, such as shawms, sackbuts, trumpets, and drums, were used outdoors for street processions and dancing, to herald the royal presence, or to urge troops into battle. The role of the *bas* (soft) instruments, such as harps, lutes, rebecs, vielles, recorders, and flutes, was generally more intimate, to accompany songs and to provide background music or entertainment during banquets and other indoor gatherings.

Music for every occasion

In his *De musica* (*On Music*) of around 1300, French theorist Johannes de Grocheio expected instrumentalists not only to play a wide range of instruments but also to have a wide repertory: "A good fiddler generally performs every kind of *cantus* [Latin for song or melody] and *cantilena* [song or melody beginning and ending with a refrain], and every musical form." Throughout the medieval period, stringed instruments, both plucked and bowed, were used to accompany songs, especially the epic poems and ballads

TECHNOLOGY

METAL STRINGS

Stringed instruments were strung with a variety of materials in the Middle Ages, depending on where the instruments were made and what function they would have. Sheep-gut (also known as cat gut) was the most common, twisted into a fine string for bowed instruments, but silk and horsehair were also used.

Metal wire was used on some plucked and hammered instruments, for a louder sound. The metals used on metal-strung harps and psalteries were extremely valuable: brass, silver, and occasionally gold. Iron was available from the late 14th century, and the technique of twisting brass or iron was discovered in the mid-16th century.

Wheel cover

Key box

Drone string

Tangents (wooden keys)

Crank

Body acted as a resonating chamber

Hurdy-gurdy
The hurdy-gurdy is a mechanical instrument that produces sound by a crank-turned wheel rubbing against the strings. Some strings are drones, producing a continuous, unaltered pitch, while on others, melodies are played by pressing wooden keys.

A choir and musicians
This 15th century illumination from a manuscript copied for René II, Duke of Lorraine, shows a group of singers who appear to be accompanied by musicians playing the psaltery and rebec.

with strong storytelling elements. The anonymous mid-13th century *Romance of Flamenca* describes the proliferation of such performances: "What with the hum of the viula players and the noise of so many storytellers, the hall was full of sound." Traces of this repertory accompanied by the vihuela (a small guitar-shaped instrument similar to the lute) survive in the anthologies of vihuelists from 16th-century Spain.

Tablature

The introduction of the printing press in the latter part of the 15th century would transform how music was recorded and circulated (see pp.54–55). Tablature was another innovation that became widespread. This form of notation was based on letters or numbers that indicated finger placings on the frets along an instrument's neck. Until then, instrumental accompaniments tended to be learned by ear, committed to memory, and improvised at each new performance.

Tablatures seem to have evolved around the time that players of plucked string instruments such as the vihuela and the lute began to use their nails or fingertips instead of a plectrum or pick. These players could now read and perform arrangements of polyphonic pieces (see pp.46–47), and compose new and more complex works.

Instrumental ensembles

The long lists of instruments found in medieval poems and the angelic orchestras depicted in altarpieces and carvings suggested a symphonic scale of musical accompaniment that greatly appealed to the specialist ensembles of the 20th-century early music revival. In the 1960s and '70s, many of these groups were formed by virtuoso instrumentalists and arrangers keen to make what might seem relatively simple or repetitive music more interesting through kaleidoscopic instrumental scorings of surviving vocal works.

In reality, medieval ensembles such as the *alta capella* (bands that played shawms and slide-trumpets in courts and cities of continental Europe) were employed to accompany banquets and dancing but, it seems, rarely singers. Indeed, songs may often have been performed *a cappella* ("in church style") and therefore unaccompanied.

Instrumental groups varied from region to region. Wind bands of shawms, sackbuts, and dulcians found particular favor in Spain from at least the early 16th century, when groups of these instrumentalists became salaried employees of the great cathedrals.

Musical angels

In addition to regional variations, certain combinations of instruments may also have performed on certain occasions. For example, an ensemble of three or four *bas* instrumentalists, generally dressed as angels, took part in the annual Corpus Christi procession, as the host was carried through the streets. Yet little is known about exactly what kind of music these angelic musicians might have played on these important civic occasions. The same is true of the less formal groups of musicians who accompanied the medieval mystery, or miracle-plays—popular dramas that reenacted cycles of biblical stories, often on wagons as part of a procession.

These ensembles were usually made up of amateur musicians who had learned their skills informally. Professional instrumentalists often came from musical dynasties or contracted apprenticeships. Many players also attended the international minstrel schools held in northern Germany and Flanders in the years around 1400, at which techniques and repertory were exchanged. From dusty streets to courts and cathedrals, Europe was humming with continually evolving musical accompaniment.

City waits
Wind bands called waits were a familiar sight in medieval towns. Their duties grew from providing the night watchman's signal at daybreak to announcing royal entries and accompanying civic processions.

AFTER

New instruments and instrumental groupings soon widened the scope of musical accompaniment in the late 15th century.

NEW TECHNOLOGY

Improved metal working led to the invention of the slide trumpet so that players could achieve a greater range of notes by extending the tube length. The double-slide sackbut, an early form of the trombone, evolved to provide low notes in the wind ensembles that began to accompany **sacred polyphony in church** **46–47 ››**.

The advent of **music printing** in the 1470s **54–55 ››** created a demand for songs with instrumental accompaniment that could be performed by **amateurs at home**.

INSTRUMENTAL FAMILIES

As instrumentalists began to play polyphonic music, instruments of the same family were made in several sizes to form **consorts** (groups) **68–69 ››** with a wider range. The viol consort was a common example, playing music for three to seven parts, as were consorts of wind instruments, such as recorders or crumhorns.

در خلوت باز گردند که حالی طاری شده مطلقا اظهار نفرمودند

و کسی از ایشان هم خبر نکرد و در همان روز حضرت سلطان ابو سعید

در جمع درویشان ایشان بقوالی اشتغالی نمودند و سماع زدند

در میان آن سماع آن حال بر حضرت سلطان ابو سعید منکشف شد

اظهار فرمودند و رسم توبه از روی فقر بجای آوردند حضرت

شیخ ابو الحسن فرمودند که اینچنین ریشی را اینچنان مرهمی می بایست

Islamic Music

During the Middle Ages, the Islamic world stretched across the Middle East, the Far East, Africa, and Spain and absorbed many regional traditions. Attitudes to music were equally diverse and still shape many of the oral traditions handed down to the present day.

BEFORE

The birthplace of Islam, the Arabian peninsula in the Middle East, traced its music back to the Bible.

ARABIAN ROOTS
Pre-Islamic writers credited **Old Testament** figures with the **invention of music**: Jubal was the inventor of song and Lamech was the creator of the *'ud*, or *oud* (see pp.42–43).

As early as the 6th century CE Arabic poetry refers to instruments such as the lute, frame-drum, end-blown flute, and cymbals, and to contrasting musical styles—"heavy" and ornate or "light" and cheerful. Poets and composers were thought to be inspired by ***jinns* (spirits)**, but it was **women** who **sang** and **performed their music**.

COURT CULTURE
In the more affluent courts of the Umayyad dynasty in 7th-century Syria and the Abbasid dynasty in 9th-century Baghdad, poetry and music were indispensable.

Transcendent states
Dervishes and other Sufi ascetics chanted, drummed, and danced to reach a state of religious ecstasy. This miniature from a 16th-century Persian manuscript shows whirling dancers accompanied by musicians.

> "**Ecstasy** is the state that comes from **listening to music.**"
>
> PERSIAN THEOLOGIAN AL-GHAZALI (1059–1111), IN HIS "REVIVAL OF RELIGIOUS SCIENCES"

The muezzin's call to prayer and the recitation of the Qur'an dominate the Islamic sound world, but over the centuries attitudes to music have varied, largely because of its ambiguous status in Islamic law. From the 7th century CE, not long after the Prophet Muhammad's death, Islamic orthodoxy largely condemned music for its ability to arouse desire, grief, and other "base" passions. The use of instruments in devotional music was *haraam*, or forbidden, as was the participation of women.

Music as entertainment may have been condemned by Islamic law, but early scholars such as Al-Farabi and Ibn Sina (*c*.980–1037 CE), the 11th-century Persian known as Avicenna in the West, discussed the healing properties of music. In the Sufi tradition of Islam, whose followers were drawn to mysticism, writers in the 11th and 12th centuries defended listening to music as a spiritual exercise that could draw the listener nearer to the Divine.

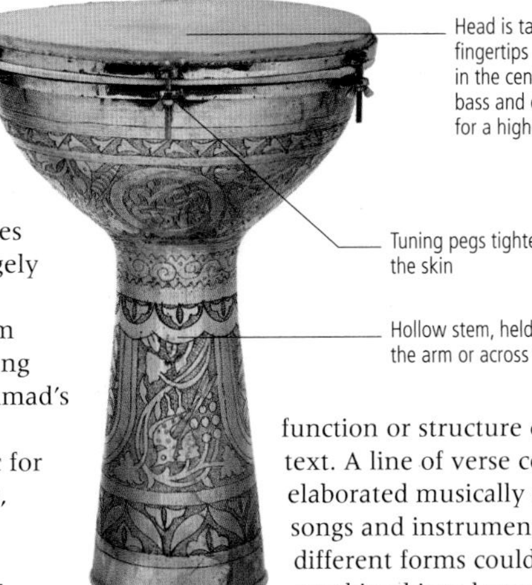

Dumbek drum
Widely used across the Middle East, North Africa, and Eastern Europe, goblet-shaped *dumbek* drums are traditionally made from clay, with a goatskin head. This ornate example in nickel is from Syria.

Musical patterns

As with the early, oral traditions of music in the West, music that was *halal*, or permitted, in the Islamic world was improvised around formulaic patterns, whether melodic or rhythmic. These musical building-blocks could be combined and repeated in different ways according to the function or structure of the text. A line of verse could be elaborated musically and, in songs and instrumental pieces, different forms could be combined into longer cycles known as *nawba*.

Drums and strings

The principal instrument of the Arab world was the *'ud* (see pp.42–43). This pear-shaped, short-necked, plucked-string instrument is the ancestor of the European lute (see pp.62–65) and has a fretted fingerboard. Arabic melodic modes, or groupings (known as *maqam*), related primarily to the frets on the *'ud*'s strings.

The *'ud* and other Arabic instruments such as the *rabāb* or *rebāb* (a simple bowed instrument) and the *naqqarā* (a pair of small drums) filtered along trade routes, through Muslim Spain into the Western music of medieval minstrels and troubadours (see pp.32–35).

Sufi music

Unlike orthodox Islam, Sufi devotional music included not only vocal pieces but instruments—such as reed-pipes, flutes, and drums—and dancing.

The most popular and enduring tradition of Sufi devotional music is *qawwali*, which originated in 8th-century Persia. This fused with Indian traditions by the late 13th century to create the form that is now known on the Indian subcontinent. Singers recite Sufi verses, ranging from love poetry to songs praising Allah and the Prophet Muhammad. All are seen as spiritual—the desire expressed in love poetry is interpreted as the longing for spiritual union with the Divine. Musical accompaniment includes the *sarangi* (a bowed string instrument), percussion instruments such as the *tabla* (a small drum) and *dholak* (a two-headed drum), and a chorus of four or five men who repeat key verses and add hand clapping to the percussion.

Qawwali musicians
These musicians are playing at Nizamuddin Dargah, the mausoleum of the Sufi saint Nizamuddin Auliya in Delhi, India, which is visited by thousands of Muslims and other pilgrims every week.

MUSICIAN (*c*.872–951 CE)

AL-FARABI

The philosopher, cosmologist, and musician Al-Farabi was born either in Kazakhstan or (according to some sources) in Afghanistan. He appears to have spent most of his life in Baghdad, although he is also known to have visited Egypt and Syria, where he died in Damascus in late 950 or early 951 CE. A leading intellectual in the golden age of Islam, Al-Farabi studied the writings of Aristotle, and is said to have invented the Arabic tone system that is still in use today. His *Great Book of Music* focused on Persian musical traditions, and in his *Meanings of the Intellect* he discussed the therapeutic qualities of music.

AFTER

From the 16th century, the more orthodox communities forbade instruments and dancing altogether, although other traditions flourished.

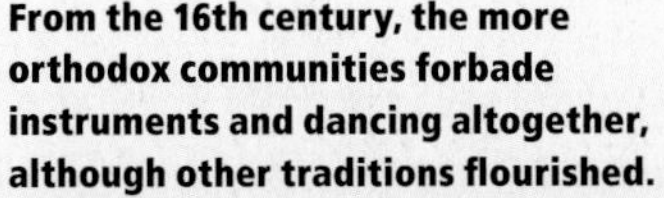

MALOUF MUSICIANS FROM LIBYA

CONQUEST AND DISPERSAL
The living Arabic musical genre of **malouf 366 ››** began in Andalusia in Spain under Islamic rule, and was displaced to **North Africa** after the 1492 reconquest of Spain. In the **Ottoman Empire** following the fall of Constantinople (now Istanbul, Turkey) in 1453, Eastern musical traditions diverged completely from Western, and Istanbul remains a hub of Islamic music. Court music continued to flourish in **Mogul India 340–43 ››** where Akbar the Great (1542–1605) had an orchestra of at least 50 musicians.

1 'UD
Height
28 in (70 cm)
2 ZITHER
Length of longest side 33 in (83 cm)
3 TĀR
Height 37 in (95 cm)
4 EGYPTIAN
REBĀB AND BOW
Height approx. 35 in
(90 cm)
Height 18–24 in (45–60 cm)
5 GIMBRI
Height 3 ft 4 in (1 m)
6 BAĞLAMA
Height approx. 28 in (70 cm)
7 ANDALUCIAN
REBĀB AND BOW

8 NAQQĀRA
Diameter 6 in (16 cm)

9 TAMBOURINE
Diameter approx. 12 in (30 cm)

10 MOROCCAN REBĀB

11 KAMANJAH
Height approx. 28 in (70 cm)

12 MOROCCAN REBĀB
Height approx. 24 in (60 cm)

13 ZUMMARĀ

14 SORNA

15 DUMBEK

16 DARABUKA

Islamic Instruments

The wide range of regional musical traditions of the Islamic world is reflected in the variety of instruments that developed from North Africa to East Asia in the Middle Ages. Most are still played in traditional music today.

1 'Ud The most important instrument in the Islamic world, the 'ud, with its pear-shaped soundboard, influenced the development of the lute. 2 Zither This instrument is set up for 72 gut strings grouped in threes, although several are missing. Commonly heard in Eastern Asia, the zither can be played on the lap or on a table. 3 Tār This Persian plucked-string instrument has a horn bridge and a wooden neck inlaid with bone. Its sound was believed to relieve headaches and insomnia. 4 Egyptian rebāb and bow A bowed instrument made from wood and animal skin, it is still played in Southern Egypt. 5 Gimbri Of Moroccan origin, this lutelike instrument has a tortoise-shell resonator and accompanies singing and clapping. 6 Bağlama Carved from a single piece of hardwood, the baglama has a giraffelike neck and a deep round back, and contributed to the distinctive sound of court music in the Ottoman Empire. 7 Adalucian rebāb and bow Having influenced the development of the medieval rebec, it can be considered an ancestor of the violin. 8 Naqqarā The rounded section of this kettle drum is made from baked clay over which a treated animal skin is fastened. 9 Tambourine Decorated with bone and ebony, this Egyptian instrument has five sets of brass disks. 10 Moroccan rebāb This plucked-string instrument is made from hollowed-out wood covered with a camel skin. 11 Moroccan rebāb Although the Arabic word "rebāb" means "bowed," this *rebāb* is played in Afghanistan and Pakistan, where it is generally plucked. 12 Kamanjah This Turkish spiked fiddle is played with a bow and has a wooden resonator with skins on both sides. 13 Zummara This reed instrument has two pipes, one of which is sounded as a drone. 14 Sorna Still played in Iran and Azerbaijan, this double-reed instrument is similar to the shawm. 15 Dumbek This drum has a distinctive, chalicelike shape and is generally made of ceramic or metal. 16 Darabuka Essentially the same as a *dumbek*, this is a particularly beautiful and ornate example.

Music in Ancient China

Music has always held a central place in Chinese culture. The Tang dynasty of 618–907 CE saw the Golden Age of music, but traces of popular theater involving dance, song, comedy, acrobatics, and puppetry still survive in Chinese opera today.

BEFORE

A CAMEL CARAVAN ON THE SILK ROAD

Over thousands of years, as ruling dynasties rose and fell, China absorbed many musical influences.

FROM BAMBOO TO BUDDHISM

Legend has it that long ago the music master of the **Yellow Emperor Huangdi** cut bamboo tubes to form 12 perfect pitches to echo the birdsong of the fabled phoenix. **Buddhism**, a new religion from India, spread eastward **along the Silk Road** through Central Asia and reached China in the 1st and 2nd centuries CE. With it came new musical repertory and instruments, such as the lute and harp. After 300 years of uprisings, China reunited under the **Tang dynasty** in 618 CE, and music reached new heights.

According to the ancient Chinese philosopher Confucius (*c.*551–479 BCE), "to educate somebody, you should start with poems, emphasize ceremonies, and finish with music." The centrality of state ceremonial in Confucian and Daoist teaching meant that music had a complex ritual function. By the time of the Tang dynasty, there were ten different bodies of musicians at court, including the Office of Grand Music and the Office of Drum and Wind Music. Elaborate rituals were developed for military exercises and religious sacrifices. Banquet music (*yanyue*) entertained guests with extended suites (*daqu*) that included dances made up of five or six movements, each differently choreographed, and even longer instrumental suites for the revered Chinese zither, the *qin*.

Diverse musical traditions flourished outside the court, and court music was often influenced by the folk traditions of song, instrumental music, and dance that successive emperors made a point of collecting. Many of the instruments used in early court music are still played in folk music today.

After the Golden Age

When the last Tang emperor was assassinated, China split apart once more. Yet elements of Tang ritual music survived, notably a syllabic singing style and ceremonial bell chimes, and scholars preserved the ancient traditions. In the great intellectual revival under the Song dynasty (960–1279), Chen Yang presented his 200-volume *Yueshu* (Book of Music) to the emperor around 1100, and later Zhu Xi (*c.*1130–1200), the creator of neo-Confucianism, published what he took to be Tang melodies for 12 texts from the ancient *Shijing* (Book of Songs).

While long-held traditions were maintained, major developments occurred in song composition. Classical *shi* (lyric poetry) was combined with more popular traditions, and shorter pieces were grouped into longer suites,

Music fit for a feast

These elegantly dressed women are members of a court banquet orchestra, playing at an imperial feast depicted in a tenth-century painting from the Tang dynasty.

Sheng players
The *sheng* is a mouth-blown reed instrument, similar to a mouth organ with long vertical pipes. It is one of the oldest Chinese instruments and is traditionally played with the *suona* (shawm) and *dizi* (flute) in outdoor festivities.

"Music is joy... This is why men **cannot do without** music."

CONFUCIAN PHILOSOPHER XUN ZI, 312–230BCE

particularly in the song form called the *changzhuan*, which was performed to the accompaniment of drum, flute, and clappers. One of the few early Chinese poet-composers whose life can be documented in some detail is Jiang Kui (1155–1221). A calligrapher by training, he composed a number of songs, some of which—for example, the "Song of Yangzhou"—are still popular today. He also discussed the tuning of the *qin* instrument in *Ding xian fa* (Tuning strings method) and transcribed his melodies using a notation method known as *gongche*. The vocal traditions cultivated during the Song dynasty, with melodies being subject to variation and then joined together to form longer works, continued to flourish in the Yuan (1279–1368) and Ming (1368–1644) dynasties.

The Mongols, who began their attack on China under the leadership of Genghis Khan in 1215 and eventually formed the Yuan dynasty, established huge ritual orchestras made up of more than 150 musicians. This sumptuous scale continued under the Ming dynasty and spilled over into the development of Chinese opera.

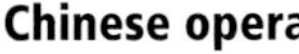

Chinese lute
The *yueqin* is a traditional Chinese lute with a round, hollow body—giving rise to the nickname "moon guitar"—and has four strings and a fretted neck.

Chinese opera

During the Tang dynasty, the Emperor Xuanzong (685–762 CE) had created a theater troupe known as the "Pear Garden." In the Song dynasty, enormous theaters capable of holding audiences of up to 3,000 people had staged variety acts that included song, dances, and comedy sketches.

These lavish entertainments formed the basis of a new kind of music theater in the Ming era—operas that elaborated heroic themes from China's past. The new genre was so popular that officials constantly sought to control it and even attempted to ban performances by threatening the actors with the death penalty.

There were hundreds of regional variations in Chinese opera, but the dominant form of the 16th–18th centuries was the *Kunqu* of southern China. This form emerged in the 14th century, early in the Ming dynasty, from a specific kind of melody known as the Kunshan *diao*. *Kunqu* would in turn influence the world-famous Peking opera (see pp.198–199), but by the early 20th century, it had all but disappeared, although it is now enjoying something of a revival.

China has long had a huge variety of instruments, in both popular and art music, and some types of instrument from ancient times are still used in traditional music, including Chinese opera. The *sheng* is a reed instrument with 19 pipes, and examples made as long ago as the 8th century still survive. It was a prominent instrument in *Kunqu* music theater, as was the *xiqin*—a fiddle with two silk strings, played with a thin strip of bamboo, which is a distant relative of the fiddle played in Chinese opera today.

Instrument of the sages

One of Ancient China's most distinctive instruments is the *guqin* or *qin*. Scholars were expected to master four art forms: calligraphy, painting, chess, and the *qin*. Known as "the father of Chinese music," this seven-string zither was so central to Chinese culture that *qin* schools were founded from at least the 11th century, and its music was copied in a special tablature—a form of notation for fingering rather than notes.

9,000 **YEARS OLD The age of the world's oldest playable flute, found in China and made from the bone of a crane.**

The *qin* is played in a different manner from Western stringed instruments. Instead of its strings of twisted silk being pressed down, or stopped, by the fingers to produce different notes, they are lightly touched, or dampened, to produce the different harmonics, or overtones, of each note. The Confucian love of systems of numbering is reflected in the so-called Twenty-Four Touches, or ways of playing vibrato to slightly vary the pitch. Often richly decorated, the finest examples of the *qin* were prized by the Chinese elite as collectable objects.

KEY WORKS

Zhu Xi *Shijing* (Book of Songs)
Jiang Kui "Song of Yangzhou"
Yang Zuan Qin anthology *Purple Cloud Cave*
Zhu Quan Qin anthology *Manual of the Mysterious and the Marvellous*
Tang Xianhu *Kunqu* opera *The Peony Pavilion*

Musicians and dancers
In the Yungang Buddhist grottoes, 252 cave chapels carved in the 5th and 6th centuries CE, these painted sculptures of musicians and dancers decorate the walls of Cave 12.

AFTER

Respect for China's musical heritage did not prevent significant advances in music theory and practice.

MUSIC FROM MING TO QING

Ming prince Zhu Zaiyu (1536–1611) is famous for his pioneering description of the **equal temperament**—a tuning system in which the 12 notes of the octave are all tuned in exactly the same ratio to one another. This is the system most commonly used, since the late 19th century, to **tune instruments in Western classical music** so that they can be played in any key. Zhu Zaiyu's concept preceded European theory by several decades and was possibly transmitted to Europe by Jesuit missionaries, such as Matteo Ricci. Under the Qing dynasty (1644–1911), ***GONGCHE***, a Chinese form of **NOTATION**, became the most widespread of several forms in use across the country. Although less popular now, it still appears in sheet music for traditional instruments and operas.

UNDERSTANDING MUSIC

CHINESE MODES

Early in the 7th century CE, during the Tang dynasty, a system of 84 classified modes, or groupings of notes, was approved by the emperor, with seven possible modes beginning on each of the 12 different pitches.

The 84 modes were not thought of as scales, or step-by-step sequences of notes as in Western music. They related to certain instruments' strictly regulated position in performance and had a strong functional identity. Later, the number of modes was reduced, and although Chinese music theory continued to refer to 12 fixed pitches, the actual pitches varied over time.

CHINESE MODE OF FIVE PITCHES, STARTING ON *GONG*, OR C IN WESTERN NOTATION

Many Voices

When musical notation made it possible to represent not just pitch but rhythm, too, it paved the way for polyphony. This new style of richly layered and rhythmically complex music for multiple voices altered Western music forever.

Patron of polyphony

In this 15th-century miniature, Philip the Good, Duke of Burgundy, listens to a mass sung in the court chapel, with singers gathered around the lectern. His court became the musical center of Europe.

Many of the innovations that would establish the course of music history in the West are found in the 13th-century polyphonic repertory of the so-called Notre Dame School in Paris.

The Cathedral of Notre Dame de Paris was completed in about 1250 and the polyphonic music composed to solemnify the liturgy celebrated there was gathered in the *Magnus liber organi* (Great Book of Organum). This impressive anthology not only contains works by the first named composers of polyphony—Léonin and Pérotin—but also includes pieces written using the newly devised system of notating rhythm: the organization of groups of notes into clearly defined rhythmic patterns called modes.

At first, polyphonic music was only written down in triple time (three beats in a bar), stressing the first beat. By the 14th century a way to notate duple time (two beats in a bar) had emerged, a breakthrough explained in Philippe de Vitry's *Ars nova notandi* (A New Art of Writing Music).

A new art

The tenor, which at first formed the lowest voice in the vocal texture, drove the structure of the piece, and was usually based on an existing melody, drawn from the plainchant for a particular feast or occasion. The tenor part was often organized into repeating patterns, both rhythmic and melodic, known as isorhythm. A second voice was then added above the tenor to form a two-voice piece, a third for a three-voice piece, and so on. These additional voices sang different texts, often secular and in Latin or French, which generally related to or commented on the sacred Latin text of the tenor. They had to be harmonious with the tenor, but not always with each other, resulting in harmonic clashes

> "Just hearing music makes people **rejoice.**"
>
> COMPOSER GUILLAUME DE MACHAUT, 1372

KEY WORKS

Pérotin *Sederunt principes* (For Princes Sat)

Guillaume de Machaut *Messe de Notre Dame* (Mass of Notre Dame)

Jacob Senleches *La harpe de mélodie*

John Dunstable *Alma redemptoris mater* (Sweet Mother of the Redeemer)

Guillaume Dufay *Missa Se la face ay pale* (If My Face Seems Pale)

Josquin Desprez *De profundis* (From the Depths)

BEFORE

For centuries, Western music had been monophonic, with a single melodic line. Between 700 and 900, a second line was added to plainchant.

ROOTS IN IMPROVISATION

Known as *organum,* early forms of polyphony were improvised, not written down. The added voices duplicated the chant melody at a different pitch and moved in parallel, note for note. The rules for composing *organum* appear in a late 9th-century French treatise, *Musica enchiriadis*, suggesting polyphony was already an established practice. Guido of Arezzo's **invention of the stave** **« 36–37** in the 10th century led to more accurate notation of pitch. By around 1100, the added voices began to move more freely and independently.

COMPOSER (*c.*1300–1377)

GUILLAUME DE MACHAUT

Born in Champagne, northern France, Machaut was appointed a canon of Reims Cathedral in 1337, where his duties included singing the Offices and Mass. His patrons were King John of Bohemia, Charles of Navarre, Charles V of France, and Jean, Duke of Berry, for whom, toward the end of his life, he compiled several anthologies of his compositions. His works include the first cyclic mass and numerous polyphonic motets and chansons.

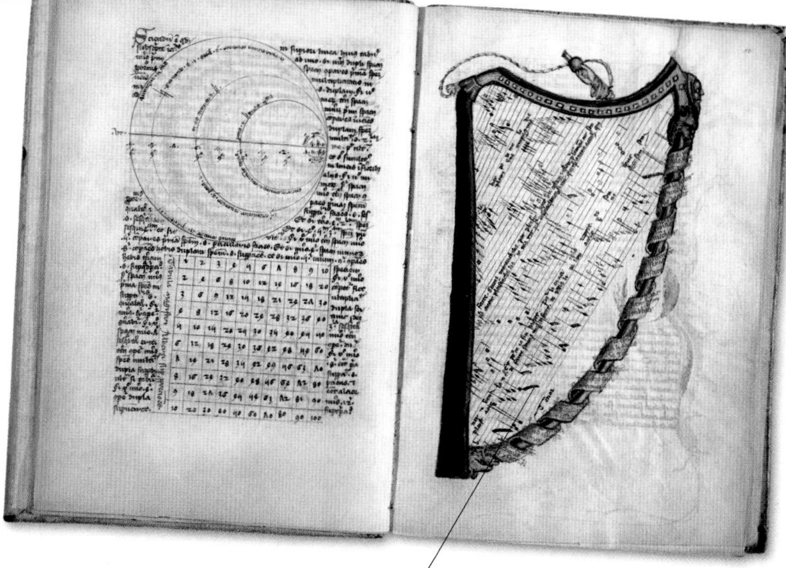

Notation on the strings

The Harp of Melody
In this manuscript of Jacob Senleches's *La harpe de mélodie*, two of the voices are notated on the harp's strings, while the scroll around the column explains how to create a third.

that sound distinctly modern even today. Polyphony called for great skill and subtlety on the part of the performers, and made considerable demands on the listener, too. It also required the substantial financial commitment of patrons—wealthy individuals and city guilds and corporations who commissioned new works (see pp.84–85).

Patterns and refrains

The *Ars Nova* culminated in the works of Guillaume de Machaut (see left) who composed in every form and style available to the 14th-century poet-composer. He established several new secular song forms, each with its own rules and pattern of repeated verses and refrains. An Italian *Ars Nova* evolved in parallel, spearheaded by the Florentine composer Francesco Landini, while a third way, the *Ars Subtilior* (More Subtle Art) developed among the musicians who clustered around the papal court in Avignon, where composers such as Jacob Senleches exploited the potential of polyphonic notation to create works of great sophistication. Mathematically complex structures and polyphonic settings involving different texts persisted into the early 15th century, but a new trend toward simpler vocal textures and harmonies spread through Europe with the circulation of works by the English composer John Dunstable (1395–1453). He championed the use of consonant harmonies that give a sense of resolution rather than dissonance and tension. Composers associated with the powerful Duke of Burgundy's court, such as Gilles Binchois (1400–1460) and Guillaume Dufay (1397–1474), incorporated Dunstable's "sweet harmonies" to produce a polyphonic style that spread across Europe—notably to Italy where rival princes and patrons vied for the best musicians from north of the Alps.

1322 The year in which Pope John XXII banned the use of polyphony in the liturgy, although the "devil's music" was tolerated by most of his papal successors.

Masses and motets

Binchois and Dufay cultivated the secular and sacred polyphonic genres established by Machaut. Particularly important in this period was the cyclic mass, which used a plainchant or secular melody in the structural voice (usually the tenor) to link the five sections of the mass: the Kyrie, Gloria, Credo, Sanctus, and Agnus Dei. This linking device was known as the *cantus firmus*, or "fixed melody."

By the second half of the 15th century, such cycles were generally composed in four voice parts, with the fourth voice below the tenor. Mass settings by Ockeghem, Busnois, Obrecht, La Rue, Josquin, and many other Franco-Netherlandish composers used complex devices such as the canon (in which one voice repeats another after a short space of time, as in a round) and imitation (in which a short phrase sung in one voice is copied in the other voices) to create large-scale works of astounding beauty.

In addition to masses, shorter pieces known as motets were composed. At first these used existing melodies in the manner of the cyclic mass, but by the 16th century they were being composed more freely, with each phrase of the text corresponding to a musical phrase. This, too, was seen as a "new art" and reflected the growing awareness of the importance of a close relationship between music and words.

Notre Dame, Paris
With soaring gothic architecture and spectacular stained glass, the great cathedral of Notre Dame (Our Lady), built in 1163–1250, mirrors the dazzling new complexity of its school of polyphony.

AFTER

In the age of Humanism, when Man and his emotions became central to art, musicians sought a closer relationship between text and music.

GOLDEN AGE OF POLYPHONY

By the 16th century, a coherent European style of polyphony had emerged—partly thanks to the invention of the **printing press**, which allowed for the widespread dissemination of music **54–55 ››**.

At the same time, the religious reforms of Martin Luther and the Council of Trent **58–59 ››** placed new emphasis on a style of music that allowed greater textual clarity. Renaissance polyphony peaked in the 16th century in the works of **Josquin des Prez** and **Palestrina** **60–61 ››**.

JOSQUIN DES PREZ

3

RENAISSANCE AND REFORMATION

1400–1600

While this period saw huge growth in the quality and style of sacred music, the Renaissance witnessed the Catholic Church's influence wane with the Reformation. The arrival of printed music made it available to people outside the Church, and musicians were able to learn from other traditions. The rise of instrumental music inspired composers to write more complex sacred and secular music and demanded new techniques and sounds.

« Cello made by Andrea Amati in 1538 and decorated for King Charles IX of France.

RENAISSANCE AND REFORMATION 1400–1600

1400

1400
The music of the *Old Hall Manuscript*—a large collection of sacred polyphony—shows that English composers are beginning to develop a distinctive, simpler style.

c.1400
Birth of Gilles Binchois, one of the great Franco-Flemish composers of the 15th century; at the Duke of Burgundy's court, he will create sacred works and *chansons* (songs in French) that are miniature masterpieces of the early Renaissance.

1410
Johannes Ockeghem is born; for much of his 80 years, this remarkable composer will be at the forefront of developments in Franco-Flemish polyphony—music with several independent voices, or parts, that are performed simultaneously.

1420

c.1430
The earliest known diagram of a harpsichord is drawn by the Dutch physician, astronomer, and astrologer Henri Arnaut de Zwolle, who studied with Jean de Fusoris, instrument-maker to Philip the Good, Duke of Burgundy. Keyboard music survives from before this time, although no instrument is specified.

≈ Florence, Italy—regarded as the birthplace of the Renaissance

» An early music printing press, depicted in a French songbook

1434
Cosimo de Medici, head of the richest bank in Florence, gains political control of the city-state. Under the Medici dynasty, the arts flourish and the city commissions countless new works of music for church and civic ceremonies.

1436
The great Franco-Flemish composer Guillaume Dufay writes a motet (choral work) for the consecration of Florence Cathedral, using its architectural proportions as the structural basis for his composition.

1440

c.1440
Dufay serves at Cambrai Cathedral in northern France and develops the choir school as a major training ground for composers. Ockeghem, Tinctoris, and Obrecht all study with Dufay.

1441
Burgundian court poet Martin Le Franc recognizes the importance of English composer John Dunstable and praises Binchois and Dufay for cultivating the sonorous "English style."

1450
In Germany, Johannes Gutenberg invents the printing press, which uses movable metallic type to produce books more quickly and cheaply than copying books by hand. It takes 50 years for the new technology to be adapted to print music.

1453
Constantinople, Byzantium's capital, falls to the Muslim Turks.

1454
Music patron Philip the Good, Duke of Burgundy, holds his Feast of the Pheasant to promote a crusade against the Turks. The lavish spectacle includes 24 musicians inside a giant pie.

1460

1467
Composer Antoine Busnois joins the Burgundian court, where he writes a mass based on the song melody "The Armed Man" for the Order of the Golden Fleece—an order of knights founded by the Duke of Burgundy.

c.1472
Flemish composer Johannes Tinctoris moves to Naples, where he writes a number of treatises on music—including the first ever dictionary of music in 1475.

≈ Musicians singing to a lute, by Lorenzo Costa, c.1485–1495

1480

1489
As Italian princes and cardinals vie for the services of Franco-Flemish composers, the most celebrated of them all, Josquin Desprez, joins the papal choir in Rome.

1490
Isabella d'Este marries the Duke of Mantua. Under her patronage music flourishes—particularly the *frottola*, an Italian song form often accompanied by the lute.

« Treble lute with ivory veneer, from northern Italy

1492
Sponsored by the Spanish crown, explorer Christopher Columbus reaches the Americas. Shiploads of silver from this "New World" will bankroll the Spanish Empire and its cathedrals and choirs for the next century.

Renaissance music spans two centuries, from the early polyphonic works of Binchois, Dufay, and Dunstaple to the first experiments with opera in Florence, Italy, around the year 1600. Church reform had a profound impact on 16th-century musical developments, as did the advent of music printing. Musical repertory and new instrumental techniques became more accessible to amateur musicians outside church and court. Composers became increasingly aware of the expressive power of music, especially when writing vocal music, and sought to find structures and styles that would reflect more closely the meaning of the texts they set.

1500

1501
In Venice, Ottaviano Petrucci is the first to print a book of polyphony—*Harmonice musices odhecaton*, containing 96 *chansons*—using metallic type. The new technology revolutionizes the way music is disseminated and boosts amateur musical activities.

1507
Petrucci is the first to print instrumental music, with Francesco Spinacino's two volumes of lute music using tablature—notation that indicates the position of the fingers on the frets of the lute.

c. 1509
Music scribe Petrus Alamire of Antwerp is employed by Charles V. His workshop produces beautifully illuminated music manuscripts as princely gifts, which preserve a vast repertory that might otherwise be lost.

1516
Charles V accedes to the Spanish throne. He brings the renowned chapel of Franco-Flemish singers from the Burgundian court, who will influence the Golden Age of Spanish polyphony.

A rauschpfeife, played in wind-instrument consorts in the 16th century

1517
German monk Martin Luther's 95 theses initiate a period of church reform that will give birth to Protestantism and have a profound impact on sacred music in the 16th century.

1520

1521
Death of Josquin Desprez. His works are highly influential in the equal balance given to polyphonic voices.

1524
Martin Luther contributes to the first collection of Protestant hymns—known as the *Wittenberg Echiridion*—which provides texts in everyday German rather than Latin.

1527
Parisian music printer Pierre Attaingnant prints a collection of *Chansons Nouvelles* in a single impression, using type that combines notes and staves. This technical advance makes music printing faster and cheaper.

Petrarch's sonnets to his beloved Laura inspired madrigal composers

1530
French composer Philippe Verdelot publishes his first book of madrigals. Combining elements of the French *chanson* and Italian *frottola*, the madrigal rapidly achieves popularity across Europe.

1539
Jacques Arcadelt's first book of madrigals is a huge success.

1540

1542
Venetian recorder virtuoso Silvestro Ganassi publishes a treatise on the art of ornamentation, catering to the Renaissance craze for adding the performer's own improvised embellishments to a melody.

1545
The Council of Trent meets, driving the Counter-Reformation that will overhaul Catholic liturgy and music.

1548
Birth of Tomás Luis de Victoria, who will become one of Spain's greatest composers of sacred music in the Renaissance—alongside Cristóbal Morales and Francisco Guerrero.

1550
In the English Reformation, John Merbecke's *Booke of Common Praier Noted* becomes the standard setting for the Anglican liturgy.

1551
Palestrina, a major composer of the Italian Renaissance, is appointed choirmaster in the papal chapel by Pope Julius III, to whom he dedicates his *First Book of Masses*.

1553
The development of a highly virtuoso instrumental style is reflected in another treatise on ornamentation, Spanish composer Diego Ortiz's *Tratado de glosas*.

Violin from the Amata workshop in Cremona, Italy, c.1550.

1558
In Venice, Adriano Willaert's *Musica nova* shows the way for polychoral antiphony, using several groups of contrasted voices.

1560

1562
The Council of Trent excludes from the Catholic Church "all music tainted with sensual and impure elements." Rome now insists on simpler, syllabic settings that make the words as clear as possible.

1562
The complete *Geneva Psalter* provides simple settings for all 150 psalms.

1567
Birth of Italian composer Claudio Monteverdi, whose choral and operatic masterpieces will bridge Renaissance and Baroque music.

1573
In Florence, a group of scholars, musicians, and writers known as the Camerata first meets. Their interest in Ancient Greek drama leads to the *stile recitativo* (imitating speech rhythms instead of melody) in solo song and, later, the birth of opera.

1580

Bagpipes accompany a peasant dance, painted by Bruegel the Elder, *c.*1569

1588
The vogue for Petrarch's poetry at court in Elizabethan England leads to the publication of Nicholas Yonge's *Musica Transalpina*, which provides English texts for madrigals by Italian composers.

1589
Orchésographie—a French encyclopedia of dance, steps, and music—is one of several Renaissance anthologies that reflect the passion for dance at all levels of society.

Dowland's *First Booke of Songes*, for a consort of singers and musicians to share

1597
The art of singing to a lute accompaniment is taken to new heights by English lutenist and composer John Dowland, who publishes his *First Booke of Songes* in a large, table-book format.

BEFORE

Simple melodies have been sung since time immemorial, but the rise of songs for several voices in the late Middle Ages radically transformed the repertoire.

SONGS FOR MANY VOICES

Sacred polyphony **« 46–47** found full voice in the 12th century in church music for two or three different voices, or parts. The pioneer of **secular polyphony** was French poet-composer **Guillaume de Machaut** (1300–1377), who set three forms of lyric verse in polyphony. Known as *formes fixes*, these were each based on a set repetition of a refrain and a number of verses, and were adopted by other composers.

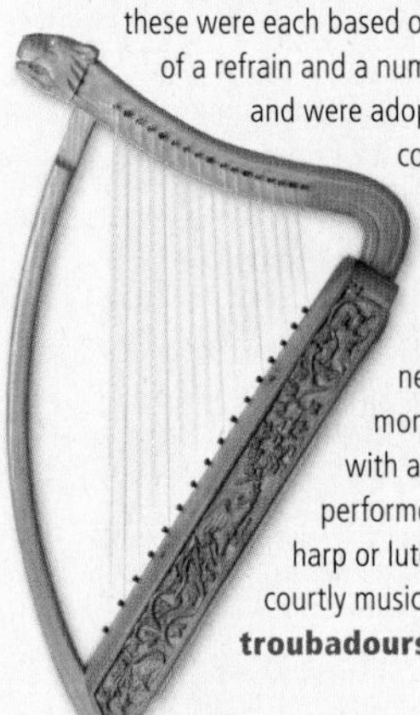

COURTLY MUSIC

Alongside the new polyphony, monophonic songs with a single part were performed, often with a harp or lute, as in the courtly music of the **French troubadours** **« 32–33**.

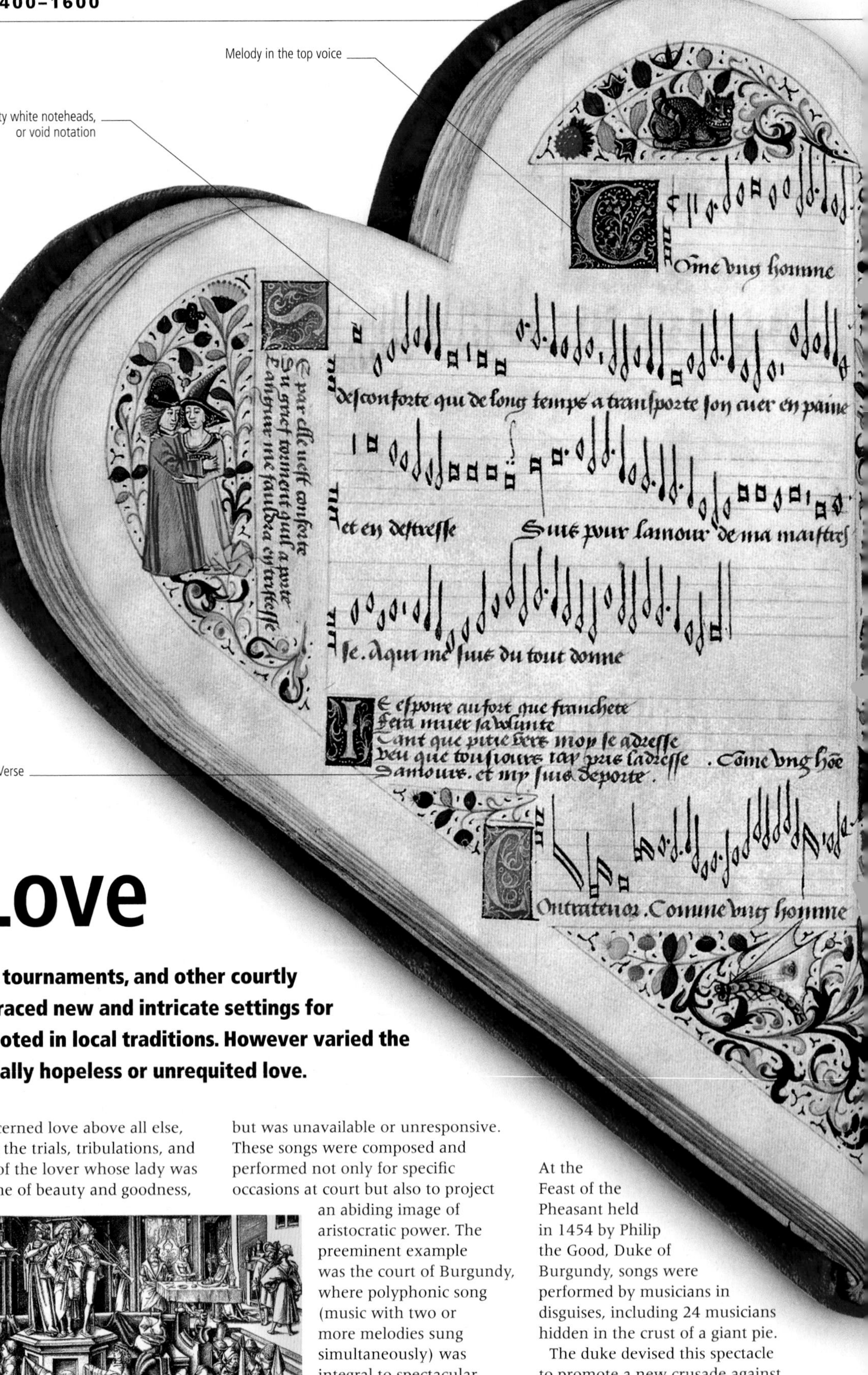

MEDIEVAL HARP

Melody in the top voice

Empty white noteheads, or void notation

Verse

Songs of Love

Performed at banquets, royal entrances, tournaments, and other courtly entertainments, Renaissance songs embraced new and intricate settings for several parts as well as simpler forms rooted in local traditions. However varied the music, its chief subject was love—especially hopeless or unrequited love.

In his *Book of the Courtier* (1528), the Italian courtier, soldier, diplomat, and author Baldassarre Castiglione revealed the importance of song in court culture. He states that every self-respecting courtier should be able to take part in singing, and preferably accompany himself or others on the lute. At the very least, he should be familiar with the substantial repertoire of songs performed in court circles and quote from them as part of witty and entertaining conversation.

Since the time of the medieval troubadours (see pp.32–33), lyric verse written and set to music at court concerned love above all else, describing the trials, tribulations, and torments of the lover whose lady was the epitome of beauty and goodness, but was unavailable or unresponsive. These songs were composed and performed not only for specific occasions at court but also to project an abiding image of aristocratic power. The preeminent example was the court of Burgundy, where polyphonic song (music with two or more melodies sung simultaneously) was integral to spectacular ceremonial occasions.

Courtly entertainment
Israhel van Meckenem's engraving of c.1500 places the Bible story of King Herod in a Renaissance setting. Three instrumentalists accompany the courtiers' stately dance.

At the Feast of the Pheasant held in 1454 by Philip the Good, Duke of Burgundy, songs were performed by musicians in disguises, including 24 musicians hidden in the crust of a giant pie.

The duke devised this spectacle to promote a new crusade against the Turks, who had captured Constantinople (modern-day Istanbul) the year before. The French song "L'homme armé" (The Armed Man") became a rallying cry for the crusade and was used as the basis for several Mass settings that were commissioned by the Duke's Order of the Golden

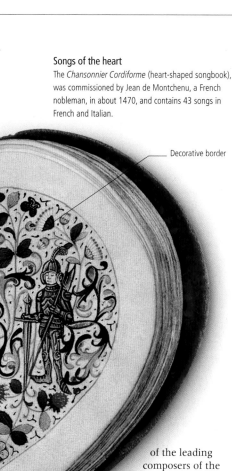

Tenor part

Decorative border

Songs of the heart
The *Chansonnier Cordiforme* (heart-shaped songbook), was commissioned by Jean de Montchenu, a French nobleman, in about 1470, and contains 43 songs in French and Italian.

Fleece, a fellowship of knights whose members vowed to protect Christendom.

Regional traditions

French and Burgundian composers such as Guillaume Dufay, Gilles Binchois, and Josquin Desprez wrote *chansons* (songs) in many interweaving parts, using the poetic forms first established by Guillaume Machaut (see p.47). These were appreciated all over Europe and fed into a rich variety of regional song traditions.

In Italy, the most common song form during the late 15th and early 16th centuries was the *frottola*. Repeating the same melody for each verse, it set lighthearted love poetry for three or four voices, or for a solo voice to the accompaniment of a lute or viols. Its two leading composers were Marchetto Cara and Bartolomeo Tromboncino at the court of Isabella d'Este in Mantua. Collections of *frottolas* by these and other, often anonymous, composers were among the first music books to be printed (see pp.54–55). They contributed to the evolution of the madrigal, the major new song form that was to emerge in 16th-century Italy (see pp.66–67).

In Germany, the main polyphonic song form was the *tenorlied*, which gave the melody to the tenor voice, with usually two voices above it and a bass line below. Meanwhile, in Spain, songs were influenced by north European composers. Johannes Ockeghem, from a small town in modern-day Belgium, is known to have visited Spain in 1470, and one of the leading composers of the Spanish *canción* (song), Juan de Urrede, was himself Flemish (Belgian). Toward the end of the 15th century the Duke of Alba's court poet, playwright, and composer Juan del Encina developed the *villancico*, turning a popular type of rustic folk song into the Spanish equivalent of Italy's *frottola*.

New influences

For most of the 15th century, songs for three or four voices were rarely heard outside the courts of Europe, yet in those courtly circles there was a growing interest in the popular songs heard in the streets and marketplaces. These were either incorporated into a longer and more sophisticated polyphonic song or used as the tune for a more refined text. Convergence between courtly and popular music continued in a burst of creativity that developed the pastoral theme in vogue from around 1500—that of the court as village, and courtiers playing the part of shepherds or shepherdesses.

Song settings of lyric poetry based on refrain-and-verse forms remained popular in the 16th century. Gradually, however, they gave way to the expressive new through-composed (nonrepetitive) solo song.

AFTER

In the 16th century, composers and performers at court and at home were increasingly drawn to expressing the meaning of the text, through new song forms such as the madrigal.

THE RISE OF THE AMATEUR
From the 1530s, **madrigals 66–67 ››** were **printed** in slim and relatively cheap **part books** (one for each voice, or part) in Venice, Italy, and in Lyon and Paris, France.

Once an aristocratic form of entertainment, secular polyphony was now available to gifted amateurs among wealthy, educated merchants. The explosion of **musical literacy** and ensembles in the home was accompanied by the rise of the virtuoso singer at court that ushered in the era of modern song **152–153 ››**.

KEY WORKS

Guillaume Dufay "Je ne vis onques la pareille" (I Have Never Seen the Equal)

Hayne van Ghizeghem "De tous biens plaine" (Possessing Every Virtue)

Clément Janequin "La bataille" (The Battle)

Juan del Encina "Triste España" (Sad Spain)

Heinrich Isaac "Innsbruck, ich muss dich lassen" (Innsbruck, I Must Leave You)

UNDERSTANDING MUSIC

SONG PERFORMANCE

In the 15th century, songs were performed in different ways according to the occasion and the musical resources available. Music manuscripts from the period give few clues as to the number and kind of musicians involved in singing polyphony. Literature and paintings, such as *The Concert* (left) by Italian artist Lorenzo Costa (*c.*1500), can offer some evidence. It seems that flexibility was the norm, from purely vocal *a cappella* performances, to solo voice and harp or lute, to wind band when songs were performed outdoors or at celebrations on a grand scale.

Music Goes to Print

Innovations in music printing by Ottaviano Petrucci in Venice in 1501 were to prove as revolutionary to music as Johannes Gutenberg's first printing press had been to literature 50 years earlier. Widely published music led to a rapid rise in musical literacy.

From the late 15th century, music was printed using the technology of woodblocks in which the notes were carved and then inked. Used in liturgical books with plainchant (unaccompanied melodies sung in church) and in some instruction manuals, this method avoided laborious copying by hand, but it was still slow and not well suited to the "white" or blank diamond-shaped note heads used in the notation of polyphony (music for multiple voices).

Avid collectors
As music books became more widespread, collecting them became a popular pastime among amateur musicians in cities all over Europe. Conrad Gesner of Zurich (1516–1565), left, was one such collector.

The printing press

In 1501, Ottaviano Petrucci (1466–1539) developed a new technique of printing music from sharply defined metallic type. It revolutionized music printing. Although the sheets of paper had to be passed through the press several times to print staves, note heads, and text to create multiple copies, Petrucci's prints of vocal and instrumental music were elegant and highly legible. However, the process was expensive, and his print-runs were small.

Movable type

By the 1520s, Pierre Attaingnant (1494–1551), a music printer in Paris, had developed a new technique that allowed music to be printed in movable type by a single impression. Each note head was cut with its own fragment of stave and could be set together with the corresponding text.

With this development, the production of music books became much more commercially viable, and the market expanded rapidly. By the 1540s, European cities such as Venice, Lyon, Antwerp, and Nuremberg had become important centers for music printing.

The spread of music

Music that had previously been the preserve of the Church and the court—masses and motets, chansons and madrigals, as well as instrumental music of all kinds—became widely available to amateur musicians, who could also learn the basics of music theory through the "teach-yourself" books that began to proliferate in print around 1500.

Anthologies of instrumental music generally provided a brief instruction manual, and pieces were often graded according to difficulty. While some books of sacred music were printed in the *folio* (large-page) format required for use at the lectern in churches and monasteries, in general music was increasingly printed in small partbooks that were cheap to produce, inexpensive to buy, and easy to accumulate and collect.

> "Their **glorious name** can be known to the **world.**"
>
> COMPOSER HERMANN FINK ON PRINTING'S IMPACT ON COMPOSERS, 1556

Music as expression

Musical genres such as motets, songs, and instrumental pieces, which were particularly attractive for performance in a private or domestic context, were soon transformed. Printing dictated a closer relationship between the placing of text and music on the page. This reflected and stimulated the notion of music serving to express the meaning of the words that lay at the heart of the madrigal (see pp.66–67) and would lead to the birth of opera at the end of the 16th century (see pp.80–81).

The spreading of musical repertories through the agency of printing and the rise of commercial book fairs brought fame to the original composers and increased the exchange of musical styles within Europe. These significant developments resulted in the transformation of the Western musical tradition.

« BEFORE

Before the advent of printing, music had to be written by hand, whether as beautifully prepared princely gifts or simply on sheets of paper that circulated between musicians.

MUSIC SCRIBES
Music was copied by **professional scribes**, usually employed by the Church or court. This was laborious and expensive, taking hours to copy a single piece. The **materials** used—parchment or paper—were also costly.

MUSIC TRANSMISSION
Manuscripts were generally copied for the use of princely chapels or cathedral choirs and rarely left those precincts. This limited their transmission but also lent them **exclusivity**.

Printing in action
Various tools and skills were required to run a press. This 16th-century miniature from *Recueil des Chants Royaux* shows the preparation of the ink (left), the compositor (seated right), operator, and proofreader.

AFTER »

Music printing from type continued into the 19th century, but the desire of composers to indicate subtleties of notation required a more flexible technology: music engraving.

MUSIC ENGRAVING
Isolated experiments with music engraving, in which **musical notation is etched onto copperplate,** began in the 16th century, but it was only in the 17th century that the technique became commercially viable. Important centers of production were established in England and the Netherlands.

MODERN TECHNOLOGY
Since the 1990s, music writing software has enabled musicians and composers to turn played or heard sounds into sheet music. The applications allow the creator to build and edit the score on screen before listening to their piece, printing it as sheet music, or sharing it with others. It is not unusual for these applications to support the sound of hundreds of instruments.
376–377 ».

1990S FLOPPY DISKS FOR STORING MUSIC

Printing music in England
This printed score is by the English composer Thomas Tallis (*c.* 1505–1585). Queen Elizabeth I granted Tallis and his fellow composer William Byrd (1539–1623) the monopoly for printing music in England.

Five-line stave
260 A Pſalme before Morning Prayer. CANTVS. T.Tallis.
Cannon 2.parts in one.
Raiſe the Lord O ye Gentils all, vvhich hath brought you into his
light: O praiſe him all people mortall, as it is moſt vvorthie and right.
TENOR, or Playnſong.
Raiſe the Lord O ye Gentiles all, vvhich hath brought you into his
light: O praiſe him all people mortall, as it is moſt vvorthie and right.
For he is full determined, on vs to poure out his mercy:
And the Lords truth be ye aſſured, abideth perpetually.
Abb. 111. Ein Pſalm vor dem Morgengebet. Von Thomas Tallis.
Diamond-shaped note head

Peasant Dance
In this scene by Bruegel the Elder, *c.*1569, peasants dance to the accompaniment of a bagpipe outside a tavern. Two couples perform what may well be a jig, a popular dance, which the piper plays by ear.

BEFORE

A few examples of notated keyboard music survive from before 1500, but until that time instrumental music was largely passed on orally.

RELYING ON MEMORY
Professionals taught students to play their instruments and passed on the pieces they knew. Some professional musicians were blind, a tradition stretching back to Homer and the bards of Ancient Greece.

EARLY NOTATION
Various methods were devised to write down instrumental music. This allowed music to circulate more freely and, once **printing** was widely available « **54–55**, to be obtained by amateur musicians.

MEDIEVAL MUSICIAN PLAYING FROM MEMORY

The **Rise** of Western **Instrumental Music**

Instrumental music developed rapidly in the 16th century, thanks in part to the availability of printed music. Composers experimented with new instrumental genres and wrote music to complement the unique characteristics of different instruments.

During the 16th century, instrumentalists participated in the performance of vocal music, but works composed specifically for instruments became increasingly important. There was also a growing tendency toward instrumental virtuosity, even when instruments accompanied voices or played vocal music. For example, in 16th-century Seville, the composer Francisco Guerrero (1528–1599) drew up guidelines to instruct the cathedral's instrumentalists how to add *glosas* (ornamentation) to the parts they were playing.

Virtuosity was also important in the instrumental sonatas and *canzonas* (pieces developed from a type of Flemish song) that were composed by the Gabrielis—Andrea (*c.*1510–1585) and Giovanni (1556–1612) —and Claudio Monteverdi (1567–1643) for St. Mark's Basilica in Venice (see pp.72–73). By the end of the century, the wealthier ecclesiastical institutions of Europe resounded with the sound of virtuoso instrumental music.

1507 **The date of Italian composer Spinacino's *Intabolatura de lauto*, the earliest known example of tablature.**

The participation of wind players in notated vocal polyphony—music with more than one melody line, for several voices or parts—shows that they read music, and did not just play from

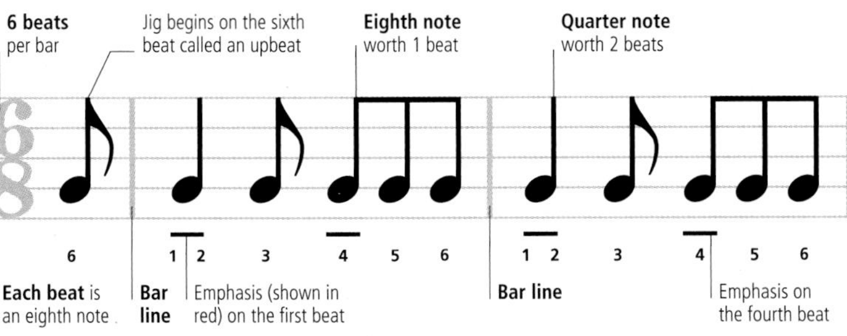

Jig
The jig is a lively dance that became popular in the 16th century. Jigs are often in 6/8 time, with two strong beats in a bar and three eighth notes to each strong beat.

memory. Improvisation was now mostly used only for virtuoso ornamentation. Several treatises on the art of ornamentation were published during the 16th century, notably in 1542 by the Venetian recorder virtuoso Silvestro Ganassi (1492–1550) and, in 1553, by the Spanish composer and viol player Diego Ortiz (1510–1570). Studying works such as these enabled dedicated amateur musicians to learn professional techniques.

The art of variation

Instrumentalists had long played music for dances, often employing techniques of improvisation and variation similar to the jamming sessions of modern jazz musicians. However, new technical skills—such as the ability to read music—meant they could develop more elaborate forms of composition that drew on their ability to improvise but which also drew on vocal forms they already knew. Another such skill was that of weaving a complex musical texture from short musical phrases that were repeated (or "imitated").

The *ricercar* was perhaps the most experimental of these instrumental forms. Even its name, meaning "to seek out" in Italian, suggests composers were exploring new territory. Some *ricercar* were chordal, centering more on harmony than melody, and featured more improvised ornamental passages. As the 16th century progressed, the style of *ricercar* that used imitation became more firmly established.

> "A **fantasia...** proceeds only from the **fantasy** and **industry** of the author who **created it.**"
>
> COMPOSER **LUIS DE MILÁN, "EL MAESTRO,"** 1536

The *canzona,* another form of instrumental music, was based on a series of contrasting sections, some of which might use counterpoint (see pp. 98–99), and others that relied more on chords. Instrumental ensembles embraced the *canzona,* especially those by Giovanni Gabrieli (see p.72) written for wind instruments. The fantasia was perhaps the least restrained of the instrumental genres developed at this time. Like the *ricercar,* it was generally free of musical material borrowed from a vocal work.

Instrumental music also became more concerned with the intrinsic qualities of specific instruments—notably the keyboard—even though music publishers favored flexibility of instrumentation as a marketing ploy. The title page of the *obras* (works) of the blind Spanish organist Antonio de Cabezón (1510–1566) proclaimed them suitable for keyboard, harp, and vihuela, while the preface also suggested they could be played by wind bands. Yet in Cabezon's sets of variations and fantasias it is clear that a highly virtuoso style of writing particularly suited to the keyboard is beginning to emerge. This more distinctive approach was taken up and developed by composers in Italy and England.

Music for dancing

Dance was considered a social grace at almost all levels of society, and a wide range of dance types went in and out of fashion throughout the 16th century. The dances were accompanied by wind band, lute, and pipe and tabor, or bagpipe, depending on the dancers' level in society and the social event or space in which it was performed.

In the 1520–1530s, the *basse* dance featured strongly in the collections of dances published by the French music printer Pierre Attaingnant. This was a stately dance that was often followed by a livelier one, and such pairings as the *passamezzo* and *saltarello, pavan* and *galliard,* and *allemande* and *courante* became common, developing into the basis for the Baroque suite.

Shawm
This replica of a shawm shows the reed, finger holes, and sound holes typical of the early instrument. The predecessor of the modern oboe, the shawm produces a strident sound well suited to outdoor performance.

Prescribed steps

In the same way that musical ornamentation was made available for the amateur instrumentalist to study and conquer through the printing of musical scores, dances could be studied and learned from published treatises. In 1551, in Antwerp, composer Tilman Susato (1500–1561) published a collection of dances titled *Danserye,* and in 1589 French cleric Thoinot Arbeau (1519–1595) published his dance treatise *Orchésographie*. This work was a veritable dance encyclopedia, presenting the dance steps carefully aligned with the corresponding musical phrase.

Similar handbooks in smaller, pocket-sized formats were published in Italy in around 1600, while in 1612 the German composer, organist, and music theorist Michael Praetorius (1571–1621) published *Terpsichore,* an anthology containing more than 300 dances.

UNDERSTANDING MUSIC

TABLATURE

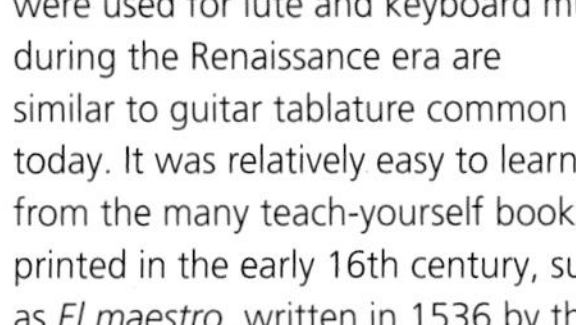

Instead of showing notes and pitch, tablature is a type of musical notation that indicates where players should place their fingers to play their instrument. Tablatures that were used for lute and keyboard music during the Renaissance era are similar to guitar tablature common today. It was relatively easy to learn from the many teach-yourself books printed in the early 16th century, such as *El maestro,* written in 1536 by the Spaniard Luis de Milán (1500–1561).

This woodcut shows the neck of a lute with tablature symbols. It comes from the 1511 book *Musica Getutscht,* written by the German Renaissance composer Sebastian Virdung (1465–1511).

Tablature was also used for keyboard music, and could use letters, numbers, or other symbols to indicate rhythmic values or notes to be sung.

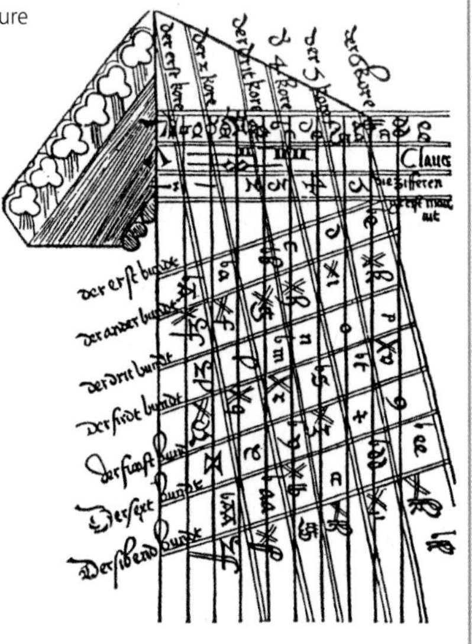

AFTER

Seventeenth-century instrumental music saw a greater emphasis on virtuosity.

VIRTUOSO VARIATIONS
Solo instrumentalists developed forms that were even more independent of vocal music. Early in the 17th century, Italian composer Girolamo Frescobaldi (1583–1643) published two volumes of *Toccatas,* while English keyboard composer William Byrd, Jan Sweelinck (1562–1621) in the Netherlands, and Juan Cabanilles (1644–1712) in Spain also focused on variation techniques. German organist Samuel Scheidt (1587–1654) drew on the art of variation in his chorale preludes.

NEW GENRES
Around 1600, a number of terms emerged to describe new styles of instrumental ensemble music. The **sinfonia, ritornello, concerto,** and **sonata** **102–103 >>** all began to be established during the 17th century, although the use of the new terminology was still quite fluid.

KEY WORKS

Francesco Spinacino *Intabolatura de lauto*
Luis de Milán *El maestro*
Girolamo Cavazzoni *Intavolatura*
Antonio de Cabezón *Obras*
Thoinot Arbeau *Orchésographie*
William Byrd *My Ladye Nevells Booke*

BEFORE

In the Roman Catholic Church, the veneration of the Virgin Mary and the saints had inspired many Latin-texted motets in the 15th century.

POLYPHONIC DEVOTIONS
Much sacred **polyphony** « 46–47 of the 14th and 15th centuries was specifically composed for services that were held on days honoring the Virgin Mary.

FRESCO OF THE VIRGIN MARY

HEARING THE WORDS
The **counterpoint** that characterized sacred music of 15th-century composers, such as that of **Johannes Ockeghem**, was already giving way to a more **syllabic** style in the works of **Josquin Desprez**.

In **Divine Service**

When the German monk Martin Luther pinned his 95 theses on the door of the castle church of Wittenberg, Germany, in 1517, he initiated a period of Church reform that was to have a profound impact on sacred music during the rest of the 16th century.

Initially Luther (1483–1546) had hoped that his reforms could be introduced from within the Roman Catholic Church. When he refused to retract his writings, however, the Pope, Leo X, excommunicated him, and he was forced to go into hiding. Luther and his followers then founded the Lutheran Church, and the incident sparked the period now known as the Reformation.

PAPAL BULL An official document with a *bulla* (lead seal). The seal served as proof that the message had come directly from the Pope.

Everyone should sing in church

Luther considered music to be second only to theology in importance in divine worship. His emphasis on the Bible as the focus of the church service meant the rejection of the cult of the Virgin Mary, and there was no place for the motets written for services held in her honor. Luther insisted that, unlike in a Roman Catholic service where congregations sat largely in silence while Mass was performed in Latin (which they did not understand), hymns or chorales were to be sung in the local language. He also encouraged every member of the congregation to sing. Luther wrote the foreword to the first collection of Protestant hymns, the *Geystliche gesangk Buchleyn* (which loosely translates as "little book of spiritual songs") composed by Johann Walther (1496–1570), and published in 1524. These were essentially simple harmonizations of well-known German melodies with which every member of the congregation would be familiar.

Anglican Book of Common Prayer, 1549
Archbishop Cranmer devised this prayer book for use in the Anglican Church. In 1550, John Merbecke set Cranmer's texts to simple melodies, based on plainchant.

Another Protestant reformer, French theologian Jean Calvin (1509–1564), firmly believed psalms should be sung. In 1539, he printed the first *Genevan Psalter* for use in the reformed churches of Switzerland and France.

Martin Luther burns the papal bull
German artist Karl Friedrich Lessing (1808–1880) recreates the scene on December 10, 1520, in Wittenberg, Germany, in which Luther, surrounded by his supporters, burned the papal bull announcing his excommunication from the Roman Catholic Church.

KEY WORKS

Johann Walther *Geystliche gesangk Buchleyn*

John Merbecke *Booke of Common Praier Noted*

Thomas Tallis "If Ye Love Me"

William Byrd *Great Service*

Vincenzo Ruffo *Missae quatuor concinate ad ritum Concili Mediolani* (Four Masses for the Milanese Rite)

Giovanni Palestrina *Missa Papae Marcelli*

Council of Trent meet in Trento, Italy, 1562
Italian artist Giovanni da Udine (1487–1564) depicts the impressive gathering of the Council of Trent, at which the subject of church music was discussed.

Rome responds

Roman Catholic Church dignitaries and theologians met to discuss Church doctrine in a series of conventions known as the Council of Trent. Lasting from 1545 to 1563, the Council never considered the use of languages other than Latin, and there was no question of congregations being allowed to sing during worship. However, it did share Luther's concern about the audibility of the sacred texts to be sung.

While there was no call to do away with the professional church choir, the Council decreed that church composers should avoid at all costs "compositions in which there is intermingling of the lascivious or impure, whether by instrument or voice." Masses or organ variations based on nonreligious melodies were in effect banned, although it seems, even in the Vatican, works based on *chansons* and madrigals were still sung (see pp.52–53).

In around 1562, Italian composer Giovanni Pierluigi da Palestrina (see pp.60–61) wrote the ***Missa Papae Marcelli*** (Pope Marcellus Mass). This setting of the Mass is significant because the text is expressed in a simpler, syllabic way, with one note per syllable. It is often cited as the work that saved the performance of polyphony (music for several voices or parts) in church, although this may be a myth.

It is clear that Palestrina, among other composers in Rome, such as Tomás Luis de Victoria (1548–1611) and Giovanni Animuccia (1520–1571), was aware of the call for the words of divine worship to be more audible. Animuccia, as music director of the choir of St. Peter's Basilica, claimed to compose "according to the requirements of the Council of Trent" and in a way that "the music may disturb the text as little as possible."

In Milan, too, Cardinal Borromeo (1538–1584), a leading Church reformer, commissioned a Mass from Vincenzo Ruffo (*c.*1508–87) in which the text "should be as clear as possible."

A desire for text to be audible was common to church music of both the Protestant Reformation and the Counter-Reformation (also known as the Catholic Reformation) set off by the Council of Trent. In Italy, Spain, and other Roman Catholic countries, it contributed to the rise of the tradition in which impressive music was created by contrasting one group of singers with another, rather than through complex compositions in which the words were easily obscured. This emphasis on the clarity of words also featured in the Reformation that took place in England in the 16th century. There, in 1544, Archbishop Thomas Cranmer (1489–1556) wrote to King Henry VIII about church music: "In mine opinion, the song... would not be full of notes, but, as near as may be, for every syllable, a note; so that it may be sung distinctly and devoutly."

> "The ... object of [churches] is **not the bawling** of choristers."
>
> LUTHER ON PRIORITIZING THE WORD OF GOD OVER THE SINGING OF CHOIRS, 1538

Anglican reform

For some time, Latin was retained as the language of the English liturgy and therefore of the music composed for church services. The brief reign of Edward VI (1547–1553) saw a wave of Protestant reform and the development of a new, simple, and unadorned Anglican liturgy in English.

The simple psalm-settings of John Merbecke (*c.*1510–1585) in his ***Booke of Common Praier Noted*** (1550) became the only music to be heard in local parish churches. In the cathedrals, anthems and services with English texts were performed by the choir—and continue to be sung today. The words were set with one note per syllable, so that they could be easily understood. Roman Catholic composers working in the Chapel Royal, such as Thomas Tallis (1505–1585) and William Byrd (see above) wrote English service music for the Anglican Church, but also composed motets with Latin texts. As hostility toward Roman Catholics intensified toward the end of the 16th century, Byrd felt compelled to compose his three settings of the Latin Mass for secret use in Roman Catholic homes.

Borromeo statue, Milan
As Archbishop of Milan, Cardinal Carlo Borromeo commissioned music for the Mass composed with one note per syllable to make the text audible.

COMPOSER (1539–1623)

WILLIAM BYRD

Byrd was born in London and studied with Thomas Tallis. As organist in the Chapel Royal, Byrd composed music for both the Anglican and Roman Catholic churches. He was a Roman Catholic, but Elizabeth I's Protestantism was moderate enough that in 1575 she granted him, along with Tallis, a monopoly on music printing. They first published a volume of Latin-texted motets, *Cantiones Sacrae*. Byrd also wrote English settings for the Anglican Church, such as his *Great Service*.

AFTER

The 16th-century reforms led new generations of composers to write sacred music of greater simplicity.

LUTHERAN MUSIC IN THE BAROQUE
The Lutheran chorale remained the basis for sacred music in the works of early **Baroque** composers, such as Johann Hermann Schein (1586–1630), and then reached its height in the chorale preludes for organ and large-scale settings of the *St. Matthew* and *St. John Passions* by **J.S. Bach** **100–01 ››**.

ROMAN CATHOLIC TRENDS
A concern for the audibility of words produced several experiments with singing styles. One style was *parlando* (sung in the style similar to speech). This was related to the idea of *falsobordone*, in which singers recited the text in a free rhythm to a single chord. Examples are found in the psalm-settings of the *Vespers* of 1610 by **Monteverdi** **81 ››**.

17TH-CENTURY ENGLAND
In the austere era of **Oliver Cromwell** **94 ››**, music for the Anglican church became largely restricted to hymns and psalms. Music flourished again with the **anthems** of **Henry Purcell**.

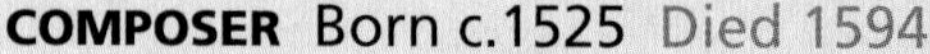

COMPOSER Born c.1525 Died 1594

Giovanni Pierluigi da **Palestrina**

"Music should **give zest to divine worship ...**"

PALESTRINA, PREFACE TO FIRST BOOK OF MOTETS, 1563

Composer Giovanni Pierluigi, known as Palestrina after his native town in Italy, spent his whole life in and around Rome, a city ruled by the Pope and dominated by the Catholic Church. The bulk of his musical output consisted of sacred music, including 104 settings of the mass and more than 3,000 motets, which represent the culmination of the Renaissance polyphonic style, with its interweaving of melodic voices.

The tranquil beauty of line and spiritual purity of Palestrina's music have been admired by composers as diverse as Wagner and Debussy. Mendelssohn said his music sounded "as if it came direct from heaven."

Renaissance composer
Palestrina, portrayed here by an anonymous painter at the age of around 50, brought Renaissance church music to its purest form. He was highly successful within his own lifetime and greatly admired by later composers.

From choirmaster to composer

Palestrina was born in troubled times. The Protestant Reformation, initiated in Germany around 1517, had rejected papal authority, splitting the Church. In response, Pope Paul III established the Council of Trent in 1545 to reform and clarify the practices and beliefs of the Catholic Church (see pp.58–59). This movement, known as the Counter-Reformation, formed the background to Palestrina's highly successful musical career.

Palestrina began his musical education as a choirboy in the basilica of Santa Maria Maggiore in Rome, and by the age of 20 was the organist and choirmaster at St. Agapito Cathedral in his hometown.

The bishop of Palestrina at this time was Cardinal Giovanni del Monte. When, in 1551, Cardinal del Monte was elected Pope Julius III, he invited the talented young musician to direct the choir of St. Peter's Basilica in Rome. Palestrina's duties included composing sacred music and directing performances during church services and ceremonies.

KEY WORKS

***Missa L'homme armé* (The Armed Man)**
***Missa Papae Marcelli* (Pope Marcellus Mass)**
Missa Assumpta est Maria
Lamentations
Song of Songs (Song of Solomon)
Stabat Mater

At this time music in Rome was dominated by the polyphony of the Franco-Flemish school (see pp.46–47), with composers hailing chiefly from what are now Belgium and the Netherlands. Palestrina became the first Italian-born composer to adopt this style successfully. It characterized his technically accomplished first book of masses, published in 1554.

Expelled from St. Peter's

Pope Julius was delighted with his protégé and brought him into the elite inner circle of the *schola cantorum* (papal choir). Shortly afterward, however, Julius died, initiating a more difficult period in Palestrina's life.

After the three-week reign of Pope Marcellus II, Paul IV became head of the Catholic Church. Whereas Julius III had been an art- and pleasure-loving pope, Paul was a severe advocate of the Counter-Reformation.

The new Pope found Palestrina wanting on two counts: he had published secular madrigals while a member of the papal choir, and he was married with children, at a time when celibacy was increasingly expected of all those working within the Catholic Church. Palestrina was consequently banned from taking papal employment.

As a musical director and composer of exceptional renown, Palestrina had no difficulty finding prominent posts elsewhere in Rome, first as the choirmaster at St. John Lateran and then at Santa Maria Maggiore.

Piety and purity

Meanwhile, the Council of Trent turned the subject of its deliberations to music. In 1562, it passed a ruling in order to exclude from the Church "all music tainted with sensual and impure elements, all secular forms and unedifying language."

It was once believed that listening to Palestrina's masses was the only thing that dissuaded Church dignitaries from imposing a complete ban on music in religious services. This is now known to be untrue, but Palestrina certainly responded to pressure for a new purity in religious music, in works such as the famous *Missa Papae Marcelli*. In 1566, he described his new book of masses as "music written in a new style and in accordance with the views of the most serious and religious-minded persons in high places."

The flowing polyphonic music that Palestrina produced from the 1560s onward sealed his fame. Its beauty attracted the private patronage of Renaissance princes, and brought Palestrina offers of employment from beyond Rome, including Vienna. But Palestrina remained in Rome and reentered papal service.

The loss of Palestrina's wife and other family members during the plague years of the 1570s almost induced him to take holy orders. Instead, in 1851 he married Virginia Dormoli, a wealthy widow, and took over the running of her husband's fur-trading business. This provided a comfortable old-age while he continued to produce compositions.

After his death in 1594, Palestrina was buried with great honor in St. Peter's Basilica.

Organ of the Basilica of St. John Lateran
Palestrina was the choirmaster at St. John Lateran, the cathedral church of Rome, from 1555 to 1560. He succeeded another renowned composer in the role, Orlande de Lassus.

> "[Palestrina's] **Stabat Mater ... captivates** the human soul."
>
> **FRANZ LISZT, LETTER TO MUSIC PUBLISHER CHRISTIAN KAHNT,** MAY 30, 1878

Palestrina score
These are the first two pages of the original edition of Palestrina's setting of the "Magnificat" (My soul doth magnify the Lord), published in 1591.

TIMELINE

- **1524 or 1525** Born as Giovanni Pierluigi in Palestrina, near Rome.
- **1537** Becomes a chorister at the basilica of Santa Maria Maggiore in Rome.
- **1544** Appointed organist and choirmaster at St. Agapito Cathedral in Palestrina.
- **July 12, 1547** Marries Lucrezia Gori in Palestrina.
- **1551** His patron, Pope Julius III, makes him choirmaster of the Julian Chapel at St. Peter's Basilica in Rome.
- **1554** Julius III makes him a member of the privileged *schola cantorum* (papal choir).
- **March 23, 1555** Julius III dies; he is succeeded, for three weeks, by Pope Marcellus II.
- **May 23, 1555** Paul IV is elected pope after the death of Marcellus. Palestrina is soon dismissed from the papal choir, but becomes choirmaster of St. John Lateran.
- **1561** Appointed choirmaster of Santa Maria Maggiore Basilica.

MEDAL STRUCK BY POPE JULIUS III

- **1562** The Council of Trent lays down new principles for church music as part of the Counter-Reformation. Probable year of the composition of the *Missa Papae Marcelli* (Pope Marcellus Mass).
- **1564** Directs musical performances at the villa of wealthy patron Cardinal Ippolito d'Este.
- **1566** Appointed music master at the newly founded Roman Seminary.
- **1568** Writes a mass and motets for Guglielmo Gonzaga, Duke of Mantua.
- **1571** Returns to the post of choirmaster of the Julian Chapel at St. Peter's. Composes the madrigal "Le selv' avea" to celebrate the Christian naval victory over the Turks at Lepanto.
- **1572–1580** Plague ravages Rome. His wife, brother, and two of his three sons die in three separate outbreaks.
- **March 28, 1581** Marries Virginia Dormoli, the wealthy widow of a Roman fur trader.
- **1584** Publishes his fourth book of motets: settings of the *Song of Solomon*.
- **1588** *Lamentations* is published.
- **1589–1590** Writes *Stabat Mater* for eight voices.
- **February 2, 1594** Dies in Rome.

Concert of Women
In the 16th century, it became more acceptable for women to be musically educated and to sing and play instruments, as depicted by a Flemish artist or studio, known as the Master of Female Half-Lengths.

The **Lute's Golden Age**

The lute developed rapidly in the 16th century, both as a solo instrument and as the principal instrument for accompanying a solo singer. Regarded as the "queen of instruments," the lute reached the height of its powers in the works of the English composer John Dowland.

By the early 16th century, the ability to sing to the lute had become an essential social requirement of the aristocratic amateur. Descriptions of court life suggest that playing and listening to lute songs were a favorite pastime. In Italy, the wealthy noblewoman and patron Isabella d'Este (1473–1539) was praised for her musicianship by the diplomat and poet Gian Giorgio Trissino in 1524: "When she sings, especially to the lute, I believe that Orpheus and Amphion ... would be stupefied with wonder on hearing her."

BEFORE

From ancient times onward, verse was spoken or sung to the accompaniment of a harp or a lyre—as exemplified by Orpheus in Greek mythology.

BARDS AND BALLADS

Epic poetry was accompanied by plucked strings throughout the Middle Ages **« 32–33**. Traces of historical ballads for soloist and *vihuela* (Spanish lute) exist in 16th-century Spanish anthologies **« 39**.

SOLO SONGS FOR ALL OCCASIONS

A solo song accompanied by a plucked-string instrument could be heard in a variety of settings in the Middle Ages. The lute and voice were used in court entertainments, dramatic performances, and pageants, and to draw attention to a royal arrival.

Love conquers all

Isabella d'Este's patronage helped to cultivate the *frottola*, a type of Italian love song that was often performed as a solo with lute (see p.53). The lute song was also favored in Spanish court circles, where it was usually performed on the *vihuela*. The printed music for this instrument was also taken up outside the noble courts,

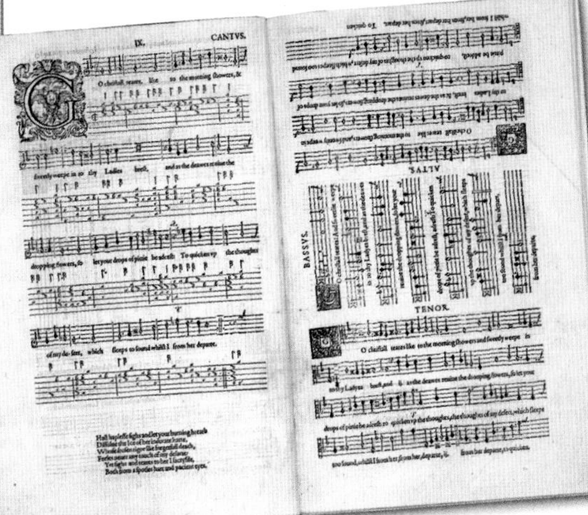

A shared first

Dowland's *First Booke of Songes or Ayres* (1597) was printed in a "table-book" format, so that the musicians who gathered to perform the songs could group themselves around a single book placed on a table.

by musical amateurs among the educated and wealthy merchant class.

Lute songs spread through France in a similar way, where *airs de cour* (court songs) were published in anthologies. The lutenist and composer Adrian Le Roy (1520–1598) had an exclusive royal warrant to print music. When he published his *Livre d'airs de cour miz sur le luth* (Book of Court Songs on the Lute), he printed the voice part with a separate bass line for the lute, supplying basic harmonies on which players could then improvise. Perhaps anxious about the quality of his composing, he focused on the beauty of the lyrics: "If the musical harmonies are not equal to the best, the words emanate from good forges ... of the century's finest poets."

75 **The number of surviving lute pieces by John Dowland.**

8 **The number of courses (pairs of strings) on a Renaissance lute.**

Expressive airs

The intimate quality of a solo song accompanied by a lute gave composers the means to write a highly expressive musical setting. One of the greatest of the English lute-song composers was Thomas Campion (1567–1620). He discussed this new relationship between the text and the music in the preface to his *Two Bookes of Ayres* (*c.*1613): "In these English ayres I have chiefly aymed to couple my Words and Notes lovingly together." This Renaissance concern with expressivity is also heard in songs by Philip Rosseter (*c.*1568–1623) and John Dowland, both lutenists to King James I.

John Dowland published four books of lute songs in London between 1597 and 1612. Having traveled to Florence in Italy, he would have been exposed to the developments there in monody (solo vocal music), and this is reflected in his later work. Although many of his songs—particularly his early work—are strophic (with repeated verses) and for several voices, he displays an instinct for capturing the precise meaning or prevailing emotional mood of a poem, and conveys it in music of great beauty and often searing intensity.

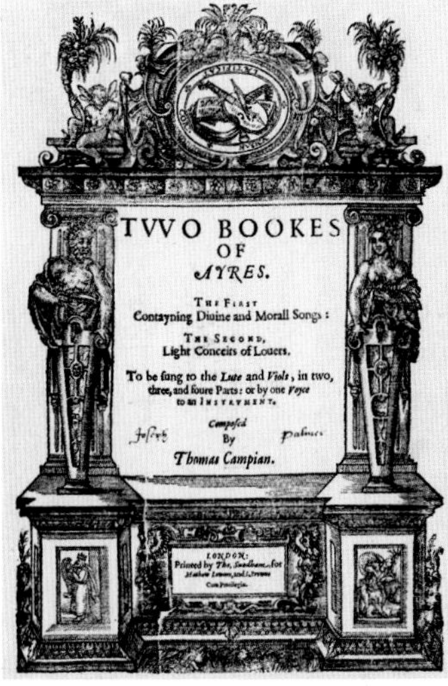
TVVO BOOKES OF AYRES.

THE FIRST Contayning Divine and Morall Songs:

THE SECOND, Light Conceits of Lovers.

To be sung to the *Lute* and *Viols*, in two, three, and foure Parts: or by one *Voyce* to an INSTRUMENT.

Composed By *Thomas Campian*.

LONDON: Printed by Tho. Snodham, for Mathew Lownes, and I. Browne

Title page from *Two Bookes of Ayres*

Published in about 1613, Thomas Campion's collection of songs contains a selection of divine and moral pieces, as well as playfully metaphorical love songs.

COMPOSER (1563–1626)

JOHN DOWLAND

Dowland was born in London, but little is known of his early training. In 1580, he went to Paris, where he became a Roman Catholic. He worked in north German courts and in Italy, and built an international reputation. He returned to England in 1596, professing loyalty to his Protestant queen, Elizabeth I, after coming into contact with a Catholic cell that plotted to kill her. From 1598, he was lutenist to King Christian IV of Denmark, but was dismissed because of his prolonged absences in London.

Dowland's Catholicism might have been a factor in his failure to secure the post of royal lutenist to Elizabeth I but, in 1612, he was appointed lutenist to her successor, James I.

KEY WORKS

Bartolomeo Trombocino "Si è debile il filo" (Yes, Feeble is the Thread)

Marchetto Cara "S'io sedo a l'ombra" (If I Sit in the Shade)

Luis Milán "Durandarte, Durandarte"

Guillaume Tessier "Le petit enfant amour" (The Little Child, Love)

John Dowland "Flow My Tears"

Thomas Campion "All Lookes Be Pale"

AFTER

The expressive potential of a song accompanied by an instrument, epitomized by Orpheus, remains a source of musical inspiration.

ITALIAN LUTE SONGS

The Italian musician **Giulio Caccini** published a hugely influential manual of lute-accompanied solo songs, *Le nuove musiche* (The New Music). He would have discussed the music of Ancient Greece as one of the group of trend-setting intellectuals, called the **Florentine Camerata** **80 »**.

EARLY ITALIAN OPERA

The theme of the earliest operas by **Caccini**, **Peri**, and **Monteverdi** **80–81 »** was also inspired by the **Greek myth** of the lutenist and singer Orpheus.

MODERN AGE

In 2006, the British singer-songwriter **Sting** attracted a modern audience to Dowland's miniature masterpieces when he released an album of Dowland songs called *Songs from the Labyrinth*.

STING PERFORMS A DOWLAND LUTE SONG

The **Lute**

The lute is one of the most important and versatile of instruments in the Western musical tradition. Played as both a solo and an accompaniment instrument, it provided backing to troubadour songs and formed part of the typical Baroque continuo ensemble (see pp.78–79).

Plucked-string instruments of the lute-type date back to ancient times in East Asia, which had the Chinese *pipa*, and the Arabic world, which had the *'ud*. These instruments share the pear-shaped form, and the system of stretching strings across a flat soundboard. Another shared characteristic is the ability to adjust the tension, and thus tuning, of the strings by movable pegs. The name lute derives, as does *'ud*, from the Arabic *al'ud*, meaning "wood," the material used to make them.

There are several ways that the Arabic *'ud* reached Europe in the early Middle Ages. The nomadic Bulgar people who settled the Balkans during the seventh century brought with them a short-necked form of lute. A century later, the Islamic occupation of Spain from 711 introduced the *'ud* there. Contemporary artwork depicting the lute suggests that it was played in Sicily in the 12th century. It is possible that it was introduced from the East through earlier conquests by the Byzantines or Saracens. From the southern and eastern reaches of Europe, the lute spread north to France and Germany. By the 14th century it was ubiquitous throughout Europe, and often referred to in medieval literature and artwork, notably as an instrument played by angelic musicians.

From quill to fingertips

The medieval instrument was played with a plectrum made from a quill of a feather. In this period it was essentially used as a melodic instrument—only one note could be played at a time. During the course of the 15th century, lute players, or lutenists, began to play with their fingertips. Flemish music theorist Johannes Tinctoris advocated playing with the fingers in around 1482. Using their fingers enabled musicians to sound more than one string simultaneously, making it possible for them to play polyphonic music—music with two or more simultaneous melodies. This change of technique coincided with writing down music for the lute in tablature, a form of notation still popular today (see p.57), which showed where the fingers should be placed on the frets.

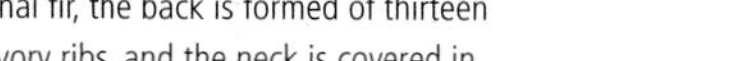

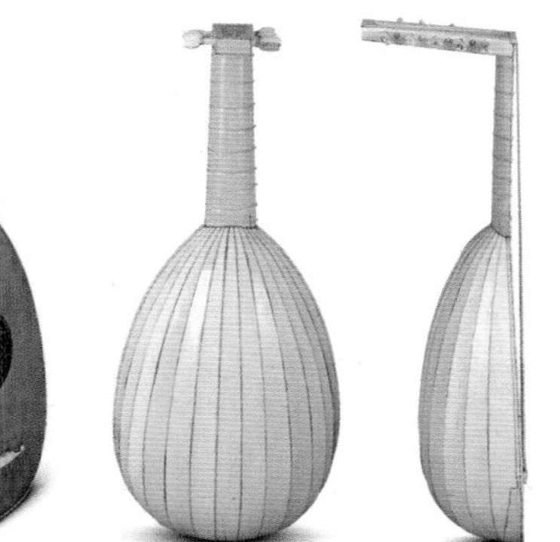

Renaissance lute
This beautiful treble lute was made in northern Italy, *c.*1500. Its soundboard is made from traditional fir, the back is formed of thirteen fluted ivory ribs, and the neck is covered in an ivory veneer. It has five courses.

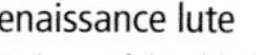

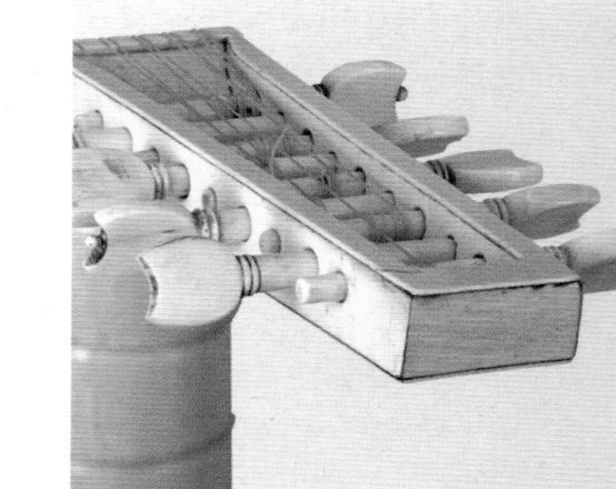

Pegs
The ivory veneer pegbox on this lute is tilted back at a right angle to the neck—on most instruments it is tilted farther. The nine ivory pegs sustain and tune the lute's nine strings.

TIMELINE

2nd century BCE
The Chinese *pipa*
The Chinese lute or *pipa* was first mentioned in Chinese texts in the 2nd century BCE, and became highly regarded as a solo and ensemble instrument in the Tang dynasty (618–907).

PIPA

711
Arabian *'ud*
The *'ud* was introduced to Spain after the invasion by Muslim forces in the early 8th century and became known in Christian court circles.

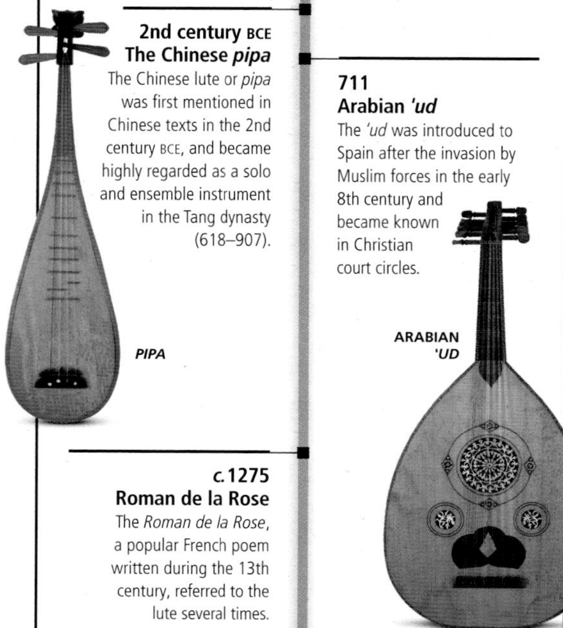

ARABIAN *'UD*

***c.*1275**
Roman de la Rose
The *Roman de la Rose*, a popular French poem written during the 13th century, referred to the lute several times.

PAINTING OF GARDEN SCENE, *c.*1490

***c.*1440**
Constructing the lute
The earliest known drawing of the construction of the lute was made by the organist Henri Arnaut de Zwolle, who worked at the French royal court.

***c.*1482**
Plectrum to plucking
A plectrum was used to sound the medieval lute until music theorist Johannes Tinctoris revolutionized lute playing by using his fingers.

CHILD PLAYS LUTE WITH PLECTRUM IN MARBLE RELIEF, ITALY, *c.*1431

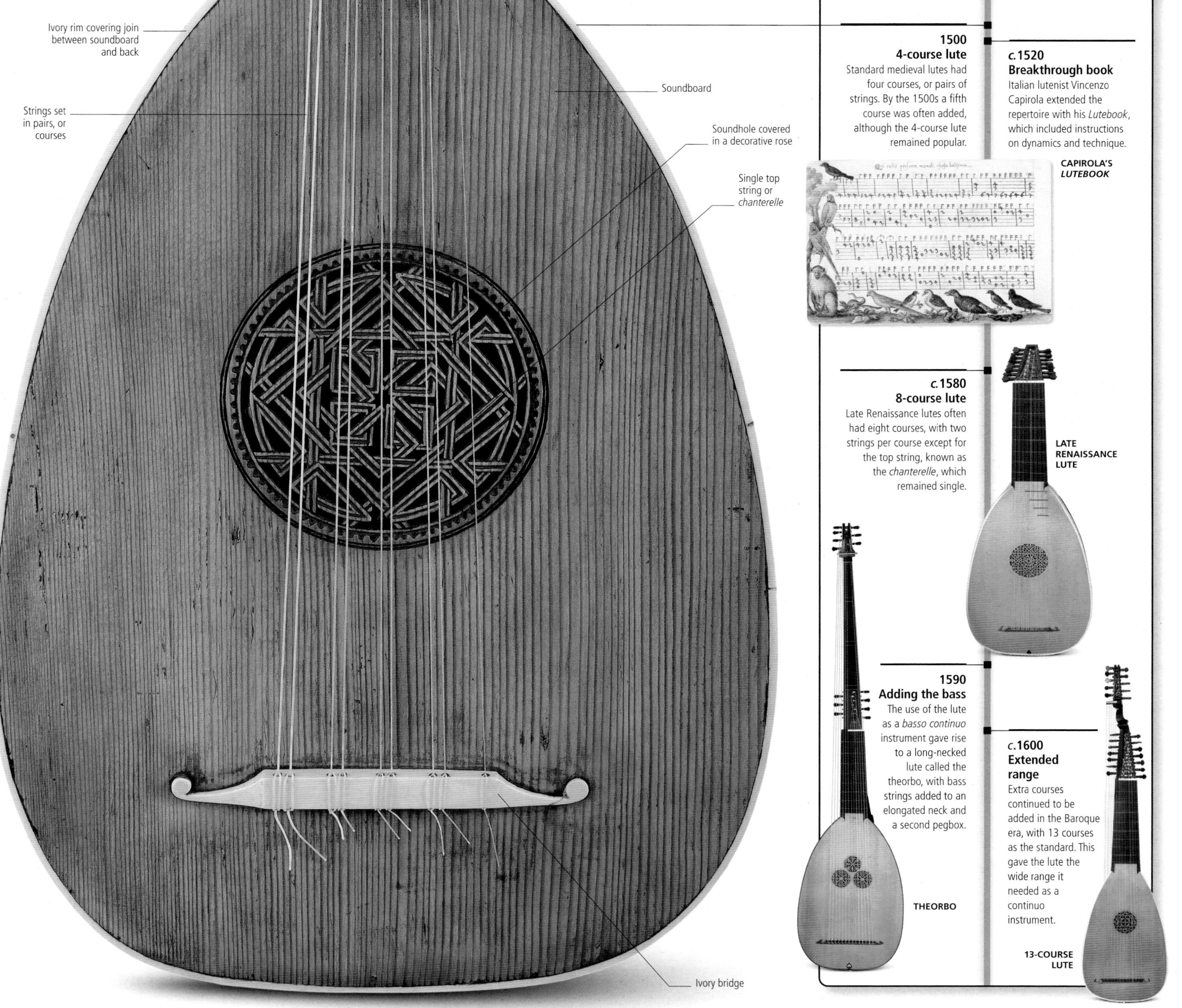

1500
4-course lute
Standard medieval lutes had four courses, or pairs of strings. By the 1500s a fifth course was often added, although the 4-course lute remained popular.

c.1520
Breakthrough book
Italian lutenist Vincenzo Capirola extended the repertoire with his *Lutebook*, which included instructions on dynamics and technique.

CAPIROLA'S *LUTEBOOK*

c.1580
8-course lute
Late Renaissance lutes often had eight courses, with two strings per course except for the top string, known as the *chanterelle*, which remained single.

LATE RENAISSANCE LUTE

1590
Adding the bass
The use of the lute as a *basso continuo* instrument gave rise to a long-necked lute called the theorbo, with bass strings added to an elongated neck and a second pegbox.

THEORBO

c.1600
Extended range
Extra courses continued to be added in the Baroque era, with 13 courses as the standard. This gave the lute the wide range it needed as a continuo instrument.

13-COURSE LUTE

The **Madrigal**

Emerging in Italy in the 1530s, the madrigal soon became popular all over Europe. The vogue for this song form was fostered by the printing of small collections of music that could be purchased at little cost and performed by amateur musicians in their own homes.

The earliest use of the word "madrigal" to refer to the setting of Italian verse to music with more than one melody line or voice occurs in the title of Philippe Verdelot's *Primo libro de madrigali* (First Book of Madrigals), published in 1530. Within a few years it had become a commonly used, standard term.

The verses favored above all others were written by the Italian poet and scholar Francesco Petrarch (1304–74). The 14-line Petrarchan sonnet of two verses of four lines, each followed by a verse of three lines, held huge appeal for composers, who relished setting the intense emotions of the text to music.

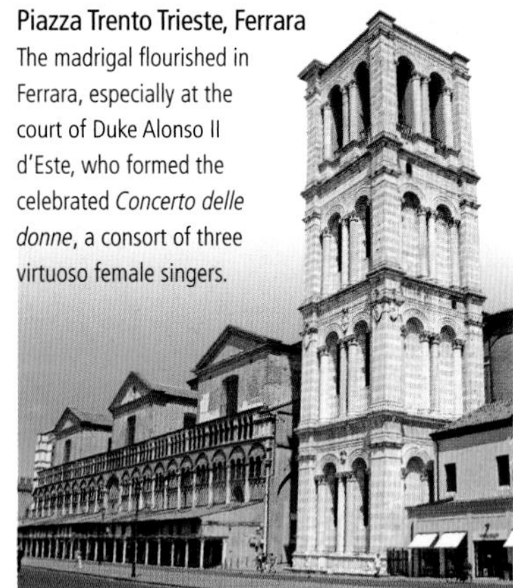

Piazza Trento Trieste, Ferrara
The madrigal flourished in Ferrara, especially at the court of Duke Alonso II d'Este, who formed the celebrated *Concerto delle donne*, a consort of three virtuoso female singers.

Torments of love

Petrarch's love affair with a lady by the name of Laura inspired many musical settings. He had given up the priesthood on meeting and falling in love with her in Avignon, France. However, she was already married and his love brought him only despair. Even after Laura's death in 1348, the poet found no respite. Such torments of love found the ideal musical expression in the madrigal.

Petrarch traveled widely but was long associated with Florence, Italy. Three composers with strong Florentine connections—Philippe Verdelot, Jacques Arcadelt, and Francesco de Layolle—were key to the development of the four-voice madrigal in the early 16th century. They combined the lively, syllabic style of the Italian *frottola* (see p.53) with the more densely woven vocal texture of the French *chanson*. Settings of poetic texts were generally through-composed (see opposite), rather than each verse being set to the same music, and they aimed to express as closely as possible the meaning of the words.

Adriano Willaert in Venice (see pp.72–73) and Luca Marenzio (1553–1599) in Rome took this compositional approach to new heights, establishing madrigals for five voices as the norm.

> "The **music ...** was so concerted, so sweet, so just, and so miraculously **appropriate** to the **words.**"
>
> WRITER ANTON FRANCESCO DONI, ON THE MUSIC OF ADRIANO WILLAERT, 1544

BEFORE

French songs of the 15th century and Italian song forms of the early 16th century influenced the development of the madrigal.

SOLO FORMS

An early song form known as the madrigal died out by about 1400 and was not directly related to the 16th-century madrigal. The Italian song form known as the ***frottola*** **« 52–53** is often held to be the immediate precursor of the madrigal. However, the *frottola* was usually sung as a solo song to a simple instrumental accompaniment, making the madrigal closer in style to the four-voice French ***chanson*** of the early 1500s.

From dance to devotion

Several forms of madrigal emerged, including the Neapolitan *villanella*, with lively dance rhythms and humorous texts, and the dramatic Roman *madrigal arioso*. The spiritual madrigal, with sacred texts set in the vernacular (local language) rather than in Latin, found champions in two composers of the Counter-Reformation: Verona's Vincenzo Ruffo (1508–1587) and the Spaniard Francisco Guerrero (1528–1599), whose two volumes of *Canciones y villanescas espirituales* (spiritual songs) were printed in 1589.

Three ladies of Ferrara

While the Italian printing presses supplied the amateur market for madrigals, music at court was characterized by professional musicians striving for technical and artistic virtuosity. This was particularly remarkable at the court of Ferrara, where composers such as Giaches de Wert (1535–1596), Cipriano de Rore (*c.*1515–1565), and Luzzasco Luzzaschi (1546–1607) wrote brilliant and complex madrigals for performance by the "three ladies of Ferrara."

According to an early historian of the court, the Duke of Ferrara, Alfonso II d'Este, ordered his trio to practice every day. The *Concerto delle donne* (Consort of Women) who performed from 1580 to 1597, became renowned throughout Europe for their vocal technique and expressive power, and were widely imitated. More women could now train as professional musicians and have more music written for them.

The three ladies' virtuosity also influenced the development of the madrigal, notably in the works by Carlo Gesualdo, Prince of Venosa (1560–1613). Gesualdo drew on extremes of musical contrast—for example, in the use of low and high voices, the juxtaposition of rapid rhetorical passages and sustained singing, and conflicting harmonies that expressed the emotional anguish or delirious joy evoked by the poetic texts. By now, a broader range of Italian poets, such as Torquato Tasso and Gian Battista Guarini, appealed to composers.

For family and friends
In England, anthologies of Italian madrigals were at first translated, but soon English verse was set to music—often for performance in the home, as shown in this woodcut.

COMPOSER (1544–*c.*1583)

MADDALENA CASULANA

The composer, singer, and lutenist Maddalena Casulana was one of the most celebrated women musicians of the Renaissance. She worked mainly in Vicenza, Italy, and is known to have performed in public on many occasions, including at a banquet in Perugia and at a meeting of the Vicenza Academy—and to have composed works for major events, such as a royal wedding in Munich, Germany. She was the first woman to publish madrigals: three volumes appeared in Venice between 1568 and 1583. In the dedication of her first book, she rails against the "foolish error of men" who think that women do not share their intellectual gifts. There is no record of her life after 1583.

KEY WORKS

Jacques Arcadelt "Il bianco e dolce cigno" (The Sweet White Swan)

Cipriano de Rore "Anche che col partire" (Although when I Part from You)

Luca Marenzio "Solo e pensoso" (Alone and Pensive)

Carlo Gesualdo "Moro, lasso, al mio duolo" (I Die, alas, in my Suffering)

John Wilbey "Draw on Sweet Night"

AFTER

After about 1600 the madrigal evolved in a number of different ways, notably into the "concerted" madrigals.

MUSICAL EXPERIMENTS

Concerted madrigals involved larger combinations of **voices** and **instruments** and contrasting musical sections. At the same time, experiments in Florence and elsewhere changed the perception of how to express the meaning of a text through music. Early 17th-century composers such as **Claudio Monteverdi** **81 ››** wrote ensemble and solo madrigals that were **operatic** in style, and over the course of the century they grew into other secular forms such as the **cantata** **82–83 ››** and **aria**. By about 1640, the madrigal as a genre had disappeared.

The spread of the madrigal

Printed anthologies of madrigals reached all corners of Europe, as did musicians traveling between courts and cathedrals. In Elizabethan England, a new interest in Petrarch's verse paved the way for a collection entitled *Musica transalpina*, published in London in 1588, in which the Italian texts of settings by composers Luca Marenzio and Alfonso Ferrabosco were translated into English.

This inspired English composers to write their own madrigals. Thomas Morley (*c.*1557–1602) developed a lighter kind of madrigal and compiled *The Triumphs of Oriana*, a book of 25 madrigals by different composers thought to be in praise of Elizabeth I. John Wilbye (1574–1638) and Thomas Weelkes (1576–1623) wrote miniature masterpieces in a more serious vein.

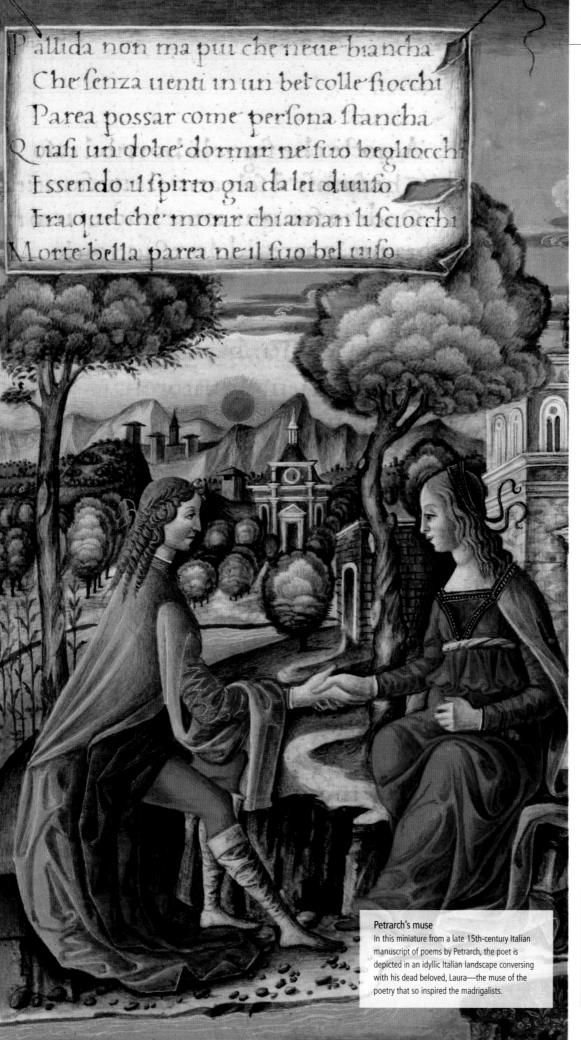

Petrarch's muse
In this miniature from a late 15th-century Italian manuscript of poems by Petrarch, the poet is depicted in an idyllic Italian landscape conversing with his dead beloved, Laura—the muse of the poetry that so inspired the madrigalists.

UNDERSTANDING MUSIC

THROUGH-COMPOSING

Song forms before the madrigal had generally followed fixed musical and poetic formats based on repetition: forms that consisted of a number of verses and a refrain (chorus). These were known as fixed forms. Since each verse was repeated to the same music, there was little scope for developing an expressive approach to setting a poem, either by shifts in the harmony or singling out words for special musical treatment. Madrigal composers increasingly set each phrase or line of verse to new music. In these "through-composed" works, the composer was now free to express the text with musical figures that reflected the meaning of the words—a technique known as word-painting.

Consort Instruments

Consorts, or small ensembles, of instruments developed rapidly in the Renaissance to accompany dancing and to provide entertainment in intimate spaces. Consorts could consist of families of instruments of different sizes.

1 **Curtal** Generally made from a single piece of wood with a double bore, the curtal is a predecessor of the bassoon 2 **Rauschpfeife** This double-reed instrument has a conical bore, increasing the sound produced. 3 **Basset recorder** Made from a single piece of wood, this 16th-century recorder was pitched between tenor and bass. 4 **Alto (or treble) recorder** This instrument is the second highest sounding member of the recorder family. It is used both in consorts and as a solo or accompanying instrument. 5 **Bass racket** This double-reed instrument combines well with other winds or string instruments. 6 **Crumhorn** The double-reed of the crumhorn is "capped," or covered, making it easier to play, as the sound it produces is not altered by lip pressure. 7 **Tenor Crumhorn** With a shapely hook, narrow bore and small finger-holes, the tenor crumhorn makes a distinctive, buzzing sound. 8 **Cornettino** The descant of the cornett family, it was often used to double the tenor voice an octave higher. The cup was usually made from animal horn. 9 **Cornett** Made from leather-covered wood, the cornett has a soft tone. 10 **Harpsichord** This Italian instrument from the 16th century has a single keyboard. The thin-walled original is here seen preserved in a substantial outer case from the 17th century. 11 **8-course lute** The standard lute in the Renaissance had eight courses of strings, with two strings per course, except for the top one, which was a single string or chanterelle. 12 **Amati viola** This 16th-century viola was made by the celebrated Andrea Amati in Cremona. 13 **Theorbo** A second peg-box allows for longer strings that provide lower bass notes. 14 **Cittern urbino** A small, quite light, metal-string instrument, this urbino is an elaborate example from Renaissance Italy. 15 **Harp** One of the oldest instrumental types, this harp has 30 strings and was made in northern Italy from a mixture of maple and walnut wood. 16 **Cittern** As popular and versatile as the guitar today, the cittern could be strummed or plucked.

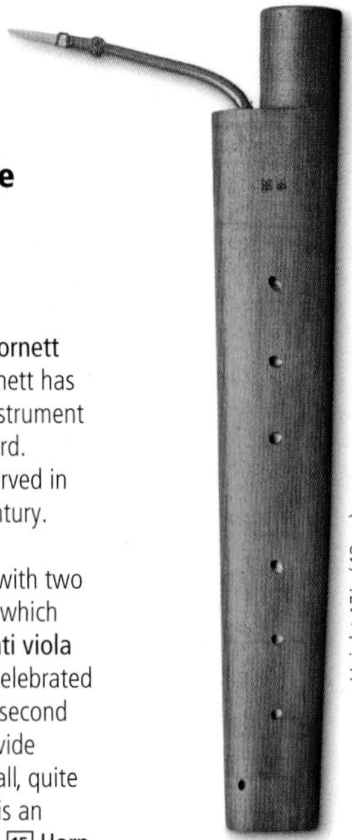

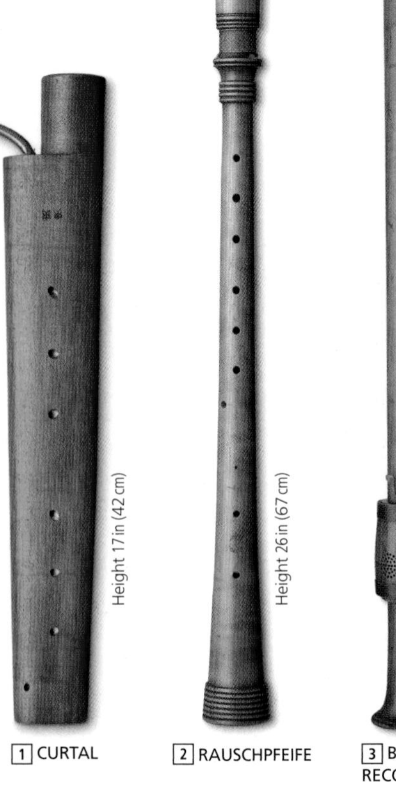

1 CURTAL

2 RAUSCHPFEIFE

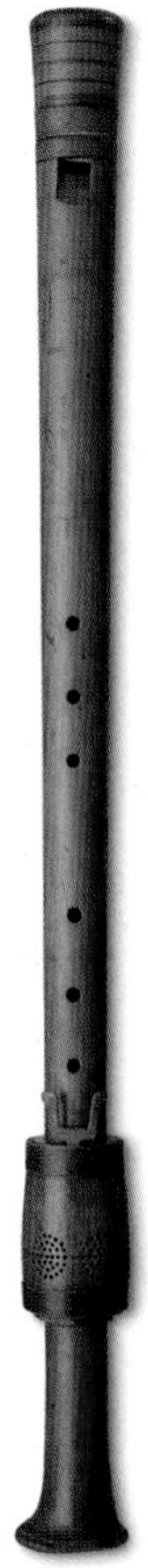

3 BASSET RECORDER

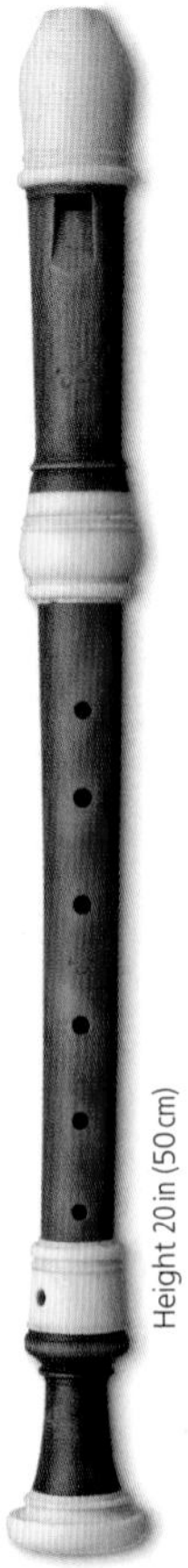

4 ALTO RECORDER

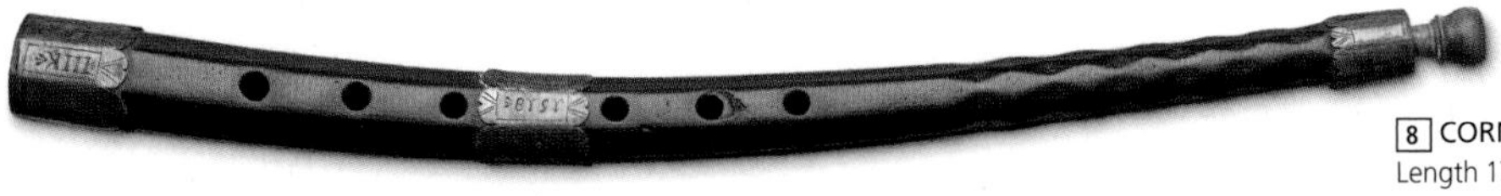

8 CORNETTINO
Length 17 in (42 cm)

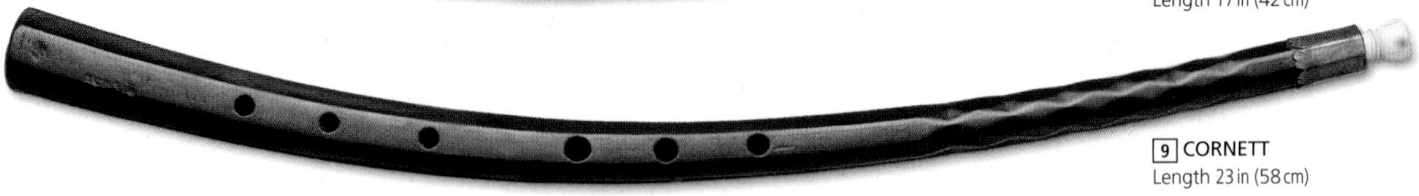

9 CORNETT
Length 23 in (58 cm)

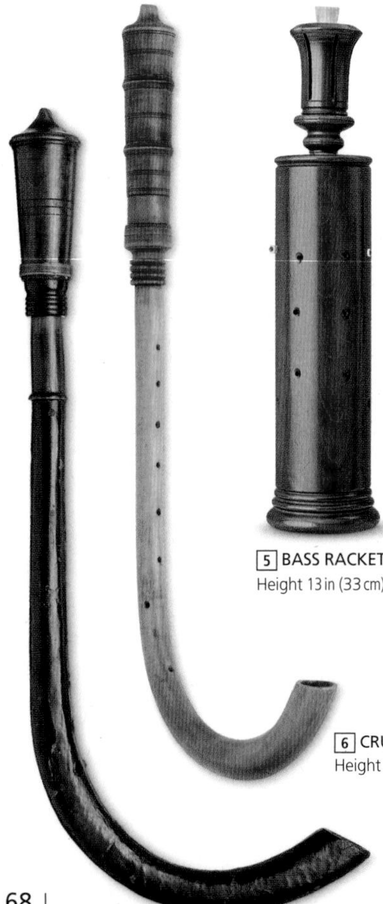

5 BASS RACKET
Height 13 in (33 cm)

6 CRUMHORN
Height 20 in (50 cm)

7 TENOR CRUMHORN
Height 26 in (67 cm)

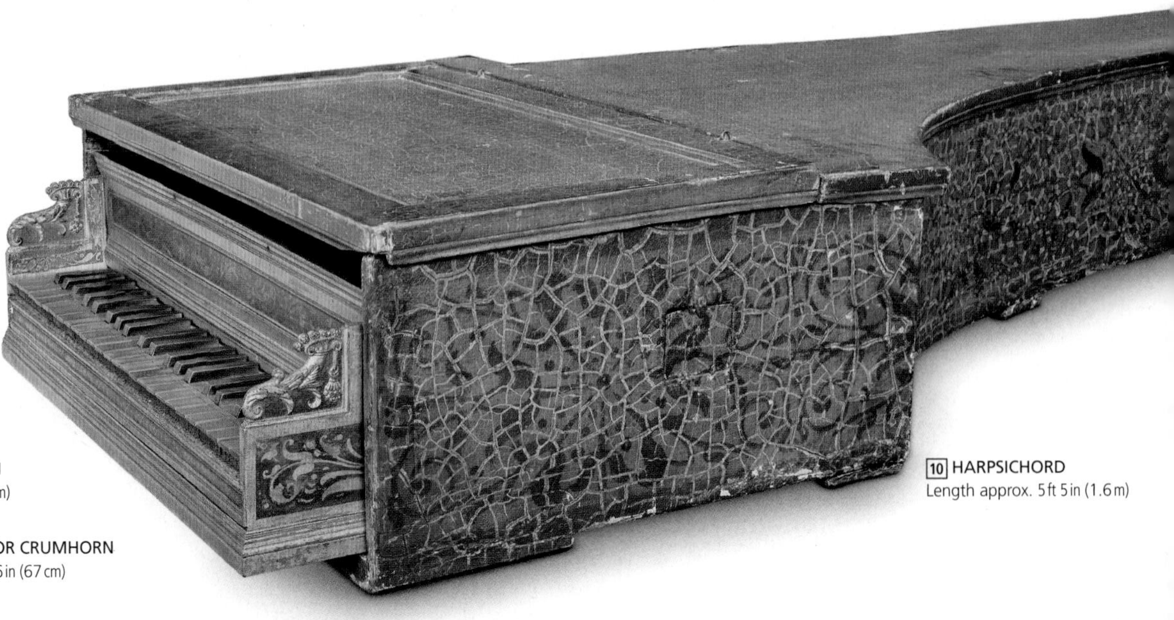

10 HARPSICHORD
Length approx. 5 ft 5 in (1.6 m)

11 8-COURSE LUTE
Total height 30 in (75 cm)

12 AMATI VIOLA
Height approx. 28 in (68 cm)

13 THEORBO
Total height 5 ft 5 in (1.6 m)

14 CITTERN URBINO
Height 38 in (97 cm)

15 HARP
Height 3 ft 7 in (1.1 m)

16 CITTERN
Height 24 in (60 cm)

Carthusian monks at Mass
The large books from which singers performed the music were set on a lectern for easy visibility. Spanish artist Francisco de Zurburán (1598–1664) shows the *facistol* (lectern) in Seville Cathedral.

BEFORE

The marriage of Ferdinand II of Aragon and Isabella I of Castile in 1469 led to the unification of Spain and a cultural revival.

ROOTS OF THE SPANISH GOLDEN AGE
Music had long played an important role in the courts of the Spanish kingdoms of Castile and Aragon. With unification of Spain in 1469 music flourished. A group of composers in the late 15th century, including Juan de Anchieta (1462–1523), Francisco de Peñalosa (1470–1528), and Juan del Encina (1468–*c.*1529), brought about a sea change in the composition of **polyphonic songs**, **masses**, and **motets** by combining local compositional techniques with those of the **Franco-Flemish school** « 46–47. Without these composers, a golden age of Spanish music would not have been possible.

An **Iberian Flowering**

The 16th century was the golden age of multi-voiced music in Spain and Portugal and their colonies in the New World. Religious reforms and Church wealth enabled a flowering of sacred music, while printed instrumental music catered to the new amateur musicians.

Thanks to ecclesiastical reforms at the turn of the 16th century, the cathedrals on the Iberian peninsula of Spain and Portugal developed polyphonic music—pieces in which two or more independent melodies are played simultaneously. As the reigning Iberian monarchs Ferdinand and Isabella traveled around their kingdoms, they recruited the best cathedral singers and rewarded them with paid jobs to encourage them to maintain close ties with the Catholic Church.

When Charles V became king in 1516, Spanish musicians in the royal chapel were forced to take cathedral posts; Charles, educated in Flanders, brought with him a renowned chapel of singers. As a result, Spanish composers working for the Church were brought into contact with the works of the best musicians of Western Europe.

Adopting new forms

The Spanish composer Mateo Flecha the Elder (1481–1553) incorporated French influences into the *ensalada*, a Spanish song style bridging several genres (see opposite). From the French *chanson* (see pp.52–53), he learned the technique of through-composing: rather than being divided into verses and choruses, his songs had non-repeated music throughout (see p.67).

Meanwhile, Cristóbal de Morales (1500–1553) and Francisco Guerrero (see opposite) absorbed the techniques of canon and imitation, where a melodic phrase is repeated (or imitated) after a brief rest, and the voices overlap to weave the counterpoint. Morales

UNDERSTANDING MUSIC

ENSALADA

Music was central to Aztec culture and inextricably linked to dance, which was termed "singing with the feet." Considered to have religious meaning and understood to be a gift to the gods, music was performed by all members of Aztec society. While priests performed with instruments, including trumpets, drums, bells, and flutes, on top of the pyramids, commoners would worship at home with rattles and small whistles. At court, music and dance were used to accompany feasts and celebrate rulers, and new sacred hymns were created to mark both mythological and historical events, such as battles and marriages. Warriors were expected to practice their singing and dancing in a dedicated building called "the house of song."

and Guerrero were trained at Seville Cathedral. Tomás Luis de Victoria (1548–1611) began his career at Avila Cathedral in Castile, but spent much of his career in Rome. On returning to Spain, he became organist at the royal convent of Las Descalzas in Madrid and published volumes of sacred polyphony. All three of these composers wrote sacred music and, through having their works printed in Italy, enjoyed European renown.

In around 1600, a number of books of sacred polyphony by other Spanish composers were published in the cities of Madrid, Salamanca, and Lisbon. The contributors included Spanish composers such as Sebastián de Vivanco (1551–1622), Alonso Lobo (1555–1617), and Juan de Esquivel (1560–1625), as well as the Portuguese composers Manuel Cardoso (1566–1650) and Filipe de Magalhães (1571–1652). Published largely with an eye to the market created by the founding of new cathedrals in the Americas, these large-format choir books contained all the polyphony required for the liturgy at that time.

The new wealth that lay behind this flourishing of polyphony largely dried up in the 17th century, which is one reason why the works of the golden age continued to form the core repertory of churches throughout the Iberian peninsula well into the 18th century.

Incan gold
The Spanish conquistadors plundered silver and gold from the Americas, including treasure from the Incan Empire. Some of it was used to fund the choirs of the cathedrals of Spain and Portugal.

Aristocrats and amateurs

Charles V employed only Franco-Flemish musicians in his chapel, but singer-composers of Spanish and Portuguese origin secured posts in the households of his consort, Queen Isabella of Portugal, and the royal children. The palaces of the nobles were also filled with music. The court of the Mendoza family in Guadalajara, for example, was said to rival that of Charles V himself, while other courts in Valencia, Seville, and Vila Viçosa were also noteworthy.

"I am **responsible** for teaching children how to **read, write, preach,** and **sing...**"

FRANCISCAN MISSIONARY PEDRO DE GANTE IN A LETTER TO CHARLES V, 1532

It was among the aristocracy that the notion of the amateur musician began to take hold, specifically with music for the *vihuela*, a guitar-shaped instrument similar to the lute. Several vihuelists exploited the lucrative potential of printing music for the well-educated gentleman *aficionado* or amateur, and brought out anthologies of pieces for *vihuela* along with manuals on how to play the instrument. These books reflect the wide range of international and local repertoire then available in Spain, in arrangements that appealed to music-lovers beyond the profession.

Music in the New World

Ferdinand and Isabella justified financing Christopher Columbus's voyage that led to the discovery of the Americas in 1492 by proclaiming the goal of bringing the peoples of the New World into the Roman Catholic fold.

Missionaries such as Pedro de Gante (1480–1572), a Franciscan monk and a relative of Charles V, used music to teach the principles of the faith. Accounts written at the time cite the innate musical skills of the native peoples as proof of their capacity to connect with the divine and be converted, and so told of the success of evangelization. Gante told Charles that many of the singers in Mexico were so skilled that "they could sing in Your Majesty's chapel, so well that it has to be seen to be believed."

Initially, the new cathedrals and churches constructed in Latin and South America—usually modeled on the cathedrals of Seville or Toledo—provided jobs primarily for musicians from the Iberian Peninsula, while its composers and instrument-makers enjoyed a rapidly expanding export market for their works. Music books and instruments were shipped across the Atlantic to Mexico and taken from there to Lima in Peru and then across the Pacific. In this way, the New World—from Mexico City to Manila in the Philippines—became a conduit for European musical culture that was adopted and adapted according to local traditions and needs.

COMPOSER (1528–1599)

FRANCISCO GUERRERO

Francisco Guerrero was part of the great triumvirate of golden-age Spanish composers, along with Cristóbal de Morales and Tomás Luis de Victoria. Guerrero was born in Seville and became choirmaster of Jaén Cathedral at the age of 17. He moved briefly to Málaga before returning to Seville and staying there for the rest of his career.

Guerrero published most of his works, including dozens of sacred songs, in Rome and Venice, incurring so many debts in the process that the Chapter of Seville Cathedral was forced to bail him out of jail. In 1589, he had leave to travel to the Holy Land, and his account of the journey became a best-seller.

KEY WORKS

Francisco de Peñalosa *Missa Ave Maria*

Cristóbal de Morales *Magnificats*

Francisco de Guerrero "Ave virgo sanctissima" (Hail, Most Blessed Virgin)

Tomás Luis de Victoria *Tenebrae responsories*

Manuel Cardoso *Requiem Mass*

Mateo Flecha the Elder *La justa* (The Joust)

AFTER

In 17th-century Iberia, music continued to thrive in cathedrals and courts but burgeoned in theaters, too.

MUSIC FOR THE THEATER

In the ***comedias*** (dramas) of the great Spanish playwrights Lope de Vega (1562–1635) and Pedro Calderón de la Barca (1600–1681), solo songs, duets, choruses, and instrumental music set the scene, symbolized heavenly and earthly characters, and **entertained the public** in *corrales* (courtyard theaters).

Despite some experiments with **opera** on the Spanish stage, the *comedia*, with its mixture of spoken dialogue and music not unlike the **semi-opera** **95 ››** of 17th-century England, was generally more popular. Opera was later imported from Italy from 1703 onward.

GUITAR MUSIC

The **guitar** had been a popular instrument in 16th-century Spain, but from about 1600 it **overshadowed the courtly *vihuela*** and spread throughout Europe **90–91 ››**.

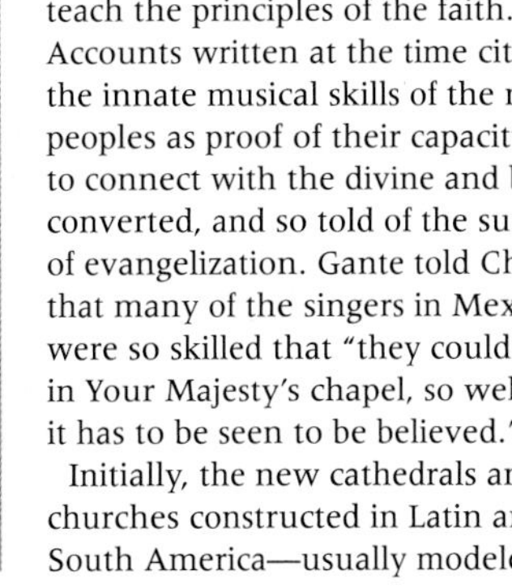

SPANISH GUITAR, 1730

BEFORE

Founded in the eighth century CE, the Republic of Venice in northern Italy grew into a powerful trading empire over the next 1,000 years. Music was an established part of the city's elaborate ceremonies.

CHARITABLE CONTRIBUTIONS

The *scuole grandi* (great schools) built by the city's major **confraternities,** or charitable organizations, became important patrons of music when, in the 15th century, they began to employ **professional musicians**

THE VENETIAN STATE was often popularly called the "Republic of Music."

instead of relying solely on the musical talents of their members. By the early 16th century, each confraternity employed eight to ten **singers**, as well as **instrumentalists**, all of whom participated in the city's many processions. Venice was one of the richest and most ceremonial cities, with music filling its churches, streets, squares, and waterways.

Venetian Glories

Music formed an integral part of the civic ceremonies of Renaissance Venice, and its great institutions of Church and state attracted some of the best musicians in Italy. Musical splendor and virtuosity soon gave rise to a new choral and instrumental style.

Music in Venice developed differently from the music in the princely courts of Italy. As the capital of a republic, Venice had its own civic authority in which state ritual and ceremonial spaces were of great importance. This required an army of accomplished musicians, who were employed by the city's churches and the five *scuole grandi* (great schools) of its confraternities. Many of the ceremonies revolved around the Doge, the republic's elected leader, who by the late 16th century took part in 16 annual processions—all involving music and displaying Venetian wealth and its sense of urban social order.

Many musical events and works were linked to St. Mark (Mark the Evangelist), patron saint of the city, whose remains were said to have been brought to Venice from Alexandria in modern-day Egypt in 827 CE. The Doge was considered to be the successor to St. Mark, just as the Pope was to St. Peter. St. Mark's Basilica celebrated its own liturgy (the *patriarchino*), which called for Venetian texts that were given polyphonic settings (with two or more melodies performed simultaneously: (see pp.46–47).

New directions

A key to the flourishing status of music in the city was the appointment in 1527 of the Flemish composer Adriano

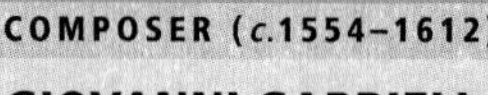

COMPOSER (*c.*1554–1612)

GIOVANNI GABRIELI

Giovanni Gabrieli was one of the great composers of the Renaissance and a pioneer of large-scale *concertato* works for opposing groups of instruments and voices. Born in Venice, he studied with his uncle, Andrea Gabrieli, and then with the composer Orlande de Lassus in Munich, Germany. He became principal organist at St. Mark's, and played the organ for the prestigious confraternity at San Rocco. He published works in the *cori spezzati* style (see opposite), notably his *Sacrae symphoniae* (a collection of sacred music, 1597). Gabrieli was highly influential: German composers Heinrich Schütz and Hans Leo Hassler studied with him in Venice.

The confraternity's riches
In 1564 the Italian painter Tintoretto was commissioned to decorate the Scuola Grande di San Rocco, where musicians of the caliber of Giovanni Gabrieli and Giovanni Croce worked.

Willaert (1490–1562) as *maestro di cappella* (music director) of St. Mark's. His appointment was part of a major overhaul of the city's musical resources and ceremonial spaces, which included the 16th-century remodelling of St. Mark's Square.

Willaert's international reputation was secured when his works were published by the major Venetian music-printing houses, including his *Musica nova* (New music, 1559), a pioneering collection of madrigals and motets (see pp.66–67). His fame attracted some of the leading composers of the time to St. Mark's Basilica, including the Italian Gioseffo Zarlino (1517–1590). He also influenced the Franco-Flemish Orlande de Lassus (*c.*1532–1594) and the Italian Palestrina (see pp.60–61).

Zarlino credited Willaert with the invention of antiphonal singing known as *cori spezzti*, which he described in 1558: "[Compositions] are arranged and divided into two choirs, or even three, each one of four parts; the choirs sing one after another, in turn, and sometimes (depending on the purpose) all together, especially at the end, which works very well. And... such choirs are placed rather far apart."

Music to amaze

Spatially and musically, this polychoral style deployed voices and instruments to exploit the magnificent scale and resonance of Venice's finest buildings. In the early 17th century, English traveler and writer Thomas Coryat witnessed the feast day of St. Roch: "[the] musicke, which was both vocall and instrumental, [was] so good, so delectable, so admirable, so super excellent, that it did even ravish and stupefie all those strangers that never heard the like ..."

Sumptuous ceremonies
Venetian love of ceremony is reflected in Gentile Bellini's *Procession in St. Mark's Square* (1496), which was commissioned by the Scuola Grande di San Giovanni Evangelista.

Music for San Marco

In St. Mark's Basilica, each upper gallery on either side of the chancel was equipped with an organ. Although it was long thought that singers were placed there to perform double-choir works, recent research suggests they performed from two large pulpits in the chancel at ground level or in two *pergole* (galleries) just inside the choir screen.

150 **The number of musicians employed for the celebration of the feast day of St. Mark in 1603. Seven organs were also required.**

Andrea Gabrieli, who was appointed organist of St. Mark's in 1566, was largely responsible for the increase in instrumental variety in the basilica's liturgy, and the development of the *concertato*—music in the style of a concerto, contrasting opposing groups of choirs and instrumentalists—that so impressed Coryat. Gabrieli's large-scale music for ceremonial occasions was published in 1587 in *Concerti*, a collection that also included works by his nephew Giovanni. Many of their choral works marked specific events in the city, such as thanksgiving for the end of a plague epidemic in 1577.

AFTER

The Venetian *cori spezzati* style continued to flourish after Monteverdi, through Giovanni Rovetta and Francesco Cavalli, his successors at St. Mark's.

MUSIC EVERYWHERE

Music became not just the preserve of the churches and confraternities, but was central to the whole of Venetian society and gained an **international reputation**, due in part to the city's many visitors. A 17th-century French tourist remarked: "**In every home**, someone is **playing a musical instrument** or **singing**. There is music everywhere." Particularly important was the development of **opera houses** from 1637 **80–81 ››**, for which **Monteverdi** and **Cavalli** composed some of their most glorious music.

KEY WORKS

Adriano Willaert *I salmi... a uno et a duoi chori* (Psalms for One and Two Choirs)

Andrea Gabrieli *Magnificat* (My Soul Magnifies the Lord)

Giovanni Gabrieli *In ecclesiis* (In Churches)

Claudio Monteverdi *Vespro de la Beata Virgine* (Vespers for the Blessed Virgin)

Francesco Cavalli *Messa concertata* (Concertato Mass)

UNDERSTANDING MUSIC

CORI SPEZZATI

The term *cori spezzati* literally means "separated choirs." The concept of singing psalms with two choirs set apart had its roots in Jewish practice, and *cori spezzati* were initially used in psalm settings. The earliest mention of the term in polyphony (see pp.46–47) is found in a volume of double-choir psalm-settings by Adriano Willaert, published in 1550 while he was chapel master of St. Mark's.

Willaert's successors, including Claudio Monteverdi who was appointed in 1613, all composed in this style. Venetian demand for large-scale ceremonial music and the vast, resonant spaces of the basilica were ideal for the development of the polychoral style that was extended to include Mass and Magnificat settings and motets, such as Giovanni Gabrieli's *In ecclesiis* or Monteverdi's 1610 *Vespers*.

4

THE BAROQUE SPIRIT

1600–1750

A period of unprecedented musical creativity, the 17th and 18th centuries saw the dominance of counterpoint—music that used multiple lines or voices—and the creation of the most dramatic musical form yet—opera. Royal courts vied with the Church to have the most glorious music. Handel's operas portrayed drama on a human scale, while the Church stormed the heavens with the sacred oratorios and masses of Bach.

« Five-course guitar made by Matteo Sellas in 1640 and decorated with ivory and ebony.

THE BAROQUE SPIRIT
1600–1750

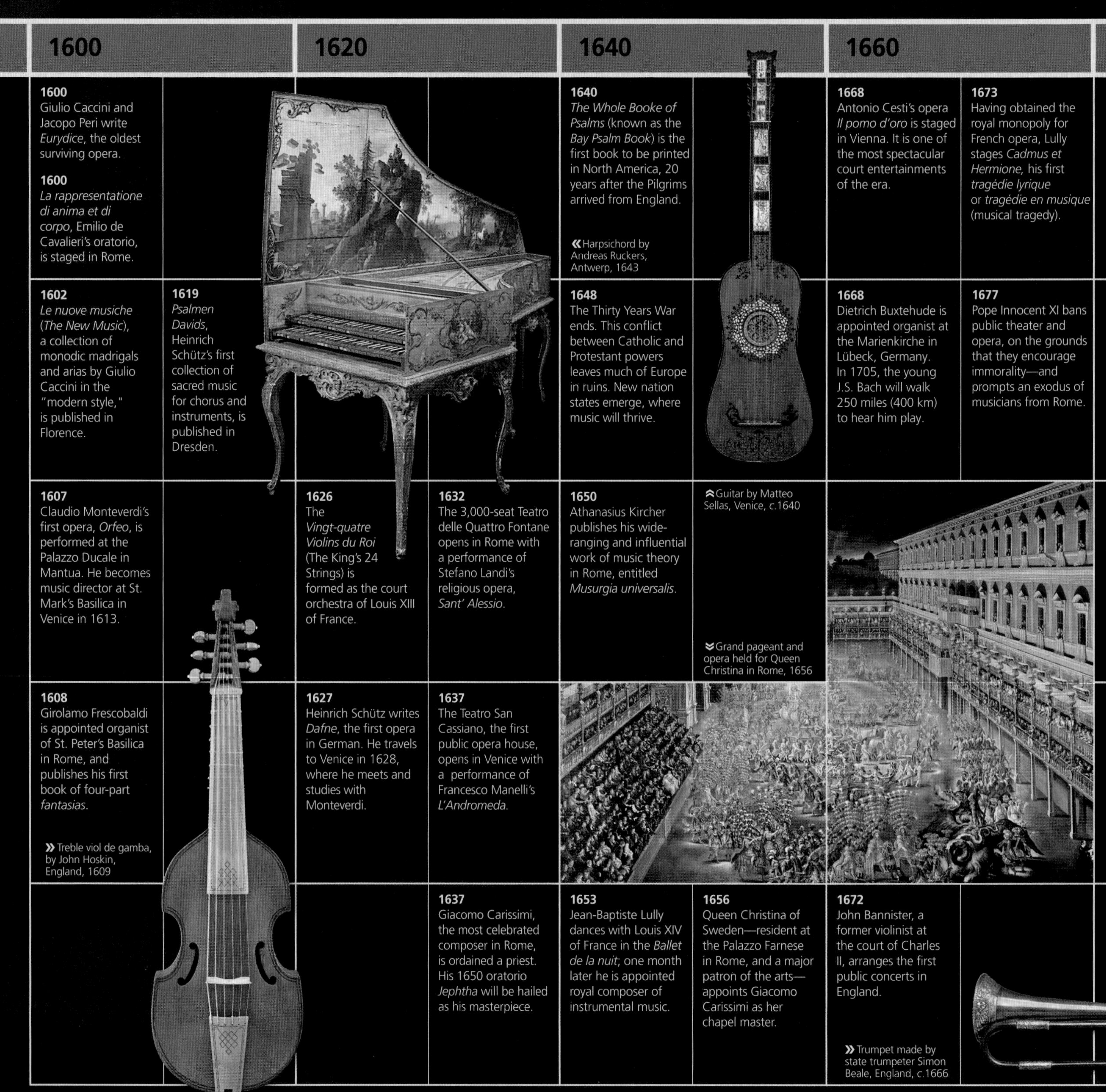

1600

1600
Giulio Caccini and Jacopo Peri write *Eurydice*, the oldest surviving opera.

1600
La rappresentatione di anima et di corpo, Emilio de Cavalieri's oratorio, is staged in Rome.

1602
Le nuove musiche (*The New Music*), a collection of monodic madrigals and arias by Giulio Caccini in the "modern style," is published in Florence.

1607
Claudio Monteverdi's first opera, *Orfeo*, is performed at the Palazzo Ducale in Mantua. He becomes music director at St. Mark's Basilica in Venice in 1613.

1608
Girolamo Frescobaldi is appointed organist of St. Peter's Basilica in Rome, and publishes his first book of four-part *fantasias*.

» Treble viol de gamba, by John Hoskin, England, 1609

1619
Psalmen Davids, Heinrich Schütz's first collection of sacred music for chorus and instruments, is published in Dresden.

1620

1626
The *Vingt-quatre Violins du Roi* (The King's 24 Strings) is formed as the court orchestra of Louis XIII of France.

1627
Heinrich Schütz writes *Dafne*, the first opera in German. He travels to Venice in 1628, where he meets and studies with Monteverdi.

1632
The 3,000-seat Teatro delle Quattro Fontane opens in Rome with a performance of Stefano Landi's religious opera, *Sant' Alessio*.

1637
The Teatro San Cassiano, the first public opera house, opens in Venice with a performance of Francesco Manelli's *L'Andromeda*.

1637
Giacomo Carissimi, the most celebrated composer in Rome, is ordained a priest. His 1650 oratorio *Jephtha* will be hailed as his masterpiece.

1640

1640
The Whole Booke of Psalms (known as the *Bay Psalm Book*) is the first book to be printed in North America, 20 years after the Pilgrims arrived from England.

« Harpsichord by Andreas Ruckers, Antwerp, 1643

1648
The Thirty Years War ends. This conflict between Catholic and Protestant powers leaves much of Europe in ruins. New nation states emerge, where music will thrive.

1650
Athanasius Kircher publishes his wide-ranging and influential work of music theory in Rome, entitled *Musurgia universalis*.

« Guitar by Matteo Sellas, Venice, c.1640

» Grand pageant and opera held for Queen Christina in Rome, 1656

1653
Jean-Baptiste Lully dances with Louis XIV of France in the *Ballet de la nuit*; one month later he is appointed royal composer of instrumental music.

1656
Queen Christina of Sweden—resident at the Palazzo Farnese in Rome, and a major patron of the arts—appoints Giacomo Carissimi as her chapel master.

1660

1668
Antonio Cesti's opera *Il pomo d'oro* is staged in Vienna. It is one of the most spectacular court entertainments of the era.

1668
Dietrich Buxtehude is appointed organist at the Marienkirche in Lübeck, Germany. In 1705, the young J.S. Bach will walk 250 miles (400 km) to hear him play.

1672
John Bannister, a former violinist at the court of Charles II, arranges the first public concerts in England.

» Trumpet made by state trumpeter Simon Beale, England, c.1666

1673
Having obtained the royal monopoly for French opera, Lully stages *Cadmus et Hermione*, his first *tragédie lyrique* or *tragédie en musique* (musical tragedy).

1677
Pope Innocent XI bans public theater and opera, on the grounds that they encourage immorality—and prompts an exodus of musicians from Rome.

Along with all the arts, music in the Baroque era possessed a new power and exuberance. Whether writing religious or secular works, composers wanted to generate an emotional response in their audience. During this period, new forms developed, such as opera and oratorio, and these put a strong emphasis on expressive melody.

There was an increase in instrumental music as an independent form, and not just to accompany dancing or singing, with the violin becoming especially popular. In both vocal and instrumental music, variety and drama were achieved by contrasting a smaller group with a larger one, a style known as *concertante*.

1680

1681
Arcangelo Corelli's Trio Sonatas opus 1 are published in Rome.

1686
Armide, the finest of Lully's *tragédies lyriques*, is staged at the Palais Royal in Paris.

Organ of St. Katharine's Cree, London, where Purcell and Handel played

1685
This year sees the birth of three major Baroque composers: Handel (February 23); J.S. Bach (March 21); and Domenico Scarlatti (October 26).

1695
English composer Henry Purcell becomes ill and dies at just 36, soon after composing the funeral music for Queen Mary.

c.1698
In Italy, keyboard maker Bartolomeo Cristofori begins building the first pianoforte, which is completed by 1700.

1700

Italian violin-maker Stradivari in his workshop

1700
A 20-year golden period begins for Antonio Stradivari, when he will make his finest violins and cellos.

Vivaldi, Italian violinist and composer

1703
Antonio Vivaldi is appointed violin master at the Ospedale della Pietà, an orphanage in Venice. He composes much of his music for its famous girls' choir and orchestra.

1716
François Couperin publishes his treatise, *L'art de toucher le clavecin*, on keyboard technique and how best to play his harpsichord music.

1711
Rinaldo, the first of Handel's operas specially written for the London stage, is performed at the Queen's Theatre in Haymarket, London.

Handel, who settled in England in 1712

1714
Gottfried Silberman completes his new three-manual organ at Freiberg Cathedral—one of many organs he builds in Saxony.

Masked actor performing a dance in 18th-century Japan

1720

1723
Appointed Kantor of Leipzig's Thomasschule, J.S. Bach also becomes the city's de facto music director.

1729
Domenico Scarlatti moves to Spain, where he writes more than 500 keyboard sonatas.

1725
Vivaldi publishes a set of 12 concertos, including *The Four Seasons*. Johann Fux's *Gradus ad Parnassum*, a highly influential treatise on mastering counterpoint, is also published.

1733
The daring harmonies of Jean-Philippe Rameau's first opera, *Hippolyte et Aricie*, cause an uproar at its Paris premiere. The term "baroque" is used as a criticism of the opera.

1728
In London, John Gay's *The Beggar's Opera* lampoons both the government and the contemporary taste for Italian opera.

1739
Theorist Johann Mattheson advises on ornamentation in *Der vollkommene Capellmeister*.

1740

1741
J.S. Bach's epic keyboard work, the *Goldberg Variations*, is published in Nuremberg.

1747
J.S. Bach visits the Prussian court of Frederick the Great (where his son C.P.E. Bach is harpsichordist) and improvises on a theme by the king—later developed as the *Musical Offering*.

1742
Handel's oratorio, *Messiah*, is first performed at a charity concert in the New Music Hall in Dublin.

1749
Handel's orchestral suite, *Music for the Royal Fireworks*, is performed at Green Park in London to celebrate the end of the War of the Austrian Succession.

1745
Rameau is appointed court composer to Louis XV. Prolific and popular at the time, his works will vanish from the repertory by the end of the 18th century.

Statue of J.S. Bach, Leipzig

1747
In Japan, *Yoshitsune and the Thousand Cherry Trees* is adapted from a puppet play to become a masterpiece of *kabuki* theater, which combines drama, music, and dance.

1750
The death of J.S. Bach, followed by Handel in 1759, marks the end of the Baroque period in music.

BEFORE

The main musical style of the Renaissance was polyphony, in which several independent musical lines were blended together.

MUSICAL REBIRTH
In the 15th century, **John Dunstable** and **Guillaume Dufay** **« 46–47** developed a new style of a **polyphony**, characterized by a sense of forward momentum. Gifted musicians traveling throughout Europe helped to spread a degree of stylistic uniformity.

MUSIC TO ENHANCE WORDS
Medieval scholars argued that music was interlinked with **mathematics**, as the **Ancient Greeks** believed **« 18–19**, but **Renaissance** scholars thought music was closer to language in its ability to **move listeners**. Finding a musical style that increased the **intelligibility** of the words being sung began to drive musical innovation.

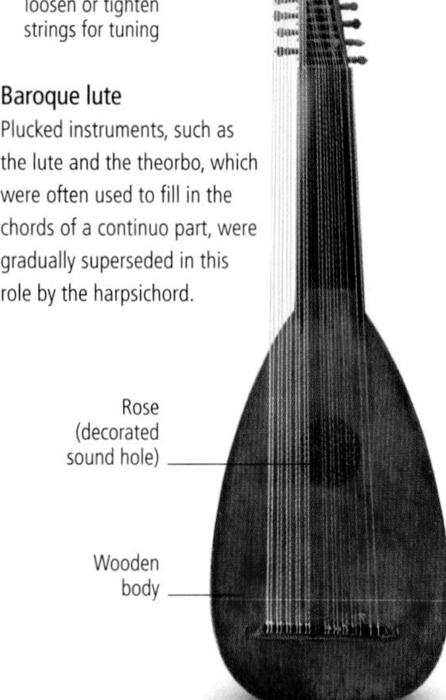

Baroque lute
Plucked instruments, such as the lute and the theorbo, which were often used to fill in the chords of a continuo part, were gradually superseded in this role by the harpsichord.

The **Baroque Style**

The term "baroque," from the Portuguese name for a misshapen pearl, was first used to describe something elaborate or unnatural. Now it refers to a period and style in which the arts displayed a newfound exuberance and theatricality that appealed directly to the emotions.

For music, the Baroque era began in Italy in around 1600, when progressive composers atttempted to make songs more expressive and better able to enhance the meaning of the words. Monody, in which a single line of melody is accompanied by one or two instruments, was considered better at communicating the text than polyphony (see pp.46–47), in which several, independent melodic lines were sung (or played) simultaneously.

This monodic style, which imitated the rhythms of speech, developed into two new forms of vocal music: recitative, a kind of speechlike, conversational singing; and the aria, an extended expressive song in which the music mirrors the emotions of the text. Both could be freely embellished by the singer and became the central elements of opera, oratorio, and cantata. Claudio Monteverdi was their first great exponent (see pp.80–83).

Support from below

The music that accompanied the soloist is called the "basso continuo," or "figured bass." As the name suggests, it is a continuous bass accompaniment to the solo melody, and is one of the hallmarks of the Baroque style.

In a written piece of music, the bass line was marked with numbers set above the notes. These "figures" indicated which chords were to be played to fill out the music between the top melodic line and the bass line. The translation of the numbers into notes—called realization—allows for a degree of flexibility in interpretation, depending on the ability of the player. The instruments that played this accompanying role were collectively known as the "continuo," and usually consisted of either a plucked string instrument, such as a lute or theorbo (see pp.90–91), or a keyboard, such as a harpsichord or small organ (see pp.104–105). The bass line was reinforced by a low instrument, such as a bass viol, cello, or bassoon.

Sculptural dynamic
This 1652 sculpture of St. Teresa of Ávila by Gian Lorenzo Bernini (1598–1680) portrays the saint experiencing a vision. Set in the church of Santa Maria della Vittoria, Rome, it displays the theatricality and sensuousness that is typical of Baroque art.

Continuo players could also accompany instrumental music, and more than one line of melody—as in a trio sonata, where the melody is shared by two instruments, accompanied by the continuo.

Composers also began to exploit the unique sound qualities of specific instruments, and became more interested in writing music for particular instruments—rather than music that could be picked up and played by any combination of instruments or voices that was available. At the same time, technical advances by instrument-makers helped increase the expressive power of instruments. Harpsichords and violins became especially popular, and there was a corresponding development of new musical forms such as sonatas, partitas, and suites (see pp.102–103).

Emotional response

Baroque artists wanted, above all, to move their listeners. Composers borrowed ideas from the art of rhetoric—the way a skilled speaker could manipulate and direct the emotions of the listeners—and transferred them to music. Composers sought to express love, hatred, sadness, or despair, as described in the words, directly through the music.

This emphasis on the emotions did not apply only to secular music. The Catholic Church, too, made use of it, in an attempt to win back the hearts and minds of believers who had abandoned Roman Catholicism for Protestantism in the early 1500s (see pp. 58–59). Church authorities encouraged composers to write music that would stir up an emotional response to their religious teachings.

However, as the new musical forms spread across Europe, the same approach was used for Protestant church music. One of the main theorists of this movement, which became known as "the doctrine of affections," was German composer and theorist Johann Mattheson (1681–1764). In 1739, he wrote *Der Volkommene Capellmeister* (The Perfect Chapelmaster), in which he outlines the correct way for a musician to perform a basso continuo, with advice on ornamentation. On the subject of the role of music itself, he declares that

Head of a bass viol
Instead of the more conventional scroll, instruments of the viol and violin families often had peg boxes with carved figurative heads at the top, either of people or animals.

UNDERSTANDING MUSIC

ORNAMENTATION IN MUSIC

To vary a written piece of music, particularly when a passage was repeated, embellishments, also called ornaments, were added to individual notes, or even sequences of notes. This is known as ornamentation and, in the Baroque era, it was either left to the performer to improvise or marked on the music by the composer. One of the most common types of ornament is the trill, which is the name for a rapid alternation between two adjacent notes.

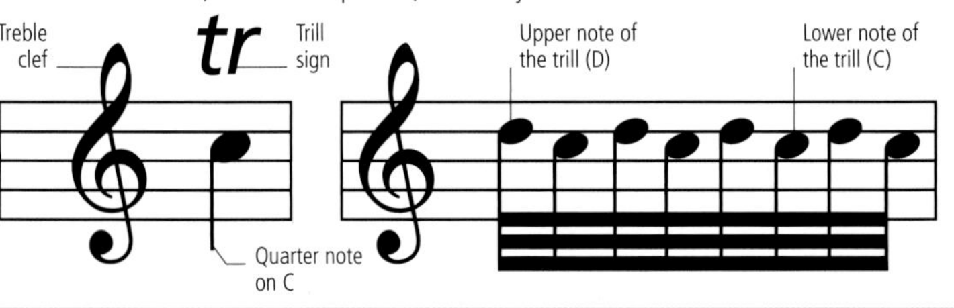

KEY WORKS

Claudio Monteverdi *Orfeo* (Orpheus)

Antonio Vivaldi *L'estro armonico* (Harmonic Inspiration), Op. 3

J. S. Bach Brandenburg Concertos (BWV 1046–1051); Cantata No.140 (BWV 140); *The Art of Fugue* (BWV 1080)

Lid, raised to help the sound travel

Strings

Stops

Manual (keyboard)

English double-manual harpsichord, 1700
The harpsichord was used as both a continuo and a solo instrument. This one, built by Frenchman Joseph Tisseran in London, is exquisitely painted to imitate panels with gold spangles that resemble Chinese lacquer.

AFTER

In the 18th century, as the Age of Enlightenment championed reason over superstition, musical complexity gave way to order and clarity.

MOVING AWAY FROM COMPLEXITY
The Baroque era ended in the 1750s with the deaths of **J. S. Bach** **100–101 ››** and **G. F. Handel** **108–109 ››**. While both continued to be admired, the music of the next generation was in the ***galant*** style—simpler, more elegant, and less demanding to listen to.

THE CLASSICAL STYLE
A **new clarity** **116–117 ››** emerged with the works of **Joseph Haydn** **126–127 ››** and **Wolfgang Amadeus Mozart** **136–137 ››**. Both wrote music in which order and balance were given equal importance to beauty. New forms, such as the **symphony** and **string quartet**, replaced the ***concerto grosso*** and **trio sonata**.

"Everything [in music] that occurs without praiseworthy Affections, is nothing, does nothing, is worth nothing."

Harmony from diversity

Another defining musical characteristic of the Baroque era is the use of contrasting groups in the same work, either by alternating singers and instrumentalists or a large group of musicians and a smaller one.

The idea was to produce a harmonious whole out of diverse elements and it was called the *stile concertato* (concerto style), from the Italian *concertare*, meaning to agree or come together. The *stile concertato* originated in the mid- to late-16th century in Venice where Andrea Gabrieli and his nephew, Giovanni Gabrieli (see pp.72–73), dramatically exploited the acoustics of St. Mark's Basilica by placing different musical groups around the church to perform.

By the 18th century, the word "concerto" was used in two ways. A *concerto grosso* (large concerto), such as the Brandenburg Concertos by J. S. Bach (see pp.100–101), divided the players between the full orchestra and a smaller solo group. In a solo concerto, the full orchestra was contrasted with an individual solo instrument, as in the many violin concertos of Antonio Vivaldi (see pp.92–93).

1733 The year the word "Baroque" was first applied—as a criticism—in relation to Rameau's opera *Hippolyte et Aricie*.

Counterpoint

The new *stile concertato* combined with the basso continuo to create a melody-led music with a strong sense of forward momentum. At the same time, Western music was moving towards the system of major-minor tonality, in which a key note, called the tonic, acted as the gravitational center around which a composition revolved.

All of these developments led composers to produce ever more complex works in which several independent melodic lines were woven together in a dynamic whole—a technique known as counterpoint (see pp.98–99). J.S. Bach was the outstanding exponent of Baroque counterpoint—whether writing elaborate, multi-voiced fugues, or works in which just one melody is set against another, as in his Cantata No. 140, *"Wachet Auf"* (Sleepers, Wake).

"**Baroque ...** meaning irregular, **bizarre,** uneven."

"DICTIONAIRE DE L'ACADÉMIE," 3RD EDITION, 1740

Orpheus and Eurydice
The story of how the musician Orpheus tried to rescue his wife, Eurydice, from the underworld, taken from Greek mythology, inspired several operas in the Baroque era. This painting of the couple is by the Italian artist Jacopo Vignali (1592–1664).

BEFORE

During the Renaissance, composers tried to find better ways of making their music serve the words' meaning.

EXPRESSING MOOD WITH MUSIC
Vocal settings of love poetry, such as **madrigals** **« 66–67**, were an ideal genre for expressing strong emotions. Italian composers **Carlo Gesualdo** and **Claudio Monteverdi** used clashing notes (dissonances) to signal the pain of love, or a falling melody to indicate a sigh.

NEW AND OLD COMPOSITION STYLES
In 1600, critic **Giovanni Artusi** (1540–1613) attacked Monteverdi for putting the demands of the poetry above the rules of composition. Monteverdi defended himself in his fifth book of madrigals (1605), writing that there were two writing styles: the old style, where music ruled the words, and the new, where **music served the words**, and so the rules of the old style must be broken.

The **Birth** of **Opera**

Though sung religious dramas had existed in the Middle Ages, opera's true origins derive from meetings held by a group of intellectuals, noblemen, and musicians, known as the Florentine Camerata, who met at the house of Count Bardi in Florence in the late 16th century.

Out of the Camerata's discussions about how Ancient Greek drama might have sounded, an idea emerged that the clearest way of expressing words set to music was through monody—a single line of sung music that followed the natural rhythm of speech.

Two composers in the Camerata, Giulio Caccini (1551–1618) and Jacopo Peri (1561–1633), put the idea into practice in *intermedi* (dramatic musical scenes) performed between the acts of a play. They were common in Florence during celebratory events, such as the wedding of Duke Ferdinando de' Medici to Christine of Lorraine in 1589.

Florence, the cradle of early opera
Opera evolved out of musical dramas shown between acts of plays performed during private entertainments that were paid for by the city's powerful Medici family.

The first operas

In 1594, Peri joined the poet Ottavio Rinucinni (1562–1621) to create a new genre—opera—that merged drama with music. The first result was *Dafne*, followed, in 1600, by *Euridice*. They were sung in a declamatory manner, halfway between speaking and singing, called recitative. The singers were accompanied by a harpsichord, lute, or other instruments capable of playing a simple chordal accompaniment. Claudio Monteverdi (1567–1643) was probably familiar with *Euridice* when, in 1607, he wrote his first opera, *L'Orfeo*. Considered the first operatic masterpiece, recitative dominates it, but he brought greater variety to the opera by including madrigal choruses and sumptuous instrumental pieces, called *ritornelli*, that return throughout the drama.

The earliest operas were written for the court but something more populist was needed for the first public opera house, the Teatro San Cassiano, which opened in Venice in 1637. By this time plots were being drawn from history as well as mythology, comic elements appeared, and a more melodic form of recitative, called *arioso*, was introduced.

Monteverdi wrote only a few operas for the Venetian opera houses. The most prolific composer was his pupil Pier Francesco Cavalli (1602–1676), whose opera *Giasone* (1648) was one of the century's most performed works. By now singers had become the stars of opera, and solos known as arias were written to show off their skills.

Beyond Italy

Opera spread rapidly throughout Italy and farther afield. Rome was an early center, though most operas there were religious and performed in churches. German court opera appeared as early as 1627 and, in 1678, an opera house opened in Hamburg. French opera did not emerge for another 30 years.

KEY WORKS

Jacopo Peri *Euridice*
Claudio Monteverdi *L'Orfeo*, *L'incoronazione di Poppea* (The Coronation of Poppea)
Francesco Cavalli *Giasone* (Jason)
Henry Purcell *Dido and Aeneas*
Alessandro Scarlatti *Il Mitridate Eupatore*
George Frideric Handel *Rinaldo*

"An **exotic and irrational** entertainment which has always been combated, and always has **prevailed.**"

DEFINITION OF OPERA, FROM "DR. JOHNSON'S DICTIONARY," 1755

ITALIAN COMPOSER (1567–1643)

CLAUDIO MONTEVERDI

The music of Monteverdi led the way from the Renaissance into the Baroque era. His experimental nature is seen in his many madrigals where, in pursuit of musical expressiveness, he broke new ground.

Much of his career was spent in Mantua, Italy, as a court composer. Eventually he wanted to move on, and in 1610 he published his *Vespers*, a setting of the evening prayer service. To advertise his versatility he wrote the *Vespers* using both traditional and newer musical styles. Three years later he was made music director at St. Mark's in Venice, where he composed most of his church music. He was ordained in 1630, but this did not prevent him from writing for the new public opera houses.

AFTER

Early in the 18th century, a group of intellectuals, led by the librettist Pietro Metastasio (1698–1782), devised *opera seria*, a more serious art.

NEW FORMULAS AND SETTINGS
To make opera less frivolous, the plots of ***opera seria*** **130–133 »** were often based on stories from ancient history. **The characters** were conventional, such as a pair of lovers and a kind-hearted tyrant, and the drama depended on a character making the right moral choice.

Opera houses sprang up throughout Italy and the rest of Europe, among them the beautiful Teatro di San Carlo in Naples.

TEATRO DI SAN CARLO OPENED IN NAPLES IN 1737

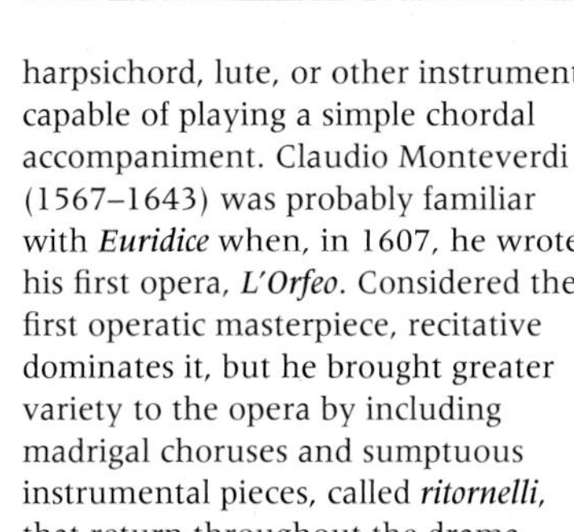

BEFORE

There are many examples of extended storytelling through song prior to the Baroque era. Sacred and secular texts had been set to music since the Middle Ages.

LITURGICAL DRAMAS

Easter week—during which Christians remember the events of Christ's crucifixion and death, followed by his resurrection—is the most important event in the Christian calendar. Beginning in the **Middle Ages**, the Gospel accounts of Christ's suffering (referred to as **The Passion of Christ**) were set to music and, eventually, dramatized, with individual singers enacting certain roles and a chorus taking on the role of the crowd. Bible stories were also dramatized and set to music.

L'AMFIPARNASO

At the same time that opera was emerging in the late 16th century, a new genre, called **madrigal comedy**, also appeared. These were comic narratives created by combining a sequence of **madrigals** « 66–67. The most famous example, entitled *L'Amfiparnaso* (The Slopes of Parnassus) was composed by Orazio Vecchi (1550–1605). The plot tells how an elderly character called Pantalone attempts to marry off his young daughter to the pompous Dr. Gratiano.

Oratorios and **Cantatas**

In addition to the music that was being composed for the motet and the mass, two new types of sacred vocal music emerged during the first half of the 17th century—the oratorio and the cantata. Both employed the new solo style of singing and were influenced by opera.

An early example of the oratorio, a musical form that originated in Rome, was *La rappresentazione di anima et di corpo* (The Representation of the Soul and Body). A morality play with music, it was a kind of sacred opera with solo singers and instrumentalists. It was produced in February 1600 with music by Emilio de' Cavalieri (*c.*1550–1602), a Roman nobleman, and was intended to be performed as part of the religious services during the weeks leading up to Easter (known as Lent).

Sacred singing

In Domenico Zampieri's 16th-century oil painting, St. Cecilia, patron saint of musicians, accompanies a choir of angels. In reality, church music was performed only by men.

Emotional impact

The oratorio was performed at the church of Santa Maria in Vallicella in Rome. This was the headquarters of a community of priests founded by St. Philip Neri (1550–1595). In his lifetime, Neri wanted to use a form of worship involving not only the usual prayers and a sermon but also a musical performance on a sacred subject. This type of service took place in an oratory—another name for a chapel—and the musical performance itself eventually became known as an oratorio.

Oratorios were almost identical to operas, apart from having a narrator, and were intended to make the same emotional impact. Their goal was to strengthen the faith of the audience. Texts were usually derived from the Bible and were written either in Latin or—in order that more people could understand the words—Italian.

Carissimi's Jephtha

By the middle of the 17th century, the most celebrated composer working in Rome was Giacomo Carissimi (1605–1674). His best-known work was an oratorio entitled *Jephtha* (1648). The oratorio retells the Old Testament story of how Jephtha promises God that he will sacrifice the first person to greet him on his return home if he is granted victory in battle. He triumphs

> "His **compositions** are truly imbued with the **essence and life** of the **spirit.**"
>
> ATHANASIUS KIRCHER, 17TH-CENTURY SCHOLAR AND "MASTER OF A HUNDRED ARTS," ON GIACOMO CARISSIMI, 1650

Cultural capital

Rome was a flourishing center of art and music during the Baroque era. Wealthy aristocrats founded artistic academies and acted as patrons supporting artists of all kinds. At the same time, the Roman Catholic Church employed many of the same artists to build and decorate churches, and compose music for church services.

Strozzi manuscript
A cantata by Barbara Strozzi for piano and voice. Strozzi was a singer and prolific composer of solo cantatas, most of which were published during her lifetime.

but, tragically, when he arrives home he is met by his daughter. The story is largely told through a narrator, but soloists are given different roles; for example, Jephtha is sung by a tenor, and the music is written to portray the emotions of the soloist. Carissimi's colleagues were deeply moved by the final chorus, a lamentation written for six voices.

Dramatic intensity

Alessandro Stradella (1639–1682), who also worked in Rome, was an outstanding composer of the second half of the century and his oratorio *San Giovanni Battista* (St. John the Baptist, 1675) is his masterpiece. The characters, and the relationships between them, were so highly developed that the composer no longer needed a narrator to move the story along. However, the most striking aspect of the work is the dramatic intensity of the music, with swift changes of mood within the same aria.

Secular entertainment

In its early form, the *cantata* (meaning "to be sung") was a short, dramatic vocal work for a solo voice and an instrument, with several sections that included arias and recitatives. Sometimes the subject was dramatic, but it was always secular. The cantata took over the pastoral and romantic themes of the madrigals, which had by now largely disappeared. Cantatas were mostly performed at private gatherings of cultured aristocrats and patrons of the arts, rather than in public theaters, and Carissimi produced many of his cantatas for this type of venue in Rome. In Venice, the cantata composer and singer Barbara Strozzi (1619–1677) wrote and performed cantatas, mostly for soprano soloists, for the same kind of select audience.

The most prolific Italian cantata composer was Alessandro Scarlatti (1660–1725). He wrote about 600 cantatas, as well as serenatas, which were extended cantatas composed in honor of major events. Cantatas written for two voices were known as *duetti di camera* (chamber duets). Strozzi wrote some cantatas for two voices, as did the Venetian composer Agostino Steffani (1654–1728), who was, in fact, largely known for them.

KEY WORKS

Giacomo Carissimi *Jephtha* (oratorio)
Alessandro Stradella *San Giovanni Battista* (oratorio)
Barbara Strozzi *L'astratto* (cantata)
Alessandro Scarlatti *Nel silenzio comune*
Agostino Steffani *Placidissime catene* (chamber duet)

COMPOSER (1605–74)

GIACOMO CARISSIMI

Highly regarded by his contemporaries, Carissimi was offered several prestigious posts during his lifetime. One of these came from the St. Mark's Basilica in Venice, which asked him to take over as music director—a highly prestigious position in charge of music. However, Carissimi preferred to stay in Rome. Here, from the age of 23 until he died 46 years later, he held the post of chapel master at Saint Apollinare, the church of the Jesuit Collegio Germanico. In 1637, he was ordained a priest. He was described as "tall, slender, and inclined to melancholy." Little else is known of his life.

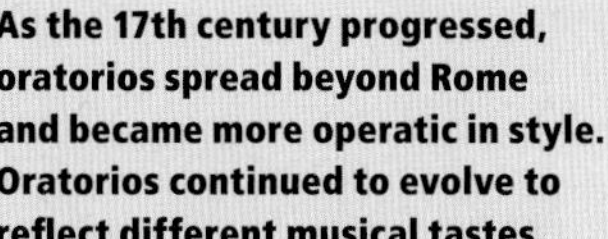

AFTER

As the 17th century progressed, oratorios spread beyond Rome and became more operatic in style. Oratorios continued to evolve to reflect different musical tastes.

HANDELIAN ORATORIO

The greatest composer of oratorios in the 18th century was German-born **George Frideric Handel** **108–109 ››**. He began to compose oratorios when opera writing was no longer profitable. Handel's texts were mostly taken from the Old Testament. He became a British citizen in 1727 and wrote his oratorios in English. His **Messiah** (1741) is the most famous oratorio ever.

SACRED CANTATAS

In Germany, the cantata was usually a sacred composition with a chorus as well as soloists. It was performed as part of the main Sunday service in Lutheran churches, and the words were based on that day's Gospel reading. During his 27 years as cantor at the Thomaskirche in Leipzig, **Johann Sebastian Bach** **100–101 ››** wrote the music for more than 200 cantatas.

Patrons and Composers

At the beginning of the 17th century it was possible for musicians and composers to achieve fame and fortune, but it was not common. Musicians depended on the Church and the aristocracy for employment, and sometimes worked for both.

BEFORE

In the Middle Ages and during the Renaissance musicians relied on the Church, nobility, and state for income.

NEW OPPORTUNITIES

Printers across Europe found better ways to reproduce sheet music during the Renaissance. After the 15th century, printed music became more widely available and affordable, and by 1501 Venetian printer **Ottaviano Petrucci** **« 55** successfully printed music using moveable type. For composers, having their music printed and published provided some income and widened their audience.

THE MATTER OF COPYRIGHT

Until the 19th century, there were no effective copyright laws to protect musicians from having their work pirated, and publishers frequently printed music under a different composer's name to enhance sales. A few composers were protected by **royal patents**, but they were exceptions.

COMPOSER (1632–1687)

JEAN-BAPTISTE LULLY

Born in Florence, the son of a miller, Lully was spotted at the age of 11 by the Duke of Guise, who took him back to Paris to help his niece improve her Italian. Lully studied with her music teacher. In 1652, he befriended the young King Louis XIV of France.

Lully eventually achieved unrivaled control over music in France. He held positions ranging from Superintendent of Music of the King's Chamber to director of the Academy of Music, and worked with French playwright Molière on a series of *comédies-ballets* (plays with music) from 1664–1671. In addition to ballet music, he wrote music for the Royal Chapel. He died of an abscess after jabbing his foot with a pole he used to beat time.

Some opera composers, such as Antonio Vivaldi and George Frideric Handel, gained some financial and musical independence by mounting performances of their own works in public theaters. However, this was a risky, often loss-making, business. Similarly, while having their music printed and published could spread a composer's fame and influence, it tended to enrich the publisher more than the composer. Many published works included a page with a lengthy dedication written by the composer addressing either an existing patron or a potential one. For example, Monteverdi's *Vespers*, a setting of the evening prayer service published in 1610, was dedicated to Pope Paul V. It was even presented to him, almost certainly in the hope of gaining employment. In any event, though, this never materialized.

Henry IV Violin
Made by the Italian instrument-maker Girolamo Amati, this violin was made for the chapel of Henry IV of France in 1595. The back of the violin is painted with the royal coat of arms between two letters H.

The glory of Rome

As the headquarters of the Roman Catholic Church, Rome was an obvious magnet for Italy's aspiring musicians. In addition to the papal chapels and many churches and monasteries that needed music, there were also several wealthy and powerful aristocratic families in Rome who patronized the arts on a lavish scale. Many of these families also supported academies—gatherings of intellectuals—at which the discussion and performance of music were common.

141,784 **The population of Rome in 1702, according to the census of that year. Of these, 8,666 were either bishops, priests, monks, nuns, or other *religiosi*.**

81 **The number of parish churches in Rome.**

Welcoming Queen Christina
The former Swedish queen's conversion to Catholicism and self-exile to Rome was a coup for the Church. She was welcomed at the Barberini palace with a grand display and an opera watched by 6,000 spectators.

At this time, the Barberini were a leading Roman aristocratic family. In 1623, Maffeo Barberini was elected Pope Urban VIII, and under his patronage, opera became Rome's most important theatrical entertainment. In 1632, the family added a 3,000-seat theater, the Teatro Quattro Fontane, to the Barberini palace. They opened it with the premiere of a sacred opera, *Il Sant'Alessio* (St Alexis), composed the previous year by Stefano Landi (1587–1639).

Swedish patroness

Another great patron of the arts was Queen Christina of Sweden (1626–1689) who lived in Rome in self-imposed exile from 1655 until her death. She presided over two academies and was influential in the opening of Rome's first public opera house, the Teatro Tordinona, in 1671. Among the notable composers who worked for her were Giacomo Carissimi (1605–1674), Alessandro Stradella (1639–1682), and Arcangelo Corelli (1653–1713), although Corelli was poached by Cardinal Pamphili before moving to the palace of Cardinal Ottoboni to lead the orchestra. The composer and organist Alessandro Scarlatti (1660–1725) was employed by all three patrons before going to Naples in 1684 to work for the Spanish viceroy.

Many churchmen, including several popes, were worldly individuals at this time, but there were some exceptions. In 1677, Pope Innocent XI banned public performances of opera on the grounds that it encouraged immorality. For this reason the Teatro Tordinona was closed down until 1689, when Pietro Ottoboni became Pope Alexander VIII and reopened it.

French absolutism

The court of Louis XIII and Louis XIV was the center of French musical life, and provided the setting for grand spectacles. In Paris, and later Versailles, music accompanied feasts, firework displays, balls, and theatrical events. All music, including religious music, served to reinforce the authority and magnificence of the monarch.

The expense could be enormous. When Cardinal Mazarin, France's First Minister, mounted two Italian operas at court he paid for them by raising taxes, causing a popular revolt in 1648.

Musicians at the French Court

In this painting by François Puget (1651–1707), the violinist is thought to be Lully and the man holding the theorbo, Philippe Quinault (Lully's principal librettist), or the lutenist Robert de Visée.

Louis XIV loved dancing and, when young, appeared in several *ballets de cour*, spectacular court entertainments that combined dance with singing. Dancing with him was the young Italian composer Jean-Baptiste Lully (see panel) who, through his subsequent friendship with the king, went on to dominate French musical life during the second half of the 17th century.

KEY WORKS

Stefano Landi *Il Sant'Alessio*

Alessandro Scarlatti *Amore, Pace, Providenza* (Love, Peace, and Providence)

Jean-Baptiste Lully *Armide*

Marc-Antoine Charpentier *David et Jonathas* (David and Jonathan)

Michel Richard de Lalande *De profundis* (From the Depths)

In 1672, Lully purchased the right to produce *tragédie lyrique*, as opera was then called in France. Lully virtually created the genre by fusing the courtly ballet with the conventions of French tragedy as written by dramatists, such as Jean Racine (1639–1699) and Pierre Corneille (1606–1684). The most famous *tragédie lyrique* Lully composed is *Armide*, which he wrote in 1686.

Lully's successors

Other French composers were subservient to Lully, at least at court, but among his most talented successors were Marc-Antoine Charpentier (1642–1704) and Michel Richard de Lalande (1657–1726). Charpentier was a versatile composer and probably studied with Giacomo Carissimi in Rome and subsequently melded the Italian style into his own work, which was mostly religious. Based in Paris, he served many patrons including the Duchess of Guise. He also wrote the music for *Le malade imaginaire* (The Imaginary Invalid), the last play of the French playwright Molière (1622–1673). By 1714, de Lalande was sole director of music of the Chapel Royal. Among his best known compositions are 64 grand motets, works for a large chorus, soloists, and orchestra.

LOUIS XIV obtained his nickname "The Sun King" after dancing the role of the Sun god Apollo in *Le Ballet de la Nuit*.

"[Lully] merits with good reason the title of **Prince of French Musicians.**"

FRENCH WRITER ÉVRARD TITON DU TILLET IN "LA PARNASSE FRANÇOIS," 1732

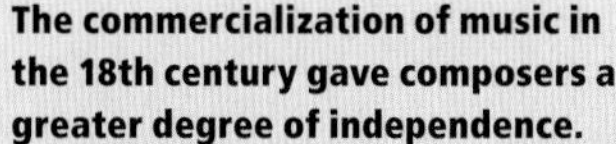

The commercialization of music in the 18th century gave composers a greater degree of independence.

NEW OPPORTUNITIES

The 18th century saw the emergence of public concert halls. These opened up the range of opportunities available to musicians.

After a life spent toiling away as music master to the Esterháza family **Joseph Haydn** **126–127 ››** experienced financial success and widespread public renown when he was invited, in 1790, by German impresario Johann Peter Salomon (1745–1815) to London to compose and conduct six symphonies.

FREEDOM AND STATUS

At the start of the 19th century the most talented musicians had a status unimaginable 50 years earlier. Virtuosos such as the violinist **Niccolò Paganini** and the pianist **Franz Liszt** **160–161 ››** were acclaimed and feted, like today's rock stars.

Fit for a virtuoso
Made by Antonio Stradivari, this violin is a well-preserved example of his work. It was once owned by Italian virtuoso Giovanni Battista Viotti (1755–1824)—the finest violinist of his generation.

TIMELINE

9th century
Rebec
Related to the North African *rebab*, this bowed ancestor of the violin had three strings and was often made from a single piece of wood. It was widely played during the Middle Ages and the Renaissance.

Medieval fiddle
Also known as a *vielle*, this instrument varied in shape but was closer to the violin than the *rebec,* with a distinct body and neck. It had up to five strings.

***c.*1520**
Three-stringed violin
Violin-like instruments with three strings—distinct from the *rebec*—date from this period and may have been known even earlier. They were probably played in a group, called a consort.

16th century
Lira da braccio
A Renaissance relative of the violin, the *lira da braccio* had seven strings attached to a pegbox. Two of the strings were set away from the fingerboard and functioned as a drone.

16th century
Amati family
The Amati family were outstanding string instrument makers, based in Cremona, Italy. They operated from *c.*1540 to 1740. The founding member, Andrea, established the classic form for the violin, but his grandson Nicolò is regarded as the greatest craftsman of the family.

1626
Violin orchestra
One of the first permanent orchestras, the *24 Violons du Roi* at the French court, featured five sizes of violin. They fell out of favor when Stradivari perfected the violin as a solo instrument.

17th century
Violino piccolo
A smaller version of the violin, the violino piccolo was tuned a fourth higher and was occasionally used to play high violin parts during the Baroque period, for example, in works by J.S. Bach.

Scroll
A side view of the violin showing the peg box, into which the four pegs attach. The strings are wound around the pegs and can be loosened or tightened as the pegs are turned.

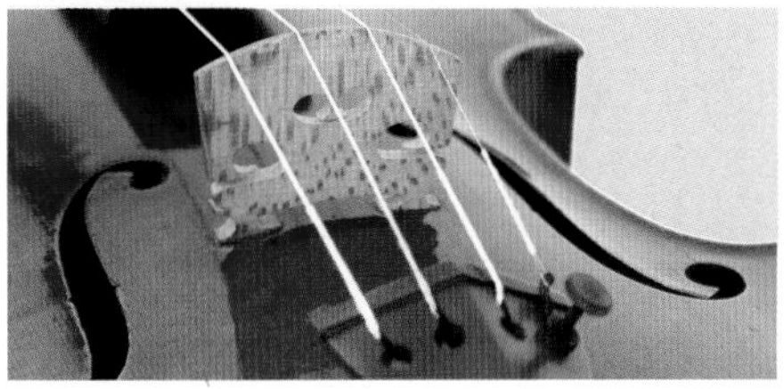

BOW

SIDE VIEW

BACK VIEW

Purfling, decorative, inlaid edge

Bridge
The bridge, a carved wedge of wood, supports the strings and carries the vibrations into the resonating body of the violin. The f-shaped sound holes amplify the sound.

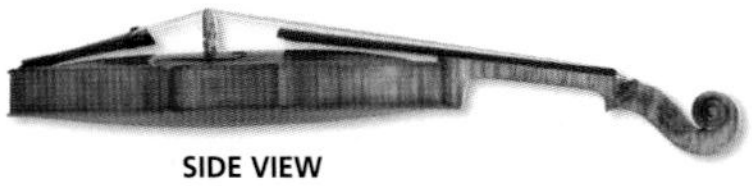

Peg

Pegbox

Scroll

Body

Neck

Fingerboard

Upper bout

The **Violin**

The violin was first developed in the 1500s. It was perfected by Italian makers and by the mid-17th century had become the preeminent bowed string instrument, prized for its rich sustained tone and its capacity for rapid playing.

The standard form of the violin, and of the related viola and cello, was established by Italian lute- and violin-maker Andrea Amati in the mid-16th century. The wooden body of the instrument acts as a sound box. The synthetic or gut strings, often wound with wire to produce a clean sound, are vibrated by drawing a horsehair bow across them. A small piece of arched wood, called the bridge, supports the strings and transmits their vibrations into the sound box. The first violinists held the instrument to the chest—as some folk fiddlers still do—but it is usually rested between the left shoulder and chin, with the right arm operating the bow.

At first the violin was primarily used as a consort instrument—its agility was thought especially appropriate for accompanying dancing. A solo repertoire only emerged in the early 17th century, much of it written by virtuoso violinists, such as Corelli and Vivaldi. By this time the instrument had spread throughout the world and was equally popular for both concert and folk music. Later instruments had minor modifications in order to produce a bigger sound, such as a longer fingerboards and a higher bridge, but essentially the violin has remained largely unchanged for almost 500 years.

1709
Stradivarius violin
Antonio Stradivari (1644–1737) is widely regarded as the greatest string instrument maker, or luthier. His design of the violin served as the basic model for violin makers for more than 250 years.

1805–1834
Paganini
The Italian virtuoso violinist and composer Niccolò Paganini achieved new heights of technical brilliance. His 24 Caprices Op.1 (1820) for solo violin are notoriously difficult for players to master.

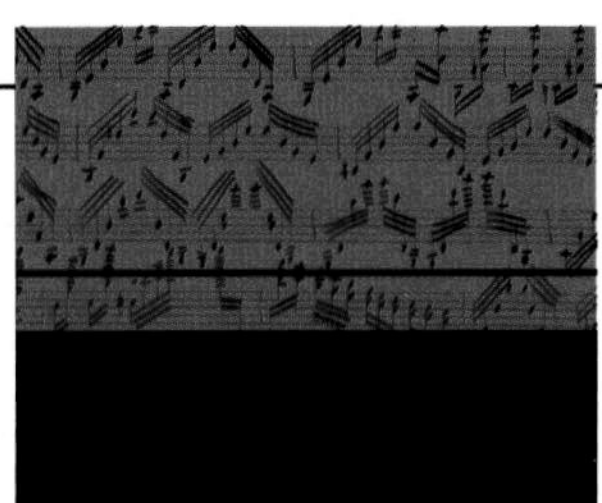
PAGANINI SCORE

2000s
Nicola Benedetti
The violin continues to be highly popular in the 21st century, with many brilliant players, such as the Scottish violinist Nicola Benedetti, inspiring young people to take up the instrument.

NICOLA BENEDETTI

c.1822
Chin rest
The composer and violinist Louis Spohr (1784–1859) invented the chin rest. Spohr's device is positioned in the middle of the base of the instrument; later versions (shown here) are placed to the left of the tailpiece.

CHIN REST

QUINTETTE DU HOT CLUB DE FRANCE

1930–1980s
Stephane Grapelli
One of the greatest jazz violinists was the Frenchman Stephane Grapelli (1909–1997) who, with guitarist Django Reinhardt, performed with the Quintette du Hot Club de France.

1930s
Electric violin
Electric violins with built-in pickups have been around since the 1930s, mostly used by jazz, folk, and rock violinists. They usually have a solid body and produce a rawer sound than their acoustic equivalents.

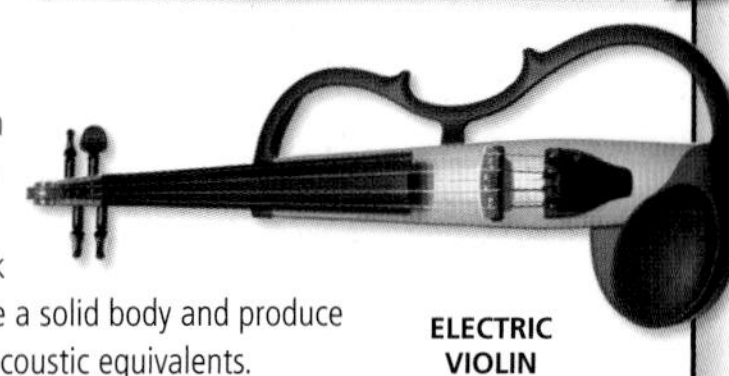
ELECTRIC VIOLIN

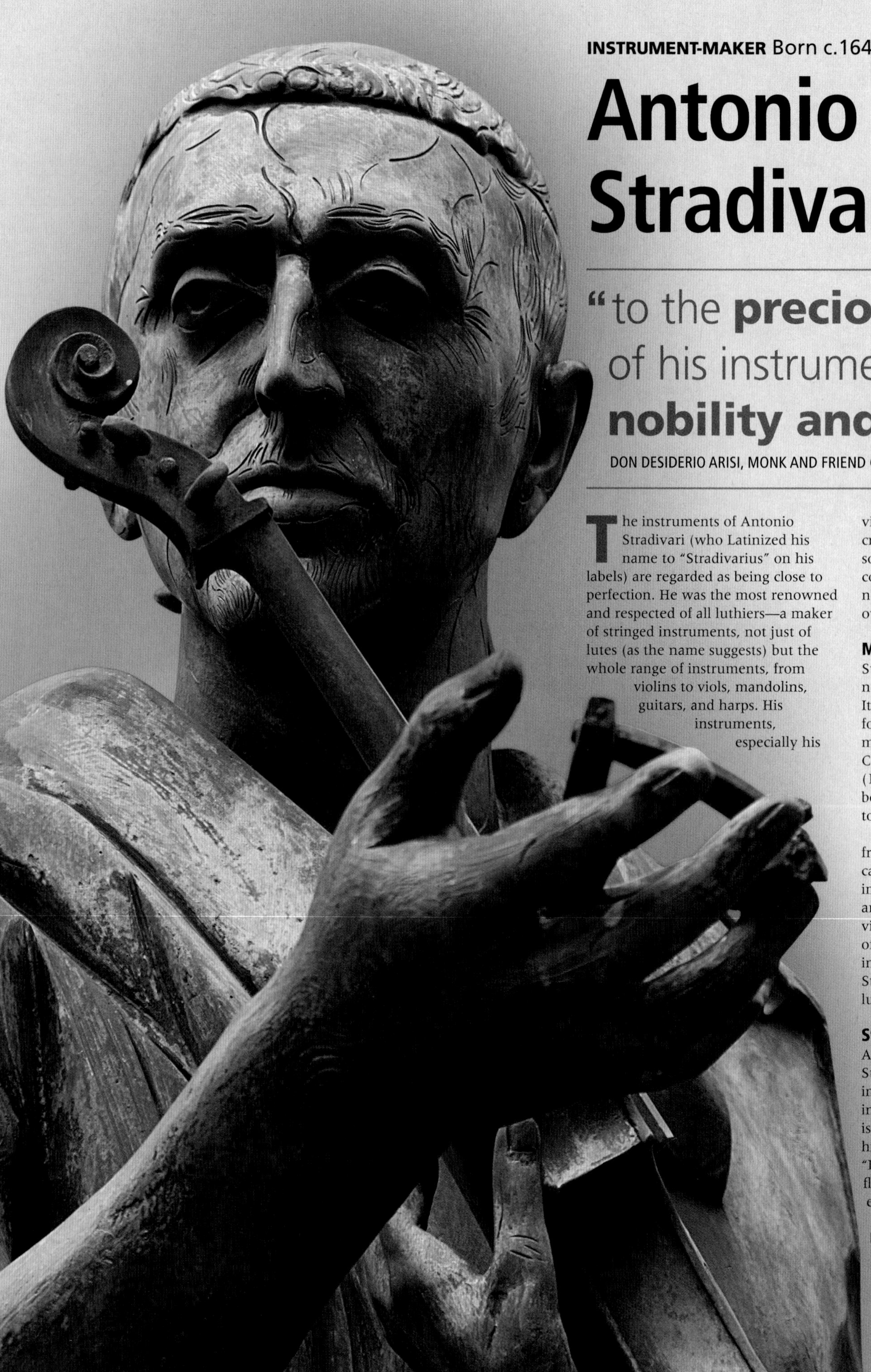

INSTRUMENT-MAKER Born c.1644 Died 1737

Antonio Stradivari

"to the **preciousness ...** of his instruments he **adds nobility and allure.**"

DON DESIDERIO ARISI, MONK AND FRIEND OF STRADIVARI, c.1720

The instruments of Antonio Stradivari (who Latinized his name to "Stradivarius" on his labels) are regarded as being close to perfection. He was the most renowned and respected of all luthiers—a maker of stringed instruments, not just of lutes (as the name suggests) but the whole range of instruments, from violins to viols, mandolins, guitars, and harps. His instruments, especially his violins, are prized for their elegance, craftsmanship, and the beauty of their sound. They are sought after by collectors and performers alike, and nearly every top violinist and cellist owns, or wishes to own, a "Strad."

Master of Cremona

Stradivari was born about 1644, in or near the city of Cremona in northern Italy, already a well-established center for stringed instrument-makers. He may have been a pupil of the leading Cremonese luthier Nicolò Amati (1596–1684) or he may—as some believe—simply have been apprenticed to a general woodworker.

Few instruments have survived from the early part of Stradivari's career. Those that have are very close in style to the instruments of Amati and are referred to as his Amatisé violins. They include a handful of violins with beautiful decorative inlay. With Amati's death in 1684, Stradivari became the preeminent luthier in the region.

Striving for perfection

A naturally experimental maker, Stradivari always looked for ways to improve the look and sound of his instruments. From around 1690, there is a temporary change in the design of his violins, with the invention of the "Long Strad"—an instrument that was flatter, slightly longer, and had a more elegant profile.

Master of his craft
This modern sculpture of Antonio Stradivari in Piazza Roma, Cremona, shows him holding a violin and a pair of calipers. Stradivari would have used calipers, an essential tool in instrument-making, to measure the thickness of wood.

Cremona workshop
No contemporary images of Stradivari exist, but this 19th-century oil painting by an anonymous artist shows him as an old man at work on a violin. The painting hangs in the Violins Room in Cremona's town hall.

The period 1700 to 1720 is regarded by most experts as Stradivari's "golden age" as a maker, when he produced his finest and most famous instruments. By this time he had reverted back to the Amati length of 14in (35.5cm) but continued to look for subtle improvements in construction. He was assisted in his work by two of his sons, Francesco and Omobono.

A typical Stradivarius of this period has slightly different proportions, noticeably a broader center curve (or bout), and the varnish has changed from the golden brown of his earlier instruments to a deep red color. In addition, the maple wood used for the backs of the instruments is often selected for its "flamed" markings. Experts also discern a noticeable richness in tone and greater power.

Among the most prized violins of the golden age are the "Betts" (1704), purchased for about $5 by John Betts in 1820, and the "Messiah" (1716). Although both these instruments are now museum pieces (and rarely, if ever, played), plenty of the estimated 600 or so surviving Stradivari violins are owned by, or loaned to, leading players. Among violinists, Anne-Sophie Mutter plays the Lord "Dunraven" (1710), Joshua Bell the "Gibson" (1713), and Izthak Perlman the "Soil" (1714), to name just three. The odd nicknames that the finest instruments have usually refer to a previous, distinguished, owner.

> "A **Strad violin ...** has **memory and loyalty."**
>
> LOUIS KRASNER (1903–1991), VIRTUOSO VIOLINIST AND TEACHER

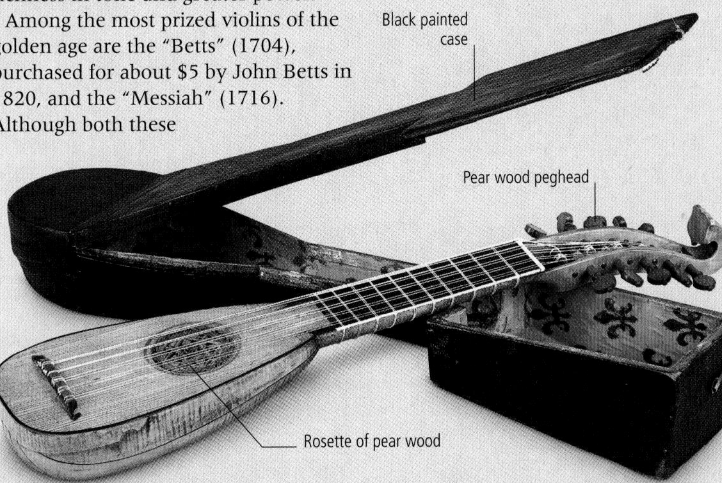

Stradivarius mandolin
This choral mandolin, known as the Cutler-Challen, is one of only two such Stradivari mandolins known to be in existence. It dates from around 1680 and is now in South Dakota's National Museum of Music.

Unsurprisingly, when Stradivarius violins of the highest pedigree appear on the market they fetch very high prices. In 2011, the "Lady Blunt" Strad was auctioned for $15.9m.

Commercial pressures

There were plenty of other distinguished luthiers in the Baroque era. Amati was part of a dynasty of makers, as was Giuseppe Guarneri (1698–1744), also known as Guarneri del Gesù, a man whose violins are now regarded by many as on a par with those of Stradivari. The reputations of Stradivari and Guarneri expanded in the 19th century, as concert halls grew larger and soloists needed the bigger sound these instruments provided in order to be audible above the rest of the orchestra. As the status of Stradivari's violins increased, so unscrupulous dealers started passing off inferior violins as his. At the same time, makers and scientists became obsessed with finding the "secret" that made his instruments so superior. Some credited a mysterious ingredient in the varnish; others thought the wood was the key. Was there a "mini ice age" during the 1680s that slowed the growth of trees, giving them a unique density? Or was it the microorganisms soaked up by the trees as they were transported downriver?

It is also worth remembering that the mystique surrounding Italian instruments of the 17th and 18th centuries is encouraged by dealers in order to maintain high prices. There are plenty of fine instruments being made by modern luthiers, but they do not come with the pedigree and history of a Stradivarius.

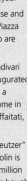

Authentic label
The peghead of this guitar, known as the Rawlins Guitar, was made by Stradivarius in around 1700. Smaller than modern guitars, it has five double strings. It is now in the collection of the National Music Museum, South Dakota.

KEY WORKS

- **"Hellier" violin (1679)**
- **"Sabionari" guitar (1679)**
- **"Servais" cello (1701)**
- **"Betts" violin (1704)**
- **"Duport" cello (1711)**
- **"Alard" violin (1715)**
- **"Messiah" violin (1716)**
- **"Cassavetti" viola (1727)**

TIMELINE

- **c.1644** Born in or near Cremona, Italy, the son of Alessandro Stradivari and Anna Moroni.
- **1666** The first known Stradivarius to be made. The label inside the violin states that it was made by a pupil of Nicolò Amati.
- **1667** Marries Francesca Feraboschi, a young widow, who goes on to bear him six children.
- **1671** Birth of his eldest son, Francesco, who later becomes a significant instrument-maker in his own right.
- **1679** Makes the "Hellier" violin, one of a handful of beautifully inlaid instruments. Birth of his son, Omobono, who also later works for his father.
- **1680** Purchases a house in Cremona's Piazza San Domenico. It is his home and workshop until his death.
- **1684** The renowned luthier Nicolò Amati dies. Stradivari is now recognized as Cremona's leading luthier.
- **1690** Develops the "Long Strad" design, a slimmer and longer style of instrument.
- **1698** Wife dies.
- **1699** Marries Antonia Costa, who goes on to bear him five more children.
- **1700** Beginning of what experts consider a 20-year "golden age," when he produces his finest instruments. Around this time, he begins working on a smaller cello design.
- **1704** Makes the violin now known as the "Betts," considered by many experts to be among his very best instruments.
- **1737** Dies and is buried in the church of San Domenico, Cremona.
- **1742** Death of his second son, Omobono Stradivari.
- **1743** Death of his first son, Francesco. The Stradivari workshop closes.
- **1773** The connoisseur and collector Alessandro Cozio, Count of Salabue, purchases 10 Stradivari violins, along with tools and molds from Paolo Stradivari, a son from Stradivari's second marriage.
- **1869** The church of San Domenico is torn down and Stradivari's tomb is destroyed.
- **1928** The house and workshop in Piazza San Domenico are demolished.
- **1930** The Stradivari Museum, inaugurated in 1893, finds a permanent home in the Palazzo Affaitati, Cremona.
- **1998** The "Kreutzer" Stradivarius violin is sold for $1.6 million in London; it is bought for violinist Maxim Vengerov
- **2011** The "Lady Blunt" violin, made in 1721, is sold for $15.9 million.

THE STRADIVARI MUSEUM, CREMONA

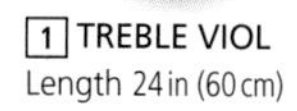

1 TREBLE VIOL
Length 24 in (60 cm)

2 TENOR VIOL
Length 35 in (90 cm)

3 BASS VIOL
Length 4 ft (1.2 m)

4 VIOLA
Length 27 in (68 cm)

5 VIOLA D'AMORE, 1736
Length 27 in (68 cm)

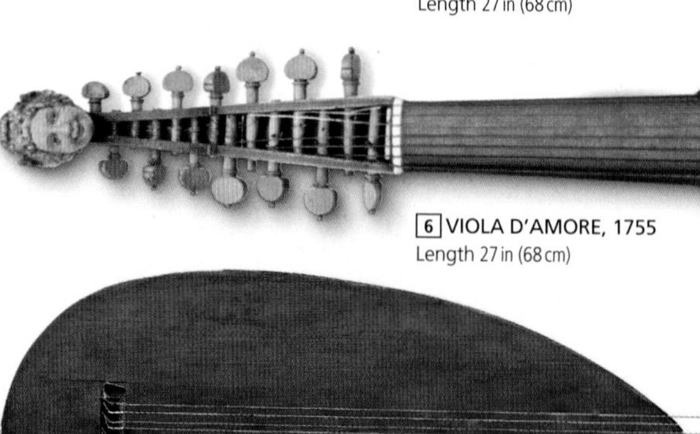

6 VIOLA D'AMORE, 1755
Length 27 in (68 cm)

String Instruments

Many of the string instruments that were widely used at the start of the Baroque era, such as the family of viols, had fallen from fashion by its end, while others, in particular the violin and cello, rose to prominence.

1 **Treble viol** The viol, dating from the 15th century, usually has six strings, a fretted fingerboard, and is held upright between the knees. The treble is the smallest of the family. 2 **Tenor viol** The tenor is usually played as part of a group of viols. 3 **Bass viol** Like the cello, the bass viol was popular as both a solo and a continuo—bass part—instrument, and outlasted the smaller viols. 4 **Viola** Similar to a violin, and played in the same way, tucked under the chin, the viola is larger and produces a deeper sound. 5 **Viola d'amore, 1736** This bowed instrument is the same size as a viola but with a more slender outline and six or seven strings. 6 **Viola d'amor, 1755** In addition to its regular strings, the viola d'amore has a set of "sympathetic" strings running beneath, and tuned to complement their tone, which produces a particularly sweet sound. 7 **Lute** Related to the Arab *'ud*, the lute was the most popular plucked instrument of the Renaissance and Baroque periods. 8 **Stradivari guitar** The great Italian violin maker Antonio Stradivari produced this instrument around 1700. 9 **Guitar** Baroque guitars, like this example from 1640, had a less pronounced figure-eight profile than modern instruments and were often highly decorated. 10 **English kit violin** A small violin with an extra long neck used by dancing masters to accompany their pupils. 11 **Kit violin** A kit was often truncheon-shaped, convenient for slipping into the back pocket of a tail coat. The French called it a *pochette*, from the word *poche* for "pocket." 12 **Piccolo violin** A smaller version of the violin and tuned to a higher pitch. 13 **Mandolin** A pear-shaped, wire-strung instrument, plucked with a plectrum, which originated in the Naples area of Italy. This one was made by Stradivari in 1680. 14 **Baryton** A bass viol with six strings for bowing, and up to 20 sympathetic strings, which could be plucked by the left thumb through an opening at the back. The name is the French word for "baritone," and the instrument originated in the early 17th-century, possibly in England. 15 **Baroque cello** Similar to a modern cello, but with a fingerboard closer to the body, gut strings, and no endpin.

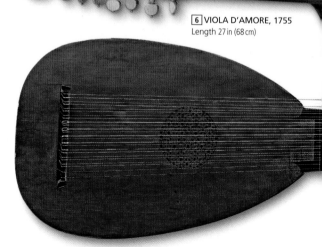

8 STRADIVARI GUITAR
Length 3 ft 3 in (1 m)

9 GUITAR
Length 38 in (96 cm)

10 ENGLISH KIT VIOLIN
Length 16 in (40 cm)

11 KIT VIOLIN
Length 16 in (40 cm)

15 BAROQUE CELLO
Length 4 ft (1.2 m)

12 PICCOLO VIOLIN
Length 21 in (54 cm)

13 MANDOLIN
Length 14 in (35 cm)

14 BARYTON
Length 4 ft 3 in (1.3 m)

7 LUTE
Length approx. 31 in (80 cm)

Born 1678 Died 1741

Antonio Vivaldi

"He can **compose** a concerto ... **more quickly** than a copyist can **write.**"

CHARLES DE BROSSES, IN A LETTER DESCRIBING VIVALDI, 1739

Man of music

This striking portrait of a violinist in the act of composing is thought by many to be of Vivaldi. Some have even discerned a hint of red hair beneath the light-colored wig.

With its dramatic contrasts of dynamics and use of motor rhythms—a regular and persistent pulse that drives the momentum of a piece—Vivaldi's music is among the most exciting of the late Baroque. As a violin virtuoso he helped to extend the technical boundaries of his instrument and as a composer he was important in extending the expressive range of the solo concerto. His set of atmospheric violin concertos, *Le quattro stagioni* (*The Four Seasons*), is an early example of painting a scene using music. Since their rediscovery during the 20th century, they have been among the most performed and recorded pieces ever.

The Red Priest

Born in Venice, the youngest of six children, Vivaldi was taught the violin by his father, a leading violinist at St. Mark's Basilica, and may have studied with Giovanni Legrenzi, the *maestro di capella* (music director) at St. Mark's. He was also educated for the priesthood and was ordained in 1703, earning the nickname *Il prete rosso* (the Red Priest) due to his striking red hair. Because of an illness, possibly asthma, he rarely celebrated mass, and as a young man his reputation was first and foremost as a brilliant violinist.

That same year Vivaldi took up the job of violin teacher at the Ospedale della Pietà (Hospital of Mercy), an institute in Venice for orphaned

KEY WORKS

L'estro armonico, Op. 3

Le quattro stagioni (*The Four Seasons*), Op. 8, Nos.1–4, RV271

Juditha triumphans, RV644

Gloria in D, RV589

Stabat Mater, RV621

Farnace, RV711

and abandoned girls. Although this was run like a convent, special emphasis was placed on music, and the Pietà had an outstanding orchestra and choir. The institute employed Vivaldi on and off until his death in 1741.

Artistic output

Much of Vivaldi's music is undated, but it is known that in 1705 he published a set of 12 sonatas for violin. However, it was an exuberant collection of concertos, *L'estro armonico* (*Harmonic Inspiration*), published in 1711, that won him wide renown. Lively, flamboyant, and challenging for both the soloist and orchestra, these 12 works replaced the stately concerto model of the day, and set the style for the future. Johann Sebastian Bach (1685–1750) admired *L'estro armonico* so much that he copied and arranged six concertos for other instruments.

In 1713, Vivaldi went to Vicenza to supervise the first of his operas, *Ottone in Villa*. He continued to travel even after becoming general superintendent of music at the Pietà in 1716. But he was allowed leave to compose operas in other cities as well as manage two theaters in Venice.

From 1718 to 1720, he was music director to the court of Mantua. While in Mantua he began an association with the contralto Anna Girò, who often sang the leading role in his operas. Rumors spread about the relationship and this, along with Vivaldi's refusal to take Mass, later caused the Archbishop of Ferrara to bar him from that city.

It was in the early 1720s that Vivaldi wrote *The Four Seasons*, music that attempts to reproduce specific sounds, such as a barking dog in "Spring" or a thunderstorm in "Winter."

Concert at the Ospedale della Pietà, Venice
Vivaldi wrote nearly all his choral music for the choir of the Pietà. The fine musical reputation of the all-girl institution drew large audiences from all over Europe.

Along with his other work, Vivaldi continued to write sacred music for the Pietà. The best known is his *Gloria* in D, in which lively choruses alternate with solos and duets. Vivaldi's moving *Stabat Mater*, written for solo voice and orchestra, reveals his ability to write expressive, slowly paced music.

> "Vivaldi's **music ... is wild and irregular.**"
>
> JOHN HAWKINS, "A GENERAL HISTORY OF THE SCIENCE AND PRACTICE OF MUSIC," 1776

Final years

Returning to Venice in 1738 to oversee a festival in honor of a visit from the King of Poland, Vivaldi found that his reputation had waned. In 1740, he left for Vienna to seek the patronage of Charles VI, but the emperor died shortly after he arrived. Vivaldi stayed in Vienna but died himself less than a year later, at the age of 63. He was buried in a pauper's grave.

After his death, Vivaldi's music was largely forgotten. In the early 20th century, scholars unearthed a number of his scores. More works are still coming to light and being performed and recorded.

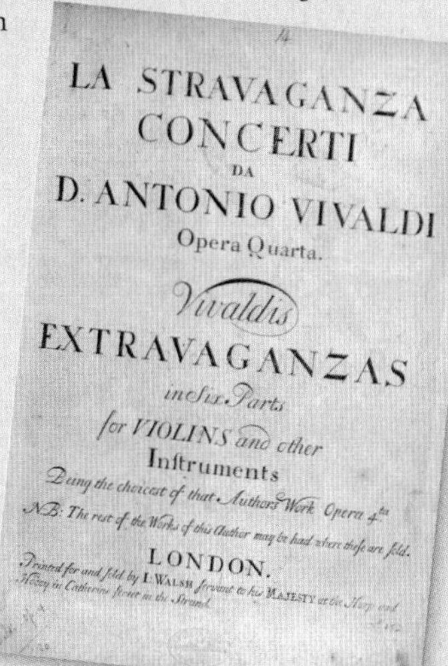

LA STRAVAGANZA
CONCERTI
DA
D. ANTONIO VIVALDI
Opera Quarta.
Vivaldi's
EXTRAVAGANZAS
in Six Parts
for VIOLINS and other
Instruments
Being the choicest of that Authors Work Opera 4th
N.B: The rest of the Works of this Author may be had where these are sold.
LONDON.
Printed for and sold by I. WALSH servant to his MAJESTY at the Harp and Hoboy in Catherine street in the Strand.

Vivaldi's extravaganzas
A London reprint of Vivaldi's *La Stravaganza*, written in 1716, dating from around 1740. It was a collection of concertos for solo violin, strings, and harpsichord.

TIMELINE

- **1678** Born in Venice to the musician Giambattista Vivaldi and his wife, Camilla.
- **1692** Begins studying to become a priest.
- **1703** Ordained as a priest and begins teaching violin at the Ospedale della Pietà (Hospital of Mercy), Venice.
- **1705** His first published music is a set of trio sonatas.
- **1711** Publishes *L'estro armonico* (Harmonic Inspiration), his musically influential collection of concertos.
- **1713** Travels to Vicenza to supervise the production of the first of his operas, *Ottone in Villa*. Begins managing the opera house Teatro Sant'Angelo in Venice.
- **1716** Oratorio *Juditha triumphans* performed at the Hospital of Mercy.
- **1717** Finishes managing the Teatro Sant'Angelo and takes over at the Teatro San Moisè.
- **1718** Begins two-year employment in Mantua as music director to the court of Prince Philip of Hesse-Darmstadt.
- **1724** His opera *Il Giustino* is performed in Rome during Carnival.
- **1725** Publishes *Il cimento dell'armonia e dell'invenzione* (The Ordeal of Harmony and Invention), a collection of 12 concertos that includes *Le Quattro Stagioni* (*The Four Seasons*).
- **1727** First performance at the Teatro Sant'Angelo in Venice of *Farnace*, one of his most successful operas.
- **1728** Around this time meets Holy Roman Emperor Charles VI, to whom he dedicates his collection of concertos, *La cetra*.
- **1730** Travels with his father to Vienna and then Prague to see a performance of *Farnace*.
- **1732** Opera *La fida ninfa* (The Faithful Nymph) opens the new Teatro Filarmonico, Vicenza.
- **1735** Employs the playwright Carlo Goldoni to adapt the existing libretto of *Griselda*.
- **1737** Cardinal Ruffo, Archbishop of Ferrara, bans Vivaldi from entering the city and, as a result, his opera *Siroe* fails there.
- **1740** Travels to Vienna to seek work at the court of the Holy Roman Emperor Charles VI.
- **1741** Dies in Vienna of an "internal inflammation" and is buried in a cemetery owned by the public hospital fund.

VIOLIN USED IN VIVALDI'S ORCHESTRA

BEFORE

Music was important in the English court and continued to thrive in the early 17th century, although it was frowned upon by the Puritans, a group of Protestants who rebelled against Church and crown.

ROYAL MUSICIAN
Black trumpet player **John Blanke** probably came to England with Catherine of Aragon in 1501. He is the only Black person in Tudor England to be identified in an image.

JOHN BLANKE, TRUMPETER

NATIVE TALENT
Notable composers included Orlando Gibbons (1583–1625) and **John Dowland** **« 63**.

CROMWELLIAN AUSTERITY
Under Oliver Cromwell, Puritan ruler of England after the Civil War (1642–1651), music in church was restricted and theaters closed. Music was featured at state events.

The **English Revival**

In 1660, King Charles II was restored to the throne of England, bringing nearly 20 years of republicanism to an end. The new king's love of spectacle meant that music and theater could once more take on an important role in the life of the nation, both at court and in public.

Charles II (1630–1685) was eager to reinstate music at court on a lavish scale. During the rule of Oliver Cromwell, he and his brother James, Duke of York, had spent much of their exile in France and had enjoyed the music at the court of Louis XIV. The challenge in England was that many of the musical institutions that served previous monarchs had been disbanded and needed to be revived.

The Chapel Royal

Foremost among these institutions was the Chapel Royal, the choir that served the monarch and sang the music for his daily services wherever he was in residence. After the restoration of the monarchy, the training of choirboys fell to Captain Henry Cooke (1616–1672), who held the title of Master of the Children of the Chapel Royal. Under his tutelage, several gifted composers emerged.

One of the most talented was the lutenist and composer Pelham Humfrey (1647–1674). Aged 17, he was sent to Italy and France to study, where he absorbed the Italianate style of Giacomo Carissimi (*c.*1605–1674), and the grand manner of Jean-Baptiste Lully (see pp.84–85). On his return, his superior air—diarist Samuel Pepys called him "an absolute monsieur"—and his music made their mark. Humfrey's early death was a great loss to English music. He was succeeded at the Chapel Royal by another Cooke protégé, John Blow (1649–1708). Blow was organist of Westminster Abbey from 1668 and is mostly remembered for the anthems he wrote, such as "Sing Unto the Lord, O Ye Saints" (1685). He is unlucky in that his fame has largely been eclipsed by Henry Purcell (1659–1695), the greatest of the post-Restoration generation of composers (see p.95). In 1680, Blow relinquished the post of organist at Westminster Abbey in order to make way for his brilliant younger colleague.

1672 **The year in which England's first public concert was held, in the Whitefriars district of London.**

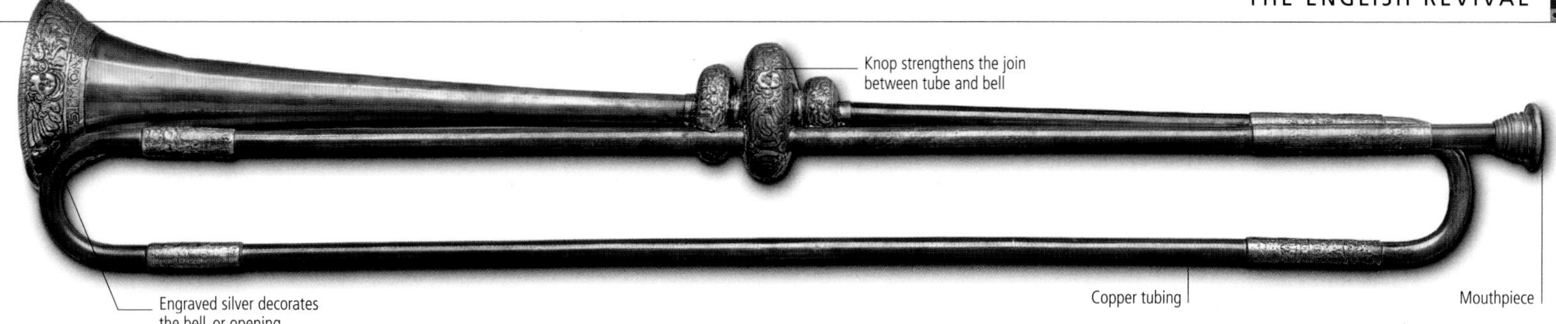

The Beale trumpet
This trumpet was made in 1667 by Simon Beale, who was state trumpeter to Oliver Cromwell and played at his funeral. Following the Restoration, he was then appointed state trumpeter to King Charles II.

Music for the court

The choir of the Chapel Royal also had court duties, such as performing the numerous odes written for special—usually royal—occasions.

The other musicians employed by the court were mostly instrumentalists. They were divided into different bands, or consorts. Matthew Locke (*c.*1621–1677) was the outstanding composer at the court of Charles II, though not always the most favored. Already a well-established figure by the time of the Restoration, his best known works include *Music for His Majesty's Sagbutts and Cornetts,* which was probably written for Charles II's coronation in 1661.

Around this time, Locke became composer for the Private Musick ensemble, who played for the king at Whitehall Palace. Sadly, the king, in the words of the historian and amateur musician Roger North (1651–1734) had "an utter detestation of Fancys"—the music Locke was so skilled at —much preferring the dance music provided by the violin band. But Locke had other roles, including organist of the private chapel of the queen, Catherine of Braganza, who was a Roman Catholic.

Saintly muse
In 1683, London musicians instigated an annual celebration in honor of Cecilia, patron saint of music, shown here playing a bass viol in a painting by Italian artist Domenichino (1581–1641).

Theater music

The principal theatrical entertainment at the court of Charles I had been masques—elaborate allegories that combined poetry, music, dance, and scenic effects to celebrate the king or a state event. They were rarer at Charles II's court, partly because he preferred the entertainments he had seen in France, including opera (see pp.80–81).

In 1660, Charles II allowed public theaters to reopen and women to perform (until then female roles had been played by boys with unbroken voices). Restoration audiences enjoyed bawdy comedies but also dramas that had plenty of singing and dancing.

Thomas Shadwell's version of Shakespeare's *The Tempest* had lavish incidental music by several composers, including Locke. An adaptation of Shakespeare's *A Midsummer Night's Dream*, renamed *The Fairy Queen* (1692), placed music by Purcell and dances between the acts in a series of masquelike scenes with no link to the plot. This form, now called semi-opera, was very popular for a short time.

Opera took time to gain popularity in England, but there were two notable examples. The first was Blow's *Venus and Adonis* (*c.*1683), which had continuous music (called "through-composed"; see p.67) and no dialogue. *Venus and Adonis* provided the model for Purcell's *Dido and Aeneas* (*c.*1689). Both works contain recitative (speech-style storytelling) and reveal an awareness of French operatic style.

Court ball
Like his cousin Louis XIV at Versailles, where he had spent much of his exile, Charles II was passionate about dancing. He is shown in the center of this painting by Flemish artist Hieronymus Janssens (1624–1693).

KEY WORKS

Pelham Humfrey "By the Waters of Babylon"

John Blow "Sing Unto the Lord, O Ye Saints"; *Venus and Adonis*

Matthew Locke *Music For His Majesty's Sagbutts and Cornetts*; *Psyche*

COMPOSER (1659–95)

HENRY PURCELL

Until the beginning of the 20th century, no British-born composer had achieved the fame of Henry Purcell. Born in London, he trained as a chorister at the Chapel Royal and studied composition with John Blow, the organist at Westminster Abbey, whom he later succeeded. He wrote his first anthems while he was at the abbey and also composed for the theater. The final scene of his most notable success, *Dido and Aeneas*, is one of the best-known moments in Baroque opera. He wrote anthems for the coronations of James II and William and Mary, but his final work was for the funeral of Queen Mary.

AFTER

Enthusiasm for semi-opera did not last long. By the first decade of the 18th century, its popularity waned as people began to favor Italian opera.

OPERATIC IMPORTS
English impresarios realized that imported talent from the continent, such as star Italian singers Faustina Bordoni (1697–1781) and the castrato Francesco Bernardi Senesino (1686–1758), attracted large audiences.

MUSIC SOCIETIES
Public concerts and music societies thrived in England in the 18th century. **Concertos 138–139 ››** began to prove popular, particularly those by Francesco Geminiani (1687–1762). The English **oratorios of Handel 108–109 ››** also became well established.

The **Organ**

The earliest keyboard instrument, the organ can produce a greater variety of sound than any other instrument. Used in churches for centuries, it is also popular as a concert instrument in both classical and popular music.

VIEW WITH DOORS CLOSED

The organ has its origins in the *hydraulis*, or water organ, of the Ancient Greeks and Romans. By the 8th century, similar instruments had reached Western Europe, and from the Middle Ages onward, they played an important role in church music. The Renaissance and Baroque eras saw many technical improvements to the instrument, which enabled more ambitious music to be written. The German composers Dieterich Buxtehude, J.S. Bach, and Pachebel achieved new heights of inventiveness. In the 19th century, large organs were built, and the range of sounds they could produce was orchestral. Composers such as Liszt and Saint-Saëns wrote symphonic pieces to include the organ.

The king of instruments

The organ is a keyboard instrument that works on a similar principle to woodwind and brass: air blown through a hollow pipe—by the bellows—produces sound. The organ consists of three main parts: the pipes, the bellows, and the controls. The pipes differ in size and shape and produce different sounds. Manuals (keyboards) control different rows of pipes (divisions). Each row is called a rank and has a pipe for each note. Each division is like a separate organ and has its own character. A typical three-manual church organ has four divisions. The stops direct the air into the correct set of pipes. When the organist pulls out a stop, all the pipes in that rank become available to play. A one-manual chamber organ may have a few stops, and a six-manual cathedral organ may have over 150. Some older organs also have a pedal to operate the bellows, though most modern organs are electrically winded. Even a small organ has a rich variety of sounds, which is why it is called "the king of instruments."

UNDERSTANDING MUSIC

SILBERMANN ORGANS

The early 18th century was a golden age of German pipe organ building in churches, and its greatest exponents were Andreas Silbermann (1678–1734) and his brother Gottfried (1683–1753). Andreas built around 34 organs in the Alsace region, and Gottfried built 46 in Saxony, including the organs of Freiberg cathedral (pictured) and Dresden's Hofkirche. The Silbermann tradition was continued by Andreas's son, Johann Andreas (1712–1783).

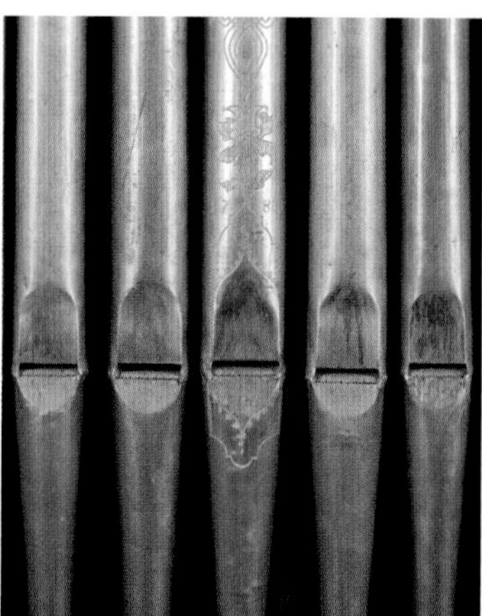
Pipes
Despite its small size and domestic function, this chamber organ contains a remarkable 294 pipes, some as long as 8 ft (2.4 m) in length.

Keyboard
This organ has just one manual, or keyboard (left), whereas larger church organs often have several. Reversing the conventional black and white arrangement of the keys was not unusual in this period.

Levers (above and right)
There are six lever-operated stops on this organ, three on each side of the keyboard. When pulled, they enable the organ to produce different sounds.

TIMELINE

c.300 BCE
Hydraulis
This illustration shows a water organ, in which air was pumped into a funnel in a tank of water and then forced into the pipes.

HYDRAULIS

826
Europe's first organ
Built by Georgius, a Venetian priest, for Louis I, King of the Franks, Europe's first organ was an important status symbol.

13th century
Portative organ
A pipe organ small enough to be held and played by one person, the portative was employed mostly in secular music during the 13th–16th centuries.

FRESCO OF A MUSICIAN AND A PORTATIVE

16th century
Regal organ
A small portable organ, the regal was popular during the Renaissance. Air from a pair of bellows was driven through metal reeds behind the keyboard.

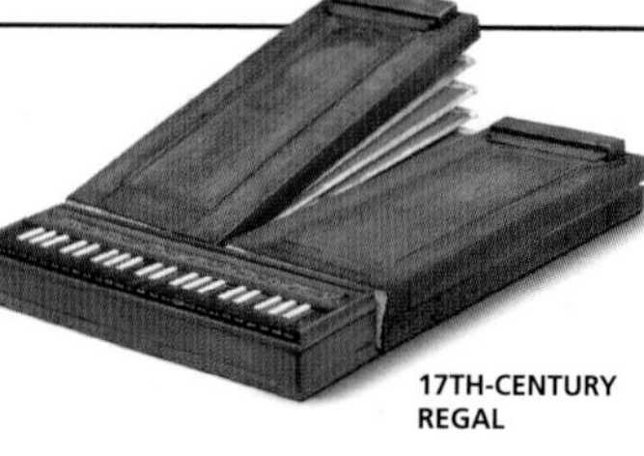
17TH-CENTURY REGAL

16th century
Positive organ
The positive was a movable organ that was blown with a bellows by one person and played by another. It was used for both domestic and religious music from 1500 onward.

16th century
Organ music
An increasingly sophisticated solo organ repertoire was developed by composers such as Claudio Merulo, Jan Sweelinck, and Girolamo Frescobaldi during the Renaissance and Baroque periods.

17th century
Chamber organs
A small one-manual pipe organ built like a piece of furniture, the chamber organ was derived from the positive organ and became popular for private, domestic use and concert halls until the 19th century.

1780
Free reeds
German engineer Christian Gottlieb Kratzenstein built a free-reed organ in which sound is made by reeds. It developed into the melodeon.

MELODEON, 1845

Chamber organ
This house, or chamber, organ was built in 1786 in Switzerland. It has the characteristic single-manual (keyboard) of this type of smaller organ, intended for domestic use.

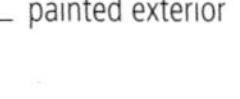

1929
First electric organ
Invented in France, electric organs became- popular in jazz, gospel, and rock music in the 1960s and '70s. They enabled stars such as Booker T. Jones to imitate other instruments.

1786
Swiss house organ
This house or chamber organ was built by Josef Loosser. Such organs were built for domestic use to accompany hymn singing.

1855
Steam organ
Inspired by locomotive steam whistles, Joshua C. Stoddard invented an organ operated by steam or compressed air and named it a calliope.

CALLIOPE

1915
Cinema organ
Special organs were developed to accompany silent films. Their many stops imitated orchestral instruments. Wurlitzer was the most famous company to produce them.

BOOKER T. JONES

Counterpoint and **Fugue**

In a piece of music, when two or more melodies are combined in such a way that they sound harmonious, it is known as counterpoint. At its most sophisticated, as in the multilayered fugues of J.S. Bach, several independent melodies, or voices, interact yet maintain a cohesive harmony.

Counterpoint can be quite simple, for example in the Two Part Inventions for keyboard of J.S. Bach (see pp.100–01), in which just two lines of music are set against each other. These melodic lines are also referred to as parts or voices.

In counterpoint, each melody is heard as something continuous rather than as a series of isolated tones, so there is a sense of forward momentum. The skill of the composer lies in weaving together all the strands so that they can be heard individually and as a whole.

Baroque counterpoint is distinguished from Renaissance polyphony (meaning "many sounds") because it focuses on the melodic interplay between the separate voices rather than their harmonic interaction. It tends, too, to be more rhythmically dynamic.

STRUCTURE: THE FUGUE
Some fugues imitate sonata form and have three sections: exposition, development, and recapitulation. Voice 1 begins by stating the subject, or theme (blue). Voice 2 enters with the answer (green), which is the same melody as the subject but five notes (a fifth) higher. At the same time, Voice 1 accompanies the answer with new material, either a countersubject (purple) or a free part (orange). Voice 3 then enters with the original subject. The development is freer and consists of "episodes" (pink), alternating with entries of the subject. This fugue ends with the recapitulation—a statement of the subject in the home key.

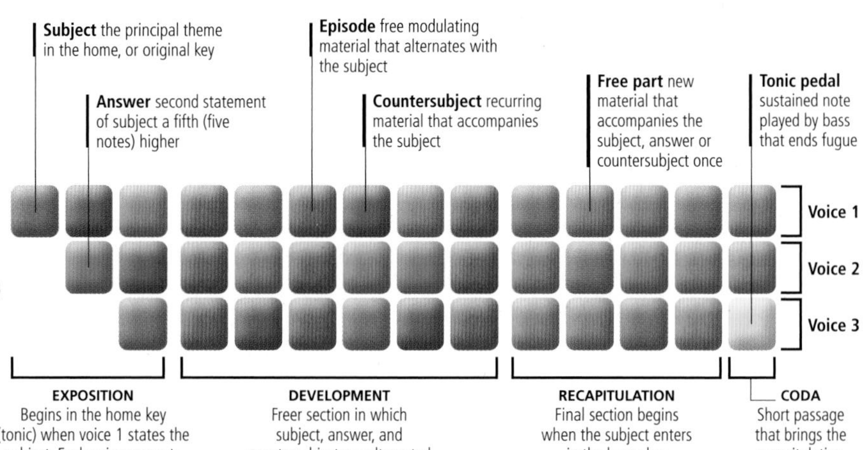
Subject the principal theme in the home, or original key
Answer second statement of subject a fifth (five notes) higher
Episode free modulating material that alternates with the subject
Countersubject recurring material that accompanies the subject
Free part new material that accompanies the subject, answer or countersubject once
Tonic pedal sustained note played by bass that ends fugue
Voice 1
Voice 2
Voice 3
EXPOSITION
Begins in the home key (tonic) when voice 1 states the subject. Each voice presents the subject or answer once.
DEVELOPMENT
Freer section in which subject, answer, and countersubject are alternated with episodes.
RECAPITULATION
Final section begins when the subject enters in the home key once more.
CODA
Short passage that brings the recapitulation to an end.

Step to Parnassus

In 1725, the Austrian composer and theorist Johann Joseph Fux (see panel opposite) published a treatise on counterpoint called *Gradus ad Parnassum* (*Step to Parnassus*). The title refers to Mount Parnassus, the home of the Ancient Greek goddesses, the Muses, who inspired the arts. Fux's treatise, which set down the rules of counterpoint, was one of the most influential of all musical textbooks.

Fux took the works of Palestrina (see pp.60–61) as his model and established a method for students to follow, based on five "species" of counterpoint. In the first species, the student had to write a new melody against a *cantus firmus* (preexisting melody) note for note. The second species set two notes against each note of the *cantus firmus*, and the third set four notes. In the fourth species, notes of equal length were sustained across the beats of the *cantus firmus* to create syncopations, or interruptions to the rhythm. The fifth species, called florid counterpoint, was a combination of the other four species with an occasional embellishment.

Using imitation

Another method of writing counterpoint is to use imitation. Here, a composer provides a melody for one voice, which is imitated by one or more other voices in succession. These voices often enter on a different pitch, usually a fifth above or a fourth below.

> "He [Bach] considered **his parts** as if they were **persons** who **conversed** together."
>
> MUSICOLOGIST JOHANN FORKEL DESCRIBING J.S. BACH'S COUNTERPOINT, 1802

A canon is a common example of imitation: one voice states the melody and the others follow at a fixed point, either at the same or different pitch, possibly reversing the melody, and lengthening or shortening the notes. The simplest canon is a round, such as "Three Blind Mice," where the imitation repeats the exact melody.

The most complex form of imitative counterpoint is the fugue, a word that suggests the idea of flight or pursuit. Fugues begin with one voice playing a melody, the subject, followed by another voice with the same melody, but at a different pitch, called the answer. The first voice continues with music accompanying the answer—either a secondary melody, the countersubject, or a free part. The pattern of subject and answer

GRANDE FUGUE
tantôt libre, tantôt recherchée
pour
2 Violons, Alte & Violoncelle
Dediée avec la plus profonde vénération
à
Son Altesse Impériale et Royale Éminentissime
MONSEIGNEUR LE CARDINAL
RODOLPHE
Archiduc d'Autriche, Prince de Hongrie et de Bohême, Prince Archevêque d'Olmütz etc. etc.
Grand Croix de l'Ordre Hongrois de St. Étienne etc. etc.
PAR
L. VAN BEETHOVEN
Oeuvre 133.
(Propriété de l'Éditeur)
VIENNE
chez
Math. Artaria
Kohlmarkt No. 258.

Technical challenge
The most famous of Beethoven's fugues is the *Grosse Fuge* (Great Fugue). It had been composed as the finale of his string quartet Op. 130, but contemporary musicians found it too difficult to play.

BEFORE

The Latin phrase *punctum contra punctum* (point against point) occurs in a medieval treatise. It is one of the earliest references to counterpoint.

12TH-CENTURY BIRTH OF POLYPHONY
From the **Notre Dame School** « 46–47 to the composer **Palestrina** « 60–61, music with many parts, or **polyphony**, grew more elaborate.

15TH-CENTURY CHIGI CODEX

SACRED POLYPHONY
The Chigi Codex, a lavishly decorated music manuscript of the late 15th century, is one of the richest sources of Franco-Flemish polyphonic masses.

Subject begins

Answer begins

Counter-subject accompanies subject

Subject enters again

Key work
This page comes from a manuscript copy, in J.S. Bach's own hand, of an A flat major fugue from his collection *The Well-Tempered Clavier*, which comprised preludes and fugues in each of the 12 major and minor keys.

continues until all the voices—usually between 3 and 6—have entered. This introduction of all the voices is known as the exposition and is the most strictly ordered section of the fugue.

The exposition is followed by the development, a new section of music that usually develops material from the exposition. It is composed more freely, with "episodes" that can take the music into different keys. This is followed by further entries of the subject, and the fugue then continues by alternating entries and episodes until it reaches a final statement of the subject in the original key. Any music that follows after this point is called a coda. A fugue often builds to a pedal point toward the end, which is a sustained note in the bass on the main note of the key (the tonic), which reinforces the original key. From this point on there is a sense of the melody coming home.

Ever increasing complexity

In the treatment of the subject after the exposition, composers could use various devices to raise the complexity. The subject could be turned upside down (inversion), played back to front (retrograde), or be repeated so rapidly by another voice that the two statements overlap (*stretto*). In his last great work, *The Art of Fugue* (1750), J.S. Bach brilliantly displays the range of these transformational techniques.

AFTER

The elaborate and complex counterpoint written by J.S. Bach and Handel had largely disappeared by the second half of the 18th century.

FUNDAMENTALS OF COMPOSITION
From the **Classical era 112–145 ››** onward, learning the rudiments of counterpoint and fugue became an essential part of a musical education. Composers were familiar with the theory of counterpoint, but generally worked in a freer style. Fugues occasionally occurred in the works of **Mozart 136–137 ››**, **Joseph Haydn 126–127 ››**, **Beethoven 142–143 ››**, and **Hector Berlioz 162–163 ››**.

COMPOSER (1660–1741)

JOHANN FUX

Although born into an Austrian peasant family, Johann Fux benefited from a privileged education. He studied music, logic, law, and language with the Jesuits at two universities.

Beginning in the 1690s, he held important musical posts in Vienna, at both the Imperial court and at St. Stephen's Cathedral. Fux was a highly prolific composer, and wrote around 95 masses and 22 operas.

His great admiration of Palestrina (c.1525–1594) is reflected in his own, rather conservative, church music. Fux's 1725 treatise on counterpoint, *Gradus ad Parnassum*, also takes the Palestrina style as its starting point.

COMPOSER Born 1685 Died 1750

Johann Sebastian Bach

"The man from whom **all true musical wisdom** proceeded."

COMPOSER JOSEPH HAYDN ON JOHANN SEBASTIAN BACH

In an era of outstanding musical achievement, Bach is, for many, the greatest of all the late Baroque composers. A master of the formal intricacies of counterpoint, he created outstanding pieces in every musical genre except opera. Although he never traveled outside Germany, he was responsive to wider musical developments in Italy and France.

Early life

Bach was born into a family of musicians in Eisenach, Germany, in 1685. His first teacher was his father, Johann Ambrosius Bach, a church organist and violinist. After his father's death in 1695, the 10-year-old Bach went to study music with his older brother, Johann Christoph, the organist in Ohrdruf, 30 miles (50 km) away. From there, he was sent to St. Michael's school at Lüneberg, where he may have studied with the organist Georg Böhm.

Following a period as a violinist at the ducal court in Weimar in 1703, Bach became organist at the Neue Kirche in nearby Arnstadt. He does not appear to have taken his duties that seriously, however, and annoyed the authorities by failing to return promptly from Lübeck, where he had gone on foot to hear Dietrich Buxtehude play the organ. His next job, as organist at Mühlhausen, was cut short when he returned to Weimar.

The Weimar years were highly productive. He composed much of his finest organ music there, including the

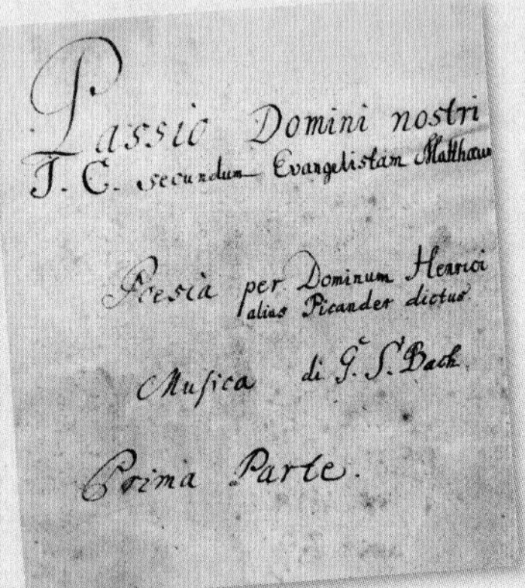

Passio Domini nostri
J. C. secundum Evangelistam Matthæum
Poesia per Dominum Henrici alias Picander dictus
Musica di G. S. Bach
Prima Parte.

Original of an oratorio
The title page of the original score of *St. Matthew Passion* shows Bach's name after that of Picander, the pseudonym of the librettist Christian Friedrich Henrici.

In pursuit of perfection
During his lifetime, Bach was admired as a virtuoso organist, but he was also a brilliant harpsichordist and a fine string player. His pursuit of the highest musical standards often put him in conflict with his employers.

KEY WORKS

Toccata and Fugue in D minor, BW V565
***Brandenburg Concertos*, BWV 1046–1051**
Violin sonatas and partitas, BWV 1001–1006
***St. Matthew Passion*, BWV 244**
***Goldberg Variations*, BWV 988**
Mass in B minor, BWV 232

Toccata and Fugue in D minor and the Passacaglia in C minor. It all ended badly, however, when Bach, having been overlooked for promotion to Kapellmeister (musical director), repeatedly requested permission to leave in order to take up a position at the court of Prince Leopold of Anhalt-Cöthen. His employer, Duke Wilhelm Ernst, responded by imprisoning him for one month before letting him go.

Fruitful period

At Cöthen, Bach had a sympathetic patron who, as a Calvinist, required no music for church services. Instead, Bach was free to compose instrumental and orchestral works, producing several of his masterpieces, including his solo violin partitas and sonatas, the solo cello sonatas, a wealth of keyboard music, including *The Well-Tempered Clavier*, and six *concerti grossi* (grand concertos) dedicated to the Margrave of Brandenburg.

In 1720, Bach's wife unexpectedly died, leaving him with four children to raise. The following year he married Anna Magdalena Wilcke, the daughter of a court musician. He went on to have thirteen children with Anna Magdalena, only six of whom survived to adulthood.

Around the same time as Bach's second marriage, Prince Leopold also married. His wife lacked the prince's love of music and Bach's position as Kapellmeister was terminated. Bach then applied to be cantor of the Thomasschule (School of St. Thomas) in Leipzig, a less prestigious position.

The Leipzig years

Bach duly secured the job at Leipzig but only after George Philipp Telemann and Christoph Graupner were unable to accept the position. For the next 27 years Bach labored under a demanding workload: his duties included teaching music at the Thomasschule, providing and directing the music at the churches of St. Thomas and St. Nicolai, as well as composing and directing music for Leipzig's important civic occasions.

During his first six years in Leipzig he composed no less than five cycles of cantatas for the main services in the Lutheran Church calendar and at least two settings of the Passion for the main Good Friday service.

Church setting
Many of Bach's great choral works were first performed at the Lutheran church of St. Thomas in Leipzig, where Bach was cantor from 1723.

By 1729, Bach, a highly skilled organist, began performing more church music by other composers while varying his own compositional activities by writing for the Collegium Musicum of Leipzig. This musical society of students and professionals, originally founded by Telemann, met and performed in Zimmermann's coffee house.

Death and legacy

Bach's last unfinished project was a complex and theoretical exploration of counterpoint entitled *The Art of Fugue*. Now in his sixties, Bach was almost blind from cataracts and his health was deteriorating. In 1750, he died of a stroke, before *The Art of Fugue* could be published.

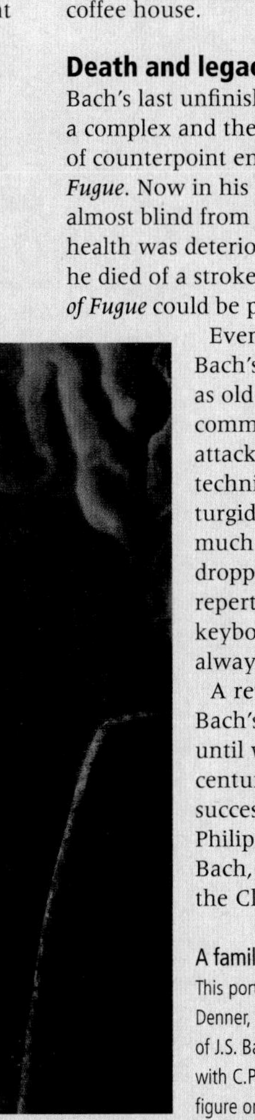

Even before his death, Bach's music was regarded as old-fashioned by many commentators and was attacked in the press for its technical difficulty and turgidity. After his death, much of his music dropped from the repertoire, although the keyboard works were always valued by pianists.

A revival of interest in Bach's music did not occur until well into the 19th century. The most successful of his sons, Carl Philip Emanuel (C. P. E.) Bach, was a forerunner of the Classical style.

> "[They] are … **hard to please** and **care little** for **music.**"
>
> J.S. BACH, COMPLAINING ABOUT HIS EMPLOYERS AT LEIPZIG, 1730

A family business
This portrait, ascribed to Balthasar Denner, is thought by some to be of J.S. Bach and three of his sons, with C.P.E. Bach suggested as the figure on the right.

TIMELINE

- **March 21, 1685** Born in Eisenach, the son of musician Johann Ambrosius Bach.
- **1695** His father dies and Bach moves to Ohrdruf to live with his brother, Johann Christoph, also a musician.
- **1703** Appointed court musician at Weimar and later organist at the Neue Kirche, Arnstadt.
- **1705** Granted leave to visit Lübeck to hear Dietrich Buxtehude play the organ.
- **1707** Appointed organist at Mühlhausen and marries his second cousin, Maria Barbara.
- **1708** Appointed organist and chamber musician to Duke Wilhelm Ernst at Weimar.
- **1717** Appointed Kapellmeister (musical director) to Prince Leopold of Anhalt-Cöthen to the annoyance of Duke Wilhelm Ernst, who reacts by imprisoning him for a month.
- **1720** Wife dies, leaving him with four children to raise.
- **1721** Marries the singer Anna Magdalena Wilcke. Presents a copy of the *Brandenburg Concertos* to the Margrave of Brandenburg in the hope of gaining patronage. The margrave has insufficient musicians to play the work and does not acknowledge the gift.
- **1723** Appointed cantor of the Thomasschule in Leipzig and also responsible for music in the city's churches and at civic events.
- **1727** The first performance of *St. Matthew Passion* is held on Good Friday.
- **1729** Argues with the council about the number of unmusical pupils entering the Thomasschule. Takes over the direction of the Collegium Musicum.
- **1737** The composer and critic Johann Adolf Scheibe publishes an attack on Bach's music, criticizing it for being turgid and confused.
- **1738** His son Carl Philipp Emanuel is appointed harpsichordist to the crown prince of Prussia, the future Frederick the Great.
- **1741** *The Goldberg Variations*, named after Johann Gottlieb Goldberg, a virtuoso harpsichordist who may have been the work's first performer, are published by Bach's friend Balthasar Schmid of Nuremberg.
- **1747** Visits Frederick the Great at Potsdam, where he improvises on a theme provided by the king. The music is developed into *A Musical Offering*. This is presented to the king, possibly in the hope of preferment.
- **1750** Undergoes a cataract operation by the renowned English oculist John Taylor. It brings only temporary relief. On July 28, he dies from a stroke while preparing *The Art of Fugue* for publication.

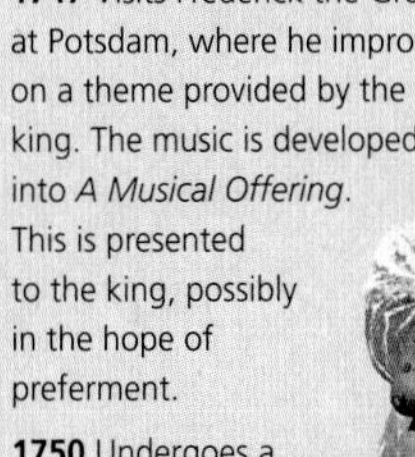

BACH MEMORIAL, LEIPZIG

Sonatas, Suites, and **Overtures**

It was during the Baroque era that instrumental music finally emerged as an independent form; previously it had mainly been played to accompany singers or dancers. As enthusiasm for instrumental music grew, so new genres began to develop.

« BEFORE

In the 16th century, before the Baroque era, instrumental music was still largely used to accompany singers or played as dance music.

CANZONAS

One increasingly widely heard form of instrumental music was the **canzona**, a transcription of the French *chanson* (song), which became highly popular during the 16th century.

Giovanni Gabrieli « 56 developed the form in Italy for Venice's many grand church and state events, with the music to be performed by the large instrumental forces of St. Mark's Basilica.

FIRST DYNAMICS

Gabrieli called one of his instrumental pieces *Sonata pian e forte* (Soft and Loud Sonata). This was one of the earliest examples of a composer specifying how the dynamics of a piece should be played.

UNDERSTANDING MUSIC

LA FOLIA

The first mention of this wild Portuguese folk dance, the name of which suggests insanity, was in the 15th century. However, it probably dates from much earlier.

In 17th-century Spain, a version of *La Folia* became popular as a sung dance, performed with guitar accompaniment. It was soon known across Europe, and a version of the music by Jean-Baptiste Lully (see pp.84–85) became particularly well-known, with a specific chord progression and a ground bass. Several Baroque composers were inspired to write variations on *La Folia*, including Corelli, Vivaldi, and Handel. Centuries later, in 1913, Russian composer Sergey Rachmaninoff (see pp.222–223) wrote a set of variations for piano based on the theme of *La Folia*.

Two of the most important of the Baroque period's instrumental genres were the *concerto grosso* (see p.79) and the trio sonata. The term sonata (the Italian word for "played") was applied fairly flexibly at this time. Domenico Scarlatti (see p.107) used "sonata" to describe his short keyboard pieces, while J.S. Bach (see pp.100–101) called his collections of dance pieces for solo violin by the same name.

What the name sonata most commonly denoted was a piece in several movements for a small group of instruments plus continuo—a continuous chordal bass line, often played by a harpsichord and cello. A trio sonata, for example, consisted of four instruments: two treble instruments (usually violins) and a bass instrument (which made up the trio), accompanied by continuo. A solo sonata was made up of bass plus continuo and just one treble instrument playing the solo part.

The composer who did most to establish these genres was Arcangelo Corelli (see opposite), who published five sets of highly influential sonatas. Many composers, including François Couperin (1668–1733), Georg Philipp Telemann (1681–1767), and Dietrich Buxtehude (1637–1707), followed his lead. Their small-scale instrumental works were known collectively as chamber music because they were intended for performance in the home or in small halls. When performed in religious services, such works were known as *sonata da chiesa* (church sonatas), and tended to be more serious in tone, with the continuo played by a small organ.

Pocket violin

This pocket-sized kit violin, also known by its French name *pochette* (meaning pocket), was mainly used by dancing masters to accompany their pupils as they practiced their steps.

KEY WORKS

Arcangelo Corelli 12 Sonatas, Op 1; 12 Concerti Grossi, Op 6

G.P. Telemann Trio Sonatas

J.S. Bach Sonatas and Partitas for Solo Violin (BWV 1001–1006); English Suites (BWV 806–811)

Dietrich Buxtehude "La Capricciosa" Variations for harpsichord

Dancing music

The suite, which could also be called a partita, was an instrumental work consisting of a series of contrasting movements based on dance forms, usually preceded by a prelude. All the movements were in the same key, which served to unify the piece.

A suite could be composed for any combination of instruments but was commonly a solo instrumental work. By the time that J.S. Bach and Handel (see pp.108–109) were composing, the movements tended to follow a set pattern. The introductory prelude, which often had an improvisatory feel to it, was followed by the *allemande*, a moderately paced dance of German origin, usually in duple time (two strong beats in a bar). This was in marked contrast to the next movement, the faster *courante* (which translates as "running"), and was usually in triple time (three main beats in a bar). Next came the stately and somber *sarabande*, which was followed by lighter, sprightly dances, such as a pair of minuets, *bourrées*, or *gavottes*. The suite was rounded off by a lively *gigue* (jig) in 6/8 time (six eighth notes in a bar, with emphasis on the first and fourth beats), which demanded great virtuosity. Handel's *Water Music* (1717) and *Music for the Royal Fireworks* (1749) are examples of the Baroque orchestral suite.

Creative variations

As an alternative to using a *gigue* to end a suite, composers began to write a set of alternating variations, known by the French term *double*, in which the original melody (the *simple*) is elaborated while the harmony remains the same.

Variations also existed as pieces in their own right, beginning with either an existing or a newly

Social dancing

In *Dancing the Minuet* by Giandomenico Tiepolo (1727–1804), an elegant reveler at the Venice Carnival takes part in a minuet, the most popular social dance of the 18th century.

composed melody. This melody was used as a theme that the composer would transform in a series of often highly elaborate variations. In some variations, the outlines of the theme would be easily recognizable; in others, it would be more difficult to discern the connection with the original.

Composers could use certain forms to structure their variations. Two almost identical ones, popular in this period, were the *chaconne* and the *passacaglia*. In both, the variations were unified by a bass line (called a ground bass), which was continuously repeated.

> "The special quality of English **jigs** is **hot** and hurried **eagerness.**"
>
> GERMAN COMPOSER AND MUSICAL THEORIST JOHANN MATTHESON, 1739

Development of the overture

The primary meaning of the word "overture" was an orchestral introduction to an opera, ballet, or oratorio. In France, this took the form of a slow and stately first section—usually in duple time with jerky dotted rhythms—followed by a faster, second section, which was often written as a fugue (a composition style in which a principal theme is repeatedly imitated).

In Italy, Alessandro Scarlatti (1660–1725), father of Domenico, established a new form for his operas, consisting of three movements (fast-slow-fast), of which the last movement was usually a lively dance.

The Italian overture, also known as a *sinfonia*, had an independent life as an occasional concert piece and paved the way for the Classical symphony (see pp.124–125). Occasionally, the name overture was used as an alternative name for a suite, notably in the case of J.S. Bach's four orchestral suites.

COMPOSER (1653–1713)

ARCANGELO CORELLI

An outstanding violinist who did much to raise playing standards in Italy, Corelli is even more influential as the composer who established the model for the *concerto grosso*, the trio sonata, and solo sonata.

From 1675, he was based in Rome, where he became the city's most renowned musician. His patrons included Queen Christina of Sweden and Cardinal Pamphili, and from 1689 he served Cardinal Ottoboni. Little of Corelli's music was published, but it had a huge impact on his contemporaries.

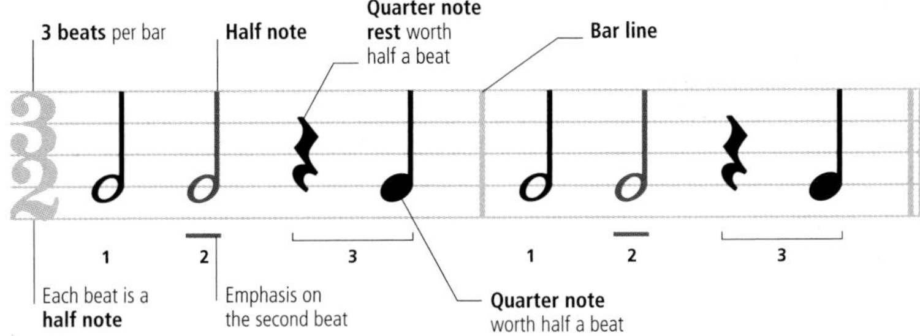

Sarabande rhythm
Originally a lively dance from Latin America, the *sarabande* was transformed at the French court, and in instrumental music, into a slow stately piece in triple time (three beats per bar), with an emphasis on the second beat.

AFTER

Several instrumental genres declined in popularity after the Baroque era, while others developed into new, more tightly structured, forms.

SYMPHONIES
By the late 18th century, the *concerto grosso* and the orchestral suite had been superseded by the **symphony** **124–125 »**.

> **Although Haydn did not invent the string quartet, he was responsible for creating the first masterpieces of the genre.**

NEW FORMS FOR CHAMBER MUSIC
Genres like the trio sonata were replaced by new forms, such as the string quartet and the piano trio, in chamber music compositions.

1 QUEEN ELIZABETH'S VIRGINAL
Length 6 ft 3 in (1.9 m)

2 MINIATURE VIRGINAL
Length 12 in (30 cm)

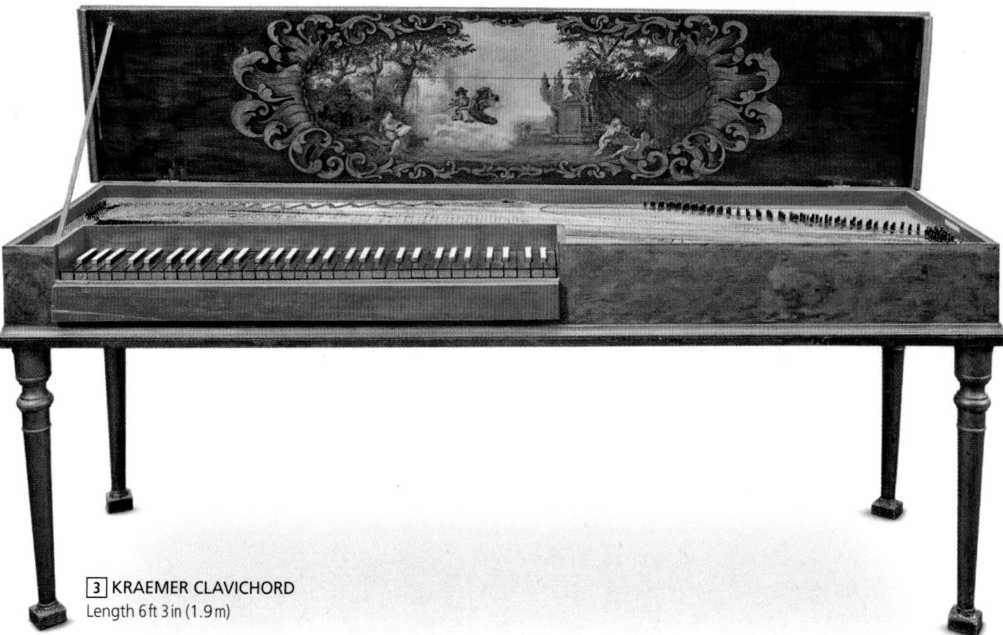

3 KRAEMER CLAVICHORD
Length 6 ft 3 in (1.9 m)

4 HASS CLAVICHORD
Length 5 ft 9 in (1.8 m)

Keyboard Instruments

Throughout the Baroque period, keyboard instruments greatly improved in their range and power. The harpsichord was the main concert instrument, but by the mid-18th century it had a rival in the new fortepiano.

1 **Virginal** (1594) This small keyboard instrument for domestic music-making was placed on a table. This richly decorated Venetian example, made by Giovanni Baffo, once belonged to England's Queen Elizabeth I. 2 **Virginal** (1672) The virginal's strings run at right angles to the keys and are plucked by quills. This miniature version, made by Franciscus Vaninus in Italy, was probably intended for a child. 3 **Clavichord** (1804) The clavichord's strings were struck, not plucked, and the note sounded for as long as a key was held down, making it more expressive than a harpsichord. This late example was made by Johann Paul Kraemer and Sons in Germany. 4 **Clavichord** (1743) The clavichord is the only stringed keyboard that can be played with vibrato. This beautifully decorated example was made by H.A. Hass in Germany. 5 **Fortepiano** (1720) The first piano, so-called because it could play loud (forte) and soft (piano), was built in Italy *c.*1700 by Bartolomeo Cristofori. The strings were struck by hammers and sounded until the key was released. Only three Cristofori pianos survive, including this one. 6 **Spinet** (1723) Smaller than the harpsichord, the spinet has plucked strings set diagonally from the keys. This one was made by Thomas Hitchcock of London. 7 **Harpsichord** (*c.*1720) With plucked strings similar to the virginal and spinet, the harpsichord is much larger and its strings lie parallel to the keys. Made by William Smith of London, this example almost certainly belonged to Handel. 8 **Spinet** (1689) Having only one string per note made spinets quieter than harpsichords, which had two, and ideal for home enjoyment. This one was made by Charles Haward in London. 9 **Spinet** (1785) This is a rare example of a spinet made by Johann Heinrich Silbermann, from a German family famous for organ building. 10 **Harpsichord** (1643) This instrument was made by Andreas Ruckers the Elder—one of three generations of a Flemish family whose instruments were prized for their sound and became a model for subsequent makers. 11 **Harpsichord** (1659) Made by Ruckers, this example—unlike many early keyboards—has its original casing.

5 FORTEPIANO
Length 7 ft 7 in (2.3 m)

6 HITCHCOCK SPINET
Length 6ft (1.8m)

7 SMITH HARPSICHORD
Length 6ft 7in (2m)

8 HAWARD SPINET
Length 4ft 7in (1.4m)

9 SILBERMANN SPINET
Length 6ft (1.8m)

10 DOUBLE- MANUAL HARPSICHORD
Length 7ft 7in (2.3m)

11 SINGLE-MANUAL HARPSICHORD
Length approx. 6ft 7in (2m)

The Harpsichord Lesson
Playing the harpsichord was a fashionable accomplishment for the well-to-do in 17th-century Europe, as is suggested by this painting, by Dutch artist Jan Steen (*c.* 1626–1679).

« BEFORE

Instrumental music to be played on its own, rather than to accompany a song, emerged in the late 16th century.

EARLY KEYBOARD COMPOSERS
Claudio Merulo (1533–1604), organist of **St. Mark's Basilica** **« 72–73**, elevated keyboard music from simple works based on vocal music to something more complex. In England, a whole school of outstanding composers emerged, including **William Byrd** (1540–1623), Orlando Gibbons (1583–1625), and John Bull (1563–1628).

RISE OF PRINTED KEYBOARD MUSIC
The availability of **printed music** **« 54–55** helped circulate ideas around Europe, as did important teachers such as Italian Girolamo Frescobaldi (1583–1643) and Dutch organist Jan Pieterszoon Sweelinck (1562–1621).

Keyboard Maestros

By the end of the 17th century, keyboard instruments had become popular with both professional and amateur musicians. Demand for music grew and as technological advances improved the quality of instruments, composers produced increasingly sophisticated pieces.

Nearly all the great keyboard composers were outstanding keyboard players. The instrument for which they wrote—harpsichord, clavichord, or organ—was not always specified. The German word *clavier* means keyboard, and for public concerts this usually meant a harpsichord, either as a solo instrument or as part of an ensemble.

The brilliance of Bach

Johann Sebastian Bach (1685–1750) had a career as a Kappelmeister (music director), teacher, and organ virtuoso, which meant he wrote a wide range of keyboard music, from simple teaching manuals to technically demanding toccatas, fugues (see pp.98–99), and suites. One of Bach's best-loved masterpieces is the *Goldberg Variations,* a set of 30 variations on a slow and stately theme, which was published in 1741. It is an epic work that is endlessly intriguing because of the highly imaginative way in which Bach transforms the material using a variety of styles and with unexpected shifts of mood. The whole set of variations is held together by the underlying presence of the theme's bass line and its harmony.

CORRESPONDENCE between J.S. Bach and the French composer François Couperin has not survived. Their letters ended up as jam-pot covers.

According to Bach's first biographer, the German musician and theorist Johann Nikolaus Forkel (1749–1818), the Russian ambassador to Saxony, Count von Keyserlingk, commissioned the variations to be played to him by his

"His **whole heart** and **soul** were in his **harpsichord ...**"

FRENCH PLAYWRIGHT ALEXIS PIRON (1689–1773) ON RAMEAU

harpsichordist, Johann Goldberg (a pupil of Bach's), in order to relieve the count's frequent bouts of insomnia.

Handel's harpsichord music

Bach's great German contemporary, George Frideric Handel (1685–1759), was also a brilliant player, but his keyboard music was secondary to his operas and oratorios—although several of his organ concertos were first played during performances of the oratorios. The majority of his best harpsichord music is contained in a collection of eight suites from 1720.

Handel used several styles—Italian melody, Germanic counterpoint, and French refinement—within the same suite. The most famous is the four-movement Suite No. 5, which ends not with the usual *gigue* (jig) but with a set of variations on a melody known as "The Harmonious Blacksmith."

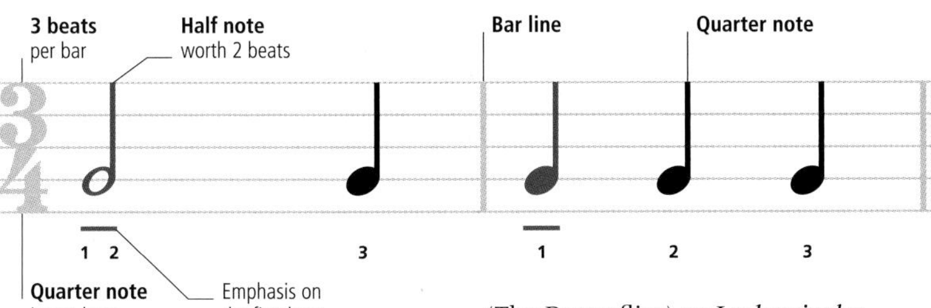

The minuet
This is a moderately paced and elegant dance in triple time (three beats per bar), usually 3/4. Baroque composers wrote minuets as independent pieces and as part of a suite.

French masters

The French style of keyboard writing was more florid and less contrapuntal (see pp.78–79) than its German equivalent, especially solo harpsichord music. Performers favored a method of playing called *style luthé* (lute style) in which chords were broken up into their component notes (or arpeggiated) instead of sounded simultaneously.

The greatest of the French keyboard masters was François Couperin (1668–1733), who wrote four books of *Pièces de clavecin* (Harpsichord Pieces) between 1713 and 1740. The books consisted of 27 suites in total, which he called *Ordres* (Orders). Although based on dance forms, they are collections of evocative miniatures rather than conventional suites (specific sets of dances). Each piece is given a name, such as *Les papillons* (The Butterflies) or *Les barricades mystérieuses* (The Mysterious Barricades); some are descriptive while others may have had a personal meaning. In the score, he specifies exactly how the piece should be ornamented, instead of leaving it up to the player to improvise.

The finest of Couperin's French contemporaries was Jean-Philippe Rameau (1683–1764) who, although better known as an opera composer (see pp.130–131), wrote around 60 outstanding harpsichord pieces, mostly arranged into suites. Some are character pieces, such as *La poule* (The Chicken), which imitates a hen's clucking, or *Les sauvages* (The Savages), inspired by seeing Native Americans from France's new colony in Louisiana dancing—both from the Suite in G minor (1726–1727). But Rameau also used traditional dance forms, such as the *allemande, courante,* and *sarabande* (see pp.102–103).

Rameau's pieces are more technically demanding than Couperin's and his harmonies are more daring. His Suite in A minor (1726–1727) closes with six particularly difficult variations on a *gavotte* (a French folk dance), an idea he may have borrowed from one of Handel's keyboard suites.

An Italian in Iberia

During his time in the service of the Infanta Maria Barbara, Domenico Scarlatti wrote the 555 keyboard sonatas upon which his fame rests. Unlike the multi-movement works of his great contemporaries, these are single-movement pieces in two contrasting sections (known as binary form). Technically demanding and highly inventive, many of the sonatas employ such devices as hand-crossing, unexpected changes of key, and dissonance (clashing combinations of notes).

Scarlatti was inspired by the music of his Iberian surroundings, and several of the sonatas incorporate elements from Andalusian and Portuguese folklore. In some, hints of guitar strumming and foot stamping can be heard.

Scarlatti's sonatas proved very popular in England, where music historian Charles Burney (1726–1814) called them: "original and happy freaks ... the wonderful delight of every hearer who had a spark of enthusiasm about him."

COMPOSER (1660–1725)

DOMENICO SCARLATTI

Domenico Scarlatti was born in Naples, Italy. A brilliant keyboard player, his career was strictly controlled by his composer father, Alessandro (1660–1725), until he won his independence through legal action, in 1717, at the age of 31.

In 1719, he was appointed director of music to King João V of Portugal. Even though he was an opera and choral composer, Scarlatti's principal duty seems to have been teaching the king's talented daughter, Maria Barbara. When she married the heir to the Spanish throne in 1729, Scarlatti accompanied her to Spain, remaining in her service until his death. Many of his sonatas originated as keyboard *essercizi* (exercises).

UNDERSTANDING MUSIC

FANTASIAS AND TOCCATAS

A skilled keyboard player was expected to be able to improvise on the spot, and two forms—the fantasia and the toccata—reflect this. The fantasia, as the name implies, was meant to suggest music that came directly from the performer's imagination, and was often full of exaggerated or distorted effects. A toccata was a virtuoso composition for keyboard or plucked-string instrument written to show off the skill and "touch" of the performer (the word derives from the Italian verb *toccare* meaning "to touch"). Toccatas were usually fast, with rapid passage work, or runs, sometimes incorporating a fugue (see p.98).

What both fantasias and toccatas shared was a spontaneity and freedom of form that made them sound as if they were being improvised. Two keyboard composers who did much to establish both forms were the Italian Girolamo Frescobaldi (1583–1643) and his German pupil Johann Froberger (1616–1667).

KEY WORKS

J.S. Bach Toccata in C minor (BWV 911)

George Frideric Handel Suite de pièce Vol. 1, No. 5 (HWV 430)

François Couperin Ordre 25ème de clavecin in E flat major

Jean-Philippe Rameau Suite in A minor

Domenico Scarlatti Sonata in B minor (K27); Sonata in A major (K212)

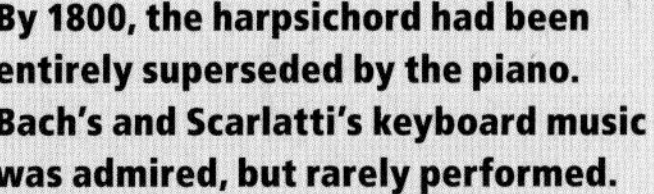

By 1800, the harpsichord had been entirely superseded by the piano. Bach's and Scarlatti's keyboard music was admired, but rarely performed.

EARLY MUSIC PIONEER

Performances of Baroque keyboard music on the type of instrument for which it was written did not reoccur again until the early 20th century. **Wanda Landowska** was a pioneering and influential figure, whose skill and tenacity helped reestablish the harpsichord as a mainstream instrument. She made several groundbreaking recordings of J. S. Bach's music, including the first complete recording of the *Goldberg Variations*, in 1933.

WANDA LANDOWSKA (1879–1959)

COMPOSER Born 1685 Died 1759

George Frideric Handel

"Handel is the **greatest composer** who **ever lived ...**"

BEETHOVEN, RECORDED BY EDWARD SCHULZ, 1823

George Frideric Handel was the Baroque period's outstanding composer of Italian *opera seria* ("serious opera"), while also being responsible for transforming the oratorio into an English and distinctly Protestant genre. His long, lyrical vocal lines combined with a dramatic instinct have ensured that many of his works have never lost their popularity.

Venerable organ
The organ of St. Katharine Cree church in the City of London was played by both Handel and Henry Purcell. Handel was noted for his exceptional command of the instrument.

Early promise

Born in the north German town of Halle in 1685, Handel showed early musical talent. His father, a surgeon at the court of Saxony, had wanted him to study law but relented under pressure and agreed to let him train with a local organist, Friedrich Wilhelm Zachow. The young Handel soon outgrew his teacher and at the age of 17 was appointed organist of Halle's cathedral. In 1703, he left to join the orchestra of the Hamburg opera house, where he wrote his first three operas.

Aware that he needed to refine his skills, Handel went to Italy in 1706 to immerse himself in composing and performing. He won acclaim in Rome, especially as a harpsichordist, haring the honors with Domenico Scarlatti in a keyboard contest at the palace of Cardinal

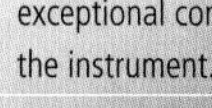

British citizen
Although born in Germany, Handel lived in London from 1711 until the end of his life. He was granted British citizenship in 1727.

Fugue by Handel
This manuscript in Handel's own handwriting is part of a fugue—a highly structured piece in which two or more voices enter one by one imitatively.

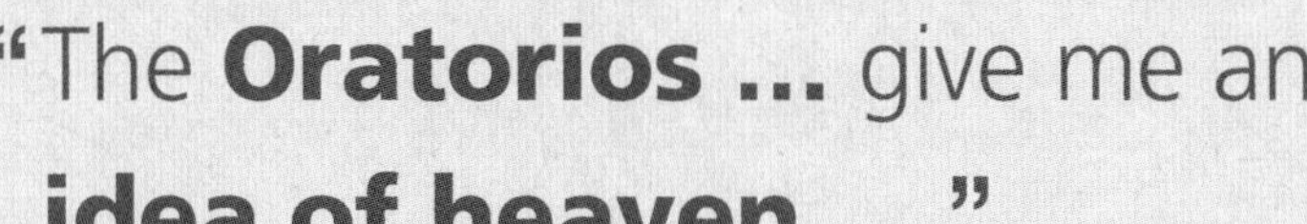

"The **Oratorios ...** give me an idea of heaven ..."

HORACE WALPOLE, LETTER TO SIR HORACE MANN, 1743

Ottoboni. Handel was quick to adopt the Italian vocal style, such as in the choral masterpiece ***Dixit Dominus***. Two operas, ***Rodrigo*** in 1707, and ***Agrippina*** in 1709, added to his reputation.

While in Italy, Handel was approached by representatives of the Hanoverian court, and in 1710 he became Kapellmeister (musical director) to the Elector of Hanover. The terms of his employment allowed him to travel, and within a few months he was in London, where Italian opera had taken hold. In 1713, he scored a hit with ***Rinaldo***, which he completed in just two weeks.

Royal commissions

Handel's absence from Hanover led to his dismissal, but he was reunited with his former employer when the Elector became King George I of England in 1714. Among Handel's royal commissions were the orchestral suites, known as the *Water Music*, written for a royal trip down the Thames River in 1717. It was around this time that Handel became composer-in-residence to the Duke of Chandos, for whom he wrote the pastoral *Acis and Galatea*, the oratorio *Esther*, and the choral Chandos Anthems.

In 1719, a group of wealthy amateurs founded London's first opera company, the Royal Academy of Music, and appointed Handel as musical director. He produced a regular supply of operas over the next nine seasons, including his most celebrated—*Giulio Cesare in Egitto* (Julius Caesar in Egypt) in 1723. Unfortunately, the Academy went bankrupt in 1728.

Handel continued to compose for royal occasions. For George II's coronation in 1727, he composed the magnificent anthem *Zadok the Priest*.

The oratorios

Despite the failure of the Academy, Handel continued to produce operas throughout the 1730s, including the masterpieces *Orlando* (1732), *Ariodante* (1734,) and *Serse* (1738). By the end of the decade, the British enthusiasm for Italian opera was fading, and Handel turned his attention to writing oratorios in English, mostly based on Old Testament stories. *Saul*, in 1738, was well received, but it was *Messiah*, in 1742, that proved his greatest success. A celebration of Christ's redemption of mankind, the music is wonderfully varied, ranging from the glorious melodic aria "Come Unto Me," and the anthem "For Unto Us a Child is Born," to the grandeur of the fugal "Amen," with which the work closes. Several more oratorios followed over the next 10 years, among them *Samson* in 1743, *Solomon* in 1749, and *Jephtha* in 1752. Handel's compositions for official occasions included, in 1749, *Music for the Royal Fireworks*, an orchestral suite to celebrate the Treaty of Aix-la-Chapelle, which ended the War of the Austrian Succession. At the king's insistence, the music included "martial instruments" to accompany the pyrotechnics.

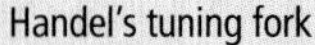

Handel's tuning fork
This tuning fork, used for ascertaining pitch, was given to Handel by the British musician John Shore, the inventor of the tuning fork.

A national figure

Blind by the end of 1752, Handel wrote no more major works after *Jephtha*. He died at his home in London's Brook Street on April 14, 1759, and was buried a week later in Westminster Abbey. He left bequests for, among others, a charity for destitute musicians and the Foundling Hospital, a children's home where he had been a benefactor and governor and also encouraged music. Handel also left £600 for the sculpture of himself by Louis François Roubiliac, still standing in Westminster Abbey.

Royal Fireworks
The first performance of the *Music for the Royal Fireworks*, depicted in this lithograph, was in London's Green Park.

KEY WORKS

- ***Water Music***
- ***Giulio Cesare in Egitto* (Julius Caesar in Egypt)**
- ***Zadok the Priest***
- **Concerti Grossi Op. 6 (Twelve Grand Concertos)**
- ***Messiah***
- ***Music for the Royal Fireworks***

TIMELINE

- **January 23, 1685** Born in Halle, northern Germany.
- **1703** Moves to Hamburg and writes his first operas.
- **1706** Travels to Italy and stays for three years.
- **1710** Appointed music director to the Elector of Hanover.
- **1711** Travels to London.
- **1713** His opera *Rinaldo* is performed at London's Queen's Theatre.
- **1714** Elector of Hanover becomes King George I of England.
- **1717** Writes *Water Music* and *Chandos Anthems*.
- **1719** Becomes music director of the newly founded Royal Academy of Music.
- **1723** Appointed composer to the Chapel Royal and leases a house in Brook Street, now the Handel House Museum, in London.
- **1724** Writes the opera *Giulio Cesare in Egitto* for the Royal Academy.
- **1727** Writes coronation anthems, including *Zadok the Priest*, for George II.
- **1732** An expanded version of *Esther* is performed at the King's Theatre.
- **1738** Becomes founding member of the Society for Decay'd Musicians. Completes *Saul*.

AT THE
THEATRE-ROYAL
In COVENT-GARDEN,
This present WEDNESDAY, FEBRUARY 19, 1777,
Will be performed a Sacred ORATORIO, called
MESSIAH.
The Music composed by HANDEL.
The Principal VOCAL PARTS by
Mr. TENDUCCI,
Mr. SAVILLE,
AND
Mr. REINHOLD.
Mifs STORACE,
AND
Mifs HARRUP,
(Being her SECOND PUBLIC APPEARANCE.)
After Part the First, a Duetto on the Tenor and Violin, by
Mr. STAMITZ and Mr. LA MOTTE.
After Part the Second, a Concerto on the Violin, by
Mr. LA MOTTE.
Boxes 10s. 6d. Pit 5s. First Gall. 3s. 6d. Second Gall. 2s.
Places for the Boxes to be taken of Mr. SARJANT, (only)
at the Stage-door.
Books of the Oratorio to be had at the Theatre.
The Doors to be opened at HALF after FIVE o'Clock,
And to begin exactly at HALF after SIX.
Vivant Rex & Regina.
On Friday, SAMSON.

ADVERTISEMENT FOR "MESSIAH"

- **1739** Twelve *Concerti Grossi*, Op. 6, considered the finest example of the genre.
- **1742** *Messiah* is premiered in Dublin.
- **1743** Composes the secular oratorio *Semele* and the *Dettingen Te Deum*, the latter to celebrate British victory over the French.
- **1748** The oratorios *Joshua* and *Judas Maccabeus* are performed to great acclaim.
- **1749** *Music for the Royal Fireworks is* performed in Green Park, London.
- **1752** First performance of *Jephtha*. Failing eyesight eventually leaves him blind.
- **1759** Dies at home in London on April 14.

Japanese Theater

The traditional theaters in Japan enjoy a high social value and are regarded as representatives for Japanese culture. Each form of traditional theater is associated with the development of a musical style that accompanies the theater productions.

Four main genres of traditional theater exist in Japan: *noh*, *kyogen*, *bunraku*, and *kabuki*.

Noh and *kyogen* are medieval forms that developed into their present shape during the late 14th century. *Bunraku* is a general term applied to puppet theater in Japan, which can be traced back to the 12th century. It originated in a traditional form on Awaji Island and was brought to Osaka by the puppet master Bunrakuken Uemura, from whose name the theater was named. The first *kabuki* performance is believed to have taken place in 1596. *Kabuki* thereafter underwent many changes and developed into the popular theater of the Edo period (1603–1868).

Noh and kyogen

Noh combines music, drama, dance, and poetry into a striking stylistic stage performance, characterized by an austere and slow pace and plays featuring beautiful women, Gods, warriors, supernatural beings, and unusual characters such as mad women. A long ramp leads the main character (*shite*) and the companion (*tsure*) from backstage onto the stage. The *shite* wear costumes consisting of extravagant silk brocades with symbolic meaning, depending on the role played. They also wear masks when portraying female, demonic, divine, animal, or some male characters.

The music of *noh* is created by a choir (*jiutai*), usually consisting of eight men, sitting to the side of the stage, who narrate the story and describe the character's thoughts or emotions by means of melodic and dynamic chanting, both song and speech. Four instrumentalists (*hayashi*), who sit at the back of the stage, accompany the choir. They comprise three drummers, who perform the rhythmic accompaniment and a *nokan* flute player, who creates the eerie atmosphere characteristic of *noh*. Two of the drummers play on hourglass-shaped drums, one held at the shoulder (*kotsuzumi*) and the other held on the lap (*otsuzumi*). The third drummer plays a barrel-shaped drum placed on a stand with two sticks.

Kyogen developed alongside *noh* from a common heritage, which separated into comedy and serious theater forms. *Kyogen* is enacted as a brief, comedic interlude between acts in *noh* plays or between two separate *noh* plays. The movements and vocal styles of *noh* and *kyogen* are very similar, although *kyogen* is more dialogue-based. The actors rarely use masks unless they play the role of animals or Gods. Their costumes are similar to *noh* costumes, albeit simpler. Actors in both theater forms use techniques such as *suriashi*, a way of sliding the feet that is derived from martial arts. The *hayashi* musicians of *noh* theater may accompany some *kyogen*.

Tuning peg

Bachi

Shamisen
The three-stringed long-necked lute, called the *shamisen*, arrived in Japan in the 16th century. It is strummed with a large plectrum, called a *bachi*.

Noh performer and mask
Actors in Noh dramas wear beautiful silk brocade costumes and also use masks for certain characters. This mask represents Hannya, a female character who is turned into a demon by anger and jealousy.

> "Important is the **tension** between their **serene presentation** and the blazing, **ravening pain** within."
>
> BEN BRANTLEY, NEW YORK TIMES THEATER CRITIC, WRITING ABOUT NOH PERFORMERS, JULY 30, 2005

Bunraku

The general term for the Japanese puppet theater is *Bunraku*, which enjoyed heights of popularity in the Kansai area around Osaka and Kyoto during the Edo and Meiji periods (1868–1912). The outstanding characteristics of *bunraku* theater are the large puppets and the *gidayu* music accompanying the play. In the early Edo period, the puppets were controlled from below and the musicians were hidden behind a bamboo curtain. In 1705, both the operator and musicians were brought into view, and in 1735, three-man puppets were introduced. The main operator controls the puppet's head and the right arm, another operator the feet, and the third the left arm. The face of the main operator is uncovered, while those of the other two operators' are covered. Using internal strings and subtle movements, the puppets can portray dramatic actions.

BEFORE

The medieval theater styles of Japan were influenced by Chinese culture imported to Japan together with literature and philosophy.

GAGAKU
The court music ***gagaku*** was imported to Japan during the **Nara Period** (710–794). It is believed that from the dance pieces of *gagaku*, an acrobatic theatrical form called ***sarugaku*** developed. Today, *sarugaku* is considered to be the root of *noh* theater.

ZEAMI MOTOKIYO (*c.*1363–1443)
Noh began to flourish in the late 14th century, when shogun Ashikaga Yoshimitsu became a major patron of **Zeami Motokiyo**. Zeami wrote many plays that are still performed.

Kabuki performance
Actors from the Ichikawa Ennosuke company perform one of the most famous *kabuki* plays, called *Yoshitsune and the Thousand Cherry Trees*. The lavish costumes and elaborate set are typical of *kabuki* theater.

Gidayu-bushi is the musical narrative of *bunraku*. It is a development of the 16th century *jouri* narrative. The *tayu*, or singer, narrates the story, speaks all the roles, including a description of their emotions, and sings all the songs. His powerful voice is aided by a special cloth tied around his stomach that holds a bag filled with sand and beans, meant to support diaphragmatic breathing. The dais where the musicians sit can rotate and the *tayu* can be changed with minimal disruption to the play. He is accompanied by a three-stringed long-neck lute *shamisen*, which is the largest of the traditional *shamisen* and which replaced the *biwa*, a short-necked bowl-lute which had previously been used. Instrumental sections may contain much information about the puppet about to arrive on stage and the setting.

The two main types of *bunraku* play are called *jidaimono*, which are historic plays, and *sewamono*, which narrate the fate of ordinary people.

> "[The artist] can give the puppet whatever **grace or dignity ... or distortion** the play demands."
>
> MARJORIE BATCHELDER, "THE PUPPET THEATER HANDBOOK," 1947

Kabuki

During the late 16th century the term *kabuki* referred to something unconventional, such as clothing or social behavior. *Kabuki* theater is a highly stylized dance-drama with elaborate costumes and make-up, and exaggerated acting—a striking contrast to the austere *noh* dramas.

In the early 17th century, *kabuki* was played by all-female troupes—often prostitutes. The Edo government then banned women on stage. This prevented women from performing, but *wakashu*, or young boys' troupes, continued, both as performers and prostitutes. This led to the government banning unshaved heads on stage (men shaved their heads after coming of age) in 1642. Finally, when *kabuki* matured as an all-male theatrical genre, it became a center of Edo social life. Audiences express their appreciation of the acting at certain points in a play by shouting, which, of course, requires expert knowledge of the plays and when and what to shout.

Kabuki music is played both onstage (*debayashi*) and offstage (*geza ongaku*). The most important elements in both groups are *shamisen* and voice. The musicians playing onstage music are placed at the back or sides of the stage and play the role of narrators of the plot and accompaniment to dance scenes. There can be up to three groups on stage. The *debayashi* groups usually consist of a *noh hayashi* (up to four *kotsuzumi* and two *taiko* players and one each of *otsuzumi* and flute) and up to eight singers and *shamisen* players.

The most important music in *kabuki* is the *geza ongaku* (offstage music played in a little room called *kuromisu*). Its task is to produce all the sounds and sound effects not produced by the musicians on stage. They use all kinds of instruments including *shamisen*, voice, and various percussion instruments such as gongs and cymbals. *Geza* music—heard but not seen—is more symbolic than realistic and can indicate a setting in the play, such as mountain or seaside. It can also indicate a mood, time, season, weather, character, and more.

Bunraku performance
The impressive puppets used in a *bunraku* may be 51–71 in (1.3–1.5 m) tall. The mouth, eyes, and ears can move and in some cases the face can transform into that of a demon.

KABUKI ACTOR (1950–)

BANDO TAMASABURO V

Bando Tamasaburo V is one of the most popular *kabuki* actors and a celebrated *onnagata* (an actor specializing in female roles). Adopted by Bando Tamasaburo IV, he made his first stage appearance at the age of seven. He is known for having dedicated his life to the study and portrayal of women. He has been bestowed with the title Living National Treasure. Tamasaburo has also acted in movies, directed drum performances, and conducted world tours.

KEY WORKS

Noh *Matsukaze*
Noh *Aoi no Ue (Lady Aoi)*
Bunraku *Noh Kanadehon Chushingura (Treasury of Loyal Retainers)*
Kabuki *Yoshitsune Senbon Zakura (Yoshitsune and the Thousand Cherry Trees)*
Kabuki *Kanjincho (The Subscription List)*

AFTER 

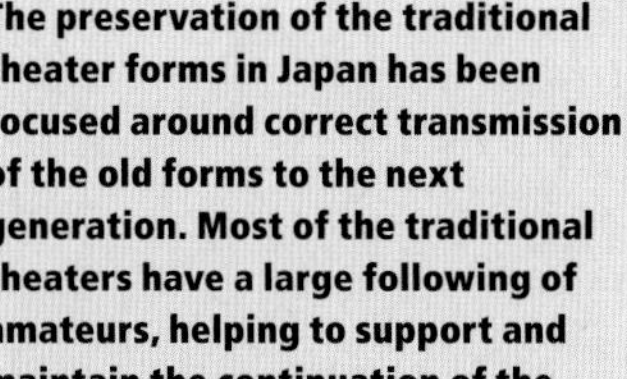

The preservation of the traditional theater forms in Japan has been focused around correct transmission of the old forms to the next generation. Most of the traditional theaters have a large following of amateurs, helping to support and maintain the continuation of the professional troupes.

EAST–WEST FUSION
After the **Meiji restoration** (1868) and the arrival of Western art forms to Japan, Japanese theater became influenced by Western realistic theater. Very quickly experiments of *kabuki* actors in realistic theater took place by, among others, theater director **Kaoru Osanai** (1881–1928). Another important figure is theater director, philosopher, and writer **Tadashi Suzuki** (1939–), who developed a method to train actors using both avant-garde and *noh* and *kabuki* concepts. This method became a major creative force in Japanese theater during the 1980s.

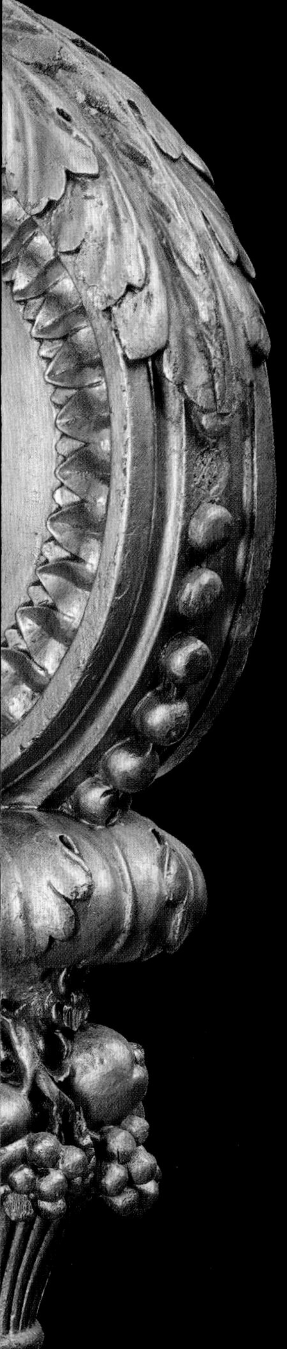

5
THE CLASSICAL AGE
1750–1820

The Enlightenment, with its emphasis on clarity and rational thinking, found its purest expression in the music of the three giants of Classical era—Haydn, Mozart, and Beethoven. The sonata, in all its forms, embodied the musical discourse that characterized this period, which scaled new heights in operas, symphonies, and concertos.

THE CLASSICAL AGE
1750–1820

1750

1750
Johann Stamitz becomes director of the Mannheim Orchestra, whose size and virtuosity will influence Classical orchestration and forms; his own work typifies the *style galante*, moving from Baroque complexity to airy grace and accessibility.

1752
In Paris, a war of words erupts between supporters of French Baroque opera and Italy's new *opera buffa*.

1753
German composer C.P.E. Bach publishes Part I of his seminal treatise, *The True Art of Keyboard Playing*, followed by Part II in 1762.

1753
Death of the German piano maker Gottfried Silbermann, who pioneered a forerunner of the damper pedal.

1754
Bretikopf & Härtel, new music printers in Leipzig, pioneer innovations in typesetting that will widen the availability of musical scores.

1759
Austrian composer Joseph Haydn writes his Symphony in D major—quite possibly his first completed work in the form—opening with a "Mannheim" crescendo.

1760

1761
Haydn becomes deputy music director to the Esterházys, who are major patrons of music.

Grand piano, built by Manuel Antunes, Lisbon, 1767

1762
At age 6, Mozart leaves Salzburg to begin his first concert tour, which includes Munich, Paris, and London.

1762
Gluck's *Orfeo ed Euridice* (*Orpheus and Eurydice*) has its world premiere in Vienna; it is the earliest opera never to have left the repertory.

1763
Mozart visits Mannheim and is impressed by its orchestra.

1764
Leading French composer Jean-Philippe Rameau dies.

1768
The first concert of piano music is given in London by J.C. Bach.

1770

1770
In Paris, François-Joseph Gossec, a former protégé of Rameau, founds the *Concert des Amateurs*, an independent orchestra; he goes on to direct the *Concerts Spirituels*, a series of public concerts established in 1725.

1771
Luigi Boccherini composes his String Quintet in E major. His most celebrated work, it is best known for the third movement, the Minuet.

18th-century chamber ensemble

1773
C.P. E. Bach is one of the first composers to write his autobiography.

The Tuilleries Palace in Paris, a venue for the *Concerts Spirituels* of 1725–1790

1775

1775
Pierre Beaumarchais' play *The Barber of Seville* is premiered in Paris; the comedy and its follow-up, *The Marriage of Figaro*, will inspire popular operas by composers such as Paisiello (1782), Mozart (1786), and Rossini (1816).

1776
Friedrich von Klinger's play *Sturm und Drang* (Storm and Stress) about the American Revolution inspires an artistic movement that challenges rationalist beliefs and portrays violent emotions, influencing composers such as Gluck, Mozart, and Haydn.

1776
Moscow's first permanent theatre company is founded; staging plays, ballet, and operas, it will become the Imperial Bolshoi Theatre.

1778
The Teatro alla Scala in Milan opens with Antonio Salieri's opera, *Europa riconosciuta* (*Europa Revealed*).

1779
Haydn's Symphony No.70 launches the rebuilding of the Esterházys' opera house after a fire.

1780

1781
The Archbishop of Salzburg releases Mozart from his employment. Mozart goes to Vienna and becomes a freelance musician.

c.1781
Johann Andreas Stein perfects a responsive hammer action for the piano.

1782
Giovanni Paisiello's opera *Il barbiere di Siviglia* (The Barber of Seville) is first performed at Catherine the Great's Imperial Court in St. Petersburg.

1784
In Vienna, Haydn and Mozart play chamber music together.

Costume sketch for Haydn's 1784 opera, *Armida*

1785

Mozart's manuscript for his "Prague" Symphony of 1786

1786
Mozart's opera *Le Nozze di Figaro* (*The Marriage of Figaro*) premieres in Vienna, with Mozart conducting. The emperor had to approve Da Ponte's libretto before the performance could go ahead.

1787
Mozart's opera *Don Giovanni* premieres in Prague.

1789
English music historian Charles Burney finishes his four-volume *General History of Music*.

The Age of Enlightenment witnessed a maelstrom of intellectual discourse and political revolution. Against this backdrop, the Classical era sought to overthrow the complexities of Baroque music and appeal to the rationality of a new generation. In so doing, it helped oversee the popularization of music through the public concert and greater availability of sheet music. New forms such as the symphony, instrumental sonata, and string quartet were developed for new, middle-class audiences by composers who now depended not only on the patronage of the elite but on the market place for their income. The legacy of the Classical era lingers on to the present day.

1790

Set design for Mozart's *Die Zauberflöte* (*The Magic Flute*)

1791
Mozart conducts the first performance of his opera *Die Zauberflöte* (*The Magic Flute*) in Vienna. He dies two months later, leaving his Requiem incomplete.

1792
Beethoven starts studying with Haydn in Vienna; he later dedicates his Op. 2 piano sonatas to Haydn.

Square piano, made in London, c.1790

1793
Daniel Steibelt gives the first piano pedalling indications, in his sixth *Pot-pourris*.

1795

1795
During Haydn's second and lucrative visit to London, he gives concerts and composes his final symphony, to great acclaim.

1795
In France, the Paris Conservatoire is founded.

1796
Beethoven completes his two cello sonatas, Op. 5, and performs them with Duport for Friedrich Wilhelm II, king of Prussia, to whom he dedicates them.

18th-century flûte d'amour

1798
Haydn's oratorio *The Creation*, first performed in Vienna, goes on to become an international success.

1798
Czech music critic and teacher, Franz Niemetschek, publishes the first full-length biography of Mozart.

1800

Prague, a hub of musical activity and Czech nationalism

c.1800
As the new century dawns, interest in Czech culture and folk traditions prompts a new note of nationalism in some composers' work.

1801
Haydn completes his oratorio *The Seasons*, and Beethoven publishes his Piano Sonata No. 14, also called the "Moonlight" Sonata.

1802
The first biography of J. S. Bach, by Johann Forkel, helps pave the way for the Bach revival in Central Europe and Mendelssohn's landmark performance of Bach's *St. Matthew Passion*.

1804
Outraged when Napoleon declares himself emperor, Beethoven changes the name of his Symphony No. 3 from the *Bonaparte* to the *Eroica* (Heroic).

1805

1805
Fidelio, Beethoven's first and only opera, receives its premiere in Vienna and is hailed as a triumph.

1808
Haydn makes his last public appearance at a gala concert performance, in his honor, of his oratorio *The Creation*. Both Salieri and Beethoven attend.

1808
Notable premieres include Beethoven's 4th and 5th symphonies, his 4th piano concerto, and his Fantasy in C minor for Piano, Chorus, and Orchestra.

1809
During a particularly hard winter, the Paris Conservatoire burns its harpsichords for firewood, considering them obsolete in the age of the pianoforte.

Ludwig van Beethoven, giant of Classical and Romantic music

1810

1813
The Philharmonic Society is founded to give the first public concerts in London. It commissions new works, including Beethoven's 9th symphony—also known as "Choral"—and Mendelssohn's "Italian" symphony.

Theater an der Wien, where Beethoven's *Fidelio* was premièred

1814
German inventor Johann Mälzel's metronome allows composers, such as Beethoven, to specify the exact speed at which their compositions should be performed.

1815

1816
Rossini writes *Il barbiere di Siviglia* (*The Barber of Seville*) in under three weeks; its first performance in Rome is a disastrous failure.

1816
Cherubini's C Minor Requiem celebrates the 30th anniversary of Louis XIV's execution in the French Revolution.

1816
Beethoven acquires a Broadwood piano from London, on which he composes his final sonatas, including Piano Sonata No. 29, known as the "Hammerklavier."

1819
Violin virtuoso Paganini dedicates his 24 Caprices for Solo Violin, Op. 1, to "the Artists," fully aware that none but he was capable of playing them.

BEFORE

The highly elaborate compositions and performance styles of the late Baroque period were confined to a court or church setting.

BAROQUE COMPLEXITY

The intricate compositions of **J.S. Bach** **« 100–101** and **Handel** **« 108–109** were losing their appeal by the mid-18th century.

LIMITED PARTICIPATION

Until the availability of **printed music** **« 54–55** and affordable instruments in the 19th century, most music was performed in church or at court by professional musicians.

CLASSICAL INFLUENCES

In art forms other than music, a new simplicity influenced by the Classical antiquity of **Ancient Greece** **« 18–19**, as well as a growing understanding of fundamental scientific principles, was taking over.

A **New Clarity**

The overthrow of the complex Baroque style in favor of the simplicity of the Classical era was one of music's most important revolutions. Its far-reaching effects still exist, not only in what we listen to and how, but even in the concept of the public concert itself.

Baroque music reached a high peak in the works of J.S. Bach and George Frideric Handel. They composed great music that was performed largely by professionals and marveled at by listeners. The emergent thinking of the Enlightenment, which encouraged simplicity and clarity, influenced the gradual development of a new, more approachable musical style. While

Europe's oldest public concert hall is the Holywell Music Room in Oxford, England, opened in 1748.

Baroque music had depended on harmonies changing on virtually every beat, the new style that was evolving often stayed with the same harmony for an entire bar or more. In addition, composers supported a single melody with simpler, chordal accompaniments.

In instrumental and vocal music, this new approach gave music a more natural, less "learned" quality. This kind of music immediately appealed to a far broader audience.

Strict instructions

To prevent performers from improvising florid embellishments (see p.78), which might interfere with the purity of the original intent, composers began to write down in the score everything that the performer needed to do. This was especially important because composers were no longer writing music just for their immediate associates. The availability and spread of printed scores meant that music was played by musicians whom the composer had never met. The instructions became ever more detailed, leaving fewer decisions regarding tempo, dynamics, and mood to the performer.

Soon, composers stopped writing an improvised continuo part (the bass line). This meant that the cadenza section of a concerto (when the orchestra pauses to allow the soloist a moment of virtuosity or reflection) was one of the few opportunities left for improvisation. Perhaps as a backlash, performers improvised cadenzas that were ever more elaborate, much to the annoyance of Beethoven who, in his last piano concerto (see pp.150–151), wrote out every note of the cadenza.

Such careful instructions left behind by composers were all part of the desire to achieve balance, which became a fundamental consideration for composers in structuring their works. For example, an opening phrase (usually four bars long) would typically be answered by a similar—but

COMPOSER (1735–1782)

JOHANN CHRISTIAN BACH

Born in Leipzig, Germany, Johann Christian Bach was the eleventh and final child of J.S. Bach. Johann studied with his father until his death, and then with his brother, Carl Philipp Emanuel. From 1756, he worked in Italy, but in 1762 went to London to premiere three operas at the King's Theatre. He settled there, earning the nickname the "London Bach." Admired by Mozart, he wrote prolifically, promoted concerts, brought the clarinet into the English opera orchestra, and became music teacher to Queen Charlotte at an annual salary of £300. He ran into debt, however, and suffered a nervous breakdown in 1781. When he died the following year, the queen funded his funeral and gave his widow a pension.

KEY WORKS

Georg Philipp Telemann Sonata for oboe in A minor, TWV 41: a3

Johann Joachim Quantz Flute Concerto in G minor, QV. 5:196

J.C. Bach Keyboard Concerto, Op.13, No. 1 in C major

C.P.E. Bach Cello Concerto in A major H. 439, (Wq 172)

Joseph Haydn Symphony No. 44 in E minor, "Trauer"

New expressiveness

This 1762 grand piano built by the Portuguese maker Manuel Antunes has a hammer mechanism based on Bartolomeo Cristofori's original invention, making it a more expressive alternative to the harpsichord and clavichord.

Natural order
The *fête galante* painting style created by French artist Antoine Watteau (1684–1721), expressed here in *Merry Company in the Open Air* (1720), inspired the *style galante* in music. Both styles share an air of clarity, simple elegance, and respect for the natural order.

slightly different—balancing phrase of the same length. Together these two would form an eight-bar "sentence," which would then usually be answered by a balancing sentence. This formula ensured that the larger sections of individual movements balanced and complemented each other as well. It also meant that composers had to consider the overall shape of their symphonies, sonatas, and concertos, ensuring that the balance and contrast of individual movements formed a coherent whole.

Style galante

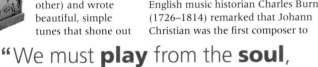

One of the first of the new Classical styles, popular from the 1720s to the 1770s, the *style galante* was valued for its freshness and accessibility at a time when the high Baroque style was still being heard. Composers of the *style galante* avoided using counterpoint (several voices playing against each other) and wrote beautiful, simple tunes that shone out over their accompaniments, which were simple and transparent. Having begun as an operatic style in Italian *opera seria* (see pp.132–133) the popularity of the *style galante* with the public ensured its use across genres by composers as diverse as Georg Philipp Telemann (1681–1767), Johann Christian Bach (see opposite), and even the young Joseph Haydn (see pp.126–127).

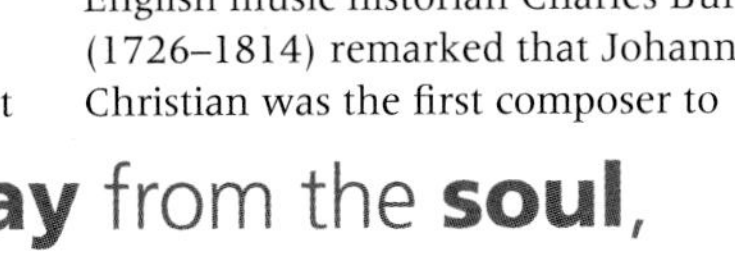

> "We must **play** from the **soul**, not like **trained birds**."
>
> C.P.E. BACH, "TRUE ART OF PLAYING KEYBOARD INSTRUMENTS," 1753

The Bach family

Two generations of the influential Bach family spanned more than a century, covering the transition from Baroque complexity to Classical clarity. Indeed, when father Johann Sebastian died (see pp.100–101), the governing body of his church celebrated the fact that they could appoint a new composer who was less old-fashioned.

His son, Johann Christian, largely rejected the complex counterpoint and polyphony of his father in favor of a single melody with accompaniment. In his many symphonies, sonatas, and operas, his supple melodies hint at the easy fluidity of the *style galante*. English music historian Charles Burney (1726–1814) remarked that Johann Christian was the first composer to observe contrast (an important aspect of balance) as a principle. Meanwhile, in Germany, his elder brother, Carl Philipp Emanuel (1714–1788), regarded the clavichord and harpsichord as excellent vehicles for refined musical expression. He set out his opinions about clarity of expression and technique in his 1753 essay, *The True Art of Playing Keyboard Instruments*.

In his keyboard works and symphonies C.P.E. Bach experimented with the so-called *Empfindsamer Stil* (sensitive style), where moods shift dramatically within single movements. This style foreshadowed not only the turbulent emotions of the *Sturm und Drang* (storm and stress) style of composition, which Haydn captured in his 1772 Symphony No. 44 in E minor, known as the "Trauer" (Mourning) Symphony, but even foretold the Romantic movement itself.

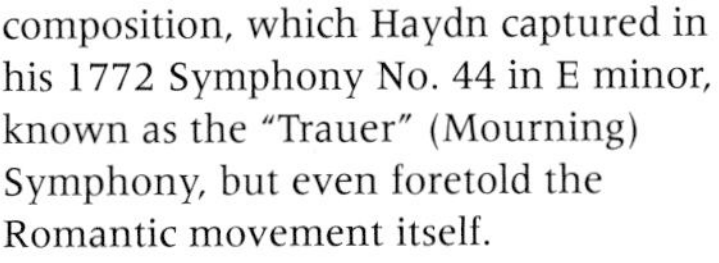

Engaging the public

Public concerts started to take place, initially in assembly rooms and meeting halls and, increasingly, in specially built concert spaces and theaters. Easier access to musical performances inspired a rise in amateur music-making. This in turn encouraged cheaper and more efficient instrument manufacture and the widespread publication of music, and eventually arrangements of concert music for domestic performance—most particularly for keyboard. To support amateur musical study, a number of self-tutor books were written by musicians including C.P.E. Bach and the German flautist Johann Quantz.

1773 **The year in which C.P.E. Bach wrote his autobiography. He was one of the first composers to do so.**

18th-century wooden printing press
With the invention of the printing press and the widespread availability of printed materials, composers could earn money selling their music, and keen amateurs could learn to play using teach-yourself books.

AFTER

Classical restraint was gradually overshadowed by the Romantic desire for emotional expression above all.

OTHER ARTS
Influences of other art forms such as **literature 156–157 ››** were evident in music composed after the 1820s.

IMPROVING INSTRUMENTS
Continuing **advances in instrument manufacture 188–189 ››** encouraged composers to write more technically challenging music.

PERFORMER AS CELEBRITY
The highly expressive, technically dazzling music of the 19th century gave **virtuoso performers 160–161 ››** celebrity status.

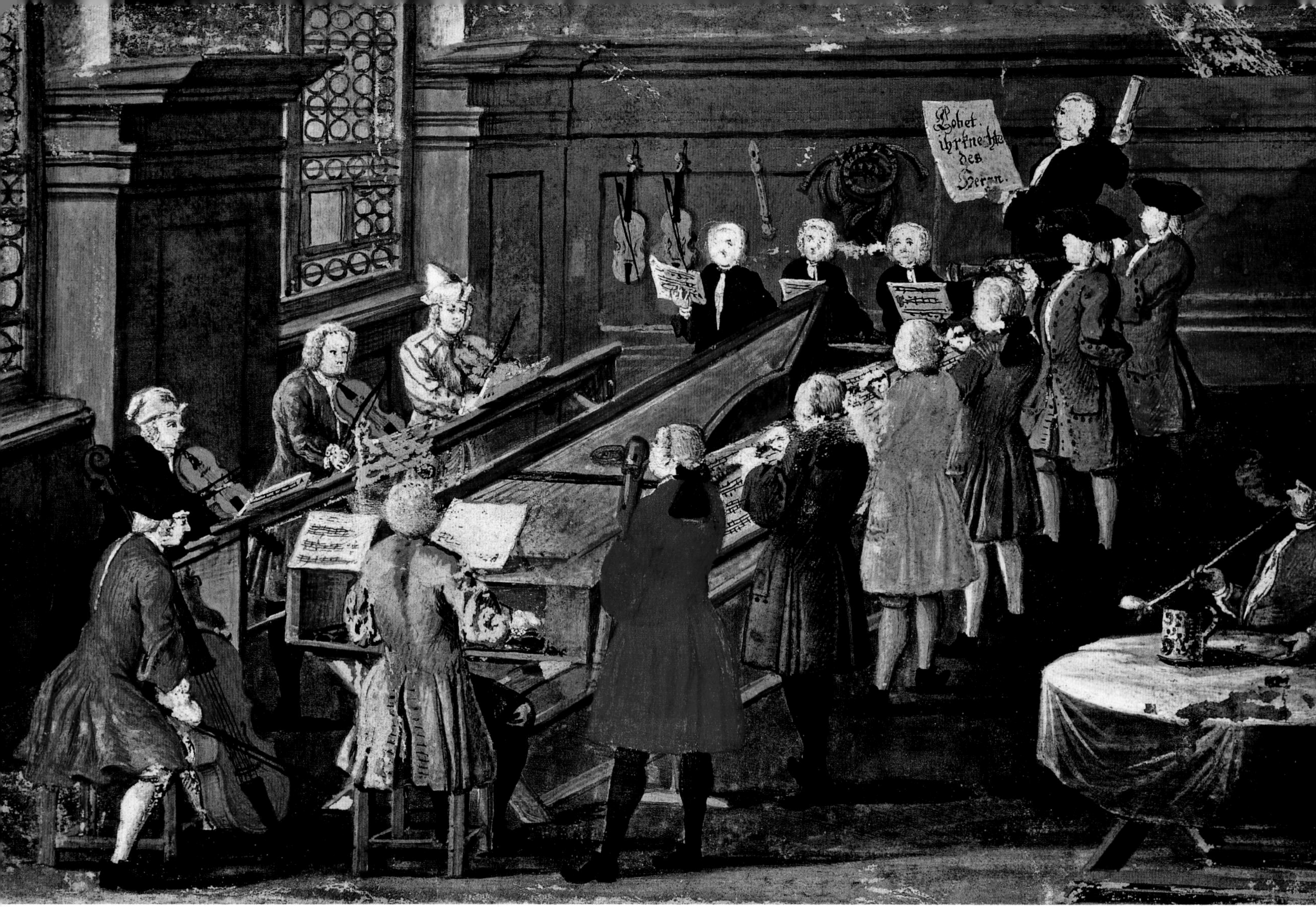

Chamber orchestra with singers
In this 18th-century ensemble, the singers, strings, and woodwind players stand. The harpsichordist and violone players, seated, play the continuo, reinforcing the bass line and filling out the harmonies.

The **Orchestra**

The evolution of the modern European orchestra began in the 17th century and continues to this day. Its development was first driven by the search for a large-scale musical medium to convey composers' emotions more expressively and a desire to impress.

« BEFORE

Before the European orchestra was established, the instruments selected for performance depended on what was available.

ITALIAN AND FRENCH BEGINNINGS
Monteverdi used combinations of various instruments to accompany his **early Italian operas « 81**. In France, at the court of Louis XIV, from 1653, **Lully** (see p.132) developed the *Vingt-quatre violons du roi* (the 24 violins of the king), an ensemble of different-sized string instruments. In his own compositions, Lully often added oboes, drums, trumpets, and bassoons to the ensemble.

18TH-CENTURY DEVELOPMENTS
The suites and *concerti grossi* of **J.S. Bach « 100–101** and **Handel « 108–109** showed the potential of the orchestra for creating complex works.

From the 1600s, many European courts maintained a group of musicians to perform music for worship in their chapel and to provide entertainment at social events. To be able to afford to employ an ensemble of instrumentalists and a composer to write and conduct high-quality music was a potent symbol of status and wealth.

The number and capability of the musicians involved depended on the enthusiasm and determination of their patron, whether king, duke, elector, or any other kind of wealthy aristocrat. Court composers tended to write music to be performed by the musicians at their disposal in their particular court, and it was not intended to be playable by others. For this reason, George Frideric Handel, who traveled widely in the first half of the 18th century (mainly to London and in Italy), had to rescore his works for the instruments that were available to him in any given location or simply compose the work all over again.

Birth of an orchestra

In 1720, the court of Charles III Philip, Elector Palatine, arrived in the small German city of Mannheim from Heidelberg, bringing with it a large ensemble of very accomplished instrumentalists.

In 1742, when Karl Theodore, Duke of

Skin drumhead

Tension mechanism

Copper bowl

Pair of timpani (kettle drums)
Used in pairs, tuned to two different notes, timpani give extra emphasis to the bass notes of the harmony and, when played with rapidly rolling sticks, add increasing musical excitement.

COMPOSER AND CONDUCTOR (1745–1799)

CHEVALIER DE SAINT-GEORGES

Already a cavalry colonel and a celebrated fencer, Saint-Georges stunned Paris society when he became a violinist in a new orchestra, Le Concert des Amateurs, in 1769. Within four years, this illegitimate child of a French plantation owner and an enslaved African woman had become the orchestra's conductor, and it was performing his own violin concertos to great acclaim. Saint-Georges went on to publish string quartets, symphonies concertantes (which appear to have influenced Mozart on his visit to Paris in 1778), and a number of operas. Queen Marie Antoinette often attended his performances.

Saxony, succeeded Charles Philip as elector, he appointed violinist and composer Johann Stamitz (1715–1757) as concertmaster. The duke had ambitions to establish the greatest orchestra in Europe, so he instructed Stamitz to find the finest musicians.

By 1777, the Mannheim Orchestra consisted of 20–22 violins (grouped into first and second violins), four violas, four cellos, four double basses, two flutes, two oboes, two clarinets, four bassoons, two horns, and timpani. While earlier 18th-century ensemble performances were directed from the keyboard by the player providing the continuo, at Mannheim the leading violinist assumed the role, using the bow to indicate starts and finishes of pieces, and to give the pulse of the music to the other players.

Stamitz and other composers, notably Christian Cannabich, Ignaz Holzbauer, and Franz Xaver Richter, formed a group of composers now known as the Mannheim School. Their unique approach to performance and composition had two far-reaching consequences. The Mannheim Orchestra was soon known and emulated across Europe, and the symphony dominated orchestral music for a century (see pp.124–125).

1763 **The year of Mozart's first visit to Mannheim.**

90 **The number of Mannheim Orchestra members in 1778.**

Mannheim mannerisms

Stamitz and his fellow composers gradually developed the symphony from the three-movement Baroque sinfonia, adding an extra movement before the finale. They also used compositional "special effects," which are now regarded as trademarks of the Mannheim School. The Mannheim Rocket, apparently inspired by a Roman candle firework, was a swiftly ascending melody, while a gradual buildup in volume by the entire orchestra, often followed by an abrupt *piano* (quiet) or a long pause, was called a Mannheim Crescendo. The Mannheim Roller featured a gradual crescendo through a rising melody over an *ostinato* (repeating) bass line, while the Mannheim Sigh consisted of a falling two-note phrase with the emphasis on the first note. There was even the twittering Mannheim Bird.

Other features included sudden and unexpected *fortissimo* (very loud) music, *tremolo* (rapid repetition of the same note), and the playing of rapid arpeggios (notes of a chord played in sequence) to create a growing sense of musical urgency.

Mozart (see pp.136–137) visited Mannheim and was very impressed by the orchestra, writing to his father: "The orchestra is very good and numerous... and should give fine music." The influence of the Mannheim School appears in the carefully managed dynamics of Mozart's Sinfonia Concertante for violin and viola (1779) and in the rocketlike opening of the finale of his 40th symphony (1778).

While the special effects were exciting to listen to, the compositions themselves were not particularly innovative. Individual instrumental parts were musically uninteresting but difficult to play, so the highly skilled orchestra members relished the challenge. Fast music was played at top speed—the faster the better—and the exaggerated mannerisms were even more overplayed for dramatic effect.

Lasting legacy

Mannheim's influence continued with a new generation of composers, including Johann Stamitz's son, Carl (1745–1801). A violin and viola virtuoso, Carl left Mannheim in 1770 for Paris, where he composed for the court and performed at the city's famous *Concerts Spirituel*, one of the first-ever series of public concerts.

Inspired by the success of the Mannheim Orchestra, other European cities established identical ensembles. Music could now be played by any orchestra other than the one for which it had originally been composed, and concert promoters were soon cashing in on the new demand among audiences for orchestral concerts.

KEY WORKS

Johann Stamitz Symphony in D major, Op. 3, No. 2

Christian Cannabich Symphony No. 59 in D major

Ignaz Holzbauer Symphony in D minor

Franz Xaver Richter Sinfonia No. 63 in B flat major (No. 1 of Grandes Symphonies)

Carl Stamitz Symphony in G, Op. 13, No. 4

Mozart Symphony No. 40 in G minor, K550

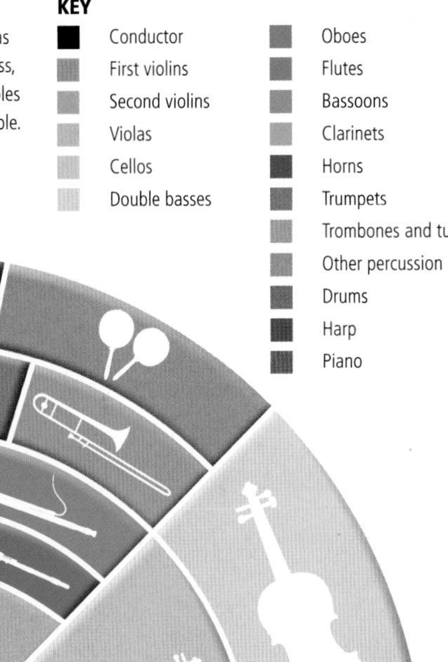

Mannheim seating arrangement

The basic orchestral seating plan still used today was established in Mannheim. Positioning the wind, brass, and percussion instruments behind the strings enables the instrumentalists to play effectively as an ensemble.

KEY

Conductor
First violins
Second violins
Violas
Cellos
Double basses
Oboes
Flutes
Bassoons
Clarinets
Horns
Trumpets
Trombones and tubas
Other percussion
Drums
Harp
Piano

AFTER »

The desire to compose more varied, expressive, and complex music drove the development of the orchestra.

MORE SUBSTANTIAL SOUND

Extra weight was given to the 19th-century orchestra by adding more string instruments. Whereas Haydn had written for orchestras with six first violins playing the same part, **Mahler 192–193 »** called for as many as 16. Composers also added new instruments to their scores, including piccolo, cor anglais (English horn), E flat and bass clarinet, tuba, contrabassoon, and trombone, including the unusual 19th-century French valve trombone.

19TH CENTURY AND ONWARD

Percussion instruments, such as gongs, xylophone, celeste, and exotic drums, added extra bite to orchestral music. Maurice Ravel used the saxophone in his 1922 arrangement of Modest Mussorgsky's *Pictures at an Exhibition*. **Gustav Mahler** and **Vaughan Williams 214 »** occasionally included choruses in their orchestral works, while **Richard Strauss 223 »** and **Edward Elgar 214 »** added orchestral organ. Later, **Pierre Boulez** and **Karlheinz Stockhausen 270–271 »** introduced **electronic effects**.

TENOR VALVE TROMBONE

BEFORE

Music often served as a backdrop to other activities, such as prayer, dance, or dining. Only aristocrats could afford music in the home.

BAROQUE HARPSICHORD SONATAS
Domenico Scarlatti « 107 wrote one-movement sonatas for harpsichord.

CHURCH SONATAS
Corelli « 102–103 wrote *sonatas da chiesa*, four-movement instrumental works often, but not exclusively, used during church services.

TRIO SONATAS
Telemann « 117 and **J. S. Bach « 100–101** used the term sonata, or trio sonata, for four-movement works written for two melody instruments plus continuo.

The **Sonata**

The term *sonata*—Italian for "sounded"—appeared around 1650 and was used to indicate that a piece of music was for instruments rather than for the voice. As the sonata developed, it proved to be one of the most far-reaching and enduring compositional forms in Western music.

During the 18th century, the term sonata became almost entirely associated with solo works, in up to five movements, but typically in three (fast-slow-fast), for either a keyboard alone or a keyboard accompanying another instrument.

The popularity of the sonata was fueled by the rise of a middle class able to afford instruments and eager for lessons. However, they were not drawn to the courtly dance suites that had been so popular in the Baroque era. They wanted really to listen to music, and not just remain vaguely aware of it in the background. By the middle of the century, it was obvious that a new approach to composing and performing music was needed.

The sonata principle

The solution was the sonata principle—music that could hold the attention of listeners over a longer period of time and that did not rely on too much repetition. The form starts with an "exposition" where, a bit like a debate, the listener is introduced to two contrasting musical themes, the first in the home key of the piece (for example, C major), and the second in a different key, usually five notes

Imperial sonatas
Frederick the Great of Prussia (1712–1786) wrote more than 100 sonatas for the flute. In Adolphe von Menzel's 1852 painting, *Flute Concert of Sanssouci*, C.P.E. Bach accompanies him on the keyboard.

SIX SONATES
Pour le Clavecin, ou Pianoforte avec
l'accompagnement d'un Violon
Dédiés
A Mademoiselle
JOSEPHE D'AURNHAMER
par
WOLFG. AMADEE MOZART
Oeuvre 2

Mozart violin sonatas
At the age of eight, Mozart wrote the early sonatas "for keyboard with violin accompaniment" to perform with his father and sister.

higher (G major). This section is often repeated to familiarize the listener with the musical themes. Next is the "development," which is the "argument," where the themes from the exposition are broken up and played in different keys and moods. The music of the "recapitulation" is similar to the exposition, but this time the second music is in the home key, so the argument is resolved.

Originally reserved only for the first movement of a sonata, this approach proved so successful that it was also used for the opening music of symphonies, string quartets, trios, and concertos. Eventually, it could even be found, in slightly different forms, in the slow and final movements as well.

The first important composer of these new sonatas was Carl Philipp Emanuel Bach (1714–1788). He was a key figure in the transition between the high Baroque style of his father, Johann Sebastian Bach (see pp.100–101), and the new Classical style that followed.

C.P.E. Bach's sonatas, which were published over 40 years starting in 1742, include music for various instruments, such as the flute, clarinet, and violin, but are mostly composed for solo keyboard. These were ideally suited to the intimate sound world of the clavichord, C.P.E. Bach's favored keyboard instrument. The later works, probably written for the newly invented pianoforte, anticipate the works of Beethoven (1770–1827), who openly acknowledged the musical debt he owed to C.P.E. Bach.

Sonatas to rival the symphony

It was Haydn (see pp.126–127) who established the sonata as a musical form to rival the symphony in the Classical era. While other composers made their slow movements reminiscent of slower Baroque dances, such as the minuet, Haydn expanded this movement into something far darker and dramatic. Equally, his finales, although vivacious, shocked listeners with their surprising harmonies and dramatic contrasts, which echoed the vivid effects famously created by the Mannheim Orchestra in the 1770s (see pp.118–119). The grandeur of Haydn's last sonatas, with their expansive and dramatic opening movements, had a profound effect on Haydn's former student Beethoven.

Public and private music

Although Mozart (see pp.136–137) wrote a number of important sonatas for violin, piano, and even piano duet, he was perhaps more interested in writing concertos than sonatas. It could be said that for him both forms of music showed a similar approach to the new Classical style. In fact, as a child he had turned some of J.C. Bach's sonatas into concertos, already realizing at an early age that these two apparently different forms were two sides of the same coin, one more private, the other more public.

However, it was undoubtedly Beethoven (see pp.142–143) who turned the piano sonata into a truly "public" form. For his very first published sonata, he chose a work in four movements. In doing so, he made a statement that this once "private" form of music was now the equal of the four-movement symphony, and that the piano, the instrument on which it was performed, was no longer an instrument for the corner of the drawing room but powerful enough to take center stage in the concert hall.

The sonata at full power

Beethoven's sonatas, whether for piano, violin, or cello, were far longer and more substantial than any sonatas that had appeared before. With works such as the "Moonlight" and "Appassionata" sonatas pointing the way forward to the Romantic era, Beethoven changed expectations of what a sonata was meant to be.

While the sonata principle continued to underpin the first movement, Beethoven introduced tragedy into the traditionally lyrical second movement, livened up the old-fashioned minuet into a blustering *scherzo*, and interjected both elation and despair into the finale. For his final sonatas, Beethoven even blurred the boundaries between movements and introduced variations and fugues (see pages 98–99).

By pushing the boundaries of the sonata form, Beethoven made a powerful impression not only on his audiences but also on the generation of composers and virtuoso players who followed in his wake.

STRUCTURE: SONATA
The sonata principle was a great creation of the Classical period. Echoing the new interest in balance, proportion, and clarity, it's three-section form uses melodic themes ("subjects") and harmonies in patterns that the listener is able to recognize.

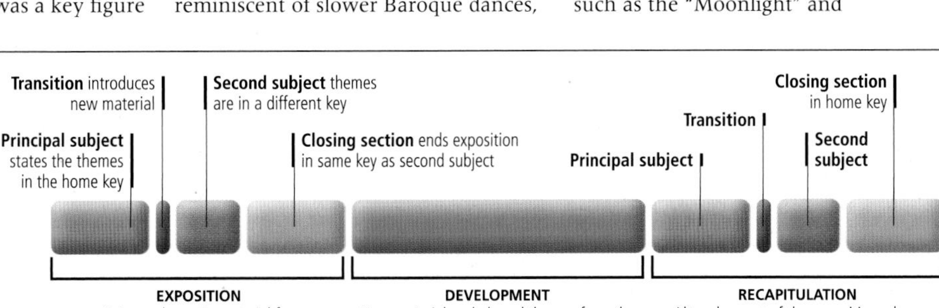
Transition introduces new material
Second subject themes are in a different key
Principal subject states the themes in the home key
Closing section ends exposition in same key as second subject
Principal subject
Transition
Closing section in home key
Second subject
EXPOSITION
Primary thematic material for the movement is presented in the exposition.
DEVELOPMENT
New material and altered themes from the exposition are developed in keys other than the home key, creating a feeling of tension.
RECAPITULATION
Altered repeat of the exposition where all the themes are restated in the home key giving a feeling of resolution.

KEY WORKS

C.P.E. Bach "Württemberg" Sonata No. 1 in A minor

Haydn Sonata in A flat major, Hob. XIV/46(1)

Mozart Piano Sonata No.16 in C major, K545

Beethoven Piano Sonata No. 23 in F minor, Op. 23, "Appassionata"; Violin Sonata No. 5 in F major, Op. 24, "Spring"

AFTER

The sonata principle governed the organization of much instrumental music, while the sonata became the foremost form of chamber music.

POPULAR FORM
After 1800, the piano sonata flourished, reflecting the instrument's rising popularity. Beethoven's 32 piano sonatas became enduring favorites for recitals.

88 **The number of piano sonatas composed by Muzio Clementi (1752–1832).**

ROMANTIC ERA
As composed by Schubert **154–155 »**, Schumann **158–159 »**, Chopin **158–159 »**, Liszt **160–161 »**, and Brahms **172–173 »**, the sonata evolved into forms as diverse as each composer's own aesthetic outlook.

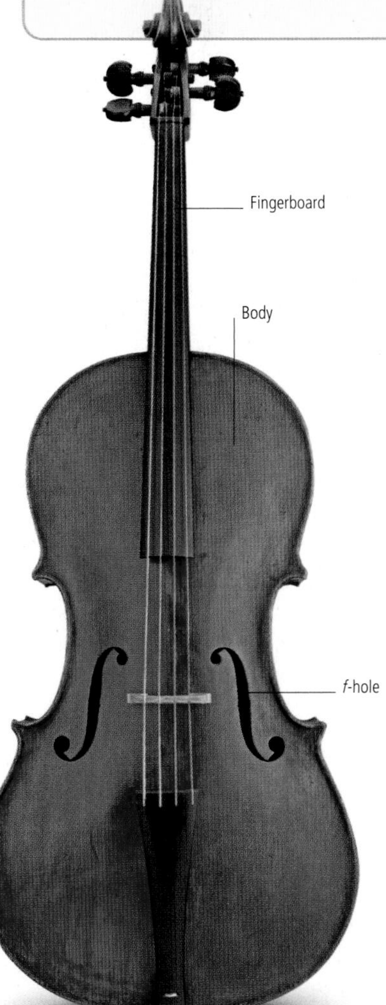
Fingerboard
Body
f-hole

The cello comes of age
In the Baroque era, the cello's role in the sonata was to provide part of the continuo accompaniment to other instruments. In the sonatas of Beethoven, Brahms, and others, the cello became an expressive solo instrument in its own right.

Orchestral Woodwind

Unlike string and brass sections, where instruments share similar sounds, the woodwind section is full of variety. Composers artfully exploit the different tone colors of its four main members—flutes, oboes, clarinets, and bassoons.

[1] **Bass flute** The metal tubing on this 20th-century bass flute is around 57 in (146 cm) long, and looped into a J-shape to bring the mouthpiece within easy reach of the player. [2] **Key flute** A soft-toned, four-piece flute with a single key, this instrument was widely played in the 18th century. [3] **Flute** This type of simple wooden flute was popular at the turn of the 19th century in Europe and the United States for home and dance music. [4] **Alto flute** In this 19th-century wooden example, an angled head lengthens the tubing to create lower notes. [5] **Piccolo** The highest-pitched wind instrument, the piccolo sparkles at the top of the orchestra. [6] **Modern concert flute** This three-piece design has remained largely unchanged since 1847, when German flautist Theobald Boehm (1794–1881) devised a new system of keys that allowed for more precise playing. [7] **Pratten system flute** The designs of English flautist and inventor Robert Sidney Pratten (1824–68) attempted to perfect a simple key system. [8] **Oboe** Dating from 1680, this three-keyed boxwood oboe is the kind used for early Baroque music. [9] **English horn** Neither English nor a horn, the English horn is a large oboe with a bulbous bell. [10] **Bassoon** A 100 in (254 cm) long tube produces low notes in the main wind group. [11] **Bassoon, 1776** The limited number of keys on the 18th-century bassoon restricted its range of notes. [12] **Contrabassoon** Larger and lower than the bassoon, the contrabassoon produces an edgy buzz. [13] **Octavin** Resembling a saxophone, the rare 19th-century octavin has a conical, bent wooden tube, and is played with a single reed. [14] **Contrabass clarinet** A late 19th-century French example of the largest and lowest-pitched of all the clarinets, it has a simple system of keywork. [15] **B flat clarinet** The most common modern clarinet, the B flat uses the same Boehm key system that was developed for the concert flute. [16] **Clarinet d'amour** Popular in the 18th century, this clarinet has a large, bulbous bell that gives its sound a veiled beauty.

[8] OBOE
Height 24 in (60 cm)

[10] BASSOON
Height 4 ft (1.2 m)

[9] COR ANGLAIS
Height 34 in (87 cm)

[1] BASS FLUTE
Length 33 in (84 cm)

[2] ONE-KEYED FLUTE
Length 24 in (60 cm)

[3] FLUTE
Length 23 in (59 cm)

[4] ALTO FLUTE
Length 28 in (70 cm)

[6] MODERN CONCERT FLUTE Length 26 in (67 cm)

[5] PICCOLO
Length 13 in (33 cm)

[7] PRATTEN SYSTEM FLUTE
Length 26 in (67 cm)

12 CONTRABASSOON
Height 5ft 7in (1.7m)

11 BASSOON
Height 4ft (1.2m)

13 OCTAVIN
Height 17in (43cm)

14 CONTRABASS CLARINET
Height 3ft 7in (1.1m)

15 B FLAT CLARINET
Height 26in (67cm)

16 CLARINET D'AMOUR
Height 30in (77cm)

BEFORE

The word symphony, or *sinfonia*, was used long before the Classical era to describe different kinds of musical collections.

EVOLVING CONCEPT
The first mentions of symphony are In the 16th century, when it referred to collections of **sacred vocal works with instrumental accompaniment**. After the 16th century, the term related to particular movements played within works such as **operas**, **concertos**, and **sonatas**.

THREE-MOVEMENT FORM
In 17th-century **Neapolitan opera** **« 80–81**, composers used three movements in a quick-slow-quick pattern in overtures or in instrumental interludes. These served as the basis for **three-movement symphonies**.

The **Symphony**

In the mid-18th century, the symphony, until then a serious three-movement work, acquired a fourth movement and took center stage. It means "sounding together," which, on both practical and artistic levels, has inspired composers ever since.

Concerts at the Tuileries
The symphonies of Joseph Haydn and other Classical composers were performed at the *Concerts Spirituels*, public concerts held in Paris in the 18th century. Among the venues was Tuileries Palace.

"Haydn's **symphonies** are ... full of **love** and **bliss,** as if before the Fall."

GERMAN MUSIC CRITIC E. T. A. HOFFMANN, 1810

In the 1740s, in the German city of Mannheim, Johann Stamitz (see below) gathered around him a group of musicians who developed the symphony into the most important form of orchestral music.

The Mannheim composers (see pp.118–119) inherited from the Baroque period the model of a three-movement symphony. Wanting to inject some lighthearted elegance into what was then a serious and substantial musical form, the Mannheim composers began to insert an extra dance-inspired movement before the finale. This was usually a graceful minuet (a kind of dance) with a contrasting "trio" middle section (so called because it was designed for three musicians to play). Thereafter, the resulting four-movement symphony (see below) became the norm.

STRUCTURE: SYMPHONY
During the Classical period, the symphony grew from three into four movements. These movements use different musical forms and are designed to incorporate variety and contrast to create a musical whole. The substantial first movement is rich in melodic material, while the second is more relaxed. A lighthearted and dancelike third movement prefaces an emphatic finale.

1ST MOVEMENT	2ND MOVEMENT	3RD MOVEMENT	4TH MOVEMENT
Sonata-allegro A fast-paced variation of sonata form (see p.121)	**Ternary form** Follows a simple ABA pattern with three sections where the third repeats the first	**Minuet and trio** Two minuets separated by a contrasting trio section in ternary (ABA) form	**Rondo form** Section A is repeated with new sections between each repetition, in an ABACADA pattern
Presents several themes and develops them in different keys, ending in the main key.	Slower, with lyrical songlike melodies presented simply and expressively.	Brisk movement in minuet form—a dance form from the Baroque era.	Fairly fast and in a variety of forms—usually either a rondo or a sonata-allegro.

COMPOSER AND VIOLINIST (1717–57)

JOHANN STAMITZ

Born in Deutschbrod, Bohemia, in the modern-day Czech Republic, Johann Stamitz was an influential figure in the development of the symphony. He moved to Mannheim in Germany in 1741, where he helped to found the Mannheim School. As director of instrumental music at the Mannheim court, he achieved exceptionally high performance standards from musicians. In his compositions, he helped to move the symphony toward its eventual four-movement form.

Stamitz had five children. His two sons, Carl and Anton, also became important Mannheim School composers.

Strings dominate

Symphonies were still predominantly string-based, although significant parts for flute, oboe, bassoon, horn, trumpet, and timpani were added. A continuo part on cello and harpsichord (see pp.78–79) filled in the harmonies, although this practice began to disappear as composers wrote fuller orchestral parts for second violins, violas, cellos, woodwind, and brass.

Early master

In the latter half of the 18th century, Joseph Haydn (see pp.126–127) seized on this new four-movement format, writing more than 100 symphonies between 1759 and 1795, each one more inventive, and occasionally daring, than the previous one. Haydn's final 12 symphonies were written in London, at the request of the composer and musical impresario Peter Salomon (1745–1815). With titles such as "Surprise" (No. 94), "Miracle" (No. 96), "Military" (No. 100), "Clock" (No. 101), and "Drum Roll" (No. 103), Haydn demonstrated how, unlike his predecessors, he used the symphony as a vehicle for dramatic expression.

Latest fashions

A cosmopolitan traveler, Wolfgang Amadeus Mozart (see pp.136–137) earned his living from commissions. Ever eager to attract new customers, he built into his 41 symphonies all the newest musical fashions picked up on his travels. His penultimate symphony, No. 40, also called his Great G Minor Symphony, is on a grand scale, lasting 40 minutes. Mozart conjures a stormy atmosphere, not just in the first movement with its urgent opening, but also in the driving finale inspired by the Mannheim "Rocket" (a series of rapidly ascending broken chords, (see p.119).

104 The total numbered symphonies written by Joseph Haydn, not including two that are unnumbered.

Mozart's final, 41st Symphony (also called the "Jupiter" Symphony), completed in 1788, is in the sunny key of C major. In it, all Mozart's technical and artistic wizardry is used to create a triumphantly jubilant conclusion to his symphonic output.

Score of Mozart's Symphony No. 41
German impresario Johann Peter Salomon is thought to have come up with the nickname "Jupiter" for Mozart's 41st Symphony, to promote the work's triumphant, magisterial spirit.

Beethoven's Seventh

In the compositions of Ludwig van Beethoven (see pp.142–143, 150–151), the symphony was expanded both physically and psychologically, as he used the form to express every human emotion. His Seventh Symphony, written in 1813, opens with an extended slow passage before easing into a dancelike rhythm. Series of repeated notes are a feature of both the slower second movement and the joyous, lively third, with its hymnlike trio. Two arresting chords open the finale, unleashing a torrent of exuberance that leads to a whirling conclusion. Beethoven's final Ninth "Choral" Symphony, completed in 1824, was revolutionary, breaking the standard mold of the symphonic form by including vocal soloists and a chorus. Using the uplifting text of German poet Friedrich von Schiller's "Ode to Joy," Beethoven's music touches the extremes of human emotion, alternating turbulence, tranquility, and triumph in a testament to the power and vulnerability of the human spirit.

Symphonic beauty

Franz Schubert (see pp.154–155) died young, with his works relatively unknown. And yet, his symphonies offered a different approach to symphonic writing. Still staying with the four-movement format, which included a minuet, Schubert tended to be most concerned with melodic beauty of his music, particularly in his C major symphony in which an expansive opening is followed by a slower, lyrical section, then a bubbling, light movement, and ends with an urgent, driven finale.

Responding to Schubert's spacious and expansive Ninth Symphony, Robert Schumann (see p.152) eulogized over its "heavenly length." Schubert's symphonies offered an escape for the Romantic composers who felt trapped by Beethoven's legacy, and anticipated the work of Anton Bruckner (see pp.162–163) 50 years later.

KEY WORKS

Johann Stamitz Symphony in E flat major, Op. 11, No. 3

Joseph Haydn Symphony No. 100 in G major

W.A. Mozart Symphony No. 40 in G minor, K. 550; Symphony No. 41 in C major, K. 551

Ludwig van Beethoven Symphony No. 7 in A major, Op. 92

Franz Schubert Symphony No. 9 in C major

AFTER

From around 1830, while some composers continued the old symphonic tradition, others moved away from its formal structure.

CARRYING ON THE CUSTOM
Robert Schumann 158–159 ››, **Felix Mendelssohn 158–159 ››**, **Johannes Brahms 172–173 ››**, and **Tchaikovsky 182–183 ››** upheld the traditional symphony.

INTO THE 20TH CENTURY
The flexible approach of **Anton Bruckner 162 ››** and **Gustav Mahler 193 ››**, along with an expanded orchestra and the gradual move away from orthodox harmonies, carried the symphony into the 20th century.

Influenced by nationalism, nostalgia, **Antonín Dvořák 193 ››**, **Edward Elgar 214–215››**, **Sergey Rachmaninoff 222–223››**, and **Dmitri Shostakovich** continued to use the symphonic form.

COMPOSER Born 1732 Died 1809

Joseph Haydn

> “I was set **apart** from the **world...** so I was forced to become **original...**”
>
> FRANZ JOSEPH HAYDN, TO HIS BIOGRAPHER, GEORG AUGUST VON GRIESINGER

The life of Haydn spanned almost 80 years of unprecedented musical activity in Europe. A key figure in the development of the Classical style, he laid the foundations for the symphony and string quartet, and paved the way for Beethoven and Mozart. His prodigious output included music in almost every genre.

Modest beginnings

Born into a musical but not musically educated family in Rohrau, Austria, the young Haydn had an excellent singing voice. This earned him a place at the choir school in Vienna’s St. Stephen’s Cathedral. After his voice broke, he made a modest living from teaching, and from serenading partygoers, and continued his education by studying musical theory and taking lessons in composition from his teacher, Nicola Porpora.

Esterházy employee
A livery coat worn by Esterházy servants rests on the chair in Haydn’s study in his house (now a museum) in Eisenstadt, Austria. Haydn wore such livery while employed by the Esterházy family.

The Esterházys

In 1761, Haydn was appointed Vice-Kapellmeister (deputy music director) at the court of the Esterházys, an aristocratic Hungarian family. Promoted to Kapellmeister in 1766, he took full charge of music, running the orchestra, playing chamber music, and composing and presenting operas.

Most summers were spent at the Esterházy summer palace at

Admired and respected
Widely considered hard-working, generous, and popular, Haydn enjoyed convivial relations with fellow composers and patrons alike. His marriage, however, was a failure.

Sketch for *Armida*
Giacomo Pregliasco's costume sketch for Haydn's *Armida*. Between 1784 and 1788, the opera was performed 54 times at the Esterháza Court Theater.

Esterháza in rural Hungary, where Haydn developed his own particular musical voice, largely unaffected by Viennese fashions. He composed fluently, and his early symphonies, though breaking little new ground, show graceful wit and charm. In his Symphony No. 45, "Farewell," for example, he set out to show his employer, Prince Nikolaus Esterházy, that the court musicians were exhausted. In the finale, the musicians stop playing one by one, snuff out their candles, and leave the room. The prince took the hint and the following day the musicians were allowed to go home for a vacation.

Haydn excelled in the string quartet, a medium he effectively invented and enjoyed playing with other court musicians. In the combination of two violins, viola, and cello he found the perfect vehicle for musical argument, deep emotional expression, and pleasurable social engagement—described by Goethe as "four rational people conversing." Over 40 years he wrote 68 quartets, gradually giving the four instruments equal importance, with the first violin no longer always having the limelight. These developments were noticed and copied by Mozart, who dedicated his six 1785 quartets to Haydn.

London calls

After Prince Nikolaus's death in 1790, an invitation to visit London came from the violinist and impresario Johann Salomon. It included a commission to provide six symphonies, one new opera, and 20 smaller works for a fee of £1,200. Haydn readily accepted. He made two visits, in 1791–1792 and 1794–1795, both of which were artistic and financial, triumphs. While there, he wrote the 12 London Symphonies, the last of his 104 symphonies. They completed a development of increasingly independent instrumental lines that exploit the distinctive tone of each instrument, as well as the development of melodic themes, and bold use of keys, especially minor. The symphonies became more ambitious, expanding from an orchestra of 20 to 60 musicians.

Choral works

Haydn returned to Vienna as an international star. He resumed working for the Esterházys but mostly pursued his own projects, such as writing choral works that included a new mass each year for September 8, the name day of Princess Maria Theresa. During this period he also composed his oratorio *The Creation*, regarded as his greatest masterpiece and widely performed today. The darkly dramatic orchestral opening, "Representation of Chaos," is followed by a sequence of robust, joyous choruses interspersed with beguiling arias depicting scenes from nature.

> "That will **make the ladies scream!**"
>
> HAYDN, ON THE UNEXPECTED MOMENT IN HIS "SURPRISE" SYMPHONY, 1791

KEY WORKS

Piano Sonata in C
Piano Trio No. 39 in G, "Gypsy"
Symphony No. 44 in E minor, "Trauer"
Symphony No. 104 in D, "London"
Concerto for Trumpet in E flat
Concerto No. 1 for Cello in C
Harmoniemesse (Wind band Mass) No. 14 in B flat
The Creation

Last performance

By 1803, Haydn's health began to fail. On December 26 of that year, he conducted his final public concert, his oratorio-like *Seven Last Words*. Five years later, he attended a celebration of his 75th birthday in the Old University in Vienna in which Antonio Salieri conducted *The Creation*. The concert was attended by Beethoven, who is said to have knelt down and kissed the hands of his former teacher.

Haydn died quietly at home in 1809. The diary of Joseph Carl Rosenbaum, a former secretary of the Esterházys, records that the memorial service held two weeks later included a performance of Mozart's Requiem: "The whole art-loving world of Vienna was present. Everything was very solemn, and worthy of Haydn."

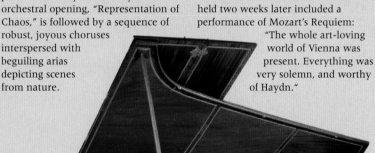

Haydn's harpsichord
More than 60 keyboard sonatas are attributed to Haydn. The early ones were for harpsichord, but markings in the scores of later works indicate they were written for the new, more versatile pianoforte.

TIMELINE

- **1732** Born in Rohrau, Austria, near the modern-day border with Slovakia and Hungary. He is the second of 12 children born to a wheelwright and the daughter of a market inspector.
- **1740** Becomes chorister at St. Stephen's Cathedral, Vienna.
- **1753** The composer and teacher Nicola Porpora gives him instruction in composition.
- **1759** Composes Symphony No. 1.
- **1760** Marries Maria Anna Keller, but the marriage is unhappy and childless.
- **1761** Appointed as Vice-Kapellmeister (deputy musical director) to the Esterházy family.
- **1766** Promoted to Kapellmeister (musical director).

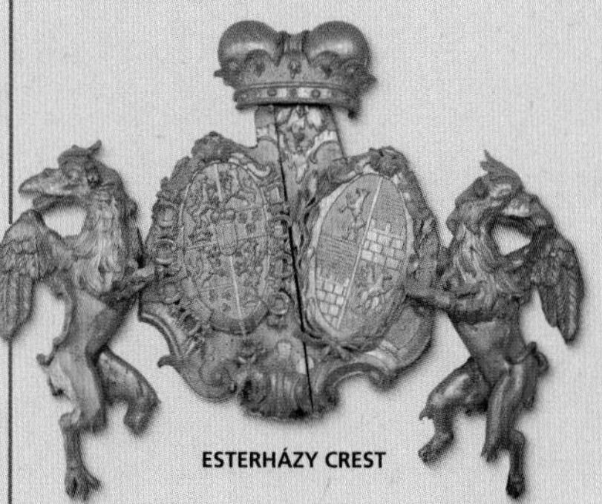

ESTERHÁZY CREST

- **1772** "Farewell" Symphony No. 45 is premiered.
- **1784** Meets and befriends Mozart in Vienna. They play chamber music together.
- **1791** Visits London, where he is commissioned by the violinist and impresario Johann Salomon. Writes and directs numerous works, including an opera, six symphonies—among which is the "Surprise" Symphony—and smaller pieces. Arranges around 400 English, Welsh, and Scottish folk songs.
- **1792** Returns to Vienna, where he meets and starts to teach Beethoven.
- **1794** On another invitation from Salomon, he returns to London and composes his final set of symphonies, including the set known as the "London" symphonies. Commissioned to write the oratorio *The Creation*.
- **1795** Period of prolific choral writing begins, including the masses *Maria Theresa* and *In tempore belli* (In Time of War).
- **1796** Writes Trumpet Concerto for Anton Weidinger's new keyed trumpet, which makes high notes, rapid runs, and lyrical melodies more easily playable.
- **1798** *The Creation* is first performed in Vienna. It becomes an overwhelming success in both England and Germany.
- **1803** Begins his final string quartet, but it is left unfinished. His health declines, and he ceases most work for the Esterházy family, although continues to attend occasional performances.
- **1809** Dies in his sleep on May 31, attended by a guard of honor outside his house.

BEFORE

Before the 18th century, ensembles of musicians performed mostly for the rich and on instruments that had evolved during the Middle Ages.

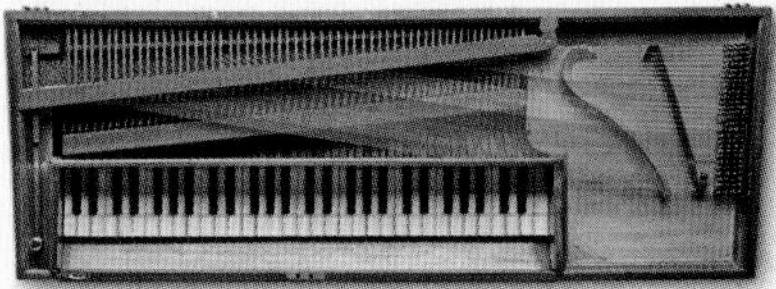

ENGLISH SQUARE PIANO

SOUNDS ON THE VERGE OF CHANGE

Courtiers in the 16th and 17th centuries listened to **consort music** **« 68–69** that was often played by groups of **viols**—fretted instruments related to the guitar and played with a bow **« 90–91**. The **harpsichord** and **early piano** **« 106–109** took a background role in ensembles, since they lacked the capability to project sustained melody lines unless supported by other instruments.

Playing Music Among **Friends**

By the 18th century, music-making had already begun to spread from the courts of kings and nobles into the home. A confident new class had the desire, means, and ability to play together and entertain each other in duets, trios, quartets, or quintets.

Small groups of varied instruments in which each player has an individual part define chamber music. It grew in the late 18th century as an amateur pursuit when players met together in a room ("chamber").

The Industrial Revolution helped to trigger chamber music's popularity. Instruments were better made, their cost was lower, and the growing middle classes, with more money and leisure time, wanted to raise their status by playing music. It became fashionable to play chamber music in ensembles, and composers responded by writing for combinations of instruments that worked well together.

German-speaking countries in particular embraced this communal activity—above all in Vienna, where a genteel Sunday's entertainment was incomplete without a group performance. Eventually, chamber music became so important as a genre, and so loved by the public, that it moved on to the professional recital platform. It remains a treasured amateur pastime the world over and composers continue to write chamber ensemble pieces.

Music for string quartets

The similar sounds of stringed instruments blend so harmoniously that the string quartet (two violins, viola, and cello) has proved the most

All eyes on the leader
Joseph Haydn is credited with inventing the string quartet. This fanciful painting by German artist Julius Schmid (1854–1935) depicts Haydn examining the score while guests listen attentively.

UNDERSTANDING MUSIC

HARMONIE

From the 1770s, diners at banquets were serenaded by pairs of oboes, clarinets, horns, and bassoons in a type of ensemble called *Harmonie*, playing *Harmoniemusik*. This became so popular in the Classical period that Emperor Joseph II founded an "Imperial Wind Ensemble" in Vienna. A *Harmonie* group appears in the banquet scene in Mozart's opera *Don Giovanni*, playing well-known melodies scored for wind instruments. Mozart expanded on this in his *Gran Partita*, a seven-movement serenade for 13 players—*Harmonie* plus two additional horns, two basset horns, and double bass. *Harmonie* not only led to the emergence of the military and concert band, but also encouraged a more prominent role for woodwind instruments in the orchestra.

LATE-18TH-CENTURY CLARINET

enduring chamber music combination. Recognizing its intrinsically beautiful sound, the composer Joseph Haydn (see pp.126–127) wrote around 70 string quartets, most of which have four movements like the Classical symphony (see pp.124–125). Mozart (see pp.136–137) also enjoyed performing and writing quartets, and dedicated six of them to Haydn. In the last of these, the "Dissonance," he experimented with the form by opening it with clashing harmonies.

Beethoven (see pp.142–143) extended the emotional range of the string quartet. His final works, a series of quartets written in the 1820s, are considered to be some of the finest musical achievements, and inspired composers as diverse as Schoenberg, Shostakovich, and Robert Schumann.

Music for two or three parts

The growing popularity of the piano spawned a new form of chamber music—the piano duet for two players at one instrument. Mozart wrote several works for four hands, while Schubert's output often required players to become better acquainted by crossing hands with one another. Many symphonies were transcribed for piano duet, which became the standard means of experiencing new orchestral works until the advent of recording.

The piano's popularity encouraged the development of the accompanied sonata and the piano trio. Both had roots in the Baroque keyboard sonata (see pp.102–103) and used the stringed instruments to double the melody and bass of the piano part to cover the rapidly dying sound of early keyboard instruments. The frontispieces of Beethoven's early violin sonatas state that they are for piano accompanied by violin, but by the 1820s, the balance between the instruments had evened out as performers became more skilled. When Beethoven premiered a new sonata, George Bridgetower, a violinist who was of African descent, felt comfortable making changes during the performance. These were immediately adopted by Beethoven, who embraced him and exclaimed, "Once more my dear fellow!"

Meanwhile, as the piano sound grew in power and individuality, composers such as Schubert and Mendelssohn exploited and celebrated the different timbres. In *Notturno*, the charming piano trio by Schubert (see pp.154–155), violin and cello alternate with the piano in a lyrical melody, delighting in the contrast between the sustained string sound of the violin and the piano's chords.

BEETHOVEN'S last piece before he succumbed to illness was a string quintet.

"The most perfect **expression** of **human behavior** is a string quartet."

BRITISH CONDUCTOR JEFFERY TATE, WRITING IN *THE NEW YORKER*, APRIL 30, 1990

A fifth element

The addition of another instrument to the string quartet produced a surprisingly richer sound. In Schubert's "Trout" Quintet, a double bass underlies the watery rippling of the piano part, bringing with it a delicate gravitas.

Further combinations included woodwind quintets (flute, oboe, clarinet, bassoon, and horn), and diverse combinations of strings and wind instruments with or without the piano. Anton Reicha's quintets show his understanding of the special quirks of woodwind, while Beethoven and Schubert wrote pieces for various combinations of wind and strings. However, mixed ensembles were in the minority, since not all composers could rise to the challenge of taming the fundamental differences in tone between wind, strings, and piano.

First violin often has the melody

Second violin supports and harmonizes

Viola adds depth and rhythmic support

Cello provides bass line

Notes of a master
Mozart's 1787 serenade "Eine Kleine Nachtmusik" ("A Little Night Music") is usually performed by a string chamber ensemble. The quartet becomes a quintet if a double bass joins in with the cello part.

KEY WORKS

Mozart Serenade No. 10 in B flat major, "Gran Partita," K.361

Haydn Quartet No. 53 in D major, "The Lark," Op. 64, No. 5

Anton Reicha Wind Quintet in E flat major, Op. 88, No. 2

Beethoven Septet in E flat major, Op. 20; String Quartet in C sharp minor, No. 14, Op. 131

Schubert Octet in F major, D.803; *Notturno* (Nocturne), Op. 148, D.897

AFTER

Chamber music became a favorite medium for listeners and performers, both amateur and professional.

ON THE PUBLIC STAGE

In the mid-19th century, professional ensembles emerged, including the **Hellmesberger** and the **Joachim** string quartets, founded by the violinists Joseph Hellmesberger Sr. and Joseph Joachim. They premiered chamber works by **Brahms** **172–173 »** and **Dvořák**, whose popular Slavonic and Hungarian Dances for piano duet also underlined the growing interest in **musical nationalism** **176–177 »**.

POPULARITY OF THE PIANO

The piano continued to evolve, gaining a more sonorous note and winning **equal status** with other instruments. The invention of the **upright piano** allowed more households to own the instrument **170–171 »**.

GALLIC FLAIR

New instruments added novelty to the genre in the 20th century, especially through French composers such as **Francis Poulenc** and **Darius Milhaud** **204–205 »**.

COMPOSER (1770–1836)

ANTON REICHA

Composer, theorist, and flute player, Anton Reicha was one of many Bohemian musicians who left Prague (see pp.146–147) in search of wider musical horizons. At 15, he joined the Bonn Court orchestra, before moving to Vienna, where he befriended Mozart and Beethoven. He was appointed professor of theory at the Paris Conservatoire in 1818 and taught Berlioz, Liszt, Gounod, and César Franck. Reicha applied his views on theory and composition in his many fugues and studies for piano. He also wrote substantially for wind quintets.

Age of Reason

By the mid-18th century, a new creative dawn was breaking over Europe as intellectuals embraced science and logic and moved to change society through the spread of knowledge. There was a new emphasis on structure and clarity in the arts, including music.

The Age of Reason, or the Enlightenment, transformed European culture. Sweeping away superstition and old beliefs, it promoted the idea that education based on reason, truth, and logic could improve humanity.

The time was right: the Church and the aristocracy were losing their influence; the scientific discoveries of Isaac Newton (1643–1727) were becoming widely accepted; interest in Classical architecture was reviving; and the Industrial Revolution was gaining momentum. The emerging middle classes, with their increased wealth and leisure, were no longer content to be onlookers on the lives and experiences of others—they wanted to be involved.

28 The number of volumes in the *Encyclopédie*, edited by Diderot. Another seven volumes were added later.

Spreading the word

Since the Renaissance, European philosophers and theorists had become increasingly preoccupied with this new humanitarian outlook. Interest was particularly strong in France, where a group of intellectuals, led by Denis Diderot (1713–84), created the *Encyclopédie*, a groundbreaking dictionary that presented information about science and the arts, including music, in a clear and systematic fashion. The *encyclopédistes*, as the compilers became known, wanted to change the way people thought, and believed that their dictionary would spread knowledge to the masses far and wide.

The new enthusiasm for knowledge had an immediate impact on music. In 1768, the philosopher Jean-Jacques Rousseau (1712–78) published his *Dictionnaire de musique*, while English historian Charles Burney's *General History of Music* provided an account of composers, their works, performances, and audience reactions.

Although the arts were regarded as key to human development, music was not considered the most important. Indeed, in his 1781 *The Critique of Pure Reason*, the philosopher Immanuel Kant (1724–1804) likened music to a perfumed handkerchief, which, being pulled from a pocket, forced others to enjoy the owner's choice of scent.

Harmony in stone
The majestic proportions and elegant balance of classical architecture, such as that found at the Roman town of Baelo Claudia in southern Spain, influenced the structure of 18th-century musical forms.

Musical transformation

In music, enlightened principles encouraged a shift away from the complex, ornamented Baroque style (see p.78). Balance, logic, structure, clarity of thought, and simplicity of expression became the new norms. Composers were now eager to draw in listeners with music that was pleasingly expressive without being overemotional, and simple melodies with straightforward accompaniments predominated.

New forms of sonata (see pp.120–21), symphony (see pp.124–25), and concerto (see pp.138–39) were established, with clear, logical structures, and rules that made music easier for the listener to follow, and more approachable for amateur players. Rather than presenting complex music to be admired, composers wanted to lead audiences by the hand with more accessible composition structures.

New French and Italian opera

In France, the light and airy grace of the rococo style, with its emphasis on jocularity, intimacy, and poise seemed a more "human" art compared with the strictness of the old-fashioned Baroque. In the elegant opera-ballets of the period, especially those by French composer Jean-Philippe Rameau (see opposite), intricate plots based on Classical mythology were abandoned in favor of narratives focusing on more human traits. Rameau's 1739 opera *Les fêtes d'Hébé* (The Festivities of Hebe), celebrating the role of the arts in freeing the human spirit, captures the ethos of the Age of Reason.

Similarly, the labyrinthine plots of Italian Baroque opera (see pp.80–81) were simplified to focus on human experiences and emotions—most commonly love, jealousy, and betrayal—rather than relying on interventions of the gods. The librettos of the poet Pietro Metastasio (1698–1782)—such as his work for Mozart's opera *La clemenza di Tito* (The Clemency of Titus)—are built on narratives of enlightened leadership and the triumph of reason, while those of Carlo Goldoni (1707–93), who collaborated with the composer

"Good music is very close to **primitive** language.**"**

PHILOSOPHER DENIS DIDEROT, "ELEMENTS OF PHYSIOLOGY" (1774–80)

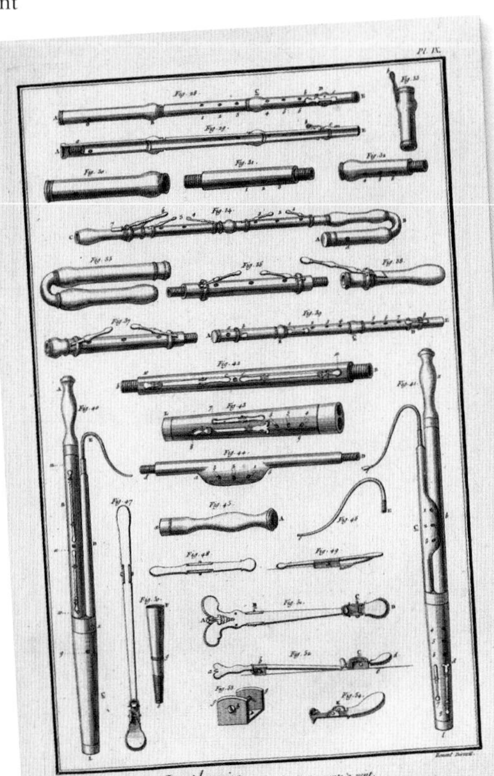

Enlightened musical record
An engraving by Robert Bénard from Diderot's *Encyclopédie*, published between 1751 and 1772, shows a range of wind instruments. The page was part of one of 11 volumes of illustrations.

BEFORE

Baroque music of the 17th and early 18th centuries was decorative and complex, with several parts playing against each other in counterpoint.

MUSIC FOR THE ELITE
For centuries, **the court and Church** dictated musical life, commissioning works that were performed by professional musicians. With the rise of **chamber music ensembles « 128–29**, amateur participation in domestic music-making became more common.

RARE SOUNDS
Instruments were expensive. Instrumental ensembles were, therefore, based at court and seldom heard by the public.

KEY WORKS

Jean-Philippe Rameau *Les fêtes d'Hébé (The Festivities of Hebe)*

Baldassare Galuppi *Il filosofo di campagna (The Country Philosopher)*

Joseph Haydn Symphony No. 22 in E flat major, "The Philosopher"

Wolfgang Amadeus Mozart *Die Zauberflöte (The Magic Flute)*

COMPOSER (1683–1764)

JEAN-PHILIPPE RAMEAU

Now best remembered for his operas, French composer Jean-Philippe Rameau was also an influential music theorist. He settled in Paris in 1722. Despite making himself unpopular with his brusque manner, and having a reputation for greed and insensitivity, he mixed with court aristocracy and the intelligentsia. Although his theoretical treatises regarded music as a science, Rameau's compositions were expressive and emotional. The revolutionary harmonies of his early operas were regarded as alarmingly modern, leading to criticism from those who favored the earlier French Baroque style of Jean-Baptiste Lully (see p.84).

Baldassare Galuppi (1706–85) in more than 20 of the latter's 109 operas, mocked arrogance, intolerance, and the abuse of power. Even Rousseau turned his hand to opera in his one-act *Le devin du village* (The Village Soothsayer), in which anxious young lovers are united after advice from the soothsayer.

The merit of an opera began to be judged not on florid singing and impressive virtuosity, but on whether the composer's music had truly encapsulated the human drama on stage (see pp.132–33).

Darkness and light

Some, such as the German poet Johann Wolfgang von Goethe (1749–1832), felt that Enlightenment rationalist beliefs failed to capture the human condition's violent emotions and senses. Their movement became known as *Sturm und Drang* (storm and stress), from the 1776 play of the same name by Friedrich Klinger. Promoting pessimism, gloom, and terror, this almost Romantic outlook caught the imagination of composers such as Gluck and Haydn. But it was a short-lived backlash, as classicism soared to new levels of expressive beauty in the music of Mozart and his contemporaries.

In Mozart's opera *Die Zauberflöte* (*The Magic Flute*), premiered only 10 weeks before his death in 1791, the forces of evil and magic represented by the Queen of the Night are overcome by the enlightened principles of justice and wisdom shown by Sarastro.

AFTER

Classical principles and forms were cast aside as the influence of Romanticism grew.

ROMANTIC IDEALS PREVAIL

Expressing strong personal emotions became more important than celebrating the collective betterment of humanity. Other art forms began to inspire composers to write descriptive "program" music **156–57 ››**.

GREATER ACCESS TO MUSIC

Musical instruments became cheaper and more widely available in the 19th century **188–89 ››**. Orchestras began to be established, and the public thirst for music **160–61 ››** resulted in the opening of concert halls.

Taming the force of magic

The story of Mozart's *The Magic Flute* encapsulates Enlightenment values with its journey from superstition to reason by trial and error. In this 1818 set design, the Queen of the Night stands at the center.

BEFORE

Once opera was launched as an art form in Italy in the late 16th century, it quickly spread to other European countries.

STYLES BEFORE 1750
Classical themes prevailed in the first Italian operas ‹‹ **80–81**. Less formal styles, including the German ***Singspiel***, the English **masque**, and the French **vaudeville** included dialogue, dancing, and comic interludes.

17TH-CENTURY FRANCE
The operas of **Jean-Baptiste Lully's** ‹‹ **84–85** were performed all over Europe. His court entertainments for King Louis XIV inspired **Charpentier's** 1693 opera *Medée*.

ENGLISH REVIVAL
Henry Purcell's opera *Dido and Aeneas* evolved from the masque, a festive courtly entertainment, and **semi-opera** ‹‹ **95**—plays in which the acts were interspersed with lavish music and dancing.

EARLY NEAPOLITAN OPERA
Allesandro Scarlatti ‹‹ **106–107** initiated a new style of opera in the 1690s, known as the Neapolitan school. His drama with music, *Il Pirro e Demetrio* (Pyrrhus and Demetrius; 1694), was a great success across Europe.

Opera Comes Alive

After its early days in Renaissance Florence, opera captured a central role in European music. The opening of opera houses in the 17th century moved it from a courtly pursuit to a public one, while 18th-century reforms readied opera for Romantic developments.

By the beginning of the 18th century, composers had developed styles of opera with elements that appealed to the tastes of their fellow countrymen and carried on traditions set out in previous generations in that country. However, Italian *opera seria* (serious opera) was still considered the standard form for opera—for instance, most of the 42 operas of George Frideric Handel (see pp.108–109) were *opera serie*.

In *opera seria*, a major role was usually allocated to a castrato (a high-voiced male singer). Mythological or historical stories were retold to a set formula, with elaborate arias as highlights. Recitative (speechlike singing that advances the plot) was accompanied only by a continuo (cello and keyboard playing a bass line). Arias were mostly *da capo* (meaning "from the top"). In these, a first melody was followed by a contrasting middle section, before the singer returned to the opening section again (back to the top). This time, the singer would decorate the melody with improvised virtuoso ornamentations.

Humanizing opera plots

Although widely appealing, the otherworldly style and stop-and-start format of *opera seria* were far removed from everyday life. Venetian court poets Apostolo Zeno (1669–1750) and Pietro Metastasio (1698–1782) attempted to "humanize" *opera seria*. Rather than using characters simply as vehicles through which singers could deliver empty virtuosity, they wrote librettos focusing on the drama and emotions of the individual characters. As a result, by the middle of the 18th century, operas had tighter plots, rounded-out characters in credible situations, more dramatic energy, and more varied music.

In Paris, this was epitomized by the German-born composer Christoph Willibald von Gluck (see below), whose work for the Paris Opéra, including *Orfeo ed Euridice* and *Iphigénie en Tauride*, helped France to overtake Italy as the spiritual home of opera.

Gluck took the reforms of Zeno and Metastasio even further. To drive the plot more seamlessly, he favored what he called "beautiful simplicity." He transformed the traditional overture into an appropriately dramatic introduction to the whole opera. Gluck abandoned the *da capo* aria, with its formulaic repetition of the opening melody, and wrote recitatives that were accompanied and enhanced by the orchestra, rather than recitatives that were simply supported by a continuo.

These alterations made each act a coherent union of music and drama and, although Gluck's plots remained classical, his characters are vibrantly human and recognizable. The roles of Orpheus and Eurydice in his 1762 opera *Orfeo ed Euridice* are not distant figures written to conform to a set formula, but seem to be living, breathing people who experience authentic and familiar emotions. In Greek mythology, Orpheus (see p.20) journeys to Hades, the underworld, to reclaim his love, Eurydice. To succeed he must leave Hades without looking at her, but at the last moment he glances back and so loses her forever. The poignant simplicity of Orpheus's aria "Che faro senza Euridice?" ("What Will I Do Without Eurydice?") only emphasizes the tragedy.

Theater poster for *The Beggar's Opera*
John Gay's 1728 opera was an early example of English ballad opera, a lighthearted, satirical entertainment inspired by vaudeville comedies brought to London by the French.

Comic opera

Alongside the developing *opera seria*, comic opera was finding its feet. Comic scenes had been popular in some early operas, and by the 1720s a new style, *opera buffa* (comic opera) took hold in Italy. With more flexibility of structure than *opera seria*, the action romps along, with songlike arias, chattering recitative, and ensembles (songs for two or more singers) that develop into musical discussions between characters.

The first example of *opera buffa* is generally regarded to be *La serva padrona* (*The Servant Turned Mistress*) by the Italian composer Giovanni Battista Pergolesi (1710–1736). Performed by an itinerant troupe of Italian comic actors (*buffoni*) in Paris in 1752, it sparked a two-year press war known as the *Querelle des bouffons* (Quarrel of the Comic Actors). One faction supported the new lighter Italian music, while the other championed the traditional French operatic style. Philosopher Jean-Jacques Rousseau

> "The most **moving act** in all **opera.**"
>
> WRITER AND MYSTIC ROMAIN ROLLAND (1866–1944) ON ACT II OF GLUCK'S OPERA, "ORFEO ED EURIDICE"

KEY WORKS

Giovanni Battista Pergolesi *La serva padrona (The Servant Turned Mistress)*

Handel *Julius Caesar*; *Xerxes*

John Gay *The Beggar's Opera*

Christoph Willibald Gluck *Alceste*; *Orfeo ed Eurydice*

W.A. Mozart *The Clemency of Titus*; *The Marriage of Figaro*

COMPOSER (1704–87)

CHRISTOPH WILLIBALD VON GLUCK

Christoph Gluck was born in Erasbach, Upper Palatinate, Bavaria, the son of a forester. He ran away from home to Prague, where he studied organ and cello. In 1745, after studying with the Milanese composer Giuseppe Sammartini (1695–1750), he went to London, where he composed operas for the King's Theatre, and met Handel. After writing operas for various countries, he settled in Vienna.

With Ranieri de' Calzabigi (1714–1795), librettist of Gluck's 1767 opera *Alceste*, he wrote a manifesto challenging prevailing operatic conventions and called for better integration between music and drama.

Gluck died in 1787 and was buried in Vienna, Austria.

Il Parnaso Confuso, Vienna, 1765
Johann Franz Greipel's painting depicts Gluck's one-act theatrical serenade being premièred by four young archduchesses as a surprise to celebrate the remarriage of their brother, Joseph II.

(1712–1778) was at the forefront as the debate continued, opposing Gluck's principles of "beautiful simplicity."

In London, John Gay (1685–1732) mocked the artifice of Italian *opera seria* in his 1728 ballad opera, *The Beggar's Opera*. The composer dropped recitative altogether, and favored popular tunes and bawdy characters. Gay's controversial plot satirized the British government and pointed to the corruption of the governing class. Produced by John Rich, the opera was a huge financial success, and newspapers joked that it had made the "rich gay and Gay rich."

Operas of Mozart

Mozart (see pp.136–137) wrote both *opera seria* and *opera buffa*, often blurring the boundaries between the serious and comic elements. *La Clemenza di Tito* (The Clemency of Titus), is an *opera seria* with a Classical subject, formal arias, and recitatives, as well as a castrato role. By contrast, *Le Nozze di Figaro* (*The Marriage of Figaro*) has a social-comedy plot with "serious" aristocratic characters contrasting with the "comic" roles of servants and villagers. Instead of a castrato part, there is an important role for the bass voice. Mozart's fairy-talelike opera *Die Zauberflöte* (*The Magic Flute*) is a *Singspiel* (a type of German comic opera with spoken dialogue) in which serious and comic elements meld and contrast. Written in 1791, only nine weeks before Mozart's death, the success of the opera offered the composer some small consolation.

1753 **The year Jean-Jacques Rousseau published his essay, *Lettre sur la musique française*, in response to the *Querelle des bouffons.* He concluded that opera was impossible in the French language.**

AFTER

Romantic composers relax the formal structures of opera to better serve the narrative and the characters.

THE SUPERNATURAL

The plot of **Weber's** 1821 opera *Der Freischütz* (*The Freeshooter*, also called *The Magic Marksman*) featured a supernatural dimension in the form of seven magic bullets **164–165 ››**.

FRENCH SPECTACLE

Operas became grand. **Berlioz 156–157 ››** made exceptional use of the orchestra in his 1856 opera *Les Troyens*, based on Virgil's *Aeneid*.

BEL CANTO

While the operas could be serious or comic, the Italian *bel canto* (beautiful singing) style favored by **Rossini**, **Donizetti**, and **Bellini** demanded an extensive vocal range, a full, resonant tone, and great powers of lyricism.

GRITTY PLOTS

Puccini 196–197 ›› made opera more personal, with intense emotional music and plots involving everyday people and their struggles.

PLAYBILL FOR THE 1829 ROSSINI OPERA "WILLIAM TELL"

BEFORE

Music performed by choirs was largely sacred, used in worship, and sung unaccompanied or with an organ.

EARLY GROUP SINGING
In the 13th century, religious **plainchant** began to develop into **organum** (two voices) and **polyphony** (many voices) « 46–47.

GLORIOUS EFFECT
The 16th-century works of **Thomas Tallis**, **William Byrd**, and **Palestrina** « 60–61 were admired for their serenely beautiful vocal lines, which were suited to large churches.

40 **The number of vocal parts in Thomas Tallis's motet *Spem in Alium*, arranged in eight groups of five voices each.**

BAROQUE DEVELOPMENTS
Instruments were used to accompany sacred subjects to sublime effect in the Mass and Passion settings of **J.S. Bach** « 100–101. **Handel** « 108–109 developed the **oratorio** form, dramatizing biblical stories in operatic fashion, using an orchestra, solo singers, and a choir. His *Messiah* was premiered in a theater rather than a church.

Choral Music

In the 18th century, choral music took a significant leap. From its traditional role in church worship, it began to shift gradually into the concert hall, inviting composers to shake off spiritual sobriety and inject distinctly secular influences into their work.

During the first half of the 18th century, only a privileged few heard choral music outside a place of worship. But with the Enlightenment, which began in the mid-1700s, people were encouraged to formulate their own beliefs and codes of behavior, which, across Europe, challenged the influence of the established churches.

Following tradition

However, composers continued to write choral music for church worship, especially settings of the Latin text of the Roman Catholic Mass. These were sung by professional singers, with little congregational involvement.

Haydn, Mozart, and many others made settings of the Mass, and the special Requiem Mass for the dead, each in their own particular musical style. Luigi Cherubini even composed a Requiem Mass, in D minor, to be played as his own funeral. Mozart's D minor *Requiem* was intended for church performance, but from the early 19th century it began to be staged in concert halls, where the somber beauty and power of its orchestration could be appreciated aesthetically as well as spiritually.

New forms

Short religious works such as the cantata and motet also increased in popularity. These were sequences of choral and solo numbers normally accompanied by the organ, and occasionally by a small ensemble of instruments to provide variety and color. The words for such forms were chosen by the composer, allowing much more musical freedom than the strict texts of the Mass. These pithy musical "sermons" often appeared between sections of the Mass, but were performed increasingly as concert pieces. Mozart's three-movement motet *Exsultate, Jubilate* has a religious text but is operatic in style.

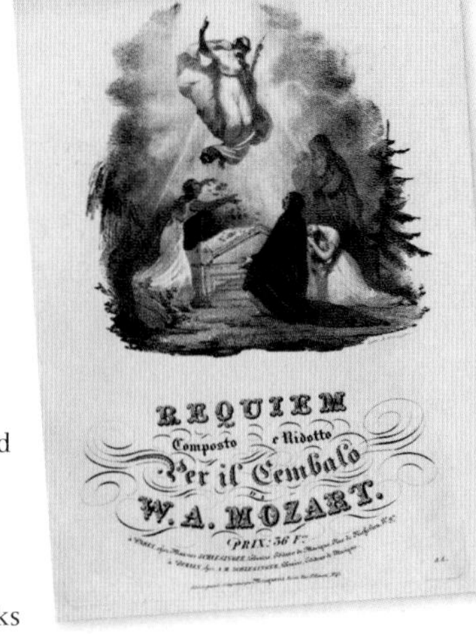

Memorial masterpiece
Mozart died before he could finish his *Requiem* in 1791. It was hurriedly completed by Franz Xaver Süssmayr and first performed in 1793.

Choral ambition grows

Beyond the church, music was developing apace. Composers began to address the wider dramatic potential of sacred texts and religious stories, their eyes fixed not only on the altar but also, increasingly, on the concert platform. Opera at this time was flourishing, orchestras were being established, and the public was developing an appetite for concert-going.

Inspired by Handel's oratorios (musical dramas on sacred themes designed for concert performance), Haydn's 1798 oratorio, *The Creation*, uses a libretto based on words from the Bible, Psalms, and John Milton's epic poem *Paradise Lost*. The words go beyond the spiritual to celebrate light, earth, plants, animals, and nature itself. The highly descriptive music for three soloists, chorus, and orchestra was intended for the biggest stages, rather than churches. The impact of *The Creation* pointed confidently towards the Romantic age.

Twenty-five years after *The Creation*, Beethoven returned to the traditional theme of the Mass with his *Missa Solemnis* (Solemn Mass). Now, however, he used his experience as a composer of operas and symphonies to inject new drama into the familiar text. Soloists, chorus, and orchestra were equal partners, setting an overall mood of profound intensity. Long—some 80 minutes—and complex, this was sacred music fit for the grandest concert hall. Beethoven's 9th Symphony, Choral Fantasy, and Mass in C are further examples of his innovative writing for choruses.

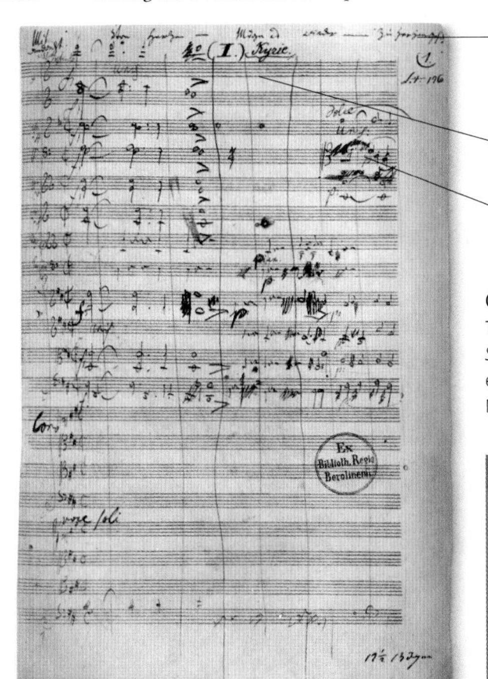

Composer's impassioned plea
The first page of Beethoven's score for his *Missa Solemnis* has the inscription: "Von Herzen—möge es wieder—zu Herzen gehen!" (From the Heart—May it Go Again—to the Heart!).

KEY WORKS

Joseph Haydn *The Creation*; *Nelson Mass* in D minor

Mozart Mass in C minor; *Requiem* in D minor

Luigi Cherubini *Requiem* in C minor

Beethoven *Missa Solemnis* in D major, Op. 123

COMPOSER (1760–1842)

LUIGI CHERUBINI

Born in Italy, Luigi Cherubini worked mostly in Paris, France, as a composer, conductor, and teacher, becoming director of the Conservatoire (college of music) in 1822. Although bad-tempered, he managed to acquire well-connected friends, such as Chopin and Rossini. In 1805, Beethoven declared him to be "Europe's foremost dramatic composer." Patriotic and politically astute, Cherubini supported the upheavals of the French Revolution and weathered its aftermath, writing his C minor *Requiem* to celebrate the 1816 anniversary of Louis XVI's execution. In his later years he wrote sacred works.

End of an era
Haydn made his last public appearance, at a performance of *The Creation* in Vienna, in March 1808. This painting by Austrian artist Balthasar Wigand depicts the event.

AFTER

Composers took an increasingly flexible approach to setting sacred texts to music, bringing in new styles.

MOVING WITH THE TIMES

Composers continued to work with traditional liturgies but used up-to-date compositional techniques and novel instrumentation **162–163 ››**. In his *Grande Messe des morts* (Requiem) of 1837, French composer **Berlioz** employed a huge chorus and orchestra, including four brass bands. In 19th-century Germany, **Mendelssohn** and **Brahms** used passages from the Bible for sacred works, and Italian composer **Verdi** brought grand-scale operatic style to choral music with his *Requiem*. From the late 19th century onward, composers such as **Mahler** and **Vaughan Williams** occasionally added choruses to their symphonies **192–193 ››**.

PUBLIC PARTICIPATION

From the 1820s, choral societies grew up in towns and cities, reviving existing works and encouraging composers to write new pieces.

COMPOSER Born 1756 Died 1791

Wolfgang Amadeus Mozart

"The **music** is not in the **notes**, but in the **silence** between."

WOLFGANG AMADEUS MOZART

One of the most respected, loved, and performed composers in Western classical music, Wolfgang Amadeus Mozart displayed a prodigious musical talent from an early age. He went on to excel in all major musical genres, from masses and requiems to symphonies and concertos. The dramatic intensity of his operas broke new ground.

Child prodigy

Inspired by his gifted older sister Nannerl, Wolfgang was picking out chords on the piano at the age of three and composing keyboard minuets at five. At age eight, he wrote his first symphony, as a simple entertainment piece. The children's father, Leopold, a noted violinist and composer, ruthlessly exploited his astonishingly talented children and abandoned his own career to promote them. Wolfgang and Nannerl performed for royalty and high society gatherings throughout Europe, including a concert at Versailles before the king and queen of France and Madame de Pompadour, the king's mistress. In 1761, Leopold wrote: "All the ladies are in love with my boy."

While in London in 1765, Mozart's father opened up the family lodgings for lunchtime recitals at which members of the public paid to witness Wolfgang improvise on the piano, his hands covered with a cloth as they dashed along the keys.

The experiences gained on these tours, and the people Mozart met, affirmed his genius and spurred him on to even greater achievements.

As he became older, Mozart focused on composition. He received commissions and in 1772, at the age of 16, was appointed Konzertmeister to Salzburg's court.

Master of emotion

Two key qualities earn Mozart his unique place in musical history: astonishing ability as a composer and performer, combined with a profound understanding of human emotions.

Traveling instrument

Mozart composed his late piano concertos on this piano, now on display in the Mozart Museum, Salzburg. He often had it carried to and from concert venues.

Italian tour
A three-year tour of Italy with his father from 1769 took Mozart to most of its major cities. In Milan, in 1770, he was commissioned to write his first *opera seria*, *Mitridate, re di Ponto*.

KEY
- Outward journey
- Detours made on return journey

Although this provided an income, he was frustrated in the position, finding Salzburg—and its people—provincial. His employer, the Prince-Archbishop of Salzburg, gave him little opportunity to compose the elaborate choral and orchestral music to which he felt drawn. Bored, Mozart began to undertake tours once again.

Mozart's repeated absences from court infuriated the Prince-Archbishop, who eventually dismissed him. In 1781, the composer left Salzburg for the larger and more vibrant city of Vienna in search of artistic freedom, becoming one of the first freelance professional musicians. He settled in the city and married Constanze Weber, a musician's daughter, in 1782.

New musical sounds

Mozart's years in Vienna were astonishingly productive. Much of his time there was devoted to composing operas, in which his capacity for illuminating the complexities of humankind found perfect expression. He blurred the boundaries between *Singspiel* (in which music is interspersed with spoken dialogue), *opera buffa* (comic opera), and *opera seria* (serious opera).

In 1786, Lorenzo da Ponte, the librettist for three of his last four operas, inspired him to write *The Marriage of Figaro*, a masterpiece of dramatic and musical characterization, psychological insight, and somber emotions, with playful diversions.

Mozart steered instrumental music toward the brink of Romantic expressivity. He adopted the well-established forms of the concerto, sonata, and symphony with few changes, but his influence was evident in the emotionally charged content of the pieces.

Fascinated by individual instrumental colors, Mozart relished giving woodwind and horns characterful solos. He also experimented with new combinations of instruments. The *Sinfonia Concertante for Violin and Viola*, the *Quintet for Piano and Woodwind* (oboe, clarinet, bassoon, and horn), and the *Kegelstatt Trio* for clarinet, viola, and piano, created new sound worlds for audiences.

Mozart's 41 symphonies chart his development as a composer in their increasing musical invention, technical refinement, instrumental brilliance, and dramatic content, culminating in his final three, all written in 1788.

Popular pauper

Without the financial security of a salaried position, Mozart gave concerts, published music, and received commissions, particularly for opera. In 1784, he became a Freemason. But despite constant composing, his debts mounted, not helped by Constanze's poor household management. To make ends meet, he offered music lessons, took in boarders, and borrowed.

Mozart died at the end of 1791, at the age of 35, not poisoned by his rival Antonio Salieri, as was suggested, but probably of rheumatic fever. He was buried in a pauper's grave outside the city, a practice not unusual at the time. Despite this, the obituaries unanimously proclaimed him a genius.

One of his best-loved choral works, the Requiem Mass, was unfinished at the time of his death. His friend, the composer Franz Xaver Süssmayr, completed it the following year at the request of Mozart's widow.

KEY WORKS

- **Sinfonia Concertante for Violin and Viola in E flat major, K364**
- **Symphony No. 35 in D major, "Haffner," K385**
- **String Quartet No. 19 in C major, "Dissonance"**
- ***The Marriage of Figaro***
- **Horn Concerto No. 4 in E flat major, K495**
- **Serenade for strings in G major, "Eine kleine Nachtmusik," K525**
- ***The Magic Flute*, K620**

"The most tremendous **genius** raised **Mozart** above all masters, in all centuries and in all the **arts**."

RICHARD WAGNER, "ON GERMAN MUSIC," 1840

Magical opera
Christopher Maltman (front left) and Dina Kuznetsova perform Mozart's last opera, *The Magic Flute*, in a production by the San Francisco Opera in 2007. The opera is known for its theatrical flamboyance.

TIMELINE

- **January 27, 1756** Born in Salzburg, Austria.
- **1761** Produces earliest keyboard compositions: Andante, K1a, and Allegro, K1b. First public appearance at Salzburg University. Begins playing violin.
- **1763** Begins a three-year tour of Germany, Paris, and London with his father and sister.

MOZART WITH HIS FATHER AND SISTER

- **1764** Arrives in London for 18-month stay. Gives public concerts and performances.
- **1766** Contracts rheumatic fever in Munich.
- **1768** The Singspiel *Bastien und Bastienne is* premiered.
- **1769** Begins three-year tour of Italy.
- **1772** Appointed Konzertmeister at Salzburg.
- **1773** Moves to Vienna, where he meets Haydn. Composes many string quartets, symphonies, and the motet *Exsultate Jubilate*.
- **1778** Visits Paris to hear his "Paris" Symphony performed.
- **1779** Composes *Sinfonia Concertante* for Violin and Viola, K364, and *Coronation Mass*.
- **1780** The opera *Idomeneo* is commissioned by the Elector of Bavaria.
- **1781** Moves permanently to Vienna.
- **1782** The opera *The Abduction from the Seraglio* triumphs. Marries Constanze Weber. Composes "Linz" Symphony.
- **1783** Completes "Haffner" Symphony.
- **1784** Composes piano concertos Nos. 14–19 for public concert series. Becomes a Freemason.
- **1785** Completes six string quartets dedicated to Haydn, including the *Dissonance*.
- **1786** *The Marriage of Figaro*, K492, is performed in Vienna to great acclaim. Composes "Kegelstatt" Trio, K498, and Symphony No. 38, "Prague."
- **1787** Writes "Eine kleine Nachtmusik." *Don Giovanni* is produced in Prague.
- **1788** Composes final three symphonies: Nos. 39 (K543), 40 (K550), and 41 (K551).
- **1789** Fails to achieve commissions or position. Travels to Dresden, Leipzig, Potsdam, and Berlin. Plays organ at Thomaskirche in Leipzig.
- **1790** *Cosi fan tutte*, K588, premieres in Vienna.
- **1791** Writes Clarinet Concerto; *The Magic Flute* premieres in Vienna. Dies on December 5, leaving his Requiem Mass unfinished.

Conductor, soloist, and orchestra
In this 2006 performance of Magnus Lindberg's Violin Concerto in New York's Avery Fisher Hall, Louis Langree conducts while violinist Lisa Batiashvili performs as the soloist.

BEFORE

A new kind of orchestral work, the "concerto" first appeared in the final two decades of the 17th century.

FIRST EXAMPLES
Earlier in the 17th century, ensembles accompanied soloists in **canzonas** **« 56**. The most important type of orchestral music after 1700 was the **Baroque** concerto, which evolved from the **concertato** **« 79**.

CHRISTMAS CONCERTO
A concerto was played in the Roman Catholic Church as an **overture before the Mass**. For the Mass at Christmas, composers often inserted an extra movement written in a pastoral style. **Arcangelo Corelli's** **« 103** *Christmas Concerto*, composed in around 1690, is a famous example of this.

The **Concerto**

A concerto displays the unique qualities of a solo instrument in dialogue with an orchestra. By the late 18th century, the popular soloists piano and violin had been joined by wind and brass, with composers pitting their distinctive colors against rich orchestral accompaniments.

By the 19th century, composers no longer wrote the orchestral part of a concerto as a mere accompaniment to enhance the solo instrument, but as an equal element. This shift of emphasis opened up new, unimagined possibilities.

New drama

Advances in musical instrument design shaped the concerto, creating new technical and expressive possibilities. Stringed instrument construction had changed little since the 1600s. The violin was fully formed by the Baroque era, for example, and so became the concerto's natural solo instrument. Woodwind and brass instruments were simple in structure and limited in the notes they could play. As a result, they were rarely used as solo instruments in any significant way before 1700. During the 18th and 19th centuries, advances were made in their design, with keys for woodwind and valves for brass. These refinements made it possible to play a greater range of notes at faster speeds, and produced a more resonant sound.

27 **The number of piano concertos written by Mozart.**

1811 **The year of the first performance of Beethoven's "Emperor" Concerto.**

Of all instruments, the greatest strides were made with the piano—the box-shaped fortepiano of the early 1700s gradually evolved into the mighty concert grand. New mechanisms meant that the keys responded more quickly

STRUCTURE:
CLASSICAL CONCERTO

The opening movement of the Classical concerto is the most musically substantial. The slow, songlike second movement invites tender expressive playing before the technically dazzling virtuosity of the finale brings the work to a crowd-pleasing conclusion.

Cadenza An improvised solo section (orchestra silent) designed to showcase the soloist's creative and virtuosic skills

1ST MOVEMENT
The longest movement and a fast-paced variation of sonata principle—sonata-allegro. Begins in home key, presents and develops several themes before ending in the home key.

2ND MOVEMENT
Always slow and lyrical-sounding in a key closely related to the home key.

3RD MOVEMENT
In rondo form, where a section A is repeated with new sections between each repetition, modified to contain features of sonata-allegro form.

when struck, allowing the pianist to play rapidly. Metal bracing ensured the frame was more robust, allowing for sustained chords powerful enough to be heard over the blast of a full orchestra.

Instrumentalists could play a greater range of notes and dynamics on the improved instruments, unleashing previously unheard levels of expressiveness as well as virtuosity. Composers exploited these new capabilities to the full.

The three-movement format had already been established in the 18th century. By the 19th century, however, the music became more dramatically contrasting. The fast opening movement was in broad sonata form (see pp.120–121), the second was reflective and slow, and the finale was fast and furious.

Mozart and the concerto form

Mozart (see pp.136–137) wrote 27 concertos—a significant part of his output—for the piano. He premiered many of them himself, improvising impressive cadenzas at the climax of each movement. In his woodwind concertos, Mozart's genius for writing melody radiates from the arching lyricism of the solo part. His concerto for flute and harp celebrates both the flute's limpid beauty and the elegance and flexibility of the mechanized pedal harp. In the four-horn concertos, Mozart's ambitious melodies push the soloist and instrument to their limits. They were inspired by remarkable works by Antonio Rosetti (1750–1792), who wrote challenging passages in which the soloist's playing is required to imitate hunting horns.

Mozart also admired the smooth, soft-toned clarinet playing of Anton Stadler, who invented an extension to the instrument that made it play lower. It was for this basset clarinet that Mozart wrote his famous clarinet concerto, which Stadler premiered in Prague just seven weeks before the composer's death in 1791.

New innovations

In the classical concerto, the orchestra often introduces the main themes, and then the soloist takes over. However, the openings of Beethoven's Fourth and Fifth ("The Emperor") Piano Concertos move into Romantic territory. The former opens quietly on the piano with a series of mysterious, repeated chords answered by the orchestra in a similar style, but in an unexpected key. The latter opens with three huge orchestral chords separated by flourishes on the piano. Both of these openings set the scene for a high-octane "conversation." Although both concertos proceed with the usual three movements—fast-slow-fast—the delicate, filigree piano writing in the sublime slow movement of the "The Emperor," written only three years after the Fourth, seems to point toward the Romantic period.

Romantic struggle

As Romanticism took hold in the mid-19th century, the concerto became a major musical form. With ever more challenging solo parts and adventurous orchestral writing, the concerto became the perfect musical expression of one of Romanticism's preoccupations—the individual's struggle against the world. Piano and violin were the favored soloists because they had the tonal variety and power to shine through dense orchestral textures. Mendelssohn, Brahms, Tchaikovsky, and Bruch all exploited this quality in their concertos for violin. In each, the orchestration is rich and dense, but dissolves magically when the solo violin must be heard.

Salon favorite
Often elegantly carved and gilded—like this 1797 pedal harp by Parisian maker Jean Henri Naderman—the harp was a favorite solo instrument in the salons of Europe, and was sometimes the soloist in concertos.

KEY WORKS

- **Antonio Rosetti** Concerto for horn in D minor, C. 38
- **Mozart** Oboe Concerto in C major, K314; Horn Concerto No. 3 in E flat major, K447; Piano Concerto No. 21 in C major, K467
- **Beethoven** Piano Concerto No. 4 in G major, Op. 58
- **Johannes Brahms** Concerto for Violin in D major, Op. 77
- **Max Bruch** Violin Concerto No. 1 in G minor, Op. 26

UNDERSTANDING MUSIC

CADENZA

The cadenza is an elaborate version of a cadence, the chord progression that normally ends a phrase, a movement, or an entire composition. Most end with a long trill before the orchestra return briefly to end the movement.

In the Baroque style, singers embellish the cadence at the end of an aria. Composers, including Vivaldi, began to incorporate the cadenza in the concerto, where it is now most commonly heard. Mozart improvised cadenzas in his piano concertos (usually at the end of the first movement), which developed the movement's themes.

Some composers wrote cadenzas down rather than letting performers improvise, including Brahms in his violin concerto in D major.

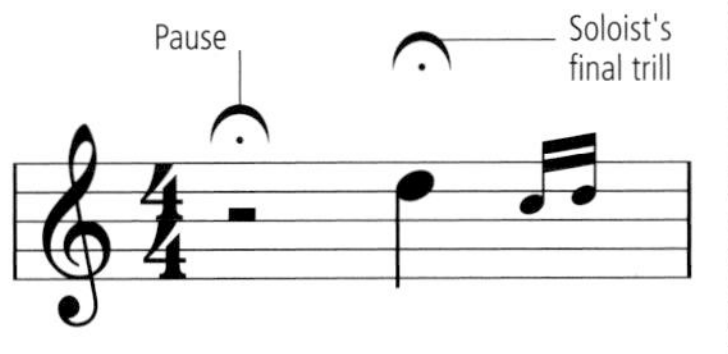

AFTER

Composers continued to write concertos well into the 20th century.

REVISITING AN OLD FORM
Rachmaninoff 222–223 ›› wrote four piano concertos at the start of the 20th century. No. 2 in C minor has been used as a soundtrack for several films and is instantly recognizable. **Sibelius's** violin concerto (1904) was inspired by the beauty of the Finnish landscape **185 ››**. In 1935, **Alban Berg** wrote a violin concerto built on a **tone row**—an arrangement of the 12 notes of a chromatic scale **210 ››**.

JAZZ BAND CONCERTO
In 1924, **Gershwin 232–233 ››** wrote his *Rhapsody in Blue*, a concerto for piano and jazz band fusing classical music with jazz.

JOSEPH JOACHIM
in Freundschaft zugeeignet.

Concert für die Violine
(Vorspiel, Adagio und Finale)
componirt von
MAX BRUCH.
Op. 26.

LEIPZIG,
C.F.W. SIEGEL'S Musikalienhandlung.
(R. Linnemann.)

Clavierauszug zu 4 Händen von RICHARD KLEINMICHEL

Bruch's violin concerto
The second movement of Bruch's first violin concerto is a touching dialogue in which the violinist's soaring line seems to be embraced by the orchestra.

The **Piano**

The piano has become the foremost icon of Western music. At turns approximating a whole orchestra or inspiring a composer's most intimate confessions, no other instrument has proved as versatile or as influential.

Meaning "soft and loud" in Italian, instrument-maker Bartolomeo Cristofori's *pianoforte* brought a new subtlety to keyboard instruments in the early 18th century. Relatively easy and intuitive to learn, and offering as wide a range of notes as an orchestra, a piano became an important symbol of status.

Composing for this domestic environment was lucrative, and there was soon a steady stream of sonatas, variations, and fantasias. Further possibilities opened up in the 1780s when English piano-maker John Broadwood produced a model with a far broader and longer-lasting sound. It was played by both Beethoven and Chopin.

In the Romantic age, virtuoso performers such as Liszt (see p.160) gave the piano a new role as a solo concert instrument. Now fortified with iron and offering such a variety of tone, pianists could astonish their audiences with piano recitals. Meanwhile, with the popularity of the upright piano, domestic music continued to thrive, catapulting composers such as Chopin, Robert Schumann, and Grieg to international fame.

By the 20th century, the piano had embraced ragtime and jazz, while the most experimental composers, including Bartok, Schoenberg, and Busoni, used it to test out the newest musical ideas. Further developments included the prepared piano. From 1940 onward, composers such as John Cage wrote works for pianos with metal and rubber items between the strings in order to create new, percussive sound worlds.

THREE–QUARTER VIEW

Internal strength
Until the advent of the one-piece cast iron frame, metal bracing such as this allowed greater string tension, which led to improved tuning stability and greater volume and sustaining power.

Keyboard
As early pianos had lighter, shallower, and narrower keys than modern instruments, students were encouraged to practice with coins balanced on the backs of their hands in order to acquire suitably gentle hand movements.

TECHNOLOGY

ENGLISH PIANO ACTION

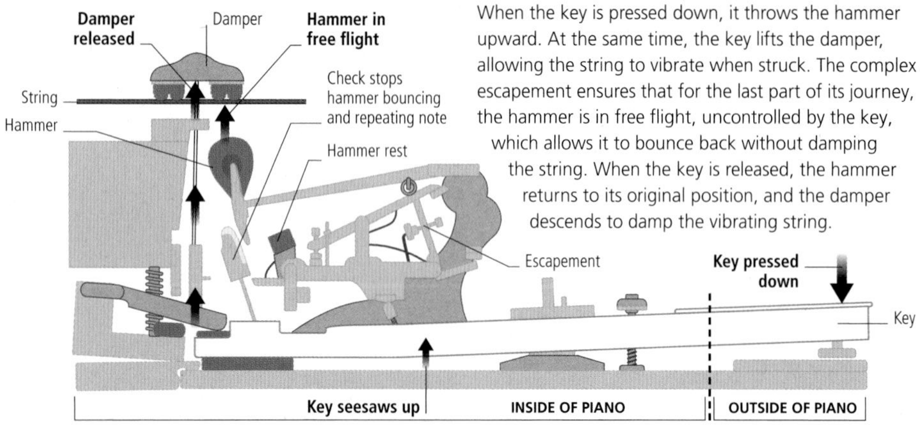

Damper released
Damper
Hammer in free flight
String
Hammer
Check stops hammer bouncing and repeating note
Hammer rest
Escapement
Key pressed down
Key
Key seesaws up
INSIDE OF PIANO
OUTSIDE OF PIANO

When the key is pressed down, it throws the hammer upward. At the same time, the key lifts the damper, allowing the string to vibrate when struck. The complex escapement ensures that for the last part of its journey, the hammer is in free flight, uncontrolled by the key, which allows it to bounce back without damping the string. When the key is released, the hammer returns to its original position, and the damper descends to damp the vibrating string.

TIMELINE

16th century
Harpsichord
Plucking the strings with uniform force, the harpsichord provided a penetrating but quickly decaying and somewhat monotonous sound. Solo works exist for the instrument, but it was commonly used as an accompaniment.

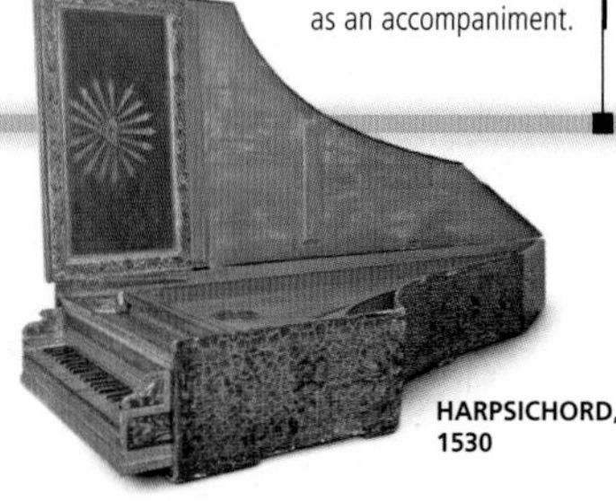
HARPSICHORD, 1530

SQUARE PIANO

1700
Cristofori piano
The first mention of the piano is in a Medici family inventory dated 1700. An extraordinary invention by Bartolomeo Cristofori, the piano spread slowly. It was expensive and not as loud as the harpsichord.

1767 PIANO WITH CRISTOFORI ACTION

18th century
Square piano
The equivalent of the modern upright piano, from the 1760s onward, the cheaper and more conveniently shaped square piano fueled the boom in home music making, sometimes doubling as a dining room table.

18th century
Beethoven
Unlike many of his contemporaries, Beethoven never owned a harpsichord. He explored the capabilities of the new piano, literally pushing them to breaking point.

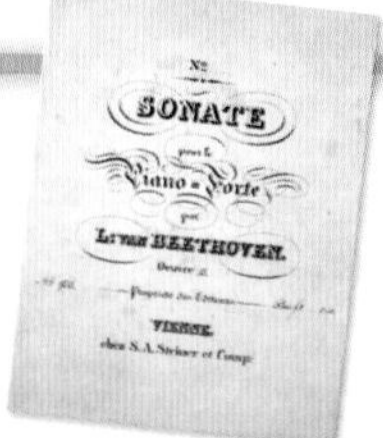
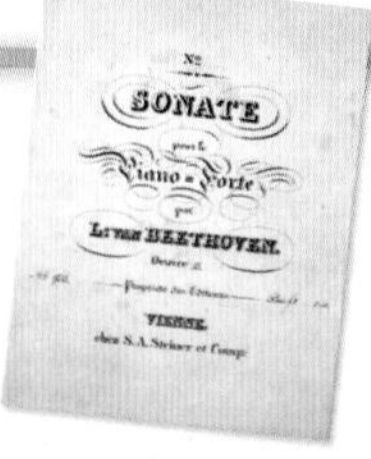

BEETHOVEN PIANO SONATA OP.13

1828
Early grand piano
Early examples of grand pianos included metal bracing to allow for increased string tension and sonority, but by modern standards, the sound was still quite thin and died far more quickly.

Early 19th century
Chopin
Writing extensively for the piano as a solo instrument, Chopin broadened the repertoire with technically demanding sonatas and works inspired by folk dances.

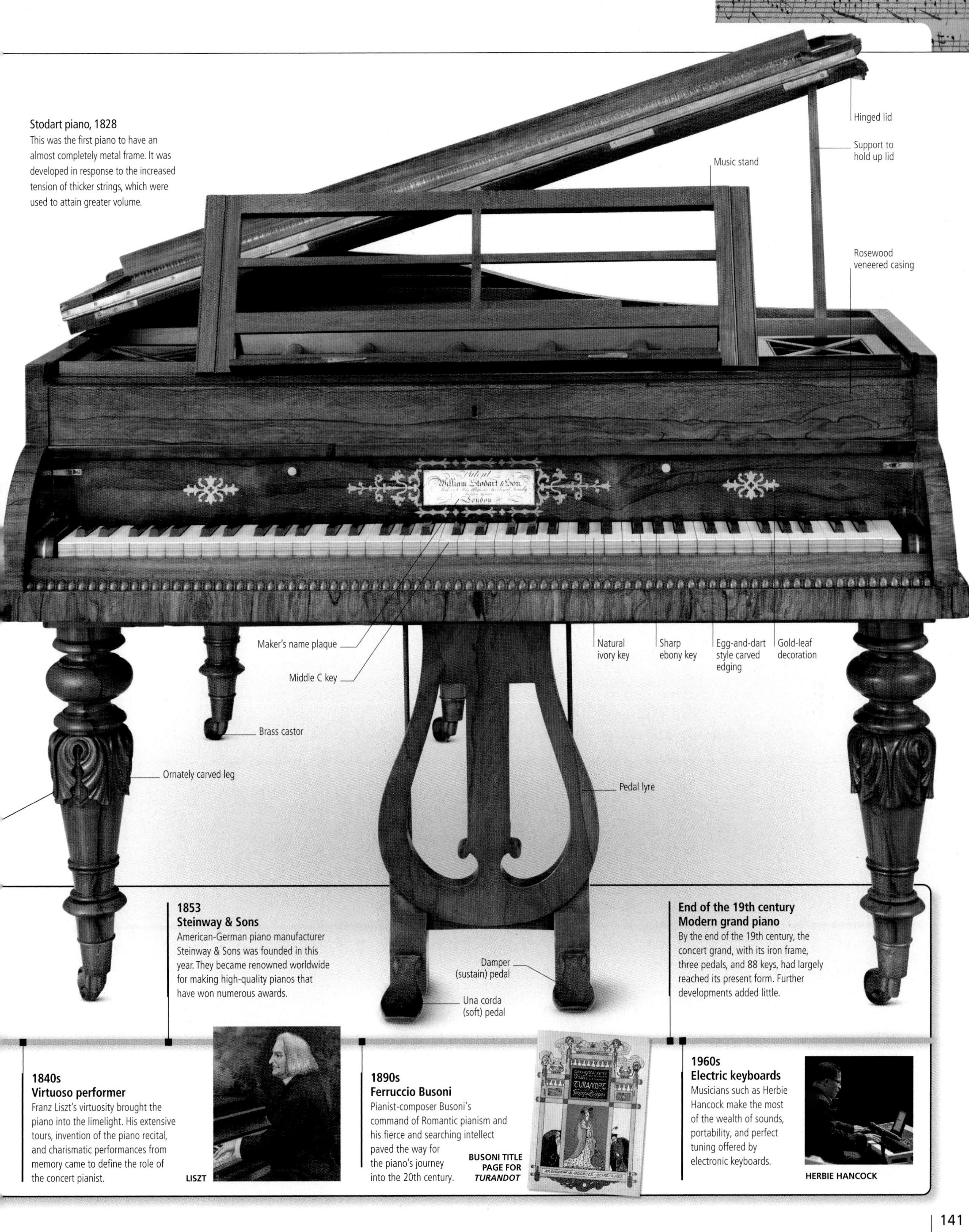

Stodart piano, 1828

This was the first piano to have an almost completely metal frame. It was developed in response to the increased tension of thicker strings, which were used to attain greater volume.

1853
Steinway & Sons

American-German piano manufacturer Steinway & Sons was founded in this year. They became renowned worldwide for making high-quality pianos that have won numerous awards.

End of the 19th century
Modern grand piano

By the end of the 19th century, the concert grand, with its iron frame, three pedals, and 88 keys, had largely reached its present form. Further developments added little.

1840s
Virtuoso performer

Franz Liszt's virtuosity brought the piano into the limelight. His extensive tours, invention of the piano recital, and charismatic performances from memory came to define the role of the concert pianist.

LISZT

1890s
Ferruccio Busoni

Pianist-composer Busoni's command of Romantic pianism and his fierce and searching intellect paved the way for the piano's journey into the 20th century.

BUSONI TITLE PAGE FOR *TURANDOT*

1960s
Electric keyboards

Musicians such as Herbie Hancock make the most of the wealth of sounds, portability, and perfect tuning offered by electronic keyboards.

HERBIE HANCOCK

COMPOSER Born 1770 Died 1827

Ludwig van Beethoven

"I came near to **ending my own life**—only **art held** me **back....**"

BEETHOVEN ON HIS DEAFNESS, IN A LETTER TO HIS BROTHERS, 1802

Beethoven's titanic talent transformed our understanding of music forever. An individual who cared little for conformity, he believed himself to be a "Tondichter"—a poet in sound. He epitomized the Romantic artist for whom the expression of emotions was more important than the observation of traditional structures. His musical voice speaks as persuasively to listeners today as it did during his lifetime.

Court musician

Born into a musical family in Bonn, Germany, Beethoven followed his father and grandfather into court service by becoming assistant court organist at the age of 11. The following year he became harpsichordist to the court orchestra and began composing his first works, including three sonatas, one concerto, and some short pieces, of which "Für Elise" is the best known.

Wanting to escape provincial Bonn, Beethoven went to Vienna in 1729, where his performances delighted audiences, who were astonished by his extraordinary improvisation skills.

Building on his success as a performer, Beethoven began writing numerous piano works: the first three of his five piano concertos, and piano sonatas. Despite Beethoven's brief period of study with Haydn, these early sonatas are more in the spirit of Muzio Clementi (1752–1832), with showy pianistic writing and thicker

Romanticism personified
A towering giant in Western music, Beethoven linked the dying embers of Classicism with the dawn of a new, expressive Romanticism.

KEY WORKS

- Piano Sonata in C Minor, "Pathétique," Op. 13
- Violin Sonata in F, "Spring," Op. 24
- Piano Concerto No. 5 in E flat, "Emperor," Op. 73
- Violin Concerto in D, Op. 61
- *Fidelio*, Op. 72
- Symphony No. 9 in D, "Choral," Op. 125
- *Missa Solemnis* (Mass in D), Op. 123

Pastoral marathon
A sketch for Beethoven's Sixth Symphony, the *Pastoral*. This groundbreaking piece of descriptive music was first performed in Vienna in 1808, in a concert lasting over four hours.

harmonies. Later sonatas from the early period include the masterpieces "Moonlight" and "Pathétique," both of which show Beethoven's distinctively personal musical voice developing.

The chamber music of the 1790s included string trios and quartets. Building on the approach of Haydn and Mozart, Beethoven began to imbue his chamber music with a new symphonic grandeur. This was to become increasingly evident as the years went by, especially in the string quartets, which are regarded as his most intense and personal works.

Deafness strikes

In 1802, the deafness that overshadowed Beethoven's life became profoundly troubling, signaling the end of his public performances. Taking a break in the village of Heiligenstadt, he wrote a statement to his brothers in which he described his affliction as "an infirmity in the one sense which ought to be more perfect in me than in others."

Overcoming depression, however, he returned to Vienna determined to "seize fate by the throat" and embarked on a period of creativity inspired by ideas of heroism. Symphony No. 3, "Eroica," was inspired by Napoleon, whom he admired. Its scale is grand—50 minutes—and it displays new developments in structure and instrumentation. The Fifth "Emperor" Concerto and the Fifth Symphony share the "Eroica's" sense of nobility. The Fifth Symphony was used as a "Victory" anthem by the Allied Forces in World War II, the four-note rhythm of its opening motive representing "V" in Morse code.

Fluctuating fortunes

As he approached 40, Beethoven's interest in heroic themes waned. The devaluation of the Austrian currency in 1811 caused him financial uncertainty, while unsuccessful love affairs left him introspective.

In spite of these personal difficulties, his new symphonies and his only opera, *Fidelio*, which premiered in 1805, were triumphantly received. By the time of the Congress of Vienna in 1814, Beethoven was the toast of the city.

The arrival in Vienna of the Italian operatic composer Rossini changed all this. Beethoven suddenly fell from favor, and he became eccentric and uncommunicative.

New creativity

Miraculously, his indomitable spirit again triumphed over adversity. In his last years, he concentrated on chamber music, producing string quartets and piano sonatas of exceptional dramatic intensity. The late quartets written in the last two years of his life, especially the "Grosse Fuge," Op. 133, first performed in 1826, are regarded as the most concentrated and deeply personal statements of all his output.

Beethoven returned to his interest in heroism, in his magnificent Ninth, the "Choral" Symphony, this time with a more compassionate spirit.

Taken as a whole, Beethoven's body of work represents the greatest evidence of man's triumph over adversity. Repeatedly recovering his spirit after periods of despair, he communicated the most profound human emotions, conveying a sense of consolation to all who listen. The portrait of Beethoven as a withdrawn individual is only partly true, and almost certainly the result of deafness. A deeply religious man, he also enjoyed company, had a sense of humor, and was kind to friends, although his relationships with women tended to be turbulent.

> "[His] **tirades** were explosions of his **fanciful imagination.**"
>
> FRIEDRICH ROCHLITZ, GERMAN WRITER AND MUSIC CRITIC, 1822

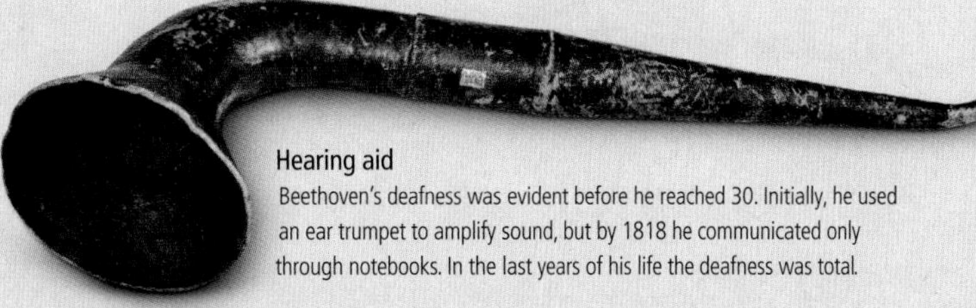

Hearing aid
Beethoven's deafness was evident before he reached 30. Initially, he used an ear trumpet to amplify sound, but by 1818 he communicated only through notebooks. In the last years of his life the deafness was total.

Beethoven's death, from edema and pneumonia in 1827, was widely mourned. The funeral was magnificent. Franz Schubert, a particular admirer of Beethoven, was among the torch bearers, and more than 10,000 people lined Vienna's streets to witness the procession.

Single opera
The Theater an der Wien in Vienna was the setting for the premiere of Beethoven's only opera, *Fidelio*, in 1805. This watercolor of the theater dates from 1825.

TIMELINE

- **1770** Born in Bonn, capital of the Electorate of Cologne.
- **1781** Appointed assistant court organist. Takes lessons in organ and violin.
- **1782** Becomes harpsichordist to court orchestra.
- **1783** Composes *Three Piano Sonatas*.
- **1787** Visits Vienna briefly, possibly to study with Mozart. He returns to Bonn within two weeks, greatly distressed when his mother becomes sick and dies.
- **1790** Composes cantata on the death of Emperor Joseph II. This material is reused later in his only opera, *Fidelio*.
- **1792** Father dies. Moves back to Vienna to study with Haydn.
- **1794** Lessons with Haydn cease.
- **1795** Writes Piano Trios, Op. 1. Gives first public concerts in Vienna, performing Piano Concerto No. 1.

PLAQUE OF BEETHOVEN IN PRAGUE

- **1796** Visits Prague to give several public concerts.
- **1798** Completes the "Pathétique" piano sonata.
- **1800** Symphony No. 1 and Septet in E flat are performed in Vienna. Composes Piano Concerto No. 3.
- **1801** Publishes "Moonlight" Sonata.
- **1802** Failing hearing causes severe depression. Writes the "Heiligestadt Testament," a letter to his brothers Carl and Johann. Composes Symphony No. 2 and "Kreutzer" Violin Sonata.
- **1804** Finishes Symphony No. 3, "Eroica"; writes "Waldstein" Piano Sonata.
- **1805** Composes "Appassionata" Piano Sonata; opera *Fidelio* premiered.
- **1806** Completes Violin Concerto, Symphony No. 4 and "Razumovsky" String Quartets.
- **1808** Writes Symphonies Nos. 5 and 6. Piano Concerto No. 4 and *Choral Fantasy* are premiered together in a four-hour concert.
- **1809** Composes "Emperor" Concerto.
- **1811** Completes "Archduke" Piano Trio.
- **1812** Finishes Symphonies Nos. 7 and 8.
- **1816** Writes song cycle *An die Ferne Geliebte*. On the death of his brother Carl, he obtains custody of his 10-year-old nephew, Karl, resulting in a legal battle with his sister-in-law.
- **1818** Completes "Hammerklavier" sonata.
- **1822** Finishes his last Piano Sonata, No. 32.
- **1823** Completes *Missa Solemnis* (Mass in D) and *Diabelli Variations*.
- **1824** Premiere of Symphony No. 9, "Choral."
- **1826** Completes String Quartet, Op. 130.
- **1827** Dies from edema and pneumonia at his home in Vienna.

Magnet for musicians
Prague has been an important musical center since the 1600s, attracting the finest performers and composers, including Muzio Clementi, Niccolò Paganini, Richard Wagner, and Clara Schumann.

BEFORE

Prague blossomed when it became the seat of the Habsburg court between 1583 and 1611. Although the capital then moved back to Vienna, the city remained a cultural center.

MUSICAL DEVELOPMENTS

Rudolf II (1552–1612), King of Bohemia and Holy Roman Emperor, established an "Imperial Ensemble" in Prague. Here, talented musicians were given education and musical training.

Christian liturgical music with a folk accent was the forerunner of classical music in the Czech lands. Songs by the composer **Adam Michna z Otradovic** (1600–1676) were later transformed into hymn tunes.

The prominent Czech composer, organist, and poet **Jan Dismas Zelenka** (1679–1745) began as a double bass player in Prague. His chamber music, especially the trio sonatas, are showpieces of melodic invention and harmonic daring.

Bohemian Rhapsody

The Kingdom of Bohemia, in today's Czech Republic, produced more than its share of notable musicians during the late 18th and early 19th century. Most of them embraced established German forms, but a few introduced a specifically Czech voice to their music.

Along with Paris and Vienna, Prague was one of the most important capitals on the European music circuit. Eminent musicians came to perform to the city's enthusiastic and well-educated audiences, bringing with them new, enlightened values based on reason, truth, and logic (see pp.130–131). These included interest in the newly established forms of sonata and symphony, a growing affection for Mozartian elegance, and a passion for Italian opera. Bohemian composers occupied themselves by writing music in these fashionable styles.

6 The number of concerts given by Niccolò Paganini on a visit to Prague in December 1828.

The comfortable atmosphere in Prague did little to encourage innovation or experimentation in music. Despite being a renowned center for music research and education, the city proved too staid for some native composers. Many left in search of a more stimulating environment. Thus Prague acquired a reputation as a hub of musical endeavor rather than an exciting incubator of new musical forms. The effect of this was not wholly negative, however. The spread of talent led to the cross-pollination of musical ideas, especially among instrumentalists. In 1800, most European orchestras had at least one player trained in Prague.

Musical backbone

Most of the native composers who chose to stay in Prague had studied in Vienna or Leipzig, Germany, and had embraced the conventions of the Germanic style. They presided over the city's musical life—writing music, giving concerts, and entertaining

CZECH COMPOSER (1737–1781)

JOSEF MYSLIVEČEK

Originally a master miller by trade, the Prague-born Josef Mysliveček studied composition in Venice, with the Italian composer Giovanni Pescetti (1737–1781). Famous for his operas, which featured Bohemian melodic touches, he was a close friend of Mozart. His premiere of *Il Bellerofonte* in 1767 led to commissions from theaters throughout Italy. The Neapolitans adored him, but had difficulty pronouncing his name, referring to him as *Il Divino Boemo* (The Divine Bohemian). However, his celebrity eventually waned, and he died in Rome in1781 after years of near-destitution.

> "Bohemia is the **conservatoire of Europe ...**"
>
> ENGLISH MUSICAL HISTORIAN CHARLES BURNEY, 1771

visiting luminaries. Bohemian-born František Dušek (1731–1799) studied in Vienna before settling in Prague. He composed more than 40 symphonies, piano works, and chamber music in traditional style. He befriended celebrated musicians, including Mozart, who completed his opera *Don Giovanni* at Dušek's country house.

Václav Tomášek (1774–1850) took over Dušek's role as the leading light in Prague and opened a music school in the city in 1824. Europe's musical elite, including composers such as Clara Schumann and Richard Wagner, and violinist Niccolò Paganini, called on Tomášek as they passed through Prague, and their influence is heard in the lyrical style of his piano music.

Mozart's "Prague" Symphony
Prague attracted many visiting musicians, including Mozart, whose Symphony No. 38, known as the "Prague" Symphony, premiered in the city. This score of the work is signed by Mozart (see pp.136–137).

Czech champions

Around 1800, as an interest in national history, culture, and folk traditions began to grow among the Czech-speaking communities in Bohemia and neighboring Moravia, traces of a Czech "voice" began to show in the music of some composers. Jakub Jan Ryba (1765–1815) was a passionate Bohemian composer. Trained in music by his father, he studied organ, cello, and theory in Prague and eventually became a teacher and choirmaster in Rožmitál in rural Bohemia. Ryba was among the first composers to set Czech texts as songs. *Christmas Mass,* his most performed work, has a rustic feel, the organ accompaniment imitating the drone of the bagpipes and hurdy-gurdy of Czech folk music.

In 1817, Ryba wrote a treatise called *The First and General Principles of the Entire Art of Music,* in which he tried to introduce Czech terms into music (Italian was the norm). However, his attempts as a musical modernizer were thwarted by Bohemia's tendency to follow tradition.

Mouthpiece

Musical exports

One of the many Bohemian musicians to leave Prague to pursue an international performing career was Dušek's son, Jan Ladislav (1760–1812). A virtuoso pianist and gifted composer, Jan wrote mainly for the piano, and his later pieces are full of unusual harmonies, runs, and trills. Their virtuosic demands and harmonic freedom anticipated Romanticism, in particular the work of Franz Liszt (see pp.160–161).

Jan was influential both on and off the concert platform. A natural entrepreneur, he settled in London, where he became associated with the piano manufacturer Broadwood, encouraging the firm to extend the range of the keyboard from five octaves to five and a half in 1791, and six in 1794.

Composer Johann Baptist Vanhal (1739–1813) grew up in rural Bohemia, where he took lessons with the village organist. His talent was spotted by Countess Schaffgotsch, who took him to Vienna when he was 22 to study with Austrian composer Carl Ditters von Dittersdorf (1739–1799). Though he never again lived in his homeland, Vanhal shared many of his compatriots' qualities. He had several celebrated musical friends, including Mozart and Haydn, was a formative influence on the development of the symphony and sonata, and included touches of Czech folk melody in his symphonies, chamber music, and piano pieces for the amateur.

One of the most significant Bohemian-born musicians to leave his homeland was violinist and composer Jan Václav Stamic (1717–1757). Trained in Jihalva and Prague, he pursued a solo touring career, before settling at the Court of Mannheim in Germany. Known by the German form of his name, Johann Stamitz, he became central in both the development of the symphony (see pp.124–125) and the establishment of the Court Orchestra (see pp.118–119), the basis of the standard orchestra today.

Folk influences
Jakub Jan Ryba used the "outdoor" sounds of wind instruments to suggest rustic folk music. A bassoon, for example, could be used to imitate the sustained drone of the bagpipe or hurdy-gurdy.

AFTER

Czech music struggled against German and Italian influences, but gained new prominence in the mid-19th century.

NEW BLOOD
František Skroup's 1826 *Singspiel Dratenik* (*The Tinker*), set to a Czech text by Josef Chmelenský, was the first truly **Czech opera**. From the mid-19th century, **Antonín Dvořák 193 ››, Bedřich Smetana, and Leoš Janáček 214–215 ››** brought Czech music center-stage with their symphonies, tone poems, and operas.

MUSIC EDUCATION
Prague remained a musical center, especially for theory, composition, and scholarship. The **Prague Conservatory** opened in 1811 and the **Prague Organ School** in 1830. The institutions were merged in 1890, and Dvorák was appointed to teach composition.

KEY WORKS

Jan Dussek Sonata for piano, Op. 69, No. 3 in D major, "La Chasse" (The Hunt)

Václav Tomášek Concerto for piano and orchestra No. 1 in C major

Jakub Jan Ryba *Christmas Mass*

Josef Mysliveček *L'Olimpiade*

NATIONALISM AND ROMANCE

1820–1910

The French Revolution put individual rights at the forefront of society, which exalted the cult of the Romantic artist. A musical era of extremes, the 19th century found composers creating psychologically charged symphonies and writing concerti that featured an unprecedented virtuosity. The epic music-dramas of Wagner, Verdi, and Strauss made this a golden age of opera.

1820	1830	1840	1850	1860	1870

1821
Carl Maria von Weber's opera *Der Freischütz* (*The Marksman*, or *Freeshooter*) premieres, establishing a German Romantic approach to opera. The opera is an instant success, especially for its depiction of the supernatural.

1824
Premiere of Beethoven's Symphony No. 9. In introducing a choral finale, it challenges the boundaries of the genre for later composers.

1825
Frédéric Chopin composes the first of almost 70 mazurkas, based on Polish folk dances—an early and influential example of musical nationalism.

« Ballerina Marie Taglioni *en pointe*

1827
Franz Schubert meets Beethoven and composes his last song cycle, *Die Winterreise* (The Winter Journey), based on poems by Wilhelm Müller.

1828
Italian violinist Niccolò Paganini's sensational tour of Austria and Germany launches his international career and creates the mold for the traveling virtuoso.

1830
In Paris, the premiere of Hector Berlioz's semi-autobiographical *Symphonie fantastique* introduces the concept of a program symphony that conveys an idea, image, or story.

1831
The tenor Gilbert-Louis Duprez sings a high C in Rossini's opera *Guglielmo Tell* (*William Tell*); this is the first time the high note is sung not in a breathy falsetto register but in the more powerful chest voice.

1832
Marie Taglioni, the first to dance *en pointe*, performs in her father's *La Sylphide* at the Paris Opéra.

1838
The first tenor tuba is invented by Carl Wilhelm Moritz, adding to the orchestra's instrumentation.

« Brass tuba, first patented c.1835–1838

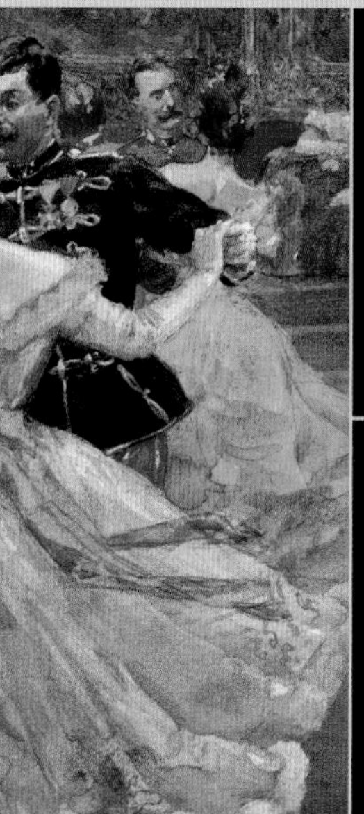

1840
Franz Liszt adopts the word "recital" for his concert at the Hanover Square Rooms, London. He breaks with convention by dispensing with any assisting artists.

1841
Adolphe Adam's *Giselle*, an early classical ballet, is first staged in Paris.

1842
The New York Philharmonic and Vienna Philharmonic orchestras are founded, becoming two of the earliest professional orchestras in the world.

1846
Adolphe Sax invents the saxophone in his quest for an instrument that would offer a middle ground between the brass and woodwind sections of the orchestra.

1848
Revolutions across Europe inspire nationalist themes in music and the rediscovery of folk genres.

1853
The Steinway company is founded, and, through extensive development of patents and numerous prizes at international exhibitions, soon becomes the preeminent piano manufacturer.

« Noted composer and pianist Clara Schumann (1819–1896)

1854
Clara Schumann writes her *Variations on a Theme of Robert Schumann* for her husband's birthday.

1860
Johannes Brahms and Joseph Joachim issue a manifesto against the music of "The New German School," whose leading exponents include Franz Liszt and Richard Wagner.

1865
The first performance of Wagner's opera *Tristan und Isolde* (*Tristan and Isolde*) heralds the emancipation of music from tonality, until then the building blocks of musical structure.

« An imperial ball in Vienna, where Strauss was waltz king

1866
Johann Strauss composes the *Blue Danube Waltz*.

1868
The Joachim Quartet forms. It is one of the first and foremost professional quartets to give public concerts. First performance of Brahms's *German Requiem*.

» Score of Brahms's Alto Rhapsody, 1869

1870
Pianist Anton Rubinstein tours the United States, sponsored by Steinway & Son.

1874
Premiere of Johann Strauss's operetta, *Die Fledermaus*.

1875
Edvard Grieg composes his *Peer Gynt Suite*, incorporating Norwegian folk influences.

« Norwegian folk fiddle

1876
First complete performance of Wagner's *Ring Cycle* at the purpose-built Bayreuth Opera House.

The music of the Romantic era was a continuation of—rather than a rebellion against—the Classical aesthetic of the previous era. Composers extended and reinvented many of the same compositional forms, with some looking to the natural and supernatural worlds for inspiration. Talent and struggle were glorified, creating the idea of the genius composer or virtuoso performer who distilled the extremes of human experience. In an effort to make art music relevant to the ordinary listener, the Romantics created the public concert, program music that tells a story, and opera inspired by realistic themes, and responded to the rise of national fervor across Europe.

1880

1880
Tchaikovsky completes the *1812 Overture* celebrating Russia's defense against Napoleon. It includes "*La Marseillaise*," "God Save the Tsar," and live cannon fire.

1881
Richard D'Oyly Carte builds the Savoy Theatre in London, where, starting with *Patience*, he presents the next ten Gilbert and Sullivan operettas. The premiere of Brahms's Second Piano Concerto introduces a new symphonic approach to the genre.

Russian folk dancing

1882
Bedrich Smetana's symphonic poem *Má Vlast* (My Country), with its overt nationalist themes, establishes a Czech national style without the need for word setting.

1885

1885
Liszt experiments with atonality in his solo piano piece, *Bagatelle Sans Tonalité*, in his quest to "hurl a lance into the future."

1887
The gramophone is patented, enabling artists to transcend time and place and changing forever where and how music is heard.

1888
Nicolay Rimsky-Korsakov writes the *Russian Easter Festival Overture*, inspired by Russian themes. Handel's *Oratorio* is the earliest surviving recording.

Virtuoso pianist and composer Franz Liszt, who died in 1886

1890

Sousaphone, first developed in the 1890s

1890
Tchaikovsky's ballet *Sleeping Beauty* is first performed at the Imperial Mariinsky Theatre in St. Petersburg.

1892
Czech composer Antonín Dvorák moves to New York as director of the National Conservatory of Music, where he researches indigenous music and writes his Ninth Symphony "From the New World."

1893
The premiere of Giuseppe Verdi's final opera, *Falstaff*, takes place at La Scala, in Milan, Italy, to immediate critical and popular acclaim.

1895

1895
The first ever "Promenade" concert is given in the Queen's Hall, London, under the direction of Henry Wood—starting a tradition that continues to the present day.

1896
The premiere of Giacomo's Puccini's opera *La Bohème* establishes the young composer as the successor to Verdi in the Italian opera tradition. John Philip Sousa writes "Stars and Stripes Forever."

1897
Edvard Grieg publishes his Op. 65 *Lyric Pieces*, which includes "Wedding day at Troldhaugen," celebrating his 25th wedding anniversary.

1899
The premiere of Elgar's *Enigma Variations* in London brings him to the attention of a wider public, which will eventually make him the most famous British composer since Henry Purcell.

1900

1900
Puccini's opera *Tosca* opens in Rome. Arturo Toscanini conducts massed orchestras and choirs at Verdi's funeral—Italy's largest-ever public gathering.

Score of Samuel Coleridge-Taylor's cantata *Hiawatha*, c.1900.

1901
Sergey Rachmaninoff gives the first performance of his Piano Concerto No. 2, one of his most popular works.

1902
Italian opera tenor Enrico Caruso makes the first of more than 290 recordings, subsequently becoming the first musician to sustain a career as both a concert and recording artist.

1905

1908
Camille Saint-Saëns becomes the first composer to write a film score, for Henri Lavedan's *The Assassination of the Duke of Guise*.

1909
Richard Strauss's opera *Elektra*, one of the most dissonant works of the late Romantic era, premieres in Dresden, in Germany.

Cartoon of Gustav Mahler conducting his own work

1910
Mahler premieres his Symphony No. 8, "The Symphony of a Thousand." The first radio broadcast of a live performance—from the Metropolitan Opera House, New York, of Mascagni's *Cavalleria Rusticana* and Leoncavallo's *I Pagliacci* with a cast led by Enrico Caruso.

BEFORE

The only true precedent for the expanded size and emotional depth of Beethoven's later works was the example already set by the composer himself.

FORCEFUL YOUTH

A revolutionary figure from the start **<< 142–143**, the rhythmic power and forceful manner of the young Beethoven's musical idiom had quickly outstripped the lighter Classical style of **Haydn** **<< 126–127** and **Mozart** **<< 136–137**.

INSPIRATION FROM THE PAST

In 1801, Beethoven disclosed to a friend in a letter that he was becoming deaf. As his hearing impairment became more complete and his sense of isolation deepened, he increasingly looked to earlier generations for musical inspiration. Beethoven was impressed by the keyboard works of **J.S. Bach** **<< 106–107** and by the large-scale choral music of **Handel** **<< 108–109**. He was also influenced by the spiritual purity of the choral style of **Renaissance** masters, such as **Palestrina** **<< 60–61**.

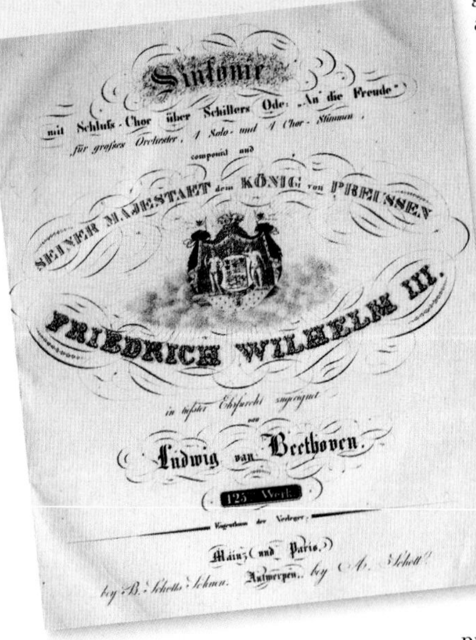

A symphony fit for a king

The first edition of Beethoven's Ninth Symphony, also called the "Choral" Symphony, was published by Schott in Mainz, Germany. It shows Beethoven's dedication to "His Majesty, King of Prussia, Friedrich Wilhelm III."

KEY WORKS

Piano Sonatas: No. 29 in B flat, Op. 106 ("Hammerklavier"); No. 32 in C minor, Op. 111

33 Piano Variations on a Waltz by Anton Diabelli, Op. 120

Missa Solemnis (Mass in D minor), Op. 123

Symphony No. 9 in D ("Choral"), Op. 125

String Quartets: No. 13 in B flat, Op. 130; No. 14 in C sharp minor, Op. 131

Beethoven's Later Works

The music Beethoven had written by his mid-40s would have ensured his place among the greatest of composers, but there was more to come. His later works, combining enormous scale and deep inward calm, surpassed even his earlier masterpieces.

For two years after 1815, Ludwig van Beethoven's legendary creative drive seemed to have stalled. He had family worries: his brother, Carl, dying of tuberculosis, left his only son, Karl, under Beethoven's guardianship, a responsibility he took seriously. Then he himself was very ill with rheumatic fever, taking months to recover. While there were isolated moments when he could hear things, his deafness was now otherwise total, accompanied by screeching tinnitus in both ears. The once outgoing and gregarious composer was trapped in a solitary world of his own, unable to appear in public either as conductor or pianist.

Yet his indomitable spirit found a new sense of direction for his music. In a sustained burst of energy, from 1817–1818 he composed his Piano Sonata No. 29 in B flat, with the subtitle "For the Hammerklavier," the name of the powerful new type of grand piano.

The Imperial and Royal Court Theatre, Vienna

This 19th-century engraving shows the Imperial Theatre near the Kärntnertor (Carinthian Gate) in Vienna, where Beethoven's "Choral" Symphony was first heard.

> "From **the heart**—may it **return to** the heart."
>
> BEETHOVEN'S INSCRIPTION ON THE FRONT PAGE OF HIS "MISSA SOLEMNIS"

The Sonata's monumental four-movement design proclaimed Beethoven's instinct to push musical possibilities to extremes. While the two outer movements are technically more demanding than any yet written, the enormously long, slow third movement opens up a new interior world of quiet and deep musical imagination. A further trilogy of piano sonatas followed. The last of these, No. 32 in C minor (1821–1822), concludes its highly unusual two-movement design with another immense slow movement, in an exploration of serene beauty.

Turkish relation

The *zurna* is an Eastern cousin of the oboe, a standard member of the orchestra in Beethoven's later works. This is a 19th-century Turkish example.

Creative struggle

Beethoven was also wrestling with the two largest symphonic works he had ever composed. The *Missa Solemnis* in D minor was a huge expansion of the traditional setting of the Roman Catholic Mass, whose familiar outlines could nonetheless still be made out. However, the Ninth Symphony was a new idea altogether.

For many years, Beethoven had been preoccupied by the poem "An die Freude" (Ode to Joy) by the German dramatist Friedrich Schiller (1759–1805). The poem's call for all men to become brothers chimed with his own belief in human comradeship and aspiration. He had also been struggling with a new orchestral Symphony in D minor, commissioned by London's Royal Philharmonic Society. Then he began to wonder about crowning the Symphony with, as its finale, a choral setting of "An die Freude."

The problem was how to attach this to the preceding movements so that it would not feel merely bolted on. Beethoven's solution was a masterstroke. The finale's introduction restates each of the main ideas from the first three movements, and the orchestra's cellos and basses punctuate these with new music of their own, imitating voices in a kind of unaccompanied recitation. Then, after the finale's own main tune has been introduced, the baritone soloist enters, taking over the chantlike music that had come before; the chorus gradually joins in, and the transition to a grand choral finale is complete.

Besides the Symphony's groundbreaking interplay of voices and instruments and its unprecedented length (it lasts for well over an hour), it also encompasses a genuinely global

Intensity personified

Like many paintings of Beethoven, this sculpture of him in the Palace of Catalan Music, a concert hall in Barcelona, Spain, captures the composer's high forehead and intense expression of concentration.

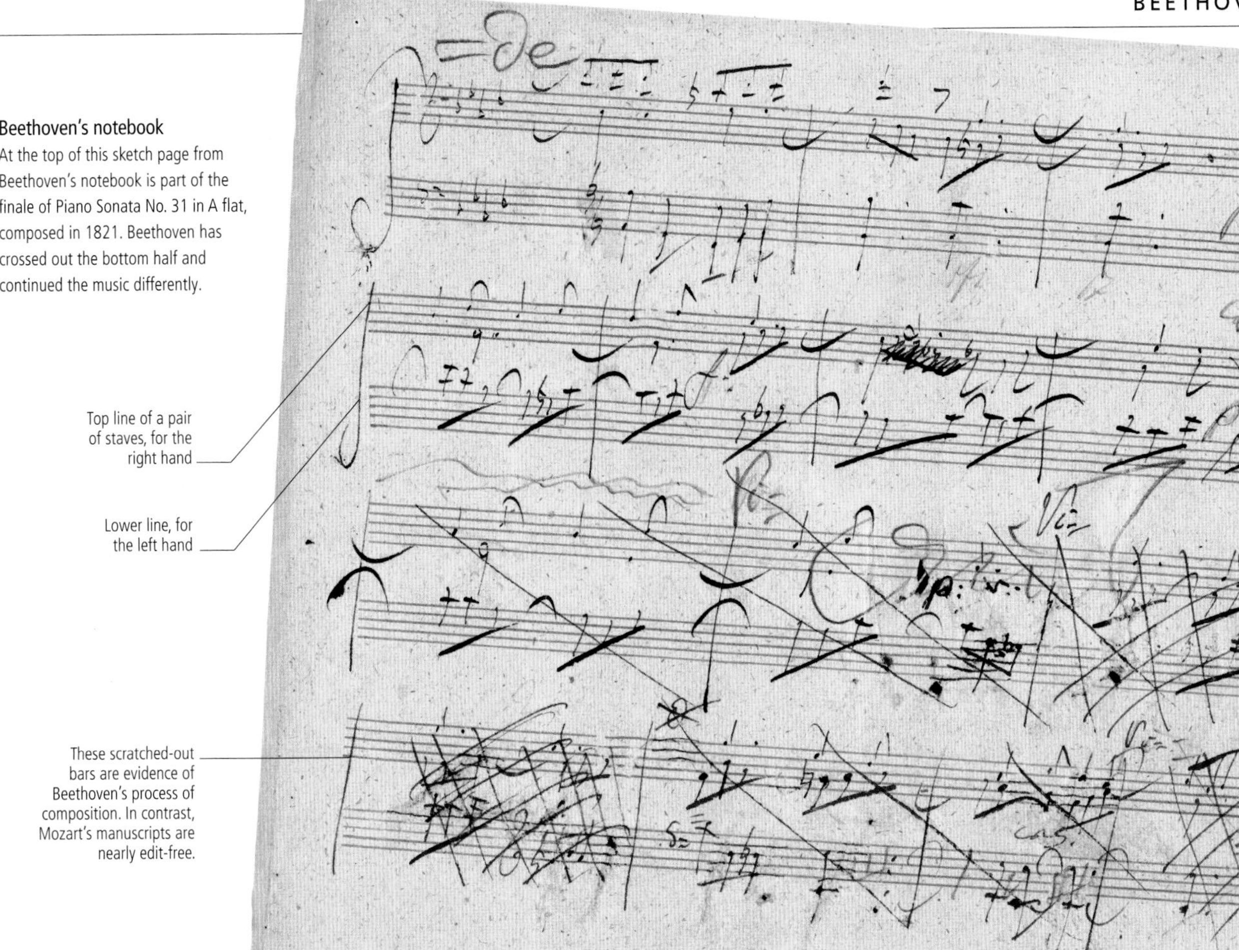
Top line of a pair of staves, for the right hand
Lower line, for the left hand
These scratched-out bars are evidence of Beethoven's process of composition. In contrast, Mozart's manuscripts are nearly edit-free.

Beethoven's notebook
At the top of this sketch page from Beethoven's notebook is part of the finale of Piano Sonata No. 31 in A flat, composed in 1821. Beethoven has crossed out the bottom half and continued the music differently.

cultural vision. The Western orchestra's expanding percussion section had begun to feature exotic Eastern instruments, such as the booming bass drum and clashing cymbals that traditionally accompanied Turkish military bands.

In the finale of the Ninth ("Choral") Symphony, these unusual percussion instruments spur on a jaunty orchestral "Turkish march," symbolizing the joyful, world-embracing progress of collective humanity. The "Choral" Symphony had its tumultuously successful première at Vienna's Imperial and Royal Court Theatre in a concert that also featured sections of Beethoven's *Missa Solemnis*.

Last quartets

Beethoven had a new commission by this time. Prince Nikolas Galitzin of Russia, an admirer of the composer since his own childhood in Vienna, wrote to Beethoven from St. Petersburg. The prince asked for a set of string quartets, and Beethoven's response was an intimately expressive set of compositions for that most harmonious grouping of instruments: two violins, viola, and cello. First came the Quartet No. 12 in E flat, in 1825. It was written on a large scale that was then dwarfed the same year by the evolving design of No. 13 in B flat. This had already extended to five movements, which include a deeply introspective slow adagio, when its finale grew into a *Grosse Fuge* (Great Fugue)—the relentlessness and sheer length of which bewildered audiences.

1824 **The year in which the "Choral" Symphony and *Missa Solemnis* were both first performed.**

Beethoven was persuaded to publish the fugue as a separate work (Op. 133); the shorter finale that replaced it was his last substantial musical statement before his death during a thunderstorm on March 26, 1827. The year before he died, he had also composed the Quartet in C sharp minor, whose seven movements are played in a single continuous sequence—another of his unprecedented achievements.

Wagner and Beethoven
In this 1872 color lithograph by Louis Sauter, Richard Wagner conducts Beethoven's "Choral" Symphony at Margrave's Opera House, in the German town of Bayreuth. Wagner was a huge admirer of Beethoven.

AFTER

The impact of Beethoven's "Choral" Symphony on later generations of composers was immense.

SYMPHONIC LEGACY

The symphonies of **Johannes Brahms** **172–173 »** and **Anton Bruckner** **192–193 »** overtook Beethoven's "Choral" Symphony in length, yet these composers still confined themselves to writing orchestral forms without voices. The first true followers of the "Choral" Symphony were the Second Symphony ("Resurrection") by **Gustav Mahler** **192–193 »**, with its choral finale, and his Eighth, which was choral throughout.

4 **The number of symphonies composed by Brahms.**

9 **The number of symphonies composed by both Bruckner and Mahler.**

For **Richard Wagner** **164–165 »**, the "Choral" heralded his concept of a *Gesamtkunstwerk* (total work of art), bringing together every aspect of music and drama in his operas.

Age of Song

During the Romantic era, song provided an ideal vehicle for expressing profound emotions. Composers set the words of carefully selected poetry to music with increasingly dramatic intensity, and the piano was used to partner the voice, reflecting and enhancing the singer.

Postcard advertising a song theme

Very much the popular music of its day, the imagery from songs found its way on to everyday objects, such as postcards. This one depicts "Death and the Maiden," the title of a Schubert song written in 1817.

BEFORE

Between the Middle Ages and the early 19th century, songs gradually became more complex, with more sophisticated accompaniment.

SONG THROUGH THE CENTURIES

In the **Middle Ages**, wandering musicians **❮❮ 32–33** sang simple melodies accompanying themselves on a stringed instrument. During the **Renaissance**, the lute songs written by **John Dowland ❮❮ 62–63** were highly popular. Around 1600, as **opera** began to evolve, the singer's melody was no longer made up of simple repeated verses and became more complex **❮❮ 80–81**.

By the time of **Mozart ❮❮ 136–137**, the piano usually accompanied the voice, and the music was written out rather than **improvised**. Songs were mostly written in verses or in three sections, at the end of which the opening musical theme was repeated.

BEETHOVEN'S SONG CYCLE

The first hint of the Romanticism in German song occurred in a composition by **Beethoven ❮❮ 142–143**, in a **song cycle** entitled *An die ferne Geliebte* (To the Distant Beloved). Written in 1816, it consists of six songs linked by piano music, which forms a kind of bridge between the songs. The texts conjure up visions of misty hilltops, soft winds, and wistful longing for reunion with the beloved. The piano accompaniment reflects the words, and the assertive return of the opening theme at the end of the cycle provides a satisfyingly optimistic musical conclusion.

Eager to overthrow the rules and limitations of the Classical age, the composers and performers of the Romantic era embraced new musical forms. Among these were German songs, known popularly as *Lieder* (pronounced "leader").

Germany was also home to many great poets who were undergoing their own Romantic rebellion, and their works formed the perfect vehicle for the new style of song writing. The poems of Johann Wolfgang von Goethe (1749–1832) and Friedrich Schiller (1759–1805) were set to song by a number of composers.

Emotional demands

Romantic composers rebelled by using new styles of melody, harmony, and rhythm to portray ever more complex emotions and moods. Alongside simple songs, in which each verse is set to the same tune (like most folk songs or ballads), a new style, the "through-composed" song, emerged. Here, the text was set freely according to the ebb and flow of the poem, rather than being tied to many verses repeating the same melody.

Composers also began to link songs together into a song cycle, based on a group of poems that told a longer, more complex story. By using more than one song, this new form offered composers a way to explore more emotions as the story unfolded. Typically, the poetry and the music rose high in the hope of finding perfect happiness, but the story ended tragically.

Master song writers

Even though so many new options for writing songs were open to composers at the time, the simplest songs could still make a great impact. In 1817, Franz Schubert (see pp.154–155), perhaps the best known of the German *Lieder* composers, wrote "An die Musik" (To Music). This approachable song is in only two verses. In less than three minutes the song tells how music has comforted, sustained, and inspired Schubert in such a way that the listener instantly understands. Some of Schubert's finest song writing is found in his two song cycles—*Die schöne Müllerin* (The Fair Maid of the Mill), in 1823, and *Winterreise* (Winter Journey) from 1827, both based on poetry by Wilhelm Müller (1794–1827). In all, Schubert wrote more than 600 songs, all demonstrating a deep understanding of human emotion and psychology.

An important song composer who came after Schubert was Robert Schumann (1810–1856), an edgy genius who suffered lifelong depression. Schumann took the musical possibilities of Romantic song to a new level. In his songs, the piano is no longer a mere accompanist to the voice but a true partner playing an equal role in expressing the meaning of the words through music. Schumann wrote short piano preludes to set the scene for his songs, and postludes at the end to summarize the mood. He wrote the song cycle *Dichterliebe* (Poet's Love) in 1840, based on a set of 16 poems by Heinrich Heine (1797–1856). The cycle, which he completed in an astonishing nine days, starts off with the elation of a newfound love but then descends into the failure of the relationship and rejection. His setting of Heine's words is heartbreaking and very real, while the piano part is intensely expressive.

> "I am **heartily sick** of the word **'Romanticist' ...**"
>
> ROBERT SCHUMANN, IN A REVIEW OF STEPHEN HELLER'S OP. 7, 1837

Robert and Clara Schumann

In 1840, the year of his long-delayed marriage to pianist and composer Clara Wieck, Robert Schumann composed more than 150 songs—one-third of his total song output.

Home entertainment

Music publishers capitalized on the growing interest in home music-making. As this title page from a 19th-century Lieder suggests, songs were published for families and friends to perform together.

Folk songs and lullabies

Johannes Brahms (see pp.172–173) was a great friend of Clara and Robert Schumann and is regarded as the natural successor to Schubert and Schumann. He wrote more than 260 songs altogether. Although he set texts by Heine and Goethe to music, his preferred medium was the folk song.

One of Brahms's most famous songs *Wiegenlied* (Lullaby or Cradle Song), written in 1868, has the simple charm of a folk song and a lilting melody for rocking a baby to sleep. His two sets of *Liebeslieder* Waltzes (1869), a group of 18 graceful waltzes for four voices and four hands at one piano, are a delightful example of drawing-room music. The texts are translations of folk poetry from Russia, Poland, and Hungary, covering the emotional range from despair to rapture, although the music maintains a folklike quality throughout.

Brahms did write a few lighthearted songs in his career, but most were restrained and serious. As he aged, his songs became slower, with dense piano accompaniments. In 1896,

Music practice
During the Romantic era, the affluent middle classes began to buy pianos and take music lessons. Singing provided both edification for the learner and drawing-room entertainment for family and guests.

the year before he died, Brahms reflected on mortality in his song cycle *Vier ernste Gesänge* (Four Serious Songs). Written for the bass voice and piano, they are settings to words from the Old Testament and St. Paul's 1 Corinthians.

New voice

Hugo Wolf (1860–1903) was born in the Austrian Empire, in what is now Slovenia. He wrote 250 songs, carrying on the Romantic song tradition but using an unusual, almost declamatory style of vocal writing paired with unexpected harmonies. In addition to setting poems of Goethe and Eduard Mörike (1804–1875), he used Spanish and Italian texts in the song books *Spanisches Liederbuch* (1891) and *Italienisches Liederbuch* (1892–1896).

KEY WORKS

Franz Schubert *Die schöne Müllerin* (The Fair Maid of the Mill), D795: An die Musik (To Music), D547; *Winterreise* (Winter Journey), D911

Robert Schumann *Dichterliebe* (Poet's Love), Op. 48

Johannes Brahms "Wiegenlied" (Lullaby), Op 49, No. 4

AFTER

Composers abandoned the piano and voice pairing and began to accompany the voice with the full orchestra.

ORCHESTRA REPLACES THE PIANO

In 1908, **Gustav Mahler** **192–193 ››** wrote a six-movement symphony for voice accompanied by orchestra called *Das Lied von der Erde* (Song of the Earth).

ENDURING POPULARITY

German *Lieder* are recorded by artists and performed in concert halls before large audiences to this day. German baritone **Dietrich Fischer-Dieskau** was one of the great recording artists and interpreters of German *Lieder* of the 20th century.

DIETRICH FISCHER-DIESKAU (1925–2012)

COMPOSER Born 1797 Died 1828

Franz Schubert

"I **compose like a God...** Thank God I **live at last,** and it was high time."

SCHUBERT ON HIS APPOINTMENT AS MUSIC TEACHER TO THE ESTERHÁZY FAMILY, 1818

A supreme melodist and highly productive, Schubert composed transcendently optimistic music in stark contrast to his tragically short, often bleak, life. Dead at the age of 31, he never achieved international recognition in his lifetime.

Modest beginnings

Schubert was born in a poor suburb of Vienna, the son of a school assistant. His father taught him to play the piano and violin, and later the viola, and at the age of 10 Schubert received a scholarship to Vienna's Imperial College (a religious seminary), where his talent blossomed. By the age of 15 Schubert had attempted his first opera and completed a series of string quartets.

After leaving the college, Schubert taught in his father's school, and embarked on a period of intense productivity. During the next three years he wrote five symphonies, four masses, three string quartets, three piano sonatas, six operas, and hundreds of songs. The settings of these songs ranged from simple, folklike tunes such as the setting for Goethe's *Heidenröslein* (Wild Rose) to extended, lyrically expressive lines of the song cycles, especially *Winterreise* (Winter Journey), inspired by 24 poems of Wilhelm Muller.

KEY WORKS

- Piano Sonata in G major, D894
- Piano Trio No. 1 in B flat, D898
- Piano Quintet "Die Forelle" ("Trout"), D667
- String Quartet in D minor ("Death and the Maiden"), D810
- Symphony No. 9 in C major ("Great"), D944
- Song cycle *Winterreise*, D911
- Mass in G major, D167

Prodigious output
Schubert achieved a remarkable amount in his short lifetime. Although primarily known for his songs, he created masterpieces in every major genre except opera.

Romantic interest
Schubert fell in love with Therese Grob, soprano soloist in his F Minor Mass. His precarious financial situation, however, meant he was considered an unsuitable choice of husband, and he never married.

Commissions and patronage

In 1816, Schubert moved into central Vienna to live with his friend Franz von Schober, who was well connected. Life opened up for Schubert, but without the security of a salaried court appointment he was forced to rely on irregular commissions and patronage. Not a great performer, he was unassertive in promoting himself, and avoided the limelight as much as possible. His main income came from the publication of songs and piano pieces.

Above all, Schubert was a songsmith, creating the German *Lied* (art-song), a fusion of words and music that was at the heart of German Romanticism for half a century. Fueled by his emotional life, and inspired by some of the greatest poets of the day—Goethe, Heinrich Heine, Johann Mayrhofer, Friedrich Schiller, and others (see pp.156–157)—Schubert wrote more than 600 *Lieder*.

Poor health and financial worries

The success of his musical life was short-lived and not reflected in his personal circumstances. Financial problems mounted and his health began to fail. A rare public concert in 1821 earned useful money for him, but the following year he noticed signs of venereal disease.

New tranquillity

Nonetheless, from 1823, Schubert entered a new period of creativity. His piano music—solo sonatas, impromptus, *moments musicaux*, dances, and works for four hands (duets), notably the Fantasie in F minor—delights both performer and listener. Schubert made no significant alterations to Classical forms inherited from Joseph Haydn (see pp.126–127), but did introduce a hallmark harmonic device—a temporary shift downward by a major third while retaining a common note—which created an effect of tranquillity.

In all, Schubert produced eight complete symphonies and several others that are unfinished. The "Great" Symphony No. 9 in C major, completed in 1828, is an extended work, Classical in style but Romantic in spirit. Its four-movement structure is familiar, but the large scale of the piece was new at the time, as was its harmonic invention. Lyrical melody prevails, but the rhythmic drive of the fast movements is compelling.

Of the unfinished symphonies, the best known and most complete is No. 8 in B minor. Its opening movement is turbulent in character, with passages of lyrical melancholy interrupted by fierce interjections. The second movement, outwardly serene, has hints of agitation. Only a sketch for the third movement exists.

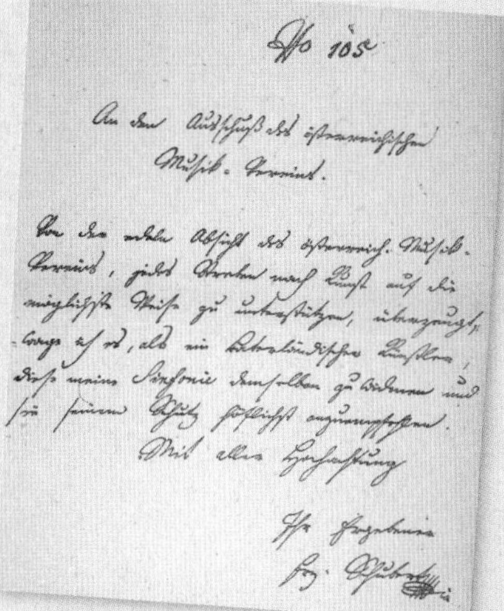

Letter from Schubert
On completing his Symphony No. 9, the "Great," Schubert sent the score with this cover letter to the Austrian Musical Union for their consideration.

The last flourish

In 1828, the last year of his life, Schubert was fervently energetic. He produced several sacred works and a number of masterpieces, including the song "Der Doppelgänger," his last three piano sonatas, and the String Quintet in C. Unlike in his early work, a sense of bleak introspection pervades them all. Confined to bed during the last week of his life, Schubert asked for a string quartet to play Beethoven in his room. Already suffering from syphilis, he was diagnosed with typhoid and fell into a coma, dying on November 19.

Despite his popular songs and enormous output, Schubert was largely uncelebrated during his lifetime. It was left to Schumann, Mendelssohn, Liszt, Brahms, and others to champion his achievements after his death.

"Truly in **Schubert** there dwells a **divine spark.**"

LUDWIG VAN BEETHOVEN, ON HEARING SCHUBERT'S WORKS, FEBRUARY 1827

Source of inspiration
Schubert and friends perform a charade of Adam and Eve and the Fall at a "Schubertiad"—an evening of fun and intellectual stimulation. This close circle of poets, musicians, and radical thinkers was a support and inspiration for Schubert.

TIMELINE

- **1797** Born in Vienna to a school assistant and domestic servant.
- **1802** Begins to study piano and violin with his father and brothers.
- **1808** Receives choral scholarship to the Imperial College, a religious seminary in Vienna. Receives instruction from Antonio Salieri.
- **1812** Composes first string quartets.
- **1813** Completes Symphony No. 1, D82. Trains as a teacher.
- **1814** Writes song "Gretchen am Spinnrade," D118. Also writes Mass in F, D105, to celebrate centenary of Lichtenal parish church, premiered with soprano soloist Therese Grob.
- **1815** Becomes a schoolmaster. Composes Symphonies Nos. 2 and 3, and the song "Erlkonig" (Erl King), D328.
- **1816** Completes Symphony No. 5, D485 and more than 100 songs including "Der Wanderer," D493.
- **1817** Composes songs including "Die Forelle" (The Trout) and "Ganymede." Meets Johann Michael Vogl, renowned baritone at Vienna Court Theater, an admirer of his songs who does much to spread his name. Writes piano sonatas in A minor, D537, and B major, D575.
- **1818** Abandons school teaching and becomes music teacher to the Esterházy family. Overture in C "in the Italian style," his first orchestral work, is performed in Vienna.
- **1819** Spends summer in Steyr. Commissioned to write "Trout" Quintet, D667.
- **1820** *The Twin Brothers*, a *singspiel* (short play with songs) is staged. Writes *Lazarus* oratorio.
- **1822** Writes "Unfinished" Symphony No. 8, D759, and "Wanderer" Fantasy, D760.
- **1823** Forms an influential circle of friends in Vienna. Musical interludes for Helmina von Chezy's *Rosamunde* is warmly received. Composes *Die Schone Mullerin*, D795. Admitted to hospital with syphilis.
- **1825** By now he is known and published in Vienna. Beethoven requests a meeting.
- **1826** Writes String Quartet No. 15 in G, D887.
- **1827** Composes the first part of the song cycle *Winterreise*, D911. In March, he Is a torch bearer at Beethoven's funeral in Vienna.
- **1828** In a year of unprecedented creativity, he completes "Great" C major Symphony No. 9, D944; *Winterreise*, D911; F minor Fantasie for piano four hands, D940; and C major String Quintet, D956. After an extended period of poor health, he dies of typhoid at his home in Vienna on November 19, leaving behind substantial debts.

MEMORIAL IN VIENNA

Literary Links

The composers of the Romantic age used a new and personal voice to express emotion. They were inspired by nature, Classical myths, and medieval legends, as well as works of literature such as Shakespeare's plays and Goethe's and Byron's poems.

BEFORE

Tales from history and Classical myths influenced opera composers of the Baroque period.

LITERATURE AND OPERA
The **Orpheus legend**, in which the musician hero attempts to rescue his beloved Eurydice from the Underworld, inspired works by several composers, beginning with **Claudio Monteverdi**'s *L'Orfeo* in 1607 **« 80–81**. A century later, **Handel** **« 108–109** based his opera *Rinaldo* (1711) on "La Gerusalemme Liberata," an epic poem about the First Crusade by the Italian poet Torquato Tasso.

STURM UND DRANG
The German literary movement **Sturm und Drang** (storm and stress) emerged as a force in music from the 1770s **« 130–31**. It was most ferociously evident in the terrifying final scene of **Don Giovanni** (1787), written by Mozart **« 136–37**, in which the wicked Don, engulfed in smoke and fire, is swept to hell.

Literature was the inspiration behind some of the greatest music written in the 19th century, from settings of the works by the great Romantic poets such as Goethe and Lord Byron to Verdi's *Rigoletto*, based on Victor Hugo's *Le roi s'amuse*.

Setting stories to song

The most common marriage of literature and music was in song. The German *Lieder* became a major art form in the hands of Franz Schubert, Robert Schumann, and Hugo Wolf (see pp.152–153). They set texts by Germany's great poets, including Goethe, Wilhelm Müller, Heinrich Heine, and Joseph von Eichendorff, using the piano part both to color individual words or phrases and to depict the mood of the song.

The fascination of Faust

Goethe's greatest work was *Faust*, a two-part drama interpreting the story of the legendary figure who sold his soul to the devil in return for worldly pleasures and supreme knowledge. The Faust legend was taken up eagerly by composers, including Hector Berlioz (see p.188), who wrote *The Damnation of Faust* (1846), a dramatic work for four soloists, seven-part chorus, and a huge orchestra.

Faust was also the inspiration for Franz Liszt's (see p.160) in his *Faust Symphony* (1857). Rather than telling the whole complex story, Liszt created in each of the three movements a musical portrait of a central character. The first movement, "Faust," is in sonata form, its strong conclusion thought to represent the composer himself. The second movement portrays the gentle Gretchen, the heroine, while the third, "Mephistopheles," takes themes from the first movement and transforms them into diabolical mutations.

Looking to the past

The Romantic Movement also looked back to the past, especially to Classical civilizations and the medieval period. Hector Berlioz wrote his own libretto based on *The Aeneid* by Roman poet Virgil for his five-act grand opera of 1858, *Les Troyens* (The Trojans). Unlike the shallow glamour of Parisian grand opera, *Les Troyens* was distinguished by the depth of characterization conjured in the key roles of Aeneas and Dido.

Dante's legacy
A fascination with the Middle Ages was a feature of Romanticism. *The Divine Comedy* by the Italian poet Dante (1265–1321), depicted here by Luca Signorelli, inspired many Romantic composers, including Liszt.

Byron's narrative poem *Childe Harold's Pilgrimage* is the basis for Berlioz's four-movement symphonic work for orchestra, *Harold in Italy*, written in 1834. A dark-toned solo viola—called "a melancholy dreamer" by the composer—represents Harold himself. The composer's own travels through Italy inspired the work's melodies, colors, and textures. Berlioz believed passionately in the power of music to embody precise images, ideas, and intense feelings.

The English essayist Thomas De Quincey's *Confessions of an English Opium Eater* were the inspiration for Berlioz's *Symphonie Fantastique—Episodes in the Life of an Artist* (1830). Elements of the story are graphically described by the music, such as a waltz in a grand ballroom in the second movement, and mournful shepherd's pipes (English horn and oboe) calling to one another as though across a valley in the third. In the fourth, even the sound of an execution is captured—the guillotined head falls into the basket to the menacing sound of *pizzicato* (plucking) double bass, followed by tumultuous *tutti* (whole orchestra) cheering from the crowd.

> "This marvelous **book fascinated me...** I read it at meals, at theater, in the street."
>
> HECTOR BERLIOZ ON READING GOETHE'S "FAUST," 1828

The descriptive power of music

The financial and amorous excesses of English poet Lord Byron (1788–1824) befitted his image as the epitome of the Romantic poet, and his poems influenced many composers. The supernatural aspect of his poem *Manfred*, about a man tortured by guilt, triggered Schumann's *Manfred: Dramatic Poem in Three Parts* (1852) and Tchaikovsky's *Manfred Symphony* (1885).

UNDERSTANDING MUSIC

THE LIBRETTIST

Many literary works have formed the basis for operas. The texts are not used intact, but adapted by writers called librettists, not least because words take longer to sing than to speak.

Shakespeare's works have given rise to more than 400 plays and countless instrumental pieces, from Schubert's "Who is Sylvia" and "Hark, Hark, the Lark," based on two sonnets, to Mendelssohn's and Britten's *A Midsummer Night's Dream*. Verdi and his librettists Arrrigo Boito and Francesco Piave created narratives centered on a single character, such as in *Macbeth* (1847) and *Otello* (1887), as well as a new story for *Falstaff* (1893) based on the character in *The Merry Wives of Windsor* and *Henry IV*.

Dramatic effects

Berlioz's *Damnation of Faust* uses a huge orchestra. This cover of the score was illustrated in suitably dramatic manner by French artist Georges Fraiponi (1873–1912).

AFTER

Literature continues to inspire popular and classical music today.

POETIC ORIGINS

Stravinsky's opera-oratorio *Oedipus Rex* (1927) **212–213 ››** has text by French poet and dramatist Jean Cocteau (in Latin), based on Sophocles' Greek drama. **Britten**'s opera *Peter Grimes* (1945) **280 ››** was influenced by the work of poet George Crabbe.

BERNSTEIN'S "WEST SIDE STORY"

SHADES OF SHAKESPEARE

Bernstein's musical *West Side Story* (1957) updated *Romeo and Juliet*'s Veronese romance by setting it on New York's Upper West Side in the 1950s **292 ››**. Coupled with Bernstein's score, lyrics by **Stephen Sondheim** **360 ››** perfectly captured the tragic intensity of the original relationship.

Felix Mendelssohn (1809–1847) was skeptical about music's descriptive ability. In a letter to his friend Baroness Pereira in 1831, he criticizes Schubert's "Erlkönig" for imitating "the rustlings of willow trees, the wailing of the child and the galloping of the horse… this kind of thing seems like a joke, like paintings in children's spelling books where the roofs are bright red to make the children realize they are indeed supposed to be roofs."

Despite this view, Mendelssohn was commissioned to write a concert overture based on Victor Hugo's tragic drama *Ruy Blas*, and his interpretation of Shakespeare's *A Midsummer Night's Dream* is one of his best-loved works.

KEY WORKS

Hector Berlioz *Symphonie Fantastique*, Op. 14; *The damnation of Faust*, Op. 24

Felix Mendelssohn *Ruy Blas Concert Overture*, Op. 95; *A Midsummer Night's Dream* incidental music, Op. 61

Franz Liszt Dante Symphony S109; *Faust* Symphony S108

Tchaikovsky *Romeo and Juliet*

Verdi *Macbeth*; *Otello*; *Falstaff*

Chopin at the piano
A pianist who prized refinement, Chopin was welcome at exclusive society gatherings. Pictured here in 1829, he entertains guests in the Salon of Prince Radziwill in Berlin.

BEFORE

A yearning for emotional intensity and self-expression began to produce a new intimacy in music.

MUSICAL EXPLORERS
Beethoven had pushed the Classical piano sonata to its limits **« 150–z151**. His constant quest for new heights of **emotional expression and technical challenge** opened the door for further musical exploration after his death. Meanwhile, the Irish composer and pianist **John Field** (1782–1837) wrote natural, unaffected music for piano. His Nocturnes, with their filigree melodies hovering over delicate, left-hand writing, directly influenced Chopin in his own works of the same name.

THE DEVELOPMENT OF THE SOLO
Schubert's fascination with poetry led him to discover new ways of using the piano expressively in **song settings « 152–153**. This marked the start of an interest in small, perfectly formed musical entities—the solo.

Expressive Piano

The dawn of Romanticism, coupled with improvements in piano manufacture, offered new opportunities for emotional expression and technical brilliance. The compositions of Chopin, Mendelssohn, and Schumann helped propel the piano into the spotlight.

As Romanticism took hold in Europe, interest in the traditional sonata and its rigid form (see pp.102–103) ebbed away. Instead, smaller pieces became popular, suiting the Romantic urge to distill intense emotion or conjure a mood.

Small is beautiful

The piano repertoire of the period includes a cluster of "miniature" genres. Among them were the waltz, impromptu, moment musical, prelude, nocturne, bagatelle, berceuse, fantasia, polonaise, barcarolle, mazurka, tarantella, ballade, scherzo, rhapsody, novelette, and song without words. Popular with piano composers seeking new vehicles for their artistic imagination, they were also favorites with listeners. Larger-scale pieces consisting of several shorter, linked items also found favor in this period, often inspired by literature.

> "Hats off, gentlemen! A **genius.**"
>
> ROBERT SCHUMANN'S REVIEW OF CHOPIN'S VARIATIONS ON "LÀ CI DAREM LA MANO" FROM "DON GIOVANNI" BY MOZART

Fashionable salons

Most piano recitals took place in the private salons of the well-to-do. Musical performances for small groups of guests were a popular form of entertainment, and some composer-performers, including Chopin, found wealthy patrons among the guests at such events.

Waltzes and nocturnes

In many ways, Polish-born Frédéric Chopin (1810–1849)—complex, effete, abandoned by his lover, and, like his German contemporaries Mendelssohn and Schumann, short-lived—epitomizes the modern view of a Romantic-composer-performer. His

music, most of which was composed for the piano, is characterized by delicacy, deeply felt expressive passion, and lyrical melody. Yet the limpid, spontaneous beauty of his music masks a strong grasp of musical structure that gives all his works, however modest in scale, a satisfying completeness.

Chopin's 17 waltzes cover almost the entire range of his genius. The subdued, haunting simplicity of the A minor Waltz, for example, contrasts with the *Grande Valse Brillante* in E flat major, which conjures images of whirling dancers at a ball.

Inspired by the Irish composer John Field, Chopin wrote 20 nocturnes (compositions evocative of the night). Melancholy in mood, most feature a simple legato (sustained) melody in the right hand, floating above a gentle left-hand accompaniment of simple chords or arpeggios (broken chords). In the Nocturne in E flat major Op. 9, No. 2, the exquisite melody is decorated with ornate trills and elaborate runs each time

Frontispiece of Chopin's mazurkas
A traditional Polish dance, the mazurka's triple time is characterized by bouncing rhythms. Mazurkas were hugely popular in 19th-century ballrooms and salons—Chopin wrote more than 50 for the piano.

it returns, reaching a climax of intensity before subsiding into quiet, repeated chords.

Master of harmony

Born into a wealthy and cultivated Jewish family, the composer and pianist Felix Mendelssohn (1809–1847) was less adventurous than Chopin in his use of established musical forms. Preserving the values and forms of the Classical period, he wrote three well crafted sonatas and various keyboard concertos.

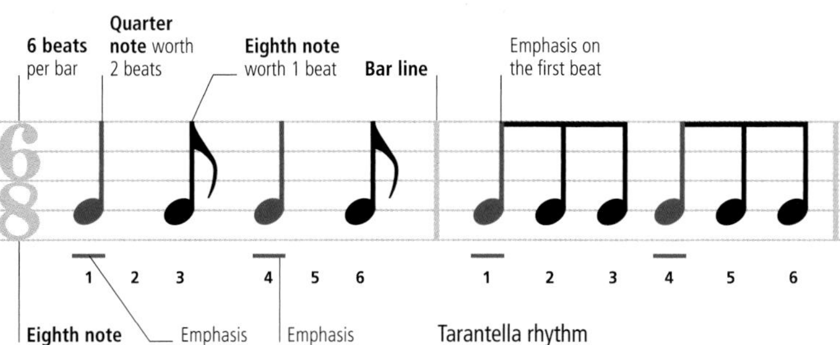

Tarantella rhythm
The fast and furious dance tarantella has two beats each subdivided into three, with the strongest emphasis on the first beat of the bar. Its name derives from the Italian town of Taranto, home to a poisonous spider called the tarantula. It was believed that frenzied dancing of the tarantella could drive out the venom.

The first of Mendelssohn's *Songs without Words* set in E flat major, of 1829, demonstrates the composer's simple, direct appeal. Perhaps his greatest legacy to pianists, it opens with a broken-chord bass in the left hand, over which an attractive right-hand melody gently unfolds. A contrasting middle section, harmonically more adventurous, is followed by a brief flight of fancy—like a tiny cadenza—in the right hand, before a final reprise of the opening section.

Mendelssohn did not ornament his melodies or use harmonies with the freedom or imagination of Chopin, nor did he exploit fully the potential of the newly improved piano or take technique to new heights, but his piano works delighted audiences with their descriptive charm and harmonic sweetness.

Musical explorer

Robert Schumann (1810–1856) composed in all genres, but was at his most inspired when writing for piano and the voice (see p.152). He had a passion for literature, evident in the literary allusions of *Carnaval* and the delicate mood pictures of *Scenes from Childhood* from which the tender "Traumerei" (Dreaming) is the best known. *Papillons* (Butterflies) is a series of pieces depicting a masked ball, a concept inspired by the novel *Flegeljahre* by the German Romantic writer Jean Paul.

Schumann's strength as a piano composer lay less in structure than in mastery of the new possibilities offered by the instrument. He enjoyed exploring musical textures, especially relishing the rich sonorities of the piano's middle register, sometimes neglecting the upper register (which was so brilliantly exploited by Chopin).

Schumann also wrote skillfully for the piano's new sustaining pedal (see pp.140–141), making the piano a well matched partner for the voice and other instruments that can naturally sustain notes. These qualities work well in Schumann's chamber music with strings, such as the Piano Quintet in E flat major, written in 1842, a year of intense creative energy for the composer.

KEY WORKS

Frédéric Chopin Piano Concerto No. 2 in F minor, Op. 21; Waltz in A minor, Op. 34, No. 2

Felix Mendelssohn *Songs without Words* in E flat major, Op.19; *Variations sérieuses*, Op. 4

Robert Schumann *Scenes from Childhood*, Op. 15, No. 7, "Traumerei" (Dreaming); Piano Quintet in E flat major, Op. 44

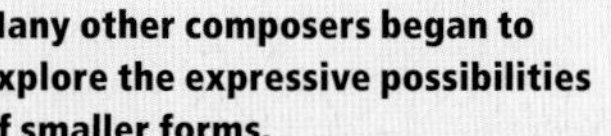

AFTER

Many other composers began to explore the expressive possibilities of smaller forms.

MINIATURE MASTERPIECES
Johannes Brahms's rhapsodies and intermezzi 172–173 ›› echo the new fashion for smaller musical works. Aria arrangements—"songs without words"—were made by **Charles-Valentin Alkan** and **Edvard Grieg 185 ››**, whose *Chants* and *Lyric Pieces* reflect the desire for intense and lyrical emotional expression.

THE UPRIGHT PIANO

MUSIC IN THE HOME
The development of the **upright piano** in the 1780s led to a significant rise in **domestic music 170–171 ››**. Composers and publishers responded to this by producing a range of **teaching and practice materials** for the amateur pianist.

BEFORE

The notion of the musical virtuoso existed as early as the 17th century, but it took on new meaning with Mozart and the advent of opera.

THE DESIRE TO AMAZE

In the 17th century, courts hired the **most accomplished musicians**, often singers, to impress guests on ceremonial occasions. In 1710, the singer Senesino, a favorite of Handel, was offered £2,000, a staggering sum at the time, to sing in London. **Instrumentalists**, too, wanted a share of the limelight. The **violinist Giuseppe Tartini** (1692–1770) was renowned for his exciting performances, not least when playing his famous "Devil's Trill" violin sonata, featuring a fiendishly difficult trill in the final movement.

TOURS AND PUBLIC PERFORMANCE

In the 18th century, Mozart's European concert tours with his father and sister while still a child **« 136–137** promoted his virtuosity widely. But it was the rise of **public concerts**, and **opera** **« 132–133**, that ushered in a more tangible virtuosity.

TARTINI'S VIOLIN AND CASE

The **Virtuosos**

Virtuosity was a natural consequence of the Romantic ideals spreading through Europe in the mid-19th century. With its new emphasis on emotional expression, music began to exist for its own sake, not just to serve a ceremonial purpose, and required brilliant performers to match.

Liszt the showman

Hungarian-born Franz Liszt perfectly captured the Romantic spirit. An astounding pianist and composer, he sometimes assumed a monk's habit while imitating the demon Mephistopheles at the piano.

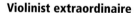

Brilliant performers were elevated to almost godlike status during the 19th century. Instruments were becoming more versatile and powerful, composers were more daring and open-minded, and the public was becoming increasingly musically informed and curious.

The opening of new concert halls brought live music to a wider audience, and it was no longer the preserve of the court or wealthy households. The Industrial Revolution had nurtured a middle class with ambitions, aspirations, and money to spend. They wanted to participate in the pursuits of the privileged, including experiencing the arts.

People were also interested in learning how to make music for themselves and so took lessons. With their new understanding, they could admire accomplishment in others. They craved spectacle and wanted to be amazed.

The first two musical superstars of 19th-century Europe were the violinist Niccolò Paganini (1782–1840) and the pianist Franz Liszt (1811–1886). Composers as well as performers, they delighted audiences throughout Europe with their brilliance.

Violinist extraordinaire

Born into modest circumstances in Genoa, Paganini was taught to play the violin by his martinet father, whose methods were rigorous. The young boy was even deprived of food as a punishment for insufficient practice. Niccolò's prodigious progress took him to Parma to study with the composer and violin virtuoso Alessandro Rolla. On hearing the young Paganini sight-read a manuscript copy of his new violin concerto, Rolla exclaimed: "I can teach you nothing, my boy."

12 The age at which Paganini made his first public appearance.

In 1810, Paganini embarked on a long concert tour of Italy. His phenomenal technique enabled him to play his own music incomparably well. The well-known *Caprices* for unaccompanied violin feature all Paganini's trademark devices: very high notes, multiple stopping (bowing more than one string at once), multiple trills, double-stopped octave runs, scordatura (changing the tuning of some strings), "ricochet" (bouncing) bowing, left-hand pizzicato (plucking the string), and simultaneous bowing and pizzicato.

Paganini traded upon his demoniac appearance to enhance his reputation as a virtuoso. The calculated iciness of his music, which relies on technical bravura for its effect, is worlds apart from the highly charged outpourings of his peers. Although he was a philanderer and gambler (he invested in the Casino Paganini in Paris, which ultimately failed), he amassed a substantial fortune. When he died in 1840, he left 22 immensely valuable stringed instruments by the esteemed makers Stradivari, Amati, and Guarneri.

The brilliant pianist

Franz Liszt is regarded as one of the most sensational pianists in history, as well as one of music's most complex figures. Like Mozart, he had an ambitious father who exploited his son's gift. In 1823, the family moved from Vienna to Paris, where Liszt gave 38 recitals in three months, a schedule that was typical for the young Liszt over the next four years.

Although lucrative, the tours organized by his father eventually exhausted Liszt, causing his health to break down. At the age of 15, and after his father's death, he retreated from the public gaze and started to teach.

Liszt was inspired to return to the platform after hearing Paganini perform in 1831. Astonished by the violinist's extreme virtuosity and bizarre demeanor, Liszt created his own showman's persona, delighting audiences by playing a variety of pieces from memory, including his own elaborate arrangements and fantasies. He was the first pianist to lift the lid of his instrument on stage and sit sideways to his audience.

The touring resumed and, alongside his celebrity performing career, Liszt

> "My **great rule** in art is **complete** unity in diversity …"
>
> PAGANINI TO HIS BIOGRAPHER JULIUS MAX SCHOTTKY

Showcase for Paganini

Nicolò Paganini's triumphant debut at La Scala, Milan, in 1813 included his *Le Streghe* (Witches' Dance), confirming his supreme virtuosity. La Scala remains one of the world's finest musical venues.

A master at work
Violinist and composer Niccolò Paganini, whose cadaverous and sinister appearance is captured in this caricature, made virtuosity an acceptable element in music.

AFTER

Following the triumphs of Paganini and Liszt, a wave of new performers attracted the label "virtuoso."

MASTER INSTRUMENTALISTS

The violin was a natural vehicle for musical pyrotechnics, and **Pablo de Sarasate**, **Henryk Wieniawski**, and **Joseph Joachim** were the top violin virtuosos in the late 19th century. They were followed by **Fritz Kreisler** and **Jascha Heifetz** in the 20th century. The brilliance of pianists **Ignaz Moscheles**, **Anton Rubinstein**, and **Vladimir Horowitz** influenced the piano repertoire for the next generation.

VOCAL VIRTUOSOS

Twentieth-century singers such as **Enrico Caruso** continued the concept of the **vocal virtuoso** promoted in the 19th century by Jenny Lind, Adelina Patti, Nellie Melba, and Fyodor Chaliapin. Virtuosity still exists but has to some extent been eclipsed by media-led celebrity.

composed prolifically. Idiomatic and thrilling piano writing came naturally, whether in original works such as the Sonata in B minor, or in taxing transcriptions and fantasies on popular operatic tunes. Features of these works include rapid octaves, wide spread chords, multiple trills, and ferociously fast passages for both hands—technical aspects that amaze audiences and challenge performers to their limits.

Cult status

Liszt's private life was as colorful as his platform presence. He eloped with a married woman in 1835 and had amorous alliances, but this proved no barrier to him achieving cult status. His fame was celebrated in "Lisztomania," a term coined by the poet Heinrich Heine in 1844 to describe Liszt's impact on the Paris music scene.

Despite this, Liszt provoked criticism throughout his life. Some disliked his exhibitionism, while others found incongruity in his nationalism, Roman Catholicism (he was ordained as an abbot in 1865), and his relationships with women. He eventually became a depressive alcoholic and died of pneumonia in 1886.

KEY WORKS

Niccolò Paganini Caprices for unaccompanied violin, Op. 1

Franz Liszt *Hungarian Rhapsody* No. 2 in C sharp minor; Piano Sonata in B minor

Pablo Sarasate *Zigeunerweisen,* Op. 20

Henryk Wieniawski *Scherzo-Tarantelle*, Op. 16

BEFORE

In the early 19th century, everything about choral music had started to expand—including the size of choirs and orchestras, and the dimensions of the works composed for them.

GRAND FRENCH CHORAL WORKS

France had a long-standing tradition of commissioning grand choral works for special occasions. The 1816 Requiem setting by **Luigi Cherubini** **« 134–135,** composed for a service in memory of King Louis XVI, was much admired by Beethoven, who considered the Italian-born, French-resident composer the greatest of his contemporaries.

UNPRECEDENTED DEMANDS

The impulse toward large-scale choral music was spurred on by **Beethoven** **« 150–151**, in his 1824 Choral Symphony and *Missa Solemnis*. Both works were unprecedented in their length and in the technical demands they made on choirs. The mood of heightened and sustained emotional intensity in Beethoven's writing for voices was to be eagerly taken up by the next generation of composers.

Baritone voice part (Elijah)

Condensed sketch of orchestral music

Alteration to sketch

Separator between grouped lines of music

Note for orchestral phrasing

Bracket grouping lines of music together

Mendelssohn's *Elijah*

This page shows the musical line to be sung by the baritone soloist in the role of Elijah. The orchestral part is not fully written out but only sketched in below because Mendelssohn left full orchestration until later.

COMPOSER (1824–1896)

ANTON BRUCKNER

Bruckner was born in the village of Ansfelden, near Linz, in Austria. Before the age of 40, he never traveled more than 25 miles (40 km) away. He began as a schoolteacher, but became one of the greatest composers of his time.

Bruckner was the organist at the monastery of St. Florian before moving to Vienna, where his music's extreme originality combined with his diffident nature to limit his success. He finished the first three movements of his colossal Ninth Symphony by 1894, but died before completing the finale.

Sacred Choruses

More than any other classical genre, large-scale choral music embodied the 19th century's spirit of Romantic grandeur. Performed before audiences of ever-growing size, sacred choral works increasingly reflected the confidence of the newly prosperous urban scene.

For classical music, 19th-century Romanticism was about expansion into new areas of psychological intensity and dramatic effect, using much enlarged forms.

In France, Hector Berlioz (see pp.156–157) wrote choral music on a grand scale and, in 1837, he was commissioned to write a Latin Requiem setting. The new work, entitled *Grande messe des morts* (Great Mass of the Dead), was performed in the magnificent basilica of the Dôme des Invalides in Paris. Berlioz assembled a much enlarged chorus of more than 400 voices and an orchestra that included a battery of massed timpani (tuned kettle drums), and four extra brass ensembles distributed around the interior of the basilica. However, the thunderous effect of the biggest moments was cannily offset by many quiet passages—Berlioz knew that soft sounds carry through an enormous church acoustic as vividly as loud ones.

High drama and gentle intimacy

In his 1874 *Messa da Requiem*, Italy's Giuseppe Verdi (see pp.164–165) completed one of the greatest of all Requiem settings. Verdi's music brings the high drama of his operatic style into a sacred choral work, and while the chorus and orchestra are not as large as those demanded by Berlioz, their combined effect is equally thrilling.

The approach of French composer Gabriel Fauré (1845–1924) to setting

> "The Requiem text was a **prey** that I had long **coveted.**"
>
> BERLIOZ IN HIS MEMOIRS, 1865

a Requiem was the polar opposite of Verdi and Berlioz. He showed that a choral Requiem could also convey a more private world of feeling. The chorus and orchestra for his setting are small, and the tone of the music is quiet and songlike. "Someone has called my Requiem 'a lullaby of death,'" Fauré remarked later. "But that is how I see death: as a welcome deliverance, an aspiration toward happiness above."

When Johannes Brahms (see pp.172–173) wrote *Ein Deutsches Requiem* (A German Requiem) in 1865–1868, he based his libretto on the Lutheran Bible in German rather than following the traditional Latin text of the Roman Catholic Requiem Mass. The work, while sacred, is not actually liturgical.

Rise of the choral society

Brahms was an experienced conductor of a kind of amateur choral society that had risen across Northern Europe. This trend reflected how society itself was changing, and with it classical music. In previous centuries, sacred music had been the preserve of the Church and royalty, with a central command structure to match. Now, the growth of an industrialized society gave an educated middle class the wealth and leisure to pursue its own artistic interests, as amateur musicians and as a paying audience. In the new concert halls that were built to mark civic success, choral music flourished.

In England, the amateur choral tradition took off in spectacular style during Queen Victoria's reign (1837–1901), with the rise of the large-scale oratorio. An English appreciation of German culture contributed to eager demand for the music of Felix Mendelssohn (1809–1847). His 1846 oratorio *Elijah* was commissioned by the Birmingham Festival, and Mendelssohn himself conducted its successful premiere.

When England produced a great native-born composer in Edward Elgar (1857–1934), he found a full-fledged choral tradition ready for his music. His largest work, *The Dream of Gerontius*, was first performed in 1900 and is considered a masterpiece. Fellow Briton Ralph Vaughan Williams (1872–1958), scored his breakthrough success with *Toward the Unknown Region* (1906), followed by *A Sea Symphony* in 1910. Both works opened up new possibilities for English choral music by setting the words of American poet Walt Whitman (1819–1892).

230 The chorus size required by Berlioz in his Requiem. A note in the score states: "If space permits, the chorus may be doubled or tripled, and the orchestra proportionally increased."

European epics

In mainland Europe, the Roman Catholic tradition of choral music was thriving. In Austria, the genius of Anton Bruckner (see opposite) flowered in the first of his three great Mass settings (1864–1868). In these works, he found a way to express his deep Catholic faith through powerful harmonic expression. He also wrote a number of unaccompanied choral motets, and made settings of the Te Deum (1884) and Psalm 150 (1892).

Another Roman Catholic composer was Hungary's Franz Liszt (see p.160). A serene and devotional tone dominates his two large-scale choral oratorios, *St. Elisabeth* (1862), based on the life of Hungary's national saint, and *Christus* (1866), an enormous three-part story of the life of Christ.

Berlioz conducting "Tuba Mirum"
French painter Henri Fantin-Latour (1836–1904) dramatically depicts Berlioz conducting the "Tuba Mirum" from his *Grande messe des morts* (Great Mass of the Dead), encircled by trumpet-playing angels.

Cathedral of sound
Built by King Louis XIV for French army veterans, the Dôme des Invalides in Paris, with its enormous interior space and massive acoustic, was the scene of the 1837 première of Berlioz's Requiem *Grande messe des morts*.

KEY WORKS

Hector Berlioz *Grande messe des morts*; Te Deum

Felix Mendelssohn *Elijah*

Johannes Brahms *Ein deutsches Requiem*

Anton Bruckner Masses in E minor and F minor; Te Deum

Giuseppe Verdi *Messa da Requiem*

Gabriel Fauré Requiem in D minor Op. 48

AFTER

Composers writing oratorios in the 20th century drew on a range of new influences.

NEW INSPIRATION

In England, **William Walton** (1902–1983) brought the **jazz age 234–235 »** into his 1931 oratorio, *Belshazzar's Feast*. **Michael Tippett** (1905–1998) incorporated American spirituals **294–295 »** into his 1942 pacifist oratorio *A Child of Our Time*. For his *War Requiem* in 1962, **Benjamin Britten 280–281 »** combined the Requiem liturgy in Latin with World War I poetry by Wilfred Owen.

COVER OF THE SCORE OF "BELSHAZZAR'S FEAST"

In France, the 1948 Requiem by Maurice Duruflé (1902–1986), was inspired by Fauré's setting and plainchant. **Olivier Messiaen 270–271 »** combined advanced modernism with the Berlioz-led tradition of choral music on a huge scale in his *La Transfiguration de Nôtre-Seigneur Jésus-Christ* (1969).

BEFORE

Near the end of the 18th century, as unrest and revolution swept across Europe, the artistic response started what was called the Romantic era.

A NEW CAST OF CHARACTERS

In the Romantic era, composers looked for fresh material and new ways to express themselves. In opera, characters from antiquity and **Classical mythology** **« 20–21** gave way to more contemporary heroic figures, from wronged, innocent peasant girls to supernatural characters.

LONGING FOR LIBERTY AND FREEDOM

The chief precursor of the Romantic movement in opera was **Beethoven** **« 142–143**, in his three-act opera, *Fidelio*. Its was premiered in Vienna in 1805. The story and music embody the spirit of longing for liberty and freedom in the face of oppression that was to become a key characteristics of Romantic opera.

Romantic Opera

Certain elements characterize Romantic opera: a fascination with the beauty of nature, the power of evil, and the supernatural; patriotism and the desire for liberty; an admiration for rural simplicity; and the development of the *bel canto* (beautiful) singing style.

The first opera to feature most of these characteristics, and seen as the founding work of this movement, was *Der Freischütz* (The Freeshooter, but the opera is also sometimes called The Magic Marksman) by German composer Carl Maria von Weber (1786–1826). His music conjured up the dark German forests, and he used folk tunes and hunting horns to provide color.

Exotic settings are a constant in Romantic opera. In 1819, Italy's Gioachino Rossini (1792–1868) wrote *La donna del lago* (The Lady of the Lake). The heroine, Elena, makes her first appearance while crossing a Scottish loch by boat. The heroine of the 1831 opera *Norma* by Vincenzo Bellini (1801–1835) is a druid priestess, in Roman Gaul while *La sonnambula* (*The Sleepwalker*), written the same year, is set in the Swiss Alps. The action of Bellini's 1835 opera *I Puritani* (*The Puritans*) takes place in the England of the Civil War (1642–1651). These settings were considered highly exotic, and had rarely been visited by the composers.

Inspirational landscape
The Romantic Movement sought inspiration in dramatic landscapes and the distant past, qualities encapsulated by Eilean Donan Castle on Loch Duich, one of the most photographed views in Scotland.

Literary sources reflected the same interest in far-flung places, with the novels and narrative poems of Sir Walter Scott providing rich material. Gaetano Donizetti (1797–1848) loosely based his opera *Lucia di Lammermoor* (*Lucy of Lammermoor*) on Scott's historical novel, *The Bride of Lammermoor*.

The German Heinrich Marschner (1795–1861) evoked the supernatural, as Weber had done, in his 1828 opera *Der Vampyr* (*The Vampire*). However, the macabre plot was mocked mercilessly in London, in 1887, by Gilbert and Sullivan in their operetta *Ruddigore* (see p.195).

The 1831 opera *Robert le diable* (*Robert the Devil*) by Giacomo Meyerbeer (1791–1864) features a hero who is drawn towards evil by the mysterious Bertram (his own father) and narrowly avoids eternal damnation.

While there were differences in style and subject matter between Romantic operas in Germany, France, and Italy, some composers crossed national lines. Meyerbeer, a German, had his greatest successes with operas written to French texts for the Paris Opéra.

> "Operas must **make people weep**, feel horrified, **die** through **singing.**"
>
> ITALIAN COMPOSER VINCENZO BELLINI'S EDICT ON OPERA

Meyerbeer's creations were told on a grand scale, played out against sweeping historical canvases. His 1836 opera *Les Huguenots*, for example, culminates in 1572 in the St Bartholomew's Day Massacre.

Bellini, Rossini, and Donizetti, followed for the next 50 years by Giuseppe Verdi (1813–1901), are the chief representatives of the Italian vein of Romanticism, while Wagner led the way in Germany.

Exquisite singing in extremis

Bellini and Donizetti created female characters pushed to extremes caused by their situations. In the title role of

1831 theater poster for *La Sonnambula*
This poster depicts the soprano Giuditta Pasta as Amina and tenor Gian Battista Rubini, as Elvino, advertising a production of Bellini's opera *La sonnambula* at the Teatro Carcano, in Milan, Italy.

Bellini's opera of the same name, Norma kills her own children in revenge for being betrayed by her lover. Lucy, the heroine of Donizetti's *Lucia di Lammermoor* is driven insane by being forced into marriage.

Technically skilled, exquisite singing was required to depict insanity and hysteria, along with ever more agile soprano and tenor voices possessing a plangent, consciously beautiful quality designed specifically to play upon the emotions of the listener. The Italian soprano Giuditta Pasta (1797–1865) was the first to sing the title roles in *Norma* and *La sonnambula,* while the Swedish soprano Jenny Lind (see pp.166–167) was greatly admired by Queen Victoria and was famous throughout Europe and North America. The French tenor Adolphe Nourrit (1802–1839) was the first Robert in *Robert le diable* and Raoul in *Les Huguenots.* Such singers attracted huge followings and earned considerable amounts of money. Their interpretations were considered definitive and were inordinately admired, or loathed, by rival fans.

LA VALKYRIE
POÈME ET MUSIQUE DE
RICHARD WAGNER
PARIS: P. SCHOTT & Cie, 70, Rue du Faubourg St Honoré

Wagner's Valkyrie
In this 1893 color lithograph, Eugene Grasset (1841–1917) depicts the final act of Wagner's *Die Walküre* (The Valkyrie). Brünnhilde, a warrior maiden, is put into an enchanted sleep by her father, the god Wotan. She will be awoken by the kiss of Siegfried in the next opera of Wagner's epic *Der Ring des Nibelungen* (The Ring Cycle)—a series of four monumental operas retelling Norse legends.

Peak of Romantic opera

Though they never met, Verdi and Wagner (see below) were actively composing at the same time; Wagner wrote his first opera, *Die Feen* (*The Fairies*), in 1833, and Verdi wrote his first opera, *Oberto,* in 1839.

Wagner brought German Romantic opera to its ultimate form in the same way Verdi had for Italian Romantic opera. Wagner, one of the towering figures of the 19th century, wrote voluptuous yet mystical Romantic operas. His only significant works are those for the theater, and few could imitate his genius for creating colors in his powerful orchestrations.

For Wagner, the music served the drama, and he wrote all of the librettos of his operas (although not the stories), himself. Staying in the Romantic mainstream, his 1843 opera, *Der fliegende Holländer* (*The Flying Dutchman*), is based on the legend of a man doomed to sail the world until he finds a woman who will give up everything to love him. His three-act opera *Lohengrin* (1850) retells a medieval legend of the son of Parsifal (who also inspired an eponymous opera), and is considered the last important German Romantic opera.

Lohengrin points the way to developments in Wagner's next period. His orchestration, for example, is more dense and somber than his previous operas, with less noticeable divisions between separate musical numbers. This foreshadows his compositional system of writing continuous music, also called endless melody. In the vocal line, the music is written in free-flowing melody, rather than staying with the formula of balanced, symmetrical phrases that were heard in the Classical era (see pp.116–17).

To hold this free-flowing music and drama together, Wagner used the *leitmotif* (a short, concentrated musical theme) to acts as a kind of musical label for an idea, a person, place, or thing in the drama. The *leitmotif* is played at the first appearance or mention of an object, place, or person, and whenever it reappears, is mentioned, or has an influence on the drama, even when it may be unseen.

Wagner also developed the theory of *Gesamtkunstwerk,* which translates loosely as "universal artwork." In his theory, opera is a meaningful work of drama, and the text, stage setting, acting, and music must all work together closely as a single all-encompassing unit to serve the central dramatic purpose of the opera.

Verdi wrote 26 operas and never abandoned the past or tried out radical new theories. His goal was to refine Italian Romantic opera to perfection. An aspect of the Romantic ideal most associated with Verdi is his sense of patriotism. Many of his early operas contain choruses that some interpret as being barely disguised appeals to Italians to resist foreign domination. However, he firmly believed every nation should foster its own native music and keep to its independent style. He deplored any foreign influence being exerted on young Italian composers. This meant that while composers in Germany romanticized the natural world and built their operas around mythology and legends, Verdi was resolutely unsentimental about it. Nature was there to make use of, not adore.

Verdi's interest was in humanity. He saw opera's ultimate role as portraying the human drama, telling the story using a simple, direct solo line, rather than using the lush orchestral and choral indulgences of French grand opera. Except for that of *Falstaff* (1893), most of his opera plots are serious, and many take their inspiration from works by Romantic authors.

COMPOSER (1813–1883)

WILHELM RICHARD WAGNER

Born into a theatrical family in Leipzig, Wagner began composing while working part-time as chorusmaster in Würzburg, and he published his first operas at his own expense. It was not until 1864, when King Ludwig II of Bavaria recognized Wagner's unique artistic vision and settled his debts, that the composer knew financial stability—he had previously relocated on several occasions to avoid his creditors.

After a difficult marriage to the actress Wilhelmine Planer, he married Cosima Liszt (daughter of Franz Liszt) in 1870. With Cosima, he founded the Bayreuth Festival, which continues to perform his operas on a yearly basis.

KEY WORKS

Carl Maria von Weber *Der Freischütz*
Vincenzo Bellini *La sonnambula; Norma*
Gaetano Donizetti *Lucia di Lammermoor*
Richard Wagner *Der Fliegende Hollander*
Giuseppe Verdi *Falstaff*
Donizetti *Luci*

AFTER

Wagner continued to fascinate composers in the late 19th century, who struggled not to imitate him.

GERMAN FAIRY-TALE OPERA
In late 19th-century Germany, there was a revival in the *Märchenoper* (fairy-tale opera), as seen in the 1893 opera *Hänsel und Gretel* (*Hansel and Gretel*) by Engelbert Humperdinck (1854–1921). He used Wagnerian orchestration and *leitmotifs* blended with folklike music.

POST-ROMANTIC GERMAN OPERA
Richard Strauss **222–223 »** embraced Wagner's theories, while pushing the boundaries of **chromatic harmony** even further. Wagner's styles of continuous music and the systematic use of the *leitmotif* can be heard in Strauss's operas.

TELEVISED SATELLITE CONCERTS
Placido Domingo, José Carreras, and the late Luciano Pavarotti gained huge commercial success singing a Romantic opera repertoire in popular concerts in the 1990s and 2000s.

THE THREE TENORS

BEFORE

Female musical talent had very few opportunities for expression before the 19th century.

EARLY PIONEERS
German abbess **Hildegard of Bingen** (1098–1179) wrote hymns and liturgical sequences in **plainchant « 30–31**. The cult of the **operatic diva** had its roots in the Italian Renaissance **« 66**.

SALON PERFORMERS
In the 18th century, women began performing in private salons. **Marianne von Martines** (1744–1812), born in Vienna, studied singing, piano, and composition with **Nicola Porpora** and **Joseph Haydn « 126–127**.

HILDEGARD OF BINGEN

Women Composers and Performers

Until the 20th century, women in the music world were mostly known for supporting the musical endeavors of others, as wife, teacher, hostess, or diarist. However, during the Romantic era, a handful of celebrated female composers and performers emerged.

Suppressed by social convention and burdened with domestic responsibility, women rarely became serious musicians. The emerging middle classes prized musical education, but this was limited to the performance of songs or piano pieces for entertainment.

For women with musical ambition, the obstacles to success were immense. Employment, even for male musicians, was hard to find. Court positions dwindled in number in the 19th century, and the Church offered no opportunities for female musicians. Marriage was regarded as a full-time occupation, and, for the unmarried, a life spent in the public eye was considered improper.

Female vocalists

The women who did succeed musically tended to be all-arounders—pianists, singers, and composers. The popularity of salon society in the 19th century offered more opportunities for them. In Paris, mezzo-soprano Pauline Viardot (1821–1910) became a society figure on her marriage to writer Louis Viardot. She made her operatic debut as Desdemona in Verdi's opera *Otello* in London (1839), triumphed in Rossini's *Barber*

Salon soirée
Pauline Viardot's soirées, one of which is depicted in this woodcut, were famous. Attending one of her salons in 1843, the Russian writer Turgenev fell in love with Pauline and went on to join her household.

COMPOSER (1867–1944)

AMY BEACH

One of the first significant American art music composers, Amy Beach was born and raised in New England. Her precocious talent, even as a child, was immediately recognized: she studied piano and made her debut as a professional pianist as a teenager. Two years later, in 1885, she performed with the renowned Boston Symphony Orchestra. Unable to pursue formal composition studies because of her gender, Beach learned the art through self-study. After her marriage, she performed less often and focused on composition instead, publishing her works under her married name, Mrs. H.H.A. Beach. Her oeuvre spans all genres common in the 19th century, from large-scale concert works to intimate character pieces.

of Seville in Russia (1843), and premiered the role of Fidès in Meyerbeer's opera *Le prophète* (1849). Also a composer, she wrote operas and songs to texts by Russian writer Ivan Turgenev and made vocal transcriptions of Chopin's mazurkas.

Soprano Jenny Lind (1820–1887), known as the Swedish Nightingale (see p.167) hit the headlines in 1838 with her performance in the opera *Der Freischütz* by German composer Carl Maria von Weber. She enjoyed commercial success, and in 1850 the American showman Phineas Taylor Barnum invited her to tour the US, where she gave 93 concerts.

$350,000 The sum earned by Jenny Lind on her 1850 tour of the US.

Family talents

A comparison of brother and sister Felix and Fanny Mendelssohn (1805–1847) illustrates the limitations experienced by women musicians. Both were talented pianists and received similar training, but their father was keen to suppress his daughter's ambition.

Fanny rarely performed in public, apart from in a few family salon concerts in Berlin, but she wrote more than 500 works, including around 120 pieces for piano, chamber music, *Lieder* (songs), and oratorios.

Her family initially prevented her from publishing her works, so six of her songs were first published under her brother's name. Many of her compositions remained in manuscript. When a small number finally reached print, *Die neue Zeitschrift*, a music magazine cofounded by Robert Schumann, expressed surprise that they were by a woman. Fanny Mendelssohn's piano pieces are occasionally heard in recitals today.

Clara Wieck (1819–1896; see pp. 168–169), the wife of Robert Schumann, was one of the few female instrumentalists widely celebrated in her own time.

Scholar-composer

One of the first women to achieve prominence as a scholar-composer was Louise Farrenc (1804–1875). She studied at the Paris Conservatoire and was later appointed professor of piano there, at age 38. A century before interest in early music began in earnest, Farrenc firmly established her scholarly credentials by publishing the 24-volume *Trésor des Pianistes*, an annotated collection of keyboard music of the three preceding centuries.

Her marriage to the music publisher Aristide Farrenc made her reputation as it ensured publication of her compositions. Her work includes piano pieces and large-scale works that were admired by Hector Berlioz for their sparkling orchestration.

"As far as **art is concerned**, you are **man enough.**"

VIOLINIST JOSEPH JOACHIM TO CLARA SCHUMANN, 1870

KEY WORKS

Louise Farrenc Symphony in C minor, Op. 32; Nonet in E flat, Op. 38

Fanny Mendelssohn Piano Trio, Op. 11

Clara Schumann Piano Concerto in A minor, Op. 7

Ethel Smyth *The Wreckers*

Amy Beach Piano Concerto, Op. 45; Symphony in E minor, "Gaelic"

AFTER

Several successful female composers emerged in Europe and the US in the first half of the 20th century.

SUCCESS STORIES

In Britain, **Dame Ethel Smyth** (1858–1944) premiered her opera *The Wreckers* in 1906. In France, **Lili Boulanger** (1893–1918) and her sister **Nadia Boulanger** (1887–1979) were influential composers as well as teachers to Philip Glass, Virgil Thomson, and Astor Piazzolla.

In the US, notable composers included **Amy Beach** (1867–1944), who produced large-scale art music, and modernist **Ruth Crawford Seeger** (1901–1953).

NADIA BOULANGER

Travel journal

In 1839, Fanny Mendelssohn embarked on a concert tour of Italy. She copied pieces of music into her travel journal, and her husband, the artist Wilhelm Hansen, illustrated them and added the title vignette at the top.

COMPOSER Born 1819 Died 1896

Clara Wieck Schumann

"What a **sublime feeling** to pursue art so that one gives **one's life** for it."

CLARA SCHUMANN

Clara Wieck Schumann was born in Leipzig, Germany, in 1819, the daughter of musical parents. Her mother, an accomplished pianist and singer, was ill-suited to her father, Friedrich Wieck, a well-known piano teacher. The couple separated while Clara was quite young, and despite her mother's objections, she was raised almost entirely by her father.

The young Clara received her early piano training from her father, but other music instruction—in violin, counterpoint, fugue, orchestration, and harmony—was provided by various other teachers.

Long duet

Clara and Robert Schumann were united by their musical talents, but they also had eight children together, and even kept a joint marriage diary.

Early career

Schumann's first public performance was in Leipzig's Gewandhaus at nine years old. At 11, she gave her first solo performance there, which included a work of her own composition. Around this time, she first met the man who would one day become her husband, Robert Schumann. A student of Wieck, he lived briefly in the family home.

Prodigious talent

Clara's skills as a young pianist led Paganini to predict that she had a great future before her and would put many great musicians in the shade.

Handwritten score
In addition to performing and composing herself, Clara helped her husband in his work. This is her handwritten score for *Variation for Pianoforte on a Theme* by Robert Schumann.

The 1830s were an incredibly productive time for Schumann. In addition to becoming well known as a concert pianist, she began composing and publishing more of her music, beginning with a set of Polonaises, her Opus 1. Other prominent compositions such as her Piano Concerto in A minor and Scherzo, Op. 10, are also products of this fruitful time.

Composer, performer, teacher

In 1840, Clara married Robert Schumann after overcoming legal obstructions placed in the way by her father. During their marriage, which lasted until Robert's death in 1856, she continued to compose, perform, and teach. Her performing repertoire gradually changed from virtuosic technical showpieces to works by Chopin, her husband, and those of earlier composers, such as Schubert, Beethoven, and Johann Sebastian Bach. Later in her career, she changed course again and focused on piano works and Lieder—German songs with piano accompaniment.

While her husband supported her compositional career, it always came second to his own; her practice time was chosen when it would not be an inconvenience to him. Because Robert had injured his finger and could no longer perform, Clara regularly premiered his works.

Robert did not enjoy traveling, but in the early 1840s, he accompanied Clara on a financially successful tour of Russia. Following their return, his mental health deteriorated, and they relocated to Dresden, where she supported the family financially. Their time in Dresden was cut short by the May Uprising of 1849, causing the family to flee to Düsseldorf; her most important chamber work, the Piano Trio, Op. 17 for piano, violin, and cello, dates from the Dresden years.

Robert's health continued to decline, and the final years of his life were spent in an asylum. After his death at the age of 46, Clara, though still a young woman at 37, ceased composing altogether but remained active as a performer and teacher. She worked tirelessly to promote her husband's music, and edited his works.

In 1878, she became the first woman to teach at the Hoch Conservatory of Music in Frankfurt. She remained active as both a performer and teacher until the 1890s.

Late life and legacy

Clara's compositions primarily comprise solo piano works and Lieder, with texts by German poets such as Friedrich Rückhardt and Heinrich Heine. Her private life was also full, with eight children and many close friendships with prominent singers and composers. Of particular note are her friendships with Hungarian violinist Joseph Joachim and composer Johannes Brahms, who helped her extensively after Robert's death.

Clara herself died in 1896, at the age of 76, following a stroke. Interest in her life and music reemerged only in the 1960s, when significant but forgotten achievements of women were rediscovered and celebrated by the feminist movement. Today, Clara Schumann is probably the most recognizable female composer in Western art music history.

KEY WORKS

Piano Concerto in A minor
Piano Trio in G minor
Scherzo in D minor (piano solo)

Clara's grand Stein
In 1828, Clara gave her first concert on this piano by André Stein, which was specially commissioned by her father.

TIMELINE

- **1819** Born in Leipzig, Germany.
- **1828** Gives her first public performance, at age nine.
- **1831** Publishes Op.1, four Polonaises for solo piano.
- **1832** Performs in Paris.
- **1833–1835** Composes Piano Concerto in A minor.
- **1838** Gives a concert tour in Vienna. *Souvenir de Vienna* and *Scherzo* are published.
- **1840** Marries Robert Schumann.
- **1841** The Schumanns' first child, Marie, is born.
- **1843** Performs in St. Petersburg and Moscow; daughter Elise is born.
- **1844** Family relocates to Dresden.
- **1845** Daughter Julie is born.
- **1846** Writes Piano Trio in G Minor, Op. 17 for piano, violin, and cello. Son Emil is born.
- **1848** Son Ludwig is born.

CLARA WITH FIVE OF HER CHILDREN

- **1848** Son Ferninand is born.
- **1850** Family relocates to Düsseldorf.
- **1851** Daughter Eugenie is born.
- **1853** Composes her last work, the three Romances for violin and piano, Op. 22.
- **1854** Robert attempts suicide. Son Felix is born.
- **1856** Robert dies.
- **1857** Family moves to Berlin.
- **1867** Gives a concert tour of Scotland and England.
- **1878** Becomes the first woman hired at Hoch Conservatory in Frankfurt.
- **1891** Performing career ends.
- **1896** Dies and is buried with Robert in Bonn.

CLARA SCHUMANN MEMORIAL, BONN

Music in the **Home**

During the 19th century, a rapidly growing middle class had the money, education, and leisure to perform and appreciate music. It became indispensable in the domestic sphere both as a principal form of entertainment and for social advancement.

Technological and industrial advances in the 19th century made instruments cheaper and more compact. This created a demand for music for solo instruments and ensembles that could be performed at home, and it led to an explosion in chamber music works, transcriptions for different instruments, and solo pieces.

BEFORE

Until the emergence of a substantial middle class, the difference between the domestic music-making of the wealthy and the poor remained fixed.

MELODIES AND BALLADS

The **harpsichord**, **lute**, or even a small private **orchestra** provided music for the wealthy; the **fiddle**, the human voice, and perhaps a caged bird was for almost everyone else. Composers wrote for the Church, the court, and the stage. Music sung or played in the home would typically have been **folk melodies** handed down the generations, or popular **ballads** that were known as "**broadsides**," which proliferated between the 16th and 18th centuries.

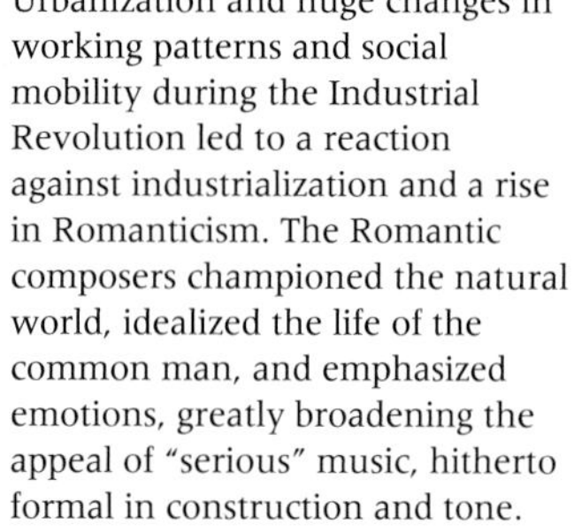

Invitation to a dance

"The Sparkling Polka" by Thomas Baker was published by Horace Waters in New York City in 1850. As well as playing and singing, people also danced at home.

Urbanization and huge changes in working patterns and social mobility during the Industrial Revolution led to a reaction against industrialization and a rise in Romanticism. The Romantic composers championed the natural world, idealized the life of the common man, and emphasized emotions, greatly broadening the appeal of "serious" music, hitherto formal in construction and tone.

More leisure time

At the same time, the rise of a large and wealthy middle class in Europe and the United States saw improved levels of education and increased leisure time. As education led to a greater appreciation of, and interest in, music, musical accomplishment became prized as a way of furthering social aspirations. It was also a source of entertainment during long evenings in the parlor or drawing room.

Methods of mass production enabled a vast proliferation of sheet music, which fed this new hunger for music in the home. This greatly expanded market coincided with the end of the traditional model of aristocratic patronage supporting composers and music-making (see pp.84–85). Lacking the opportunities at princely courts that their 18th-century predecessors had relied on, musicians turned instead to performing solo in public recitals or private parties, further fueling the creation of music for chamber performance.

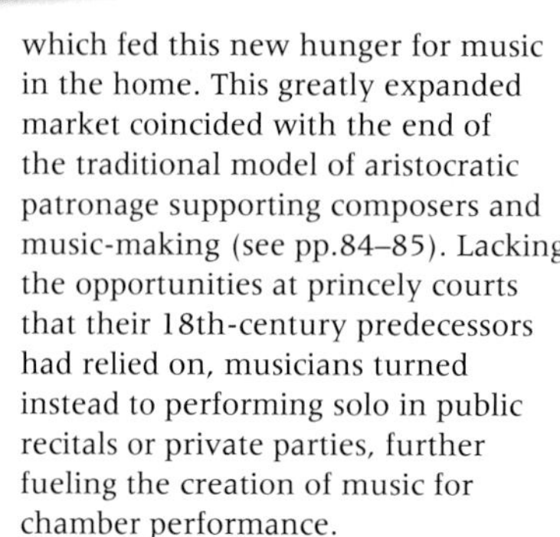

Solo instruments

Proficiency in a musical instrument was an important feature of a well-rounded education, particularly for girls. The range of instruments that were played at home was extensive and included the harp, violin, cello, harmonium, woodwind, and, in the United States, the concertina and banjo. But none was as important or popular as the pianoforte, ideal for solo performance and accompanying other instruments, singers, and dancing.

As cheaper and more compact pianos were developed, suitable even for small rooms, every respectable home had one, and the piano remained a major component of domestic life until well into the 20th century. The proliferation of works for solo piano saw a surge of challenging pieces, with new names coined to describe them: sonatas were joined by nocturnes, polonaises, mazurkas, impromptus, and études. Schubert (see pp.154–155), Chopin (see pp.158–159), and Liszt (see pp.160–161) were preeminent among the composers writing for solo piano. At the same time, duets and pieces for four hands became hugely popular.

With the piano as the principal tool of music-making, transcriptions became the main means of spreading serious music, from arias to oratorios. Liszt raised the art to new levels of sophistication with transcriptions of symphonies by Beethoven and Berlioz

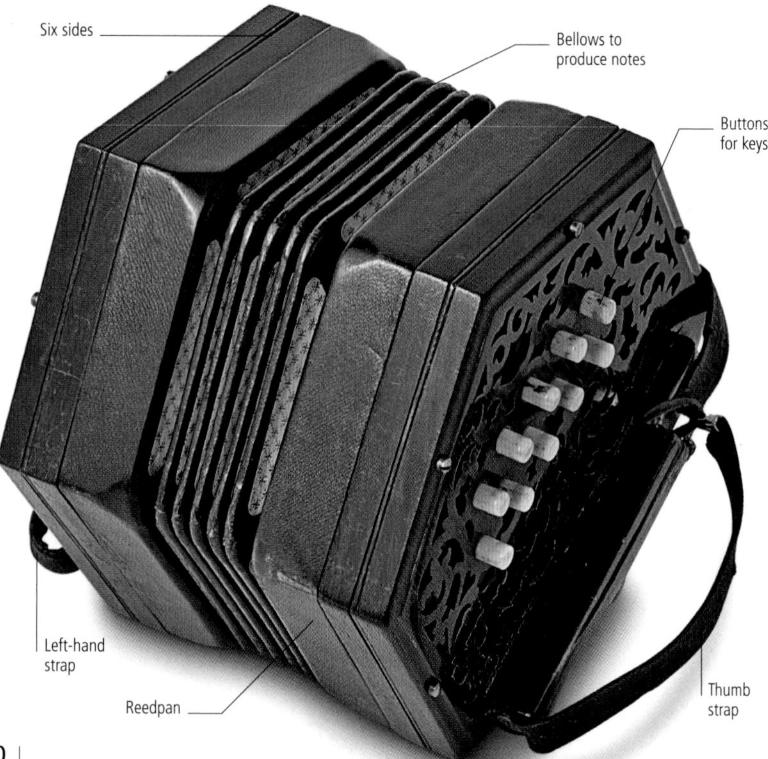

Family favorite

A concertina was a popular home instrument, invented in England and Germany in the 1830s and 1840s. It belongs to the accordion family, but its buttons are pressed individually, rather than as chords.

KEY WORKS

Henry Bishop "Home Sweet Home"
Franz Schubert *Winterreise (Winter Journey)*
Frédéric Chopin *Nocturnes*
Franz Liszt Piano transcription of Berlioz's *Symphonie Fantastique*
Sir Arthur Sullivan "The Lost Chord"
Johannes Brahms *Three Violin Sonatas*
Max Bruch Eight Pieces for clarinet, viola and piano, Op. 83

COMPOSER (1810–1849)

FRÉDÉRIC CHOPIN

Exiled from his native Poland at the age of 21, Chopin moved to Paris. He hated public concerts and largely performed in the salons of the aristocrats, whose daughters he taught for the highest fees in the city. In 1836, he started a relationship with the female novelist George Sand and went on to write his most important works. His health declined rapidly after their separation in 1847, and he died in 1849.

The Victorian parlor
Christmas Carols by the British artist Walter Dendy Sadler (1854–1923) shows an idealized family singing around the piano. Everyone in the family was expected to play an instrument or add their voices to the gatherings.

and highly original variations on operatic scores that popularized the original works. Since small ensembles could be formed in large families or with friends, or engaged to perform at soirées, chamber music was in demand.

The piano was joined by other instruments to form duets or trios. These—with or without piano—were easily managed in the parlor; larger ensembles formed the focus of more formal gatherings.

The new passion for chamber music created an insatiable demand for quartets, and most composers catered to this huge market, even those not usually identified with instrumental music, such as Italian opera composer Gaetano Donizetti (see p.164).

The versatile voice

The Romantic era was a golden age of song, from popular ballads, hymns, and folk songs to sophisticated song cycles and operatic arias. Singing was popular, and "parlor songs," often sentimental and requiring little vocal skill, were published in their thousands. Settings of poems, songs commemorating major events, and the latest hits of music-hall and vaudeville stars were also much in demand.

> "Music washes away from the **soul** the **dust** of everyday life."
>
> GERMAN POET AND AUTHOR BERTHOLD AUERBACH (1812–82)

AFTER

Homemade music was gradually replaced by devices that, with the turn of a handle or the flick of a switch, brought music into the home.

CYLINDER TO DISC

The rise of Thomas Edison's **phonograph** (1877) started to bring outside music into the home. The oldest surviving music recordings are of Handel's choral music, made in 1888 at the Crystal Palace in London. The **gramophone**, with discs recorded on one side, replaced wax cylinders from around the start of the 20th century. For many homes, the sound of an orchestra, or of leading singers, could be heard for the very first time. From the 1920s, radio **260–261 >>** replaced music-making as the main form of home entertainment. At the same time, people increasingly found entertainment outside the home, such as at the cinema.

PORTABLE INSTRUMENTS

The **piano** remained a symbol of respectability and accomplishment in the home, but space and expense made portable instruments such as the **guitar** popular.

GRAMOPHONE

COMPOSER Born 1833 Died 1897

Johannes Brahms

"Someone … destined to give **ideal expression** to **the spirit** of the **times.**"

ROBERT SCHUMANN ON BRAHMS IN "NEUE ZEITSCHRIFT FÜR MUSIK," 1853

Brahms stood at the culmination of a German musical heritage reaching back to Bach and Beethoven. His music blended Romanticism and the Classical tradition in works of intellectual and emotional scope, rich in melody, thrusting and dynamic.

Family encouragement

The second child of a double-bass player who had married a seamstress 17 years his senior, Brahms grew up in modest circumstances in Hamburg. Nonetheless, when Johannes revealed a precocious interest in music, his father placed him with a gifted piano teacher, Friedrich Wilhelm Cossel. Impressed by his pupil's talent, Cossel passed him on to Eduard Marxsen, a composer, pianist, and teacher, who encouraged Brahms to compose as well as play piano. Marxsen instilled in his pupil a reverence for the great works of Beethoven, Mozart, Haydn, and Bach.

Humble birthplace
Brahms spent his infancy in this overcrowded apartment block near the docks in Hamburg. Money was in short supply and his parents struggled to support Brahms and his siblings.

As a teenager, Brahms contributed to the family finances by playing piano in Hamburg's taverns. But he aspired to a higher level of performance, and in 1853 embarked on a concert tour with Eduard Remenyi, a young violinist. It was a turning point in his life.

The Schumanns

Through Remenyi, Brahms met the violinist Joseph Joachim, who enthused over the "originality and power" of Brahms's compositions and introduced him to the pianist and composer Franz Liszt (see p.160). Liszt and Brahms did not get along, but an introduction to the Romantic composer Robert Schumann and his pianist wife, Clara, was more successful (see p.152).

Young Brahms
As a young man, Johannes Brahms impressed people with his physical presence as well as his musical talent. Nonetheless, he did not achieve fame until his mid-30s.

Score of the *Alto Rhapsody*
Composed in 1869, the *Alto Rhapsody* was a wedding gift for Clara Schumann's daughter, Julie. Brahms revised scores repeatedly, in search of perfection.

The Schumanns instantly liked the young man and his music. Robert Schumann published an article entitled "New Paths" in the magazine *Neue Zeitschrift für Musik* (New Journal of Music), describing the 20-year-old Brahms as a "man of destiny."

In 1854, Robert Schumann's fragile mental health collapsed. After a suicide attempt, he was confined to an asylum. Brahms put his career on hold in order to aid Clara in this crisis. After Schumann's death in 1856, Brahms and Clara remained close, but whether any physical relationship occurred is unknown. Loyalty to Clara may have stood in the way of other attachments, such as to Agathe von Siebold, to whom he was briefly engaged.

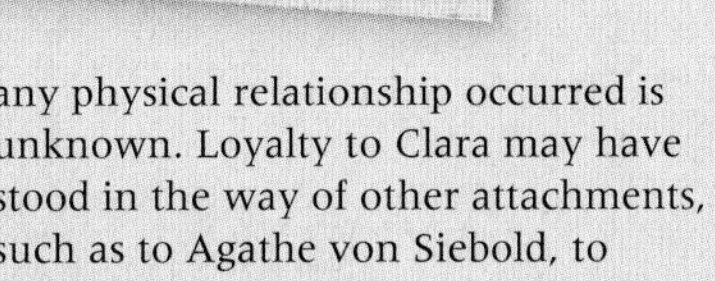

Highs and lows

Between 1857 and 1859, Brahms undertook three seasons as musical director to Count Leopold III. His emotional turmoil during this period was reflected in his First Piano Concerto of 1859. Audience response to its first performances ranged from unenthusiastic to hostile. In 1860, he launched a public attack on the New German school led by Richard Wagner and Franz Liszt. Their espousal of new forms, such as the symphonic poem, offended Brahms and others attached to Classical forms, such as the four-movement symphony and the sonata.

Brahms's piano
A renowned pianist as well as a composer, Brahms played this piano as a court musician. However, this instrument was already outdated and he preferred grand pianos.

Favorite haunt
The sign of the Red Hedgehog tavern in Vienna, where Brahms dined daily during the 1870s. Brahms maintained a modest lifestyle and regular habits.

By the 1860s, Brahms was earning a good living from concerts and composition but had no great reputation. This changed with the performance of his *German Requiem* in 1868. Inspired by his grief at the death of his mother, this large-scale choral work established Brahms as one of the leading composers of the day. Working with renewed confidence, he embarked on a series of symphonies and concertos, assuming the mantle of Beethoven. A perfectionist, he struggled to bring his works to completion, but a substantial body of work accumulated—orchestral and choral pieces, works for piano and chamber ensembles, organ preludes, and songs.

Wealth flowed from the success of his compositions and demand for his service as conductor and pianist. He sought inspiration in journeys abroad, especially to Italy. His final years were darkened by illness and the death of old friends, including Clara. Late works such as the *Four Serious Songs* of 1896 reflect on the transience of life.

After a battle with cancer, Brahms died in April 1897. He was buried in Vienna's Central Cemetery, close to the graves of Beethoven and Schubert.

KEY WORKS

- ***A German Requiem*, Op. 45**
- ***Variations on a Theme of Paganini*, Op. 35**
- ***Academic Festival* Overture, Op. 80**
- **Symphonies: No. 1 in C minor, Op. 68; No. 2 in D major, Op 78; No. 3 in F major, Op. 90; No. 4 in E minor, Op. 98**
- **Piano Concertos: No. 1 in D minor, Op. 15; No. 2 in B flat major, Op.83**
- **Violin Concerto in D major, Op. 77**

> **"He ... comes** as if sent **straight from God."**
>
> CLARA SCHUMANN ON BRAHMS, DIARY ENTRY, SEPTEMBER 1853

TIMELINE

- **May 7, 1833** Born to a musician and a seamstress in Hamburg, northern Germany.
- **1843** Begins lessons in composition and piano with Viennese musician Eduard Marxsen.
- **September 21, 1848** Gives his first solo piano recital in Hamburg.
- **April–May 1853** On his first concert tour he meets Franz Liszt, who performs his *Scherzo*.
- **September–October 1853** Visits Robert and Clara Schumann in Düsseldorf.
- **February 1854** Robert Schumann is confined to an asylum. Brahms becomes Clara Schumann's closest companion.
- **July 29, 1856** Death of Robert Schumann.
- **September–December 1857** The first of three seasons as musical director to Count Leopold III.
- **1859** Soloist at the premiere of his First Piano Concerto, Op. 15, in Leipzig.
- **1860** Publishes a manifesto attacking the influence of the New German School of Richard Wagner and Franz Liszt.
- **1863** Completes his virtuoso piano work, *Variations on a Theme of Paganini*, Op. 35.
- **February 2, 1865** Death of his mother.
- **April 10, 1868** First performance of *German Requiem*, Op. 45, in Bremen Cathedral establishes his reputation as a major composer.
- **1869** Publishes two books of Hungarian Dances, which are a popular success.
- **1871** Takes up residence in Vienna, becoming the conductor of the Gesellschaft der Musikfreunde (Society of Friends of the Music of Vienna).
- **November 4, 1876** The First Symphony, Op. 68, is premiered in Karlsruhe.
- **December 30, 1877** The Second Symphony, Op. 78, is performed in Vienna.
- **1878** Completes his Violin Concerto in D Major, Op. 77.
- **January 4, 1881** First performance of the *Academic Festival* Overture, Op. 80, at the University of Breslau.
- **November 9, 1881** First performance of the Second Piano Concerto, Op. 83, in Budapest, Hungary.
- **December 2, 1883** First performance of the Third Symphony, Op. 90, in Vienna.
- **October 25, 1885** Conducts first performance of the Fourth Symphony, Op. 98, at Meiningen.
- **1889** Records one of his Hungarian Dances on the newly invented phonograph.
- **May 20, 1896** Death of Clara Schumann.
- **April 3, 1897** Dies of cancer. He is buried in the Zentralfriedhof in Vienna.

BRAHMS IN HIS FINAL YEARS

The **Viennese Waltz**

The waltz, a dance for couples in 3/4 time, reached the height of its popularity in Vienna in the middle of the 19th century. Of the many composers then meeting the demand for dance music, none was more successful than Johann Strauss II, known affectionately as the "Waltz King."

The Blue Danube
Johann Strauss II's most popular waltz, *An der schönen blauen Donau* (By the Beautiful Blue Danube, 1867), was originally written as a choral work but the words were soon dropped.

« BEFORE

In the late 18th century, folk dances were for ordinary people, while upper-class dances were more stately.

CLOSE EMBRACES
The **origins of the waltz** are unclear, but dances where couples held each other in a close embrace were popular in southern Germany and Austria. There were several regional variants, such as the Weller and Spinner, known collectively as *Deutsche Tänze* (German dances).

AUSTRIAN PEASANT DANCE
The closest of these dances to the waltz was the *Ländler*, from upper Austria. This was a slow peasant dance in triple time that sometimes included clapping and stamping. **Haydn « 126–127, Mozart « 136–137,** and **Schubert « 154–155** all utilized the distinctive rhythm of the *Ländler* as an alternative to the more stately minuet in their compositions.

The waltz (from the Latin *volvere,* to turn or spin), emerged as a social dance in Austria and Germany in the second half of the 18th century. By 1800, it had taken Europe by storm. Some regarded it as immoral because of the close physical contact involved, and unhealthy because of its speed. The moves were free at first but dance manuals, such as Thomas Wilson's *A Description of the Correct Method of Waltzing* (1816), soon laid down precise steps.

Composers of the waltz

Michael Pamer (1782–1827) was one of the first composers to specialize in waltzes. He performed every evening at Vienna's Golden Pear Inn. Joseph Lanner (1801–1843) and Johann Strauss (1804–1849), two young members of Pamer's band, built on his success and each formed his own orchestra. Between them, the two men composed a huge number of dances, and by touring abroad regularly, they took their music to ever wider audiences. It was Johann Strauss who transformed the waltz from a rural peasant dance into the more elegant waltz format: a slow introduction, then five repetitions of the main waltz tune followed by a short coda (end section). Strauss's best-known work is not actually a waltz but the *Radetzky March* (1848), named after an Austrian general.

Musical dynasty

Three of Strauss's sons all became musicians, but the eldest, Johann II (1825–1899), became the most famous waltz composer of all. He extended the middle section of the waltz, and varied the orchestral writing. By this time, composers had already started writing waltzes as recital pieces rather than purely as dance music. Carl Maria von Weber's *Invitation to the Dance* (1819), for piano, was among the first grand concert waltzes, and was later orchestrated by Hector Berlioz. Schubert, Chopin, Liszt, and Brahms all wrote waltzes for the piano, but the dance also appears in Délibes' ballet *Coppélia* (1870) and in the opera *Eugene Onegin* (1879) by Tchaikovsky.

THE YOUNG Johann Strauss II backed the 1848 Vienna Revolution but changed his mind when his political views threatened his career.

In the ballroom, however, few composers could rival the Strauss family. Two who came close were the Austrian Karl Michael Ziehrer (1843–1922), whose waltz *Wiener Bürger* (Viennese Citizens) was a big hit in 1890, and Frenchman Émile Waldteufel (1837–1915), whose 1882 waltz *Les Patineurs* (The Skaters) remains a favorite to this day.

KEY WORKS

Joseph Lanner "Die Schönbrunner" waltzes
Johann Strauss I *Lorelei Rheinklänge* (Sounds of the Lorelei on the Rhine)
Johann Strauss II *By the Beautiful Blue Danube; The Emperor Waltz*
Josef Strauss *Perlen der Liebe* (Pearls of Love)
Karl Michael Ziehrer *Wiener Bürger* (Citizens of Vienna)

AFTER »

The heyday of the Viennese waltz ended with World War I, but it is still popular with 21st-century audiences.

MODERN PASTICHE
Modern composers used the waltz sometimes nostalgically—**Richard Strauss 222–223 »** paid operatic homage to his namesake in his 1911 opera *Der Rosenkavalier*—and sometimes more ironically, as in the 1920 orchestral work *La valse* by **Maurice Ravel 204–205 »**.

BALLROOM WALTZES
The slow waltz survives as part of the repertoire of competitive ballroom dancing, with new tunes provided by composers of light music, such as Eric Coates (1886–1957).

POPULAR MUSIC
Richard Rodgers of Rodgers and Hammerstein **286 »** was the 20th century's star composer of waltzes, with "Lover," "Falling in Love with Love," and "Oh, What a Beautiful Mornin'."

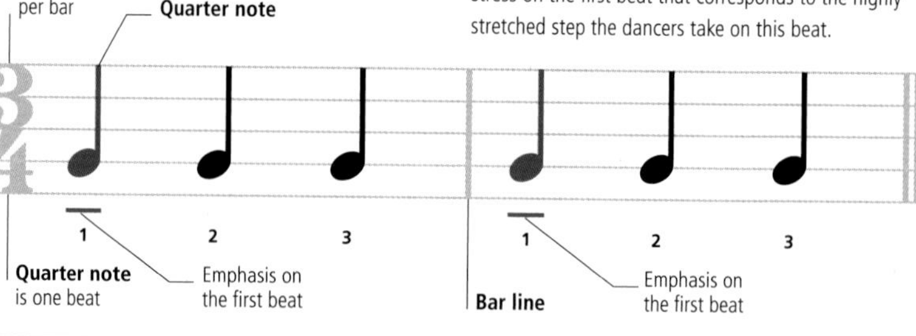

Waltz rhythm
The waltz always has three beats in a bar, with a heavy stress on the first beat that corresponds to the highly stretched step the dancers take on this beat.

COMPOSER (1825–1899)

JOHANN STRAUSS II

The son of composer Johann Strauss I, Johann Strauss II was born near Vienna. His father wanted him to have a career in banking, so as a child he studied the violin in secret. He was briefly a bank clerk but by 1844 was conducting his own ensemble in Vienna. On Johann I's death, Johann II merged his father's orchestra with his own and was soon even more popular than his father. Although based in Vienna, he toured Europe and regularly performed in Russia. When Johann II's health suffered, his brother Josef became conductor of his orchestra, and Johann was able to focus on composing. In addition to his waltzes, Strauss wrote polkas, such as the *Tritsch-Tratsch-Polka* (1858), and operettas, including, in 1874, *Die Fledermaus* (The Bat).

Imperial Ball, Vienna
Wilhelm Gause's painting shows a couple dancing the waltz at the annual Imperial Ball. This glittering event was held at the Hofburg Palace in Vienna and attended by Emperor Franz Josef I (1830–1916).

BEFORE

Interest in national folk culture grew in Europe from the early 1800s, when composers found ways to weave folk idioms into their music.

GERMAN TRIGGER

There were glimmers of interest in national characteristics in music in the 18th century, but they were eclipsed by enthusiasm for the new forms of **symphony « 124–125**, **sonata « 120–121**, and **concerto « 138–139**. Among the first "national" works was Carl Maria von Weber's 1821 German opera *Der Freischütz* (The Marksman). Based on a German legend, it was full of elements that appealed to the **German Romantic spirit**, such as a pure heroine, humble village folk, a villain, the supernatural, and a prince.

A PERFORMANCE OF *DER FREISCHÜTZ*

National Stirrings

The cult of the individual was a characteristic of the Romantic period, and the individuality of nations became a theme in European culture. Composers found inspiration in unique aspects of their country, especially folk songs and landscapes.

Wars and political upheaval across Europe during the 19th century triggered a large appetite for "national" qualities in music. The results of this ranged from the superficial application of local color in the form of folk dance rhythms to a raw, passionate expression of national character.

At first, nationalism was most noticeable in central and eastern European music, where folk culture and song were fundamental aspects of peasant life. It was slower to take hold in western and southern Europe and Scandinavia. Part of the appeal of nationalist music was the glimpse it gave of distant cultures.

1892 The year Dvořák was appointed Director of the National Conservatory of Music in New York, earning $15,000 per annum.

And a new genre evolved to express these ideas. The single-movement symphonic poem was established by Franz Liszt in the 1850s, as an orchestral vehicle for subject-matter encompassing literature, painting, dramatic historical events, and ancient mythology. And Felix Mendelssohn's earlier "overtures" *The Hebrides* and *Calm Sea and Prosperous Voyage* are nature-depicting symphonic poems in all but name.

Eastern Europe

Czech composers were particularly preoccupied with creating musical portraits of their national landscape (see pp.144–145). The six symphonic poems forming Bedřich Smetana's *Má vlast* (My Homeland, 1874–1879) describe specific scenes, including Prague Castle, woods and fields, and the mountains where the mythical army of patron saint St. Wenceslas sleeps. Best known is the second movement, *Vltava*, which describes the river running through Prague.

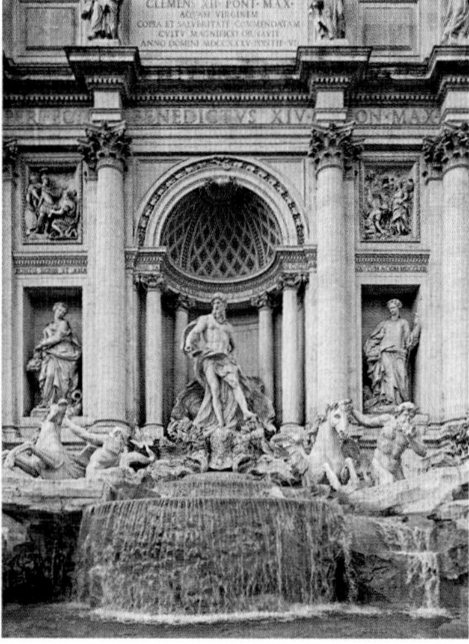

Water music

Italian nationalism, evident in Verdi's operas, inspired the music of Ottorino Respighi (1879–1936). His *Roman Trilogy* celebrated Rome's festivals, pine trees, and fountains, such as the Trevi Fountain in Piazza di Trevi.

Also Czech, Antonín Dvořák (1841–1904) is among the most successful of the nationalist composers. His *Slavonic Dances*, modeled on the *Hungarian Dances* by Brahms, make clever use of Slavic rhythms while the melodies are his own creation. Of Dvořák's nine symphonies, the seventh is darkly Slavonic in flavor, while the glorious eighth feels like a joyful folk celebration. The ninth symphony, "From the New World," was written when the composer was in America. Although Dvořák maintained that American folk music could be woven into new compositions, the slow movement's cor anglais (English horn) tune, which resembles a Negro spiritual, was his own creation.

The spread of ideas

In Paris, catering to a taste for the foreign and exotic, Frédéric Chopin (see pp.160–161) played mazurkas and polonaises inspired by Polish folk dance. Franz Liszt's Hungarian persona—expressed in the *Hungarian Rhapsodies*—added to his cult following (see pp.160–161).

National stirrings in Russia may have been slow to materialize but were deeply powerful once they had taken root. Before Russian nationalism came to the fore through Mikhail Glinka and the composers known as the "Big Five" (see pp.180–181), non-national composers such as the Italian Catterino Cavos (1775–1840) began to write operas to Russian texts, going against the prevailing preference for Italian words. Inspired by Russia's 1812 victory over Napoleon, Cavos produced the ballet *The National Guard* in the same year and in 1816 wrote the opera *Ivan Susanin*, based on a story that Glinka later used in his opera *A Life for the Tsar*.

Southern flavors

The music of Spanish composer Isaac Albéniz (1860–1909) is a far cry from the often dark-hued sounds of northern Europe. Born in Catalonia, northern Spain, Albéniz was a talented pianist who gave his first public performance at the age of four. In 1880, he traveled across Europe, and in 1883, he began to study with the Spanish musicologist Felipe Pedrell and was inspired by his interest in folklore and folk song. The suite *Iberia*, Albéniz's masterpiece, is a 90-minute

"My **fatherland means more to me** than anything else."

BEDŘICH SMETANA, LETTER TO A FRIEND

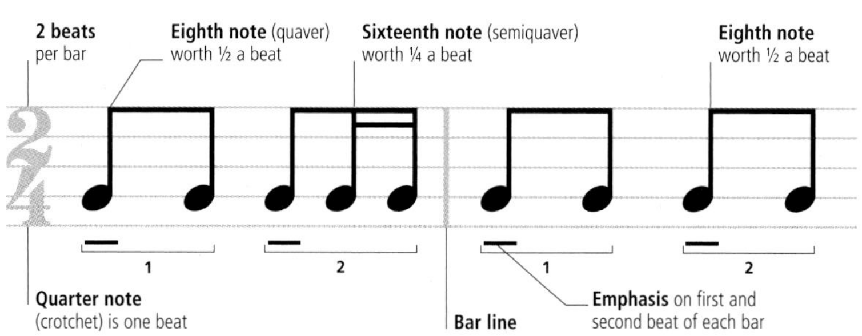

Polka rhythm

Originally a Bohemian peasant dance, the polka has two strong beats in each bar, inviting dancers to step in lively, bouncing fashion. It became a popular ballroom dance in 1830s Prague and spread across Europe.

COMPOSER (1875–1912)

SAMUEL COLERIDGE-TAYLOR

The son of an English mother and a father from Sierra Leone, Samuel Coleridge-Taylor grew up in the London suburb of Croydon. At 15, his violin playing won him a scholarship to the Royal College of Music. His composition teacher there, overhearing a racial insult, retorted that his pupil had "more music in his little finger" than the speaker had "in his whole body." Coleridge-Taylor is remembered mainly for his Longfellow-inspired cantata *Hiawatha's Wedding Feast*, whose melodic appeal, derived from European late Romanticism, made it a favorite of choral societies. Had he lived longer—he died at age 37—his deepening awareness of African-American music might have taken British classical music into new and uncharted territory.

AFTER

Nationalism remained important—especially in Czech, Hungarian, and Russian music.

THE NEW NATIONALISTS

From around 1870, the **breakdown of structures** and traditional **harmonic patterns** impacted across Europe, and nationalism was no longer an end in itself. **Josef Suk** followed in Dvořák's footsteps with the symphonic poem *Prague*, while Czech composer **Vítězslav Novák** studied Moravian and Slovakian folk music. These and other nationalists paved the way for the genius of **Leoš Janáček, Bohuslav Martinů, Béla Bartók,** and **Zoltán Kodály**. In Russia, the **"Big Five"** **180–181 ››** nationalist composers held sway from the mid-19th century. Landscape and myth remained at the heart of **Scandinavian music** **184–185 ››**, while Spanish composers **218–219 ››** such as **Manuel de Falla** and **Joaquín Turina** continued to fly their musical flag.

KEY WORKS

Bedřich Smetana *Ma Vlast*

Antonín Dvořák Slavonic Dance, Op. 46, No. 1

Jean Sibelius *Finlandia*, Op. 26

Isaac Albéniz *Suite Espagnole*, Op. 47, No. 5, "Asturias," arranged for guitar

Enrique Granados *Goyescas*, No. 1, "Los Requiebros" ("Compliments")

Manuel Ponce 24 Preludes for Guitar, No. 1 in C major

The sounds of Spain
Isaac Albéniz's *Suite Espagnole* included several pieces inspired by Spanish regions and cities. Like those in his later work, *Iberia* (1906–1908), they evoke the many of the sounds of Spain, including guitar and flamenco.

set of four books, each with three pieces, among them "Almería," "Málaga," and "Jerez." These intrinsically Spanish pieces, dazzlingly complex and technically challenging, are washed with the impressionistic color that Albéniz admired in Debussy and Ravel.

The major achievement of Albéniz's compatriot Enrique Granados (1867–1916), who regarded himself as an artist rather than a composer, was the piano suite *Goyescas*, based on paintings by the Spanish artist Francisco Goya. The pieces range from wildly virtuosic to romantically lyrical, their unusual modulations (changes of harmony) rooting them firmly in the Moorish-inspired Spanish folk tradition. The cellist Pablo Casals (1876–1973) maintained that he had been greatly influenced by the music of Granados. Manuel Ponce (1882–1948) was influenced by the harmonies and forms of songs from his native Mexico. A scholar and music teacher as well as a composer, Ponce is remembered for integrating popular song and folklore with classical music, especially in his *Cuban Suite* and *Mexican Rhapsody*.

A Czech national opera
Smetana wrote his 1866 opera *The Bartered Bride*, shown here in a 2005 production at Glyndebourne, England, to counter accusations of "Wagnerism" in his previous opera *The Brandenburgers in Bohemia*.

BEFORE

No one is sure of the exact origins of flamenco, but there is no doubt it grew out of a troubled past.

JOURNEY FROM THE EAST
Scholars disagree over the roots of flamenco. One theory is that it was brought by migrating populations from **India to Egypt** (the etymological root of the word "Gypsy") and to Eastern Europe (home of the Romany culture), eventually arriving in Andalusia in Spain in the 16th century.

4 **The number of flamenco museums in Andalusia.**

12 **The number of beats to a *uleria* flamenco rhythm.**

PROTEST AND ANGUISH
An alternative theory states that during the reign of the "Catholic Monarchs" Ferdinand V and Queen Isabella **<< 70–71**, outlawed minorities such as Romany and Muslims came together and flamenco was born as a collective expression of protest and anguish. What is certain is that flamenco contains elements of **Jewish, Romany, and Moorish musical traditions** and that its seedbed is the Andalucian cities of Jerez, Granada, Seville, and Malaga.

Flamenco

The signature sound of Spain is passionate and pained. Much of flamenco's power derives from the way the structure of the music constrains, though never quite contains, the intensity of emotions.

Flamenco is the music of the Gypsy soul, and for the people of Andalucia in the south of Spain, it represents the dreams and disappointments of the long-suffering lower classes. It springs from close, often family-based communities, and both performers and *aficionados* are fiercely proud of its history.

Key characteristics

Three components make up flamenco: voice, guitar, and dance. To this might be added the hand claps (*palmas*), as well as foot stomping and assorted hand-percussion instruments (typically the box-shaped *cajón*).

Flamenco is a single musical genre but its repertoire is made up of more than 60 individual song styles (*palos*). The most popular of these styles are *siguiriyas, soleares, tangos,* and *fandangos*. There are also a large number of dance styles and rhythmic cycles—each cycle, or *compas*, is technically complex, with strong accents distributed differently over, in a typical example, a 12-beat cycle.

Popular appeal
Advertising a flamenco show from Seville in 1887, this French poster captures the growing appeal of flamenco.

Solos to ensembles

Traditionally, flamenco was performed by a solo singer, backed by one or more guitarist with additional musicians and/or a dancer or dancers. Today it is often

"**Duende** is simply a **momentary burst** of inspiration, the **blush** of **all that is truly alive...**"

FEDERICO GARCÍA LORCA (1898–1936)

Drama of music and dance
Flamenco has captured the imagination of many writers and artists. This 1882 oil painting by John Singer Sargent is titled *El Jaleo*, which describes the spontaneous clapping and shouting.

KEY WORKS

Manolo Caracol *"El Florero"*
La Niña de los Peines *"El Corazon de Pena"*
Camarón de la Isla *"Sube al Enganche"*
Niño Ricardo *"Sevilla es mi tierra"*
Son de la Frontera *"Buleria de la cal"*
Estrella Morente *"Calle del aire"*
Paco de Lucía *"Entre dos Aguas"*

performed by ensembles, with nontraditional instruments, such as the piano and flute.

Flamenco can be divided into three vocal forms: *cante chico, cante intermedio,* and *cante jondo*. The first two generally deal with lighter, humorous subjects, which is echoed in the style of delivery, while the third translates as "deep song." For singers, *cante jondo* presents an opportunity to express deep emotions and stretch technical abilities to the limit.

Gypsy roots

After the expulsion of the Moors from Spain in 1492, the *cante gitano* singing of the itinerant Gypsies of Spain and Portugal merged with the musical rhythms and singing styles of the indigenous Andalucian peoples. Between 1765 and 1860, flamenco schools were established and the dance appeared. Early flamenco was probably a vocal form, accompanied by clapping, but as classical musicians such as Julián Arcas (1832–1882) placed guitar playing at the center of their repertoire, so flamenco artists began to do the same. In the first decade of the 19th century, Antonio Fernández, a Romany blacksmith known as El Planeta, is said to have invented the form known as the *martinet*, which sometimes uses the smith's hammer and anvil as percussion instruments.

UNESCO has declared flamenco a Masterpiece of Oral Heritage.

Lorca's influence

In the early 20th century, radio and the record player popularized flamenco, and the Spanish poet and playwright Federico García Lorca, who used the word *duende* (passion) to describe flamenco's soul, added to the tradition and its mythology through poetry. Also a talented pianist, García Lorca compiled the important *Colección de Canciones Populares Españolas* (Collection of Early Popular Songs), which included flamenco.

Paco de Lucía
Born in Algeciras, in southern Spain, Paco de Lucía (1947–2014) was one of a generation of musicians who created new sounds by fusing flamenco with classical music and jazz.

National unity

After the Spanish Civil War (1936–1939), dictator General Francisco Franco promoted flamenco as a symbol of national unity, giving it institutional respectability. However, by the 1960s, the live music scene had become something of a tourist trap, and it took a group of unorthodox artists to give it new life. Camarón de la Isla (José Monje Cruz) was a young Romany rebel who achieved rock star status and broke with tradition in his use of an electric bass. Other performers were open to fusions of flamenco with jazz, blues, rock, and reggae, a sound that became *nuevo flamenco*. Flamenco had become part of the world music scene.

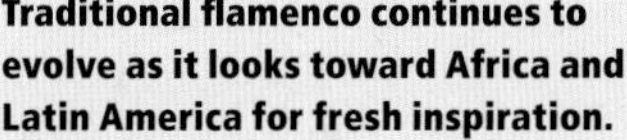

AFTER

Traditional flamenco continues to evolve as it looks toward Africa and Latin America for fresh inspiration.

NEW FUSIONS

Recording artists such as Son de la Frontera, Mayte Martín, and Diego Amador have taken the mantle from 1980s singer Camarón de la Isla and guitarist Tomatito. Córdoba-born Paco Peña, who shared the bill with Jimi Hendrix in the 1960s, found audiences with **flamenco shows**, some exploring fusions.

"JIP-JOP FLAMENKILLO"

The band **Radio Tarifa** has emphasized ties with North Africa, while bands such as Ojos de Brujo have melded **hip-hop** **370–371 »** with flamenco in "jip-jop flamenkillo."

OJOS DE BRUJO

Folk roots
In the Russian countryside, villagers celebrated festivals with music and dance. Folk tunes collected by 19th-century music scholars at such events fueled interest in nationalism.

BEFORE

Peter the Great regarded European music as a mark of civilization and invited German musicians to work in his newly founded capital of St. Petersburg.

WESTERN INFLUENCES

The Russian czar Peter the Great (1682–1725) founded the city of St. Petersburg in 1703 as a "window on the West." Seeing European music as a means of Westernizing the country, he hired German musicians to train his military bands to provide music for banquets and dancing. His successors introduced **ballet** to Russia, and under Catherine the Great **Italian opera** **« 80–81** took hold in the court. This European domination of Russian culture gave rise to a **nationalist backlash** in literature and music by the 1830s.

PETER THE GREAT

Russia's Big Five

The "Big Five" was the name given to a group of major composers who wanted to create a Russian nationalist school of composition. Their music conjured up the distinctive history, landscape, and emotions of their beloved country.

Part of a bigger group of Russian musicians, sometimes referred to as the "Mighty Handful," the "Big Five" were a distinctive group of composers, all based in St. Petersburg, whose commitment to Russian nationalism went beyond simply introducing Russian folk tunes into traditional European Classical forms. The group comprised Mily Balakirev, Aleksandr Borodin, César Cui, Modest Mussorgsky, and Nikolay Rimsky-Korsakov. Their main inspiration was Mikhail Glinka.

The catalyst

Brought up on a country estate, where folk music was often played, Mikhail Glinka (1804–1857) attended house-orchestra concerts at his uncle's home and took piano lessons from the Irish composer John Field, who spent long periods in Russia. On a visit to Italy in 1830, Glinka met Gaetano Donizetti and Vincenzo Bellini and recognized the Italianate lyricism of their music. Not wanting simply to emulate Italian opera, however, Glinka resolved to cultivate a truly Russian musical style. He chose the 1613 invasion of Russia by the Poles as the subject for *A Life for the Czar*. This landmark opera is thoroughly imbued with distinctively Russian moments, unusual five-in-a-bar rhythms, and polonaises (Polish folk dances) to represent the Poles.

Glinka's next opera, *Ruslan and Lyudmilla*, was based on a story by the Russian poet Pushkin. Echoing Russian romantic composers' interest in all things exotic, Glinka's use of vivid harmonies and non-Western scales suggests a range of musical idioms, including Arabian as well as Russian.

Driving force

Mily Balakirev (1837–1910) took up Glinka's mantle. A domineering individual, he hunted down stories and folk songs and forced other composers in the group to use them in their work, sometimes supervising progress bar by bar. His best-known orchestral work, *Tamara*, is skillfully orchestrated, but his strength was in piano writing. The "Oriental" fantasy *Islamey* owes much to Liszt in its virtuosity, but proved too difficult for Balakirev himself to play.

Balakirev's domineering character earned him enemies, while overwork contributed to periods of exhaustion. In 1871, he withdrew from public life

KEY WORKS

Mikhail Glinka *A Life for the Czar*

Mily Balakirev *Islamey* for piano, Op. 18

Aleksandr Borodin *Prince Igor; In the Steppes of Central Asia*

Modest Mussorgsky *Boris Godunov*

Nicolay Rimsky-Korsakov *Russian Easter Festival Overture*, Op. 36

RUSSIAN CRITIC (1824–1906)

VLADIMIR STASOV

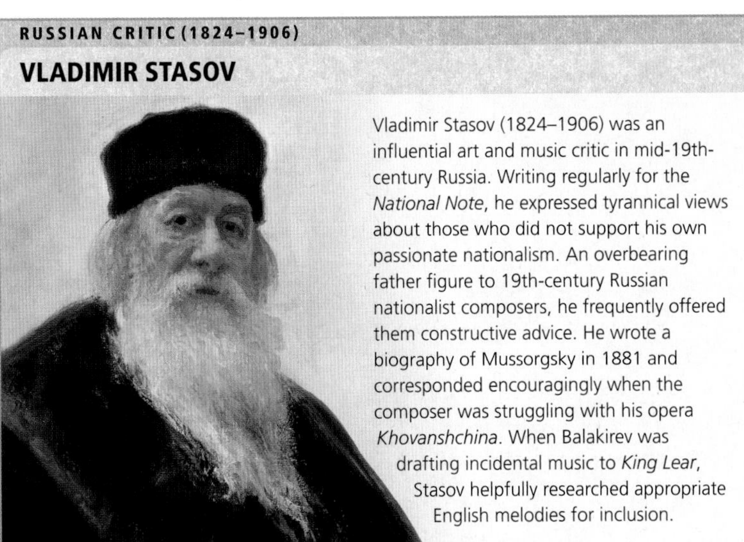

Vladimir Stasov (1824–1906) was an influential art and music critic in mid-19th-century Russia. Writing regularly for the *National Note*, he expressed tyrannical views about those who did not support his own passionate nationalism. An overbearing father figure to 19th-century Russian nationalist composers, he frequently offered them constructive advice. He wrote a biography of Mussorgsky in 1881 and corresponded encouragingly when the composer was struggling with his opera *Khovanshchina*. When Balakirev was drafting incidental music to *King Lear*, Stasov helpfully researched appropriate English melodies for inclusion.

> "A **love** for my own **country** led me to the idea of **writing** in the **Russian style.**"
>
> MIKHAIL GLINKA, AFTER VISITING ITALY, 1830,

and explored mysticism, reappearing in 1883 to direct the music for St. Petersburg's Imperial Court Chapel.

Master of instrumentation

Aleksandr Borodin (1833–1887) was a scientist and part-time musician. He studied with Balakirev in 1863 and acquired exceptional mastery of orchestral color, often incorporating Russian folk tunes into classical forms. He wrote two symphonies, three string quartets, songs, piano music, and the political opera *Prince Igor* (completed after his death by Rimsky-Korsakov and Aleksandr Glazunov), about the Russian prince's campaign against invading Polovtsian tribes in 1185.

Prince Igor's Polovtsian Dances, in which the captured prince is entertained by his opponents, is a sequence of dances for orchestra and chorus. The cor anglais (English horn) and oboe melody of the women's dance ("Gliding Dance of the Maidens") later found fame in the song "Stranger in Paradise" in Robert Wright and George Forrest's musical *Kismet* (1953), which was based on Borodin's music.

Musician and critic

Born in Vilnius, in modern-day Lithuania, César Cui (1835–1918) was an expert on military fortifications who taught at the St. Petersburg Academy of Military Engineering. The least well known of the Big Five, he was essentially a miniaturist, producing many small-scale piano pieces and songs. Cui is remembered now for the opera *William Ratcliff*, with a libretto by the poet Aleksey Plescheyev. Russian influences in his own music are rare, although the first movement of his opera *A Prisoner in the Caucasus* includes nationalist references. His nationalism was more evident in his work as a critic, where his wit was used to lacerating effect.

Inspired by the past

The music of Modest Mussorgsky (1839–1881) was on a big scale, brash and brilliant, and less refined than that of the other members of the "Five."

A visit to Moscow, which was far less Westernized than St. Petersburg, in 1859 inspired his nationalist imagination. In a letter to Balakirev, he wrote: "I have been a cosmopolitan but now I have undergone a sort of rebirth: I have been brought near to everything Russian." Mussorgky's nationalism was most evident in his choice of subject matter rather than in the music itself. His opera *Boris Godunov* was based on the Pushkin play about a member of the *Oprichnina*, the secret police founded to eradicate enemies of the Russian czar Ivan the Terrible. The coronation scene and magnificent settings (including the Kremlin and St. Basil's Cathedral), coupled with dramatic arias, massive choruses, and rich orchestration, spoke powerfully to the Russian people.

Mussorgsky died on his forty-second birthday, leaving many works to be finished by other composers. These included the opera *Khovanschina*, about the rebellion of Ivan Khovansky against the Westernizing reforms of Peter the Great, which was completed by Rimsky-Korsakov.

Master orchestrator

Originally a naval officer, Nicolay Rimsky-Korsakov (1844–1908) wrote part of his first symphony while on duty. A brilliant orchestrator (he wrote treatises on the subject), he also composed prolifically, including symphonic suites, symphonies, operas, and songs. In his autobiography, he revealed how his *Russian Easter Festival Overture* portrayed a real event: an Easter mass in a cavernous church, in which several priests are celebrating communion simultaneously. The listener is taken through Good Friday reflections to hints of Orthodox liturgy, to the spiritual ecstasy of the festival—not forgetting the hubbub of revelers looking on. An equally effective work is *Capriccio Espagnol*, which demonstrates Rimsky-Korsakov's interest in national color outside Russia.

1862 **The year in which St. Petersburg Conservatory was founded by the pianist, composer, and conductor Anton Rubinstein.**

The Russian *balalaika*

Popular since the 18th century, the *balalaika* has a triangular body, three strings, which are plucked, and frets. Originally a folk instrument, it was incorporated in concert performances in the late 19th century.

AFTER

Interest in nationalism had waned by 1900, but the impact of the "Big Five" moved Russian music on to new and distinctive paths.

CHIEF HEIR

The legacy of the "Big Five" was inherited by **Aleksandr Glazunov** (1865–1936). Essentially a polished traditionalist, Glazunov balanced Russian and European elements. His sophisticated ear for color or timber, a common trait among the "Big Five," is evident later in the **tonal language** of **Claude Debussy** and **Maurice Ravel** **204–205 >>**.

NEW APPROACHES

Nationalism declined as a characteristic of European music after about 1900. In Russia, **Sergey Prokofiev** and **Dmitri Shostakovich** took forward the national spirit of Russia, while **Igor Stravinsky** **212–213 >>** forged a new approach to composition in the 20th century. **Sergey Rachmaninoff** **223 >>**, who left Russia for the United States after the 1917 revolution, harked back to a Romantic style, in which expressive melodies soar over romantic harmonies. Of the more eccentric composers, **Alexander Scriabin** (1872–1915) stands out. His interest in mysticism inspired *The Mysterium*, a synthesis of music and dance with incense and a procession—sadly incomplete, but possibly the earliest multimedia "happening."

Music and medicine

Borodin was also a professor of chemistry at St. Petersburg's Medical Academy. The tiles behind his bust at his tomb in St. Petersburg depict notation from the "Gliding Dance of the Maidens" from Polovtsian Dances.

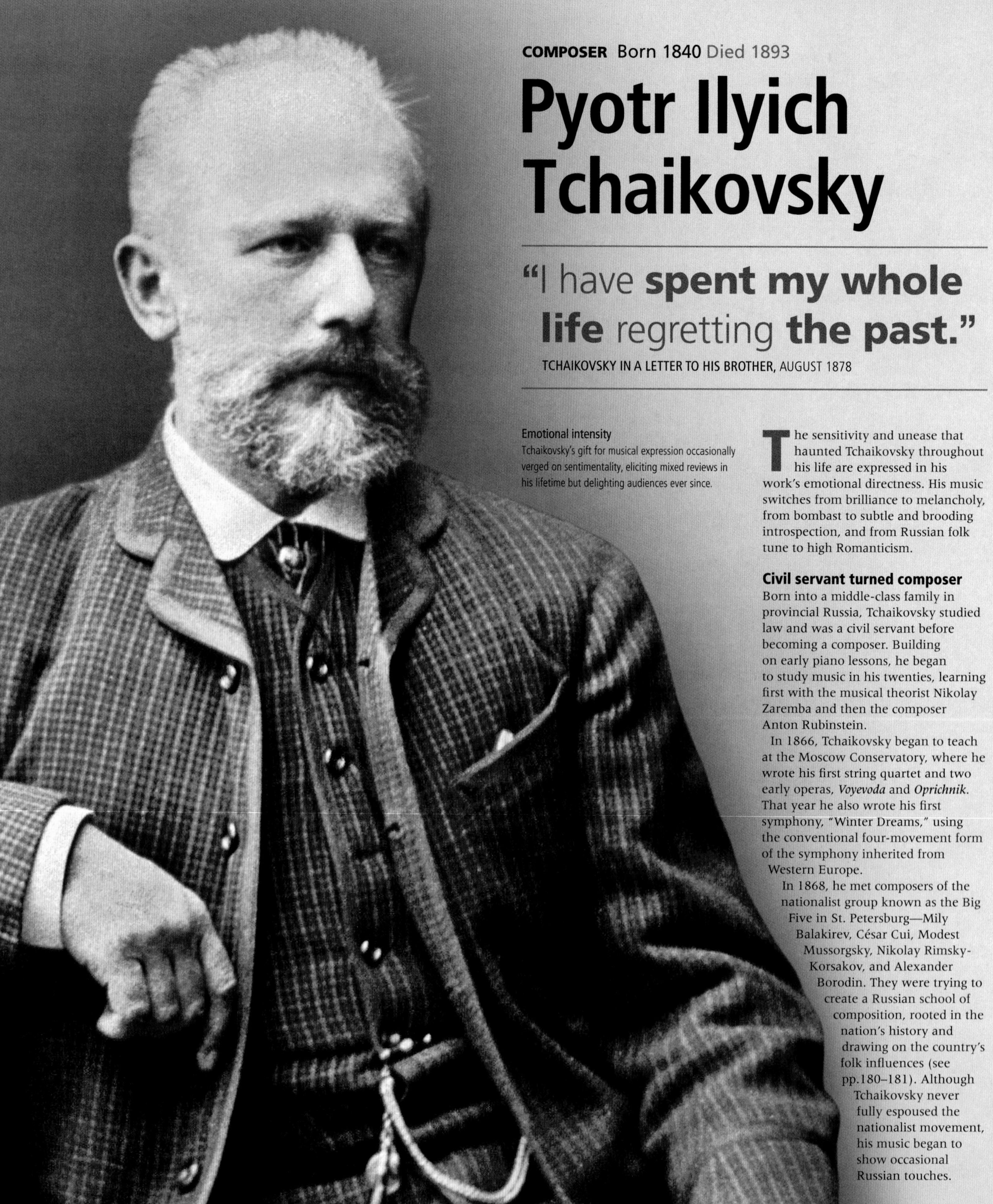

COMPOSER Born 1840 Died 1893

Pyotr Ilyich Tchaikovsky

"I have **spent my whole life** regretting **the past.**"

TCHAIKOVSKY IN A LETTER TO HIS BROTHER, AUGUST 1878

Emotional intensity
Tchaikovsky's gift for musical expression occasionally verged on sentimentality, eliciting mixed reviews in his lifetime but delighting audiences ever since.

The sensitivity and unease that haunted Tchaikovsky throughout his life are expressed in his work's emotional directness. His music switches from brilliance to melancholy, from bombast to subtle and brooding introspection, and from Russian folk tune to high Romanticism.

Civil servant turned composer

Born into a middle-class family in provincial Russia, Tchaikovsky studied law and was a civil servant before becoming a composer. Building on early piano lessons, he began to study music in his twenties, learning first with the musical theorist Nikolay Zaremba and then the composer Anton Rubinstein.

In 1866, Tchaikovsky began to teach at the Moscow Conservatory, where he wrote his first string quartet and two early operas, *Voyevoda* and *Oprichnik*. That year he also wrote his first symphony, "Winter Dreams," using the conventional four-movement form of the symphony inherited from Western Europe.

In 1868, he met composers of the nationalist group known as the Big Five in St. Petersburg—Mily Balakirev, César Cui, Modest Mussorgsky, Nikolay Rimsky-Korsakov, and Alexander Borodin. They were trying to create a Russian school of composition, rooted in the nation's history and drawing on the country's folk influences (see pp.180–181). Although Tchaikovsky never fully espoused the nationalist movement, his music began to show occasional Russian touches.

> "... that **appalling day** is as **vivid** to me **as if it were yesterday.**"
>
> TCHAIKOVSKY ON THE DEATH OF HIS MOTHER 25 YEARS EARLIER, 1879

Tchaikovsky's piano
The composer's piano is in the Tchaikovsky Museum in Klin, near Moscow. His piano concertos show exceptional understanding of the instrument.

His second symphony, "The Little Russian," uses three Ukrainian folk songs, and in 1873 he composed incidental music to Ostrovsky's play *The Snow Maiden*, based on a Russian folk tale. The opening of the finale of Symphony No. 4 is punctuated by the folk tune, "In a field stood a little birch tree."

Complicated relationships

Toward the end of the 1870s, Tchaikovsky's life reached a turning point. Seeking to avoid the negative social implications of his homosexuality, he married a young student, Antonina Milyukova. The marriage immediately failed, and they separated. Meanwhile, Tchaikovsky had begun a 14-year correspondence with an admirer, Madame Nadezhda von Meck. By mutual agreement they never met, but she provided financial support, and Tchaikovsky was devastated when she abruptly terminated the liaison in 1890.

The symphonies

Tchaikovsky's six symphonies, spanning 27 years, chart his development as a composer. The comparative innocence of the First Symphony contrasts starkly with the turbulence of the Sixth, "Pathétique" (Passionate), of 1893, which was an apt summary of his tormented personal life. After a brooding opening played by bass instruments, the first movement eventually opens out into one of Tchaikovsky's most moving melodies, in which yearning strings sing out over a gently throbbing accompaniment, used later in the popular song "Story of a starry night," made famous by Glenn Miller. The Sixth's second movement is a charming five-in-a-bar waltz—ironically undanceable—while the finale is an adagio of tragic intensity, beginning with a cry of anguish. The composer conducted its premiere just nine days before his death, sparking rumors that it was a musical suicide note.

The operas

Although Tchaikovsky's ballet music—*Swan Lake, The Sleeping Beauty, The Nutcracker* (see p.187)—is better known, Tchaikovsky's operas form an important part of his output. *Eugene Onegin* (1878) is based on a story by Pushkin, and features Onegin, a Byronic aristocrat, who breaks the heart of the young Tatyana by coldly rejecting her declaration of love. The expressive harmonies, graceful melodies, ballet scenes, and brilliant orchestral writing root the work firmly in the tradition of old-fashioned lyric opera. The famous "letter scene," in which Tatyana writes a love letter to Onegin, echoes the composer's perplexing relationship with his patron, Madame von Meck.

In the *Queen of Spades*, also based on a story by Pushkin, French song, Russian folk music, and hints of Orthodox liturgy weave through a dense plot to great dramatic effect.

Pen pal and patron
Madame Nadezhda von Meck's correspondence with Tchaikovsky shed light on his creative processes and innermost thoughts.

Disease and death

Tchaikovsky's last years were miserable. He was plagued by depression, and in 1892 contracted cholera, apparently by drinking a glass of water against official advice. Rumors that he committed suicide spread after his death and linger to this day, with some commentators suggesting he swallowed arsenic. This untimely death in mysterious circumstances reflected the underlying tragedy of his life.

KEY WORKS

Piano Concerto No. 1 in B flat minor, Op. 23

Violin Concerto in D, Op. 35

Symphony No. 2 in C minor ("The Little Russian"), Op. 17

Capriccio Italien for orchestra, Op. 45

***The Queen of Spades*, Op. 68**

Fantasy overture *Romeo and Juliet* Suite

***The Nutcracker*, Op. 71a (entire ballet Op. 71)**

Beloved ballet
Tchaikovsky's ballets are among the best loved in the repertoire. Here, dancers of the English National Ballet rehearse Tchaikovsky's *Swan Lake* at London's Coliseum in August 2012.

TIMELINE

- **1840** Born in Votkinsk, Viatka province, Russia, to a mining inspector father.
- **1850** Moves with his family to St. Petersburg. Enters the School of Jurisprudence.
- **1859** Joins the civil service.
- **1860** Begins study with Nikolay Zaremba.
- **1863** Studies with Anton Rubinstein.
- **1866** Moves to Moscow. Appointed professor of harmony at the Conservatory. Composes Symphony No. 1, Op. 13.
- **1868** Meets the composers of the Big Five group in St. Petersburg.
- **1869** St. Petersburg premiere of symphonic poem *Fate*. Opera *Voyevoda*, Op. 3, produced. Begins fantasy overture *Romeo and Juliet* with the help of Mily Balakirev, conductor of *Fate*.
- **1872** Publishes textbook, *Guide to the Practical Study of Harmony*. Becomes music critic for the Russian newspaper *Russkiye vedomosti*.
- **1873** Symphony No. 2, Op. 17, performed to great acclaim in Moscow. Composes *The Snow Maiden*, Op.12.
- **1874** Opera *Oprichnik* (The Guardsman) is produced. Composes Piano Concerto No. 1, Op. 35 and String Quartet No. 2, Op. 22.
- **1875** Piano Concerto No. 1, Op. 23, premiered in Boston. Symphony No. 3, Op. 29, premiered in Moscow.

TCHAIKOVSKY'S HOUSE IN KLIN, NEAR MOSCOW

- **1876** Begins correspondence with wealthy widow Madame Nadezhda von Meck.
- **1877** *Swan Lake* is produced. Begins opera *Eugene Onegin* and Symphony No. 4, Op. 36. Marries student Antonina Milyukova and embarks on eight years of international travel.
- **1878** Resigns from Conservatory to devote himself to composition.
- **1880** Writes *1812 Overture*, Op. 49.
- **1881** Violin Concerto, Op. 35, premieres in Vienna to disastrous reception.
- **1888** Symphony No. 5, Op. 64, premieres successfully.
- **1890** Relationship with Madame von Meck ends. *The Sleeping Beauty* is produced in St. Petersburg. Premiere of the opera *The Queen of Spades*, Op. 68. Composes *Souvenir de Florence*, Op. 70.
- **1891** Travels to the US, leading concerts of his work in New York, Baltimore, and Philadelphia.
- **1892** *The Nutcracker*, Op. 71, is produced.
- **1893** Premiere in St. Petersburg of Symphony No. 6, *Pathétique*. Dies suddenly in Moscow.

Northern Lights

The most profound and distinctive influences on the Nordic composers were the rich mythology, folk culture, and bleakly beautiful landscapes of their native countries. These preoccupations imbued their music with a stark, rough-hewn quality, especially in the case of the Finnish and Norwegian composers.

From the 1820s, it was common for Nordic musicians to train in Austro-German traditions, with many of them going to study in Vienna, Berlin, or Leipzig. This solid grounding in Classical compositions is evident in their loyalty to the tried-and-tested established forms of symphony, sonata, and concerto even after they began to embrace nationalist themes in their own music.

Great Danish composers

The first nationalist tendencies in Denmark were evident in songs, especially the 1840–1842 folk song settings made by Christophe Weyse (1774–1842), a Danish composer of German extraction. But Niels Gade (1817–1890) was the most influential Danish composer of the 19th century. The son of an instrument-maker, he played the violin and studied composition with Andreas Peter Berggreen, a folklore enthusiast who awoke in Gade an interest in Danish folk music and literature. After completing a concert tour of Norway and Sweden in 1838, he began to turn to Danish poets rather than the German Goethe for his inspiration.

In 1843, Gade went to Leipzig where Felix Mendelssohn (see pp.158–159), who was to become a friend, conducted the premiere of Gade's first symphony. The outbreak of war between Prussia and Denmark in 1848 took Gade back to Copenhagen.

After this period, the influence of Mendelssohn is evident in Gade's music. As a teacher, however, Gade was himself influential. He taught both Carl Nielsen and Edvard Grieg, inspiring in them a curiosity about their national folk heritage.

Carl Nielsen (1865–1931) had little musical training outside his native Denmark. He was not immersed in the Austro-German Classical tradition as many of his contemporaries were, so his raw, natural talent was left intact. This may explain his unorthodox use of harmony, such as moving unexpectedly from one key to another, juxtaposing keys that were regarded as opposing, and eventually resolving them. His music is dramatic, sometimes aggressive, often exuding a sense of struggle—the fourth of his six symphonies is named "The Inextinguishable."

In Nielsen's *Wind Quintet* (1922), written for the Copenhagen Wind Quintet, he not only wrote idiomatically for each instrument—flute, oboe, clarinet, bassoon, and French horn—but also reflected the different personalities of the musicians. In a program note he wrote: "At one moment they are all talking at once, at another they are quite alone." The second movement opens with an aggressive-sounding "conversation" for bassoon and clarinet, wryly suggesting an offstage relationship that was less than harmonious.

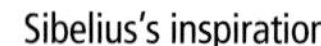

Sibelius's inspiration
In Finland, nationalism was inspired by the *Kalevala*, an epic poem based on Finnish mythology. The story of Lemminki, who was drowned while trying to capture the black swan in the river of Tuonela (the Underworld), inspired Sibelius's *Lemminkäinen Suite*.

Finland and Sibelius

The greatest national voice in the Nordic countries was that of the Finnish composer Jean Sibelius (1865–1957). Born to a Swedish-speaking family in Hämeenlinna, a Russian garrison town in central Finland, Sibelius attended the country's first-ever Finnish-speaking grammar school. Here, he became immersed in Finnish mythology and folklore through the *Kalevala*, a 19th-century work of epic poetry based on Finnish mythology.

10 **The age at which Sibelius started composing. He stopped 30 years before his death.**

Abandoning law studies, Sibelius turned to music, studying in Berlin and then Vienna. Back in Finland, he astonished audiences in 1892 with *Kullervo*, an extended symphonic poem (a piece inspired by a nonmusical source). Its massive scale—five movements with soloists and a male chorus—was reminiscent of the work of the Austrian composer Mahler, although the underlying mood was Finnish. Since Finland was still a Grand Duchy under Russian control, the public took the work, and its composer, to its heart.

In 1899, Sibelius's first symphony and the symphonic poem *Finlandia* underlined his commitment to national pride and self-determination, and brought him international recognition. He went on to compose six more symphonies, each one a major step forward in development. The symphonies share a unique harmonic language and

Finnish composer
Pictured here as a student in Vienna, Sibelius won lasting acclaim overnight after the first performance of his symphonic poem *Kullervo* in 1892.

BEFORE

The Nordic countries had a vigorous folk tradition, but national influences were slow to filter through to classical music.

ISOLATED FROM EUROPEAN TRENDS
The **wave of nationalism** « 176–177 that spread through Central Europe in the mid-19th century took longer to reach the Nordic countries. The **influence of Germany**, still felt in political and cultural ties, took time to recede, and the individual identities of Denmark, Sweden, Norway, and Finland were slower to emerge.

NATIONAL BODY
In Sweden, the **Swedish Royal Academy of Music** was founded by King Gustav III in 1771 to promote musical education among the native people.

FOLK INSTRUMENTS
The Nordic countries had long had their own instruments. The **Finnish *kantele***, a zither plucked with the fingers of both hands producing a bell-like sound, is taught in Finnish music conservatories to this day.

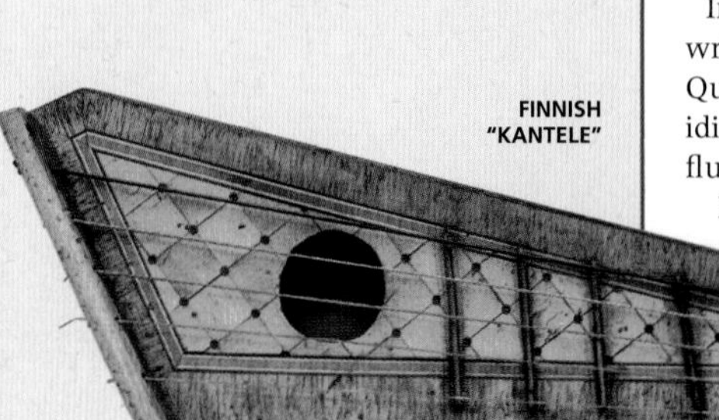

FINNISH "KANTELE"

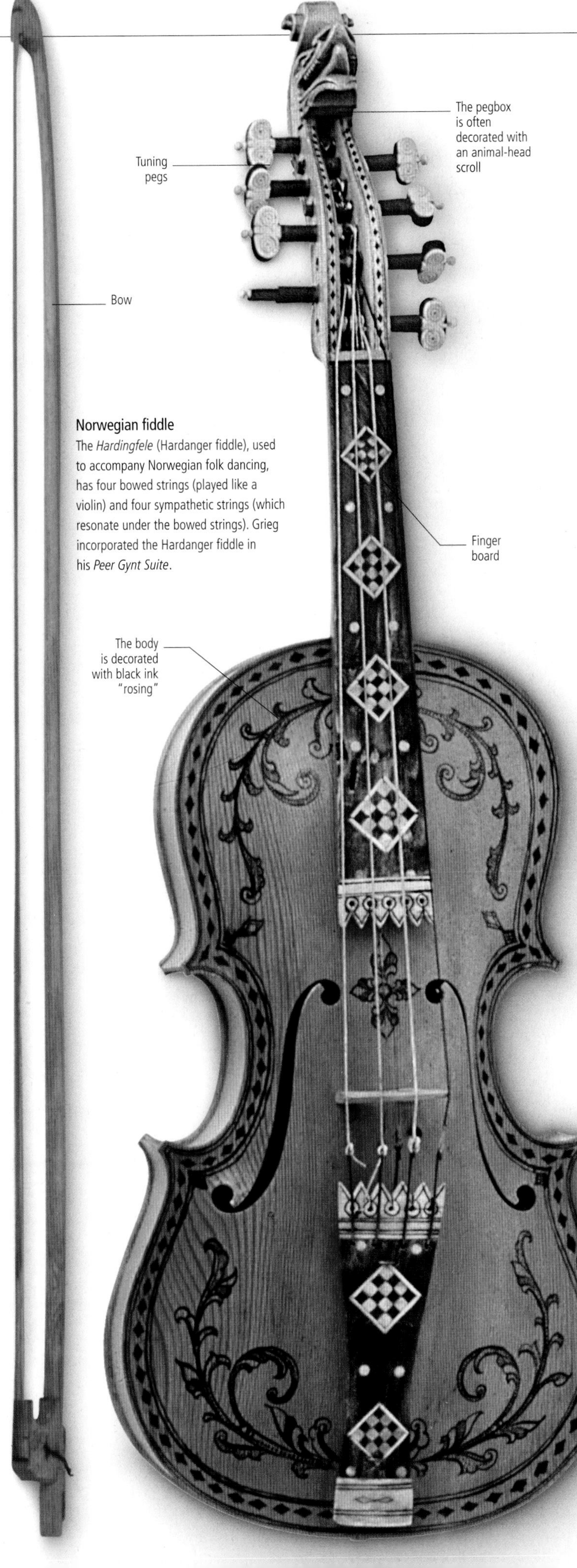

The pegbox is often decorated with an animal-head scroll

Tuning pegs

Bow

Finger board

The body is decorated with black ink "rosing"

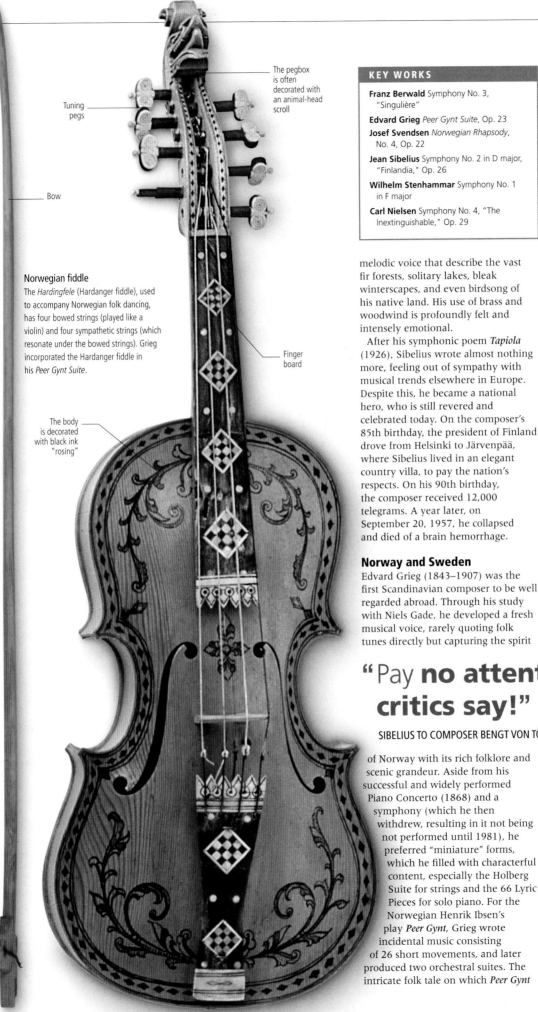

Norwegian fiddle
The *Hardingfele* (Hardanger fiddle), used to accompany Norwegian folk dancing, has four bowed strings (played like a violin) and four sympathetic strings (which resonate under the bowed strings). Grieg incorporated the Hardanger fiddle in his *Peer Gynt Suite*.

KEY WORKS

Franz Berwald Symphony No. 3, "Singulière"

Edvard Grieg *Peer Gynt Suite*, Op. 23

Josef Svendsen *Norwegian Rhapsody*, No. 4, Op. 22

Jean Sibelius Symphony No. 2 in D major, "Finlandia," Op. 26

Wilhelm Stenhammar Symphony No. 1 in F major

Carl Nielsen Symphony No. 4, "The Inextinguishable," Op. 29

melodic voice that describe the vast fir forests, solitary lakes, bleak winterscapes, and even birdsong of his native land. His use of brass and woodwind is profoundly felt and intensely emotional.

After his symphonic poem *Tapiola* (1926), Sibelius wrote almost nothing more, feeling out of sympathy with musical trends elsewhere in Europe. Despite this, he became a national hero, who is still revered and celebrated today. On the composer's 85th birthday, the president of Finland drove from Helsinki to Järvenpää, where Sibelius lived in an elegant country villa, to pay the nation's respects. On his 90th birthday, the composer received 12,000 telegrams. A year later, on September 20, 1957, he collapsed and died of a brain hemorrhage.

AFTER

As wider influences were absorbed, so the impact of nationalism dwindled in the Nordic countries.

NEW HORIZONS

Folk influences lingered, but composers began looking beyond national borders to developments in the rest of Europe and the US. **Dag Wiren**'s *Serenade for Strings* (1880) and **Christian Sinding**'s piano miniature *Rustle of Spring* (1896) represent the **dying embers** of Nordic nationalism.

But music continues to flourish at the heart of Nordic life and audiences remain impressively large. Recent significant composers include **Magnus Lindberg** (Sweden), **Per Norgard** (Denmark), and **Poul Ruders** (Denmark). In Finland, Sibelius's bright torch is carried forward by **Einojuhani Rautavaara**, **Aulis Sallinen**, and **Kaija Saariaho**.

DANISH OPERA HOUSE, COPENHAGEN

Norway and Sweden

Edvard Grieg (1843–1907) was the first Scandinavian composer to be well regarded abroad. Through his study with Niels Gade, he developed a fresh musical voice, rarely quoting folk tunes directly but capturing the spirit of Norway with its rich folklore and scenic grandeur. Aside from his successful and widely performed Piano Concerto (1868) and a symphony (which he then withdrew, resulting in it not being not performed until 1981), he preferred "miniature" forms, which he filled with characterful content, especially the Holberg Suite for strings and the 66 Lyric Pieces for solo piano. For the Norwegian Henrik Ibsen's play *Peer Gynt*, Grieg wrote incidental music consisting of 26 short movements, and later produced two orchestral suites. The intricate folk tale on which *Peer Gynt* is based has a large cast of characters, including trolls, witches, gnomes, madmen, dairymaids, a mountain king, a skipper, and Anitra, the daughter of a Bedouin chief. This eclectic cast list inspired Grieg to lofty descriptive heights, especially in the gentle, flute-led "Morning Mood" and the haunting "Solveig's Song." According to the composer, the latter was the only occasion when he used an original folk tune unaltered.

> "Pay **no attention** to what the **critics say!**"
>
> SIBELIUS TO COMPOSER BENGT VON TÖRNE, 1937

Norway's national flame was also fueled by Josef Svendsen (1840–1911). His four symphonies and Norwegian Rhapsody fuse Viennese Classical traditions with Norwegian folk influences and forms more explicitly than Grieg's.

Meanwhile, in Sweden, Wilhelm Stenhammar (1871–1927), though an admirer of Wagner, Brahms, and Anton Bruckner, was also influenced by the gentle reflectiveness of Gabriel Fauré and Edward Elgar.

BEFORE

The word "ballet" is French, from the Italian *balletto* ("little dance"), reflecting ballet's roots in the opera of Renaissance Italy and France.

FIRST STEPS

On her marriage to King Henry II of France in 1533, **Catherine de Medici** brought with her the Italian tradition of *intermedii*—spectacular interludes of music and dance at **court celebrations ❮❮ 52–53**.

FRENCH DIVERSIONS

Appointed to the French court of King Louis XIV in 1653, composer **Jean-Baptiste Lully** included ballet sequences in his **operas ❮❮ 84**. With the playwright Molière, he created the *comédie-ballet*, blending drama, music, and dance. His first danced drama without singing was *Triomphe d'amour* (Triumph of Love) in 1681. André Campra featured dance more prominently. His 1697 *L'Europe galante* (Europe in Love) inspired **Jean-Philippe Rameau ❮❮ 130–131** to include extended *divertissements* (dances as diversions) in *Les Indes galantes* (The Indies in Love) in 1735 and *Les Fêtes d'Hébé* (The Festivities of Hebe) in 1739.

1661 The year Louis XIV established the Académie Royale de Danse to set standards for teachers and dancers.

"Dance is the **hidden language** of the **soul.**"

US DANCER AND CHOREOGRAPHER MARTHA GRAHAM IN HER AUTOBIOGRAPHY, *BLOOD MEMORY*, 1991

KEY WORKS

Adolphe Adam *Giselle*
Léo Delibes *Coppéia; Sylvia*
Tchaikovsky *Swan Lake; Sleeping Beauty; The Nutcracker*
Frédéric Chopin (orchestrated by Alexander Glazunov) *Les Sylphides*
Igor Stravinsky *The Firebird; Petrushka; The Rite of Spring*
Maurice Ravel *Daphnis and Chloé*
Sergei Prokofiev *Romeo and Juliet*
Aaron Copland *Appalachian Spring*

Pioneering ballerina
Italian-Swedish ballet dancer Marie Taglioni (1804–1884) wore pointe shoes, allowing her to dance on tiptoe. She also wore a lighter skirt (which became the tutu) and a center-parting in her hair.

Ballet Music

Originally a string of entertaining courtly dances and pleasing diversions in early opera, ballet came of age in the mid-19th century. Composers now wrote original scores in which dance and drama came together to tell a story to some of the most memorable music of all.

While opera had become a fully fledged art form by the middle of the 18th century, ballet was slower to find its own identity as a musical genre. Opera composers of the day continued the tradition of including dance sequences in each act, but these entertaining *divertissements* (diversions) did not drive the action forward.

Dance in public theaters had also become popular, but the music was often based on favorite opera tunes thrown together by a staff composer at the theater. The dancing became more showy (many of the most celebrated dancers were men), music was secondary, and narrative was virtually nonexistent.

Orchestra at the Paris Opéra
Musicians take center stage in Edgar Dégas' 1870 painting of the Paris Opéra Orchestra accompanying a ballet sequence.

Ballet takes flight

In Paris around 1700, a new kind of entertainment had begun to emerge, distinct from opera. *Ballet d'action* was a story told in music, dance, and mime, without words. Jean-Georges Noverre, Ballet Master at the Paris Opéra from 1775, dropped empty virtuosic display in favor of telling a coherent story but still preferred to create dances before the music was written.

The conventions of 18th-century ballet staging and costumes—with long coats, heavy skirts, and high heels—had made dancing difficult. In the 18th century, Marie-Anne Camargo, a dancer at the Paris Opéra, switched to soft ballet slippers and raised the hemline of her skirt to reveal ankles clad in special ballet tights, while Marie Sallé adopted light, flowing muslin dresses and abandoned the formal wig. These adaptations allowed dancers to move more freely, with fewer contrived frolics and more expressive gestures. In 1832, when Marie Taglioni first appeared at the Paris Opéra, dancing the role of a forest sylph in *La Sylphide*, she amazed the audience with her elegant lightness and grace.

The birth of Romantic ballet

These new dancers opened composers' eyes to ballet's expressive possibilities. Adolphe Adam (1803–1856), a French composer famed for his operas, created one of the first original Romantic ballet scores, *Giselle* (1841), for the dancer Carlotta Grisi. *Giselle* is based on a poem about a peasant girl who falls in love with Duke Albrecht, dies of a broken heart, and makes a ghostly return. In his music, Adam associated *leitmotivs* (short melodic themes) with Giselle and Albrecht, changing their key, speed, and mood to move the plot forward.

Adam's pupil Léo Delibes (1836–1891) based his 1870 comic ballet *Coppélia* on a story by E.T.A. Hoffmann about a toy maker who builds a doll so lifelike that it is thought to be his daughter. Delibes and Adam greatly influenced the first major symphonic composer to write for ballet—Tchaikovsky (see pp.182–183)—and Russia now supplanted France as the new driving force in ballet.

> "*Dance can reveal the* **mystery** *that* **music conceals.**"
>
> CHARLES BAUDELAIRE, FRENCH POET, ESSAYIST, AND ARTS CRITIC (1821–1867)

A Russian revolution

Tchaikovsky's three ballet scores were choreographed by Marius Petipa and Lev Ivanov, whose work would crystallize the Classical ballet style. The first, *Swan Lake* (1877), tells the story of a princess turned into a swan by an evil magician. With its haunting melody, it remains the most performed ballet.

The composer regarded his second ballet, *Sleeping Beauty* (1890), as his best. The score has a new fluency, and even minor characters are vividly depicted. The individual dances move the action forward, and it culminates in a spectacular *grand divertissement* for the royal wedding.

The Nutcracker (1891), Tchaikovsky's last ballet, is based on a story by Hoffmann. Petipa's scenario hangs a series of set-pieces on a flimsy plot, but the score is brilliantly orchestrated. The tinkling celeste in the Sugar Plum Fairy's solo and the flutes in the Dance of the Mirlitons still enchant today.

When Russian impresario Serge Diaghilev (1872–1929) brought his Ballets Russes company to Paris in 1909, ballet's image changed overnight. Audiences were startled by the Russian-inspired costumes and sets and by the visceral physicality of the dancing. Composers clamored to write for the company, and a string of original ballet scores soon appeared, with sets created by the most radical artists of the day, not least Picasso. Modernized, reinvigorated, and provocative, ballet was all the rage.

AFTER

In the 20th century, Classical ballet gave rise to two new forms: modern dance and jazz-ballet.

OLD THEMES, NEW FORMS
Evoking primeval sacrifice, Stravinsky's ***The Rite of Spring*** **210–213 ››** caused a near riot at its premiere in 1913. He went on to create a new tradition in ballet with US choreographer **George Balanchine.** Shakespeare's play *Romeo and Juliet* inspired brilliant new scores, with **Prokofiev**'s ballet *Romeo and Juliet* in 1938 and **Leonard Bernstein**'s musical ***West Side Story*** in 1961 **282–283 ››**. Founded in 1926, the Martha Graham Dance Company pioneered contemporary dance with **Aaron Copland**'s *Appalachian Spring.*

GEORGE BALANCHINE, 1935

COMPOSER (1891–1953)
SERGEY PROKOFIEV

Born in a remote district of Ukraine, musical prodigy Prokofiev became the youngest student at the St. Petersburg Conservatoire at the age of 13. His first published works were boldly modern, and the debut of his Piano Concerto No. 2 in 1913 caused a minor scandal. Prokofiev emigrated to the US in 1918 but returned to Europe two years later, earning a reputation as a musical innovator. His ballet *Chout* (The Buffoon), commissioned by impresario Sergei Diagalev, debuted to acclaim in Paris in 1921. He moved to the Soviet Union in 1936, where he wrote *Romeo and Juliet*, classical masterpieces such as his Violin Concerto No. 2, and the children's story *Peter and the Wolf.*

New Tones and **Timbres**

The 19th century was a period of unprecedented developments in the history of musical instruments. Inspired by the Industrial Revolution, craftsmen and composers used their skills and imagination to transform the way musical instruments sounded.

This surge of invention went hand in hand with composers' search for new, expressive sounds to inject greater emotional intensity into their music and was further fueled by the need for reliable and affordable instruments for amateurs. With the major forms of symphony, sonata, concerto, and opera firmly established, and the romantic principle of descriptive (program) music finding acceptance, the quest for a varied palette of colors and textures was the obvious next step for composers.

Using their growing understanding of acoustics and mechanization, makers focused on developing keywork and valve systems for woodwind and brass that made an instrument's full range of notes easily playable.

Music on the march

At one time, armies used brass instruments and drums to signal going into battle. Since the 19th century, military bands have mainly supplied music for ceremonial occasions.

BEFORE

In the 17th and 18th centuries, woodwind and brass instruments had limited range and tone quality, and could be unreliable.

EARLY PERCUSSION

Percussion, generally limited to **timpani**, was often paired with **trumpets**.

LIMITATIONS AND SOLUTIONS

Woodwind instruments **« 122–123** had few keys and many open holes. Highly skilled players used complex "cross-fingering" to create more than the few basic notes that the tube allowed.

As for brass instruments, the **horn** and the **trumpet** had no valves, limiting their choice of notes, though **extra lengths of tubing**, known as crooks, could be added, to change the basic key of the instrument and extend its tonal range.

SIMPLE ONE-KEY IVORY FLUTE

Woodwind developments

At the end of the 18th century, flutes, oboes, clarinets, and bassoons were used regularly as solo and orchestral instruments, but they were technically limited. It was difficult to play rapid passages and to move smoothly from one note to the next. Keys operated by the little fingers worked pads that opened and covered holes lower down the tube that the fingers could not reach, restricting the number of notes, and limiting the keys in which an instrument could easily be played.

A number of inventors worked to improve woodwind instruments. For example, to extend the extremes of pitch of the woodwind family, bigger and smaller versions were developed. One of the most notable of these inventors was Theobald Boehm (see opposite). His innovations were revolutionary, especially for the flute.

Once they had been improved, unusual instruments could take solo parts in orchestral works. In 1830, for example, the soulful English horn moved center stage as somber soloist. Its rustic quality is heard in the slow-movement dialogue with the reedy oboe used by Hector Berlioz (see below) in his *Symphonie fantastique*. The dark-hued bass clarinet featured in the 1849 opera *Le prophète* by German composer Giacomo Meyerbeer (1791–1864), while the smaller E flat clarinet screeches in the "Witches' Sabbath" finale of Berlioz's *Symphonie fantastique*. The lowest of the woodwind, the contrabassoon, adds a gravitas to the symphonies of Austrian composer Gustav Mahler (see pp.192–193), and a gruff comedic element in the 1896 symphonic poem *The Sorcerer's Apprentice* by French composer Paul Dukas (1865–1935).

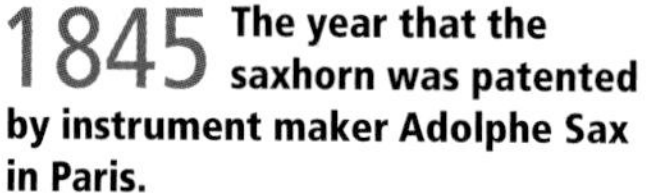

1845 **The year that the saxhorn was patented by instrument maker Adolphe Sax in Paris.**

Brass inventions

Improvements to brass instruments, which began in the 1700s, continued apace. The range of notes a brass instrument can play depends on the basic length and shape of the tube (conical or cylindrical), and the shape and size of the mouthpiece.

With a fixed length of tubing, it is possible to play only a certain number of notes. The crooked horn, in which extra lengths of tubing (crooks) were inserted, increased the number of playable notes. This system was cumbersome, however, so makers devised numerous solutions to lengthen the tube more efficiently.

The use of valves or pistons to direct the column of air into built-in extra tubing, as required, was the most successful solution, and also proved useful for the trumpet and tuba. However, the simple slide mechanism of the trombone proved hard to better.

There were also experiments with new mouthpieces. The cornet (similar to the trumpet but actually a post horn with valves) was popular because its deep-cupped mouthpiece allowed the performer to play fast-moving tunes more accurately.

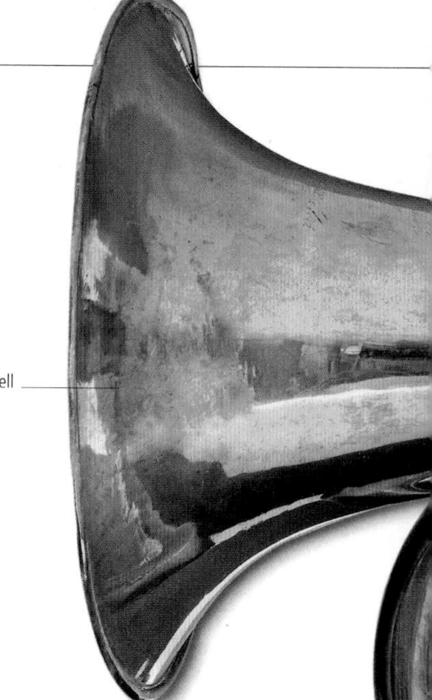

KEY WORKS

Giacomo Rossini Overture to *William Tell*

Hector Berlioz *Symphonie Fantastique*

Richard Wagner *Das Rheingold* (The Rhine Gold) from *Der Ring des Nibelungen* (The Ring of the Nibelung)

Camille Saint-Saëns *Danse Macabre*; Symphony No. 3 (Organ), Op. 78

COMPOSER (1803–1869)

HECTOR BERLIOZ

Berlioz was born in France and began studying music at the age of 12. Defying his doctor father, he abandoned medical studies in Paris to pursue a musical career and to indulge himself in literature and passionate love affairs. His obsession with actress Harriet Smithson (her initial rejection of him inspired the *Symphonie fantastique*) led to a destructive nine-year marriage.

Berlioz's compositions were little appreciated in his lifetime, but his understanding of instrumentation and orchestral settings was revolutionary.

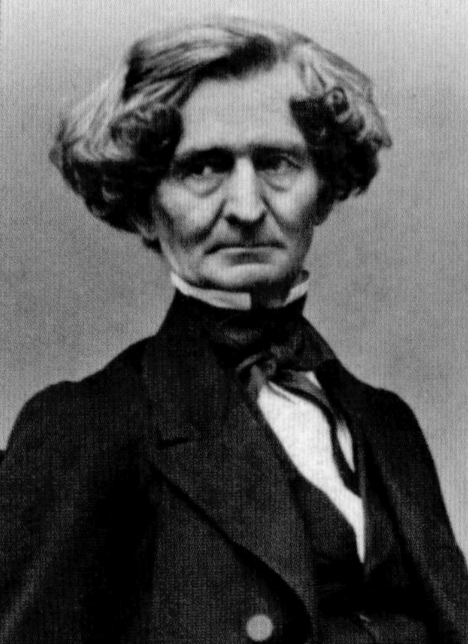

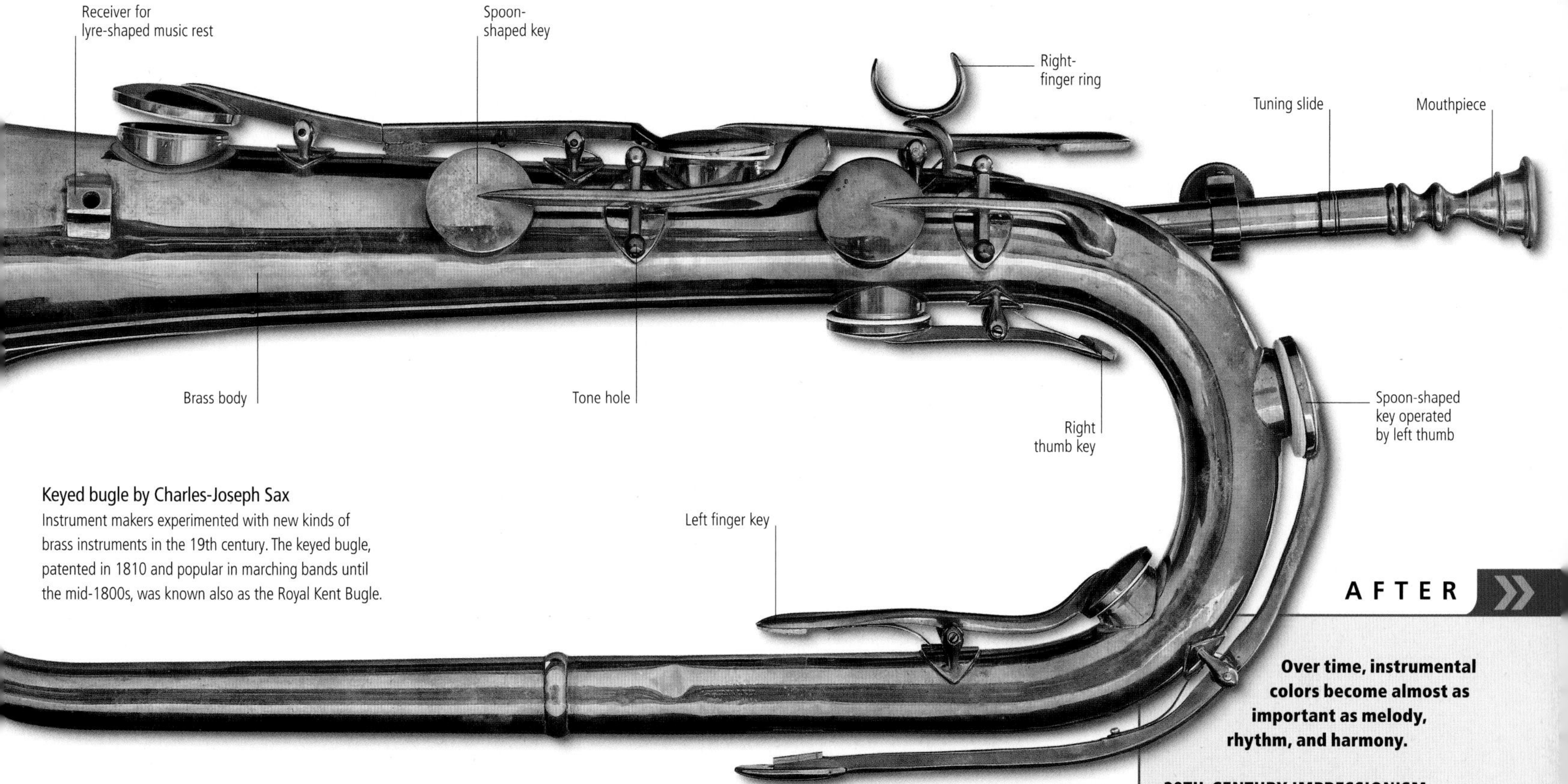

Receiver for lyre-shaped music rest

Spoon-shaped key

Right-finger ring

Tuning slide

Mouthpiece

Brass body

Tone hole

Right thumb key

Spoon-shaped key operated by left thumb

Left finger key

Keyed bugle by Charles-Joseph Sax
Instrument makers experimented with new kinds of brass instruments in the 19th century. The keyed bugle, patented in 1810 and popular in marching bands until the mid-1800s, was known also as the Royal Kent Bugle.

In addition to improvements to existing instruments, new ones were invented. Some of these were short-lived, but others survived. Among the inventions of the Belgian instrument-maker Adolphe Sax (1814–1894), best known for the saxophone, the brass saxhorn was very successful (see pp.200–201).

The rise of brass and marching bands demanded new instruments that were easier for amateurs to play, and in different sizes so players could change easily from one to another. For this reason other 19th-century creations, including the flugelhorn, sousaphone, and euphonium, found enduring popularity among band members.

New sounds and effects

Many experiments were short-lived, but not the Wagner tuba. Seeking a mellow brass tone for his *Ring* cycle of operas, Richard Wagner (see pp.164–165) devised an elliptical kind of French horn. The instrument was also used by German composer Anton Bruckner (1824–1896) to great effect in his Seventh Symphony. Inspired by new capabilities of wind and brass, string players and composers found new ways of playing their instruments. These effects are heard to mesmerizing effect in Italian Niccolò Paganini's *24 Caprices* for violin (see p.178). The harp was further mechanized in the 19th century and features in the music of Berlioz (who used four in his *Symphonie fantastique*) and in the ballet music of Igor Tchaikovsky (see p.187).

6 The number of harps used by Wagner to depict the Rhine River in his opera *Das Rheingold*.

Percussive adventures

The exponential expansion of the percussion section began in the 19th century, with the addition of side and bass drums, gongs, bells, triangle, cymbals, celesta, and xylophone. Each of these unique instruments gave composers extra sonorities to use. Berlioz, Nikolay Rimsky-Korsakov (see p.181), and Tchaikovsky (see pp.182–183) had a special talent for using a range of percussion instruments to add expressive beams of light and color to their compositions for orchestra. Above all, though, it was Berlioz who drove forward the imaginative use of instruments. He wrote a work entitled the *Treatise on Instrumentation*. This was a technical study of Western instruments, first published in serial form and then as a whole in 1843. In it, he vividly describes the special character of each instrument. His own preferences are clear, and there is little doubt that Berlioz favored orchestral instruments. He described the oboe as "melodic, rustic, tender, and shy," the horn "noble and melancholy," but the organ was "jealous and intolerant."

> "**Instrumentation** is at the **head** of the **march.**"
>
> BERLIOZ, TREATISE ON INSTRUMENTATION, 1843

AFTER

Over time, instrumental colors become almost as important as melody, rhythm, and harmony.

20TH-CENTURY IMPRESSIONISM
French **Impressionist composers 204–205 ››** focused on the unique tonal qualities of woodwind instruments.

INSTRUMENT INVENTION CONTINUED
The Heckelphone, a bass oboe invented in 1904, was heard in the 1905 opera *Salome* by **Richard Strauss 222–223 ››**.

EXPERIMENTAL ELECTRICAL MUSIC
Electronics 212–213 ›› enabled the development of new, distinctive sounding instruments such as the vibraphone, **electric guitar**, and **theremin**.

UNDERSTANDING MUSIC

BŒHM SYSTEM

Flautist, goldsmith, and craftsman, Munich-born Theobald Boehm (1794–1881) developed a novel system of keying woodwind instruments. Boehm's invention allowed the holes to be cut in the tube at the correct acoustical position to produce notes that were perfectly in tune.

Some holes were too for apart for the fingers to reach, so Boehm created rings around the open finger holes. When pressed down, these rings opened and closed distant holes by a coupling mechanism of rods and springs, allowing performers to play easily in most keys.

Developed in the 1830s and '40s, this solution was most successfully applied to flutes and clarinets, some of which still use a version of the Boehm System today. It inspired composers to write more elaborately for wind instruments.

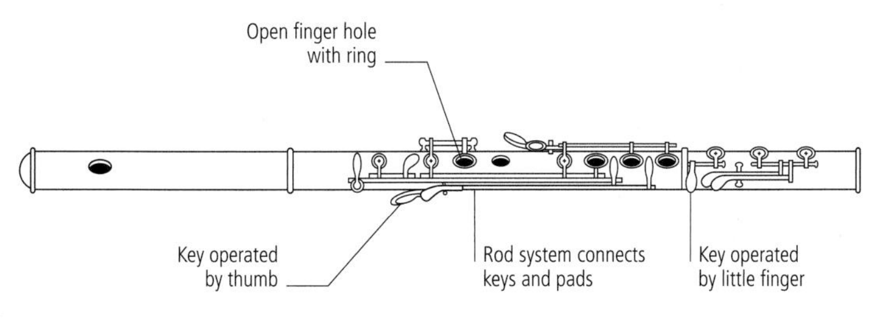

Wooden mouthpiece

Ligature holds reed in place

Upper octave key

Single reed

Neck cork

Neck

Lever activates upper octave key

Lever connects to upper octave key lever

Adjustment screw to raise or lower pads

Pad that controls E

Rod on which keys are mounted

Pad lowers when keys pressed

Cork pad under keys

Octave key lever

B key

A key

G key

G-sharp key

B key

C-sharp key

Neckstrap ring

The Saxophone

The saxophone is a magnificent invention of a 19th-century Belgian musician-craftsman. Blending the best qualities of both brass and woodwind instruments, this unique hybrid was an instant hit in bands in Europe and America and remains a central pillar in today's diverse music scene.

At a time of fast and furious invention in the instrument world, maker Adolphe Sax was eager to find ways of extending the power and bass range of woodwind instruments. He was constantly experimenting in his Paris workshop. In 1842, Sax's friend composer Hector Berlioz wrote of "a brass instrument rather like a ophicleide [a large keyed bugle played upright] in shape but with a mouthpiece like that of the bass clarinet… there is not a bass instrument to compare with it." He was describing the first saxophone.

Family members

Although Sax designed 14 instruments, modern players tend to use one of six saxophones. The smallest, the sopranino and soprano, are straight, while the alto, tenor, baritone, and bass have bent tubing and upward-tilted bells. Despite the variation in size, all saxophones are made of conical brass tubes and have keywork and a mouthpiece like the clarinet. The shape of the body allows a large body of air to vibrate in the instrument, creating a full, hornlike sound. One benefit of building families of instruments is that players can easily swap to different sizes—this is useful in bands. Clarinetists occasionally double on saxophone.

Sound success

The saxophone's elegant design makes it ideal for virtuoso playing. Its keywork facilitates rapid soloistic playing, while its natural, near-vocal expressiveness allows players to create their own individual sound.

Immediately popular in marching bands where its versatility was highly prized, orchestral composers, including Bizet, Mussorgsky, Vaughan Williams, and Prokofiev, were also quick to seize on its unique timbre for solos.

Sax supremacy

The saxophone is most at home in jazz. Its sound, alternately mellow and abrasive, is perfectly suited for improvisation. Whether in dizzying technical pyrotechnics or achingly mournful melancholy, the saxophone has become the "voice" of some of the greatest musicians of the last 120 years.

TIMELINE

1841
Creation
Adolphe Sax first made the main members of the saxophone family, which he patented in 1846: soprano, alto, tenor, baritone, and bass.

1844
Berlioz the champion
Within three years of its invention, Hector Berlioz used a bass sax in an arrangement of his choral work *Chant sacré*.

B FLAT BASS SAX

1866
Patent expires
Sax patented 14 models of the saxophone in 1846. The patent lasted for 20 years, and when it expired, other instrument-makers quickly brought their own versions to the market. Sax extended his original patent in 1881.

ALTO SAX

1868
Classical premiere
The alto saxophone featured in a virtuoso but expertly written solo *obbligato* part in Amboise Thomas's 1868 opera *Hamlet*.

1872
French pioneer
Georges Bizet becomes one of the first composers to give the alto saxophone a prominent orchestral role, in his piece *L'Arlésienne* (*The Girl from Arles*).

BIZET

SOUSA'S BAND CONCERT PROGRAM

1892–1931
Sousa's saxes
John Philip Sousa's celebrated military band included several alto saxophones. Saxes continued to play important roles in American and British military and marching bands.

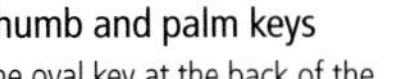

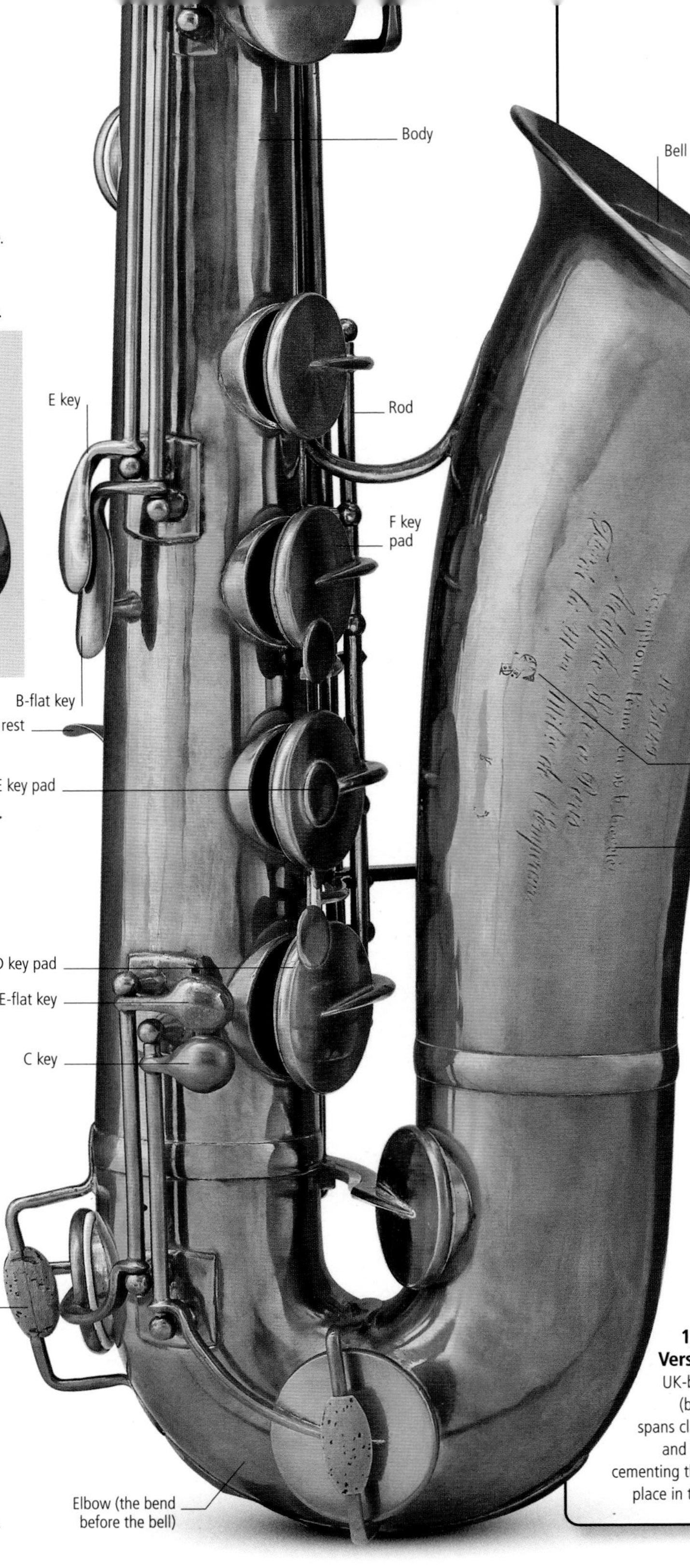

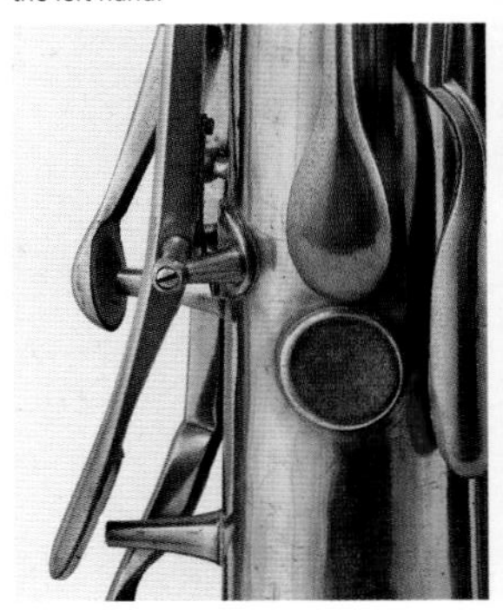

Thumb and palm keys

The oval key at the back of the saxophone is pressed by the left thumb to make notes an octave higher. The keys on the left-hand side are played by the palm of the left hand.

Keywork

Each key has a round touchpiece for the fingers to push down on when playing a note. The height at which a key sits over a hole affects the note's tone.

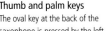

Bell

The saxophone's upward-facing bell projects the sound highly effectively, helping it penetrate through noisy environments.

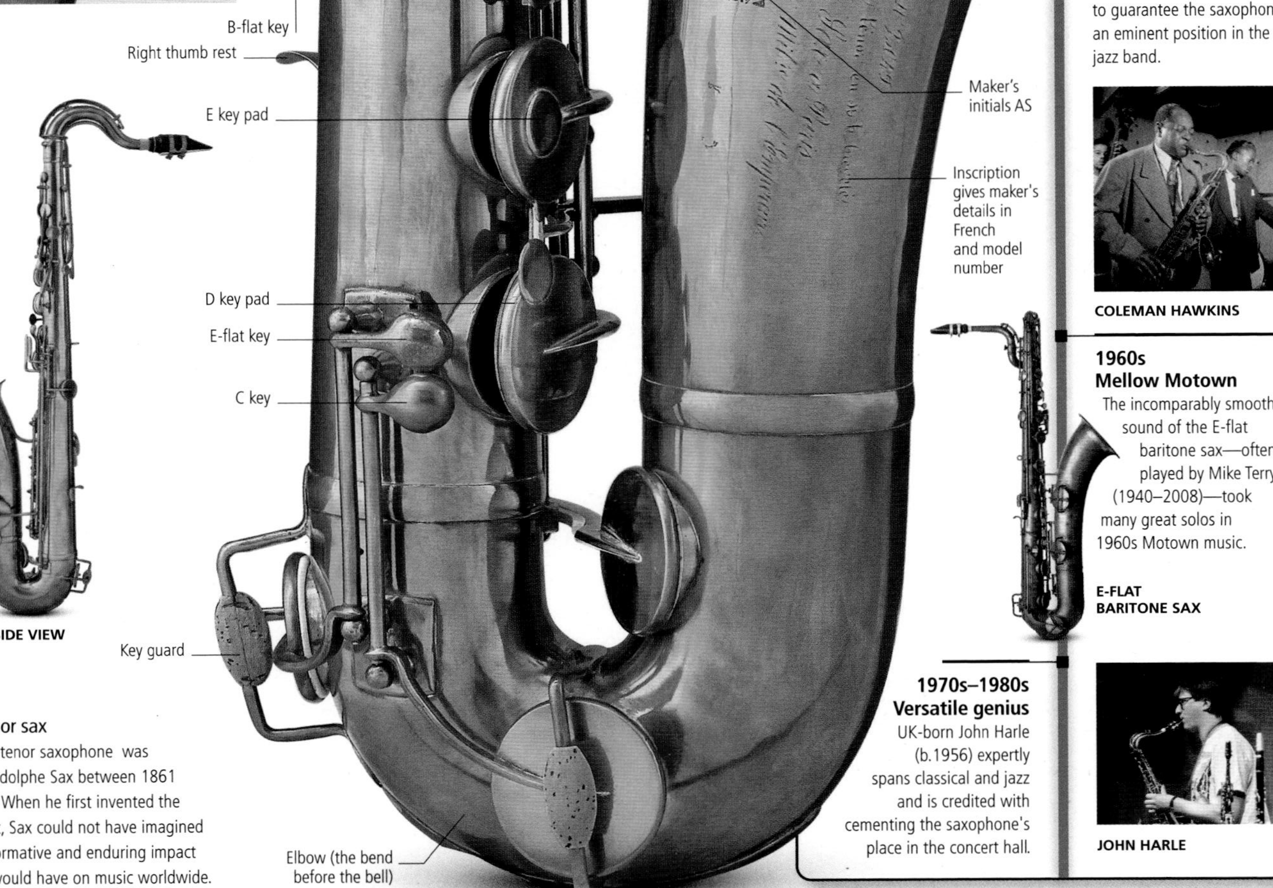

B-flat tenor sax

This B-flat tenor saxophone was made by Adolphe Sax between 1861 and 1862. When he first invented the instrument, Sax could not have imagined the transformative and enduring impact his work would have on music worldwide.

INSTRUMENT-MAKER (1814–1894)

ADOLPHE SAX

Adolphe Sax was an extraordinary musical inventor whose finest creation, the saxophone, remains central to music to this day. Born in Brussels, Sax moved to Paris in 1842, where he exhibited an early model of his saxophone. He invented saxhorns and saxtubas for brass bands, but it was the saxophone, patented in 1846, that earned him lasting fame. The originality of his inventions was challenged in a series of lawsuits but, undeterred, Sax continued inventing. His Paris-based firm continued for some years after his death in 1894.

1920s
Doubling up
Originally a New Orleans clarinetist, Sidney Bechet (1897–1959) excelled on soprano saxophone with spectacular solos and his distinctively wide vibrato.

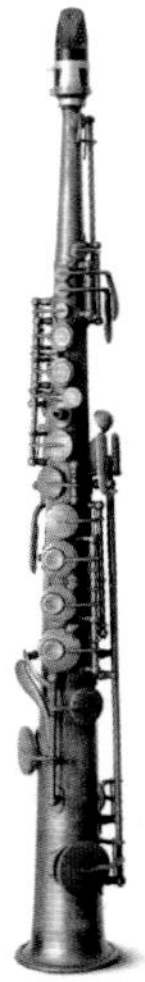

SOPRANO SAXOPHONE

1930s
The new jazz
American Coleman Hawkins (1904–1969), a renowned tenor sax soloist, helped - to guarantee the saxophone an eminent position in the jazz band.

COLEMAN HAWKINS

1960s
Mellow Motown
The incomparably smooth sound of the E-flat baritone sax—often played by Mike Terry (1940–2008)—took many great solos in 1960s Motown music.

E-FLAT BARITONE SAX

1970s–1980s
Versatile genius
UK-born John Harle (b.1956) expertly spans classical and jazz and is credited with cementing the saxophone's place in the concert hall.

JOHN HARLE

BEFORE

The Classical symphony fell out of favor in the Romantic era. However, composers who continued to work in the form were able to take advantage of new orchestral developments.

THE CLASSICAL SYMPHONY

In the early 19th century, the symphonies of **Beethoven « 142–143** and **Franz Schubert « 154–155** followed the four-movement structure of the **Classical symphony « 124–125** but the musical content became more wide-ranging melodically, harmonically, and rhythmically.

EXPRESSING EMOTION

Romanticism encouraged composers to express personal and nationalist feelings. Many turned to more flexible structures, such as the **tone poem « 156–157**.

NEW INSTRUMENTS

The **expansion of the orchestra « 118–119** from around 1800 offered greater musical variety. Instruments such as the piccolo brought piquancy to the upper register, while new brass and percussion added further colors to the orchestral palette.

Symphonic Supremacy

While the impact of Romanticism tempted composers to try new musical forms, several major figures revived the Classical symphony from the 1870s. They used its large-scale, formal structure as a framework for working out new ideas.

After Schubert, most composers were using their energies in opera and song or in music with a story (program) inspired by literature or art. However, the symphony enjoyed a new lease of life in the hands of composers rooted in the Austro-Germanic musical tradition. These included Brahms, Bruckner, and Mahler, who embraced the creative opportunities that the larger orchestras of the age provided.

Austro-German symphonists

Johannes Brahms (1833–1897) deplored the idea of program music, and preferred music that had no descriptive element. In his four symphonies, he wrote conservatively for an orchestra, with a large group of strings, pairs of woodwind instruments, horns, trumpets, trombones, and percussion. Their rich-hued instrumentation and strong melodies made his symphonies eternally popular.

Brahms's contemporary Anton Bruckner (1824–1896) took a more innovative approach to symphonic writing and to the orchestra. An organist, who was largely self-taught as a composer, he was 40 before he tackled a symphony, but he went on to write nine. He was an admirer of Richard Wagner (1813–1883), in particular his extreme harmonies, imaginative instrumental colors, and extended,

Bruckner's Ninth

The last movement of Bruckner's Ninth Symphony was unfinished at the time of his death in 1896. Although there have been seven "completions" by other composers, it is usually performed as a three-movement work.

China National Symphony Orchestra
New instruments and a public eager to hear large orchestral works such as symphonies led to an increase in the number and size of professional orchestras from the late 1800s. The China National Symphony Orchestra was founded in 1956.

unfolding melodies. Bruckner incorporated Wagnerian features into his work. Rather than developing themes in the symphonic tradition of four distinct movements, he preferred to juxtapose several extended ideas in a sequence, often separating them with a pause.

These blocks of sound and abrupt changes became hallmarks of Bruckner's symphonic writing. His Fourth Symphony in E flat major, the "Romantic"—alluding to the medieval romances used by Wagner in the music-drama *Lohengrin*—is typical. From the opening solo horn call over trembling strings to the brass call-and-answer sequences of the third movement and the exciting finale, it forms a work of transcendent appeal.

New sounds

Czech composer Antonín Dvořák (1841–1904) wrote nine symphonies, all in the Classical four-movement tradition, with occasional cyclic repetitions of a theme across the movements to bring cohesion. He relished the sounds of the newer additions to the orchestra, writing parts for all instruments.

In France, the symphony was a rarity, as grand opera was the preoccupation. César Franck's D Minor Symphony (1888) was successful, while the third of Camille Saint-Saëns's three symphonies (1886) included a large part for the organ, celebrating a revival of interest in the instrument in Paris.

Pushing the boundaries

At the point when Romanticism was in rapid decline, the Austrian conductor and composer Gustav Mahler (1860–1911) transformed the symphony. In his nine symphonies (and a part of a tenth), he created tension by using harmonic and rhythmic inventions and unusual juxtapositions of style. He used the voice in four symphonies and expanded the orchestra—the eighth symphony is called the "Symphony of a Thousand," referring to the huge orchestra and chorus that it requires.

The German folk-story anthology *Des Knaben Wunderhorn* (The Boy's Magic Horn) was a lifelong influence on Mahler, its satire appealing to his own tendencies. Its impact is evident even in his First Symphony, the "Titan," whose innocent second-movement dance, Ländler, subtly distorts into a parody of itself. The third movement opens with a high solo double bass transforming a folklike tune (akin to the children's song "Frère Jacques") into a spooky portent. The finale opens with an orchestral screech followed by a sinister march and yearning melody, before reaching a triumphal, brassy conclusion. Twenty-four years later, Mahler died while working on his Tenth Symphony, having pushed the form to the utmost extreme.

Master of invention
This caricature of Gustav Mahler from a 1900 edition of *Illustrirtes Wiener Extrablatt* depicts him conducting his Symphony No. 1, "Titan." Mahler employed unexpected juxtapositions in his music to suggest parody and irony.

KEY WORKS

Johannes Brahms Symphony No. 2 in D major, Op. 73

Anton Bruckner Symphony No. 4 in E flat major, "Romantic," WAB 104

Gustav Mahler Symphony No. 1 in D major, "Titan"

César Franck Symphony in D minor

Camille Saint-Saëns Symphony No. 3, "Organ," Op. 78

Crook horn
Detachable coils of tubing were added to the horn to change the length of the tube and hence its pitch, introducing a greater variety of brass notes to the orchestra. Even after the invention of the valve in the 1820s, many players and composers continued to prefer the tones of the crook horn.

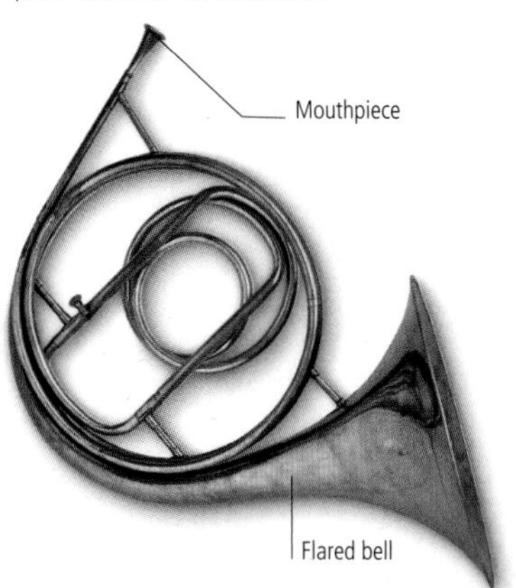

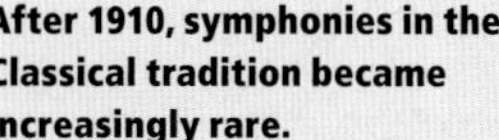

AFTER

After 1910, symphonies in the Classical tradition became increasingly rare.

SYMPHONIC ISLANDS

In Finland, **Jean Sibelius** « 184–185 wrote seven symphonies. Deviating from the symphonic norm (the seventh consists of a single movement), he explored the sounds of landscape and nature.

In Russia, **Sergey Rachmaninoff**'s three symphonies are anachronistic in feel, with heart-rending melodies 222–223 ». By contrast, **Shostakovich** used the symphony to express his profound differences with the Soviet regime.

Britain clung to the symphony longer than most countries. **Edward Elgar**'s are intense and brooding, while **Vaughan Williams**'s have a pastoral feel 214–215 ».

UNDERSTANDING MUSIC

PROGRAM SYMPHONIES

A longer version of the 19th-century tone poem (symphonic poem), program symphonies are inspired by nonmusical ideas, often with the aim of telling a story or producing a mood. Richard Strauss's *Sinfonia Domestica* (1903), for example, was inspired by his family life. It features children playing, parental happiness, a love scene, and an argument. Other examples include Alexander Scriabin's *Poem of Ecstasy* (1908), inspired by theosophy, and Sir Arthur Bliss's *A Colour Symphony* (1922), with the four movements based on the colors purple, red, blue, and green.

BEFORE

The development of comic opera in the 18th century delighted audiences in several countries.

FRANCE AND ITALY

In early 18th-century France, **opéra comique**, with its farces and satires, were popular. In Italian opera in Naples, comic *intermedi* (lighthearted contrasting sections) were inserted into serious operas, and Italy's own version of comic opera, **opera buffa** **« 132–133**, emerged in the 1720s.

PARODY AND SATIRE

Ballad opera **« 132–133** became popular in Britain with John Gay's *The Beggar's Opera* (1728), which parodied Italian opera while satirizing the British government.

THE MAGIC FLUTE

Mozart's **« 136–137** singspiel (opera with spoken dialogue) *Die Zauberflöte* (*The Magic Flute*) of 1791 blended sublime music with bawdy jokes and comic repartee.

A **Lighter Touch**

Operetta, meaning "little opera," arose in Paris, Vienna, and London toward the middle of the 19th century. Lighthearted entertainment for educated, cosmopolitan audiences, it was sung in the local language, and was full of dancing, choruses, and witty dialogue.

The first significant operetta was written by the French composer and critic Adolphe Adam (1803–1856). Entitled *Le Chalet,* it had only one act. It was premiered in 1834 at Paris's Théâtre Opéra-Comique and was such a success that by 1873 it had been performed 1,000 times.

The German-born cellist and conductor Jacques Offenbach (1819–1880) is considered the undisputed first master of operetta. The Opéra-Comique, where he was a cellist in the orchestra, was not at all interested in Offenbach's operettas. Taking advantage of the influx of visitors to Paris's great International Exhibition of 1855, he hired a small theater on the Champs-Elysées and mounted a series of short, one-act comic pieces. The move was a triumph that launched him as a composer.

> "**Orpheus** was a **profanation** of **holy** and **glorious antiquity ...**"
>
> JULES JANIN ON ORPHEUS IN THE UNDERWORLD, "JOURNAL DES DÉBATS," 1859

Operatic outrage

Offenbach's *Orpheus in the Underworld,* written in 1838, is regarded as the first full-length operetta. Not only did it mock the classical myths that many serious operas had been based upon, but it also featured the risqué can-can, a dance seen more often in vaudeville revues at that time.

While audiences loved the scandalous plot and lighthearted music, critics were outraged, declaring it profane and blasphemous. This notoriety caused all performances to sell out and for the next 10 years Offenbach

MUSICAL PARTNERSHIP

GILBERT AND SULLIVAN

Librettist William Schwenk Gilbert (1836–1911) was born in London and had several careers. By the time of his first collaboration with Sullivan in 1871 he was a playwright, poet, illustrator, and theater director. In 1889, he built the Garrick Theatre in London.

Composer and conductor Sir Arthur Sullivan (1842–1900) was also born in London. He studied piano at the Royal Academy of Music in London and then received a scholarship to study at the Leipzig Conservatory. In addition to operettas, he composed ballets, piano pieces, choral works, and orchestral works.

Soap cards for collectors

The comic operas of Gilbert and Sullivan captured the popular public imagination. To mark the opening night of *The Mikado* in 1885, fans could collect soap cards showing a range of characters and scenes.

Parisian home
The Théatre des Bouffes in Paris premiered the operettas of Jacques Offenbach in the mid-19th century. The theater still hosts premieres of new operas and ballets today.

dominated the operetta scene in Paris. He went on to compose more operettas, notably *La belle Hélène* (1864) and *La Périchole* (1868). Near the end of his life Offenbach worked on the more serious opera *Les contes d'Hoffmann* (*Tales of Hoffmann*), completed in 1877.

Viennese operetta

In 1874, Austrian composer Johann Strauss II (1825–1899), already famous for his supreme waltz music, wrote the comic opera *Die Fledermaus* (The Bat). The plot, which makes fun of life in high-class Viennese society, is full of twists and turns. The elegant waltzes and lively polkas performed in the lavish ballroom scene have gone on to find popular appeal, and some of the arias have become widely famous in their own right, in particular Adele's "Laughing Song" from Act Two.

Gilbert and Sullivan

The English partnership of W.S. Gilbert and Arthur Sullivan, known as "Gilbert and Sullivan," resulted in 14 light comic operas between 1871 and 1896. The plots bristle with satire, the absurd, parody, and burlesque. Sullivan's arias allow the singer to portray a range of emotions while Gilbert's witty rapid-fire patter songs require outstanding diction and impressive feats of memorization. The success of *Trial by Jury* (1875) persuaded producer Richard D'Oyly Carte (1844–1901) to form a company to perform Gilbert and Sullivan's works. In 1881, he built the Savoy Theatre in London to house them.

A string of unparalleled triumphs followed, including *Iolanthe* (1882), *The Mikado* (1885), and *The Gondoliers* (1889). The works still enjoy an enthusiastic following around the world. A large part of their popularity is due to the fact that the dialogue and songs can be updated and reworded as needed to satirize current events.

Austro-Hungarian revival

Interest in operetta waned in the 1890s in Europe, but Austro-Hungarian military bandmaster and composer Franz Lehár (1870–1948) revived it. His first major operetta success came in 1905 with *Die Lustige Witwe* (*The Merry Widow*). Rather than following the tradition of inserting songs for comic actors to sing, he composed music for singers who could be amusing. He was skilled at slipping waltzes and other dances smoothly into the story, so his operettas were seamless.

Lehár wrote 42 operas and operettas. Although some are still performed today, none have surpassed the popularity of *The Merry Widow*.

Operetta Poster, 1900
The popularity of operetta crossed national boundaries, and the vocal music and dialogue were regularly translated into other languages. In French, Strauss's operetta *Die Fledermaus* is known as *Le Chauve-Souris*.

KEY WORKS

- **John Gay** *The Beggar's Opera*
- **Adolphe Adam** *Le Chalet*
- **Jacques Offenbach** *Orpheus in the Underworld*
- **Johann Strauss** *Die Fledermaus*
- **Gilbert and Sullivan** *The Mikado, The Gondoliers, Trial by Jury*
- **Franz Lehár** *The Merry Widdow*

AFTER

A few composers continued to write operettas, but the musical began to replace the form by the mid-20th century.

LATER OPERETTA

Franz Lehár wrote six tailor-made operetta roles for Austrian tenor **Richard Tauber** (1891–1948), including *Das Land des Lächlens* (*Land of Smiles*) in 1923. In 1928, **Kurt Weill** **256–257 ››** composed *The Threepenny Opera* based on John Gay's *The Beggar's Opera* of two centuries earlier.

BROADWAY MUSICAL

Alan Jan Lerner and Frederick Loewe's musical *My Fair Lady*, based on George Bernard Shaw's 1914 play *Pygmalion*, opened on Broadway in 1956. It became a movie in 1964 **293 ››**.

Italian Opera Gets Real

At the end of the 19th century, inspired by a new literary realism, a group of Italian composers began writing operas that reflected the lives and hardships of ordinary working people, especially those in the poorer south of Italy.

« BEFORE

Only a few earlier composers had attempted to make opera more of a true reflection of contemporary life.

THE FALLEN WOMAN
For the 1853 première of the Romantic opera *La traviata* (*The Fallen Woman*), **Verdi** **« 164–165** altered the contemporary setting to an earlier era to keep from scandalizing the audience. The heroine of the opera is a high-class prostitute who gives up the man she loves out of a sense of moral duty.

CARMEN'S FINAL SCENE OUTSIDE THE BULL RING, USED HERE TO ADVERTISE BEEF EXTRACT

THE INCARNATION OF VICE
Carmen (1875), the masterpiece of French composer Georges Bizet (1838–1875), was regarded as immoral because its central character, a fiercely independent Romany woman working in a cigarette factory in Seville, uses her sexual powers to ensnare men and openly defies conventional morality and the law. One critic called her the "incarnation of vice."

"I love **Italian opera**—it's so reckless. I like the Italians who all run on **impulse,** and don't care about their immortal souls…"

ENGLISH WRITER D. H. LAWRENCE, IN A LETTER TO HIS FIANCÉE, LOUIE BURROWS, 1911

Against the mid-19th century backdrop of revolution and industrialization, a new spirit of anti-Romantic realism swept through the arts, from France to Russia. In Italy, a new style of opera called *verismo*, the Italian for realism, can be traced to 1888, when the publisher Edoardo Sonzogno offered a prize for a one-act opera by an Italian composer. One of the winners was Pietro Mascagni (1863–1945) whose entry, *Cavalleria rusticana* (Rustic Chivalry), was based on a play by the Sicilian realist Giovanni Verga. Set in Sicily, *Cavalleria rusticana* is a tale of infidelity, jealousy, and revenge.

The story sees Turiddu, a local heartthrob back from military service, seduce a girl while resuming his affair with a former lover who is now married. The music is immediate and intense, matching the emotions of the characters. There are many powerful melodies, such as the orchestral *intermezzo* (interlude) and the final aria that Turiddu sings as he faces death in a duel.

True to life

Cavalleria rusticana was an almost instant hit, with subsequent performances in several other countries. The opera started a trend for greater realism among a new generation of Italian composers. Stories were usually set among poor, working-class people, and often involved a crime of passion. There was a regional flavor to several of these operas, as composers incorporated local songs and dances, and instruments such as the mandolin.

The next opera to adopt this approach was by a runner-up in the Sonzogno competition, Umberto Giordano (1867–1948). His three-act opera *Mala vita* (Wretched Life), set in Naples, tells the story of how a laborer, Vito, vows to rescue a prostitute by marrying her if he is cured of tuberculosis.

In the same year, the composer and librettist Ruggero Leoncavallo (1857–1919) wrote a two-act opera, *I pagliacci* (The Clowns), inspired by the example of *Cavalleria rusticana*. The action takes place among a company of traveling performers whose leading actor, Canio, discovers that his wife, Nedda, is having an affair. Mid-performance, Canio—taking the part of a clown—stabs Nedda when she refuses to name her lover. Although Canio is a murderer, it is his suffering that is the focus of the work, and his aria, *"Vesti la giubba"* (Put on your costume), is one of the opera's high points.

The love of a true story
This edition of Mascagni's opera *Cavalleria rusticana* has been translated into French, proving how popular the Italian opera was in other European countries.

French successes

The success of these new, *verismo* operas beyond Italy led to the trend for grittier stories in contemporary settings being taken up by composers in other countries. In 1890, the Paris première of *La navarraise* (The Girl from Navarre), by French composer Jules Massenet (1842–1912), took place. This was another tragic love story, but the setting was Spain, in 1874, against the background of civil war.

Ten years later, Massenet's student, Gustave Charpentier (1860–1956), completed *Louise*. The simple story tells the tale of a poor Parisian dressmaker. Still living with her parents, she longs for freedom, and is also in love with a young artist named Julien.

The young school

Both Mascagni and Leoncavallo went on to write several more operas, but only *Cavalleria rusticana* and *I pagliacci* are regularly performed today, usually as a double bill. Giordano, too, finished up as a one-hit composer, not for *Mala Vita* but for a later work *Andrea Chénier* (1896). This opera tells the stirring tale of a real-life poet at the time of the French Revolution (1789–1799), and combines a historical setting with the fast and naturalistic action typical of *verismo* opera.

Francesco Cilea (1866–1950) also adapted the *verismo* style to a historical subject with *Adriana Lecouvreur* (1902), a melodrama loosely based on the life of a famous French actress who lived in the 18th century.

Among these trailblazing Italian composers, known as the *giovane scuola* (young school), was Giacomo Puccini—measured by how often his works are performed, probably the most popular opera composer of all.

The works of Puccini

It is debatable whether Puccini is truly a *verismo* composer—only his one-act opera *Il tabarro* (The Cloak) entirely conforms to the *verismo* style. But his operas do make use of the same emotionally heightened musical style and one of his biggest successes, *La bohème* (The Bohemiam Girl), in 1896, offers a glimpse into the lives of a group of poverty-stricken young people in Paris.

KEY WORKS

Pietro Mascagni *Cavalleria rusticana*
Ruggero Leoncavallo *I pagliacci*
Giacomo Puccini *La bohème; Tosca; Madama Butterfly; Turandot*

What makes Puccini's operas so effective is his ability to interweave beautiful melodies with powerful emotions yet maintain a tight dramatic structure. In *La bohème*, the love affair between Rodolfo, a struggling poet, and Mimì, a poor seamstress with tuberculosis, is convincingly set against the busy, chaotic lives of his friends. The next and highly popular opera by Puccini, bearing all the hallmarks of the *verismo* style, is *Tosca* (1900). Set in the church of Sant' Andrea della Valle in Rome in 1800, the plot focuses on the struggles of two lovers, painter Cavaradossi and singer Floria Tosca, who defy the villainous police chief, Scarpia. The brutal plot includes a torture scene and a murder, and finishes with a dramatic suicide.

Madama Butterfly (1904) is another tragic story, this time set in Japan in the 1890s. A US naval officer, B. F. Pinkerton, woos and marries a young geisha, Cio-Cio-San, before abandoning her and sailing back home. She bears him a son and waits for his return. Several years later, Pinkerton reappears, with his American wife. Cio-Cio-San agrees to give up her child to the couple, before killing herself with her father's sword. Puccini died before he could complete his last opera, *Turandot*, set in ancient Beijing, but not before he had written the famous tenor aria "Nessun dorma" (None shall sleep).

La bohème proved to be one of the most popular operas of all time, but nearly all of Puccini's operas are performed regularly on the world's opera stages.

$4 MILLION The sum earned by Puccini during his own lifetime. His operas were performed in cities across Europe and in the United States.

OPERA COMPOSER (1858–1924)

GIACOMO PUCCINI

Born in Lucca, Tuscany, into a family of musicians going back five generations, Puccini was spotted by the music publishers Ricordi and wrote his second opera, *Edgar* (1888), for them. It was not a success but his next opera, *Manon Lescaut* (1893), was. A run of triumphs followed, almost unbroken, until his death.

Puccini's private life was not so easy. He lived with a married woman, who bore him a son, and was only able to marry her on her husband's death in 1904. He still managed to enjoy the fruits of his success, however, indulging a passion for duck shooting and motor cars. While his operas have been criticized for brutality and sentimentality, Puccini's ability to compose great melodies and his vivid orchestration are indisputable.

AFTER

***Verismo*'s interest in more realistic and contemporary subject matter in opera plots continues to this day.**

OPERA GLASSES

CHALLENGING CONVENTION

A woman's customary role in society was challenged by operas such as *Jenůfa* (1904) by **Leoš Janáček** **214 ››** and *Lulu* (1935) by **Alban Berg**, while *Peter Grimes* (1945) by **Benjamin Britten** **284–285 ››** looked at an outsider's struggles with a community. **John Adams** **280–281 ››** has used news events for plots in *Nixon in China* (1987) and *The Death of Klinghoffer* (1991). **Mark-Anthony Turnage**'s *Anna Nicole* (2011) considers a modern obsession with celebrity.

Bohemian tragedy
The last act of Puccini's opera *La bohème* sees the main characters gather together as Mimì and Rodolfo are finally reunited, only for her to die of tuberculosis shortly thereafter.

BEFORE

From its earliest days, Chinese opera was presented for the entertainment of the country's elite—the emperor, his court, and the intelligentsia.

SOURCES OF MUSIC AND WORDS

The root of operatic tunes is the ***Qinqiang***, which means "Qin tune," a form of **folk opera** from northwest China. It traces its history to the establishment of the Qin dynasty, and the unification of China, in 210 BCE. Earliest opera librettos date from the Yuan dynasty, when the Mongols ruled China (1271–1368). Musical notations, though, were lost.

A POPULAR STYLE EMERGES

The first flowering of Chinese opera was ***Kunqu*** ("songs from Kun Mountain"), which developed in the 14th century in the Kunshan district, between Suzhou and Shanghai in eastern China. *The Peony Pavilion* by Tang Xianzu (1550–1616), first performed in 1598, is one of its most enduring works **« 45**.

Kunqu reached its peak in the early Qing dynasty, in the late 17th century, with *The Peach Blossom Fan* (1699), a love story by Kong Shangren (1649–1718). By the middle of the 19th century, **Peking opera** took over as the most popular form.

Chinese Traditional Opera

An art form that comprises singing, acting, dialogue, and martial arts, Chinese traditional opera has spawned numerous regional varieties in the past two centuries. With simple staging, vibrant costumes, and elaborate physicality, its appeal has reached far and wide.

In the Western operatic tradition, a composer and a librettist usually collaborate to develop a new work. Chinese traditional operas are created primarily by fitting new texts to existing types of tune and melodic formulas, known as *qupai* ("labeled tune") and *changqiang* ("vocal patterns"), although new music is also added over time.

There are as many regional varieties of Chinese traditional opera as there are regional dialects. Typical plots range from myths and legends to historical events, scenes from major literary classics, to specially written stories, often teaching moral lessons of fidelity and filial piety.

To those not familiar with the style, the singing sounds high-pitched, mostly in falsetto for male performers, and as equally stylized for females. In certain regional operas, male actors play female roles and vice versa. Another distinguishing feature is the musical arrangement. Melodic instruments in the ensemble, such as lutes and fiddles, embellish the vocal line, and the operas are more or less "conducted" by the lead percussionist.

Getting into character
The designs and colors of the face makeup of Chinese opera artists send out messages to the audience. Here, the prominent teeth drawn above the lips are typical of demigods and demons.

Color and cross-dressing
A scene from the opera *Meng Lijun*, set in an imperial court, features women playing the parts of men. This form of opera, called *Yue*, emerged in the early 20th century and flourishes in the area around Shanghai.

Regional styles take shape

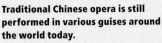

The *Kunqu* musical style, which sprang up along the eastern reaches of the Yangzi River, achieved its height of popularity in the late 17th century. Several librettos survive with details of tune types and the names of melodic formulas. In this form, there was a keen focus on the core script, making it the most "literary" of the regional varieties. Authentic *Kunqu* productions can be performed with as few as five actors, and only four to five instrumentalists in the ensemble, with much less emphasis on percussion. Vocal lines are usually mirrored by the mellow, pastoral-sounding bamboo flute, and accompanied by plucked Chinese lutes.

Kunqu opera is still widely performed, but other varieties, following regional dialects, have also flourished. *Chuanju* (Sichuan opera), from southwestern China, dates, like *Kunqu*, back to the Ming dynasty (1368–1644), but was reformed and formalized in the early 20th century. It is noted for a high-pitched singing style, fire-spitting stunts, and lightning-speed face changes. There are also other noted lyrical varieties, such as the graceful and colorful *Chaoju* (from Chaozhou, in the southern Guangdong province) and *Gaojiaxi* (from the Fujian coastal area of the southeast).

In southern China, the tradition of Cantonese opera took root only from the mid-19th century onward, influenced by the more formalized styles of the north. Emigrants from Canton exported this form across the globe, as far as the west coast of North America, where Cantonese opera troupes have performed since the early 20th century.

20 The number of hours it takes to perform all 55 scenes of *The Peony Pavilion*.

KEY WORKS

The Peony Pavilion
Peach Blossom Fan
The Three Kingdoms
The Water Margin
Journey to the West
Dream of the Red Chamber
Romance of the West Chamber

Peking opera

By far the most prominent "national" Chinese form, and the most familiar to Western audiences, is Peking opera, or *jingju*, which draws on many earlier styles in a combination of instrumental music, oration, singing, stylized movement, and acrobatics. Brought originally by artists from the eastern Anhui province around 1790, the style became popular in the capital during the 19th century. The Empress Dowager Cixi (1835–1908), who effectively ruled China for 47 years until her death, was a supporter and had a theater created for her in the Summer Palace for private performances.

In Peking opera, the leading string instrument in a small ensemble is the *jinghu*. Its two strings, played with a bow, create a piercing quality that cuts through the open air. Resonant gongs, with rising and descending tones, and woodblocks provide intricate rhythmic patterns to accompany movement and punctuate melodies.

Making a distinctive sound
The *huqin* (left) comes in various sizes and pitch ranges. While the *jinghu* possesses the most piercing sound that distinguishes Peking opera, larger *huqins* can be found in many other regional Chinese operas.

Characters, costumes, action

The roles in Peking opera are generally divided into four main types, according to the gender, age, social status, and profession of the character. *Sheng* refers to male roles, subdivided into *lao sheng* (middle-aged or old men), *xiao sheng* (young men), and *wu sheng* (men with martial skills). *Dan* denotes female roles and is subdivided into *qing yi* (women with a strict moral code), *hua dan* (vivacious young women), *wu dan* (women with martial skills), and *lao dan* (elderly women). *Jing* refers to the roles with painted faces, usually warriors, heroes, statesmen, or even demons. *Chou* is a comic character and can be recognized from his makeup, which includes a distinctive patch of white paint on his nose.

The colors used on faces and costumes symbolize and exaggerate aspects of each character's personality. On faces: red often signifies loyalty; white, treachery; blue, courage; black, a sense of justice; and green, cruelty. The embroidery on the silk costumes is also highly symbolic: red signifies high-ranking officials; green, a virtuous person; and yellow, royalty. Stylized hand gestures and footwork embody the gracefulness of gymnastics, with fight scenes including much tumbling and jumping. Emotions are expressed with such gestures as hands and body trembling (anger), rapid flicking of a silk sleeve (disgust), and covering the face with a sleeve (embarrassment).

AFTER

Traditional Chinese opera is still performed in various guises around the world today.

STAR PERFORMER
The most renowned Peking opera star was **Mei Lanfang** (1894–1961), a specialist in *qing yi* (virtuous female) roles. He traveled to the West in the 1930s and inspired such modern dramatists as the German **Bertolt Brecht** **257 ❯❯**.

MEI LANFANG IN 1930

HIGH ACCOLADE
UNESCO recognized both *Kunqu* and Cantonese opera as Masterpieces of the Oral and Intangible Heritage of Humanity in 2001 and 2009, respectively.

> "We have the **responsibility** of **connecting** the **past** and the **future.**"
>
> YU KUIZHI, ARTISTIC DIRECTOR, PEKING OPERA, 2020

Venue to entertain an empress
During the final 11 years of her life, the Empress Dowager Cixi spent 262 days in the Summer Palace in Peking (now Beijing), watching performances in the opera theater built for her in 1891–1895.

BEFORE

Military bands sounded a threat to their enemies and synchronized the movement of the armies they served.

TURKS AND MARTIAL MUSIC

There are records of military **instruments in the Turkish court** from the late 1200s. By the time of the Ottoman empire, military bands, known as Mehter, meaning "crescent," reflecting their formation, comprised five different instruments and up to 100 players. They played in peacetime at the palace and outside the sultan's tent in times of war.

OTTOMAN MARCHING BAND, C.1720

Marching to the **Beat**

The military has long needed music, not only to signal commands but also to steel the troops, strike fear into the enemy, and honor the fallen. It also brings color and dignity to public ceremonies, acting as a powerful bond between the armed forces and civilians.

Drums were the favored instrument of command in the British infantry until the late 19th century, when the bugle began to take precedence. Every day drummers beat out the reveille (the call to wake up), troop (assemble), retreat (return to quarters), and tattoo (lights out)—the four cornerstones of the military day—as well as other calls that would have been instantly recognizable to the men. The customs of the United States military were similar, with trumpet and bugle-calls supplanting drum beats after the Civil War (1860–1865).

In time to the music

In the 19th century the role of band music—military music not directly connected to communication—began to expand. Improved roads meant that most armies now marched in line and in step over long distances. Boosted by rapid advancements in brass instrument technology, marching bands and music developed to accompany armies on the march and on parade, not just in battle. Soon individual regiments were adopting a regimental march, such as "The British Grenadiers" of the

Roll up! Roll up!
The 1901 "Thunder and Blazes" arrangement by Canadian Louis-Philippe Laurendeau of "Entrance of the Gladiators" became the classic circus march.

Part for piccolo, a small flute

Julius Fučík, the original composer

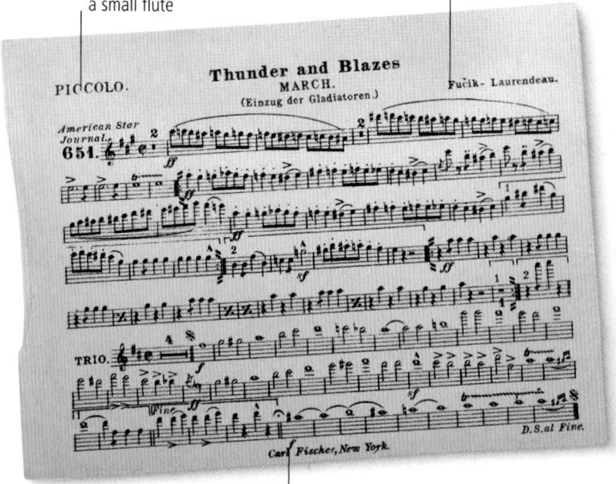

Music publisher Carl Fischer of New York

Bringing the march to the masses
The band of John Philip Sousa—Sousa's Band—performs in Calgary, Canada, in 1919. Nine years before, Sousa and his 100 musicians covered 60,000 miles (100,000 km) on a 14-month world tour.

COMPOSER (1854–1932)

JOHN PHILIP SOUSA

"The March King," born in Washington, D.C., began his musical career in the US Marine Band at the age of 13. Sousa composed more than 130 marches, including "Stars and Stripes Forever" and "The Liberty Bell," earning him wealth and lasting fame. With his band, he toured tirelessly around the world from 1892 to 1932, notching up more than 15,000 concerts.

Grenadier Guards and *Semper Fidelis* of the United States Marine Corps, to symbolize their history and values and create a camaraderie among the troops.

Big sounds for big stages

March music reached its peak in the late 19th and early 20th centuries, with composers throughout Europe and the US adopting the form and bringing it to concert halls, bandstands, and parades. The chief exponents included John Philip Sousa (see above), Julius Fučík (1872–1916)—a Czech bandmaster in the Austro-Hungarian army, best known for "Entrance of the Gladiators"—and in Britain the prolific Kenneth J. Alford (1881–1945), whose 1914 march "Colonel Bogey" was an international success long before its use in the 1957 movie *The Bridge on the River Kwai*.

Military bands were also able to increase their concert repertoire thanks largely to further advances in the development of instruments. Makers such as Adolphe Sax in Paris contributed to improvements to the valve, allowing the brass section to explore a fuller range of sounds. New instruments, such as the cornet and tuba, with tubing that increases in diameter throughout its length, also improved projection—vital for outdoor performance—and tone quality. Sax's great contribution—the saxophone and its family (patented in 1846)—also moved military music on, filling out the sounds in the middle of the band.

With the varied instrumentation, pitches, and tone colors available in the brass and wind families, music from the classical and operatic repertoire could now be adapted to military bands. Alongside this, a new repertoire of virtuoso works began to flourish, as soloists pushed the technical boundaries of their instruments. Superstar soloists, such as US cornetist and bandleader Patrick Gilmore (1829–1892), performed pieces written specifically for them, drawing huge audiences.

> "...essential to the **credit and appearance** of a regiment."
>
> "QUEEN'S REGULATIONS AND ORDERS FOR THE [BRITISH] ARMY," ON THE NEED FOR BANDS, 1844

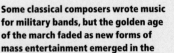

Keeping in step with royalty
The bands of the Household Division (Life Guards, Blues and Royals, Grenadier, Coldstream, Scots, Irish, and Welsh Guards) lead the Queen down The Mall in London during the Trooping of the Color ceremony.

KEY WORKS

Johann Strauss "Radetzky March"
John Philip Sousa "Stars and Stripes Forever"; "The Liberty Bell"; "The Washington Post"; "Semper Fidelis"
Julius Fučík "Entrance of the Gladiators"
Kenneth J. Alford "Colonel Bogey"
Gustav Holst Suite No. 1 and Suite No. 2 for military band (1909 and 1911)

AFTER 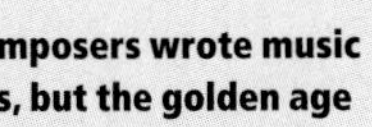

Some classical composers wrote music for military bands, but the golden age of the march faded as new forms of mass entertainment emerged in the early 20th century.

CLASSICAL FANS
Gustav Holst opened the door to new, serious writing for military bands, followed by others, such as **Ralph Vaughn Williams** and **Percy Grainger**.

THE BANDS GO MARCHING ON
Music remains at the core of the military's ceremonial and social roles, and its musicians have become increasingly professional. **Brass bands** began to form in the 1840s, often from community cooperatives. Employers also financed brass bands, partly to distract employees from political activity. By 1860, there were more than 700 bands in England.

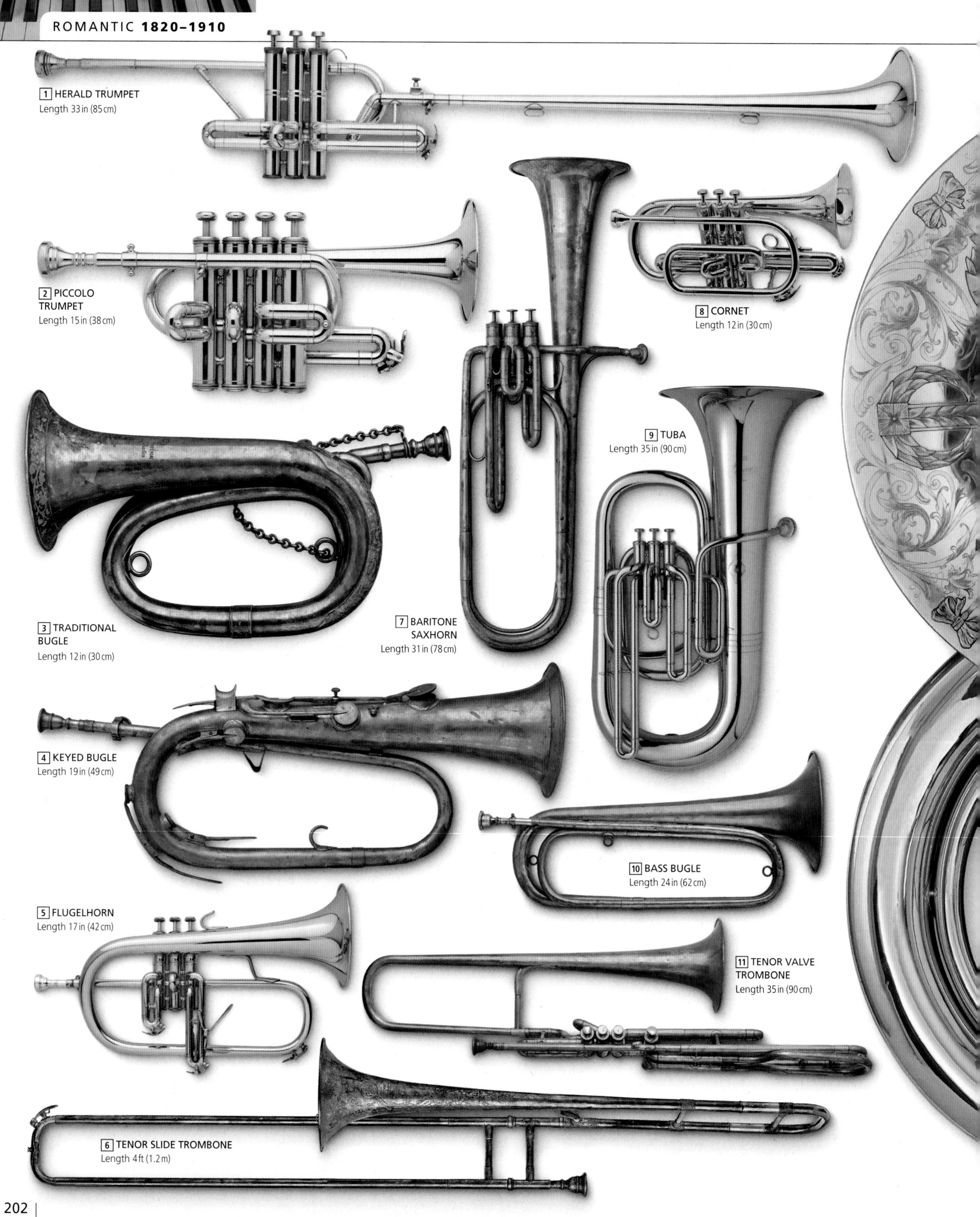

1 HERALD TRUMPET
Length 33 in (85 cm)
2 PICCOLO TRUMPET
Length 15 in (38 cm)
3 TRADITIONAL BUGLE
Length 12 in (30 cm)
4 KEYED BUGLE
Length 19 in (49 cm)
5 FLUGELHORN
Length 17 in (42 cm)
6 TENOR SLIDE TROMBONE
Length 4 ft (1.2 m)
7 BARITONE SAXHORN
Length 31 in (78 cm)
8 CORNET
Length 12 in (30 cm)
9 TUBA
Length 35 in (90 cm)
10 BASS BUGLE
Length 24 in (62 cm)
11 TENOR VALVE TROMBONE
Length 35 in (90 cm)

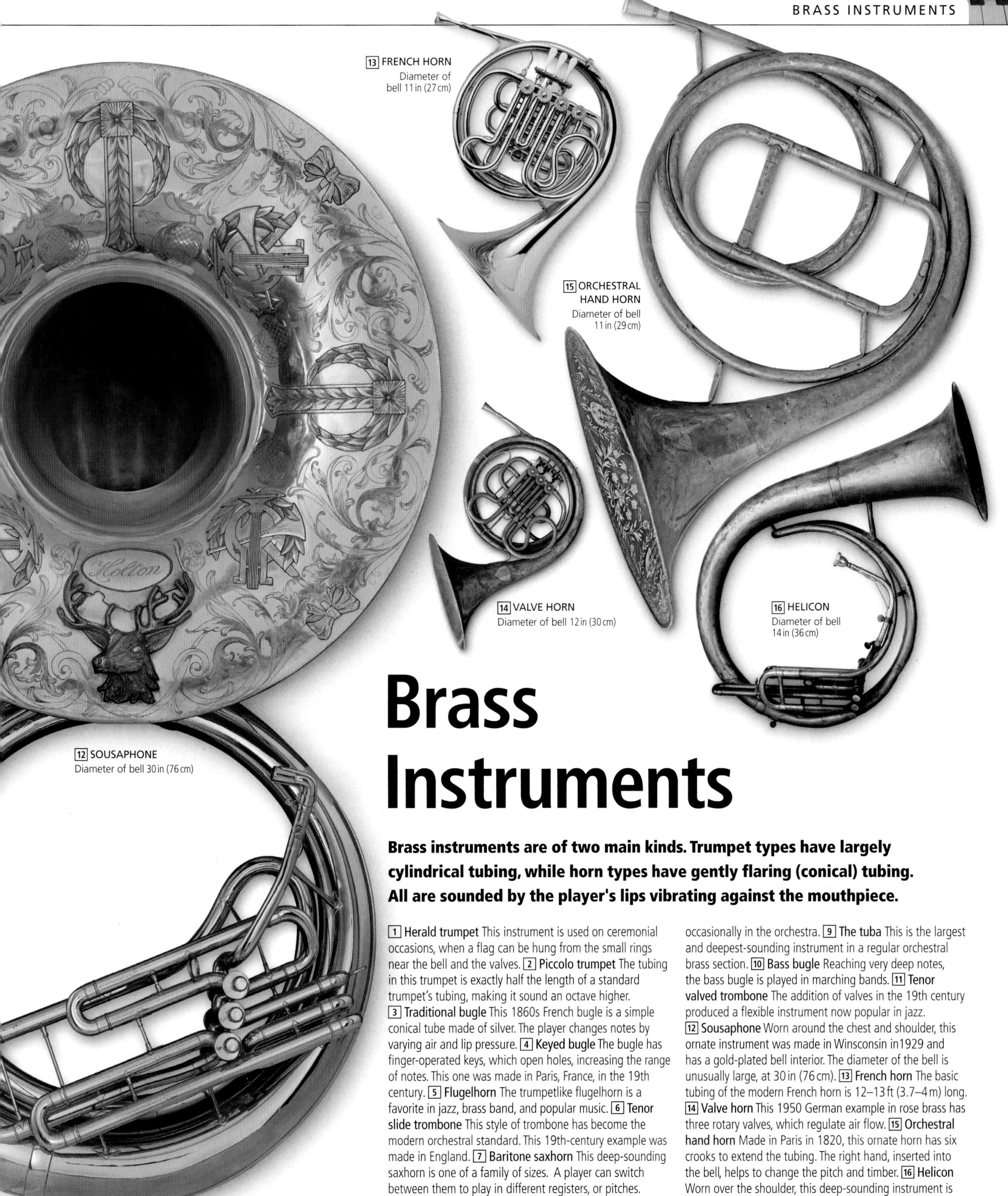

13 FRENCH HORN
Diameter of bell 11 in (27 cm)

15 ORCHESTRAL HAND HORN
Diameter of bell 11 in (29 cm)

14 VALVE HORN
Diameter of bell 12 in (30 cm)

16 HELICON
Diameter of bell 14 in (36 cm)

12 SOUSAPHONE
Diameter of bell 30 in (76 cm)

Brass Instruments

Brass instruments are of two main kinds. Trumpet types have largely cylindrical tubing, while horn types have gently flaring (conical) tubing. All are sounded by the player's lips vibrating against the mouthpiece.

1 **Herald trumpet** This instrument is used on ceremonial occasions, when a flag can be hung from the small rings near the bell and the valves. 2 **Piccolo trumpet** The tubing in this trumpet is exactly half the length of a standard trumpet's tubing, making it sound an octave higher. 3 **Traditional bugle** This 1860s French bugle is a simple conical tube made of silver. The player changes notes by varying air and lip pressure. 4 **Keyed bugle** The bugle has finger-operated keys, which open holes, increasing the range of notes. This one was made in Paris, France, in the 19th century. 5 **Flugelhorn** The trumpetlike flugelhorn is a favorite in jazz, brass band, and popular music. 6 **Tenor slide trombone** This style of trombone has become the modern orchestral standard. This 19th-century example was made in England. 7 **Baritone saxhorn** This deep-sounding saxhorn is one of a family of sizes. A player can switch between them to play in different registers, or pitches. 8 **Cornet** This instrument plays melodies in bands and occasionally in the orchestra. 9 **The tuba** This is the largest and deepest-sounding instrument in a regular orchestral brass section. 10 **Bass bugle** Reaching very deep notes, the bass bugle is played in marching bands. 11 **Tenor valved trombone** The addition of valves in the 19th century produced a flexible instrument now popular in jazz. 12 **Sousaphone** Worn around the chest and shoulder, this ornate instrument was made in Winsconsin in1929 and has a gold-plated bell interior. The diameter of the bell is unusually large, at 30 in (76 cm). 13 **French horn** The basic tubing of the modern French horn is 12–13 ft (3.7–4 m) long. 14 **Valve horn** This 1950 German example in rose brass has three rotary valves, which regulate air flow. 15 **Orchestral hand horn** Made in Paris in 1820, this ornate horn has six crooks to extend the tubing. The right hand, inserted into the bell, helps to change the pitch and timber. 16 **Helicon** Worn over the shoulder, this deep-sounding instrument is played in marching bands. This helicon is from the 1890s.

BEFORE

Romantic composers often evoked powerful narratives and emotions through their music.

19TH-CENTURY ROMANTICS

Symphonie fantastique composed by **Hector Berlioz's « 156** in 1830 described the story of an artist's life, while **Modest Mussorgsky's « 180–181** *Night on a Bare Mountain*, dating from 1867, is an orchestral portrayal of a terrifying witches' sabbath. **Edvard Grieg « 184** depicted landscape in his 1875 *Peer Gynt* suites, especially in the tranquil flute tune of "Morning" and the heavy rhythms of "In the hall of the Mountain King."

FORESHADOWING IMPRESSIONISM

Gabriel Fauré's « 163 interest in **modality « 31** and his use of mild discords anticipated the unusual **scales** used by Debussy, which were hallmarks of his music.

Impressionism

By the late 19th century, European music was at a crossroads. Traditions were crumbling, conventional harmony was dissolving, and old forms were being pushed to the breaking point. From France, a completely new approach emerged.

The Impressionist movement of the late 19th century influenced music as well as art. Composers, like painters, became preoccupied with conjuring up an atmosphere through suggestion and allusion, rather than by objectively telling a story or directly conveying an emotion. Just as, decades earlier, painters had experimented with new techniques, composers began to depart from the harmonic system that had been in use since J.S. Bach.

"**Music** is made up of **colors** and **barred rhythms**."

DEBUSSY TO HIS PUBLISHER, AUGUSTE DURAND, 1907

The press was quick to label the Parisian composer Claude Debussy (see below right) an Impressionist, but he refuted it. In 1908, he wrote: "I am trying to do 'something different' ... what the imbeciles call 'impressionism' is a term which is as poorly used as possible, particularly by arts critics." Debussy was naturally drawn to the piano. As an accomplished performer,

Music at Le Chat Noir

In 1874, Adolphe Willette painted *Parce, domine* (Spare, Lord, your people) for the Parisian cabaret-café Le Chat Noir. Frequented by Debussy, Satie, and many of their contemporaries in the arts, the café became a hub of Impressionism.

Naming a movement
When Claude Monet (1840–1926) named this 1872 painting of a sunrise at Le Havre, France, "*Impression, soleil levant*," critics seized upon the word "Impressionism" as a label for the emerging art form.

he was able to use the instrument to create in sound the textures, colors, and degrees of light and shade that artists could achieve using paint.

Revolutionary effect

As a composer, Debussy's unique approach to the fundamentals of melody, harmony, rhythm, texture, and color changed music forever. The mysterious parallel harmonies opening his 1910 piano prelude *La cathédrale engloutie* (The Sunken Cathedral) reflect his interest in medieval chanting, while the exotic-sounding pentatonic melodies (like the piano's five black notes) evoke the sounds of the Javanese gamelan (gong orchestra; see pp.302–303). The chimes of the submerged bells ring through the texture, while the ascending melodic figure suggests the cathedral's slow rise from the sea.

The orchestral palette offered Debussy great stimulus. The unusual combinations of instruments in his three symphonic sketches, *La mer* (The Sea, 1905), create new orchestral colors and are works of art in sound.

Fluttering moths

Debussy and his compatriot Maurice Ravel (1875–1937) were friends as well as rivals. Ravel wrote polished, sophisticated music with technical precision. In the first of his five *Miroirs* (Reflections) for piano (1904–1905), he creates a dark, nocturnal atmosphere broken by the quietly intense fluttering of moths. The fourth movement, the Spanish-inspired *Alborada del gracioso* (The Jester's Morning Song), exploits the piano's extremes of pitch, tonal color, dynamics, and touch, and demands staggering skill to perform.

Satie and "Les Six"

Erik Satie (1866–1925) was a lone but fascinating voice. He played the piano in the Parisian cabaret-café Le Chat Noir, an important meeting place for artists, musicians, and writers. In 1888, he published his three piano compositions, entitled *Trois Gymnopédies*. The modal harmonies and repetitions of the first of the three pieces invokes a trancelike state in the listener. In 1917, Satie collaborated with artists Jean Cocteau (1889–1963) and Pablo Picasso (1881–1973) on the ballet *Parade* for the Ballets Russes, the innovative dance company run by Serge Diaghilev (1872–1929).

In 1920, Satie and Cocteau inspired a group of six composers, including Georges Auric, Louis Durey, Arthur Honegger, Darius Milhaud, Francis Poulenc, and Germaine Tailleferre, called "Les Six." They were united around the anti-Impressionist idea that music should be spare and "modern." Of the six, it was Poulenc (1899–1963) and Milhaud (1892–1974) who made the biggest impact on European composers who were, once again, going separate ways.

Java comes to Paris
In 1889, an *Exposition Universelle* (World Fair) was held in Paris. Here, Claude Debussy first heard Javanese musicians playing a gamelan. The influence of this experience can be heard in his later compositions.

KEY WORKS

Claude Debussy *Clair de lune*; *Prélude à l'après-midi-d'un faune*; *La mer*

Maurice Ravel *Miroirs*; *Daphnis et Chloé*, Suites Nos. 1 and 2

Erik Satie *Parade*; *Trois Gymnopédies*

Darius Milhaud *Scaramouche Suite* for two pianos, Op. 165b

COMPOSER (1862–1918)

CLAUDE DEBUSSY

Claude Debussy's parents ran a china shop in a Paris suburb, but in 1871 his father was imprisoned for revolutionary activities. Despite an unconventional start in life, Debussy showed early promise as a concert pianist at the Conservatoire in Paris. In 1884, he won the Prix de Rome and studied in Italy. In 1888–1889, he heard Wagnerian operas at the Bayreuth festival and was struck by their adventurous harmonies.

Debussy absorbed influences from all quarters: nature, art, and literature. He died of cancer in Paris while the city was under bombardment during World War I.

AFTER

Impressionistic colors continued to feature in musical composition after the Impressionist movement had ended.

ENGLISH ORCHESTRAL COLORING

English composer **Frederick Delius** **« 223**, a superb orchestral colorist, used Impressionism in his 1912 **tone poem** *On Hearing the First Cuckoo in Spring*. A two-note **motif** on the clarinet imitates the song of a cuckoo, while sliding chromatic harmonies evoke an atmosphere of calm stillness. In 1933, Delius published two string pieces entitled *Aquarelles* (Watercolors).

SOURCES OF INSPIRATION

In his orchestral work *Roman trilogy*, Italian composer **Ottorino Respighi** (1879–1936) created impressions using music to evoke the sights and sounds of Italy's capital city. Meanwhile, Polish composer **Karol Szymanowski** (1882–1937), inspired by Debussy, composed "Fountains of Arethusa," the second of his three chamber pieces, *Myths* (1915). The rippling piano part and yearning melody create an elegant impression of flowing water.

7

MUSIC IN THE MODERN AGE

1910–1945

The frenetic 20th century sped ahead with the inventions of the radio, phonograph, and telephone, and music blossomed with new rhythms that created ragtime, blues, and jazz. While musical theater became the driving force in popular song, in classical music, the accepted traditions established by Bach, Beethoven, and Brahms were challenged by Stravinsky, Bartók, Hindemith, and the Second Viennese School led by the visionary Arnold Schoenberg.

« Shure Model 55 Unidyne Microphone introduced in 1939.

MUSIC IN THE MODERN AGE 1910–1945

1910 | 1915 | 1920 | 1925

1910
Composer Arnold Schoenberg writes his influential *Harmonielehre* (Theory of Harmony). Richard Strauss's opera *Salome* is performed in London after a British ban is lifted.

Poster for Richard Strauss's opera *Salome*

1911
Irving Berlin's hit song "Alexander's Ragtime Band" is published.

Sheet music for Irving Berlin's first hit song

1913
Audiences riot during the Paris premiere of Igor Stravinsky's *Rite of Spring*, performed by the Ballets Russes.

Igor Stravinsky

1914
Vaughan Williams, inspired by English folk songs, composes *A Lark Ascending*. In the United States, the song "St. Louis Blues" by W. C. Handy is published.

1917
In New Orleans, the Original Dixieland Jass Band records the first jazz single, "Livery Stable Blues." In Argentina, Carlos Gardel records "Mi Noche Triste," which becomes a hit throughout Latin America.

Hot-air gramophone, made in 1910

1918
London premiere of *The Planets*, Gustave Holst's orchestral suite. Sergey Rachmaninoff and Sergey Prokofiev emigrate to the United States in the wake of the Russian Revolution.

1919
London première of Manuel de Falla's *El sombrero de tres picos* (*The Three Cornered Hat*) for the Ballets Russes. English composer Edward Elgar writes his Cello Concerto.

1920
"Crazy Blues," the first African American blues record, is recorded by Mamie Smith and her Jazz Hounds on Okeh Records.

1921
Arnold Schoenberg composes his Piano Suite, Opus 25 based on his 12-tone theory. "Ory's Creole Trombone" is recorded by Kid Ory's Sunshine Band in Los Angeles.

1922
Czech composer Leoš Jánácek writes the choral piece *The Wandering Madman*. Al Jolson's "Toot Toot Tootsie (Goodbye)" is the year's biggest song.

1923
New York's Cotton Club opens, where top African American jazz musicians play for white-only customers.

1924
Jean Sibelius's 7th and final symphony premieres in Stockholm. George Gershwin's *Rhapsody In Blue* premieres in New York.

1925
The Grand Ole Opry radio show begins, showcasing country music in the United States. Premiere of Alban Berg's avant-garde, atonal opera *Wozzeck*.

Early radio

1927
Jánácek composes his *Glagolitic Mass*, a choral setting of the mass written in Old Church Slavonic.

1927
Hoagy Carmichael and Mitchell Parish write "Stardust." Country artists Jimmie Rodgers and The Carter Family make their first recordings. Jerome Kern and Oscar Hammerstein's musical *Show Boat* opens on Broadway, New York.

1928
Premiere of Maurice Ravel's orchestral piece *Bolero* in Paris. Louis Armstrong's Hot Five record "West End Blues" is recorded. Kurt Weill and Bertolt Brecht's *Threepenny Opera* opens in Berlin.

Louis Armstrong's trumpet

1929
Fats Waller releases "Ain't Misbehavin."

Composers and theorists in thrall to modernism—the aesthetic upheaval sweeping through early 20th century arts—challenged and redefined the prevailing structural, tonal, sonic, melodic, and rhythmic principles established by the preceding Classical and Romantic eras. Jazz music evolved from bordellos through dance halls to concert halls, while its rhythmic and harmonic influence impacted on the development of popular song. The invention of the microphone and amplification had an immeasurable effect on recording technology and performance styles, and with the rise of the gramophone and radio, the modern age of music was heard throughout the world.

1930

c.1930
The blues migrate from the Mississippi Delta to northern cities such as Memphis and Chicago. Première of Prokofiev's Symphony No. 4 in Boston. Cole Porter publishes the song "Love For Sale."

⌃ Tango goes global with Carlos Gardel's tours and films in the '30s

1931
Folk singer-songwriter Woody Guthrie leaves Oklahoma during the Great Dust Storm and takes to the road in search of work; he reaches California in 1937, singing on KFVD radio station, and New York in 1940, where he writes "This Land is My Land."

» Mississippi blues in the 1930s

1932
Fletcher Henderson begins arranging for the Benny Goodman Orchestra. Francis Poulenc's *Concerto for Two Pianos and Orchestra* premières in Venice.

1933
In Germany, the Nazi regime begins to ban the work of some composers, including Paul Hindemith, Alban Berg, and Igor Stravinsky. Fleeing the Nazi threat, Austrian composer Arnold Schoenberg emigrates to the United States. Louis Armstrong tours Europe and gains the nickname Satchmo.

1934
Benny Goodman and his Orchestra begin performing on the NBC radio series *Let's Dance*, paving the way for the swing boom a year later. Aged 17, Alan Lomax begins traveling the United States to collect folk music with his father, recording thousands of songs and interviews.

1935

1935
Duke Ellington composes jazz's first extended composition *Reminiscing in Tempo*. Carlos Gardel releases "*El Dia Que Me Quierasi*," one of Argentina's most popular tangos; he dies in a plane crash in the same year.

⌃ Concert program for Prokofiev's *Peter and the Wolf*

1936
Prokofiev returns to live in the Soviet Union; his *Peter and the Wolf* premieres in Moscow. Rachmaninoff composes his Symphony No. 3. Blues singer Robert Johnson records 16 songs in San Antonio, Texas.

1938
The first concert of music of African American origin, *From Spirituals To Swing*, takes place in Carnegie Hall, New York. Samuel Barber's *Adagio For Strings* premieres in New York. Gene Autry stars in *Man from Music Mountain*, one of many B-movie Westerns featuring the country singer.

⌃ Poster for a Gene Autry film about a singing cowboy

1939
Joaquín Rodrigo's *Concierto de Aranjuez* premieres in Barcelona, Spain. Swing music spreads from the United States to Europe, helping to boost morale among civilians and troops.

1940

⌃ Cuban rumba dancer Zulema performs in Havana in the 1940s

1940
Latin jazz musician Machito forms his Afro-Cubans band in New York. Bandleader Glenn Miller's "In The Mood" tops the US charts.

1941
Les Paul designs the first solid-body electric guitar. Olivier Messiaen's *Quartet for the End of Time* is first performed in a German prisoner of war camp.

1943
Holocaust victims write and perform a children's opera in the Terezín concentration camp in Czechoslovakia.

1944
Coleman Hawkins records the first bebop record with Dizzy Gillespie, "Woody 'n' You." Première of Aaron Copland and Martha Graham's ballet *Appalachian Spring*.

1945
Premiere of Symphony No. 9 by Shostakovitch, who is later denounced by Soviet censors.

⌄ 1940s drum kit, essential to bebop music

The **Shock** of the **New**

Modern music—or what still sounds like it to many of today's listeners more than a century later—did not appear overnight. But it felt like that to the first audiences of some of the early 20th-century masterworks that revolutionized music.

A process of musical evolution that had been under way for decades reached a tipping point in the early 20th century. A disturbing new world of sound seemed suddenly to open up, shocking and scandalizing those who heard it first.

Throughout the 19th century, modern-sounding moments in music had been happening more often: for example, in the compositions of Mahler, Liszt, and Wagner. However, they took place within a broadly traditional language whose basis would still have been familiar to Mozart and Beethoven. In that sense, the sounds that would soon be unleashed by Stravinsky and Schoenberg were not as unfamiliar as they seemed. What was new, however, was the context. The seemingly unstable (dissonant) modern harmony was no longer being deployed just at key moments to spice up a musical work. Now it was the musical work.

« BEFORE

The slow-burning fuse leading to the explosion of "modern music" had been lit by composers such as Liszt and Wagner.

COMMEMORATIVE ENGRAVING OF WAGNER'S *DIE WALKÜRE*

MOMENTS OF MODERNISM

In the 19th century, **Franz Liszt « 160–161** explored ferocious-sounding modernism in his *Totentanz* (Dance of Death) for piano and orchestra. The emotional impact and incredible complexity of the music of **Wagner « 165** were a sign of things to come.

Crossing the threshold

Richard Strauss's operas *Salome* (1906) and *Elektra* (1909) confronted their first audiences with long passages of musical dissonance so extreme that melody and harmony, as traditionally understood, seemed to be disintegrating. However, the familiar boundaries were still there: for example, *Elektra* ends in the conventional key of C major. Sensing that modernism was about to go where he did not want to follow, Strauss went on to explore a personal brand of "rediscovered Romanticism" in his next opera, *Der Rosenkavalier* (The Knight of the Rose) of 1911.

Schoenberg's sensation

Something more radical was afoot in Vienna. In the fourth movement of his Second String Quartet (1908), Arnold Schoenberg (see opposite) found himself writing in a style in which the orientation points of traditional harmony and melody—the bedrock of Western classical music for 1,000 years—could no longer be made out. Besides the usual four stringed instruments, a solo soprano voice sings words by the Austrian poet Stefan George, telling of distant regions from which the music seems to have arrived. Schoenberg's idiom, no longer anchored by familiar harmonies, floats free in a new world of sound.

> "I feel the **air** from **another planet.**"
>
> WORDS BY STEFAN GEORGE (1868–1933), SET IN SCHOENBERG'S STRING QUARTET NO. 2

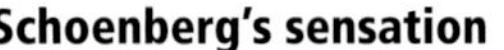

Open to ridicule
This caricature from the German weekly magazine *Lustige Blätter* depicts Strauss inducing "electric" convulsions in his captive by blowing the music into the back of his head through a trumpet.

The Quartet's premiere, in Vienna in 1908, polarized its audience into two groups—enthusiastic supporters and outraged opponents. The furious shouting of the latter camp almost halted the performance. Undaunted by this mixed reception, Schoenberg pushed further ahead into a new musical territory.

The same was true of two of his former pupils, both fellow Austrians. In his compositions, Anton Webern (1883–1945) searched for new extremes. His *Five Pieces for Orchestra* of 1911–1913 (the "orchestra" is a medium-sized chamber ensemble) together last fewer than four minutes, one of them for a scant 19 seconds. In 1914–1915, his *Three Pieces for Orchestra*, Alban Berg (1885–1935) went to the opposite extreme. Composed on a larger scale, and for a huge symphony orchestra, the work takes up the late-Romantic idiom of Gustav Mahler (see p.193) and propels it into a new era of modernism.

Russian spring

Igor Stravinsky (see pp.212–213), a former pupil of Nikolay Rimsky-Korsakov (see pp.180–181), was famous for his music for the Diaghilev ballets *The Firebird* and *Petrushka* when, in 1913, at Paris's Théâtre des Champs-Elysées, he unveiled his latest work,

KEY WORKS

Charles Ives *Central Park in the Dark*
Richard Strauss *Elektra*
Arnold Schoenberg String Quartet No. 2 in F sharp minor, Op. 10; *Pierrot Lunaire*, Op. 21
Anton Webern *Five Pieces for Orchestra*, Op. 10
Igor Stravinsky *The Rite of Spring*
Alban Berg *Three Pieces for Orchestra*, Op. 6

UNDERSTANDING MUSIC

TWELVE-NOTE COMPOSITION

As his style became more free-floating and complex, Schoenberg felt that the music he and his followers were composing risked falling apart, and that no existing technical procedure could solve the problem. So Schoenberg invented a new system. His idea was to generate music from a specific ordering of the 12 notes of Western music, making a "set" or "row." The row in prime form (P, in the example below) can then be manipulated: reversed, or played backward (R); inverted, or set upside down (I); or both inverted and reversed (IR).

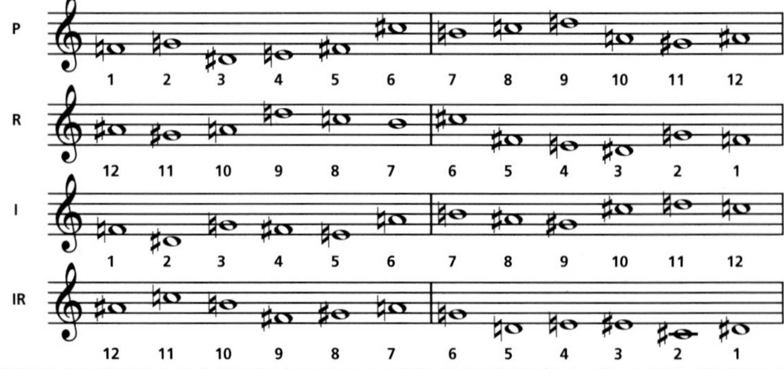

Instruction to play *Allegretto giovale* (medium-fast cheerfully)

1. Geige (First violin)

Composer's signature

Berg's *Lyric Suite*

This is the manuscript of the first violin part of the *Lyric Suite* by Alban Berg. Completed in 1926, Berg's work was one of the first string quartets to use the 12-note method of composing.

AFTER

After Schoenberg and Stravinsky, music could never be the same again. Others would follow or reject their example, but few would ignore it.

NEW WAYS

DMITRI SHOSTAKOVICH

Benjamin Britten **281 ››**, **Leoš Janáček** **214–215 ››**, and **Dmitri Shostakovich** (1906–1975) felt that Schoenbergian modernism offered little that related to their own music. But Schoenberg's 12-note method inspired Stravinsky **212–213 ››** and **Aaron Copland** **225 ››** to write masterworks.

RADICAL DEVELOPMENTS

The rhythmic power of Stravinsky's *The Rite of Spring* was a beacon for the French composer **Edgard Varèse**, whose *Ionisation* was the first work for an all-percussion orchestra.

The Rite of Spring. The premiere generated the most notorious riot in the history of classical music. Outraged by the choreography, large parts of the audience protested so loudly that Stravinsky's score could hardly be heard at all. This meant that the dancers could not hear it either, so the performance was close to chaos. But the concert premiere (an orchestra performance of the piece without any dancers) of *The Rite of Spring* in Paris in 1914 was an outright triumph for Stravinsky. His masterwork had taken music to new levels of orchestral firepower and rhythmic invention.

American pioneer

The young Charles Ives (1874–1954) was isolated from the early modernist European scene, yet his compositions at this time were in some ways ahead of it. In Ives's 1906 chamber-orchestra piece *Central Park in the Dark*, different sections of the ensemble play various kinds of music independently of one another, and at different speeds. The string section (effectively a separate orchestra) quietly evokes the nocturnal scene, undisturbed by the surrounding noises of New York City nightlife, including tunes whistled by passersby, music played by a ragtime band, and a pianist playing in a bar. His music portrayed space, time, and memory in a way that had never been achieved before.

COMPOSER (1874–1951)

ARNOLD SCHŒNBERG

Born into a Jewish family in Vienna, and virtually self-taught as a composer, Schoenberg became a leading composer of his era and an influential teacher—his students included Anton Webern and Alban Berg.

Having lived in Vienna and Berlin, Schoenberg emigrated to the United States with his second wife and three children in 1933. He taught at the University of California, in Los Angeles, and pioneered a new technique of 12-tone composition (see p.210).

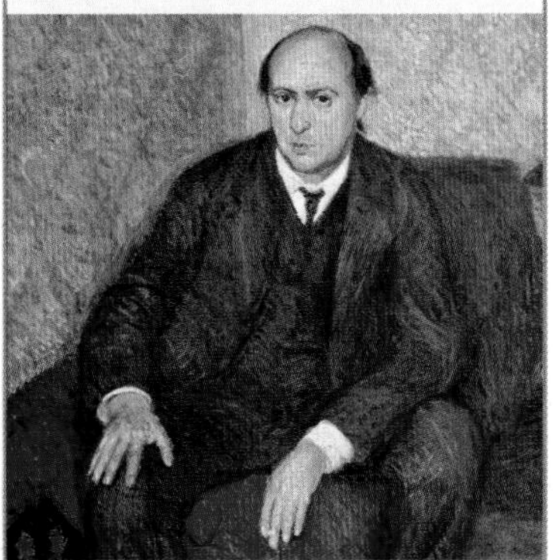

COMPOSER Born 1882 Died 1971

Igor Stravinsky

"**Music** [is] a form of **communion** with our fellow **man** and with the **Supreme Being.**"

IGOR STRAVINSKY, "POETICS OF MUSIC," 1942

Stylish composer
This portrait of Stravinsky was painted by Jacques-Émile Blanche in 1915. A stylish figure, courteous, and urbane, Stravinsky was a radical in aesthetics but a social conservative.

One of the great 20th-century modernists, Igor Stravinsky has been compared to the artist Pablo Picasso in his restless inventiveness and exploration of diverse styles. In his early ballet scores he restored complex rhythms to the forefront of Western music. Through 60 years of composition, he was never predictable and always attempted something new.

A chance meeting

Born into the cultured elite of St. Petersburg, the capital of czarist Russia, Stravinsky had a passion for opera and ballet. But his father, an opera singer, was not eager to push his sickly third son into a musical career. Instead, Igor enrolled in college as a student of criminal law.

In 1902, however, on a family trip to a German spa, Igor met the prominent Russian composer Nikolai Rimsky-Korsakov, who gave him lessons in composition.

Explosive talent

In the early 20th century, St. Petersburg was a center of modernist innovation in the arts, and Stravinsky was soon exploring ideas alien to the elderly Rimsky-Korsakov. The orchestral piece *Fireworks*, premiered in 1908, revealed a young man in touch with the latest trends in French music—Debussy and Ravel (see pp.204–205)—but with his own explosive feel for rhythm and timbers (qualities of sound). The

KEY WORKS

The Firebird
Petrushka
The Rite of Spring
Oedipus Rex
Symphony of Psalms
Symphony in Three Movements
The Rake's Progress
Agon

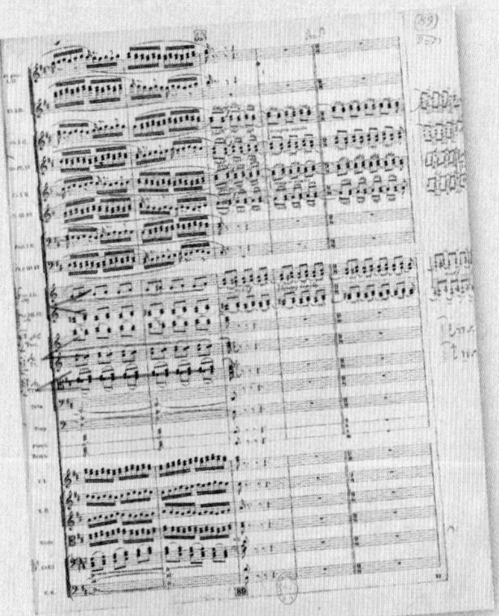

Score for *Petrushka*
First performed in 1911, the *Petrushka* was Stravinsky's second ballet. Like Tchaikovsky, Stravinsky wrote some of his greatest music for ballet, which occupies a fundamental place in Russian art.

Russian artistic impresario Serge Diaghilev attended the performance. Seeking to promote Russian talent in Paris, he commissioned Stravinsky to write the score for a ballet, *The Firebird*, to be performed by his new company, the Ballets Russes. Choreographed by Mikhail Fokine, this was a sensational success, making Diaghilev's company and Stravinsky the darlings of the Parisian cultural elite.

Stravinsky's next ballet score, *Petrushka*, was more innovative in its use of bitonal harmony—chords from contrasting scales played together. It was another popular and critical success. The music fit Diaghilev's

Conductor at work
Stravinsky conducts his own music in rehearsal in 1958. He had strong views on conducting, rejecting the view that music was open to "interpretation" and insisting on rigorous adherence to the score.

winning formula of cutting-edge dance and colorful spectacle, exploiting French interest in Russian exoticism.

Two years later, the ballet *The Rite of Spring*, inspired by pagan Russian folk rituals, seemed set to continue the successful sequence. But while the score was more radical than *Petrushka* in its use of dissonance and dislocation of rhythm, it was the choreography that gained a reaction from the audience. The first performance in Paris in 1913 saw a rain of missiles thrown from the crowd. The scandal confirmed Stravinsky's standing as a leader of the musical avant-garde.

Time of upheaval

In 1914, World War I broke out, and Stravinsky moved to Switzerland with his family. He suffered deep personal loss when his younger brother died on the Eastern Front in 1917. In the same year, the Russian Revolution erupted. Despite his move to Paris and then Switzerland, Stravinsky remained emotionally rooted in his homeland. The installation of a Communist government turned Russia into an alien country for him. He redefined himself as a "cosmopolitan" and did not return to Russia for half a century.

New turnings

The course that Stravinsky now charted disoriented many who had admired his pre-1914 masterpieces. Living in France through the 1920s and '30s, he became part of the trend known as Neoclassicism, governed by principles of order and emotional restraint.

Stravinsky's first postwar ballet score, *Pulcinella*, was based on music by the 18th-century Italian composer Giovanni Pergolesi. Stravinsky's assertion that "music is... essentially powerless to express anything at all" seemed to justify critics who found his music formal and cold. Yet there was no decline in his musical originality. He experimented with jazz and explored the use of small ensembles, wrote the austerely monumental opera-oratorio *Oedipus Rex* (1927) and the faith-inspired *Symphony of Psalms* (1930).

> "My **music** is best **understood** by **children** and **animals.**"
>
> IGOR STRAVINSKY, INTERVIEW, 1961

The late 1930s were a difficult time for Stravinsky. One of his daughters, his wife, and his mother died in the space of six months, and he was sick with tuberculosis. In 1939, he moved to the United States, becoming a resident of Hollywood. His *Symphony in Three Movements*, premiered in 1946, was a commentary on the horrors of World War II. Its brutal ostinatos (repetitions of equal sounds) recalled the shock of *The Rite of Spring*.

Losing the edge

The opera *The Rake's Progress*, with a libretto by the poet W. H. Auden, exemplified Stravinsky's Neoclassical style. By the time it was premiered in 1951, Stravinsky was no longer regarded as a leader of modernism, which by then was dominated by the 12-tone serial technique (see pp.210–211) of Arnold Schoenberg. Although cautious about its merits, Stravinsky used the 12-tone system in the ballet *Agon* and the choral piece *Threni*. This did not prevent new composers, alienated by his political conservatism as well as his musical style, from seeing him as outdated.

In 1962, Stravinsky received an invitation to visit Soviet Russia, where his work had been banned since the 1930s. This homecoming completed the arc of his life. He continued composing until his death in New York in April 1971.

The Rite of Spring
The Royal Ballet perform *The Rite of Spring* at London's Royal Opera House in 2011. The premiere in 1913 provoked outrage in some quarters.

TIMELINE

- **June 17, 1882** Born at Oranienbaum, outside St. Petersburg.
- **1901** Enters St. Petersburg University to study law.
- **1902** His father dies. Nikolai Rimsky-Korsakov becomes his musical mentor.
- **January 24, 1906** Marries his cousin, Katya Nossenko.
- **April 1907** His first orchestral work, Symphony in E flat, is performed.
- **1909** Serge Diaghilev commissions *The Firebird* for the Ballets Russes.
- **June 1910** *The Firebird* is performed in Paris.
- **June 1911** *Petrushka* is premiered.

PROGRAM FOR "THE FIREBIRD," 1926

- **May 1913** The premiere of *The Rite of Spring* causes an uproar in Paris.
- **1915** Moves to Switzerland.
- **November 1917** Russian Revolution.
- **September 1918** *The Soldier's Tale* is performed in Lausanne, Switzerland.
- **1920** Moves to Paris. Premiere of *Pulcinella*.
- **May 1927** First performance of *Oedipus Rex*.
- **1928** *Apollon Musagète* is the last Stravinsky ballet produced by Diaghilev's Ballets Russes.
- **December 1930** The *Symphony of Psalms* premieres in Brussels.
- **1934** Takes French citizenship.
- **March 1939** Wife dies of tuberculosis.
- **September 1939** Moves to the US following the outbreak of World War II in Europe.
- **1940** Marries Vera de Bosset and settles in Los Angeles. A version of *The Rite of Spring* is used in the Disney film *Fantasia*.
- **1945** Becomes a US citizen.
- **January 24, 1946** *Symphony in Three Movements* is premiered in New York.
- **September 11, 1951** Conducts the first performance of *The Rake's Progress* in Venice.
- **1957** Premiere of the ballet *Agon*, which shows the influence of 12-tone technique.
- **March 1962** *The Flood*, his last dramatic work, is premiered in a television production.
- **September 1962** Visits the Soviet Union.
- **April 6, 1971** Dies in New York and is buried on the island of San Michele, Venice.

National Flavors

At the start of the 20th century, the Austro-Hungarian empire extended from northern Italy and Czech Bohemia across to Romania and Serbia. The colorful folk music of these varied regions and cultures now became a major source of inspiration to their composers.

Folk music was a product of the countryside, where communities did not have opera houses, orchestras, or concert halls. There, people made their own music, with the few instruments that they had and with their singing. They sang for pleasure and to express deeper feelings in the only musical way they could.

To a new generation of composers sensing the rise of nationalist awareness, folk music had a refreshing directness and urgency. Classical music, they felt, was in danger of becoming an overly sophisticated, self-absorbed art form—perhaps folk music offered a means of renewal. If so, it had to be sought out and listened to, then collected and written down.

Finding national voices

The early works of Hungarian Béla Bartók (see right) were influenced first by German composer Richard Strauss (see pp.210–211), and later by France's Claude Debussy (see pp.204–205). Then, like his compatriot and fellow composer Zoltán Kodály (1882–1967), Bartók began to feel that these influences were not enough for the musical needs of a proud Hungarian. As a result, he and Kodály started visiting remote village communities for inspiration, making on-the-spot recordings of the local songs and dances on an early phonograph. Then they meticulously wrote these down, often also making vocal or piano arrangements of them.

Classical music deals in large forms, such as the extended movements of symphonies or sonatas or the different acts of an opera. A folk tune tends to be short and is not designed to be extended and developed on a larger scale. Bartók and his contemporaries started looking for a way of solving this musical conundrum. While a folk tune might not itself generate a whole musical movement, it could color it, determine its atmosphere, and enrich its blend of ideas.

> "A nation **creates music**. The composer only **arranges** it."
>
> HUNGARIAN COMPOSER, BÉLA BARTÓK

Bartók's music had an uncompromising, modernist streak that seemed worlds apart from a simple folk song. However, he succeeded in bringing the two together in his darkly powerful 1911 opera *Bluebeard's Castle*.

Between World Wars I and II, from 1919–1939, Bartók's international career as a pianist flourished, and he composed two piano concertos to perform himself, both of which were strongly influenced by the driving rhythms of Hungarian folk dance.

Kodály's more benign musical style produced national masterpieces in both his 1923 choral work *Psalmus Hungaricus*, and his comic Hungarian folk opera *Háry János*, which premiered in 1926. He also devised the so-called Kodály Method of music education, based on his belief that every child is born with an instinctive capacity to sing and can achieve remarkable standards if taught early enough.

Táragotó

Much used in Hungarian and Romanian folk music, this instrument resembles the saxophone or orchestral clarinet with its single-reed mouthpiece but has a much more forceful and penetrating sound.

Sung speech

The son of a village schoolteacher in Czech Moravia (modern-day Czech Republic), Leoš Janáček (1854–1928) was another composer who collected and transcribed local folk songs, in his case, simply using a notebook. He also took to writing down sentences overheard from passersby in the streets of Brno, the Czech city where he worked as a music teacher. Janáček sensed that the shapes and rhythms of these suggested a new way of singing, which might be effective in the opera house.

The triumphant result was his 1904 opera *Jenůfa*, brilliantly deploying this personal brand of folk-influenced "sung speech." *Jenůfa* eventually swept the operatic world off its feet, and triggered an astonishing creativity in Janáček's old age. Among a torrent of late masterpieces was his 1927 *Glagolitic Mass*, a choral setting of the Mass written in Old Church Slavonic, which was the first literary Slavic language.

Like Bartók, in Hungary, Poland's Karol Szymanowski (1882–1937) was much influenced in his early music by the powerful examples of Richard Strauss and then Debussy. However, he differed from Bartók in that he was only drawn to his nation's folk music later in his career. His ballet-pantomime *Harnasie*, written between 1923–1931, was based on songs and dances from the region of southern Poland's Tatra Mountains.

BEFORE

A sense of musical nationalism in Eastern Europe was already on the rise in the late 19th century.

NORWAY'S VOICE

Farther north, Norway had found its own musical hero in **Edvard Grieg** **« 184.**

AUSTRO-GERMAN DOMINANCE

In Eastern Europe, in the 19th century, a reaction against the supremacy of **Wagner** **« 165** and **Brahms** **« 172–173** was growing. The Austro-Hungarian Empire covered diverse regions and peoples. Czech-speaking Bohemia, for example, produced composers **Antonín Dvořák** and **Bedrich Smetana** **« 176–177.**

FLAG OF AUSTRO-HUNGARIAN EMPIRE (1867–1918)

KEY WORKS

Leoš Janáček *Jenůfa*

Ralph Vaughan Williams *A Sea Symphony*

Béla Bartók *Bluebeard's Castle*, Piano Concertos Nos.1 and 2

Igor Stravinsky *Les Noces*

Ottorino Respighi *Pines of Rome*

Frederick Delius *Brigg Fair*

English uprising

The arrival of a gifted new generation of English composers was announced in 1899 by an orchestral masterpiece, *Enigma Variations* by Edward Elgar (1857–1934). It was followed a year later by his choral work, *The Dream of Gerontius*. Elgar's distinctively English idiom had grown from a traditional, German-style musical training, and folk music did not much interest him.

However, it did interest Ralph Vaughan Williams (1872–1958) and his friend Gustav Holst (1874–1934). Like Bartók and Kodály, they set about collecting and transcribing English folk songs before emigration from countryside to city led, as they feared, to their disappearance.

COMPOSER (1881–1945)

BÉLA BARTÓK

Bartók was born in a Magyar-speaking Hungarian community, in what is now Romania. At age 4, he could play 40 piano pieces, and gave his first recital at age 11. He studied in Budapest and, by 1903, had written his first major orchestral work. His ballet *The Miraculous Mandarin* was thought so violent that it was banned after its 1926 premiere. In 1940, outraged that Hungary backed Nazi Germany, Bartók moved to the United States. Despite having leukemia, he composed until he died.

In orchestral compositions such as Vaughan Williams's 1906 *Norfolk Rhapsody No. 1*, and his work for chorus and orchestra, *A Sea Symphony* (1903–1909), the English folk song influenced his style. Holst also shows evidence of being under the same influence in his orchestral masterpiece *The Planets* (1914–1916).

Russian Influences

By 1900, interest in Russian folk music was waning, leading Rimsky-Korsakov to say that it was "getting harder and harder to say something original in a folk style." However, his student Stravinsky was soon to prove him entirely wrong by including a memorable Russian folk tune in his landmark ballet of 1910, *The Firebird*. Perhaps concerned that his music would seem insufficiently Modernist, Stravinsky usually denied using actual folk music, instead claiming that, in works such as *The Rite of Spring*, he had written original music simply inspired by folk music traditions. In fact, he had even used a Lithuanian folk song for the iconic bassoon melody that begins the piece, and he used and adapted other folk melodies in the rest of the work, as well as for his ballets *Petrushka* and *Les Noces*. As such, some of the most revolutionary musical sounds of the early 20th century turned out to be ancient Russian folk melodies.

Folk inspiration
As well as the music, tradition inspired the scenery and costumes for the original production of Stravinsky's *The Rite of Spring*, shown here in a revival for its centenary.

AFTER

The years after World War II saw national styles wane, as an increasingly global world led to similar trends among composers.

20TH-CENTURY CLASSICS

National fingerprints can still be detected in the music of **Benjamin Britten** **280–281 ››**, who wrote several popular volumes of English folk-song arrangements. In the USSR, **Shostakovich** used traditional Jewish songs and tunes, identifying with Jews oppressed by the Soviets, and wrote the song-cycle *From Jewish Folk Poetry*.

WILLIAM GRANT STILL

EUROPEAN AVANT-GARDE

For French modernist composer **Pierre Boulez** **266–267 ››**, music based on folk song was an outdated irrelevance.

THE AMERICAN SCENE

American voices made themselves heard: Aaron Copland used folk tunes in his opera *The Tender Land* (1952–1954), while William Grant Still's *And They Lynched Him to a Tree* (1940) spoke to the issue of **racial violence** in America. Composers also looked to contemporary history for inspiration **376–377>>**.

The **Flute**

The modern metal flute has its roots in simple instruments of primitive societies thousands of years ago. Now a sophisticated, finely honed metal instrument, its smooth, bright sound adds a lustrous gleam at the top of the woodwind group.

The earliest flutes were made of bone, wood, or clay, held vertically, and most common in South and Central America. The modern flute originated from early side-blown bamboo versions in India and the Far East.

In Renaissance Europe, a cylindrical, keyless flute became popular, usually made from maple or boxwood. It was used as a military instrument from the 1300s, when German and Swiss soldiers marched to a fife (pipe) and drum band. The fife remains a popular children's and folk instrument.

Around 1670, a single key was added to the Renaissance flute, and the tube was slightly tapered toward the foot. This became the standard flute of the Baroque period, and a version remained in production into the 19th century as a beginner's model. By the end of the Baroque era, eight keys were common, and the flute's soft, clear sound was used to great expressive effect, notably by J.S. Bach in his *obbligato* writing (important solos in partnership with a solo voice).

From the early 19th century, makers experimented with new key systems in the search for a more powerful, well-tuned instrument. The most successful was Theobold Boehm, whose system (see p.189) is used on most modern flutes, which, with their metal, usually cylindrical, bodies, produce a bright, resonant tone. Gentler-toned wooden flutes are still used for authentic performances of early music and in traditional celtic music. The modern flute has just over three octaves and is usually pitched in C. Of its alternative sizes, alto and piccolo are the most common, heard in orchestral and chamber music as well as in jazz.

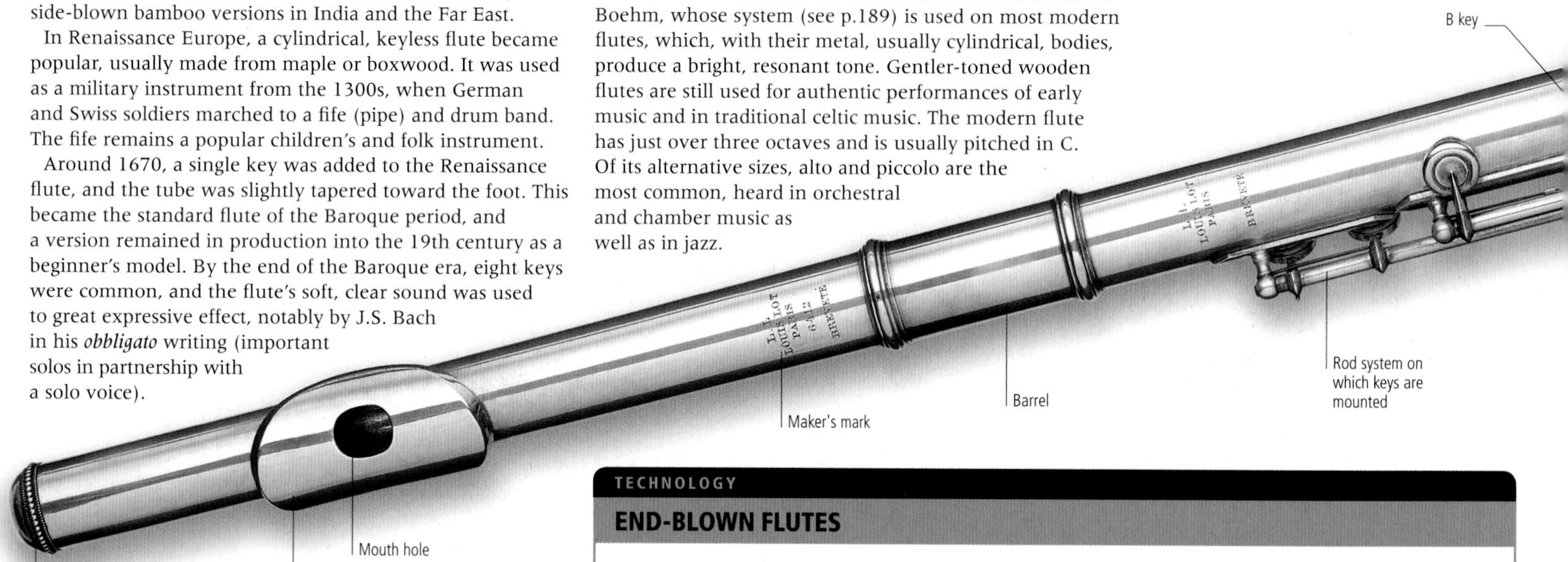

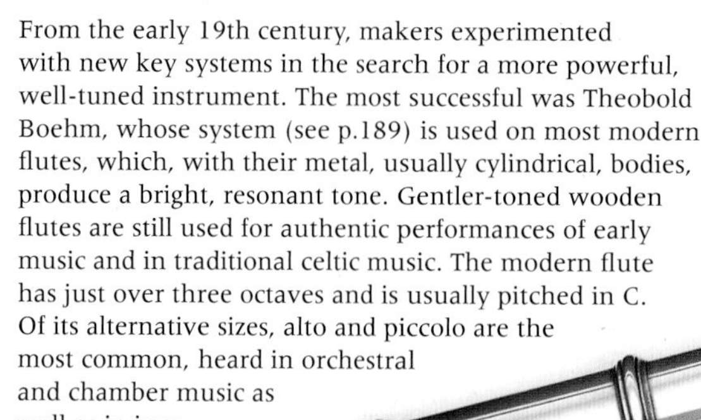

Open-holed flute
The modern flute is usually made of silver or a silver alloy, which gives it a brilliance in its upper notes and a sonorous clarity in the lower. This flute made by Louis Lot in 1867 uses the Boehm system of keywork that was completed in 1847 and has five open holes.

TECHNOLOGY

END-BLOWN FLUTES

End-blown flutes are most commonly used as folk instruments and, despite their apparent simplicity, are very difficult to play. The player directs the airstream against the sharp rim of the open upper end of a pipe, rather like blowing across the top of a bottle. Usually made of wood, bamboo, or metal, the pipe is normally quite long with only a small number of holes and no keys. It is held pointing downward, its head resting against the chin. End-blown flutes are especially common in South America, parts of Africa, and Eastern Europe, but perhaps the best known is the Japanese *shakuhachi*. Originating from a Chinese instrument, it is a slightly curved bamboo tube, with four front and one back fingerholes. Originally used for Zen meditation, its breathily expressive sound is occasionally heard in European pop music.

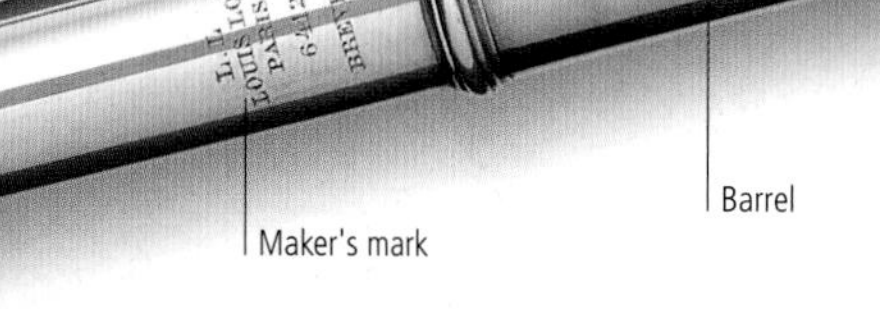

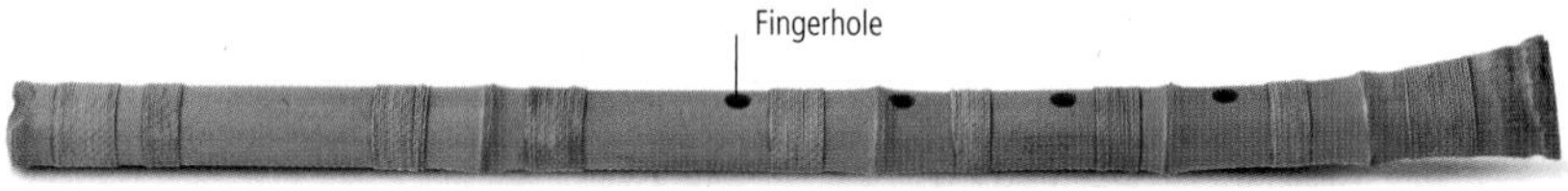

SHAKUHACHI

TIMELINE

14th century
Medieval military beginnings
Fifes, simple side-blown flutes, began to be used in military bands during the medieval period, typically in conjunction with drums. This traditional combination continues in bands to this day.

MILITARY BAND WITH FIFE

1700
First piccolo outing
In use from around 1700, the piccolo's first orchestral appearance was in Handel's 1711 opera *Rinaldo*. By 1800 it was established as a regular addition to the orchestral flute section.

MODERN PICCOLO

1707
First flute treatise
Born to a family of woodwind makers, French composer, flautist, and teacher Jacques-Martin Hotteterre (1674–1763) published "Principles of the transverse flute," the first such work in Europe.

HOTTETERRE

FLUTE D'AMOUR

***c.*1730**
Flute d'amour appears
Slightly wider and softer-toned than the regular flute, yet clearer than the alto flute, the flute d'amour was briefly popular in the 1730s when composers wrote specifically for it.

1752
Johann Joachim Quantz
An influential German flautist, flute maker, and composer, Quantz (1697–1773) published "On Playing the Flute," which became a key source of information about 18th century music.

QUANTZ

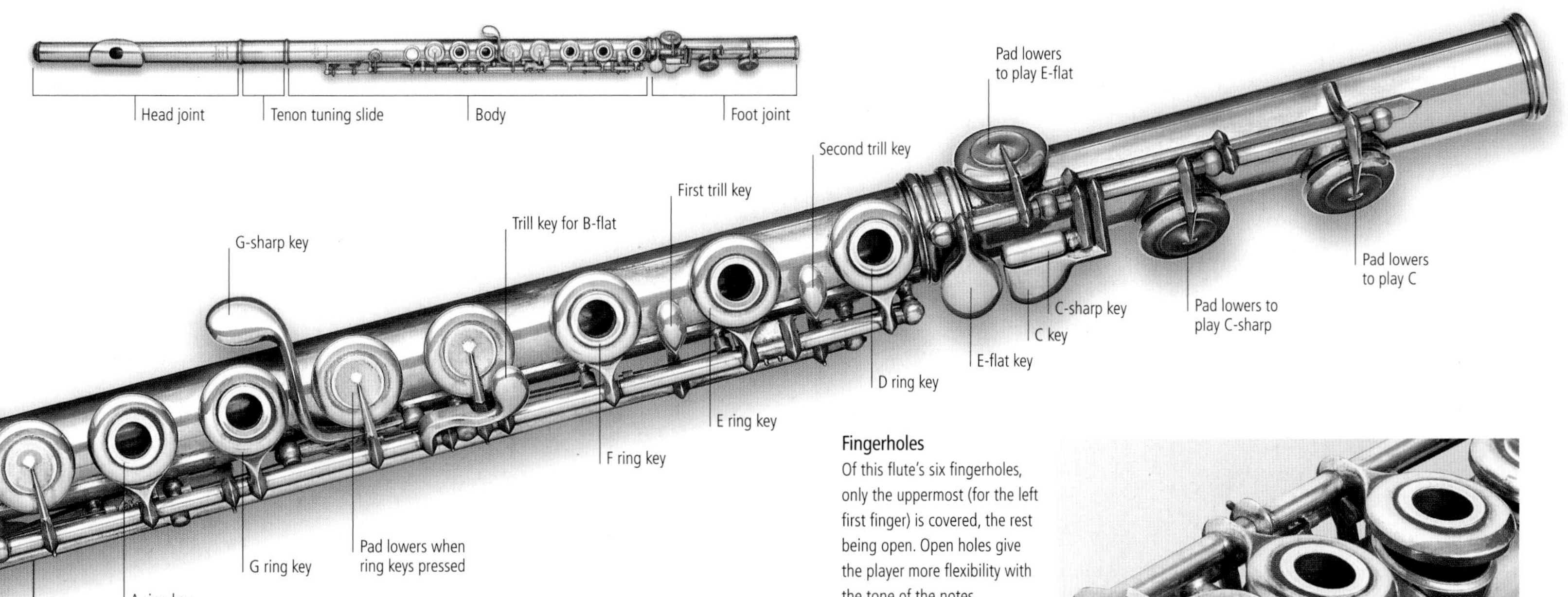

Fingerholes
Of this flute's six fingerholes, only the uppermost (for the left first finger) is covered, the rest being open. Open holes give the player more flexibility with the tone of the notes.

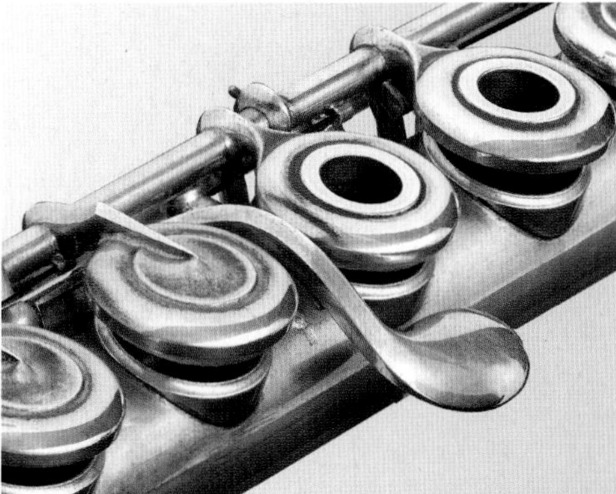

Embouchure (lip) plate
The flautist blows across (rather than into) the hole in the embouchure plate. "Embouchure" is the shape of the lips and facial muscles used to create a sound on wind or brass.

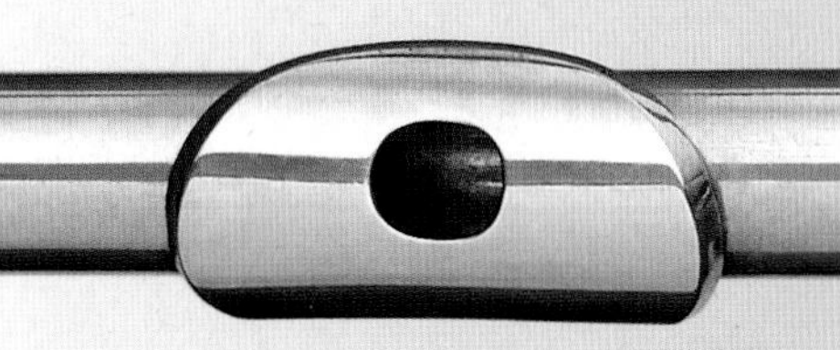

Crown
The crown is the cap or stopper at the head of the flute, which ensures that the stream of air is directed correctly down the tube.

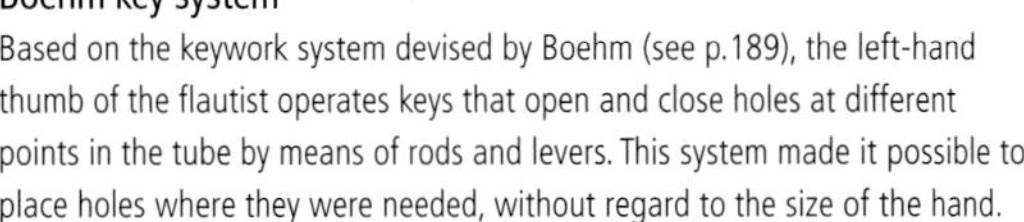

Boehm key system
Based on the keywork system devised by Boehm (see p.189), the left-hand thumb of the flautist operates keys that open and close holes at different points in the tube by means of rods and levers. This system made it possible to place holes where they were needed, without regard to the size of the hand.

Sound
When the player blows air across the embouchure hole, the airstream causes a vibration in the tube that flows down the body to the foot. The player can vary the flute's sound from soft-toned to bright by subtly adjusting the embouchure and the force of the air stream.

1847
Boehm system
By 1847, inventor and flautist Theobold Boehm completed his system of keywork for the flute. It was gradually and almost universally adopted. This Louis Lot flute is made with a high percentage of pure silver, rather than sterling silver, and bears hallmarks on each section.

19th century
Alto flute
The larger, lower alto flute was developed in the 19th century. Altos are usually metal with a head that curves to extend the length of the tubing—this lowers the pitch while keeping the keys in reach.

19TH-CENTURY WOODEN ALTO FLUTE

20th century
Jean-Pierre Rampal
Celebrated French flautist Jean-Pierre Rampal (1922–2000) helped put the flute on the map as a virtuoso solo instrument, and also brought its forgotten 18th century repertoire to life.

JEAN-PIERRE RAMPAL

***c.*1855**
Pratten system
English flautist Robert Sidney Pratten developed different key systems for the flute as an alternative to Boehm's system, which some thought too complex. The Pratten system is still used today for playing Irish music.

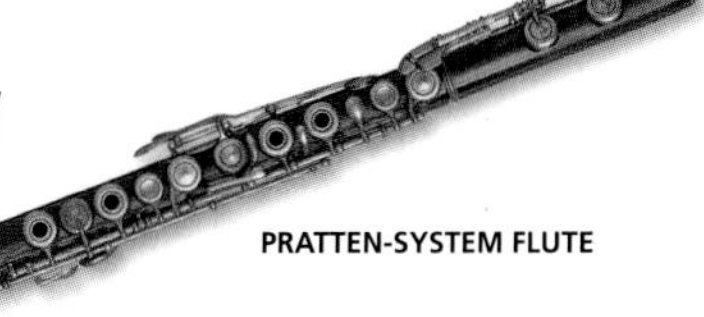

PRATTEN-SYSTEM FLUTE

20th century
Bass flute
Since the 18th century, inventors had experimented with large-sized flutes, generally unsuccessfully. This 20th-century example was created by Rudall Carte in London.

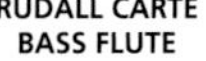

RUDALL CARTE BASS FLUTE

Spanish Classical Music

Despite two world wars convulsing Spain's neighbors, and a bloody civil war of its own that had repercussions for all aspects of society—including the arts—Spanish classical music flourished in the 20th century, inspired by folk traditions and three great musicians.

BEFORE

The legacy of Moorish rule, a Catholic monarchy, and a far-flung empire in the Americas set Spain apart from other European countries.

A COUNTRY OF MANY PARTS
While Spain's **golden age** of classical music was dominated by the Catholic Church **« 70–71**, the country's patchwork of regions, each with its own musical identity, gave rise to many folk forms—from the guitar and dance-based **flamenco « 178–179** of Andalusia to the bagpipes of the northwest.

RISE OF THE GUITAR
In Renaissance Spain, the ***vihuela***—like a **lute** but with a flat back—preceded the guitar **« 38–41**. The **guitar** evolved in the Baroque era **« 90–91** and came of age when composer Gaspar Sanz (1640–1710) published the first playing manual in 1674.

Perhaps the best-known musical work from the 19th century with a distinct Spanish flavor is the opera *Carmen*. Yet it was written by a Frenchman, Georges Bizet. Germany, Italy, and France dominated opera in Spain, and Spanish orchestras mainly played foreign repertoire.

Folk and the man from Cádiz

The 20th century started on a more assertive note, with the founding of a symphony orchestra in Madrid, the capital, in 1903. Then, as the century progressed, three musical innovators showed the world that sublime classical music could be fashioned from Spain's rich folk history. The first, Manuel de Falla (1876–1946), learned piano in his native Cádiz and moved to Madrid at the age of 20 to study the instrument at the Royal Conservatory. Here, he also had composition lessons and used his free time to write musical comedies.

Strongly influenced by Gypsy music, de Falla's early works explored the rhythms of Andalusian flamenco (see pp.178–179) and the traditional *zarzuela* form of part-spoken, part-sung drama, which led to his first success, *La vida breve* (The Brief Life), in 1904. A move to Paris in 1907 allowed him to study with, and fall under the Impressionist spell of, the French composers Ravel, Debussy, and Paul Dukas. Once back in Madrid, de Falla wrote the *Noches en los jardines de España* (*Nights in the Gardens of Spain*), a series of three nocturnes, each depicting a famous Spanish garden and

> "The guitar is a small **orchestra.** Every string is a different color."
>
> ANDRÉS SEGOVIA, CLASSICAL GUITARIST

Spanish music meets Spanish art
A 1920 program for a production of Manuel de Falla's ballet *El sombrero de tres picos* (*The Three-Cornered Hat*) at the Paris Opera shows two costume designs by Pablo Picasso, who also designed the sets.

Royal setting
The Palacio Real de Aranjuez is a Spanish royal palace, south of Madrid, built in the 16th–18th centuries. Its vast gardens inspired Joaquin Rodrigo to write his *Concierto de Aranjuez*.

KEY WORKS

Manuel de Falla *Homenaje À Claude Debussy* (*Elegía de la guitarra*); Seven Popular Spanish Songs, as sung by Montserrat Caballé

Joaquín Rodrigo *Concierto de Aranjuez*; *Fantasia para un gentilhombre*

Enrique Granados Campiña *12 danzas españolas* (12 Spanish Dances)

bringing in elements of Andalusian folk music. It was given its premiere by the Madrid Symphony Orchestra in 1916.

Two years later, the ballet impresario Sergei Diaghilev commissioned de Falla to write a piece for his Ballets Russes company. The result was *El sombrero de tres picos* (The Three-Cornered Hat), which, infused again with Adalusian folk styles, was staged to critical and popular acclaim in London in 1919.

De Falla settled in Granada in 1920 and began composing a vast oratorio, *Atlántida*, based on an epic Catalan poem about the mythical land of Atlantis. He continued the work in Argentina, where he moved after the Spanish Civil War, but *Atlántida* remained unfinished at his death.

A blind visionary

While de Falla was in Paris, a boy from Sagunto, near Valencia, Joaquín Rodrigo (1901–1999), was mastering the piano and violin despite his virtual blindness, which had been caused by an attack of diphtheria at the age of three. In his late twenties, Rodrigo moved to Paris, where he studied with Paul Dukas and mixed with artists, writers, and other Spanish musicians, including de Falla.

Rodrigo's music, noted for its rich melodies, drew on a wide range of his country's traditions, from folk music to the works of Cervantes, the author of *Don Quixote*. He wrote songs, concertos, piano pieces, and music for the theater and films, but while he never mastered the guitar as a performer, his most enduring achievements are two concertos for guitar, the *Concierto de Aranjuez* (1939), and *Fantasia para un gentilhombre* (Fantasia for a Gentleman), composed in 1954. These, perhaps more than any other works, raised the profile of the guitar as an instrument worthy of serious orchestral treatment.

The classical guitar hero
Andrés Segovia holds the instrument that he popularized the world over. His technique of plucking strings using both fingertips and nails revolutionized guitar playing.

Taking the guitar to the world

If Rodrigo raised the stakes for composers, Andrés Segovia (1893–1987) was the man who established the guitar as a concert instrument to rival the piano and the violin.

Born into a humble family in Linares in Andalusia, Segovia spent most of his youth in Granada. His family opposed his interest in music, so Segovia taught himself guitar and learned to read music, giving his first concert, in Granada, at the age of 16.

Early concerts met with mixed reviews, but Segovia achieved his goal of getting the guitar into the spotlight.

He even persuaded composers who were not guitarists, such as de Falla, Granados (1867–1916), the Brazilian Heitor Villa-Lobos (1887–1959), and the Mexican Manuel Ponce (1886–1948), to write for him.

Segovia toured the world tirelessly, introducing new audiences to the classical guitar. He also inspired, and sometimes taught, a new generation of concert guitarists, including Julian Bream and John Williams.

AFTER

After 1945, a fresh generation of composers experimented with new forms and instruments, while Spain's classical traditions were promoted by world-class performers.

NEW AUDIENCES

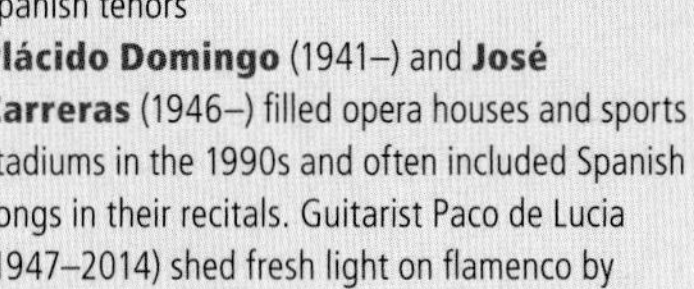

MONTSERRAT CABALLÉ WITH LUCIANO PAVAROTTI

The Spanish singer **Montserrat Caballé** (1933–2018) recorded the album *Barcelona* in 1988 with Freddie Mercury from the band Queen, while Spanish tenors **Plácido Domingo** (1941–) and **José Carreras** (1946–) filled opera houses and sports stadiums in the 1990s and often included Spanish songs in their recitals. Guitarist Paco de Lucia (1947–2014) shed fresh light on flamenco by fusing it with jazz.

AVANT-GARDE

Madrid-born composer **Miguel Ángel Coria** (1937–2016) mixed traditional and modern forms, and confounded Spain's first laboratory for electronic music. Another native of Madrid, **Carlos Cruz de Castro** (1941–), wrote the unconventional *Menaje (para dos grupos de utensilios de vajilla de cristal y metal)*, played not on orchestral instruments but on dishware, glassware, and metal utensils.

Music of Mexico

There is much more to Mexican music than "La Bamba," "La Cucaracha," and *mariachi* bands. The largest Spanish-speaking nation has a proud and independent musical tradition that runs the gamut from raucous *ranchera* to gushing *bolero* and mass-market Latin pop.

BEFORE

Mexican music is often thought of as being Spanish based, but there was a lively musical tradition in the region before the European settlers arrived.

EARLY MUSIC SCHOOLS

When the Spanish conquered Mexico in 1519, the **Aztec and Mayan peoples** already had a significant musical legacy, with both cultures using music for **sacred** as well as **secular** purposes. The Aztecs used a range of **percussion** instruments, including the ***ayotl*** (a drum made from a turtle shell) and ***huehuetl*** (upright skin drum), and had formal music schools called ***cuicalli***.

THE INFLUENCE OF SPAIN

During the colonial era, **Spain's regional forms** were introduced at the court of the colonial ruler and among the population.

MESTIZO MUSIC

Modern Mexican music is a combination of Spanish, indigenous, *mestizo* (mixed), and foreign influences. The rhythms of the pre-Columbian peoples continue to resonate—both as distinct folk music and as elements of *mestizo*.

Mexican music is widely known through the distinctive *mariachi* bands and popular songs that have found audiences around the world. But few people realize the diversity of Mexico's music or that it is one of the most musical nations in Latin America.

Epic ballads

By the early 19th century, as Mexico pushed for independence from Spain, Mexicans began to embrace other genres of European and Caribbean music, including the German polka and the Viennese waltz.

In the 1840s, a homegrown epic musical ballad, the *corrido*, came out of the Mexican-American War of the 1840s. These recorded heroic exploits, battles, crimes, and acts of betrayal. The instrumental accompaniment ranged from a single guitarist to a small ensemble. The *corrido* continued to serve as a vehicle of musicalized oral history during the revolutionary period of 1910–1917, which established Mexico's status as an independent nation.

The most famous *corrido*, "La Cucaracha," is said to have been a marching anthem used by the forces of Pancho Villa, whose many accomplishments included the attack on Columbus, New Mexico, in 1916. In time, each state or region adapted the form to suit its own musical traditions.

Baroque meets folk

The word *son* is used to describe music that combines elements from Spanish baroque and Mexican folk, with guitar and violin as the prominent instruments. In the 1930s, regional *son* flourished,

COMPOSER (1897–1970)

AGUSTÍN LARA

Agustín Lara was born in Mexico City, although he claimed Veracruz as his birthplace. At the age of 13, he played his first concert at a local brothel. A natural-born bohemian, he excelled in a variety of styles, from the foxtrot, tango, and waltz to blues, jazz, *ranchera*, and—above all—*bolero*. Between 1930 and 1939, while hosting his radio show, *La Hora Intima*, he wrote most of his 700 or so songs, including "Veracru." In 1943, Lara made his debut with his own orchestra and toured Europe in the 1950s. Spanish opera singer Placido Domingo has recorded an album of his songs.

Buttons on the right hand are for playing the melody

Push-button accordion

This decorative push-button accordion was used by the band Los Tigres del Norte. Buttons take the place of piano keys on this type of accordion.

Classic *mariachi*
With sombreros and black-and-white costumes, *mariachi* musicians present a classic image of Mexico. Their instruments include the six-string acoustic bass *guitarrón mexicano.*

with each state or even town producing its own arrangements with instruments such as the African marimba (in Oaxaca) and the harp (in Veracruz).

Son jarocho, from the state of Veracruz on the Gulf of Mexico, displays lyrical improvisation and other elements of Afro-Cuban music; the song "La Bamba," made famous by Mexican-American singer Richie Valens, comes from this tradition. *Son jaliciense*, from the state of Jalisco, northwest of Mexico City, gave us the *mariachi*, groups known for their *charro* suits, popularized as patriotic costumes during the dictatorship of General Porfirio Díaz (1830–1915).

GUITARRÓN MEXICANO

Mexican fusions

During the US Prohibition era (1920–1933), many Germans migrated to the Mexico-Texas border. There the German button accordion came together with the Mexican *bajo sexto*—a 12-string guitar used in the northern regions—to create *música norteña*, or *norteño* music. Small groups called *conjuntos*, with a snare drum, double bass, and occasionally a saxophone, play this hybrid form, which mixes Mexican *son* with Bohemian and Czech folk rhythms. From this melting pot, Tex-Mex emerged, pioneered by accordionist Narciso Martinez (1911–1992) and singer-guitarist Lydia Mendoza (1916–2007).

Sound boards each side of the bellows hold the reeds

Buttons on the left hand play the accompaniment

Bellows draw and suck air across internal reeds

> "She has the **rough** voice of **tenderness.**"
>
> FILM-MAKER PEDRO ALMODÓVAR ON THE SINGER CHAVELA VARGAS

The main repertoire for all *norteño* groups includes the *corrido* and the *ranchera*. The latter genre is a traditional country tune, often depicting everyday activities and events—from life on the farm to domestic tragedies—and idealizing the life of rural Mexicans.

Today, most kinds of Mexican ensemble will perform *rancheras*, which have enjoyed notable success across the border in the US. The *ranchera* is frequently associated with the large brass band, the *banda*, which is a descendant of Spanish municipal bands.

The undisputed king of the *ranchera* is José Alfredo Jiménez (1926–1973), born in the town of Dolores Hidalgo. The so-called *grito de Dolores*, the call of Mexican Independence, which took place there on September 16, 1810, lives on in the whooping call of many patriotic *rancheras*. Sometimes likened to the 20th-century American folk musician Woody Guthrie, Jiménez had no musical training but is a musical icon in Mexico. His 1,000-plus songs, including "Ella," "Paloma querida," and "Cuando el destino," are much-loved. Jiménez also made numerous films during the 1950s.

Deep emotion

With her deep, gravelly voice, Chavela Vargas (1919–2012) is known as a singer of *rancheras*. Vargas, who smoked cigars and wore masculine clothes, added a new twist to this masculine genre, appealing to audiences beyond Mexico. Her songs celebrated rural values and explored the emotional subjects of love and longing, sorrow and mortality.

Vargas is also known for her performances of the *bolero* (a slow-tempo romantic song suited to dancing). It is perhaps associated more with Cuba than Mexico, but the modern *bolero* boom started in 1927 when young composers Guty Cárdenas and Agustín Lara penned entries for a song contest in Mexico City. From then on the genre became popular across Latin America, aided by its use in films. *Bolero* has helped the reputations of Trio Los Panchos, Celia Cruz (see pp.278–279), and pop crooner Luis Miguel.

KEY WORKS

José Alfredo Jiménez "Camino de Guanajuato"
Agustín Lara "Veracruz"
Ritchie Valens "La Bamba"
Pedro Infante "Bésame Mucho"
Chavela Vargas "La Llorona"
Lila Downs "La Cucaracha"

AFTER

Mexican music is more diverse than ever, but its themes are still the gritty realities of life. Today, they confront poverty, drugs, violence, and emigration.

LILA DOWNS

FEMINIST ANGLE
The singer-songwriter Lila Downs performs witty feminist songs to music that mixes Mexican folk forms with African-influenced **cumbia**, **pop**, **rap**, and **flamenco**.

CLUB MUSIC
In Tijuana, on the border with California, **Nortec Collective**, an electronic club music band, explores *frontera* themes such as gun-running and the influence of the US. A subgenre is the ***narcocorrido***, which narrates tales of drug gangs. **Los Tigres del Norte** are leading exponents of this music.

The sound of *ranchera*
Chavela Vargas sang songs traditionally performed by men. She also appeared in films by the Spanish director Pedro Almodóvar.

The **Last Romantics**

As the 19th century ended and the 20th began, a new age of musical modernism dawned. For some composers, this radical upheaval confirmed, more deeply than ever, their own affinity with Romanticism—a movement from an era they were now beginning to outlive.

The developing story of classical music involves several historical movements—Romanticism, Impressionism, modernism—whose respective composers, however individual their musical styles, shared a broad set of goals and values. For the "Last Romantics"—notably Richard Strauss and Sergey Rachmaninoff, but also Jean Sibelius (see pp.184–185) and Frederick Delius—the situation was different. They had little in common, either with one another, or with the winds of change in the musical world around them. Their achievement was to extend the values of 19th-century Romanticism deep into a modern age that increasingly considered those values outmoded.

BEFORE

The great age of Romanticism in the 19th century produced composers of a magnitude to match the times.

MARKERS LEFT BY MAESTROS

Germany's **Richard Wagner** took opera into new regions of turbulent drama and expressive power **« 164–165**. Hungarian **Franz Liszt** invented the orchestral symphonic poem as a vehicle for the soaring Romantic imagination **« 160–161**, and Russia's symphonic tradition was raised to greatness by **Pyotr Ilyich Tchaikovsky** **« 182–183**. For the next generation of Romantic composers, their own musical course was largely determined by the influence of these powerful predecessors.

Change of tone

Austrian composer Richard Strauss (see opposite) was only 24 when the spectacular success of his orchestral symphonic poem *Don Juan*, first performed in 1889, won him instant fame. Like Wagner and Liszt before him, the young composer saw himself as a bold musical progressive. Each of his symphonic poems that followed *Don Juan* deployed richly expressive harmony in music of virtuoso invention and panache, orchestrated with phenomenal mastery, and seemingly leading toward the turbulent new world of musical modernism.

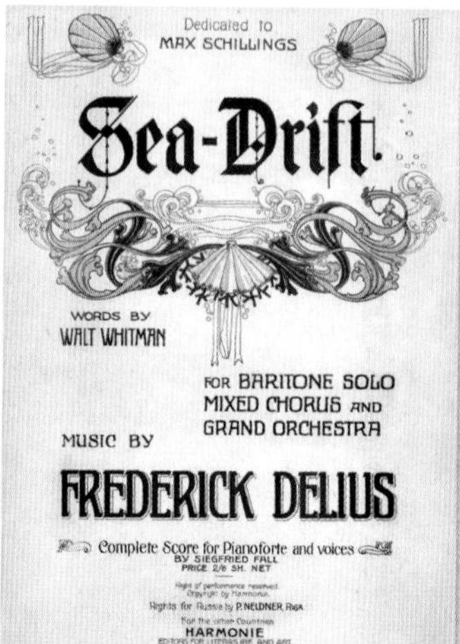

Dedicated to
MAX SCHILLINGS
Sea-Drift
WORDS BY
WALT WHITMAN
FOR BARITONE SOLO
MIXED CHORUS AND
GRAND ORCHESTRA
MUSIC BY
FREDERICK DELIUS
Complete Score for Pianoforte and voices
HARMONIE
BERLIN W.

Music of love and loss
A score from 1906 offers Delius's setting of words from the *Sea-Drift* section of Walt Whitman's poetry collection *Leaves of Grass*.

Strauss's third opera, *Salome* (1905), based on the play of the same name by Oscar Wilde, was followed three years later by *Elektra*, his first collaboration with the Austrian writer Hugo von Hofmannsthal. Both operas were full of musical tensions, and dealt with sex, violence, and emotional extremes.

Then came a shift of style, perhaps surprising even to Strauss himself. His next opera with Hofmannsthal, *Der Rosenkavalier* (The Rose Cavalier), first performed in 1911, was a winsome comedy set in 18th-century Vienna. Its music was written in a warmly benign style, featuring Viennese waltzes, and glowing lyrical arias for the singers. Instead of pushing further into modernism, he had found a way to bypass it.

> "I am a **first-class** second-rate **composer.**"
>
> RICHARD STRAUSS, DURING A CONCERT REHEARSAL IN LONDON, 1947

By the 1930s, Strauss was still composing operas in the late-Romantic style, almost as if the 20th-century musical world around him did not exist. For Strauss, the end of his own era came with the Allied bombing of the grand opera houses of Germany and Austria during World War II. In 1945, he wrote *Metamorphosen* for string orchestra as a lament for a culture destroyed by barbarism and violence.

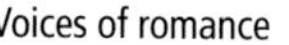

Voices of romance
A painting by Alexander Fyodorovich Lushin, from 1938, shows costume and scenery designs for a production of *Aleko* (1892), the first of three operas written by Rachmaninov.

Russian master of melody

Besides his gift as a composer and conductor, Sergey Rachmaninoff (1873–1943) was one of the greatest pianists of all time. In his first works he quickly discovered his late Romantic style, whose natural conservatism (like that of Russian society itself) was already out of step with the more progressive European scene. The premiere of his First Symphony in 1897 was a disaster, and for the next few years Rachmaninoff composed nothing. Therapy by the hypnotist Nikolai Dahl then led to the creation of the hugely successful Second Piano Concerto (1901).

Stretching his keyboard skills
Rachmaninoff sits at the piano around 1931. He was a tall man and had enormous hands, with a span much wider than that of most other pianists, making his music a particular challenge for others to play.

In the years before the Russian Revolution in 1917, Rachmaninoff's prolific output included his Third Piano Concerto and the sumptuously melodic Second Symphony. But Russia after the revolution was a hostile world for a late Romantic with deep roots in the musical past. Rachmaninoff emigrated to the United States, where homesickness made composing difficult, and his style was widely denounced as old-fashioned. He spent much of his time in his new country giving piano concerts, but still managed to complete some last masterpieces, full of romantic nostalgia—among them the concerto-style *Paganini Rhapsody* (1934) and the Third Symphony (1936).

Haunting harmonies

Finland's Jean Sibelius (1865–1957) continued to epitomize Romantic nationalism into the 1920s, when he wrote the last of his seven, uniquely haunting symphonies. English-born Frederick Delius (1862–1934) was another "one-of-a-kind" whose style owed little to the wider musical world. Aside from Wagner's expressive power, the only real influence on Delius's work was the fresh-air Romanticism of his friend Edvard Grieg (see pp.184–185). The son of a wool merchant, Delius eventually settled in the French village of Grez-sur-Loing. Here, he composed his finest works, remarkable for their darkly glowing sonority and powerful atmosphere, including the choral and orchestral *Appalachia* (1903). By the late 1920s, Delius was blind and paralyzed. He dictated his last works, among them the choral *Songs of Farewell,* to his assistant, Eric Fenby. They explore an unchanged, late-Romantic sound-world, far from contemporary modernism.

Salome's dance of the seven veils
A poster by German artist Max Tilke advertises a 1910 performance of Strauss's opera in Paris—the city that saw the premiere of Oscar Wilde's play *Salomé* in 1896.

COMPOSER (1864–1949)

RICHARD STRAUSS

Born in Munich, Strauss (no relation to the composer Johann Strauss) was the son of Bavaria's leading horn player. Alongside conducting positions, he found early acclaim for his tone-poems, such as *Also sprach Zarathustra* (Thus Spoke Zarathustra, 1896), and wrote more than a dozen operas. In the 1930s, Strauss refused to leave Nazi Germany, but he despised the regime and successfully protected his Jewish daughter-in-law. His orchestral *Four Last Songs* were first performed in London's Royal Albert Hall in 1950, a year after his death.

KEY WORKS

Richard Strauss *Don Juan*; *Till Eulenspiegel*; *Der Rosenkavalier*

Sergei Rachmaninoff Piano concertos: No. 2 in C minor, Op. 18, and No. 3 in D minor, Op. 30; Symphony No. 2 in E minor, Op. 27; *Vespers* (All-Night Vigil)

Frederick Delius *A Village Romeo and Juliet*; *Sea Drift*

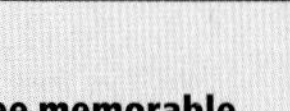

AFTER

Alongside these three memorable "Last Romantics," other composers with the same traditional values continued to carry the banner of Romanticism into the 20th century.

KEEPING THE FLAME ALIVE

Austria's **Erich Wolfgang Korngold** (1897–1957) moved to the United States and composed romantic Hollywood movie scores, including *Robin Hood* (1938) and *The Sea Hawk* (1940) **290–291 ››**. The late-Romantic style of England's **William Walton** (1902–1983) developed early, in works such as his Viola Concerto (1929), and changed little even by the late 1970s. In *Knoxville: Summer of 1915* for soprano and orchestra (1947), American **Samuel Barber** composed a warmly nostalgic portrait of the past.

American **Voices**

Although the American colonies were primarily settled by Europeans, by the late 19th century, American composers were beginning to find their own sound that was distinct from that of Europe. American music is now one of the most important sources of Western art music.

The 19th century was a turning point for music in America, beginning with Louis Moreau Gottschalk (1829–1869), the New Orleans composer/pianist who became the country's first international performer. His music, which is imbued with the African syncopations and rhythms that he heard as a child, fascinated Europeans.

Popular music

The most prolific songwriter of the mid-19th century was Stephen Collins Foster (1826–1864); his most popular songs, "Oh! Susanna," "Camptown Races," and "Old Folks at Home" (more commonly known as "Swanee River"), were written for the minstrel stage prior to the American Civil War (1861–1865). Although Foster also penned sentimental songs for the parlor, such as "Jeannie with the Light Brown Hair" and "Beautiful Dreamer," his fame rests primarily on his minstrel contributions.

After the American Civil Rights movement (1954–1968), Foster's music was performed less frequently due to its connection to the racist stereotypes perpetuated by minstrelsy. Despite this, the state of Kentucky still uses his minstrel song "My Old Kentucky Home, Goodnight," intended as the lament of an enslaved person separated from his family, as their state song, with some changes to the lyrics.

Finding an American School

In the 1890s, Jeannette Meyers Thurber, an important patron of music, brought Czech composer, Antonín Dvořák (1841–1904) to the National Conservatory of Music in New York City in the hope that he would be able to establish an American style of music. Dvořák, who had successfully created a distinctly Czech style of music in his homeland, suggested Americans tap into the musical traditions of the populations that made the country distinct from Europe: namely those of Native Americans and Black Americans. Because these populations were highly discriminated against, there was a mixed reaction to this suggestion. Some people wondered whether classical music composers should use the music of the disenfranchised in the concert hall.

Other musicians embraced Dvořák's ideas. Scholars had already started to research Native American music. Theodore Baker's doctoral dissertation, *Über die Musik der nordamerikanischen Wilden* was published in 1882, followed by Alice Cunningham Fletcher's transcriptions of melodies of the Omaha tribe, in 1893. Composers turned to these sources for new themes, launching what became known as the "Indianist" School. The movement's most prominent champion was the composer and music critic Arthur Farwell (1872–1952), who established the Wa-Wan Press, which was dedicated to publishing American composers who used folk music elements in their works.

Indigenous sounds
An Omaha tribesman performs a traditional dance. The music of the Omaha helped create a distinctly American sound.

Charles Ives

One of America's most influential composers in the late 19th and early 20th centuries, and still popular today, was Charles Ives (1874–1954). Taught music as a child by his bandleader father, Ives went on to study music with composer Horatio Parker at Yale University. Ives's compositions are characterized by stark dissonance and quotations of art music, hymns, and patriotic music. They are frequently related to specific aspects of American history or culture, such as *Three Places in New England* and *Central Park in the Dark*. His *Second Piano Sonata (Concord Mass: 1840–1860)*, published in 1920, was inspired by the transcendentalist movement, a school of literature that developed in the eastern US in the 1820s and 1830s. Each of its four movements is named after one of the school's leading writers: "Emerson," after Ralph Waldo Emerson; "Hawthorne," after Nathaniel Hawthorne; "The Alcotts," after Louisa May Alcott and Amos Bronson Alcott; and "Thoreau," after Henry David Thoreau. Ives's sonata celebrated the spirit, people, and landscapes of Massachusetts.

Harlem Renaissance

In the 1920s, exciting new sounds in classical music sprang out of the Harlem Renaissance, a flowering of African American culture that touched all the arts. Among its leading lights was composer and conductor William Grant Still (1895–1978). His *Afro-American Symphony* (1931) was the first symphony by a composer of color to be performed by a major orchestra, the Rochester Philharmonic. Still prefaced each of the four movements with a quote from the Black American poet Paul Laurence Dunbar; incorporated blues notes (or lowered tones); and utilized a tenor banjo in the ensemble. Still's later work, *And They Lynched Him on a Tree*, a collaboration with Katherine

KEY WORKS

Louis Moreau Gottschalk, *Le Banjo*
Arthur Farwell, *Pawnee Horses*
William Grant Still, *Afro-American Symphony*
Florence Price, *Symphony No. 1 in E minor*
Charles Ives, *Three Places in New England*

BEFORE

A unique American compositional style began to emerge in the colonies in the 18th century.

ONE VOICE
Singing schools were introduced in New England in the 1720s as a way to improve the quality of **church singing**. The students were usually taught by an itinerant master who held classes for several months.

CHORAL COMPOSER
America's first professional composer, **William Billings** (1746–1800) wrote more than 300 pieces of choral music, which were published in tune books. Among his works are the **rousing anthem** "The Lord is Risen Indeed" and the patriotic anthem "Chester."

SINGING PROCESSION

> "All of us on the scene at that time were **making a contribution** to something uniquely and **definitely American.**"
>
> WILLIAM GRANT STILL, 1954

First in line
Florence Price was the first Black American woman to have a work performed by a leading ensemble.

Garrison Chapin, was uniquely scored for "white chorus," "Negro chorus," a soloist, the narrator, and orchestra.

Composer and pianist Florence Price (1887–1953), a native of Arkansas, was also connected to the Harlem Renaissance. After studying composition at the New England Conservatory and working as a teacher in various Southern cities, she moved to Chicago, Illinois, to continue her studies at the American Conservatory. Her *Symphony in E minor*, the winner of the 1932 Wanamaker Foundation Competition, received its world premiere with the Chicago Symphony Orchestra the following year. It was widely lauded. The *Chicago Daily News* described the work as a "faultless work that speaks its own message with restraint yet passion." Price's other notable works include songs with texts by Black American poets Langston Hughes and Paul Laurence Dunbar, spiritual arrangements, and keyboard works for solo organ and piano.

Mid-Century to minimalism

During World War II and in the postwar period, composers were drawn to more patriotic subjects, a trend seen in the works of Aaron Copland (1900–1990) who incorporated folk tunes, such as the Shaker tune "Simple Gifts," in his ballet *Appalachian Spring*.

In the 1960s, a new style termed minimalism emerged as a reaction to the complexity of music; it is characterized by musical fragments that are repeated with subtle changes over long periods of time.

Appalachian Spring
Martha Graham (1894–1991), who commissioned and choreographed Aaron Copland's ballet, dances one of its lead roles. The story is set in a newly built farmhouse in 19th-century Pennsylvania.

AFTER

Women composers are a strong voice in American music, creating some of the country's most interesting work.

APPALACHIAN INFLUENCE

Jennifer Higdon (1962–) has won the Pulitzer Prize and three Grammy Awards for her work. Her experience of living in Appalachia as an adolescent is evident in her *Concerto 4-3* and her first opera, *Cold Mountain*, **based on the novel** of the same name by American author Charles Frazier.

NEW MEETS OLD

Caroline Shaw (1982–) won the 2013 Pulitzer Prize for *Partita for Eight Voices*, which includes a **uniquely American dimension** by quoting 19th-century hymn writer George Frederick Root.

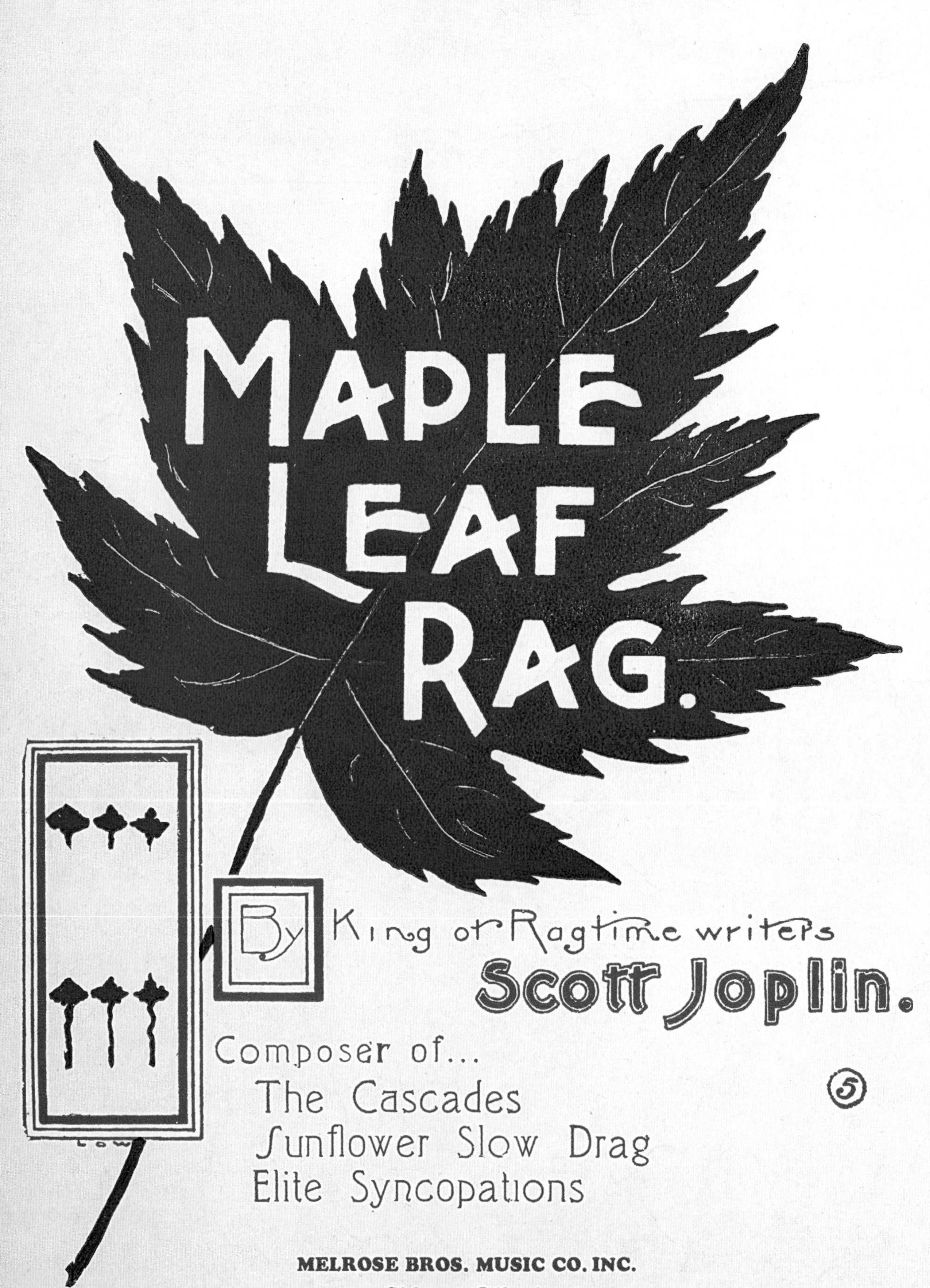
MAPLE
LEAF
RAG.
By King of Ragtime writers
Scott Joplin.
Composer of...
The Cascades
Sunflower Slow Drag
Elite Syncopations
5
MELROSE BROS. MUSIC CO. INC.
Chicago, Illinois

BEFORE

Music was one of the cultural expressions the millions of enslaved people transported to North America from Africa were able to retain.

THE ROOTS OF RAGTIME
Before the American Civil War (1861–1865), free and enslaved African Americans reconstructed African instruments and adapted European ones to create a **unique rhythm**. This laid the foundation for several genres, including ragtime.

MINSTRELSY OPENS DOORS
The first **minstrel shows** emerged in the 1830s, with white performers like Thomas Rice, who blackened his face and sang in an exaggerated vernacular while dancing a jig. Black performers joined minstrel shows in the mid-1860s, introducing their musical innovations to wider audiences.

Ragtime

Three new musical genres emerged in the final quarter of the 19th century among African Americans—ragtime, jazz, and blues. This creative surge happened as the first generation born after the end of slavery grew to adulthood, and introduced the world to syncopated rhythm.

Among the African-American performers who took to the minstrel stage after the Civil War was musician, dancer, and comedian Ernest Hogan (1865–1909). Translating the rhythms played by Black musicians to accompany the cakewalk dance, he published two hit songs. "La Pas Ma La" (1895), which he labeled a "rag," established Hogan's reputation as an innovator. His 1896 song "All Coons Look Alike to Me" initiated a flood of similar degrading "coon" songs that stereotyped African Americans. Although he later regretted the racist tone of the songs, he praised them for popularizing ragtime and creating opportunities for Black Americans.

Marching to a new beat

The term "ragtime" refers to the "ragging" or raggedly informal reinterpretation of a melody—a rhythmic approach in which a steady pulse is decorated by melodic accentuation of surprising, weaker beats (or off-beats). This technique, known as syncopation, creates a spirited, dancing sound that inspires listeners to move to the music.

> "Syncopations are **no indication** of light or trashy music."
>
> COMPOSER SCOTT JOPLIN, IN "SCHOOL OF RAGTIME," 1908

Originally developed on banjos and fiddles, this idiosyncratic syncopated approach soon became associated with the piano. Composers William Krell (1868–1933), Scott Joplin (see left), Joseph Lamb (1887–1960), and James Scott (1885–1938) adapted the Sousa march style (see pp.200–201), and applied African-American-derived polyrhythms. These elegant piano rags often feature a steady oom-pah in the left hand while the right plays three or four distinct syncopated themes, the first being the catchiest.

Hitting the big time

The popularity of ragtime piano, especially Joplin's, helped create a musical craze that spread across the United States and into Europe. Ragtime was incorporated into dance band styles, ragtime ensembles were formed, and the songwriters of Tin Pan Alley (see pp.230–231) were quick to capitalize on the fad.

Cakewalk capers
A minstrel-show entertainer in 1903 performs the cakewalk, an exaggerated dance originally invented by enslaved people to mock white plantation owners.

Stravinsky, stomping, and stride

Though ragtime is a distinctly American idiom, it also infiltrated European music, notably in pieces by Debussy (see pp.204–205), Satie (see pp.210–211) and Stravinsky (see pp.212–213).

Piano rags such as Joplin's archetypal "Maple Leaf Rag" (1899) were meant to be played precisely as written, like classical pieces. However, pianists often used these technically challenging pieces to assert their prowess, and performance speeds gradually increased way beyond the composer's intentions. A new generation of players, notably Jelly Roll Morton (see p.234), took ragtime as an inspirational starting point for their own improvisatory, "stomping" style. This is turn led to the development of "stride piano" as practiced by jazz masters James P. Johnson (1894–1955) and Fats Waller (1904–1943).

Fats Waller
The popular jazz singer, pianist, organist, and entertainer Thomas "Fats" Waller was a student of stride maestro James P. Johnson and composed his first rags at age 15.

COMPOSER (*c*.1868–1917)

SCOTT JOPLIN

Born in Texas, the son of a railroad worker who, before emancipation, had played violin at plantation parties, the young Scott Joplin traveled with a vocal quartet, and played cornet, guitar, and violin, although his specialty was the piano. He later settled in Sedalia, Missouri, and wrote a string of ragtime pieces that he said aimed for a "weird and intoxicating effect." Living off his royalties, he later diversified into composing full-length operas such as *Treemonisha*. Joplin did not believe in improvisation, insisting that "each note will be played as it is written."

Rag to riches
First published in 1899, the sheet music for "Maple Leaf Rag" provided Scott Joplin with a steady income for the rest of his life. Joplin himself played his rags more slowly than modern pianists tend to do.

KEY WORKS

William Krell "Mississippi Rag"
Scott Joplin "Maple Leaf Rag"; "Easy Winners"; "The Entertainer"
James Scott "Frog Legs Rag"
Joseph Lamb "Sensation"

AFTER

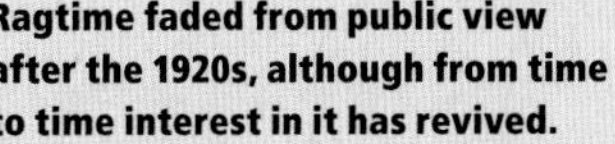

Ragtime faded from public view after the 1920s, although from time to time interest in it has revived.

LEFT BEHIND BY JAZZ
Ragtime was both an influential strand in the development of jazz and a popular musical style in itself for more than 20 years. But when **jazz swept the world** in the 1920s **234–235 ››**, ragtime was suddenly regarded as old-fashioned and it faded from view.

MAKING A COMEBACK
Audiences rediscovered ragtime with Joshua Rifkind's Grammy-winning Scott Joplin album in 1971 and Joplin tunes such as "The Entertainer" in the 1973 movie ***The Sting***.

BEFORE

Country evolved from the gradual cross-fertilization of several musical strands. Two major influences were Celtic folk music introduced by European settlers and the songs and music of cowboys.

APPALACHIAN FOLK MUSIC

Rooted in **ballads** brought to the eastern US by Scottish and Irish settlers in the 18th and 19th centuries, Appalachian folk music was characterized by emotional, often harmonized vocals, accompanied by banjo, guitar, fiddle, and mandolin. These **stringed instruments** still form the basis of most acoustic country styles.

COWBOY MUSIC

Otto Gray & His Oklahoma Cowboys, formerly McGinty's Oklahoma Cowboy Band, were the first nationally known western music group. The original members were real cowboys, later replaced by professional musicians. They sang traditional material of the sort documented in *Cowboy Songs and Other Frontier Ballads* by folk-song collector John Lomax in 1911.

Country's Roots

Until the late 1940s, country and western was known variously as Appalachian, old-time folk, mountain, cowboy, rural, and western music. This reflected its rich variety of acoustic American folk traditions and musical traits.

Roy Acuff and his Smokey Mountain Boys
The bigger country stars featured in hillbilly movies about rural life in the southeastern United States. Here, Roy Acuff and his Smokey Mountain Boys perform in the film *Night Train to Memphis* (1946).

The earliest commercial recordings of country music were made by Eck Robertson from Texas ("Sallie Gooden" in 1922) and Fiddlin' John Carson ("The Little Old Log Cabin in the Lane" in 1924). Both recordings, made by fiddlers with informal, nonclassical technique, reveal the Celtic influence on American folk.

Following trained singer Vernon Dalhart's 1924 recording of "The Wreck of the Old 97," which sold a million copies, the Victor record company went in search of authentic Southern country sounds. American producer and talent scout Ralph Peer, responsible for recording Fiddlin' John Carson, recorded 19 performers at the famed "Bristol Sessions" that he set up in Tennessee in 1927, inviting local musicians to showcase their music. The event was pivotal in the history of country music, and the royalty system that Peer devised at the sessions remains the basis for music business contracts to this day.

"Country music is the **people's music.** [It is] about **real life** and… **truth** and it tells things how they **really are.**"

COUNTRY SINGER FAITH HILL (1967–)

Early country stars

Among the artists recorded at the Bristol Sessions was Jimmie Rodgers (1897–1933), a Mississippi-born rail worker who developed a distinctive singing style. His trademark yodeling—suddenly flipping his voice to falsetto register—led to his nickname "The Blue Yodeler." His blend of blues, folk, and country styles on recordings such as "Blue Yodel," "Waiting for a Train," and "Mule Skinner Blues" was influential.

Another act exposed on the Bristol Sessions was the Virginia-based Carter Family. Their close harmonies over folk material and the self-taught guitar style of Maybelle Carter, in which she strummed chords with her fingers while picking out low-register melodies with her thumb, had a big impact on country's development. Tunes such as "Wabash Cannonball" and "Keep on the Sunny Side" are country standards.

Acoustic king
First made in 1937, Gibson's J200 was favored by Roy Rogers and Gene Autry. It became known as the "king of the flat-tops," prized for its deep and powerful sound.

COUNTRY BAND (1920s–1990s)

THE CARTER FAMILY

Born and raised in Virginia, Alvin Pleasant "A. P." Delaney Carter, his wife Sara, and sister-in-law Maybelle sang American folk and gospel in tight harmony accompanied by innovative guitar work from Maybelle. They sang as a group and, from 1927, recorded standards such as "Wildwood Flower," "Engine 143," and "Can the Circle Be Unbroken." They disbanded in 1943, but Maybelle continued to perform with her daughters as The Carter Sisters, reverting to The Carter Family in 1960. After Maybelle's death in 1978, the group continued with next generation Carters until 1998.

Country's heart

The *Grand Ole Opry* is a country radio show that began in 1925 and became the single most influential country broadcast in the United States. At the same time, Nashville, where it took place, became America's country capital. Early performances included upbeat music for country square dancing known as "hoedown," as played by the Binkley Brothers' Dixie Clodhoppers, and comic monologues by Minnie Pearl, a regular Opry performer between 1940 and 1991.

26 **The number of times artists had to perform in the Grand Ole Opry show in one year to remain a "member" in 1963.**

The program also introduced a new generation of singer-songwriters. Tennessee-born Roy Acuff (1903–1992) played fiddle with the Smokey Mountain Boys and developed a clear, loud singing style that immediately connected with listeners. He went on to have a 50-year career and became known as the "King of Country." Alabama-born Hank Williams (1923–1953) had a rockier relationship with the program due to his unreliability caused by alcoholism, but his body of storytelling songs (including "Cold, Cold Heart," "Hey Good Lookin'," and "Your Cheatin' Heart") is the most revered in country music.

Musical Westerns

Another mass media outlet for country music in the 1930s and '40s was the musical western, or B-Western. These low-budget movies presented the "good guys" as genial, upstanding characters with a penchant for a guitar and a western song. They starred actor-singers such as the hugely influential Texas-born Gene Autry (1907–1998), who was already a successful

Singing cowboy
This 1938 movie poster advertised one of 93 B-Westerns starring Gene Autry. In *Man from Music Mountain*, Autry is trapped in a gold mine before bringing a swindler to justice.

singer, having sold a million copies of "That Silver-Haired Daddy of Mine" in 1931. His smooth, hillbilly-style crooning helped him become the biggest-selling country artist of the period. Other singing cowboys included Tex Ritter and Roy Rogers. Ritter, who appeared in 85 movies between 1936 and 1945, went on to have a successful recording career that included the hit "Do Not Forsake Me Oh My Darling," the theme from the 1952 movie *High Noon*.

Subgenres of country

Though American folk roots could be heard in all types of country music, the many distinct styles made for rich diversity. A dance music that rose to popularity in the West and South in the 1930s blended rural folk, cowboy song, jazz, and blues and became known as Western Swing, using fiddle, banjo, and steel guitar. Its reliance on acoustic stringed instruments and improvised arrangements made it distinct from big band swing (see pp.242–243). Notable Western Swing groups included the Texas-based Light Crust Doughboys and Bob Wills and the Western Playboys.

Another strand was developed by Kentucky-born mandolin player Bill Monroe (1911–1996) in the 1940s. With fast tempos, tight vocal harmonies, and instrumental "breaks" (short unaccompanied flourishes by a soloist), he and his band, the Blue Grass Boys, created the style known as bluegrass.

The California-based Maddox Brothers and Rose specialized in a raucous country sound that became known retrospectively as hillbilly boogie, a fusing of country style and driving bass lines associated with the piano-based blues of boogie-woogie. Another influential and blues-inflected variation on the country sound was dubbed honky tonk, and featured love-lorn songs and vocals with a nasal twang. Ernest Tubb's best-selling 1941 hit "I'm Walking the Floor Over You" exemplifies the style. Both styles pointed the way to a vigorous country variant called rockabilly, an early version of rock 'n' roll (see pp.314–315).

KEY WORKS

The Carter Family "Worried Man Blues"
Jimmie Rodgers "Blue Yodel"
Roy Acuff "The Wabash Cannonball"
Gene Autry "Back In The Saddle Again"
Hank Williams "Your Cheatin' Heart"
Bob Wills and the Texas Playboys "Steel Guitar Rag"
Maddox Brothers and Rose "Water Baby Boogie"

AFTER

New fusions emerged from the 1950s, and country music now outsells any other genre in the United States.

NEW HYBRIDS
Continuing the country tradition of blending with other genres, a **country-pop hybrid** with lush orchestrations and glossy production values was developed in the 1950s and '60s by producers Chet Atkins and Owen Bradley. This became known as the **Nashville Sound** or **Countrypolitan**.

MUSIC FOR OUTSIDERS
In the 1970s and '80s, **Outlaw Country** favored traditional musical values to express the outlook of the outsider, as in the work of singer-songwriters Waylon Jennings and Willie Nelson, and the late career of Johnny Cash **346–347 ››**.

Tin Pan Alley

The music of Tin Pan Alley largely comprised catchy popular songs with a sentimental or lighthearted tone. At their worst, the songs were ephemeral and crass, but the best are American Songbook classics that have a timeless appeal.

Tin Pan Alley was a New York-based community of publishers and songwriters dedicated to commercial music. Their business involved calculating what might appeal to the public, writing appropriate songs, and then publishing and selling the sheet music.

"I would **rather** have written the **best song** of a nation than its **noblest epic.**"

AMERICAN AUTHOR EDGAR ALLEN POE

BEFORE

Printed music arrived in the US at the end of the 18th century. Without radio or telephone, the popularity of songs relied on word of mouth.

SHEET MUSIC

In the mid-1800s, US **piano sales** exploded and self-made entertainment was based on singing at home and in schools and churches. This provided a market for **sheet music**. By the end of the Civil War (1861–1865), several thousand pieces of popular music had been sold. With loose **copyright** laws, publishers were at liberty to compete with each other in publishing the same song. Civil War songs were adapted from **folk hymns** such as "Battle Hymn of The Republic" by Julia Ward Howe. Imitations of **African-American vernacular** included "Camptown Races" (1850) by Stephen Foster, while Irish-style **ballads** included "I'll Take You Home Again Kathleen" (1876) by Thomas P. Westendorf.

JEWISH INFLUENCE

A sizeable proportion of the key Tin Pan Alley songwriters were the offspring of **Jewish immigrants**, including George and Ira Gershwin, Lorenz Hart, Irving Berlin, Jerome Kern, and Harold Arlen. Although their work reflected the American idioms of ragtime, blues, and jazz, Cole Porter detected enough of a plaintive quality to declare to composer Richard Rodgers that all he had to do to compose hit songs was to "write Jewish tunes."

Geographically, Tin Pan Alley was located in Manhattan on West 28th Street between 5th and 6th Avenue. It was active between around 1885 and the mid-1930s. The term "Tin Pan Alley" relates to the metallic clatter made by dozens of out-of-tune pianos heard on the street through the open windows of the publishers' offices, as songwriters composed and demonstrated their ditties. However, the wider meaning of the term Tin Pan Alley refers to a popular song industry.

Alley origins

Charles K. Harris, an opportunistic songwriter from Milwaukee, Wisconsin, is often referred to as the Father of Tin Pan Alley. A sign outside his office read, "Songs Written To Order."

Harris moved to New York City and in 1906 wrote a book entitled *How To Write A Popular Song*. It featured copious tips on writing songs in popular genres such as the Comic Song, and the "Home" or "Mother" Song. It also included advice on how to stay abreast of the public's taste in music and current subject matter. This handbook for commercial songwriting holds much advice that remains useful to songwriters today.

Father of Tin Pan Alley
Charles K. Harris had his biggest hit with "After the Ball," set in waltz time. Published in 1892, the sheet music sold 5 million copies, and he went on to produce a best-selling book about songwriting.

Popular themes

A popular commercial songwriting technique was to turn a topical news item into a sentimental song. Edward B. Marks and Joseph W. Stern wrote "The Little Lost Child" (1894) after reading a story about a lost child in a newspaper, while the invention of the telephone inspired Charles K. Harris to pen the tearjerker "Hello Central, Give Me Heaven" (1901).

The latest dance crazes such as the Cakewalk or the Charleston were commonly name-checked, while current musical trends—often African American—were diluted and adapted into songs for mass consumption. Irving Berlin's "Alexander's Ragtime Band" (1911), for example, was an exuberant popular song and an enormous hit, but it had little to do with the refined and stately works of the ragtime composer and pianist Scott Joplin (see pp.226–227).

W. C. Handy's "St. Louis Blues" (1915), although by an African-American composer and self-published, was a cleaned-up Tin Pan Alley version of the blues, complete with a fashionable tango introduction (see p.240).

World War I opened a rich new source of subject matter for songwriters, inspiring the Alley to produce a glut of songs designed to rally the troops—providing a good marching tempo—as well as raise spirits on the home front. Popular wartime songs included "Over There" by George M. Cohen and "Goodbye Broadway, Hello France" by C. Francis Reisner, Benny Davis, and Billy Baskette.

Live performance

Teams of energetic and outgoing song-pluggers were employed by music stores to sell the publishers' sheet music by performing the numbers live on a piano.

The formation of ASCAP (the American Society of Composers and Publishers) in 1914 ensured that any songs performed publicly were due royalties, which made the song business more lucrative and even more feverish. Popular vaudeville performers such as Al Jolson (1886–1950), who were guaranteed to make a song a hit, were paid and credited as cowriters by song publishers so that they would perform their songs in their acts. As recordings became more popular, well-known bandleaders and vocalists were courted by song-pluggers using similar tactics.

1,800 The number of ragtime tunes published on Tin Pan Alley between 1900 and 1910.

A touch of stardust
Self-taught, with abundant talent, Hoagy Carmichael had a distinctive jazz piano style. He was a prolific songwriter, whose hits included "Stardust," "Georgia On My Mind," and "The Nearness Of You."

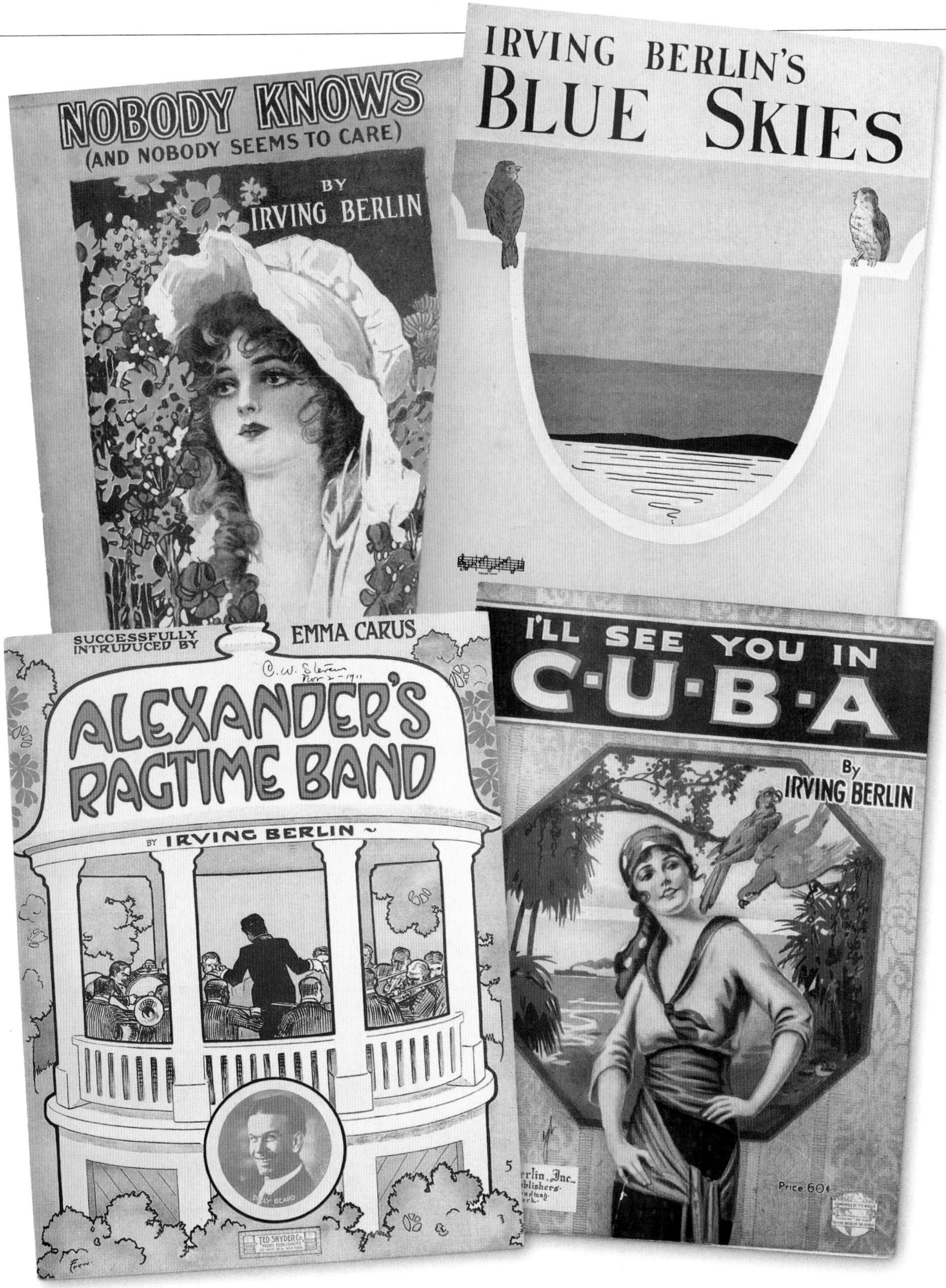

Ragtime to big time
One of the most successful songwriters was Irving Berlin, whose first major hit was "Alexander's Ragtime Band" (1911), included among this selection of Berlin sheet music. Berlin went on to write some 1,500 songs, as well as scores for films and Broadway shows.

KEY WORKS

George M. Cohen "Over There;" "Give My Regards To Broadway"

Irving Berlin "Blue Skies"

Johnny Green "Body and Soul"

Paul Dresser "On the Banks of the Wabash, Far Away"

Nora Bayes/Jack Norworth "Shine On Harvest Moon"

New York and beyond

Most major American composers and lyricists of the 1920s and '30s were associated with Tin Pan Alley, and although New Yorkers such as George Gershwin (see pp.232–233) were indelibly linked to the city, talent arrived from across the United States, bringing different outlooks, experiences, and musical styles. Self-taught musician Hoagy Carmichael (1899–1981), for example, came from Indiana, while songwriter, singer, and composer Johnny Mercer (1909–76) was influenced by the African-American music that he heard during his childhood in Savannah, Georgia.

But it is perhaps the lesser-known characters who provided the authentic sound of Tin Pan Alley. Songs such as "Some Of These Days," "Ain't She Sweet," and "My Blue Heaven" are remembered long after the names of their composers Shelton Brooks, Jack Yellen, and Walter Donaldson. The advent of the radio and phonograph (see pp.260–261) led to the gradual decline of sheet music sales through the 1920s and 1930s, while the most gifted and sophisticated of the new generation of songwriters headed west to Hollywood or focused their efforts on Broadway musicals, hoping to see their names in lights.

From then on, American popular songs were as likely to originate from the stage or big screen as from the pianos of Tin Pan Alley.

AFTER

Tin Pan Alley may no longer exist as a place in New York City, but it remains a name to tag on to any hothouse of popular songs.

BRILL BUILDING
New York's Brill Building was a Tin Pan Alley-style community of writers and publishers that existed in the 1930s. It revived during the **rock'n'roll** and **pop** eras of the 1950s and 60s **318–319 ››** eras thanks to songwriters such as Burt Bacharach, Neil Diamond, and Carole King.

THE BRILL BUILDING'S CAROLE KING

UK EQUIVALENT
During the 1950s, Britain's own Tin Pan Alley sprang up in Denmark Street in London's West End, its offices populated by music publishers and songwriters such as **Lionel Bart** and **Elton John**.

SINGERS AND SONGWRITERS
Since the **Beatles** **324–325 ››** and the arrival of writer-performers, commercial songwriters have been less in demand. But there will always be some noncomposing performers who need composers with an ear for a hit and a Tin Pan Alley attitude.

COMPOSER Born 1898 Died 1937

George Gershwin

"Life is a **lot like jazz ...** it's best when you **improvise."**

GEORGE GERSHWIN, 1929

American composer George Gershwin is unique in having achieved durable success both as a writer of popular songs and as the composer of works that have a permanent place in the classical repertoire. His inventiveness brought a new sophistication to Broadway, while his melodic gift drew a wider audience to the serious concert halls.

Early influences

Gershwin grew up on Manhattan's Lower East Side, the son of Russian Jewish immigrants. Although he was a streetwise city kid, his family was not poor and he listened to composers such as Antonín Dvořák alongside jazz and popular songs. His talent for piano was evident by the time he was 10.

Charles Hambitzer, a successful composer and pianist, became Gershwin's mentor in 1912, introducing him to a broad classical repertoire, including works by Claude

Elegant composer
By his mid-20s, Gershwin was a prosperous and fashionable figure on the New York social scene. Also a workaholic, he often had three musicals on Broadway at the same time.

Songwriter in the making
Gershwin's first published song was "When You Want 'Em You Can't Get 'Em," in 1916. Sales of the sheet music earned the 17-year-old composer a meager advance of $5 and no royalties.

French connection
Gershwin (right) watches French composer Maurice Ravel at the keyboard. The American was heavily influenced by contemporary French music in his classical works.

Debussy and Maurice Ravel (see pp.204–205). At the same time, Hambitzer did not discourage Gershwin's interest in ragtime and the songs of Irving Berlin. The young Gershwin was already conceiving the idea of writing American symphonic music that built on these popular genres.

At 15, Gershwin worked as a pianist playing in stores to promote the sales of sheet music. He was soon selling his own songs to the publishers of Tin Pan Alley, the hub of New York's song industry (see pp.230–231). His first hit, "Swanee," popularized by singer Al Jolson, outsold all his other songs.

> "Why be a **second-rate Ravel** when you are a **first-rate Gershwin?**"
>
> MAURICE RAVEL, IN CONVERSATION WITH GEORGE GERSHWIN, 1928

Broadway to Paris

In his mid-20s, Gershwin teamed up with his brother, Ira, as lyricist to write a string of Broadway musicals, combining innovative harmonies and syncopated jazz rhythms with catchy tunes. However, he never lost sight of his desire to write "serious" music. In 1922, he tried inserting a one-act jazz opera, *Blue Monday*, into a Broadway revue, but the experiment was abandoned after a single performance.

In 1924, he was commissioned by dance band leader Paul Whiteman to write a piece that bridged the gap between the jazz and classical genres. The result was *Rhapsody in Blue*. The first performance of this "jazz piano concerto," with the composer at the keyboard, involved a large element of improvisation. A success from the start, *Rhapsody* encouraged Gershwin to pursue his serious musical ambitions.

While continuing to be one of America's most successful tunesmiths, Gershwin took lessons in composition and studied the works of avant-garde composers. Tireless, he wrote Piano Concerto in F and *Three Preludes* without interrupting the flow of hit musicals. On a visit to Europe in 1928 he was feted by the French cultural elite. Performances of *Rhapsody in Blue* and the Piano Concerto in F received a rapturous response. He met composers such as Ravel, Darius Milhaud, and Francis Poulenc, who were as eager to be influenced by Gershwin as he was to learn from them. The tone poem *An American in Paris*, inspired by the trip, showed Gershwin coming to grips with larger-scale musical forms.

Fusion of genres

Gershwin invested immense effort in the creation of *Porgy and Bess*, a long-contemplated project on which he finally settled to work in 1934. It was the result of his attempt to fuse melody, jazz, and the modern classical tradition. The work was not initially well received by the public or critics. Later on, it became the first American work to enter the international operatic repertoire.

Gershwin did not live to see the fulfillment of his ambitions. From 1934, he began experiencing blackouts. Undiagnosed, these were, in fact, symptoms of a brain tumor that killed him at the tragically early age of 37.

SAMUEL GOLDWYNS FILMPRODUKTION
PORGY und BESS
Prädikat: BESONDERS WERTVOLL
SIDNEY POITIER · DOROTHY DANDRIDGE
SAMMY DAVIS JR · PEARL BAILEY
MUSIK VON GEORGE GERSHWIN · LIBRETTO VON DuBOSE HEYWARD
REGIE: OTTO PREMINGER
IM VERLEIH DER COLUMBIA · CinemaScope · TECHNICOLOR-STEREO-TON

International hit
Porgy and Bess, which contains the songs "Summertime" and "It Ain't Necessarily So," was made into an internationally successful movie by Otto Preminger in 1959. This poster advertised the film in Germany.

KEY WORKS

- ***Rhapsody in Blue***
- **Piano Concerto in F**
- ***Three Preludes***
- ***An American in Paris***
- **Stage musicals *Lady Be Good, Funny Face, Girl Crazy***
- ***Porgy and Bess***
- ***Shall We Dance***

TIMELINE

- **September 26, 1898** Born in Brooklyn, New York, the son of Jewish immigrants from Ukraine. His original name is Jacob Gershovitz.
- **1912** Begins music lessons with pianist and composer Charles Hambitzer.
- **1916** Publishes his first song at the age of 17.
- **May 26, 1919** His first complete musical, *La La Lucille*, opens at Henry Miller's Theatre on Broadway, New York.
- **1920–24** Provides the music for George White's annual *Scandals* revue on Broadway.
- **1923** Makes his first visits to London and Paris.
- **February 12, 1924** *Rhapsody in Blue* is premiered at the Aeolian Hall in New York with the composer as soloist keyboard player.
- **December 1, 1924** The stage musical *Lady Be Good* opens at the Liberty Theatre on Broadway. It stars Fred and Adele Astaire, with lyrics by George's brother, Ira Gershwin.
- **December 3, 1925** Piano Concerto in F has its first performance at Carnegie Hall in New York, again with the composer at the keyboard.
- **November 4, 1926** Gives first performance of his Three Preludes for Piano at the Hotel Roosevelt in New York.
- **November 8, 1926** Musical comedy *Oh, Kay!* opens at Broadway's Imperial Theatre.
- **November 22, 1927** Musical *Funny Face* opens at the Alvin Theatre on Broadway.
- **1928** Visits France, meeting Ravel, Prokofiev, and other European composers.
- **December 13, 1928** First performance of the orchestral piece *An American in Paris* at Carnegie Hall.
- **July 2, 1929** Musical *Show Girl* premieres at the Ziegfield Theatre.
- **January 14, 1930** Opening of musical *Strike Up the Band* at the Times Square Theatre.
- **October 14, 1930** Musical *Girl Crazy* opens at the Alvin Theatre on Broadway. It stars Ethel Merman and Ginger Rogers.

GEORGE (LEFT) AND IRA GERSHWIN, 1930s

- **1931** Writes his first movie music for *Delicious*.
- **January 29, 1931** *Second Rhapsody* is premiered in Boston.
- **1932** *Girl Crazy* is the first Gershwin stage musical adapted for film.
- **September 30, 1935** The opera *Porgy and Bess* premieres at the Colonial Theater in Boston.
- **1936** Moves to Hollywood, where he writes the score for the Astaire-Rogers movie musical *Shall We Dance*.
- **July 11, 1937** Dies in Hollywood while working on the score for the film *The Goldwyn Follies*.

Beginnings of Jazz

Toward the end of the 19th century in New Orleans, the music that became known as "jazz" was created when African and Caribbean rhythms were incorporated into both brass-band and popular dance music. Twenty years later, jazz took the world by storm.

New Orleans was the crucible that forged this red-hot new music. The city—owned in turn by France, Spain, and (from 1803) the United States—was home to a vibrant African-American population and well placed to synthesize the disparate musical traditions of its citizens.

Before the Civil War, New Orleans was the only American city that allowed enslaved people, including new arrivals from Africa or the Caribbean, to gather together freely. At weekly sessions in the city's Congo Square, enslaved and free people of color sang in African languages, played African instruments, and performed African dances.

BEFORE

New Orleans was already home to many African-American musicians. However, jazz could only develop freely after the end of enslavement.

BRASS BANDS
New Orleans's first **brass-band parade** took place in 1787; in 1838, the city's *Picayune* newspaper described "a real mania in this city for horn and trumpet playing."

CLASSICAL TRADITIONS
The classically trained orchestras that played the latest European dance tunes in New Orleans's ballrooms had many **Creole** (mixed-race) members.

RAGTIME
This **syncopated** style, derived from African musical traditions, accentuated the off-beat, creating a new musical genre **« 226–227**.

Mardi Gras
New Orleans's marching brass bands featured in parades of all kinds, including the city's annual Mardi Gras celebrations preceding the start of Lent, the Christian period of penance.

Melting pot

Following the abolition of enslavement, mixed-race and African-American musicians found themselves competing for work, and, inevitably, playing together.

New Orleans had long shown a passion for brass-band music, which was boosted further after the Civil War by the national craze for the rousing tunes of John Philip Sousa, such as "The Liberty Bell" and "Stars and Stripes Forever" (see pp.200–201). Marching bands were hired for public occasions of all kinds—including, famously, funerals.

3 **The number of valves in a cornet. It has the same pitch as a modern trumpet, and the two terms "cornet" and "trumpet" are often used interchangeably in jazz.**

Ad-hoc instruments

Unschooled street musicians formed "spasm" bands, playing homemade instruments created out of anything they could find, such as washboards, bottles, spoons, and saws. They grew up to join formal brass bands, and, in turn, brass-band musicians joined the ad-hoc groups that played in the dance halls. To supply the sheer volume essential in crowded indoor venues, trumpets, cornets, trombones, and clarinets replaced the violin as lead instruments, playing over a typical rhythm section of guitar, bass, drums, and piano.

Defining jazz

Coming up with a precise definition of what constitutes jazz has taxed musicians and fans alike. In a sense, it is easier to say what went into the pot—blues, ragtime, and Black work songs and spirituals—than what came out of it, but broadly speaking the key components are the rhythm and the use of improvisation, with the emphasis on the performer as interpreter. Legend has it that the defining moment in jazz history came when the smooth, sophisticated dance orchestra led from 1893 onward by Creole multi-instrumentalist John Robichaux (1866–1939) was rendered passé by the new sounds of the flamboyant cornet player Buddy Bolden (1877–1931), who founded his own band in 1897. A spellbinding performer heralded as the first jazz trumpeter—

Early jazz great
Joe "King" Oliver and his Creole Jazz Band play in San Francisco, in 1921. The mentor and first employer of Louis Armstrong, cornet player Oliver achieved huge success in the 1920s. He used a battery of mutes—cups, glasses, buckets—to create a distinctive sound that was widely imitated.

JAZZ MUSICIAN (1885–1941)

JELLY ROLL MORTON

Notorious for his claim that he created jazz, Jelly Roll Morton was always a hustler. Wild claims aside, his contribution to early jazz ranks second to none. Born Ferdinand Joseph La Menthe in 1885—although there is some dispute about the date—he grew up playing ragtime piano in the brothels of New Orleans. By 1906, he was on the road, crisscrossing the United States and Canada and introducing countless pickup bands of hired musicians to the new sounds of jazz. The first great jazz composer, responsible for such tunes as "Doctor Jazz Stomp" and "Wolverine Blues," he always stressed the importance of improvisation.

Cool cornet
Louis Armstrong learned to play on this battered cornet when he was sent to the Colored Waif's home in New Orleans in about 1913; just five years later, he was a professional jazz musician.

no recordings of his work survive—contemporary accounts praise Bolden's big sound and bold improvisations.

Raised under a red light

An attempt to restrict prostitution to a single area of New Orleans in 1897 resulted in a thriving red-light district called Storyville. The name came from the New Orleans city alderman Sidney Story, who forced all places of vice into a prescribed number of blocks. During the next 20 years, both cheap and elegant brothels sprang up, employing many musicians.

1898 The year when Buddy Bolden is said to have recorded the first jazz track on an Edison cylinder, which is now lost.

Although it is often said that jazz was born in Storyville, most brothels preferred to employ a solo pianist, or "professor," rather than a full band. Storyville was more the incubator for a particular kind of jazz—piano-based, ragtime-derived, and full of what Jelly Roll Morton (who got his start playing piano in the Storyville brothels) called "Spanish tinges," or rather Cuban habanera rhythms.

Jazz leaves town

When the brothels of Storyville were closed down in 1917, jazz musicians departed en masse to Chicago and then New York, where they helped to kick-start the worldwide "jazz age" of the 1920s.

No one now knows what the first jazz bands sounded like because no early recordings survive. Cornet player Freddie Keppard (1890–1933), whose band took Chicago by storm in 1914, refused to be recorded at that time, reportedly on the grounds that other musicians would be able to steal his style. As a result, the first jazz band to make a record—The Original Dixieland Jass Band—in New York in 1917, were white New Orleanians.

Million-seller

Their million-selling record "Livery Blues/Dixie Jass Band One-Step" inspired African-American New Orleans bandleaders such as Edward "Kid" Ory (1886–1973), in California, and Joe "King" Oliver (1885–1938), based in Chicago, to try their hands at cutting tracks, too. Oliver's Creole Jazz Band cut the first definitive jazz classics in 1923, before breaking up acrimoniously. However, the band's second trumpeter, Louis Armstrong (see pp.248–249), went on to form his seminal Hot Five and Hot Seven groups in New York. Jelly Roll Morton was also in Chicago by 1923. He reached his creative peak there, recording early jazz classics with the Red Hot Peppers in 1926.

AFTER

Jazz is very much alive a century or more after its birth. It has diversified in that time into many forms.

BIG BANDS AND SWING
The emergence of the "big bands" toward the end of the 1920s ended the first heyday of jazz. They used great jazz musicians like **Bix Biederbecke** but shunned improvisation. The more sophisticated "swing" bands **242–243 ››** supplanted them from the 1930s onward.

JAZZ FUSION
In the mid- to late 1960s, jazz embraced two new influences: rock music and amplification, creating jazz fusion **334–335 ››**. Trumpeter **Miles Davis** led the way. At the same time, rock bands began to incorporate jazz elements.

KEY WORKS

Louis Armstrong "West End Blues"
Freddie Keppard "Stock Yards Strut"
Miff Mole And His Little Molers "Imagination"
Joe "King" Oliver "Dippermouth Blues"
Kid Ory's Sunshine Orchestra "Society Blues"

"I myself happened to be the **creator** of **jazz** in the year of **1902.**"
JAZZ MUSICIAN JELLY ROLL MORTON

Born 1915 Died 1959

Billie Holiday

"Without **feeling**, whatever you do amounts to **nothing.**"

BILLIE HOLIDAY, "LADY SINGS THE BLUES," 1956

Acknowledged as one of the finest jazz singers of all time, Billie Holiday forged a path from a disadvantaged background to global fame. Her life was a constant struggle against a racist and misogynistic society, as well as against inner demons that drove her to addiction, but she found an inexhaustible source of joy in musical performance. A songwriter as well as a singer, she was most famous for the depth of emotion she could bring to dark, poignant numbers such as "Strange Fruit" or "Gloomy Sunday," but she excelled at being light, upbeat, and inventive. Her nuance of expression and feel for rhythmic variation lifted popular love songs to the status of art.

The details of Holiday's early life are obscure, but there is no doubt she had an extremely difficult childhood and youth. Her father was probably the jazz guitarist Clarence Halliday (or Holiday) but he played no part in her upbringing. As a child she was known as Eleonora Fagan. Struggling with poverty, her mother, Sadie, left the child with relatives in Baltimore, and it is there that Holiday grew up. She was probably abused in childhood and certainly allowed to run wild. Because she was frequently absent from school, a juvenile court sent her to a Catholic reformatory, the House of the Good Shepherd for Colored Girls, at the age of nine. Soon after her release she gave up school altogether. Her musical education came from hearing musicians in Baltimore bars, and the early records of Louis Armstrong and Bessie Smith.

Classic collaboration
Pianist Teddy Wilson, pictured here in a recording studio, first worked with Holiday in the 1930s. Some of the songs they recorded became signatures for Holiday, including "What a Little Moonlight Can Do."

Early breakthrough

Holiday became a singer in Harlem, New York. She went to join her mother there at the age of 14, scraping together a living as a waitress, maid, and sex worker before finding employment singing in bars. She took the name Billie Holiday, combining her father's name with the first name of Hollywood actress Billie Dove. Her natural talent and unique smoky voice soon made her a sought-after performer at venues such as Pod's and Jerry's, a speakeasy serving alcohol, at that time banned under Prohibition. It was there that she was spotted by John Hammond, a wealthy jazz enthusiast who was actively promoting new talent on radio and record. Hammond arranged for Holiday to make her first recordings with clarinetist Benny Goodman, whom Hammond was also promoting. Her real breakthrough, however, came when she teamed up with pianist Teddy Wilson. They made a series of recordings from 1935 onward that turned standard popular songs of the day into jazz classics through originality of phrasing, expression, and rhythm.

Big band vocals

This was the era of big band music. With her growing reputation, Holiday landed

Lady Day
Billie Holiday achieved both commercial success and critical acclaim in her short lifetime. Her ability to convey intense emotion and her groundbreaking improvisations left a lasting legacy that stretches far beyond the world of jazz.

Leading lady
This movie still from a musical short shows Holiday performing with the Count Basie band. Basie described working with Holiday as "getting her tunes like she wanted them" rather than collaborating on them.

the role of vocalist first with the Count Basie band and then with Artie Shaw. Racial segregation was the norm in the 1930s, and strictly enforced in the South, and Holiday's appearance with Shaw's band as its vocalist led to problems on tour. Staying with the other musicians at one hotel, for example, she was made to use the staff entrance since Black people were not admitted as guests. She did not stay long with Basie or Shaw, partly because her highly individual style of interpretation did not match the needs of the big band scene and its popular audience.

Unmatched emotional force

In 1939, Holiday found a more welcome ambiance at the Café Society in New York's Greenwich Village, a racially mixed venue frequented by left-wing thinkers. There she made "Strange Fruit" a part of her repertoire, delivering this graphic depiction of a lynching with acute emotion. Some of her own best music dates from this period, like "Fine and Mellow," a song she wrote as a reflection on the mistreatment she had received from men in the course of a complex love life. Along with "Strange Fruit," the success of Holiday's recording of "Gloomy Sunday" in 1941—called the "suicide song" because listening to it was said to have driven people to kill themselves—confirmed the impression that she was a singer of melancholy and tragic material. Yet she rarely sang blues and her stock-in-trade remained popular love songs and jazz standards, delivered with a flexibility of vocal improvisation that made her performance resemble a saxophone solo. She regarded herself as one of the musicians in a jazz ensemble.

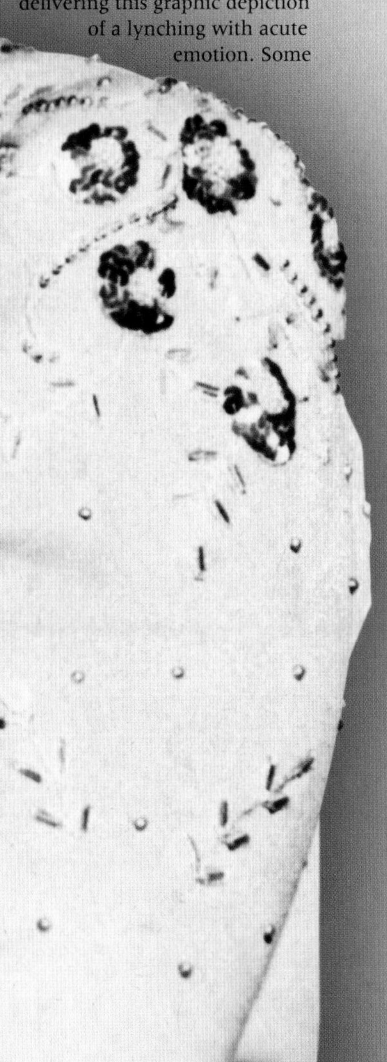

Personal problems

By the mid-1940s Holiday was a famous singer of hit records enjoying high earnings, but her personal problems grew in step with her wealth. In 1947 her heroin addiction led to a conviction for possessing narcotics, for which she served almost a year in prison. Upon her release she was feted by her fans, but her criminal record barred her from employment in clubs and thus she lost her much of her income.

In the last decade of her life she was frequently ill and in financial difficulties. Her voice deteriorated and her interpretations of familiar songs became more mannered, yet some of her performances during her later years were still of remarkable quality. Her frailty increased the sense of vulnerability that had always been one of her charms. Some of her friends and collaborators stuck with her to the end, notably the saxophonist Lester Young, her most faithful companion in a long, platonic relationship. Battered by drugs and alcohol abuse, Holiday's body finally succumbed to cirrhosis of the liver in a New York hospital at the end of May 1959. She was only 44 years old when she died.

Jazz drama
In 1946, Holiday appeared in the jazz movie *New Orleans*, as advertised on this Swedish poster, with her idol, Louis Armstrong. The film includes her tracks "Do You Know What It Means to Miss New Orleans" and "Blues are Brewin'."

TIMELINE

- **April 7, 1915** Born in Philadelphia; she moves at an early age to Baltimore.
- **1925** A juvenile court in Baltimore sends her to a Catholic reform school.
- **1929** Joins her mother in New York City.
- **1930** Begins singing regularly in the clubs of Harlem, New York.
- **November 1933** Makes her recording debut with Benny Goodman.
- **1935** Appears in a short film, *Symphony in Black*, made by Duke Ellington.
- **July 2, 1935** Begins recording with jazz pianist Teddy Wilson.
- **1936** Forms a lifelong friendship with saxophonist Lester Young, who nicknames her "Lady Day."
- **September 1936** Makes the first successful recording of the Gershwins' "Summertime."
- **1937** Joins the Count Basie band as vocalist.
- **1938** Tours with Artie Shaw's swing band, as the first Black vocalist to front a white orchestra.
- **1939** Performs the song "Strange Fruit" at Café Society in Greenwich Village, New York.

ALBUM WITH LESTER YOUNG OF MUSIC FROM 1937–46

- **1941** Records "Gloomy Sunday," known as "the suicide song."
- **August 25, 1941** Marries trombonist and nightclub owner Jimmy Monroe.
- **October 1944** Records "Lover Man" for the Decca label; it is a major hit.
- **1946** Appears in the movie *New Orleans* alongside Louis Armstrong.
- **January 22, 1946** Makes the first recording of the song "Good Morning Heartache."
- **May 1947** Arrested in New York for possession of narcotics, she is sentenced to a term in a federal prison camp.
- **1956** Publishes a ghostwritten autobiography *Lady Sings the Blues*; releases an album of the same name.
- **November 1956** Performs in two sell-out concerts at Carnegie Hall.
- **March 28, 1957** Marries Louis McKay.
- **May 15, 1959** Last public performance at the Phoenix Theater, New York.
- **July 17, 1959** Dies in the Metropolitan Hospital, New York City, of cirrhosis of the liver.

The **Clarinet**

The clarinet is a versatile woodwind instrument beloved for its warm tone and expressive capabilities in a variety of musical styles, including classical, jazz, and klezmer. The large clarinet family ranges from the contrabass (lowest) to the piccolo clarinet (highest).

Though related to older instruments like the *alboka*—a Basque single-reed instrument from the Middle Ages—the modern clarinet was developed in the early 1700s. German instrument maker Johann Christoph Denner added a register key to the *chalumeau*, a baroque single-reed instrument, to invent the clarinetto.

Different developers, notably Russian clarinettist Iwan Müller (1786–1854) in the early 1800s, added further keys, refined the mechanics, and amended the pads, using leather and felt to close the sound holes. This improved intonation, ease of fingering, and melodic flexibility.

Although Müller's basic design was at the instrument's core, the clarinet was further developed by Eugène Albert (1860–1890) into the Albert, or simple, system. This was favored by 19th-century clarinet virtuoso Henry Lazarus and is still used today by klezmer, New Orleans jazz, and eastern folk musicians for easy slurring (gliding smoothly over several notes).

The modern standard clarinet comes from a different arrangement of tone holes and keys called the Boehm system (see p.189). Inspired by Theodore Boehm's ring-key concept for flute, it was devised by French clarinettist Hyacinthe Klosé (1808–1880) in 1839. This is the most common clarinet system for both jazz and classical, except in Germany and Austria where an 1880s derivation of the Müller system developed by clarinettist Oskar Oehler (the Oehler system) prevails. The standard Boehm system clarinet is pitched in B flat and used in most styles of music. The clarinet pitched in A is frequently used in orchestral and chamber music.

From classical to jazz

Austrian composer Wolfgang Amadeus Mozart (see pp.136–137) was especially attracted to the clarinet and composed several pieces for it in the 1780–1790s. The clarinet became an established part of the orchestra by the early 1800s and many composers showcased its qualities as a solo voice over the next 200 years. The various clarinets and their distinctive range of sounds, from deep woody tones to sweet high register notes, remain valuable colors in the orchestral palette. Meanwhile, in jazz, the clarinet has become associated with New Orleans, swing, and revivalist styles.

TECHNOLOGY

CONSTRUCTION MATERIALS

The body of the clarinet has been made from a variety of substances over the years, each with their own characteristics. Wood was common in early clarinets, but intonation was affected by humidity and temperature. Larger clarinet bodies are constructed partially or entirely from metal. Cheaper instruments are made from plastic resin while professional clarinets are often made from grenadilla (African blackwood). The shortage caused by over-harvesting grenadilla (pictured) has led instrument makers to develop eco-friendly alternatives.

TIMELINE

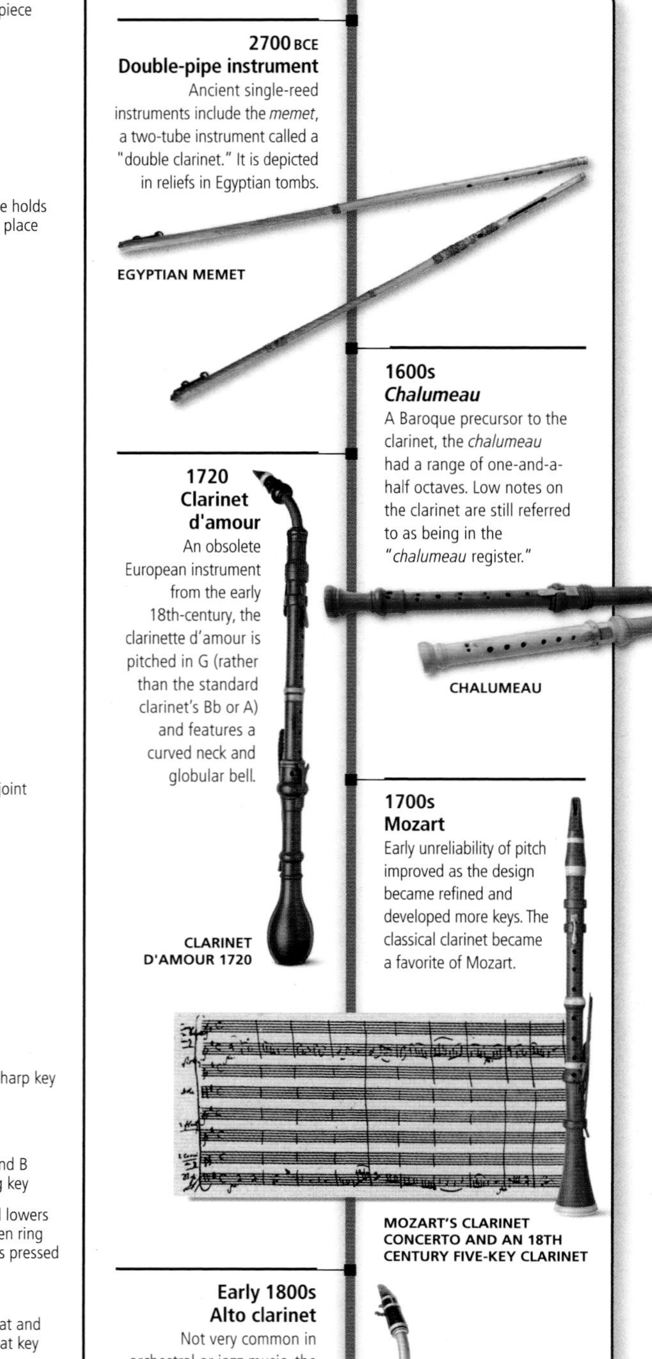

2700 BCE
Double-pipe instrument
Ancient single-reed instruments include the *memet*, a two-tube instrument called a "double clarinet." It is depicted in reliefs in Egyptian tombs.

EGYPTIAN MEMET

1600s
Chalumeau
A Baroque precursor to the clarinet, the *chalumeau* had a range of one-and-a-half octaves. Low notes on the clarinet are still referred to as being in the "*chalumeau* register."

CHALUMEAU

1720
Clarinet d'amour
An obsolete European instrument from the early 18th-century, the clarinette d'amour is pitched in G (rather than the standard clarinet's Bb or A) and features a curved neck and globular bell.

CLARINET D'AMOUR 1720

1700s
Mozart
Early unreliability of pitch improved as the design became refined and developed more keys. The classical clarinet became a favorite of Mozart.

MOZART'S CLARINET CONCERTO AND AN 18TH CENTURY FIVE-KEY CLARINET

Early 1800s
Alto clarinet
Not very common in orchestral or jazz music, the alto clarinet, invented by Iwan Müller and Heinrich Grenser and developed by Adolph Sax, is still used in wind bands.

ALTO CLARINET FROM LATE 19TH-CENTURY

“The beauty of the clarinet lies in its sweet sound; this is its essence ...”

FLEMISH CLARINETTIST AND TEACHER, AMAND VANDERHAGEN, 1785

Classical clarinet
A Boehm-system clarinet in A. The “standard” clarinet is in B flat but the A clarinet is widely used in orchestras for ease of fingering in sharp keys and is perceived by some to have a warmer tone.

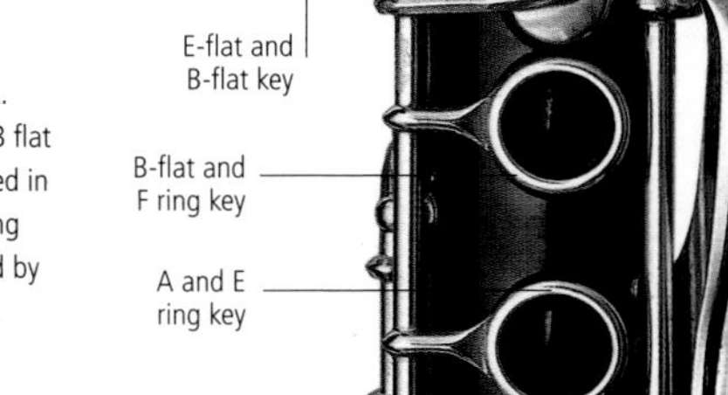

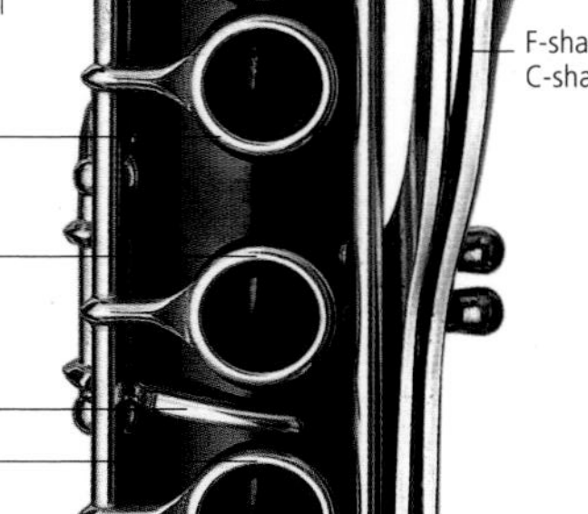

Upper joint
On the upper joint, the key in the middle lifts both pads above it when pressed with the left index finger. The key on the right is pressed with the inside knuckle of the index finger and lifts only the left pad.

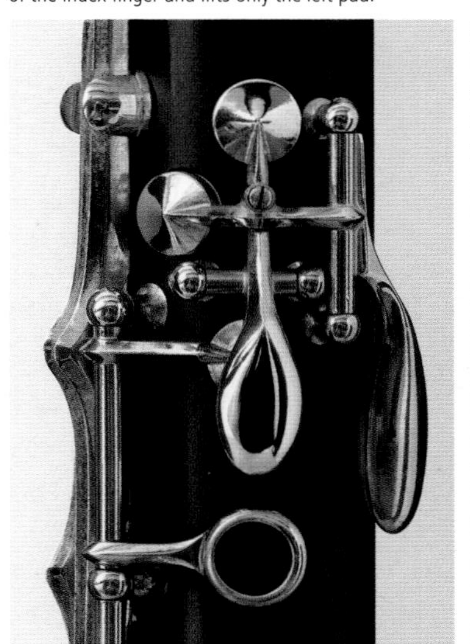

Ligature and reed
The clarinet’s reed is held in place on the mouthpiece by a modern metal ligature, a device invented by Iwan Müller to replace twine.

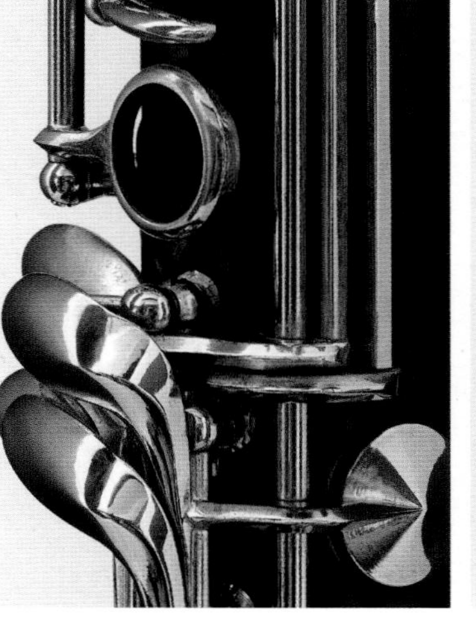

Lower joint
The group of four keys clustered midway down the lower joint of the clarinet are manipulated by the little finger of the right hand. They are connected to a system of rods and levers that open or close pads.

Back of clarinet
The teardrop-shaped register key on the back of the upper joint is manipulated by the left thumb and switches octaves. The thumb hole (below) remains closed for most notes in most registers.

1808
Contrabass clarinet
Sounding two octaves below the standard Bb clarinet, the first contrabass clarinet appeared in 1808. It was favored by avant-garde composers.

CONTRABASS CLARINET 1890

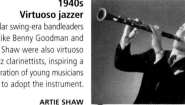

1830s–1840s
Bass clarinet
With its rich, earthy tone, the bass clarinet became a solo instrument. Hector Berlioz wrote a solo part for it in his *Grande Symphonie* (1840).

BASS CLARINET 1885

1839
Hyacinthe Klosé
French clarinet player Hyacinthe Klosé and instrument maker Auguste Buffet developed the Boehm system clarinet, based on his concept of ring keys. It remains the standard clarinet design.

1840s
Size and tone
By the 1840s, the clarinet became more standardized in both size and tone. Different pitched clarinets were made in standard sizes, while the bores of clarinets were refined to produce more even notes.

1840s
Albert system
Although relatively sidelined these days, the Albert, or simple, system clarinet was much prized by the leading clarinet virtuoso of his day, Henry Lazarus (1815–95).

HENRY LAZARUS

1920s
Arundo donax
From the 1920s onward, most clarinet reeds were made from the Asian cane plant *Arundo donax*. Different thicknesses of reed are available to suit different playing styles and situations.

1940s
Virtuoso jazzer
Popular swing-era bandleaders like Benny Goodman and Artie Shaw were also virtuoso jazz clarinettists, inspiring a generation of young musicians to adopt the instrument.

ARTIE SHAW

"Mother" of the Blues
Ma Rainey and her Georgia Jazz Band pose for a photograph in the studio in around 1925. She discovered blues music early in the 20th century while working as a professional musician.

Birth of the **Blues**

While much about the roots of the blues remains mysterious, there is no doubt as to where and when it first emerged as a distinct musical genre: in the Deep South of the United States, at the start of the 20th century.

BEFORE

The music that became the blues incorporated not only African-American elements but also influences from farther afield.

FROM AFRICA TO MISSISSIPPI
The call-and-response **chanting of enslaved people** on the plantations of the Deep South were direct echoes of their African heritage. After the **American Civil War** (1861–1865), Black musicians could earn a living performing for Black audiences. Ideas spread via touring "medicine," minstrel, and "tent" shows.

HAWAIIAN CONNECTION
The **slide or bottleneck technique** of playing guitar originated in Hawaii and was popularized by touring Hawaiian musicians.

There is no record of anything that we would now recognize as the blues being performed during the 19th century. Instead, it seemed to appear fully fledged, just after 1900, among the poorest African-American people of the South. It was an amalgamation of songs and styles from various sources, reinterpreted with an emphasis on raw, personal experience. Both Gertrude "Ma" Rainey (1886–1939) and W.C. Handy (1873–1958), credited as the "Mother" and "Father" of the blues, described encountering it as an unfamiliar music when they were traveling as professional musicians at the turn of the century—Rainey with variety troupe the Rabbit Foot Minstrels in Missouri in 1902, and Handy in Mississippi in 1903.

The Delta Blues

Now regarded as the most celebrated form of the blues, the Delta Blues grew to prominence from around 1900. The flood plain of the Mississippi river below Memphis was farmed in the postslavery era by African-American sharecroppers, working on white-owned plantations, in return for a share (often tiny) of the crop. So many sharecroppers worked on the larger plantations that musicians could make a living from playing weekend dances in bars known as "juke joints."

For an accomplished musician such as Charlie Patton (1891–1934), music offered the chance to escape a life of back-breaking labor. A master of both bottleneck and finger-picking guitar, he was also a consummate showman with an unfailing ear for rhythm, stamping out complex patterns with his feet, banging his hands against his guitar, or barking out lyrics in staccato bursts.

Patton's music was not recorded until 1929, but he was playing such signature pieces as "Pony Blues" as early as 1910. The style he pioneered was characterized by the interplay between words and music, with the guitar aiming to parallel and complement the singing rather than simply provide a backing. Patton lived for several years at the Dockery Plantation, which was also where electric bluesman Howlin' Wolf and Roebuck "Pops" Staples, patriarch of the Staples Singers gospel group (see p.294–295), grew up.

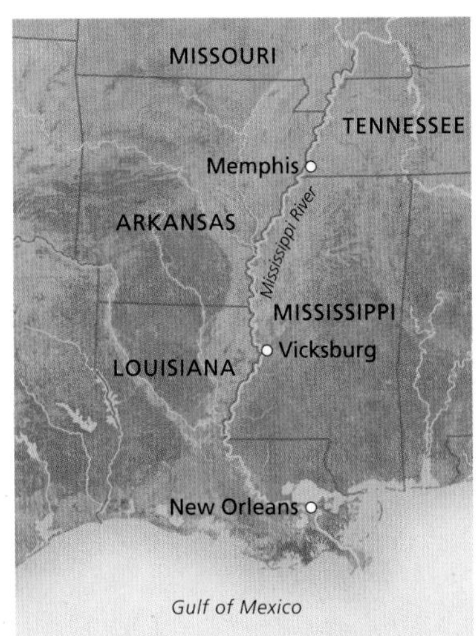

The spread of the blues
The Mississippi Delta—from Memphis, Tennessee, in the north to Vicksburg, Mississippi, in the south—is considered to be the birthplace of the blues. In the 1930s, the music spread to urban centers in the north.

The songs that Patton played came from all sorts of sources, including Irish- and Scottish-derived folk tunes and even vaudeville showstoppers. The most characterful Delta musicians to emerge in his wake—including blues legends such as Tommy Johnson, Robert Johnson (see above right), and Skip James—used their own preoccupations and daily concerns to create powerful and deeply personal styles. While largely recorded as solo artists, they would often perform live in ad hoc groupings. There was also a handful of established groups, such as the Mississippi Sheiks.

Divas and the classic blues

The first blues performers to attract mass attention, from the early 1920s, were not impoverished Delta farmers but gorgeously attired, nationally known divas, such as Mamie Smith (1883–1946)—whose 1920 "Crazy Blues" is the earliest recording of the blues—Bessie Smith (1894–1937), and "Ma" Rainey.

These female vocalists outsold the Delta bluesmen, and they were much more significant in establishing the genre with the record-buying public. To modern ears, however, their so-called classic blues sound more like early jazz than the blues. This is hardly surprising, since their small backing groups featured the same instrumental lineups—and often the same musicians, including such giants as Louis Armstrong (see pp.248–249)—as are heard on the first jazz recordings.

Blind blues musicians

As the Delta Blues gained momentum, differing blues styles emerged in other regions of the American South. Many of the greatest performers were blind street musicians. The biggest-selling artist of all was Blind Lemon Jefferson (1883–1929) from Texas. Even as early as 1926, Paramount Records was marketing his raw, intense work as being "real, old fashioned blues by a real, old-fashioned blues singer." By the time he died in 1929, Jefferson had sold more than a million records—a huge number at the time, and enough for him to employ his own chauffeur.

Jefferson's contemporaries included Blind Willie Johnson, a Texan slide guitarist with an exclusively religious repertoire; the mellifluous, ragtime-influenced Blind Blake, from the East Coast; and the Georgian singer and guitarist Blind Willie McTell, whose recording career lasted into the 1950s.

BLUES MUSICIAN (1911–1938)

ROBERT JOHNSON

According to the most famous legends about the blues, Robert Johnson sold his soul to the devil at a remote Mississippi crossroads to become the greatest Delta bluesman of all time. Barely known in his lifetime, he was only 27 when he died in 1938, poisoned by the jealous husband of a woman friend. Folk purists who rediscovered his recordings in the early 1960s admired doom-laden songs such as "Hellhound on My Trail." However, Johnson was not so much a songwriter as a skilled interpreter of existing material. His guitar playing, combining a constant "boogie bass" with the standard voice-guitar dialogue on the upper strings, laid down a template for amplified blues.

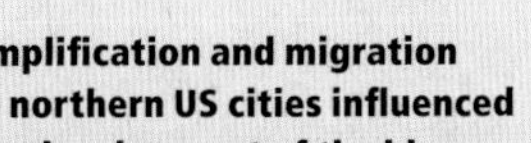

KEY WORKS

Bessie Smith with Louis Armstrong "St. Louis Blues"
Blind Lemon Jefferson "Matchbox Blues"
Blind Willie McTell "Statesboro Blues"
Charlie Patton "Pony Blues"
Skip James "I'm So Glad"
Robert Johnson "Cross Road Blues"

"[He] pressed a knife on the **strings of the guitar...** the **weirdest music** I had ever heard."

W.C. HANDY, IN HIS AUTOBIOGRAPHY *FATHER OF THE BLUES*, 1941

Making music
A man and a child play the blues in Mississippi in the 1930s. During this era, the blues were very much a rural, acoustic music, with each different region of the South developing its own idiosyncratic style.

AFTER

Amplification and migration to northern US cities influenced the development of the blues.

DECLINE OF THE RURAL BLUES
Collapsing record sales during the 1929–1933 Great Depression ended many blues careers. However, **amplification** and the electric guitar **312–313 ››** enabled the blues to shift from country juke joints to **city clubs**. Beale Street in Memphis became a magnet for blues musicians, including B.B. King in the 1940s. Musicians such as Skip James and Mississippi John Hurt were rediscovered in the 1960s.

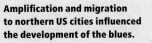

BB KING'S, BEALE STREET, MEMPHIS

CHICAGO BLUES
Muddy Waters' 1943 move from Mississippi to Chicago epitomized the Black migration from the rural South to the urban North. A new form of blues emerged in **Chicago 306–307 ››**, led by Memphis Minnie, Big Bill Broonzy, and Lonnie Johnson.

Swing session

Young people jive up a storm at a swing session at the Savoy Ballroom, Harlem, New York, in 1938. Visitors were able to dance to music played by the world's finest jazz musicians.

BEFORE

When jazz caught the ear of arrangers in the 1920s, the big band was born. It included rhythm, brass, and woodwind instruments.

JAZZ ENSEMBLES

In the mid-1920s, bandleaders such as **Duke Ellington** and arrangers such as **Don Redman** began arranging music for 12- to 24-piece **jazz ensembles**. At the same time, sweeter-toned **dance bands** incorporated jazz elements into their commercial style. They both contributed to the development of swing.

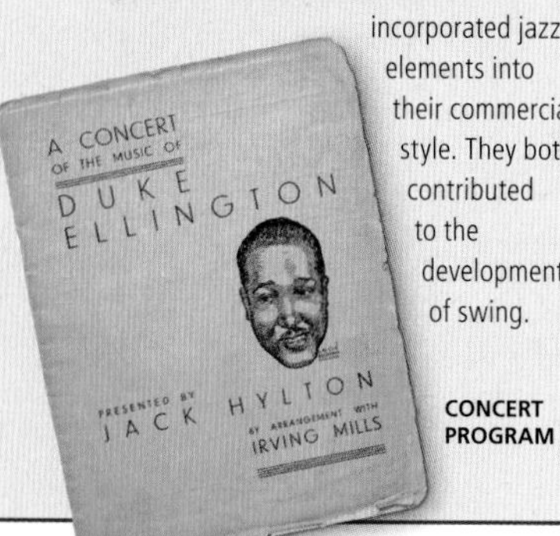

CONCERT PROGRAM

Let's Swing

From around 1935 to 1946, a smoothly arranged version of jazz called swing was wildly popular. This big band music had people dancing and romancing in dance halls across America, while its bandleaders and instrumental stylists were nothing less than superstars.

Swing music evolved from small-group jazz styles as ensembles became larger and a greater proportion of their music was arranged rather than improvised. Improvisations, when present, tended to feature individual musicians rather than the collective improvisations of earlier styles. The drummer's rhythmic accompaniment moved from the snare drum to the cymbals; the guitar replaced the banjo, creating a smoother accompaniment, and the double bass replaced the tuba. This allowed jazz to develop a more even four-in-a-bar feel. Band lineups commonly featured sections of two to four trumpets, trombones, and saxophones, with a four-piece rhythm section.

"[The] rhythm causes a **bouncy buoyant,** terpsichorean urge."

BANDLEADER DUKE ELLINGTON, DEFINING SWING, 1939

Commercial breakthrough

A pivotal moment in the development of swing was when bandleader and clarinetist Benny Goodman (see above right) began using arrangements bought from Fletcher Henderson, the leader of a popular African-American

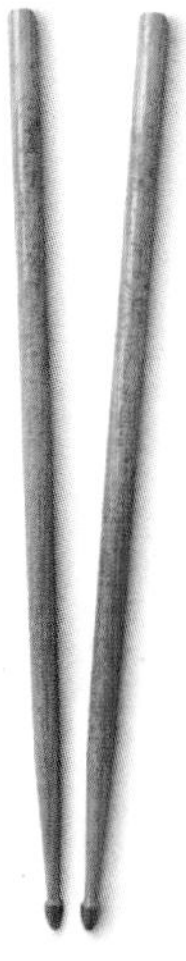

Gene Krupa's drumsticks

Percussionist Gene Krupa's explosive tom-tom feature, "Swing Swing Swing," with the Benny Goodman band, was the first extended drum solo to be recorded and released commercially. It is a classic of the swing era.

BANDLEADER (1909–1986)

BENNY GOODMAN

"King of Swing" Benny Goodman, the commercially savvy bandleader, was renowned for his instrumental prowess as a clarinetist. He was also a pioneer in musical racial integration, hiring African-American musicians Teddy Wilson and Lionel Hampton in 1936. He embraced new developments in music, using electric guitar prodigy Charlie Christian for his sextet in 1939–1941 and recording with bebop musicians in the 1940s (see pp.246–247). In 1949, Goodman premiered classical works for clarinet and orchestra.

orchestra in the early 1930s. This created the widely appealing music that combined the excitement and danceable rhythms of African-American jazz with a commercial sensibility. Goodman's band had struggled to connect with an audience more used to the sweeter sounds of the likes of the Canadian-American bandleader Guy Lombardo. However, regular appearances on America's NBC radio series *Let's Dance* in 1934 and 1935 led to a historic broadcast from the Palomar Ballroom, Los Angeles, in August 1935 that met with acclaim.

This occasion is often cited as the birth of the swing era. In January 1938, Goodman led his own orchestra and members of the Duke Ellington and Count Basie bands at a swing concert at Carnegie Hall, an event that did much to encourage mainstream acceptance of jazz.

The Glenn Miller sound

Although Goodman was soon dubbed "King of Swing," many other bands and their leaders forged strong identities. The bandleader and trombonist Glenn Miller (1904–1944) pioneered a signature clarinet-led ensemble sound. His fellow trombonist Tommy Dorsey (1905–1956) established a musical personality based on his smooth trombone style and the arrangements of jazz trumpeter and composer Sy Oliver. Artie Shaw (1910–2004) was a sufficiently distinctive clarinetist and musician to lead a popular band that provided a viable alternative to the all-conquering Goodman.

African-American bands

Though the most popular bands were led by white players, African-American bands of the swing era were as distinctive and at least as important historically: Jimmie Lunceford led one of the top bands of the era; Count Basie had a looser, riff-based style

New rhythms
The introduction of the double bass to the rhythm section in the 1920s precipitated a four-in-a-bar walking bass style, which replaced the two-beat "stomping" feel of earlier jazz.

with a deep feeling for the blues; and Duke Ellington's superior compositions and arrangements set him and his work apart from mainstream swing.

Virtuoso performers

The big bands often produced musical heroes from their ranks who developed followings of their own. Notable figures include the drummer Gene Krupa (with Benny Goodman), known for his explosive playing; trumpeter Harry James (also with Goodman), famed for his brassy tone and matinée idol looks; and alto saxophonist Johnny Hodges (with Duke Ellington) with his gliding-between-the-notes approach, a style known as portamento.

Important musicians who made their mark in the swing era but were not affiliated with big-name orchestras include pianist-singers Fats Waller (see p.227) and Nat "King" Cole, guitarist Django Reinhardt (see p.277), pianist Art Tatum, and tenor saxophonist Coleman Hawkins.

Getting into the swing
Music is said to "swing" if it is played with an underlying triplet (group of three notes played in the same amount of time as two notes of the same value) feel. Musicians "swing" if they play with persuasive rhythmic feel.

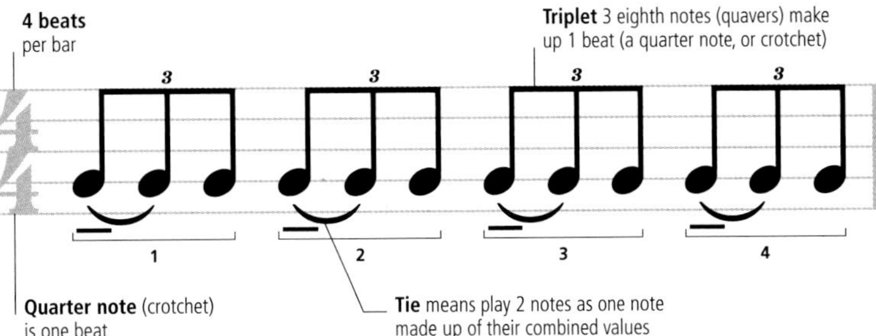

The spread of swing

European dance bands soon incorporated swing into their style of music, and its popularity spread through dance halls in Europe. The music even played a part in boosting morale during World War II (1939–1945).

However, America's entry into the conflict in 1941 ultimately had a detrimental impact on big bands, as musicians were drafted into the military. Glenn Miller was killed when his plane disappeared on the way to France to entertain US troops. Many big bands folded during the mid-1940s, and only a few (notably Ellington and Basie) reconvened after the war.

The rise of the singer as personality, exemplified by the success of former Tommy Dorsey vocalist Frank Sinatra (see pp.288–289), heralded the popularity of swing-oriented pop music but marked the end of the era when the big band was king.

Signature sound
The Count Basie Orchestra was known for its powerful, blues-flavored swing and "head arrangements"—riffs and patterns that evolved spontaneously from within the band rather than from an arranger's pen.

AFTER

The musical values of swing were upheld by small groups and the "mainstream" movement.

NEW STRANDS
Following the end of the swing era, big bands no longer felt an obligation to provide dance music. **Stan Kenton** and **Boyd Raeburn** favored a progressive direction, while **Duke Ellington** created several long-form masterpieces for jazz orchestra.
Bands such as **The Count Basie Orchestra** upheld their swing values, while small groups played an ultra-danceable form of swing called **jump**. Soloists attracted to swing-style improvisation evolved a melodic style dubbed "mainstream", as exemplified by saxophonist **Scott Hamilton**.

KEY WORKS

Count Basie "One O'Clock Jump"
Benny Goodman and His Orchestra *Live at Carnegie Hall*
Glenn Miller and His Orchestra "In the Mood"
Artie Shaw and His Orchestra "Stardust"
Duke Ellington and His Orchestra "Take the 'A' Train"

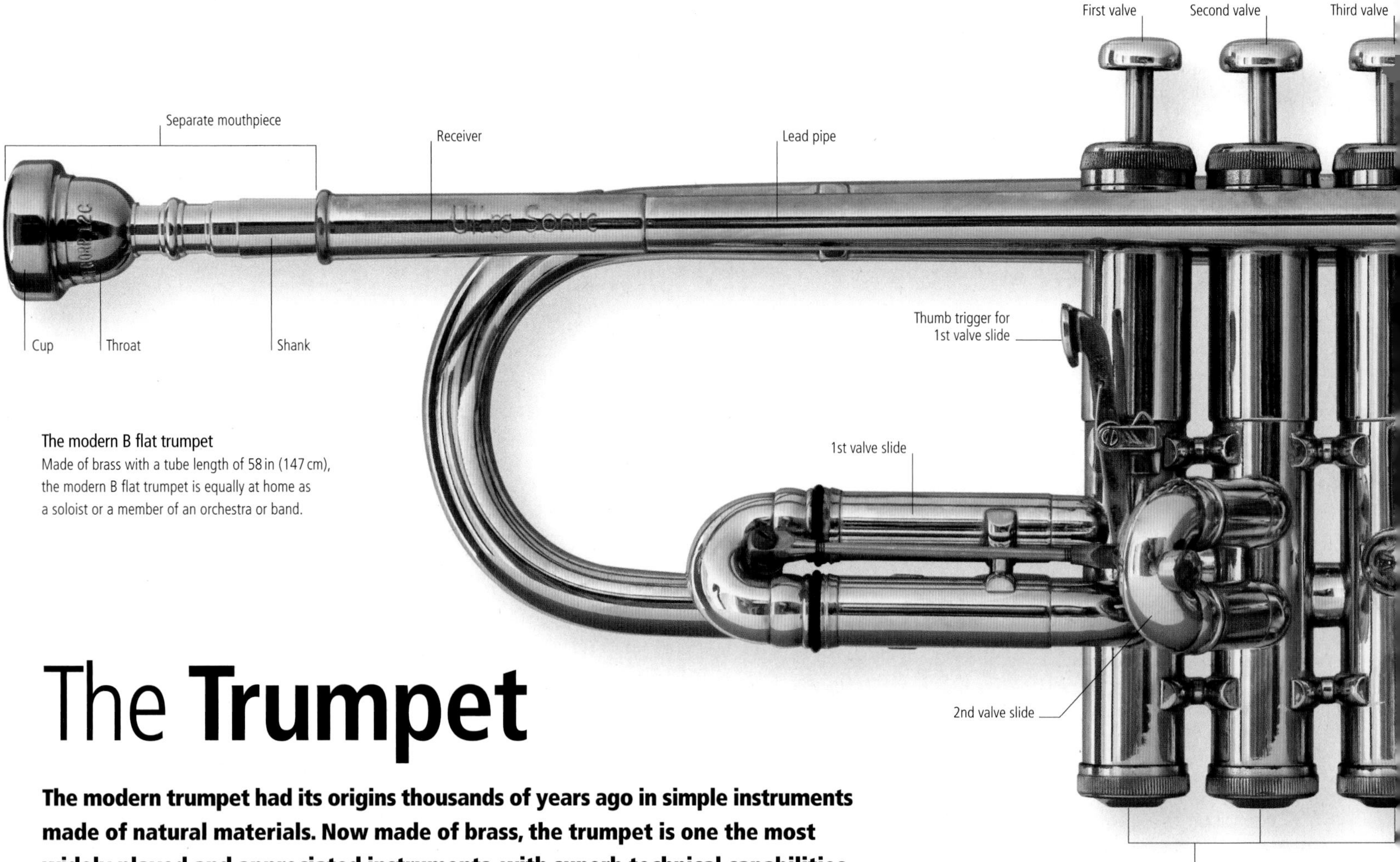

First valve
Second valve
Third valve
Separate mouthpiece
Receiver
Lead pipe
Cup
Throat
Shank
Thumb trigger for 1st valve slide
1st valve slide
2nd valve slide
Valve caps

The modern B flat trumpet
Made of brass with a tube length of 58 in (147 cm), the modern B flat trumpet is equally at home as a soloist or a member of an orchestra or band.

The **Trumpet**

The modern trumpet had its origins thousands of years ago in simple instruments made of natural materials. Now made of brass, the trumpet is one the most widely played and appreciated instruments, with superb technical capabilities.

The trumpet shines out in music of all types. Affordable, portable, and accessible, it is an instrument for all people—whether screaming out a jazz solo or playing its part in an orchestra. Early examples were simple tubes of wood, clay, shell, or bone. Found in primitive societies on every continent, they were used for signaling, ritual, and ceremony.

The ancient civilizations of Assyria, Egypt, Greece, and Rome developed metal trumpets, which were longer lasting and produced a more far-reaching sound. From the Middle Ages, straight trumpets became the European norm and their continuing military and ceremonial associations were established.

Transforming the sound

The notes available on a trumpet depend on the length of the tubing and the air pressure applied through the mouthpiece. As a result, the last three centuries have seen numerous experiments to extend the basic length of tubing and its coiling. The most successful solution—the valve—transformed the instrument's fortunes in the 19th century. This made it easier to play rapid passages and wide-ranging melodies, allowing for extreme technical virtuosity. The extra tubing lengths can each be further finely tuned by adjusting the slides. The result of these innovations is one of music's best-loved creations.

TIMELINE

c. 2200 BCE
Ancient trumpet
The earliest trumpets date from the third millennium BCE and were simple metal tubes. Later examples were found in Tutankhamun's tomb, decorated with depictions of Egyptian gods.

TRUMPETS FROM KING TUTANKHAMUN'S TOMB c. 1500 BCE

ANGEL PLAYING TRUMPET

Early 13th century
Medieval trumpets
Retaining the straight shape of ancient times, medieval trumpets feature widely in artwork of the period, often associated with angels.

18TH-CENTURY SLIDE TRUMPET

1410
Slide trumpet
The addition of a slide mechanism to a natural trumpet (now seen in the modern trombone) was an early attempt to increase the range of notes available to the player.

ORNATE NATURAL TRUMPET

17th century
Baroque trumpet
The natural trumpet with no keys, slides, or valves continued to be popular during the Renaissance and Baroque periods. This example was made by Simon Beale, court trumpeter to Charles II of England, in 1666.

SIX-KEYED TRUMPET

1770
Keyed trumpet
A further attempt to improve the pitch selection on the trumpet was the addition of key-covered holes. Notes were found by opening or closing keys.

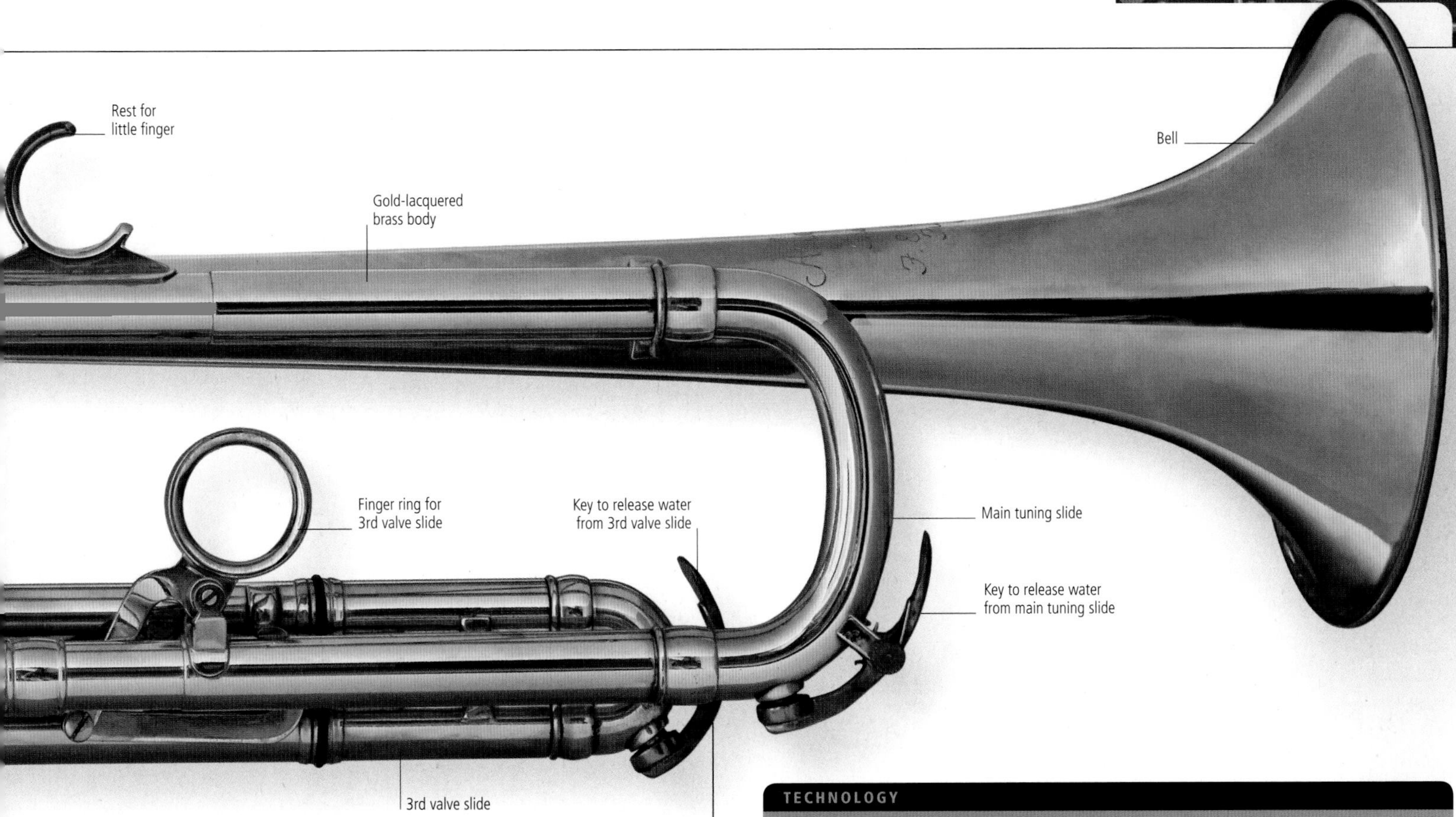

Rest for little finger

Gold-lacquered brass body

Bell

Finger ring for 3rd valve slide

Key to release water from 3rd valve slide

Main tuning slide

Key to release water from main tuning slide

3rd valve slide

Valves
Most trumpets have three valves, which can be depressed individually or in any combination to make a whole new range of pitches available.

TECHNOLOGY

TRUMPET VALVE MECHANISM

When a valve is at rest, air blown into the trumpet passes directly through the main tube of the instrument. When the valve is depressed by the finger, holes in the valve stock align with holes in the casing, diverting air into an extra length of tubing. This extends the total length of the tubing to make a new series of pitches available. A spring returns the valve from the casing to its normal resting position.

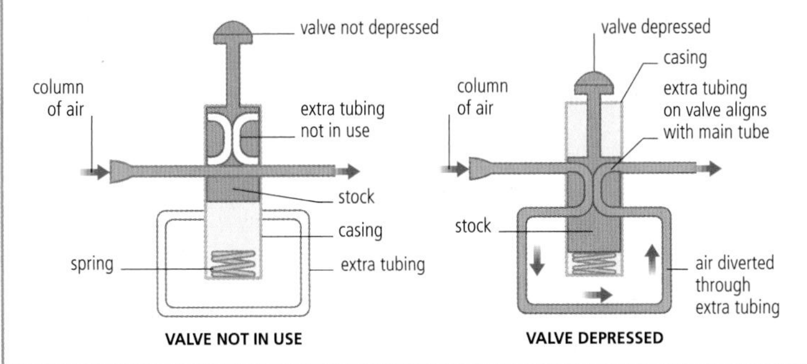

1796
Favorite solo
Joseph Haydn's Trumpet Concerto, written in 1796 for his friend Anton Weidinger, remains one of the most popular pieces in the trumpet repertoire.

JOSEPH HAYDN

18th century
Tibetan trumpet
This *rkang-gling* is an ornate 18th-century trumpet that dates back to 9th-century Tibet. It was usually made from a human thighbone and used in Buddhist rituals.

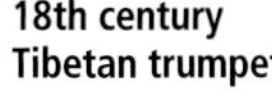

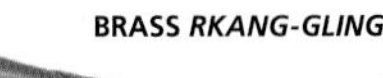

BRASS *RKANG-GLING*

19th century
B flat valve trumpet
The most common type of trumpet today is the modern B flat valve trumpet. Since the development of valves in the 19th century, three valves became the standard for modern trumpets.

***c.*1890**
Piccolo trumpet
The piccolo trumpet, pitched an octave higher than standard B flat trumpet, is useful for playing high passages, especially in jazz and modern Baroque performances.

HIGH-PITCHED TRUMPET

20th century
Hybrid invention
A creation of the early 20th century, the Jazzophone was a brass instrument shaped like a saxophone and played with a trumpetlike mouthpiece.

JAZZOPHONE

1926–1991
Miles Davis
American trumpet-player Miles Davis pushed the boundaries of jazz and of the instrument itself. He amplified it, bent it, and pointed the bell downward to experiment with the sound.

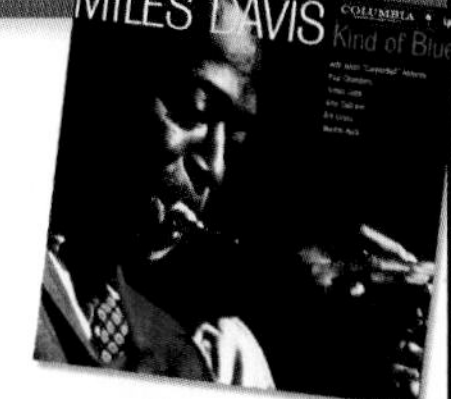

MILES DAVIS'S ALBUM *KIND OF BLUE*

OOP BOP SH-BAM

by DIZZY GILLESPIE, "GIL" FULLER and JAY ROBERTS

BE-BOP

(THE NEW JAZZ)

DIZZY GILLESPIE

Series of

PIANO SOLOS

Arranged by FRANK PAPARELLI

Published by J. J. ROBBINS & SONS Inc.
1585 Broadway, Manhattan, New York, U.S.A.

BOSWORTH & CO. LTD.
14/18, Heddon Street, Regent Street, London, W.1.
For the British Empire and Europe
(excluding Canada, Newfoundland and Australasia)
Made in England Imprimé en Angleterre

PRICE 3/-

From bopping to bebop
This is the cover of a piano arrangement of one of trumpeter Dizzy Gillespie's memorable bop anthems, "Oop Bop Sh-Bam." Gillespie put a fun-loving face to the new music.

BEFORE

Jazz styles that influenced the foundation of bebop included Dixieland, Chicago, and swing.

EARLY JAZZ AND SWING
The 1920s were dominated by banjo-driven **Dixieland**, **New Orleans** **« 234–235**, and **Chicago** jazz styles, while the 1930s and early 1940s were characterized by the swing music of the **big bands** **« 242–243**, in which the emphasis was on danceable rhythms.

After World War II, most big bands broke up and were replaced by smaller groups. Swing musicians influenced the architects of bebop through their instrumental prowess and **harmonic** and **melodic** thinking.

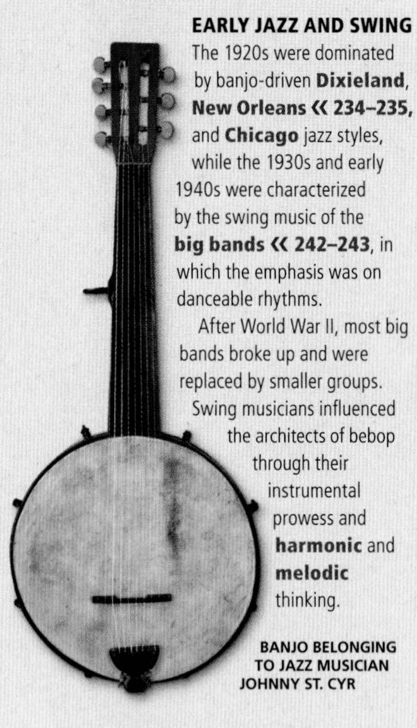

BANJO BELONGING TO JAZZ MUSICIAN JOHNNY ST. CYR

KEY WORKS

Dizzy Gillespie Quintet "Shaw 'Nuff"
Dizzy Gillespie Sextet "Groovin' High"
Charlie Parker's Reboppers "Koko"
Charlie Parker Quintet "Embraceable You"
Bud Powell Trio "Indiana"
Thelonious Monk "Misterioso"

Jazz Goes Bebop

Bebop was an exciting new style of jazz that emerged in the mid-forties in New York City. This startling music introduced and popularized several harmonic, melodic, and rhythmic innovations and remains the foundation for what is often called "modern jazz."

Bebop, known earlier as rebop and later simply as bop, was the onomatopoeic name given to the jazz that emerged in New York City in the mid-1940s. The term originated when singers imitated quick two-note figures of the instrumentalists by scatting the syllables "re-bop" and "be-bop."

To the record-buying public, bebop appeared seemingly from nowhere. Actually, it had evolved in the hot house jams and after-hours sessions at New York nightclubs such as Minton's on West 118th Street. These sessions were peopled by young musicians such as Dizzy Gillespie, pianist Thelonious Monk, alto saxophonist Charlie "Bird" Parker (see opposite), and drummers Kenny Clarke and Max Roach.

New intricacy

It was at these sessions that harmonic concepts involving altered chords, chord substitutions, and re-harmonization of standard tunes were exchanged among musicians. Improvisations tended to feature complex and intricate syncopation (where rhythmic stresses fall in unexpected places) and "double-time" (twice as fast) sixteenth-note runs than in earlier jazz styles. Musicians with a more traditional approach were baffled and excluded from proceedings, which was the intention.

Although the jazz patrons of New York City heard prototype bebop in 52nd Street clubs, such as the Three Deuces

Hot-house jams
Bebop grew out of sessions at nightclubs such as New York's Minton's Playhouse. Pictured outside in about 1947 are, from left, Thelonious Monk, Howard McGhee, Roy Eldridge, and Teddy Hill.

and the Spotlite, a two-year musicians' union recording strike starting in 1942 meant that when the first records of the new music actually arrived on the market in 1944–1945, they hit the wider listening world like bolts of lightning.

Old school reaction

Recordings by the Gillespie/Parker Quintet set the standard. While some musicians were excited by the brilliance of the music, others were suspicious. A jazz hero of an earlier style, Louis Armstrong (see pp.248–249) referred to bebop as "Chinese music."

Those who rose to the challenge set by bebop to become important figures in the development of 1940s modern jazz included pianist Bud Powell, tenor saxophonists Dexter Gordon and Stan Getz, and drummer Art Blakey.

Musical style

The quintet (trumpet, saxophone, plus a rhythm section of piano, double bass, and drums) was quickly established as the default bebop lineup. A standard performance would comprise trumpet and saxophone playing in unison or in harmony on the "head" (the composed melody or theme) followed by individual melodic improvisations and a closing head.

Although often based on the harmonic sequence of an established standard—favorites included George Gershwin's "I Got Rhythm," Fats Waller's "Honeysuckle Rose," and the 12-bar blues—bebop heads featured angular, witty, and unpredictable eighth-note melodies and elaborated chords—where the chord is broken out into an arpeggio or extra harmonies are added).

34 The age at which leading bebop musician Charlie Parker died.

A signature sound of the music was the overt use of the "flattened fifth" interval, a mildly dissonant sound that gave the music an air of playful danger. This can be heard, among many other places, on the introduction to Gillespie and Parker's dazzling 1945 recording of the album *Shaw 'Nuff*.

A further distinction between bebop and earlier jazz was the rhythmic behavior of the instruments. While the bass maintained a steady four-to-the-bar pulse, the piano and bass drum and snare of the drum kit were at liberty to offer spontaneous, syncopated punctuation of the beat. This resulted in a propulsive and fluid dialogue between the rhythm section and the soloist, which could inspire a confident performer and also provide a more complex rhythmic listening experience for an attentive audience. Bebop's unhummable tunes and its idiosyncratic rhythmic approach announced that it was not jazz that could be sung along with or danced to. This was jazz to be listened to, to be "dug," to be "sent" by; this was jazz as art.

70 The number of works by jazz pianist Thelonious Monk.

Intellectual appeal

Despite Gillespie's audience-friendly persona, a brief flurry of commercial interest, and bebop's faddish sartorial accoutrements of berets, horn-rimmed glasses, and goatee beards, bebop was never a popular music. Its intellectualism and exclusivity appealed to ambitious and capable jazz musicians and the bohemian intelligentsia much more than it did to the general public. What is more, bebop's association with the birth of "modern jazz" frequently meant that fans of earlier styles of jazz were positively hostile toward it.

> "Bebop is a **music of revolt ...** against commercialized music **in general.**"
>
> ROSS RUSSELL, CRITIC, 1948

1940s drum kit
For bebop, steady rhythms were supplied by the ride and hi-hat cymbals, while the snare and bass drums were free to drop "bombs," which were spontaneous emphases of beats.

AFTER

While the more extreme mannerisms of bebop faded as the 1950s approached, its core musical values remained central to modern jazz in the next decade and beyond. It was still bop, but with a new haircut.

COOL JAZZ
A lighter-toned style of bebop, cool jazz evolved on the **west coast of America** in the early to mid-1950s. Its emphasis was on counterpoint and sometimes harmonies, as exemplified by the **Miles Davis Nonet**, the **Gerry Mulligan/Chet Baker Quartet**, and the Modern Jazz Quartet.

HARD BOP
A muscular, driving offshoot of bebop, hard bop had an emphasis on explosive, **blues**-inflected themes and **improvisation**, and was a central jazz style of the mid-1950s to the early 1960s. Key exponents were saxophonist **Cannonball Adderley** and drummer Art Blakey and his band the **Jazz Messengers**.

JAZZ SOLOIST (1920–55)

CHARLIE PARKER

One of jazz's most conspicuously prodigious and iconic improvisers, Kansas City-born Charlie Parker played music full of unexpected, modernistic shapes, profound swing, and a deep feeling for the blues.

"He was a genius," his erstwhile partner Dizzy Gillespie observed. His virtuosity was so persuasive and startling that most modern jazz musicians of the era came under his influence. Unfortunately, his use of heroin was also imitated, resulting in many stalled careers, even early deaths. Parker himself died at the age of 34, a victim of his self-destructive tendencies.

Born 1901 Died 1971

Louis Armstrong

> "He is the **father of us all,** regardless of style or how **modern we get.**"
>
> JAZZ TRUMPETER NICHOLAS PAYTON

Trumpeter and vocalist Louis Armstrong, known as "Satchmo," is generally regarded as the man who transformed jazz from a folk music tradition into a sophisticated musical form focused upon solo improvisation. A supremely talented instrumentalist and a major innovator in the 1920s, he went on to enjoy a long career as an ambassador for jazz music and a much-loved celebrity.

Streets of New Orleans

Armstrong grew up in New Orleans, the birthplace of jazz (see pp.234–235). The illegitimate son of a boiler stoker and a laundress, he was brought up in poverty. From the age of five he lived with his mother in the city's red-light district, where she sometimes worked as a prostitute. It was from listening to bands in this notorious area that Armstrong received his first musical education. At the age of 12, he was sent to a Colored Waifs' Home after firing a pistol loaded with blanks in the street. In this institution, run on quasi-military lines, he was formally taught to play the cornet. After his release, he spent four years doing backbreaking work delivering coal before opportunities opened up for him to become a professional musician.

Armstrong played cornet with a string of New Orleans bands in the years immediately after World War I, performing in clubs and cabarets and on board Mississippi paddle steamers. He quickly established a reputation as a player of exceptional promise.

Heading north

At this time African Americans were migrating en masse to northern cities such as Chicago and New York, taking their music with them. In 1922, Armstrong's hero, cornettist Joe "King" Oliver, was signed up for a two-year residency at Lincoln Gardens in Chicago. Oliver sent for Armstrong to join his

Great entertainer
Armstrong's popularity owed as much to the sunny warmth of his personality as to the quality of his musicianship. He moved effortlessly between the roles of jazz trumpeter and mass-market entertainer.

KEY WORKS

Hot Five "Hotter Than That"

With Earl Hines "Weather Bird"

Louis Armstrong and his Orchestra "Star Dust"

With Ella Fitzgerald "Stompin' at the Savoy"

Louis Armstrong "What a Wonderful World"

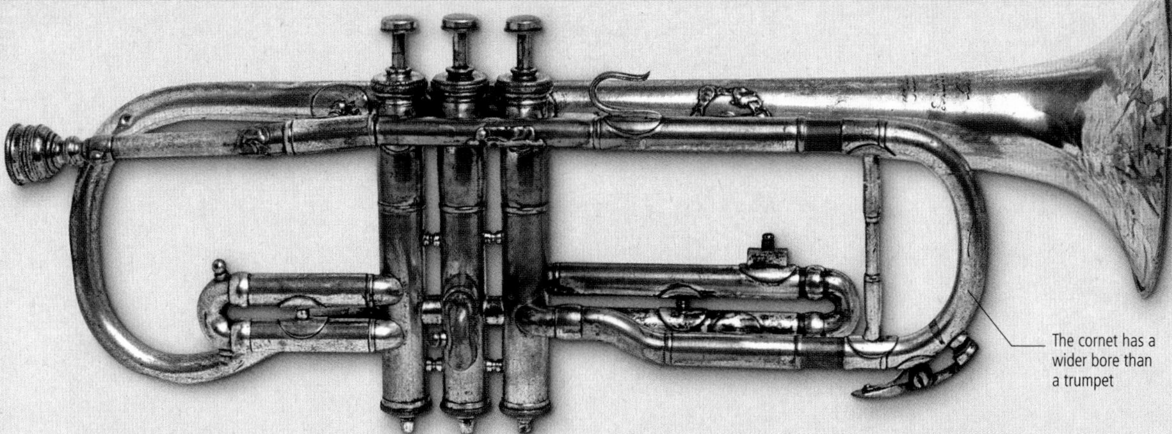

First notes on the cornet
Now in the Smithsonian's National Museum of American History in Washington, DC, this cornet belonged to Peter Davis, Armstrong's teacher. It is believed that Armstrong took lessons on this horn.

Creole Jazz Band. Armstrong's role was as second cornet, which was often uncomfortable, since he played with a more powerful tone and greater technical proficiency than the leader, Oliver. He formed a liaison with the band's pianist, Lil Hardin, whom he married in 1924. Hardin had a driving ambition that the relaxed Satchmo lacked, and she pushed him to move beyond a subordinate role.

The Hot Five

Jazz records were a booming business in the 1920s. In 1925 Armstrong made a series of outstanding records with singer Bessie Smith. He then put together his own band, the Hot Five, for a series of recording sessions. Over the following three years the Hot Five and expanded Hot Seven produced performances that redefined jazz. Armstrong used the band to showcase his talent for individual improvisation. In recordings such as the 1927 classic "Potato Head Blues," his trumpet solo freely interprets the underlying chord progression of the song, rather than simply embellishing the melody. His playing showed outstanding rhythmic subtlety and expressiveness. Armstrong blazed an exciting new trail that jazz musicians followed for the next four decades.

In addition to starring on trumpet, Armstrong reinvented jazz vocals. He was far from the first performer to sing "scat" nonsense syllables, but he did establish scat singing as central to jazz improvisation. His distinctive expressive vocal style was to have a profound influence on popular song as well as on jazz, with Bing Crosby in particular learning from his example.

It was typical of Armstrong that he saw no difficulty in combining jazz with popular entertainment. He took easily to the big band swing (see pp.242–243) that predominated in the US during the 1930s and '40s, happily showing off his virtuosity on trumpet in endless variations on the same stock of tunes, and making hit records as a popular singer.

When Armstrong returned to playing a small combo, founding his All Stars in 1947, the move was greeted with enthusiasm by jazz aficionados. With a series of scintillating recordings, the All Stars showed that traditional New Orleans jazz could still be a live, creative form in the age of Bebop and modernism.

A wonderful legacy
An album including the song "What a Wonderful World" was released in 1968. The biggest-selling single in the UK did not become famous in the US until after Armstrong's death.

Touring All Stars

Armstrong was a popular figure with white Americans. The US government sponsored All Stars tours abroad as an advertisement for the American way of life. As confrontation over African American civil rights became acute in the 1950s, Armstrong faced accusations from fellow African Americans of being an "Uncle Tom," the term, appropriated from the novel *Uncle Tom's Cabin*, given to African Americans accused of collaborating with white power. Although he made clear in the strongest terms his opposition to white racism, Armstrong could never be a confrontational figure. "What a Wonderful World," a popular song that he recorded late in life, expressed the warm and optimistic attitude that infused his music from start to finish.

Creole Jazz Band
Armstrong plays slide trumpet with Joe "King" Oliver's Creole Jazz Band, one of the leading combos of the 1920s. He regarded Oliver—standing in the center of the picture, on cornet—as his mentor. The pianist is Lil Hardin, who became Armstrong's second wife.

"You can't **play** anything on a **horn** Louis hasn't played."

MILES DAVIS, IN AN INTERVIEW, 1958

TIMELINE

- **August 4, 1901** Born in New Orleans, Louisiana.
- **November 1918** Becomes a professional musician with New Orleans bands.
- **August 1922** Moves to Chicago to join the King Oliver Creole Jazz Band, making its first recording the following year.
- **May 1924** Joins the Fletcher Henderson band in New York City, switching to trumpet.
- **November 12, 1925** First recording as leader of the Hot Five; recording of "Heebie Jeebies" breaks new ground with scat singing.
- **May 7–14, 1927** Classic recordings as leader of the Hot Seven, with masterpieces such as "Potato Head Blues."
- **June 1928** Records with a revamped Hot Five, including pianist Earl Hines; the recordings include a famous version of "West End Blues."
- **1929** Established as a popular singer, performing "Ain't Misbehavin" in the Broadway musical *Hot Chocolates*.
- **1930** Moves to Los Angeles, playing at the New Cotton Club.
- **1931** Begins recording popular songs such as "Body and Soul" and "The Peanut Vendor."
- **1932** Travels to perform in England.
- **1933–34** Visits Europe on tour. Acquires the nickname "Satchmo."
- **1935** Joe Glaser becomes his manager. Takes over as leader of the Luis Russell band.
- **1937** Becomes first African American to host a national network radio show.
- **1943** Settles in Queens, New York, with his fourth wife, Lucille Wilson.
- **1947** Switches to a small band format, leading to the founding of the Louis Armstrong All Stars.
- **February 21, 1949** Becomes the first jazz musician to appear on *Time* magazine's cover.
- **1956** Performs in newly independent Ghana.
- **1957** Movie documentary *Satchmo the Great* is released.
- **1957** Withdraws from a government-organized tour of Russia in protest of racism in the American South.

ARMSTRONG'S SHOW SONG WAS A HIT

- **1964** Records "Hello, Dolly!"—it is a huge hit.
- **1967** Records "What a Wonderful World."
- **July 6, 1971** Dies of a heart attack in New York.

Latin Beats

Much of the music of South America, Central America, and the Caribbean is rooted in dance, but the myriad rhythms that evolved on the island of Cuba before its 1950s revolution have had perhaps the greatest influence on dance styles across the world.

Long before Fidel Castro and Che Guevara brought Communism to Cuba, the musical world knew the island partly through the 1930 hit ("The Peanut Vendor"). At the time, success was measured by sheet-music sales, and this song, written by orchestra leader Moisés Simons, sold more than a million copies. The rhythm of the song was *son* (from the Spanish for "sound" or "rhythm"), the source of many Cuban dance styles.

The beat begins

Spanish settlers brought folk and flamenco (see pp.178–179) to Cuba, and the guitar soon became a popular instrument with provincial musicians. In the eastern province of Oriente, this Iberian mixture combined with African rhythms and percussion to produce *son*, which then migrated to the capital, Havana, in the early 20th century.

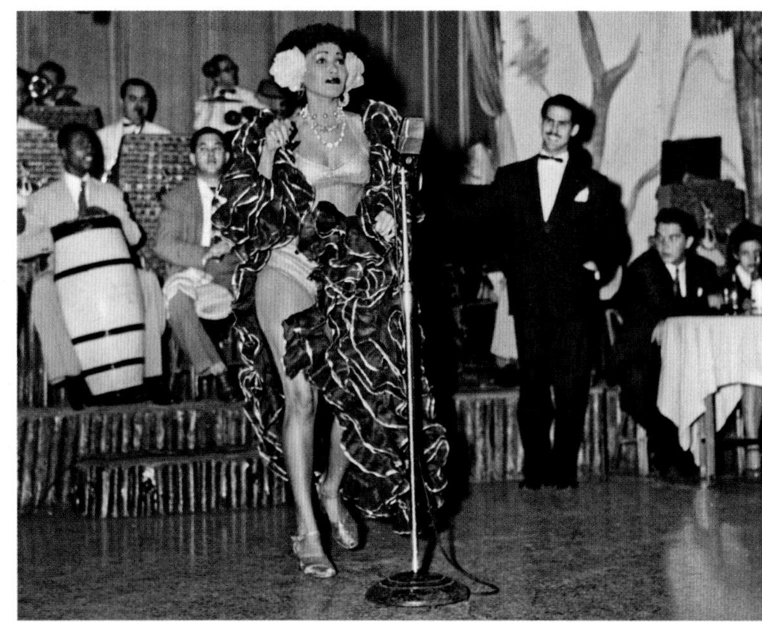

Getting hot in Havana

Zulema, a Cuban rumba dancer, performs on stage with a band at the Zombie Club on Zulueta Street, in February 1946. The years after World War I saw a tourism and nightlife boom in Cuba.

BEFORE

Latin American folk rhythms and many of the hybrid musical forms that emerged during the course of the 19th century, such as Argentine tango and Cuban *son*, can be traced back to Africa as well as to Spain.

ROOTS OF THE RHYTHMS

The dance styles *danzón*, rumba, mambo, and salsa have their origins in West Africa. The five-stroke pattern of Latin dance music, known as *clave*, has its counterpart in **sub-Saharan African music** and is the element that binds the rhythms in both musical traditions.

THE ENSLAVED IN CUBA

Cuba's prominence in the world of Latin dance music is a direct result of the island's role as a Spanish base where many enslaved people arrived, often via other countries, from Africa. Dances evolved as a social outlet for the enslaved and in musical theater.

AFRICAN CONGA DRUM

The first *son* ensembles varied in their choice of instruments but usually consisted of guitar, tres (a guitar with its six strings in three groups of two), bongos, maracas, claves (two wooden sticks knocked together in rhythm), and a *marimbula* (a boxlike plucked instrument) or *botija* (jug)—later replaced by the double bass. Early artists included the Cuarteto Oriental, who first recorded in 1917, and Isaac Oviedo, a self-taught tres player who helped to place that instrument at the center of the *son* sound.

When radio arrived in Havana in the 1920s, the music took off, coinciding with an influx of Americans, who were escaping the anti-alcohol Prohibition laws at home. The best bands began to tour abroad, and Cuban singer Rita Montaner's first version of "El Manisero" in 1928, followed by bandleader Don Azpiazú's 1930 hit recording in New York, sealed *son*'s status as the music of the moment.

Dancing to different tunes

The flexibility of the *son* beat led to its influencing other Cuban styles, such as the *danzón*. This folk dance grew in the late 19th century from the *contradanza*, which in turn had evolved from the *contredanse*, introduced by French colonists in the late 18th century and performed by couples in a line or a square. The *danzón* was one of the first Cuban dance styles where couples faced each other, its slow pace encouraging proximity and sensuous moves. But rather than gliding round the floor, the dancers stayed in a small area—a template that modern salsa and other Latin dances have followed.

Early *danzón* stars included clarinetist and composer José Urfé (1879–1957), who fused it with *son* in his 1910 dance "El Bombín de Barretto" (named after a friend's bowler hat), and pianist and composer Antonio María Romeu (1876–1955), who, in the same year, formed a *son*-influenced *danzón* orchestra. Romeu was still performing *danzón* in the early 1950s, when Cuban violinist, Enrique Jorrín, playing in the Orquesta America, took the style and turned it into the "cha-cha-cha"—the name mirroring its shuffling rhythm. The dance soon traveled to the United States, where it became a craze and was soon established in the ballroom dancing repertoire.

Messing with Cuban roots

When "The Peanut Vendor" was released as a record, the label called it a "rumba," a name that stuck as a catch-all for the fast-paced Cuban-style dancing that gripped the United States in the early 1930s. In fact, rumba (from the Spanish word for "party") had been the name of a Cuban folk dance since the late 19th century.

Another craze began during the late 1930s, when a popular Havana-based *danzón* band, Arcaño y sus Maravillas, featuring cellist Orestes Lopez (1908–1991), invited couples to improvise during rehearsals. The resulting hard-edged dance style became known as *danzón mambo*, named after a song, "Mambo," written by Orestes and his brother, Cachao, in 1938.

The style was picked up by Cuban musician Pérez Prado (1916–1989), who moved to Mexico in 1948 and began to record for the RCA label. In 1949, he released "Que Rico Mambo" and "Mambo No. 5"—the hits that set off the mambo fever of the 1950s.

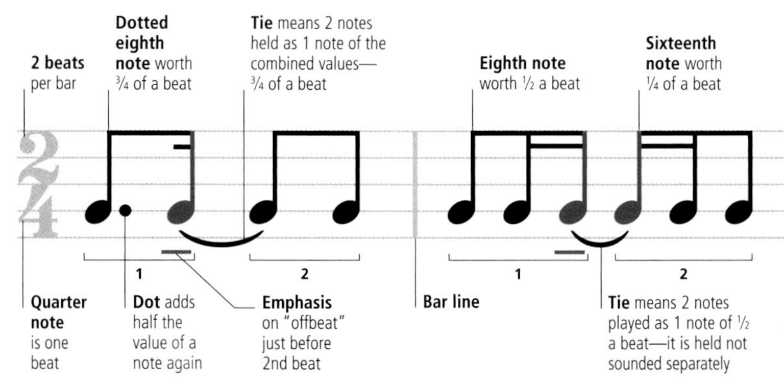

Rumba rhythm

Rumba is a generic term for a family of percussive rhythms, written in 2/4 or 4/4 time. These patterns are syncopated and stress the offbeat. Ties are used to hold notes across the onbeat, effectively skipping over it.

The moves of the moment
A couple dance cheek to cheek on the cover of sheet music for Emilio de Torre's translation of American jazz lyricist Walter Hirsch's "Poor Pedro," with music by the Cuban pianist Eliseo Grenet. The song was published in 1939, at the height of rumba mania.

KEY WORKS

Don Apiazú "El Manisero"
Beny Moré and Pérez Prado "Bonito y Sabroso"
Tito Rodriguez "Mama Guela"
Tito Puente and Celia Cruz *Cuba y Puerto Rico Son*
Fania All Stars *Cross Over*

AFTER

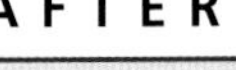

Salsa fills nightclubs across the world, and there are salsa classes in most towns from the United States to China. Cuba, meanwhile, keeps its beats alive.

CUBA CONTINUES TO EVOLVE
Despite its revolution, Cuba never stopped dancing—though some stars, most notably **Celia Cruz 278–279 ››**, went into exile. Nearly 50 years after it closed in the 1940s, the Havana-based **Buena Vista Social Club** of musicians became the subject of a film and album that were global sensations, putting Cuban music back in the spotlight. Beyond the traditional, since the late 1960s bands such as **Los Van Van** and **NG La Banda** have explored *son*, jazz, and *timba* (local Cuban music mixed with styles like rock and funk).

"SON" IN THE GYM
In the 1990s, Colombian dancer Alberto Perez forgot his usual workout tapes, put on some salsa and *merengue* (a fast-paced Afro-Hispanic style) music, and the dance-based Zumba exercise program was born.

The king of Latin percussion
Tito Puente sits at his drum kit during one of his many shows. Puente performed right to the end of his life, dying of a heart attack in 2000, shortly after a performance in Puerto Rico, his family's homeland.

Everybody salsa

Two gifted percussionists—New York-born Puerto Rican Tito Puente (1923–2000) and the blind Cuban multi-instrumentalist Arsenio Rodriguez (1911–1970)—are often credited with melding mambo and other Cuban styles into a form that became known as salsa. A product of the New York melting pot of immigrants—and often dubbed Nuyorican because of its popularity among Puerto Ricans—salsa, like rumba before it, was used as an umbrella term for a mix of Cuban genres. Since the 1950s, the dance has become popular far beyond the Americas, spawning sub-genres such as *rueda de casino*—in which dancers swap partners in the round—and the Colombian and Miami styles.

Salsa has produced many singing stars from the 1960s onward, including Puerto Rican Tito Rodríguez, or "El Inolvidable" (The Unforgettable One), Panamanian Rubén Blades, and Cuban Celia Cruz (see pp.278–279). These, and many other salsa artists, were promoted by Fania Records, a New York-based label founded in 1963 by Dominican musician Johnny Pacheco and Brooklyn native Jerry Masucci.

160 The number of versions of the *son*-style hit "The Peanut Vendor" recorded between 1930 and the late 1980s.

The salsa phenomenon is now embraced across the world, often by those without a Latin bone in their body. But at its heart is the beat of Cuban *son*.

Latin Percussion

From the syncopated sophistication of Afro-Cuban son to the festive fervor of samba, rhythm drives Latin American music, and an array of percussion instruments has evolved around immigrant, creole, and indigenous cultures.

1 *Cajón* This boxlike instrument was introduced into Peru by enslaved Africans. 2 Timbau This tall, tapered drum was first found in the Brazilian state of Bahia. 3 Tan tan Small samba groups use this low-volume cylindrical hand drum. 4 Surdo drum Worn with a waist belt or shoulder strap, the surdo—made of wood or steel—provides the main beat and syncopated flourishes in Brazilian samba and axé music. 5 Bongo drums Played in pairs, the Afro-Cuban drums are divided into a bigger *macho* (male) and smaller *hembra* (female) drums. 6 Conga drum The tall conga originated in Africa and developed among formerly enslaved people in Cuba. 7 Caixa de Guerra The "war drum" produces lively cross-rhythms for marches and carnival parades. 8 Timbales and cowbells The shallow metal timbales were first played by Cuban danzón musicians; cowbells are used to keep time when the drums are silent. 9 Triangle The triangle has a key role in Brazil's forró music, where it provides a constant, hypnotic pulse. 10 Chekere The Cuban chekere is a gourd covered with beads, seeds, or shells woven into a net; it can be shaken or patted for a fast, soft-sounding beat. 11 *Ganzá* Basketlike, and filled with beads, the ganzá provides a back beat to Brazilian samba. 12 Maracas Originally made from the shells of plants such as gourds, maracas are rattlelike instruments played in pairs. 13 Cabasa Based on an African gourd instrument, the cabasa's rattlesnake hiss is a staple of Latin jazz and bossa nova. 14 Chocalhos When shaken by samba performers, this simple metal frame covered in jingles produces a frenzied "dirty" sound. 15 Goat hoof rattle From Bolivia, where goat hooves are plentiful, the rattle produces a dry, clacking rhythm. 16 Marimba The xylophone-like marimba is popular in Mexico and throughout Central America. 17 Claves This ancient percussive instrument, used in genres such as son and guaguancó, a kind of rumba, provides the *clave*—or key—pattern of beats. 18 *Clavéfono* Cuban composer Roberto Bonachea Entrialgo invented this combination of güiro, woodblock, and maracas in the 1990s. 19 *Güiro* Made from a hollow gourd, the güiro produces a harsh, scraping sound, used in cumbia and salsa music. 20 Rainstick Probably an Aztec invention, this hollow tube is filled with beans or pebbles, producing a sound like rain.

1 CAJÓN
Height approx. 20 in (50 cm)

8 TIMBALES AND COWBELLS
Diameter of two drums 16 in (40 cm) and 12 in (30 cm)

5 BONGO DRUMS
Diameter of two drums 8 in (20 cm) and 6 in (15 cm)

2 TIMBAU
Diameter of head 14 in (35 cm)

3 TAN TAN
Diameter of head 14 in (35 cm)

4 SURDO DRUM
Diameter of head 24 in (60 cm)

6 CONGA DRUM
Diameter of head 12 in (30 cm)

7 CAIXA DE GUERRA
Diameter of head 12 in (30 cm)

9 TRIANGLE
Length 4–10in (10–25cm)

10 CHEKERE
Diameter 8in (20cm)

11 GANZÁ
Height 9in (23cm)

12 MARACAS
Diameter 4in (10cm)

13 CABASA
Diameter of head 5in (13cm)

14 CHOCALHOS
Length 15in (38cm)

15 GOAT HOOF RATTLE
Height 10in (25cm)

16 MARIMBA
Length 84–100in (2.1–2.6m)

17 CLAVES
Length 10in (25cm)

18 CLAVÉFONO
Length approx. 10in (25cm)

19 GÜIRO
Length 15in (38cm)

20 RAINSTICK Length 47in (1.2m)

Melancholy music

Melancholia is a common theme in tango, as the elegant cover of this 1915 sheet music, entitled *Desdichas* (meaning "sorrows"), illustrates. The music was written by Pascual Contursi and Augusto Gentile.

BEFORE

Tango's genesis has been appropriated by Argentine historians, but the dance is rooted in West Africa.

AFRICAN CONNECTIONS
Drawings from the early 19th century show African-Argentines walking with a tangolike gait carrying a coffin. The word "tango" may have its roots in the African word for a place where people danced, and the Niger-Congo word "tamgu" (to dance).

20 **The number of newspapers for African-Argentine readers in the 1880s.**

CONGO-BASED MOVES
Tango moves, such as *quebradas* (a hip twist) and *sentadas* (when the woman sits on the man's thigh) have been likened to the bumping of bellies, hips, or rears known as *bumbakana* in the Congo.

AFRICAN-ARGENTINE TANGO STAR
One early star of tango was pianist Rosendo Mendizabal (1868–1913), composer of the classic song "El Entrerriano," which became one of the most famous tango songs ever.

KEY WORKS

Gerardo Matos Rodríguez, Pascual Contursi, and **Enrique Pedro Maroni** "La Cumparsita" (Tango Song)

Carlos Gardel and **Pascual Contursi** "Mi Noche Triste" (My Sad Night)

Osvaldo Pugliese "La Yumba"

Enrique Santos Discepolo and **Edmundo Rivero** "Yira Yira"

Let's Tango

One of the earliest examples of a genuine world music, the tango had its genesis in humble areas on the outskirts of Buenos Aires, but it was later embraced by the middle classes and soon conquered dance halls all over the world.

The tango evolved from a mixture of local and imported dance rhythms. Native guitar-based *milonga* rhythms blended with West African *candombe* rhythms, introduced by the descendants of enslaved people in Argentina and Uruguay.

The music first became popular in Buenos Aires in the last 20 years of the 19th century. It was originally performed with violin, guitar, and flute, and soon the *bandoneón* (accordion) was added, bringing a somber sensuality to the music.

Tango evolved first as dance music. Early photographs show pairs of men practicing the steps in the streets, and the first tango halls were probably bars and general stores on the poorer margins of Buenos Aires, where gauchos (South American cowboys) and African and European immigrants of humble origin socialized. Tango is often associated with the bordello, and may have been performed in the waiting rooms to keep impatient clients entertained.

The tango evolves

In the 1900s, the basic *orquesta típica*—a sextet made up of two violins, piano, double bass, and two *bandoneóns*—became the standard lineup. In Buenos Aires venues such as the Café de Hansen and El Velódromo, pioneering bandleaders such as Roberto Firpo and Vincente Greco introduced the tango sound to the lower middle classes.

Voice of the tango

Argentine baritone Carlos Gardel (1890–1935) visited the United States many times during his career. Here he is seen making a broadcast on the NBC network during a trip in 1934.

4 beats per bar — **Dotted quarter note** worth 1½ beats — **Quarter note** worth 1 beat — **Bar line** — **Eighth note** worth ½ a beat

1 2 3 4 1 2 3 4

Quarter note is one beat — Emphasis on the first beat — Emphasis on the third beat

The tango beat

Tango can be written in 2/4 or 4/4 time, with the top number denoting the number of dance steps as well as beats per bar. The attacking downbeat—the first beat in the bar—and the regular, almost martial pulse of the music reflect the serious character of the dance.

Across the Plate, River, tango was also being performed in the Uruguayan capital, Montevideo.

Most well-to-do South Americans had rejected the new dance, perhaps because of its unseemly embrace and footwork. Many bands decided to go abroad and enjoyed success in Europe, the United States, and Russia. When it became fashionable in Paris, the smart set of Buenos Aires also took it up.

Crossing class boundaries

Tango provided a rare neutral space in which the so-called *compadritos* (street hoods) could mingle with the higher echelons of society, and soon the tango could be heard all over the Argentine capital. Elegant venues, such as the Palais de Glace and Armenonville, attracted the sons and daughters of the landed *estancieros*, creole landowners who had grown rich thanks to booming meat exports.

Musicians such as Agustín Bardi, Osvaldo Fresedo, and Pedro Maffia, and songwriters such as Rosendo Mendizábal and Angel Villoldo, became local legends. In 1916, Firpo rewrote a march composed by Uruguayan musician Gerardo Matos Rodríguez: "La Cumparsita" became the most famous orchestral tango ever. The early orchestras and songwriters are often grouped together as *La Guardia Vieja* (The Old Guard), and this first flourishing of tango lasted from approximately 1900 to 1924.

New tango sounds

The rise of the radio played a decisive role in spreading tango's popularity, as did the appearance of the first gramophones (see below). This helped the career of Carlos Gardel, a French immigrant known for his tremulous baritone voice. In 1917, he recorded "Mi Noche Triste" (My Sad Night) for the Nacional-Odeon label, and from this time on, singers became a key part of the tango scene. Meanwhile, Gardel became tango's first superstar, touring Latin America and appearing in films.

With the *orquesta típica* established as the classic format, some daring bandleaders began to experiment. Julio de Caro was a virtuoso violinist and talented songwriter whose polished musical language and subtle melodies added a new intelligence to orchestral tango. Juan Carlos Cobián, who toured widely and helped popularize the tango in North America, was another innovator. He was the first arranger to fill in the bass line with embellishments during rests in the melody, and is widely regarded as the precursor of avant-garde tango.

Tango maestros

In the golden age of tango that lasted from the mid-1930s to the early '50s, three giants stood out—the *bandoneón* players Aníbal Troilo and Astor Piazzolla, and the pianist Osvaldo Pugliese, all of them popular bandleaders who wrote and performed as much for the music-lover's ear as for the dancer's feet. Troilo's mesmerizing performances on the *bandoneón* tested the limits of the instrument, while Pugliese wrote slower but challenging arrangements.

Piazzolla (see p.277) was one of the first global superstars of tango. Born in the coastal city of Mar del Plata in 1921, his family moved to New York when he was a child. Given a *bandoneón* by his father, young Astor excelled as a soloist, and when he returned to Buenos Aires he played with several leading orchestras, including the one fronted by Troilo.

Piazzolla was an iconoclast and his experimental style was not suited to the dance hall. After studying with classical composers Alberto Ginastera (1916–1983) and Nadia Boulanger (1887–1979), he began writing classical movements with tango motifs and later wrote jazz-inflected works, tangos for synthesizers, and a tango-themed opera. Collaborations with saxophonist Gerry Mulligan, vibraphone-player Gary Burton, and Uruguayan poet Horacio Ferrer led him to increasingly daring experiments.

While Piazzolla had detractors among the conservative Buenos Aires tango establishment, songs such as "Adiós Nonino" (Goodbye, Grandad) and "Vuelvo al Sur" (I return South) are recognized as classics. When Piazzolla died in 1992, tango lost its last true maestro.

Street sign in Buenos Aires

This sign, painted in a style called *fileteada*, is typical of Buenos Aires. In addition to being the name of a street in La Boca district of the city, *Caminito* is the name of a 1926 tango and the Argentine word for "little street."

Bandoneón

This double-action accordion, known as a *bandoneón*, was made by Wilhelm König in 1914. Its Argentine name is a corruption of Band Union, the name of a German manufacturer.

TECHNOLOGY

VICTROLA

In the 1900s, the United States Gramophone Company, and then the Victor Talking Machine Company, started to sell windup phonographs in Buenos Aires. Cafés and bars unable to afford to employ a house orchestra could buy a talking machine (or *victrola*, in Spanish) for the entertainment of clients, thus helping to popularize tango more widely. The Victor Talking Machine Company later became RCA Victor. It was to be a major record label for tango, along with other musical genres.

In Argentina's collective memory, *la victrola* is associated nostalgically with the golden age not only of tango, but also of Buenos Aires itself.

AFTER »

The golden age of tango is long past, but the music survives as a marginal dance scene, in stage shows, and as a hybrid popular form.

VICTIM OF IDEOLOGY

Piazzolla apart **277 »**, tango faded after the 1950s. Some blame the government of Juan Perón (1895–1975), which promoted rural folk music as part of its populist ideology.

MODERN REVIVAL

Tango went through a revival in the 1980s after the global success of the stage show *Tango Argentino*.

TANGO TODAY

A handful of Argentine tango stars, including singer Adriana Varela and pianist Sonia Possetti, keep the tango beat alive today.

Top hats and stockings
The 1930 film *Der Blaue Engel* (*The Blue Angel*) made Marlene Dietrich famous and defined cabaret. This nightclub scene from the movie captures the decadent style.

BEFORE

Censorship in Germany under Kaiser Wilhelm II kept the first Parisian-style *kabarett* clubs underground.

BERLIN
In Berlin in 1901, satirist and author Ernst von Wolzogen opened *Überbrettl* (Ultra-Cabaret), a venue which became known for its literary parodies and satirical songs. **Arnold Schoenberg « 210–211** and Viennese composer Oscar Straus directed shows there.

MUNICH
Also in 1901, theater producer Otto Falckenberg founded *Die Elf Scharfrichter* (The Eleven Executioners) in Munich, a politically charged entertainment that included works by subversive playwright Frank Wedekind.

Come to the **Cabaret**

The period between the wars was marked by an explosion of vibrant and subversive popular art in Germany. Part of this cultural renaissance was manifest in sexually charged cabaret and ferociously satirical musical theater.

The establishment of the Weimar Republic in Germany at the end of World War I led to a lifting of censorship restrictions and an eruption of artistic and political expression. The 1920s and '30s saw a growth in popularity of *kabarett*—satirical, antiestablishment entertainment in cafés, nightclubs, and bars. Performed by dancers, singers, and comedians, it displayed a distinctive black humor along with an air of hedonism, sexual liberalism, and decadence. Against the backdrop of hyperinflation and an impending sense of panic, cabaret was part of the era's feverish artistic activity, known as the "Dance on the Volcano." Cabaret's heydey was brief because the form was banned in Hitler's Third Reich.

"Alles Schwindel" ("All's a Swindle") is a typical song of the era. Composed by the Russian-born Mischa Spoliansky (1898–1985), the jolly "oom-pah" music is matched by lyrics expressing political cynicism and grim humor.

Falling in love again

Movie director Josef von Sternberg discovered Marlene Dietrich performing in Spoliansky's 1929 Berlin revue *Zwei Krawatten* (*Two Ties*). He cast her in his 1930 film *Der Blaue Engel* (*The Blue Angel*), set in the Weimar cabaret world. It made the actress a star. Her signature song, "Ich bin von Kopf bis Fuß auf Liebe eingestellt"—"Falling In Love Again (Can't Help It)"—was written by Friedrich Hollaender (1896–1976), a composer involved in Berlin cabaret.

After the rise of the Nazis in Germany from 1933, *kabarett* was outlawed and its practitioners hounded. Both Spoliansky and Hollaender left Germany to become movie composers, the former in London, the latter in Hollywood in the United States.

One writer who witnessed these dangerous, heady days in Germany was Christopher Isherwood, whose 1939 novel *Goodbye To Berlin* was made into the 1966 musical, *Cabaret*, by John Kander and Fred Ebb. It later became a hit movie starring Joel Grey and Liza Minnelli.

Political slant

Elsewhere in Weimar Germany, the Novembergruppe—a community of Berlin-based, left-wing artists with a social and political agenda—included in their number the composer Kurt Weill (1900–50). Through the 1920s, Weill divided his efforts between modernist orchestral and chamber works and abrasive, jazz-influenced musical theater, most successfully with the dramatists Georg Kaiser (1878–1945) and Bertolt Brecht (1898–1956).

With Brecht, Weill produced several works, including his most famous and popular piece, *The Threepenny Opera* (1928), a loose adaptation of John Gay's 1728 *The Beggar's Opera* (see p.133). A provocative critique of capitalism, it was set in a stylized, amoral Victorian London. The dour threat of the opening tune, "Die Moritat von Mackie Messer," was diluted somewhat when translated as "Mack The Knife" to become a jazz standard 25 years later. The *Moritat* in the song's original title was a medieval murder ballad performed by troubadours. Success came with Brecht and Weill's epic opera parody *Rise And Fall Of The City Of Mahagonny* (1930), from which comes "Alabama Song," covered by US rock group The Doors in 1966.

Another prominent composer of the period was Austrian-born Hanns Eisler (1896–1962). Trained in 12-tone serialism, a new mathematical technique for composing by Arnold Schoenberg (see pp.210–211), Eisler became drawn instead to cabaret and jazz styles. "I am bored by modern music," said Eisler. "It is of no interest to me since much of it is devoid of all social relevance." A fellow Marxist, Eisler collaborated with Brecht on the hard-hitting *Die Massnahme* (*The Measures Taken*, 1930) and a host of plays, movies, and protest songs.

6.5 **The percentage of votes for the Nazi Party in the 1924 election.**

43.9 **The percentage of votes for the Nazis in the 1933 election.**

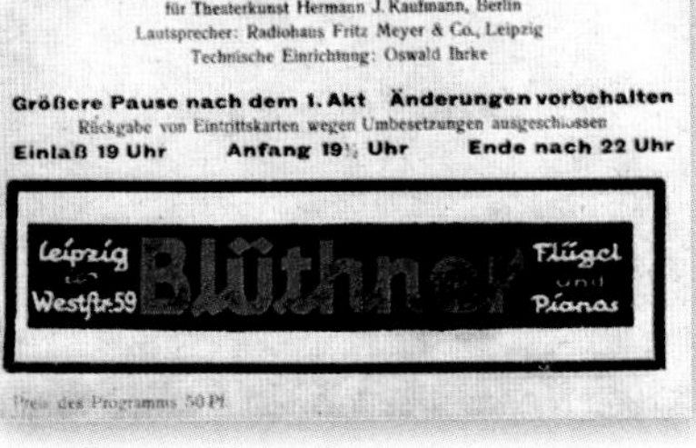
NEUES THEATER

Sonntag, den 9. März 1930

Außer Anrecht

Uraufführung

Aufstieg und Fall der Stadt Mahagonny

Oper in drei Akten — Musik von Kurt Weill — Text von Bert Brecht

Bühnenbilder und Projektionen: Caspar Neher

Musikalische Leitung: Gustav Brecher — Spielleitung: Walther Brügmann

Leokadja Begbick	Marga Dannenberg
Willy, der „Prokurist"	Hanns Fleischer
Virginia-Moses	Walther Zimmer
Jenny	Mali Trummer
Johann Ackermann	Paul Beinert
Jacob Schmidt	Hanns Hauschild
Heinrich (genannt Sparbüchsenheinrich)	Theodor Horand
Josef Lettner (genannt Alaskawolfjoe)	Ernst Osterkamp
Tobby Higgins	Alfred Holländer
Ein Liebespaar	Ilse Koegel Hans Lißmann

Acht Mädchen von Mahagonny, Männer von Mahagonny

Chöre: Konrad Neuger

Kostüme nach Entwürfen von Caspar Neher angefertigt in den Werkstätten für Theaterkunst Hermann J. Kaufmann, Berlin

Lautsprecher: Radiohaus Fritz Meyer & Co., Leipzig

Technische Einrichtung: Oswald Ihrke

Größere Pause nach dem 1. Akt **Änderungen vorbehalten**

Rückgabe von Eintrittskarten wegen Umbesetzungen ausgeschlossen

Einlaß 19 Uhr **Anfang 19½ Uhr** **Ende nach 22 Uhr**

Leipzig Westftr. 59 Blüthner Flügel und Pianos

Preis des Programms 50 Pf

Banned by the Nazis
The premiere of the Kurt Weill/Bertolt Brecht satirical opera *Rise and Fall of the City of Mahagonny*, advertised on this play bill, opened at the Neuestheater in Leipzig in 1930. It was banned by the Nazis in 1933.

America-bound

As popular, left-leaning Jewish artists, Eisler and Weill were targets for the Nazis, and they left Germany in 1933. Eisler combined choral composing with a return to serialism and a successful career as a Hollywood composer before being deported as a communist and settling in East Berlin.

Weill went to New York City, where he studied American popular music styles and wrote successful musicals with American lyricists Maxwell Anderson and Ira Gershwin. Several of Weill's later songs became standards, including the "September Song" (from the musical *Knickerbocker Holiday*, 1938).

Singer and composer
Kurt Weill's wife, the Austrian actress and singer Lotte Lenya, played Jenny in the 1928 production of Weill's *Threepenny Opera* and later had a role in *Cabaret* on Broadway.

Banned music

Germany's liberal musical arts, including the work of Paul Hindemith, Alban Berg, and Igor Stravinsky (see pp.212–213), were largely banned by the Nazis. American swing and jazz were considered *Negermusik* ("Negro Music") and its white practitioners and composers were ostracized as "degenerates."

However, in Hamburg and Berlin, a faction of rebellious teenagers resisted the pressure to become Hitler Youth and instead defined themselves as pro-British, pro-American, and pro-jazz. The *swingjungend* ("swing-kids") organized clandestine dance parties and became associated with antiauthority subversion.

Although the movement was largely stamped out by the mid-1940s by the Nazi authorities, chief among them the Propaganda Minister Goebbels, the *swingjungend* can be seen as part of a German tradition of musical and social nonconformity in the face of official disapproval.

KEY WORKS

Kurt Weill/Bertolt Brecht *Mahagonny; Die Dreigroschenoper (The Threepenny Opera); Happy End*

Spoliansky *Zwei Kravatten (Two Ties); Es Liegt in der Luft (It's in the Air)*

Friedrich Hollaender *Der Blaue Engel (The Blue Angel)*

"There is only **good music** and **bad music.**"

COMPOSER KURT WEILL (1900–1950)

Musical imports
A linen postcard showing the skyline of 1930s New York City, the view that greeted Kurt Weill, Bertolt Brecht, and other German artists escaping persecution.

AFTER

While *kabarett* went West, notably in the show *Cabaret*, a national identity was retained in postwar Germany in two particular styles.

LEIDERMACHER

Related to the French ***chanson*** **268–269 >>** and American **troubadour** styles, songs sung by the *liedermacher* (German singer-songwriters) often provide **social commentary** and/or **protest.** Notable practitioners of the form include the sporadically political Reinhard Mey and the erudite, Berlin-based Klaus Hoffman. A vegetarian concerned with animal rights, Hoffman composes songs about everyday life as well as more politically charged subjects in songs such as "Alles OK in Guantanamo Bay."

SCHLAGER

A folk-derived, sentimental **ballad** style, *schlager* was popularized by Heino and Rex Gildo in the 1960s and '70s, and remains distinct from other European **pop** styles.

LIZA MINNELLI AND JOEL GREY IN THE 1972 MOVIE OF "CABARET"

Recording and **Listening**

Though recorded music is taken for granted today, the privilege and convenience of enjoying music without being in the presence of musicians performing live has only been available to the listening world for around a century.

From Josef Hoffman's piano recordings onto a cylinder in inventor Thomas Edison's laboratory in 1887, through electronic recording equipment in acoustically engineered studio spaces, to the latest dance track created on a home computer, the story of recorded music is one of technological innovation. The incredible science involved in capturing and reproducing sound has driven the development of recorded music from crackly, ghostly echoes to pristine, larger-than-life sonic experiences. Composers largely relished the prospect of their music being captured in "a complete and meticulous immortality," as Claude Debussy described it in 1904.

From novel to normal

Consumption of recorded music has taken many forms. A fashionable, fascinating novelty in the early days, recordings were collected by music lovers. Today, easy access to inexpensive, high-quality recorded music is taken for granted. This evolution has been driven by technology. Earlier recorded music formats, such as wax cylinders that contained sound recordings in the grooves on their surface (*c.*1888–1915), were available mainly to the privileged classes. These were followed by 78rpm discs (*c.*1903–1958) that played at a frequency of 78 revolutions per minute. However, it was not until cheaper record players became available that recorded music on LPs (*c.*1948–present) and 45rpm singles (*c.*1949–2000) were accessible to more households. The advent of CDs (*c.*1983–present), legal and illegal digital downloads (*c.*1994–present), and digital streaming sites on the Internet has seen the dissemination of recorded music on a scale unimaginable by Thomas Edison.

Early recording studio
Musicians crowd around a single acoustic horn during a recording session at an early purpose-built recording studio in the United States in 1921.

Modern recording studio
Engineers sit at a mixing desk monitoring the recorded sound through speakers while musicians record in a separate room.

"The most **surprising,** the most **beautiful...** and the most interesting among all **inventions.**"

RUSSIAN COMPOSER TCHAIKOVSKY DESCRIBING THE PHONOGRAPH

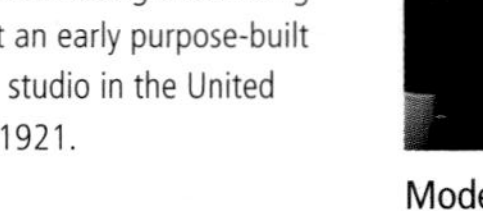

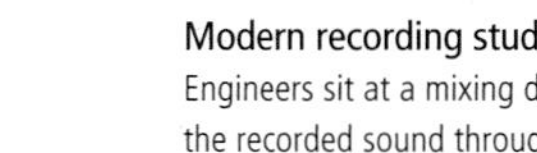

Hot air gramophone
Swiss manufacturer Paillard produced a wide range of gramophones. In 1910, it brought out this ornate model that was powered by burning alcohol.

TIMELINE

1857
The phonautograph
French inventor Édouard-Léon Scott de Martinville's phonautograph was the first device that could record sound, but it was unable to play it back.

1877
The phonograph
Thomas Edison invented the phonograph. This was the first device that could reproduce recorded sound, via a stylus creating indentations in tinfoil wrapped around a grooved cylinder.

PHONOGRAPH AD, 1901

1887
Berliner gramophone
Building on Edison's innovations, Emile Berliner invented both the gramophone and a method for mass-producing copies of a recorded disc.

BERLINER GRAMOPHONE

c.1903
78rpm discs
Usually made of shellac, 78s came in a variety of sizes. The grooved surface stored recordings compactly, but they were very fragile, and the format largely died out by the mid-1950s.

1910
Gramophone
From 1910–1914, Swiss manufacturer Paillard produced the hot-air powered gramophone as a labor-saving alternative to earlier wind-up models.

1920
Electrical recordings
The development of the microphone led to traditional acoustic recording methods being replaced by superior quality electronic recording by the end of the 1920s.

1934
Magnetic tape
German company BASF refined and manufactured magnetic recording tape. It came to dominate recording for the next 50 years.

1948
LP
The Columbia record label introduced long-playing albums playing at 33rpm as an alternative to 78rpm discs. The 45rpm single followed a year later.

EARLY MICROPHONE

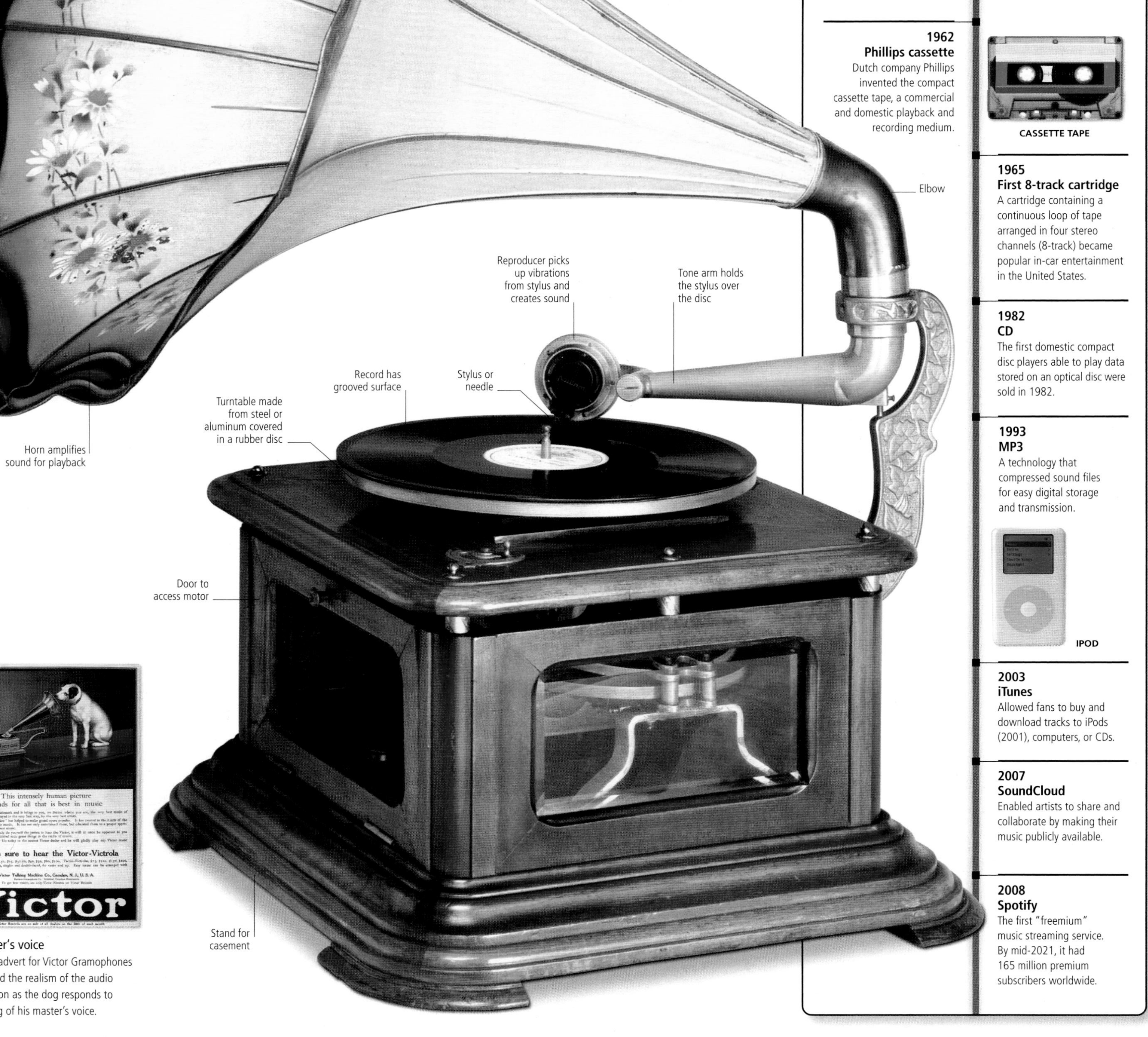

1962
Phillips cassette
Dutch company Phillips invented the compact cassette tape, a commercial and domestic playback and recording medium.

1965
First 8-track cartridge
A cartridge containing a continuous loop of tape arranged in four stereo channels (8-track) became popular in-car entertainment in the United States.

1982
CD
The first domestic compact disc players able to play data stored on an optical disc were sold in 1982.

1993
MP3
A technology that compressed sound files for easy digital storage and transmission.

2003
iTunes
Allowed fans to buy and download tracks to iPods (2001), computers, or CDs.

2007
SoundCloud
Enabled artists to share and collaborate by making their music publicly available.

2008
Spotify
The first "freemium" music streaming service. By mid-2021, it had 165 million premium subscribers worldwide.

His master's voice
The 1910 advert for Victor Gramophones emphasized the realism of the audio reproduction as the dog responds to a recording of his master's voice.

BEFORE

It seemed miraculous to listeners when they first heard words and music at the touch of a button.

INVENTOR ON THE FIDDLE

On Christmas Eve 1906, the world's first radio program was broadcast by a Canadian inventor named Reginald Fessenden. He played a **phonograph recording** of the opening aria of **Handel's opera** *Serse*, followed by the song "O Holy Night," played by himself on the **violin**. The broadcast was heard hundreds of miles away.

THE FIRST commercial broadcast in the United States was in 1920.

ONLY OPERA was broadcast on KYW, Chicago's first radio station.

US NETWORKS

Commercial radio was set up in the United States on networks that had been established during World War I. The first entertainment programs were broadcast in 1922, when one million radios were in use in the country.

The ribbon microphone

Invented in the 1920s, the iconic, chunky-looking ribbon microphone became a staple of radio broadcasts at stations such as NBC. It was known for its smooth sound and the authority it gave to a voice.

Golden Age of Radio

The vast continent of North America was brought together when radio broadcasting began. Within just a few years, hundreds of stations were bringing all kinds of music into the homes of ordinary people and giving musicians vast audiences.

Before television, radio was the leading form of home entertainment across the world, as people clustered around their radio sets to listen to music, news, drama, and information. Popular music could never have become the phenomenon it did without the huge US radio networks. They turned local singers into national celebrities, and popularized all kinds of music, crossing barriers of genre, race, and class.

The growth of radio was explosive. Licensed public radio stations in the United States went on air in 1920, and by 1922, there were 600 stations. Between 1923 and 1930, 60 percent of American families bought radios.

Commercial sponsorship

Companies soon realized that advertising on radio would win customers and the sponsored music feature became the leading entertainment format. These broadcasts, recorded live, made stars out of the musicians who presented them. Comedy routines, corny one-liners, and old-fashioned vaudeville entertainment added variety. But classical music was not forgotten, and some stations built orchestra-sized recording studios.

82 **The percentage of Americans who owned a radio by 1947.**

50 **The percentage of recorded music played on radio in the United States in the 1940s that was by Bing Crosby.**

The big bands

The mass takeup of radio coincided with the mainstream popularity of jazz (see pp.242–243). Paul Whiteman, the American big-band leader, known as the "King of Jazz" in the 1920s, had regular broadcasts, such as *Paul Whiteman's Musical Varieties* and *Kraft Music Hall*. His genteel, symphonic arrangements gave the music a newfound respectability, but also earned him criticism from some quarters for overly formalizing jazz and downplaying the role of improvisation in favor of written-out arrangements. Whiteman introduced the airwaves to composer, bandleader, and trombonist Jack Teagarden and singers Mildred Bailey and Bing Crosby (1903–1977).

The crooner

Bing Crosby's voice became, in many ways, synonymous with radio's golden age. His soft and intimate vocal style was ideal for the medium. In the radio recording studio, performers could get unprecedentedly close to a microphone so that it picked up every lip-smacking detail. The gentle, sophisticated singing style of the "crooner" was perfect for this (see pp.288–289).

Indeed, Crosby became fascinated with recording technology and invested his own money in the development of reel-to-reel tape recorders, which enabled him to

Early radio

Designed as elegant pieces of furniture, early radios used valves, which were like electric bulbs, that took a few minutes to heat up before they could receive any sound. At first these used AM signals; in the late 1930s, FM signals were introduced.

record his radio shows in advance, rather than having to broadcast them live. Crosby's entrepreneurial flair, easygoing vocal style, and assurance made him a forerunner of the pop star, setting the stage for Frank Sinatra (see pp.288–289), whose mass appeal to the teenagers of America would prove to be even more media-savvy.

Grand Ole Opry stars

Country music had its own commercially sponsored shows. The most famous of the long-running country radio programs remains the *Grand Ole Opry*, a weekly broadcast from the Nashville venue that first aired in 1925 (see pp.228–229). The biggest star of the show's early years was Uncle Dave Macon, a larger-than-life folk singer who played banjo, sang, and performed skits. He bridged the gap between the old-time traditional music of the mountains, and the slick entertainment demanded by commercial broadcasting.

The *Grand Ole Opry*, recorded before a live audience, proved so popular that it was soon hosting top-charting country music stars such as Roy Acuff, Hank Williams, and Lefty Frizzell.

Cloth-covered speaker

Radio kings

Another sponsored music show, the African-American-oriented blues and R&B show *King Biscuit Time* was first broadcast in 1941, and continues to be broadcast each weekday on KFFA Radio in Helena, Arkansas. It was first presented by blues harmonica player Sonny Boy Williamson II (1912–1965), financed by King Biscuit Flour, a local company, and broadcast throughout the Mississippi Delta (see pp.240–241).

The half-hour program featured Williamson and the guitarist Robert Lockwood playing live, backed up by the house band, the King Biscuit Entertainers, featuring Pinetop Perkins on piano and James Peck Curtis on drums. The show aired at 12:15 p.m. each day—a slot that was chosen to coincide with the lunch break of African-American workers.

Winning format

Radio played a vital role in raising troop morale during World War II, when American bandleader Glenn Miller put a little extra swing into marching tunes and the Andrews Sisters became the Sweethearts of Armed Forces Radio Service (see pp.242–243). Miller himself perished in the conflict—he was declared missing in action in 1944 after the plane flying him to Paris to perform for the troops disappeared over the English Channel.

In 1949, the 26-year-old Hank Williams (1923–1953), already a huge star of country music, struck a deal with the makers of Hadacol, a vitamin supplement, to sponsor his first syndicated radio series. The program became known as the *Health and Happiness Radio Show.*

As television eclipsed radio in popularity in the 1950s, the golden age of radio drew to a close. But TV used many popular radio formats, including variety hours and opries.

Made for the maestro
The Italian conductor Arturo Toscanini became an American household name conducting the NBC Symphony Orchestra—put together especially for him—on weekly transmissions between 1937 and 1954.

> **"The voice of Bing Crosby has been heard by more people than the voice of any other human who ever lived."**
>
> DECCA RECORDS PRESS RELEASE, 1954

AFTER

Changes in radio went hand-in-hand with changes in society. Radio became the dominant medium for the youth culture that would give rise to rock 'n' roll and pop music.

MUSIC ON THE MOVE

The **transistor radio** revolutionized the world's listening habits. Invented in the late 1940s, it was smaller, battery-powered, and portable. This allowed **teenagers** to take music wherever they wanted. The boom in sales meant an explosion in the number of **radio stations**, which became less formal during the 1950s. Radio helped spread and mix the musical influences of **R&B 310–311 ››** with **country music 346–347 ››**. **Pop music 350–351 ››** and 1960s youth culture were just around the corner.

THE TRANSISTOR RADIO

KEY WORKS

Hank Williams "Happy Rovin' Cowboy"
Uncle Dave Macon "Go Long Mule"
Sonny Boy Williamson "V-8 Ford"
Bing Crosby "You Go to My Head"
Nat King Cole "I've Got the World On a String"
Arturo Toscanini Shostakovich Symphony No. 7

JAZZ MUSICIAN (1919–1965)

NAT KING COLE

One of the most seductive voices in jazz, the singer and pianist Nat King Cole had several hits in the 1940s with his distinctive trio—piano (played by Cole), bass, and drums. His smooth baritone stood out in the big-band age. Cole secured a 15-minute radio show on the NBC station. The show, *King Cole Trio Time*, was the first radio program to be led by an African-American performing artist. In the 1950s, his sound moved toward stately, highly orchestrated love songs, such as "Mona Lisa" and "Unforgettable."

8

GLOBAL MUSIC

1945–PRESENT

After World War II, mass communication via radio, television, and film produced a truly global music. All kinds of music found wider audiences, and musicians melded what they heard to create exciting new genres, from Congolese *soukous* to Korean pop. In the 21st century, this trend exploded: high-speed Internet allowed popular and classical musicians to collaborate remotely, and consumers could stream music directly to their ear.

« Gibson Les Paul electric guitar made in 1952

GLOBAL MUSIC
1945–PRESENT

1945	1950	1955	1960	1965	1970

1945
Benjamin Britten's *Peter Grimes* establishes modern opera in Britain.

Irving Berlin's 1946 hit musical *Annie Get Your Gun*

1946
Igor Stravinsky's Symphony in Three Movements premieres in New York City. The first Darmstadt summer school attracts a new wave of avant-garde composers.

1947
Patti Page is the first pop artist to overdub her own voice to provide harmonies on her hit "Confess."

1948
Pierre Schaeffer coins the term *musique concrète*, for music made up of electronic recordings of natural sounds. *Four Last Songs*, by Richard Strauss, laments the culture destroyed under the Nazis. Olivier Messiaen's *Turangalîla-symphonie* wins global fans.

1950
Pierre Boulez' early masterpiece, the notoriously difficult Second Piano Sonata, is given its world premiere. Muddy Waters records "Rollin' Stone," a Chicago Blues classic.

A Les Paul1952 solid-body electric guitar—the instrument of rock 'n' roll

1952
John Cage composes *4′33″*, whose performers remain silent for 4 minutes and 33 seconds.

1953
Frank Sinatra signs with Capitol Records, where he will record a string of hits.

1954
Karl Stockhausen produces *Studie II*, the first published electronic music score. "Shake, Rattle and Roll" is rock 'n' roll's first big hit, for blues shouter Big Joe Turner and for Bill Haley and the Comets.

1955
Ali Akbar Khan and Chatur Lal introduce Indian classical music to America, at the Museum of Modern Art, New York.

1956
RCA releases Elvis Presley's "Heartbreak Hotel," a rock 'n' roll landmark.

1957
The radically modern musical *West Side Story* opens on Broadway. "Chega de Saudade" is the first bossa nova recording.

1959
Miriam Makeba, the "Voice of Africa," makes her debut on American TV on *The Steve Allen Show*. Motown Records is founded in Detroit.

Elvis on stage in his home town of Tupelo, 1956

Fanzine cover from 1964, when the Beatles toured the United States

1960
Bernard Herrmann's film score adds to the horror in *Psycho*. After the Cuban Revolution, salsa star Celia Cruz and her band defect to the United States.

1961
Brian Epstein sees the Beatles at the Cavern in Liverpool and offers to manage the group.

1962
The Rolling Stones play their first gig and the Irish folk group the Chieftains form; 50 years later, both bands are still performing.

1963
Bob Dylan's "Blowin' in the Wind" resonates with the civil rights movement.

1964
The jazz/bossa nova album *Getz/Gilberto* achieves global fame with the song, "The Girl from Ipanema."

1965
Bob Dylan first plays electric guitar on stage, at London's Royal Albert Hall. Opera legend Maria Callas performs for the last time, as Tosca, in London.

1967
Sgt. Pepper's Lonely Hearts Club Band is released by the Beatles. Soul diva Aretha Franklin's "Respect" becomes a civil rights anthem.

Woodstock, 1969

1968
Luciano Berio's *Sinfonia* is premiered in New York. Tammy Wynette takes country mainstream with "Stand by Your Man."

1969
The Woodstock music festival draws half a million people; Glastonbury follows a year later. Neil Armstrong walks on the Moon, and David Bowie releases "Space Odyssey."

1970
Rock heroes Led Zeppelin release "Whole Lotta Love".

1971
Marc Bolan appears on BBC television's *Top of the Pops* with glitter on his face, ushering in the glam era. As the Cold War and Vietnam War drag on, John Lennon writes "Imagine".

1974
Reggae goes global as Eric Clapton has a No. 1 hit in the United States with Bob Marley's "I Shot The Sheriff". Abba win the Eurovision Song Contest with "Waterloo".

Reggae superstar Bob Marley

...the postwar period produced classical, jazz, and popular music that challenged the notion of what music actually was. Some modern classical composers and jazz artists explored ever more intricate tonality and lyricism; others jettisoned traditional musical values in pursuit of the new and provocative. Rock 'n' roll linked youth-oriented popular music to an insubordinate subculture that alienated the older generation—as did punk and hip-hop. The broad notion of "mainstream" and "alternative" music appeared as popular music fragmented into a diverse array of subgenres, while technology transformed the way music was produced, distributed, and consumed.

1975

1975
Electronic pioneers Kraftwerk promote their *Autobahn* album on a world tour.

1976
The Ramones release their debut album in the US, while the Sex Pistols explode on to the UK scene; together they spawn the punk movement.

Sex Pistols' 1977 single, "God Save the Queen"

1977
Giorgio Moroder produces "I Feel Love" for disco diva Donna Summer, creating the electronic dance music genre.

Dolly Parton topped pop and country music charts in 1977

1978
Steve Reich's *Music For 18 Musicians* gives minimalism a higher profile.

1979
"Rapper's Delight" by the Sugarhill Gang introduces hip-hop to the world.

1980

1980
The Linn LM-1 drum computer goes on sale, defining the sound of 1980s pop.

African djembe

1981
Andrew Lloyd Webber's *Cats* opens in the West End; London's longest-running musical plays for 21 years. MTV launches in the United States.

1982
The compact disc (CD) is introduced in Japan. Minimalism goes to the movies with Michael Nyman's score for Peter Greenaway's *The Draughtsman's Contract*. The annual WOMAD festival is first held in the UK, celebrating world music, art, and dance.

1983
Michael Jackson does his "moonwalk" for the first time on the *Motown 25* TV special. When the Warehouse club opens in Chicago, locals coin the term "house" for its DJs' distinctly new style of electronic dance music.

1985

1985
Live Aid concerts in London and Philadelphia attract a TV audience of almost two billion people to raise funds for famine relief in Ethiopia.

1987
John Adams's opera *Nixon In China*—about the 1972 meeting between the US president and Chairman Mao—premieres in Houston, Texas.

1988
In *Different Trains* for string quartet and tape, minimalism's Steve Reich contrasts the trains of the United States and the Holocaust by using prerecorded interviews to generate musical phrases.

1989
Bosnian musician Goran Bregović provides the Romani soundtrack to the film *The Time of the Gypsies*.

James Maddalena playing Richard Nixon in *Nixon in China*

1990

Nirvana's front man, Kurt Cobain

1991
Nirvana releases *Nevermind*, popularizing grunge. London's Ministry of Sound opens in an unused bus garage, as the UK's first nightclub for American house music.

House and rave spawned a new club culture in the '80s–'90s

1993
Arvo Part records his "Te Deum" in post-Soviet Estonia, winning a new audience for "holy minimalism."

1994
MP3 files begin to appear on the Internet, compressing a huge amount of audio data in a digital format for music streaming and storage. Youssou N'Dour and Neneh Cherry sing "7 Seconds."

1995

1995
Michael Jackson's *HIStory* is the best-selling double album ever. Rock band Grateful Dead perform their final show.

1996
The Spice Girls' debut single "Wannabe" is released.

Kendrick Lamar

1999
Mamma Mia, Abba's jukebox musical, opens in London. Wim Wenders' movie *Buena Vista Social Club* popularizes Cuban music. Death of Amália Rodrigues, Portugal's queen of fado.

2000

2001
Apple's online music store iTunes opens for business.

2004
Influential reality talent show *The X Factor* debuts on UK TV.

2005
YouTube video-sharing website is launched.

2007
The first *High School Musical* film is released.

2008
The music-streaming site Spotify is launched.

2012
YouTube uploads the video for "Gangnam Style" by Korea's Psy, whose horse-riding dance moves go global. Amanda Palmer dispenses with her record company by raising over $1 million from almost 25,000 backers on her website to release her album *Theatre Is Evil*.

2020
Spotify, founded in 2008, now claims 60 percent of music downloads. A number of artists, including Kendrick Lamar, garner tens of millions of monthly listeners.

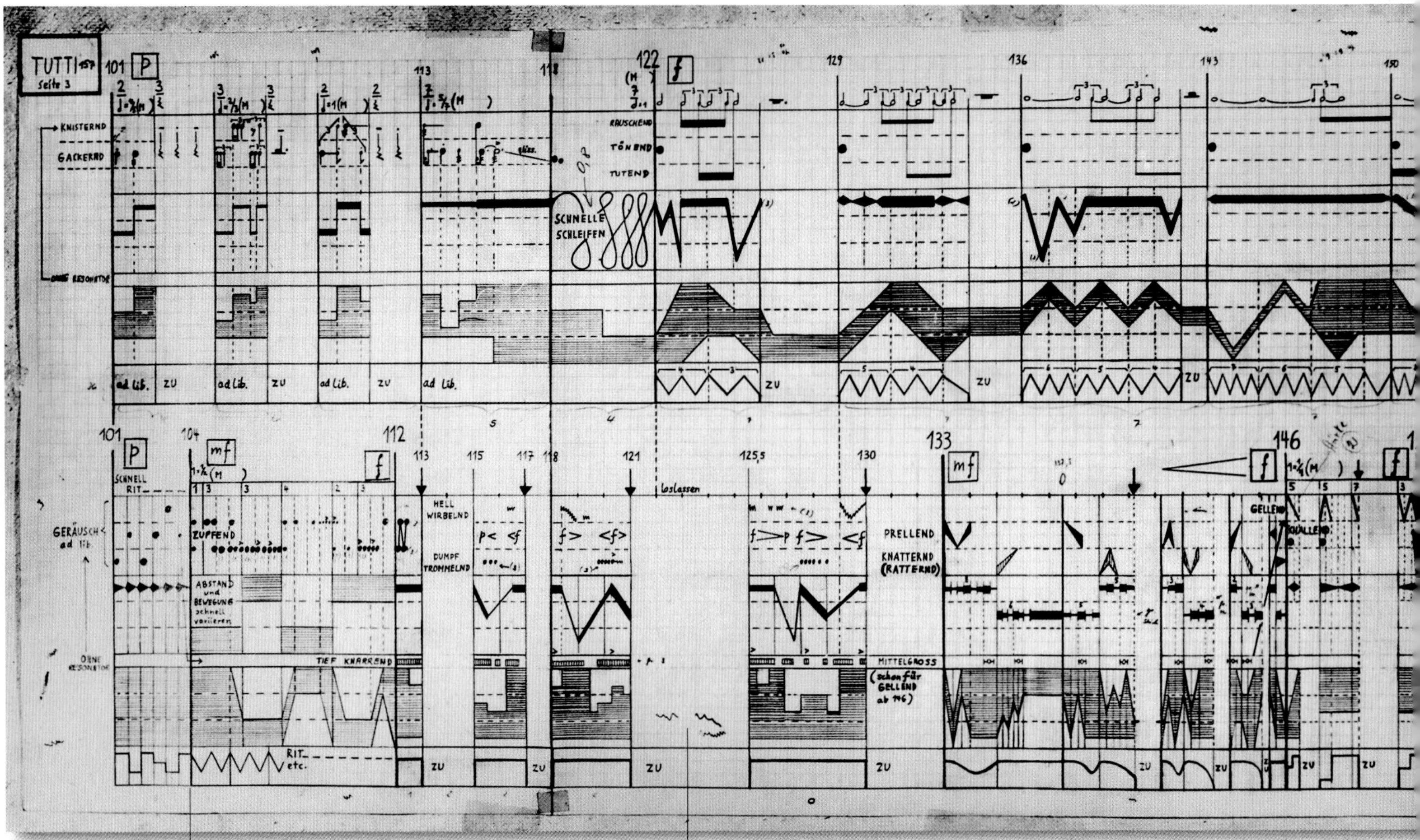

Piece divided into 33 "moments," or structural units, separated here by vertical lines

Section with very little sound detected

BEFORE

Like many revolutions, postwar experimental music was the latest stage in a process of evolution, with strong roots in the recent past.

LIFE IN THE RUINS OF DRESDEN, 1946

CLEARING THE MUSICAL RUBBLE

For a new generation of composers, the destruction caused by World War II (1939–1945) signified the erasing of an old musical world. To launch a new one, they looked to the radical example set by their prewar modernist forerunners, **Schoenberg**, **Webern**, and **Berg** **<< 210–211**.

Experimental Music

The end of war in 1945 heralded the rise of an uncompromising fresh generation of European modernist composers. Individually very different, they shared a common purpose: to set the tone of a new peacetime era by forging ahead with revolutionary methods of composing.

The most prominent of the new personalities was France's Pierre Boulez (1925–2016). Arriving as a student at the Paris Conservatoire with only a limited musical upbringing, Boulez quickly made a name for himself as a multitalented, furiously energetic musical voice. Besides his spectacular composing skills, his abilities as a pianist and scholar of music made a huge impact.

For Boulez, the prewar musical past was a slate to be wiped clean. Almost everything composed up to that point, he insisted, was outdated and irrelevant. He felt that the only valid path for his own generation was to develop the radical modernist possibilities opened up by the music of Austria's Arnold Schoenberg, Anton von Webern, and Alban Berg in the first decades of the 20th century (see pp.210–211). Boulez and his colleagues began to develop the idea of "serial" music. This meant extending the scope of Schoenberg's method of 12-note composition that predetermined the order of the notes in a piece of music so that no single note dominated. In serial music, the same kind of organization was now applied to the duration (rhythmic units) and dynamics (volume level) of the notes.

12 **The number of randomly tuned portable radios used in John Cage's 1951 piece *Imaginary Landscape No. 4*.**

Boulez's tumultuous, ultra-virtuoso style produced an early masterpiece in his Second Piano Sonata (1948), and in 1955 he completed *Le marteau sans maître* (The Hammer Without a Master), a work for mezzo-soprano and chamber group set to surrealist poetry. When his work *Le visage nuptial* (The Nuptial Countenance) was revised and expanded as a choral and orchestral cantata in 1958, it proved so difficult to perform that the only person capable of conducting it was Boulez himself. This was to be the start of his career as one of the world's leading conductors.

Modernists in the ascendancy

Boulez's charisma made him a dominant presence at the influential summer music school founded in 1946

Wired for sound
The "score" of *Mikrophonie 1*, written in 1964 by Karlheinz Stockhausen, shows how the sounds of a large tam-tam (gong) are electronically transformed during a live performance.

at Darmstadt, West Germany, to which leading lights of the new generation of composers made annual pilgrimages. Among these were the Germans Hans Werner Henze (1926–2012) and Karlheinz Stockhausen (1928–2007), the latter's work setting new standards of fearsome technical complexity (see pp.270–271).

Two other avant-garde composers who attended Darmstadt were Italy's Luigi Nono (1924–1990) and the American John Cage (1912–1992). For Nono, revolutionary new music was also about revolutionary political commitment. In 1956, he produced an impassioned statement in *Il canto sospeso* (The Suspended Song) for soloists, chorus, and orchestra, based on the writings of resistance fighters executed in World War II.

Inspired by the East

John Cage had a different take on modernism. His interest in Eastern philosophy and Zen Buddhism led him to examine the role that chance played in music. The creation of his *Music of Changes* (1951) for piano was determined by the *I Ching*, the ancient Chinese book of divination, and his *4′33″* (1952) was composed for any combination of performers, who remain silent for the duration of the work's title. These ideas of chance-determined "aleatory music" (from the Latin *alea*, for dice) now began to influence other composers, including Boulez, who explored it in his Third Piano Sonata (1957).

An extra string to his bow
Pierre Boulez leads Switzerland's Lucerne Festival Academy Orchestra through a rehearsal. Besides a lifetime of activity as a composer and writer, Boulez has been a top conductor since the late 1950s.

Going electric

A new musical age brought with it the electronic studio. It became possible to compose by generating electronic sounds, without having to rely on the limitations of instruments or voices. *Cinq études de bruits* (Five Studies of Noises), written in 1948 by France's Pierre Schaeffer (1910–1995), was one of the first works of *musique concrète* (concrete music), manipulating sounds from gramophone records.

Another groundbreaking electronic work was Stockhausen's 1956 *Gesang der Jünglinge* (Song of the Youths), in which a boy's tape-recorded treble voice was electronically deconstructed, transformed, and then reassembled on tape. In 1958, Italy's Luciano Berio (1925–2003) took a similar approach in *Thema: Omaggio a Joyce* (Theme: Homage to Joyce), based on electronic transformation of the voice of his wife, the soprano Cathy Berberian, reading from James Joyce's novel *Ulysses*.

Decades earlier, in prewar America, the French émigré composer Edgard Varèse (1883–1965) had dreamed of working in musical media yet to be invented. Now he could create his *Poème électronique* (Electronic Poem), a piece of electronically generated sounds transferred to four-track magnetic tape, which preceded his works for orchestra—*Ameriques*, *Octandre*, and *Arcana*. The *Poème* was played at the 1958 Brussels World Fair, channeled through 400 loudspeakers placed around the interior of the Philips pavilion.

> "All **non-serial composers** are **useless.**"
>
> PIERRE BOULEZ, IN THE ESSAY "SCHOENBERG IS DEAD," 1952

Pupils teach the master

In Frenchman Olivier Messiaen (see below right) the new musical generation had a father figure. Besides his success as a composer, he was a leading teachers of his time, with Boulez, Stockhausen, and other young talents attending his composition class at the Paris Conservatoire.

Although not sharing his students' combative and secular musical values (he was a devout Catholic), Messiaen felt an instinctive affinity with some of their progressive ideas. His early music, with its richly expressive sound, had developed from the example of Claude Debussy (see pp.204–205). Now teacher turned pupil, and Messiaen found himself being influenced by the avant-garde younger composers and their music's complex technical methods. Messiaen's *Four Rhythmic Studies*, written in 1949–1950 for his pianist wife Yvonne Loriod, drew directly on the technique of serial music pioneered by Boulez, as did the rich tapestry of colorful orchestral sounds assembled in his *Chronochromie* (The Color of Time) written in 1960.

The composer's toolbox of tricks
John Cage wrote a number of compositions, including *Sonatas and Interludes* (1946–1948), for "prepared piano," its sounds altered and adapted by objects placed on or between the strings.

AFTER »

As the Darmstadt era of the 1950s and 60s began to lose collective momentum, its leading composers went their separate ways.

FORKS IN THE MUSICAL ROAD

Stockhausen immersed himself in the 1960s musical counterculture **270–271 »**, producing in 1968 his hypnotic *Stimmung* (Tuning or Mood) for six solo voices. **John Cage** embraced electronic music, mixing it with conventional instruments, before returning in the late 1960s to more traditional notation.

For **Messiaen**, his Catholic faith and the world of nature remained central inspirations. His 1983 opera *Saint François d'Assise* (St. Francis of Assisi) depicts the life of the Italian saint in a vast musical fresco, celebrating both the composer's and the saint's love of birdsong.

KEY WORKS

Pierre Boulez Piano Sonata No. 2; *Le marteau sans maître*

John Cage *Music of Changes*; *Sonatas and Interludes*

Karlheinz Stockhausen *Gesang der Jünglinge*

Luigi Nono *Il canto sospeso*

Olivier Messiaen *Chronochromie*

COMPOSER (1908–1992)

OLIVIER MESSIAEN

Born in Avignon, France, Messiaen studied at the Paris Conservatoire in the late 1920s, composing *Le banquet céleste* (The Heavenly Feast) for organ and the piano *Préludes* while a student. Captured while on service in World War II, Messiaen was sent to a prison camp in Silesia, now in Poland, where he wrote and performed in the *Quartet for the End of Time*. The monumental ten-movement *Turangalîla-symphonie* (1948) confirmed his global reputation.

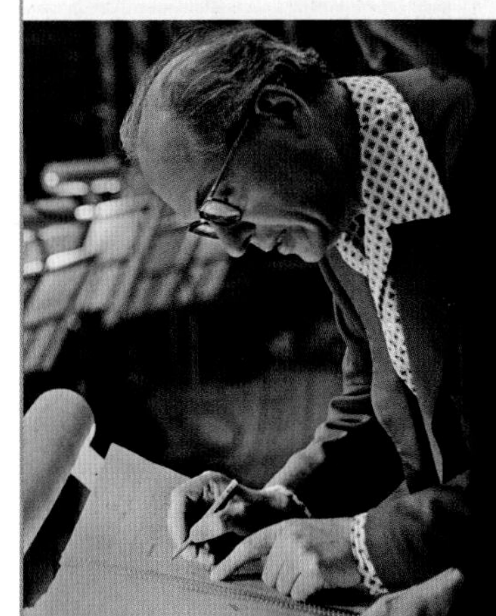

Modern Chanson

The modern *chanson* is a phenomenon of 20th-century Paris. The songs were written by literate, charismatic composer-performers who had individual political, poetic, comic, or romantic world views. In France, these *chanteurs* and *chanteuses* are considered folk heroes.

There is a saying, *"tout finit par des chansons"* or "everything ends with songs," which reflects the importance of popular song in France. *La chanson* is part of the country's national identity. In the 20th century, the ambitious, passionate *"auteur-compositeur-interprète,"* the French name for singer-songwriters, continued the centuries-long tradition of *chansons français* as a popular musical form of journalism, poetry, and storytelling.

Reaffirming the connection that French society has with this particular form of popular song, the *chanson* and its performers communicated with the French public at a deep cultural level. Yet, for the most part, *chanson* meant little to the wider popular music world.

Musically, *chanson* has no standard format, beyond being easy to listen to. It often utilizes accessible folk/pop song structures with limited harmonic movement, but often with a vigorous rhythm, whether a traditional march or waltz, or more voguish settings such as swing and tango.

The success of *chanson* lies in the effectiveness of its performance. Although there are many memorable *chanson* melodies, the musical setting always serves as support to the vivid delivery of the lyric.

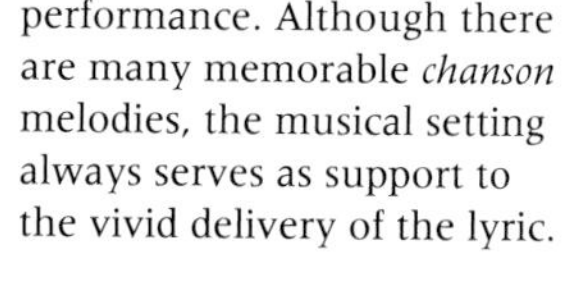

BEFORE

The provocative, irreverent founder of the modern chanson employed the artist Toulouse Lautrec to popularize his concerts with posters.

"REALIST" SONGS

The singer-songwriter **Aristide Bruant** (1851–1925) wrote and sang guttural and bawdy songs known as *chanson realiste* about the ill-fated street characters of Paris. He performed in his own Montmartre club, Mirliton, where he was well-known for insulting his guests, as well as in the famous Chat Noir. His humorous, ironic celebration of the working and criminal class made him a favorite of the petty-bourgeois intellectuals of the city.

POSTER BY TOULOUSE LAUTREC, 1892

Saved from accountancy

Although his style and subject matter are lighter than that of many of the singer-songwriters who followed, Charles Trenet is a founding father of the modern *chanson*. The Belgian singer Jacques Brel observed, "Without him, we'd all be chartered accountants."

Prominent as a performer from the late 1930s until the 1950s, Trenet was given his nickname *"Le Fou Chantant,"* the Singing Madman, while doing military service. He performed only his own material, which was unique at the time. His songs ranged from romantic and nostalgic pieces to witty, whimsical ditties, full of surreal detail, often musically set in an American-style swing. His most famous songs include the onomatopoeic "Boum!," which was used in the James Bond movie *Skyfall* (playing through speakers in the villain's bombed-out island), and "La Mer," which was translated as "Beyond the Sea" and covered by numerous artists over the years.

400 **The number of recordings of Charles Trenet's "La Mer."**

1,000 **The number of songs written by Charles Aznavour.**

Piaf and Brel

Singers Yvette Guilbert and Mireille Mathieu did much to elevate the nuanced theatricality of chanson performance during the early 20th century, but it was Edith Piaf who became best known.

S.N. PATHE-CINEMA PRÉSENTE
CHARLES TRENET
Romance de Paris
JEAN TISSIER
YVETTE LEBON
ALERME
UN FILM DE
JEAN BOYER

Father of the genre
This Charles Trenet movie poster is from occupied Paris in 1941, where Trenet continued his career after being demobilized. He made his last album at the age of 86.

One of the few figures to translate her fame beyond France, Piaf made recordings that are recognized worldwide, including "La Vie En Rose," "Je ne regrette rien," and "Milord." A dramatic performer, she was known as the Little Sparrow, due to the delicacy of her build and her tremulous portrayal of emotional fragility. Although largely an interpreter rather than a creator of *chansons*, Piaf set the standard for performance with her great stage presence, intense theatricality, and powerful voice, influencing the style of many singer-songwriters who saw her, including Jacques Brel.

Belgian-born Jacques Brel moved to Paris in 1953 at the age of 34, and was soon a popular performer in the city's clubs and cafés. He railed against what he considered the ordinary and the mediocre in both his life and in his art, and dedicated his existence to risk and adventure. Brel's vigorous performance style and provocative subject matter was sometimes characterized as "violent." He disagreed: "It's not violence," he said, "it's anger." The source of his anger was what he saw as the indolence, complacency, and ignorance of society.

Brel's obsessive, lusty *chansons* dealt with the complex adult subjects of love, death, hypocrisy, exploitation, ego, and sex, in a charged, theatrically stylized manner. Some of his work trickled into the English-speaking world via international concerts. His work was promoted by British pop-star Scott Walker, and translated in cover versions such as "Le Moribund" ("Seasons In the Sun," a UK number one for Terry Jacks in 1974) and *"Ne me quitte pas"* ("If You Go Away"), later recorded by Nina Simone and Barbra Streisand, among many others.

Inspired by literature

Georges Brassens was at least as forthright, anti-establishment, and important to modern chanson as Brel. He rarely left France, however, and his songs—inspired by his study of 19th-century French literature by Baudelaire, Hugo, and Verlaine—resisted effective translation. Like Aristide Bruant 50 years before him, Brassens took great delight in shocking

KEY WORKS

Charles Trenet "Que reste-t'il de nos amour?"

Edith Piaf "Je ne regrette rien"; "La Vie En Rose"

Jacques Brel "Ne me quitte pas"

Léo Ferré "Avec le temps"

Georges Brassens "Le pornograph"

Charles Aznavour "Apres l'amour"

Going his own way
"The Bad Reputation" (1953) is a semiautobiographical song by George Brassens in which he complains that people do not like anyone who chooses to go a different way from their own.

the French middle classes with "Le Gorille" (The Gorilla), "Le Mauvais Sujet Repenti" (The Wicked Repented), and other lewd, satirical songs.

Another singer-songwriter with radical streak was singer-pianist Léo Ferré, who began in the mid-1940s as a flamboyant cabaret performer and, with his satirical anarchic material, became popular with left-wing audiences in the 1950s. His most famous piece is the elegiac "Avec le temps."

The "chanteur" abroad

Mentored as a young songwriter by Edith Piaf, Charles Aznavour matured into an internationally popular singer, composing in German, Italian, Spanish and English. Specializing in complex love songs, Aznavour had an appealing, throaty quality to his vocals and inhabited his material to an uncanny degree. His willingness to venture onto the world stage (he was appointed Armenian ambassador to Switzerland) led to an international profile denied to his peers, most of whom did not stray far from their Parisian, or at least French, fan base.

AFTER

When Serge Gainsbourg died in 1991 at the age of 62, the president of France, Françcois Mitterand, said the singer-songwriter had "lifted the song to the level of art."

FEARLESS BOHEMIAN

SERGE GAINSBOURG AND JANE BIRKIN

Paris-born Gainsbourg started as a cabaret performer in the late 1950s and went on to compose a Eurovision song contest winner "Poupée de cire, Poupée de son." He recorded in the **reggae**, **electronica**, **art pop**, and **Africana** genres, establishing himself as one of the most individual and fearless artists in **European pop music**. Gainsbourg's love life and bohemian persona seemed only to emphasize his poetic and musical gravitas. Although perhaps best known internationally for "Je t'Aime, Moi Non Plus," the risqué 1969 duet with Jane Birkin, his influence has been considerable.

"**I don't** write **poetry,** I'm no poet. **I write songs.**"

JACQUES BREL IN A TV INTERVIEW

The Little Sparrow sings
Edith Piaf began singing at the age of 14, and her extraoraordnary life was part of the *chanteuse*'s appeal. It was made into a movie, *La Vie en Rose*, the title of one her songs, in 2007. This photograph was taken during a recording session in 1937.

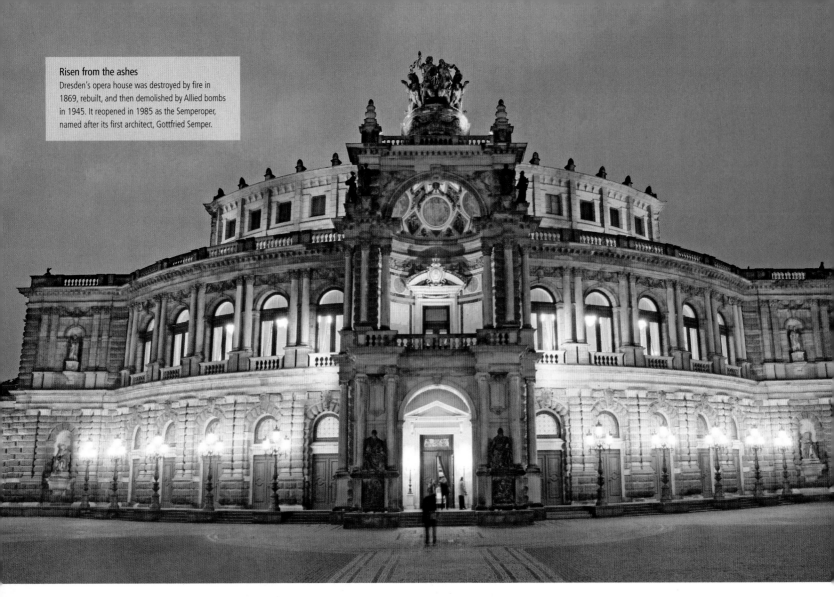

Risen from the ashes

Dresden's opera house was destroyed by fire in 1869, rebuilt, and then demolished by Allied bombs in 1945. It reopened in 1985 as the Semperoper, named after its first architect, Gottfried Semper.

BEFORE

When the Nazis came to power in Germany, Jewish composers fled and some forms of music were banned.

MUSICAL EXILES

In 1933, Hitler became Chancellor of Germany and introduced anti-Jewish laws. Composers fled, many to the United States—among them **Arnold Schoenberg « 210–211, Kurt Weill « 261**, and **Erich Korngold 291 »**.

AN UNEASY HOME FRONT

Nazis censorship of Entartete Musik, or "degenerate music," included **jazz** and **Romany** music (due to their non-Aryan roots) and **modernist** compositions **« 266–267**.

KEY WORKS

Richard Strauss *Four Last Songs*

Hans Werner Henze *Boulevard Solitude*

Karlheinz Stockhausen *Gruppen*

Hanns Eisler *German Symphony*

Karl Amadeus Hartmann *Concerto funèbre*

The **German Revival**

After the shame of war, defeat, and the full exposure of Nazi crimes, there was an urgent need to rebuild German culture—including classical music, the most Germanic of art forms. This was complicated by the splitting of the old country into two new, ideologically different states.

The postwar division of Germany into the Democratic Republic (East Germany, under Soviet influence) and the Federal Republic (West Germany) created separate nations with little shared cultural contact. In terms of modern classical music, West Germany dominated, but many East German musical institutions remained world-class—notably its orchestras, such as the Dresden *Staatskapelle* (meaning "state chapel"), and the Leipzig *Gewandhaus* (named after the hall where textile merchants once traded in cloth).

In the aftermath of war, many citizens of both countries underwent a shaming process for those suspected of having played any part in the defeated regime. Among the musicians forced to submit were Richard Strauss (see pp.222–223), whose *Four Last Songs* (1948) are the dying breath of a culture destroyed by the war, and the conductors Wilhelm Furtwängler (1886–1954) and Herbert von Karajan (1908–1989).

Some composers emerged untainted by any Nazi association, including Karl Amadeus Hartmann (1905–1963), who throughout the Nazi era refused to allow his music to be performed. After the war, he revised his prewar music to reflect a changed world: his 1939 *Trauermusik* (Mourning Music) reemerged in 1959 as the *Concerto funèbre* (Funeral Concerto). He also curated a concert series entitled Musica Viva, reviving music suppressed by the Nazis. First held in Munich in 1945, the concerts continue to champion new music to this day.

Opera on the grandest scale

A stark cover fronts a recording of Bernd Alois Zimmermann's *Die Soldaten* (The Soldiers). First seen in 1965, it was an ambitious antimilitaristic satire, requiring a huge orchestra and multiple screens.

Among the new breed of composers there was an overwhelming urge to break with the past. A generation younger than Hartmann, Hans Werner Henze (see right) had reluctantly served as a soldier during the war, including a period as a prisoner of the British. For a time he was part of a loose-knit group of composers who congregated at a summer school held in Darmstadt, West Germany. There, he encountered new ideas, music, and composers from Europe and the rest of the world.

14 **The number of helicopters needed for a performance of Stockhausen's 1993 "Helicopter String Quartet," part of his massive opera cycle *Licht* (*Light*).**

Forging a new beginning

"Darmstadt school" became shorthand for an international avant-garde style that took the modernist ideas of Arnold Schoenberg and Anton von Webern (see pp.210–211) to an extreme. Henze's war experiences had made him wary of a rigid musical approach. His first full-scale opera, *Boulevard Solitude*, acknowledged inspiration from such disparate sources as Kurt Weill (see pp.158–159) and jazz.

Henze became disillusioned with Darmstadt, but the school continued to play a vital role in the regeneration of German music. Among those who attended was Bernd Alois Zimmermann (1918–1970), who during the war had served in France, where he was struck by the energy he heard in the music of Stravinsky (see pp.212–213) and Darius Milhaud (see p.205). After the war, he continued to draw not only on the vast history of Western classical music, including his contemporaries, but also on non-classical forms, including jazz. Such eclecticism made him unpopular in some circles, but it was part of a wider movement to reshape German music without completely rejecting the past.

Cutting-edge technology

Hardly less important than the Darmstadt school were regional radio stations such as Westdeutscher Rundfunk (WDR), based in Cologne, and Hessischer Rundfunk (HR) in Frankfurt. In 1951, WDR established an electronic studio to take advantage of technological advances in recording equipment. Among the composers who flocked to the studio was another Darmstadt visionary, Karlheinz Stockhausen (see pp.270–271).

From the very beginning of his career, Stockhausen was a composer of epic ambition. His vast *Gruppen* (Groups), composed in 1955–1957, required three separate orchestras and three conductors. It received its premiere from the Cologne Radio Symphony Orchestra, the in-house orchestra of WDR.

Making waves

Stockhausen experimented in the "Studio for Electronic Music" at the WDR radio station, shown here in around 1960. It was in this studio that he produced a new musical language.

By the 1960s, a generation of composers was emerging whose development had hardly been touched by Nazism and war. Prominent among them was Helmut Lachenmann (1935–), who from as early as his 1972 string quartet *Gran Torso* showed a capacity to extend musical expression to include all manner of scraping, creeping, and scratching sounds in a sound world that has its own strange and intricate beauty.

The postwar revival saw the building or rebuilding of many German opera houses and concert halls, including in Berlin, Munich, and Leipzig. The new auditoriums reflected German music's renewed confidence, with cutting-edge acoustics to match (see below).

Pulling aside the Iron Curtain

Few composers who fled Germany in the 1930s were inclined to return to communist East Germany. One who did was Hanns Eisler (1898–1962). He had studied with Schoenberg in the 1920s, but as a Communist he sought to compose serious music that ordinary listeners could enjoy, with influences drawn from jazz and cabaret (see pp.256–257). In exile, he worked in Hollywood with fellow émigrés, playwright Bertolt Brecht and film-maker Fritz Lang. After the war, Eisler was put on the Hollywood studios' blacklist, accused of being the "Karl Marx of music." Expelled from the United States in 1948, he returned to East Germany, composing the new nation's national anthem. His greatest work is the *German Symphony* (using texts by Brecht), begun in the 1930s as "an antifascist cantata" but not completed until the 1950s.

It is opera, though, that may have seen East Germany's most enduring contribution to postwar musical life. Austrian director Walter Felsenstein (1901–1975) pioneered an innovative, precise production method at Berlin's Komische Opera from 1947 that stressed acting as much as music, and put the words in the local language. The style gradually transformed the staging of opera around the world.

COMPOSER (1926–2012)

HANS WERNER HENZE

Influenced by his youth in Nazi Germany, from early in his career Hans Werner Henze showed an abiding commitment to left-wing politics, often reflected in his music. Visits to Cuba inspired the music theater piece *El Cimarrón* (1970), about a person who escapes enslavement, while his opera *We Come to the River* (1976) outraged many with its strident antiwar position. Yet, as his ten symphonies show, Henze was equally committed to lyricism and melody.

"It's about **breaking the old context,** by whatever means, **to break the sounds,** looking into their anatomy."

HELMUT LACHENMANN, COMPOSER, IN A MAGAZINE INTERVIEW, 2003

UNDERSTANDING MUSIC

ACOUSTICS

How a room distributes sound—its acoustics—is a challenge for every concert hall. Instead of scale models, most acousticians now use computers to work with an auditorium's shape, materials, and soundproofing. Some designers opt for a shoe-box form for the auditorium, others prefer fanlike structures. The revolutionary design of Berlin's Philharmonie (opened in 1963) has the orchestra encircled by rising terraces of seats for the audience.

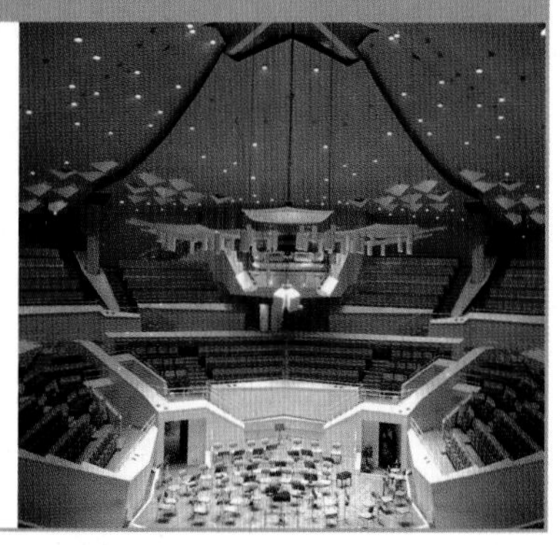

AFTER 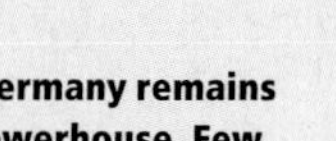

Reunited in 1991, Germany remains a classical music powerhouse. Few other countries are so committed to the making of challenging new music.

COMPOSER BABY BOOMERS

Part of Hans Werner Henze's music legacy is the **Munich Biennale**, set up in 1988 as a festival and showcase for contemporary opera. Although he has never performed at the Biennale, **Wolfgang Rihm** (1952–) is among the most prolific German composers: since composing his First Symphony in 1968, he has written hundreds of works in every genre from solo piano to grand opera. Just as versatile is **Heiner Goebbels** (1952–), whose pieces such as *Eislermaterial* (a tribute to Hanns Eisler) and *Black on White* mix theater and installation art, improvization and traditional notation, classical and popular.

LEIPZIG'S GEWANDHAUS CONCERT HALL (1981)

BEFORE

The Romany people have spent a millennium on the move, adapting and influencing the music of countries along the way.

INDIAN ROOTS
The Romany people have their roots in India. Some historians trace their origins to Rajasthan in the 11th century and claim elements of Romany music can be heard in the music of modern **Rajasthani bands**. The musical culture of the Roma traveled via Turkey and Egypt, from which the term "gypsy," sometimes considered derogatory, derives—to spread across Europe, Arabia, North Africa, and the Americas.

4 MILLION **The number of Roma thought to live in Europe.**

200 **The number of beats per minute played by Fanfare Ciocărlia band.**

FUSING CULTURES
Although the musical heartland of the Romany is, at present, in Central and Eastern Europe, their music is a **fusion** of elements from many cultures, including Greece, Turkey, and Spain. **Flamenco « 178–179** is considered to be a music with a debt to the Romany people.

Romany Music

The spirited and spontaneous music of the Romany people has traveled from East to West, only to be marginalized and oppressed. Now it is admired all over the world, attracting large audiences and winning awards.

The Romany musical tradition is strongest in Hungary, Romania, and the countries of the Balkan peninsula, where it taps the roots of indigenous folk music—including slow, plaintive singing, fast melodies for dancing, hand claps, mouth clacking, and wooden spoons—and combines it with Eastern elements such as glissandi (sliding between notes), timbral manipulation, and improvisation.

Historically, the Roma have often lived as wandering entertainers and traders, and their music is most at home in a live, festival setting. Across the Balkans and Central Europe, Romany musicians often earned their living by playing for village weddings.

As they traveled, they became familiar with the local folk sound, added their own flourishes, and

UNDERSTANDING MUSIC

GLISSANDI

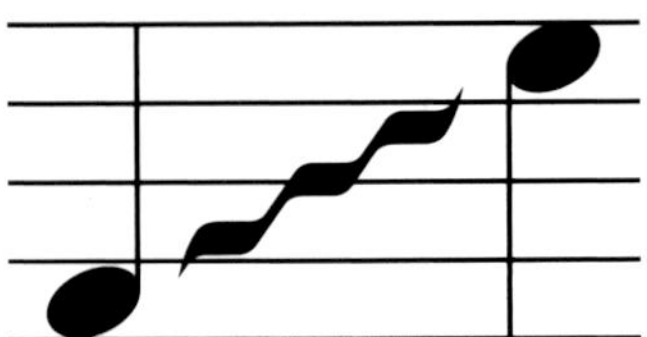

A straight or squiggly line between two notes on sheet music represents a *glissando*, an instruction that one note should glide (from the French *glisser*) to another. The device is frequently heard in Romany music—typically on string instruments. On the guitar, for example, a finger of the left hand slides up the string while the fingers of the right hand hurriedly pick out the notes, resulting in a feverish, virtuosic sound. The technique is not confined to stringed instruments. One of the best-known examples of *glissandi* are the opening bars of George Gershwin's *Rhapsody in Blue*, played on a clarinet.

French Romanies
A boy dances to Romany music in France. There are more than half a million Romanies in the country, and they have produced a number of musicians, including the popular Gypsy Kings.

KEY WORKS

Django Reinhardt "St. Louis Blues"

Emir Kusturica & The No Smoking Orchestra *Time of the Gypsies* (Punk Opera)

Taraf de Haidouks *Musiques de Tziganes de Roumanie*

Esma Redzepova *Songs of a Macedonian Gypsy* (with Usnija Jasarova)

Fanare Ciocarlia *World Wide Wedding*

produced a crowd-pleasing hybrid. Romany would frequently play with Jewish klezmer musicians from Eastern Europe.

Historically, Roma lived on the edges of towns and villages due to discriminatory policies that prevented full integration, and this setting has given the music its themes—romance and revelry, drinking, rural life, and country games.

Emotional variety

Romany music can be heartbreakingly sad, and there are subgenres of slow-paced lyrical songs that function as a kind of catharsis or shared outpouring of grief.

At the same time, fast-paced dances such as the Bulgarian *horos* and *trite pati* or the Hungarian *xuttjadi djili* (leaping song) and spirited ensemble playing of the fiddle, drums, and *zurna* (a woodwind instrument similar to a shawm) are joyous. They provide the kind of energetic drive that can power the days-long celebrations that accompany Romany weddings and festivals.

Ottoman legacy

The violin is the central instrument of Romany music, and the hammered dulcimer, or cimbalom, is also popular. The brass bands of modern Romany music are a legacy of the military bands of the Ottoman occupation of the Balkans and the massive Trumpet Festival of Guca, in modern-day Serbia, where more than 200 groups compete, now draws audiences from across Europe.

Influencing other music

In the 19th century, nationalist stirrings in Central and Eastern Europe exploited Romany culture. Musicians such as the virtuoso pianist Franz Liszt (see pp.160–161) and, later, the composer Béla Bartók (see pp.214–215) borrowed elements of the Romany tradition in their classical compositions.

During the 20th century, however, Romany culture was subject to assimilation and oppression in the Nazi, Soviet, and Eastern Bloc regimes. An estimated 600,000 Roma were exterminated during the Holocaust.

The 1988 film *The Time of the Gypsies*, by the Serbian director, actor, and musician Emir Kusturica, educated Western audiences about the Romany and provided a platform for the music of the Bosnian composer Goran Bregovic, who fronts a 40-piece band made up of a brass contingent, bagpipers, a string ensemble, and an all-male choir.

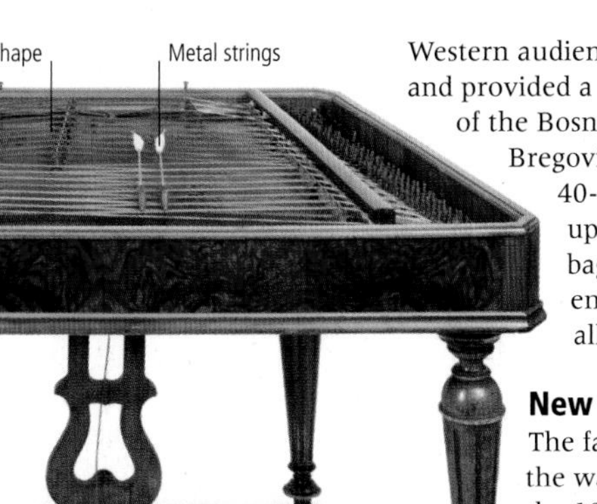

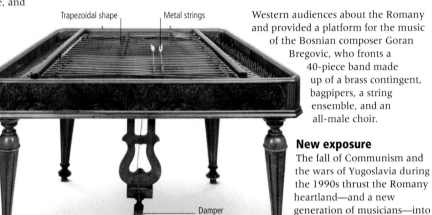

The percussive sound
A European folk instrument, the cimbalon is played by striking two hand-held beaters on the strings. It is a variant of the concert hammered dulcimer and can be found in many countries around the world.

JAZZ GUITARIST (1910–1953)

DJANGO REINHARDT

A brilliant soloist who forged a distinctive style rooted in his Romany origins, Django Reinhardt was the first outstanding European jazz musician. He grew up in a Romany settlement outside Paris and learned violin and guitar. In 1928, a fire resulted in the mutilation of his left hand, after which he devised a special fingering method to overcome his handicap. He performed in cafés in Paris, and in 1934 was a founding member of the Quintette du Hot Club de France. He toured the United States as a soloist with Duke Ellington's band, and his short compositions, such as *"St. Louis Blues"* (1937), are masterpieces of rhythm and inflection.

New exposure

The fall of Communism and the wars of Yugoslavia during the 1990s thrust the Romany heartland—and a new generation of musicians—into the spotlight. The film *Latcho Drom* (1993), directed by Tony Gatlif, a French filmmaker of Romany extraction, told the story of the great journey of the Roma from India to Eastern Europe. Shortly afterward, Emir Kusturica's film *Underground* (1995), which won the prestigious Palme d'Or at the Cannes Film Festival, provided Goran Bregovic with a hit soundtrack album.

Romania's Fanfare Ciocărlia, Serbia's Boban Marković, and Macedonia's Kočani Orkestar have all played a role in bringing the bold brass and woodwind Romany sound to Western ears. In Spain and France, guitar and voice dominate, but in the recordings of the Camargue-based Gitano Family or the late genius Django Reinhardt (see above), the Romany roots of the music are clearly audible.

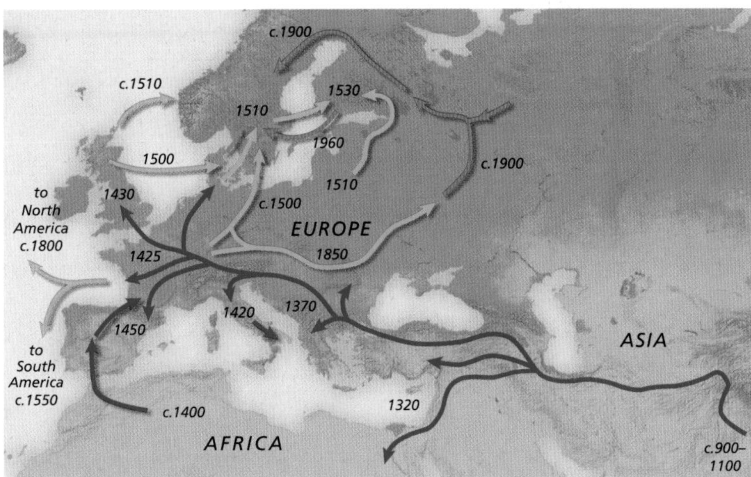

Migration to Europe
The first documented evidence of Romany peoples in Europe is in 14th-century Greece, where they are thought to have come from Egypt. They also migrated to Europe from Asia via Turkey.

KEY
- 1900 onward
- 1500–1900
- 900–1500

AFTER

The rise of "world music" has brought new interest in Romany festivals and bands, and tour firms promote vacations that include music events.

TAKING ON THE WORLD
There is room in the modern Romany scene for every shade of Romany-influenced music, from the **traditionalist** Rajkó Orchestra and Folk Ensemble to Bregović, who has collaborated with **rock** star Iggy Pop. It embraces other musical genres, with Slovakia's Vera Bílá melding her impassioned native singing style with **Brazilian melodies** and rhythms.

A NEW SHOWCASE
The legacy of Django Reinhardt lives on in the work of French guitarist **Birelli Lagrene**, and the inclusion of Macedonian diva Esma Redzepova—**"Queen of the Gypsies"**—in the 2013 Eurovision Song Contest gave Romany traditions a new audience.

Loud and invigorating
The award-winning 12-piece Romany brass band Fanfare Ciocărlia is renowned for its incredibly energetic, virtuosic performances, old instruments, and random interruptions.

Brazilian Beats

Brazil's musical landscape is one of the most vibrant in the world. Influences from indigenous folk culture, Africa, and Europe combine to make a unique musical language. Since the 1960s, samba and bossa nova beats have seduced musicians and audiences worldwide.

BEFORE

Brazil's musical history dates back thousands of years, to when clapping and stamping first provided a powerful rhythmic energy.

MANY INFLUENCES
Music and dancing formed a central aspect of festivals and celebrations throughout Brazil. From 1500, **Portuguese settlers** brought influences from Europe, North Africa, the Middle East, and India, including instruments—**tambourine**, the **accordion**, the simple **clarinet**, and stringed instruments—and European modes and scales patterns.

The slave trade introduced characteristics of **African music**, including certain melodic devices (notably a **flattened seventh** note in a major scale) and elaborate **off-beat** (syncopated) rhythmic patterns. Africans in Brazil also developed **capoeira**—a mixture of martial art and rhythmic dance, with associated call and response songs.

Music is part of everyday life in Brazil, heard in cafés, concert halls, sports grounds, and at the annual pre-Lent Mardi Gras carnivals held all over the country. Rhythm is at the heart of all Brazilian music, especially the use of syncopation—where the accent is shifted unexpectedly from a strong to a weak beat. Inspired by the complex rhythms of African drumming, it gives Brazilian music the irresistible sway that makes everyone want to dance.

Traditional music

Music and dance are intertwined in Brazilian traditional music, as is the terminology: samba, for example, can mean a dance, a musical style, and a rhythm. Folk and popular cultures have melded together, and regional variations of musical styles survive alongside urban versions.

Each region of Brazil has evolved its own musical traditions and styles, which are still heard at local festivals. In Recife and Olinda in the northeast, for example, colorful parades take place against a backdrop of African-inspired maracatu performances by drummers accompanying a singer and chorus, dancers, and stock characters, including a king and queen and tribal deities. The fast and furious frevo is a popular dance number, played on brass at carnivals and soccer games. It transforms the martial art of capoeira into a contest between dancers leaping and lunging with umbrellas.

Brazil's oldest style of popular urban instrumental music is choro, often called *chorinho* ("little cry" or "little lament"). Blending African rhythms and European dance genres, it started in Rio de Janeiro around 1870, when groups of *chorões* (serenaders) performed dances and sentimental songs in the street. Despite its name, it is usually cheerful, fast, and virtuosic, with showy improvisation. It traditionally has a trio of instruments—flute, guitar, and *cavaquinho* (a small four-stringed instrument resembling a ukulele)—although today bands often add a mandolin, clarinet, brass, and a rhythm section of bass guitar and *pandeiro* tambourine. Composer Villa-Lobos (1887–1959) defined *choro* as the true incarnation of Brazilian soul.

300 **The approximate number of street bands that take part in the carnival in Rio de Janeiro each year.**

Samba and bossa nova

Beginning in villages as a folk dance for a couple, the urbanized samba is the best-known musical form in Brazil, popular in the eastern cities of Rio de Janeiro, São Paolo, and Salvador. The easy, singable melodies are often performed in simple harmony with call and answer between soloist and vocal ensemble. The swaying, syncopated rhythm in the accompaniment is articulated by a particular set of percussion instruments associated with samba: the *berimbau* (single-stringed bow); *tamborim* and *pandeiro* (tambourines); *surdo, timba,* and *caixa* (drums); *agogô* (double-headed bell); and *reco-reco* (scraper), *ganza* (rattle), and *chocalho* (shaker).

The less percussive, more languid bossa nova ("new trend") emerged from the samba in the 1950s and '60s. The melody can be deliberately at odds with the harmony, the resulting dissonance creating an expressive tension—as in Carlos Jobim's famous number "Desafinado" (Off-key). The lyrics tend to be reflective, about love, beauty, and loss. The typical setup is piano, classical guitar, and vocals, although there are also arrangements for full orchestra. The gently syncopated rhythm creates an air of easy suavity.

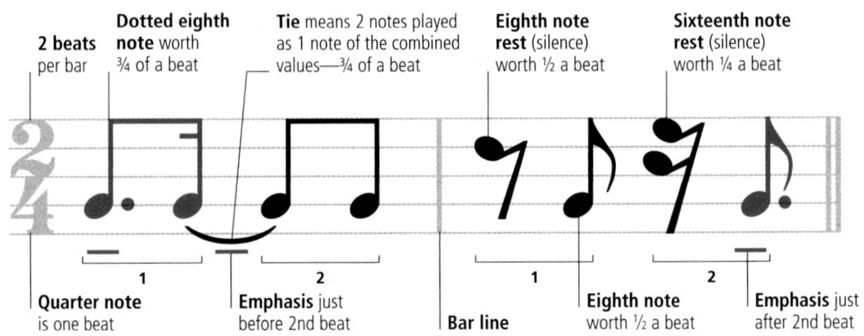

Bossa nova beat
Shifting the emphasis from a strong to a weak beat (syncopation) gives the bossa nova its special swing. The second note of the first bar unexpectedly anticipates the second beat, while in the second bar, the second note sounds delayed.

> "For me **Brazilian music** is the perfect mix of **melody** and **rhythm...** If I had to pick just **one music style** to play it would be Brazilian."
>
> AMERICAN JAZZ FLAUTIST HERBIE MANN

Ipanema beach
Rio de Janeiro's spectacular Ipanema beach was made famous overnight in 1965, when "The Girl from Ipanema," sung by Astrud Gilberto, earned a Grammy Award. The hit became one of the most recorded songs in history.

KEY WORKS

Quincy Jones "Soul Bossa Nova"
Heitor Villa-Lobos *Bachianas Brasileiras No. 5*
Antonio Carlos Jobim "Desafinado"; "The Girl from Ipanema"; "Agua de Berber"
Stephen Sondheim "The Ladies Who Lunch"
Beth Carvalho "Camarão Que Dorme a Onda Leva"
Zeca Pagohino "Maneiras"

Samba spectacular

During Rio de Janeiro's annual carnival, the city's samba schools parade in the 765 yd (700 m) street inside Rio's Marquês de Sapucaí Sambadrome, designed by Brazilian architect Oscar Niemeyer.

BRAZILIAN MUSICIAN (1927–1994)

CARLOS "TOM" JOBIM

Multitalented Carlos Jobim is best known for creating the bossa nova ("new trend") style. In 1962, he partnered US guitarist Charlie Lee Byrd (a disciple of Django Reinhardt) in the successful album *Jazz Samba*, but it was the 1963–1964 recordings with US saxophonist Stan Getz, Brazilian guitarist João Gilberto, and his wife, Astrud Gilberto, that made Brazilian music an international sensation.

AFTER

After Brazil's military coup in 1964, new kinds of music emerged, including one that combined samba, bossa nova, folk, and protest genres.

BEYOND BOSSA NOVA

As a counter to the country's 1964–1985 dictatorship, **Música Popular Brasileira** (MPB) sought a distinctive Brazilian sound that drew on bossa nova and samba but also incorporated folk, protest, rock, and jazz. The song "Arrastão" sung by **Elis Regina** (1945–1982) marked the beginning of the genre. Regina was also important in **Tropicália**, which merged Brazilian and African styles.

VOICE OF RIO

In recent years, the easy-listening songs of **Zeca Pagodinho** (1959–), which are inspired by his childhood in Rio, have made him a best-selling artist worldwide.

SINGER ZECA PAGODINHO

The man with the maracas
The Latin jazz singer and bandleader Machito fronts his band, the Afro-Cubans, around 1940. The middle of the three trumpeters is his brother-in-law and musical director, Mario Bauzá.

Jazz Goes Latin

A fluid musical form, jazz is always evolving. But Latin jazz, also called Afro-Latin jazz, is a distinct genre, which is most recognizable by the *habanera* beat that found its way to the United States from Africa, via the Caribbean island of Cuba.

BEFORE

Some of the early jazz played in New Orleans at the beginning of the 20th century incorporated rhythms that came from nearby Cuba.

A SPRINKLING OF LATIN SPICE

Jazz pioneer and ragtime legend **Jelly Roll Morton** used the term "Spanish tinge" to refer to **Afro-Latin** elements in jazz during its early **New Orleans** days « 234–235. With the motto "You've got to have that Spanish Tinge", he popularized a jazz sound that featured the ***habanera*** (named for Cuba's capital, Havana, but known in Cuba as the *contradanza*) and **tresillo** rhythms, which have their roots in sub-Saharan African music. Morton's "Spanish Tinge" referred not to any influences from Spain, but rather to the ones that came out of its former island colony of Cuba.

PAIR OF CLAVES, USED IN CUBAN PERCUSSION

As early as 1914, the blues composer W. C. Handy (see p.240) had used the slow two-beats-to-the-bar *habanera* rhythm as a bass line in his song "St. Louis Blues." However, it was not until 1943 that a certain tune heralded the arrival of a new musical form.

"Tanga"—written by Havana-born Mario Bauzá (1911–1993) and performed by his brother-in-law and fellow Cuban Machito (1908–1984) and his band—is regarded as the first example of true Latin jazz, as it fused together African-inspired Cuban rhythms with jazz improvisation. Machito (real name Francisco Raúl Gutiérrez Grillo) grew up singing and dancing with his three older sisters and the employees of his father, a cigar manufacturer. By his late teens, he was an established singer and maracas player, and both he and Bauzá, a trumpeter, began to make a name for themselves playing in local bands.

15 The age of the saxophonist Stan Getz when he started to play professionally in New York jazz bands.

America calls

In 1937, the pair moved to New York City to record with the growing community of Cuban musicians. They introduced Cuban musical elements while performing with the big bands of Chick Webb and Cab Calloway. In 1940, they formed their own band, the Afro-Cubans, led by Machito on vocals and maracas, with trumpets, saxophones, and a rhythm section of piano, double bass, timbales, bongos, and congas.

A rehearsal of "Tanga" at the Park Palace Ballroom on May 29, 1943, using jazz instruments and with solo improvisations, marked the birth of Latin jazz.

In March 1946, the jazz pianist and bandleader Stan Kenton (1911–1979) recorded a tribute tune "Machito," widely considered to be the first Latin jazz recording by American jazz musicians. Then, in December of the same year, Kenton recorded an instrumental arrangement of the Afro-Cuban classic "The Peanut Vendor" with members of Machito's own rhythm section.

The first live concert to feature an American band playing Afro-Cuban jazz took place in September 1947, when trumpeter and bandleader Dizzy Gillespie (see pp.246–247) collaborated with Machito's conga player Chano Pozo to perform the "Afro-Cuban Drums Suite" at Carnegie Hall, New York City. Pozo remained in Gillespie's orchestra and together they recorded "Manteca," which went on to become the first jazz standard with a distinct Cuban beat.

Laying down the beat
The conga is a tall, narrow Cuban drum that originated in Africa. It is usually played as a pair, using the fingers and palm of the hand, and forms an essential part of the Latin jazz sound.

A musical melting pot

Gillespie is also credited with inventing the Cuban bop, a melding of Cuban rhythms and the jazz bebop style. During his long career, Gillespie went on to explore a range of Latin American musical traditions in his music, and in 1956 even shared a stage in Buenos Aires with the tango orchestra of the Argentine songwriter Osvaldo Fresedo (see pp.254–255).

Chart topper
The *Getz/Gilberto* bossa nova album, released in March 1964 on the Verve label, won the 1965 Grammy Award for Best Album of the Year. It was the first time a jazz record had achieved that honor.

A separate jazz tradition grew out of the mambo, a high-energy Afro-Cuban rhythm that sparked a dance craze in the 1950s. The most notable exponent of this connection was the musician Tito Puente (1923–2000), a New Yorker of Puerto Rican extraction. In the 1960s, Puente collaborated widely with other New York-based musicians, playing with jazz big-band leader Woody Herman, and Cuban singers Celia Cruz (see pp.278–279) and La Lupe. His molding of a range of Latin rhythms, including mambo, son, and salsa, with that of jazz, epitomized the Latin-jazz fusion.

That influence took a step further in 1970, when his 1963 song "Oye Como Va" became a hit for the Latin-infused rock band Santana. By this time Latin jazz had adopted New York City—home to large communities of Puerto Ricans, Cubans, and African Americans—as its base.

A flute-based jazz, originally from Cuba, called *charanga*, was briefly popular, and the funk, soul, and mambo-influenced boogaloo burned brightly for a brief time in the mid-'60s. New Yorker Joe Cuba, "the father of boogaloo," had a big hit in 1966 with "Bang Bang," and helped to export the boogaloo book back to Puerto Rico.

Flying down to Rio

The Brazilian sound of bossa nova ("the latest thing") that had grown out of samba in Rio de Janeiro in the 1950s (see pp.278–279) was embraced in the early 1960s by many American jazz artists, including Charlie Byrd and Stan Getz. Getz was invited by the founding fathers of bossa nova—musicians João Gilberto (1931–2019) and Antônio Carlos (aka Tom) Jobim (1927–1994)—to collaborate on what became one of the best-selling jazz albums of all time, *Getz/Gilberto*. Gilberto's wife, Astrud, who sang on the record, became an international star, and the track "The Girl from Ipanema" was a global hit.

New tango, new fusions

In Argentina, the composer Astor Piazzolla (1921–1992) revitalized the tango (see pp.254–255). He incorporated jazz elements and styles into his *nuevo tango* ("new tango"), and collaborated with American jazz musicians, most notably the baritone sax player and composer Gerry Mulligan (1927–1996).

Jazz continued to absorb Latin American elements. Brazilian percussionist Airto Moreira, one of the pioneers of jazz fusion, played with Miles Davis (see pp.334–335), and participated in the recording of Davis' 1970 album *Bitches Brew*. Joe Zawinul, a founding member of the jazz fusion band Weather Report, and the fusion group led by guitarist Pat Metheny, also played an ambassadorial role in the 1970s and '80s, taking Latin jazz back to Latin American audiences.

The beat goes on

Meanwhile, Machito, the man who had been at the start of Latin jazz, back in 1943, pressed on with his brass-led ensembles. He toured the world in the 1970s and died just before going on stage at Ronnie Scott's jazz club in London in 1984. Playing the classic Cuban percussion instruments—timbales, conga, and bongo—in Machito's orchestra was his son, Mario Grillo. Since then, Mario has lead the orchestra, helping to keep the Latin jazz big band style alive.

AFTER

"The Girl from Ipanema" casts a long shadow, with much smooth jazz underpinned by its easy beat, while Latin jazz continues to evolve.

FRESH LATIN STYLES
Puerto Rican saxophonist **Miguel Zenón** incorporates native folk music into his Latin jazz compositions, while French quartet **Sakésho** plays jazz inspired by the **bigusine** style of Martinique and Guadeloupe.

BOSSA KEEPS GOING POP
The Brazilian singer **Bebel Gilberto**, daughter of João Gilberto, followed her *bossa nova* lineage into her *Tanto Tempo* album (2000). Since 2004, the French band **Nouvelle Vague** has produced *bossa nova* covers of **punk 356–357 ››** and New Wave songs.

KEY WORKS

Machito and His Afro-Cubans "Tanga"
Dizzy Gillespie and Chano Pozo "Manteca"
Astrud Gilberto, with Joáo Gilberto and Stan Getz "The Girl from Ipanema"
Astor Piazzolla and Gerry Mulligan "Twenty Years Later"
Dizzy Gillespie and Machito "Pensativo"

"...to **change the tango,** you had better **learn boxing...**"

ASTOR PIAZZOLLA, ARGENTINE MUSICIAN AND COMPOSER, IN AN INTERVIEW WITH THE UK'S "THE GUARDIAN" NEWSPAPER

Tango revolutionary
Astor Piazzolla, photographed in 1989, injected jazz into the tango, but he was also a virtuoso player of the *bandoneón*, a kind of accordion and an instrument long at the heart of the traditional Argentine dance.

Born 1925 Died 2003

Celia Cruz

> "When **people hear me sing** I want them to be **happy, happy, happy.**"
>
> CELIA CRUZ, INTERVIEW WITH THE "NEW YORK TIMES," 1995

Glamorous, flamboyant, strident, proud of her Afro-Cuban roots, and supremely talented, Celia Cruz was the Queen of Salsa for more than five decades—and of rumba and of crossover Latin music, too. An ambassador for the variety and vitality of the music of her native Havana, after the revolution she became a symbol of artistic freedom for Cuban-American exiles.

The band that got away

Cruz and La Sonora Matancera were touring Mexico in 1960 when they decided to defect from Cuba to the US. Soon after, she married trumpeter Pedro Knight.

Natural virtuosity

Latin America's music has traditionally been male dominated. But Cruz, through sheer energy and a formidable work ethic, rose to the very top of her genre. Her shows were exuberant and her costumes extravagant, but she had a natural virtuosity, and her jazzlike improvisations were likened to those of Sarah Vaughan and Ella Fitzgerald.

KEY WORKS

- **"Cao Cao, Mani Pcao"** (with La Sonora Matancera)
- **"Burundanga"** (with La Sonora Matancera)
- **"Yerbero Moderno"** (with La Sonora Matancera)
- **"El Paso del Mulo"** (with Johnny Pacheco)
- **"Quimbara"** (with Johnny Pacheco)
- **"Loco de Amor"** (with David Byrne)
- **"Mi Tierra"** (with Martika)
- ***Azúcar Negra***

Over the decades Cruz would play alongside many Latin and global superstars, from Tito Puente to Dionne Warwick to David Byrne. She recorded more than 60 albums—23 of which went gold—and won seven Grammy awards.

Born Úrsula Hilaria Celia de la Caridad Cruz Alfonso de la Santísima Trinidad, the singer grew up in the working-class barrio of Santo Suarez in Havana. One of the eldest among 14 children—brothers, sisters, and lots of cousins—she would often have to put the younger ones to bed, singing them to sleep.

Thriving music scene

While still a child, Cruz won first prize in a radio contest, singing the tango "Nostalgias." As she grew older, she began entering other amateur singing contests. Cuba's salsa scene, based on a musical tradition that mixed elements of Spanish music with African

Cuban days

The singer photographed in Cuba in the 1950s, where she began singing with La Sonara Matancera. She was not tall, but her energy and stage presence were powerful.

Salsa spectacular
Cruz's brilliant costumes, some of which are now in the Smithsonian's National Museum of American History, were a major part of her show.

rhythms, was thriving at the time. It symbolized the island's history of enslavement and embodied the national character traits of exuberance and romantic melancholy. But being a singer was not viewed as an entirely respectable career. Her father, who wanted her to become a teacher—and who persuaded her to attend teacher training college for a time—disapproved of her ambition.

Nonetheless, from 1947, Cruz studied music theory, voice, and piano at Havana's National Conservatory of Music. Her big break came in 1950 when Myrta Silva, the singer with Cuba's Conjunto Sonora Matancera, returned to her native Puerto Rico. In need of a new singer, the band decided to give young Cruz a chance. Some fans wrote to the radio station that broadcast her performances to complain, but she persevered, won the support of Sonora's band leader, Rogelio Martínez, and went on to record hits such as "Yembe Laroco" and "Caramelo" with the band. Soon Cruz had a bigger name than they did.

Defection

Cruz became famous across Cuba, and during the 15 years she spent with Sonora, the band became a regular at Havana's famous *Tropicana* nightspot, appeared in several movies, and toured all over Latin America.

> "The most **influential** female figure in **Cuban** music history."
>
> LEILA COBO, "BILLBOARD" MAGAZINE

In July 1960, following the revolution in Cuba, La Sonora Matancera was on a tour of Mexico when the band members decided to defect en masse and settle in the United States. Castro vowed that none of the artists would ever be allowed back into the island. Cruz attempted to return when her mother died in 1962, but was not granted government permission.

Settling in the US

Cruz became a US citizen in 1961 and a year later married Sonora's trumpet player Pedro Knight, who became her manager and musical director. She recorded several albums with the established Tito Puente Orchestra, and began to hone her stage show. Fans adored her extravagant stage outfits. Her high heels and towering wigs added to her allure. But there was depth in the delivery: her powerful, gravelly voice was a match for any rhythm section, and she was a tireless dancer and audience-rouser.

In the 1970s, salsa attracted a new generation of Latin American exiles. Cruz signed to the Fania label, a promoter of salsa, and performed with the Fania All-Stars. In 1974, she recorded the album *Celia y Johnny* with All-Stars founder, the Dominican band leader Johnny Pacheco.

Throughout this period, Cruz lived in New Jersey, but was also a major star in Miami, where she sang the jingle for the WQBA radio station declaring: "I am the voice of Cuba... I am liberty, I am WQBA, *Cubanísima*!."

It was only during the 1980s and '90s that Cruz began to garner the international recognition that was her due. She picked up Grammy awards, appeared in movies and a Mexican soap opera, and became, with hits such as "La Vida es un Carnaval," a fully fledged crossover artist. In 1987, she was honored with a star on Hollywood's Walk of Fame, and in 1994 President Clinton presented her with an award from the National Endowment of the Arts.

Celia Cruz died in Fort Lee, New Jersey, in 2003. Her body was taken to lie in state in Miami, before being returned to New Jersey, where tens of thousands of fans paid tribute to her. Cruz, who had collaborated with countless Latin American legends and music superstars, appeared posthumously on the 2006 Dionne Warwick album *My Friends and Me.*

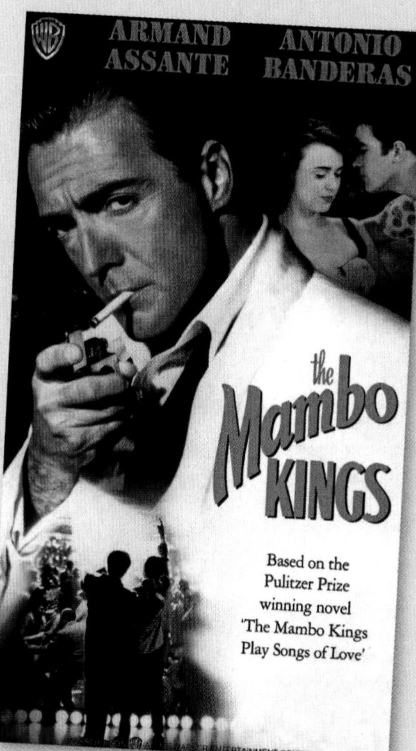

Fiction follows fact
Cruz starred in the 1992 film *The Mambo Kings*, based on Oscar Hijuelos's 1989 novel, in which two brothers (played by Armand Assante and Antonio Banderas) flee Cuba for the US to pursue their musical careers.

TIMELINE

- **October 21, 1925** Born in Havana, Cuba, the daughter of a railroad stoker.
- **1935** Wins a talent contest on the radio show *La Hora del Té Serra.*
- **1950** Joins La Sonora Matancera.
- **January 1951** Makes her recording debut with La Sonora Matancera on the song "Cao Cao, Mani Picao."
- **1959** Revolution in Cuba.
- **1960** Defects to the US while on tour with her band in Mexico.
- **1961** Becomes a US citizen.
- **1962** Marries Pedro Knight.
- **1965** Leaves La Sonora Matancera and signs to Tico Records; she goes on to release 12 albums with Tico.
- **1966** Begins working with Tito Puente.
- **March 29, 1973** Appears live at Carnegie Hall, playing the part of Divine Grace in Larry Harlow's *Hommy, A Latin Opera.*
- **Summer 1974** Album *Celia y Johnny* is released by Vaya Records for the Fania label and goes gold, kicking off a new salsa revolution.
- **1976** Takes part in *Salsa*, a documentary film, along with Desi Arnaz, Willie Colon, Manu Dibango, and Dolores del Río. Double album of a concert in New York's Yankee Stadium is released.
- **1982** Reunited on record with La Sonora Matancera on *Feliz Encuentro.*
- **1987** Awarded a star on Hollywood's Walk of Fame.
- **1988** Cameo appearance in the movie *Salsa.*
- **1990** Shares Grammy for Best Tropical Latin Performance with Ray Barretto for the album *Ritmo en el Corazón.*
- **1992** Movie *The Mambo Kings* is released. Cruz acts alongside Antonio Banderas.
- **1994** US President Bill Clinton presents her with the National Medal of Arts.
- **1995** Wins *Billboard* magazine's Lifetime Achievement Award.
- **1998** Releases the hit single "La Vida es un Carnaval."
- **2002** Wins Grammy for best salsa album for *La Negra Tiene Tumbao.*
- **2003** Wins Grammy for best salsa/merengue album for *Regalo del Alma.*
- **2003** Dies of brain cancer in Fort Lee, New Jersey.
- **2004** Her last album, *Regalo del Alma*, wins a posthumous award at the Premios Lo Nuestro for best salsa release.

CELIA CRUZ

STAR ON HOLLYWOOD'S WALK OF FAME

BEFORE

Earlier in the 20th century, composers had brought daring new subjects and styles to the tradition of grand opera.

SOCIAL REALISM

In 1904, **Leoš Janácek « 214** brought a new social realism to opera with *Jenůfa*, which he set in a Czech-Moravian village.

AUSTRIAN AVANT GARDE

In his 1925 opera, *Wozzeck*, **Alban Berg « 210** created a dark modernist masterwork.

THE SURREAL

Soviet Russia produced a great young talent in **Dmitri Shostakovich**, whose operas *The Nose* (1928) and *Lady Macbeth of Mtsensk* (1932) explored a surreal world.

MARIA JERITZA PLAYING JENUFA, 1924

Operatic Rebirth

When World War II ended in 1945, the future of opera looked unpromising. The era of its leading prewar composers was long gone. Then, in one bound, an English composer from Suffolk, named Benjamin Britten, transformed the operatic world.

No musical medium places greater demands on a composer than opera. It has to fill an entire evening in a theater, making it the largest of musical forms. The quality of the musical score has to be matched by that of the libretto (dramatic text).

The range of skills required from an opera composer is huge: the ability to write effectively for solo voices alone or in groups, also for chorus, for orchestra, and for every combination of these together.

In England, no great opera had been composed since Henry Purcell's *Dido and Aeneas* (see pp.96–97) in 1688.

15 **The total number of operas composed by Britten.**

1970 **The year Britten wrote the opera *Owen Wingrave*, for television.**

A new British voice

Benjamin Britten (see opposite), undeterred by this absence of an operatic tradition in England, was drawn to the medium that gave full scope for his brilliant range of gifts.

His first attempt, *Paul Bunyan*, was written in 1941 during an extended stay in the United States. The result was closer to operetta (see pp.194–195), but provided its composer with useful opera-staging experience.

Britten's return to England then brought the creation of *Peter Grimes* and, on June 7, 1945, its successful premiere at London's Sadler's Wells Theatre. This tragic story of an unpopular fisherman in a North Sea village community drew from Britten a score of masterly sweep, atmosphere, and invention. *Peter Grimes* established a modern English opera tradition in a single stroke and, almost overnight, its composer became world famous.

Britten's achievement in *Peter Grimes* was to propel the genre of full-length opera into the modern postwar era, while also reconnecting it with its

A modern drama

In this scene from the 1945 London premiere of Britten's opera *Peter Grimes*, apothecary Ned Keene (played by Edmund Donlevy) rouses the townsfolk of The Borough to a vigilante-style hunt for Grimes.

COMPOSER (1913–1976)

BENJAMIN BRITTEN

Born in Lowestoft and the son of a dentist, Britten studied at the Royal College of Music, in London, but he grew frustrated by England's musical life. In 1939, he moved to the United States with his life partner, tenor Peter Pears (1910–1986), before returning home in 1942. Following the success of *Peter Grimes*, he settled with Pears in the Suffolk coastal town of Aldeburgh, founding its Festival in 1948.

In addition to composing, Britten was an exceptional conductor and pianist. His deep pacifist beliefs inspired him to write the 1962 choral work *War Requiem*.

Weakened by a partial stroke during heart surgery in 1973, he died three years later.

traditional roots. Compared to the modernist style of Alban Berg's 1925 opera *Wozzeck* (which Britten deeply admired), the style of *Peter Grimes* is conservative in terms of the orthodox "operatic" sweep of its melodies, and its deployment of the chorus in spectacular, big-scale crowd scenes. Britten's mastery of the genre's technical demands was linked to his music's ability to involve an audience with the story and its characters. He and tenor Peter Pears, for whom the opera's title role was composed, were homosexual and pacifist. So Britten naturally identified with the character of Peter Grimes, the suspect outsider on whom a community might turn at any moment. And his music had the expressive power to engage the listener's sympathetic response.

Britten composed many other operas of different kinds. These ranged from further large-scale, full-length works with chorus, such as *Billy Budd* (1950), to more "portable" operas for a small number of singers and a reduced ensemble. A masterwork of this type is the opera *The Turn of the Screw*, which premiered in Venice, Italy, in 1954.

Britten's success in re-creating English opera was both a beacon and a challenge to his contemporaries in Britain and abroad. His lyrically expressive idiom was too individual to be imitated successfully.

Britten's success was followed by fellow pacifist Michael Tippett (1905–1998), whose compositional style was more complex than Britten's. His 1953 opera *The Midsummer Marriage*, is an optimistic blend of compassionate humanism, Jungian psychology, and idyllic English pastoralism. Four more operas followed, including the sharply outlined drama of contemporary relationships, *The Knot Garden* (1970).

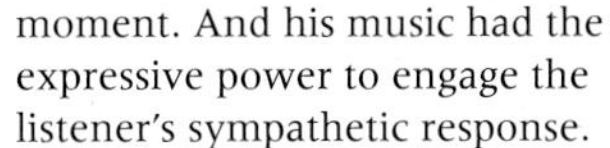

"As an **artist** I want to **serve** the **community.**"

BENJAMIN BRITTEN, PRESENTED WITH THE FREEDOM OF LOWESTOFT, 1951

A political stand

The modernist, post-*Wozzeck* idea of opera that dominated in Europe differed from Britten's traditionally focused style. For many composers working in Europe, the role of opera in society was to reject entertainment values and replace them with intellectual and political confrontation.

Repelled by Italy's fascist leadership, Luigi Dallapiccola (1904–1976) led an underground existence during World War II. Soon afterward, in 1948, he completed his tumultuous masterpiece *Il Prigioniero* (The Prisoner), a parable of human courage and hope destroyed by totalitarian power. Later, the stridently polemical one-act opera *Intolleranza 1960* (Intolerance 1960), by the Communist-supporting Luigi Nono (1924–1990), triggered rioting between left- and right-wing groups at its premiere in Venice, in 1961.

American developments

America's lack of a truly homegrown operatic tradition was even more marked than England's before Britten. Then, with *Nixon in China*, first performed at Houston Grand Opera in 1987, John Adams (1947–) created a new type of political opera-as-reportage, portraying US President Richard Nixon's historic visit to Mao Zedong's People's Republic of China in 1972, at the height of the Cold War. In a traditional-sounding operatic style, although of a kind quite different from Britten's, the characters are presented almost as cartoon figures, unwittingly caught up in the wider forces of politics and fate.

Adams' next opera, *The Death of Klinghoffer*, was about the real-life hijacking by Arab terrorists of the cruise ship *Achille Lauro* in 1985. By presenting the story from the terrorists' viewpoint, alongside that of the Jewish passenger they killed, the opera's premiere in 1991 provoked furious controversy in the United States.

KEY WORKS

Benjamin Britten *Peter Grimes; The Turn of the Screw*

Luigi Dallapiccola *Il Prigioniero* (The Prisoner)

Michael Tippett *The Midsummer Marriage*

Luigi Nono *Intolleranza 1960* (Intolerance 1960)

John Adams *Nixon in China*

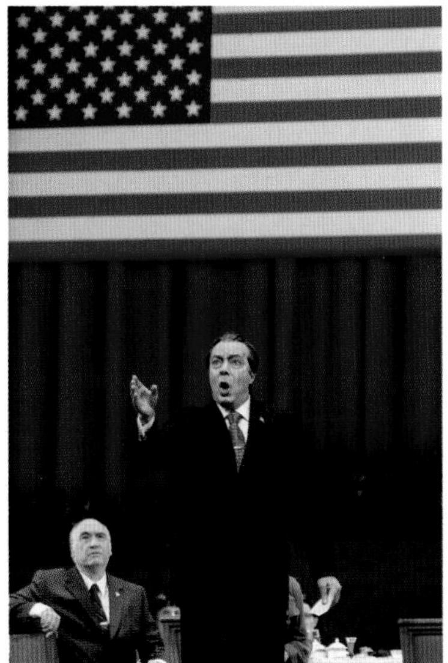

The politics of opera
American baritone James Maddalena reprised the part of Richard Nixon in the Metropolitan Opera production of John Adam's opera *Nixon in China* in 2011. Maddalena originated the role in 1987.

AFTER

The twin traditions originated by Britten and Adams have proved to be fertile territory for new operas by English and American composers.

NEW ENGLISH GENERATIONS
In 1986, **Harrison Birtwistle** **376–77 ››** created a huge-scale, multifaceted retelling of Greek mythology in *The Mask of Orpheus*. Thomas Adès's *The Tempest*, based on Shakespeare's play, met with global acclaim following its 2004 premiere at London's Royal Opera House.

AMERICAN BREAKTHROUGH
In 2021, Terence Blanchard's *Fire Shut Up in My Bones*, based on Charles M. Blow's memoir of his traumatic coming-of-age in **small-town Louisiana**, became the first opera by a Black composer to be staged at the Metropolitan Opera in New York.

THE TEMPEST

Early Musical Theater

As the 20th century progressed in the United States, theatrical entertainment featuring the coherent integration of drama, music, and dance was developed into a great and enduring popular art form known as the musical.

Popular early 20th-century musicals included British Edwardian light musical comedies, such as *The Orchid* (1903) and *Our Miss Gibbs* (1909), the Viennese operetta *The Merry Widow* (1907), and the American operetta, *Naughty Marietta* (1910). But it was the vaudeville-flavored shows of Rhode Island-born George M. Cohan (1878–1942) that brought a distinctly American energy to the musical. Shows such as *Little Johnny Jones* (1904), featuring the song "Give My Regards To Broadway," ensured Cohan's reputation as the founder of the American musical.

Sentimental, operetta-style shows such as *Rose-Marie* and *The Student Price* (1924) held on to their popularity in the 1920s. However, it was the work of composers such as Jerome Kern (1885–1945) that introduced the American musical genres of ragtime and jazz to the stage, giving the Broadway musical a fresh musical palette.

George and Ira Gershwin's *Lady Be Good* (1924), Vincent Youmans' *No No Nanette* (1925), and Richard Rodgers' and Lorenz Hart's *A Connecticut Yankee* (1927) were all major hits. Lighthearted in tone and frothy of plot, these shows brought to light many enduring, popular songs, later known as "standards."

« BEFORE

The infusion of music and drama has ancient origins, but two key influences on 20th-century musical theater come from the 19th century.

ENGLISH LIGHT OPERA
The comic operas of **Gilbert and Sullivan** « 194–195 feature absurd, satirical plots integrated with witty, memorable songs.

19TH CENTURY ON BROADWAY
The **vaudeville sketches** and comic songs of American actor-writer Edward Harrigan, as performed by Harrigan and Tony Hart, developed into popular social and ethnic satires set in New York. Shows included *The Mulligan Guards' Ball* (1879) and *The Mulligans' Silver Wedding* (1883).

Musical revues

Running parallel to developments in the "book musical" (musical shows with plots and characters) was the musical revue. These were variety-style presentations without any plot, which featured glamorous, scantily dressed showgirls, singers, dancers, and comedians.

The more famous revues included *Follies* (1907–1931), presented by theater producer Florenz Ziegfeld; *Scandals* (1919–1939), produced by George White; and, the most risqué of them all, *Vanities* (1923–1932), produced by Earl Carroll. Many composers of the day contributed songs to the revues. Future movie-musical star Fred Astaire established his career in *The Band Wagon* (1931), a revue by Howard Dietz and Arthur Schwartz.

Soaring success
Oscar Hammerstein wove his Broadway hit *Carousel* (1945) around a 1909 play called *Liliom*, by Hungarian Ferenc Molnár. When it opened, Jan Clayton played Julie Jordan and John Raitt played Billy Bigelow (seen here).

Oklahoma! poster (1943)
The New York Times hailed *Oklahoma!* (based on the 1931 play *Green Grow the Lilacs* by Lynn Riggs), as "the most thoroughly and attractively American musical comedy since Edna Ferber's *Show Boat*."

A "musical play"

Show Boat (1927), by Jerome Kern and lyricist Oscar Hammerstein, was dubbed a "musical play" by some commentators in order to distinguish it from its lightweight predecessors. Its skillfully crafted dialogue and plot, based on a best-selling book by Edna Ferber, and sensitive integration of the thoughtful, lyrical songs, including "Old Man River" and "Can't Help Lovin' Dat Man," set the standard for other book musicals to emulate.

Irving Berlin's *As Thousands Cheer* (1933) had similarly powerful moments, while George Gershwin's "folk opera" *Porgy And Bess* (see pp.232–233), of 1935, did much to raise the artistic bar for the musical. However, the public's appetite for escapist, upbeat entertainment was also fed by the musicals of Cole Porter, such as *Anything Goes*, in 1939, and those by Richard Rodgers and Lorenz Hart, such as *On Your Toes* (1936) and *Babes in Arms* (1937). Rodgers' and Hammerstein's *Oklahoma!* (1943) continued the thoughtful amalgamation of song, story, and dance established by *Show Boat*, which bravely tackles racial prejudice. Songs such as "Oh What A Beautiful Mornin'" and "People Will Say We're In Love" shine out from its rich score.

Golden era

Oklahoma! heralded the so-called "golden era" of musical theater. The era was dominated by several huge hits by Rodgers and Hammerstein through the 1940s and '50s, but also featured significant contributions from composers Leonard Bernstein (*On The Town*, 1944), Burton Lane (*Finians's Rainbow*, 1947), Kurt Weill (*Street Scene*, 1947) and Cole Porter (*Kiss Me Kate*, 1948), among others.

The Rodgers and Hammerstein scores emphasized a luxuriously melodic style, an approach that was adopted by another hit team of the period, Alan Jay Lerner and Frederick Loewe. The pair wrote *Brigadoon* (1947), *My Fair Lady* (1956), and *Camelot* (1960).

By contrast, Bernstein favored jazz influences for *West Side Story* (1957). Stephen Sondheim (1930–2021), the lyricist on *West Side Story*, worked with

MUSICAL TEAM (1943–1960)

RICHARD RODGERS AND OSCAR HAMMERSTEIN

Composer Richard Rodgers (1902–1979) and librettist Oscar Hammerstein (1895–1960) were the most successful songwriting team in American musical theater. Rodgers' extraordinary melodic facility and Hammerstein's sincere romanticism and social conscience produced some of the world's most beloved musicals, including *Carousel* (1945), *South Pacific* (1949), *The King And I* (1951), and *The Sound Of Music* (1959). Famous songs include "If I Loved You," "Some Enchanted Evening," and "Getting To Know You."

Musical legend
Rodgers and Hammerstein produced Irving Berlin's 1946 musical *Annie Get Your Gun*, a fictionalized tale based on real-life Wild West sharpshooter Annie Oakley. This is the cover of the sheet music.

KEY WORKS

Kern and Hammerstein *Showboat*
Cole Porter *Anything Goes*
Rodgers and Hammerstein *Oklahoma!*
Irving Berlin *Annie Get Your Gun*
Lerner and Loewe *My Fair Lady*
Bernstein and Sondheim *West Side Story*
Stein and Sondheim *Gypsy*

Jule Styne on another Broadway classic, *Gypsy* (1959), before finally producing the entire score for the hit *A Funny Thing Happened On The Way To The Forum* (1962). Sondheim became the most significant musical-theater composer of the late 20th century.

British musical theater

Although British musical theater was largely overshadowed by its American counterpart, the UK continued to produce the occasional transatlantic hit. Ivor Novello's *Perchance To Dream* (1945) contained music that seemed to belong to another era; *The Boyfriend* (1954) by Sandy Wilson was itself a pastiche of early Rodgers and Hart musicals; and Julian Slade's unsophisticated but irrepressible *Salad Days* (1958) evoked more innocent times.

17,162 **The number of performances of *The Fantasticks* off Broadway between 1960 and 2002.**

9 **The number of performances of Stephen Sondheim's *Anyone Can Whistle* (1964) before closing.**

Off Broadway

Although they were traditional fare for large commercial theaters, musicals were also popular "Off Broadway," where smaller venues showed scaled-down productions. Mark Blitzstein's 1954 modernization of *The Threepenny Opera* was a hit show that set the trend for other off-Broadway musicals. Of these, *The Fantasticks* (1960) ran for 42 years, the longest run for a musical.

A number of blockbuster musical-theater hits of the 1960s signposted a growing diversity in musical styles. *Fiddler On the Roof* (1964), by Jerry Bock, Sheldon Harnick, and Joseph Stein, made use of traditional Yiddish musical styles for the story of Tevye, a poor Russian living in 19th-century czarist Russia, while *Man Of La Mancha* (1965), by Dale Wassermann, Joe Darion, and Mitch Leigh, used Spanish idioms to tell the tale of 17th-century knight Don Quixote. Later in the decade, it was rock music that would make its impact on Broadway.

AFTER

After the golden era of musicals ended in the mid-1960s, the sounds of rock and pop music dominated.

POP-ROCK MUSICALS

Hair (1967) opened the door for the pop operas of **Andrew Lloyd Webber** **360–361 ››**. Next-generation composers such as **Jason Robert Brown** display a versatility that takes in classic Broadway, rock, and everything in between.

JUKEBOX MUSICALS

The opposite of a "book musical," where the music serves the story, the "jukebox musical" contrives a plot to string together an established catalog of popular songs, often by a pop group. Notably popular shows include *Mamma Mia* (1999), based on the songs of Abba, and *We Will Rock You* (2002), which uses material by Queen.

A PERFORMANCE OF "WE WILL ROCK YOU"

Born 1923 Died 1977

Maria Callas

"When you **interpret** a role you have to have a **thousand colors** to portray happiness, joy, sorrow, fear."

MARIA CALLAS, QUOTED IN JOHN ARDOIN'S "CALLAS, THE ART AND THE LIFE", 1974

Maria Callas was one of the outstanding operatic divas of the 20th century. Her dramatic personality on and off the stage attracted a wide public to the experience of opera, helping ensure its future as a popular musical form in a rapidly changing world. She is credited with almost single-handedly reviving the tradition of *bel canto*—the melodious, florid operatic style of Rossini, Bellini, and Donizetti, whose works she reinstated as central to the repertoire. But she is perhaps best remembered for her performances as the eponymous heroine of Puccini's *Tosca*, a role she played with an alternation of fierceness and vulnerability that drew on the roots of her own conflicted personality.

La Divina
Callas's prodigious talents led the opera world to call her "La Divina" ("the divine one" in Italian). Her exquisite voice, dramatic skill, and perhaps her well publicized temper, made her the very definition of a diva—which she remains, decades after her death.

An ugly duckling

Callas was born in New York City in December 1923 to Greek parents who had emigrated to the United States the previous August. She was christened Anna Maria

Venetian sensation
Callas burst on to the international opera scene at La Fenice in Venice, Italy. Named "the phoenix," the theater has burned down and been rebuilt twice at its current site.

Calling down the Moon
Callas made the title role in Bellini's *Norma* her own. She is shown here playing the druid priestess who evokes the Moon with the aria "Casta diva" in a performance at the Metropolitan Opera, New York.

Sophia Cecilia Kalogeropoulos. Her father simplified the family name for American use to Callas, although the singer did not consistently employ the name Maria Callas until the 1940s.

Growing up in the borough of Manhattan, Maria did not have a happy childhood. She said of herself that she was "the ugly duckling, fat and clumsy and unpopular." Her mother Evangelia was a woman of drive and ambition. Discovering Maria's talent for music, she forced her to work at both the piano and singing from the age of five. When Evangelia split with her husband in 1937, she took Maria and her sister back to Athens, Greece, where she harried the local Conservatoire into taking the teenager as a pupil.

Greek tragedy
In 1969 Callas starred in a non-singing role in the film *Medea*, as advertised in this poster. Directed by Pier Paolo Pasolini and based on the play by Euripides, it was to be Callas's only movie appearance, for which she received mixed reviews.

A guiding hand

At the Athens Conservatoire, Callas encountered the major influence in her development as a singer, the Spanish soprano Elvira de Hidalgo. It was through de Hidalgo that she learned the almost lost art of *coloratura*, the elaborate ornamentation of melody required to sing the operas of the *bel canto* tradition. The young Callas nonetheless also possessed the statuesque build, dramatic presence, and powerful voice demanded by the lead roles in the Wagner and Puccini works that dominated opera houses.

Taking center stage

Callas built an impressive reputation in Athens under the tough circumstances of the Nazi occupation of Greece from 1941–1944. Moving that reputation to the international stage proved more difficult. She first set her sights on the US, but the Metropolitan Opera in New York, while acknowledging her talent, failed to agree to a contract, and a projected staging of Puccini's *Turandot* in Chicago fell through.

It was in Italy that she achieved her breakthrough. The famed Italian opera conductor Tullio Serafin spotted Callas's potential and arranged for her to perform at the Verona Arena, a large open-air venue that showcased the power of her voice. In Verona she caught the attention of wealthy industrialist Giovanni Meneghini, whom she married. With emotional and financial support from Meneghini and professional backing from Serafin, she was ready for fame.

In 1949 she created a sensation at Venice's La Fenice opera house by performing as Brünnhilde in Wagner's *The Valkyrie* and as Elvira in Bellini's *The Puritans* in the same week. Brünnhilde is a demanding soprano role in the forceful Wagnerian tradition, Elvira a *bel canto* role requiring gentle warmth and grace. Opera buffs were astounded by her stamina and by the fact that the same singer could perform with such brilliance in such contrasted styles.

Dramatic diva

Years of triumph followed. For seven years from 1951 she was a star of the season at La Scala in Milan. Her talent as a dramatic actress, which was always as important an element in her career as a fine singing voice, made her a favorite of the most innovative opera directors of her time. Franco Zeferelli, Luchino Visconti, and Margarete Wallmann all staged operas at La Scala in the 1950s with Callas in the lead soprano role. She became especially associated with Donizetti's *Lucia di Lamermoor*, Bellini's *Norma*, and Verdi's *La Traviata*, her performances regarded as a revelation of the potential of works that had long suffered neglect. From 1954 onward she conquered the United States, becoming a Hollywood-style celebrity, feted for her glamour but subject to media intrusion in her private life. She also became a major recording artist. The version of *Tosca* that she made for EMI in 1953 with tenor Tito Gobbi is considered one of the finest of all operatic recordings.

Definitive record
Puccini's *Tosca* provided Callas with one of her most celebrated roles, which she first performed at the age of 19. In 1953, she recorded a version of the opera—LP cover shown above—to great acclaim.

Leaner and meaner

From the late 1950s Callas's career declined. She became slimmer and more glamorous, but this weight loss adversely affected her voice. She had always been a fiery personality who argued with other singers, directors, and theater managers, but such clashes grew more serious. A falling out with manager Rudolf Bing ended her involvement with the New York Metropolitan Opera and she ceased to appear at La Scala. Her relationship with Greek tycoon Aristotle Onassis led to divorce from her husband Meneghini. Callas gave her last operatic performances in 1965, by which time she was past her best. A final recital tour in the 1970s met with rapture from audiences but was scorned by critics. She died Paris in 1977, a withdrawn, reclusive figure.

TIMELINE

- **December 2, 1923** Born Anna Maria Sophia Cecilia Kalogeropoulos in New York City.
- **1932** Given her first piano lessons.
- **1937** After her parents separate, she moves to Athens, Greece, with her mother.
- **April 11, 1938** Studying under Maria Trivella at the Greek National Conservatoire, she gives her first public performance.
- **1939** Learns the technique of *coloratura*, taught by Spanish soprano Elvira de Hidalgo.
- **February 1942** Makes her professional debut in Athens with a minor role in Suppé's *Boccaccio*; later in the year she performs Puccini's *Tosca* for the first time.
- **August 2, 1947** Appears for the first time in Italy, singing the title role in *La Gioconda* at the Verona Arena.
- **1949** Causes a sensation with performances in Wagner's *The Valkyrie* and Bellini's *The Puritans* at La Fenice in Venice.
- **April 21, 1949** Marries Italian industrialist Giovanni Meneghini.
- **December 1951** Opens the opera season at La Scala, Milan, in Verdi's *The Sicilian Vespers*, to general acclaim.
- **1952** Appears for the first time at Covent Garden in London; signs a recording contract with EMI.
- **1954** Makes her American debut in Bellini's *Norma* at the Lyric Theater in Chicago.
- **October 29, 1956** Makes her first appearance with the Metropolitan Opera in New York.
- **1958** Her career runs into difficulty as she quarrels with the directors of La Scala and the Metropolitan Opera.
- **1960** Divorces her husband Meneghini after becoming involved with Greek shipping magnate Aristotle Onassis.
- **July 5, 1965** Makes her final operatic performance in *Tosca* at London's Covent Garden, after which she retires.
- **1968** After Onassis's marriage to Jacqueline Kennedy, she adopts a reclusive lifestyle in Paris, France.
- **1971** Performs in a non-singing role in the movie *Medea*, directed by Pier Paolo Pasolini.

CONCERT WITH DI STEFANO IN LONDON, 1973

- **1973–1974** Returns from retirement for an international recital tour with tenor Giuseppe di Stefano.
- **September 16, 1977** Dies of a heart attack at her home in Paris, aged 55.

The **Acoustic Guitar**

From serving as a primitive percussion instrument to providing the other "voice" in Spanish flamenco and folksong and then taking the spotlight as a solo instrument in classical works, the history of the acoustic guitar mirrors the history of Western music.

The origins of the European guitar lie in western Asia, where harps with up to a dozen strings were made using tortoise shells as resonators. Early predecessors of the guitar, with between three and five strings, appear on illustrated manuscripts and carved in stone in churches and cathedrals from Roman times right up to the Middle Ages. By the Renaissance, the four-course (four pairs of strings) guitar had become dominant in Europe, and Spanish composers began to write music specifically for the *vihuela*, the forerunner of the Spanish guitar.

The modern classical guitar

During the 17th and 18th centuries the guitar had a prominent role in flamenco (see pp.218–219) as it began to share the lead role with the singer's voice. The "modern" guitar with six single strings evolved gradually during this period. By the 1850s, Spanish guitar maker Antonio de Torres Jurado redefined the instrument, giving it a far louder sound. He perfected a fan-bracing system inside the guitar to strengthen it, increased the size of the body, and altered the proportions.

Toward the end of the 19th century, Spanish guitarist Francisco Tárrega (1852–1909) transcribed the music of Bach, Mendelssohn, and Albéniz for the guitar and composed important works for the instrument too.

During the 20th century, composers such as Manuel de Falla, Heitor Villa-Lobos, and Manuel Ponce gave the guitar a central role in their orchestral works. The acoustic guitar—in its six- and 12-string incarnations—has also enjoyed immense popularity in folk, rock, and jazz music.

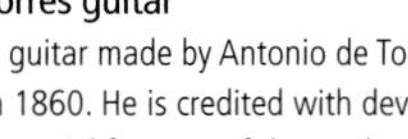
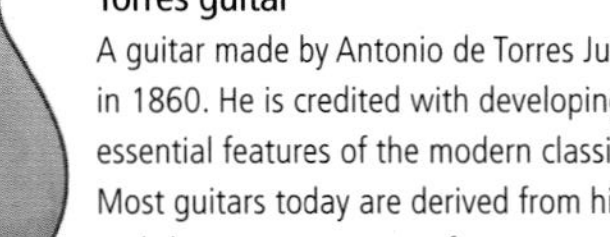
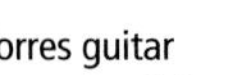
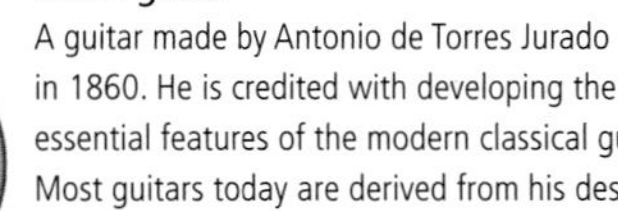
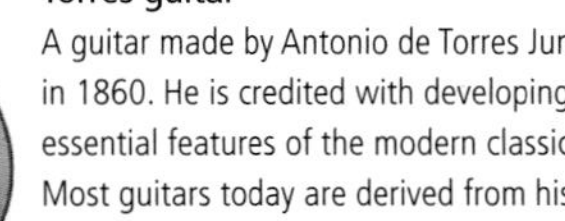
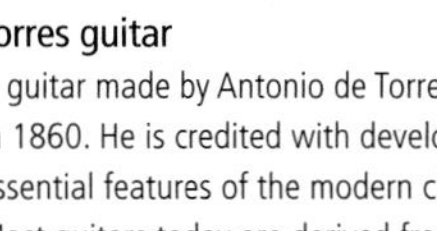

Torres guitar

A guitar made by Antonio de Torres Jurado in 1860. He is credited with developing the essential features of the modern classical guitar. Most guitars today are derived from his design and share many common features.

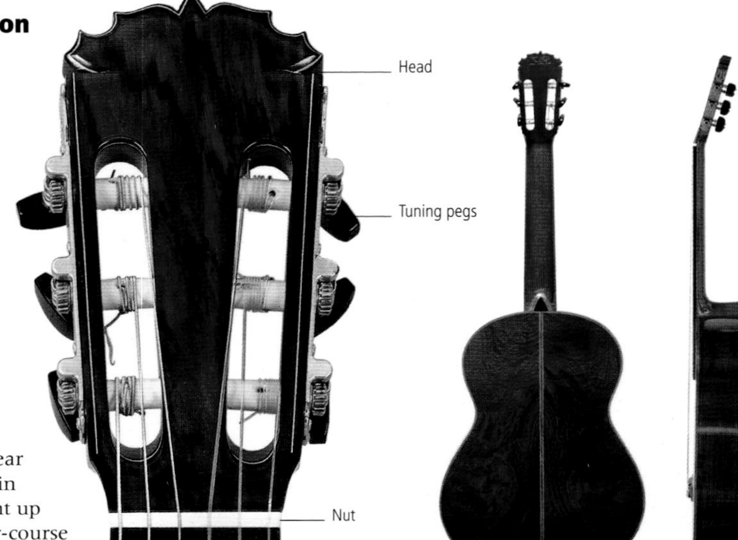

BACK

SIDE

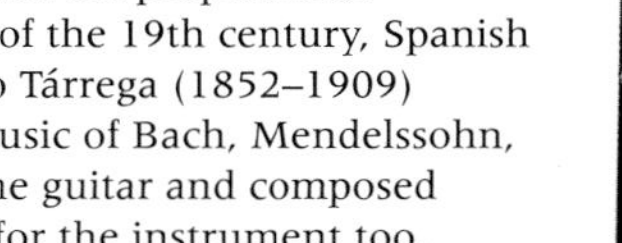

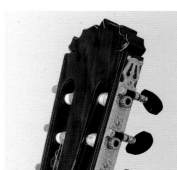

Tuning pegs

The open strings on a standard guitar are tuned EBGDAE. This is achieved using a tuning fork, an electronic tuner or the harmonics—using each string to tune the next one along. The pegs are turned until the string is at the optimum tension.

TIMELINE

4000 BCE
Egyptian *tanbur*
The *tanburs* of western Asia have a long, straight neck or fingerboard. They are one of the earliest known stringed instruments and may have developed from the bowl harp.

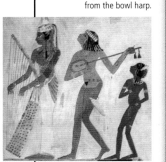

EGYPTIAN TANBUR

c.2750 BCE
Sumerian lyre
Many of the earliest harps were of primitive manufacture, perhaps with a calabash shell or tortoise shell to magnify the sound, but this Sumerian lyre from the royal cemetery at Ur, in modern-day Iraq, is an artistic masterpiece.

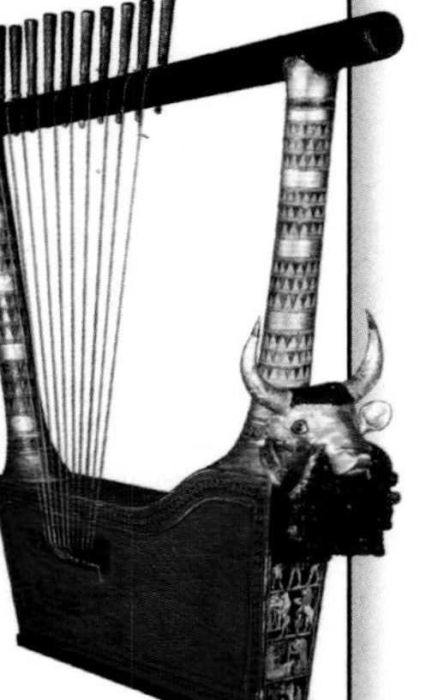

LYRE

15th century
Spanish *vihuela*
A clear precursor to the guitar, the *vihuela* established the guitar in Spain. With equivalents in Italy and Potugal, the instrument usually had six double strings. Spaniard Luis de Milán was the first to compose music for the *vihuela*.

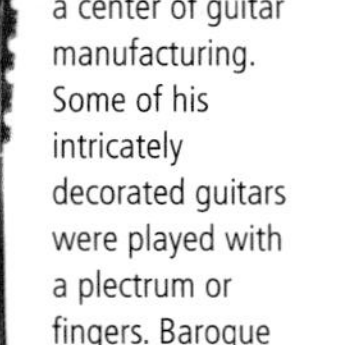

SPANISH VIHUELA

1640
Matteo Sellas guitars
German-born Matteo Sellas and his brother Giorgio helped establish Venice, Italy, as a center of guitar manufacturing. Some of his intricately decorated guitars were played with a plectrum or fingers. Baroque guitars often had five courses (10 strings).

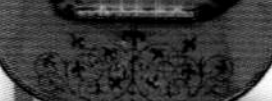
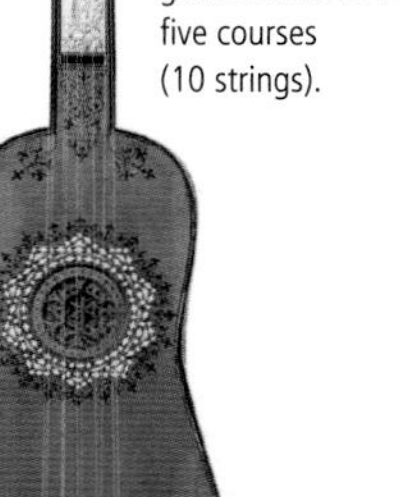

MATTEO SELLAS GUITAR

1615–81
Francesco Corbetta
Born in Pavia, Italy, Corbetta was an influential guitar virtuoso, teacher, and composer. Five collections of his music for the five-course guitar, which includes strummed music for dancing, have survived.

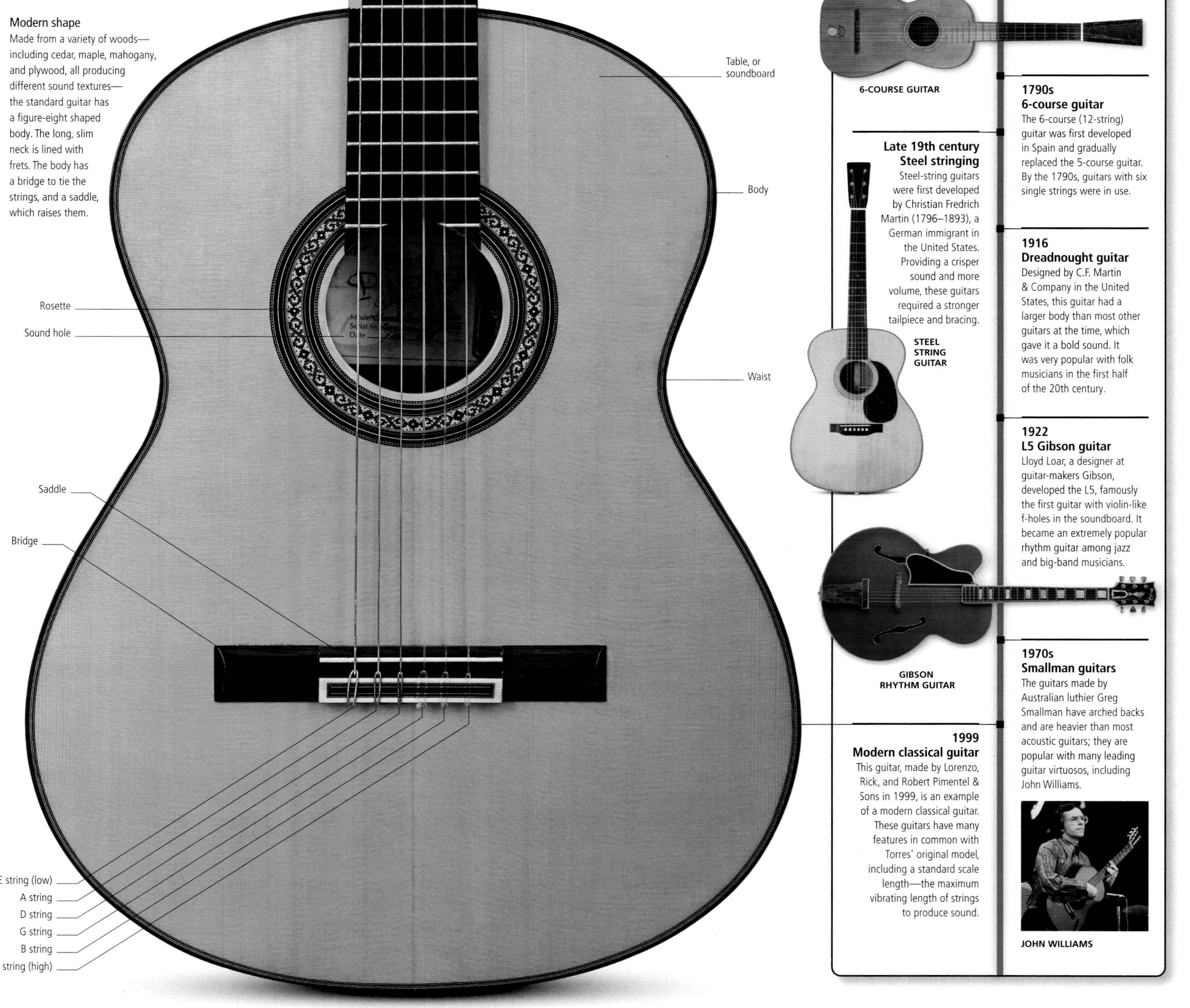

Modern shape

Made from a variety of woods—including cedar, maple, mahogany, and plywood, all producing different sound textures—the standard guitar has a figure-eight shaped body. The long, slim neck is lined with frets. The body has a bridge to tie the strings, and a saddle, which raises them.

1790s
6-course guitar

The 6-course (12-string) guitar was first developed in Spain and gradually replaced the 5-course guitar. By the 1790s, guitars with six single strings were in use.

Late 19th century
Steel stringing

Steel-string guitars were first developed by Christian Fredrich Martin (1796–1893), a German immigrant in the United States. Providing a crisper sound and more volume, these guitars required a stronger tailpiece and bracing.

1916
Dreadnought guitar

Designed by C.F. Martin & Company in the United States, this guitar had a larger body than most other guitars at the time, which gave it a bold sound. It was very popular with folk musicians in the first half of the 20th century.

1922
L5 Gibson guitar

Lloyd Loar, a designer at guitar-makers Gibson, developed the L5, famously the first guitar with violin-like f-holes in the soundboard. It became an extremely popular rhythm guitar among jazz and big-band musicians.

1970s
Smallman guitars

The guitars made by Australian luthier Greg Smallman have arched backs and are heavier than most acoustic guitars; they are popular with many leading guitar virtuosos, including John Williams.

1999
Modern classical guitar

This guitar, made by Lorenzo, Rick, and Robert Pimentel & Sons in 1999, is an example of a modern classical guitar. These guitars have many features in common with Torres' original model, including a standard scale length—the maximum vibrating length of strings to produce sound.

BEFORE

Before microphones, singers needed volume and presence to make themselves heard.

BELTING IT OUT

Opera singers have long been trained to project their voices by using techniques affecting posture, breathing, and resonance—in other words, the way the sound vibrates within the vocal cavity. Vaudeville-style performers like **Al Jolson** **« 230** were also expected to "hit the back of the theater" and many developed a full-voiced vocal sound known as the "belt" through sheer vitality.

BREATHY QUALITIES

The **microphone** **« 258–259** allowed smaller voices to be heard over acoustically overbearing musical ensembles. It put paid to loud singing, encouraging a more intimate style. Indeed, too loud a note could damage early microphones. **Radio** **« 260–261** was a prime force in developing microphones.

Smooth Operators

The advent of the microphone and the rise of radio broadcasts made possible a more personal approach to popular singing and a new breed of vocal star. The laid-back style defined the music of the first half of the 20th century and remains influential.

From the mid-1920s, American popular singing, as heard on recordings and radio broadcasts, began to sound different from what had gone before. Vocalists adopted a softer, more conversational style of singing known as "crooning."

The American saxophonist and bandleader Rudy Vallée (1901–1986) was the most prominent crooner of the late 1920s and went on to become a matinée idol at the movies. Other popular American crooners included Art Gillham, known as "The Whispering Pianist," and Gene Austin, composer of the 1925 hit "When My Sugar Walks Down The Street." In the UK, the style caught on thanks to the popularity of South African-born vocalist Al Bowlly, who sang with British dance bands led by Ray Noble and Lew Stone.

Crosby's winning style

The light-toned tenor style of the 1920s crooners was overshadowed in the 1930s by the rich baritones of American composer, actor, and singer Russ Columbo (1908–1934) and Washington-born singer Bing Crosby (1903–1977). Along with Louis Armstrong (see pp.248–249), Crosby was the father of jazz-inspired popular singing. Although initially influenced by Rudy Vallée, Crosby's relaxed, warm style was only superficially related to the early crooners. A jazz fan, Crosby brought rhythmic vitality and easygoing melodic variation (including his trademark trills) to popular singing with a vocal sound that was substantial but not overbearing, and mellow without being

Ol' Blue Eyes, the Old Groaner, and Dino
Bing Crosby (center) was a source of inspiration to younger singers Frank Sinatra (left) and Dean Martin (right). The three are shown recording together in this photograph dating from the early 1960s.

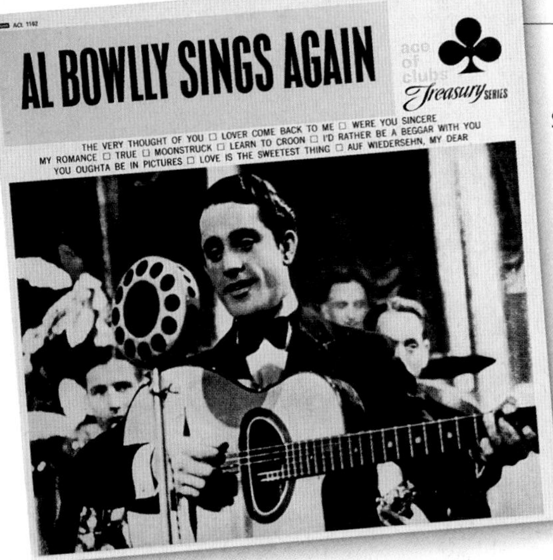

AL BOWLLY SINGS AGAIN
ace of clubs
Treasury SERIES
THE VERY THOUGHT OF YOU □ LOVER COME BACK TO ME □ WERE YOU SINCERE
MY ROMANCE □ TRUE □ MOONSTRUCK □ LEARN TO CROON □ I'D RATHER BE A BEGGAR WITH YOU
YOU OUGHTA BE IN PICTURES □ LOVE IS THE SWEETEST THING □ AUF WIEDERSEHN, MY DEAR

Sentimental songs
Between 1930 and 1933, Al Bowlly recorded more than 500 songs with the bands of Roy Fox and Ray Noble. They included "Love Is The Sweetest Thing" and epitomized British dance band sounds of the period.

effete. Crosby's wide repertoire of popular songs and his genial persona on radio and film established him as an American icon and the most popular male entertainer of the 1930s and '40s. Before his early death in 1934, Columbo was Crosby's rival, but it was Crosby who influenced the next generation of singing stars.

Going solo

Many popular vocalists in the 1930s were employed by bandleaders. Crosby, as an established solo singer, was an exception. By the early 1940s, band singers ventured into solo careers and a few endured. Perry Como (1912–2001), an even more laid-back singer than Crosby, left the bandleader Ted Weems in 1942 and went on to be a popular recording and TV performer for several decades into the 1990s. Frank Sinatra (1915–1998) left the bandleader and trombonist Tommy Dorsey in 1942 and became an idol to swooning teenagers through the war years. Sinatra developed an influential and much-imitated mature style in the 1950s on albums such as *Only The Lonely*, in which his ballads showcased detailed musical phrasing and sensitive reading of lyrics, while his swing numbers on *Songs For Swingin' Lovers* displayed an exciting rhythmic vivacity.

Many female singing stars of the 1940s who employed a natural, post-crooning delivery also came from big bands. Smooth-voiced Jo Stafford (1917–2008), for example, was with Tommy Dorsey as part of the Pied Pipers vocal group and became the first artist to sign to Capitol Records, the home of superior vocal pop in the 1950s. Peggy Lee (1920–2002) sang with Benny Goodman before becoming a successful solo singer known for her restrained and sophisticated style. Doris Day, perhaps the most gifted of all, was the female singer with bandleader Les Brown before movie stardom refocused her career.

The jazz singers

Popular African American vocalists of the period often came from the jazz world. Nat "King" Cole (see p.269) was a major jazz pianist who had to be coaxed into singing. His lush ballads "Smile" and "Unforgettable" with his distinctive honeyed baritone were among the most popular records of the 1950s. Billy Eckstine (1914–1993) had run a groundbreaking bebop band before going solo in 1947 and selling millions of records that featured his impressive, vibrato-adorned singing.

Billie Holiday (see pp.236–237) developed an effective vocal style that blended a grainy timber with a jazz-informed ability to reform a melody. She influenced many singers, including Sinatra. Ella Fitzgerald (see above) and Sarah Vaughan (1924–1990)displayed conspicuous improvisational skills but were equally at home with easy-on-the-ear, swing-derived pop as with out-and-out jazz.

Nice 'n' easy

Other famous performers in the 1950s such as the singer-songwriter and pianist Johnny Ray were slightly outside the crooning tradition, although even after the dawn of rock 'n' roll, the ballads of Elvis Presley (see pp.316–317) displayed the distinct influence of Dean Martin (1917–1995), himself a crooner in the Crosby tradition.

In the 1960s and '70s, music with a relaxed approach to an American songbook standard was labeled "easy listening," exemplified by performers such as Matt Monro and Jack Jones, although later, rich-voiced pop-era singer-songwriters such as Scott Walker, Bryan Ferry, and Elvis Costello exhibited crooner characteristics.

KEY WORKS

Rudy Vallée "Deep Night"
Al Bowlly "The Very Thought Of You"
Bing Crosby "Pennies From Heaven"
Frank Sinatra "I've Got You Under My Skin"
Doris Day "Secret Love"
Ella Fitzgerald "Ev'ry Time We Say Goodbye"

252 **The number of songs recorded by Ella Fitzgerald for her *Songbook* series.**

7 **The number of albums released by Sinatra after his "retirement."**

SINGER (1917–1996)

ELLA FITZGERALD

Ella Fitzgerald had many hits with novelty swing numbers in the late 1930s and early 1940s, but it was her later bebop-influenced scat skills that marked her as a major jazz talent. From 1957 to 1964, under manager and producer Norman Granz, Ella recorded a series of eight refined *Songbook* albums in a swing style that emphasized the craft of the great American composers, setting a benchmark for all vocalists venturing into similar territory.

> "**Bing** sings like all **people think** they **sing in the shower.**"
>
> AMERICAN SINGER AND ACTRESS DINAH SHORE, ON BING CROSBY

TECHNOLOGY

RIBBON MICROPHONE

The essential function of the microphone is to capture ambient sound and translate it into electrical signals that can be recorded or converted back to sound via amplification and loudspeakers. This process is achieved with various acoustic-electro methods. Early microphones struggled to capture the nuance of real sound, and initial efforts, including those of American inventor Thomas Edison, were directed at developing the microphone as a telephone voice transmitter. In 1878, American-Welsh scientist and musician David Edward Hughes patented the carbon microphone, establishing the microphone technology in use today. More advanced versions transformed the possibilities for radio as well as live and recorded sound, enhancing singers' voices and cutting out background noise.

Microphones appeared on bandstands from the early 1920s. This picture shows a ribbon microphone, a refinement developed in the early 1940s and known for its smooth sound.

AFTER

Since the 1980s, a new generation of jazz and swing singers has revived the crooning style.

THE RAT PACK COMEBACK

Jazz pianist Harry Connick Jr. became popular in the late 1980s with a **swing style** that revived an interest in the "Rat Pack" music of Frank Sinatra, Dean Martin, and Sammy Davis Jr. British pop star **Robbie Williams** recorded the Rat Pack tribute *Swing When You're Winning* in 2001, and the Sinatra-derived work of Canadian **Michael Bublé** has fans worldwide. The influence of 1950s songbirds is also evident in the songs of **Norah Jones** and **Melody Gardot**.

HARRY CONNICK JR.

Recording a soundtrack
English composer Sir Malcolm Arnold (1921–2006) conducts the orchestra during the recording of the soundtrack composed by Sir William Walton (1902–1983) for the 1969 film *The Battle of Britain*.

BEFORE

Early silent films were often accompanied by a piano or organ soloist playing a random score.

ORCHESTRAL ACCOMPANIMENT
As early as 1908, **Camille Saint-Saëns** produced an 18-minute orchestral piece to accompany the film *The Assassination of the Duke of Guise*, and in 1916, American composer **Victor Herbert** provided an entire symphonic score for *The Fall of a Nation*, a sequel to D.W. Griffith's *The Birth of a Nation* (1915). Otherwise, cinema orchestras played from compilation scores aided by cue sheets compiled from the cinema's stock of music cues. These orchestras disbanded when "talkies" arrived.

CINEMA ORGAN, 1927

Music for the Screen

Film music was once regarded by critics as commercial writing by composers subsidizing their earnings from more serious endeavors. Increasingly, however, the quality of soundtrack music casts its practitioners as fine composers and musicians.

The film industry recognized early on that musical accompaniment enhanced the moviegoer's experience. When silent films were supplanted by "talkies" in the late 1920s, music soundtracks continued the mood-heightening work that live music accompaniments had begun—but under the much closer control of the filmmaker.

Still, it took a few years for filmmakers to become comfortable with the notion of "nondiegetic" music in film—music that does not occur naturally within a dramatic situation: for example, from a visible band or orchestra. However, by the mid-1930s, the symphonic film score had become an integral part of a movie and working practices were established.

Procedures and techniques

Scores were commonly created from a list of cues negotiated at an initial "spotting" session when the composer and director viewed a rough-cut of the film. Quantity, location, length, and type of cue were agreed upon. The composer then had to work to produce the score quickly, as the music was usually composed toward the end of the filmmaking process. Recording was done while the film was being shown, so the conductor (often the composer) could time the music appropriately. Aids to this process included audible "click-tracks" that were punched into the film, or visual scratches and flashes on the frames.

Composers soon learned numerous techniques suitable for film scoring. One was an adaptation of Wagner's *leitmotif* technique, the name for a recurring, short melodic theme associated with character, idea, or significant event. This served two useful purposes. First, there was appropriate, often subliminal reinforcement of a storyline or theme, and, second, the repetition of previously written musical material

High Noon sheet music
"Do Not Forsake Me—Oh My Darlin'," the song written by Dmitri Tiomkin and sung by Tex Ritter over the titles of the 1952 Western *High Noon*, encouraged the rise of the film theme song.

saved precious moments for the time-strapped film composer. Composers became adept at supporting the narrative—for example, using rhythmic and vibrant cues for images of galloping horses or moody and dissonant sounds for scenes of tension. If the music reflected the screen images too literally—for instance, a timpani hit as someone falls over—this was referred to as "mickey mousing" after the highly synchronized cartoon scores.

Europeans in Hollywood

Although the vast majority of films in the 1930s and '40s were made in Hollywood, a striking number of film composers originated from overseas. This helped establish late-19th-century European romanticism as Hollywood's default musical style, though with various genres to write for, many composers became known for particular styles. Viennese-born Max Steiner, for example, was best known for dramatic, melodious music and creating landmark scores for *King Kong* (1933) and *Gone With the Wind* (1939), while Austrian Erich Korngold wrote rich, passionate music, notably for *The Adventures Of Robin Hood* (1938). Hungarian Miklós Rózsa was as effective at moody scoring for the film-noir classic *Double Indemnity* (1944) as for epics calling for grandeur, such as *Quo Vadis* (1951) and *Ben-Hur* (1959). Bernard Herrmann produced some of cinema's most memorable scores in this period, including for Alfred Hitchcock's *Vertigo* (1958) and *Psycho* (1960). Orson Welles specifically edited parts of *Citizen Kane* (1941) to fit in with Herrmann's score.

"He only finishes **60 percent** of the **picture;** I have to **finish it for him.**"

BERNARD HERRMANN, COMPOSER, ON FILM DIRECTOR ALFRED HITCHCOCK

Although they were highly trained musicians who produced accomplished concert works as well as film scores, these professional Hollywood composers received little respect from the classical music establishment. British composers William Walton and Ralph Vaughan Williams and the American Aaron Copland, who only dabbled in film music, received the critical plaudits during this period.

Enter the moderns

Alex North's jazz-influenced, dissonant score for *A Streetcar Named Desire* (1951) helped create the first Hollywood movie that sounded like modern America. There were further explorations of jazz idioms in Leonard Bernstein's tough *On The Waterfront* (1954) score, Elmer Bernstein's startlingly brash *Man With the Golden Arm* (1955), and the work of Quincy Jones, Henry Mancini, and Lalo Schifrin through the 1960s and '70s. Italian composer Ennio Morricone found fame with Sergio Leone's western *Fistful of Dollars* (1964) before going on to work with Bernardo Bertolucci and Quentin Tarantino, picking up an Oscar for the score of *The Hateful Eight* in 2015.

Scores for electronic instruments grew in popularity through the 20th century. German disco producer Giorgio Moroder won an Oscar for the score of *Midnight Express* (1978), as did Greek rock musician Vangelis for *Chariots of Fire* (1981). In the 21st century, composers Atticus Ross and Trent Reznor were highly praised for the electronic score of *Gone Girl* (2014).

Electronic composing and editing have also changed the way film scores are produced. The technology enables composers to create "mock-ups" using sample libraries of instruments, so that the directors can listen to a soundtrack before it is recorded by musicians.

The return of the orchestra

Although Elmer Bernstein, Jerry Goldsmith, and others continued to provide traditional film scores through the 1960s and '70s, it was the vivid music for *Jaws* (1975) and *Star Wars* (1977) by John Williams that revived the orchestral score. His strong melodic themes and lush orchestrations remain influential to this day. Rachel Portman, who was awarded an Oscar for the score of *Emma* (1996), hardly uses electronic instruments at all, while fellow Oscar winning composer Anne Dudley (*The Full Monty*, 1997) combines electronic and orchestral music to thrilling effect.

COMPOSER (1932–)

JOHN WILLIAMS

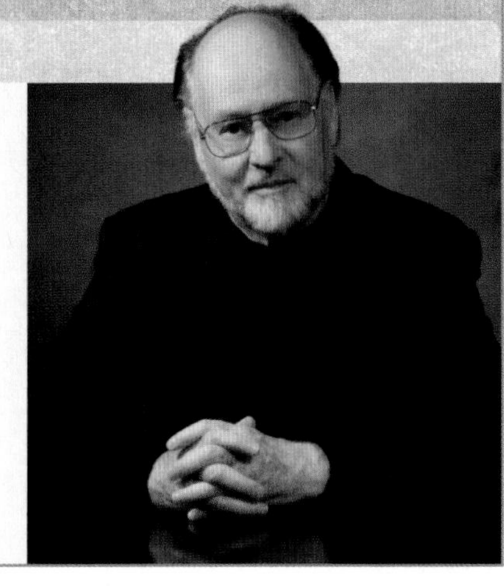

The most successful composer in the history of film, John Williams has written the scores for *Jaws* (1975), *Star Wars* (1977), *Close Encounters of the Third Kind* (1977), and the first three Harry Potter films (2002–2004). His strong melodic scores have won five Oscars (52 nominations), two Emmys, three Golden Globes, 25 Grammys, seven BAFTAs, and innumerable other accolades. In addition to composing music (classical as well as for film and TV), Williams works as a conductor and pianist. He is renowned for writing scores by hand.

AFTER

Screen composing embraced new opportunities, but progress on the inclusion of diverse talent was slow.

VIDEO GAMES

Japanese composers Koichi Sugiyama (*Dragon Quest*, 1986) and Nobuo Uematsu (Final Fantasy series, 1987–present) introduced grand **orchestral scores** to the video game world.

UNDERREPRESENTED

In 2016, composer Katheryn Bostic became the first Black American woman to join the Academy of Motion Picture Arts and Sciences. In 2019, Icelandic composer Hilda Guðnadóttir won an Oscar for *The Joker*, only the third awarded to a woman for a musical score.

The orchestral score of *Psycho*
This page is from the score used to conduct the orchestra in the recording of Bernard Herrmann's soundtrack for the Hitchcock film *Psycho*. The harrowing, piercing writing for the violins to accompany the infamous shower scene is visible here.

KEY WORKS

Erich Korngold *The Adventures of Robin Hood*
Max Steiner *Now, Voyager*
Franz Waxman *Sunset Boulevard*
Bernard Herrmann *Psycho*
Ennio Morricone *The Good, the Bad, and the Ugly; The Mission*
John Williams *Jaws*

Hollywood Musicals

Hollywood musicals not only brought virtuoso performances, stage hits, and grandiose spectacle to moviegoers, but they also attracted the world's finest composers, songwriters, and lyricists, who found that movies offered limitless opportunities for musical innovation.

Amid the misery of the economic depression and wartime horrors of the 1930s and '40s, movie audiences yearned for escapism—song and dance, comedy and romance. It is no coincidence that the first great movie musical coincided with the Great Depression. The musical *42nd Street* (1933) established a bankable movie format, while also defining the "backstage musical" genre (a musical with a plot that revolves around the production of a play or musical revue) that endures to this day. Its score established the Hollywood career of the composer and songwriter Harry Warren and its stars, Dick Powell and Ruby Keeler, became the first performing partnership that enthralled audiences.

Fred and Ginger

The screen partnership of Fred Astaire and Ginger Rogers epitomized the glamour, romance, and sheer virtuosity of dance on film.

BEFORE

As soon as the movies could talk, they also sang. The first "talkie," *The Jazz Singer* (1928), featured Al Jolson singing six songs, with "Toot Toot Tootsie" the first musical number committed to sound film.

THE VERY FIRST MUSICALS

The **first all-sound musical** was *The Broadway Melody* (1929), which was also the first MGM musical and the first "talkie" to win the **Oscar for Best Picture**. Its success prompted a glut of movie musicals, as other studios rushed to exploit the public's appetite for sound movies and **Broadway composers** were lured to Hollywood. Yet the public's appetite for these early movie musicals was quickly satiated. More than 100 musicals were released in 1930; 1931 saw just 14.

The success of *42nd Street* inspired a succession of movies. More sophisticated were the movies of Fred Astaire and Ginger Rogers, who embodied elegance and romance in a succession of hugely popular vehicles that are valuable not only as a showcase for the duo's dancing, but also for the succession of standards they introduced—"A Fine Romance" and "The Way You Look Tonight" from *Swing Time* (1936); George Gershwin's "They Can't Take That Away From Me" from *Shall We Dance* (1937); and Irving Berlin's "Cheek to Cheek" from *Top Hat* (1935).

Production values soared as the 1930s progressed, with mammoth set pieces and innovative camerawork pushing the capabilities of both movies and musical performance. The studios' music departments made Los Angeles a hub of international talent at a time when leading composers and instrumentalists were fleeing Nazism in Europe.

Under the direction of such musicians as Alfred Newman (at 20th Century Fox) and Herbert Stothart (at MGM), in-house orchestras and teams of arrangers and orchestrators provided a pool of musical talent that could fulfill every musical requirement. Arrangers and orchestrators such as Leo Arnaud, George Bassmann, and Conrad Salinger were instrumental in achieving the richness and variety of the Hollywood musicals' sound.

The decade culminated with one of the most expensive movies made to date, *The Wizard of Oz* (1939), whose score by Harold Arlen and E. Y. Harburg included the Academy Award-winning song "Over the Rainbow." Financial constraints and the looming war, however, put an end to these extravaganzas. The 1940s saw wholesome, lower-key movies, such as MGM's "let's put on a show" musicals starring Mickey Rooney and Judy Garland, which included *Babes in Arms* (1939), *Strike Up the Band* (1940), and *Babes on Broadway* (1941).

Screen star

Judy Garland, MGM's leading musical star in the 1940s, achieved stardom as Dorothy Gale in one of the best-loved movies of all time, *The Wizard of Oz.*

Singin' in the Rain
Performer, director, and choreographer, Gene Kelly redefined the role of dance in movies. This scene from the movie *Singin' in the Rain* remains an iconic image of the entire genre.

"It's an era that will **never come back** again, and it's a **treasure:** a true **American art form."**

AMERICAN DANCER, SINGER, AND ACTRESS ANN MILLER, SPEAKING IN 1996

Dancing on screen

The American director and choreographer Busby Berkeley (1895–1976) was noted for his kaleidoscopic set pieces featuring dozens of dancers. In movies such as *Gold Diggers* (1933) and *Dames* (1934), he redefined the cinematic potential of choreography and led the way for choreographers such as Charles Walters (1911–1982), Hermes Pan 1910–1990), Stanley Donen (1924–2019), and Bob Fosse (1927–1987).

Undoubtedly, the movies' greatest dance partnership remains that of Fred Astaire (1899–1987) and Ginger Rogers (1911–1995), who epitomized glamour and romance in a string of 1930s hits. Meanwhile, Eleanor Powell popularized solo tap-dancing, paving the way for later stars such as Ann Miller.

The greatest movie dancer was Gene Kelly (1912–1996), who elevated dance to an integrated part of film's dramatic momentum in *An American in Paris* (1951) and *Singin' in the Rain* (1952).

COMPOSER (1894–1973)

HARRY WARREN

Harry Warren's career embraced the golden age of the Hollywood musical, from the groundbreaking *42nd Street* to the finest achievements of the Freed Unit. Born in Brooklyn, he wrote songs for all the major studios. He received eleven Academy Award nominations for Best Song and won three times. His hits included "Lullaby of Broadway" (*Gold Diggers of Broadway*, 1935), "You'll Never Know" (*Hello, Frisco, Hello*, 1943) and "On the Atchison, Topeka and the Santa Fe" (*The Harvey Girls*, 1946).

The golden age

The movie company MGM was to become the undisputed home of the Hollywood musical, but earlier in the 1940s it was the exuberant Technicolor musicals of 20th Century Fox that did most to lift war-weary spirits. The decade's biggest moneymaking star was Fox's Betty Grable (1916–1973), known as "Queen of the Hollywood Musical." Her movies were often nostalgic, and some of her biggest hits, such as *Sweet Rosie O'Grady* (1943), *Coney Island* (1943), and *Mother Wore Tights* (1947), featured 1890s settings that revived old vaudeville and parlor songs.

The 1940s saw a breathtaking array of talent in movie musicals, often with a unique style or selling point—raucous Betty Hutton, aquatic Esther Williams, and exotic Carmen Miranda. Now firmly established as the prime showcase of popular music, movie musicals produced some of the biggest song hits of the time, including Harry Warren's "Chattanooga Choo-Choo" from *Sun Valley Serenade* (1941), and Hugh Martin's and Ralph Blane's "Have Yourself a Merry Little Christmas" and "The Trolley Song" from *Meet Me in St. Louis* (1944).

As World War II ended, musicals became less about pure escapism, although nostalgia and spectacle were still vital. At MGM, the producer Arthur Freed assembled a coterie of superb talent that became legendary as the "Freed Unit" and established MGM as Hollywood's musical powerhouse. He transformed musicals into more integrated, character-driven works, such as *Easter Parade* (1948).

Off Broadway

As Hollywood battled the rise of television in the 1950s, musicals grew in scale and ambition. This was the decade of the blockbuster Broadway musical, an obvious source of material on which to lavish the latest cinematic developments, such as Cinemascope and 3-D technology. The 1950s were therefore dominated by adaptations of Broadway musicals. Irving Berlin's *Annie Get Your Gun* (1950) was the first of a highly successful string of movies that included Cole Porter's *Kiss Me Kate* (1953); Frank Loesser's *Guys and Dolls* (1955); and Rodgers and Hammerstein's *Oklahoma!* (1955), *The King and I* (1956), *Carousel* (1956), and *South Pacific* (1958).

The leading musical star of the 1950s was Doris Day, whose movies ranged from musical comedies such as *Calamity Jane* (1953) to dramatic musical biopics like *Love Me or Leave Me* (1955). Day was the last of the truly great movie musical stars; as she turned to romantic comedy at the end of 1950s, movie musicals had already begun to diminish.

Genre in decline

Despite the success of several movie musicals, notably *West Side Story* (1961), *Mary Poppins* (1964), *My Fair Lady* (1964), and *The Sound of Music* (1965), the rise of rock 'n' roll heralded changing tastes in the 1960s. Elvis Presley made several movie musicals, but the genre failed to keep up with the transformation of popular culture. The failure of big-budget movies such as *Jumbo* (1962), *Camelot* (1967), and *Doctor Dolittle* (1967) contributed to the studios' financial problems, while the decline of the studio system dismantled the teams of visionaries that had made the movie musical the epitome of Hollywood glamour and imagination. *Hello Dolly!* (1969) was the last of the lavish Hollywood musicals in the classic mold. It flopped.

My Fair Lady
This poster advertised the movie *My Fair Lady*. Adapted from Lerner and Loewe's stage hit in 1964, it was one of a series of adaptations of Broadway shows, and one of the last of Hollywood's big hit musicals.

KEY WORKS

Harry Warren and Al Dubin *42nd Street*
Irving Berlin and Max Steiner *Top Hat*
Hugh Martin and Ralph Blane *Meet Me in St. Louis*
Arthur Freed and Nacio Herb Brown *Singin' in the Rain*
George Gershwin *An American in Paris*
Rogers and Hammerstein *The Sound of Music*

AFTER

After the failure of *Hello Dolly!* in 1969, the Hollywood musical was no longer bankable. Yet they continued to find an audience, from nostalgia-soaked Grease (1978) to a string of hits from Disney.

STILL FROM THE MOVIE *GREASE*

STAR POWER

New-wave Hollywood musicals frequently cast stars who have made their names on the stage or small screen. Meryl Streep steals *Mamma Mia!* (2008), Ryan Gosling stars in *La La Land* (2016), and Andrew Garfield leads *Tick, Tick... Boom!* (2021).

DISNEY REVIVAL

In the 1990s, **Disney** kept the movie musical alive, with major hits such as *Beauty and the Beast* (1991) and *The Lion King* (1994). *Beauty* was reprised in 2017 with Emma Watson, while *The Lion King* was given a CGI makeover in 2019. Will Smith as *Aladdin* (2019) gave Disney the top three highest-grossing movie musicals of all time.

One Voice

Black gospel music is one of the major contributions of African Americans to American music. Gospel blues united the Negro Spiritual with the blues to give a new flavor to traditional hymns. Moving on from its golden age in the 1950s, gospel continues to evolve.

Gospel music came from churches. Traditional hymns, brought over from England to the United States, were sung every Sunday by white Americans. Enslaved people, influenced by West African call-and-response techniques, grafted a "call-and-response" format on to them, and they evolved into what came to be known as the "Negro spiritual." During the 1920s and '30s, classically trained singers Marian Anderson and Paul Robeson included spirituals in their repertoires.

In concert halls attended by the upper crust of society, operatically styled Negro spirituals arranged by Harry T. Burleigh (1866–1949) became popular. They were a world away from the call-and-response songs sung by enslaved people during an arduous workday on cotton plantations and chain gangs who used the call-and-response model in their work songs. One singer would sing a line and it would be repeated, often in harmony, by the group.

Gospel blues

Thomas A. Dorsey (1899–1993) was a ragtime and blues pianist who became known as the Father of Gospel Music. He and Willie Mae Ford Smith (1904–1994) were pioneers of gospel blues, a style of singing at the intersection of the blues and gospel music. Its musical characteristics included improvisation, free timing, sermonette style, and call-and-response, all delivered in an emotional and passionate manner.

Willie Mae Ford Smith often used the sermonette style, in which a sermon was delivered within the context of a song. Because women were discouraged from being preachers, "sermonetting" allowed them to embed spiritual messages into songs. With the formation of the National Conference of Gospel Choirs and Choruses (NCGCC) in 1932, Dorsey introduced the music to a broader audience.

Blues is the backbone of gospel, and Sister Rosetta Tharpe's (1915–1973) gospel style was heavily blues-influenced. She was unique among gospel singers of the 1930s and '40s in accompanying herself with a raucous amplified guitar. Meanwhile her contemporary, Mahalia Jackson (1911–1972), became one of the first Black gospel superstars. In the 1940s, her song "Move On Up a Little Higher" sold over eight million copies.

The golden era to urban beats

The Staple Singers were a family who sang together. Comprising Roebuck "Pops" Staples and his daughters, Cleotha, Pervis, Mavis, and Yvonne, they started off performing gospel songs acoustically, in a rural and folksy style, in Chicago churches in the early 1950s. Pops Staples was a blues guitarist who played a traditional Mississippi Delta style, and they employed musicians from soul and funk backgrounds to provide instrumental backup, leading to a heavier tone than most gospel. While religious in nature, their lyrics spoke of liberation and better times to come, themes with political resonance in the days of unequal rights for African Americans.

In the 1970s, Black gospel artists from earlier generations, including Willie Mae Ford Smith and Albertina Walker, recorded albums, received awards, and gained recognition from newly established artists, inspiring another generation of commercially successful Black gospel artists.

A showbiz act
Gertrude Ward and her daughters Willa and Clara established the Ward Singers in the 1930s. The all-female troupe was celebrated for its showbiz approach to gospel performance.

KEY WORKS

Charles Albert Tindley "The Storm Is Passing Over"
Shirley Caesar "Satan We're Gonna Tear Your Kingdom Down"
Tonéx "Make Me Over"
Jonathan Butler "Falling in love with Jesus"
Le'Andria Johnson "Better Days"
LaShun Pace "I Know I've Been Changed"
The Clark Sisters "Is My Living in Vain"
Marvin Sapp "Never Would Have Made It"

« BEFORE

Gospel music evolved in the 19th century and went on to incorporate elements of early soul and jazz.

THE FIRST GOSPEL STARS
In the late 1800s, Fisk University's **Jubilee Singers** brought Negro spirituals to a wider audience around the world. The blues emerged during Reconstruction (1865–1877) in the Mississippi Delta. Devout churchgoers referred to it as "the devil's music."

THE FISK JUBILEE SINGERS, 1871

GOSPEL SINGER (1904–1994)

WILLIE MAE FORD SMITH

Willie Mae Ford Smith was born in Mississippi to a religious musical family and grew up listening to the blues. The family relocated to St. Louis, Missouri, where Willie Mae and her sisters formed The Ford Sisters. In 1934, Mother Ford's performance of Thomas A. Dorsey's song "If You See My Savior, Tell Him That You Saw Me" was a turning point. Dorsey rushed to the venue and sold over 4,000 sheet copies of the song. This sparked a partnership that lasted until Dorsey's death. Smith, who had an aversion to commercialism, was virtually unknown until the 1970s, when she began recording.

The Father of Gospel
The son of a revivalist preacher, Thomas A. Dorsey became known as the "Father of Gospel Music" thanks to his up-tempo blues arrangements of gospel hymns.

Interviewed in the 1982 documentary, *Say Amen, Somebody* (directed by George T. Nierenberg), Willie Mae Ford Smith speaks about the difficulty she faced singing gospel blues. Because she believed that commercializing the music would be ungodly, she lacked financial resources, making day-to-day life on the road very difficult.

Urban contemporary gospel combines Black gospel with various secular styles, such as electronic beats, hip-hop, R&B, Reggae, and other commercial forms. In "Stomp," Kirk Franklin (1970–) uses techniques popular in hip-hop, including a rap feature and a funky groove. This groove is reminiscent of the 1970s groups Chic and Sly and the Family Stone. Tye Tribbett (1976–) is known for fusing hip-hop, soul, and odd time signatures in his music and live arrangements, such as his track "We Gon' Be Alright."

> "**This rhythm** I had, I brought with me to **gospel** songs."
>
> THOMAS A. DORSEY (1899–1993)

Leader of the choir
Choir director Kirk Franklin is the most successful contemporary gospel artist of his generation, winning his 16th Grammy Award in 2021.

AFTER

Gospel music moves beyond the confines of the church and the traditions of the genre.

THE FUTURE OF GOSPEL
Chicago-born contemporary gospel artist **Jonathan McReynolds** (1989–) has a spellbinding tenor textured vocal timbre. He often sings about the conflict between worldly and spiritual matters.

B.SLADE
Tonéx's (1975–) alter ego, B.Slade, takes his music beyond the church. Known for his flamboyant garb, he has abandoned gospel's traditions. The ballad "Make Me Over" catapulted him to nationwide fame. He has worked with **secular artists** such as Patti Labelle, Snoop Dog, and Janet Jackson.

B.SLADE

The **Music** of **Indonesia**

The Republic of Indonesia is spread across 17,508 islands. Not surprisingly, it has a wide range of musical styles, but its signature genres are all based on the gamelan orchestra—a percussion ensemble made up of gongs, xylophones, flutes, and drums.

A gamelan orchestra is chiefly made up of tuned metal percussion, including gongs, metallophones (metal bars), and drums (see pp.298–299). Unlike Western orchestras, it has no conductor, no sheet music, and no soloists. Gamelan music is a community-based music based upon practice and performance. Each player learns all the different instruments and during a long performance musicians will frequently change places and roles.

BEFORE

The origins of the gamelan orchestra date back centuries. The music was embraced by Hindu, Buddhist, and Muslim religions.

EARLY ORCHESTRAS
The largest gamelan orchestras, **gamelan Sekaten**, are thought to have been built during the early days of **Islam** in 12th-century Indonesia, on the island of Java. They play once a year, on Muhammad's birthday.

SHADOW PLAYS
A centuries-old tradition in Indonesia is the *wayang kulit*, essentially an **all-night puppet show** accompanied by a gamelan orchestra. Stories from the **Hindu epics** *Ramayana* and *Mahabharata* are enacted by shadow puppets—the silhouettes of figures manipulated by a puppeteer behind a screen.

JAVANESE SHADOW PUPPET

The structure of gamelan music is reflected in its layout. Metallophones in the center of the ensemble play a melody, the instruments at the front then play variations on this, and the gongs at the back add slow, weighty interjections. There are two main modes, or scales, in which gamelan music is played: the five-note *laras slendro* and the seven-note *laras pelog*.

The main types of gamelan music come from the Indonesian islands of Java and Bali.

Frame

Large tube

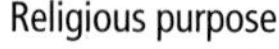

Religious purpose
The *angklung* is a four-note gamelan instrument. It is played by the older boys of the Balinese villages during the annual island-wide festival of Galungan, in which family processions take offerings to the temple.

Gamelan in Java

The most important instrument in a Javanese gamelan ensemble is the *gong ageng*. It is the largest gong at the back of the ensemble. Typically forged from a single piece of bronze, it is surrounded by several smaller hanging gongs called *kempul* and various horizontally mounted gongs called *ketuk* and *kenong*, which play shorter, more melodic phrases.

At the front of a Javanese gamelan lie the main melody instruments: two small kettle-gongs called *boning*, several metallophones known as *gender*, wooden xylophones, zithers, spike-fiddles, and *suling* (flutes). All of these play the most nimble and lithe melodies. A complete ensemble also includes a chorus of male singers and one of female singers—known respectively as *gerong* and *pesindehen*.

"Fantastically rich **melodically, rhythmically, texturally ...**"

BENJAMIN BRITTEN, BRITISH COMPOSER, DESCRIBING GAMELAN, 1956

Javanese styles

The gamelan music of Java has two main styles, which date back to the 19th century and the two royal courts based in the cities of Surakarta and Yogyakarta—the two styles are known as the Solonese and Yogyanese. The ruling Javanese sultans commissioned pieces from their in-house gamelan orchestras and dancers, and there was a creative rivalry between the two royal schools, in both dance and gamelan playing.

There is also a tradition of gamelan called *calung*, in Banyumas, the western part of the province of Central Java, where the instruments are made of bamboo rather than bronze. They were initially constructed to provide portable substitutes for the metal gamelan instruments. Even the sounds of the heaviest gongs are imitated—by blowing down a huge bamboo tube.

Farther west lie Javanese regions that are ethnically Sundanese, the second-largest ethnic group (after Javanese) in Indonesia. *Degung* gamelan is one traditional Sundanese form, and its key distinguishing feature is its particular use of the *suling*. The predominance of this bamboo flute lends *degung* a gentler ambience to Central Java's gamelan, despite the fact that it still uses similar clanging gongs and metallophones. *Degung* gamelan gave rise to a vocal-led music known as *pop sunda*, performed by stars such as Detty Kurnia (1961–2010) who began her career in the mid-1970s and recorded more than 150 albums.

Gamelan orchestra
Each orchestra has a unique character, for its instruments are tuned to each other rather than to a standard. Sets of instruments are often given fanciful names such as "Venerable Spirit of Perfection."

KEY WORKS

Gamelan Gong Kebyar of Belaluan "Kebyar Ding"

Court Gamelan of the Pura Paku Alaman "Ketawang: Puspawarna"

Sekaa Genggong Batur Sari "Angklung Sekar Jati"

Gesang "Bengawan Solo"

Rhoma Irama "Santai"

Hetty Koes Endang "Cinta"

Balinese gamelan

On the Indonesian island of Bali, gamelan playing is an essential part of village life, and most communities have several gamelan ensembles, generally made up of nonprofessional players. The two scales of *slendro* and *pelog* are played, but the tunings may vary, leading to distinct differences in sound between Balinese and Javanese gamelan. In general, Balinese gamelan

Dance and the gamelan
Accompanied by a gamelan orchestra, Batak dance was traditionally used to invoke spirits and ward off disaster. Today, it is performed at weddings, celebrations, and to welcome guests.

music is louder and more ebullient than Javanese gamelan, which is slower and softer.

A style known as *kebyar*, which translates as "blossoming," became very popular in Bali after the dissolution of the Balinese courts in the early years of the 20th century. The rhythms and tempos of the courtly gamelan had been slow and elegant, whereas *kebyar* was fast and dynamic.

In a parallel to the *calung* style of Java's Banyumas area, the impoverished Balinese villages began to construct gamelan instruments from bamboo. In order to replicate the massive bass sonorities of the largest bronze gongs, lengths of bamboo were suspended over a huge earthenware pot to amplify the sound.

Folk and pop

Kroncong is a folk style that evolved from the use of Western instruments brought by the Portuguese to Indonesia in the 16th century. It shares its name with a ukulele-like instrument used in this form of music and is usually played in small ensembles on instruments such as guitar, bass or cello, flute, and—most importantly—accompanied by a singer.

Kroncong had its commercial golden age from the 1930s to the 1960s. The lush, melancholic style of singers such as Hetty Koes Endang can at times sound like an exotic distant cousin to the slow, jazzy American ballad, and at other times resemble Hawaiian music. *Dangdut* is the popular form that rivals gamelan in being a definably Indonesian music.

It developed in the 1960s and the name derives from the sound made by the two-headed *kendang* drum—a percussion instrument similar to the Indian *tabla*.

Dangdut's eclectic blend of Indonesian, Arabic, and Latin American music with jazz and pop instruments made it a fresh and entertaining sound, groovily evocative of its time. Rhoma Irama and Elvy Sukaesih became famous as *dangdut*'s king and queen in the 1970s. Like most Indonesian pop legends, however, they have also experimented in many other styles during their long careers.

METALLOPHONE A xylophone, with metal keys rather than wood.

SULING A flute made from bamboo, one of gamelan's main melody instruments.

AFTER

The creative fusions of the 1960s and 70s laid the foundations for the cosmopolitan sounds heard across Indonesia today.

LEADING LIGHTS

SambaSunda, an Indonesian ethnic music fusion group, has had international success at world music festivals in Europe and the US. Based in Bandung, the cultural center of Sundanese culture in West Java, the 17-strong group plays a kind of **modern-day gamelan** that mixes and matches styles from across the Indonesian islands. As the name suggests, the band is also influenced by the thunderous percussion of Brazilian samba bands.

RITA TILA, SINGER WITH THE SAMBASUNDA ENSEMBLE

INDONESIAN HIP-HOP

Another musician to have sprung from Bandung is the rapper **Iwa K**, who recorded the first Indonesian hip-hop album, *Ku Ingin Kembali*, in 1992. It was an overnight success.

[1] KENDHANG KETIPUNG
Length 20 in (50 cm)

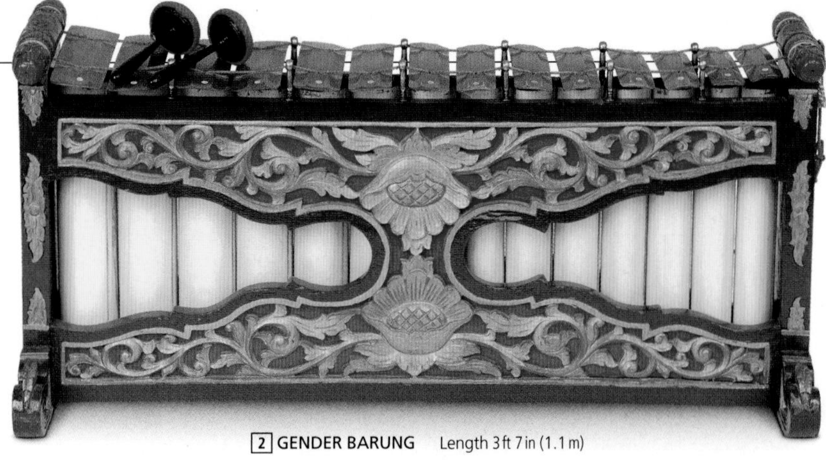

[2] GENDER BARUNG Length 3 ft 7 in (1.1 m)

[5] KENONG
Height 16 in (40 cm)

[6] KEMPYANG
Height 11 in (28 cm)

[7] KETHUK
Height 11 in (28 cm)

[8] SARON BARUNG Length 34 in (86 cm)

Gamelan

Bronze gongs and metallophones make up the instruments of this traditional Indonesian orchestra. There are many types of gamelan, which vary from area to area. The set shown here is from Central Java.

[1] *Kendhang ketipung* Located at the center of the orchestra, this drum controls the tempo of the music as well as signaling a change of section and the end of a piece. Different styles of drumming are used for livelier or more serious pieces. [2] *Gender barung* Played with two soft mallets, the gender barung is one of the "soft instruments" of the ensemble, along with the gender panerus, gambang, and rebab. They are used to create a shimmering layer of elaborations over the lower, more percussive instruments. [3] *Gender panerus* This instrument plays running patterns at twice the speed of the larger and deeper gender barung. The keys are suspended on strings over bamboo or metal resonators. [4] *Slenthem* Struck with a soft mallet, the slenthem produces a sustained and resonant sound. It is used to play the same part as the sarong barung and saron demung. [5] *Kenong* These large pot gongs mark out the structure of a piece, alternating with the kempul and gong suwukan. [6] *Kempyang* and [7] *Kethuk* are two pot gongs played by one player to mark the beats. [8] *Saron barung* Like the saron demung, the saron barung plays the central melody of the piece. [9] *Saron demung* Played with a hard mallet, this instrument is particularly important in loud and fast sections. [10] *Gambang* The only wooden instrument in the gamelan, this is played in octaves and struck with horn-handled mallets. [11] *Rebab* This two-stringed spike fiddle plays a continuous, ornamented melody. Originating in the Middle East, the body was once made from a coconut shell. [12] *Saron panerus* Tuned to play an octave higher than the saron barung, the saron panerus is also played twice as fast. [13] *Bonang barung* A single player strikes this set of pot gongs using two mallets. [14] *Bonang panerus* Sounding an octave higher than the bonang barung, this instrument is often used to play interlocking patterns with its larger brother. The sound of these patterns is often said to be like "golden rain." [15] *Gong ageng* The largest, lowest, and most revered instrument of the gamelan, the gong ageng is struck once to mark the end of a section or piece. Considered sacred, this gong is given offerings of flowers and rice. [16] *Gong suwukan* and *gong kempul* One player plays this collection of gongs, working in tandem with the kenong to mark out the structure of the piece.

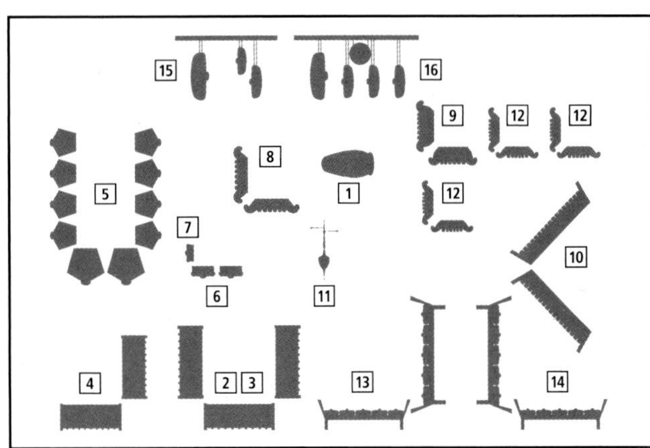

Gamelan orchestra arrangement
This diagram shows the typical seating arrangement of instruments in a gamelan orchestra. The drum player is situated at the center, with the softest instruments placed in positions at the front. The largest—and loudest—gongs are at the back.

[12] SARON PANERUS
Length 66 cm (26 in)

[14] BONANG PANERUS
Length 5 ft (1.5 m)

[15] GONG AGENG
Length 9 ft 2 in (2.8 m)

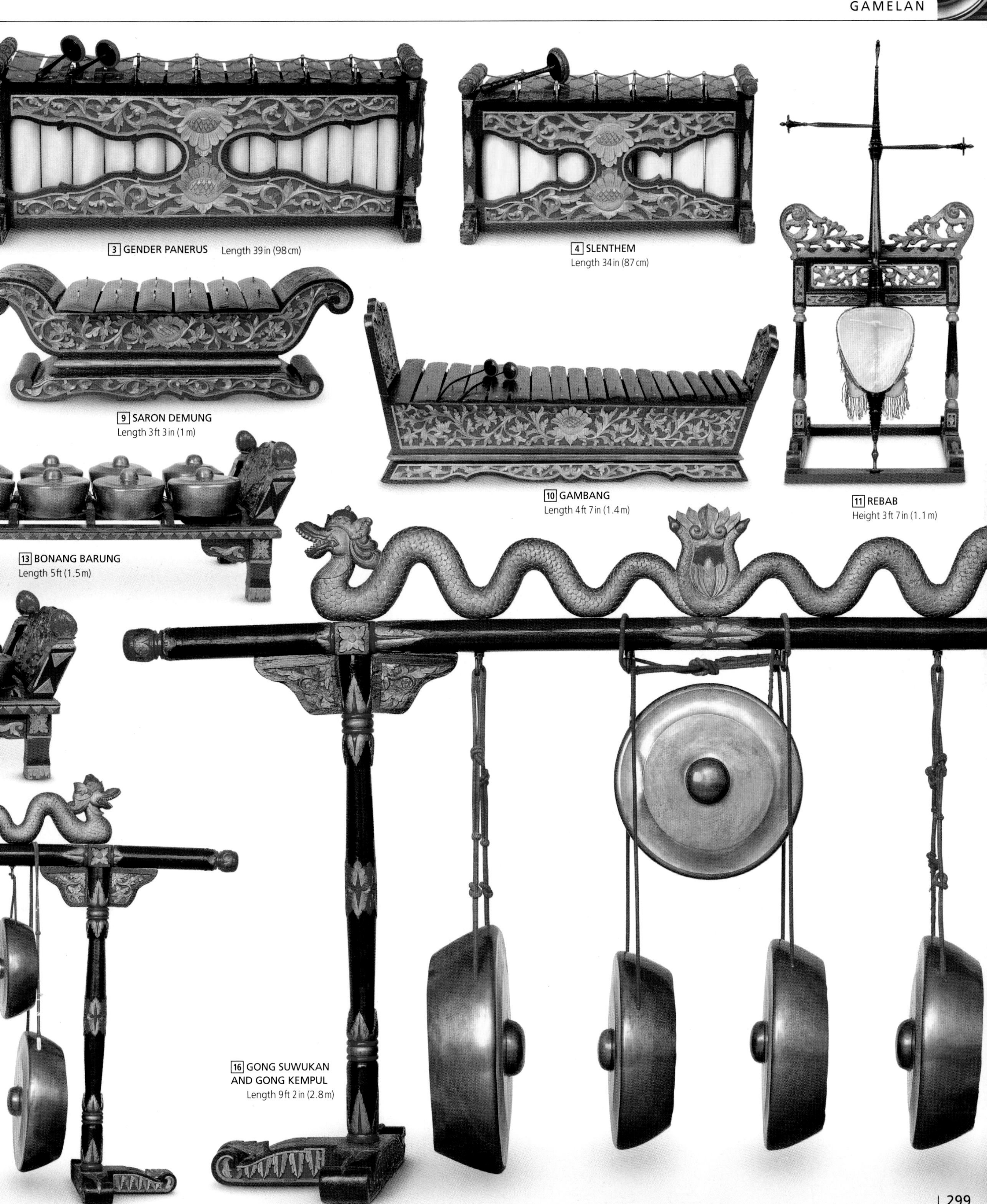

3 GENDER PANERUS Length 39 in (98 cm)

4 SLENTHEM
Length 34 in (87 cm)

9 SARON DEMUNG
Length 3 ft 3 in (1 m)

10 GAMBANG
Length 4 ft 7 in (1.4 m)

11 REBAB
Height 3 ft 7 in (1.1 m)

13 BONANG BARUNG
Length 5 ft (1.5 m)

16 GONG SUWUKAN
AND GONG KEMPUL
Length 9 ft 2 in (2.8 m)

BEFORE

The culture, language, and music shared by the voyagers who spread from Southeast Asia into the Pacific took differing forms throughout the islands of Polynesia.

FIRST CONTACT
Polynesian peoples first reached Fiji around 3,000 years ago, Hawaii less than 2,000 years ago, and New Zealand within the last thousand years.

EUROPEAN ARRIVALS
Europeans first explored Polynesia in the 18th century, while **Christian missionaries** arrived early in the nineteenth. Less than 10 percent of Hawaii's population count as **native Hawaiians**.

HULA INSTRUMENTS: IPU AND IPUHEKE

Island Music

The music of Hawaii and the Pacific is an intriguing hybrid of ancient Polynesian traditions and the influences introduced by migrants—and tourists—from around the globe.

In the many centuries that elapsed between the peopling of the Pacific islands and the arrival of the first European explorers, the Polynesians established a rich and complex culture that took subtly different forms on different islands.

The inhabitants of the remote Hawaiian archipelago were typical in basing their music on chanting rather than singing. The art took two basic forms—*mele hula*, when the chant was composed for, and performed alongside, dance, and *melo oli*, when it stood alone. Musical accompaniment was largely percussive; the large *pahu* drum, made from a hollowed-out palm trunk topped with a tautly stretched shark skin, spread throughout Polynesia from Tahiti, while Hawaii was unique in having the smaller *ipu* drums, made from gourds. The drum bodies themselves also served as a percussive instruments; conch shells could be blown; and in New Zealand, Samoa, and elsewhere, wooden flutes and trumpets were also commonly used.

A royal tradition

Hawaiian music stopped being purely Hawaiian the moment Captain Cook encountered the islands in 1778. It was under foreign influence that islanders started to sing melodies in addition to chanting in rhythm. The two main initial sources were the hymns taught by Christian missionaries from the United States, and the folk

Queen Lili'uokalani
Hawaii's last monarch, Queen Lili'uokalani remains its most famous composer. She wrote "Aloha Oe" in 1878, 13 years before she ascended to the throne.

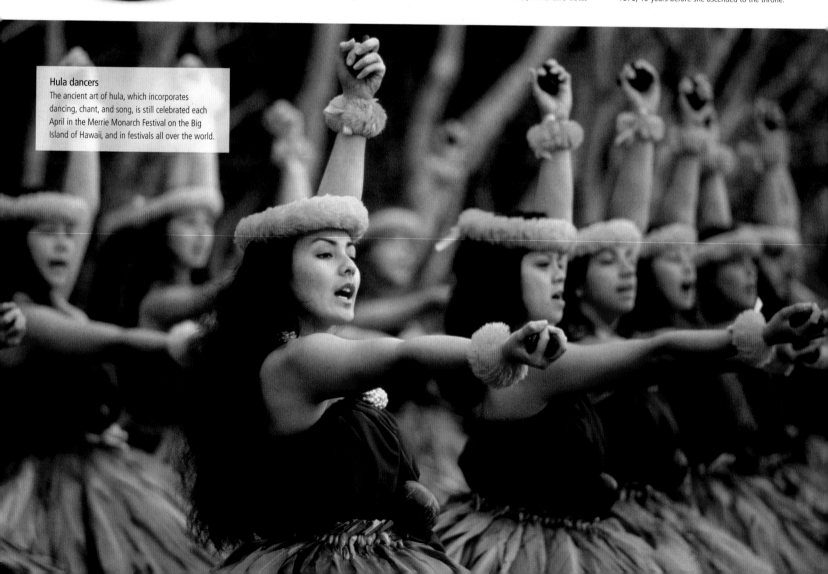

Hula dancers
The ancient art of hula, which incorporates dancing, chant, and song, is still celebrated each April in the Merrie Monarch Festival on the Big Island of Hawaii, and in festivals all over the world.

Founding father
For his solo recordings as well as his role in founding the Sons of Hawaii, slack-key guitarist Philip Kunia "Gabby" Pahinui is the founding father of modern Hawaiian music.

songs (and guitars) brought by Mexican cowboys who came to tend the islands' new cattle herds. Later in the 19th century, immigrants arrived from all over the world to work on extensive sugar plantations. One Portuguese party, in 1878, brought with them the diminutive, four-string guitarlike *braguinha*, which in Hawaiian hands became the ukulele.

The first missionaries denounced hula as being lascivious and immoral. In 1883, however, King David Kalakaua (1836–1891), a proud nationalist determined to reinvigorate Hawaiian culture in the face of foreign encroachment, came to the throne. The so-called "Merrie Monarch" set about encouraging island music, and even formed his own ukulele group. By then, another element had also entered the mix: Prussian bandleader Henry Berger had set up the Royal Hawaiian Band, and Hawaii was going crazy for brass bands. Berger also taught yodeling, which added an idiosyncratic twist to the already established local tradition of falsetto singing, in which the *hai*, or the break between falsetto and "ordinary" voice, is deliberately emphasized rather than hidden.

Both King David and his sister Queen Lili'uokalani (1836–1917), who succeeded him in 1891 only to be deposed in a United States-inspired coup in 1894, were enthusiastic music composers. Many of the songs they wrote remain Hawaiian standards, including the Queen's haunting "Aloha Oe."

> "The **hula** is the **heartbeat** of the Hawaiian people."
>
> KING DAVID KALAKAUA, THE "MERRIE MONARCH"

MUSICIAN AND SINGER (1959–1997)

ISRÆL KAMAKAWIWO'OLE

The biggest Hawaiian star of recent years, Israel Kamakawiwo'ole had a singing voice of stunning power and delicacy, equally at home with militant political anthems and gentle love songs. Best known for his medley of "Somewhere Over the Rainbow/What a Wonderful World," he succumbed to the same obesity-related issues that had previously claimed his elder brother.

Birds of paradise

Even more than lilting melodies and strumming ukuleles, the defining sound of Hawaiian music is the steel guitar. The technique in which a metal rod or knife is pressed onto guitar strings was started by an Oahu schoolboy, Joseph Kekuku (1874–1932), in 1889. After leaving Hawaii in 1904, he toured the United States popularizing the style. It played a major role in the development of the Delta blues, and also provided an essential component of country music.

Many Hawaiian musicians followed in Kekuku's wake, and their music became widely known thanks to the 1915 Panama-Pacific Exposition in San Francisco, and a touring Broadway musical *The Bird of Paradise*. To suit American audiences, and the increasing number of tourists visiting Hawaii, Hawaiian songs were often translated partly or completely into English. A new hybrid genre, *hapa haole*, was born—*hapa* meaning "half," and *haole* "foreign." Part Hawaiian and part American, *hapa haole* songs were frequently performed for comic or novelty effect, emphasizing the supposedly nonsensical sound of Hawaiian words—as in the many versions of the "Hawaiian War Chant," which had originally been a love song—and soon they were being written by Tin Pan Alley songwriters who had never been to Hawaii (see pp.230–231). However, the finest Hawaiian musicians, such as steel guitar masters "King" Bennie Nawahi and Sol Ho'opi'i, achieved world renown for their skills.

While the first *hapa haole* songs drew heavily on ragtime, the genre shifted with each shift in popular taste, thus moving toward jazz and blues in the 1920s and 1930s, big-band swing in the 1940s, and rock 'n' roll in the 1950s. Although the label is not applied to more recent music—the preferred term is "contemporary Hawaiian"—in a sense much modern Hawaiian music is still *hapa haole*, having taken on strong elements of California-style soft rock in the 1970s and 1980s, and later still, in a style also known as "Jawaiian," incorporated reggae.

Postwar pop and purity

Hawaiian tourism boomed in the late 1950s and early 1960s, when Hawaii became the fiftieth state of the United States, jet planes cut down flight times to the islands, and Elvis Presley filmed a string of Hawaii-themed movies. Local musicians who set out to preserve the integrity of authentic Hawaiian music included Gabby Pahinui (1921–1980), a maestro of the then little-known art of slack-key guitar, in which the strings are "slackened" to create an open chord. He joined with ukulele wizard Eddie Kamae (1927–2017) to create the Sons of Hawaii, who recorded a series of sublime albums. That musical revival came to coincide with a larger cultural renaissance from the 1970s onward, in which Hawaiian musicians sang proudly in their own language, and frequently advocated Hawaiian sovereignty, or independence from the United States.

Quintessentially Hawaiian
Modeled originally on small Portuguese instruments, the ukulele is the quintessential Hawaiian instrument. Its name means either "the gift that came here" or "jumping flea."

Blue Hawaii
Elvis Presley, whose looks could convincingly pass for Hawaiian, filmed a string of Hawaii-set musicals, including 1961's *Blue Hawaii* and *Paradise, Hawaiian Style* in 1965.

KEY WORKS

Kanui & Lula "Oua Oua"
Genoa Keawe "Alika"
Israel Kamakawiwo'ole "Hawaii '78"
Lena Machado "E Ku'u Baby Hot Cha Cha"
Sol Ho'opi'i "Uheuhene"
Mahi Beamer "Kahuli Aku Kahuli Mai"
Sons Of Hawaii "Hanohano Hawai'i"

AFTER

While Hawaii is today home to as diverse a musical scene as that of any American state, Hawaiian music as a distinct genre remains very much alive.

MODERN VOICES
Many contemporary performers have **reincorporated chant** into their music, including the Maui-based *kumu hula* (hula teacher) Keali'i Reichel, and the Big Island chanter, dancer, and singer, Kaumakaiwa Kanaka'ole. The tradition of **female falsetto** singing has been reinvigorated by the likes of Amy Hanaiali'I Gilliom.

STRING STARS
Acclaimed **slack-key guitarists** include Dennis Kamakahi and Ledward Ka'apana, while the impressive fingerwork of the virtuoso Jake Shimabukuro has reintroduced the ukulele to the **YouTube generation**.

BEFORE

The rise of nationalism in the 19th century led to a surge of interest in ancient Celtic culture.

ANCIENT CELTIC CULTURE
The Celts were a group of tribal societies, probably with a shared language, that flourished in Europe during the **Iron Age** (from 800 BCE). The domination of the **Roman Empire** **« 24–25** led to a decline in Celtic influence, but Celtic culture survived in Ireland, the west and north of Britain, and western France. It then evolved along different lines.

IRISH REVIVAL
The rise of **nationalism** **« 176–177** in the 19th century resulted in a new interest in Celtic culture and identity. Ireland's Home Rule movement inspired the poet **W. B. Yeats** to rediscover Irish folklore and song, giving it a newfound political significance and artistic boost.

BAGPIPES ARE COMMON TO MANY CELTIC CULTURES

Celtic Music

The traditional music of the ancient Celtic areas of Britain, France, Ireland, and Spain have many similarities, including common instruments. In recent years, these have inspired striking pan-Celtic collaborations and musical cross-pollination.

Celtic music means different things to different people. It often simply refers to traditional Irish music, but it is also a term used to describe musical traditions from nations with a Celtic history, such as Ireland, Scotland, the Isle of Man, Wales, Cornwall, Wales, Brittany, and Galicia in northwest Spain.

Breton revival

The Breton musician Alan Stivell, born in 1944, is probably Celtic music's best spokesperson. He is a master of the Celtic harp, which he began playing at the age of nine when he was given a re-creation of an ancient Celtic harp made by his father.

Stivell's musical career took off in the mid-1960s. The release of his album *Renaissance of the Celtic Harp* sparked a grassroots revival of Breton culture in northern France. His immersion in Celtic mythology, art, and history inspired him to master the Scottish bagpipes, Irish tin whistle, and the bombarde, a fearsome instrument from the oboe family with a piercing tone. On albums such as *Brian Boru*, named after the Irish chieftain who vanquished the Vikings in the 11th century, Stivell demonstrated the similarities between his own traditions and those of the Celtic British Isles.

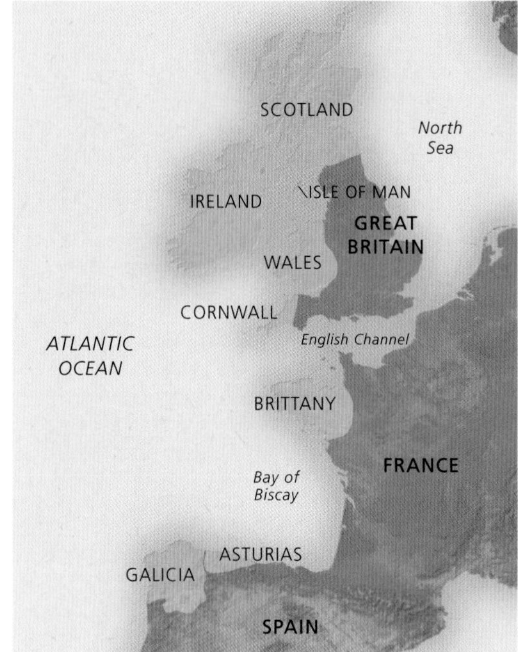

Celtic culture
During the Roman conquest of western Europe, the Celts were driven back to Scotland, Wales, Cornwall, the Isle of Man, Ireland, Brittany in France, and northwest Spain. Elements of Celtic culture, including music, survive in these areas today.

> "The **chain of tradition** was broken. But what we are seeing now is the **rebirth of it all...**"
>
> GALICIAN MUSICIAN CARLOS NÚÑEZ

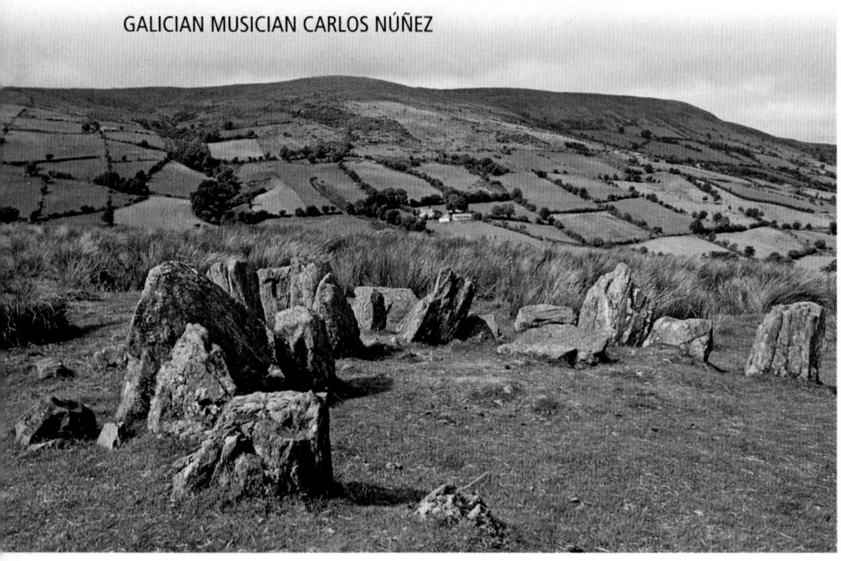

Looking to the past
The 19th-century revival of Gaelic culture led to an interest in Celtic myths, such as that of Ossian, a third-century poet-warrior. Ossian's burial site was said to be this cairn in Cloughbrack, Northern Ireland.

The Chieftains

While Stivell championed Celtic music in France, Ireland's Paddy Moloney was raising the profile of traditional Irish music. His band, the Chieftains, formed with master whistle player Sean Potts and flute player Michael Turbridy in 1962, became one of the most influential and respected traditional music groups in Ireland.

Almost entirely instrumental, the Chieftains' music was based on Ireland's folk dance repertoire of jigs, reels, and hornpipes. It comprised the same rich and varied material that pipers, fiddlers, accordionists, and banjo players were performing in pub sessions throughout Ireland.

220 **The number of pieces composed by the 17th-century Irish harpist Turlough O'Carolan. This blind and itinerant musician is considered to be the godfather of Irish music, and many of his pieces form a core part of Irish music today.**

Over their long career, Moloney took the Chieftains in often surprising, pan-Celtic directions, investigating Brittany's music on albums such as *Celtic Wedding*, for example, and inviting the Galician musician Carlos Núñez to collaborate on the album *Santiago*, released in 1996.

Celtic pipers

Paddy Moloney plays both tin whistle and uilleann pipes. These small bagpipes produce a haunting but nimble sound, as essential to the atmosphere of Irish music as the fiddle or Irish banjo.

Moloney learned the uilleann pipes from the great Irish piping master Leo Rowsome (1903–1970), who came from a long line of virtuoso pipers. A child prodigy, Rowsome became a teacher at Dublin's Municipal School of Music at the age of just 16. He impressed audiences with his Pipe Quartet, a small-group format he favored throughout the 1930s and '40s.

Pipe bands are common to many Celtic regions. Early in his career, Alan Stivell played in a traditional Breton music group called Bagad Bleimor—a *bagad* being the name for the Breton version of the pipe band.

Galician notes

The pipe band has also been adopted for the *gaita*—a bagpipe played in the Galician region of northwest Spain. The instrument, in existence since the Middle Ages, was revived by Núñez and fellow Galician Susana

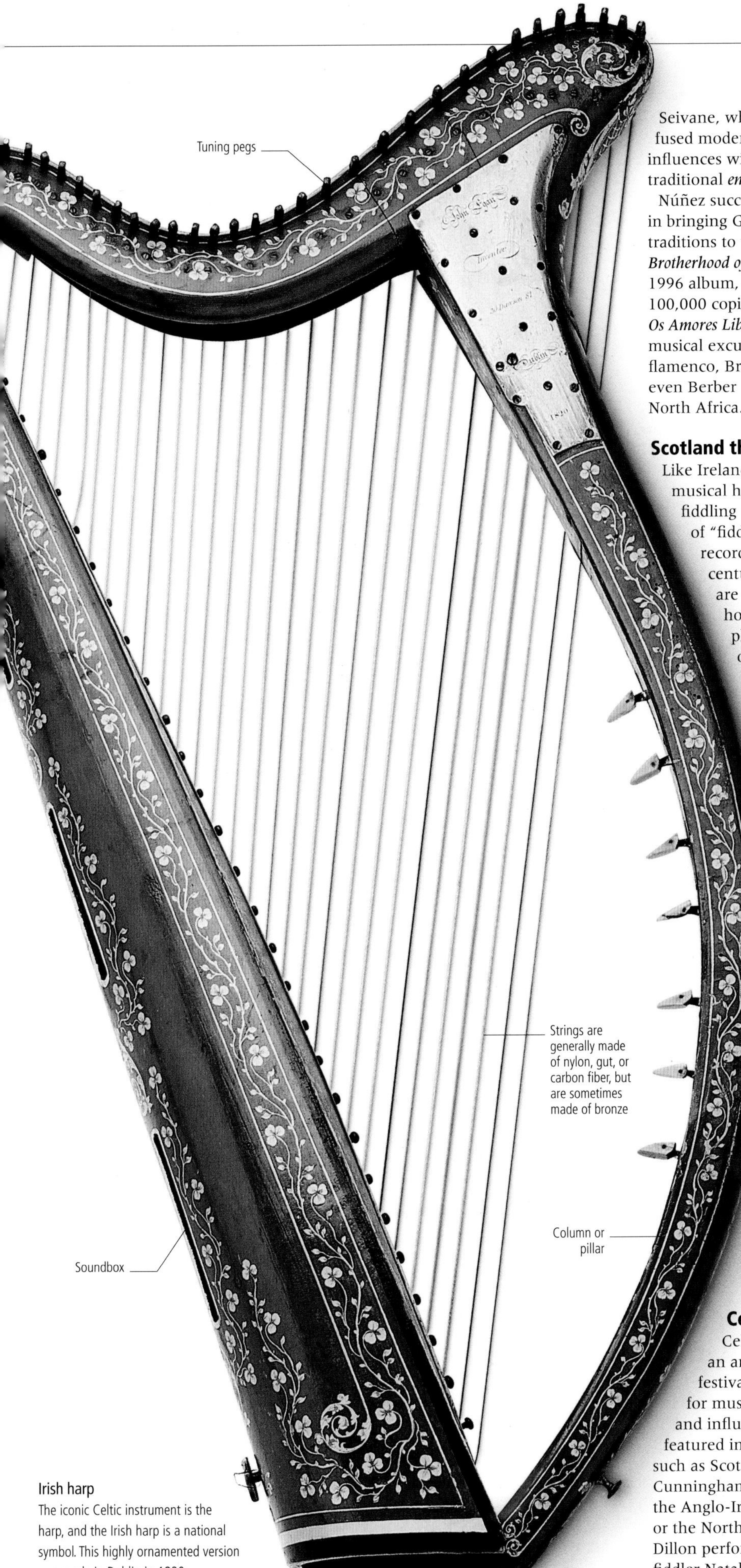

Tuning pegs

Strings are generally made of nylon, gut, or carbon fiber, but are sometimes made of bronze

Column or pillar

Soundbox

Irish harp
The iconic Celtic instrument is the harp, and the Irish harp is a national symbol. This highly ornamented version was made in Dublin in 1820.

Seivane, who have fused modern musical influences with Galicia's traditional *enxebre* style. Núñez succeeded in bringing Galician traditions to the masses. *Brotherhood of Stars*, his 1996 album, sold over 100,000 copies, while *Os Amores Libres* featured musical excursions into flamenco, Breton, and even Berber music from North Africa.

Scotland the brave

Like Ireland, Scotland has a rich musical heritage, including a strong fiddling tradition, with thousands of "fiddle tunes" collected and recorded over the last two centuries. These tunes are usually jigs, reels, or hornpipes, and can be played on instruments other than the fiddle.

Scotland also has its own type of fiddle music, known as the Strathspey, a majestic-sounding folk form that some claim developed from a mimicry of the rhythms of Scots Gaelic—Scotland's form of the Celtic language. Modern Scottish fiddlers include Alasdair Fraser, Ali Bain, and Catriona MacDonald, and Duncan Chisholm. One of the leading lights in the younger generation is the singer and multi-instrumentalist Julie Fowlis, who sings Scots Gaelic songs and plays fiddle tunes on the Scottish smallpipes—another variant on the Celtic bagpipe design.

Celtic platform

Celtic Connections, an annual Scottish music festival, provides a platform for musicians to exchange tunes and influences. The event has featured innumerable collaborations, such as Scottish accordionist Phil Cunningham sharing a stage with the Anglo-Irish folk group Flook, or the Northern Irish singer Cara Dillon performing with Cape Breton fiddler Natalie MacMaster.

Beating the Irish *bodhran*
The *bodhran*, an Irish frame drum, made from taut goatskin, is played with a beater. The player can adjust the pitch by placing their hand inside the drum.

While it is impossible to pinpoint what all these different national musics owe to the ancient Celts, the existence of similar instruments, and the ease with which so many musicians borrow from each other, suggest a shared heritage.

KEY WORKS

The Chieftains "The Ace and Deuce of Pipering"
Alan Stivell "Marv Pontkalleg"
Alasdair Fraser "Cuillin Nights"
Carlos Núñez "Brotherhood of Stars"
John Doherty "Roaring Mary/Stormy Weather"
Susana Seivane "Dous Mares"

AFTER

New generations of musicians are fusing Celtic traditions with pop, rock, and dance forms.

CELTIC ROCK AND DANCE FUSION
In the 1970s, many young bands began infusing traditional Celtic music with **elements from rock music**. In Ireland, the band **Horslips** brought electric rock band arrangements to Irish folk music and wrote lyrics inspired by Irish mythology. Some 10 years later, the Scottish band **Capercaillie**, singing in Scots Gaelic, created their own blend of different Celtic influences. They invited dance remixers to take on their material, embraced drum'n'bass beats, and experimented with pop production.

In the 1990s, the **Afro-Celt Sound System** proved popular at European festivals, melding West African influences with Celtic tunes, dub reggae, and electro. The band invited Senegalese singer **Baaba Maal** to perform with Irish singers, and then dance producers to provide remixes.

BEFORE

Fado may have Afro-Brazilian roots, and can be used to describe any kind of music about mourning or loss.

THE FIRST FAMOUS SINGER
Perhaps from the Latin *fatum* (fate), fado may be traced to the time when **Portugal's court** was in **Rio de Janeiro** (1804–1822). Lisbon prostitute Maria Severa Onofriana (1820–1846), known as A Severa, was the first famous singer, and her romance with aristocrat Count Vimioso established fado as a musical genre of marginalized people.

SHIPS ARRIVE IN LISBON HARBOR

Longing for Fado

Portugal's urban folk music sings of the sea, of longing, of melancholy, and of life among the poor. Accompanied by the Portuguese guitar, fado is deeply rooted in the port district of Lisbon, but it also has a strong tradition in the university town of Coimbra.

A musical form characterized by mournful tunes and lyrics, fado contains elements of Brazilian and North African music as well as Portuguese poetry and the native ballads known as *modhina*.

The roots of the music are often traced to Brazilian immigrants who brought *fofa* and *lundu* dance music to Portugal in the early 1800s. Like tango (see p.254), fado was initially perceived by the bourgeoisie to be a disreputable, lower-class music but was later embraced by all classes. There is even a subgenre of aristocratic fado.

Fado evolved in the port district of Lisbon, and it evokes the rhythms and sounds of the sea and the lives of the poor and working classes who lived and worked as fishermen and docker workers. But the most distinctive note in fado is a sentiment of resignation, fatefulness, and melancholia—loosely captured by the Portuguese word *saudade* (longing). Typically, fado songs take their lyrics from classical poems, such as the works of the 16th-century poet Luís Vaz de Camões, the "Shakespeare of Portugal," and deal with lost or unrequited love, existential sadness, and death. It is this emotional quality that has led to fado being called the blues of Portugal.

12 **The number of strings on a Portuguese guitar.**

17 **The number of verses in a Manuel Alegre fado.**

From Congo via Brazil

The key instrument of fado is the *guitarra portuguesa*, a guitar derived from a lute common to the Congo region of Africa. It was carried to the Portuguese colony of Brazil in the 15th century during the early years of the trafficking of enslaved people and eventually made its way back to Portugal, where it was modified over the years.

In African and Afro-Brazilian music, lutes were mainly used to provide music for dancing, but in Portugal it was adopted by balladeers as the favored instrument of accompaniment. Bass, violin, viola, and cello are also often used for accompaniment by modern fado bands, as are percussion instruments.

African elements imported into Lisbon waned in importance during the 19th century, and the key

A captivating sound
O Fado, painted by Portuguese artist José Malhoa (1855–1933) in 1910, shows fado being played in a tavern. The musician's face echoes his plaintive song, which has captivated the woman at the table.

performers in fado became the singers. Fado was generally sung by one person called a *fadista* and, when performed in bars or impromptu, it was normally accompanied by the teardrop-shaped Portuguese guitar

> "Fado only **brings tears** to those who have **heart.**"
>
> DOM ANTÓNIO DE BRAGANÇA (1895–1964), FADO POET

or the classical guitar.

Fado was the means by which Lisbon's urban poor paid homage to their hometown. The songs celebrated the light, the Tagus River, the old days, and the daily rhythms of the street. Visual beauty served as a counterweight to the trials of life, and the sweet, often soothing melodies and rhythmic music show fado to be more complex than its somber stereotype. Some fados were even accompanied by dancing, with the hips moving in time to the music.

Distinctive dress

Among the Lisbon middle classes, *fadistas* were viewed as outsiders, and the singers and musicians adopted a dress code that made them stand out from normal society. In her 1874 travelogue, ***Fair Lusitania***, Lady Catherine Charlotte Jackson, the wife of a British diplomat, wrote: "*Fadistas* wear a peculiar kind of black cap, wide black pants with close-fitting jacket, and their hair flowing low on the shoulders. They are held in very bad repute, being mostly *vauriens* [good-for-nothings] of dissolute habits."

Portugal's 1926 military coup, led by General Manuel Gomes da Costa, caused the fado scene to retreat further onto the margins of society. Despite this, the expansion of radio in the 1930s allowed a number of fado artists and groups to reach new audiences and flourish, including Berta Cardoso (1911–1997), Madalena de Melo (1903–1970), Júlio Proença (1901–1970), and the Troupe Guitarra de Portugal, with Ercília Costa (1902–1985).

Queen of Fado
Lisbon-born singer Amália Rodrigues had a 50-year recording career and starred in a number of movies, including *Fado* (1947). Here, the Queen of Fado, as she was known, performs in France in 1960.

Modern fado

Fado is largely the musical legacy of Lisbon and Coimbra. In the capital, the music enjoys a lot of support among the working class. Amália Rodrigues (1920–1999) is widely regarded as the pioneering voice of modern fado and is known as the *Rainha do Fado* (Queen of Fado). She performed all over Europe, Japan, and South America, and visited the United States in the 1950s to sing at New York nightclub La Vie en Rose. Rodrigues also acted in a number of movies, and a biopic, ***Amália***, was released in 2008.

Guitarra portuguesa
This 19th-century Portuguese guitar is made of walnut and spruce. Guitars made in Lisbon are larger and usually tuned to D, while those made in the town of Coimbra are tuned to C.

Watchkey tuning pegs
12 strings strung in 6 courses of 2 strings each
Spruce soundboard
Movable bone bridge

Rodrigues is credited with defining the modern style of fado music, and when she died in 1999, the Portuguese government declared three days of national mourning and awarded her a state funeral. A national icon, she is buried in Lisbon's National Pantheon, alongside former presidents.

The districts of Lisbon most associated with fado are Mouraria and, especially, Alfama, the old Arab quarter spreading below the castle, where there are dozens of *casas de Fado*, or Fado restaurants, in which both established and emerging artists perform. As with Spanish flamenco, the local tourism sector exploits fado.

The Coimbra sound

Northeast of Lisbon is the university town of Coimbra, known for its intellectual climate. Its more stylized fado has attracted a middle-class audience and has produced a large number of male artists, including singers Alberto Ribeiro, Adriano Correia de Oliveira, and Josè Afonso, and guitarists Artur Paredes and Carlos Paredes. In keeping with the academic setting, singers and musicians wear old-fashioned garb of dark robes, capes, and leggings. Their guitars have larger soundboards, which gives a more accentuated bass sound. According to tradition, to applaud fado in Lisbon the audience clap their hands; in Coimbra, they cough, as if clearing their throats.

KEY WORKS

Ana Moura "Amor Em Tons De Sol Maior"
Amalia Rodrigues "Coimbra"
Mariza *Transparente*
Alberto Ribeiro "Coimbra"
Adriano Correia de Oliveira "Fado de Promessa"
Madalena de Melo "Fado Amandinho"

Pop alternative

During the 1980s, several artists associated with the Portuguese rock scene started to show an interest in fado, partly as a means of challenging the prominence of Anglo-American pop. Bands such as Variações and Mler Ife Dada, and singers such as Anabela Duarte and Paulo Bragança dressed casually, sang about contemporary themes, and loosened up the sound to create what became known as *novo fado* or new fado. "We need to take the fado further," said Duarte. "Cut its corsets, let it breathe."

AFTER

Unlike jazz, tango, and rock, which have flourished as hybrid forms far beyond their places of origin, fado has remained an indigenous musical tradition.

FADO MUSICIANS IN A PORTUGUESE TAVERN

AN INTERNATIONAL FOLLOWING
In recent years, fado artists such as Misia, Mariza, António Zambujo, Artur Paredes, and Ana Moura have kept the sound alive and won fame abroad. Mariza has introduced fado to fans of **pop** as well as **world music**. She duetted with Sting at the 2004 Olympic Games, and her 2005 album *Transparente* was a Top 10 hit in several European countries. Madredeus, who play a Portuguese **folk music** only loosely linked with fado, have also gained an international following.

A CREOLE VARIATION
Morna, a creole music that is sometimes considered the national music of Cape Verde (once a Portuguese colony), is an offshoot of fado. Cape Verdean singer Cesária Évora (1941–2011) made it famous worldwide.

GUITARIST (1910–1976)

HOWLIN' WOLF

Compressing the passion of the Delta and the electric urgency of Chicago into one mighty frame, Howlin' Wolf was the most essential bluesman of all. Born Chester Burnett in Mississippi in 1910, and taught guitar by Charlie Patton, he possessed an awe-inspiring singing voice, bristling with menace yet suffused with vulnerability. A farmer until 1948, Wolf recorded for Sun Studios in Memphis before being lured north by Chicago's Chess Records. There, spurred by a fierce rivalry with Muddy Waters, he cut such classics as "Smokestack Lightnin'," "Evil," and "Forty Four."

Bright Lights, Big City Blues

After World War II, the blues ceased to be primarily identified with solo acoustic performers, and became the preserve of small groups playing amplified electric instruments. It was a shift between the old "country blues" and the new "city blues."

The epicenter of the electric blues was Chicago. In that city alone, the African American population increased by more than half a million between 1940 and 1960. With so many migrants heading up from the South in search of well-paid work, musicians naturally followed, and Chicago became the heart of a thriving entertainment industry. Blues clubs opened up throughout the city's South Side, where the new arrivals could listen to the music they had grown up with back home.

Finding a voice

Much like the ordinary migrants who made the transition from farm laborers to factory workers, many of the earliest Southern bluesmen to reach the North arrived as unknowns, hoping to find new opportunities and prepared to leave their old ways behind. Muddy Waters (1913–1983), for example, drove a truck when he first reached Chicago in 1943. He later avowed that when he acquired an electric guitar and formed his own band two years later, he was simply doing what he had to do to make himself heard in his new environment. Waters soon became the biggest star on the fledgling Chess record label, playing what was basically an amplified version of the Delta blues on songs such as "Rollin' Stone." Founded by Polish brothers Leonard and Phil Chess, the American record company established itself during the 1950s as the definitive home of Chicago blues.

In addition to recording Chicago-based artists, Chess licensed records made elsewhere—the relationship with Sam Phillips' Sun Records in Memphis was particularly fruitful. It then moved on to sign up artists all over the South, and bring them to Chicago. Names on the roster that later became giants included Howlin' Wolf, Etta James, and Sonny Boy Williamson II, as well as artists more closely associated with rock 'n' roll (see pp.314–315), such as Bo Diddley and Chuck Berry.

Characteristic set-up

The Chess sound was created in the studio by the same four- to five-man groups that played the clubs at night. The core combination of one or two guitars, plus bass and drums, formed the template for the rock bands of the 1960s and ever after. Rather than highlighting horns or saxophones, they tended to feature a single harmonica. Little Walter (1930–1968), who first developed the technique of cupping both a harmonica and a microphone with its own amp in his hands and playing the two together, was the greatest harmonica player of the period and had a string of hits.

STRUCTURE: 12-BAR BLUES

The 12-bar blues progression has a distinctive form: the first four bars state the theme, the second four repeat it, and the final four resolve it. It is usually in 4/4 time and uses three chords based on the 1st, 4th, and 5th notes of an eight-note scale. The first four bars are chord 1, then two bars of chord 4 and two bars of chord 1, and the last four bars are chord 5, chord 4, and two bars of chord 1.

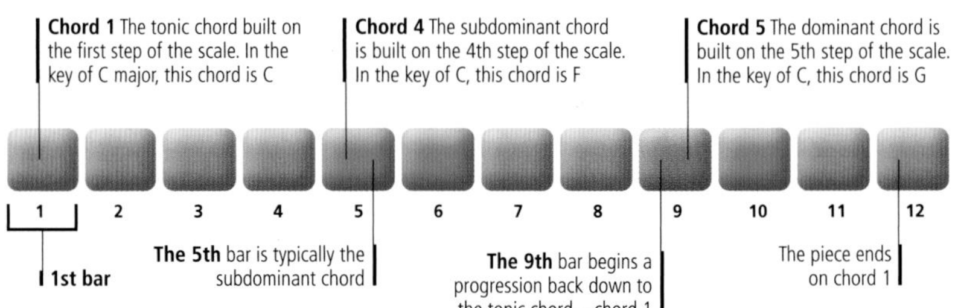

Chord 1 The tonic chord built on the first step of the scale. In the key of C major, this chord is C
Chord 4 The subdominant chord is built on the 4th step of the scale. In the key of C, this chord is F
Chord 5 The dominant chord is built on the 5th step of the scale. In the key of C, this chord is G
1 2 3 4 5 6 7 8 9 10 11 12
1st bar
The 5th bar is typically the subdominant chord
The 9th bar begins a progression back down to the tonic chord—chord 1
The piece ends on chord 1

BEFORE

The Great Depression of the 1930s caused many African Americans to move from the Deep South to the northern cities in search of work. They took their music with them and adapted it to its new setting.

NORTH AND SOUTH

The **blues** **« 240–241** played in Chicago in the 1930s was already more sophisticated than that played in the South. The recordings of stars such as Lonnie Johnson and Big Bill Broonzy owed as much to **jazz** **« 234–235** as to the Delta. Although prewar **Delta bluesmen** were recorded as solo performers, they frequently performed live in small groups. A six-minute recording of the blues singer and guitarist Son House warming up with a band in the studio, recorded in 1930 and discovered in 1985, sounds like a **pre-electric** version of Chicago blues.

INTERRUPTED BY THE WAR

The American recording industry all but closed down during World War II (1939–1945). However, the postwar years were a boom period for new sounds and new labels.

CHICAGO
"The City Beautiful"

"The City Beautiful"
A color postcard shows a view of the lakeshore area of Chicago, Illinois, dubbed "The City Beautiful" for the 1893 World Columbian Exhibition. In the Great Depression, it became a magnet for workers from the impoverished South.

Playing with the master
Muddy Waters performs with harmonica player Isaac Washington in New York in 1959. Blues greats who served their apprenticeships in Muddy's band included Little Walter, Otis Spann, Junior Wells, and Buddy Guy.

Willie Dixon (1915–1992) was another linchpin of the Chess success story, anchoring Muddy Waters' band with his stand-up bass. He wrote songs such as "Hoochie Coochie Man" for Waters, "My Babe" for Little Walter, and "Little Red Rooster" for Howlin' Wolf.

Trailblazing label

In the 1950s, Chicago was also home to the entirely African American-owned Vee Jay Records. Its biggest star, Jimmy Reed (1925–1976), who was originally from Mississippi, far outsold all the Chess artists. Unlike Dixon's songs, which tended to have an undercurrent of pre-rap arrogance, Reed's material was imbued with a warm, lazy charm, and singles such as "Baby What You Want Me to Do?" and "Bright Lights, Big City" actually reached the US pop charts.

While Reed himself played the harmonica, his records were rooted in a hypnotic boogie style, propelled by the kind of "walking bass lines" that Robert Johnson (see p.241) had pioneered back in the Delta.

Putting the boogie into the blues

Singer, songwriter, and guitarist John Lee Hooker (1917–2001), another Mississippi migrant, recorded "Boogie Chillen" for Modern Records in Detroit in 1948. The song talks about the Henry Swing Club on Hastings Street, where many of the clubs were located. Hooker, who joined Reed at Vee Jay a few years later, and was hailed by jazz great Miles Davis (see pp.334–335) as "the funkiest man alive," continued to play endless idiosyncratic and entertaining variations on the boogie theme until well into the 21st century.

Beale Street blues

The blues never left the South behind, however. For every postwar bluesman who used Memphis as a stepping-stone to Chicago, plenty more built their careers in Memphis. The clubs of Beale Street spawned Junior Parker, who cut "Mystery Train" at Sun Studios the year before Elvis; Bobby "Blue" Bland; and "Beale Street Blues Boy" B.B. King—which is where he got the "B.B." from. The Memphis connection remained strong into the 1970s, with Stax Records producing landmark recordings by guitarist Albert King.

The South goes electric

Texas, too, had a strong blues scene. T-Bone Walker (1910–1975), the first electric blues guitarist, started out collecting tips for Blind Lemon Jefferson (see p.241) in Dallas, while Houston was home to the Duke and Peacock labels, where both Bobby Bland and Junior Parker enjoyed ten-year runs of success from the mid-1950s. Meanwhile, Louisiana was home to its own distinct subgenre, known as "swamp blues," and kept chugging along with a laid-back but infectious boogie. The style was epitomized by Slim Harpo (1924–1970), whose recordings for the Excello label included "I'm a King Bee" and "Shake Your Hips," both of which were swiftly—and reverentially—covered by the Rolling Stones (see pp.326–327), the former on their eponymous 1964 debut album.

Reviving the blues

Even after the blues had all but disappeared from the national stage, Mississippi's Malaco Records kept the flame alive, with the success of Z. Z. Hill's "Downhome Blues" in the early 1980s. Mississippi also produced a couple of unlikely latter-day blues heroes as late as the 1990s, when two cantankerous, uncompromising grandfathers, R. L. Burnside and Junior Kimbrough, boogied their way out of the juke joints of the state's Hill Country, which had its own North Hill Country blues.

KEY WORKS

Howlin' Wolf "Smokestack Lightnin'"
John Lee Hooker "Boogie Chillen"
Jimmy Reed "Bright Lights, Big City"
Muddy Waters "I've Got My Mojo Working"
Slim Harpo "Shake Your Hips"
Sonny Boy Williamson "Don't Start Me to Talkin'"
T-Bone Walker "Call It Stormy Monday"

Veteran bluesman
Raised in rural Mississippi, B. B. King started his career as a radio DJ in Memphis in the late 1940s. He has been a successful recording artist for more than 60 years.

"I have **heartache,** I have **blues.** No matter what **you got,** the blues is there."

BLUES MUSICIAN JOHN LEE HOOKER (1917–2001)

AFTER

While the blues played a crucial role in the evolution of popular music, and continues to inspire musicians, the genre declined rapidly in popularity from the mid-1960s.

A NEW ERA

With few exceptions, the **electric blues** seldom addressed the social or political issues of the day. With the advent of the Civil Rights Movement in the 1960s and the popularity of **soul music** **320–321 »** and musicians such as Ray Charles, the blues came to be seen by African American audiences as out of date and out of touch. However, as the heyday of Chicago blues drew to a close, it was given unexpected longevity by the acclaim of young white audiences in the US and musicians in Europe.

JOHN LEE HOOKER

DYING OUT

Veteran performers John Lee Hooker (1917–2001) and B.B. King (1925–2015) enjoyed success into old age, but no new generation of blues stars has emerged to follow in their footsteps.

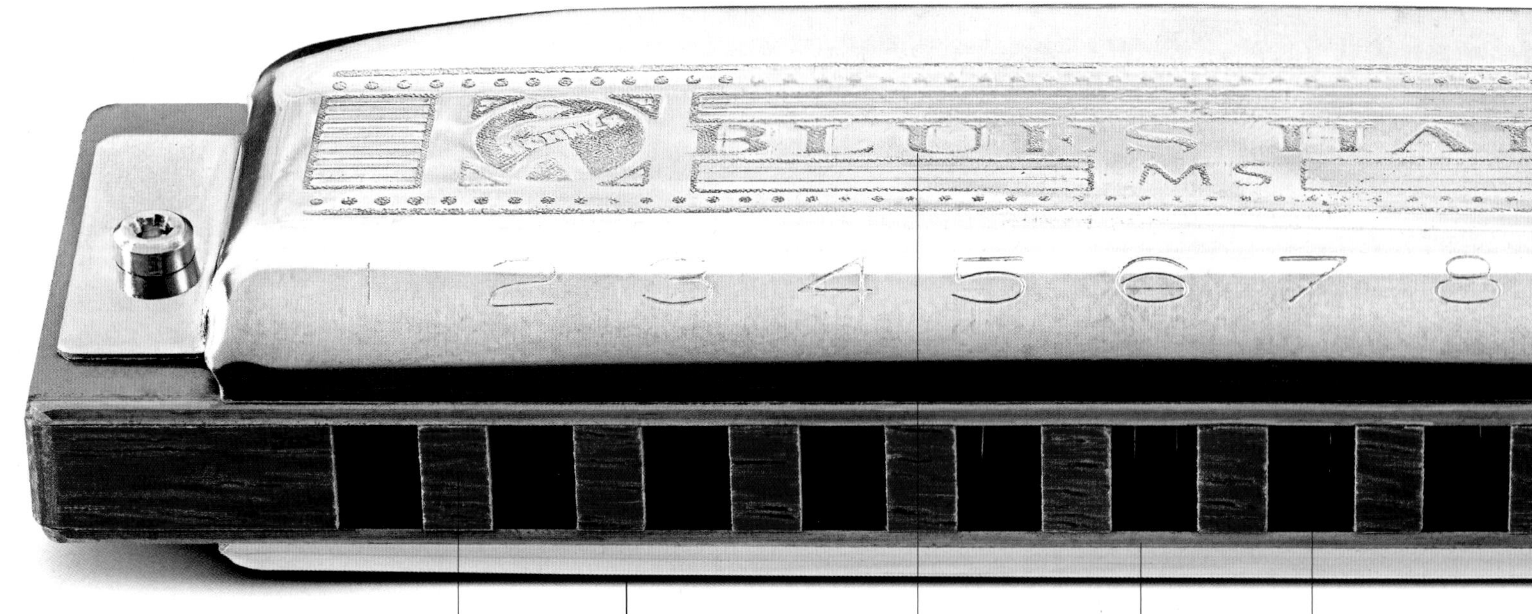

Blues harp
The blues harp is a 10-hole example of a diatonic harmonica. It has a wooden comb, which gives the notes a fuller tone and brass reed plates. This model was made by Hohner in 1995 and played by Stevie Wonder.

> "The **harmonica** is the world's **best-selling musical instrument.** You're welcome."
>
> BOB DYLAN ON HIS ROLE IN POPULARIZING THE INSTRUMENT

SINGER-SONGWRITER (1950–)

STEVIE WONDER

The legendary soul singer-songwriter was revealed as a gifted harmonica player aged 12 in 1962 with his record "Fingertips" and thereafter throughout his remarkable 50-year career. Stevie Wonder mostly played a chromatic harmonica, performing beautifully nuanced solos with melodic exuberance and jazzy decoration in "For Once In My Life" (1967), "Creepin'" (1974), and "Isn't She Lovely" (1976). The blues-drenched solo on "Boogie On Reggae Woman" (1974) was a rare Stevie outing on a diatonic harmonica.

TIMELINE

1857
Hohner factory opens
German clockmaker Matthias Hohner began mass-producing harmonicas in 1857, eventually building the biggest harmonica factory in the world.

HOHNER CATALOG

1900s
Diatonic harmonica
The standard diatonic harmonica (with no sharp or flat notes) was developed in the 1900s. Although experiments with different materials have been undertaken over the years, the design has remained largely unchanged since its earliest days.

1920s
Chromatic harmonica
Unlike the fixed-key models, the chromatic harmonica (with sharp and flat notes), manufactured by Hohner, opened up a whole range of melodic possibilities because it was capable of playing in any key.

THE CLOVER, c.1900

Early 1900s
Diatonic funnel harmonica
Developers experimented with the harmonica's design. The Clover Harmonophone by German firm Ferdinand Strauss projected the sound to the side of the instrument, rather than from the back.

TREMOLO HARMONICA WITH BELLS

1920s
Tremolo harmonica
In the 1920s Hohner developed the basic models of harmonica, producing a tremolo with bells. Its two reeds sound together, one tuned sharp and one flat.

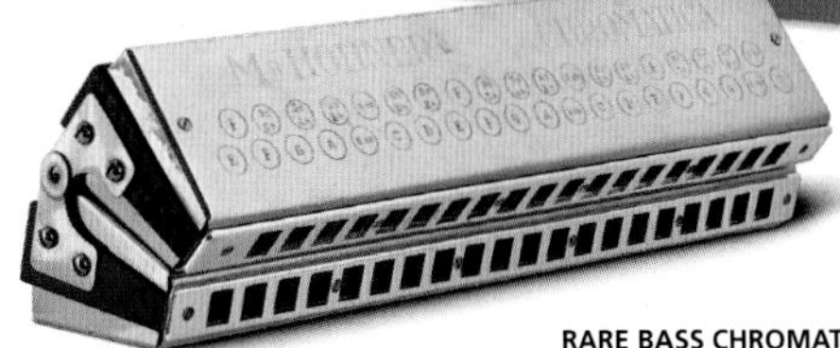
RARE BASS CHROMATIC HARMONICA AND COURSE POSTER

The **Harmonica**

Capable of the simplest of chords and the most intricate melodic expression, the harmonica is as versatile as it is portable. Effective across a range of musical genres, it is playable by everyone.

Also known as the mouth organ, the harmonica is a free reed instrument, which requires a player to move air across tuned reeds that vibrate and produce sound. This is achieved by blowing and drawing air while the mouth is pressed to the holes of the air chambers (the comb). Each air chamber can vibrate two reeds, one on a blow, the other on a draw. Single-note melody playing is achieved by moving the mouth to different air chambers and careful manipulation of the embouchure (the jaw, tongue, and lips). More than one note can be sounded simultaneously on either a blow or draw by ensuring the mouth covers more than one air chamber on the comb.

Elaborations on the basic harmonica sound can be achieved by various techniques. Embouchure adjustments and breath techniques can produce a characteristic bending of pitch to allow access to notes that would otherwise be unavailable on the instrument.

An instrument for every genre

First appearing in Vienna, Austria, in the early 19th century, the harmonica lent itself immediately to European folk music. Subject to a myriad of modifications and variations over the years, the harmonica has endured in country, folk, blues, rock, and jazz music. It has a plaintive, expressive quality that evokes an earthy, nostalgic feeling, whatever the musical context.

Popular in America from the mid-19th century, the instrument was reportedly played by president Abraham Lincoln, and soldiers of the Civil War. Instrumental pioneers include DeFord Bailey, the old-time country harmonica solo specialist, heard on record as early as 1927, and Belgian jazz master Jean "Toots" Thielemans, who featured on many famous movie soundtracks including Midnight Cowboy (1969). American virtuoso Larry Adler (1914–2001) was the inspiration behind several concert pieces, including those composed by Vaughan Williams, Malcolm Arnold, and Darius Milhaud.

BOTTOM VIEW

FRONT VIEW

BACK VIEW

Hohner harmonicas
These early 20th-century advertisements from German harmonica manufacturer Hohner, featured the latest designs including the Trumpet Call Harmonica, which had five bell-shaped sound horns.

1920s
Novelty harmonicas
Instrument makers invented and developed novelty harmonicas as well as more practical designs. The pictured Koh-i-Noor model is an ornate example with jeweling and a painted comb.

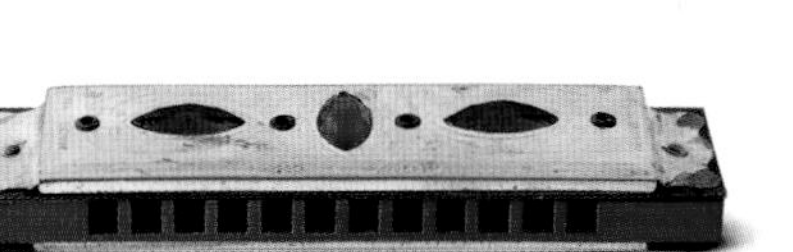

JEWELED HARMONICA

1930–1940s
Sonny Boy Williamson
Mississippi-born Williamson was one of the most influential blues players to demonstrate the blues harp technique (playing a fifth below the key of the song) to create a distinctive "bluesy" sound.

SONNY BOY WILLIAMSON

1950
Double harmonica
A Hohner innovation was the double harmonica, playable in different keys from the front and back. The Echo Elite model featured tuned tremolo reeds and a futuristic 1950s design.

"ECHO ELITE" HARMONICA AND BOX

LITTLE WALTER AND BULLET MICROPHONE

1950s
Little Walter
Frustration with competing with amplified guitars in electric blues bands led Little Walter to experiment with a small public address "bullet" microphone to amplify and distort the sound of the blues harp.

1960s
Bob Dylan
Influenced by American folk singer Woody Guthrie, Bob Dylan punctuated his early protest songs with a rough, emotionally powerful harmonica style.

BOB DYLAN

Rhythm and **Blues**

The term "Rhythm and Blues" was introduced by *Billboard* magazine in 1949 to rename what was previously called its "Race Records" chart. A catch-all label for popular African-American music, it remains current, in its abbreviated form of "R&B."

Although it is hard to pinpoint when R&B either started or stopped being a single, readily identifiable genre, music historians generally use the term to describe the African-American artists and recordings that dominated the US market between the mid-1940s and mid-1950s. It is often retrospectively applied to those musicians who did not become identified with the genres that evolved from R&B, such as rock 'n' roll, soul, Chicago blues, and pop. Thus some of the biggest names—Ray Charles, Sam Cooke, Bobby Bland, and "Fats" Domino—are often regarded as "belonging" to more recent genres, while the label R&B tends to remain attached to largely forgotten names.

Shouting the blues

The "rhythm" component of R&B came as much from jazz and big-band swing (see pp.242–243) as it did from the blues. The best-known pioneers of the genre tended to be big-voiced singers who had started out shouting to make themselves heard before microphones were invented and saw no reason to stop once amplification enabled them to bellow even louder. Big Joe Turner (1911–1985), the definitive "blues shouter," epitomized the style. Having begun his career as a singing barman in Kansas City in 1932, he shot to fame with "Roll 'Em Pete" in 1938. Backed by no fewer than three pianists at once—Pete Johnson, Albert Ammons, and Meade "Lux" Lewis—he sparked a national mania for boogie-woogie.

After the war, Turner moved to California where, just as his career seemed about to tail off, an opportune linkup with the newly formed Atlantic Records triggered his most successful period. A string of blues-based hits culminated with "Shake, Rattle and Roll," which topped the R&B charts in 1954. Even if some called Turner's 1950s' output rock 'n' roll, he insisted it was "a different name for the same music I [*sic*] been singing all my life."

With its boastfulness and overt sexual references, R&B was very much adult music. Other prominent shouters with a line in double entendres included Wynonie Harris and Bull Moose Jackson, whose hits included the tongue-in-cheek "All She Wants to Do Is Rock" and "I Want a Bowlegged Woman." To add extra punch to these big voices, the musical backing would feature horns and saxophones rather than just the guitars favored in the blues of Chicago (see pp.306–307).

Jack of all trades

Louis Jordan and the Tympany Five perform in 1940. As well as leading the band and taking the vocals, Jordan played alto, tenor, and baritone saxophone and could also play piano and clarinet.

A lighter touch

R&B also had its gentler side, thanks to softer-voiced vocalists such as Amos Milburn, whose "Chicken Shack Boogie" was a hit in 1948; Ivory Joe Hunter, who recorded "I Almost Lost My Mind" in 1950; and Percy Mayfield, best known for "Please Send Me Someone to Love," also from 1950. African-American singers who found themselves tagged as "Sepia Sinatras," on the basis of their perceived musical resemblance to Frank Sinatra, included Billy Eckstine and Nat King Cole (see p.261), a smooth balladeer who had his own TV show between 1956–1957.

The most consistent R&B hit-maker of all was Louis Jordan (1908–1975). Originally a ballad singer who billed himself "Louis Jordan, his Silver Saxophone, and his Golden Voice," Jordan emerged from the big-band era. From 1942 onward, he enjoyed a 10-year run of number-one R&B singles, most of which were novelty songs, including "What's the Use of Getting Sober?" and "Is You Is or Is You Ain't My Baby?"

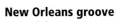

Piano man

Although "Fats" Domino never abandoned his signature R&B style, with its swing rhythms on the piano, he paved the way for rock 'n' roll.

KEY WORKS

Big Joe Turner "Shake, Rattle, and Roll"
Bo Diddley "I'm a Man"
Johnny Otis "Willie and the Hand Jive"
Percy Mayfield "The River's Invitation"
Professor Longhair "Tipitina"
Louis Jordan "Caldonia"
Fats Domino "The Fat Man"

Sound of the South

Although Los Angeles was the principal home of R&B during its heyday—where bandleader and drummer Johnny Otis made his name in the 1940s—no city had a longer or more fruitful connection with the style than New Orleans. One of its bar-room pianists, Antoine "Fats" Domino (1928–2017) came to be associated with the birth of rock 'n' roll, but that lay several years ahead when he released "The Fat Man" in 1949. Working with arranger Dave Bartholomew, Domino sold 100 million records of what essentially remained R&B, with titles including "Ain't That a Shame" and "Blueberry Hill."

Prompted by Domino's success, the Californian record label Specialty turned its attention to New Orleans. Using the same studio and musicians as Domino, Specialty recorded sound-a-likes, such as Lloyd Price, whose "Lawdy Miss Clawdy" went to No. 1 in 1952, and Georgia native Little Richard (1932–2020), on signature tracks such as "Tutti-Frutti" (1955) and "Rip It Up" (1956). Another Georgian, Ray Charles (1930–2004), spent a formative year in New Orleans in 1953, working with Specialty on such songs as blues artist Guitar Slim's "The Things That I Used to Do."

New Orleans groove

Around the same time, New Orleans's most idiosyncratic R&B artist, Henry Roeland Byrd (1918–1980), emerged. Byrd, a former tap dancer who reinvented himself as pianist Professor Longhair, failed to find significant fame beyond the South, despite being acclaimed by

BEFORE

The immediate antecedents of R&B were the big bands, swinging jazz orchestras, and the boogie-woogie pianists of the 1930s.

SHEER HOKUM
"Hokum," or "party blues," was an exuberant form of innuendo-laden blues popularized from the late 1920s by the likes of **Tampa Red** and the **Harlem Hamfats** band.

335 The number of songs recorded on 78 rpm records by Tampa Red, one of the most prolific bluesmen.

BOOGIE-WOOGIE BOYS
America's prewar craze for piano-based **boogie-woogie** blues was kick-started by **Big Joe Turner** and **Pete Johnson** at New York's Carnegie Hall in 1938.

MOOCHIN' AND MISBEHAVIN'
The 1930s work of artists such as **Cab Calloway** and **Fats Waller** led the way for the hip novelty songs of **Louis Jordan**.

Jerry Wexler of Atlantic Records as "the Picasso of keyboard funk." He did, however, write and record three of the genre's classics—"Tipitina," "Big Chief," and the carnival anthem "Go to the Mardi Gras"—all characterized by Afro-Latin rhythms and dazzling piano triplets.

By the 1960s, R&B barely existed outside New Orleans, but it was a golden era for the genre in that city. Songwriter and pianist Allen Toussaint (1938–2015) was almost single-handedly responsible for this. His hits included ex-boxer Lee Dorsey's "Working in the Coal Mine" and Irma Thomas's "Ruler of My Heart." Toussaint collaborated with another New Orleans pianist, Mac Rebennack, who adopted a new persona as Dr. John in the late 1960s.

$4 The amount the teenage Ray Charles earned per night playing piano in Jacksonville (about $10 in today's money).

Rhythm and Blues Review

Filmed at the Apollo Theater in Harlem, this 1955 feature film includes performances by jazz singers and musicians, such as Cab Calloway, Nat King Cole, Count Basie, and Big Joe Turner.

UNDERSTANDING MUSIC

FUNK

By the 1970s, a new four-letter phenomenon had taken hold across the United States. Funk music was defined by its heavy grooves, hard-hitting horn lines, and sun-soaked soul from the Bayou. Key groups include The Meters, whose self-titled debut was produced by Allan Toussaint; Ohio Players; Sly and the Family Stone; and George Clinton's Parliament Funkadelic. Its most famous exponent is James Brown (1933–2006), whose hit records "The Payback" and "The Boss" became the blueprint for the genre. Brown's track "Funky Drummer" was also foundational, featuring an iconic drum break from Clyde Stubblefield (1943–2017) that was later sampled by hip-hop producers Marley Marl and Dr. Dre.

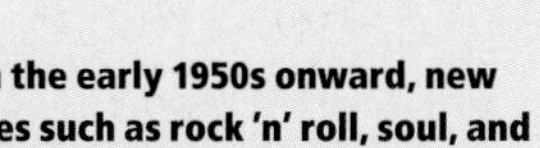

AFTER

From the early 1950s onward, new genres such as rock 'n' roll, soul, and hip-hop eroded the identity of R&B as a separate genre.

FROM R&B TO ROCK 'N' ROLL

Bill Haley and the Comets 314–315 ›› rerecorded Big Joe Turner's "Shake, Rattle, and Roll" in 1954, establishing a pattern in which rock 'n' roll musicians appropriated R&B hits.

SOUL BROTHER

Shunning categorization as an R&B artist, Ray Charles is considered to have invented **soul music 320–321 ››**.

RAY CHARLES, FATHER OF SOUL

WHAT'S IN A NAME?

From the 1980s and '90s, the term R&B was applied increasingly to the pop—infused with soul and hip-hop—of **Michael Jackson 350–351 ››**, **Beyoncé**, and **Ne-Yo**.

BEFORE

Makers have always tried to give instruments as much volume as possible, fashioning the design to optimize the projection of sound.

EARLY AMPLIFICATION

Musicians of the early 20th century often struggled to make themselves heard at the dances, bars, and fairs where they played. **George Beauchamp**, a Texan and vaudeville musician who played violin and lap-steel guitar, solved the problem by teaming up with guitar-maker **John Dopyera** to **develop the resonator** (or resophonic guitar) in 1927. These had conical aluminum resonators inserted into the body to **amplify the sound**. Some examples kept the wooden body, while others were made of metal. Musicians such as the Romany guitarist **Django Reinhardt** **<< 273** attached microphones to their instruments.

RESOPHONIC GUITAR

Plugged-in for Sound

Rock 'n' roll changed music forever, and in turn transformed the whole of popular culture. Defining what it meant to be a teenager, it created a new generation gap. But rock 'n' roll could not have existed without the powerful thrill provided by electric instruments.

With the invention of the electric guitar (see pp.332–333), a revolution in sound took place. As the guitarists of the 1950s discovered, when a guitar is plugged into an amplifier and the volume is turned up loud, the sound changes: it begins to distort. Unexpectedly, guitarists and audiences discovered that they liked the new sound, and amplification meant that it was no longer necessary to have a large band in order to make an impact.

Bill Haley & His Comets
Formerly a country music performer, Bill Haley embraced the amplified sounds of rock 'n' roll and changed his musical direction. With his band the Comets, Haley was one of the first performers to bring these new sounds to mainstream audiences.

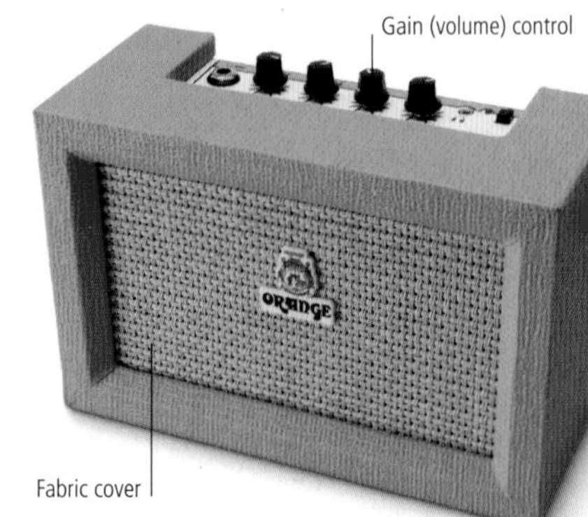

Hear it loud
This portable guitar amplifier is made by Orange, a British manufacturer founded in 1968 whose larger stacks are favorites of heavy rockers such as Sunn O))).

Faster and louder

The music of white and black rural American musicians—country and blues—changed when they moved into the cities in search of work (see pp.306–307). Most abandoned their acoustic guitars for electric ones, a transformation that can be heard in the music of blues players such as Willie Dixon, Howlin' Wolf, Sister Rosetta Tharpe, and Muddy Waters. The music became simpler, faster, and louder. Blues became rhythm and blues (see pp.310–311), and country rockabilly (see p.347). The four-piece of guitar, bass, drums, and vocals became the standard setup for a band.

It was only a matter of time before the black rhythm and blues acts such as Chuck Berry, Bo Diddley, and Little Richard crossed over to white audiences. Bill Haley's worldwide hit

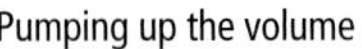

"**The design** of each element should be **thought out** in order to be easy to make and **easy to repair.**"

LEO FENDER, INVENTOR AND DESIGNER, 1954

of 1954, "Rock Around the Clock," was a watershed. It turned rock 'n' roll into a youth craze. The song—a celebration of staying up late—proved that rock 'n' roll was here to stay. In terms of sound, however, it was more restrained than the black R 'n' B that inspired it.

Wray and Hendrix

The best demonstration of the impact made by distorted amplification was Link Wray's "Rumble" from 1958. This rock 'n' roll instrumental had a gritty, twangy guitar sound that many have cited as a precursor to heavy metal. Wray went to the extreme of poking holes into his guitar's amplifier because it didn't sound sufficiently "fuzzy."

Many radio stations refused to play the track, even though it had no lyrics, alleging that it glorified juvenile delinquency—a testament to its atmosphere of brooding teenage menace.

The link between loud electric guitars and rebellion was to prove timeless. In the 1960s, Jimi Hendrix (1942–1970) experimented with guitar feedback in his guitar solos—moving his guitar dangerously close to his amplifier in order to make high-pitched wails and squeals feed back—in much the same spirit as Link Wray. Hendrix's use of devices such as the wah-wah pedal and the tremolo arm brought a new sonic palette to the instrument, and to rock music.

Pumping up the volume

Jimi Hendrix played at an unprecedented volume and intensity. He worked with British audio engineers Jim Marshall and Roger Mayer to develop high-powered guitar amplifiers and exotic-sounding audio effects.

Bass and keyboard

It was not just guitarists who went electric. The electric bass had been invented by Leo Fender in 1951 and was taken up by many jazz double-bassists. But the man who did the most to popularize the electric bass was Bill Black, bass player for Elvis Presley (see pp.316–317), who played Fender's Precision model.

Keyboard players were not to be outdone, however. The Wurlitzer Company's first electric piano in 1955 found a fan in Ray Charles. Portable electric organs, made by Farfisa and Hohner, became popular in the 1960s. The garage-pop classic "96 Tears," a 1966 hit for the Mexican-American band Question Mark & the Mysterians, features a perfect example of the Farfisa's quaint but tough sound, which became a hallmark of many psychedelic bands of the era. Keyboard players were also enthralled by the exotic, watery noises produced by the Fender Rhodes electric piano, used by both The Doors and Miles Davis in the 1960s and early '70s.

Recording innovations

The 1960s also witnessed radical developments in the technology used in recording studios. These developments turned the humble recording engineer into an artist, and the hallmark sounds of George Martin, Brian Wilson, and Phil Spector were as important a factor in the sound of the music. The British record producer Joe Meek improvised weird and wonderful futuristic noises to spice up the chart hits of his pop artists. His album *I Hear a New World*, crammed with space age sonic gimmickry, has proved to be an enduring influence on many of today's electronica acts.

137 **The number of decibels achieved by British electronica band Leftism in Brixton in 1996, setting a record for the loudest concert ever.**

GUITARIST (1915–2009)

LES PAUL

A teenage prodigy, Lester Polfus started out playing R 'n' B and country under the name Rhubarb Red before adopting the name Les Paul. He had a string of hits in the 1940s and '50s with his girlfriend, the singer Mary Ford. His invention of the multitrack tape recorder allowed him to stack electric guitar parts on top of each other and to record high-pitched, superfast passages by recording at different speeds. His greatest legacy was "the Log," the chunky, solid-body electric guitar that he designed for Gibson Guitar Corporation. Called the Gibson Les Paul, it became one of the most popular guitars of all time. Its powerful sound presaged the heavy rock of the 1970s.

KEY WORKS

Sister Rosetta Tharpe "Up Above My Head"

Bill Haley & The Comets "Rock Around the Clock"

Link Wray "Rumble"

The Kinks "All Day and All of the Night"

Jimi Hendrix "Star Spangled Banner"

Joe Meek "I Hear a New World"

AFTER

Thanks to electrification, musicians continue to wring new sounds out of their instruments.

GUITAR EXPERIMENTALISTS

The **Velvet Underground, Sonic Youth**, and **My Bloody Valentine** have all used feedback, distortion, reverb, and other effects to build up startling walls of noise. **Robin Guthrie** (The Cocteau Twins) and **Robert Fripp** have taken the guitar into **ambient music**, making it sound shimmering and atmospheric.

ELECTRONIC MUSIC

The 1970s band **Kraftwerk** was a pioneer of **synthesizer pop 336–337 ››**. Their clean, clinical electronic music celebrated and satirized the industrial age, and their influence can be heard in **house 372–373 ››**, **drum 'n' bass**, and **dubstep**. In the 1990s and 2000s, acts such as **The Prodigy** and **The Chemical Brothers** brought rock influences into electronic music.

THE GERMAN BAND KRAFTWERK

BEFORE

Rock 'n' roll emerged as a specific genre in the 1950s, helped by the "wild child" image portrayed by certain movie stars.

R&B ROOTS

Rock 'n' roll was often created by the same musicians who were pumping out blues and R&B in cities such as **New Orleans, Memphis**, and **Chicago** **« 306–307**. The term "rock 'n' roll" was already being applied to music during the 1940s. Cleveland DJ **Alan Freed** first used it to identify a specific genre in 1951 on his nightly *Moon Dog House Party Rock and Roll* radio show, which led to the **first rock 'n' roll concert**, held in Cleveland on March 21, 1952.

ROCK 'N' ROLL MODELS

Marlon Brando in *The Wild One* (1953) and **James Dean** in *Rebel Without A Cause* (1955) epitomized rock 'n' roll attitude on screen even before music tracks to go with them had appeared.

MUSICIAN (1926–2017)

CHUCK BERRY

Born in St. Louis, Missouri, Chuck Berry served time for armed robbery while a teenager. In 1955, he performed both R&B and country with pianist Johnnie Johnson, traveling to Chicago to audition for Chess Records. The string of worldwide rock 'n' roll hits that ensued was characterized by dazzling wordplay, a close identification with teenage preoccupations, and, above all, electrifying guitar riffs, modeled on Johnson's keyboard flourishes. "Johnny B. Goode" and "Too Much Monkey Business" remain standards to this day.

Rock 'n' Roll Models

As much social phenomenon as musical genre, rock 'n' roll was very much more than the sum of its parts. Its roots are recognizable in blues and R&B, but the way it transcended the racial divide was a new development in popular music in 1950s America.

Perhaps even more important than the fact that rock 'n' roll amalgamated Black and white musical traditions was that it targeted an entirely new audience—teenagers. Thanks to the high postwar birth rate, known as the Baby Boom, a third of the US population was under the age of 15 in 1958.

The beginning

There is no real dispute as to where rock 'n' roll was born—Sun Studios, in Memphis, Tennessee. From the late 1940s onward, the African American-oriented programming of Memphis radio stations such as WDIA lured musicians to the city from all over the South. Sun itself started out as a blues record label, but swiftly became a melting pot of different musical ideas.

Some argue that Jackie Brenston's "Rocket 88," a No. 1 R&B hit created by Ike Turner in 1951, was the first rock 'n' roll record; others claim that it was Junior Parker's "Mystery Train," from 1953. Certainly, by 1954, when the unknown 20-year-old Elvis Presley (see pp.316–317) cut his own version of "Mystery Train" at Sun Studios, rock 'n' roll was here to stay.

> **"The blues** had a **baby,** and they named the baby **rock 'n' roll."**
>
> MUDDY WATERS, SONG TITLE, 1977

In musical terms, while rock 'n' roll clearly evolved out of R&B, it also introduced new elements into the mix. This is illustrated by the song "Shake, Rattle and Roll," the first huge rock 'n' roll hit, which sold a million in 1954 for both Big Joe Turner and Bill Haley and the Comets. Turner's original was firmly rooted in the "blues shouter" R&B tradition. Country singer Haley gave the song an extra vigor by adding a brisk slap bass and powerful sax riff; and Elvis recorded the song twice, first at Sun in 1955, when he gave it a light, rockabilly feel, and then, bursting with exuberant energy, at RCA in 1956.

Rocket take-off

Though credited to Jackie Brenston, "Rocket 88" was largely the work of 19-year-old bandleader and Sun Record scout Ike Turner. Released in 1951, it has been described as "the first rock 'n' roll song."

A younger audience

Above all, it was the emphasis on youth and fun that gave rock 'n' roll its explosive appeal. Mainstream popular music was traditionally made by men in suits, with neatly combed hair—grown-ups, to put it simply. Now, young, wild-looking white singers were belting out the kind of innuendo-laden lyrics that had previously been the preserve of world-weary, aging bluesmen.

America's older generation tended to see rock 'n' roll as a menace, threatening to overturn conventional standards of social order and sexual behavior, and to disrupt the long-established racial segregation of the South. Frank Sinatra decried rock 'n' roll (which usurped his kind of music and audience) as "sung, played, and written for the most part by cretinous goons... the martial music of every sideburned delinquent on the face of the Earth."

Something more was happening than whites playing Black music. For the first time, radio audiences were uncertain as to which performers were Black and which white, and Black and white musicians mingled on cross-country tours, performing to hordes of screaming teenagers.

Teen-oriented movies spread the music. *Blackboard Jungle* in 1955 and *The Girl Can't Help It* in 1956 triggered riots in Britain.

Elvis, Cochran, and Holly

The rock 'n' roll pantheon was peopled by a remarkable cast. Elvis Presley was the closest musical equivalent to movie

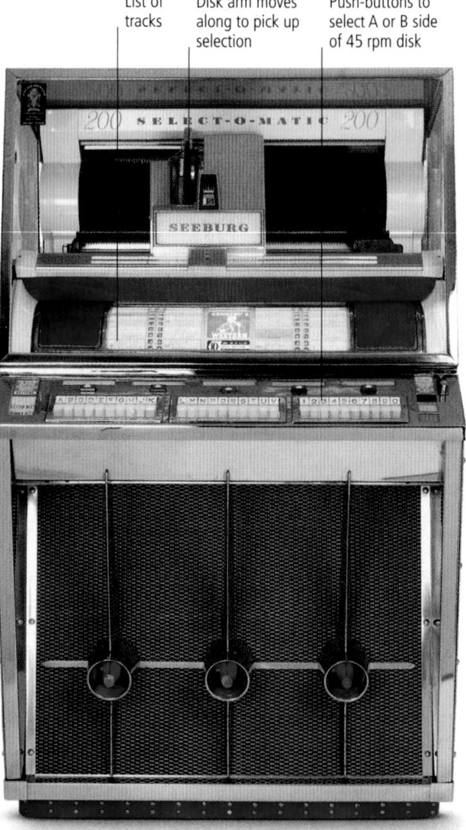

The music machine

Jukeboxes like this American Seeburg made in 1957 blasted out 45-rpm singles, which were first released eight years earlier. Jukeboxes were perfect for delivering rock 'n' roll to jiving teenagers.

Rock 'n' roll goes to the movies
Gene Vincent and his Blue Caps perform "Be-Bop-A-Lula" in the 1956 movie *The Girl Can't Help It*, starring Jayne Mansfield. *Rolling Stone* magazine called them "the first rock and roll band in the world."

stars such as Marlon Brando and James Dean, but in both their looks and their lyrics, young white singers such as Eddie Cochran, with "Summertime Blues" and "Somethin' Else," and Gene Vincent, with "Be-Bop-A-Lula," suggested a new sense of identity for American teenagers.

Perhaps the greatest of the new breed of rock 'n' rollers was a young, bespectacled Texan, Charles Hardin "Buddy" Holly. A precursor of the singer-songwriters of the 1960s, he might not have fit the mold of a conventional rock 'n' roll star, but songs such as "Oh, Boy" and "Not Fade Away" perfectly captured the spirit of the age.

KEY WORKS

Buddy Holly "Peggy Sue"
Chuck Berry "Roll Over Beethoven"
Elvis Presley "That's All Right"
Gene Vincent "Be-Bop-A-Lula"
Jerry Lee Lewis "Great Balls Of Fire"
Little Richard "Tutti Frutti"
Eddie Cochran "Summertime Blues"

A whole lotta shakin'

There were also rock 'n' roll's eccentrics. One of these was the original "Wild Child," Jerry Lee Lewis, a shock-haired, shrieking, piano-pumping kid from Louisiana, who arrived at Sun Studios a couple of years after Elvis and set the charts alight with singles such as "Whole Lotta Shakin' Going On" and "Great Balls of Fire." Before him was Georgia's outrageous, sexually ambiguous Little Richard, another performer with a penchant for kicking his keyboard, who injected doses of gospel and New Orleans R&B into classics such as the song "Lucille."

End of an era

Rock 'n' roll ended catastrophically at the close of the 1950s. Buddy Holly was killed in a plane crash on February 3, 1959—"the day the music died," as Don McLean sang in "American Pie." Eddie Cochran died a year later, age 21, in a car accident in Britain that also curtailed Gene Vincent's career. Jerry Lee Lewis, meanwhile, had scandalized the press by marrying his 13-year-old cousin, and Chuck Berry was charged with immorality in 1959 and jailed. In 1958, Elvis was drafted into the US army.

Million seller
Recorded by Jerry Lee Lewis in October 1957, "Great Balls Of Fire" sold a million copies in its first 10 days and eventually sold five million. Lewis's records far outsold Elvis Presley's releases on the Sun label.

AFTER

Rock 'n' roll ceased to exist as a living genre after the early 1960s, and rock 'n' roll musicians have largely been confined to the "oldies" circuit ever since.

A PARTING OF THE WAYS
While their original recordings remained popular and influential, musicians who are primarily identified with rock 'n' roll are now mainly listened to by older generations.
To some extent, the end of the rock 'n' roll era saw Black and white musicians fall back into separate camps, with Black artists moving toward **soul** **320–321 ››**, and white artists to what became **rock**, taking in influences from **folk music** and **jazz**.

ROCK GOES POP
In the aftermath of rock 'n' roll, American popular music entered an especially bland phase, dominated by "teen idols" such as **Frankie Avalon** and **Bobby Vee**.

SINGER Born 1935 Died 1977

Elvis Presley

"He introduced the **beat to everything** and **changed** everything."

LEONARD BERNSTEIN TO RICHARD CLURMAN, EDITOR AT *TIME* MAGAZINE

In some ways, the world was ready for Elvis Presley when he came roaring out of Memphis in the mid-1950s. The emerging mass market of American teenagers was demanding new forms of entertainment. What better way to capture their hearts, and their money, than by reworking the energy of the blues to suit younger, white listeners? As the man credited with discovering Presley, Sam Phillips (1923–2003)—a lover of rhythm and blues who was the owner of Sun Records, Elvis's first record label—repeatedly stated in the early 1950s: "If I could find a white man who had the Negro sound and the Negro feel, I could make a billion dollars."

Elvis with his parents in 1938
Not long after this picture was taken, Elvis's father, Vernon, was sent to the notorious Parchman Farm penitentiary for forging a check.

Elvis, however, not only had a new sound but also a whole new way of moving—not to mention movie-star looks. He could also sing: purely as an instrument, with a range of almost three octaves, his voice was superb.

The boy from Memphis

Born in Tupelo, Mississippi, in 1935, Elvis moved to Memphis, Tennessee, at the age of 13. Despite the racial segregation of the time, his dirt-poor origins ensured that he grew up exposed to both Black and white culture. At age 18, and working as a truck driver, he arrived at Sam Phillips's Sun Studio in the summer of 1954, to cut a demo record. He made enough of an impression for him to be called back the following year to work with a small band.

New tape-recording technology had made it possible to experiment in a studio, and Elvis was one of the first musicians to "fool around," swiftly establishing the template he followed for the rest of his life, of repeatedly reworking whatever came into his head until it sounded right. Gifted with a superb musical memory, he would assemble fragments drawn from all kinds of sources, ranging from bluegrass and country swing to gospel and even light opera. Thus, in an interlude between country ballads, he released "That's All Right."

To bluesman Arthur Crudup's sedate, world-weary 1946 original, Elvis added much that was unique and new. His vocal style—at some moments sly, at others bursting with exuberance—supported by

Screen idol
Presley starred in 31 movies, beginning with *Love Me Tender* in 1957. This picture was taken to promote the movie *Jailhouse Rock*, released in the same year.

Local boy made good
The electrifying young Elvis Presley returns to his hometown of Tupelo as a national star for the Mississippi-Alabama State Fair in September 1956.

the sparse but swinging arrangement (no drums), made the record an overnight sensation.

Storming to success

Over the next year, Elvis had a string of hit singles on Sun, each of which coupled blues-derived material such as "Mystery Train" with more conventional country songs.

Touring in the Deep South, he hooked up with a manager, "Colonel" Tom Parker, who, in 1955, negotiated Elvis's transfer to the huge RCA label. There, Elvis set about producing worldwide hits such as "Heartbreak Hotel" and "Don't Be Cruel." His hip-swiveling stage act transfixed TV audiences, and he swiftly became a Hollywood movie star as well.

Army and marriage

Elvis took an enforced break between 1958 and 1960, stationed with the US Army in Germany. While there, he met the 14-year-old Priscilla Beaulieu, the daughter of a US officer, whom he was to marry in 1966. On his return to the US, Parker decided Elvis should concentrate on his movie career.

Although Elvis continued to release records, Parker steered him toward ballads rather than rock 'n' roll. Parker also insisted that songwriters surrender their copyrights for the privilege of working with Elvis, a move that resulted in a drastic decline in material for him.

Comeback special

In 1968, with audiences tiring of Elvis's increasingly formulaic movies, the "King" came back. A television special for NBC revealed him at a new peak—slimmed down, dressed to kill in tight black leather, and giving the performance of his life. The next year he returned to Memphis to record at Chip Moman's American Studios, sessions that resulted in classics such as "Suspicious Minds" and "In The Ghetto." He also returned to live performances, making the first of hundreds of appearances at the International Hotel (later the Hilton) in Las Vegas.

Terminal decline

It is the Elvis of the 1970s, karate-kicking his way across stages in tight jumpsuits, booming out ballads such as "My Way" and "Unchained Melody," who is best remembered today. While that Elvis is easy to mock, he could still command a global audience, and he still recorded gems such as "Burnin' Love" and "Promised Land."

Tragically, however, Elvis's life went into decline after his marriage to Priscilla ended in 1972. For many fans, Parker was the villain of the piece—refusing to let Elvis play overseas and forcing him to follow endless Las Vegas engagements with grueling national tours, although Elvis seemed happy to become a crooner. Elvis succumbed to his own weaknesses as well, bingeing on food and becoming dependent on drugs and prescribed medicines.

Elvis kept on touring to the end. His final gig was in Indianapolis on June 26, 1977, and he died at his home in Memphis on August 16.

To this day Elvis is often depicted as an idiot savant who played no part in his own success, or a thief who appropriated the creativity of others. Neither his physical deterioration and early death, however, nor the stagnation of his career in the 1970s, should obscure the talent that enabled him to transform popular music forever.

> "This boy had... the **looks,** the **moves,** the **manager,** and **the talent...**"
>
> CARL PERKINS, FELLOW SUN RECORDING ARTIST

Aloha From Hawaii
Elvis performs in Honolulu in 1973, the peak of his worldwide popularity. He sports his signature white, jeweled jumpsuit.

KEY WORKS

"That's All Right"
"Mystery Train"
"Heartbreak Hotel"
"Hound Dog"
"Jailhouse Rock"
"It's Now or Never"
"Guitar Man"
"Suspicious Minds"
"American Trilogy"

TIMELINE

- **January 8, 1935** Born in Tupelo, Mississippi.
- **October 1945** Comes second in talent contest at Mississippi-Alabama Fair & Dairy Show.
- **1948** The Presley family moves to Memphis, Tennessee.
- **1953** As a gift for his mother, Elvis pays $3.98 to record "My Happiness" and "That's When Your Heartaches Begin" at Sun Studio.
- **1954** Invited back by Sun Records owner Sam Phillips, records "That's All Right," with Scotty Moore on guitar and Bill Black on bass.
- **1955** RCA buys his contract from Sun Records for $35,000.
- **1956** "Heartbreak Hotel" reaches number one in the US singles charts. Releases first album, *Elvis Presley,* which includes Carl Perkins' song "Blue Suede Shoes." Flies to Hollywood for a screen test.

BLUE SUEDE SHOES

- **1957** "Jailhouse Rock" released. Performs "Don't Be Cruel," by African-American Otis Blackwell, on *The Ed Sullivan Show* in the US.
- **1958** Drafted into the US Army and sent to Germany, where he meets Priscilla Beaulieu.
- **1958** Mother dies in Memphis.

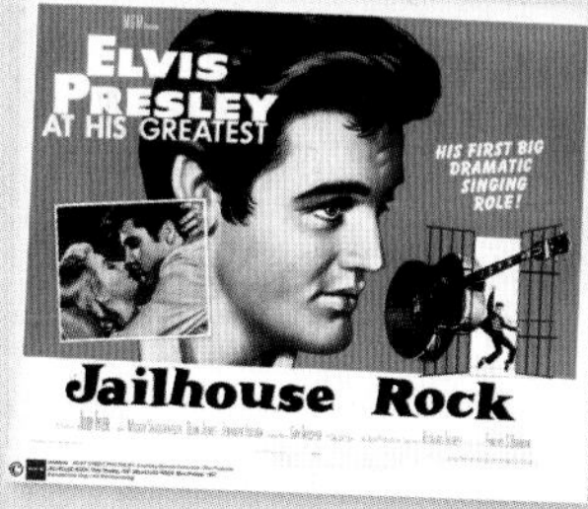

POSTER FOR THE MOVIE "JAILHOUSE ROCK"

- **1960** Returns home from the army. Records the ballads "Are You Lonesome Tonight?" and "It's Now or Never"—a specially commissioned English-language version of "O Sole Mio." Movie *GI Blues*.
- **1963** Shoots *Viva Las Vegas*, costarring Ann-Margret.
- **1966** Marries Priscilla in Las Vegas.
- **June 1968** Makes a stunning "Comeback Special" for NBC TV.
- **January 1969** "Suspicious Minds" becomes his first US number one hit for seven years.
- **July 1969** Returns to live performance in Las Vegas, with the first of 837 appearances at the International Hotel (later the Hilton).
- **1972** Marriage to Priscilla falls apart.
- **July 1973** A worldwide TV audience of over one billion people watch Elvis perform his *Aloha From Hawaii* concert in Honolulu.
- **August 16, 1977** Dies at his Memphis home, Graceland.

BEFORE

Earlier music hubs had existed in New York and the Brill Building itself was home to a community of publishers, performers, and songwriters in the 1930s and 1940s.

TIN PAN ALLEY
This was a collection of New York City music **publishers and songwriters** who dominated US popular music in the early 20th century. The name referred to a specific place: West 28th Street between 5th and 6th Avenue in **Manhatten** **« 230–231**.

EARLY PUBLISHING TENANTS
The Brill Building had housed a jazz-oriented publisher and Crawford Music in the 1930s. Bandleaders such as **Duke Ellington** and **Tommy Dorsey**, and songwriters **Johnny Burke** and **Jimmy Van Heusen** also had offices there.

KEY WORKS

Ben E. King & The Drifters "Save The Last Dance For Me"
The Shirelles "Will You Still Love Me Tomorrow?"
Neil Sedaka "Breaking Up Is Hard To Do"
The Crystals "Da Doo Ron Ron"
The Ronettes "Walking In The Rain"
Shangri-Las "The Leader Of The Pack"

The Brill Building
The Victor Bark-designed art deco-style building is still home to many music-business-related companies. The bust is of Alan Lefcourt, son of the builder Abraham Lefcourt, who died at age 17.

Leaders of the Pack

Between the late 1950s and early '60s, post-Elvis and pre-Beatles, a group of talented young writers and music business professionals based in and around a New York building—the Brill Building—crafted an era-defining string of pop hits for solo singers and groups.

Located at 1619 Broadway on 49th Street, Manhattan, New York, the Brill Building housed dozens of song publishers' offices and songwriters, often composing in tiny songwriting cubicles furnished with little more than a piano and chair. The Brill Building was a more contained musical community than Tin Pan Alley (see pp.230–231) but was very much a continuation of the Alley's businesslike, commercial music ethos, and produced dozens of pop hits in the late 1950s and early 1960s. This music became known as the Brill Building Sound.

Top 40 pop

Although several of the songwriters and publishers associated with the genre were actually located nearby at 1650 Broadway, the term Brill Building Sound has come to represent a generic approach to a style of pop music in a particular period rather than simply a specific geographical location.

The music was well-crafted, post-rock 'n' roll pop. It had memorable "hooks" such as catchy title melodies or vivid instrumental moments. Songs had refined rhythm and blues influences and, often, Latin American-flavored rhythms.

404 **The number of Brill Building songs out of the 1,200 played on US radio show *Your Hit Parade* from 1935–1958.**

Brill building teams

The work of songwriter/producer partners Jerry Leiber and Mike Stoller, such as "Searchin" and "Yakety Yak" for The Coasters and "Stand By Me" for Ben E. King, has become synonymous with the Brill Building Sound.

Spurred on by hit-hungry publishers such as Don Kirshner of Aldon Music, other professional songwriters, often in established teams of two, worked prodigiously to provide hits for pop artists. An early team of Kirschner's comprised Doc Pomus and Mort Schuman who from 1959 to 1961 created such hits as "Teenager In Love" (by Dion and The Belmonts), "Save The Last Dance For Me" and "Sweets For My Sweet" (both by The Drifters). Then in 1961, Elvis Presley recorded their "Little Sister" and "Surrender."

Phil Spector and The Ronnettes
The fortunes of family vocal group The Ronettes were transformed in 1963 by their association with producer Phil Spector, though Spector's romantic obsession with lead singer and future wife Ronnie (holding music) complicated matters.

Composer Burt Bacharach met and began collaborating with lyricist Hal David at the Brill Building in 1957. Although outside of what is considered the Brill Building Sound—Bacharach never considered himself a rock 'n' roll writer—Bacharach and David nevertheless applied themselves with the same hit-driven ethos to produce dozens of hits including "Magic Moments" for Perry Como, and a string of classics for Dionne Warwick.

Shangri-Las album cover
The youngest of the girl-groups, the Shangri-Las specialized in intense teenage dramas, imaginatively produced and written by George "Shadow" Morton from 1964–66.

While Leiber/Stoller, Pomus/Schuman, and Bacharach/David were experienced professionals, other Brill Building teams were mere teenagers. Neil Sedaka and Howard Greenfield resurrected Connie Francis's career with the novelty rocker "Stupid Cupid" in 1958 before Sedaka went on to be a teenage star singer with such "shoo-be-do" pop hits as "Oh Carol" and "Happy Birthday Sweet Sixteen."

Several key Brill Building writers were young married couples; Gerry Goffin and Carole King married in 1958 and composed in the evening after their day jobs before their breakthrough hit "Will You Still Love Me Tomorrow," recorded by The Shirelles in 1960. Later, they wrote hits including "Some Kind Of Wonderful" (recorded by The Drifters), "The Loco-Motion" (for Little Eva), and "Chains," covered by The Beatles on their 1963 debut album.

Another husband and wife team, Barry Mann and Cynthia Weil, peaked a little later in the mid-60s with their moodier pieces "You've Lost That Lovin' Feelin'," recorded by the

$50 Little Eva's weekly pay at the height of her fame.

16 The average age of the Shangri-Las when signed to Red Bird Records in 1964.

Righteous Brothers, and The Animals' "We Gotta Get Out Of This Place."

Meanwhile, Ellie Greenwich and Jeff Barry succeeded with several girl-group epics including "Be My Baby" for the Ronettes in 1963, "Da Doo Ron Ron" for the Crystals, and "Leader Of The Pack" for the Shangri-Las.

Quality sounds

Although the Brill Building Sound had much to do with the pop sophistication of the writing, it was also about the striking quality of the records. Producers such as Leiber and Stoller, George "Shadow" Morton, and Phil Spector ensured that pop records of the period were musical events with memorable and compelling arrangements and dynamic production. Phil Spector referred to his overstated "wall-of-sound" record production style as: "A Wagnerian approach to rock 'n' roll: little symphonies for the kids."

Girl groups

While some of the acts supplied by the Brill Building professionals were writers themselves (notably singers Gene Pitney and Bobby Darin), these were exceptions. Noncomposing solo performers like the clean-cut rockers who arrived in Elvis Presley's wake—Fabian, Bobby Vee, and Dion among them—were always on the lookout for new songs.

But it was the young female vocal groups with their naïve, attractive sound that were the defining vehicles for the Brill Building machine, with several groups becoming associated with particular writers/producers. The Crystals and The Ronettes were overseen by Phil Spector, The Cookies were supplied with songs by Dave Goffin and Carole King, while The Shangri-Las were signed to Leiber and Stoller's Red Bird Records.

However, the master-servant relationship between the creators and artists meant that when the hits stopped and the writer/producers lost interest, with no creative impulse beyond singing and no publishing royalties to accrue, few of the performers had the artistic or financial resources to maintain a significant career.

The rise of self-contained composer-performers such as Bob Dylan and The Beatles, and the admiration these performers inspired in the next generation of artists, changed the music business: the proportion of musicians relying on "professionals" reduced dramatically. Today, only the singers participating in X-Factor-style TV talent shows have a comparable relationship with the music business as those in the Brill Building era.

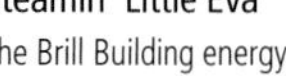

Steamin' Little Eva
The Brill Building energy is captured in this 1962 publicity photo with (L-R), the publishers Don Kirschner and Al Nevins, the singer Little Eva, and the writers Gerry Goffin and Carole King promoting "The Loco-Motion."

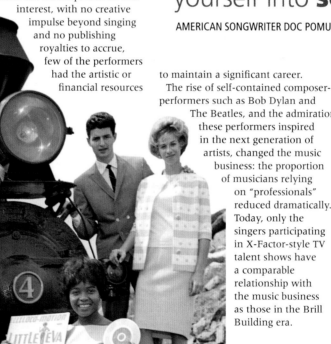

SINGER-SONGWRITER (1942–)

CAROLE KING

Married at age 17 to songwriter Gerry Goffin, at 18 she co-wrote "Will You Still Love Me Tomorrow," a number one for The Shirelles in 1960. Other Brill Building-era hits included "Take Good Care Of My Baby" and "Up On The Roof," recorded by The Drifters in 1963. Splitting with Goffin in 1968, King continued as a solo singer-songwriter, releasing "Tapestry" in 1971, one of the biggest-selling albums of all time. She wrote a million-seller for Celine Dion in 1997 ("The Reason") and toured with fellow singer-songwriter James Taylor as recently as 2010. She was fêted at a tribute concert at the White House in 2013.

"If you're not **writing songs** for a teenage audience, you can get yourself into **serious trouble.**"

AMERICAN SONGWRITER DOC POMUS, "THE JOURNALS OF DOC POMUS"

AFTER

Music publishers and writing teams moved on with the rise of singer-songwriters, and geographically based music hubs were less common.

DON KIRSCHNER

The driving force behind several of the significant writing teams of the Brill Building era, Kirschner found lucrative output for his abilities in the mid-to-late 1960s with made-for-TV pop creations **The Monkees** and animated bubblegum group **The Archies**.

SONG FACTORIES

Nashville, Tennessee, is known for its proliferation of songwriters and musicians. Notable examples of later hit factories include Berry Gordy's team of writers and producers at Detroit's **Motown Records** **>> 320–321** and British producers/songwriters **Stock, Aitken & Waterman**, who produced a string of multi-artist successes in the 1980s, including a Kylie Minogue cover of "The Loco-Motion."

KYLIE'S LOCOMOTION

The **Sounds** of **Soul**

During the 1960s, amid the turmoil of civil rights protests, the war in Vietnam, and a spate of assassinations, a new kind of Black music came to the fore in the United States. Impassioned, personal, immediate, and political, it became known by a single word—soul.

BEFORE

Soul's foundations had already been laid in the R&B and gospel of the '50s.

BROTHER RAY
By incorporating disparate elements ranging from country to jazz into his music, the R&B artist **Ray Charles** paved the way for soul **« 310–311**.

THE GOSPEL TRUTH
Even those soul stars who had not previously sung with gospel groups consciously adopted the vocal mannerisms of singers like **Claude Jeter** (1914–2009) of the **Swan Silvertones**.

To specify a precise moment when soul was born is impossible. As much a movement as a genre, it drew on the fundamental building blocks of Black American music, set down since the early years of the 20th century. Above all, it was the vocal and choral emphasis of gospel (see pp.294–295) that influenced soul and set it apart. The transition from gospel to soul could at times be quite explicit; not only would singers draw vocal styles and inflections from the church, but they would even take the actual songs. In 1956, for example, Ray Charles turned the hymn "This Little Light Of Mine" into a love song, "This Little Girl Of Mine."

From church to charts

Gospel music was not restricted just to the church. Big-name gospel artists toured the United States performing to huge audiences, and were mobbed by enthusiastic teenagers. By recording a pop single in 1956, though, Sam Cooke (1931–1964), then the lead singer with the gospel group the Soul Stirrers, crossed a significant line. He went on to become a major pop star, with light, strings-dominated hits like "You Send Me" (1957) and "Only Sixteen" (1959).

Motown hit machines
Stevie Wonder and Marvin Gaye share a microphone at the Motown studios in 1965. That year, Gaye (right) released his first million-selling record, "I'll Be Doggone."

Here come the girls
Martha and the Vandellas perform on a US television show in 1965. Their 1963 hit "Heat Wave," written by one of soul music's great songwriting teams, Holland-Dozier-Holland, helped establish the Motown sound.

Then, after hearing the 1963 song "Blowin' in the Wind" by Bob Dylan (see p.322), Cooke decided that he too should be addressing issues of social concern. In a prime example of pop moving toward soul, he wrote "A Change Is Gonna Come," which became a civil rights anthem.

Another founding father of soul, Solomon Burke (1940–2010), was literally born into the church—consecrated at birth in Philadelphia as a bishop in his grandmother's own church. He started recording in his teens, but Burke's role in the genesis of soul began when he signed to Atlantic Records in 1960.

12 The age of Stevie Wonder when he recorded his first US number 1 hit, "Fingertips," for Motown in 1962.

Co-founded by Ahmet Ertegun, a Turkish American, in the 1940s, Atlantic had swiftly become the main source for R&B (see pp.310–311), and with Ray Charles in particular, the label had done much to establish the soul template. Burke had a string of hard-driving hits for Atlantic in the 1960s, including "Got To Get You Off My Mind" and "Home In Your Heart"; and it was Burke, reluctant to be categorized as a blues singer, who first used the term "soul" to describe his music.

Joining Atlantic similarly served to propel Aretha Franklin to the status of "Queen of Soul." A hugely gifted singer, pianist, and arranger, Franklin struck gold in 1967 with the song "Respect" (see p.322).

Songs of the South

With his sexually charged lyrics and dancing, no one could ever have mistaken James Brown (see below) for a gospel singer. But Brown's vocal delivery and onstage persona owed a great deal to the religious ecstasy of an African American Baptist minister. Brown came to be known as the "Godfather of Soul." He started his career as the singer for the Famous Flames, a romantic doo-wop influenced soul band, but later adopted a more muscular and minimal hard funk sound. Thanks in no small part to the punchy horn arrangements of Fred Wesley and the bass lines of Bootsy Collins, James Brown turned songs about personal and racial freedom into powerfully danceable music.

Broken band of soul brothers
The Bar-Kays pose for a group portrait outside the Stax Records "Soulsville USA" headquarters in Memphis in 1967. That same year, four band members died in the plane crash that also claimed Otis Redding.

Motown magic in "motor city"

Even though its music aimed from the start at the pop charts, shunning the vocal flourishes and roars of most soul created elsewhere, Motown Records is inseparable from the history of the genre. Founded in Detroit by African American entrepreneur Berry Gordy in 1959, Motown—an abbreviation of the city's nickname, "motor town"—set out to find the common ground between pop and soul, deliberately mixing its catchy three-minute singles to sound good on car radios, and the new portable transistor radios. Motown soon dominated the global charts, thanks to the array of largely local talents who streamed through its doors. These included Diana Ross, lead singer of the Supremes; songwriter Smokey Robinson; male vocal group the Temptations, known for their harmonies, choreography, and stylish outfits; and the Four Tops, a group fronted by the baritone Levi Stubbs.

As the 1960s progressed, many performers who had at first been happy, and highly successful, working within the standard Motown formula grew increasingly influenced by changes in the world at large—social and political, as well as musical. Motown thus served as a spawning ground for some of the greatest achievements in soul, including the 1971 album *What's Going On* by Marvin Gaye (1939–1984), and the two 1972 albums, *Music Of My Mind* and *Talking Book*, by Stevie Wonder.

> "Motown is the **greatest** musical event... in the history of music."
>
> SMOKEY ROBINSON, INTERVIEW WITH "CHRISTIANITY TODAY," 2004

The Stax label in Memphis proved to be a hotbed of soul music, thanks especially to its house band, Booker T and the MGs, comprising two Black members, organist Booker T. Jones and drummer Al Jackson, and two white guitarist Steve Cropper and bassist Donald "Duck" Dunn. In addition to recording their own hits, like the electrifying instrumental "Green Onions" (1962), the MGs backed a superb roster of soul talent, including Eddie Floyd ("Knock On Wood") and Wilson Pickett ("In The Midnight Hour"). The greatest of all, though, was the Georgia-born Otis Redding, a magnificent vocalist who died in a plane crash at the age of 26, shortly after recording his soulful signature hit "(Sittin' On) The Dock Of The Bay" in 1967.

SOUL SINGER (1933–2006)

JAMES BROWN

Born in Augusta, Georgia, James Brown was a true pioneer, first of soul and then funk. His reputation rests primarily on the radical reappraisal of rhythm that went into the irresistible dance music he created, and his injection of raw, gospel-infused passion into ballad singing. In its presaging of soul, his first recording, "Please, Please, Please" in 1955, was a decade ahead of its time, while the 1963 album *Live At The Apollo* immortalized the energetic performing style that made him the "hardest working man in show business."

AFTER

Soul as a separate genre had largely disappeared by the late 1970s, along with the heated social and political climate that had helped define it.

LOSS AND RELOCATION
Stax never quite recovered from Otis Redding's death and the assassination in Memphis in 1968 of civil rights leader Martin Luther King. Motown left its best soul days behind when it moved from Detroit to Los Angeles in 1972.

DANCE FEVER
Disco, a lighter and much less personally intense form of dance music, dominated the charts in the late 1970s **354–355 ››**.

OUTPOST IN ENGLAND
In the 1970s, DJs in northwest England championed some of the more obscure American soul records of the 1960s, in a movement known as **northern soul**.

The queen conquers
Aretha Franklin appears on the cover of her 1967 record *I Never Loved A Man The Way I Love You*. It reached number 2 in the US albums chart and marked her breakthrough as a top soul artist.

KEY WORKS

Solomon Burke "Cry to Me"
Marvin Gaye "What's Goin' On"
Otis Redding "These Arms of Mine"
Wilson Pickett "In the Midnight Hour"
Stevie Wonder *Talking Book*
Aretha Franklin "Respect"
James Brown "Please, Please, Please"

Time for a Change

While the 1960s were the decade in which pop music came of age, they were also a time of political upheaval. Folk and gospel singers raised their voices in protest against the Vietnam War and in support of civil rights.

BEFORE

For centuries, musicians have expressed discontent through political songwriting and satire.

THE ALMANAC SINGERS
Alarmed by the rise of fascism in the late 1930s, Pete Seeger, Woody Guthrie, Lee Hays, and Millard Lampell formed the Almanac Singers. They wrote songs in support of worker's unions, **protesting against racial segregation** **« 240–241**, and opposing Adolf Hitler. They wore working men's street clothes at their performances and played at protest marches and union meetings.

GODFATHER OF US PROTEST MUSIC
Because of earlier involvement in left-wing and labor politics, and his refusal to answer questions from the US House Committee on Un-American Activities, **Pete Seeger was blacklisted** in the 1950s during a time of increased **fear of communists** among Americans. Unable to perform professionally, Seeger went underground, appearing only unofficially. He is now regarded as the godfather of American protest folk music.

1939 **The year the anti-lynching ballad "Strange Fruit" was recorded, by US jazz singer Billie Holiday.**

American folk music experienced a huge revival in the late 1950s. Acts such as Peter, Paul and Mary and the Kingston Trio found success singing new versions of traditional folk songs. Joan Baez was the first folk act to crack the pop charts and maintain a political agenda. She sang folk ballads and gospel songs at political rallies. In 1963, she brought international attention to the young Bob Dylan by inviting him on stage with her and by performing his songs.

Political anthems

Bob Dylan made his name with protest songs such as "The Lonesome Death of Hattie Caroll" and "Blowin' in the Wind," which became an anthem of the civil rights movement. His rasping voice, aggressive harmonica playing, and surreal sense of humor quickly set him apart. Dylan's peers, who performed in the coffee houses, of Greenwich Village in New York, included the singer-songwriters Tom Paxton and Phil Ochs. The latter was also known as "The Singing Journalist" due to his songs that satirized US policy in Vietnam and the Cuban missile crisis.

Protest singers were not unique to New York City. Bruce "Utah" Phillips and Rosalie Sorrels, two folk singers from Utah, made their names in the 1960s. Their songs were influenced as much by anarchist politics as by the people and landscape of their home state.

Joan Baez
A highly politically motivated singer, committed to the African American civil rights movement in the 1950s and '60s, Baez sang at anti-Vietnam War and workers' solidarity marches. She was arrested several times.

Music with a message

Gospel singers had long made their voices heard in the struggle for civil rights. Mahalia Jackson sang at many civil rights events in the 1950s. When Dr. Martin Luther King Jr. invited her to sing in Montgomery, Alabama, in 1956, in protest against racial segregation on buses, the house in which she was staying was firebombed. She escaped without injury.

> "... the **world is run** by those who **never listen** to **music ...**"
>
> BOB DYLAN IN *TARANTULA*, HIS BOOK OF EXPERIMENTAL PROSE POETRY, 1966

At the March on Washington for Jobs and Freedom in 1963, more than 250,000 people stood in front of the Lincoln Memorial to hear the speakers. Gospel and folk singers sang out a message of freedom and hope. On the bill were Marian Anderson ("He's Got the Whole World in his Hands"), Mahalia Jackson ("How I Got Over"), Odetta ("I'm On My Way"), Peter, Paul and Mary ("Blowin' in the Wind"), Bob Dylan ("When the Ship Comes In"), and Joan Baez, who led the crowd in singing "We Shall Overcome," the anthem of the civil rights movement. Dr. Martin Luther King Jr. spoke last. Behind him, Mahalia Jackson prompted, "Tell 'em about the dream!"

Soul singers

In 1967, Aretha Franklin, who was blessed with one of the most powerful voices of the 20th century, released "Respect," giving soul singer Otis Redding's 1965 song such gospel-influenced flourishes as spelling out the letters "R-E-S-P-E-C-T" and adding a chorus of her sisters singing "sock it to me, sock it to me." While ostensibly the complaint of a woman bemoaning her lover's treatment of her, its title and lyrics, demanding respect, had an obvious wider social import. Franklin bridged the gap between gospel and soul and performed at civil rights benefit concerts throughout the 1960s.

James Brown (see p.321) was a soul sensation with a social conscience. His "Say It Loud (I'm Black and I'm Proud)" was an unambiguous statement of Black pride, containing the defiant lyric "we'd rather die on our feet/than be living on our knees." The song used the age-old call-and-response technique of gospel, for which Brown brought a group of children into the recording studio.

While James Brown had a gruff bark of a voice, Curtis Mayfield (1942–1999) had a high falsetto. Mayfield's music favored lush string and brass orchestrations, backed

SINGER-SONGWRITER (1941–)

BOB DYLAN

Born Robert Allen Zimmerman in Duluth, Minnesota, Dylan is considered, musically and culturally, one of the most influential people of the 20th century. The grandchild of Jewish immigrants, he spent his early years listening to radio and formed bands while still in high school. He dropped out of college after one year.

Musically, he was influenced by Woody Guthrie (1912–1967) and first made his name playing folk and blues standards at coffeehouses in New York. In 1965, he "went electric," taking his music in a rock 'n' roll direction, which many folk fans regarded as a betrayal. Dylan continues to tour and has vowed never to stop writing songs.

KEY WORKS

Bob Dylan "Blowin' in the Wind"
Pete Seeger "We Shall Overcome"
Phil Ochs "I Ain't Marching Anymore"
Sam Cooke "A Change Is Gonna Come"
The Temptations "Ball of Confusion"
Nina Simone "I Wish I Knew How It Would Feel to be Free "
Marvin Gaye "What's Goin' On"
Aretha Franklin "Respect"

What's Going On

Marvin Gaye's album was a melodic cry of protest from the titular first track to the last, covering Vietnam, civil rights, and ecology.

by African percussion and funky bass lines. The music may have been more orchestral, but the messages in his lyrics were no less militant than Brown's. Mayfield found fame with The Impressions, a soul vocal group, and the songs he wrote for them—such as "Keep on Pushing" (1964), "People Get Ready" (1964), and "We're Rolling On" (1967)—helped keep up the momentum of the civil rights movement.

Mercy, mercy me

Unlike the uplifting, defiant mood of the music of many of his peers, Marvin Gaye's songs focused on specific issues, such as the indignities and struggles of people in Black neighborhoods, drug dependency, and lack of education. Gaye (1939–1984) had an established reputation as a singer of love songs, and he had to fight the boss of his record label, Berry Gordy, to get his protest songs recorded. Gaye was proved right, however. "What's Going On" sold more than 100,000 copies in its first week, paving the way for the phenomenal success of his album of the same name.

One of the most popular African American entertainers to involve herself in the civil rights movement was Nina Simone (1933–2003). Coming from a background in jazz and classical music, Simone wrote songs in response to day-to-day events, penning "Mississippi Goddam" following the 1963 bombing of a church in Birmingham, Alabama, which killed four African American children. The single was boycotted in certain southern states. On her 1968 album, *Silk and Soul*, she recorded the classic song "I Wish I Knew How It Would Feel to be Free," which became an anthem for the civil rights movement, and was rerecorded by both Black and white musicians of the time. Simone was in favor of violent revolution during the 1960s, in contradiction to the peaceful protest advocated by Dr. Martin Luther King Jr. However, on King's death in 1968, she wrote an entire album in his honor.

Jazz singer

Nina Simone's jazz background and powerful voice gave an edge to the literate and evocative songs she penned.

AFTER »

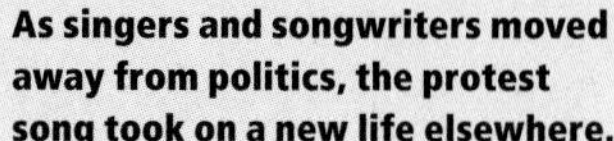

As singers and songwriters moved away from politics, the protest song took on a new life elsewhere.

PUNK AND PROTEST

Punk rock took the protest song's anti-establishment spirit to notoriously nihilistic extremes in the late 1970s. "I don't know what I want, but I know how to get it," sang Johnny Rotten in "Anarchy In the UK." **Punk 356–357 »** protested against everything. Celebrating attitude over ability, anyone who knew a few guitar chords could start a band. The voice of punk was working class and angry.

HIP-HOP AND SOCIAL ISSUES

In the 1980s and '90s, **hip-hop 370–71 »** brought the stark reality of life in Black America to the world's attention. Confronting social issues such as racism, poverty, crime, gangs, and drug abuse head on, acts such as **Public Enemy**, N.W.A, Ice T, Schoolly D, and the Geto Boys told the world what life for many African Americans was really like.

BEFORE

The Beatles took their main inspiration from the giants of American rock 'n' roll.

GENIUS IN SPECTACLES

Texas singer-songwriter **Buddy Holly** **« 314–315** exemplified the self-contained rock 'n' roll artist, playing guitar, and taking lead vocals on his own compositions. His band, the Crickets, influenced the Beatles' choice of name, while his music made an indelible mark. "What he did with three chords," enthused John Lennon, "made a songwriter out of me."

LITTLE RICHARD AND "THE KING"

Paul McCartney based his ballad-singing style on **Elvis** **« 316–317** and his rock delivery on **Little Richard** **« 315**. At the Beatles' induction into the Rock and Roll Hall of Fame, in Cleveland, Ohio, in 1988, George Harrison thanked all the "rock 'n' rollers," especially Little Richard, saying, "It's all his fault, really."

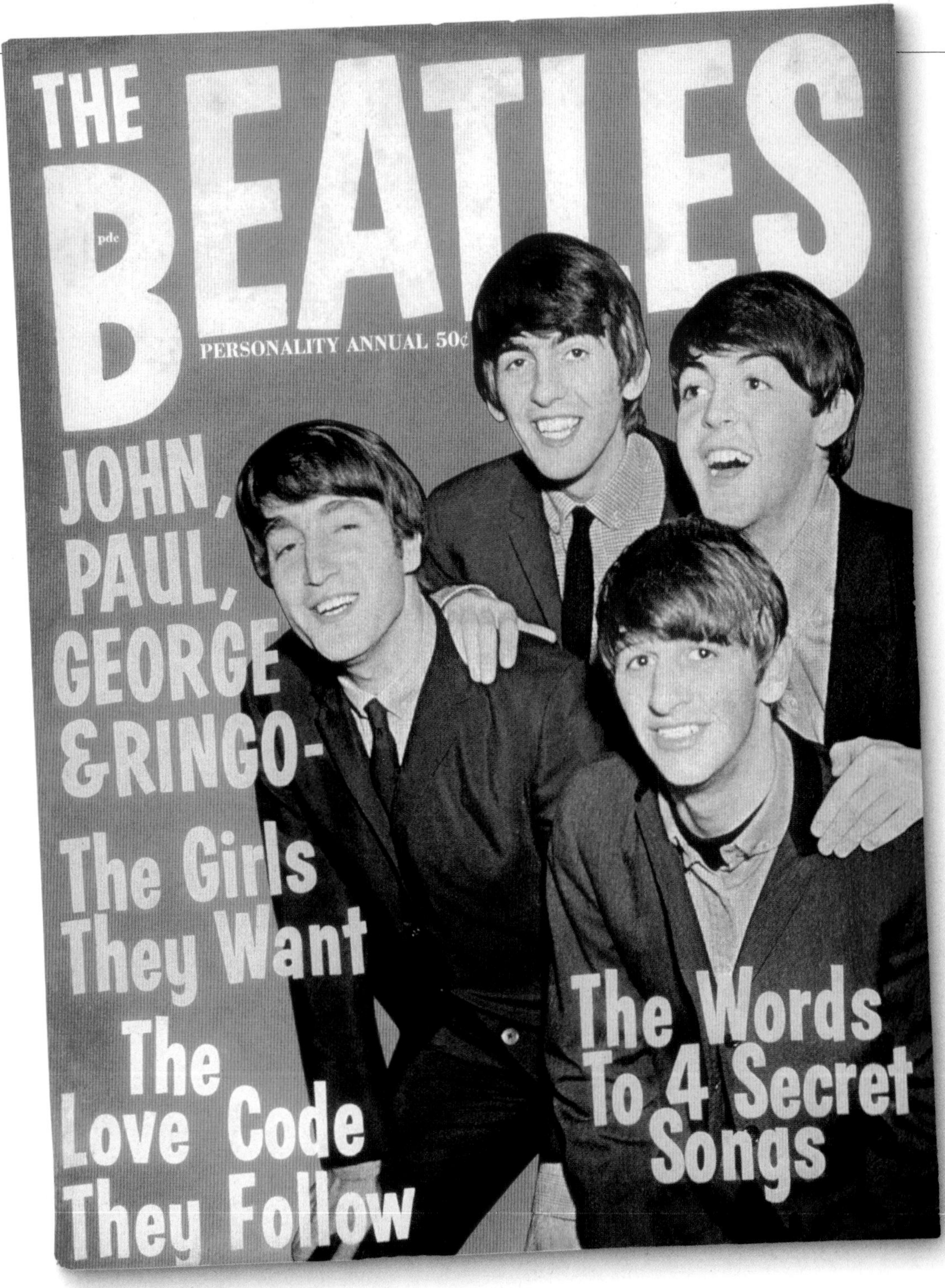

THE BEATLES
PERSONALITY ANNUAL 50¢
JOHN, PAUL, GEORGE & RINGO-
The Girls They Want
The Love Code They Follow
The Words To 4 Secret Songs

The fab foursome
An American magazine cover from 1964 features (clockwise from left) John Lennon, George Harrison, Paul McCartney, and Ringo Starr. It is typical of the cheery, Beatle-related paraphernalia of the period.

RECORD PRODUCER (1926–2016)

GEORGE MARTIN

Before joining EMI, George Martin studied the piano and oboe. He produced most Beatles' recordings from 1963 to 1969 and was a trusted steward in the studio. Increasingly in thrall to the group's musical creativity, he coped with the contrasting demands of Lennon, McCartney, and Harrison with discreet authority and good-humored flexibility. His subtle and versatile musicianship created some memorable arrangements, including the atmospheric double string quartet of "Eleanor Rigby" and the sinister cello of "I Am the Walrus."

Beatlemania

The Beatles were the best-loved group of the 1960s and possibly the most influential musical entity of the 20th century. The band's recordings between 1963 and 1970 remain popular music benchmarks, while their spirit of lighthearted invention continues to inspire.

The impact of the Beatles was earthshaking. Yet the four mischievous mop-haired lads from Liverpool began their domination of 1960s popular culture by simply being themselves. It was their sassy personal charm rather than their music that ensnared producer George Martin. "When you meet someone… and they give you a kind of glow, when they leave you, you feel a bit little lost," explained Martin. "The Beatles had that effect on me." Via top TV shows, British and American teenagers were exposed to that same indefinable magnetism and Beatlemania ensued.

Early impact

Of course, the music helped. It was upbeat pop with a rock beat, chiming guitars and tight vocal harmonies, unforgettable melodies, and hints of American R&B, Tin Pan Alley, and British folk. The songs spoke a universal language about holding hands or

Closely followed and watched
The Beatles' movements were followed avidly by their fans and the media. On February 7, 1964, photographers scramble for the best pictures as the Beatles prepare to leave London Airport, bound for the United States.

holding you tight, and money not being able to buy you love, all shot through with infectious, exciting yeah-yeah-yeah positivism. Early Beatles music captured the spirit of the new decade, representing the possibilities of a classless society peopled by a smart, irreverent, young generation.

They also impressed the musical establishment. A critic on Britain's *The Times* newspaper, for example, called Lennon and McCartney "the outstanding English composers of 1963," while American composer Leonard Bernstein talked of their "flawless intonation, the utterly fresh lyrics, the Schubert-like flow of musical invention."

> "The Beatles **saved the world** from boredom."
>
> GEORGE HARRISON, INTERVIEW WITH AMERICAN WRITER GEOFFREY GIULIANO, 1984

Varied influences

Although not trained musicians, both John Lennon and Paul McCartney had musical parents. They were also sensitive to a wide range of 20th-century popular music through movies, records, and the radio, and they developed an instinctive awareness of technique and craft. Their sense of melody and intuitive recall of chord sequences, along with a friendly but competitive interpersonal chemistry when writing "eyeball to eyeball" (as Lennon put it), produced a string of pop masterpieces.

The Beatles' musical growth was further encouraged by their being open to outside influences and possessing the technical ability to exploit them. Lennon was quick to incorporate something similar to the obscurity of Bob Dylan lyrics ("You've Got To Hide Your Love Away") or a groove from a Wilson Pickett record ("When I Get Home"). McCartney would adapt the bold bass lines on Beach Boys' records ("Fixing a Hole") or, after hearing experimental composer Stockhausen (see pp.270–271), experiment with tape loops ("Tomorrow Never Knows").

String of firsts

The Beatles were the first group to play a stadium concert (Shea Stadium, New York, 1965), put lyrics on an album jacket (*Sgt. Pepper's*, 1967), and form their own company (Apple Corps Ltd., 1968). But it was perhaps the self-contained power of the Beatles as composers and performers that was most influential on the music business. Previously, most pop performers relied on professional songwriters and musicians. After the Beatles, groups that wrote and played their own songs became routine, leaving many professional songwriters out in the cold.

The Beatles' interest in influences outside the norm, whether drugs, Indian gurus, or avant-gardism, contributed to the group constantly refreshing its musical palette, often taking fans by surprise. Throughout the 1960s, many looked to the Beatles to show them what was happening "out there." The group introduced ordinary people to psychedelic experiences ("Tomorrow Never Knows," "A Day In The Life"), and love-and-peace philosophy ("All You Need Is Love"), while George Harrison's interest in the sitar ("Norwegian Wood," "Within You Without You") brought the exotic sound of Indian music to millions of Western listeners.

On the bandwagon
The Animals, formed in Newcastle, England in 1963, were quick to follow the Beatles across the Atlantic in 1964, part of the "British invasion" of pop bands that took the United States by storm.

Touched by greatness

As early as 1966, the group decided to stop touring and concentrate on writing and recording. This produced mature work that redefined what pop music could be. The dizzying band-within-a-band soundworld of *Sgt. Pepper's Lonely Hearts Club Band* (1967) mesmerized a generation during the Summer of Love. The hugely varied double *White Album* (1968) swung from raw blues to avant-garde collage to schmaltz; and their swansong, *Abbey Road* (1969), displayed almost symphonic tendencies. Each of these albums was widely admired and imitated.

From the early appeal of a good tune, an optimistic sentiment, and a dash of genius to the emotionally complex, musically advanced work of their middle and late period, the Beatles represent one of the few times in musical history when the most popular was perhaps also the best. Despite the band's split in 1970, after barely 10 years together, new generations of pop groups, guitar combos, and singer-songwriters continue to be in thrall to their achievements.

Iconic design incorporating the initials S. P. enclosed by a heart

The Sgt. Pepper Trumpet
Sgt. Pepper's Lonely Hearts Club Band inspired a film of the same name in 1978. The film featured many well-known musicians, 29 Beatles songs, and this heart-shaped trumpet.

AFTER

The Beatles never re-formed, but they continued to influence music and remain much imitated today.

NEW BANDS
After disbanding in 1970, the Beatles went on to have solo careers or to form new bands: **John Lennon** with his wife Yoko Ono **326–327 ››**, and Paul McCartney with Wings. Only Paul McCartney and Ringo Starr survive today; Lennon was murdered in 1980, and George Harrison died of cancer in 2001.

A BIT LIKE THE BEATLES
Many bands, including Badfinger, ELO, Jellyfish, and Oasis, have presented variations on a Beatles-like chord sequence, melody, vocal harmony, or production technique.

KEY WORKS

"I Want to Hold Your Hand"
"Help"
"Eleanor Rigby"
"She Said She Said"
Sgt. Pepper's Lonely Hearts Club Band
"Revolution" (B-side of "Hey Jude")
Side two of *Abbey Road*

A taste for the blues
The Rolling Stones took up the blues cause. Here they are rehearsing for a British TV appearance in 1964, with (from left) Bill Wyman, Brian Jones, Mick Jagger, Charlie Watts, and Keith Richards.

BEFORE

By the start of the 1960s, when British audiences were discovering the blues, African American audiences were already moving on.

HOMEMADE SKIFFLE
In the 1950s, **electric blues « 306–307** and **rock 'n' roll « 314–315** were developing side by side at Chicago's Chess studios, while in Britain many musicians were influenced by Lonnie Donegan, who played blues-based **skiffle** using homemade instruments on hits such as "Rock Island Line" (1954) .

LONNIE DONEGAN was the bestselling UK artist until the Beatles.

FOLK REVIVAL
While musicians in the UK were looking for authenticity in the blues, an equivalent search for authenticity had started among young white Americans that would lead to the **folk revival**. These trends would expose international audiences to the raw intensity of prewar **Delta blues « 240–241** rooted in the plantations of the American South.

Blues Rock

In the 1960s, just as the blues seemed to be losing relevance in the United States, it was enthusiastically adopted by young British musicians on the other side of the Atlantic, including Fleetwood Mac and the Rolling Stones.

Among the least predictable developments in popular music history was the way in which during the early 1960s the blues was taken up by British musicians, who then exported it to the United States, where it seemed to have lost its relevance.

When a wave of British bands carried their new take on the blues back to the land where it originated, it was embraced just as eagerly by young Americans and found a mass white audience there, too.

Trading the blues

The blues served as the initial inspiration for almost all the British "beat groups" of the 1960s. The typical pattern was for young fans to fall in love with the music they heard on prized, imported records; to learn to play their instruments by copying the sounds as closely as possible; to form bands playing cover versions of blues songs; and eventually to perform with their American idols on European tours. Those who achieved lasting success, however, tended do so by evolving further still, writing their own songs and leaving the blues behind.

Unlike jazz, which rapidly spread across the world, the blues remained for the first half of the 20th century closely identified with its original core audience. Although Black migrants from the deep South took the blues to America's cities, many then discarded it in favor of more sophisticated—and politicized—urban genres. Had it not found acclaim in Europe, the blues might have withered away altogether.

The first major blues figures to visit Europe were Lead Belly, in 1949, and Big Bill Broonzy, in 1951. European

"What's the **point** of hearing **us** do 'I'm a King Bee' when you can hear **Slim Harpo** doing it?"

MICK JAGGER, "ROLLING STONE" MAGAZINE, 1968

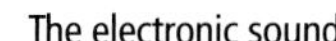

audiences idealized blues singers as straight-from-the-fields folksters. Broonzy had been recording with groups since the 1930s, but duly donned workingmen's overalls and recast himself as an acoustic bluesman. Muddy Waters followed in 1958, the first electric bluesman to make the crossing, and returned several times with other Chess Records stars such as Sonny Boy Williamson II and Howlin' Wolf (see pp.306–307).

Embracing the electric blues

Some European fans felt that electric guitars and amplification sullied the "authenticity" of the blues. For many British musicians, however, the live power of the electric blues was a revelation. London jazz stalwarts spurred to form their own blues bands included John Mayall, Alexis Korner, and Graham Bond. Graduates of Mayall's Bluesbreakers included Mick Taylor, who went on to join the Rolling Stones, and Eric Clapton.

When guitarist Peter Green left Mayall in 1967, he took bassist John McVie and drummer Mick Fleetwood along with him. As Fleetwood Mac, they were perhaps the finest British blues band of all. B.B. King later said of Green: "He has the sweetest tone I ever heard; he was the only one who gave me the cold sweats."

What was to become rock music evolved rapidly away from the blues, especially in the wake of the psychedelia-infused "Summer of Love" of 1967. That said, many of rock's biggest names owed a considerable debt to the blues, even if it was not always acknowledged. Led Zeppelin, founded by former Yardbirds Jimmy Page and John Paul Jones in 1968, modeled much of their material on blues templates (see pp.328–29).

The electronic sound
For blues players, the electric guitar was all important, and was often customized to meet top players' needs. This red Gibson Les Paul guitar is from the 1960s, named after its designer. Les Paul was a pioneer of this kind of instrument.

The Rolling Stones

The story of the archetypal British blues band began at Dartford station, in Kent, in October 1961, when guitar-toting art student Keith Richards ran into his former classmate Mick Jagger. Jagger was carrying LPs by Chuck Berry and Muddy Waters, bought by mail from the United States. Taking their name from a Muddy Waters song, they played their first gig as the Rolling Stones in 1962, and finalized their five-piece lineup in 1963.

Even if the Rolling Stones originally saw themselves as blues purists, they brought many more flavors to the pot. Covers on their first album, released in 1964, ranged from rock 'n' roll to Motown, Marvin Gaye to Buddy Holly.

The Stones are often characterized as recording "old" blues songs, but, in fact, during the 1960s, those songs were still very current. Howlin' Wolf recorded "Little Red Rooster" in 1961, and Slim Harpo "Shake Your Hips" in 1966.

Much like Elvis 10 years before, the Stones in their early days brought an exuberant teenage energy to what had originally been powerful adult songs, such as Muddy Waters' "I Just Want To Make Love To You." Jagger and Richards grew to discover that they could express themselves even better by writing their own material, but their classic albums continued to include at least one bona-fide blues gem.

John Mayall
For his work on the seminal 1966 album with the Bluesbreakers' John Mayall (far left), the 21-year-old Eric Clapton (reading the *Beano* comic) acquired the burdensome nickname "God."

The blues go home

While there had been a small contingent of white blues enthusiasts in the United States ever since the 1930s, most focused on the blues as an acoustic, folk tradition rather than the latest sounds from Chicago. During the folk revival of early 1960s, for example, white fans were instrumental in "rediscovering" aging Delta bluesmen, and Bob Dylan's debut album consisted largely of acoustic blues covers.

The story that the Rolling Stones, during their first US tour in 1964, found Muddy Waters painting the walls of Chess Records studios to earn a few extra dollars, perhaps best illustrates the lack of US interest in electric blues. The huge success of the Stones and other British bands, however, coupled with Dylan's 1965 decision to hook up with the Paul Butterfield Blues Band, encouraged the emergence of more white US blues bands, such as Canned Heat. In addition, veteran Black bluesmen suddenly found themselves playing for—and adapting their music to suit—predominantly white audiences.

12 **The number of weeks the Stones' first album, entitled *The Rolling Stones*, stayed at No. 1 in the UK album charts.**

GUITARIST (1945–)

ERIC CLAPTON

Born in Surrey in 1945, and always devoted to the blues, Eric Clapton established his reputation in a bewildering succession of bands. He joined the Yardbirds as a guitar prodigy in 1963, nicknamed "Slowhand"; moved to John Mayall's Bluesbreakers in 1965, and then formed two short-lived "supergroups," Cream, with Jack Bruce and Ginger Baker, and Blind Faith. At the end of the 1960s, he recorded "Layla" in the United States with Derek and the Dominoes. Since then he has toured and recorded under his own name, performing his own compositions as well as classics by the likes of Robert Johnson, and collaborating with veterans such as B.B. King.

KEY WORKS

The Animals "House of the Rising Sun"

Fleetwood Mac "Need Your Love So Bad"

The Rolling Stones "I Just Want to Make Love to You"

John Mayall's Bluesbreakers "Ramblin' on My Mind"

Canned Heat "On the Road Again"

AFTER

Many white stars of the blues rock era remain household names, and Black originators had lasting careers. But blues rock music passed from the mainstream at the end of the 1960s.

FLEETWOOD MAC'S "RUMOURS"

ROLLING ON

Among the most enduring legacies of blues rock were American **boogie bands** such as ZZ Top, and so-called **Southern Rock** bands like the Allman Brothers and Lynyrd Skynyrd.

Peter Green suffered a breakdown and left Fleetwood Mac in 1970, after which the band, abandoning its blues roots, produced bestselling albums such as *Rumours*. Green returned to performing under his own name in the 1990s. The Rolling Stones continue to release albums and undertake world tours.

Heavy Rock

Bigger music festivals and larger concert halls required ever larger loudspeaker systems and amplifier stacks. With rock bands delighting in their new sonic power, and audiences clamoring for louder and longer songs, a musical behemoth was born: heavy rock.

BEFORE

A mix of blues-rock and psychedelia occurred in the late 1960s that would give birth to hard rock in the early 70s.

DRUMMING UP A STORM

Jimi Hendrix and **Eric Clapton 312–313 ››** wrote the rulebook for the extended guitar solo. Drummers such as Ginger Baker of the British band **Cream** and Keith Moon of their compatriots **The Who** helped ratchet up the volume of bands to stadium-rock levels, and the instrumental arrangements of their songs grew increasingly complex.

WILD MAN KEITH MOON OF THE WHO

BLUES ROCKERS

The United States had its own blues rockers who bridged the gap between **psychedelia** and **heavy metal**. Vanilla Fudge had its biggest hit in 1968 with an overhaul of **the Supremes 320–321 ››** soul-pop classic "You Keep Me Hangin' On," slowing it down and rocking it up. That same year, Blue Cheer, a trio from San Francisco inspired by the Jimi Hendrix Experience, had a hit with a similarly beefed-up cover version of **Eddie Cochran's** "Summertime Blues."

In the late 1960s, rock players who had idolized acoustic blues guitarists such as Robert Johnson, Son House, and Leadbelly developed their own powerful electric version of the blues. Singer Robert Plant and guitarist Jimmy Page were, much like their slightly older peers, the Rolling Stones, big fans of the blues (see pp.306–307) and early Black rock 'n' roll (see pp.314–315). Their band, Led Zeppelin, took these musical forms on to the world stage, louder and heavier than ever, setting the heavy-rock template for decades to come.

The world's biggest band

Unlike the majority of Black blues vocalists—or, indeed, most white rock singers—Robert Plant eschewed his natural vocal range in favor of a high-pitched yet powerful shriek. It cut across the crunchy electric guitar of Jimmy Page, powerhouse drums of John Bonham, and inventive bass

126 The number of decibels reached by The Who in the loudest concert on record, at Charlton Athletic Football Ground in London, in 1976.

of John Paul Jones. Led Zeppelin's larger-than-life shows, consummate rock stagecraft, and relentless touring made them the biggest band in the world in the early 1970s.

Although Led Zeppelin is routinely cited as the band that invented heavy metal, their characteristic volume and machismo were not their only talents. On tracks such as "Stairway to Heaven" and "Black Mountainside," the band let their softer psychedelic and folk influences show. The lyrics of Robert Plant often referenced folklore and magic, while John Paul Jones's guitar playing owed a debt to British acoustic folk

Heavy themes
Pink Floyd's *Dark Side of the Moon* was an intense and highly focused album. The heaviness of its themes—money, time, and mental illness—was matched by the music on tracks such as "Brain Damage" and "On the Run."

The godfathers
Led Zeppelin's Robert Plant (far left) and Jimmy Page (far right) have altered their image over their many albums, as the band dabbled in funk and even reggae. They remain the godfathers of heavy metal, although their music has been adapted to hip-hop and rap.

LED ZEPPELIN FAN BUTTONS

guitarists such as Bert Jansch and Davey Graham. The phenomenal worldwide success of Led Zeppelin spawned a wave of bands heavily influenced by them.

Classical grandeur

Fellow Britons Deep Purple had an operatic vocalist in Ian Gillan and a dexterous guitar hero in Ritchie Blackmore, but they set themselves apart from being mere Zeppelin copyists with their leanings toward progressive rock: their keyboard player Jon Lord added distorted Hammond organ and quasi-symphonic grandeur to their sound on their breakthrough album of 1970, *In Rock*. They shared

TECHNOLOGY

DISTORTION PEDAL

Often known as a fuzz box, the distortion pedal first appeared in 1962, in the shape of the Maestro Fuzz Tone pedal. It became an essential item of equipment among '60s rock guitarists after it was used in the classic riff of the Rolling Stones song "I Can't Get No) Satisfaction." Distortion pedals boost an electric guitar's signal, causing a signal to "clip," or distort. Vintage pedals of the 1960s and '70s are highly sought-after. The Seattle-based grunge band Mudhoney named its mini-album *Superfuzz Bigmuff* after two '60s fuzz boxes.

Stacked for sound
The iconic "Marshall stack" amplifier was invented after drummer and store-owner Jim Marshall heard complaints from Deep Purple's Ritchie Blackmore and The Who's Pete Townshend that there were no guitar amplifiers with a big enough sound and impact.

their classical pretensions and prog-rock tendencies with the British band Queen, led by the flamboyant Freddie Mercury and propelled by Brian May's irrepressible guitar solos. Over the years, Queen would embrace pop and disco, obscuring the fact that their early albums were no-holds-barred heavy rock: hard, loud, self-indulgent, and lots of fun. Theatrical hard-rock pioneer Arthur Brown had given an earlier masterclass in stagecraft when he topped UK charts with "Fire" and his flaming helmet in 1968.

> "Hippies wanted **peace** and **love.** We wanted **Ferraris, blondes,** and **switchblades.**"
>
> AMERICAN ROCK SINGER ALICE COOPER

Detroit horror

Heavy rock was by no means just a British invention. Alice Cooper was a band formed in Detroit in 1969, and fronted by singer Vincent Furnier, who later adopted the group's name as his own stage name. "I'm Eighteen" and "School's Out," with their big, anthemlike choruses, were huge hits for Alice Cooper in 1971 and 1972 respectively. The songs celebrated adolescent rebelliousness and were vaguely anti-authority in a manner that resounded with America's suburban middle-class youth at the time.

A key element in Alice Cooper's appeal was the outrageous horror image projected by his band. His stage show featured copious amounts of fake blood, mock beheadings using plastic guillotines, and "executions" using pretend electric chairs.

Action-packed performance

The hard-rock American four-piece band KISS followed a similar musical formula: the guitars were loud and rocky, but the songs had catchy, melodic choruses. The band's onstage antics were even more spectacular than those of Alice Cooper. Gene Simmons, the band's lead singer, was the ringmaster of the show, and their circuslike performances included breathing fire and spitting blood, while guitars set off fireworks and drum kits levitated. All members wore harlequin-like black-and-white face makeup. Going to a pyrotechnic KISS concert became something of a rite of passage for male American teenagers of the 1970s.

The extravagances of heavy rock inevitably had a backlash. The Australian band AC/DC brought the music back to basics in the mid-1970s. Angus Young, the band's guitarist, returned hard rock to the tight riffs and no-nonsense solos of the Rolling Stones. While singer Bon Scott had a high, rough voice that he probably would never have adopted were it not for Led Zeppelin's Robert Plant, the band's overall musical aesthetic was toward economy.

Kiss of gold
The band KISS has been awarded more gold albums than any other US rock band. Here, band members (from left) Gene Simmons, Peter Criss (behind, on drums), Paul Stanley, and Ace Frehley perform in 1992.

KEY WORKS

Led Zeppelin "Whole Lotta Love"
Deep Purple "Smoke on the Water"
Alice Cooper "School's Out"
Black Sabbath "Paranoid"
Queen "Liar"
Kiss "Parasite"
AC/DC "Back in Black"

AFTER

Hard rock became known as heavy metal—or simply "metal"—in the late 1970s. It is a musical subculture that remains popular with generations of (male) teenagers.

GUITAR HEROES
The peculiar mix of **camp** and **machismo** epitomized by Led Zeppelin and KISS became the defining quality of American **heavy metal** in the 1980s. Los Angeles was a hotbed of aspiring guitar heroes, and the uniform of tight leather pants and big, permed, hairsprayed hair earned the music the nickname **hair metal** or **poodle rock**. Typical of these bands were Mötley Crüe, Twisted Sister, and, most successful of them all, **Guns N' Roses**.

Hair metal was essentially **pop music** played with very loud guitars, although Guns N' Roses distinguished themselves by sounding as authentically sleazy as the Rolling Stones did during their prime. The 1987 Guns N' Roses album *Appetite For Destruction*, the definitive heavy-metal record of the 1980s, was chock-full of chest-beating vocals and grandstanding guitar riffs.

COVER ART FOR GUNS N' ROSES' FIRST STUDIO ALBUM

Revolutionary instrument

This 1952 Gibson Les Paul guitar has a solid body made from mahogany with a maple veneer. The all-over metallic gold finish on this model is rare. The fingerboard is made from Brazilian rosewood with mother-of-pearl inlays and 22 metal frets.

String retainer

Tail piece (bridge)

Bridge (lead) pickup

Neck (rhythm) pickup

Strap button

Strap button

Pick guard

Neck pickup tone (rhythm)

Neck pickup volume (rhythm)

Bridge pickup tone (lead)

Bridge pickup volume (lead) control

TIMELINE

1931
The Frying Pan
Texan musician George Beauchamp invented this first electric guitar in 1931. He mounted a magnetic pickup on his Hawaiian lap-steel guitar.

BEAUCHAMP'S A-22 FRYING PAN

GIBSON ES150

1936
Gibson ES150
Early electric guitars were acoustics with transducers to convert vibrations into electrical signals. Made in 1936, it was played by jazz guitarist Charlie Christian.

CHARLIE CHRISTIAN

1951
Fender Telecaster
This iconic solid-body guitar ushered in the rock 'n' roll era. Country musicians loved its aggressive sound because it cut through noisy bars, transforming country into rockabilly.

FENDER TELECASTER

1952
Gibson Les Paul
Gibson enlisted jazz guitarist Les Paul to design this heavy solid-body guitar. Used in rock music, it remains one of the most popular electric guitars of all time.

1954
Fender Stratocaster
This was a more sophisticated relative of the Telecaster with three pickups, allowing for more control over the tone. A tremolo arm meant all the strings could be bent at once.

BUDDY HOLLY PLAYING A STRATOCASTER

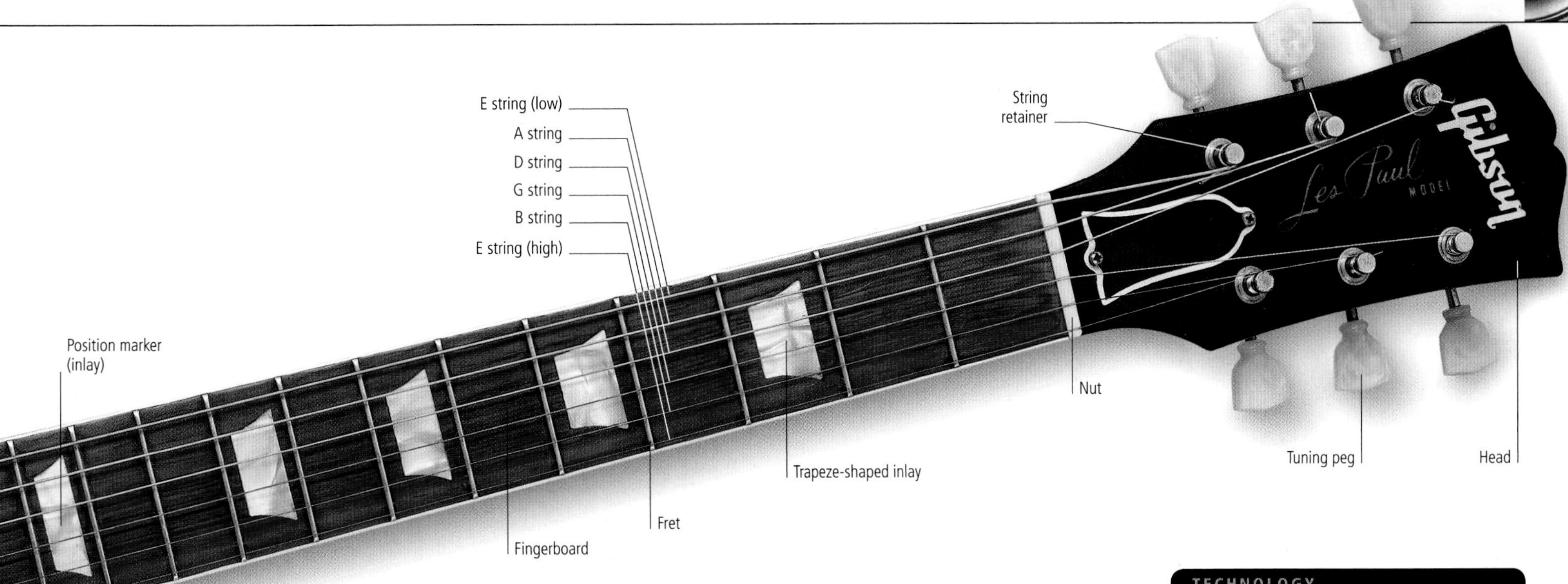

The **Electric Guitar**

It's impossible to imagine 20th-century music without the electric guitar. Developed for purely practical reasons—to allow a guitar to be heard alongside large musical ensembles—it utterly transformed music, defining the sound of rock and pop.

The electric guitar dates back to the 1930s, when jazz musicians began amplifying their instruments. They soon discovered that their acoustic guitars were prone to howling feedback when amplified—they were simply too effective at resonating and projecting sound. These acoustic properties were considered undesirable at the time and guitar makers of the 1950s, such as Leo Fender and Les Paul, came up with electric guitars with entirely solid bodies.

The first solid bodies

When Leo Fender put his Telecaster electric guitar on sale in the mid-50s, it flew out of the stores. Simplicity itself, the Tele was the first production-line guitar to be made from a solid plank of wood. It was much slimmer than the big jazz guitars, and its cutting sound was modern and fresh. Fender then brought out the more sophisticated Stratocaster. The rock 'n' rollers loved it and both Dick Dale in the United States and Hank Marvin in England conjured up a modish "surf guitar" sound from its heavy twang.

In 1952, Gibson approached jazz guitarist Les Paul to design a guitar. Its fat, warm tone proved popular among blues-rock guitarists of the '60s, including Peter Green of Fleetwood Mac and Eric Clapton of The Yardbirds and later, Cream. The Les Paul's big sound and curvy shape made it the favorite ax of rockers such as Led Zeppelin's Jimmy Page and Slash from Guns N' Roses, allowing them to play solos at dazzling speeds and look effortlessly cool while doing so.

TECHNOLOGY

PICKUPS

It is the guitar's pickups that make a steel-string electric guitar audible. These are magnets, mounted on the guitar near the bridge, that have been wrapped up with a coil of many thousand turns of fine copper wire. When the guitar strings are hit, their magnetism alters that of the coil, which induces an alternating current through it. This signal can then be amplified.

1958
Twin-necks
Gibson introduced the first twin-neck model in 1958. They became popular in the 1970s with heavy metal and prog rock guitarists, enabling them to play technically challenging solos.

GIBSON DOUBLE-12, 1958

1964
Rickenbacker 12-string
Developed in response to folk music's new popularity, the Rickenbacker 12-string provided George Harrison's sound on mid-1960s Beatles albums.

RICKENBACKER 12-STRING

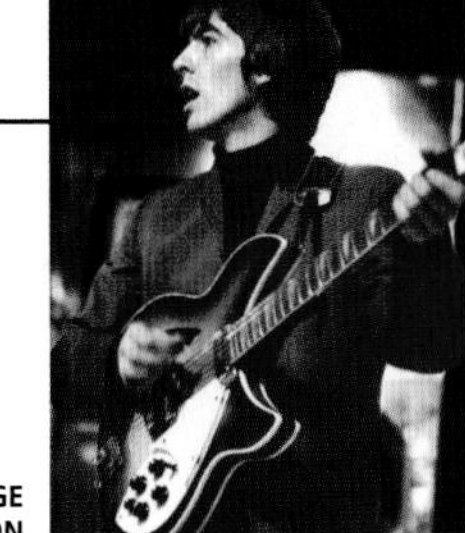

GEORGE HARRISON

1962
Distortion pedal
In 1962, the first portable, standalone distortion pedal, called the Fuzz Tone, was introduced. Many other effects pedals soon followed.

MODERN EFFECTS PEDAL

1963
Gibson SG special
The SG special is a variant on the Les Paul that is lighter in tone and weight. It became popular with rockers and indie bands, such as Radiohead.

GIBSON SG SPECIAL

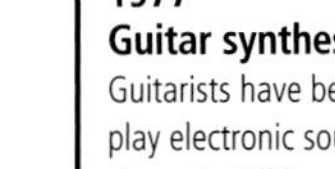

1977
Guitar synthesizers
Guitarists have been able to play electronic sounds since the early 1980s, using guitar synths such as the Roland G707. However, these never entirely caught on.

ROLAND G707

Rebel Music

Musicians around the world have provided a voice for the voiceless by singing about oppression, often at great personal cost to themselves. Their records were often banned, many performers were forced into exile, and some were even killed.

Bob Dylan's protest songs influenced a new generation of British singer-songwriters in the 1960s, including Bert Jansch, Ralph McTell, and Steve Tilston. As well as conventional love songs, they sang about homelessness, drug abuse, and apartheid. The Irish singer Christy Moore (1945–) also began his career in the 1960s, with songs reflecting his Republican views. He sang of the Irish volunteers in the Spanish Civil War, and expressed support for the Irish Republican prisoners who were on hunger strike in Northern Ireland's Maze Prison during the 1980s.

New Spanish song

The socially conscious *nueva canción* (new song) movement first rose up in Chile, before spreading throughout Latin America. It reenergized Spanish folk music with lyrics criticizing the right-wing dictators who ruled Spain, Argentina, and Chile. As well as acoustic guitars, singers played traditional instruments, such as the *charango* (lute), Andean flute, and panpipe.

Chilean Violeta Parra (1917–1967) was a pioneer of the new song movement. From the 1940s until her death, she sang stark, guitar-accompanied songs describing the worsening plight of Chileans. Inspired by Parra, Victor Jara (1932–1973), a communist, teacher, theater director, and poet, became a well-known singer. His songs included "Plegaria a un Labrador" (Prayer to a Worker), and "El Aparecido" (The Ghost), in which he correctly predicted the death of Che Guevara, the Argentinean revolutionary. A military coup brought Augusto Pinochet to power in Chile in 1972 and, in 1973, Jara was arrested, tortured, and shot dead along with many others.

In Argentina, Mercedes Sosa was the figurehead of *nueva canción*. Known as *La Negra* ("The Black Woman"), she wrote from a feminist perspective. Well-known for her left-wing views, she was harassed after the military took over and her songs were banned. She fled Argentina in the mid-1970s, only returning when its military junta collapsed in 1982.

Ralph McTell
McTell's hit "The Streets of London" (1969) moved crowds for decades. In 2020, he wrote an additional new verse in response to the COVID-19 pandemic.

« BEFORE

Music gives voice to the anger and frustration of people struggling to free themselves from foreign rule.

MOTHER INDIA
Although "Vande Mataram," which translates as "I Praise the Motherland," was banned by the British after the poem was set to music in 1896, Indian nationalists continued to sing it, although some were jailed by the British for doing so. It became the **national song** of an independent India in 1950.

THE IRISH STRUGGLE
Ballads told the story of the fight for Irish freedom from British rule. "The Grand Old Dame Britannia," written during World War I, was an anti-enlistment song, while in "The Row in the Town," Peadar Kearney writes with understated bitterness of the Easter Uprising of 1916. Many ballads memorialize fallen Irish **freedom fighters**.

ALGERIAN INDEPENDENCE
Rai, a rhythmic Algerian folk music of the early 20th century, usually deals with sensual pleasures, but during Algeria's war of independence against the French (1954–1962), rai musicians sang out in support of the **liberation movement**. The legendary Cheikha Rimitti (1923–2006) performed songs dedicated to the struggle.

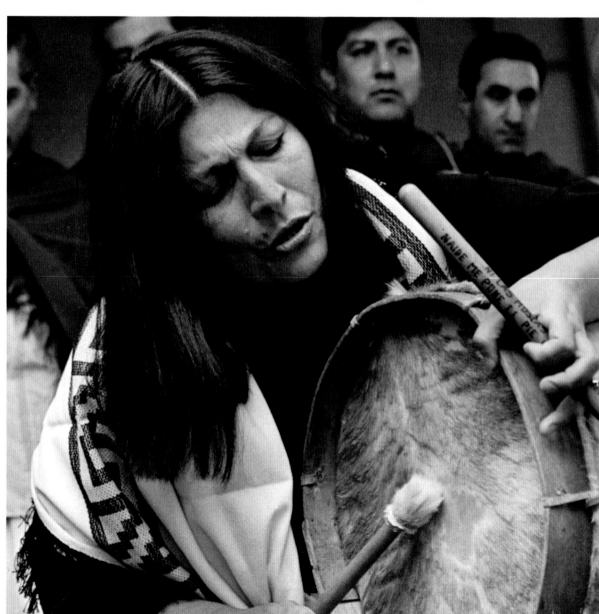

African music with a message

Thomas Mapfumo (1945–) is Zimbabwe's best-known musician. In the 1970s, he and his band, Black Unlimited, pioneered a politically charged genre of music called *chimurenga* (which means "struggle"), with lyrics about the country's battle for liberation from British rule. Chimurenga took Zimbabwe's ancient and much-loved instrument, the *mbira*—a type of thumb piano—into the rock band format. Mapfumo achieved this by duplicating the sound of the *mbira* itself, and the rhythms of *mbira* music, on an electric guitar. Mapfumo was a huge influence on Oliver Mtukudzi (1952–) who, with his band Black Spirits, blended *chimurenga* with South African township jive, rumba, and soul. In the 1980s, this became known as 'Tuku" music. Like Mapfumo, Mtukudzi wrote hard-hitting lyrics and was the first Zimbabwean singer to address the AIDS epidemic in the country.

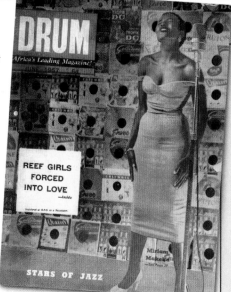

Mama Africa
Miriam Makeba, here pictured on a magazine cover in 1957, had her citizenship revoked by the South African government for speaking out against its apartheid policy to the United Nations in 1963. She remains an iconic figure in South Africa.

"**Would you** keep silent and **do nothing** if you were in our place?"

MIRIAM MAKEBA, SINGER, SPEAKING AT THE UN IN 1963

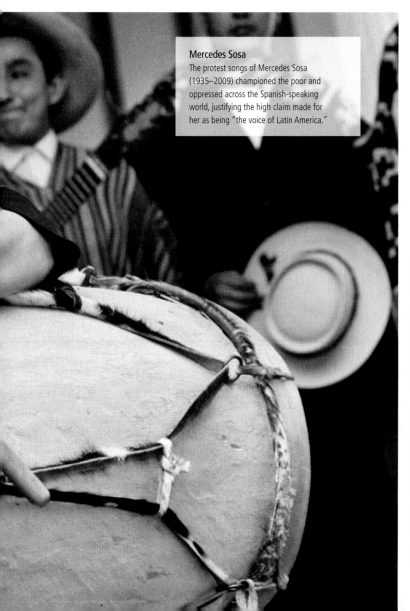

Mercedes Sosa
The protest songs of Mercedes Sosa (1935–2009) championed the poor and oppressed across the Spanish-speaking world, justifying the high claim made for her as being "the voice of Latin America."

Ending Apartheid

Music that expressed sentiments of resistance, protest, and unity played a major role in the struggle against apartheid in South Africa. Trumpeter, singer, and composer Hugh Masekela wrote anti-apartheid songs, while singer-songwriters Miriam Makeba and Johnny Clegg doubled as political activists. Their voices were censored and suppressed by the government; in 1961, Makeba had her passport revoked. Clegg, a white South African who spoke fluent Zulu, formed the bands Juluka and Savuka, comprising Black and white musicians, which defied racial segregation. His song "Asimbonanga" ("We Have Not Seen Him") was a tribute to the jailed leader of the anti-apartheid movement, Nelson Mandela. Banned in South Africa, it was a hit in France. Anti-apartheid music remains a powerful tool for change, playing a significant part in the development of the country.

AFTER

From mass singing to music videos that call for change, songs continue to provide hope for change.

THE SINGING REVOLUTION
From 1986–1991, Estonia, Lithuania, and Latvia sought freedom from the Soviet Union, and thousands **gathered to sing** banned patriotic songs. In 1989, about 700,000 Estonians, 500,000 Latvians, and one million Lithuanians joined hands and sang. They gained independence in 1991.

BOBI WINE
Ugandan pop star-turned-politician Bobi Wine used his **political status** to challenge the leadership of Ugandan President Yoweri Museveni. He expresses his views through Afropop music, which he popularizes online.

BOBI WINE IN HIS TRADEMARK RED BERET

KEY WORKS

Victor Jarra "Plegaria a un labrador"
Mercedes Sosa "La Maza"
Johnny Clegg "Asimbonanga"
Neneh Cherry and Youssou Ndour "Seven Seconds"
Bob Marley "Africa Unite"
Bobi Wine "Freedom"

MUSICIAN (1938–1997)

FELA KUTI

Born in Abeokuta, Nigeria, to a feminist and labor activist mother, Kuti took piano and percussion lessons before studying classical music at Trinity College, London. There, he played piano in jazz and rock bands and discovered various musical styles.

Returning to Nigeria in 1963, Kuti formed a band, Koola Lobitos. Alongside percussionist Tony Allen, he invented Afrobeat, a blend of American heavy funk with Nigerian influences.

Kuti released a prolific string of enormously successful albums in the 1970s. His songs had radical political lyrics, sung in Pidgin English. Kuti's music made him a thorn in the side of the Nigerian government, and he was frequently harassed and arrested.

Jazz Fusion

The amplified hybrid known as jazz fusion or jazz-rock evolved in the United States during the mid-to-late 1960s. Widely embraced, it diversified into many subgenres, incorporating folk, Latin, and ethnic influences.

BEFORE

Jazz fusion grew out of funk and R&B rhythms and the electronic effects of rock.

SOUL JAZZ
Between the late 1950s and the early 1960s, jazz with a **gospel**, **blues**, and **R&B** feel, influenced by the small-group recordings of **Ray Charles** **« 311**, was dubbed "soul jazz." Records such as Horace Silver's "Song For My Father" and Herbie Hancock's "Cantaloupe Island" exemplify the style. What separated soul jazz from funky hard bop was the change in the underlying pulse from the swing feel in jazz to a "straight-eight"(rocklike) feel.

Meanwhile, UK R&B artists, such as the **Graham Bond Organisation**, incorporated jazz and progressive rock elements into their music.

SOULFUL ALTO SAX

Jazz fusion consists of two main strands—jazz that incorporates rock elements, and rock music that adopts jazz improvisation or extended and altered harmony. While there is some crossover between these two kinds of fusion, essentially they remain distinct.

In the mid-1960s, jazz musicians began to experiment with amplified sounds. Joe Zawinul, pianist with the American soul jazz group Cannonball Adderley Quintet, pioneered the use of electric piano in jazz on the 1966 song classic "Mercy Mercy Mercy," while guitarist Larry Coryell favored a rock-flavored sound on the 1967 album *Duster*.

13 **The age at which jazz musician Miles Davis began learning the trumpet.**

Inspired by Hendrix

The following year, star jazz trumpeter Miles Davis heralded what became known as his electric period by using electric guitar, electric bass, and electric piano on the album *Miles In The Sky*. Before long, Davis was playing his horn into a stack of Marshall amplifiers via a wah-wah pedal (an electronic attachment that changed the sound) inspired by the psychedelic rock of Jimi Hendrix.

At the same time, the rhythmic underpinning of some jazz began to show a rock and funk influence. Tracks such as "Miles Runs The Voodoo Down," on Miles Davis's 1969 album *Bitches Brew*, feature propulsive grooves and electric bass ostinatos (repetitions) supporting long, semi-abstract improvisations.

In the wake of the artistic achievement and the commercial success of *Bitches Brew*, many of Miles Davis's collaborators of the 1960s went on to lead a diverse range of era-defining fusion groups in the 1970s in which synthesizers became an essential instrumental texture. Keyboardist Chick Corea abandoned the avant-garde in order to reach a wider audience and formed Return To Forever, which explored Latin fusion possibilities in its early incarnations before developing into distinctively intricate jazz rock.

Guitarist John McLaughlin, who also collaborated on *Bitches Brew*, formed the Mahavishnu Orchestra, which featured a heavily amplified, rhythmically and melodically complex approach to jazz-rock while keyboardist Herbie Hancock formed The Headhunters, a popular jazz-funk group influenced by the psychedelic soul of Sly Stone.

The most enduring fusion outfit of the 1970s and '80s was Weather Report, a group put together by Joe Zawinul and saxophonist Wayne Shorter. Beginning with experimental space-jazz, the group evolved into a popular electric jazz group displaying pop and funk inspirations.

"Jazz is... **open** enough to borrow from any other form of **music.**"

AMERICAN JAZZ MUSICIAN HERBIE HANCOCK

Tremolo control
Volume control
Keyboard
Sustain pedal

Electric keyboard
A key element in the transition of jazz into jazz fusion was the electric piano. Its bell-like tones were an essential ingredient in the sound of the genre.

Rock and pop elements

In the mid-1960s, British rock bands such as Traffic and Cream and the American band Grateful Dead adopted extended, jazzlike improvisation as part of their jamming approach. Other rock musicians went further by incorporating jazzlike improvisation and harmony into their own disparate styles. The composer-guitarist Frank Zappa used advanced jazz harmony in his work between 1966 and 1986 and often employed jazz-oriented musicians in his band, including keyboardist George Duke.

The British rock band Soft Machine blended psychedelia and free jazz on their early 1970s albums, while fellow Brits Colosseum evolved a muscular prog rock/jazz hybrid in the same period. In the United States, Steely Dan used jazz players and composed songs with jazz harmonies, giving their progressive R&B a distinct fusion flavor, notably on their album *Aja*, in 1977.

Comparatively few pop and rock singer-songwriters have utilized jazz elements in their work beyond surface pastiche. Notable exceptions include Northern Irish musician Van Morrison, who trusted jazz musicians to make sense of his cryptic songs for the album *Astral Weeks* (1968), and American singer-songwriter Joni Mitchell, whose Shadows and Light band in 1980 included jazz musicians Michael Brecker, Jaco Pastorius, and Pat Metheny, representing the summit of jazz-informed, song-based pop.

Jazz fusion classic
John McLaughlin's 1971 debut album as leader of the Mahavishnu Orchestra, *The Inner Mounting Flame*, was a classic of the genre. It was loved by rock-oriented listeners who like their guitar fast and loud.

KEY WORKS

Miles Davis *Bitches Brew, Live Evil*
Mahavishnu Orchestra *Inner Mounting Flame*
Tony Williams *Lifetime Emergency!*
Herbie Hancock *Headhunters*
Pat Metheny *Bright Size Life*
Weather Report *Heavy Weather*
Chick Corea Elektric Band *Chick Corea Elektric Band*

AFTER

In the 1980s, jazz fusion became smooth and commercial. Later crossovers, however, turned to hip-hop for inspiration.

SMOOTH JAZZ
Producer Creed Taylor's jazz/pop of the late 1960s and early 1970s paved the way for a soft-edged fusion called crossover or smooth jazz, with **light funky grooves** and melodic improvisation. The music of saxophonists David Sanborn and Kenny G are typical of the style.

HIP-HOP
In the 21st century, jazz has been melded with hip-hop. Artists such as Roy Hargrove and pianist Robert Glasper have had considerable success combining **laid-back** beats with extended harmony and rap lyrics from Common, Lupe Fiasco, and Jean Grae.

Miles Davis magic
Already influential in the development of post-bop jazz styles, jazz trumpeter Miles Davis's enthusiasm for blending jazz, rock, and funk styles was crucial to the growth of jazz fusion.

BEFORE

By the late 1960s, the long-playing record was the defining artistic statement of the rock band. It was used to showcase novel sounds provided by new instruments.

ROOTS OF ELECTRONIC ROCK

Rock groups such as the **Beatles « 324–325**, Beach Boys, and the **Rolling Stones « 326–327** all pushed the boundaries of the sounds they could produce in the studio. On the 1967 single "Good Vibrations," singer and arranger Brian Wilson of the Beach Boys used an electronic instrument known as the **Electro-Theremin**, or **Tannerin**, to produce the unearthly wail heard in the song's chorus.

MELLOTRON KEYBOARD

It was also in 1967 that the Beatles used a **Mellotron** on "Strawberry Fields Forever." This was a keyboard instrument that used keys to trigger spools of magnetic tape, producing **atmospheric string and flute sounds**. It was later used by **Led Zeppelin « 326–327** to give a sense of the epic to "Rain Song" and "Kashmir."

Electronic Rock

Ever since the dawn of rock 'n' roll in the 1950s, the electric guitar has been the rock band's main instrument. However, from the early Moog synthesizers of the 1960s to today's laptop, electronic sound has been a significant feature in rock's musical lexicon.

If there were one band that could be said to bridge the psychedelic rock of the 1960s and the electronic rock experiments of the 1970s (see pp.328–329), it is Pink Floyd. In the band's early years, keyboard player Rick Wright (1943–2008) conjured exotic, spacey electronic sounds on a Farfisa organ (an inexpensive electric keyboard) through a Binson Echorec device. As its name suggests, it produced an echo effect that perfectly complemented the psychedelic lightshows for which Pink Floyd was famous.

Pink Floyd's electronic explorations were not confined to Rick Wright's keyboards. For their *Animals* album, released in 1977, they created extended "audio collages" using recordings of sounds—some exotic, some everyday—and then processing them in the studio to render them strangely musical. Pink Floyd had a significant impact on the progressive (prog) rock bands of the early 1970s, which took their sprawling instrumental passages to symphonic extremes.

Electronic film music
Composer Vangelis (Evangelos Odysseas Papathanassiou) began his career in a prog rock band but found wider success writing film soundtracks. His score for *Blade Runner* is a masterpiece of early-1980s electronic music.

Synthesizer devotee

The prog rock band Yes owed much of its success to its flamboyant keyboard player, Rick Wakeman. A seasoned session musician, he joined Yes in 1971, and his tenure with them produced the band's most successful and ambitious albums. The songs grew longer and the arrangements ever more overblown, culminating in the epic concept album *Tales From Topographic Oceans* (1973). Wakeman was a devotee of the Moog

Keeping the sound alive
The band Kraftwerk was a pioneer of electronic rock. Kraftwerk's lineup has changed since the early days, but its sound remains popular and the band still sells out live shows.

synthesizer and, in performance, there would often be several of them among the banks of keyboards he played.

Robotic aesthetic

For some bands, electronic rock meant far more than simply adding novel synthesizer parts to a standard rock-band lineup. The German group Kraftwerk, for example, wanted to dispense with the traditional concept of a band. Ralf Hütter and Florian Schneider formed the group in 1970, but it was not until they fully embraced a robotic aesthetic in 1974 that they had a hit with "Autobahn," a paean to the German highway set to repetitive electronically generated music.

Kraftwerk gained two more members, who played electronic percussion, while the bulk of the music relied on synthesizers such as the Minimoog and the EMS Synthi AKS. Meanwhile, Kraftwerk's vocals were processed through vocoders, which "robotize" a singer's voice. On later albums, such as *Radio-Activity* (1975), *The Man-Machine* (1978), and *Computer World* (1981), Kraftwerk refined its electronic sound.

Electronic visionary
Brian Eno, here pictured during the recording of his 1973 album, *Here Come the Warm Jets*, is a visionary producer and electronic musician. He collaborated on the most innovative rock albums of the 1970s.

In 1977, David Bowie (see pp.338–339) met Hütter and Schneider. Bowie was a huge fan of Kraftwerk's music, and its influence can clearly be heard on the mid-70s albums Bowie recorded in Berlin: *Low*, *Heroes*, and *Lodger*. These albums were made with the electronic music impressario Brian Eno. His musical curiosity and experiments with studio gadgetry added a hint of the avant-garde to Bowie's songs.

Kraftwerk also influenced Japan's Yellow Magic Orchestra (YMO), led by Haruomi Hosono. YMO produced cutting-edge music using synthesizers, such as the ARP Odyssey and the Yamaha CS80, but with a childlike pop sensibility featuring motifs derived from Japanese music. Their 1978 debut album, *Yellow Magic Orchestra*, used electronic sounds to poke fun at Western preconceptions of Japanese culture. YMO sparked a huge "techno pop" craze in Japan, spearheaded by synth-loving groups, such as Plastics, Hikashu, and P-Model.

Punk sensibility

The American band Suicide, a duo consisting of Alan Vega and Martin Rev, brought a punk sensibility to electronic rock. They became infamous for their raucous and confrontational live shows: Vega declaimed, screamed, and howled to Rev's incessant, deliberately repetitive synthesizer bass lines. While their music was distorted and challenging, it also paid homage to the rock 'n' roll of Jerry Lee Lewis and Bo Diddley. Applying the basic rock 'n' roll template to electronic instruments, it made the synthesizer sound dirtier and more like an electric guitar.

Suicide and late-'70s punk (see pp.356–357) paved the way for "industrial" music, influencing bands such as Throbbing Gristle, Cabaret Voltaire, Whitehouse, Nurse With Wound, and Einstürzende Neubauten. Many industrial musicians also had backgrounds in performance art or movies and knew the electronic music of classical composers such as Varese, Ligeti, and Stockhausen. Ever eclectic, industrial music featured drones, distorted vocals, and noise that might be deemed unmusical—deployed as shock tactics to challenge not only musical but social norms.

KEY WORKS

Pink Floyd "Chapter 24"
Kraftwerk "The Robots"
David Bowie "Be My Wife"
YMO "Behind the Mask"
Suicide "The Ballad of Frankie Teardrop"

TECHNOLOGY

MOOG SYNTHESIZER

American electronics expert Robert Moog (1934–2005) was fascinated by voltage-based instruments such as the Theremin. He began developing the Moog synthesizer in the mid-1960s.

By today's standards the Moog was cumbersome, but after it was heard at the 1967 Monterey Pop Festival, its palette of electronically generated space-age sounds, grainy white noise, and burbling bass tones caught on.

Rock acts of the late 1960s loved the moog synthesizer for the psychedelic textures it could produce, and the Doors, Rolling Stones, Byrds, and Monkees all used it in recordings. The Beatles used a Moog on their last album, *Abbey Road*, in the song "Because."

AFTER

Every generation of synthesized pop musicians finds new ways to marry electronic sound with rock music.

ELECTRONIC HEIR

The collaborative albums of Bowie and Eno were a huge influence on **Gary Numan**, singer with the band Tubeway Army. Numan used heavily amplified synthesizers and a vocal style not unlike Bowie's to score chart hits with songs such as "Cars" and "Are 'Friends' Electric?." Numan wrote lyrics about the industrial age with a militaristic bent.

SYNTH-BASED GROUPS

Bowie and Numan's influence is heard in the music of more **recent electronic rock bands**, such as SCUM, Nine Inch Nails, Marilyn Manson, and Add N to X.

GARY NUMAN, 1980

Born 1947 Died 2016

David Bowie

> "My whole professional life **is an act...** slip from one guise to another very easily."
>
> DAVID BOWIE, IN AN INTERVIEW WITH "PEOPLE" MAGAZINE, 1976

Although David Bowie's career spans half a century, he owes his place in history to his remarkable ten-year creative burst during the 1970s, in which he redefined rock stardom—in persona and performance as well as music—in ways that have reverberated ever since.

Like many British rock stars, Bowie was raised in the dreary suburbs of postwar London. Born David Jones in 1947, he was inspired by American rock 'n' roll to learn the saxophone—one youthful ambition was to join Little Richard's band. From his teens onward he devoted himself single-mindedly to becoming a star. Working in an advertising agency by day, in the heart of "Swinging London," he spent the mid-1960s both as a solo artist and in several quickly discarded groups, experimenting with genres ranging from R&B to Broadway musicals. Crucially, he also withdrew repeatedly from music to explore other avenues. Thus he studied mime, set up an "Arts Lab" in a South London pub, and spent months in a Buddhist monastery.

Starman
Bowie's Ziggy persona and album has had a lasting impact on popular and rock music. This special edition of the *NME* music magazine celebrated the 40th anniversary of the record's release. Ziggy himself had a shorter lifespan—Bowie killed him off in 1973.

A man of many faces

Even after success arrived, when his ethereal single "Space Oddity" hit the British charts at the time of the first moon landings in 1969, Bowie continued to reinvent himself. Two innovative and very different albums, the hard-rocking *The Man Who Sold The World* and the more introspective, singer-songwriter-style *Hunky Dory*, made little impact before the 1972 release of the sci-fi concept album *The Rise And Fall Of Ziggy Stardust And The Spiders From Mars*. Eschewing the willfully drab jeans-and-T-shirt dress code then prevalent on the rock

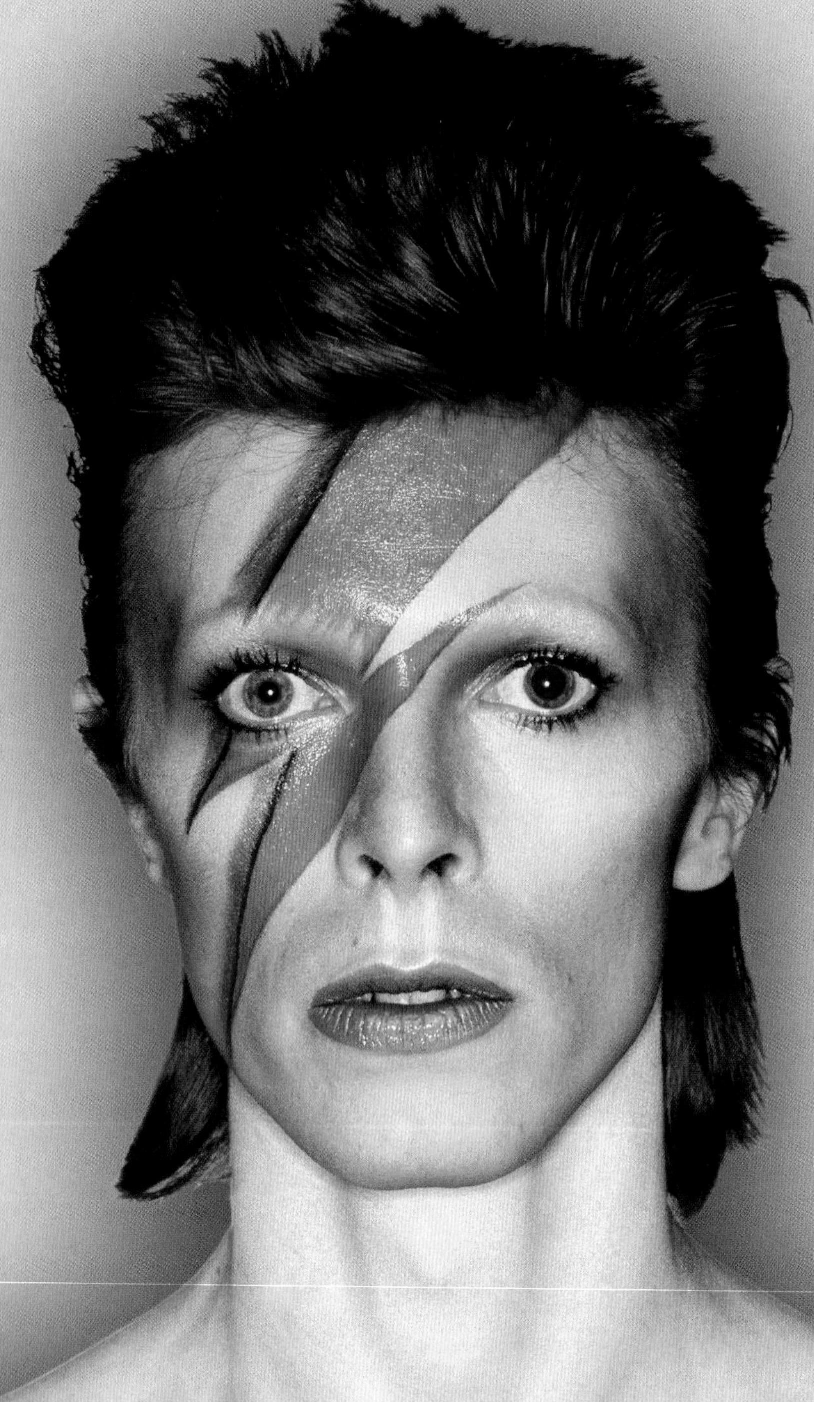

Identity crisis
This portrait of Bowie captures him in the character of *Aladdin Sane*. The name is a play on "a lad insane"; Bowie has repeatedly explored themes of madness and multiple identities throughout his career.

scene, Bowie embraced color and costume, presenting himself off- as well as on-stage as a futuristic, androgynous creature from some other, more exciting and flamboyant, world. His physical stagecraft, drawing on elements from the Kabuki theater of Japan and the Italian *Commedia del Arte*, as well as mime, enthralled live audiences, and he was a pioneer in transforming rock concerts into extravagant spectacles. He also attracted huge attention by telling the media he was bisexual; while that may have been more of a marketing ploy than a lasting statement about his sexuality, it empowered many young fans to explore and express their own sexual identities.

By 1973 David Bowie was enough of a global superstar to become a Svengali-style producer, resuscitating the careers of American proto-punk heroes like Lou Reed, and Iggy and the Stooges, for whom he produced the *Transformer* and *Raw Power* albums respectively. So thoroughly had he come to identify himself with his own creation, the doomed Ziggy Stardust, that he "killed off" the character on the last night of a world tour, vowing that he would never perform as Ziggy

Pale imitation
Bowie's Thin White Duke character, seen here on stage in 1976, was unveiled on the *Station to Station* album. The Duke was modeled on crooners and matinee idols—Sinatra visited Bowie in the recording studio.

himself from the crucible of punk in Britain by relocating to edgy, decadent Berlin in 1976. There he recorded 1977's experimental electronic album *Low*, in collaboration with Brian Eno, formerly of Roxy Music, and under the influence of German "Krautrock" bands such as Kraftwerk and Neu! Two more Berlin albums followed—the self-consciously epic *Heroes* in 1978, and the rockier *Lodger* in 1979. Iggy Pop was very much part of this scene; Bowie produced, played on, and even toured as a band member to promote Iggy's first two, acclaimed solo albums in 1977, *The Idiot* and *Lust For Life*.

> "It was **just the songs** and the trousers. That's what sold Ziggy."
>
> DAVID BOWIE, INTERVIEW WITH "MOJO" MAGAZINE, 2002

again. By then, however, he had already introduced a new persona on his next album, *Aladdin Sane*, and he soon resumed touring. An abortive attempt to stage a musical version of George Orwell's *1984* was stymied by copyright laws, but he used much of the material for his next album, *Diamond Dogs*.

Bowie's next shift was to experiment with American soul music, cutting the funky *Young Americans* album in Philadelphia in 1975. Yet another persona followed soon afterward, in the sticklike, slick-haired, and deathly pale figure of the Thin White Duke, the part-crooner protagonist of the starker 1976 album *Station to Station*.

The Berlin years

By now increasingly fragile, thanks in part to a heavy dependence on cocaine, Bowie removed

Bowie goes pop

With his first album of the 1980s, *Scary Monsters and Super Creeps*, he seemed to be still ahead of the game, outdoing the upcoming New Romantics. While it sold in greater quantities than its immediate predecessors, it arguably marked the end of his great run as one of rock's true innovators. There is no disputing the global success of his next release, *Let's Dance*, made in 1983 in conjunction with guitarist/producer Nile Rodgers—the title track was the biggest hit of his entire career, and his only single to top the charts in both the UK and the United States. Musically, it slotted comfortably into the over-produced, disco-influenced pop of the era.

Cover girl
Co-written with, and previously recorded by, Iggy Pop, "China Girl" was a huge hit for David Bowie when he rerecorded it for 1983's *Let's Dance* album. It was released as a picture disc as shown here.

Bowie continued to write and record through the 1980s and 1990s, and also carried on dabbling in styles, without attracting the huge audiences he was accustomed to. In 1988, he briefly stopped identifying himself as a solo artist and became the lead singer of a four-man rock band, Tin Machine. Further albums under his own name followed, including the 1997 *Earthling*, on which he created an idiosyncratic take on drum 'n' bass. Probably his most radical innovation of the 1990s was to make $55 million by selling all future income on his existing recordings in the form of "Bowie Bonds" in 1995—a move that proved prescient when digital downloading prompted music sales to collapse a few years later.

Still surprising

The early years of the 21st century saw Bowie release two more albums, *Heathen* in 2002 and *Reality* in 2003, which were considered by many to be a return to form. Despite the lack of any official announcement, he was considered to have retired after he suffered a heart attack during a concert in Germany in 2004. The 2013 release of a new, rock-oriented album, *The Next Day*, came as a huge surprise, therefore, marking an end to his hiatus as a New York–based art collector.

In January 2016, Bowie released his final album, *Blackstar*, on his 69th birthday. Two days later, he died of liver cancer. According to Tony Visconti, the album's co-producer, Bowie intended the album as something of a swan song.

TIMELINE

- **January 8, 1947** David Robert Jones is born in Brixton, South London.
- **1962** Joins his first band, the Kon-Rads, playing alto sax and singing.
- **1963** Having left school with one "O" Level, in Art, he starts work as an ad-man.
- **1964** Releases his first single "Lisa Jane" with the King Bees, then joins the Manish Boys.
- **1965** Changes his name to David Bowie, to avoid confusion with the English singer with the newly famous Monkees, Davy Jones.
- **June 1, 1967** First album, *David Bowie*, released.
- **1969** "Space Oddity" is a top ten hit in the UK, and coincides with the first moon landings.
- **1970** Records *The Man Who Sold The World*.
- **November 1971** Releases *Hunky Dory*; Peter Noone has a hit with "Oh, You Pretty Things."
- **1972** Performs "Starman" on UK music show Top of the Pops; tours as Ziggy Stardust to promote *Ziggy Stardust & the Spiders From Mars*; produces *Transformer* for Lou Reed.
- **1973** Ziggy Stardust announces his retirement at London's Hammersmith Odeon; Bowie has already released the album *Aladdin Sane*.
- **1974** Copyright issues thwart plans to write a musical based on the novel *1984*, but much of the music feeds into the album *Diamond Dogs*.
- **1975** "Fame," co-written with John Lennon and taken from the album *Young Americans*, is Bowie's first UK number one hit.
- **1976** Releases *Station To Station*; plays an alien in the Nicolas Roeg movie *The Man Who Fell To Earth*; and moves to Berlin.

MOVIE POSTER

- **1977–1979** Releases his "Berlin Trilogy"—*Low*, *Heroes*, and *Lodger*; works with Iggy Pop; and records "Little Drummer Boy" with Bing Crosby.
- **1980** In the video for "Ashes to Ashes," Bowie resuscitates Major Tom from "Space Oddity."
- **1983** *Let's Dance* is a commercial success.
- **1988** Forms Tin Machine.
- **1992** Marries Somalian model Iman.
- **1993–2003** Five more studio albums follow: *Black Tie, White Noise*; *Outside*; *Earthling*; *Heathen*; and *Reality*.
- **2004** Has a heart attack on stage in Germany and abandons his final concert tour.
- **March 8, 2013** Unexpectedly releases his first album in 10 years, *The Next Day*.
- **January 8, 2016** Releases final album, *Blackstar*, two days before dying of liver cancer.

BEFORE

Indian classical music is founded on sacred Hindu hymns and theoretical principles established in antiquity.

ORAL TRADITION

The earliest Indian music is found in the **Vedas, sacred Hindu hymns** thought to have been written in 1500–1200 BCE by Indo-European peoples who settled in India in the 2nd millennium BCE. Handed down orally, they are still in use today.

POEMS AND BARDS

Early in the 1st millennium CE, a system of art music emerged in India, incorporating **poetry and dance**. The tradition flourished between the 3rd and 6th centuries CE.

Poetic bards in southern India performed songs with harp accompaniment in royal and domestic settings. **Invasions from Central Asia**, and the rise of **Islam** **« 40–41**, influenced the music.

SITARIST (1920–2012)

PANDIT RAVI SHANKAR

A legendary sitarist and composer, Shankar was born in Benares (now Varanasi) into an orthodox Brahmin family. Hearing Vedic chants as a child awakened Shankar's passion for music.

Shankar danced in his brother's classical Indian dance company in Paris from 1930–1932 but took up the sitar on his return from India. He studied for seven years with Vilayat Khan (1928–2004) and married his daughter.

Shankar gave his first concert in 1939, and began writing scores for Indian films in 1946. He was founder-director of All India Radio's first National Orchestra. A consummate showman with flawless technique, he was showered with awards. The daughter of his second marriage, Anoushka, is a well-known sitarist, and his other daughter, Norah Jones, is a singer who has won several Grammy awards.

Ragas and Talas

With its hypnotic rhythms, elaborate melodies, and alluring mysticism, Indian classical music enjoys a worldwide following. Many are captivated by the music's links with spirituality and meditation, and a number of Western composers and performers have fallen under its spell.

Ancient philosophical ideas and Hindu spiritual principles provide the rules for the composition and performance of Indian classical music. Starting in the 12th century, the music divided into two main categories: Hindustani from northern India, and Carnatic from the south. Hindustani music is more expressive, while Carnatic music remains traditional and untouched by foreign influence. Though viewed as entertainment, Indian music retains its links with Hinduism, with the songs retelling the stories of the Hindu gods.

Patterns of melody and rhythm

The most popular musical form in both northern and southern India is the *raga*, a musical form usually for voice and typically accompanied by *tabla* (drums) along with a plucked stringed instrument, often a sitar. Cycles of rhythmic patterns, known as *talas*, underpin the *raga*. These *talas*, along with the shimmering sitar, give the music its particular sound quality. The mood and style of the piece depends on the choice of *raga* and *tala*.

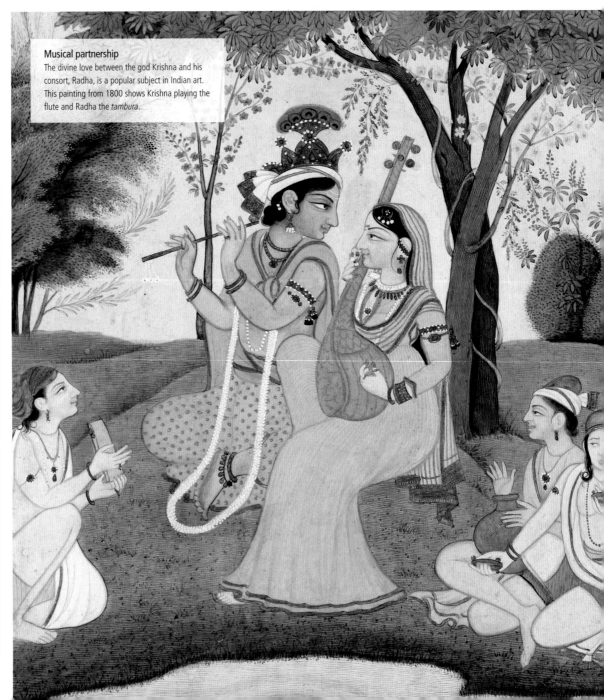

Musical partnership
The divine love between the god Krishna and his consort, Radha, is a popular subject in Indian art. This painting from 1800 shows Krishna playing the flute and Radha the *tambura*.

Music to the ear

Ragas are patterns of notes from which melodies are constructed. However, performers frequently utilize idiosyncratic tunings of their instruments and voices to create an individual take on a classic raga.

In tandem with the complex beauty of the 22-tone scale upon which Indian music is based, this individuality gives Indian musicians a great variety of sounds and techniques to express themselves in their music.

This freedom of expression is further enhanced by liberal use of ornamentation, including vibrato, trills, and grace notes. Underlying the melody, the rhythmic patterns of the *tala* are played in repeating cycles. These patterns can be very complex, and a single *tala* may contain up to 15 beats. Often the beats are clapped. In addition, a performer in the ensemble (usually the drummer) emphasizes the first of each *tala* to let other musicians know that the cycle has begun again and to help them keep time. In Carnatic music, the drummer may have an independent part. This rhythmic complexity and the focus on the solo raga means that large ensembles performing Indian music are very rare due to the difficulty such groups would have in preserving the clarity of the soloist.

While systems for writing down music have existed in India for centuries, players of classical Indian music perform without following written music because, as students, they learn by example directly from masters, and commit the music to memory. Even today teachers prefer to instruct their students orally.

Within the parameters of set notes and beats, the ability to improvise is a highly prized skill, and there are many approaches or styles. Performers freely use ornamentation. In northern India, the performance of a piece can last up to an hour and often has three parts: an improvised prelude; a traditional composition on the *raga* and *tala* accompanied by *tabla*; and a final improvisation. Carnatic performances are built around the popular *kritis* (songs), and concerts can last for up to three hours. The centerpiece may be a *ragam-tanam-pallavi*, a type of composition that allows the singer to improvise. The practice has been passed down from ancient times when competitions were held to showcase the ability of singers to perform dazzling improvisations.

Carnatic diva
Regarded as the finest exponent of Carnatic song, Madurai Subbulakshmi (1916–2004) made her first recording at age 10. During the 1960s, she sang in London, in Moscow, and at Carnegie Hall in New York.

> **"Unforgettable...** a music-making that I could have **only dreamt of."**
>
> YEHUDI MENUHIN, 1997, ON HIS COLLABORATION WITH RAVI SHANKAR

40,000 The number of people who attended Ravi Shankar's two Concerts for Bangladesh in New York, in 1971.

Rhythmic drivers
The tabla, which consists of two small drums played by one seated performer, provides the rhythmic foundation of Indian music. One drum is conical, the other is bowl-shaped, and each is tuned to a different pitch.

Captivating the West

Legendary sitarist Ravi Shankar almost single-handedly introduced northern Indian music to the West and, at a time of a spiritual reawakening, the music spoke directly and powerfully to new audiences. In 1967, festival-goers heard Shankar play at Monterey, in California, and at Woodstock, New York, in 1969 (see pp.344–345).

Inspired by Indian music, Beatle George Harrison (see pp.324–325). learned to play the sitar. In 1965, he used it in the Beatles' song "Norwegian Wood" and, in 1966, on the album *Revolver*. Harrison studied sitar with Shankar, and performed and recorded with him in the 1970s.

Classical violinist Yehudi Menuhin (1916–1999) recorded three albums of violin-sitar works with Shankar between 1966 and 1976, with both artists gliding in and out of each other's styles.

Shankar also worked with the American opera composer Philip Glass, co-composing a chamber music album in 1990. Titled *Passages*, the music blended Hindustani classical music with Glass's classical American minimalist style (see pp.376–377).

Evolution at home

In India, after centuries of adhering to classical traditions and religious associations, Indian music is evolving. New styles of classical music are emerging that keep pace with India's fast-changing global environment.

And while Indian classical music continues to absorb new influences from its own culture, it adapts ideas from others. Although the films of Bollywood (the Mumbai-based film industry), for example, have long featured classical Indian music, Bollywood producers are now leaning toward using other styles of music for the soundtracks of films that have a modern theme.

KEY WORKS

M.S. Subbulakshmi *Madhuraashtakam*
Ustad Vilayat Khan *Jalsaghar* (soundtrack)
Shankar and Menuhin *West Meets East*
Nikhil Banerjee *Total Absorption*
Zakir Hussain and Alla Rakha Tabla Duet
Ravi Shankar and Philip Glass *Passages*
A.R. Rahman *Slumdog Millionaire* (soundtrack)

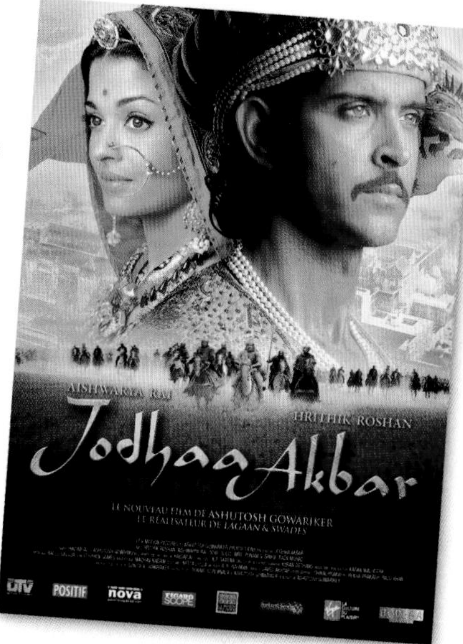

Bollywood soundtrack
The well-known Indian composer A.R. Rahman is known for integrating classical Indian music with electro and Western genres. His soundtrack for the 2008 Bollywood epic *Jodhaa Akbar* won many awards.

AFTER

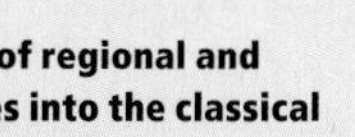

The assimilation of regional and outside influences into the classical traditions has taken Indian music in a number of new directions.

REGIONAL INFLUENCES
Performances of authentic Indian classical music have become less common in recent years. India's rich **regional folk traditions** and **Western popular music** have blurred the boundaries with the strict classical system.

WORLD MUSIC
The unique sonorities of Indian music, especially the rhythmic pulsing of the *tabla* and hypnotic, shimmering sitar music, have become staple additions to the broad genre of **world music**.

Indian Instruments

The richness and diversity of India's history and cultural heritage is reflected in the dazzling variety of its musical instruments. Strings, wind, and drums play distinctive roles in ceremonial occasions, classical music, and dance.

1 **Ornate *Shehnai*** North India's shehnai has a double reed (attached on a cord) that is inserted into the mouthpiece to play. This rosewood example has a shapely, engraved bell made from nickel and brass. 2 **Wooden *Shehnai*** This ceremonial instrument is played in temples, processions, and weddings. 3 **Wooden Flute** The finger holes on this side-blown flute can be partially covered, creating slight variations of pitch. 4 **Bamboo flute** This pipe is an expressive solo instrument in Indian classical music. 5 **Ankle bells** Worn by dancers, these bells add rhythmic jingling as well as striking decoration. 6 ***Manjira*** Pairs of small metal hand cymbals often accompany folk music and religious ceremonies. 7 ***Dholak*** Cotton cords are strung across this wooden drum to maintain the tension across the two drum heads. It is played with the same subtle hand techniques as the tabla (see p.341). 8 ***Veena*** Richly decorated gourd resonators amplify the sound of the ***veena's*** plucked strings. 9 ***Saraswati veena*** Saraswati, the Hindu goddess of knowledge, arts, and music, is often depicted playing this instrument. This example has an ornately carved head. 10 **Sitar** When the main strings of the sitar are plucked, its "sympathetic" strings resonate, too, enhancing the sound. This richly decorated sitar has a small second resonator behind the long, hollow neck. 11 ***Esraj*** Like the sitar, the esraj has sympathetic strings, which add a shimmering aural halo. 12 ***Rewāp*** Resembling a long-necked lute, this rewap has five metal strings and geometric decorations in ivory and camel bone. 13 ***Tambura*** This elegant lute provides a drone accompaniment to solos on other instruments. 14 ***Sarangi*** Expressive melodies are the specialty of this bowed fiddle, which resembles the human voice in its beautiful timber. 15 ***Sarinda*** The unusual shape of the sarinda, with its conveniently cutout sections, allows for easy movement of the bow across the strings. 16 ***Pamir robāb*** A long-necked lute from the Pamir mountains, this historic example dates from around 1650. 17 ***Mandar bahar*** Similar to a bowed double bass, this instrument is used in orchestras. 18 ***Sarinda*** The front of this folk fiddle's sound box is made from animal skin. 19 ***Mayuri veena*** Resting on birdlike feet, this bowed "peacock" veena has a hollow body and up to 30 strings.

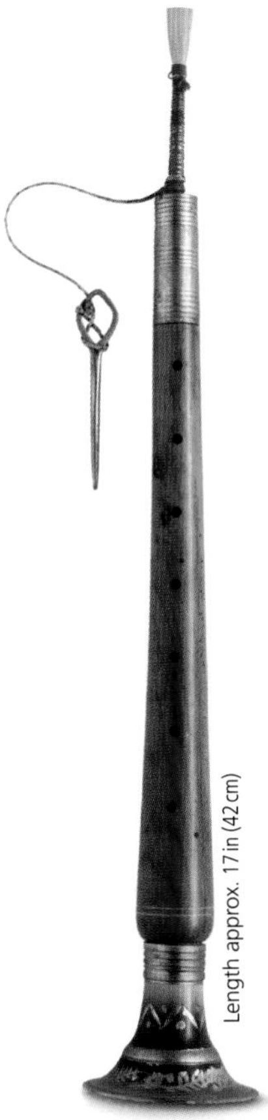

Length approx. 17 in (42 cm)

1 ORNATE SHEHNAI

Length approx. 17 in (42 cm)

2 WOODEN SHEHNAI

Length approx. 15–38 in (38–96 cm)

3 WOODEN FLUTE

Length approx. 15–38 in (38–96 cm)

4 BAMBOO FLUTE

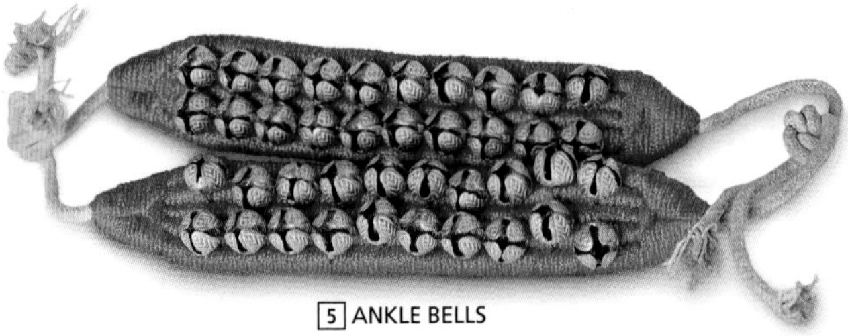

5 ANKLE BELLS
Length 6 in (15 cm)

6 MANJIRA
Diameter 4 in (10 cm)

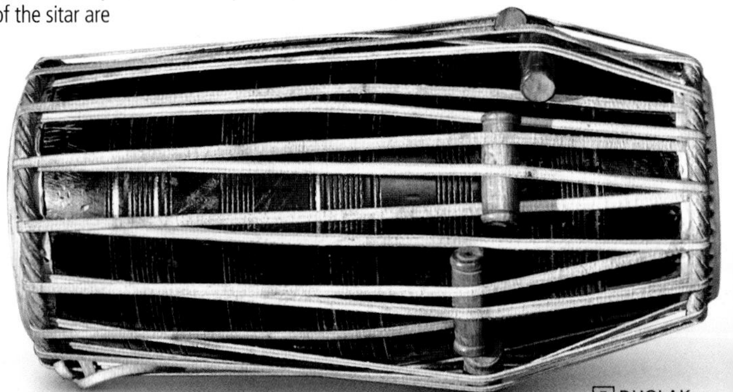

7 DHOLAK
Length 14 in (35 cm)

8 VEENA
Length approx. 5 ft (1.5 m)

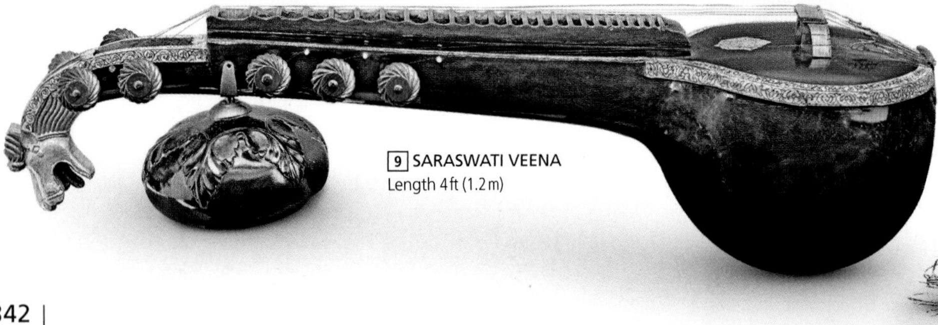

9 SARASWATI VEENA
Length 4 ft (1.2 m)

[10] SITAR
Height 4 ft (1.2 m)

[11] ESRAJ
Height 36 in (91 cm)

[12] REWĀP
Height approx. 3 ft 3 in (1 m)

[13] TAMBURA
Height 4 ft (1.2 m)

[14] SARANGI
Height approx. 26 in (65 cm)

[15] SARINDA
Height approx. 25 in (63 cm)

[16] PAMIR ROBĀB
Height 31 in (80 cm)

[17] MANDAR BAHAR
Length 4 ft (1.2 m)

[18] SARINDA
Height approx. 25 in (63 cm)

[19] MAYURI VEENA
Length approx. 4 ft 3 in (1.3 m)

BEFORE

Woodstock and Glastonbury had their precursors in the great festivals of folk and jazz, the popular music of the 1950s and '60s.

IT STARTED IN NEWPORT

The **Newport Jazz Festival** in well-to-do Newport, Rhode Island, began in 1954. Students came to listen to jazz greats, including Miles Davis, Thelonious Monk, Ella Fitzgerald, and Billie Holliday. **A Newport Folk Festival** followed in 1959.

ACOUSTIC GUITAR

SUMMER OF LOVE

The three-day **Monterey Pop Festival** in the Monterey's County Fairground in 1967, with **Janis Joplin, Otis Redding**, and **Ravi Shankar**, is regarded as the first rock festival and was a highlight in the Californian "Summer of Love." That same summer, jazz fans in Europe were rewarded with the **Montreux Jazz Festival** by Lake Geneva in Switzerland. Attracting top names, it became an annual event and was the world's biggest jazz festival until the 10-day Festival International de Jazz de Montréal, started in the French-Canadian city in 1980.

Music Festivals

Camped among like-minded music lovers in the open air, with nobody to complain about the noise, young festivalgoers experience a right of passage. Rooted in the 1960s, an age of peace and love, festivals are now vast commercial events that have sprung up all over the world.

The utopian image of the music festival as free, spontaneous, and uninhibited by scheduling or big business was defined forever by Woodstock in 1969. Captured on film by director Martin Scorsese, footage of the festival conjures up a world of brightly colored teepees and long-haired young American hippies wearing tie-dye T-shirts.

It was not originally intended that the festival, held on a sprawling dairy farm in the Catskills region of New York state, would be free of charge. Devised by a small group of entrepreneurs, Woodstock was declared free at the last minute, when it became clear that the security costs of policing entry and fencing off the area were unaffordable. The festival had become national news, and thousands of music fans flocked toward the three-day event. The site was deluged with rain and there was little in the way of sanitation or food facilities. At one point over the weekend, the governor of New York considered mobilizing 10,000 National Guardsmen to enforce order.

In all, 32 acts played in front of more than 500,000 people. Folk singer and guitarist Richie Havens opened the festival, and the very last act to perform was the Jimi Hendrix Experience, which ended up playing at the un–rock 'n' roll hour of 8:30 a.m. on Monday.

Isle of Wight and Glastonbury

One absentee from Woodstock was Bob Dylan, who was at the time on a ship bound for the UK, where he had been booked to headline the Isle of Wight festival. Around 10,000 people had attended the festival the previous year when Jefferson Airplane and The Pretty Things were on stage. This time 200,000 turned up, and the following year more than half a million music fans—"the biggest human gathering in the world"—boarded a ferry to the small island to hear a festive mix of Jimi Hendrix, The Who, Joan Baez, Miles Davis, and Leonard Cohen.

The baton for the big summer festival was handed on to Glastonbury in the west of England in 1970. It was started by idealistic farm owner Michael Eavis, who had been inspired by Led Zeppelin's epic performance—three and a half hours and five encores—at the nearby Bath Festival of Blues and Progressive Music. Admission cost £1 and Tyrannosaurus Rex (later T-Rex)

> "An **Aquarian** exposition: Three Days of **Peace** and **Music.**"
>
> SLOGAN FROM POSTER ADVERTISING WOODSTOCK, 1969

A milestone in music history

A sea of fans, several hundred thousand strong, at Woodstock in 1969, with Joe Cocker and the Grease Band on stage. The festival started a demand for large-scale outdoor performance.

Overcrowded island
The Isle of Wight was so heavily attended in 1970 that an Act of Parliament was passed banning gatherings of more than 5,000 on the island without a licence.

headlined. It has since become a multimillion-pound business run by Michael Eavis's daughter Emily. The world's major artists have headlined—Paul McCartney, David Bowie, The Killers, Coldplay, The Rolling Stones, Stormzy, and Bruce Springsteen.

Flowering of festivals

The fairground atmosphere of Glastonbury, with its food stalls, camping, and close company, created a rush for more festivals in farmers' fields, in spite of the wet and muddy conditions for which such festivals are famous. Others that started as idealistic, hippie events have also become big business. Roskilde Festival in Denmark, which began in 1970, has become one of the biggest festivals in Europe and is staffed by 30,000 volunteers. The same year, in the city of Milwaukee, the not-for-profit Summerfest entered the record books as the world's largest music festival, with 700 bands attracting a million people. It has now been dwarfed by Austria's Danube Island Festival, which regularly attracts more than 2 million people.

International music

The WOMAD festival was founded in 1980 as an international arts foundation. Its first live festival was in 1982. Today, it is best known as the biggest celebration of global music, arts, and dance in the world with multiple performance events in the UK, New Zealand, Gran Canaria, Chile, and Australia.

Touring festivals

Music festivals do not have to be stationary. One of the biggest annual touring events is Big Day Out, started in 1992, which tours Australian and New Zealand cities. Bob Dylan set the template for the touring festival with his Rolling Thunder Revue in the early 1970s. He assembled a loose band of musicians, including Joan Baez, Roger McGuinn, and Bob Neuwirth. All played their own sets, but collaborated on one another's songs.

Several decades later, Perry Farrell, the frontman of bohemian funk-rock band Jane's Addiction, set up a similar festival, Lollapalooza, which first toured North America in 1991. It featured Siouxsie and the Banshees, Nine Inch Nails, Living Colour, Ice-T, Butthole Surfers, and Rage Against the Machine. Some years later, the feminist touring festival, Lilith Fair, organized by Canadian musician Sarah McLachlan, raised more than 10 million dollars for women's charities in three years. Her line-ups included Tracy Chapman, Fiona Apple, Suzanne Vega, and Emmylou Harris.

AFTER

Festivals continue to pop up around the world. Some attract a few hundred cult followers, others audiences of hundreds of thousands.

YEAR-ROUND CELEBRATION

Whatever the time of year it is, music fans can enjoy a festival somewhere in the world, such as **Mad Cool Festival** in Madrid; Rock in Rio in Lisbon; Lollapalooza in Paris; Pärnu in Estonia; Morro de São Paulo in Brazil; and the **Berlin Festival** in Tempelhoff Airport.

ROCKING THE DESERT

Coachella has become the world's best-known bohemian boutique festival. Founded in 1999 by rock band Pearl Jam, it takes place over **two weekends** in April in Indio, California. The festival has moved beyond music into art installations and become a center for bohemian fashion.

LIZZO PERFORMING AT COACHELLA

The Nashville Sound

It began as rural folk music. But over the 1940s, '50s, and '60s, country absorbed the influences of jazz, swing, R&B, rock 'n' roll, and pop. What became known as the "Nashville Sound" developed—essentially the blueprint for today's mega-selling country music hits.

BEFORE

Nashville had been the center of country since the *Grand Ole Opry*—country music's top radio show—began broadcasting there in 1925.

FROM OLD-TIME TO COUNTRY

The ***Grand Ole Opry*** **<< 228–29** started off featuring resident acts such as **Uncle Dave Macon** and **Bill Monroe**. They were steeped in the folk traditions of the previous century—old-time ballads and fiddle tunes of the **Appalachian Mountains**, played on banjos, mandolins, violins, and acoustic guitars which were passed down through the years.

THE NEXT GENERATION

Blues-influenced **Hank Williams** and **Jimmie Rodgers** bridged the gap between old-time music and the streamlined country sound that was to come.

HOME OF THE "GRAND OLE OPRY" UNTIL 1974

The tuneful and unashamedly populist "Nashville Sound" had its real beginnings in the 1950s, the decade in which country became a commercial phenomenon that swept the United States. A host of musicians contributed to this musical shift, but the producers Chet Atkins and Owen Bradley made the most significant changes. Both brought a smooth production style to country, influenced by the orchestrations of the crooners of the late 1940s and '50s—velvet-voiced balladeers such as Frank Sinatra (see pp.288–289) and Rosemary Clooney.

Two stars of the new sound

Patsy Cline (1932–1963), one of the most successful country singers of the 1950s, had just as tough an upbringing as any of her country forebears, but the sound of hits such as "She's Got You," "Crazy," and "Walking After Midnight" was opulent and sophisticated, helped by Cline's assured, clear-as-a-bell contralto voice. Although she was initially reluctant to move away from the traditional, banjo-inflected country sound, she eventually embraced a "torch song" (bluesy love song) style, and swapped her tasseled cowgirl outfits for cocktail dresses. It was then, in the late 1950s, that she became a nationwide star, reaching the upper heights of both the country charts and pop charts.

14 The age of Dolly Parton when she signed for Mercury Records, two years after her first television appearance.

Cline had a stylistic counterpart in Jim Reeves (1923–1964), whose soft baritone made him country's answer to Bing Crosby (see pp.288–289) in sentimental but suave songs such as "He'll Have to Go." Reeves, who was older than Cline, had begun his musical career in the late 1940s, singing in a traditional loud, hollering country music voice. But after he signed to the record label RCA, he was paired with the producer Chet Atkins, who encouraged Reeves to sing lower and more intimately, with his mouth much closer to the microphone. His first big hit in this new style was "Four Walls," recorded in 1957 and reaching No. 11 in the US pop charts.

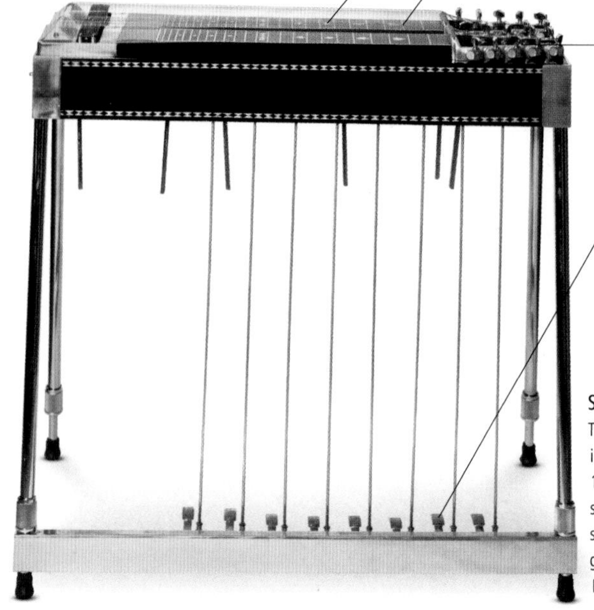

Sounds like country The pedal steel guitar, introduced in the late 1940s, produces a smooth, sustained sound, with each note gliding into the next. It is played seated.

Moving with the times

Country performers and producers were studying the popular music of the time and tailoring themselves to fit. The same approach was adopted by the next generation of country singers such as Dolly Parton(1946–), who had begun performing in the late 1950s. She made pop-chart-friendly songs—such as "9 to 5," a countrified take on disco from a 1980 comedy movie of the same name—while also continuing to perform authentic rural music. She won critical acclaim for traditional country music on albums such as *My Grass Is Blue*.

Tammy Wynette (1942–1998) followed a similar path. A Nashville-based single mother of three, she struck gold from the 1960s into the '70s with a string of anthemic country-pop songs with choruses that resonated with the experiences of ordinary people, such as "Stand by Your Man" and "D-I-V-O-R-C-E."

Top billing for Johnny Cash A 1960 poster advertises a country music show in Des Moines, Iowa, hosted by Johnny Cash. He always introduced himself with the deadpan catchphrase "Hello—I'm Johnny Cash."

COUNTRY MUSICIAN (1932–)

LORETTA LYNN

A coal-miner's daughter, Loretta Lynn was married at 15 and a mother by the following year. Her husband bought her a cheap guitar when she was 21, and she eventually made her first record in 1960, at the age of 28. Her colorful songs concerned the day-to-day struggles of the poor and hard-working, with lyrics about unfaithful husbands, put-upon women, and gender inequality. In her 1960s and '70s heyday, Lynn brought a new topicality to country, singing about the Vietnam War on "Dear Uncle Sam," and birth control on "The Pill," which proved too controversial for many conservative country radio stations.

Multitalented country star
Dolly Parton not only plays the banjo, piano, drums, and numerous other instruments but has also written many of her own hits, including "Backwoods Barbie," "Jolene," and "I Will Always Love You."

But country's acceptance by the mainstream was not simply a matter of going pop. The Bakersfield sound (from Bakersfield, California) was a no-frills, up-tempo style of country that sprang up in the 1950s in rowdy working men's honky-tonk bars, and was popularized by the singers Buck Owens and Merle Haggard.

Rock'n'roll also made its presence felt in the music, attitude, and image of bad-boy country singers such as Johnny Cash, Waylon Jennings, and Willie Nelson. Cash (1932–2003) began his career playing rockabilly—a mix of country and rock 'n' roll—at Sun Records in the 1950s, alongside Elvis Presley (see pp.316–317). But it was his songs about prisoners, murderers, love, religion, and redemption that made him one of the most influential figures in 20th-century popular music, recording up to his death.

KEY WORKS

Jim Reeves "He's Got to Go"
Patsy Cline "Walkin' After Midnight"
Johnny Cash "Folsom Prison Blues"
Dolly Parton "In My Tennessee Mountain Home"
Tammy Wynette "Stand by Your Man"
Loretta Lynn "Don't Come Home a Drinkin'"

AFTER

Country is part of American—and world—pop culture. It continues to feed off pop and rock, creating new mainstream stars like Taylor Swift.

COWBOY-BOOTED MEGASTARS

The biggest country acts of the 1980s and '90s, such as **Garth Brooks** and **Billy Ray Cyrus**, sold albums by the million. Brooks and Cyrus both emphasized country's working-man appeal, taking influences from rock singer-songwriters like **Bruce Springsteen**. Cyrus's "Achy Breaky Heart" brought line-dancing to the world in 1992.

GARTH BROOKS PERFORMING IN 2009

Reggae

Being an island, Jamaica developed its music in relative isolation. But, being close to the United States, it has also been heavily influenced by R&B, soul, and funk. Reggae processed all of these genres in its own irresistibly rhythmic and laid-back way.

There is a blurry line between early reggae and "rocksteady," a mid-1960s Jamaican popular music that emphasized the bass, with a clipped lead guitar often doubling the notes of the bass line. The music was made by bands at studios such as Duke Reid's Treasure Isle and Sir Coxsone's Studio One.

Rocksteady was enjoyed, and often made, by "rude boys"—disaffected, unemployed, young Jamaican men. Lyrically, it took inspiration from action films, for instance, Desmond Dekker's hit single "007."

The Upsetters in the studio
The in-house band of Lee "Scratch" Perry's Upsetter label, the Upsetters featured on Bob Marley's early albums – which many consider to be his best.

BEFORE

Reggae took a long time to brew. Several proto-reggae musical forms had recognizable reggae elements, but they hadn't quite settled into the bass-heavy "skanking" off-beat rhythm that came to define the genre.

SKA SOUNDS OF THE SIXTIES

The **uptempo** sounds of **ska** dominated Jamaica in the mid-1960s. It was a distinctly Jamaican form. American **R&B** **«« 310–311** was the inspiration behind the music, but ska was choppier: the guitar or horns stabbed the **off-beats,** whereas R&B was smoother. Ska became popular with Jamaican immigrants in the UK, and the Skatalites, featuring the explosive trombone player Don Drummond, were its most deft exponents. Many of reggae's leading acts started off in ska bands. Ska could be said to be to reggae what **skiffle** was to **rock 'n' roll** **«« 314–315.**

Reggae emerges

Toots Hibbert was a veteran of earlier reggae-related forms who performed in The Maytals, a 1960s Jamaican group. Toots's soul-drenched voice, reminiscent of the American soul singer and songwriter Otis Redding, rendered tracks such as "Pressure Drop" and "Sweet & Dandy" particularly powerful.

Around the turn of the 1970s, true reggae was born—it was rocksteady but rootsier. Reggae took the heavy shuffle of mento (a style of Jamaican folk music that is similar to calypso) and applied it to rocksteady, while slowing the tempo and rendering the bass more prominent by leaving it plenty of space. Emphasis was on the off-beat (or the "skank") and the head-nodding rhythm that it created.

Messages in the lyrics were growing more militant, and Rastafarianism was becoming more of an influence. The leading studios—Treasure Isle and Studio One—started to notice that they had some competition in the form of producers such as Lee Perry, Joe Gibbs, Winston "Niney" Holness, and Winston Riley.

The singer Lee Perry established the Upsetter label in 1968, named after his hit "I Am the Upsetter," a song that was roundly dismissive of his former studio employer, Coxsone Dodd. On an early release, "People Funny Boy," he incorporated both the sound of a baby crying and glass breaking. Even more radical techniques and gimmicks would later be employed in his dub reggae mixes of the 1970s. Perry also produced the Wailers in the late 1960s, and his sparse arrangements on the albums *Soul Rebels* and *African Herbsman* are a revelation for anyone who has only heard Bob Marley's later recordings.

Star singer and actor
Jamaican reggae star Jimmy Cliff had his first hit record at the age of 14 and helped popularize reggae around the world. Cliff starred in the 1972 reggae movie *The Harder They Come*.

Going global

Bunny Wailer, Peter Tosh, and Bob Marley—the Wailers—had known each other since childhood, and had honed their art through the ska and rocksteady years. They had had their first hit, "Simmer Down," a comment on gang violence, in 1964. The band signed to Island Records in 1972 and recorded two classic albums—*Catch A Fire* and *Burnin*—that are known as the first reggae albums.

In 1974, the trio dissolved, with each member chasing a solo career. Marley kept the name, however, and Bob Marley and the Wailers now featured a chorus of female backing singers, the I-Threes. Marley found success in the UK with the song "No Woman No Cry" in 1975, and the following year he cracked the US market with the *Rastaman Vibration* album. He was the first bona fide music superstar in the developing world.

Strings are tuned like a double bass: E, A, D, G

Four strings

Distinctive sound
The electric bass guitar is a dominant instrument in reggae. With the drum, its simple chord progressions underpin the dance rhythm. "Drum and bass" becomes more evident in dub music.

Dub reggae

In the early to mid-1970s, dub reggae came of age. It was a product of the recording studio, and the fascination with tinkering with technology that has always been a facet of Jamaican music. Lee Perry's experiments were key, but even more important was King Tubby. He ran a sound system for reggae dances, but he was also a studio engineer and could strip vocal recordings to a minimum to give DJs the opportunity to speak over records. In this way, the dub (instrumental) version was born. DJs such as U-Roy, Prince Jazzbo, and Big Youth entered recording studios, their improvisations growing more complex. This was the start of "toasting"—a forerunner of rapping.

Vocal trios

As a response to the heaviness of dub, a new wave of vocal trios emerged in the mid-1970s. The Wailing Souls, the Gladiators, and the Mighty Diamonds

KEY WORKS

Dave and Ansell Collins "Double Barrell"
The Wailers "Small Axe"
Lee "Scratch" Perry "People Funny Boy"
Bob Marley "One Love"
Burning Spear "Marcus Garvey"
Toots and the Maytals "Pressure Drop"
Horace Andy "Night Nurse"

Reggae's superstar
Bob Marley (1945–1981) performs live at the Rainbow Theatre in London, in June 1977, four years before his death. His posthumous album, *Legend*, issued in 1984, has sold more than 25 million copies worldwide.

all sang impeccably tight harmonies over tracks laid down by—or inspired by—producers such as Augustus Pablo and Sly and Robbie. The latter—drummer Sly Dunbar and bassist Robbie Shakespeare—are probably the most prolific rhythm section in the world, and have played on literally thousands of records.

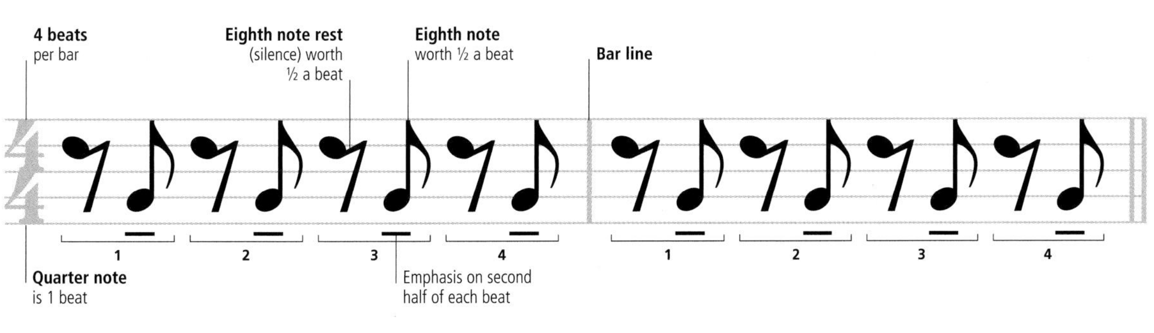

Ska stroke
Common to ska, rocksteady, and reggae, ska strokes have a bouncing rhythm played on the downstroke in a chord, typically in four-four time, rising and falling in pitch. The upstroke may have a "ghost note," achieved by lifting the fingers slightly off the frets.

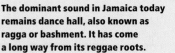

4 beats per bar

Eighth note rest (silence) worth ½ a beat

Eighth note worth ½ a beat

Bar line

1 2 3 4 1 2 3 4

Quarter note is 1 beat

Emphasis on second half of each beat

All-digital dance hall

The 1980s saw a steady evolution in the sounds and techniques that the dub reggae producers and DJs used in the 1970s. Witty DJs became known for their ribald rhymes. The style became generally known as "dance hall," and during the 1980s its music gradually shifted toward a programmed, synthesizer and drum-machine based sound that was a far cry from the skank and depth of classic Jamaican reggae. Wayne Smith's hit single "Under Me Sleng Teng," recorded in 1985, proved to be a turning point in the genre. Reggae's first all-digital rhythm, it has been covered by numerous bands since.

AFTER

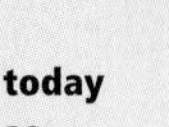

The dominant sound in Jamaica today remains dance hall, also known as ragga or bashment. It has come a long way from its reggae roots.

DIGITAL DEVELOPMENT

Contemporary dance hall is entirely digitally produced using punchy **drum machines** and **synths**, with deep sub-bass played on large speakers, or through the **bass-bins** of a sound system.

DANCE HALL DJS

The 1990s resounded to the tones of the operatic Buccaneer, gravel-voiced Capleton, and the baritone bark of Shabba Ranks. More recently, the label VP records had a stable of charismatic **dance hall DJs** such as Queen Ifrica, Jah Cure, Spice, and Romain Virgo.

BEFORE

The idea of putting together a few good-looking singers to manufacture a band that could sell large numbers of records took off in the 1960s.

BIRTH OF THE BOY BAND
The first "boy band" is generally considered to be the **Monkees**, a four-piece group put together by TV producer Bob Rafelson in 1965 for a TV series based on the adventures of a band much like the Beatles. The group was given first-rate songs such as "Daydream Believer" and "Last Train to Clarksville" by top American songwriters.

NOVELTY ITEM—A PUZZLE FOR YOUNG FANS

KEY WORKS

The Osmonds "Crazy Horses"
Duran Duran "Girls on Film"
Madonna "Get Into the Groove"
Michael Jackson "Billie Jean"
The Spice Girls "Spice Up Your Life"
Justin Timberlake "Rock Your Body"
Rihanna "Work"

Music Goes Pop

From the classic songs of the king and queen of pop—Michael Jackson and Madonna—to the instant hits of manufactured bands who just want to be famous, pop is universally appealing, with strong melodies, simple lyrics, and straightforward fun.

If there were a golden age for the pop pinup, it was the 1970s. At that time, a brace of boy bands, all featuring improbably young singers, and often comprising members of the same family—for example, the Osmonds, the Bay City Rollers, and the Jackson 5—ruled the charts. The music was a softer version of the type of glam rock performed by T-Rex or David Bowie, or, in the case of the Jacksons, preteen-friendly disco and soul. The Swedish four-piece ABBA became pop royalty in Europe during the 1970s. Their inventively arranged songs, such as "Dancing Queen," "The Name of the Game," and "Money, Money, Money" used bold harmonies over soft rock and disco, and dominated the charts.

Huge sounds

In the 1980s, pop's general trajectory was toward bigger, brighter, and ever more over-the-top sounds and images. By then, recording studios had 24 tracks of available recording space (previously there had only been eight; the Beatles had only four). This allowed producers such as Trevor Horn and Bob Clearmountain to give a huge sound to British pop groups like ABC and Frankie Goes To Hollywood.

The American club scene was a hotbed of talent in the early 1980s. Madonna's million-selling 1984 album *Like A Virgin* was reminiscent of the late-1970s disco sound of Chic. Her music was initially disco-oriented, with lyrics addressing such time-honored subjects as dancing, love, sex, and, more unusually, the conflicts of her Roman Catholic upbringing.

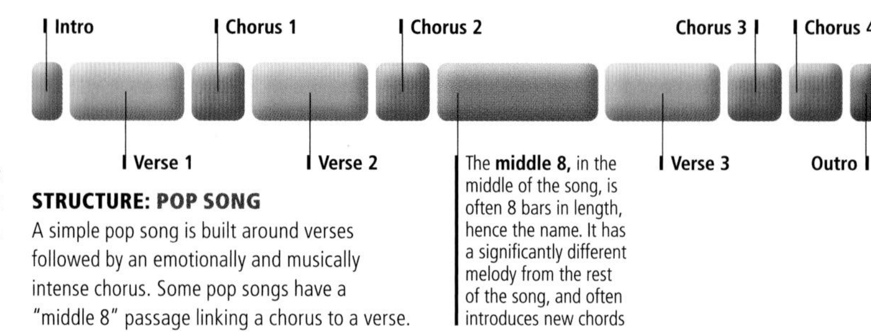

STRUCTURE: POP SONG
A simple pop song is built around verses followed by an emotionally and musically intense chorus. Some pop songs have a "middle 8" passage linking a chorus to a verse.

> "I **won't be happy** until I am as **famous as God.**"
>
> MADONNA, AT THE START OF HER CAREER

The brash, hedonistic '80s welcomed the British duo Wham! with open arms. George Michael and Andrew Ridgeley became pop pinups and had a string of hits, including "Wake Me Up Before You Go Go" and "Edge of Heaven," that were influenced by the poppy soul of 1960s Motown—their music was perfect for teenage discos and wedding-reception dance floors.

Another megastar of the 1980s indebted to disco was Michael Jackson. Having found fame as a child star in the 1970s, he towered over the world's pop scene in the 1980s. His 1979 album *Off The Wall* sold more than 20 million albums worldwide, helped by songwriting from Stevie Wonder and Paul McCartney (see pp.324–325).

Jackson was labeled the "King of Pop," and his mock horror-movie video for his 1982 song "Thriller" was perfectly timed for the video-hungry audiences of 1980s MTV. His albums *Bad* (1987) and *Dangerous* (1991), with their heavy drum machines and synthesized soul-pop, proved that he could move with the times.

Boy bands and girl bands

The 1990s saw the rise of the manufactured boy band specializing in up-tempo dance-pop with catchy choruses. The effervescent Take That and their more staid successors, Boyzone, enjoyed surprisingly long-lived careers, considering their appeal was carefully targeted at teenage girls. Other boy bands that

Abba's meteoric rise
Swedish pop group Abba perform their song "Waterloo" at the Eurovision Song Contest held in Brighton, UK, 1974. They won the competition and went on to achieve global superstardom.

Bad world tour
In 1987, Michael Jackson embarked on his first world tour as a solo artist. Called the *Bad* tour, after his newly released album, and lasting 16 months, it was the most successful concert tour ever. Here, Jackson performs at London's Wembley Stadium, in July 1988.

exploded in the 1990s, such as New Kids On The Block, Backstreet Boys, East 17, Five, and Blue, had less time in the spotlight.

It wasn't just the boys having all the fun. The Spice Girls burst into the charts around the world in 1996 with the childlike hip-hop pop of "Wannabe," and followed it up with fizzy and enjoyable self-referential hits like "Spice Up Your Life" (1997). They had worthy successors in Girls Aloud, winners of the British TV talent show *Popstars: The Rivals*, whose albums are written and produced by the inventive British production duo Xenomania (Brian Higgins and Miranda Cooper).

Pop goes hip-hop

Hip-hop (see pp.370–71) had a huge influence on pop music in the 1990s and 2000s. The innovative production techniques of producers such as Timbaland, The Neptunes, and Dr. Dre on albums for singers like Justin Timberlake, Britney Spears, Nelly Furtado, Kelis, and Beyoncé brought a new weight and adventurous rhythm to the pop charts, with stripped-down percussion and heavy bass lines.

Timberlake made the leap from being in a manufactured boy band ('N Sync) to becoming a soul singer, heavily influenced by prime Michael Jackson.

Fantastic album cover
George Michael (right) and Andrew Ridgeley formed Wham! in the early 1980s and had worldwide hits. Michael went on to a successful solo career.

TECHNOLOGY

AUTO TUNE

When Exxon engineer Andy Hildebrand developed software for interpreting seismic data, he realized that his system could analyze and alter the pitch of vocals or instruments.

Released in 1997 as Auto Tune, the software was first used to correct out-of-tune vocals. But, after Cher's 1998 hit "Believe," producers found they could use Auto Tune to give vocals a radical, futuristic distortion, making them sound synthesizer-like. Auto Tune became a must-have effect for artists, such as Kanye West (who used it extensively on his 2008 album *808s And Heartbreak*) and the rapper T-Pain.

But while pop was influenced by hip-hop, the bombastic sound of late-1980s Euro pop also crept into hip-hop. The thumping disco heard in German nightclubs became an unlikely influence on African American music, and the dividing lines between pop, R&B, and hip-hop has blurred over time. Rihanna, a Barbadian singer, embraced the synthesizers of Euro pop on her risqué tracks "S&M" and "Only Girl (In The World)." Lady Gaga, who came close to replicating Madonna's success in the 21st century, has also courted controversy by setting sexually explicit lyrics to 1980s-influenced music. Very much a product of YouTube and social media, she is arguably more famous for her radical dress sense than her music.

AFTER

Many have lamented the decline in music sales in the face of online music streaming and download piracy. Nevertheless, pop music thrives in the 21st century, helped by television talent shows.

FAST LANE TO POP FAME

British **music mogul Simon Cowell** has made lucrative franchises out of his talent shows *The X Factor, Pop Idol*, and *American Idol*. Often, the personality and background of the winning contestants are the deciding factor. The shows have led to successful careers for previous winners, such as Leona Lewis, Will Young, One Direction, Carrie Underwood, and Kelly Clarkson.

SIMON COWELL

GLEE CLUB

The American TV series *Glee* has also bolstered global pop music sales. Centered on the lives and loves of a high school music and drama group, the hit show's cast perform covers of pop classics, such as Journey's "Don't Stop Believin'" and Britney Spears's "Toxic."

BEFORE

Though new technology often initially disrupted established income streams, the music business soon adapted to capitalize on new sources of revenue and opportunities for promotion.

EARLY MUSIC BUSINESS
In the early days of the music business, it was music publishers who generated revenue with sales of **printed sheet music**. In the early 18th century, this domination of the music industry was diluted by the invention of commercially available recordings on cylinder and disc, and spending on music was gradually redirected to **record companies**.

POWER OF THE RADIO
Sheet music and record sales were knocked by both the Great Depression and the **rise of radio** in the 1920s **« 260–261**, which changed forever the way the public could access music. Ultimately, however, radio assisted the rise of the record industry by broadcasting music nationwide and **creating demand**. The power of radio made the medium a key target for record company's **promotional strategies**.

KEY WORKS

Queen "Bohemian Rhapsody"
Michael Jackson "Thriller"
Dire Straits "Money for Nothing"
Talking Heads "Once in a Lifetime"
Peter Gabriel "Sledgehammer"
Madonna "Like a Prayer"
Britney Spears "...Baby One More Time"

Chart Toppers

Popular music has always been a money-making business, but with rising record sales in the latter half of the 20th century, the increasing importance of sales charts and awards, and the emergence of video as a marketing tool, the commercialization of pop went into overdrive.

In the 1920s, the record business overtook the sheet music publishers as the dominant force in the music industry. The following decades saw many record companies come and go, with a select few—Decca and Columbia among them—emerging as enduring businesses. As companies competed with each other to sell the most records, it became increasingly important to assess and promote how records performed in relation to each other, which led to the rise of the bestsellers chart.

Pop charts

Though early song popularity charts were based on sheet music sales, record sales were soon incorporated. Weekly radio shows such as *Your Hit Parade* (1935–1955), which presented live performances of what it judged to be the fifteen most popular songs in the country, became very influential. Claiming to base their song selection on information from several sources—sample figures from the songs' sheet music and record sales, radio requests, and jukebox plays—the program's actual methods of calculation remained unscrutinized, leaving them open to unscrupulous industry manipulation. This question mark hung over all "bestseller" charts for many years.

In the 1940s and 1950s, America's music industry magazine *Billboard* had three charts: Best Sellers (as reported by record shops), Most Radio Plays (as reported by the radio stations), and Most Jukebox Plays. This last category was essential in gauging the popularity of records among the youth, especially as certain genres—rhythm and blues and rock 'n' roll—were often not part of radio's playlists. In 1958, Billboard created the Hot 100, which tracked each single's popularity with information from a range of sources, across the genres. The chart remains the US music industry standard today.

Video pioneers
The chart-topping rock group Queen was one of the pioneering acts in the use of promotional music videos. Here they are shown shooting the famous video for their single "Radio Ga Ga."

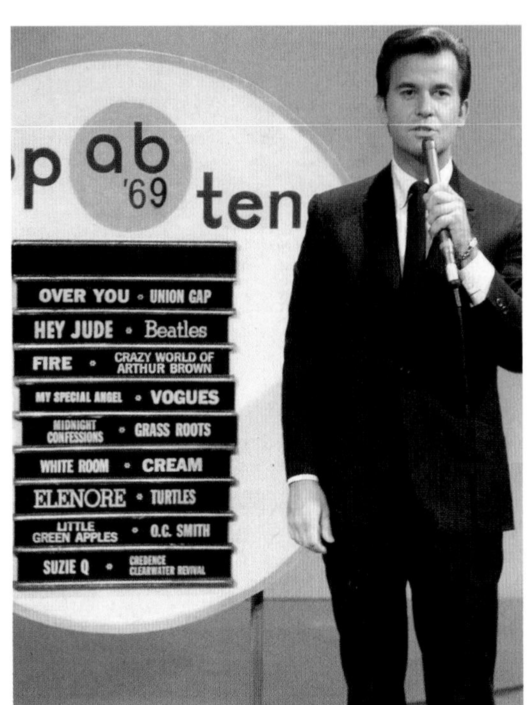

American Bandstand
Begun in 1952, *American Bandstand* was presented and produced by Dick Clark from 1956 until 1989. Its format of dancing teenagers and guest artists was mimicked by several similar shows around the world.

> "They don't **honor** the **arts** or the **artist** for what he **created.** It's the music business **celebrating itself.**"
>
> LEAD SINGER OF GRAMMY-WINNING BAND TOOL, MAYNARD JAMES KEENAN, ON WHY HE BOYCOTTED THE GRAMMYS, 2002

Most countries had their own popularity charts, sometimes several. In the UK, the BBC based its chart on sampled sales figures, which invariably differed in detail from those in music papers such as *Melody Maker* and the *New Musical Express*.

Today, with the advent of digital communication, the modern charts have reached a consensus and incorporate a wide range of sales information, including digital downloads.

Music awards

Functioning both as inter-industry approbation and further promotional opportunity, American annual entertainment business awards began in 1929 with the Academy Awards, or "Oscars" (for film). They

The Grammy
Named after inventor Emile Berliner's 1895 disc-playing gramophone, the Grammy trophy retains the same design today as at the first awards ceremony in 1959.

continued in 1947 with the "Tonys" (for theater), which were followed by the "Emmys" (for TV) in 1949, before finally in 1959, the "Grammy" awards appeared, rewarding outstanding achievements in the music industry. With many strands of the music business clamoring for an award, or a nomination, the number of Grammy categories ballooned from 28 in 1959 to 109 in 2011, though they were scaled back to 78 categories for 2012. In the UK, the British Phonographic Industry (BPI) Awards were established in 1977 and renamed "the Brits" in 1989.

While these, and the many other award ceremonies that have sprung up in their wake, are often glitzy, entertaining, celebratory affairs, the awards themselves, though ostensibly given on merit, are regarded with some suspicion by some commentators and artists as self-serving, conservative, and slow to reflect the fast-moving trends and tastes of modern popular music and its audience.

18 MTV AWARDS were won by "Sledgehammer" by Peter Gabriel in 1986, the most played video in MTV's history.

Film and TV promotion

Musical artists have been promoted in short films since the advent of sound-capable film, known as the "talkies." In America in the 1940s, hundreds of early versions of the music video, known as "Soundies," were produced to be played by the Panoram, a coin-operated video jukebox found in many bars, restaurants, and amusement arcades.

As television became more popular and affordable in the 1950s and 1960s, music-based TV shows became an important part of music promotion. Shows such as *American Bandstand* (1952–1989) began by showing Soundie-style promotional films—a precursor to MTV-style programming 30 years later—before concentrating on artist's in-person appearances to deliver lip-synched performances.

Producer Jack Good introduced rock 'n' roll television to the UK in the late 1950s with *Six Five Special* and *Oh Boy*, but it was the chart-based, *Bandstand*-style *Top Of The Pops* (1964–2006) that endured through several generations.

Music video

Though the important music TV shows required artists to make in-person appearances, Soundie-style promotional films continued to be made, not least by artists in France and Italy where the Skopitone and the CineBox were popular visual jukeboxes.

Bestseller Madonna's *Like a Virgin* (1984) was her first number-one album in the United States and a huge international hit. It has sold 21 million copies worldwide, making it one of the bestselling albums of all time.

Classic movie musicals and rock-era films starring musical stars such as Elvis Presley all made their mark, but it was the inventive song sequences in The Beatles' movies *A Hard Day's Night* (1964) and *Help* (1965), directed by Richard Lester, and the Bob Dylan documentary *Don't Look Back* (1965), directed by D. A. Pennebaker, that helped establish standards for the filming of musical performance.

While *The Monkees* (1966–68) TV show based its visual style on The Beatles' movies, several 1960s British acts, including The Rolling Stones, The Who, and Pink Floyd, produced inventive filmed inserts for use on TV, often abroad. However, with much music TV still requiring personal appearances, music promo films remained relatively rare. It was not until after the startling promotional film for Queen's "Bohemian Rhapsody" (1975), shot and edited on videotape, that the pop video became an increasingly important marketing tool.

MTV

As pop video developed in quality and appeal, established music TV shows began to incorporate videos into its programming, and new TV programs entirely devoted to pop video appeared. In 1981, Music Television (MTV), the first 24-hour music video channel, launched in the United States with the promo film for The Buggles' "Video Killed the Radio Star." As the channel's impact grew in the next few years, video play was established to be at least as important a marketing technique as radio play.

The music industry spent money to ensure videos were noticed and those made to accompany certain records became events in themselves. Michael Jackson's "Thriller" (1983), directed by the Hollywood filmmaker John Landis, was an elaborate short movie that cost $500,000, while Dire Straits' "Money for Nothing" (1985), directed by Steve Barron, featured ground-breaking computer animation.

20 MINUTES The length of Michael Jackson's "Thriller" video.

40 PERCENT of adolescents are exposed to music videos daily.

Controversial videos, including Duran Duran's "Girls on Film" (1981), Frankie Goes to Hollywood's "Relax" (1983), and several Madonna videos, were banned or heavily edited. Such censorship generated much welcome publicity.

Other music channels followed MTV to reflect the diversity of music genres, origins, and audience demographics. As satellite and cable television became more common, music television spread all over the world.

Video star
An homage from one pop culture icon to another, Madonna's "Material Girl" video (1984) aped Marilyn Monroe's performance of "Diamonds Are a Girl's Best Friend" from *Gentlemen Prefer Blondes* (1953).

AFTER 

The growth of the music streaming industry means that more music is available to more people than before.

INTERNET REVOLUTION
In recent years, many stars have kick-started their own careers without a record label, enabled by cheap recording equipment and the Internet. This democratization of music hit new heights when Nathan Evans topped the UK charts with his TikTok rendition of "The Wellerman."

ENDURING LEGACY
Even after decades, chart-topping records are still cultural milestones, with blockbuster films like Marvel's *The Guardians of the Galaxy* (2014) and Netflix's *Umbrella Academy* (2020) showcasing classic hits, such as Blue Swede's "Hooked on a Feeling" and Frank Sinatra's "My Way."

Disco Inferno

In the early '70s, the inner-city nightclub came into its own as the cosmopolitan place to be. Disco music was its soundtrack, bringing elegance and sophistication to those who wanted to look impressive on the dance floor. It took over nightclubs across the world.

Fueling the craze
The 1977 film *Saturday Night Fever* was a box-office smash, cementing disco's popularity, and making a star of actor John Travolta. The soundtrack album revived the careers of the Bee Gees.

The hallmark of disco was a constant, on-the-beat kick-drum. It made things as simple and as smooth as possible for dancers, with a thump that was not at all difficult for their feet to follow, and a handclap on every second beat. It is a rhythm that has become a staple of mainstream dance music ever since.

The sound evolved gradually. Many have pointed to the 1972 track "Soul Makossa," by Cameroonian jazz saxophonist Manu Dibango, as being the first. It certainly uses most of disco's trademarks: up-tempo and largely instrumental, with a simple chanted refrain. It has plenty of Afro-Latin percussion and, most importantly, uses the classic disco beat.

Disco beat
Most disco songs have a steady four-on-the-floor beat. This is a uniformly accented beat in 4/4 time in which the bass drum is hit on every beat.

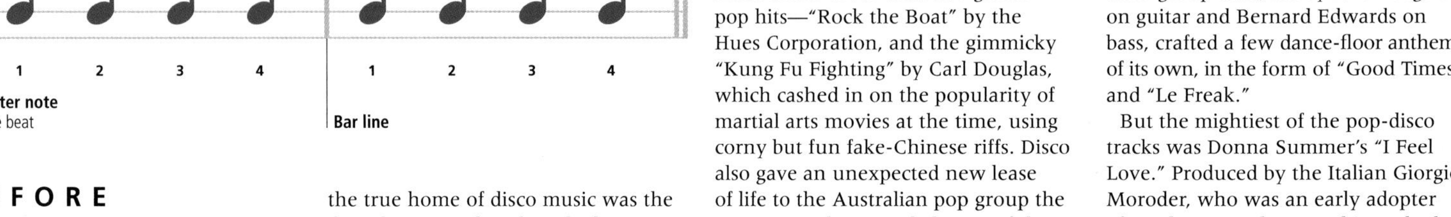

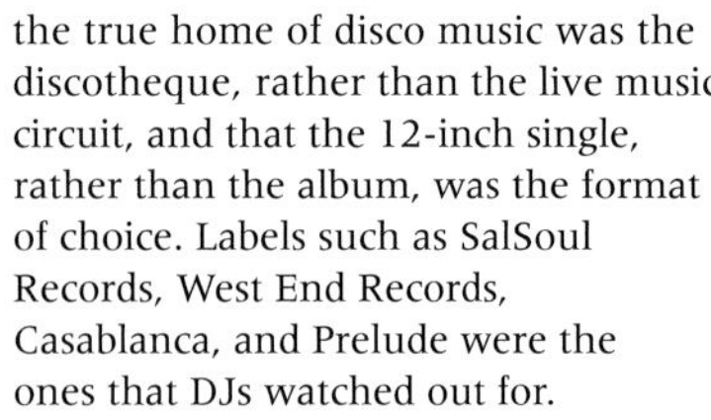

A legend on the decks
Larry Levan was a DJ at New York's Paradise Garage between 1974 and 1984, where he incorporated drum machines into his sets. His nights were celebrated for the tolerance and diversity of the crowd they attracted.

Record labels

The craze was slow to give rise to any star performers. Before disco became big business, it was the record labels, rather than the artists, that attracted the attention of disco aficionados. This was hardly surprising, given that the true home of disco music was the discotheque, rather than the live music circuit, and that the 12-inch single, rather than the album, was the format of choice. Labels such as SalSoul Records, West End Records, Casablanca, and Prelude were the ones that DJs watched out for.

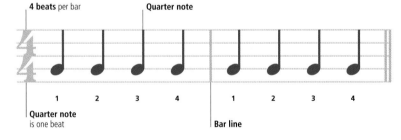

SalSoul records was run by Ken Cayre, an entrepreneur and a fan of the in-house musicians who played for the Motown-influenced record label Philadelphia International. Their rhythm section in particular—Ronnie Baker on bass and Earl Young on drums—laid down the rock-steady disco beat that all others copied. Young's prominent use of the hi-hat cymbal (see p.247), playing 16th notes, was easy to make out in a deafening nightclub, and made it easier for DJs to seamlessly mix records without a pause, thus never disappointing an eager dance floor. Their signature style can be heard on the disco-soul classic "Love is the Message" by MFSB.

Keep on moving

To be a successful disco DJ, you had to keep the crowd moving. Skillful DJs matched the tempo of one record with another, and blended the end of one with the beginning of the next. It was only a matter of time before these DJs—David Mancuso, Shep Bettibone, Frankie Knuckles, and Larry Levan—began making recordings. They became famous for their remixes, or rather "re-edits," whereby the tape of existing recordings would be physically cut and spliced on reel-to-reel tape machines in order to extend the most danceable parts of disco tunes.

Taking the world by storm

Disco broke cover with two global pop hits—"Rock the Boat" by the Hues Corporation, and the gimmicky "Kung Fu Fighting" by Carl Douglas, which cashed in on the popularity of martial arts movies at the time, using corny but fun fake-Chinese riffs. Disco also gave an unexpected new lease of life to the Australian pop group the Bee Gees, who provided most of the songs on the soundtrack for the movie *Saturday Night Fever*. Their piercing falsetto singing on top of thumping bass lines and tough drums was irresistible, and songs such as "Stayin' Alive" remain popular.

The Swedish pop group ABBA, who dominated the European pop charts in the 1970s, also jumped on the disco bandwagon. The tight vocal harmonizing on "Dancing Queen" rendered it an instant anthem for disco-dancers everywhere. Meanwhile, the African American disco group Chic, led by Nile Rodgers on guitar and Bernard Edwards on bass, crafted a few dance-floor anthems of its own, in the form of "Good Times" and "Le Freak."

But the mightiest of the pop-disco tracks was Donna Summer's "I Feel Love." Produced by the Italian Giorgio Moroder, who was an early adopter of synthesizers, the 1977 hit pushed

High society
Nile Rodgers and Bernard Edwards were inspired by the decadent high-society image of British glam rock band Roxy Music to form Chic in 1976. They influenced Queen, hip-hop crew Sugarhill Gang, and the indie-dance band New Order.

BEFORE

The Motown Record Corporation, founded in 1960 in Detroit, steered African American soul music toward pop. It is impossible to imagine disco's arrival without it.

THE MOTOWN SOUND
Known as "The Hit Factory," Motown perfected its own house sound in the 1960s, taking **soul** **« 320–321** and funk and fashioning them into pop music **« 350–351**. Acts such as **the Supremes** and **the Four Tops** sang over lush violin and horn orchestrations to a driving, up-tempo beat that was far from the hip-swinging groove of soul and funk. It anticipated the four-on-the-floor rhythm of disco. The **Jacksons**, led by a young Michael Jackson, were one Motown act that went on to have global disco hits.

disco in an electronic direction. Donna Summer (1948–2012) was an American soul singer living in Europe and appearing in musicals when she met Moroder. The pairing of her angelic voice with Moroder's relentless and slightly menacing synthesizer bass line resulted in a unique record. This electronic disco sound was the shape of things to come.

Electric buzz
The erotically charged vocals of Donna Summer combined with Giorgio Moroder's synthesizer-based tracks were a huge hit and proved that programmed electronic music was the future for disco.

KEY WORKS

Manu Dibango "Soul Makossa"
The Trammps "Disco Inferno"
The Bee Gees "Stayin' Alive"
ABBA "Dancing Queen"
Donna Summer "I Feel Love"
Anita Ward "Ring My Bell"

AFTER

Disco gradually evolved into the electronic dance music that dominated the DJ sets of nightclubs of all kinds for the next few decades.

THE BIRTH OF HOUSE MUSIC

DJs such as Larry Levan and Frankie Knuckles transformed original songs for the dance floor, and the "re-edit" became known as the "extended remix." These were so common in the 1980s that even **rock** and **heavy metal** songs were affected.

At New York's Paradise Garage, Larry Levan contributed to the birth of **house music 372–373 ››**, and the instrumentation of disco became electronic and stripped down. In other American cities, similar changes were taking place. Detroit's Juan Atkins and Derrick May were playing eclectic DJ sets that included **electronic music** by **Kraftwerk** (see pp.336–337). They began making their own music, using the powerful bass tones of drum machines such as the Roland 808 and 909 to lend dance music a visceral new sound.

ROLAND 808 DRUM MACHINE

BEFORE

Punk did not come from nowhere. The garage rock of 1960s America could be said to have been punk before the term was invented.

IGGY POP

AMERICAN ROOTS

When the Rolling Stones became successful in the United States, they inspired teenagers across the country to start rock bands. **Garage rock** gained its name because most of the people who made it still lived with their parents, and the garage was the only place they could rehearse.

Garage rock was primitive R&B **« 310–311**, and could be cheaply recorded. The Sonics, a raucous five-piece garage band from Tacoma, Washington, were punkier than most of their peers, as was singer **Iggy Pop** and his band The Stooges, whose nihilistic lyrics and driving R&B were a great influence on punk.

MC5

The most political of the proto-punks was the Detroit-based band **MC5**, famed for their live album *Kick Out The Jams*. The band played at anti-Vietnam protests **« 322–323**, and they often brandished unloaded rifles onstage.

"My **favorite** artists have always been **Elvis** and **The Beatles.**"

JOEY RAMONE, 1984

KEY WORKS

The Ramones "Blitzkrieg Bop"
Sex Pistols "Anarchy In The UK"
The Clash "London Calling"
The Damned "New Rose"
The Buzzcocks "Boredom"
X-Ray Spex "Oh Bondage Up Yours!"

Punk Explosion

Few movements in 20th-century music has been as distinctive as punk. Loud, raw, and irreverent, it appealed to a disaffected generation, and was defined as much by its disregard for musical traditions as by anything that was deemed fashionable.

Punk rock is generally thought of as being a negative, aggressive music—an anti-establishment music of rebellion. So it is perhaps ironic that the band often cited as being the first punk group was, in many ways, an old-fashioned bunch of guys. The Ramones, in essence, just wanted to play rock 'n' roll music in the traditional way. "By 1973, I knew that what was needed was some pure, stripped-down rock 'n' roll," said drummer Tommy Ramone.

In line with their back-to-basics approach, each member of the New York band adopted the stage last name of Ramone and wore a uniform of a black leather jacket and skinny jeans. Their music was punishingly fast and abrasively loud. Few Ramones songs had more than three chords, and few of them lasted longer than two minutes. Their signature song, "Blitzkrieg Bop," lived up to its name, while "Teenage Lobotomy" and "Sheena is a Punk Rocker" celebrated a trashy American popular culture of high-school loners, schlocky horror films, and Cold War paranoia.

Essentially, they had taken the romantic, rebellious, teenage spirit of rock 'n' rollers such as Eddie Cochran and Chuck Berry and added a large dash of healthy cynicism and cocky attitude.

155 The duration in seconds of the longest track on the Ramones' debut album.

Glamorous and raucous

The Ramones had glamorous soulmates of sorts in the form of The New York Dolls. They, too, were interested in taking rock back to a no-nonsense format, and were in thrall to the spit 'n' sawdust R&B sound of the Rolling Stones (see pp.326–327)—they had a theatrical Jagger-esque front man in David Johansen and their own Keith Richards in guitarist Johnny Thunders.

The energy and raucousness of their delivery made their music more than the sum of its parts on songs such as "Personality Crisis," with lyrics hinting at mental breakdown married to

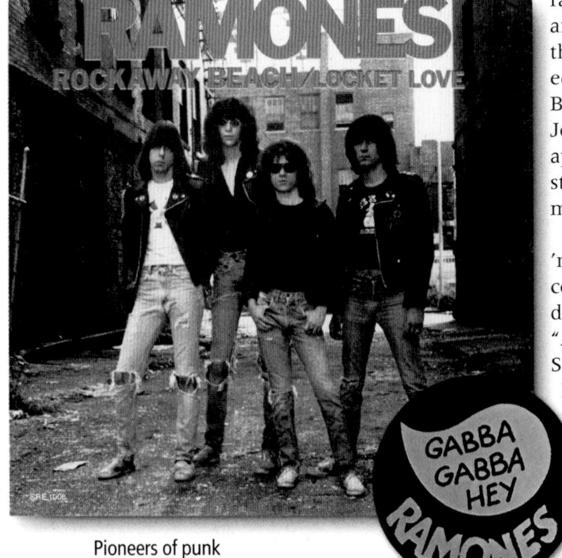

Pioneers of punk
Rolling Stone magazine described the Ramones as "authentic American primitives" and ranked their debut album 33rd in their all-time greatest albums.

good-time, backroom-bar rock. Thanks to their gender-bending stage outfits and their reputation for dangerous live concerts, their notoriety spread.

Sounds of disenchantment

Meanwhile, there were similar stirrings happening in Britain. The Sex Pistols came together in August 1975 after a green-haired John Lydon, wearing an "I Hate Pink Floyd" T-shirt, met guitarist Steve Jones and drummer Paul Cook who used to hang out in Sex, the fashion boutique on London's King's Road owned by Malcolm McLaren and Vivienne Westwood. By way of an audition, Lydon sang along to Alice Cooper's song "I'm 18" on a jukebox.

McLaren wanted to put together a band partly as a brand extension for his shop and partly as an artistic experiment. Managed by McLaren, the Sex Pistols started playing at art colleges and attracted die-hard fans from the very beginning. With their ragged, anti-fashion image and anti-establishment lyrics, they struck a chord in an economically depressed Britain. Lydon was rechristened Johnny Rotten—because of his appalling teeth—and adopted a stage persona that seemed to mock the idea of being onstage.

The music was a wall of rock 'n' roll guitar—the perfect counterpart to Rotten's snarling delivery. Songs such as "Anarchy in the UK" and "God Save the Queen" sealed the Pistols' reputation as the most polarizing band in Britain. Released at the height of Queen Elizabeth II's Silver Jubilee preparations in 1977, "God Save the Queen" was banned by almost all British radio stations. This did record sales no harm at all, sending the single to No. 2 in the UK charts.

The group did not last long. It split up after a traumatic American tour in January 1978, and Sid Vicious, the band's bassist, died of a drug overdose in 1979. The band only recorded one album, *Never Mind The Bollocks... Here's the Sex Pistols*, but its influence was huge and continues to be so.

Punk goes viral

The Sex Pistols were not the first British punks to release a record. "New Rose" by The Damned was the

An English banshee
Inspired by the Sex Pistols, Kent-born Susan Janet Ballion formed Siouxsie and the Banshees with guitarist Steven Severin in 1976 after an impromptu gig improvising on the Lord's Prayer for 20 minutes.

AFTER

Punk music rushed off in radically new directions, but in some countries it remained a form of protest.

POST-SEX PISTOLS
John Lydon continued to make music with a new vehicle, **Public Image Limited**. With Jah Wobble on bass and Keith Levene on guitar, the band moved away from rock toward a fusion of dub reggae and Middle Eastern music with dissonant guitar.

STILL PROTESTING
Punk's do-it-yourself aesthetic savvy was absorbed by a new wave of British bands. Former Clash member Mick Jones formed Big Audio Dynamite, which mixed punk with **hip-hop 370–371 ››** and **reggae 348–349 ››** influences. His bandmate Joe Strummer went on to play with The Mescaleros, fusing punk with world music, country, and jazz.

A NEW YORK MURAL OF JOE STRUMMER OF THE CLASH

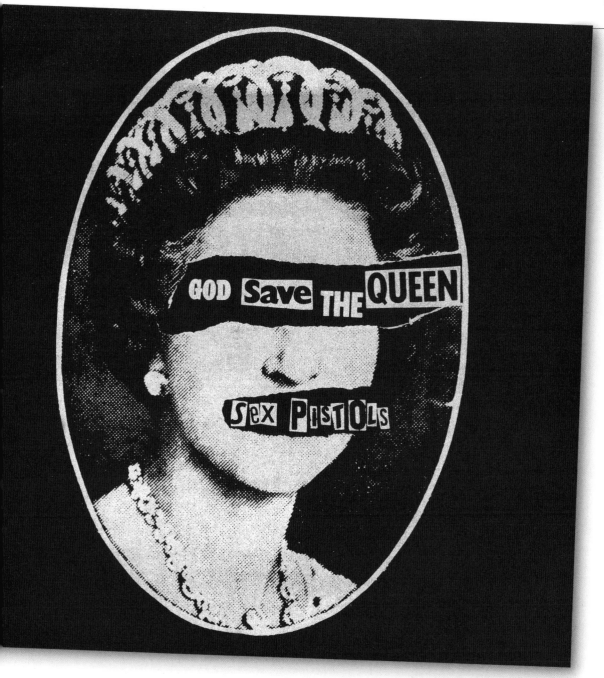

Royal shock
The cover of the Sex Pistols' controversial single "God Save The Queen" was designed by punk artist Jamie Reid. The lyrics rhymed "queen" with "fascist regime."

first UK punk single. Influenced by the Stooges and other 1960s garage bands, The Damned's music was fast and chaotic, while its image was inspired by horror movies— lead singer Dave Vanian appeared onstage dressed like a vampire.

Commune Clash

Seeing the Sex Pistols live prompted Joe Strummer to form The Clash with Mick Jones and Paul Simonon. Strummer had been living in a commune-based squat in West London and was a member of The 101ers, a group that played R&B and blues tracks and was named after their London street address. The Clash became one of the more musically diverse punk bands, and over the course of several albums they incorporated reggae influences—most notably in their anthem "London Calling"—and rockabilly—on the single "Should I Stay or Should I Go?" from the band's fifth album *Combat Rock*, in 1982.

In Manchester, in northern England, Peter McNeish (whose stage name became Pete Shelley) and Howard Traford (later Devoto) formed the Buzzcocks in 1975. They brought emotional vulnerability and pop melodies to the punk template, singing about sex, love, loneliness, and boredom. The Buzzcocks were at heart a pop group, but they celebrated teenage awkwardness, and the juxtaposition of their lovelorn lyrics with raging guitars made them a major inspiration for British indie bands during the 1980s.

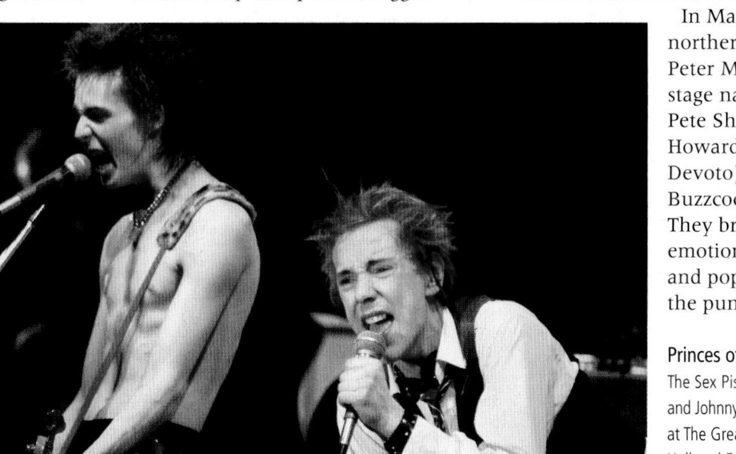

Princes of Punk
The Sex Pistols' Sid Vicious (left) and Johnny Rotten (right) perform at The Great South East Music Hall and Emporium, Atlanta, on the band's final tour in 1978.

Female punk acts

The Slits, an all-female band led by Ari Up (German-born Ariane Daniela Forster, who was just 14 when she formed the band), set confrontational songs about conventional gender roles to a quirky, ramshackle, reggae-influenced backing.

Also fronted by a teenage female singer, Poly Styrene, the British band X-Ray Spex dared to add a wailing saxophone to their lineup, which worked perfectly on their controversial debut 1977 single "Oh Bondage, Up Yours!" With teeth braces and a war helmet, Poly Styrene did not take herself particularly seriously and she brought some lightheartedness to the punk scene.

Alternative Rock

The do-it-yourself legacy of punk rock led to an unprecedented number of independent record labels springing up in the early 1980s. A new generation of bands—uninterested in chart success—recorded cheaply and toured college circuits with what was also called indie or college rock.

Over the course of the 1980s and '90s, so-called alternative rock moved from being a largely underground music, written about in obscure magazines and listened to by a devoted student following, into an international commercial entity.

At the forefront

The same could be said about alternative rock's leading light, the American band R.E.M. Formed in Athens, Georgia, in 1981 and fronted by the singer Michael Stipe, R.E.M. had a highly individual sound. The band's guitarist, Peter Buck, rejected a traditional distorted rock guitar style in favor of clean, chiming playing while Stipe sang his abstract, politically informed lyrics low and indistinctly.

As R.E.M. grew more and more popular, its sound became more conventional, taking on folk influences on the album *Green* in 1988 and country on 1991's massively successful album *Out of Time*, which featured the anthemic ballad "Everybody Hurts."

The Violent Femmes from Milwaukee, Wisconsin, were another band that emerged from the post-punk early-1980s era, and their debut album was an unexpected international hit in 1983, thanks largely to the sarcastic but undeniably catchy single "Blister in the Sun." The band's singer, Gordon Gano, had a petulant, whining voice that complemented the group's brittle, punky acoustic instrumentation.

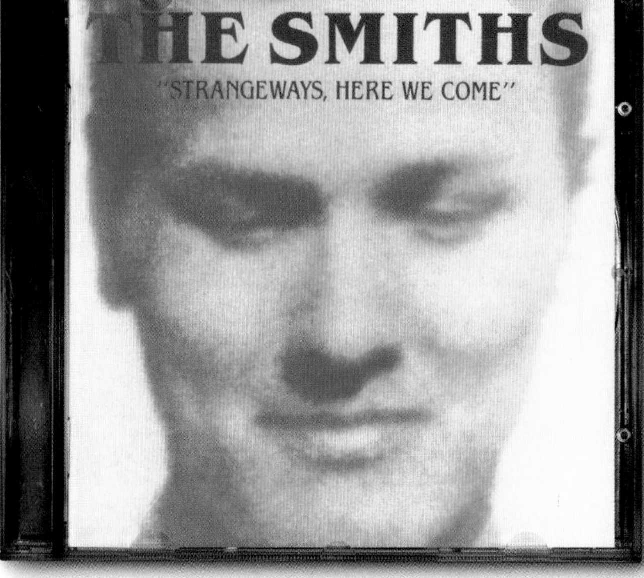

Jail bait
The Smiths' last studio album was *Strangeways, Here We Come*, released in 1987. The title of the album referred to a high security prison near Manchester in northern England .

Going hardcore

Elsewhere in the United States, the punk of the late-1970s mutated into a superfast, purist genre known as hardcore. One of the more innovative of these bands was California's Minutemen, who adopted the shouted vocals and abrasive guitars of hardcore but were heavily influenced by the atonal, jazzy blues of Captain Beefheart and the punk-funk of British band The Pop Group. The band's sprawling, danceable grooves would later be co-opted in the early music by California's favorite funk-rock band, Red Hot Chili Peppers.

The Minnesota trio Hüsker Dü began as a typical hardcore band, with barked lyrics and unremittingly fast tempos, but their music grew progressively sunnier and more lyrical. The band's songs were, at heart, classic pop in the style of the Beatles or Neil Young—albeit with loud, punishing guitars and fast-paced tempos.

Championing the outsider

The UK's most significant alternative rock band in the 1980s was undoubtedly the Smiths. Like R.E.M., the band had an innovative guitar player—Johnny Marr—who also avoided a traditional rock sound. His clean, jangly playing influenced a whole generation of guitarists in bands such as Suede, Radiohead, the Stone Roses, and the Strokes. However, the Smiths' greatest asset was Lancashire-born Stephen Patrick Morrissey, who called himself simply Morrissey. He was perhaps the most idiosyncratic lead singer in rock's history. His singing was arch and stylized, with frequent use of falsetto, and his lyrics flirted with bisexuality, addressing small-town teenage concerns from the outsider's perspective. In the wake of the Smiths came a wave of other bands specializing in songs about literature, heartbreak, and shyness.

At the same time, however, the highly influential Dublin group My Bloody Valentine emerged. While their lyrics had something in common with the jangly indie bands, their music could not have been more different. Their guitarist, Kevin Shields, used punishingly loud, excessively distorted guitars to create dreamlike textures. They inspired groups such as Ride, the Telescopes, and Catherine

"If your **hair** is **wrong**, your **entire life** is wrong."

MORRISSEY, LYRICIST AND SINGER WITH THE SMITHS

SINGER AND GUITARIST (1967–1994)

KURT COBAIN

No one imagined how successful the grunge band Nirvana would become, least of all the band's lead singer and guitarist, Kurt Cobain. Backed by the propulsive rhythm section of Dave Grohl on drums and Krist Novoselic on bass, Cobain became the most famous rock star on the planet when *Nevermind*, their second album, took the world by storm in 1991. It was a position he was extremely uncomfortable with. *In Utero* (1993) was a bleaker album, as if the band were attempting to rid itself of its fame. Cobain took his own life in 1994.

BEFORE

Rock music has had a history of experimentation since its beginnings in the 1960s.

UNDERGROUND BEGINNINGS

The first self-consciously alternative rock band was New York's **Velvet Underground**, which married simple pop melodies to droning, open-tuned guitars and minimalist viola parts. Their technique of using guitar feedback as musical texture was employed later by Sonic Youth and My Bloody Valentine.

In 1970s New York, **artier punk** and new wave acts **« 356–357**, such as Patti Smith and Talking Heads, took a highly individual approach to lyric-writing and music-making, avoiding the clichés of mainstream rock.

VELVET UNDERGROUND

Body has a crescent-moon cutaway shape

Six-stringer was also available in a 12-string version

Fretboard of varnished maple

Pickup with tone and volume controls

Rickenbacker's best-seller
The Rickenbacker 330 guitar was designed by the German Roger Rossmeis. It became the alternative rock instrument of choice in the 1980s, played by Peter Buck of R.E.M. and the Smith's Johnny Marr.

Wheel, which became known as the "shoegaze" movement, due to the bands' self-deprecating tendencies to look down and away from the audience while onstage.

Britpop

Alternative rock went overground in Britain in the 1990s, in the form of Britpop. Assured indie bands such as Blur, Oasis, and Pulp found themselves at the top of the charts. Oasis discovered a winning formula; their guitarist, Noel Gallagher, had a knack for Beatle-esque melodies, which his brother Liam delivered with rock 'n' roll ferocity. Blur and Pulp were more inventive, with a magpielike attitude toward the British songwriting heritage of the 1960s, '70s, and '80s, and the influences of the Kinks, David Bowie, Magazine, and Pink Floyd could be detected across their many albums.

The grunge sound

The US also had its own alternative-rock heyday in the 1990s, when the hard rock of grunge exploded. Seattle, Washington, was the apex of the grunge storm, being the city where Nirvana, Mudhoney, Soundgarden, and Pearl Jam were formed. The grunge sound mixed 1960s garage music, with the '70s hard rock of Black Sabbath and the no-nonsense attitude of punk. Nirvana was grunge's most infamous success story, becoming the world's biggest band in the early 1990s. The mighty production and powerful dynamics of their classic album *Nevermind* juxtaposed stripped-down verses with explosive guitar-laden choruses. It was a dynamic technique borrowed from the Pixies, a group that mixed surf guitar and Tex-Mex influences with noisy art-rock on the late 1980s albums *Surfer Rosa* and *Doolittle*.

Spearheaded by Nirvana, grunge usurped heavy metal's dominance of the American teenager's bedroom stereo. Suddenly the guitar solos and posturing of bands such as Guns 'N Roses seemed passé. Even long-lived alternative rock bands gained a share of the spotlight. Sonic Youth had been playing since the early 1980s, honing an experimental brand of rock that was inspired by the modern classical music of composer Glenn Branca as much as the primitive punk of the Stooges. Their unconventional guitar tunings and wall-of-noise sound found a champion in MTV and they gained a major label record deal for their breakthrough album *Goo* (1990). Alternative rock was no longer alternative. It was clear that rock music in the United States would never be the same again.

175 MILLION The number of records by Nirvana sold worldwide, a third of them in the United States.

College friends.
Dropping out of the University of Georgia to form R.E.M., Byrds-inspired guitarist Peter Buck (left) and singer Michael Stipe (second left) took the band from college radio to stadium concerts.

KEY WORKS

The Smiths "What Difference Does it Make?"
R.E.M. "It's the End of the World as We Know it"
Violent Femmes "Blister in the Sun"
Nirvana "Smells Like Teen Spirit"
Blur "Song 2"
Sonic Youth "100%"

AFTER

Once grunge had stolen heavy metal's throne in the United States, and Britpop had taken hold in the UK, alternative rock became mainstream.

INDIE ANTHEMS
Coldplay's album *A Rush of Blood To the Head* (2002) picked up R.E.M.'s baton, with **anthemic songs** perfect for grand **sing-alongs** by vast audiences at concerts. The bands Keane, Snow Patrol, and Mumford & Sons followed in their wake.

CHRIS MARTIN OF COLDPLAY

EMO'S YOUTH APPEAL
Grunge's teenage nephew—emotional hardcore, or **Emo**—kept the loud guitars and **anti-authoritarian spirit**, but brought glossy production and **self-obsessed** lyrics. Young bands such as My Chemical Romance, Jimmy Eat World, and Fall Out Boy provided millions of teenage listeners with just the right mix of angst, aggression, and sentimentality.

BEFORE

The 1940s to 1960s witnessed a golden age of musicals on Broadway and in London's West End, dominated by sophisticated, melodious shows.

VINTAGE CLASSICS

Rodgers and Hammerstein **« 282–283** released albums of original cast recordings or movie soundtracks of their musicals. *The Sound of Music, Oklahoma!,* and *South Pacific* were among the highest-selling records of their day.

ENCHANTED MELODIES

Every successful musical of the period featured crafted lyrics, memorable melodies, and fine harmonies. Individual songs from the musicals, such as "Some Enchanted Evening," from *South Pacific* (1949), also won widespread popularity.

SHEET MUSIC FROM "SOUTH PACIFIC"

Musical Revival

The influence of pop and rock invaded musical theater in the 1960s and '70s, transforming the genre and attracting new audiences. The search for new themes and musical innovation continued through the 21st century, culminating in the hip-hop hit *Hamilton*.

Throughout the modern era of musicals, old-school composers still flew the flag for traditional musical theater. The work of Jerry Herman, who wrote *Hello Dolly* (1964) and *La Cage aux Folles* (1983), exemplified an exuberant, high-kicking style whose heart belonged in another era, while the versatile John Kander and Fred Ebb wrote *Cabaret* (1966) and *Chicago* (1974) in German cabaret and hot jazz styles, respectively.

Musical hub

New York's Broadway has the highest concentration of commercial theatres in the world. Musicals commonly occupy more than half of the available Broadway theatres.

Rock and pop

In 1967, rock invaded Broadway and stayed. *Hair*, advertised as an "American Tribal Love-Rock Musical," broke the mold with Galt MacDermot's vibrant numbers reflecting the idealism of hippie counterculture. Songwriter Burt Bacharach's *Promises Promises* (1968) set the composer's lofty pop music into musical theater. Even the composer and lyricist Stephen Sondheim (see right) wove rock flavors into his 1970 musical *Company*.

It was *Jesus Christ Superstar* (1971) by British songwriting team Andrew Lloyd Webber and Tim Rice, however, that revolutionized musicals. Beginning life as a rock concept album, the score's grand themes, highly emotional tone, and lack of dialogue led *Superstar*, and similar shows, to be called "rock opera."

Another contributor in this style was the American Steven Schwartz, who wrote the similarly biblical *Godspell* (1971). More than 30 years later, Schwartz's witty pop score for *Wicked* (2003) helped make it one of the most successful musicals of modern times.

Musicals in the 1970s and '80s displayed a noticeable diversification of genres. *Grease* (1972), *The Rocky Horror Picture Show* (1974), and *Little Shop Of Horrors* (1982) harked back to vintage rock 'n' roll, while *The Wiz* (1974) and *Dreamgirls* (1981) featured soul-style scores. Marvin Hamlisch's score for the perennially popular *A Chorus Line* (1975) blended traditional Broadway swing ("One") with catchy pop songs ("What I Did For Love"), though Lloyd Webber/Rice's *Evita* (1976) was the smash of the era and its pop-aria style hit song "Don't Cry For Me Argentina" set the tone for the future.

The 1980s saw the rise of the European "pop opera" spectacle, as exemplified by Andrew Lloyd Webber's *Cats* (1981), *Starlight Express* (1984), and *Phantom of the Opera* (1986). These popular, long-running shows featured elaborate staging, dramatic story lines, and forceful scores with memorable melodic themes that sometimes became hit records.

French songwriting team Alain Boublil and Claude-Michel Schönberg developed their own highly intense pop opera style with *Les Misérables* (1985), which, even before it was made into an award-winning movie in 2013, became one of the most lucrative musicals of all time.

> "[Hamilton] is a story of **America then,** told by **America now.**"
>
> LIN-MANUEL MIRANDA

Jukebox musicals

Capitalizing on the public's taste for feel-good nostalgia and a catchy tune, the "musical revue" or "jukebox musical," threaded a story through an existing catalog of popular songs. These were sometimes biographical; *Buddy* (1989) tells the story of ill-starred rock 'n' roll singer-songwriter Buddy Holly, while

KEY WORKS

Stephen Sondheim *Company; Sweeney Todd*
John Kander and Fred Ebb *Chicago*
Andrew Lloyd Webber *Cats*
Jerry Herman *La Cage aux Folles*
Boublil and Schönberg *Les Miserables*
Steven Schwartz *Wicked*
Lin-Manuel Miranda *Hamilton*

Poster for the musical *Hair*

Featuring anti-war protest, a racially integrated cast, and rock music, *Hair* caused controversy by depicting drug-taking and nudity. Its 2009 Broadway revival confirmed the show as a vital, exciting musical.

COMPOSER AND LYRICIST (1930–2021)

STEPHEN SONDHEIM

Born in Manhattan, New York, Sondheim was the acclaimed lyricist of *West Side Story* (1957) and *Gypsy* (1962). As a composer, he was also responsible for some of musical theater's most admired (if not always the most successful) scores, including *Company* (1970), *A Little Night Music* (1973), *Sweeney Todd* (1977), and *Sunday in the Park with George* (1983).

For many, Sondheim represents the artistic conscience of musical theater—highly literate, profoundly musical, and provocatively creative, with little regard for wide instant commercial appeal or current trends. His blend of late romantic/early modern classical music may be an acquired taste, but his work continues to be revered and discovered by each new generation.

Jersey Boys (2005) charts the rise of 1960s vocal group The Four Seasons. Often the plots are fictional; *Mamma Mia* (1999) weaves a romantic tale around songs by Swedish pop group ABBA.

New audiences

In the aughts, a new audience that had grown up watching animated films on TV, iPads, and phones were eager to see those same shows on stage and sing along to the familiar tunes. Disney's take on Hans Christian Andersen's *The Snow Queen* started as the film *Frozen* (2013), before being turned into a musical and opening on Broadway in 2018 to critical acclaim.

Contemporary musical composers have continued to contribute to the musical theater repertoire, often finding young audiences along the way. *Legally Blonde* (2007) and *Hairspray* (2002) with their scores full of upbeat pop-rock songs packed theaters. Jonathan Larson's rock-oriented *Rent* (1995), based on Puccini's *La Bohème*, inspired a cult following before its mainstream success. The musicals of Jason Robert Brown, such as *Songs for a New World* (1995) and *Last Five Years* (2002), and David Yazbek's *The Full Monty* (2000) and *Dirty Rotten Scoundrels* (2005), display influences from Billy Joel to British band XTC. Most significant, in recent years, however, has been Lin-Manuel Miranda's *Hamilton* (2015). The first major hip-hop musical on Broadway, its race-reverse casting—depicting America's founding fathers as Latino, Black, and Asian—caused a sensation. In 2016, it won 11 of the 16 Tony Awards for which it was nominated and has gone on to become one of the most critically successful musicals of all time.

Founding Father center stage
Lin-Manuel Miranda wrote and starred in the title role of *Hamilton*, which used hip-hop to tell the story of America's founding fathers and won multiple awards.

AFTER

New ways are continually being found to capture new audiences and promote new ventures.

NEW THEMES
The topics and stories covered by musicals are becoming ever broader. No themes are seen as too serious, in spite of the genre's light image. *The Book of Mormon* (2011) concerns the ethics of imposing religion on others, *Fun Home* (2013) is about a dysfunctional home, in which the father commits suicide, and *Dear Evan Hansen* (2015) deals with depression.

$1.43 BILLION The amount generated by Broadway musicals in 2018–2019.

REMOTE VIEWING
During the worst of the COVID-19 pandemic in 2020–2021, theaters around the world were forced to close. Some shows were **streamed online**, including *Hamilton* on Disney+, allowing people to view them at much lower cost. Not seen as a threat to live musical theater, online streaming of blockbusters has become common and an important revenue stream for shows.

Japanese Popular Music

The popular music of Japan displays great diversity, from the stereotypical girl and boy bands brandishing Western instruments, to emotionally engaging music based on traditional Japanese music and the technologically innovative vocaloids.

Postwar Japan experienced an influx of Western popular music. Many youngsters tuned in to the US military radio Far East Network and listened to popular music from the United States and Europe. During the 1950s, following the rise of youth culture, Japanese popular music was termed *kayōkyoku* (ballad). The music, a mixture of Latin, jazz, and rock 'n' roll, with lyrics written in Japanese, was called *mūdo* (mood) *kayōkyoku*. Many singers gained experience performing at US military bases.

In 1961, Kyu Sakamoto released the single "Ue o muite arukō" ("Will look up while walking"), which became a hit and reached the top of the US Billboard Hot 100 chart in 1963 under the alternative name "Sukiyaki." Thereafter, domestic music grew in popularity, and in 1967, Japanese artists outnumbered foreign singers.

Koto
Originally used in traditional music, the 13-stringed *koto* is the national instrument of Japan. Despite the prominence of Western music, the *koto* has proved adaptable, featuring in hip-hop, jazz, and pop tracks.

BEFORE

Japanese music is multifaceted, with traditional, Western classical, and popular music living side by side.

WOMAN PLAYING A SHAMISEN

EDO PERIOD
The traditional music heard in Japan today—traditional theater music, *sankyoku* (chamber music), *min'yō* (folk songs), *shakuhachi* (flute), and *shamisen* (lute)—originated in the Edo period (1603–1868). This was a time of isolationism, unprecedented peace, economic growth, and popular enjoyment of the arts.

19TH-CENTURY WESTERNIZATION
In an effort to modernize Japan, the Meiji government decreed in 1871 that only Western music could be taught in schools—meaning that traditional music was widely unknown.

The soul of Japan

Thought to originate from the protest songs of early-20th-century Japan, *enka* is a popular music genre that—despite using Western instruments—is often described as being the soul of Japan. The music uses a pentatonic, or five-note, scale that is also traditionally used to compose children's songs. The lyrics deal mainly with broken hearts, lost dreams, lost love, and hardship. The glamorous singers perform with a highly expressive delivery, reflecting the drama in the songs. *Enka* is often shown on television spectaculars and perhaps gets more airtime than its position in the music charts might warrant. The songs speak to people who are at a reflective age and realize that things have not turned out quite as they had envisioned when they were young. *Enka* acts as a collective outlet for the Japanese to express their worries, anger, and sorrow.

Singular success
Singer Aki Yahsiro, here performing at a trade fair in 2005, started out as a jazz singer before finding success with *enka*. She was the first female *enka* artist to have seven top 10 singles in the chart.

Japanese idol

During the 1970s and '80s, *aidoru* (idol) singers began dominating the market. They signed contracts with large recording companies that trained the young singers in vocals and dancing. The budding stars were then heavily promoted via TV shows produced by the record label's own in-house TV production companies. Pink Ladies in the 1970s and Seiko Matsuda and Masahiko Kondō in the 1980s became prominent icons of *aidoru kayōkyoku*.

J-pop

Like its predecessors in *kayōkyoku*, J-pop is characterized by female singers in their teens or twenties accompanied by Western instruments. The transition from *kayōkyoku* to J-pop is not clearly defined, but one of the key features of J-pop is the stylized English pronunciation of Japanese words. In 1988, the commercial radio station J-Wave was established, and in 1990, Tower Records defined J-pop as all music owned by the Recording Industry Association of Japan (RIAJ), excluding nonmainstream music. An interesting characteristic of J-pop is that these idols are not supposed to be too far above the average person in singing talent or in looks—they could very well be the proverbial girl next door. This is a clever marketing ploy, selling the dream that anyone can become the next idol. If the singers were too good-looking or sang too well, it might put off potential fans. Designed to maintain this intimate relationship between J-pop idols and the audience, the idols are expected to attend handshaking ceremonies where fans come to shake hands with them before a concert, get-togethers where fans and idols play games together, public photo shoots in which idols pose for amateur photographers, and to mail correspondence with fans.

TECHNOLOGY

VOCALOID

Vocaloid began as voice-synthesizer software that enabled users to synthesize singing performances by typing in the melody and lyrics. A humanoid robot was set up to react to the vocaloids. Users were then able to create videos of their songs and share them online. This has led to vocaloids, such as Hatsune Miku (pictured below) and Megurine Luka, becoming virtual idols. Hatsune Miku was the first vocaloid to reach No. 1 in the charts. She performs live concerts projected on a screen and has been on world tours.

90 **PERCENT of the Japanese music market is domestic.**

1967 **The first year that Japanese domestic releases exceeded imports.**

Pop diversifies

J-pop has spawned a multitude of subgenres incorporating independent labels, rock, and highly stylized goth varieties. J-indie is the term used for all independent music that is not associated with the RIAJ. This group also comprises musicians hoping to make it into the mainstream. One such band from the 1990s that won a contract with a major record label was

Prolific performers
The Japanese all-girl pop group AKB48 performs at a charity concert in Tokyo, 2011. Membership of the group is fluid,and girls start as trainees who work their way up into teams until they graduate and move on.

AFTER

After decades of exporting hardware, Japan has shifted its focus to selling its unique pop culture to the world.

SOFT CULTURE
Today, Japan is a major producer and exporter of "soft culture," such as animé, manga, fashion, J-pop, TV dramas, and Hello Kitty. Through **Japan festivals** that include music, dance, and martial arts, and events such as manga-drawing contests, people around the world experience the soft culture of Japan.

GOING GLOBAL
J-pop became popular in neighboring countries from the 1990s. The sound, style, management, and popularity of J-pop has influenced the popular music of other Asian countries, leading to **K-pop (Korea)** **374–375 ››**, C-pop (China), and M-pop (Malaysia), which—together with J-pop—enjoy an increasingly large following outside Asia.

Judy and Mary. They mixed punk, rock, and pop in an innovative personal style. Japanese indie music has different regional flavors. The music of the area near the city of Osaka is characterized as noise music with drums, bass, and screaming guitars and singers, while the Tokyo area offers psychedelic music, free improvisation, and such trends as radical silence. Famous alternative musicians include Haino Keiji, a noise musician, and Sachiko M, an electronic musician who creates sounds of torture.

Pop phenomenon

The Japanese girl group AKB48, which holds the Guinness Record for the biggest pop band (86 members), has achieved a popularity that is a social and musical phenomenon in a class of its own. AKB48 holds a number of records, including for the most singles sold in Japan and for becoming the first all-girl group to sell over three million units, of their hit single "Teacher Teacher." This huge band is divided into three groups, which enables them to perform on a daily basis at their own theater in Akihabara in Tokyo while also performing on tour in other locations, making them more accessible to live audiences and fans than other J-pop bands.

All members are in their early teens to mid-twenties, and their performances are highly choreographed dance shows. Aspiring trainees are always present to replace members when they "graduate" due to age or personal choice. Members of the group have to abide by strict rules of behavior set by their management company, such as not dating. This helps preserve the sense of availability to their fans. A sister group, HKT48, has been created in the town of Fukuoka in southern Japan, and several associated groups have formed throughout Asia.

Although women have always been the face of Japanese popular music, it has been men who have controlled the industry that created the music. The past decades have seen changes led by such singers as Miki Imai and the band Shōnen Knife—an all-girl band who writes their own music.

"A **freedom** to **express myself**, that's what I believe **visual kei** is."

YOSHIKI, VISUAL KEI ARTIST, IN AN INTERVIEW IN *JAME WORLD* MAGAZINE, 2011

Performance art

Another movement within J-pop or rock is a performance style known as Visual Kei. The musicians are famous for their use of heavy makeup, elaborate hairstyles, and flamboyant costumes. Due in part to the makeup, musicians of Visual Kei are often linked with androgynous aesthetics, and some of the bands keep their sexual orientation secret. Although Visual Kei is often referred to as a subgenre of Japanese popular music, the music itself is related to J-pop, glam rock, heavy metal, and punk rock, and it is the performance aesthetics that characterize the genre. The groups X-Japan and Luna Sea are some of the pioneers of this style of music.

KEY WORKS

Kyu Sakamoto "Sukiyaki"
Seiko Matsuda "The Wind Is Autumn Color"
Hibari Misora "Like the Flow of the River"
Namie Amuro "Can You Celebrate?"
Ayumi Hamasaki "Fireworks"
Shonen Knife "Super Group"
AKB48 "Manatsu No Sounds Good"
Hikaru Utada "Goodbye Loneliness"

JAPANESE MUSICIANS

YOSHIDA BROTHERS

The Yoshida Brothers have been highly influential in the rise of interest in fusing Japanese musical instruments with pop music. They first rose to prominence with their debut album in 1999 and have changed the old-fashioned image of Japanese traditional music visually and musically and made it popular with young people. With dyed hair and traditional but unusually colorful costumes, the brothers have infused traditional instruments with fresh energy. They skilfully combine their virtuosic *tsugaru-jamisen* playing with rock and pop genres and have been featured in Nintendo commercials and the Disney album *Nightmare Revisited*.

Congolese collective
The Kasai Allstars play traditional instruments, distorting the sounds with amplifiers, and yet this modern music contains echoes of Franco Luambo and the greats of *soukous*.

BEFORE

African music draws on a global heritage reaching north to Israel and across the Atlantic to Latin America.

HARP OF DAVID
One of the most ancient African instruments still being played today is the Ethiopian **begena**, a ten-stringed lyre, also called the Harp of David. The Ethiopian King Menelik I is thought to have brought it to the region from Israel in around 950 BCE.

RUMBA
This fast-paced Cuban music has a percussive rhythm written in 2/2 or 4/4 time with a stress on the offbeat. **Latin Beats 276 ››** were brought to Latin America by enslaved Africans.

19TH-CENTURY ETHIOPIAN BEGENA PLAYER

East and Central African Music

Many different forms of cultural expression can be found in the music of East and Central Africa, but it was the infectious genre of *soukous* that took the world by storm. Before the Internet, local radio stations inspired new musical genres by playing music from across Africa.

In the 1960s, almost 50 African countries became independent. At the same time, musicians around the continent were creating exciting new musical forms that reflected this turning point in their history, blending traditional and modern, African and European. The 1970s and '80s saw African music, sometimes modified for non-African audiences, reaching the four corners of the globe.

The rhythm of Africa

Originating from the Congo region of Central Africa, *soukous* developed from Congolese rumba through the 1940s, '50s, and '60s and mirrors the long history of interaction between Latin America and Africa. Enslaved Africans brought their music with them to the New World, where they then created hybrid genres, including the rumba. When the rumba made its way back to the Congo, it was reworked to create *soukous*. Singer-songwriter Tabu Ley Rochereau (1940–2013) was the first person to transform traditional rumba into modern *soukous*.

The sound of *soukous* is all about its upbeat tempo and danceable groove: a distinctive duple-time rhythm (two beats in a bar). Instruments include electric guitar, bass guitar, African hand percussion, and Western brass. Usually singing in Lingala, one of the Congo's many languages, vocalists use harmonies, interwoven melodies, and improvisations. The songs feature distinct sections, the most prominent being the *seben*, a danceable extended guitar solo that forms the climax of the song. These long dance sequences in particular distinguish *soukous* from Congolese rumba.

In "Tu m'as déçu Chouchou" (1966), Docteur Nico (1935–1986) on slide guitar provides a masterclass in *soukous*. Franco Luambo (1938–1989), another great guitarist who recorded more than 1,000 songs during his career, was another leading light of the genre.

Docteur Nico
The great guitarist and *soukous* exponent Docteur Nico performed with several bands including Orchestre African Fiesta.

Ethiopian drum
The *kebero*, a double-headed drum from Ethiopia, comes in two sizes. Large ones are used in the Ethiopian Orthodox Church; small ones are used in secular settings.

Politics and music have been intertwined in the Democratic Republic of Congo since Le Grand Kallé (the stage name of Joseph Kabasele) wrote the "Indépéndance Cha Cha" to celebrate what was then the Belgian Congo's independence from Belgium in 1960. With catchy upbeat lyrics in Lingala and French, it caught the mood of the continent, becoming the first pan-African hit.

Other Congolese stars have also used music to voice their political opinions. In the haunting "La Glas a Sonné" (The Death Knell), written after the 1991 riots in Kinshasa, Tabu Ley Rochereau (1940–2013) cries out against his country's inequality and corruption to the rhythm of African drums and the tolling of a bell. After falling foul of President Mobutu Sese Seko, Rochereau went into exile, returning after the fall of Mobutu and entering politics himself.

In the 1970s, *soukous* was widely played as dance music in clubs and bars all across Africa, alongside Ghanaian highlife (see pp.366–367). By the 1980s, it had found commercial success outside Africa, particularly in France and the UK, with the flamboyant Papa Wemba (1949–2016) at the forefront, creating some records specifically for European audiences. His "Mandola" with its disco backing beats is a prime example.

Benga blast

Drawing on the folk songs and gospel traditions of the Luo people, *benga* originated in the western region of Kenya, and in particular its capital city, Nairobi, starting in the 1940s and taking off with gusto in the 1960s. It draws on many African musical forms, including *soukous* and Cuban dance music. Its sound is characterized by intricate electric guitar picking, weaving melodies, repetitive bass lines, and danceable, syncopated percussion. Recurring musical patterns and allusions are typical. The call-and-response between the soloist and the backup singers parallels the dialogue between the instruments, while the electric guitar imitates the *nyatiti*, the traditional lyre of Luo religious music.

Although *benga* is primarily secular today, its roots are in the gospel tradition and in praise song (words and music celebrating a person, often a ruler, or something from nature), and there is still a degree of overlap. It is not unusual for musicians to play *benga* music in a religious setting during the day and then perform it in a club or bar later that night.

Said to be the grandfather of *benga*, Daniel Owina Misiani (1940–2006) discovered and developed the style when he moved to Kenya from neighboring Tanzania in 1964. A prolific songwriter known for his witty and controversial lyrics, Misiani was jailed several times for his political and social commentary.

Although the heyday of *benga* was over by the late 1980s, Misiani and his band Shirati Jazz continued to release records, including 1989's album *Benga Blast*, and perform around the world. The *benga* beat goes on today: it has been an influential predecessor to other genres, such as Zimbabwe's *kanindo*, named after Phares Oluoch Kanindo, head of the record label that exported *benga*.

Ethiopian poet-musicians

The *azmari* poet-musicians make their living as storytellers in Ethiopia, a country that retains a vibrant oral tradition. They sing a mix of traditional repertoire handed down through the generations by word of mouth, and extemporized songs. Performing at weddings and banquets, *azmari* musicians are known for their wit—it can be biting if they feel they have been underpaid. The men play easily transportable instruments, such as the *masenqo*, a single-stringed fiddle, and lutes, while female singers also dance.

The *azmari* musical tradition started when people who had received musical training through the Ethiopian Orthodox Church began to sing secular songs. In their chantlike music, they criticized the Church and commented on worldly matters.

In Ethiopia, anything related to the arts is considered shameful, and the *azmaris* make up one of the lower social castes. Through music, they are able to explore vulgar topics that normally cannot be discussed in public, giving them an "invisible power" despite their lowly status. In addition, *azmaris* serve as social critics and can promote change.

> "**Congolese** music is the **mother** of **African music**, and has influenced lots of other African countries."
>
> PAPA WEMBA, CONGOLESE MUSICIAN (1949–2016)

The Nyatiti
Ayub Ogada (1956–2019) was the foremost modern exponent of the Luo lyre. His most famous composition is a resetting of a Luo folk song "Koth Biro."

KEY WORKS

Le Grand Kallé "Indépendance Cha Cha"
Tabu Ley Rochereau "Kelya"
Docteur Nico "Tu m'as décu Chouchou"
Zaiko Langa Langa "Ndonge"
Franco "Mario"
Mbilia Bel "Kelhia"
Fenta Bele and Alemayehu "Shemanena Fetaye"

AFTER

African musical traditions are adapting to changing surroundings and musical influences.

AFRO-ELECTRO HYBRIDS
The enterprising Congolese ensemble Konono No. 1, alongside Kasai Allstars, are at the forefront of a genre dubbed **Congotronics**. Traditional instruments **368–69 ››**, such as the *likembé* (a thumb piano), are amplified until they distort, accompanied by homemade percussion instruments.

AFRICAN SOUNDS OVERSEAS
While the *soukous* played abroad still uses traditional rhythms and melodies, it transforms these into a more modern and electronic style, as in the music of American-Kenyan band Extra Golden, whose style has been dubbed "Southern-fried benga" by one critic. Its members—two from Kenya and two from Louisiana—create an exuberant interplay of rock guitar and driving Kenyan percussion.

EXTRA GOLDEN

West and Southern African Music

The musical roots of West and Southern Africa go back centuries, but their dynamic sounds, which combine the traditional and modern, are often used to unite and mobilize people politically and culturally.

BEFORE

From 14th-century Mali to 20th-century Ghana, West Africa has rich musical traditions.

THE GRIOT TRADITION
The West African *griot* (troubadour) tradition dates back to the 14th-century Mali Empire, which stretched from Central to West Africa. The *griot* tradition is a legacy of the Mande culture's **strict caste system**, where only the *griot* families made music. *Griot* children learn the craft from their fathers.

HIGHLIFE
The good time dance music called highlife was virtually the national music of Ghana in the early days of political independence in the 1950s. Its name derived from its **refined initial style**—the social elite would dress up to listen to it played by dance orchestras.

DANCING TO HIGHLIFE, LAGOS, 1959

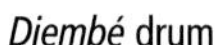

Djembé drum
A very versatile drum as it can produce three pitches, the *djembé* is played with bare hands. Initially from West Africa, and played only by *griots*, it is now one of Africa's most common instruments.

The musicians of West and Southern Africa often update traditional music by adding modern methods and Western instrumentation to create vibrant new sounds and forms.

Music of Mali and Senegal

The centuries-old *griot* (troubadour) tradition is still strong in Mali. The *griot's* most distinctive instrument is the *kora*—a cross between a harp and a lute, with 21 strings.

Modern virtuoso *kora* players have included Toumani Diabaté, Mory Kanté, Sekou Kouyaté, Sona Jobarteh, and Ballaké Sissoko. Tomani Diabaté has shown the *kora's* versatility on the world stage, collaborating with flamenco musicians. He has also demonstrated that the solo *kora* repertoire has a formal rigor and musical profundity.

The music of Malian guitarist Ali Farka Touré (1939–2006) made clear the links between West African music and American blues (see p.240–41). His sparse, modal guitar playing and nasal, parched voice often drew comparisons with John Lee Hooker, the American blues singer-songwriter. Farka Touré also played the *njarka* (a single-stringed fiddle) despite not coming from a *griot* family.

One of Mali's most famous singers is Salif Keita (1949–). Ostracized by his local community at an early age for being an albino (believed to be bad luck), he moved to Bamako, Mali's capital, in the late 1960s. Here, Keita joined the legendary Super Rail Band de Bamako, which played a form of jazzy, Cuban-influenced music made popular by Congolese bands, such as OK Jazz. He then joined another band, the Ambassadeurs, who added soul, funk, and even reggae influences to their mix. Keita's music headed in a pop-influenced direction during the 1980s, when he moved to Paris.

A very different type of West African music is associated with Senegal. *Mbalax* is a fusion of Senegalese drumming (*sabar*) with Western pop, soul, jazz, and some Latin American influences. Youssou N'Dour (1959–) started out singing *mbalax* music before becoming one of Africa's most famous singers thanks to his global hit "7 Seconds" with the Swedish singer Neneh Cherry in 1994.

Desert blues is a term that has been used for music made by Tuareg musicians—nomadic Berber tribesmen living in the Saharan regions of Mali, Niger, and Algeria. Bands such as Tinariwen, Tamasha, and Etran Finatawa have added electric guitar to the rolling percussion, single-stringed fiddle, and flute that accompanies Tuareg vocal music.

The beat goes on

Afrobeat first emerged in West Africa in the late 1960s, and its origins can largely be traced to the influence of

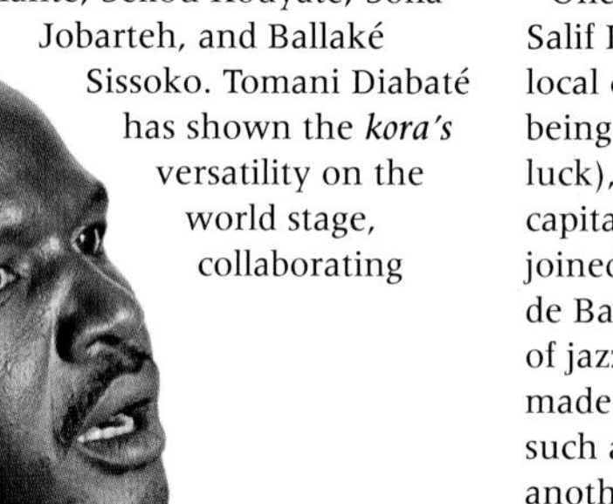

Story teller
In Burkina Faso, *griots* still ply their trade, singing and reciting family histories. Playing a traditional guitarlike instrument called *ngoni*, this man sings during the Muslim feast of Eid.

UNDERSTANDING MUSIC

MA'LUF

With strong ties to Islam and the Sufi tradition, *Ma'luf* was brought to the cities of Tunisia and Algeria by Muslims after the reconquest of Spain in 1492. The human voice is at the heart of this music, with the violin, double bass, flutes, and lyres echoing the vocal melodies. After Tunisia became independent from France in 1956, the government designated *Ma'luf* its national music, and the country is now viewed as the home of the music in its purest form. An annual festival of *Ma'luf* that attracts musicians from across the Maghreb and Spain is held in the town of Testour in northern Tunisia.

Fela Kuti (1938–1997) with the sound, style, and public image of this multi-talented artist defining the genre. In calling for Africans to reclaim and embrace the diversity of traditional African religions, the genre's spiritual connections were amplified by Kuti's powerful on- and off-stage persona.

Afrobeat needs to be seen in the context of protest and political strife in Africa, specifically against Western imperialism and cultural dominance. During this period, national figures promoting Pan-Africanism and unity had been largely subdued by governmental forces, and the fruits of liberation and decolonization once envisioned as being for all had been deferred. Well into the 1970s, collective feelings of frustration were channeled artistically into Afrobeat, with its performers acting not just as mere musicians but as legitimate political voices with a vision for change.

A new music

In its early incarnation, Afrobeat was seen as the successor of Ghanaian highlife (see left). However, while Afrobeat drew from earlier forms, it became an entirely new and unique style of music. Fela Kuti and his band created Afrobeat's signature three-guitar arrangement, in which two guitars would play rhythmic accompaniment and one would play solo. Call-and-response patterns are stylistic staples of the genre, both instrumentally and vocally. Sung in both Yoruba and Pidgin English, the lyrics speak to the cultural diversity of both Afrobeat artists and their audiences. Kuti's "Teacher Don't Teach Me Nonsense" (1986) puts all of these elements into play, from the arrangement, composition, and lyrics to the social commentary and cultural purpose.

Fela Kuti
Famous for his dramatic stage shows, his opposition to the oppressive Nigerian government, and his subversive lyrics, the legendary Fela Kuti saw himself as "playing deep African music."

The Nigerian style of Afrobeat is known for its synthesis of sounds, incorporating highlife, fuji, and Yoruba percussion with its hallmark "talking drums" (see pp. 368–369), blending them with the foreign influences of jazz and R&B and later soul and funk. Western instruments such as guitar, bass, saxophone, horns, and drum kits mesh with the complex West African rhythmic template. The Western instruments take the back seat to what is an indigenous African cultural expression. Since 2000, artists such as D'Banj, Fuse ODG, and WizKid have helped popularize afrobeats, a fusion of hip-hop, R&B, house, Afrobeat, and other styles, characterized by highly danceable rhythms.

> "Music **in Africa**... is always a vehicle for **social** connections, discussions, and **ideas.**"
>
> YOUSSOU N'DOUR, SENEGALESE SINGER-SONGWRITER AND POLITICIAN (1959–)

SINGER (1932–2008)

MIRIAM MAKEBA

Nicknamed "Mama Africa" and frequently called "the voice of Africa," Miriam Makeba developed a uniquely African take on jazz. She first came to fame in South Africa's jazz boom of the early 1950s, singing with the Skylarks, an all-female group that blended jazz and traditional African songs. She became the first Black South African musician to achieve global stardom and introduced the traditional songs of South Africa's Xhosa and Zulu peoples to Western audiences.

Southern Africa

The music of South Africa and Zimbabwe is almost inseparable from the political struggles of those countries to free themselves from colonial rule in Zimbabwe and apartheid in South Africa. More recently, music was used to challenge the authoritarian regime of Robert Mugabe in Zimbabwe.

Starting in the 1960s in South Africa, trumpeter Hugh Masekela and singer Miriam Makeba were well-known jazz pioneers in their home country before becoming global superstars. (They were married in 1964 but divorced two years later.) Both were outspoken critics of the apartheid regime. Makeba's records were banned, and she lived in exile in the US for more than 30 years. Masekela, who was also exiled, used his music to amplify the anti-apartheid message. He played his hit, "Mandela (Bring Him Back Home)" around the world to demand justice for Nelson Mandela, then a prisoner on Robben Island.

Ladysmith Black Mambazo, an all-male Zulu group led by Joseph Shabalala, was massively popular in the 1970s. They sang a style known as *isicathamiya,* which is unaccompanied by instruments and traditionally sung by men. When they sang on the American singer-songwriter Paul Simon's 1986 hit album *Graceland,* they achieved worldwide fame.

Liberation songs

In Zimbabwe, the politically charged lyrics of *chimurenga* (see p.333), which means "liberation," became the heartbeat of a national revolution against white minority rule. Thomas Mapfumo popularized *chimurenga* in the late 1970s, writing his lyrics in Shona, the language of most Black Zimbabweans. The government banned his music from the radio and briefly imprisoned him in 1977. Mapfumo's politicized music played a part in achieving Zimbabwe's independence in 1980.

Chimurenga continued to deliver a political message during the Mugabe years. "Mahororo Serewende" by the Dendera Resango Mbira Group, recorded in the Magaya village in 2005, illustrates the core features of *chimurenga,* with its distinctive use of the Shona *mbira* (thumb piano) and its polyrhythmic complexity. The genre allows artists a degree of economic security, although, as there is no established music industry in Zimbabwe, its musicians rely on live performances to get by.

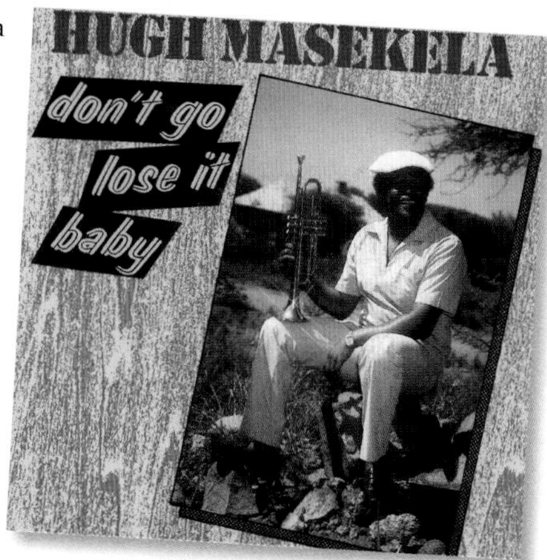

Hugh Masekela (1939–2018)
Masekela's trumpet riffs float over the top of this 1984 Afro-funk dance anthem with its driving beat. Masekela played in many different styles, from the pop jazz of his US hits, such as "Up Up and Away" (1967), to the blues jazz of "Soweto Blues."

KEY WORKS

- **Miriam Makeba** "Pata Pata"
- **Ali Farka Touré** "Biennal"
- **Fela Kuti** "Teacher Don't Teach Me Nonsense"
- **Neneh Cherry and Youssou N'Dour** "7 Seconds"
- **Sona Jobarteh** "Gambia"
- **Toumani Diabaté** "Elyne Road"

AFTER

African musical traditions are adapting to changing influences.

ELECTRO BEATS

Some rural South African musicians make electronic music associated with the **Shangaan** electro dance-music movement using speeded-up marimba samples or a synthesizer's marimba sound. Some tracks are as fast as 190 BPM.

BUBU MUSIC

In Sierra Leone, religious music played during the Muslim holy month of Ramadan has been incorporated into electronic dance music. Known as bubu, it carried a **message of peace** during the civil war of the 1990s.

1 MOROCCAN TRUMPET
Length approx. 5 ft (1.5 m)

2 SUDANESE WHISTLE
Length approx. 4 in (10 cm)

African Instruments

With 54 countries and over 2,100 spoken languages, it is not surprising that the African continent has a vast wealth of different instruments and styles of music.

1 **Moroccan trumpet** About 5 ft (1.5 m) in length, a *nfir* traditionally signals the end of Islam's holy month of Ramadan. 2 **Sudanese whistle** This instrument is carved out of gourd or nut. 3 **Balophon** Tuned wooden xylophones are associated with the noble *griot* (bardic) tradition of Guinea. 4 **Thumb piano** These "magnetophones" from Angola are played with the fingernails, producing a muted, metallic, and often buzzing sound. 5 **Agogo bell and wooden beater** The Yoruba people of Nigeria and Benin use the *agogo* in religious ceremonies. 6 **Shekere** Found in Nigeria, Ghana, and Guinea, this dried gourd is shaken and tapped to provide rhythmic vocal accompaniment. 7 **Southern African rattle** This percussion instrument from Zimbabwe is made from dried calabash plants. 8 **Kora** This 21-stringed harp has a beautiful, rippling sound. It is played in Guinea, Mali, the Gambia, and Burkina Faso. 9 **African stick zither** This bowed zither (pictured here unstrung) is an ancestor of the Brazilian *berimbau*. 10 **Valiha** Made from bamboo from the island of Madagascar, this stringed zither is plucked with the fingertips and is played either solo or in small ensembles. 11 **Raft zither** Found in Uganda, the raft zither's strings are stretched across a "raft" of bamboo and amplified by a metal gourd. 12 **Luo-style lyre** An eight-stringed lyre, this *nyatiti* is played by the Luo people in western Kenya. 13 **Beganna** This ancient *beganna* lyre (harp) is from Ethiopia and Eritrea and known as the Harp of David. 14 ***Rebāb*** An instrument of the nomadic Bedouin of North Africa, this is played like a tiny cello by a *sha'ir* (poet-singer). 15 **Congolese drum** Played standing up, with hands rather than sticks, the *ngoma* drum can be up to 4 ft (1.2 m) tall. 16 **Slit drum** Known as a *mondo* in West Africa, a *kolokolos* in Guinea, and a *mukoku* in the Congo, the slit drum is a fixed-note instrument, usually made of wood. 17 **Talking drum** Played throughout West Africa, the talking drum was used by *griots* (bards). Its hourglass shape allows it to be squeezed, making a sound mimicking human speech.

9 AFRICAN STICK ZITHER
Length 4 ft (1.2 m)

3 BALOPHON
Length approx. 3 ft 3 in (1 m)

4 THUMB PIANO
Length approx. 12 in (30 cm)

5 AGOGO BELL AND WOODEN BEATER
Length 10–11 in (25–28 cm)

6 SHEKERE
Diameter 8 in (20 cm)

7 SOUTHERN AFRICAN RATTLE
Length approx. 14 in (35 cm)

8 KORA
Height 4 ft (1.2 m)

10 VALIHA
Length approx. 3 ft 3 in (1 m)

11 RAFT ZITHER
Length 18 in (45 cm)

12 LUO-STYLE LYRE
Height 20 in (50 cm)

13 BEGANNA
Height 4 ft (1.2 m)

14 REBĀB
Height approx. 35 in (90 cm)

15 CONGOLESE DRUM
Height up to 4 ft (1.2 m)

16 SLIT DRUM
Length approx. 20 in (50 cm)

17 TALKING DRUM
Height 20–26 in (50–70 cm)

BEFORE

African American culture has a long tradition of poetry being recited over jazz, soul, or percussion.

SPOKEN-WORD POETRY
Poets such as Gil Scott Heron, The Last Poets, and The Watts Prophets, with their **critiques of American society** and pull-no-punches delivery, were direct influences on hip-hop.

ELECTRONIC FUNK
Hip-hop's drum-machine beats and **pumping bass lines** developed from the electronic funk of acts such as Afrika Bambaata, Man Parrish, and Jonzun Crew. Break dancing emerged as part of hip-hop culture.

BREAK DANCERS IN ACTION

Hip-Hop

Initially dismissed as a fad, hip-hop has existed for more than 40 years. It has progressed from being the soundtrack of America's inner-city districts into a global commercial force and is arguably the most influential musical genre today.

In the 1970s, the politically conscious soul music of Curtis Mayfield, Marvin Gaye, and James Brown became usurped by disco. Geared toward the dance floor rather than the streets, disco had a good-time ethos, and its lyrics were about dancing and having fun. For the working-class African American youth, there was no music that conveyed what life could be like in the poor and often violent neighborhoods in which they lived.

Psychedelic single
The dungaree-wearing American hip-hop trio De La Soul brought a sense of adventure to hip-hop in the late 1980s. The single "Eye Know" from the album *3 Feet High and Rising* sampled 1960s psychedelia.

The origins of hip-hop

When the young DJ Kool Herc (Clive Campbell) started playing hard funk records in the recreation room of his apartment building, he could not have foreseen that he was helping to create the foundations for a new form of music. In 1973, Herc was a teenager and all he was doing was making the crowd happy. He had figured out a way to extend the funkiest part of a song for as long as he could by using two copies of the same record, switching the sound from one turntable to another, and "rewinding" one while the other was playing. He called these sections "breaks." Herc began to hype up the crowd during the breaks with simple chants and exhortations. Although he soon assigned vocal duties to a more capable friend, Coke La Rock, he had essentially laid down the foundations of both hip-hop music and rapping.

Others were quick to copy him, and the craze spawned a chart hit in 1979 in the form of the Sugarhill Gang's "Rapper's Delight," based on Chic's disco hit "Good Times." Then the DJ Grandmaster Flash ushered in a more hard-hitting style with his global hit "The Message" in 1982. The song brought a social conscience to hip-hop in its frank discussion of poverty, drugs, and gangs. Around the same time, Melle Mel, an associate of Flash's, scored a hit with the song "White Lines," about cocaine dealing.

Hip-hop gets hard

Boasting about their rapping prowess became a staple theme for rappers (also known as MCs). In the mid-1980s, Run DMC, Ultramagnetic MCs, Cold Crush Brothers, and Eric B & Rakim specialized in dispensing combative, witty put-downs. The music that accompanied them made use of driving, stripped-down drum-machine beats, and recording devices known as samplers began to be used.

The precocious 17-year-old rapper LL Cool J put a new spin on rap by including soft, romantic raps, such as his worldwide hit "I Need Love," alongside the more usual self-aggrandizement. He was one of many acts signed to Def Jam Records, the biggest record label in hip-hop during the mid-1980s. The white rap trio Beastie Boys were also signed to the label, bringing hip-hop to mainstream white audiences.

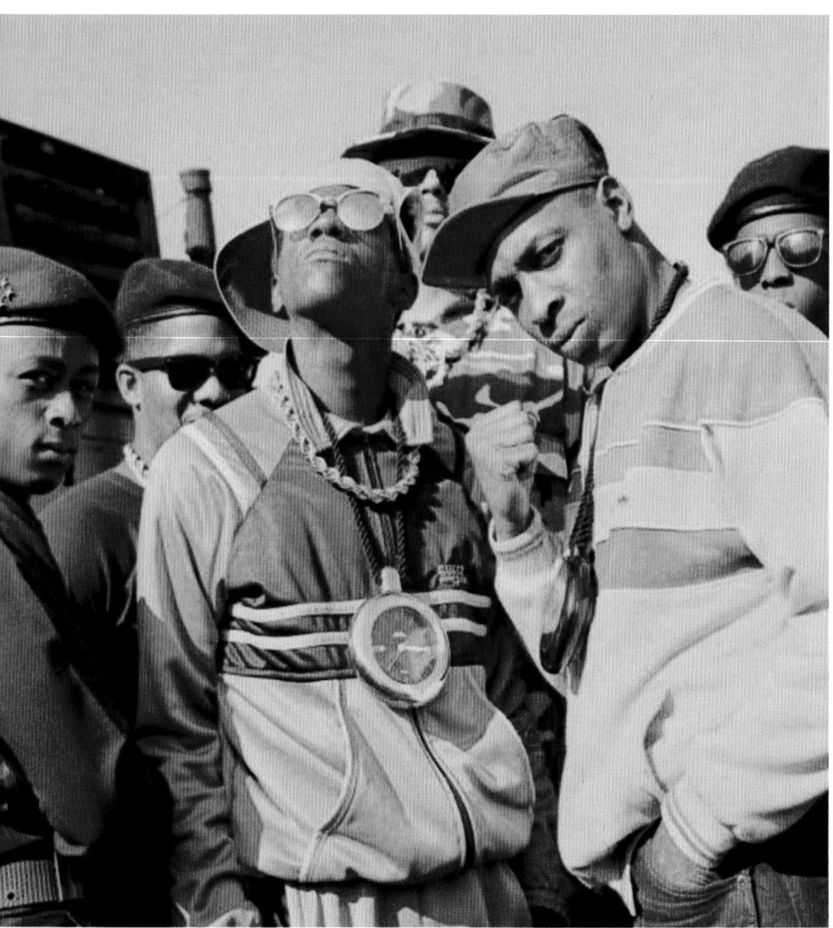

Public Enemy strikes a pose
Chuck D, Flavor Flav, Terminator X, Professor Griff, and his S1W group made up Public Enemy, a definitive hip-hop group of the 1980s and '90s. They rhymed about social problems and activism, and their musical techniques, including sampling, proved revolutionary.

TECHNOLOGY

DRUM MACHINE AND SAMPLER

Samplers such as the SP1200 Sampling Drum Machine transformed the sound of hip-hop during the late 1980s. They allowed a hip-hop producer to "sample," or record, a small excerpt of a track and then tweak, manipulate, cut, and loop it so that it repeated as a musical refrain. Hip-hop DJs were already using the records of other musicians to make music of their own, but samplers allowed producers to take the process to a more sophisticated level. Hip-hop producers such as The Bomb Squad, Ced-Gee, DJ Premier, and the RZA stacked up bits and pieces of other people's music to make entirely new, collagelike pieces of music.

Cardi B's online path to fame
One of the most recognizable voices in rap, Cardi B ascended to stardom via the internet platforms Instagram and Vine. Her single "WAP," with Megan Thee Stallion, has been streamed over a billion times.

Def Jam's most explosive act was Public Enemy, one of the most radically political groups in popular music history. Their two rappers, Chuck D and Flavor Flav, were to hip-hop what the Sex Pistols were to punk, delivering militant lyrics and comments on racial inequality in the US. Their producers, The Bomb Squad, backed them up with suitably cacophonous but eminently danceable music, using the sonic possibilities provided by samplers to turn the sounds of air-raid sirens and whistling kettles into musical instruments.

Gangsta rap, jazz cats, and indie

The militancy of Public Enemy had a counterpart in the gangsta rap that began to spring up in Los Angeles and elsewhere on America's West Coast. The rapper Ice T wrote raps about gang life, robbery, and "pimping."

The act that became synonymous with gangsta rap was N.W.A, short for "N*ggaz Wit Attitudes." Their debut album, *Straight Outta Compton*, released in 1988, caused a huge amount of controversy due to its forthright condemnation of the police. N.W.A featured the rappers Ice Cube, Eazy-E, and Dr. Dre among its number, all of whom would go on to achieve success in and out of the music industry.

By contrast, a different school of hip-hop based in New York was celebrating eccentricity, with a jazz-inspired aesthetic. De La Soul were the progenitors of this music. Their elliptical lyrics, eclectic music, and playful image made their debut album, *3 Feet High and Rising*, a classic. The early 1990s saw a boom in jazz-rap, with rappers and DJs in crews such as A Tribe Called Quest, Dream Warriors, Gang Starr, and Pete Rock & CL Smooth plundering their parents' record collections.

> **"Rap** is something **you do—hip-hop ... you live."**
>
> RAPPER KRS-ONE, 1986

Queen Latifah was initially part of De La Soul's wider circle, and they collaborated on her first album, 1991's *All Hail the Queen*, which brought a feminist angle to the genre. While better known as an actress, in the late 1980s, she was one of the most charismatic of New York's female rappers.

Rap also evolved in the 1990s. While Notorious B.I.G was flooding the charts with braggadocious singles, the Wu-Tang Clan brought hip-hop back to basics, with gritty raps inspired by kung-fu films and Buddhist philosophy. The South also started to make a name for itself, most notably through the Atlanta-duo Outkast, who blended soul and psychedelic influences, blurring the lines between what was sung and rapped.

New century, new sounds

Rappers were lauded as superstars in the late 1990s. The arrival of Jay-Z, Missy Elliott, and Eminem signaled the genre's global dominance. This was cemented in the new century by Drake and Kanye West, who brought introspection and a more urbane touch to rap. The Broadway show *Hamilton*, (see pp. 360–361) chronicled the life of a Founding Father through hip-hop.

The form continued to develop, and more intense subgenres such as trap and Chicago drill took hold. Rapper Chief Keef and his producer Young Chop pioneered the Chicago sound, juxtaposing nihilistic lyrics with incessant hi-hats and tuned Roland TR-808 kick patterns. The 21st century also saw increased representation for LGBTQIA+ rappers, with Mykki Blanco, Le1f, and Lil Nas X experiencing considerable success.

Kendrick Lamar
Hailing from Compton, South Central Los Angeles, Kendrick Lamar changed the game with his razor-sharp political commentary and storytelling capabilities. Here, he performs "King's Dead" at the 2018 Grammys.

RAPPER AND PRODUCER (1969–)

JAY-Z

Born Shawn Corey Carter in the Marcy Project estate in Brooklyn, New York, Jay-Z had a difficult family life and a misspent youth. His early experiences inspired the lyrics for his subsequent bestselling albums. From selling CDs out of his car as a teenager, he rose to become one of the most commercially successful rap artists and president of the label Def Jam in 2003. He continues to work with top rappers and has won more than 20 Grammy awards.

KEY WORKS

Grandmaster Flash & the Furious Five "The Message"
Public Enemy "Bring the Noise"
N.W.A "Straight Outta Compton"
Wu-Tang Clan "C.R.E.A.M."
Outkast "So Fresh, So Clean"
Kendrick Lamar "Alright"

AFTER

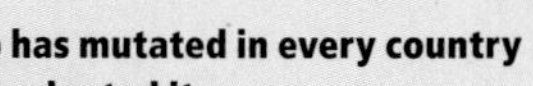

Hip-hop has mutated in every country that has adopted it.

BRITISH TAKE
In the UK, the genre known as grime has borrowed from computer-game music, cell phone ringtones, Jamaican dancehall, and UK garage to produce a savage electronic backdrop for rapid-fire rapping. Britain has also contributed to the sonics of drill, with rappers 67 and producer 808Melo at the forefront of these innovations.

LATIN AND GALLIC FLAVORS
In Latin America, **reggaeton**—a mish-mash of dancehall reggae and hip-hop with Spanish lyrics and Latin percussion—has made superstars of **Daddy Yankee** and **Ivy Queen**. The French language has also proved ideal for hip-hop, with rappers such as the suave MC Solaar, TTC, and Supreme NTM lending Gallic influences to hip-hop's beats.

BEFORE

Contemporary house and techno take their basic template from disco. Changes in music technology brought an electronic sound to the dance music that DJs spun in nightclubs.

ELECTRONIC DISCO

In the mid-1970s, synthesizers and drum machines were still primitive by modern standards. That did not stop Italian producer **Giorgio Moroder** from fashioning the electronic, six-minute disco track "I Feel Love" for soul singer **Donna Summer** « 354–355. Brian Eno correctly predicted that it would "change the sound of club music for the next 15 years."

LEE "SCRATCH" PERRY

PIONEERS

The machine-age synth pop of "Trans-Europe Express" by Germany's **Kraftwerk** was a big influence on the electro music of the early 1980s. The sonic alchemy of **Jamaican producers** King Tubby and Lee "Scratch" Perry was also foundational for later electronic experimentation.

Club Culture

Dance music exploded when nightclubbing became a lifestyle activity during the hedonistic mid-1970s and the DJ came to be seen as an artist. It continues to evolve in the 21st century, coming up with innovative subgenres at a bewildering rate.

There was no sudden point at which disco died and electro was born. In a process that would be seen time and again in genres of dance music, a new sound or style simply became a trend that, after enough DJs and music-makers caught on, ended up sounding unrecognizable to its previous incarnation. Electro was an abbreviation of "electronic funk" and was born in the Bronx, a predominantly African American area of New York City. It was one of the most significant styles of music of the past 50 years, in that it influenced hip-hop, house, and all the related music that branched off from them.

10,000 **The number of clubbers who can fit into Privilege, a nightclub on the Mediterranean island of Ibiza in Spain, known as the clubbing capital of the world.**

From electro to house

Afrika Bambaataa, a New York DJ, wrote and produced "Planet Rock" (1982), which was electro's founding anthem. It owed a debt to 1970s synthesizer pioneers such as Kraftwerk and Yellow Magic Orchestra (see pp. 336–337), borrowing riffs from both acts: white middle-class Germans and classically trained Japanese musicians were influences on a genre born out of urban African American communities.

Mantronix, Jonzun Crew, and Man Parrish all experimented in the drum-machine-led electro genre, in which proto-rap vocals would occasionally surface as encouragements to dance. Some of electro's pioneers went on to become house and techno DJs and producers, such as Detroit's Juan Atkins, who has recorded music under the names Cybotron, Model 500, and Channel One.

Chicago in the early 1980s has the best claim to being the birthplace of house. DJs there played eclectic mixes of late-1970s disco with electro and synth pop. Mr. Fingers was the leading

Rave parties
House music came to Europe in the late 1980s and led to all-night dances known as raves, often held in open fields or industrial spaces. Rave culture then went back to the United States, where it became hugely popular.

UNDERSTANDING MUSIC

HOUSE

House was a stripped-down form of dance music, using the new drum machines and synthesizers available in the 1980s, such as the Roland TB808's now iconic skeletal drum sounds. Wholly machine-generated, it dispensed with traditional song forms in favor of vocal snippets (often from older disco, soul, or gospel records) or repeated chants. Its most important elements are the drums and the bass; it is characterized by a relentless, on-the-beat, four-to-the-floor kick-drum. This was a legacy of disco (see pp.354–355)—but with house, the drums are in the foreground, taking the place of the vocal in significance.

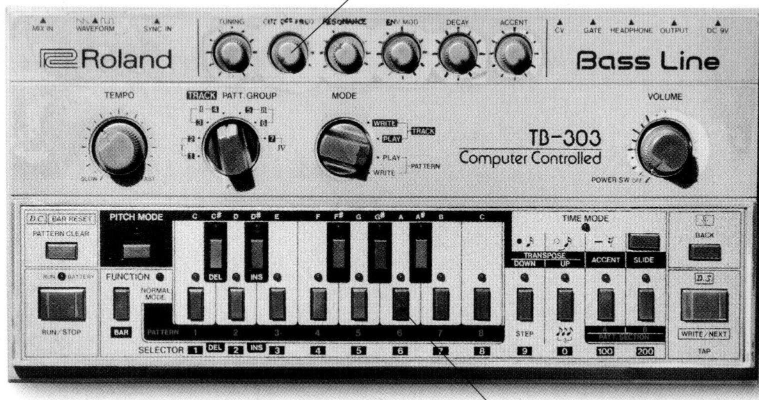

The mighty bass box
The Roland TB303 bass synthesizer was the defining noise of acid house, with a chattering electronic sound that was both comical and menacing, and with programmable filters for repetitive riffs.

light of what was known as deep house, the term used to describe house that incorporated soulful elements, such as snatches of R&B or gospel vocals. The ultra-minimal "Acid Tracks" (1987) by Phuture was particularly influential. Its use of the Roland TB303—the squelchy-sounding bass synthesizer—became the defining sound of acid house.

Detroit had its own spin-off version of house, known as Detroit techno. Juan Atkins, Derrick May, and Kevin Saunderson were the big three of Detroit techno, and May's "Strings of Life" (1987) became a global house anthem, marrying synthesized violin string arrangements to a soul vocal.

House style
One of the more long-lasting acts to graduate from the UK's 1980s rave scene, the Prodigy—led by producer Liam Howlett (above)—added a punk sensibility to their breakbeat-driven dance music.

House goes raving

House spread to Europe and became immensely popular in the UK from around 1987, adopted by acts such as Coldcut, Bomb the Bass, MARRS, and S'Express. They added pop elements and would often use collage techniques and sampling.

In continental Europe, subgenres such as Italo House (sometimes known as piano house) were popular in Mediterranean clubs, giving rise to massive dance hits such as Black Box's "Ride on Time." House in the UK grew harder and faster at clubs and raves, with acts adding sped-up breakbeats (sampled from hip-hop records) and pitch-shifted, chipmunk-sounding vocals—as typified by Altern8 and the Prodigy. DJs figure out the BPM (beats per minute) of tracks they play so as to easily mix them. While house tracks tended to be around 120 BPM, rave tunes sometimes took the speed up as far as 180 BPM.

This mutated into drum and bass in the early 1990s. A refinement of UK house style, it was characterized by high-speed drum programming, fast-paced MCing, and deep-dub reggae bass lines. The producer Roni Size (Ryan Williams) made drum and bass with a jazz-funk influence; Photek (aka Rupert Parkes) took the genre's drum-programming to extremes; and Goldie (Clifford Price) mixed in soul and ambient influences.

Clubs in Britain and the United States soon shook to the drums of big beat in the 1990s. It was inspired by funkier, danceable hip-hop tracks, with vocal hooks sampled from soul or rap songs and was typified by acts such as the Chemical Brothers and Fatboy Slim.

A lithe, funky form of house music known as garage became the new trend in the UK when drum and bass appeared to have stagnated in the late 1990s. Garage tracks by Grant Nelson, MJ Cole, and Wookie were dance-floor-friendly, taking inspiration from US house producer Todd Edwards.

Global beats and bass

The components of house music have been influential around the world. South Africa's dance music scene has offered reinventions throughout the late 20th and early 21st century. Kwaito—a slowed-down form of house combining four-to-the-floor drums with call-and-response passages—gained credence after the liberation of Nelson Mandela in 1990. Later manifestations include gqom, which took hold in Durban. Pioneered by DJ Lag, it features irregular kick patterns and macabre synth lines, providing dancers with an infectious energy.

At the opposite end of the tempo spectrum, dubstep is the most notable form to go global. Artists such as Benga, Hatcha, and Skream engineered the loping, bass-heavy form, but its heavy, reggae-influenced beats have transcended its South London roots. Los Angeles-based artist Skrillex has had massive success with dubstep, giving it a rock attitude that belies its origins as an introspective form of dance music.

Black Coffee
Durban-born DJ Black Coffee runs South African dance label Soulistic Music. In 2017, he was sampled by Canadian rapper Drake for the album *More Life*. Here, he plays at the Altitude Beach Club in Johannesburg.

AFTER

As their musical ambitions outstripped the dance floor, many house-inspired acts eventually left dance music behind. But they continued composing with the same electronic sounds.

DANCE GETS INTELLIGENT
The UK's record label WARP has become the most influential label in what is known as **electronica** (or **IDM**—intelligent dance music), with acts such as Autechre, Boards of Canada, Aphex Twin, and Squarepusher making genre-defying records that sometimes owe as much to **contemporary classical** and **ambient music** as to club culture. **Glitch music**, which creates wayward rhythms from the undesirable sounds made by a **CD skipping** or a **vinyl record popping**, became the trademark sound of the experimental label Mille Plateaux, as heard in the work of Pole and Oval.

KEY WORKS

Phuture "Acid Tracks"
Inner City "Big Fun"
A Guy Called Gerald "Voodoo Ray"
Roni Size "Brown Paper Bag"
The Prodigy "Out of Space"
Skream "Midnight Request Line"

BEFORE

Korea was once known as "The Land of the Morning Calm," but in fact it has always been a land alive with music and dancing.

AN ANCIENT TRADITION

Tomb paintings from the 4th century CE depict music and dance, and historical texts record legends about the invention of instruments and repertories. In Seoul, the **National Gugak Center**, a body that promotes traditional Korean performing arts, preserves court music dating back to the 15th century and beyond.

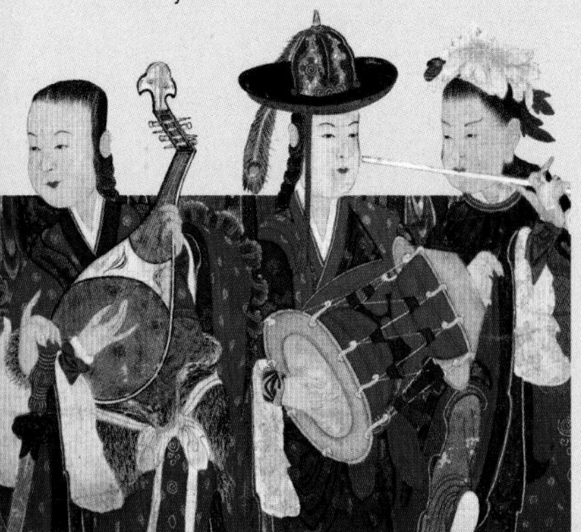

GUARDIAN DEITIES MAKE MUSIC

MUSIC OF THE LAND

Until recently, the countryside of South Korea resonated to the sound of percussion bands (*p'ungmul*) and folk songs (*minyo*), used for ritual, work, and entertainment. Professional musicians traveled the land performing *p'ansori*—a form of solo sung storytelling—and *sanjo*—hour-long pieces for a single melodic instrument accompanied by a drum.

WESTERN MUSIC

Missionaries introduced Western music to the country in the last quarter of the 19th century. Japanese occupation from 1910 suppressed its development, but after the Korean War of 1950–1953, musicians were able to perform more freely. Some composers studied music in Germany, including **Isang Yun** (1917–1995), who attended the influential avant-garde summer schools at Darmstadt « **266–267**.

The **Korean Wave**

In the early 1990s, the first ripples of something big began to spread in South Korea as new young artists put a colorful spin on Western styles like hip-hop and electro pop. Three decades later, this has built into a worldwide musical tsunami powered by the forces of social media.

It all started in March 1992, when the group Seo Taiji and Boys burst on to TV screens and into the charts with the dance song "I Know"—the first rap single ever broadcast in South Korea. Before then, the country's pop had been caught in a time warp, a place of uninspiring ballads influenced by Chinese and Japanese pop music.

Now, young Korean musicians began to look toward the United States, pulling in elements of hip-hop, techno, and other styles. To appease domestic censors, they avoided the references to sex and violence found in American rap but still appealed to a young audience by including issues such as education in their lyrics.

The girl-band production line
Members of Girls' Generation perform in August 2012 in Yeosu, South Korea. The group played their opening concert in 2007, seven years after the first member had joined S.M. Entertainment's grueling training system.

Creating a new sensation

The popular potential of this new pop was spotted by a musically astute South Korean entrepreneur. Lee Soo-man, an ambitious graduate of Seoul National University, former singer, and founder of the S.M. Entertainment company, created the country's first boy band, H.O.T. (High Five of Teenagers), in 1996. Their first album sold 1.5 million copies, and when the group disbanded seven years later, they had sold more than 10 million albums.

Soo-man soon saw the commercial possibilities of "idol bands" and repeated H.O.T.'s success by forming South Korea's first successful girl group, S.E.S. (named after its members, Sea, Eugene, and Shoo), in 1997. They were quickly followed by more girl bands, such as Fin K.L. (Fin Killing Liberty) and Baby V.O.X. (Baby Voice of Xpression), put together by other music companies who could see the potential.

By the end of the 1990s, South Korean groups had also built a massive fan base across the Far East, including Taiwan, Hong Kong, and China. And it was in China that the term *hallyu*, meaning "Korean wave," was coined in 1999 to describe the flow of South Korean film, music, and other popular culture across the region. By 2002, South Korea was the second-largest music market in Asia, with domestic sales of $300 million. Lee Soo-man's S.M. Entertainment was listed on the country's stock market and controlled around 70 stars.

> "Teenagers from Tokyo to Taipei **swoon** over … **boy band[s]**."
>
> *TIME MAGAZINE*, JULY 29, 2002

The wave builds

In 2002, 17-year-old BoA (Kwon Boa), another vocal and dance talent spotted by S.M., became the first South Korean solo artist to have both a debut single and a debut album reach No. 1 in Japan's charts. Like a number of other South Korean stars, she began to sing in English to gain international attention. After six No. 1 albums in the Japanese charts, and with fans throughout East and Southeast Asia, she launched in the United States in 2008, releasing an English-language album in 2009.

Another singing and dancing prodigy, Rain (Jung Ji-Hoon), proved just as popular. He was spotted by Park Jin-young, producer and head of the JYP Entertainment company, and his third album, *It's Raining* (2004), topped the charts around Asia. Two years later, he was performing to sell-out

Conquering the world
Fans cheer South Korean bands at the K-POP Festival in Hong Kong in 2012. Other concerts on the tour, organized by the South Korean *Music Bank* television show, took in Japan, France, Chile, and Indonesia.

KEY WORKS

BoA "Only One"
Super Junior "Sorry, Sorry"
Girls' Generation "The Boys"
Psy "Gangnam Style"
Big Bang "Fantastic Baby"
2NE1 "I Am the Best"

crowds at New York's Madison Square Garden, followed by acting roles in Hollywood films, such as *Speed Racer* (2008) *Ninja Assassin* (2009), and *The Prince* (2014).

Control through new media

All this growing global success was possible only under the strict regime of the South Korean recording companies. They created the stars by scouting young talent and training artists for up to six years, then binding them to tight contracts and controlling everything they produced. Some stars rebelled: three of S.M. Entertainment's boy band TVXQ successfully argued in a Seoul court in 2009 that their 13-year contract was too long.

Movies climb on board
Sympathy for Lady Vengeance (2005) is the third in director Park Chan-wook's trilogy of films exploring revenge, violence, and salvation. Cinema joined music as part of a broader South Korean cultural wave.

To build the global reach of the Korean Wave, music companies and the South Korean government worked closely together. Starting in 2010, the three biggest music organizations, JYP Entertainment, S.M. Entertainment, and YG Entertainment, established the labels JYP Nation, SM Town, and YG Family, expressly to make the most of social media. They tweeted news and new pictures of stars and ran contests in which foreign fans could master dance moves. Meanwhile, the Korean Ministry of Culture established "K-pop Academies" abroad to further South Korean culture by using the popularity of the country's pop music. The targeting of social media sites like Facebook and Twitter now meant that huge crowds greeted visiting artists, and demand for tickets was high.

4.259 BILLION The number of views of Psy's "Gangnam Style" video on YouTube by August 2021.

A one-man deluge

The South Korean music industry continued to grow, with sales of $900 million in just the first quarter of 2012. But it was one man, a song, and a video that would bring South Korean pop to the attention of the whole world.

In July 2012, Psy (Park Jae-sang), a 34-year-old singer, rapper, and dancer, released the single "Gangnam Style," named after a district of Seoul, his home city. It went straight to No. 1 in the South Korean charts, and once the video was uploaded to YouTube, it became an international sensation. On December 21, 2012, "Gangnam Style" became the first YouTube video to pass 1 billion views.

The wave rolls on

K-pop became mainstream in the West in 2017 when seven-piece boy band, BTS (Bangtang Boys) won Top Social Artist at the Billboard Music Awards. By 2019, they were opening *Good Morning America*'s summer concert, and in 2020, they performed at the New Year's Eve celebration in Times Square, New York, with a TV audience of over 10 million. The Korean Wave shows no signs of breaking yet.

AFTER

The influence of South Korean pop seems set to continue, thanks to heavy government investment.

CULTURAL AMBASSADORS
In 2018, K-pop stars performed in front of North Korean president Kim Jong-un as part of a **cultural delegation** to the North Korean capital, Pyongyang.

K-POP FIRST
The world's **first arena** built for K-pop is due to open in Seoul in 2024 with 20,000 seats inside, another 40,000 outdoors, as well as a digital metaverse for fans to watch virtually.

Jumping to the beat
The members of bestselling K-pop boy band BTS bring polished dance routines and high energy to their concerts.

New Voices in **Classical**

In the 1960s, a new minimalist style of composing began to spread across the United States and Europe. The slowly evolving music of repeating units was embraced by some but reviled by others. Now, composers have a choice of styles from utter simplicity to extreme complexity.

American composer Terry Riley took simplicity to a new level. His 1964 work, *In C*, has 53 musical modules, to be played any number of times, by any number of players. Riley's ideas profoundly influenced three fellow Americans—Steve Reich, Philip Glass, and John Adams—whose music became known as minimalism. Reich has stayed closest to the roots of minimalism, and his compositions demonstrate that repetition and variation can generate music of trancelike intensity. Pop musicians have often sampled his work. In moving away from minimalist austerity, Glass and Adams embraced a lusher harmonic world in which an insistent pulse is less prominent.

Glass has written 10 symphonies and two dozen operas, including a bio-opera about Walt Disney, *The Perfect American* (2013). Adams made his name with *Nixon in China* (1987), about the 1972 meeting between Richard Nixon and Mao Zedong, while *Doctor Atomic* (2005) concerned the Manhattan Project in 1945, as Robert Oppenheimer contemplated the morality of the atomic bomb.

UNDERSTANDING MUSIC

MINIMALISM

Minimalism emerged in America in the 1960s, offering simplicity, repetition, and a steady rhythm as alternatives to the complexities of many compositions of the time. Ignored by the classical establishment, Steve Reich and Philip Glass formed their own ensembles. Today, orchestras queue up to perform their work. The basic constituents remain the same, yet, while early minimalist compositions retain their raw power, stylistic possibilities have expanded, not least technologically.

Britain after Britten

Minimalism soon made its mark in Europe. The first person to apply the term "minimalism" to music may have been Michael Nyman, who converted to the cause in the 1960s after hearing Reich's music on the radio. Nyman is best known for the scores he wrote for films by Peter Greenaway, including *The Draughtsman's Contract* (1982).

Minimalism's static harmonies also played a part in John Tavener's work. Taverner composed to express his Christian faith so was labeled, often dismissively, a "Holy minimalist." His music aspired to the timelessness of religious icons, as exemplified in his eight-hour "all-night vigil "*The Veil of the Temple* (2002).

Musical module to be repeated. The same score can be used for any instrument

Phrases are numbered and should be played in order

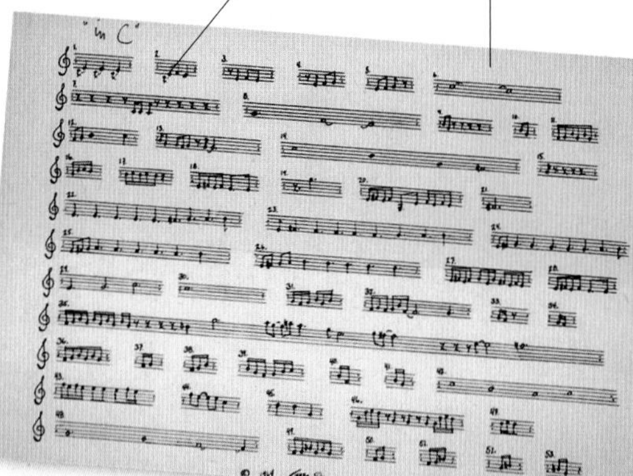

Keeping Score

Terry Riley's 1964 work, *In C*, may last just a few minutes or several hours, according to the whim of the musicians. The entire score fits on to one single page.

However, many British composers rejected minimalism, including Harrison Birtwistle, who called it "simple-minded." His own work is complex, layered, and abrasive, and the listener senses ancient, often violent, rituals unfolding through music, as in his orchestral masterpiece *Earth Dances* (1986).

The first operas of both Mark Anthony Turnage and Thomas Adès caused a furore. Turnage's opera *Greek* (1988) depicted recession-ravaged London while Adès's *Powder Her Face* (1995) relived the scandal of the 1963 divorce trial of the Duchess of Argyll. Turnage integrated jazz into *Blood on the Floor* (1994), written for improvising soloists and orchestra, while Adès found inspiration in pop for *Cardiac Arrest* (1995), an arrangement of a song by the British group Madness. More recently, composers such as Errolyn Wallen and Anna Meredith have blurred the boundaries between popular and classical music in their careers as well as their compositions.

Northern lights

In Finland, the composers Esa-Pekka Salonen, Kaija Saariaho, and Magnus Lindberg formed the "Ears Open" Society to explore avant-garde music. They each developed distinctive styles. Salonen's music is effervescent and demands virtuosity, while Saariaho's work is contemplative. She shows sensitivity to the voice: her operas include *L'Amour de loin* (Love from Afar) in 2000, based on the life of a 12th-century Provençal poet. Lindberg's early works, such as Kraft (1985), embody his statement that "Only the extreme is

"**I'll** be **dead** ...before the word **minimal** is **dead....**"

STEVE REICH, AMERICAN MINIMALIST COMPOSER, 1995

East meets West

Seen here taking up the baton, the Chinese-American composer Tan Dun brings ancient Asian traditions into fruitful collision with modern Western idioms in his works, such as *Ghost Opera* (1994).

KEY WORKS

Arvo Pärt *Tabula Rasa*
Harrison Birtwistle *Earth Dances*
Steve Reich *Clapping Music*; *Different Trains*
John Adams Chamber Symphony
Tan Dun *Ghost Opera*
Magnus Lindberg Violin Concerto

BEFORE

Dating as far back as medieval plainsong, repetition has always been central to Western musical traditions.

EXPERIMENTS WITH REPETITION

In 1893, **Erik Satie « 204–205** wrote a piece called *Vexations*, in which a simple theme is played 840 times. The work's first complete performance was organized in 1963 by **John Cage « 266–267**, whose own 1944 work *Four Walls*, using only the piano's white keys, plays with silence and repetition.

NEW INFLUENCES

American composer **La Monte Young** experimented with repetition. He studied with **Karlheinz Stockhausen « 270–271** in the 1950s, but his style changed after he heard music by Cage and **Indian music « 340–341**. Young's 1960 work, *Composition 1960 #7*, consists of two notes, "to be held for a very long time."

Atomic opera
Gerald Finley (center) sings the role of the nuclear physicist J. Robert Oppenheimer in John Adams's opera *Doctor Atomic*, staged by Penny Woolcock at the English National Opera in London in 2009.

interesting." He composed with the aid of a computer, creating complex, dense harmonies in his 2006 Violin Concerto.

Estonian classical music survived the Soviet era, although the country's most celebrated composer, Arvo Pärt, left in 1980. His early style was atonal, but in the 1970s, he began to compose music of slow, ecstatic melancholy like Tavener's for which he created the term *tintinnabuli* (Latin for bells), to denote its radiant simplicity. Works such as *Tabula Rasa* (1977), for two violins, "prepared" piano (see p.267), and orchestra, won Pärt a global audience.

COMPOSER (1936–)

STEVE REICH

Steve Reich was born in New York City. His early work included pieces manipulating tape-recorded speech or song to create overlapping rhythms and repetition.

A visit to Africa in the 1970s exerted an enormous influence, heard in *Clapping Music* (1972), in which two pairs of hands beat out overlapping patterns, while in more elaborate works, such as *Different Trains* (1988), Reich deploys prerecorded speech to generate musical phrases for his players. Using the basic building blocks of minimalism, Reich has constructed a richly varied body of work.

New millennium modernism

American Elliott Carter began composing in the 1930s and completed his last work weeks before his death in 2012, at age 103. His music could be dense, but had a lyricism that became more prominent later in his life.

The New York–based composers who make up Bang on a Can—Michael Gordon, David Lang, and Julia Wolfe—fuse minimalism with a raucous, percussive idiom that has been called "postindustrial." New York is also home to Tan Dun, who, following the pioneering work of the Japanese composer Toru Takemitsu, brings together ancient Chinese ritual and the contemporary avant-garde.

1,000 **The number of complaints the BBC received after broadcasting Birtwistle's *Panic* at the Last Night of the Proms in 1995.**

24 **The number of new works by Elliott Carter premiered after his 100th birthday.**

AFTER

Recent developments in who makes music and how it is made have disrupted some of the hide-bound traditions in classical music.

DIVERSE VOICES

Since the 1960s, women and musicians from a wide range of ethnicities have taken their rightful places in all areas of performance and composition. In addition, the Paraorchestra, based in the city of Bristol, in the UK, has demonstrated that physical disability is no obstruction to making music.

3-D FILM AND PRERECORDED MUSIC

In 2013, Michael van der Aa's *The Sunken Garden* hinted at one way in which opera might develop, with 3-D film interacting with prerecorded sound, and live singers. Orchestras will acquire new techniques and new instruments to cope with the changes.

Digital Revolution

The launch of the MP3 digital format in 1993 revolutionized the music business worldwide. By compressing songs and albums into tiny files, MP3 enabled people to store and exchange music physically and online through file-sharing applications.

Before the advent of MP3 audio files in the 1990s, music was recorded first on to acrylic and vinyl discs (records) and later onto cassette tapes and compact discs (CDs). The sound quality of records and tapes was often poor, especially when tapes were copied. CDs provided good quality digital sound and were durable, but, like their predecessors, they were expensive to produce.

In 1993, a digital audio format known as the MP3 was launched. This compressed songs and albums into very small digital files that could be downloaded to MP3 players. One of the benefits for the consumer (but a disadvantage for the record labels) is the ease with which MP3 files can be shared. They can be stored on a device, downloaded onto a recordable CD or memory stick, and quickly sent to another person over the internet.

The dedicated file-sharing service Napster, launched in 1999, made the process even easier by providing a central server that allowed its users to share, search for, and download MP3 music files. It became popular across the globe as somewhere to access huge catalogs of songs for free, including rare versions of recordings and, in some cases, unpublished demos.

It did not take long for music producers to find out that their artists' material was being unlawfully shared. In 2000, the American heavy metal band Metallica discovered that a demo of their then-unreleased song "I Disappear" was being played on the radio after someone shared it on Napster, where the band's entire back catalog could also be found.

Metallica, Dr. Dre, and Madonna sued Napster for copyright infringement, and the company was forced to close in 2001. By this time, the app had more than 20 million active users.

The year Napster closed, Apple launched iTunes. Aided by the spread of broadband internet through the aughts, this online music store enabled people to buy the tracks they wanted legally and download them to Apple's iconic iPods (designed to complement iTunes), computers, or recordable CDs.

Social media

The rise of social networking sites gave musicians unprecedented opportunities to connect with their audience. The UK's Lily Allen found fame directly as a result of Myspace, which launched in 2003 and quickly attracted young wannabe musicians looking to publicize their work. Although Allen already had a record deal, it was not until she began posting demos of her bubbly ska-influenced pop on Myspace in 2005, attracting tens of thousands of "friends," that she acquired a significant fan base.

Allen also achieved notoriety as a diarist, posting frank and informal comments about celebrities such as Amy Winehouse and Katy Perry on her account, much like any other teenager might. She therefore had a large audience when her debut album, *Alright, Still,* was officially released in 2006. In similar fashion, when the English indie rock band Arctic Monkeys had a huge British hit with their single "I Bet You Look Good on the Dancefloor" in 2005, they appeared to have come from nowhere, but they had also built up a considerable online presence. In 2003, the band had recorded 17 tracks as demos to sell at concerts, which were immediately shared online by fans, as an album under the name *Beneath the Boardwalk.* Effectively, the band's followers had released an album for them.

Building connections

The internet also enabled musicians around the world to connect with each other. The launch of SoundCloud, a Swedish audio distribution platform, in 2007, allowed musicians to collaborate and share knowledge; later, it became a music distributor.

SoundCloud still provides a platform where emerging artists can upload new tracks. American rapper Bryson Tiller released his debut single, "Don't," on SoundCloud in 2014. Commercially released in 2015, it went on to make the top 13 in that year's Billboard Top 100. Tiller continues to upload songs to his SoundCloud page and has received more than 115 million plays. Similarly, fellow American rapper Post Malone, one of SoundCloud's most successful artists of 2015, received over a million plays for his debut track "White Iverson." The song's video has obtained more than 939 million views on YouTube.

YouTube generation

In 2005, three American entrepreneurs launched the phenomenally successful website YouTube for sharing and watching videos. Now attracting up to two billion visitors each month, it massively increases exposure for new bands, though it also leads to copyright breaches. The site has proved to be a career-making vehicle for some surprising acts. "Gangnam Style" (see pp.374–75), for example, became the first YouTube video to top one billion views, thanks to the comedic sight of South Korean rapper Psy doing an absurd horse-inspired dance.

In building up advance publicity

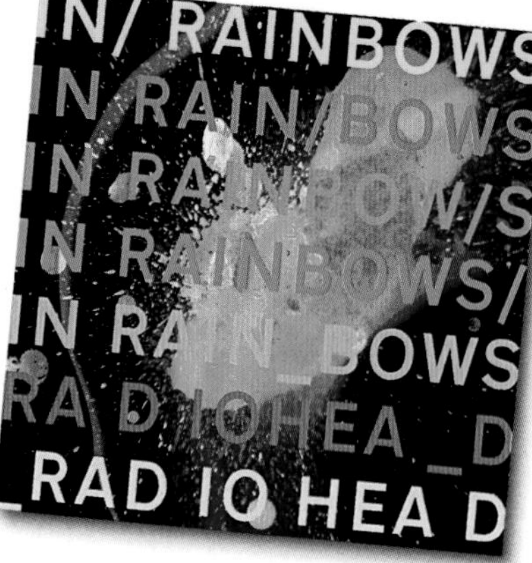

Pay-what-you-want
In 2007, the band Radiohead released the album *In Rainbows* in a pay-what-you-want download format. Only around one-third of people who downloaded the album chose to pay nothing—$8 was the average price.

Online fan base
The Arctic Monkeys won thousands of fans on the social networking site Myspace. Here, lead singer Alex Turner and drummer Matthew Helders perform at the 2012 Orion Music Festival in Detroit.

BEFORE

The invention of the compact disc (CD) in 1982 transformed the audio quality of music.

DIGITAL FORERUNNER

The CD—a 4.7 in (12 cm) diameter plastic disc holding digital data written on to it with a laser—was celebrated for its purity of sound and durability. Gone were the pops and crackles of vinyl, not to mention the slow degradation of sound quality of cassette tapes.

The CD quickly moved beyond the initial endorsement of classical music audiences, and in 1985 *Brothers in Arms*, by the British rock group **Dire Straits**, became the first CD album to sell one million copies. The format brought the record industry healthy profits as consumers began not only to buy new music but also to renew their old vinyl record and tape collections in CD form. Initially, CDs could not record music; the CD-R (Compact Disc Recordable), became affordable in the late 1990s.

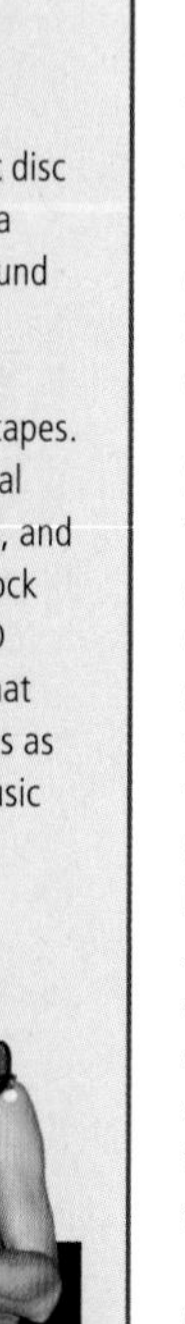

MARK KNOPFLER

TECHNOLOGY

BLUETOOTH

Music is increasingly played using Bluetooth, which sends and receives radio waves across short distances. Bluetooth earbuds and earphones connect wirelessly to songs stored on or streamed by a Bluetooth-activated smartphone, allowing music to be played straight into the listener's ear, without snagging wires.

Bluetooth technology and the ever-increasing storage capacity of smartphones also allows users to play streamed or downloaded music through speakers or a car's stereo system. The sound capacity is enough to fill a home or even a music venue.

for their 2013 album, *Random Access Memories*, the French electro duo Daft Punk used every trick in the digital marketing book, letting the public do the hard work for them. They screened a teaser advertisement for their new star-studded release, which featured Nile Rodgers of disco kings Chic (see pp.354–355) and rapper Pharrell Williams of N.E.R.D., at the huge Coachella music festival (see pp.344–345) in California. It also aired during the break on the NBC TV show *Saturday Night Live*. The ads were immediately posted on YouTube by fans, and musicians uploaded cover versions of the Daft Punk single "Get Lucky" before it was even released.

Streaming

Broadband was a significant enabler for the music business. Widely available in the US and UK from 2007–2008, it enabled consumers to download video or music files much more easily. Each new generation of broadband—2G, 3G, 4G, and 5G—brought faster connection speeds, allowing people to stream content directly from the internet instead of downloading it to an MP3 player, a memory stick, or a computer. The music-streaming service Spotify, launched in 2008, was the first to achieve a successful revenue model for this—users can either hear songs interspersed with advertising for free or pay a monthly subscription to listen to their choice of over 70 million songs without being interrupted by ads. More than 381 million people use Spotify each month, including 172 million paying subscribers. Streaming is now the fastest growing sector of the music industry. In 2020, it accounted for more than 60 percent of all music revenue.

18.5 PERCENT The increase in paid subscriptions to music streaming services in 2020.

Remote collaboration

Forced to collaborate remotely during the worst months of the COVID-19 pandemic in 2020–2022, many musicians used apps such as Zoom, Microsoft Teams, and FaceTime to create and record songs. Time lag can be a significant issue for recording songs, but with persistence, and a strong Wi-Fi connection, remote collaboration has become a viable alternative to being in the same room. Alongside virtual live collaboration, musicians are using the Cloud to upload parts of a track so that fellow band members can develop and add to it in turn. There are also apps that allow users to send incomplete songs to musicians who can provide the missing parts. These virtual production services can deliver professional sounds, albeit at a high cost.

Runaway success
Drake's phenomenal output, soundscape-like albums, and knack for promoting his work helped him to become the most-streamed artist of the 2010s, at over 28 billion streams.

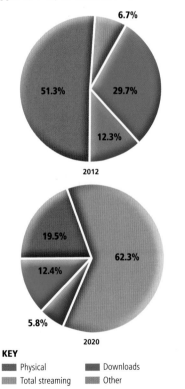

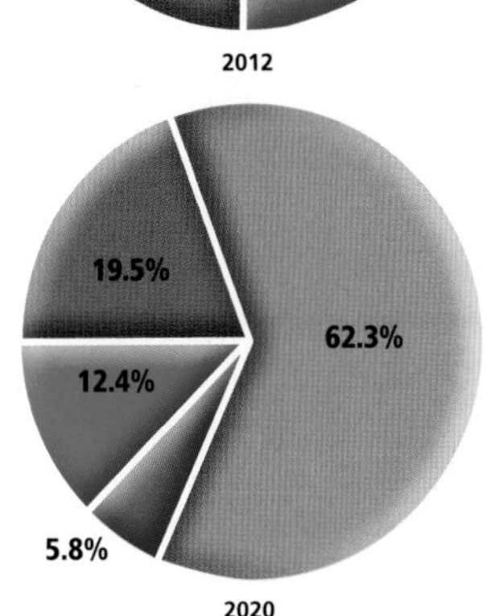

Watching the sales
These two pie charts show the global growth of digital sales, and the decline in sales of CDs in recent years. This steady change in the public's buying habits is contributing to the closure of record stores in many countries.

STREAMING STAR (2001–)

BILLIE EILISH

Born to musical parents in Los Angeles California, American singer-songwriter Billie Eilish started to write songs at the age of 11. In November 2015, she uploaded her first single, "Ocean Eyes," to the streaming platform SoundCloud. The song became a surprise hit and Eilish was signed by the label Interscope Records. By 2021, "Ocean Eyes" had been streamed over 200 million times. In 2020, she released the theme song for the 2021 James Bond film *No Time to Die*—the youngest-ever musician to write and sing a Bond soundtrack.

KEY WORKS

Ed Sheeran "Shape of You"
Luis Fonsi "Despacito"
The Weeknd "Blinding Lights"
Drake "God's Plan"
Dua Lipa "Don't Start Now"
Justin Bieber "Sorry"
Lewis Capaldi "Someone You Loved"

AFTER

Digital music costs consumers much less than records, cassettes, or CDS. The music industry therefore needs additional revenue streams.

LIVE RESURGENCE
One of the ways artists can increase their income is through doing more **live tours and festivals**. PwC Global Entertainment and Media estimates that live music is worth $31 billion worldwide.

VINYL LOVERS
Record companies have tapped into the nostalgia for the old-style sound of **vinyl records.** In 2020, vinyl accounted for one in five album sales, according to the British Phonographic Industry.

Holton

REFERENCE

This section contains a wealth of information about key musical terms, instruments, and genres and looks at the careers of some of the most important artists and composers.

« Sousaphone made in Wisconsin, 1929.

Glossary

Within an entry, terms that are defined elsewhere in the glossary appear in **bold**.

Air (Ayre) A simple tune written for voice or an instrument. The form flourished in England throughout the 16th and 17th centuries, with composers such as John Dowland writing for solo voice with lute accompaniment. The term also applies more broadly to folk songs and ballads.

Alto The highest of the male voices. The lowest of the female voices. Prefix to an instrument that is lower in **pitch** and darker in **tone** than a standard instrument – for example, alto clarinet.

Aria Literally "air" (Italian). A vocal piece for one or more voices in an **opera** or **oratorio**; more formally organized than a song. Arias written in the 17th and 18th centuries usually take the form of **da capo** arias, with a three-part structure, the third part being a reiteration of the first.

Arpeggio Literally "like harp" (Italian). A **chord** in which the notes are spread, or played, separately, either from top to bottom or vice versa.

Articulation The technique used by a musician to affect the length a note is sounded for, or the transition between notes. For example, a note may be stopped abruptly (**staccato**), or slurred smoothly into the following note (legato).

Ballet Dance form in which a story is told through the unification of music and dance. Originated in the French court of the 16th century. Used by Lully as an interlude in his **operas**, then evolved into hybrid opera-ballet. Later became an independent art form, dominated by the French until the emergence of Tchaikovsky. Since the end of the 19th century, many composers have written for ballet, notably Prokofiev and Stravinsky.

BAR

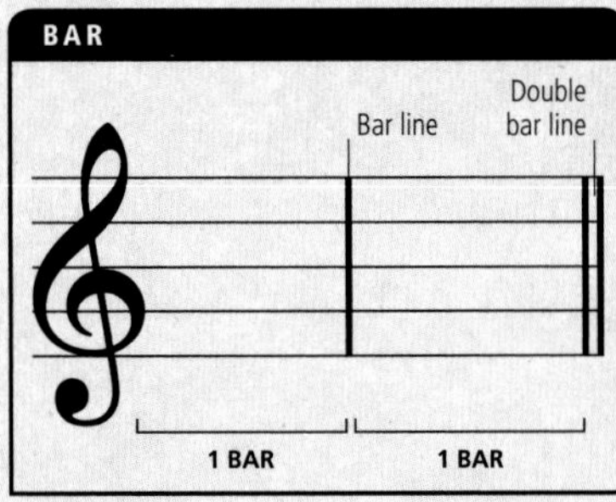

Bar ▲ A bar, also called a "measure," is a segment of time containing a fixed number of beats, each of which carries a particular **note value**. Each bar, or measure, satisfies the specified **time signature**, so a piece of music written in 4/4 time has 4 quarter note beats per bar. Bars are marked by vertical lines known as bar lines that mark the boundary between one bar and the next. A double bar line consists of two single bar lines drawn close together. It separates two sections within a piece of music and, when the second line is thicker, marks the end of the piece.

Baritone The male voice between **tenor** and **bass**, or an instrument sounding within this **range**.

Baroque Music composed between 1600 and 1750, spanning the period from Monteverdi and Gabrielli to Bach and Handel. The period before **Classical**.

Bass The lowest of the male voices. The lowest part of a **chord** or piece of music. The lowest of an instrumental family, such as bass clarinet.

Basso continuo **Harmonic**, quasi-improvisatory accompaniment extensively used in the **Baroque** period. Usually in the form of a harpsichord or organ and bass viol or cello, it was sometimes played on other instruments.

Bel canto Literally "beautiful song" (Italian). An 18th- and early-19th-century school of singing characterized by a concentration on beauty of **tone**, virtuosic agility, and breath control. Bellini, Rossini, and Donizetti are the main bel canto composers.

Bitonal Music that uses two distinct **keys** at the same time. Employed by composers such as Stravinsky in the first half of the 20th century.

Boogaloo A fusion of Latin **mambo** and African-American rhythm and blues music, and accompanying dance, that originated in Cuba but was popular in the United States in the 1960s.

Break A short, usually improvised passage in a piece of music—literally a break away from the melody. In jazz music, a soloist usually performs a break without the backing of the rhythm section. In popular music, breaks are usually instrumental, or can be purely percussive.

Bridge A passage in which there is a transition from one part of a melody to another.

Broken chord A **chord** in which the notes are played successively like in an **arpeggio**.

Broken time In jazz music, improvised playing without an obvious beat; an irregular form of **syncopation**.

Cadence The closing sequence of a musical **phrase** or composition. The "perfect cadence" gives a sense of completion; the "imperfect cadence" leaves the music hanging in midair.

Cadenza Literally "cadence" (Italian). Originally an improvised solo passage by the solo performer within a **concerto**; from the 19th century onward, cadenzas became more formalized and less spontaneous.

Call and response A musical **phrase** in which the first part (often a solo) is answered by a second part (often an ensemble part) that is heard as a direct commentary or response to the first. It is a feature of many types of music including gospel, blues, and jazz, as well as Cuban music, African religious ceremonies, and Indian classical music.

Canon **Contrapuntal** piece in which the separate voices or instruments enter one by one imitatively. If a canon is strict, the melody line is repeated exactly by all parts.

Cantata A cantata is in many respects similar to **opera**, being a **programmatic** piece generally for voice and **orchestra** that is designed to tell a story. The 17th and 18th centuries saw the rise of both the **cantata da camera** (a secular chamber piece) and the **cantata da chiesa** (its sacred equivalent).

Cantor The leader of a choir appointed by a cathedral or monastery, often with responsibility for teaching junior choristers and for selecting the music to be performed during worship.

Canzona Short, **polyphonic part song** popular in the 16th and 17th centuries. In many ways a canzona is similar to a **madrigal**, although the writing is lighter.

Capriccio Short piece in a generally free style. Capriccios written in the 17th century tend to be **fugal** in structure and rather more formalized than their **Romantic** equivalents, which tend to be solo **rhapsodic** pieces.

Castrato A male singer castrated as a child, developing a **soprano** or **contralto** voice. Very popular during the 17th and 18th centuries—the last castrato died in the 20th century.

Cavatina A lyrical operatic song or **aria** in one section, or an instrumental work in imitation of such a song—for example, the fifth **movement** from Beethoven's Quartet No.13.

Chamber music Music composed for small groups of two or more instruments, such as duets, trios, and **quartets**. Chamber music was originally designed to be performed at home for the entertainment of small gatherings, but is now more often performed in concert environments. Similarly, chamber **orchestras** and **operas** are pieces written for small numbers of instruments, although all orchestral instruments are represented.

Chord ▶ Any simultaneous combination of notes. The chords that are encountered most frequently in music are called **triads**. These consist of three distinct notes, and are built on the first, third, and fifth degree of a **scale**. In the **key** of C major, the notes of the scale are C D E F G A B and the C major triad is C, E, and G (1, 3, and 5).

Chromatic Literally "of color" (Latin), based on the **scale** of all 12 **semitones** in an **octave**, as opposed to **diatonic**, based on a scale of seven notes.

Classical The post-**Baroque** period, roughly between 1750 and 1820. Preeminent Classical composers were Haydn, Mozart, and Beethoven, who refined the **sonata**, **symphony**, and **concerto** forms. A general term used to distinguish Western music intended for a formal context, such as a church or concert hall, from more informal, popular music, such as rock and folk.

Classicism In 18th-century Europe, a movement in the arts that emulated the ideals of Classical antiquity. In music, the **Classical** era is marked by simpler, cleaner melodies and arrangements than in the **Baroque** era that preceded it.

CLEF

Clef ▲ A sign placed at the beginning of a musical **stave** to determine the **pitch** of the notes on the stave. Clefs were originally letters and there are three clefs—the letter G evolved into the modern **treble** clef and the letter F into the modern **bass** clef. The letter C evolved into the **alto** and **tenor** clefs.

Clave A **syncopated**, two-**bar rhythmic** pattern found in Afro-Cuban music. Also a wooden stick used in a pair as a percussion instrument.

Coda Literally "tail" (Italian), a final section of a piece of music that is distinct from the overall structure.

Concerto Today, the Italian term—derived from Latin words meaning both "performing together" and "struggling"—is used to describe a large piece for solo instrument and **orchestra**, designed to be a vehicle for the solo performer's virtuosity on their instrument. In the earlier **Baroque** concerto grosso, however, there was a more equal interplay between the much smaller orchestra (ripieno) and a group of soloists (concertino).

CHORD

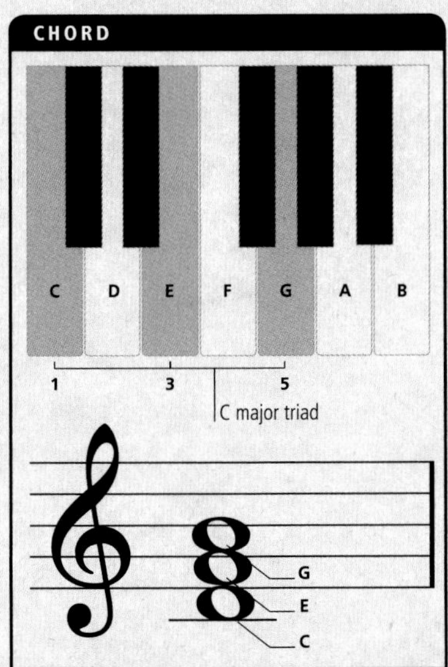

Consonance A **chord** or **interval**, such as a third or fifth, that sounds pleasing to the ear; the opposite of **dissonance**.

Consort An instrumental ensemble, popular during the 16th and 17th centuries in England. There are two types of consort: "whole" consorts, which contain instruments of one family (such as wind or stringed instruments), and "broken" consorts, which contain instruments of different families (for example, viols, lutes, and recorders). The term "consort" is also used to describe the music played by these ensembles as well as the performance itself.

Contralto The lowest of the female voices. The same as an **alto**, but alto is associated with sacred and choral music and rarely describes a solo voice, whereas contralto is applied to **opera** singers.

Contrabass A term denoting any member of an instrument family that is lower in **pitch** than the **bass** instrument of the same type—for example, contrabass clarinet. Also, another term for the double bass—the largest and lowest-pitched bowed string instrument of the violin family in the modern symphony **orchestra**.

Contrapuntal Describes music using counterpoint, the simultaneous playing or singing of two or more **melodic** lines. Contrapuntal forms such as the **ricercare**, **canzona**, and **fugue** evolved in the **Renaissance**, and reached their height in the work of composers such as Palestrina and J.S. Bach.

Counter melody A secondary melody that is played simultaneously with a lead melody, but is subordinate to it. *See also* Contrapuntal.

Counterpoint *see* Contrapuntal

Courante Late **Renaissance**- and **Baroque**-era courtly dance, originating in France. Literally meaning "running," the courante is lively but graceful and set in quick triple time.

Da capo Literally meaning "from the head," the Italian term da capo instructs the performer to repeat a piece of music from the beginning. It is often abbreviated as D.C.

Damper A mute, or any device that deadens vibrations in stringed instruments to reduce the volume of a note. More specifically, in a piano or harpsichord, a damper is a pad that deadens each note as the corresponding key is released.

Deceptive cadence A two-**chord** sequence, or **cadence**, that begins on the fifth note of the **scale** and closes on any note other than the first. This produces an unresolved feeling, as the listener expects a closing return to the first note but is left hanging by a move elsewhere.

Descant A melody or **counterpoint** that accompanies a basic musical melody and is higher in **pitch**. The **soprano** part in a piece of music. An instrument of higher-than-normal pitch—for example, a descant recorder.

Diatonic Based on a **scale** of seven natural degrees—five **tones** and two semitones—with no sharps or flats, constituting the white piano keys. The modern **major and minor** scales are diatonic.

Dissonance Sounding together of notes to produce discord (sounds unpleasing to the ear). The opposite of these terms are "**consonance**" and "concord." Dissonance is very subjective, and combinations of notes considered dissonant in one period are often heard as consonant by later audiences.

Distortion (clipping) The effect produced by overloading an amplifier so that the peaks of the sound waves are cut off or clipped, distorting the sound. This is most commonly associated with the electric guitar, and the effect can be produced in a variety of ways, including effects pedals. Distortion produces a warm, fuzzy sound that has been used in jazz, rock 'n' roll, and blues music since the 1950s.

DYNAMICS

MARKING	MEANING
<	*Crescendo*: Getting louder
>	*Diminuendo*: Getting quieter
pp	*Pianissimo*: Very quiet
p	*Piano*: Quiet
ff	*Fortissimo*: Very loud
f	*Forte*: Loud
mf	*Mezzo forte*: Fairly loud
mp	*Mezzo piano*: Fairly quiet
Sf	*Sforzando*: Sudden accent (just on that note)
>	Accent: Emphasis on a particular note

Dynamics ▲ Differences in volume of a piece or section of music. Dynamics also refers to the **notation** system of written or printed markings that indicate these relative differences in volume in a piece of music.

Equal temperament System of tuning (or "temperament") whereby each note of the **chromatic scale** is separated from its neighbors by exactly the same degree. Equal temperament was introduced in the 18th century, and the new system made it possible to play in any **key** of the chromatic scale. *See also* Temperament.

Exposition In music, the exposition is when the thematic musical material of a composition (or a part of one, such as a **movement**) is initially introduced. In **sonata form**, the exposition is the first section—it presents the principal thematic material, establishes the **tonic key**, and then ends on the dominant, or fifth note. In a **fugue**, the exposition consists of the statement of the subject by the first voice (the beginning of the fugue) and the imitation of the subject by other voices.

Falsetto A technique used by male singers to extend the top of their vocal **range** by limiting the vibration of their vocal chords, so that just the ligaments at the edges are used to produce the sound.

Fantasia A loosely structured, usually instrumental, composition, with a suggestion of improvisation, which allowed more freedom of expression than the **Classical** forms. Also associated with English viol consort music.

Fermata A fermata, or hold, is a symbol used in musical **notation** over a note, **chord**, or rest to indicate that it should be sustained for longer than its value indicates. It is up to the performer or the conductor to decide how much longer to sustain the note for, and twice as long as its **note value** is not unusual.

Figure Also "figuration." A recurring sequence of notes in a composition that acts as a musical motif. Particularly common in **variations** on a **theme**.

Figured bass A **bass** part with numbers specifying the **harmonies** to be played above it. Used extensively during the **Baroque** period for keyboard or lute accompaniments.

Fill Similar to a **break**, a short passage of music that runs between the main sections of a melody. A fill maintains the flow of the main melody and literally "fills in the gap." Not used in classical music but common in pop and jazz.

Finger-picking A style of guitar playing in which the right thumb plays the **bass** strings, maintaining a steady **rhythm**, and the index and middle fingers pick out a melody on the **treble** strings, often with the use of plastic or metal picks fitted on the fingers and thumb. This technique is used in folk, country, jazz, and blues music.

Flat (♭) A note that has been lowered by a **semitone**; for example, B lowered by a semitone is B-flat. An instrument or voice that is out of tune by being lower than the intended **pitch**.

Frottola A type of Italian secular song that was popular in the late 15th and early 16th centuries. It became popular at the courts of Northern Italy, having developed at Mantua. It usually consists of a composition for four voice parts or a solo voice with instrumental accompaniment, with the upper voice leading and singing the melody.

Fugue From the Italian "fuga," "to chase." A complex, highly structured **contrapuntal** piece, in two or more parts, popular in the **Baroque** era. The separate voices or lines enter one by one imitatively: the first voice states a subject, then the second enters with an "answer" (the subject starting on a different note), while the first voice performs a countersubject. The process continues until all the voices have entered, and may be followed by freer "episodes" or contrapuntal variations or a repeated statement of the subject.

Galant A courtly musical style of the 18th century characterized by elegance, formality, and clarity, without **ornamentation**.

Glissando Principally applied to string instruments. The sliding of a finger over a number of consecutive notes, thus creating an extended slither of sound.

Gregorian chant A type of solo and unison **plainsong** employed in the liturgy of the Roman Catholic Church. It came to dominate liturgical tradition, and is attributed to Pope Gregory I (Gregory the Great, 590–604), who founded Rome's choir school, the *schola cantorum*.

Habanera A type of Cuban dance and music, thought to have its roots in the **rhythms** of traditional African music. Written in 2/4 time with a distinctive pattern of quarter notes, the habanera —or contradanza as it was originally known in Cuba —became popular in Europe during the 19th century, and is most famous from an **aria** in Bizet's *Carmen*.

Harmonic A harmonic series consists of a fundamental (the note played) and a logarithmic, ascending progression of overtones (frequencies higher than the fundamental), which determine the individual **timbre** of an instrument.

Homophonic Describes a style of writing popularized in the **Classical** period in which a lyrical melody line is supported by chordal harmony and a solid **bass**.

Instrumentation The scoring of music for particular instruments—not the same as **orchestration**, which refers to a composer's skill in writing for groups of instruments. Thus Schubert's *Octet*, which shows a remarkable awareness of the qualities of each component, is a superb example of instrumentation.

Intermezzo Light-hearted interlude performed between the acts of an **opera seria**. The intermezzo developed from the intermedio, a short musical drama performed between the acts of spoken plays in the 15th and 16th centuries.

Interval The difference in **pitch** between two notes. Intervals are expressed numerically—thirds, fourths, and so on (though "**octave**" is used rather than "eighth"). Composers' preferred intervals are highly recognizable aspects of their style.

Intonation The **pitching** of a voice or instrument. An instrument such as a flute or violin can be tuned **flat** or **sharp** for instance—or an individual note can be sounded similarly out of tune. Intonation also refers to a musician's skill at sounding notes in tune.

Jig Today, the jig is a dance most commonly associated with traditional Celtic music, but it dates back to 16th-century England and became popular throughout Europe. It has diversified into several different forms, including the slip jig written in 9/8 time, and the double jig in 6/8 time. In Irish sessions, it is common to run two or three jigs together at a time. The jig is also the origin of the **Baroque** gigue, popular in France in the 17th century, that often closes Baroque dance **suites**.

Key The tonal center of a piece of music, based on the first note (or **tonic**) of the **scale**. A **key signature** on a **stave** tells a musician which notes to play in a piece of music. The word "key" also refers to an individual note on a piano or keyboard.

Key signature A group of accidentals—**sharps** or **flats**—at the beginning of a **stave** indicating which **key** a piece of music is played in. Rather than writing in a sharp for each F and C in D major, for example, the two sharps would be included on the stave. *See also* Major *and* Minor.

Keynote *see* Tonic

Leading note The note below the **tonic** in a **scale**, also known as the subtonic. Being one **semitone** lower than the tonic, it naturally leads back to the keynote, giving an effect of resolution.

Madrigal Secular a cappella song popular in the **Renaissance** period, particularly in England and Italy, often set to a lyric love poem.

Major and **Minor** ▶ The term major can be applied to a **key signature** or any **chord**, **triad**, or **scale** in a major **key**. The **intervals** in a major key consist of two whole **tones** followed by a half tone, then three whole tones followed by one half tone. Though it is ultimately subjective, major keys are often described as sounding happy, while minor keys are more subdued and sad. The term minor can be applied to a key signature, or a chord, triad, or scale in a minor key. There are three different types of minor scale: natural, harmonic, and melodic. A natural minor scale consists of a whole tone followed by a half tone, then two whole tones followed by a half tone and two whole tones. In a harmonic minor scale the seventh tone is raised by one semitone, whereas in a melodic minor scale the sixth and seventh tones are both raised by a semitone ascending but are usually flattened back to the natural minor on the descent.

Mambo A Latin dance and accompanying music, originating from Cuba in the 1930s, with a fast, **syncopated rhythm**.

Mazurka National dance and music of Poland, usually written in a fast-paced 3/4 time. The mazurka became popular in the 19th century and was adopted by many classical composers—Chopin composed more than 60 for the piano.

Measure *see* Bar

Meter The organization of music into a recurring, **rhythmic** pattern of stressed and unstressed beats. *See also* Rhythm.

Mezzo-soprano The lowest **soprano** voice (one **tone** above **contralto**).

Middle eight Refers to the section of a popular song that occurs in the middle of the song and generally is around eight **bars** in length. Its function is to break up the simple repetition of the verse-chorus-verse structure by introducing new melodies and **chords**.

Minimalism A predominantly American school of music, which rejected the strictures of the European avant-garde in favor of a more accessible sound-world involving a hypnotic texture of repeated short patterns. Associated with Steve Reich, Philip Glass, and John Adams.

MAJOR AND MINOR

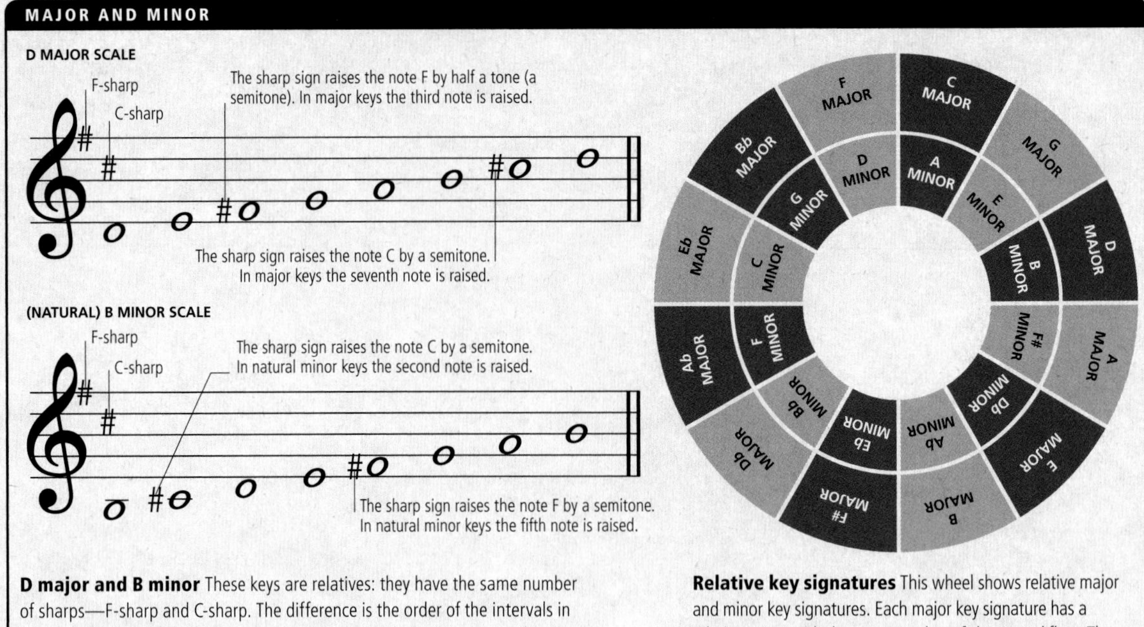

D major and B minor These keys are relatives: they have the same number of sharps—F-sharp and C-sharp. The difference is the order of the intervals in the scale and the location of these sharp notes, which is what creates the major and minor "sound."

Relative key signatures This wheel shows relative major and minor key signatures. Each major key signature has a relative minor with the same number of sharps and flats. The relative minor is found by going down three semitones.

Minuet and trio A graceful dance in 3/4 time, normally in three sections: the minuet section (either two- or three-part form), then the trio (originally intended for three musicians to play, and consisting of unrelated material), and finally a reprise of the minuet. The piece appears as a movement of **Baroque suites** and **Classical sonatas** and **symphonies**, but was replaced with the faster **scherzo** by Beethoven.

Modernism In music, this refers to the period of innovation and change that coincided with the turn of the 20th century. Older musical language was reinterpreted and confronted, and plurality was a key facet—no single musical genre was given prominence.

Modes Seven-note **scales** inherited from Ancient Greece via the Middle Ages, in which they were most prevalent, although they still survive today in folk music and **plainsong**.

Modulation A shift from one key (tonality) to another—for example, from C major to A minor.

Monophonic Describes music written in a single line, or melody without an accompaniment.

Motet A **polyphonic** choral composition based on a sacred text, usually without instrumental accompaniment. In medieval times, it was a vocal composition elaborating on the melody and text of **plainsong**. In the 15th century, it became a more independent religious choral composition.

Movement A self-contained section of a larger work; so-called because each section had a different, autonomous **tempo** indication.

Multiple stopping A musical technique that involves playing multiple notes simultaneously on a bowed stringed instrument, such as the cello or violin, by bowing or plucking different strings at the same time. Double, triple, and quadruple stopping (where two, three, or four strings, respectively, are bowed or plucked simultaneously) are collectively referred to as multiple stopping.

Natural instrument Usually refers to a woodwind or brass instrument consisting of a basic tube with no extra mechanisms for modifying the sound, other than breath control and embouchure (the positioning and use of the lips, tongue, and teeth).

Natural (♮) A natural is a note that is not **sharp** or **flat**. A natural symbol can be used to cancel a sharp or flat introduced earlier in a **bar**, or to override a **key signature**.

Neoclassicism A trend that became strong during the 1920s, in reaction to the indulgences of late **Romanticism**. Typified by the adoption of **Baroque** and **Classical** forms, and the use of heavily **contrapuntal** writing. Much of composer Igor Stravinsky's output can be classified as neoclassical.

Notation The symbols used to represent a piece of music visually. A system of musical notation can convey **pitch**, **rhythm**, harmony, **tempo**, and **dynamics**.

Note values ▼ The duration of a note—how long it should be played for. All notes are given a value: a semibreve is a whole note (held for four beats in 4/4 time); a minim is a half note (held for two beats); a crotchet is a quarter note (one beat); a quaver is an eighth note (half beat); and a semi-quaver is a sixteenth note (quarter beat). *See also* Rest values.

NOTE VALUES

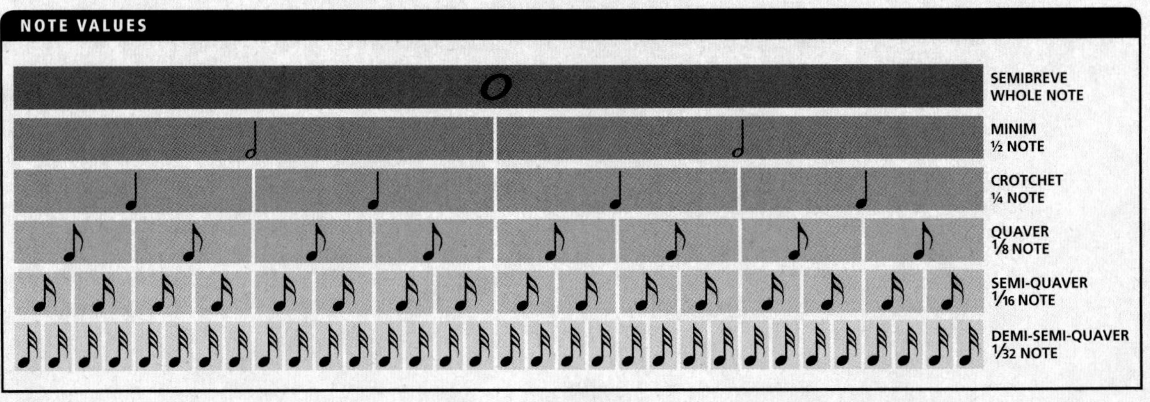

Obbligato A musical accompaniment that is important and therefore "obligatory." The term is commonly used to describe either a counter-melody played by an instrument in an ensemble (often complimenting a vocal line) or a **Baroque** keyboard accompaniment that is written out in full rather than with the standard **figured bass notation** (a written-out **bass** line with numbers indicating harmony).

Octave ▼ The interval between one **pitch** and another with double or half its frequency—for example, between the notes C and C on a keyboard. In the Western **diatonic scale** an octave consists of eight notes. The **chromatic** scale (including all the white and black—**sharp** and **flat**—notes on a keyboard) identifies 12 intervals within an octave.

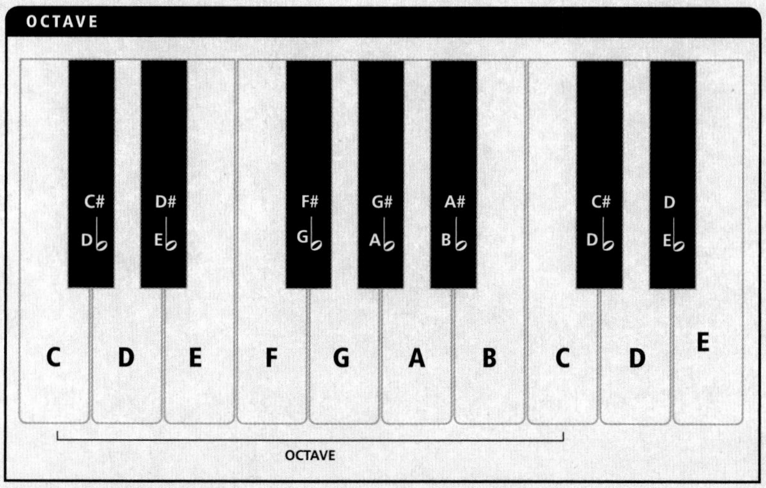

OCTAVE

C# D♭ | D# E♭ | F# G♭ | G# A♭ | A# B♭ | C# D♭ | D E♭

C D E F G A B C D E

OCTAVE

Opera Drama in which all or most characters sing and in which music is an important element. Traditionally, the writing is for full **orchestra**, soloists, and chorus, although examples exist that include fewer or more than these elements.

Opéra comique An exclusively French type of **opera** which, despite its name, is not always comic, nor particularly light. It always consists of original material, however, and always includes spoken dialogue.

Opera buffa Type of comic **opera** that was especially popular in the 18th century. Examples are Mozart's *The Marriage of Figaro* and Rossini's *The Barber of Seville*.

Opera seria Literally "serious opera," and the direct opposite of **opera buffa**. The style is characterized by heroic or mythological plots, and a formality of music and action.

Operetta Literally "little opera," and sometimes known as "light opera," a lighter style of 19th-century **opera** including spoken dialogue. It was full of dancing, choruses, and witty dialogue.

Opus A Latin word meaning "work," used when cataloging a composer's pieces. It is often abbreviated to "Op." and followed by a number to show the order in which it was published; Beethoven's Symphony No. 5 I Op.67 was the 67th piece he published.

Oratorio Work for vocal soloists and choir with instrumental accompaniment, originating in the congregation of Oratorians, founded by St. Philip Neri in the 16th century. Oratorios traditionally take biblical texts as their subject matter and are usually performed "straight," although they originally involved sets, costumes, and action.

Orchestra The first regular orchestras appeared in the **Baroque** era, and consisted of strings, oboes, and bassoons, plus a widely changing list of solo instruments. The layout became standardized during the **Classical** period, when Mozart and Haydn made specific demands regarding the number and quality of players for their **symphonies**. This Classical orchestra established the basic division of players into four sections: strings; woodwind (flutes, oboes, bassoons, and clarinets); brass (horns and trumpets); and percussion (kettledrums). Beethoven's symphonies demanded more, and better, players, and Berlioz, Wagner, and Mahler required yet further expansions of the orchestra's resources. Though some instruments have been refined over the years, the orchestra of today is not much different from that of 150 years ago.

Orchestration The art of writing for an **orchestra**, demanding an understanding of the qualities of each instrumental section and an ability to manage and combine them. Also, the scoring of a work not originally intended for the orchestra—for example, Mussorgsky's *Pictures from an Exhibition*, originally for piano, was orchestrated by Ravel.

Ornamentation An embellishment of a note or **chord**. This can be a simple added "grace" note, a trill, or a short, **melodic** fragment such as a turn—the note above the main note, the main note, and the note below, played in quick succession before the main note.

Overture Literally "opening" (French). An instrumental introduction to an **opera** or **ballet**, which presents some of the main thematic material, usually in **sonata form**. In the **Romantic** period, standalone overtures were written, such as Brahms's *Tragic Overture* and Mendelssohn's *Hebrides Overture*, and performed in their own right.

Part song An unaccompanied song with parts for two or more voices, which carry the melody.

Passacaglia Originally a slow and stately dance in a moderately slow triple **meter** appearing in 17th-century keyboard music. These pieces are based on a short, repeated **bass**-line melody that serves as the basis for continuous **variation** in the other voices. With later passacaglias, the repeated **theme** did not necessarily appear in the bass.

Passion A musical setting of the suffering of Jesus Christ from the Last Supper to his crucifixion. Famous examples include J.S. Bach's *Passions* and Part II of Handel's *Messiah*.

Pastorale A work that evokes rural, or pastoral, life. Commonly written in 6/8 or 12/8 time over a drone, the form was popular with **Baroque** composers. Notable examples include the third **movement** of Spring from Vivaldi's *The Four Seasons* and Bach's *Pastorale in F major* for the organ.

Pentatonic scale A **scale** of five notes—often without **semitones**—and the music based on these notes. Examples are found worldwide.

Phrase A group of notes that form a unit of music. Individual phrases in music can be thought of as being similar to sentences in a story and they combine to build a melody. In **notation**, a phrase mark indicates the distinct groups within a melody, and can help a musician decide how to shape a piece for performance.

Pick-up A pick-up is a transducer—a device that captures and converts mechanical vibrations from a stringed instrument, such as an electric guitar or an electric violin, into an electrical signal for amplification.

Pitch The position of a sound in relation to the whole range of tonal sounds, depending on the frequency of sound waves per second (hertz). A high frequency is heard as a high pitch, a low frequency is heard as a low pitch. In the United States and the UK, pitches are named for the first seven letters of the alphabet.

Pizzicato Literally "pinched" (Italian). A style of playing stringed instruments that are normally bowed, such as the violin or cello, by plucking the strings with the fingers.

Plainsong Also known as plainchant (from the Latin "cantus planus"), this medieval church music still survives in the Roman Catholic Church. It consists of a unison, unaccompanied vocal line in free **rhythm**, like speech, with no regular **bar** lengths. A well-known type is **Gregorian chant**.

Polka A dance with three steps and a hop, and accompanying music that follows this distinctive **rhythm**. The polka originated in Central Europe in the 19th century but became widespread, with versions found in the folk music of Ireland and the United States. The polka style was also adopted by **Classical** composers and was popular in the dance music of 19th-century Vienna, Austria.

Polonaise (Polacca) A Polish dance and accompanying music in 3/4 time that has a steady, march-like **rhythm**. Many **Classical** composers wrote polonaises but perhaps the best-known examples are by Chopin.

Polychoral A performance style of sacred music that developed in the late 16th century; polychoral music involved the use of two or more spatially separate choirs that sang in alternation.

Polychord A polychord consists of two or more **chords**, one on top of the other—for example, E minor on top of D minor. This may suggest **bitonality** or **polytonality**. They are found in the work of Stravinsky.

Polyphony Literally "many sounds." In classical music this refers to a style of writing in which all parts are independent and of equal importance, and therefore implies **contrapuntal** music. Forms that typify this style include the **canon**, **fugue**, and **motet**.

Polytonality The use of two or more **keys** at the same time. Mostly a 20th-century technique; Stravinsky's music is full of examples.

Power chord A power chord (also known as a fifth chord) is a **chord** that consists of the root note and the fifth **interval**. Power chords are an essential characteristic of many styles of rock music.

Prelude An introductory piece of music, for example one that precedes a **fugue** or an act of an **opera**. A self-contained piano piece, as in the *Préludes* of Chopin and Debussy.

Prima donna Literally "first lady" (Italian). The principal female singer in an **opera** or opera company.

Principal The lead musician in a section of an **orchestra**, who is responsible for leading that group and for playing any solos. For example, the principal trumpet player leads the brass section, while the principal violinist leads the strings and is sometimes known as the concertmaster, leading the entire orchestra after the conductor.

Programme music Any music written to describe a nonmusical theme, such as an event, landscape, or literary work.

Progression The transition from one note or **chord** to the next, especially when following a recognizable pattern. Examples of progression are **cadences**, or the structured series of chords followed in 12-bar blues.

Psalm Any of the 150 prayers or songs from the Book of Psalms in the Old Testament of the Bible. The text makes reference to music that is now lost but many composers have been inspired to write music to set Psalms to, including Mendelssohn, Brahms, and Liszt. The Psalms are widely sung as hymns, such as Jessie Seymour Irvine's setting of Psalm 23 "The Lord's My Shepherd."

Quartet A group of four instruments. The most common is the string quartet (two violins, one viola, one cello).

Raga In classical Indian music, a particular pattern of melody based on five or more notes and a **rhythm**, which a composition is based on. It literally means "tone" or "color" in Sanskrit and can be thought of as being the mood or hue of a piece of music.

Range ▼ The range of a musical instrument is the distance from the lowest to the highest **pitch** it can play. For a singing voice, the vocal range is the span from the lowest to highest note a particular voice can produce.

RANGE

Vocal range The standard ranges for singing voices are shown here shaded dark grey. Some singers with a particular voice type can sing a little higher or lower, as indicated by the lighter grey keys.

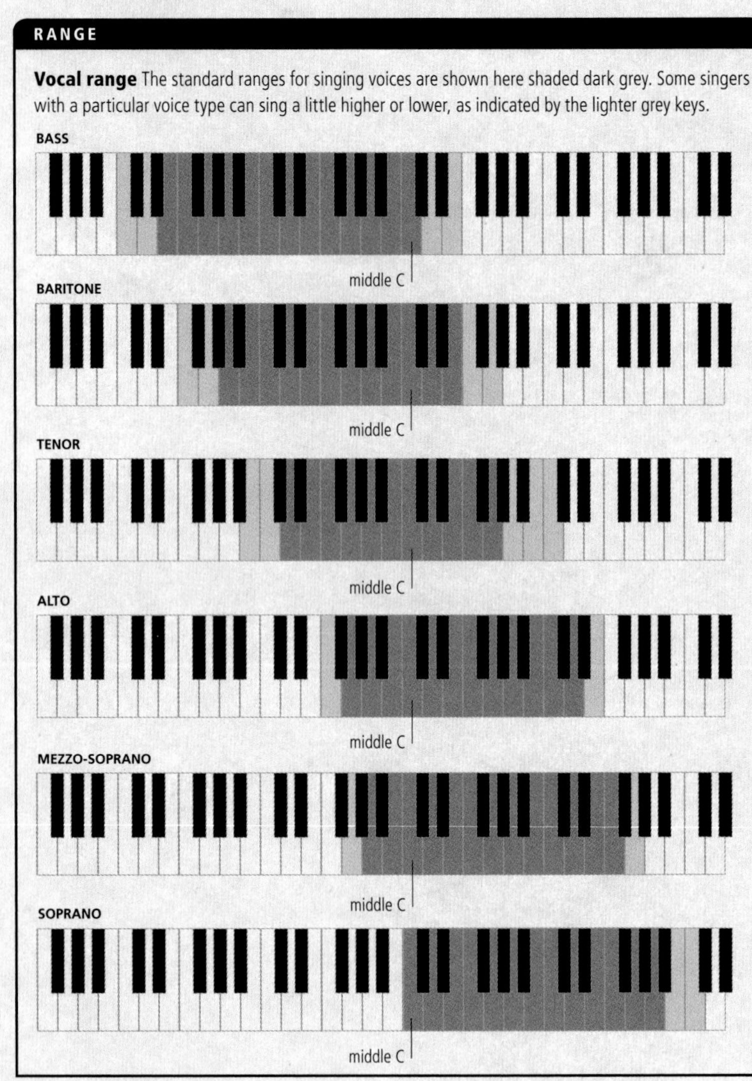

Rap In popular music, a rhythmic, rhyming speech usually delivered over a prerecorded instrumental track.

Recitative Style of singing in **opera** and **oratorio** that is closely related to the delivery of dramatic speech in **pitch** and **rhythm**. Recitative sections are often used for dialogue and exposition of the plot between **arias** and choruses.

Reel A fast-paced dance and tune common in traditional Irish and Scottish music, in 2/4 or 4/4 time. Two or three reels are usually grouped together into a set when performed or when accompanying a dance.

Refrain A refrain is the line or lines that are repeated in a piece of music (or a verse) – such as the chorus of a song. In a song, the refrain consists of both the lyrics and the melody. Sometimes refrains vary their lyrics when repeated, but they are recognizable because the melody remains the same.

Renaissance Roughly spanning the period from the 14th to 16th centuries, the Renaissance (from the French word meaning "rebirth") saw a revival of interest in learning and the arts. In music, the period was marked by the development of harmony. Instrumental and secular vocal music were popular.

Rest values ▶ Rest symbols indicate the duration for which a note should not be played. As with **note values** there are whole, half, quarter, eighth, and sixteenth symbols, which in 4/4 time would be held for four, two, one, half, and a quarter beats respectively.

Rhapsody A **Romantic** term, applied to compositions suggestive of heroic endeavor or overwhelming emotion. Best-known examples are Brahms's *Alto Rhapsody*, Rachmaninov's *Rhapsody on a Theme of Paganini*, and Gershwin's *Rhapsody in Blue*.

Rhythm The pattern of relative durations of and stresses on the notes of a piece of music, commonly organized in regular groups or **bars**. Also, any specific form of this, such as double or triple rhythm.

Ricercare A musical composition that originated in the late 15th century for instruments such as the lute or keyboard, in which one or more of the musical **themes** are developed through the use of **melodic** imitation.

Riff A series of notes that is repeated constantly, or a **chord progression** played by the rhythm section of a band or by a solo instrument.

Romantic The cultural epoch heralded in music by Beethoven, which dominated the 19th century. Characterized by the abandonment of traditional forms, a predilection for extra-musical subjects, an increase in the scale of composition, and an affection for **chromaticism**.

Rondo Piece (or **movement**) of music based on a recurring **theme** with interspersed material, following a form such as ABACADAE.

Rondo sonata form A mix of **rondo** form and **sonata form**. Like a sonata, there are three main sections: **exposition**, middle section (which may be a development), and recapitulation. However, like a rondo, the first section has an ABA format, the middle section is C, and the recapitulation goes back to ABA, although the B section is usually modified.

Sample A short extract from an existing recording that is used in a new recording. The screams of soul legend James Brown and the drummers of the Motown label recordings are among the most sampled pieces.

REST VALUES

NAME	LENGTH	SYMBOL
WHOLE NOTE/ SEMIBREVE REST	4 BEATS	
HALF NOTE/ MINIM REST	2 BEATS	
QUARTER NOTE/ CROTCHET REST	1 BEAT	
EIGHTH NOTE/ QUAVER REST	½ BEAT	
SIXTEENTH NOTE/ SEMI-QUAVER REST	¼ BEAT	

Sarabande A slow court dance in triple time, popular in Europe from the 17th century. In the **Baroque** era it was often included in dance **suites** with examples written by composers such as Bach and Handel.

Scale A series of notes that define a tune and, usually, the **key** of the piece. Different scales give music a different feeling and "color".

Scherzo Lively dance piece (or **movement**) in triple time. During the **Classical** and **Romantic** periods, the third movement of a **symphony** or one of a **sonata**'s middle movements was a scherzo, usually paired with a trio. The scherzo and trio replaced the **Baroque minuet and trio**.

Scordatura An alternative way of tuning a stringed instrument, also known as cross-tuning, altering the **pitches** produced and the **timbre** of the notes.

Semitone *see* Tone

Serenade A love song. In the 18th century, an evening entertainment for **orchestra** – for example, Mozart's *Eine kleine Nachtmusik*.

Serenata A kind of 18th-century secular **cantata**, often of an occasional or congratulatory nature, and performed either as a small quasi-**opera** or as a concert piece.

Serial music System of atonal composition developed in the 1920s by Arnold Schoenberg and others of the Second Viennese School, in which fixed sequences of musical elements are used as a foundation for more complex structures. Most commonly these sequences comprise arrangements of each degree of the **chromatic scale** – known as a "tone row" – although shorter sequences may also be used.
This tone row, or series, can then appear in four different ways: forwards, backwards (retrograde), upside-down (inversion), and upside-down and backwards (retrograde inversion).

Sharp (♯) A note that has been raised by a **semitone**, for example F raised by a semitone is F-sharp. An instrument or voice that is out of tune by being higher than the intended **pitch**.

Slapping (slap bass) A style of bass-playing used in rock and jazz music that involves plucking a string and releasing it sharply so that it hits, or slaps, the fretboard to produce a sound.

Slide (slide guitar) Also known as bottleneck guitar, a style of playing in which a metal or glass tube is fitted on to the finger, held across the strings over the fretboard, and slid up and down to produce a warm, buzzing effect. The technique originated with blues musicians who used a glass bottleneck worn on the finger to slide over the strings.

Sonata Popular instrumental piece for one or more players. Appearing first in the **Baroque** period, when it was a short piece for a solo or small group of instruments accompanied by a **basso continuo**, the **Classical** sonata adhered to a three- or four-**movement** structure for one or two instruments, though the three-instrument trio sonata was often popular. A sonata usually comprised three or four movements: an opening movement (in what later became known as "first movement" or "sonata" form), a slow second movement, a lively **scherzo**, and finally a **rondo**.

Sonata da camera Literally "chamber sonata" (Italian). A multi-instrumental piece – usually for two violins with **basso continuo** – of the late 17th and early 18th centuries that often took the form of a collection of dance **movements**, usually with a quick first movement.

Sonata da chiesa Literally "church sonata". A multi-instrumental piece similar in many respects to the secular sonata da camera, usually comprising four **movements**: a slow introduction, a **fugal** movement, a slow movement, and a quick finale.

Sonata principle/form Structural form popularized in the **Classical** period, and from this period onwards the first **movements** of **sonatas**, **symphonies**, and **concertos** were written mainly in this form. A piece written in sonata form traditionally comprises an **exposition**, comprising a subject followed by a second subject (linked by a **bridge** section and modulated to a different **key**), after which the initial material is expounded on in the development section, and finally the recapitulation restates the exposition, although remaining in the **tonic** (main key).

Soprano The highest of the four standard singing voices. A female or boy singer with this voice.

Staccato Literally "detached" (Italian). A performance technique whereby each note is **articulated** separately without slurring.

Standard tuning The usual **pitch** to which a stringed instrument is tuned. For example, the strings of a guitar would normally be tuned to E, A, D, G, B, and E (the first E is below middle C on a piano, the last is the E above it). Alternative tunings are known as **scordatura**.

Stave The grid of five horizontal lines on which music is written. Also known as the "staff".

Suite Multi-**movement** work – generally instrumental – made up of a series of contrasting dance movements, usually all in the same **key**.

Suspension A note that is held, often creating a **dissonance**, before being resolved by falling to the next note down.

Swing The **rhythmic** momentum inherent in a musical performance, especially of jazz music. The feel of the music that makes listeners want to dance or tap their feet.

Symphonic poem Extended single-**movement** **symphonic** work, usually of a **programmatic** nature, often describing landscape or literary works. Also known as a tone poem.

Symphony Large-scale work for full **orchestra**. The **Classical** and **Romantic** symphony, made popular by Haydn, Mozart, and Brahms, contains four **movements** – traditionally an **allegro**, a slower second movement, a **scherzo**, and a lively finale. Later symphonies can contain more or fewer. The first movement is often in **sonata form**, and the slow movement and finale may follow a similar structure.

Syncopation Accentuation of the offbeat, not the main beat. Characteristic of jazz, and much used in jazz-influenced early 20th century music.

Tablature A system of musical **notation** commonly used for playing the lute, guitar, and banjo that uses letters and symbols, instead of standard notation, to indicate how a piece of music should be played. It consists of a diagram of the strings from highest to lowest, with finger positions for each string indicated by numbers corresponding to the appropriate frets.

Tarantella Literally "tarantula" (Italian). Traditional folk dance and music from Southern Italy written in fast, rhythmic 6/8 time.

Temperament A way of tuning an instrument that involves adjusting the **intervals** between notes to enable it to play in different **keys**. This is of particular importance to keyboard instruments that play fixed notes, as opposed to wind or string instruments where the musician can affect the **pitch**. There are several different types of temperament but most keyboard instruments are tuned using "**equal temperament**" based on an **octave** of 12 equal **semitones**.

Tempo ▼ The pace of a work. The tempo of a piece of music is usually written at the start. In modern Western music it is usually indicated in beats per minute. Some pieces do not use a mathematical time indication. **Classical** music uses Italian words to indicate tempo (pace) and mood to the musician, since many of the key composers of the 17th century were Italian.

TEMPO

ITALIAN	ENGLISH
Grave	Very slowly
Lento	Slowly
Largo	Broadly
Adagio	Leisurely
Andante	At a walking pace
Moderato	Moderately
Allegro	Fast
Presto	Very quickly
Accelerando	Gradually speed up
Rallentando	Gradually slow down
Rubato	Literally "robbed time", where rhythms are played freely for expressive effect

Tenor The highest natural adult male voice, or an instrument that sounds in this **range** – for example, tenor saxophone.

Theme A passage of notes or simple melody that is used as a musical motif recurring in a composition. A theme may be repeated slightly differently each time in a series of **variations**.

Tie In **notation**, this is a curved line that connects the heads of two notes of the same **pitch** and name to indicate that they should be played as a single note, equal in duration to their combined **note values**.

Timbre The particular quality (literally "stamp"), or character of a sound that enables a listener to distinguish one instrument (or voice) from another. Synonymous with tone color.

Time signature ▼ The numbers at the beginning of a composition, **movement**, or section (or midway through a phrase in some 20th-century scores) to indicate the number and kind of beats in a **bar** – for example 4/4, 3/4, 9/16.

Tonic The first note, or degree, of any **diatonic** (**major or minor**) **scale**. It is called the keynote and is the most important note of the scale, providing the focus for the melody and harmony of a piece of music.

Treble The highest unchanged male voice, or the highest instrument or part in a piece of music. Also, the name for the symbol (**clef**) used to indicate notes above middle C on the piano.

Triad A three-note **chord** consisting of a root note plus the **intervals** of a third and a fifth. The four types of triad are: major (e.g. C–E–G), minor (e.g. C–E-flat–G), augmented (e.g. C–E–G-sharp), and diminished (e.g. C–E-flat– G-flat).

TIME SIGNATURE

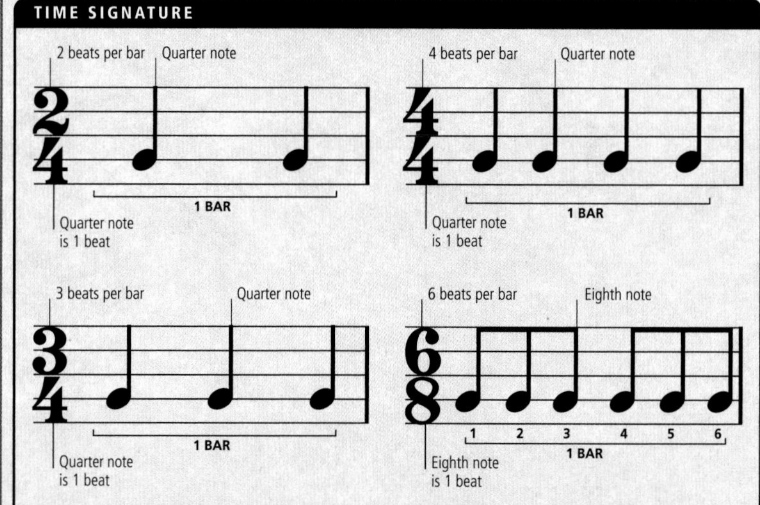

Tone and **Semitone** ▼ Tone is the quality of a note sounded. A whole tone, equal to the interval of a major second (comprising two adjacent positions on a **stave**), consists of two semitones. A semitone, also known as a half step or half tone, is the smallest musical interval between notes in Western tonal music. There are two semitones in a whole tone and twelve semitones in an **octave**. On a keyboard, a semitone is found where two keys are as close together as possible – for example, E to F is a semitone, as is F to F-sharp.

Variation The repetition of a **passage** of music or **theme** with alterations and embellishments. In a similar way, players of Celtic music modify a section of a tune on the second and third repetition, improvising changes and adding **ornamentation** so that effectively a tune is never played in quite the same way twice.

Vibrato Rapid but small vibrations in **pitch**, especially those created by string players, singers, and wind players.

TONE AND SEMITONE

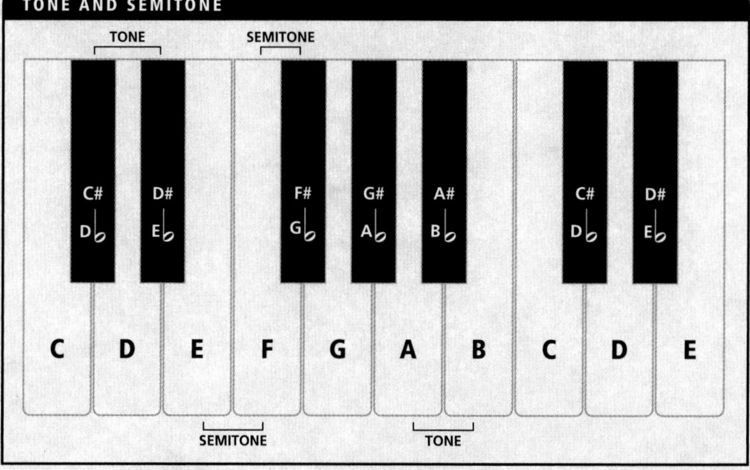

Genres

This section consists of a survey of genres from around the world and throughout musical history, from the Carnatic music of southern India to modern forms, such as hip-hop. Although many Western music genres are based around the same fundamental music theory, other cultures draw on different techniques and theories. For example, while the seven-note scale is dominant in Western music, in China the pentatonic (five-note) scale is more widely used.

Classical

Classical music is a broad tradition, encompassing everything from the religious compositions of the Middle Ages to the avant-garde art music of the 20th century. Although classical music styles vary greatly, the genre has several unifying characteristics: it is a predominantly written form, with little room for improvisation, and tends to have string instruments at the head of its sound.

Middle Ages

Spanning a period of almost 1,000 years, from the 5th century to around 1430, the music of the early Middle Ages features both secular and sacred compositions that are often monophonic in character (consisting of a single line of melody). Secular monophonic music was only considered worthy of preservation in written collections from the 12th century onward, meaning the surviving music of the period is heavily weighted in favor of the sacred. Plainsong was the most common type of religious music during the Middle Ages and was sung in every church, monastery, cathedral, and chapel, by one voice or many.

During this period, composers of music were usually employed to do something else, such as work as a priest. To compose and write music, one had to be musically literate to some degree, especially for the creation of polyphony. People who received an education were usually either part of the nobility or employed by the Catholic Church, living within a religious institution such as a nunnery or monastery. Most church musicians would have been expected to commit hundreds of chants to memory as part of their musical training, even after Guido d'Arezzo developed the music staff in the 11th century.

The most famous secular composers of the time were the troubadours, trobairitz (female troubadours), and trouvères of medieval France, whose music and poetry usually expressed ideas of courtly love. Little is known about how their music was performed, but it is possible that their songs were accompanied by the vielle, a five–stringed forerunner of the violin. One of the vielle's strings produced a drone, like that of a hurdy-gurdy or bagpipe; the instrument may have been used to simply provide a steady drone or more complex accompaniments to a solo singer.

ILLUSTRATION FROM A MEDIEVAL SONGBOOK

The rise of polyphonic (literally "many voiced") forms of composition from approximately the 12th century took place within the Church, as singers elaborated on the basic plainsong by the addition of other vocal parts on special occasions, such as Christmas or Easter. In the Cathedral of Notre-Dame de Paris, Léonin and Pérotin are credited with having written the first body of two-, three-, and four-part music to be circulated in manuscript form. By the 13th century, a large repertory of polyphony was found in major churches across Europe, and secular forms of music were also being written in more than one part.

One of the most popular sacred forms during the later Middle Ages was the motet, which was developed in the 13th century in Northern France. The plainsong was placed into a strict rhythmic pattern, above which between one and three other lines were placed; these upper parts were each given a new text, resulting in a complex texture in which many different words were sounded together.

KEY ARTISTS AND WORKS

Hildegard of Bingen *Symphonia Armoniae Celestium Revelationum* (c.1150)

Léonin (Leoninus) *Magnus Liber* (c.1200)

Pérotin (Pérotinus Magnus) *Viderunt Omnes* (c.1200)

Guillaume de Machaut *Messe de Nostre Dame* (c.1363)

Guillaume Dufay *Nuper Rosarum Flores* (1436)

Renaissance

Renaissance music is generally seen as covering a period from the mid-15th century to the beginning of the 17th century. Along with new secular forms of song in the 16th century, such as the madrigal, instrumental music rose to such a status that it was more frequently copied down than it had been in the Middle Ages and the Renaissance saw increased involvement of merchant classes in musical performance. The invention of music printing by Ottaviano dei Petrucci in 1501 meant that music could be sold and distributed more easily, cheaply, and reliably than ever before, although much was still written down in manuscript (handwritten) form.

Wealthy patrons of the 16th century demanded vocal and instrumental music for all sorts of musical combinations. In particular, "families" of instruments that comprised various sizes of one type of instrument (a consort of recorders, viols, or voices) flourished during the Renaissance period, though mixed or "broken" consorts of string, wind, and voice were also cultivated. Dances such as the stately *pavana* and the *gagliarda*—a lively dance involving leaps—became enormously popular.

Secular vocal music was written in vernacular languages, and very often had an amorous subject. The madrigal rose to prominence in the 16th century, and was notable for its use of subtle musical descriptions that matched the text—a technique known as "word-painting." Composers delighted in devising ways to set the most expressive poetic phrases to music. During the Renaissance, the majority of composers continued to come from the Church or the nobility, although the merchant classes also valued a musical education for their sons and, to some extent, daughters. There were relatively few female composers during this period, although many anonymous pieces may have been written by women, and women performed music written by men.

The Protestant Reformation of the 16th century had inevitable consequences for the music of the time. Protestant reformers destroyed as much Catholic music as possible and replaced it with new, more direct styles, particularly in England. This made extraordinary demands of English composers of the period. Thomas Tallis, for example, wrote music for four different monarchs, each of whom required compositions with a very different religious emphasis: from the direct, Protestant settings of English texts favored by Elizabeth I, to the elaborate, Latin-texted polyphony composed for her half-sister, Mary.

MARBLE RELIEF FROM CATHEDRAL OF SANTA MARIA DEL FIORE

The simplest post-Reformation religious polyphony involved straightforward chanting in harmony, with all voices working together in the same rhythm as one another (homophony). The idea of a musical texture where voices imitated one another in counterpoint became a distinguishing feature of sacred and secular music of the Renaissance. It is perhaps most recognizable in the choral music of Giovanni Pierluigi da Palestrina and the instrumental fantasies of English consort music at the end of the period. The music of the Renaissance is usually perceived as ending with the operatic innovations of Claudio Monteverdi and his contemporaries.

KEY ARTISTS AND WORKS

Thomas Tallis *Spem in Alium Nunquam Habui* (c.1570); *Puer Natus est Nobisi* (1554)

Josquin Desprez *Stabat Mater Dolorosa* (c.1480); *Missa "Pange Lingua"* (c.1515)

John Taverner *Missa "Gloria Tibi Trinitas"* (c.1520); *Magnificat à 4* (c.1540)

Giovanni Pierluigi da Palestrina *Missa "Papae Marcelli"* (1567); *Missa brevis* (1570)

William Byrd *Great Service* (c.1600)

Giovanni Gabrieli *Sacrae symphoniae* (1597); *Canzoni et sonate* (published 1615); *Symphoniae sacrae* (published 1615)

Tomás Luis de Victoria *Officium defunctorum* (1603)

Baroque

The Baroque era—dating roughly from the late 15th century to 1750—saw the genesis of opera, the growth of the orchestra, and a flourishing of instrumental music, especially the violin and keyboard. Most new fashions originated in Italy and Italian musicians dominated the field. However, by the end of the period, distinctive national styles had evolved. The word "baroque" was originally a pejorative term for a style of architecture and art produced between the end of the 16th and the mid-18th centuries, but by the time music scholars adopted the term, it had lost most of its negative connotations.

This period was one of great creativity—from the work of William Shakespeare and Miguel de Cervantes in literature to that of Isaac Newton and Galileo Galilei in science. Music too blossomed. By the 1590s, a new musical style had emerged in contrast to the lush polyphony of Palestrina and his contemporaries. Instead of complex intertwining parts, the new style—dubbed *stile moderno* to distinguish it from the *stile antico* (old style) of earlier Renaissance compositions—placed a solo voice or instrument above a simple accompaniment, consisting of a bass line with the chords lightly

BAROQUE ORGAN

filled in above it (*basso continuo*, a "continuous bass"). There were usually two instruments playing the *continuo*—a keyboard, lute, or guitar along with a low-ranged melodic instrument, such as a cello, bass viol, or bassoon, reinforcing the bass line. The term "monody" (from the Greek word for "one song") was used to describe this new combination of solo voice and *basso continuo*. Monody allowed the performer the freedom to embellish and ornament the melodic line at will, something unthinkable in the older polyphonic style. This new style of singing allowed composers to convey the text clearly through a solo voice, while singers could interpret the words more dramatically. It was monody that made musical drama, or opera, possible.

The invention of opera is credited to a group of Florentine musicians and poets known as the Camerata, particularly the composers Giulio Caccini and Jacopo Peri and the poet Ottavio Rinuccini, who were trying to recreate the singing style of Ancient Greek drama. This new style was first demonstrated in *intermedi*—short musical dramas performed between the acts of spoken plays—but in 1598 the three collaborated on *Dafne*, the first true opera. Two years later, both Peri and Caccini wrote operas on the Orpheus myth, *Euridice*, but it was Monteverdi's *L'Orfeo* (1607) that is seen as the true benchmark for early opera. The new art form would combine a variety of musical styles—speechlike recitative, moving arias, choral and instrumental interludes—into one large narrative structure.

The Catholic Church frowned on the "immoral" plots of some operas and banned their performance during Advent and Lent. The void was filled by another kind of dramatic vocal music: the oratorio. Operas and oratorios both employed recitative, arias, duets, and instrumental pieces, but oratorios were unstaged, with no costumes or sets, and tended to be about biblical subjects. Comic opera followed, gaining ground in the 1730s. It developed from short comic pieces (*intermezzi*), performed in the intervals between the acts of serious operas.

Opera was not the only musical form to flourish. Major and minor courts across Europe maintained chamber ensembles as a mark of prestige. This created a demand for instrumental sonatas and concertos to entertain the noble patrons and their guests. In the sonata, the violin (which could emulate certain qualities of the singing voice) gained a whole new repertoire and generated an increased interest in its potential. This was also the age of the great violin makers of Cremona: Amati, Stradivari, and Guarneri.

The 17th century also saw the birth of the orchestra, driven in large part by the growth in opera, the size of the ensemble growing along with the visual spectacle onstage. Keyboard music (mainly for harpsichord and organ) also flourished, and virtuosi such as Johann Pachelbel and the Couperins attracted much attention in court and church circles.

Although the innovations of early Baroque came out of Italy, distinctive national styles began to emerge. The Italian style was one of melodic dominance, virtuosity, and a strong sense of meter, while the French style, developed by Jean-Baptiste Lully at the court of Louis XIV, was strongly influenced by dance rhythms. The German style, taken to its greatest heights by Johann Sebastian Bach, was a hybrid of the two, with the addition of a contrapuntal element.

KEY ARTISTS AND WORKS

Claudio Monteverdi *L'Orfeo* (1607); *Arianna* (1608); *Il Combattimento de Tancredi e Clorinda* (1624)

Jean-Baptiste Lully *Le Bourgeois Gentilhomme* (1670); *Armide* (1686)

Arcangelo Corelli *12 Concerti Grossi* (1714)

Henry Purcell *Ode for St. Cecilia's Day* (1683); *Dido and Aeneas* (c.1688)

Antonio Vivaldi *Gloria* (c.1715); *La Quattro Staggioni* (1725); *Six Flute Concertos* (1728)

Georg Philipp Telemann *Nouveaux Quatuors en Six Suites* (c.1736); *Musique de Table* (1733)

George Frideric Handel *Water Music* (1717); *Zadok the Priest* (1727); *Messiah* (1742); *Music for the Royal Fireworks* (1749)

Johann Sebastian Bach *The Brandenburg Concertos* (1721); *St. Matthew Passion* (1727); *Goldberg Variations* (1741); *The Well-Tempered Clavier* (1722–1742)

The classical era

In Western music, the period between the 1760s and 1820 is known as the Classical era. Among its forerunners were composers such as Carl Philipp Emanuel Bach, Johann Quantz, and Baldassare Galuppi. Their works were a reaction against the complexity of Baroque music—its intricate polyphony, counterpoint, and ornamented melody. Instead, composers aimed for a style where a simple melody was accompanied by harmonic progressions.

The Enlightenment, with its focus on rational, human ideals, played a major part in this shift in aesthetic values. So, too, did interest in the simple elegance of ancient Greek and Roman art and architecture, inspired in part by the excavation of the ruins of Pompeii, in present-day Italy, in 1748. Socially and politically, the Classical era was a time of great change, with the effects of the Industrial Revolution and colonization creating a larger middle class eager to become active consumers of the arts. At the same time, the aristocracies of Europe, suffering from the ravages of the

HARMONIE

> “**Simplicity** and **truth** are the sole principles of the **beautiful in art.**”
>
> CHRISTOPH WILLIBALD GLUCK

Napoleonic Wars (1792–1815), were less able to support musicians, and the old patronage system started to crumble.

Traditionally, musicians employed by aristocratic courts were numbered among the servants. However, as public concerts became more common, they were able to earn money from their performances, and publishing their compositions produced further income. Joseph Haydn, who was employed by the Esterházy family, was given frequent leave to travel, and by the end of his life he had transcended his lowly position to become part of the court. Amadeus Mozart, on the other hand, employed by the Archbishop of Salzburg, was not given the same freedoms, and resenting his servile position, moved to Vienna to become one of the first freelance musicians. However, the music world could not yet support such an ambition, and he suffered considerable financial hardship. When Ludwig van Beethoven moved to Vienna in 1794, he gained the support of wealthy patrons and never held an official appointment.

As instrumental music became more popular than vocal music for the first time, composers had to develop ways to create larger musical canvases that could support more intense listening. The result was the "Sonata Principle" (sometimes known as the Sonata Form), a musical structure consisting of three sections. Its use became almost synonymous with the first movements not only of sonatas, but also of symphonies, and indeed, most instrumental music of the era. It has remained in use until the present day.

The symphony evolved from the small-scale Baroque *sinfonia* into an iconic art form. Usually performed in four movements, the symphony would start with a gripping *sonata allegro* movement, followed by a slow movement. The third movement was usually an elegant *minuet*, but this evolved into the *scherzo*, which could be humorous, or express a more ironic, elemental passion. The finale was frequently a *rondo*, in which repetitions of a catchy, upbeat melody were interspersed with contrasting themes.

Other genres were also redefined. The three-movement concerto, in which the ideals of balance and elegance were matched by instrumental virtuosity, became a vehicle for just one soloist. The sonata developed into a more formal composition for one or two instruments. The rise in domestic music-making created a market for new forms of chamber music, such as the string quartet—invented by Haydn—and the piano trio.

The symphony orchestra became a broadly standardized entity, smaller but not very different from the orchestra of today. With the orchestra's fuller sound, the role of the *continuo* gradually died out; instead, the first violin directed the orchestra until it was eventually displaced by a specialist conductor. Orchestras now had a far greater dynamic range. In the 1740s, the crescendos and diminuendos of the Mannheim Court orchestra, under Johann Stamitz, caused a sensation and were soon a staple of all symphonic writing.

In opera, notably in the works of Christoph Gluck and Mozart, plots were now chosen for greater dramatic realism, and music was written to serve the drama rather than decorate it. Gradually, Italian artists began to lose their dominance as important works were written in German and French.

KEY ARTISTS AND WORKS

Christoph Willibald Gluck *Artasere* (1741); *Orpheo ed Euridice* (1762); *Iphigénie en Tauride* (1779)

Carl Philippe Emanuel Bach *Magnificat* in D Major, WQ215 (1749); Flute Concerto in G Major, WQ169 (1755)

Franz Joseph Haydn Trumpet Concerto (1796); String Quartet No. 63, "Sunrise," Op. 76, No. 4 (1797); *The Creation* (1798)

Wolfgang Amadeus Mozart Piano Sonata No. 8, K310 (1778); *Don Giovanni* (1787); "*Eine Kleine Nachtmusik*," K525 (1787); Symphony No. 41, "Jupiter," K551 (1788)

Ludwig van Beethoven Piano Sonata in F Minor, "*Appassionata*," Op. 57 (1805); *Fidelio*, Op. 72 (1805); Symphony No. 9, "Choral," Op. 125 (1824); Piano Concerto No. 5, "Emperor," Op. 73 (1811)

Louis Spohr Symphony No. 6 in G major, "Historic," Op. 116 (1839); Violin Concerto in A Minor, Op. 47 (1816)

The Romantic era

The Romantic movement emerged at the end of the 18th century in art and literature, and somewhat later in music. Advocates of Romanticism rejected the confines of classical convention; for them, originality was of paramount importance. They celebrated the emotional and the instinctive, and looked toward nature for inspiration.

Beethoven cast a long shadow over the 19th century. The emotional power of his music made him the chief precursor of what we now call Romanticism. His lifetime coincided with a watershed in history—the French Revolution of 1789, which was the most visible expression of the rights of the individual in the 18th century. Despite the oppressive regimes of the post-Napoleonic period, the Romantic cult of the individual flourished, along with an increasing awareness of the rights of nations to govern themselves and take pride in their own culture. In this climate of self-expression, women came nowhere near to winning equal rights, but a few were able to become composers and publish their works—Clara Schumann and Fanny Mendelssohn being the most celebrated examples. Some music of this period was characterized by the virtuoso performer, such as Franz Liszt. A parallel trend for intimate music intended for the salon—such as the shorter works, or "miniatures," of Chopin and Schumann—developed around the same time. This created a conflict between the public character of many of the great Romantic solo and orchestral works and the solitude of works such as Schubert's song cycle *Winterreise*.The Romantic era was one of extremes, with composers not only looking to the past but also abandoning classical conventions and experimenting with new and daring harmonic language and form. This progressive style was especially evident in Hector Berlioz's *Symphonie Fantastique*, with its extraordinary narrative of desire and destruction; in Liszt's Piano Sonata in B minor, S178 of 1852, with its snakelike one-movement form; and in the strange harmonies of Liszt's quasi-impressionistic late piano pieces, such as *Nuages Gris*. The Romantic period can claim to have "rediscovered" music from the past. When Mendelssohn organized a performance of J. S. Bach's *St. Matthew Passion* in 1829, he unlocked a treasure trove of music, which was revived in the next few decades. Not only did this alert musicians and audiences to the significance of Bach's own music, but it also encouraged musicians to perform music of the past, and inspired composers such as Brahms to use its materials and forms.

THE PIANO BECAME VERY POPULAR DURING THE ROMANTIC ERA

While musicians of earlier periods had tended to concentrate on their craft alone, the Romantics blurred the lines between disciplines: Berlioz and Schumann both published criticism as well as music, Weber wrote a novel, Liszt wrote essays on a wide range of interests, and Wagner wrote his own libretti as well as the music for his operas. Romantic composers therefore frequently referred to ideas beyond music itself—for example, landscape and nature became important themes, featured in music ranging from the songs of Schubert to 20th-century works such as Richard Strauss's "Alpine" Symphony and Vaughan Williams's "Sea" Symphony.

With constant theorizing about the direction music should take, it is not surprising that the Romantic era was one of bitter disputes. One of the most celebrated feuds was between the followers of Brahms and those of Wagner. Brahms followers saw him as a traditionalist, while Liszt and Wagner were believed by their supporters to represent the musical future. In fact, Brahms's musical language was at times highly adventurous, just as Wagner often looked to the past (most clearly in the music of *Die Meistersinger von Nürnberg*).

If there is one instrument that symbolizes the Romantic period, it is the piano. Most Romantic composers wrote not only concert music for the instrument but also music meant to be

JOHANNES BRAHMS

played by amateurs. Far more homes now owned a piano, and there was a consequent demand for music that could be played in a domestic setting. As such, many orchestral and operatic works were arranged for the piano.

Music from the Romantic era has remained perennially popular with listeners. It continues to be enjoyed for the richness of its melodic and harmonic invention, its poignancy and grandeur, as well as its extra-musical associations. Many late-20th-century composers have adopted certain characteristics of the Romantic style and incorporated them into theirs—for example, for the film *Star Wars*, John Williams composed music in the Romantic symphonic style to represent the future. Likewise, some of the orchestral works of American composer John Adams, such as *Harmonielehre,* could be interpreted as neo-Romantic.

KEY ARTISTS AND WORKS

Niccolò Paganini *Le Streghe,* Op. 8 (1813); 24 Caprices , Op. 1 (1820)
Franz Schubert Piano Quintet, *"Die Forrelle"* ("The Trout"), D667 (1819); Symphony No. 8 in B Minor, "Unfinished," D759 (1822); *Winterreise*, D911 (1827)
Hector Berlioz *Symphonie Fantastique*, Op. 14 (1830); Te Deum, Op. 22 (1849); *The Trojans,* Op. 29 (1858)
Felix Mendelssohn *A Midsummer Night's Dream*, Op. 21, 61 (1826–1842); Violin Concerto, Op. 64 (1844)
Frédéric Chopin Piano Concerto No. 2 in F Minor, Op. 21 (1830); Preludes, Op. 28 (1839); *Barcarolle*, Op. 60 (1846)
Robert Schumann *Fantasy in C*, Op. 17 (1838); *Dichterliebe*, Op. 48 (1840)
Johannes Brahms *Ein Deutches Requiem*, Op. 45 (1867); Violin Concerto, Op. 77 (1878); Symphony No. 3, Op. 90 (1883); Clarinet Quintet, Op. 115 (1891)
Franz Liszt *Faust-Symphonie*, S108 (1854); Piano Concerto No. 1, S124 (1855); *Mephisto Waltz No. 1*, S110/514 (1861)
Anton Bruckner Mass No. 1 in D Minor, WAB. 26 (1864); Symphony No. 3, WAB. 103 (1873–1889)
Pyotr Ilyich Tchaikovsky Piano Concerto No. 1, Op. 23 (1875); *Swan Lake*, Op. 20 (1877); *Eugene Onegin*, Op. 24 (1878); *The Nutcracker*, Op. 71 (1892)
Gustav Mahler Symphony No. 5 (1902); *Das Lied von der Erde* (1909)
Richard Strauss *Also Sprach Zarathustra*, Op. 30 (1896); *Salome*, Op. 54 (1905); *Der Rosenkavalier*, Op. 59 (1910); *Ariadne auf Naxos*, Op. 60 (1912)

Romantic opera

Opera thrived as a full-fledged genre during the 19th century, and some of the most popular of all operas—Giuseppe Verdi's *La Traviata, Rigoletto,* and *Aïda*; Richard Wagner's *Ring* cycle; Georges Bizet's *Carmen*; and Giacomo Puccini's *La Bohème*—were created around this time. The popularity of these works was based on their universal themes, the huge emotions they generated, and the mastery of their writing for voice and orchestra.

The years between the death of Mozart in 1791 and the arrival of Gioachino Rossini on the scene two decades later were comparatively barren for opera. Europe was too preoccupied with the Napoleonic Wars to spare money for this extravagant art form. The year 1813, when Rossini had his first great successes, was also the year in which two of the greatest Romantic opera composers, Verdi and Wagner, were born. Each revolutionized opera and polarized its enthusiasts into what even today can be—though should not be—two opposing camps. Romantic opera covers more than a century of composition. Up until World War I, Europe enjoyed a long period of relative peace, broken only by the political upheavals of the revolutions of 1848. These affected Wagner directly (he was exiled for his participation in the Saxony riots) and several other composers indirectly.

The other major change of the century was the Industrial Revolution. By midcentury, railways crisscrossed Europe and steamships plied the Atlantic, allowing composers, singers, and conductors to embark on international careers. Verdi traveled to Russia, Antonín Dvořák to the United States, Pyotr Ilyich Tchaikovsky to England (to pick up a doctorate), and Puccini to his eventual death in a Brussels hospital. The soprano Adelina Patti, greatest of bel canto singers, retired to a castle in south Wales; the tenor Enrico Caruso made New York City's Metropolitan Opera like a second home; and the Russian bass Feodor Chaliapin sang to audiences in Paris and London. In a century of nationalism, opera was a truly international art form.

Opera often draws on literary sources for its plots, characters, and themes. Plays, epics, novels, and histories have always inspired librettists and composers, and 19th-century Romantic opera took its inspiration from a particular set of writers. William Shakespeare's plays, Sir Walter Scott's novels, Goethe's *Faust*, and Friedrich Schiller's historical tragedies all became sources for opera librettos. Another great source of Romantic inspiration was the legends and poems of medieval Europe. Rossini took the old Swiss tale of William Tell for his last and possibly greatest opera, and Wagner drew on the medieval German epics *Tristan und Isolde*, the *Nibelungenlied*, and *Parsifal*.

In Italy, Rossini's use of Romantic plots, often melodramatic and improbable, inspired his two immediate successors, Gaetano Donizetti and Vincenzo Bellini, who took Romanticism still further. Donizetti drew on Sir Walter Scott for *Lucia di Lammermoor*, while Bellini told tales of Druid priestesses in *Norma* and of sleepwalking girls in *La Sonnambula*. In each of these operas, the central figure was that great Romantic icon, the damsel in distress. Lucia in her bloodstained nightgown and Norma in her priestess's robes are among the most hauntingly dramatic heroines in all theater, spoken or sung.

Verdi made further revolutions in the writing of opera. His earliest works told stirring tales of nationalism and heroism (*Macbeth*, *Ernani*, and *Nabucco*), while in his middle period, in works such as *Rigoletto*, he examined the relationship between parent and child, portraying vulnerable heroines with uncomprehending, overbearing fathers. Verdi's successors, Pietro Mascagni, Ruggero Leoncavallo, and Puccini, added the new element of *verismo* or realism to their operas, telling stories in music that were none the less Romantic for being drawn from everyday life.

In Russia, composers such as Mikhail Glinka and Tchaikovsky produced operas, usually on Russian themes. In France, the Parisian grand opéra employed huge stage sets, vast orchestras and choruses, and prodigious solo voices, with Giacomo Meyerbeer being the dominant composer. Jacques Offenbach wrote in the rival form of *opéra comique*, concluding his career with a masterpiece of Romantic opera, *The Tales of Hoffmann*. Other French works that have lasted well include Bizet's *Carmen*, Gounod's *Faust*, and Massenet's *Cendrillon*.

In Germany, the first great Romantic opera was Weber's *Der Freischütz*, based on a folk tale set in the forests of Bohemia. Weber brought a new richness of orchestration to his score. *Der Freischütz*

SCENE FROM A 1980S PRODUCTION OF VERDI'S *LA TRAVIATA*

inspired Wagner, who decided that the German world needed its own form of music drama, and proceeded to invent it, writing both words and music. Richard Strauss followed the unfollowable Wagner, producing Romantic works well into the 20th century. He was the last of the great Romantic composers.

KEY ARTISTS AND WORKS

Carl Maria von Weber *Der Freischütz* (1821); *Oberon* (1826)

Gaetano Donizetti *Anna Bolena* (1830); *Lucia di Lammermoor* (1835)

Giuseppe Verdi *Macbeth* (1847); *Rigoletto* (1851); *La Traviata* (1853); *Aida* (1871)

Richard Wagner *Tannhäuser* (1845); *Lohengrin* (1850); *Tristan und Isolde* (1859); *Die Meistersinger von Nürnberg* (1867); *Der Ring des Nibelungen* (1876)

Giacomo Puccini *Manon Lescaut* (1893); *La Bohème* (1896); *Tosca* (1900); *Madama Butterfly* (1904); *Turandot* (1926)

Jacques Offenbach *Orphée aux Enfers* (1858); *Les Contes d'Hoffman* (1881)

Johann Strauss Jr. *Die Fledermaus* (1874); *Der Zigeunerbaron* (1885)

National schools

Much of the music of the Baroque and Classical periods has an international style that cannot be pinned down to a single country. In the 19th century, however, musicians began to define themselves in terms of their nationalities as well as the styles or genres in which they worked. European politics in the 19th century was dominated by nationalist movements. These were of two main kinds. There were people united by a common language, such as the Italians and Germans, whose aim was to form a single-nation state, while other people—for example, the Hungarians, Czechs, and Irish—were subject to foreign rule and sought autonomy or independence. Music, along with language and literature, became a means of expressing their aspirations.

The most clear-cut example of musical nationalism, however, did not emerge in a country ruled by an oppressive empire. Russia was itself a great empire, but historically had been made to feel culturally inferior to Western Europe. European music had been imported into Russia by and for the aristocracy; the only truly Russian music was that of the folk tradition. The catalyst for change in Russia was Mikhail Glinka. His opera *A Life for the Czar* was similar to Rossini in style, but recalled the Russian folk melodies he had heard in his childhood. In the mid-19th century, a group of Russian composers, known as "The Five," took Russian nationalism much further. Mily Balakirev composed the symphonic poem *Russia* and Aleksandr Borodin wrote *In the Steppes of Central Asia*. A third member of the group, Modest Mussorgsky, was not a formally trained musician. Unfamiliar with Western harmonic progressions, he composed music that made full use of Russian folk harmonies. Later Russian composers, such as Nikolay Rimsky-Korsakov, also used folk melodies and influenced future generations of composers, including Glazunov and Stravinsky. The fifth member of "The Five," César Cui, was a military theorist and lecturer at the military academy who wrote music in his spare time.

Czech nationalist composers were less virulently anti-Western than their Russian counterparts. Their aim was to affirm their cultural difference from the Austrian Habsburg Empire, which had ruled Bohemia and Moravia for centuries, suppressing Czech language and culture. Bedřich Smetana, Antonín Dvořák, and Leoš Janácek contributed to the development of their country's national musical style. *Má Vlast*, Smetana's cycle of symphonic poems, is not only a portrait of the Czech landscape, but also an evocation of Czech culture and history. The section *Tábor* includes a Czech Hussite chorale, "Those who are Warriors of God."

Hungarians' situation differed from that of Czechs, as their folk music had been represented (or misrepresented) by prominent Romantic composers, such as Franz Liszt, Johannes Brahms, and Joseph Joachim. It was only in the 20th century that Béla Bartók and Zoltán Kodály began to collect traditional Hungarian folk music more systematically and make use of it in a more authentic way.

Political and cultural links between Germany and the Scandinavian countries took some time to loosen; Denmark's Niels Gade, for example, spent a significant amount of time studying and subsequently conducting in Leipzig. It was left to Nordraak and Grieg (who also studied in Leipzig) to create a distinctive style of Norwegian art music. Grieg's famous Peer Gynt Suite was written as incidental music for Henrik Ibsen's verse drama about the eponymous adventurer. In Finland, the music of Jean Sibelius displayed subtle nationalist tendencies only through its quotation of Finnish folk music.

> "I love music passionately... I try to **free it from** barren **traditions** that stifle it."
>
> FRENCH COMPOSER CLAUDE DEBUSSY

In North America, most art music of the 19th century ignored folk material, although Edward MacDowell's *Indian Suite* uses American Indian melodies. Charles Ives was a more distinctively American composer, and his quotations of music from his own environment provide a highly evocative picture of his childhood in New England. Later, Aaron Copland would create a highly recognizable American music, partly by appropriating rustic styles such as the "hoedown" in Rodeo. A revival of folk music in Spain coincided with that in Britain in the early 20th century. Composers such as Enrique Granados in Spain and Vaughan Williams in England used the folk music of their respective countries in similar ways.

MIKHAIL IVANOVICH GLINKA

KEY ARTISTS AND WORKS

Alexander Scriabin Piano Concerto Op. 20 (1896); Piano Sonata No. 4, Op. 30 (1903); *The Poem of Ecstasy* Op. 54 (1908); *Prometheus (The Poem of Fire)* Op. 60 (1910)

Sergey Rachmaninoff Piano Concerto No. 2 Op. 18 (1901); Symphony No. 2 Op. 27 (1908)

Antonín Dvořák Cello Concerto, Op. 104 (1895); Symphony No. 9, Op. 95, "From the New World" (1893)

Sir Edward Elgar Variations on an Original Theme ("Enigma"), Op. 36 (1899); *The Dream of Gerontius* Op. 38. (1900). Cello Concerto, Op. 85 (1919)

Frederick Delius *A Mass of Life* (1905); *In a Summer Garden* (1908); *On Hearing the First Cuckoo in Spring* (1912)

Ralph Vaughan Williams *Fantasia on a Theme by Thomas Tallis* (1910); *The Lark Ascending* (1914); Symphony No. 5 (1943)

Claude Debussy *Prélude à l'aprés-midi d'un Faune*, L.86 (1894); *Pelléas et Mélisande* (1902)

Heitor Villa-Lobos *Choros* (1920–1929); *Bachianas Brasileiras* (1930–1945); *Five Preludes for Guitar* (1940)

Edward MacDowell *Woodland Sketches* (1896); Piano Concerto No. 2, Op. 23 (1885)

Modern music

The first half of the 20th century was dominated by two very different composers: Austrian Arnold Schoenberg and Russian Igor Stravinsky. Both these composers established themselves in Europe and then moved to California. Schoenberg and his followers—raised on the high Romanticism of composers such as Mahler and Wolf—saw themselves as building on the Austro-Germanic tradition. At the same time, his interest in painting indicates a close relationship between the Expressionism of artists such as Oskar Kokoschka and Wassily Kandinsky, and of his own music and that of his followers, such as Berg. Stravinsky rose to fame with Russian ballets, such as *The Firebird* (1910) and *The Rite of Spring* (1913). He revived music with the primitive force of his rhythmic language, mirrored in the angular lines of the paintings of Pablo Picasso from the same period.

Later, Stravinsky looked back to the past by drawing on styles and actual materials of the 17th and 18th centuries, and this spirit of "neo-Classicism" was embraced by many contemporary composers, especially in France. Stravinsky's *Pulcinella* (1920) was the seminal example of neo-Classicism, and even as late as his *The Rake's Progress* (1948–1951) there is a sense of reverting to the traditions (and plots) of the past.

In France, Maurice Ravel's music was sufficiently objective in its poise and clarity to adapt to the neo-Classical ethos, as is shown in his *Le Tombeau de Couperin* (1917–1919). Even Claude Debussy succumbs to the charms of the past in *Suite Bergamasque* (1890). In Britain, William Walton and Constant Lambert took up the neo-Classical style, while in Germany, Paul Hindemith explored the forms of earlier periods, most notably in his series of duo sonatas for orchestral instruments and piano.

Many composers turned to the past to react against Romanticism, but others found in jazz a perfect foil to the music of the previous century. Virtually no composer in Paris was immune to the influence of jazz: Stravinsky composed a Ragtime (1918); Darius Milhaud composed the first jazz fugue in his ballet *La Création du Monde* (1923); and Ravel's *Violin*

SCENE FROM A 1948 PRODUCTION OF STRAVINSKY'S *ORPHEUS*

Sonata (1923–1927) contains a blues movement. At the same time, in the United States Gershwin was creating concert works, such as *Rhapsody in Blue*, that bridged the divide between popular and "serious" music.

Elsewhere, composers explored their musical folk heritage. In Eastern Europe, Béla Bartók and Zoltán Kodály traveled extensively to make recordings of folk songs and dances. Australian composer and pianist Percy Grainger was equally industrious, collecting music from various parts of the world. In North America, Aaron Copland began to use cowboy songs, Quaker hymns, and Latin American material in his own work, creating an immediately identifiable American style. Later, European composers as diverse as Benjamin Britten and Luciano Berio would make settings of the traditional folk songs of their countries, and composers such as György Ligeti, Steve Reich, and Kevin Volans would be influenced (in very different ways) by the music of Africa.

In Russia, several distinct and important voices emerged during the 20th century. Sergey Prokofiev spent some time in the West, and was influenced by the neo-Classicism he found in Paris, whereas Dmitry Shostakovich remained in the Soviet Union and was forced to pay lip-service to the Socialist Realism of the Soviet authorities. Political interference also surfaced in Nazi Germany, where Jewish composers were banned during the 1930s and even the music of non-Jewish composers, such as Anton Webern and Alban Berg, was outlawed as "degenerate art." Among the potentially great composers who died or were killed in Nazi camps were the Moravian Gideon Klein and the Czech Viktor Ullmann.

Some composers remained resolutely independent from other movements. Olivier Messiaen took religion as an important unifying factor for his music and, at the same time, used exotic scales and birdsong. Pierre Boulez was initially influenced by Messiaen, but later rejected his teacher and became a high priest of formalism, taking the principles of serialism to a new level.

In the United States, John Cage, who had studied with Arnold Schoenberg, turned his back on serialism and looked to the music and philosophy of the East for inspiration, while bizarre conceptual preoccupations inspired the work of Karlheinz Stockhausen, one of whose works involves a string quartet performing in midair in four helicopters. Technology impacted all types of music, through recording and through the use of synthesized sound; Edgard Varèse, for example, created a tape-only piece, *Poème Électronique*, for Le Corbusier's Philips Pavilion at the Brussels Expo of 1958.

A group of composers who emerged in the late 1960s were the minimalists. Terry Riley, Philip Glass, and Steve Reich composed music based on the repetition of simple motives that many found mesmerizing. Ultimately this style was taken up by composers who sought to reintroduce elements of development, such as John Adams, who has composed orchestral music and opera of Romantic proportions both in scale and richness of expression. Just as the minimalists rebelled against the complexity of serialism, so a group of European composers, including John Tavener, Henryk Górecki, and Arvo Pärt, developed music that was equally simple in its construction, but emerged out of a spiritual calm.

KEY ARTISTS AND WORKS

Arnold Schoenberg Chamber Symphony No. 1 *Op. 9* (1906); *Gurrelieder* (1911); *Pierrot Lunaire, Op. 21* (1912)

Béla Bartók *Music for Strings, Percussion, and Celesta Sz. 106* (1936); Concerto for Orchestra *Sz. 116* (1943)

Igor Stravinsky *The Firebird* (1910); *The Rite of Spring* (1913); *Apollon Musagète* (1928); *Dumbarton Oaks* (1938); *The Rake's Progress* (1951)

Charles Ives *Three Pieces in New England* (1903–1914); Symphony No. 4 (1916)

George Gershwin *Rhapsody in Blue* (1924); *An American in Paris* (1928); *Porgy and Bess* (1935)

Aaron Copland Piano Variations (1930); *Appalachian Spring* (1944)

Sergey Prokofiev *Piano Concerto No. 2, Op. 16* (1913); *Visions Fugitives, Op. 22* (1915–1917); *Romeo and Juliet* (1935)

Dmitri Shostakovich *Lady Macbeth of the Mtsensk District*, Op. 29 (1932); Symphony No. 5, Op. 47 (1937); Symphony No. 10 (1953); Symphony No. 13 (1962)

Michael Tippett *The Midsummer Marriage* (1955); *A Child of Our Time* (1941)

Benjamin Britten *Peter Grimes Op.33* (1945); *Young Person's Guide to the Orchestra Op.34* (1945); *Billy Budd*, Op. 50 (1951)

Jazz

Developed by African-American musicians in the early 20th century, jazz encompasses a variety of styles and genres, from its ragtime origins to later more adventurous forms, such as free jazz. It is characterized by its heavy use of improvisation and brass instruments, such as the saxophone and the trumpet.

Ragtime

African American musicians developed ragtime music in the city of New Orleans, Louisiana, during the first two decades of the 20th century. Influenced by their own musical tradition, classical and minstrel music, its unorthodox approach to rhythm—especially the use of syncopation—paved the way for many of the jazz styles that followed. The piano is the dominant instrument of ragtime and, thanks to the wide dissemination of printed piano music, the genre's most prominent composers, such as Scott Joplin, enjoyed widespread influence and popularity throughout America. Although ragtime fell out of favor before 1920, its standards were incorporated into the jazz repertoire during the 1950s and 1970s. Unlike later forms of jazz, ragtime is an entirely composed genre allowing no space for improvisation.

KEY ARTISTS AND WORKS

Scott Joplin "Maple Leaf Rag" (1899); "The Easy Winners" (1901); "Elite Syncopations" (1902); "The Entertainer" (1902)

Joseph Lamb "Excelsior Rag" (1909); "American Beauty Rag" (1913); "The Bohemia" (1919)

James Scott "Frog Legs Rag" (1906); "Grace and Beauty" (1909); "Broadway Rag" (1922)

"MAPLE LEAF RAG" BY SCOTT JOPLIN

Swing

Although ragtime used syncopated rhythms, it had a formalized structure and was heavily notated, leaving musicians little opportunity for artistic license. During the 1930s, African-American musicians such as Jelly Roll Morton introduced a looser approach to composing for jazz, allowing for significant improvization. This development culminated in the Swing Era, dating from about 1935–1946. During this time, jazz-based music moved from a predominantly African American audience to become a staple of mainstream American culture.

Swing bands—also known as big bands—released popular records and staged well-received live performances. Their leaders, such as Benny Goodman and Duke Ellington, and lead singers, including Ella Fitzgerald and Frank Sinatra, became full-fledged stars. Swing bands were usually large, consisting of as many as 25 musicians separated into rhythm, woodwind, and brass sections. In addition to "swinging" rhythms, their music was defined by its accessible, repetitive, and melodic hooks and its room for improvised solos, a trait by which jazz would become defined.

KEY ARTISTS AND WORKS

Duke Ellington "Mood Indigo" (1930); "It Don't Mean a Thing (If It Ain't Got That Swing)" (1931); "Sophisticated Lady" (1932); "In a Sentimental Mood" (1935); "Take the 'A' Train" (1939)

Benny Goodman's Orchestra "Get Happy" (1935); "Sing, Sing, Sing" (1937)

Count Basie Orchestra "One O'Clock Jump" (1937); "Jumpin' at the Woodside" (1938)

Frank Sinatra *Swing Easy!* (1954); *Songs for Swingin' Lovers* (1956); *A Swingin' Affair* (1957)

Ella Fitzgerald "I'm Beginning to See the Light" (1945); *Ella Fitzgerald Sings the Duke Ellington Song Book* (1957)

Bebop

Bebop was developed in the United States—in New York, in particular—during the early 1940s by musicians such as the pianist Thelonious Monk and the saxophonist Charlie Parker. In contrast to the rhythmic solidity of swing, which was popular as dance music, bebop emphasized the importance of imagination and innovation, particularly in the use of the solo instruments—typically, the saxophone, trumpet, and piano. Unusual phrasing and rapid sequences of notes were trademarks of the genre. As a result, it was a more demanding form of jazz—for both the performer and the listener—than the styles that preceded it.

> "The **piano** ain't got **no wrong notes.**"
>
> THELONIOUS MONK, SPEAKING ON WCKR STATION

KEY ARTISTS AND WORKS

Charlie Parker "Yardbird Suite" (1946); "Ornithology" (1946); "A Night in Tunisia" (1946)

Thelonious Monk *Genius of Modern Music Volumes 1 and 2* (1947–1952); *Brilliant Corners* (1956)

Dizzie Gillespie *Groovin' High* (1945)

Bud Powell "Bouncing with Bud" (1946); "Dance of the Infidels" (1949); "Hallucinations" (1951); "Un Poco Loco" (1951)

Cool jazz

Coming to prominence after World War II, cool jazz heralded a return to some of the looser rhythms of the pre-bebop era. Pioneered by American musicians such as the trumpeter Miles Davis and the pianist Dave Brubeck, it retained bebop's emphasis on musical virtuosity but was usually less frenetic than its predecessor, adopting relaxed, resonant percussion styles and fostering a more expansive quality among soloists. Unlike bebop, which had principally been developed in the jazz clubs of New York, many cool jazz musicians were based in Los Angeles, resulting in the music being described as "West Coast" jazz. However, as a subset, West Coast jazz is closer to bebop than to "cool jazz."

DAVE BRUBECK QUARTET

KEY ARTISTS AND WORKS

Lester Young "I Want to be Happy" (1946); "Crazy Over J-Z" (1949)

Miles Davis "Jeru" (1949); "Venus de Milo" (1949)

Chet Baker "My Funny Valentine" (with the Gerry Mulligan Quartet) (1952); "Tommyhawk" (1955); "Ponder" (1955)

The Dave Brubeck Quartet *Brubeck Time* (1955); *Time Out* (1959)

Modal jazz

Popularized by American trumpeter, bandleader, and composer Miles Davis, modal jazz was an innovation of the late 1950s. It replaced chord-based song structures with modal (scale-based) progressions. This shift allowed improvising soloists to draw on a wider range of notes, enabling them to create more interesting complementary and contrasting atmospheres. The size of modal jazz groups remained similar to those of cool jazz, usually involving between four and six musicians. Miles Davis' modal jazz album, *Kind of Blue*, is regarded as a landmark in jazz and in the history of 20th-century music.

KEY ARTISTS AND WORKS

Miles Davis *Milestones* (1958); *Kind of Blue* (1959)

John Coltrane *My Favorite Things* (1960)

Free jazz

Although modal jazz offered improvisers a wider range of choice than music structured around a chord progression, it was still limited by the notes of the mode, or scale. Developed during the mid-1950s, free jazz aspired to liberate itself from all restrictions, enabling improvisers to pursue any direction, without adhering to the conventional dictates of scale or chord progressions. Pioneered in New York by the saxophonist Ornette Coleman, its formlessness often extended beyond song structure; rhythms were rarely regular and performers often used unorthodox techniques to produce unusual sounds from their instruments.

KEY ARTISTS AND WORKS

Ornette Coleman *The Shape of Jazz to Come* (1959); *Free Jazz: A Collective Improvisation* (1961)

John Coltrane *A Love Supreme* (1965)

Jazz-funk

Fusing some of the characteristics of jazz—the emphasis on soloing and improvisation, for example—with the beat-driven rhythms of funk music, jazz-funk reached the height of its popularity during the 1970s and '80s. Although many of its leading exponents, such as Herbie Hancock and Roy Ayers, were American, the genre enjoyed significant success in England during the '80s.

KEY ARTISTS AND WORKS

Herbie Hancock *Fat Albert Rotunda* (1969); *Head Hunters* (1973); *Man-Child* (1975)

Roy Ayers *Ubiquity* (1970)

Donald Byrd *Blackbyrd* (1973); *Places and Spaces* (1975)

Latin jazz

From the early 20th century, African-American musicians started incorporating Cuban rhythms into their music. However, the first formal fusions of LatinAmerican rhythms with bebop-style jazz took place during the 1940s; this was exemplified by the Cuban-born musician and bandleader Machito, who experimented with a combination of jazz arrangements and Latin percussion. The influential bebop trumpeter Dizzy Gillespie also worked with Latin American musicians during the 1940s. Latin fusion gathered momentum during the 1950s and 1960s, and bandleaders and musicians, such as Tito Puente and Stan Getz, became mainstream stars.

KEY ARTISTS AND WORKS

Machito "Tanga" (1942); "Havana Special" (1949); "Fiesta Time" (1949)

Dizzy Gillespie "Manteca" (1947); "Tin Tin Deo" (1951); *Bahiana* (1975)

JAZZ NIGHTCLUB IN HARLEM, NEW YORK CITY

Tito Puente *Cuban Carnival* (1956); *Mambo Diablo* (1985)
Stan Getz *Jazz Samba* (with Charlie Byrd) (1962); *Big Band Bossa Nova* (1962)

Fusion

Coming to prominence during the late 1960s and early '70s, fusion was a crossover between rock and jazz. Early fusion was generally performed by jazz rather than rock musicians, and was developed by groups such as Weather Report. The genre retained the extended improvisations and unusual time signatures of cool jazz and bebop, but combined them with conventional rock instrumentation, such as electric guitars. Miles Davis produced several important works in the jazz-rock genre, beginning with the electric album *In a Silent Way* (1969) and following it with *Bitches Brew* in 1970, which is notable for its use of rock, rather than jazz, rhythms.

KEY ARTISTS AND WORKS
Miles Davis *In a Silent Way* (1969); *Bitches Brew* (1970); *A Tribute to Jack Johnson* (1971)
Weather Report *Weather Report* (1971); *8:30* (1979)
Chick Corea *Chick Corea Elektric Band* (1986); *Light Years* (1987)

Blues

Developed by African-American musicians in the 20th century, blues music gained popularity from the 1920s onward, first in its acoustic, and then in its electric form. It is characterized by a prominent use of the guitar and the employment of the 12-bar blues form.

Country blues

The term "country blues" is used to describe the earliest forms of blues music. It is believed to have emerged from a fusion of folk music and African-American work song in the southern United States during the late 19th century. From the 1920s onward, it proliferated in live and recorded forms, particularly in the towns and cities of the Mississippi delta.

Although early blues music encompassed a variety of approaches and styles, it is characterized as an acoustic music, typically featuring a singer accompanied by a guitar, or similar instrument. It is usually based on a repeating 12-bar pattern of chords, accompanied by lyrics that are mournful or fatalistic. Within the music, there is usually space for improvisation, and performers such as Robert Johnson and Blind Willie Johnson were virtuoso guitarists.

KEY ARTISTS AND WORKS
W.C. Handy "Memphis Blues" (1912): "Saint Louis Blues" (1914); "Beale Street Blues" (1917)
Blind Lemon Jefferson "Black Snake Moan" (1927); "Matchbox Blues" (1927); "See That My Grave is Kept Clean" (1927)
Lead Belly "Death Letter Blues Part 1" (1935); "Packin' Trunk Blues" (1935); "T.B. Blues" (1940)
Robert Johnson "Cross Road Blues" (1936); "Ramblin' on my Mind" (1936); "Hellhound on my Trail" (1937)

Electric blues

Although blues had begun as a rural form of music, it spread to the cities during the 1920s and '30s, resulting in different styles, larger bands and louder instruments playing to larger audiences. After World War II, the use of amplified instruments grew in popularity, thanks to the efforts of

B. B. KING PERFORMS

musicians such as T-Bone Walker. Chicago was the centre of the electric blues scene throughout the late 1940s and '50s, and it was home to many electric groups, which usually consisted of one or two electric guitars, a full drum kit, and amplified vocals and harmonicas. The electric bass guitar replaced the double bass during the 1950s. Despite the change in instrumentation, many electric blues exponents retained the characteristic chord progressions and lyrical content of their acoustic predecessors. However, other performers experimented with variations in form, such as the boogie-woogie-based electric blues of the Detroit-based musician John Lee Hooker. Electric blues was highly influential in the development of the role of the lead guitar in rock 'n' roll and the rock and pop music of the 1960s and '70s.

KEY ARTISTS AND WORKS
Muddy Waters "Rollin and Tumblin'" (1950); "I'm Ready" (1954); "Hoochie Coochie Man" (1954); "Mannish Boy" (1955)
John Lee Hooker "Boogie Chillen'" (1948); "I'm in the Mood" (1951); "Boom Boom" (1962)
Howlin' Wolf "Smokestack Lightning" (1956); "Spoonful" (1960); "Back Door Man" (1960); "Killing Floor" (1964)
B.B. King "Woke Up this Morning" (1953); "When My Heart Beats Like a Hammer" (1954); "Please Accept my Love" (1958); "How Blue Can you Get" (1964)

Folk

Folk music typically refers to the indigenous shared music of a specific people or area. Although its qualities vary around the world, the word "folk" is often synonymous with the string-based music of Ireland and the Appalachian region of the United States. Traditionally an oral form, passed on through performance, it influenced the folkrock music of the second half of the 20th century.

Appalachian folk

Although folk-inspired music enjoyed a boom in popularity during the 1960s, the traditional folk music of the United States was born in the eastern Appalachian region. The music evolved from the string-based acoustic compositions of 18th-century British and Irish immigrants, who accompanied their songs of agricultural and mining life with a fiddle, guitar, dulcimer, or banjo—an instrument introduced to the area by enslaved African Americans. Original Appalachian music was not formally performed, but played for leisure and at social gatherings. During the 19th century, Appalachian folk songs were disseminated through live performances, but in the early 20th century, musicians such as The Carter Family and Dock Boggs began to record their interpretations of traditional compositions. The music reached a wider audience and influenced the development of country and bluegrass during the 1930s and 1940s. It was revived during the 1960s, when it was referenced by folk and pop artists, such as Bob Dylan.

KEY ARTISTS AND WORKS
Dock Boggs "Danville Girl" (1927); "Pretty Polly" (1927); "Country Blues" (1927)
The Carter Family "Keep on the Sunny Side" (1928); "Wildwood Flower" (1928); "Wabash Cannonball" (1929); "Can the Circle Be Unbroken (Bye and Bye)" (1935); "I'm Thinking Tonight of My Blue Eyes" (1929)

IRISH DRUM

Irish folk

Irish folk music refers to the traditional music of Ireland, played prior to the 20th century, and the folk-influenced music played in Ireland from the 1950s onward. Traditional Irish folk music—played up to the 19th century—was generally a solo art form that used the country's native instruments, such as the *feadan* (a flutelike instrument) or the *timpan* (a stringed instrument). It was disseminated through oral tradition until the 19th century, when ballad printers became established. Although it experienced a decline in popularity during the first half of the 20th century, it was revived in the 1950s and 1960s by bands such as The Clancy Brothers and The Chieftains. It now enjoys an international audience and is particularly popular in countries with large expatriate Irish communities.

KEY ARTISTS AND WORKS
The Clancy Brothers "Whiskey You're the Devil" (1959); "Haul Away Joe" (1961); "The Irish Rover" (1962)
The Chieftains "The Wind That Shakes the Barley/The Reel with the Beryl" (1978); "Boil the Breakfast Early" (1979)

Country

Developed during the 1920s, country music is one of the most commercially successful forms of music in the United States. Heavily influenced by traditional folk music, it is characterized by its use of string instruments, such as the guitar, banjo, and the fiddle. Contemporary musicians have developed the genre by including electric instruments.

Traditional country

Influenced by the folk music of the Appalachian region in the eastern United States, country music was developed by musicians, such as Jimmie Rodgers and The Carter Family, whose recordings during the 1920s established a blueprint for the genre. From the 1930s onward, the Grand Ole Opry, a

Nashville-based radio program with a large audience, provided country musicians with a nationwide platform and launched the careers of stars such as Roy Acuff and Red Foley. Although the earliest forms of this type of music consisted of traditional acoustic songs, from the 1940s onward, bands incorporated louder instruments—drum kits and electric guitars—into their setup, and often mixed ballads with more upbeat compositions.

KEY ARTISTS AND WORKS
Jimmie Rodgers "Blue Yodel No. 1 (T for Texas)" (1927); "Frankie and Johnnie" (1929); "Blue Yodel No. 8 (Mule Skinner Blues)" (1931)
Roy Acuff "The Prodigal Son" (1944); "I'll Forgive You But I Can't Forget" (1944); "The Waltz of the Wind" (1947)
Red Foley "Smoke on the Water" (1944); "Shame on You" (1945); "New Jolie Blonde (New Pretty Blonde)" (1947); "Tennessee Saturday Night" (1948)

Bluegrass

While mainstream country music became more polished, bluegrass music, developed during the mid-1940s, preserved the raw string-band roots of Appalachian folk. The leading figure in the creation of bluegrass was the guitarist, singer, and songwriter Bill Monroe and he was the driving force behind the genre's rise in popularity during the 1950s. In addition to preserving the traditional instruments and songs of folk music, bluegrass was less concise and pop-orientated than mainstream country, allowing space within the songs for improvisations. Many mainstream country artists have also produced bluegrass music, including Dolly Parton.

KEY ARTISTS AND WORKS
Bill Monroe "Footprints in the Snow" (1945); "Blue Moon of Kentucky" (1946); "Molly and Tenbrooks" (1949)
Earl Scruggs "Foggy Mountain Breakdown" (with the Foggy Mountain Boys) (1950); "Roll in My Sweet Baby's Arms" (with the Foggy Mountain Boys) (1951)
Ricky Skaggs *Sweet Temptation* (1979); *Skaggs and Rice* (with Tony Rice) (1980)

BILL MONROE

Nashville sound

During the 1950s Nashville-based producers and record labels made a conscious effort to reduce the raw folk and honky-tonk elements of country music to increase its appeal to mainstream audiences. As a result, traditional instruments such as the steel guitar and the fiddle were replaced with more conventional pop music backings, such as string sections, and smoother production techniques were used. The effort was a commercial success, and the pop influence on this music was increased in the 1960s and into the '70s with the successful chart music known as "Countrypolitan," performed by mainstream stars, including Glen Campbell and Tammy Wynette.

KEY ARTISTS AND WORKS
Patsy Cline "Walkin' After Midnight" (1957); "Crazy" (1961); "I Fall to Pieces" (1961); "She's Got You" (1962)
Tammy Wynette *Your Good Girl's Gonna Go Bad* (1967); *Stand by Your Man* (1968)
Glen Campbell "By the Time I Get to Phoenix" (1967); "Gentle on My Mind" (1967); "Wichita Lineman" (1968); "Galveston" (1969)

Outlaw country

As a reaction to the high-production values and pop ambitions of the Nashville sound of the 1960s, several high-profile country performers, including Johnny Cash and Willie Nelson, sought a rougher, more rugged aesthetic. This movement was known as "outlaw country" and was built around gritty lyrics and less polished production techniques, which matched the rebellious image of its performers. The genre enjoyed significant commercial success during the 1970s.

KEY ARTISTS AND WORKS
Johnny Cash *Johnny Cash at Folsom Prison* (1968); *Johnny Cash at San Quentin* (1969); "The Man in Black" (1971)
Waylon Jennings *Lonesome, On'ry and Mean* (1973); *Honky Tonk Heroes* (1973)
Willie Nelson *Shotgun Willie* (1973); *Wanted! The Outlaws* (with Jessie Colter, Tompall Glaser, and Waylon Jenning) (1975)

Gospel

The gospel music of African-American communities that developed during the 1930s was a form of worship music, influenced by both the African-American spirituals and blues music of the first three decades of the 20th century. A vocal-led format, gospel combined group harmonies with virtuoso solo performances designed to provoke a heightened sense of spirituality and reverence in the listener.

During the 1940s and '50s, it was a commercially successful genre and its biggest stars, including Brother Joe May and James Cleveland, sold millions of records. Gospel went on to influence later African-American genres of music, including soul.

KEY ARTISTS AND WORKS
James Cleveland "Old Time Religion" (c. 1950); "It's Me O Lord" (1957)
Aretha Franklin *Amazing Grace* (1972)

Rhythm and blues

Rhythm and blues developed from the electric blues music of the late 1940s, with a greater focus on catchy riffs and melodies as opposed to virtuoso improvisation. It also made heavy use of Afro-Cuban rhythmic styles to create a genre that appealed to dancers. Pioneered by musicians such as Ray Charles during the 1950s, rhythm and blues employed horn sections to create vibrant music that enjoyed significant mainstream success. It was highly influential in the development of rock 'n' roll, soul, and funk.

KEY ARTISTS AND WORKS
Ruth Brown "So Long" (1949); "Teardrops from my Eyes" (1950); "(Mama) He Treats Your Daughter Mean" (1953)
Ray Charles "I Got a Woman" (1954); "This Little Girl of Mine" (1955); "Lonely Avenue" (1956); "Night Time is the Right Time" (1958)
Fats Domino "Ain't That a Shame" (1955); "Blueberry Hill" (1956) "Blue Monday" (1956)

Rock music

Founded in blues and rhythm and blues music, rock music began to emerge as a popular form during the early 1960s and was fully established as a dominant cultural force within a few years. Its popularity has continued as it has fused with other styles. The electric guitar is the central instrument of rock music.

Early rock 'n' roll

Influenced by country, electric blues, and rhythm and blues, rock 'n' roll used simple song structures, prominent rhythm sections, and amplified instruments—with the electric guitar being most prominent—to create a fast-paced and exciting genre that paved the way for the popular styles of rock music that exist today.

Developed during the 1950s, it was performed by both white and African-American musicians, and gave birth to some of American music's biggest mainstream stars, including Elvis Presley, Chuck Berry, and Little Richard. It was predominantly popular with a youthful audience and the lyrical content was often concerned with teenage life.

LITTLE RICHARD WITH HIS BAND

KEY ARTISTS AND WORKS
Chuck Berry "Maybellene" (1955); "Roll Over Beethoven" (1956); "Rock and Roll Music" (1957); "Johnny B. Goode" (1958)
Elvis Presley "Heartbreak Hotel" (1956); *Elvis Presley* (1956); *Elvis* (1956)
Little Richard "Tutti-Frutti" (1955); "Long Tall Sally" (1956); "The Girl Can't Help It" (1956); "Lucille" (1957)
Buddy Holly "Not Fade Away" (1957) "That'll Be the Day" (with the Crickets) (1957); "Peggy Sue" (1957)

1960s pop-rock

Inspired by the work of American rhythm and blues and rock 'n' roll performers, British musicians formed their own groups and, during the 1960s, they achieved international success with their records and performances. They were particularly well received in the United States, where their presence was described by the phrase "British

BEATLEMANIA

Invasion"; significant bands in this movement included The Beatles, The Rolling Stones, and The Kinks. Although they were heavily indebted to the sound of American rock 'n' roll, they concentrated on writing their own music and developing a distinctive sound. This period in rock music heralded the move of the long-playing album toward being a cohesive form of artistic expression, rather than simply a collection of popular singles. In the United States, surf rock was a hugely popular form of pop-rock and The Beach Boys emerged from that scene to achieve critical acclaim later in their career.

KEY ARTISTS AND WORKS

The Beatles *Meet the Beatles* (1964); *A Hard Day's Night* (1964); *Revolver* (1966)
The Rolling Stones *Beggars Banquet* (1968); *Let It Bleed* (1969); *Sticky Fingers* (1971); *Exile on Main Street* (1972)
The Kinks *Something Else* (1967); *The Village Green Preservation Society* (1968); *Arthur (Or the Decline and Fall of the British Empire)* (1969)
The Beach Boys *Today* (1965); *Pet Sounds* (1966)

Folk rock

Inspired by politically motivated singers and songwriters like Woody Guthrie, traditional folk music enjoyed a resurgence in popularity in the United States during the 1960s. The new folk-rock artists, such as The Byrds and Bob Dylan, played a mix of original compositions and songs from the folk repertory, using both acoustic and electric instruments. These acts were influential in inspiring British folk-rock acts, such as Donovan.

KEY ARTISTS AND WORKS

Joan Baez *Joan Baez* (1960); *Joan Baez Vol. 2* (1961)
Bob Dylan *Bringing It All Back Home* (1965); *Highway 61 Revisited* (1965); *Blonde on Blonde* (1966); *Blood on the Tracks* (1975)
The Byrds *Mr. Tambourine Man* (1965); *Turn! Turn! Turn!* (1965)
Simon and Garfunkel *Parsley, Sage, Rosemary, and Thyme* (1966); *Bookends* (1968); *Bridge Over Troubled Waters* (1970)

Psychedelic rock

Rising to prominence during the mid-1960s, psychedelic rock took the electric innovations and lyrical concerns of popular rock and folk rock music and introduced an element of experimentation. Linked to a counter cultural movement in which hallucinogenic drugs were viewed as a potential source of creativity, psychedelic rock bands, such as The Jimi Hendrix Experience, The Beatles, and The Grateful Dead, experimented with unorthodox production techniques, looser song structures, and unusual instrumentation—including Indian instruments such as the sitar.

KEY ARTISTS AND WORKS

The Beatles *Rubber Soul* (1965); *Revolver* (1966); *Sgt. Pepper's Lonely Hearts Club Band* (1967); *The White Album* (1968)
The Jimi Hendrix Experience *Are You Experienced* (1967); *Axis: Bold as Love* (1967); *Electric Ladyland* (1968)
The Grateful Dead *Anthem of the Sun* (1968); *Wake of the Flood* (1973)
The Doors *The Doors* (1967); *Strange Days* (1967); *L.A. Woman* (1971)

Blues rock

Many rock bands of the 1960s and '70s were influenced by rock 'n' roll, which had in turn been influenced by blues music. During the late 1960s, some performers began to emphasize the blues aspect of their sound, creating the sub-genre of blues-rock. Their song structures were similar to those of mainstream rock music, but there was an increased emphasis on virtuosity, particularly with regard to the guitar. Many of the musicians and groups within this genre were British, and included Cream (featuring Eric Clapton) and Fleetwood Mac. In the United States, blues-rock was highly influential in the development of hard rock.

KEY ARTISTS AND WORKS

Cream *Fresh Cream* (1966); *Disraeli Gears* (1967)
Fleetwood Mac *Fleetwood Mac* (1968); *English Rose* (1969)
Jeff Beck *Truth* (1968)

Progressive rock

Popular during the late 1960s and early '70s, progressive rock, or "prog rock" as it was widely known, was a reaction against the immediacy, compactness, and disposability of much rock music. Its exponents, such as King Crimson and Pink Floyd in England and Tangerine Dream and Can in Germany, created more expansive music with an emphasis on texture and atmosphere rather than catchy choruses and energetic riffs. Although much of the music was instrumental, its lyrical content was often esoteric and less literal than mainstream rock. Many progressive rock acts were influenced by jazz music as much as they were by other rock musicians, and often displayed a high level of technical skill in composition and musicianship.

KEY ARTISTS AND WORKS

Pink Floyd *The Dark Side of the Moon* (1973); *Wish You Were Here* (1975); *The Wall* (1979)
Frank Zappa *We're Only in It for the Money* (1968)
Tangerine Dream *Phaedra* (1974); *Rubycon* (1975)

Glam rock

Characterized by the theatricality of both its music and the appearance of its performers, glam rock was a popular form of chart rock in Britain during the 1970s. Its musical and visual aesthetic was initially defined by Marc Bolan, who adopted a glamorous and androgynous style of dress, featuring platform shoes, feather boas, and makeup. His band, T. Rex, produced a catchy form of pop-rock defined by its bold melodies and repetitive overdriven guitar riffs. David Bowie took glam rock's inherent theatricality to its logical conclusion through the creation of a cast of fantastical characters, such as Ziggy Stardust.

KEY ARTISTS AND WORKS

T. Rex *Electric Warrior* (1971); *The Slider* (1972)
David Bowie *The Rise and Fall of Ziggy Stardust and the Spiders from Mars* (1972); *Aladdin Sane* (1973); *Pin Ups* (1973)
Roxy Music *Roxy Music* (1972); *For Your Pleasure* (1973); *Stranded* (1973); *Country Life* (1974)

MARC BOLAN OF T. REX

Hard rock and heavy metal

During the early 1970s, rock bands such as Led Zeppelin combined blues riffs and song structures with a louder, faster, and more overdriven sound than their blues-rock predecessors. Their template was adopted in the late 1970s by groups such as AC/DC and Aerosmith. Black Sabbath, near contemporaries of Led Zeppelin, combined similar blues-rock influences with unorthodox guitar tunings and brooding lyrics to create the genre that came to be known as heavy metal. It would later be popularized by groups such as Iron Maiden and Metallica.

KEY ARTISTS AND WORKS

Led Zeppelin *Led Zeppelin II* (1969); *Led Zeppelin IV* (1971); *Houses of the Holy* (1973)
Black Sabbath *Paranoid* (1970); *Master of Reality* (1971); *Black Sabbath Vol. 4* (1972)

AC/DC *Dirty Deeds Done Dirt Cheap* (1976); *Highway to Hell* (1979); *Back in Black* (1980)
Aerosmith *Toys in the Attic* (1975); *Rocks* (1976)
Metallica *Ride the Lightning* (1984); *Master of Puppets* (1986)

Punk and new wave

Punk emerged in the United States and Britain during the mid-1970s as a reaction against the musical virtuosity and esoteric lyrics of genres such as progressive rock. British groups including the Sex Pistols and The Clash, and American acts such as Patti Smith and The Ramones produced short guitar-based songs in which attitude and energy were more important than the technical skills of the musicians involved. These groups influenced the post-punk and new wave bands that followed them during the late 1970s and early '80s. Bands such as Blondie, Television, and Elvis Costello shared the anti-establishment attitude of punk, but expanded their musical range to accommodate different sounds, more refined musicianship, and pop-orientated melodies.

> "Punk is **musical freedom.**"
>
> NIRVANA'S KURT COBAIN

KEY ARTISTS AND WORKS
The Sex Pistols "God Save the Queen" (1977); "Anarchy in the UK" (1976)
The Clash "White Riot" (1977); *London Calling* (1979)
Blondie "X-Offender" (1976); *Parallel Lines* (1978)
Talking Heads *More Songs About Buildings and Food* (1978); *Remain in Light* (1980)
Elvis Costello *My Aim is True* (1977); *This Year's Model* (1978); *Armed Forces* (1979)

Alternative rock and indie

During the 1980s, American alternative rock was dominated by college rock bands such as R.E.M., who combined punk and new wave rock influences with a more reflective, melancholy esthetic, and rougher industrial and noise rock groups such as Nine Inch Nails, Sonic Youth, and the Pixies. Despite being alternative acts, many of these bands achieved significant commercial success in the United States and abroad. In the UK, indie-rock bands such as The Smiths combined jangling guitar riffs with poetic lyrics, while groups such as New Order and Primal Scream fused traditional guitar music with electronic influences, to create indie-dance.

KEY ARTISTS AND WORKS
R.E.M. *Murmur* (1983); *Reckoning* (1984); *Automatic for the People* (1992)
The Smiths *The Smiths* (1984); *The Queen is Dead* (1986)
New Order *Power, Corruption and Lies* (1983); *Low-life* (1985); *Technique* (1989)
Nine Inch Nails *Pretty Hate Machine* (1989); *The Downward Spiral* (1994)

Grunge

Centered around the city of Seattle on the western coast of the United States, grunge was characterized by its anticorporate, antimainstream lyrics and heavy guitar sound. Developed by cult bands such as Mudhoney and Soundgarden, it became a mainstream form of chart music during the early 1990s, thanks to the success of groups such as Pearl Jam, Alice in Chains, and Nirvana.

PEARL JAM PLAYING AT SEATTLE'S MAGNUSON PARK

KEY ARTISTS AND WORKS
Nirvana *Nevermind* (1991); *In Utero* (1993)
Soundgarden *Badmotorfinger* (1991); *Superunknown* (1994)
Pearl Jam *Ten* (1991); *Vitalogy* (1994)

Britpop and British rock

The term "Britpop" was used to describe British groups of the mid-1990s who played music that was heavily indebted to the sounds and iconography of British rock bands of the 1960s, including The Beatles, The Kinks, and The Who. This genre replaced grunge as the most popular form of rock music in the UK, but not the United States. The most high profile of these bands, such as Blur and Oasis, enjoyed success around the world, while others were limited to a largely British audience. Of the British bands that followed Britpop, Radiohead pushed rock music into more experimental directions, while others, such as Coldplay, adopted a bold stadium-rock sound, achieving mainstream success in the process.

DESMOND DEKKER

KEY ARTISTS AND WORKS
Blur *Modern Life is Rubbish* (1993); *Parklife* (1994); *The Great Escape* (1995); *Blur* (1997)
Oasis *Definitely Maybe* (1994); *(What's the Story) Morning Glory* (1995)
Radiohead *The Bends* (1995); *OK Computer* (1997); *Kid A* (2000)
Coldplay *Parachutes* (2000); *A Rush of Blood to the Head* (2002)

Ska and reggae

Although the word "reggae" is often used to describe all forms of staccato dance music produced on the Caribbean island of Jamaica, it is actually a specific genre of music derived from an earlier Jamaican form known as "ska." Ska developed during the 1960s under the guidance of Prince Buster, who reinterpreted American rhythm and blues through the perspective of Afro-Caribbean music, stressing the second and fourth beat of a four-beat bar to develop a distinctive staccato, upbeat form of dance music.

By the late 1960s, ska had been transformed into the slower, looser sound of reggae. This music transcended its Jamaican context and reached an international audience, first through the work of singers such as Desmond Dekker, and later through Bob Marley, whose highly melodic reggae songs turned him into the first Jamaican musical superstar. Ska enjoyed a resurgence in popularity in the UK during the '70s through the 2-Tone movement, while reggae continued to influence pop artists, such as UB40 and Shaggy, through the '80s and '90s. It is also influential in the contemporary genres of dancehall and ragga, which cross the rhythms and instrumentation of reggae and ska with explicit, rap-style lyrics.

KEY ARTISTS AND WORKS
Desmond Dekker "Israelites" (1968); "007 (Shanty Town)" (1967); "You Can Get It If You Really Want" (1970)
Jimmy Cliff *Wonderful World, Beautiful People* (1969); *The Harder They Come* (1972)
Bob Marley *Catch a Fire* (1973); *Burnin'* (1973); *Natty Dread* (1974); *Exodus* (1977)

Soul

Soul music evolved during the late 1950s from a combination of rhythm and blues and gospel music. The American singer and songwriter Ray Charles is regularly cited as the catalyst for the development of soul as an identifiable standalone genre. Songs such as "I Got a Woman" established a blueprint for the music that would follow, although they were labeled as rhythm and blues at the time.

The cities of Chicago, Detroit, and Memphis were the geographical centers of soul music at the height of its popularity during the 1960s and early '70s, and each area produced music that was distinctive in style. Detroit produced the Motown sound, named after the record label of the same name, and was associated with some of the genre's biggest stars, including Stevie Wonder and Marvin Gaye. Motown was nominally associated with a commercially led pop aesthetic, although Wonder and Gaye both went on to produce hard-hitting socially conscious albums. Stax Records, based in Memphis, released many of the songs that define the classic vocal-led soul sound, by artists such as Aretha Franklin and Otis Redding. Chicago-based artists, such as Curtis Mayfield and The Impressions, displayed a more prominent gospel influence in their music. Soul diversified during the 1970s toward funk and the more commercial sound that would eventually become modern-day R&B.

CURTIS MAYFIELD

KEY ARTISTS AND WORKS

Ray Charles "I Got a Woman" (1954); "This Little Girl of Mine" (1955); "Drown in my Own Tears" (1956)
Aretha Franklin "Chain of Fools" (1967); "(You Make Me Feel Like) A Natural Woman" (1967); "Respect" (1967); "Think" (1968); "Rock Steady" (1971)
Marvin Gaye "I Heard It Through the Grapevine" (1968); *What's Going On* (1971); *Let's Get It On* (1973)
Stevie Wonder *Talking Book* (1972); *Innervisions* (1973); *Songs in the Key of Life* (1976)

Funk

The genres of rhythm and blues and soul were defined by their tight song structures and catchy melodies. Keeping the same instrumental ingredients as soul—vocals, drums, bass, guitars, and a horn section—James Brown pioneered a form of music during the mid-1960s that emphasized rhythm rather than melody. He encouraged the drum and bass players to the fore, employing unusual rhythmic patterns to create a repetitive "groove." This groove was augmented with horn stabs, short guitar riffs, and Brown's distinctive gravelly vocals. Brown's funk template was imitated by many other bands throughout the 1970s, and was expanded by Sly and the Family Stone and Parliament, a band led by George Clinton. Both of these added a psychedelic twist to James Brown's funk blueprint.

KEY ARTISTS AND WORKS

James Brown "Papa's Got a Brand New Bag" (1965); "I Got You (I Feel Good)" (1965); "Get Up (I Feel Like Being a) Sex Machine" (1970); "The Payback" (1973)
Parliament *Mothership Connection* (1975)
Sly and the Family Stone *Stand* (1969); *There's a Riot Goin' On* (1971)

Disco

Fusing funk, soul, and Latin dance music, disco rose to prominence during the 1970s. Unlike the genres that influenced it, disco is characterized by its use of a "four-on-the-floor" beat, in which the kick drum is sounded on every beat in a four-beat bar of music. This repetitive rhythm, combined with prominent bass, established disco as a popular music in the nightclubs of New York. From there, it became a staple of mainstream radio and the popular charts, and several of its performers, including Donna Summer and the Bee Gees, became international stars. Although the popularity of pure disco declined during the 1980s, its innovative use of a prominent "four-on-the-floor" drumbeat was influential in much of the dance music that followed during the that decade.

KEY ARTISTS AND WORKS

Donna Summer *Love to Love You Baby* (1975); *Bad Girls* (1979)
The Bee Gees *Saturday Night Fever* (1977)

Pop

Pop is a diverse and eclectic genre and styles vary around the world. However, it is united by its use of memorable hooks and melodies and simple, usually short, song structures. It is influenced by many other genres, including dance, rock, and hip-hop, and typically enjoys significant commercial success.

C-pop

The term "C-pop" is used to describe a variety of styles of Chinese popular music. Mandarin-language standards first enjoyed significant success during the 1930s and '40s through the performances and recordings of the "Seven Great Singing Stars"—seven popular female solo singers, including Zhou Zuan and Wu Yingyin. After the Chinese Civil war ended in 1949, Chinese-language pop music experienced a decline. It was revived during the 1970s and '80s by Hong Kong–based performers such as Alan Tam and Leslie Cheung. They produced Western-style pop ballads and their fame and popularity continued into the 1990s.

KEY ARTISTS AND WORKS

Alan Tam *Love in Autumn* (1984)
Leslie Cheung "Monica" (1984); "Who Resonates with Me" (1986); "Sleepless Night" (1987)
Anita Mui *Bad Girl* (1985); "Sunset Melody" (1989)

French pop

Since World War II, French pop music has been closely linked to the tradition of cabaret, particularly in the genre of *chanson*, which was defined by literate lyrics and orchestral, rather than rhythm and blues, backings. Performers such as Edith Piaf and the Belgian Jacques Brel popularized this formula during the late 1940s and the '50s. While the popular music of the Anglophone world of the 1960s and '70s was dominated by rock influences, the pop music of France retained some of the

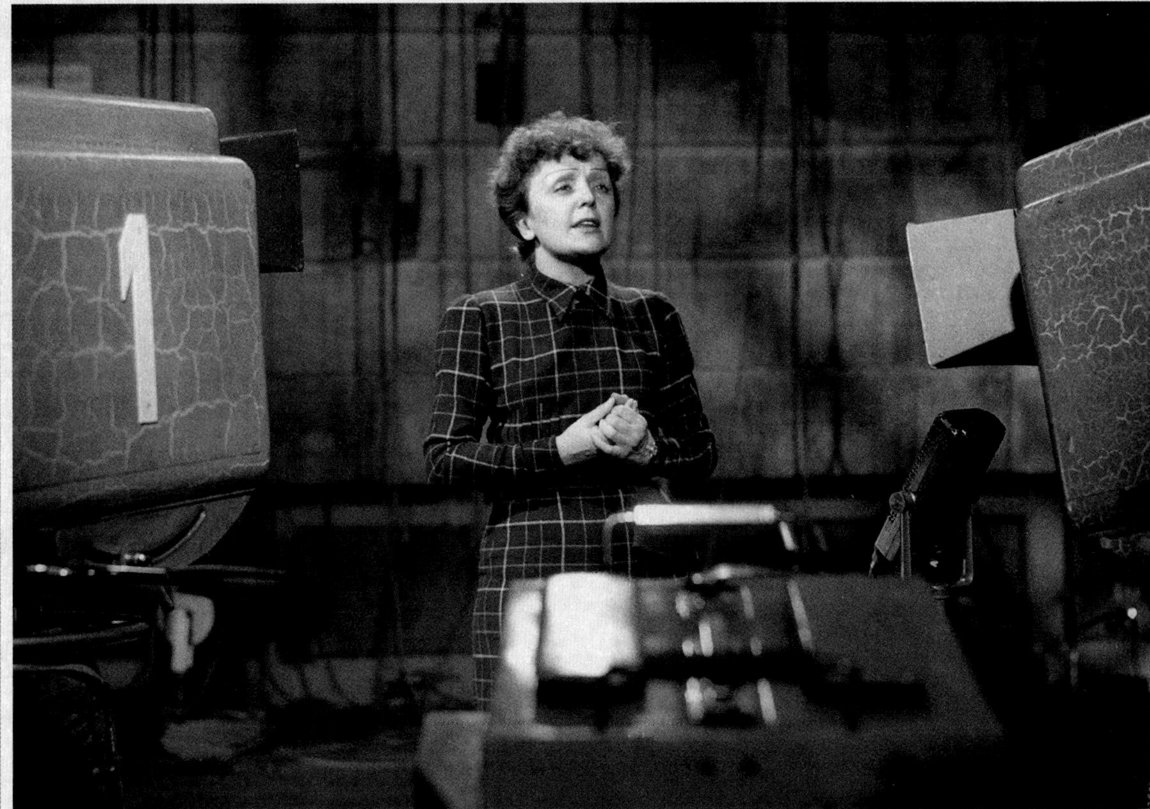

EDITH PIAF RECORDING A RECITAL

influence of *chanson* in the lush arrangements of musicians such as Francois Hardy and Serge Gainsbourg.

KEY ARTISTS AND WORKS

Edith Piaf *"La Vie en Rose"* (1946); *"Hymne à l'amour"* (1950); "La Foule" (1957); *"Non, je ne regretted rien"* (1961)

Jacques Brel *Jacques Brel 3* (1958); *Jacques Brel 6* (1964)

Serge Gainsbourg *Initials B. B.* (1968); *Histoire de Melody Nelson* (1971)

J-pop

The term "J-pop" is used to describe the pop music of Japan. Western instrumentation, combined with Japanese melodic modes, was being used in Japan in the jazz-influenced *ryūkōka* genre from the 1930s onward. The influence of rock and roll in Japan during the 1950s and '60s resulted in a decline in Japanese-language pop. However, during the early 1970s, the rock group Happy End returned Japanese lyrics to prominence, achieving mainstream success with their music. The work of the Yellow Magic Orchestra introduced electronic influences to Japanese pop music during the early '80s, though rock acts, such as Southern All Stars, continued to be popular. During the 1990s and 2000s, J-pop grew into a dominant chart presence, with teen-pop performers such as Namie Amuro selling millions of records.

PIZZICATO FIVE WITH DJ TOWA TEI

KEY ARTISTS AND WORKS

Happy End *Happy End* (1970); *Kazemachi Roman* (1971)

Southern All Stars *"Itoshi no Ellie"* (1979); *Nude Man* (1982); *Kamakura* (1985)

Namie Amuro "Chase the Chance" (1995); *Sweet 19 Blues* (1996)

K-pop

During the 1960s, enthusiasm for Western rock acts was widespread in South Korea. This resulted in a boom in the numbers of Korean folk-pop and ballad singers during the 1970s and '80s, such as Han Dae-soo and Lee Gwang-jo. However, it was the mainstream pop of the all-male group Seo Taiji & Boys that established a significant audience for K-pop music, which was maintained throughout the 1990s and into the 2000s.

KEY ARTISTS AND WORKS

Seo Taiji and Boys *Seo Taiji and Boys 1* (1992); *Seo Taiji and Boys 2* (1993)

H.O.T. *Wolf and Sheep* (1997); *Resurrection* (1998)

Dance-pop

Developed during the 1980s, dance-pop consists of simple pop music song structures typically set to an electronic backing. The earliest dance-pop artists, such as The Pet Shop Boys, Madonna, and Michael Jackson, fused disco, R&B, and electronic influences with accessible vocal melodies and bold, repetitive instrumental hooks, to create a hugely successful form of commercial music. The genre is usually producer-driven, and is dominated by the use of electronic instrumentation. During the 1990s and 2000s, dance-pop has retained its position as one of the preeminent forms of commercial music through the work of performers such as Kylie Minogue, Britney Spears, and Lady Gaga.

> "Dancers come and go... but the **dance lives on.**"
>
> MICHAEL JACKSON, FROM INLAY SLEEVE OF ***DANGEROUS***, 1991

KEY ARTISTS AND WORKS

Michael Jackson *Off the Wall* (1979); *Thriller* (1982); *Bad* (1987)

Madonna *Madonna* (1983); *Like a Virgin* (1984); *Like a Prayer* (1989)

Pet Shops Boys *Actually* (1987); *Introspective* (1988)

Kylie Minogue *Light Years* (2000); *Fever* (2002)

Electronic and dance music

The use of electronic instruments and sounds in popular music began during the 1970s and proliferated during the '80s through dance music genres such as house and techno. While dance music continues to be popular, electronic music styles have diversified and electronic instruments are now regularly used in many genres.

Early electronic music

During the mid-20th century, art music (classical) composers began to experiment with electronic sounds and instrumentation, such as looped recordings and synthesizers. The popularization of electronic instruments during the early 1970s resulted in electronic sounds being incorporated into pop- and rock-influenced acts, such as the German progressive rock band Can. Kraftwerk, another German band, were responsible for advancing electronic music during the mid-1970s and early '80s. In addition to stripping away conventional instrumentation to create an entirely electronic sound, their overall esthetic minimized human presence. Advances in electronic music were not restricted to Germany: the Yellow Magic Orchestra, led by the classically trained Japanese musician Ryuichi Sakamoto, achieved worldwide recognition, while the former Roxy Music member, Brian Eno, paved the way for ambient and chill-out music. Like Kraftwerk, these artists greatly influenced the electronic musicians that followed them.

KEY ARTISTS AND WORKS

Kraftwerk *Autobahn* (1974); *Trans-Europe Express* (1977); *The Man Machine* (1978)

Yellow Magic Orchestra *Yellow Magic Orchestra* (1978); *Solid State Survivor* (1979)

Brian Eno *Music for Films* (1978); *Ambient 1: Music for Airports* (1978)

House and Techno

House music grew out Chicago's nightclubs during the mid-1980s. Like disco, it was defined by a metronomic "four-on-the-floor" beat, with the kick drum being sounded on every beat in a four-beat bar of music. However, it was less commercial and accessible than disco. Chicago DJ's such as Frankie Knuckles played heavily edited versions of these songs in which the

YELLOW MAGIC ORCHESTRA

DAFT PUNK

drum part was prominent, increasing their appeal to dancers. As house music grew in popularity, it spread across the United States; it was particularly well received in Detroit, where several young music producers, including Juan Atkins and Derrick May, fused the rhythms of Chicago house music with instrumentation similar to that used by early electronic acts such as Kraftwerk and the Yellow Magic Orchestra. The resulting genre was known as "techno." House and techno spread across the world during the late 1980s and '90s, with different derivative genres being produced in different countries; in the UK, the synthesizer sounds of acid house achieved commercial success through artists such as the KLF, while techno proliferated in Germany, giving birth to a more melodic offshoot called trance. In France, groups such as Daft Punk fused house with funk and disco to widespread critical and popular acclaim.

KEY ARTISTS AND WORKS

Mr. Fingers "Mystery of Love" (1985); "Can You Feel It?" (1986)
Juan Atkins "No UFOs" (as Model 500) (1985); *Deep Space* (as Model 500) (1995)
The KLF *The White Room* (1991)
Daft Punk *Homework* (1997); *Discovery* (2001)

Jungle and big beat

Developed in the UK during the early 1990s, jungle substituted the "four-on-the-floor" beat of house music with syncopated rhythms, known as "breakbeats," which were created on drum machines, or sampled and speeded up to around 160 beats per minute. Although jungle (also known as "drum 'n' bass") began life as a dance music sub-culture, it increased in sophistication, and artists such as Goldie and Roni Size achieved critical acclaim. The use of syncopated rhythms rather than kick drum sequences influenced several subsequent dance music genres, including big beat, which fused samples of speeded up hip-hop and funk drum patterns with rock and house music instrumentation. The genre produced several mainstream artists, including Fatboy Slim and The Chemical Brothers.

KEY ARTISTS AND WORKS

Goldie *Timeless* (1995); *Saturnz Return* (1998)
Roni Size *New Forms* (1997); *In the Mode* (2000)
Chemical Brothers *Exit Planet Dust* (1995); *Dig Your Own Hole* (1997)
Fatboy Slim *Better Living Through Chemistry* (1996); *You've Come a Long Way, Baby* (1998)

Trip-hop and electronica

Electronica describes a diverse range of music and artists that are influenced by the sounds and production processes of dance music. Although they use electronic instruments (synthesizers and drum machines) and techniques, such as sampling, the music is usually slower than conventional dance music and intended for home listening. In the 1990s, trip-hop artists such as Massive Attack and DJ Shadow sampled funk, reggae, and soul records to create a form of brooding ambient hip-hop, while the Icelandic singer and songwriter Björk and the French band Air married ambient electronic sounds with pop melodies, achieving significant mainstream success.

KEY ARTISTS AND WORKS

Massive Attack *Blue Lines* (1991); *Protection* (1994); *Mezzanine* (1998)
DJ Shadow "In/Flux" (1993); "What Does Your Soul Look Like" (1994); *Endtroducing* (1996)
Björk *Post* (1995); *Homogenic* (1997)
Air *Moon Safari* (1998); *Talkie Walkie* (2004)

Urban music

The term "urban music" is used to describe a range of hip-hop influenced styles, usually produced by African American musicians. From its earliest underground hip-hop roots in the late 1970s and '80s, urban music has acquired a large mainstream audience, and styles such as R&B are synonymous with modern pop music.

Old school and crossover hip-hop

Hip-hop was developed in New York during the late 1970s and early '80s. In its earliest form, it consisted of a DJ playing sections of funk, soul, and electro records that were talked over by MCs, or rappers. Groups such as Grandmaster Flash and the Furious Five and The Sugarhill Gang added to the sophistication of the genre, using drum machines and samplers to produce drum-heavy backing tracks and moving beyond call-and-response vocals toward lyrics that often dealt with sociopolitical issues through rhyme and wordplay. During the mid 1980s, New York group Run-DMC's success turned hip-hop into a commercially successful form. Their success was built on by politically motivated groups such as Public Enemy, who frequently addressed race-related issues through their lyrics. Jazz, funk, and soul music were the most prominent source of samples for many groups, including A Tribe Called Quest and De La Soul. Although hip-hop was mainly produced by African American musicians, and its earliest audiences came from African American communities in New York, it quickly gained popularity as a mainstream genre with a multiracial audience.

KEY ARTISTS AND WORKS

Grandmaster Flash and the Furious Five "The Adventures of Grandmaster Flash on the Wheels of Steel" (1981); "The Message" (1982); "White Lines" (1982)
Run-D.M.C. *Run-D.M.C.* (1984); *King of Rock* (1985); *Raising Hell* (1986)
Public Enemy *It Takes a Nation of Millions to Hold Us Back* (1988); *Fear of a Black Planet* (1990)
De La Soul *3 Feet High and Rising* (1989); *De La Soul is Dead* (1991)

Gangsta rap and beyond

Although New York was the focus of rap music until the early 1990s, Los Angeles-based groups such as N.W.A. and Ice T began to establish a uniquely "West Coast" style of rap during the late 1980s and early 1990s. This genre, celebrating hedonism and often discussing criminality, came to be known as gangsta rap. The producer and rapper Dr. Dre confirmed gangsta rap as the commercially dominant force in urban music with the release of *The Chronic*, and he was followed by a number of other gangsta rap stars, including Snoop Doggy Dog and 2Pac. During the late 1990s and 2000s, rap became a prominent form of pop music, enjoying worldwide commercial and critical acclaim. With mainstream success, the traditional geographical polarization of the genre in the United States diminished; from the late 1990s onward, the southern states of the county produced several hip-hop stars, including Lil' Wayne, Outkast, and Ludacris.

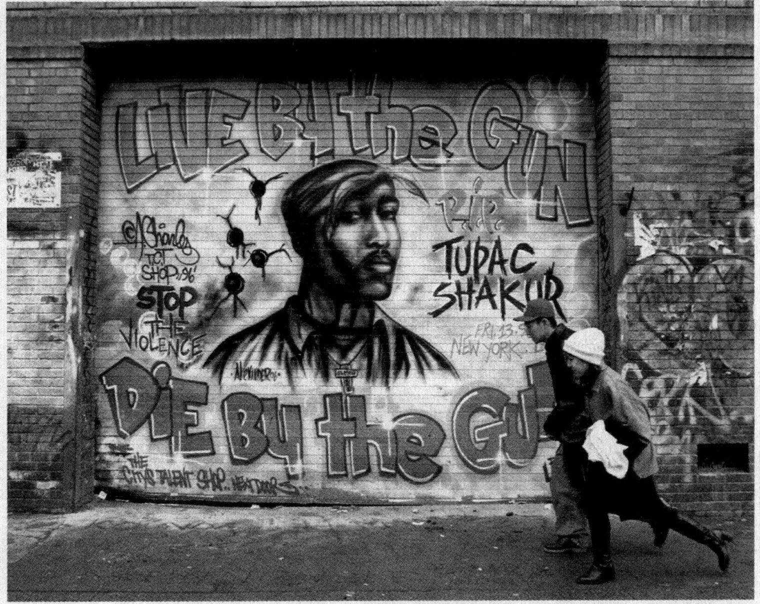

GRAFFITI DEPICTING TUPAC SHAKUR, BETTER KNOWN AS 2PAC

In addition to experiencing success in music, rappers such as Jay-Z have established themselves as dominant figures in American culture, writing soundtracks for films, running record labels, and enjoying unparalleled levels of fame and recognition.

KEY ARTISTS AND WORKS

Dr. Dre *The Chronic* (1992); *2001* (1999)
Snoop Doggy Dogg *Doggystyle* (1993); *Murder Was the Case* (1994)
2Pac *Me Against the World* (1995); *All Eyez on Me* (1996)
Jay-Z *Reasonable Doubt* (1996); *The Blueprint* (2001); *The Black Album* (2003)
Eminem *The Slim Shady LP* (1999); *The Marshall Mathers LP* (2000)

Contemporary R&B

Despite sharing its name with the rhythm and blues genre of the 1950s, contemporary R&B is characterized by a combination of hip-hop style instrumentation and soul vocals and is usually produced by African American musicians. Contemporary R&B first emerged during the late 1980s in response to the diminishing popularity of disco; some of its earliest exponents, including Marvin Gaye and Tina Turner, had enjoyed significant popularity in other genres, such as soul and funk. It became a mainstream genre in the mid-1990s, with female vocalists, such as Whitney Houston and Janet Jackson, enjoying huge commercial success. The dominance of contemporary R&B in mainstream charts in the early years of the 21st century made it synonymous with pop music, and many of its biggest stars, including Beyoncé Knowles, have achieved worldwide renown.

KEY ARTISTS AND WORKS

Janet Jackson *Rhythm Nation 1814* (1989); *Janet* (1993)
Whitney Houston *Whitney* (1987); *My Love is Your Love* (1988)
Mariah Carey *Daydream* (1995); *Butterfly* (1997)
R. Kelly *R. Kelly* (1995); *R.* (1998)
Beyoncé *Dangerously in Love* (2003); *B'day* (2006)

Iberian music

Although Spain and Portugal have produced a range of distinctive styles, they are best known for the folk genres of flamenco and fado respectively.

Flamenco

Flamenco began as a vocal-only form of Spanish music in the 18th century. During the 19th century, a guitar accompaniment was added and the instrument has been a prominent feature of flamenco music ever since—both as a solo instrument and as part of an ensemble. Castanets are the most common percussion accompaniment in the genre. The various style of flamenco, distinguished by different rhythms, melodic modes, and chord progressions, are described as *palos*. Flamenco songs are written according to the dictates of the chosen *palo* and often provide an accompaniment to the dance of the same name.

KEY ARTISTS AND WORKS

Paco de Lucía *Al Verte las Flores Lloran* (1969); *El duende flamenco de Paco de Lucía* (1972)
Camarón de la Isla *"Sube Al Enganche"* (1970)
Estrella Morente *"Calle del aire"* (2001)

Fado

Fado emerged during the 19th century as a folk form among the working classes in Portugal. There are two separate styles of fado: the looser Lisbon style and the more formal Coimbra style. Both are united by their use of melancholy lyrics and vocal melodies set to a 12-stringed acoustic guitar backing. In the middle of the 20th century, performers such as Alfredo Marceneiro and Amália Rodrigues spearheaded a golden age of fado. Although the music's popularity dwindled slightly during the 1970s it has continued to influence younger generations of Portuguese musicians.

KEY ARTISTS AND WORKS

Amália Rodrigues *"Ai, Mouraria"* (1945); *"Perseguição"* (1945); *"Novo Fado da Severa"* (1953)
Mariza *Fado em Mim* (2001); *Fado curvo* (2003)
Carlos Paredes *Guittarra portuguesa* (1967)

FADO SINGER MARIZA ON-STAGE IN GLASGOW

CALYPSO QUINTET

Music of Latin America and the Caribbean

Latin American and Caribbean music encompasses everything from the lyrically inventive calypso of Trinidad to the dance-focused Cuban mambo. Although there is a wide range of styles, the music of the region is often characterized by the prominent use of percussion.

Corrido

A Mexican form of folk song that narrates heroic or epic stories relating to the history of the country, corrido songs are set to a musical backdrop similar to a European waltz. The genre reached the height of its prominence during the early 20th century and retained its popularity during the Mexican Revolution of 1910–1920. However, its focus changed in the latter years of the 20th century to address subjects such as criminality and drug smuggling. This sub-genre is known as "Narcocorrido."

KEY ARTISTS AND WORKS

Antonio Aguilar *"El Corrido de Lamberto Quintero"* (1984)
Los Tigres del Norte *"Contrabando y Traición"* (1972) *"Pacas de a Kilo"* (1993)

Calypso

Calypso was developed from the vocal music tradition of enslaved African people in Trinidad in the 17th century. However, the modern form of the genre, characterized by rhythmic singing and witty lyrics, was developed during the first two decades of the 20th century. The steelpan instruments that now typify calypsonian percussion were added during the 1930s. At this time, calypso began to transcend its origins in Trinidad and reach wider audiences through the work of singers and songwriters, such as Roaring Lion and Attila the Hun, who traveled to the United States and England to record and perform. Calypso reached the height of its commercial popularity through the work of mainstream singers, such as Harry Belafonte. Its appeal declined during the 1960s and 1970s; however, it has influenced subsequent genres of Caribbean music.

KEY ARTISTS AND WORKS

Roaring Lion "Ugly Woman" (1934); "Mary Ann" (1945); "Netty, Netty" (1937)
Lord Kitchener "Green Fig" (1942); "The Road" (1963); *"Mama dis is Mas"* (1964); "Rainorama" (1973)
Harry Belafonte *Calypso* (1956)

Son

Son emerged in Cuba during the first two decades of the 20th century. Generally performed by Afro-Cuban musicians, it combined African rhythms with Spanish guitar and romantic or sentimental lyrics. It was popularized by the leading sextets of the genre, such as Sexteto Habanero and Sexteto Bolano. These groups usually consisted of percussion and string instruments. By the late 1920s, son was one of the most popular forms of music in Cuba, and later performers, such as Arsenio Rodríguez and Beny Moré, continued to develop the genre during the 1940s. With the rising popularity of big band Latin jazz during the 1950s, the prevalence of son declined, though it was influential in the development of new Latin styles, including mambo.

KEY ARTISTS AND WORKS

Sexteto Habanero *"Yo No Tumbo Cana"* (c.1926); *"Ahora Si"* (1930)
Arsenio Rodríguez *"Triste Soledad"* (1941); *"Sin tu Querer"* (1942); *"Triste Lucha"* (1943)

Tango

Tango evolved in Argentina in the late 19th century as a fusion of European and African musical styles. A popular form of dance music in Buenos Aires, it was initially played by a trio featuring a violin, flute, and guitar. Later, the flute and guitar were replaced by piano and bandoneon (an accordion-like instrument), then the trio became a sextet of a piano, two violins, two bandoneons, and a double bass. The size of the band continued to grow and could include a full string section and up to four bandoneons. The music is characterized by staccato rhythms and sometimes features a romantic or sentimental vocal part. Driven by bandleaders such as Juan D'Arienzo and Ástor Piazzolla, tango reached the height of its popularity between 1930 and 1960, although contemporary bands, such as the Gotan Project, continue to incorporate aspects of the genre in their music.

KEY ARTISTS AND WORKS

Juan D'Arienzo *"Desde El Alma"* (1935); *"Hotel Victoria"* (1935); *"La Puñalada"* (1937)
Rodolfo Biagi *"Indiferencia"* (1937); *"Humillación"* (1941); *"Magdala"* (1945)
Astor Piazzolla *"El Desbande"* (1946); *"Tres Tangos Sinfonicos"* (1963); *"Balada para un loco"* (1969); *"Libertango"* (1974)
Gotan Project *La Revancha del Tango* (2001); *Lunático* (2006)

Mariachi

During the late 19th century, mariachi string bands proliferated in rural Mexico, playing a form of folk music called *Son Jaliscience*. Traditional bands featured a harp, violins, guitars, and a guitarron. In the early 20th century, mariachi made a transition from a rural art form to an urban one. This led to an evolution in the makeup of mariachi ensembles, with a horn section—consisting of one or two trumpets—being added around the 1930s. Traditionally, mariachi bands were itinerant, moving from place to place to perform. They were identified by their adoption of the costume of the "charro," the traditional horsemen of Mexico.

KEY ARTISTS AND WORKS

Lola Beltran *"Cucurrucucù Paloma"* (1962)
Pedro Infante *"Acqui Vienen Los Mariachis"* (1951)

Bolero

Although "boleros" are a feature of Western classical music, the genre of bolero originated in Cuba in the late 19th century. It consisted of melancholy romantic vocal parts set to a slow backing and was usually performed as an accompaniment to dancing. The earliest Cuban stars included Pepe Sánchez and Benny Moré, though the genre spread across Latin America during the first half of the 20th century. It was adopted and performed by singers, such as the Mexican Agustín Lara. Bolero's popularity lasted until the 1960s, when it was superseded by other dance styles, such as the cha-cha-cha.

KEY ARTISTS AND WORKS

Pepé Sanchez *"Tristezas"* (1885)
Agustín Lara *"Solamente Una Vez"* (1941)

Samba

Styles of Brazilian samba vary depending on the region in which they are written and performed, but the form most typically associated with the genre evolved in Rio de Janeiro during the early 20th century. Its development was fueled by annual competitions in the city, in which samba schools—neighborhood dance and music clubs — sought to win acclaim by composing original sambas and performing them, accompanied by a choreographed dance. Some of the finest composers, such as Nelson Cavaquinho, emerged in this way. Typically, their songs were melodic and supported by complex, syncopated rhythms. Although a diverse range of instruments was frequently used, the traditional ensemble was focused around the *pandeiro*, a hand drum, and the *cavaquinho*, a guitarlike instrument. Samba has continued to be popular in Brazil, and has been fused with other genres, including rock, rap, and reggae.

GUITARRON, AN ACOUSTIC BASS GUITAR

WOMAN IN COLORFUL COSTUME AT A SAMBA DANCE SHOW

KEY ARTISTS AND WORKS

Nelson Cavaquinho *"Rugas"* (1946); *"A Flor o Espinho"* (1957); *"Luz Negra"* (1966)
Cartola *Cartola* (1974); *Cartola II* (1976)
Zeca Pagodinho *Zeca Pagodinho* (1999)

Mambo and cha-cha-cha

Danzón, a fusion of European dance music and African rhythms, was a popular form of dance music in Cuba in the early 20th century. In 1938, the brothers Orestes and Cachao Lopéz composed a danzón called "mambo," creating a new rhythm and a new genre of music. Its popularity grew during the 1940s and '50s, and the style evolved, becoming characterized by its heavy use of percussion—especially cowbells—and brass. It reached a significant audience in the United States thanks to the work of musicians and bandleaders, such as Cachao López and Tito Puente. In the 1950s, the Cuban composer Enrique Jorrín adapted the mambo to make a more accessible form of dance music that became known as cha-cha-cha.

KEY ARTISTS AND WORKS

Pérez Prado "Mambo No. 5" (1949); *"Que Rico el Mambo"* (1949); "Cherry Pink and Apple Blossom White" (1955)
Tito Puente *Cuban Carnival* (1956); *Dance Mania* (1958); *Dance Mania Vol. 2* (1961)
Enrique Jorrín *"La Enganadora"* (1953); *"El Alardoso"* (1953)

Bossa nova

Literally meaning "new style," bossa nova developed in Brazil during the late 1950s and early '60s as a fusion of samba and jazz. It was less percussive and dance-oriented than samba, employing classical guitar, light percussion, and often subtle, nuanced lyrics that dealt with youthful themes. The collaboration of bossa nova artists, such as Antônio Carlos Jobim, with notable American jazz musicians, such as Stan Getz, popularized bossa nova around the world. Although the popularity of the genre diminished during the 1970s, it has continued to influence the work of young Brazilian musicians, such as Bebel Gilberto.

KEY ARTISTS AND WORKS

Antonio Carlos Jobim *Black Orpheus* (1959)
Joao Gilberto *Getz/Gilberto* (1964); *Getz/Gilberto #2* (1966)

Zouk

Pioneered by Kassav, a Paris-based group of musicians from the islands Martinique and Guadeloupe, zouk music updated the traditional dance music of the Antilles through the use of modern production techniques and instrumentation, such as synthesizers and drum machines. With an emphasis on dance-friendly rhythms, zouk achieved popularity in France, Canada, and the francophone countries of Africa during the late 1970s and early 1980s.

KEY ARTISTS AND WORKS

Kassav *Love and Ka Dance* (1979); *Yélélé* (1984)
Zouk Machine *Sové Lanmou* (1986); *Maldon* (1989)

Soca

Soca—a portmanteau word created from a combination of "soul" and "calypso"—was developed in Trinidad during the 1960s, predominantly through the work of the calypso singer, Lord Shorty. He combined the traditional calypso of Trinidad with Indian instruments, such as the tabla, to create the early energetic soca sound. During the 1970s and '80s many soca musicians added electric instruments, including synthesizers, to his blueprint, and the genre became a popular form of dance music throughout the world.

KEY ARTISTS AND WORKS

Lord Shorty "*Ïndrani*" (1973); *Soca Explosion* (1978)

Machel Montano *Soca Earthquake* (1987); *Dr. Carnival* (1988)

Music of Africa

From the blues-style music of Sub-Saharan Africa to the buoyant dance sound of West African highlife, the music of Africa is diverse. African music has influenced the musical life of Latin and Central America, particularly the rhythms of Cuban genres, such as son.

Gnawa

A form of traditional African-Islamic music, gnawa is usually performed at religious celebrations in Morocco and Algeria. Gnawa songs typically consist of a chant accompanied by lutelike instruments, such as the *gunibri*, and light percussion. Traditional forms of the music continue to be performed in North Africa, but updated secular styles of gnawa, and fusions with Western popular genres such as rap and jazz, are also popular.

KEY ARTISTS AND WORKS

Mahmoud Ghania *The Trance of Seven Colours* (1994)

Hassan Hakmoun *Gift of the Gnawa* (1991)

Highlife

Developed in Ghana during the early 20th century, highlife began as a fusion of traditional African music and early jazz styles. From the 1930s onward, its popularity spread through Nigeria, and it eventually became one of the most widely performed styles of dance music in West Africa. The most prominent musicians and bandleaders of highlife, such as E. T. Mensah (known as the "King of Highlife"), were acclaimed outside Africa and sometimes performed with Western jazz musicians. Highlife's popularity declined at the end of the 1960s, although it is still played in Nigeria and Ghana today.

KEY ARTISTS AND WORKS

E. T. Mensah "All For You" (1955); "Nkebo Bayaa" (1955)

Dr. Sir Warrior *Nwanne Awu Enyi* (1978)

Ebo Taylor *Ebo Taylor* (1977)

Jùjú

Developed during the 1920s, jùjú is a highly percussive form of Nigerian dance music that makes extensive use of the talking drum, a popular percussion instrument of the Yoruba people. With its combination of upbeat rhythms, melodic guitar, and poetic lyrics, it achieved popularity during the 1950s through the work of musicians such as I. K. Dairo and Tunde Nightingale. Throughout the 1970s and early '80s, innovative performers such as King Sunny Adé reached a global audience.

KEY ARTISTS AND WORKS

I. K. Dairo *Ashiko* (1994)

King Sunny Adé *Juju Music* (1982); *Synchro System* (1983)

TALKING DRUM

African blues

Although blues is regarded as a quintessentially American form of music, it is widely acknowledged that the African American pioneers of the genre were influenced in part by African music. A growing presence in world music since the 1970s, African blues constitutes a response by African musicians to the influence of American blues music. Styles of African blues vary depending on the region of its origin, but it is the string-based music of artists from the Sahara region, such as the Malian African blues innovator Ali Farka Touré, that is most closely associated with the genre.

TUNING A BALAFON

KEY ARTISTS AND WORKS

Ali Farka Touré *Ali Farka Touré* (1988); *African Blues* (1990)

Tinariwen *The Radio Tsidas Sessions* (2001)

Afrobeat

Afrobeat was developed during the 1960s by the Nigerian musician Fela Kuti, who combined the upbeat rhythms and harmonies of traditional African music with aspects of African American forms, such as the scratchy rhythm guitars of funk, to create a setting for his politically and socially aware lyrics. During the 1970s, Kuti achieved stardom and, despite afrobeat's politically challenging nature, his music became popular around the world. Afrobeat influenced many forms of music, including jazz, and more recently, indie-rock. It continues to be a popular genre in its own right.

KEY ARTISTS AND WORKS

Fela Kuti *Gentleman* (1973); *Confusion* (1975)

Femi Kuti *Femi Kuti* (1995); *Day by Day* (2008)

Mbalax

Developed in Senegal during the 1970s, mbalax represents a collision between the Senegalese appropriation of Western—especially French—music and the traditional music of the native Wolof people. As a result, it combines jazz and rock with indigenous instruments, such as the *sabar* drum and the *balafon*, and lyrics written in Wolof. Performers, such as Youssou N'Dour and his band, Étoile de Dakar, gained an audience throughout the francophone world. Mbalax is still popular in West Africa and is often fused with more contemporary genres, such as hip-hop and zouk.

KEY ARTISTS AND WORKS

Etoile de Dakar "*Jalo*" (1981)

Baaba Maal and Mansour Sek *Chauffeur Bi* (1980); *Djam Leelii* (1984)

Music of Asia

The music of Asia includes a range of traditions and styles, from the kantrum folk music of Thailand to the Hindustani and Carnatic music of northern and southern India, respectively. In recent years, the commercial music of East Asia has become popular around the world.

ERHU

Chinese opera

The first Chinese opera group was formed during the 8th century to provide entertainment for the Emperor Xuanzong. From the Middle Ages onward it splintered into a variety of forms based on regional preference. The most prominent of these was Beijing opera, which was developed during the 18th century and featured song, dance, and combat on a sparse stage. Songs were simple and melodic and were usually accompanied by string and percussion instruments. Chinese Opera flourished until the Cultural Revolution (1966–1976), then it as good as disappeared.

KEY ARTISTS AND WORKS
Tang Xianzu *The Peony Pavillion* (1598)
Kong Shangren *The Peach Blossom Fan* (1699)

Hindustani classical music

Hindustani classical music is the classical music of northern India. Its present-day form was developed from the 12th century onward and consists of a wide range of styles, all united by the presence of a vocal melody, known as a *raga*, sung over a rhythmic pattern, known as a *tala*. The rhythmic accompaniments are usually provided by string instruments, such as the *veena* or the *tambura*, and drums, such as the *pakhavaj*. During the Medieval period, the Islamic rule of the Delhi sultanate in India resulted in a Persian influence on Hindustani classical music, and this is one of several features that distinguish it from Carnatic music, the classical music of southern India. Until the 19th century, the music was rarely written down and was mainly played in palaces and dance halls. However, from the early 20th century onward, performers and curators of Hindustani music, such as Vishnu Digambar Paluskar, introduced formal teaching processes and standardized systems of notation. More recently, musicians such as Ravi Shankar have brought the form to an international audience.

KEY ARTISTS AND WORKS
Ravi Shankar *Three Ragas* (1956); *India's Master Musician* (1963)
Ali Akbar Khan *The Soul of Indian Music* (1965)

> "**Spirituality** and Indian classical **music** are two **sides of the same coin.**"
>
> PANDIT SHIV KUMAR SHARMA

PANDIT RAVI SHANKAR

Carnatic music

Along with Hindustani classical music, Carnatic music is the principal subgenre of Indian classical music. While the Hindustani style proliferates in the north of India, Carnatic music is the classical music of the southern states of the country. The focus of Carnatic music is vocal, and most compositions consist of a *raga* (vocal melody) supported by a *tala (*rhythmic pattern). The vocal is usually backed by a string instrument that supplies a drone, such as a *tambura*, fiddle, or violin, and a drum, such as mridangam. Unlike Hindustani classical music, Carnatic songs are traditionally fixed compositions that are interpreted by the performer. Frequently, songs are written to include space for improvisation.

KEY ARTISTS AND WORKS
Tyagraja *Pancharatna Krithis* (c.1800)
Muthuswami Dikshitar *Kamalamba Navavarna* (c.1800)

Gamelan

A gamelan is a traditional Indonesian music ensemble mainly consisting of percussion instruments, such as gongs and metallophones, although some gamelan ensembles also feature string and wind instruments. While ensembles featuring drums, gongs, and percussion instruments are common throughout Indonesia, the gamelan is unique to Java, Bali, and Lambok. The music played by these ensembles was developed between 1300 and 1500 and consists of interlocking layers of percussion that are used to generate both rhythm and melody. Gamelan music is rarely written down, but it is a central feature of Indonesian cultural life. In its earliest years, gamelan was a feature of life in the royal courts of Indonesia, but it is now performed to accompany poetry and drama.

KEY ARTISTS AND WORKS
K.P.H. Notoprojo *Jaya Manggala Gita* (1952)
R.L. Martopangrawit *Ladrang Biwadhapraja* (1939); *Ra Ngandel (*1986)

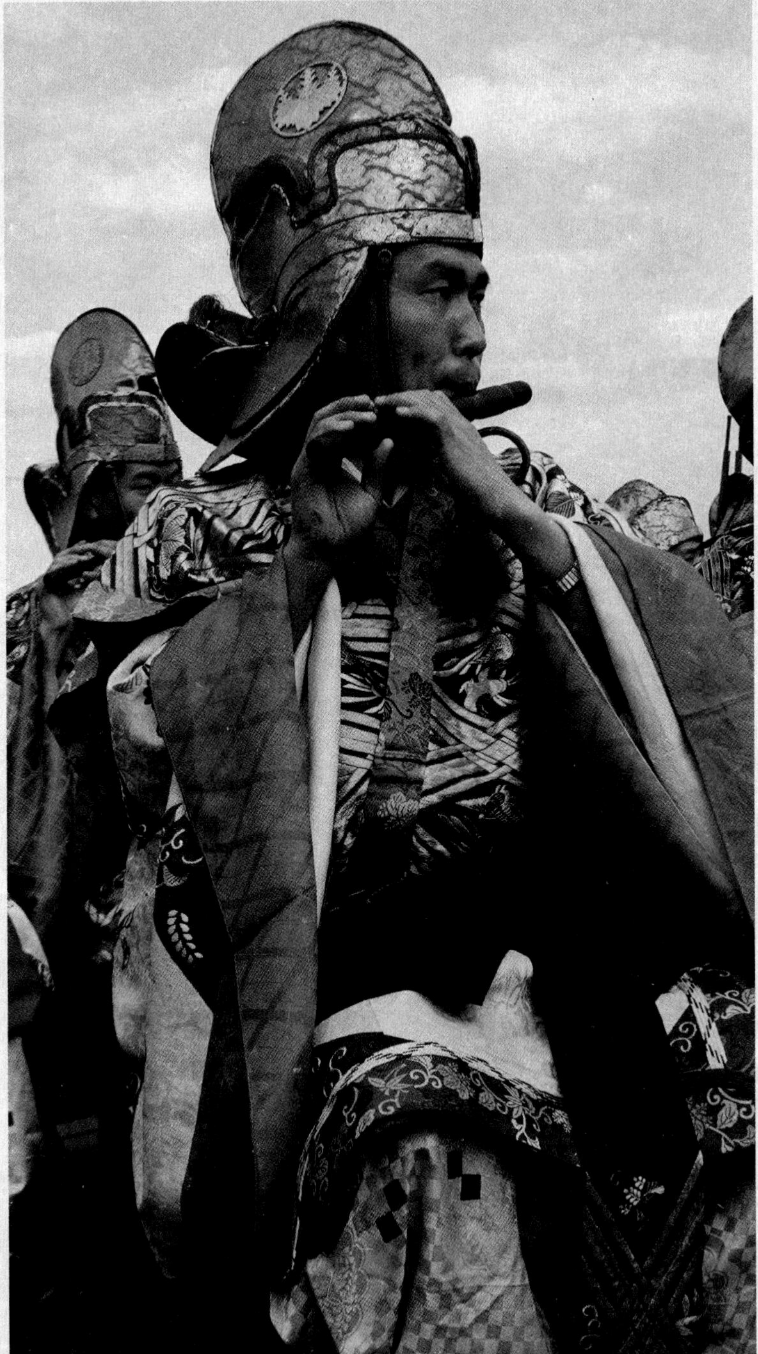

FLUTE-PLAYERS AT A GAGAKU FESTIVAL IN JAPAN

Gagaku

The oldest form of Japanese classical music, gagaku was introduced to Japan from China before the 7th century. From that time onward, it was traditionally played by ensembles of musicians who belonged to hereditary guilds based in different regions of Japan. By the 19th century, the format of these ensembles had become established, and typically consisted of three wind instruments and three percussion instruments. A regular feature of Japanese theatrical performances, gagaku is now most frequently played as a form of concert or dance music.

KEY ARTISTS AND WORKS
Reigakusha "In an Autumn Garden" (2000)
Kong Shangren *The Peach Blossom Fan* (1699)

Min'yo

A genre of Japanese folk music, min'yo usually takes the form of a work song. Originally, these songs consisted of unaccompanied solo or ensemble vocals, but between the 17th and 19th centuries they were often backed by a string instrument, such as a *shamisen*. When used as a form of dance music, min'yo compositions were typically accompanied by percussion instruments. In the 20th century, the status of min'yo changed from a folk form to a classical one. Many min'yo compositions were connected to specific towns in Japan but were often reinvented in other towns.

KEY ARTISTS AND WORKS
Takio Ito *Takio Jinc* (1986)
Tsuru To Kame *Tsuru To Kame* (2002); *Ai no Kaze (Kita no Kuni)* (2003)

WOMAN PLAYING SHAMISEN

Kantrum

A style of folk music played by the Khmer people of Thailand, kantrum is centered around ensembles consisting of a singer, percussionists, and fiddle players. It is usually performed as an accompaniment to dancing and the lyrics are sung in both Thai and the Northern Khmer dialect. Recently, kantrum musicians have introduced electric instruments to the genre, achieving mainstream pop success in the process.

KEY ARTISTS AND WORKS
Darkie *Kantrum Rock* (c.1988); *Darkie Rock II: Buk Jah* (1997)
Jane Saijai *Kantrum Dance* (c.2000)

"**Music** is the map of the **Jewish spirit...** The Torah is God's libretto, and **we**, the Jewish people, **are His choir**, the performers of His choral symphony..."

JONATHAN SACKS, CHIEF RABBI OF ENGLAND

Jewish music

Secular and spiritual music is an integral part of Judaism and Jewish culture. Religious occasions, from large formal ceremonies to family meals, are frequently observed through musical settings of sacred texts. Jewish folk music is usually performed at celebrations, such as weddings.

Klezmer

One of the most prominent forms of traditional Jewish music, the modern incarnation of klezmer was developed in Eastern Europe during the 19th century by musicians known as klezmorim. Traditional klezmer groups performed celebratory songs, usually sung in Yiddish and derived from Jewish religious music. At first, string instruments were the focus of the genre, although the clarinet later became its most recognizable feature. Klezmer's popularity declined during the early and mid-20th century, but it influenced classical composers, including Dmitri Shostakovitch and Leonard Bernstein, and enjoyed a revival during the 1970s.

KEY ARTISTS AND WORKS
Naftule Brandwein *King of the Klezmer Clarinet* (1997)
The Klezmatics *Shvaygn = Toyt* (1989)

Sephardic

The Jewish population of Medieval Iberia, known as Sephardic Jews, was expelled from Spain in 1492. Sephardic Jews settled in North Africa and the Eastern Mediterranean, and the musical settings of their spiritual and secular texts acquired the distinct character of the countries of their diaspora. Nonetheless, most Sephardic music is united by its predominantly vocal character. Instruments, when they are used, are region-specific, but usually include string instruments, such as the zither, *oud*, or violin. Traditionally, the poetic lyrics of Sephardic songs were written in Hebrew or Ladino, a form of Judeo–Spanish.

KEY ARTISTS AND WORKS
Haim Effendi *"A la una nassi io"* (1907–1908); *"Indome Para Marsiglia"* (1907–1908)
Gloria Levy *Sephardic Folk Songs* (1959)

YASMIN LEVY

Religious music

The traditional music of Judaism contains a large body of vocal-led songs and chants, such as *piyyutim*, various forms of which have existed for more than 1,000 years. These chants are usually written for specific spiritual and ceremonial functions; for example, *zemiros* are sung during religious meals, while *piyyutim* are typically sung during ceremonies. The different forms of Judaic chants and

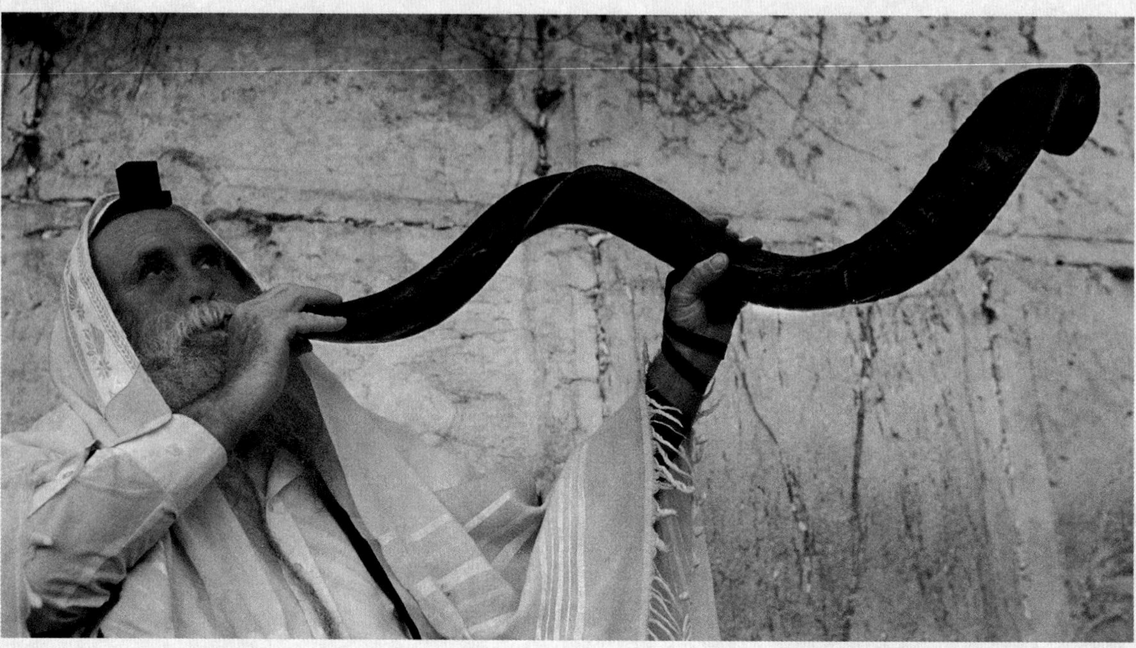

PLAYING A HORN NEAR THE WESTERN WALL, ISRAEL

A QAWWALI PERFORMANCE IN PAKISTAN

songs are often based around a poetic structure or device, such as an acrostic.

KEY ARTISTS AND WORKS

Anonymous *"Adir Hu"* (1644); *"Adon Olam"* (c.11th century CE)

Rabbi Shlomo Halevi Alkabetz *"Lekhah Dodi"* (16th century)

Music of Arabia

The Arab world has produced a range of musical styles, both secular and spiritual. Arguably, the most influential form of Arabic music was that created in Al-Andalus, also known as Islamic Iberia. This classical music spread from present-day Spain and Portugal to North Africa between the 9th and 15th centuries.

Andalusian classical music

Between the 8th and 16th centuries, parts of Spain, Portugal, and France were ruled by an Islamic caliphate. Andalusian classical music is believed to have been developed during this time by composers and court musicians, such as Ziryab and Avempace. Travel through the Medieval Islamic world, which extended to Africa, Europe, and Persia, meant that the music spread across several countries and diversified into myriad styles. However, the various styles are unified by certain characteristics, including the use of traditional string instruments such as the *rabāb* and the *'ud*, the employment of modal compositional techniques, and the presence of poetic lyrics. The music was performed across Arabic society, from aristocratic houses to communal celebrations. It is a feature of religious ceremonies even today.

KEY ARTISTS AND WORKS

Sabah Fakrhi *Mouwachah Iski Al Itash* (1970)

Amina Alaoui *Gharnati* (1995)

Qawwali

Originating in India during the 13th century, qawwalis are sung in South Asia even today. Songs feature spiritual lyrics and are typically performed by an ensemble consisting of a singer (known as a *qawwal)*, harmonium players, and percussionists, one of which is usually a tabla player. Each member of the group joins in the singing and some members clap rhythmically with the music. Compositions are generally lengthy—the longest recorded qawwali is almost two hours long—and build from a slow start to a rapid conclusion in order to inspire devotion among listeners. The *qawwals* too see themselves as conveying the message of God through their music.

KEY ARTISTS AND WORKS

Nusrat Fateh Ali Khan *Devotional Songs* (1992)

Sabri Brothers *Nazr-e-Shah Karim* (1983); *Qawwali Masterworks* (1991)

Chaabi

Chaabi is a form of Algerian folk music that evolved from Andalusian classical music during the late 19th century. A typical chaabi song involves a melancholy vocal part backed by a string band and underpinned by percussion. Although chaabi began as an underground music, performers such as El Hajj Muhammad El Anka found a mainstream audience for the music from the 1950s onward.

KEY ARTISTS AND WORKS

El Hajj Muhammad El Anka *"Ani f h'mek"* (1973; *"Touchia"* (1968)

El Hachemi Guerouabi *Le Chaabi des Maîtres* (1994)

Malhun

A traditional form of sung poetry, malhun has been performed in Morocco for more than 700 years. Initially an exclusively literary form, the music that is now a feature of malhun was influenced by the classical forms of the Islamic caliphate of Andalusia. Each malhun features separate melodies for the lyrics and the refrains that are positioned between the verses.

KEY ARTISTS AND WORKS

Thami Mdaghri *"Al-Gnawi"* (c.1800); *"Aliq Al-Masrüh"* (c.1800)

Haj Houcine Toulali *"Kassidat Damlij"* (1991); *"Kassidat Nacar Lahcane"* (1991);

Al Jeel

Influenced by other forms of Arabic music such as raï, Al Jeel was developed in Egypt during the 1970s as an alternative to Western pop and rock music. It uses synthesizers to create an electronic setting for romantic lyrics.

KEY ARTISTS AND WORKS

Hamid El Shaeri *"Lolaiki"* (1988)

Amr Diab *Nour El Ain* (1996)

Raï

Raï originated during the 1920s in Oran, the second-largest city in Algeria. However, it was not until the 1980s that the modern form of raï music—a fusion of Western instrumentation and traditional Algerian song—emerged. Notable for its challenging, often political lyrics, it became popular in France during the 1980s and performers, such as Khaled, became stars throughout the francophone world.

KEY ARTISTS AND WORKS

Khaled *Kutché* (1988); *Khaled* (1992)

Rachid Taha *Diwan* (1998)

RACHID TAHA

Biographies

This section contains biographies, arranged alphabetically, of prominent musicians and composers from musical cultures throughout the world and the history of music. From the composers of Islamic Iberia to the Western classical musicians of the Middle Ages and the Renaissance, early professional musicians usually occupied a position within the royal court or a religious institution. It was not until the Classical era that the notion of the freelance musician was properly established.

ABBA

ABBA

(active 1973–1982, Swedish)

Between 1970 and 1973, singer-songwriters Benny Andersson and Bjorn Ulvaes and their respective partners, the singers Anni-Frid Lynstad and Agnetha Faltskog, made moderately successful pop music under a number of different guises. In 1973, they took the name ABBA—an acronym of their first names. The following year, they won the Eurovision Song Contest with their performance of "Waterloo," which went on to achieve chart success around Europe and is now one of their trademark songs. During the late 1970s, ABBA dominated the European pop charts with their self-penned singles, including "Dancing Queen," "S.O.S.," and "Fernando," all of which displayed a variety of influences, from rock and disco to cabaret-style ballads. Although the group never achieved significant commercial success in the United States, they were full-fledged international stars, playing to an audience of 20,000 in Sydney, Australia, in 1977. Their popularity continued into the early 1980s, but the strained personal relationships of the two couples led to them disbanding in 1982. Nonetheless, their hook-driven compositions and glossy production techniques continued to be influential in contemporary chart music, and in 2021, they reunited and released a new album, *Voyage*.

AC/DC

(active 1973–present, Australian)

AC/DC was established in 1973 in Sydney, Australia, by two teenaged brothers, Angus and Malcolm Young. After some fluctuations in their lineup, they released their first album of hard rock, *High Voltage*, in 1976. Having earned a reputation for their energetic live shows, they reached a wider audience with their 1978 album *Powerage*, before becoming international stars in 1979 with *Highway to Hell*, which sold over one million copies. Just months after the album's release, the band's lead singer, Bon Scott, died suddenly and AC/DC considered disbanding. However, they recruited a new singer, Brian Johnson, and the ensuing album, *Back in Black*, became their most successful record, remaining on the US Billboard chart for 131 weeks. The band's mainstream popularity declined throughout the 1980s, although they reversed the trend with successful releases during the 1990s. One of the most influential hard rock groups in the history of the genre, they are the ninth highest-selling band ever in the United States.

John Adams

(1947–present, American)

John Adams studied composition at Harvard University from 1965, supporting himself by working as a reserve clarinetist for the Boston Symphony Orchestra. During the late 1970s his work, such as *Phrygian Gates* (1977), was heavily influenced by minimalism. In 1982, he was appointed composer in residence with the San Francisco Symphony Orchestra and he moved away from minimalism toward a more expressive style around the same time. In 1987, he wrote his first opera, *Nixon in China*, based on US president Richard Nixon's visit to China in 1972. He won the Grawemeyer Award for "Violin Concerto" in 1995. Now acknowledged as a major figure in modern classical music, Adams wrote the choral piece, *On the Transmigration of Souls*, in 2002 to commemorate the attacks of September 11, 2001.

King Sunny Ade

(1946–present, Nigerian)

Born into a Nigerian royal family, King Sunny Ade's enthusiasm for the guitar led him to give up a university education to become a highlife musician with the Federal Rhythm Dandies in the mid-1960s. In 1967 he formed his own band, The Green Spots, and began to build a reputation as a live performer and recording artist during the 1970s. He became a worldwide star with the release of the album *Juju Music*, created with his support band, African Beats, in 1982. As a result of its success, he began to perform in Europe and North America. Ade has continued to be a prominent force in Nigerian music, promoting and recording the work of new Nigerian musicians.

Aerosmith

(active 1970–present, American)

Formed in Boston in 1970, Aerosmith developed a local following through their impressive live shows, before signing a record deal in 1972. As a studio band, they enjoyed significant success from the outset and achieved mainstream popularity in 1975 with the album, *Toys in the Attic*. By the end of the 1970s, the band was a popular touring act and their albums and singles regularly appeared in the charts. However, drug addiction and conflicts within the band led to the departure of a founding member, the guitarist Joe Perry, and they only released one album between 1980 and 1984. Perry returned to the band in 1984, appearing with vocalist Steven Tyler on Run-DMC's cover of their song "Walk this Way" in 1986. This heralded a return to commercial popularity for the group and they produced best-selling albums during the 1990s and 2000s. They continue to tour and record, and have sold more than 150 million albums worldwide.

Louis Armstrong

(1901–1971, American)

Louis Armstrong took up the cornet while residing at a New Orleans childrens' home, where he had been sent as a punishment for delinquency. By 1922 he was working as a professional musician with the well-regarded bandleader, Joe "King" Oliver. Encouraged by his second wife, Lil Hardin Armstrong, Armstrong moved to New York in 1924, where he took up a position with the Fletcher Henderson Orchestra. It was during

LOUIS ARMSTRONG

this time that he abandoned the cornet in favor of the trumpet and started incorporating anecdotes and jokes into his stage act. However, he returned to Chicago in 1925 and began to lead his own jazz ensembles, such as the Hot Fives and the Hot Sevens. He recorded songs such as "Potato Head Blues" and "West End Blues" with these groups, and his performances on the recordings were influential in defining the course of improvization in jazz music. By the early 1930s, Armstrong was an established bandleader, touring Europe and America and achieving mainstream chart success with songs such as "All of Me" and "Love, You Funny Thing." As the taste for big band music declined during the 1940s, he reinvented himself in 1947 as the leader of Louis Armstrong and His All Stars, a group with a rotating personnel of musicians. A fully fledged mainstream star—appearing on the cover of *Time* magazine in 1949—Armstrong continued to record and play until shortly before his death in 1971.

Juan Atkins

(1962–present, American)

As a young man growing up in Detroit, Juan Atkins' interest in early electronic groups such as Kraftwerk caused him to experiment with synthesizers. He met Rick Davis while studying musical electronics and the two began to make synthesizer-based music under the name Cybotron. In 1983, they released the album *Enter*, which aligned the rhythms of the new genre of house music with synthesizer sounds, paving the way for a style that would eventually be known as techno. He left Cybotron in 1985 and began recording under the name Model 500, releasing underground dance hits such as "No UFOs" and "Night Drive." This established a blueprint for intelligent dance music and earned Atkins the nickname "godfather of techno." During the late 1980s, techno's popularity spread around the world and Atkins became an internationally renowned artist.

JOHANN SEBASTIAN BACH

organist at the Bonifaciuskirche at Arnstadt in 1703. His tenure was not without difficulties; first he almost dueled with a student, then he angered the town consistory by overstaying his leave. Bach remained in Arnstadt until 1707, when he moved to Muhlhaüsen to take up the position of organist. Within a year he had married his cousin Maria, fought with his new students, and left to become a violinist at the ducal court in Weimar. Bach thrived in his well-paid new post until internal politics made his position untenable. He left to become Kappellmeister at the Cöthen court in 1717 and many of his instrumental works were composed during this period, including the seminal chamber pieces, *The Brandenburg Concertos*. Bach's wife died in 1720 and he married singer Anna Wilcke the next year. In 1723, he became Kantor at the Thomasschule in Leipzig. This heralded a period of productivity that produced sacred and secular cantatas and motets for all occasions and church feasts, including five complete cycles of cantatas for the calendar year. In 1729, Bach became Director of the Collegium Musicum at the university in Leipzig. He continued to compose and perform until his failing eyesight made writing difficult. He died after two unsuccessful eye operations in 1750.

lyricist Hal David. He achieved early success with songs such as "Magic Moments" and became the first songwriter to achieve consecutive No. 1 singles on the UK pop chart in 1958. During the 1960s, Bacharach and David composed over 20 hit singles for the singer Dionne Warwick, including "Walk on By" and "I Say a Little Prayer." Bacharach and David's songs were also interpreted by other high profile artists, including Dusty Springfield and The Carpenters. Although he continued to work throughout the 1980s and '90s, he is best known for his jazz and soul-inflected compositions of the 1960s.

Nikhil Banerjee

(1931–1986, Indian)

The son of an amateur musician, Banerjee began to play the sitar as a five-year old in Kolkata. A child prodigy, he won a national competition and was a regular radio performer until the age of 14, before studying the instrument formally throughout the 1940s. Although he made very few recordings during his lifetime, he performed constantly during the 1950s and '60s, appearing at venues outside India for the first time in 1955. Known for his excellent improvisation skills, his distinctive style of playing has been highly influential and he was posthumously honored with the Padma Bushan by the Indian government.

Béla Bartók

(1881–1945, Hungarian)

Born in southern Hungary to a teacher and an amateur musician, Béla Bartók composed enthusiastically as a child. In 1899, he entered the academy of music, where he shone as a pianist and was soon invited to perform in Vienna, Berlin, and Manchester, among other cities. In 1905, he met Zoltán Kodály and discovered a shared interest in folk music. Eventually, they collected music from all over Eastern Europe, joined on their field trips by Bartók's first wife, Márta Ziegler. Much of the music Bartók wrote around 1910, such as the *Allegro Barbaro* for piano, was percussive in style—mirroring the primitivism of Stravinsky's music from the same period. His compositions are usually meticulously crafted, with different parts mirroring each other, a technique evident in *The Wooden Prince*, which he began writing in 1914. After World War I Bartók's music went through an expressionistic phase, demonstrated by compositions such as *The Miraculous Mandarin*. He staged his first concert tour of the United States in 1927, and he composed over 150 short piano pieces between 1932 and 39 as part of a set entitled *Mikrokosmos*. Bartók moved to the United States permanently in 1940 after the German invasion of Austria and died in New York after a long period of illness in 1945.

BÉLA BARTÓK

The Beach Boys

(active 1961–present, American)

Formed in 1961 in California, the Beach Boys originally consisted of brothers Carl, Brian, and Dennis Wilson, their cousin, Mike Love, and his friend, Al Jardine. Inspired by vocal harmony groups, they released their first album, *Surfin' Safari*, in 1962. This was followed by *Surfer Girl* (1963), which featured songs of increased sophistication and complexity, such as "In My Room." During 1964, the Beach Boys achieved a commercial breakthrough, reaching the charts on numerous occasions and touring Europe. Brian Wilson did not enjoy the exertions of touring, and from 1965 onward he concentrated on writing and producing music. This period resulted in a burst of inventive songwriting, culminating with the internationally acclaimed *Pet Sounds* in 1966. However, by the end of the 1960s, Wilson was struggling with the pressure of producing new material for the group. His plan to make an epic psychedelic album, entitled *SMiLE*, failed and he withdrew from the group in the early 1970s. Despite a renaissance in the late 1970s, the band fragmented during the 1980s, and Dennis Wilson died in 1983. The Beach Boys continued to work throughout the 1980s and '90s, individually and, occasionally, as a group.

"For the **glory** of the **most** high **God** alone, and for my **neighbor** to **learn** from."

JOHANN SEBASTIAN BACH, COMPOSER, EPIGRAPH TO THE *ORGELBÜCHLEIN*, 1717

Johann Sebastian Bach

(1685–1750, German)

Orphaned at 10, Bach lived with his brother, Johann Christoph, who taught him the organ. After studying in Lüneberg, he was appointed

Burt Bacharach

(1928–present, American)

A multi-instrumentalist and student of composition, Burt Bacharach began to write songs for popular singers during the late 1950s, in partnership with the

The Beatles
(active 1960–1970, English)

The Beatles was formed in Liverpool, England, by John Lennon, Paul McCartney, and George Harrison, former members of a rock 'n' roll group called The Quarrymen. In 1960, the three guitarists were joined by bassist Stuart Sutcliffe, and drummer, Pete Best. In the same year the band secured a seven-month residency in Hamburg, Germany, where they developed their act through intensive live performances. The Beatles returned to Liverpool in 1961 and built up a committed local following. Stuart Sutcliffe left the band in the same year and Ringo Starr replaced Pete Best in 1962. They released their first British number one single, "Please Please Me," in 1963 and the album of the same name topped the charts for 30 consecutive weeks, heralding a period of huge commercial success. In 1963 their singles "She Loves You" and "I Want to Hold Your Hand" both sold over one million copies in the UK and their live performances were rapturously received. Their success was not restricted to the UK, and in the first week of April 1964, they occupied the top five places of the US singles chart. Despite their phenomenal commercial popularity the band sought to constantly evolve their sound, experimenting with folk-rock and psychedelic electronica. In 1967, they concluded this experimental phase with *Sergeant Pepper's Lonely Hearts Club Band*, which enjoyed huge acclaim. *The White Album* of 1968 was another critical success, but personal relationships within the band had become strained, and after the release of *Let It Be* in 1970, The Beatles broke up. Paul McCartney, George Harrison, and John Lennon enjoyed successful solo careers after The Beatles, but Lennon's life ended prematurely when he was murdered on a New York City street in 1980.

Beck
(1970–present, American)

The son of a musician father and artist mother, Beck began his musical career as a busker and folk artist in Los Angeles. He moved to New York in the late 1980s but returned to Los Angeles in 1990. Having released two low-key albums, *Golden Feelings* and *Stereopathic Soulmanure*, he received critical acclaim for fusing acoustic blues and folk with hip-hop beats in the album *Mellow Gold*, an approach typified by the single, "Loser." Increasing the sample-based aspect of his music, the album *Odelay* established him as a major figure in alternative rock, producing several successful singles, including "Where It's At" and "The New Pollution." Beck continued to experiment during the late 1990s, moving towards a Prince-influenced funk sound on *Midnite Vultures* and enhancing his reputation as a witty and ambitious live performer. He continued to record and perform throughout the 2000s and dabbled with a variety of styles, including folk, hip-hop, and rock. A visual artist as well as a musician, his artistic collaborations with his grandfather were exhibited in 1998.

The Bee Gees
(active 1959–2003, English)

Born in England, the Gibb brothers—Barry, Robin, and Maurice—moved to Australia while they were children. Barry formed a group called the BG's with his friends Bill Goode and Bill Gates. When his brothers joined, and the Bills left, the meaning shifted. The group became known as the Brothers Gibb. They renamed themselves The Bee Gees in 1959 and released several rock singles during the early 1960s, regularly performing on the local music scene. Having moved to England in 1967, the group disbanded, but in 1970, they reformed as a progressive rock act, achieving success in the US. In the mid-1970s, they arrived at the sound for which they became best known, aligning Barry's falsetto vocals with synthesized disco music to create hit singles, including "Jive Talking" and "You Should be Dancing." They reached the peak of their success in 1977 through their contributions to the *Saturday Night Fever* soundtrack, which included "Night Fever" and "Stayin' Alive." These made them synonymous with the disco genre, although they remained a successful pop act for the rest of their career.

THE BEE GEES

"**Music** is the **mediator** between the **spiritual** and the **sensual life.**"

LUDWIG VAN BEETHOVEN, COMPOSER

Ludwig van Beethoven
(1770–1827, German)

Displaying an early talent for music, Beethoven received a grounding in musical principles from the Bonn court organist, Christian Gottlob Neefe, and was soon acting as his deputy. Aged 17, he visited Vienna and may have studied with Mozart, but he returned home within weeks when he learned his mother was dying. By 1792, he had already composed a number of vocal and chamber works, and an accomplished set of variations for piano. Impressed by his music, Joseph Haydn invited him to return to Vienna to resume his studies. Beethoven soon moved into aristocratic circles, where the beauty and virtuosity of his playing, and his compositional prowess, won him many patrons. During this time, his compositions, such as the "Moonlight" and "Pathetique" piano sonatas, enjoyed success. However, by 1802 he realized that he would eventually become totally deaf and, while staying in the village of Heilingenstadt, he wrote a letter revealing the depth of his unhappiness. Overcoming this crisis, he launched into a period of prolific creativity during which many of his most famous works, such as the *Kreutzer Violin Sonata* and the epic "Eroica" symphony, were produced. By 1812, his deafness had caused further depression, isolation, and a lapse in creativity. However, his final years brought forth his most spiritual and exalted music, including Symphony No. 9, also known as the "Choral," an iconic work of Western music, and one against which all subsequent symphonies have been judged. Beethoven fell ill and died in 1827; 10,000 people attended his funeral in Vienna.

LUDWIG VAN BEETHOVEN

Lola Beltran
(1932–1996, Mexican)

Lola Beltran was an aspiring singer during the early 1950s. She worked as a secretary at a major radio station in Mexico City, before making her professional debut in 1954. Beltran launched her film career in the same year and was a prolific recording artist during the 1960s and '70s, popularizing the Mexican ranchera and mariachi styles on the world stage. A renowned live performer, she was the first ranchera singer to appear at the Palacio de Bellas Artists—Mexico City's most famous opera house. A huge star in Mexico, her body lay in state to allow members of the public to pay their respects on her death in 1996.

Irving Berlin
(1888–1989, American)

Irving Berlin was born in the Russian Empire, in present-day Belarus. He moved to New York with his family at the age of five to escape persecution of the Russian Jewish community by Czar Nicholas II. At the age of 18, he taught himself to play the piano and secured a position as a songwriter with a music publishing company just two years later. In 1911, he shot to international fame with the release of his march-style composition,

"Alexander's Ragtime Band." A prolific composer, Berlin wrote many similar songs in the years that followed, several of which were hits. He continued to compose after World War I, writing stand-alone songs and music for films and musicals, including *The Jazz Singer* in 1927. He began to compose film musicals in 1935, such as *Holiday Inn* (1942) and *Easter Parade* (1948). This period culminated in 1946 with his score for the successful Broadway musical, *Annie Get Your Gun*—produced by Richard Rodgers and Oscar Hammerstein. Berlin retired from music in 1962.

Hector Berlioz

(1803–1969, French)

As a young man growing up near the town of Grenoble in southeastern France, Hector Berlioz was expected to become a doctor like his father. As a result, he received only basic training in music; lacking a piano, he was forced to study harmony in secret from theoretical treatises. In Paris, where he studied medicine, he made frequent visits to the Opéra, studied music in private, and enrolled at the Conservatoire against his parents' wishes. There he heard Beethoven's symphonies and read Goethe's *Faust*, but his most formative artistic experiences were the performances of Shakespeare that he witnessed. During this time, he fell in love with the actress Harriet Smithson, and her initial rejection of him inspired the intense *Symphonie Fantastique*, which won the Prix de Rome in 1830. The success of the *Symphohonie Fantastique* did little to increase acceptance of Berlioz's music and, in spite of a generous gift from Niccolò Paganini, he turned to music journalism to earn a living, contributing acerbic and witty articles to several journals. Unhappy with the performances of his works, he started to conduct, establishing an international reputation. For the following 20 years, he toured extensively and wrote some of his most important choral works, such as his magnum opus *Les Troyens* (*The Trojans*), based on Virgil's *Aeneid*. Berlioz's lasting legacy is his grand orchestral music, which embodies Romantic ideals.

Leonard Bernstein

(1918–1990, American)

Bernstein studied music at Harvard University, graduating in 1939. He rose to fame in 1943, when he stepped in at short notice to conduct at the New York Philharmonic after Bruno Walter became ill. From the outset of his career he divided his time between "serious" art music and works for the popular stage. In 1944, he experienced success with Symphony No. 1, the ballet *Fancy Free*, and the musical *On the Town*. During the 1950s he became an established and prominent figure in the world of music. In 1953, he became the first American to conduct at La Scala, the prestigious Milanese opera house, and enjoyed commercial success with the operetta *Candide*. In 1957, Bernstein recorded his biggest success with the Broadway musical, *West Side Story*. He simultaneously maintained a high profile career as a conductor and programmer, taking over as musical director of the New York Philharmonic in 1957 and resigning from the post in 1969. During the 1970s and '80s, he toured the world as a conductor and theorist, lecturing on the relationship between language and music.

Chuck Berry

(1926–2017, American)

Born into a large middle-class family in St. Louis, Missouri, Chuck Berry achieved his first musical success in a high-school talent contest. After serving a sentence in a juvenile detention center for car theft, he got married and supported himself with a number of jobs, including factory worker and beautician, while he developed his skills as a guitarist. A gifted showman, he experimented with numerous genres, including blues, rhythm and blues, and even country music. His first recording, a version of a folk song called "Ida Red," is regarded as the one of the founding songs of rock 'n' roll, and appealed to Black and white audiences alike. By the end of the 1950s, Berry was a nationwide star with a string of hits to his name, including "Roll Over Beethoven" and "Johnny B. Goode." However, at the height of his fame, he was convicted for transporting an under-age girl across state lines with a view to setting her to work as a prostitute. Berry appealed the conviction, citing racism and a prejudiced jury, and eventually served one-and-a-half years in prison. He left prison in 1963 to find himself lauded by influential bands such as The Beatles and The Rolling Stones. He was a popular live act and his music continued to find commercial success—the novelty song, "My Ding-a-Ling," reached number one in the charts. Berry continued to play music and is regularly hailed as an innovative and influential figure in the history of rock 'n' roll. Berry received a Grammy Lifetime Achievement Award in 1984.

Vishwa Mohan Bhatt

(1950–present, Indian)

The son of two musicians, Mohan Bhatt began his musical training under the stewardship of his father, an experienced musician and teacher. He had always displayed an interest in innovative instrumentation and his first instrument was a modified Spanish guitar. In 1970, he began to record music and went on to perform internationally, regularly performing with the world-famous sitar player, Ravi Shankar, and collaborating with other notable musicians. He is famous for inventing the Mohan veena, a modified guitar which features 13 additional strings, to allow for a combination of western techniques with sounds that are more typical of classical Indian instruments, such as the veena or sitar.

VISHWA MOHAN BHATT

GEORGES BIZET

Georges Bizet

(1838–1875, French)

The son of a music teacher, Bizet was a child prodigy who read music at the age of four, played piano at six, entered the Paris Conservatoire at nine, and composed an accomplished symphony at 17. He won the Grand Prix de Rome in 1857 with his setting of the cantata *Clovis et Clotilde* and his operetta *Le docteur miracle* was staged in the same year. In 1863, he achieved a hit with the opera *Les pêcheurs de perles* (*The Pearl Fishers*), which was inspired by his mentor, Charles Gounod. A fallow patch followed before Bizet produced a string of international successes, such as *Jeux d'enfants* in 1871, and started work on *Carmen*, which premiered in Paris in 1875. The first realistic opera, *Carmen* shocked its audiences with its graphic on-stage murder. Although its lifelike drama and sensual music were to become highly influential in French opera, the first critics received it coolly, and Bizet died before it became a hit.

Eubie Blake

(1883–1983, American)

Eubie Blake began his musical career as a teenager, playing the piano in a bordello in his native city of Baltimore. Having initially composed ragtime songs, he went on to find work as a vaudeville musician from 1912 onward. His collaboration with the bandleader and singer Noble Sissle in 1921 resulted in the musical, *Shuffle Along*, which became the first Broadway hit written by an African American. Although Blake's popularity declined after 1930, he continued to perform and record for the rest of his life, reviving many of the early ragtime songs.

Aleksandr Borodin
(1833–1887, Russian)
Born in St. Petersburg, Aleksandr Borodin was the illegitimate son of a Georgian prince who registered the child under the name of a servant. Although he excelled in both science and music from childhood, he chose a career in chemistry. He composed in his spare time, while practicing as a professor and researcher at the Academy of Medico-Surgery in St. Petersburg. Borodin studied with his compatriot Mily Balakirev in 1863, and this period had a dramatic influence on his style. In 1869, his Symphony No. 1 premiered unsuccessfully, but his Symphony No. 2 in B minor, of 1877, displayed a mastery of technique. Perhaps the most overtly Romantic of the "mighty handful" of Russian composers, Borodin is principally remembered for his opera, *Prince Igor*. Set in 12th-century Russia, it depicts the imprisonment of a Russian prince by an invading Tartar tribe, and was premiered in St. Petersburg in 1890—three years after Borodin's death.

ALEKSANDR BORODIN

Bhundu Boys
(active 1983–2000, Zimbabwean)
Formed in Harare in the early 1980s, the Bhundu Boys began their career by playing covers of Western pop music on homemade instruments. Having built a committed local fanbase with their live shows, they released their first single, "Hatisitose," in 1981. It was the first of several singles to top the charts in Zimbabwe and reflected the development of their sound toward a fusion of chimurenga—traditional Zimbabwean music—with Western pop. This style was known as "jit," and became influential throughout Africa. During the mid-1980s, the Bhundu Boys' growing catalog of music attracted the attention of several high-profile DJs in the UK, and they peaked as a critically acclaimed act with the release of their albums *Shabini* and *Tsvimbodzemoto*. This resulted in significant commercial attention and they performed as a supporting act during pop star Madonna's three-night residency at Wembley Stadium in London, in 1987.

Rodolfo Biagi
(1906–1969, Argentinean)
Born in Buenos Aires, Rodolfo Biagi's family were opposed to him pursuing a career in music. Eventually they relented, buying him a violin, the instrument in which Biagi was initially interested. During his studies at a Conservatory in his native city, he began to play the piano, providing a musical background for silent film shows at cinemas. On the strength of these performances he secured work in professional bands. He spent several years touring South America as a member of different groups. In 1935, he joined the orchestra of Juan d'Arienzo and over the next three years, played a crucial part in defining their sound, which is now inextricably linked with a boom in the popularity of tango music in Argentina. Biagi left d'Arienzo's orchestra to form his own band in 1938 and enjoyed popularity throughout South America with his live tours and appearances in Argentinean television and radio. Biagi's compositions, such as the instrumental tango "Cruz Diablo," were also well received. He made his final live appearance at the famous Hurlingham Club in Buenos Aires on August 2, 1969, and died the following month.

Björk
(1965–present, Icelandic)
Björk started her career as a singer with the Icelandic rock group The Sugarcubes in 1986. She launched her solo career with the album *Debut*, which received critical acclaim and gave rise to hit singles in both the UK and the United States. A sonic innovator, Björk's second album, *Post*, combined elements of techno and jazz with her idiosyncratic singing style. With her third album, *Homogenic*, she emphasized the rhythmic aspect of her music. In 2000, she won the Best Actress award at the Cannes Film Festival for her performance in the Lars Von Trier film, *Dancer in the Dark*. An eclectic composer and arranger, she is also famed for her inventive approach to live performances, employing a range of imaginative stage sets and elaborate and unpredictable costumes.

BLONDIE

Black Sabbath
(active 1968–present, English)
Originally a blues band, Black Sabbath's 1970 debut album, showcasing their hard rock sound, was a top-10 success in the UK and went on to sell well in the United States. However, it was their second album, *Paranoid*, also released in 1970, that propelled them to stardom—remaining in the US charts for a year. Defined by the pained vocals of Ozzy Osbourne and the abrasive guitar of Tony Iommi, the album did much to define the emerging sound of heavy metal. Between 1970 and 1975, the band released four more commercially successful studio albums, but the failure of *Technical Ecstasy* in 1976 led to Osbourne leaving the band for the first time. He returned in 1977, but internal disputes caused by drug and alcohol abuse, and the poor reception of their album *Never Say Die!*, resulted in his eventual sacking. He then embarked on a commercially successful solo career. The members of Black Sabbath changed regularly during the 1980s, but the original lineup reformed in 1997 and on several occasions since.

Blondie
(active 1974–present, American)
Blondie was formed in 1974 in New York by guitarist Chris Stein and singer and model Debbie Harry. They released a self-titled debut album in 1976, though their first commercial success came in Australia, in 1977. A year later, they became one of the first new wave bands to become popular in the UK. Their third album, *Parallel Lines*, turned them into international stars in 1978. The disco-influenced record sold 20 million copies worldwide and produced six singles, including "Heart of Glass," which topped the charts in eight different countries. Blondie continued to produce commercially successful music into the early 1980s, experimenting with different genres, including disco and rap. Chris Stein's ill health and the commercial failure of their sixth album, *The Hunter*, resulted in them disbanding in 1982. Debbie Harry pursued a solo career and the group reformed in 1997.

Dock Boggs
(1898–1971, American)
Born Moran Lee Boggs in Virginia, in 1898, Dock Boggs got his nickname from the doctor who delivered him. He acquired his love of music from his father, who took charge of the musical education of his children—teaching all of them to sing and encouraging his son to play the banjo. Boggs worked in mines before he reached his teens, married at the age of 18, and continued to improve his banjo skills by observing other musicians and playing at local dances. In 1927, he performed well at an audition held by a record label and this success resulted in recording sessions in New York later in the year. These recordings, including "Pretty Polly" and "Country Blues," have established Boggs as a seminal figure in folk music. Although he spent a brief period earning a living as a musician during the late 1920s, financial trouble forced Boggs to return to work at the mines in the early 1930s. However, a resurgence of interest in folk music in the 1960s led Boggs back to the recording studios and tours of the United States. He performed at clubs and festivals, until his health declined in the early 1970s.

Blur

(active 1989–present, English)

Blur was formed by university students Damon Albarn, Graham Coxon, and Alex James in London in 1988. Their two albums, released between 1991 and 1993, received little commercial attention. However, their third album, *Parklife*, supported by the singles "Girls and Boys" and Parklife," made them mainstream stars in the UK and cemented their reputation as one of the most famous bands of the Britpop genre. A much publicized rivalry with the British band Oasis added to their celebrity status. After the commercial disappointment of their fourth album, *The Great Escape*, Blur moved away from buoyant guitar-pop toward a rockier sound and earned critical acclaim and commercial success in the United States for the first time with their self-titled fourth album. Two more records followed but the band separated in 2003. The lead singer Damon Albarn went on to form the best selling hip-hop and pop fusion band, Gorillaz. However, in the late 2000s, Blur reformed to play a series of sell-out concerts around the world and were the headline act at the closing ceremony for the London Olympics in 2012.

Marc Bolan

(1947–1977, English)

After spending some time on the periphery of the rock scene, during the mid-1960s, Marc Bolan formed an acoustic group called Tyrannosaurus Rex in 1967. The three albums recorded under that name, in 1968–1969, were popular underground releases, but it was the introduction of an electric rock influence that raised Bolan's profile. The 1970 single "Ride a White Swan" was a chart success and was accompanied by a name change—the group was now called T. Rex—and a radical image transformation. Bolan took to wearing feather boas and glitter and his aesthetic is one of the defining images of the glam-rock genre. T. Rex's music grew in popularity during the early 1970s, with the albums *Electric Warrior* and *The Slider*, and the singles "Get It On," "Jeepster," and "Children of the Revolution." Bolan's popularity declined in the mid-1970s, and he died in a car crash in 1977.

Pierre Boulez

(1925–2016, French)

A child prodigy in math, Pierre Boulez was sent by his father to Lyon to study engineering, but he transferred to the Paris Conservatoire in 1944, where he was taught by the composer Olivier Messiaen. An iconoclast, Boulez gained a fearsome reputation for heckling at concerts of contemporary works he judged to be insufficiently radical. He made his name as a composer in 1955 with *Le marteau sans maître* and taught at the Darmstadt summer schools with Karlheinz Stockhausen during the late 1950s. Boulez began an international career as a conductor during the 1960s, becoming the chief conductor of the BBC Symphony Orchestra in 1971 and succeeding Leonard Bernstein as music director of the New York Philharmonic Orchestra the same year. He founded IRCAM—an institute dedicated to exploring the use of technology in music—in 1977 at the Pompidou Centre in Paris. In 1981, he produced Répons, his first major work in association with the institute. He continued to work on this until 1984 and received a Grammy for it in 2000.

PIERRE BOULEZ

DAVID BOWIE

David Bowie

(1947–2016, English)

A teenage jazz lover, David Jones, better known by his stage name David Bowie, started out in music as a student of the saxophone. After he left school, he performed with several bands and released a debut solo album in 1967, which garnered no attention.

> "What I like **my music** to do to me is **awaken** the **ghosts inside of me.**"
>
> DAVID BOWIE, SINGER AND SONGWRITER

Bowie produced a hit with the single "Space Oddity" in 1969, but the albums made in the following two years were only moderately successful. However, his career took off with the glam-rock album, *Ziggy Stardust and the Spiders from Mars* (1972). This heralded a prolific period during which he expanded his stylistic range as a songwriter, while maintaining his commercial popularity. In the middle of the 1970s, Bowie struggled with drug addiction but he continued to make popular and adventurous music, producing albums that encompassed dystopian rock (*Diamond Dogs*) and soul (*Young Americans*). He moved to Berlin in 1976, breaking his drug dependency and producing the "Berlin Trilogy," which experimented with minimalism and electronica. During the early 1980s, he became an established mainstream pop star, collaborating with Queen, Tina Turner, and Mick Jagger, and producing the album *Let's Dance*, with the Chic guitarist, songwriter, and producer, Nile Rodgers. He continued to experiment with different styles during the 1990s and 2000s, incorporating drum 'n' bass and industrial music into his work. He released a new album, titled *The Next Day*, in 2013. The release of his final album, *Blackstar*, coincided with his 69th birthday and came just two days before his death.

Johannes Brahms

(1833–1897, German)

Born in a poor family in Hamburg, Johannes Brahms displayed early promise as a musician. He earned extra money for his family from around the age of 13 by performing in bars and beer halls. In 1853 he toured with the violinist Eduard Reméyni in an effort to forge a career as a professional pianist. During this time, he met the violinist Joseph Joachim, the composer Robert Schumann, and Schumann's wife, Clara, a renowned pianist. Schumann, impressed with Brahms's work, wrote an article in 1853 hailing him as the heir to the famous composer Ludwig van Beethoven. The following year, however, Schumann suffered a breakdown and Brahms went to Düsseldorf to help Clara and their family. He fell in love with her, and the nature of their relationship after Schumann's death in 1856 has been the source of much speculation. Brahms regarded Clara as a close friend and adviser, and trusted her with the first reading of many of his greatest works. By the late 1860s, his reputation as a composer and conductor was secure and he considered giving up composing in 1890. However, inspired by the work of clarinetist Richard Mühlfeld, he wrote the *Clarinet Quintet* (1891), which constitutes his finest and most innovative contribution to chamber music. In 1896, Clara died, prompting Brahms to write the song cycle "Vier Ernste Geange" ("Four Serious Songs")—a late contribution to a genre in which he is an influential figure. Brahms succumbed to cancer a year later, and was buried in Vienna.

JACQUES BREL

Jacques Brel

(1929–1978, Belgian)

Jacques Brel was born in Brussels and took up the guitar at the age of 15. He became a professional musician in 1953, releasing a single and moving to Paris, where his reputation grew. In 1956, "Quand On N'a Pas Que l'Amour" became a French chart hit and Brel subsequently released an album every year between 1957 and 1959. By the early 1960s, he had moved beyond a purely Francophone audience and was an international star, appearing at Carnegie Hall in New York in 1963. During the late 1960s and the 1970s he turned his attention to cinema and theater, but interest in his music was maintained through cover versions produced by a diverse array of high-profile artists, including Frank Sinatra, Scott Walker, and David Bowie. Diagnosed with lung cancer in 1974, Brel recovered and in 1977, he released the album, *Brel*, which was a massive success, selling two million copies around the world. However, Brel's cancer returned and he died in 1978, at the age of 49.

Benjamin Britten

(1913–1976, English)

A precociously gifted child, Britten began to study with the English composer and violist Frank Bridge at the age of 11. In 1930, he entered the Royal College of Music, and in 1935, he met the poet W.H. Auden. The two became friends and would work together several times during their lives. In 1939, Britten fell in love with the tenor singer Peter Pears, and in 1947, they set up house together in the Suffolk coastal village of Aldeburgh, where Britten would live intermittently for the rest of his life. Reading the Suffolk poet George Crabbe partly fueled Britten's decision to return to England in 1942, after a period in the United States escaping World War II. Britten wrote many of his greatest roles for Pears, including the title role in his opera *Peter Grimes*, which enjoyed a hugely acclaimed premiere at Sadlers Wells in 1945. From 1947, Britten concentrated his operatic efforts on the newly formed English Opera Group, though he also received prestigious commissions from Covent Garden, such as *Billy Budd*, and from the Anglican Church—his *War Requiem* was used for the reopening of Coventry Cathedral in 1962. His last decade was clouded by ill health but his latest works are among some of his greatest—for example, the opera *Death in Venice*, which premiered in 1973, with Pears in the lead role.

Garth Brooks

(1962–present, American)

The son of Colleen Carroll, a professional country singer, Garth Brooks learned the guitar and banjo as a child, but did not begin his music career until 1985, the year after he graduated from university. He moved to Nashville in 1987, and in 1989, he released his first album, *Garth Brooks*, achieving immediate commercial success. His second album, *No Fences*, released in 1990, established him as a mainstream star, reaching number three on the pop charts. A traditional country songwriter with pop and rock influences, Brooks became well known for his energetic and theatrical live shows, which were unconventional in the tradition of country. This exuberant image helped him to reach an even wider audience and his third record, *Ropin' the Wind*, became the first country album to enter the pop charts at number one, heralding a period of international pop stardom during the late 1990s. Although Brooks announced his retirement from music in 2000, he staged a series of comeback concerts in 2007 and continues to perform and release new music.

James Brown

(1933–2006, American)

Brown began his career during the 1950s with the Georgia-based R&B vocal group The Famous Flames, eventually becoming lead singer of the band. By the early 1960s, he was famous for his energetic and charged live performances, and his music was moving toward the tight, horn-led sound that would eventually be known as funk. In 1965, he became a mainstream pop star with the single "Papa's Got a Brand New Bag," and he built on this success with "I Feel Good," which would become one of his signature songs. He maintained his commercial popularity during the late 1960s. During the early 1970s he moved toward a rougher, rawer sound, driven by his band, who were known as the J.B.'s. In part, his powerful music was the result of the size of his group, which regularly featured three guitarists, two bassists, two drummers, a horn section, and a percussionist. Brown's impact as an innovator dwindled during the 1970s, but the influence of his music on hip-hop and rap producers led to a resurgence of interest in his work during the 1980s. However, during the late 1980s, he experienced several personal crises and spent two years in prison for threatening people with a gun. After his release he continued to record and perform around the world.

Dave Brubeck

(1920–2012, American)

As a child in California, Brubeck studied the piano with his mother, a professional piano teacher, before entering the conservatory of the College of the Pacific, despite being unable to read music. Drafted into the army during World War II, he resumed his studies in 1946 and by 1951 he had released his first album as the leader of The Dave Brubeck Quartet. The quartet performed at college campuses across America, building up a large grassroots fanbase. In 1954, Brubeck became only the second jazz musician to appear on the cover of the prestigious *Time* magazine and in 1959, he released the album that would define his career, *Time Out*. A collection of pieces written in unorthodox time signatures, *Time Out* went on to sell over a million copies. "Take Five," a single taken from the album, was the first jazz single to break the 1 million sales milestone. The quartet were prolific throughout the 1960s, sometimes releasing as many as four albums a year. At the same time Brubeck experimented as a composer, even writing a musical which premiered at the Monterey Jazz Festival in 1962. He disbanded the quartet in 1967, preferring to focus on compositions that reflected his spiritual beliefs, including orchestral and choral works.

Anton Bruckner

(1824–1896, Austrian)

Born in Ansfelden, Bruckner was taught to play the organ by his father, a village schoolmaster. He was largely self-taught as a composer, and also worked as an organist, often practicing 12 hours a day. A very religious man, Bruckner's first surviving work is the *Requiem Mass*, written in 1849. His first job as an organist was at the Abbey of St. Florian near Ansfelden in 1851, and he later went on to Linz Cathedral, where he worked from 1856 to 1868. During this time he wrote Mass No. 1 in D Minor, his first piece as a fully mature composer. In 1868, he was appointed court organist and a teacher at the Vienna Conservatory. A solitary figure, he was wary of explaining or discussing his music with other people. This inclination may have been exacerbated by his strong provincial accent, a legacy of his peasant background that was looked down on by the metropolitan elite of Vienna. He went on to write eight more symphonies in addition to a number of other sacred works and substantial pieces for organ, piano, and choir, such as the *Te Deum* mass of 1884. Bruckner died in 1896, leaving his intensely spiritual Symphony No.9 unfinished.

ANTON BRUCKNER

Prince Buster

(1938–2016, Jamaican)

After several unheralded ventures as a singer during the 1950s, Prince Buster released his first single, "Little Honey," in 1961. An instrumental piece, the song is now credited with pioneering the genre that would come to be known as ska. During the early 1960s he became a one-man cottage industry, releasing a string of hits as a performer in his own right, or as a songwriter and producer working for other artists. Songs written and released during this period include "Oh Carolina" and "One Step Beyond," which was successfully covered by the UK 2 Tone band, Madness. During the late 1960s Prince Buster changed his sound, pioneering music in the slower rocksteady genre, culminating with the album *Judge Dread Rock Steady*. He stopped performing in 1973. In 2001, he was awarded the Order of Distinction by the Jamaican government.

William Byrd
(*c.*1543–1623, English)
Born in London, William Byrd is thought to have studied under the influential composer Thomas Tallis. In 1563, he was appointed master of choristers and organist at Lincoln Cathedral. Later, in 1572, he became a Gentleman of the Chapel Royal, which allowed him significant access to the court of Queen Elizabeth I. In 1575, she granted Byrd and Tallis a patent for publishing printed manuscript paper and music and in the same year they jointly published *Cantiones*, a collection of 34 motets—17 by each composer—commemorating the 34 years of her reign. A Catholic, Byrd nonetheless accepted commissions to produce religious music for the Protestant Elizabeth and *Great Service* is credited with significantly contributing to the development of the English Anthem. Between 1588 and 1589, Byrd produced two books of English songs, *Psalmes, Sonets and Songs* and *Songs of Sundrie Natures*. He died in 1623 having amassed a fortune through his music.

"When **music** fails to agree to the **ear...**the **heart** and the senses, then it has missed its **point.**"
MARIA CALLAS, OPERATIC SOPRANO

John Cage
(1912–1992, American)
Born in Los Angeles, John Cage was inspired to pursue a life in music after a meeting with the composer Arnold Schoenberg in 1934. A restless innovator, he invented the "prepared piano" in 1938, altering the sound of a conventional piano by placing objects on the strings. Ten years later he completed a sequence of sonatas and interludes for the instrument; these were well received and earned Cage a favorable reputation with fellow musicians and composers. He studied Buddhism during the 1940s and his reading of the ancient Chinese text, *I Ching*, led him to experiment with "chance pieces," stripping away intention and form by allowing chance operations into his music. In 1952, this resulted in his most famous composition, "4′ 33," which consists of 4 minutes and 33 seconds of pure silence, allowing any chance noises to become part of the piece. His collected writings, *Silence*, brought him world fame in 1961. During the 1970s, his work became more ambitious; *Roratorio*, a cacophonous work written for electronic tape and live performers, is an attempt to translate James Joyce's novel, *Finnegans Wake*, into sound. Cage continued to experiment with music until his death at the age of 79.

Maria Callas
(1923–1977, Greek)
Born in New York to Greek parents, Maria Callas moved to Athens with her mother in 1937, where she received her training as a soprano singer at the Greek National Conservatoire. Her professional career began in 1942 and in the same year she received critical acclaim for her performance in the title role of Puccini's opera, *Tosca*. After a brief and unsuccessful spell in America, Callas began to perform in Italy from 1948 onward. In 1949, she attracted the attention of the opera world when she performed the markedly different roles of Brünnhilde in Richard Wagner's *Die Walküre* and Elvira in *I puritani* by Vincenzo Bellini. Her ability to perform a wide range of operatic styles established her as a major force in the genre, and during the 1950s she performed at many of the world's most prestigious opera houses, including La Scala in Milan, New York's Metropolitan Opera, and the Royal Opera House in London. It was here that she gave her final stage performance in 1965, as Tosca, the role with which she first achieved recognition.

Mariah Carey
(1970–present, American)
Mariah Carey worked as a backing vocalist before achieving immediate and significant success with her eponymous debut album, which gave rise to four consecutive number one singles in the United States. A songwriter as well as a gifted R&B and pop vocalist, Carey continued her success as an R&B and pop performer throughout the 1990s, releasing four albums from 1991–1994. Carey collaborated with other high-profile R&B artists, such as BoyzIIMen, and in 1993, she married Tommy Mottola, an executive at her record company. Their separation in 1997 coincided with her move toward hip-hop-oriented songwriting on the album *Butterfly*. She maintained her popular and critical reputation, and in 1999 she became the first performer to have registered a number one hit in every year of the 1990s. From 2000 onward, she continued to make music and embarked on a career as a film actress. She has sold more than 200 million records around the world and has influenced a subsequent generation of R&B singers with her five-octave vocal range and use of melisma, in which several different musical notes are attached to a single syllable of lyric.

MARIAH CAREY

The Carter Family
(active 1920s–1960s, American)
Initially a husband and wife duo consisting of A. P. and Sara Carter, the definitive Carter Family group was formed when Maybelle Carter, A. P.'s sister-in-law, joined in 1926. In 1927, after a successful audition for a record company, they released several singles, including "The Wandering Boy." In 1928, they recorded several more songs for the Victor record company and these sessions featured pieces such as "Keep on the Sunny Side" and "Can the Circle be Unbroken," which did much to popularize the genre of country music in the United States. By the end of 1930, the Carter Family had sold 300,000 records, but they earned little money because of copyright issues. Financial difficulties eventually forced A. P. Carter to move to Detroit in pursuit of work, while Maybelle and her husband left Virginia for Washington D.C. Sara and A. P. separated in 1932 and for several years the group only met to record together. In 1938–1939, exposure on the radio enabled them to build a nationwide fanbase, but in 1943 Sara moved to California with her new husband, and the group disbanded. Although A. P. and Sara reunited in 1952 to form a new band with their children, they were met with indifference by the public, and the group separated again. However, in 1967, seven years after the death of A. P. Carter, Maybelle and Sara reunited to record and perform. In 1970, the Carter Family became the first group to be inducted into the Country Music Hall of Fame.

THE CARTER FAMILY

Cartola
(1908–1980, Brazilian)
Cartola was born in Rio de Janeiro, Brazil. As a child, he watched his father play the guitar and the cavaquinho, picking up a grounding in both instruments. After his mother's death in 1923, he left school and worked in a number of casual jobs while involving himself with the musical life of his native city. In 1928 he cofounded a samba school in the Mangueira district of Rio de Janeiro and some of his first sambas were composed during his tenure as a teacher there. Cartola began to sell these compositions during the early 1930s. Although he enjoyed some success, he continued to struggle financially and in addition to his work as a teacher, he supported himself by part-time jobs. Cartola composed two award-winning sambas, "Partiu" and "Sei Chorar," during the late 1930s. After this productive period, his popularity declined during the 1940s and he suffered some personal crises, including the death of his second wife, Deolinda, and a bout of meningitis. At this time, he was heavily reliant on alcohol and his creative muse deserted him. However, a journalist, Sérgio Porto, helped revive Cartola's career in 1956 and in 1963 Cartola and Zica, his third wife, opened Zicartola, a bar and concert venue that became a focal point for samba music in Rio. During the 1960s and '70s, many classic samba compositions were released on record, and Cartola benefited from this commercially. A prolific writer, Cartola is credited with the composition of approximately 600 samba songs.

Johnny Cash
(1932–2003, American)
Johnny Cash began to write his first songs as a 12-year old in Arkansas, refining his skills during a stint in the army from 1950–1954. He was married in 1954 and became a significant voice in country music with the release of his second single, "Folsome Prison Blues," in 1955. This was followed by the commercial pop hit "I Walk the Line." During the late 1950s, Cash continued to release hits that did well on the country and pop charts and refined his image as "The Man in Black." Though he continued to churn out hits, Cash experienced personal problems, including drug addiction and divorce, in 1966. June Carter, a former collaborator, helped him recover from his addictions and the breakdown of his marriage, and introduced him to Christianity—they married in 1968. Cash revived his career and released his most popular album, *Johnny Cash at Folsom Prison,* in 1968. His popularity continued throughout the 1970s and he was inducted into the Country Music Hall of Fame in 1980—the youngest person to receive that honor. The *American Recordings* albums, released between 1993 and 2002, won him critical acclaim and a new, younger audience.

RAY CHARLES

Nelson Cavaquinho
(1911–1986, Brazilian)
Nelson Antonio da Silva was born into a poor family in Rio de Janeiro, Brazil. The son of a tuba player in the military police band, he took up factory work at an early age and began to play the cavaquinho—the guitarlike instrument after which he is known. Cavaquinho enrolled with the military police at 19, and got married a year later. Initially working as a composer of *choro* (Brazilian instrumental pieces), he soon turned to samba, forming a brief writing partnership with the great sambist Cartola. During the late 1930s, Cavaquinho began to sell compositions to recording artists and started writing for the popular singer Ciro Monteiro in 1943. Their 1946 collaboration, "Rugas," was a hit. Cavaquinho formed a lifelong creative partnership with the singer, songwriter, and painter, Guilherme de Brito in 1955, and in the immediate aftermath of this he wrote some of his greatest works, such as "A Flor e o Espinho." Cavaquinho continued to write and perform throughout the 1960s and '70s, and is credited with around 600 compositions, which continue to be performed by contemporary stars of Brazilian music. He died of pulmonary emphysema in 1986.

Ray Charles
(1930–2004, American)
Blinded by glaucoma at the age of seven, Ray Charles studied classical music at school and developed his skills as a jazz pianist in his spare time. He turned professional in 1946, leaving his hometown of Albany in Georgia, first for Florida, and then Seattle.

> "**Learning** to read music in **Braille** and play by **ear** helped me develop a [very] good **memory.**"
>
> RAY CHARLES, SINGER AND SONGWRITER

During the early 1950s, he established himself as a minor rhythm and blues artists, before achieving a hit in 1955 with "I Got a Woman." His reputation, and his sound, developed through the late 1950s and the music he made then is now credited as fundamental to the evolution of soul music. Charles experienced mainstream success in 1959 with the release of "What'd I Say," and he continued to experiment with his sound, drawing on big band, jazz, and country influences. His fusion of country and pop did much to break down the racial segregations that were typically attached to the music. By the mid-1960s, Charles' success as a recording artist had peaked and his heroin addiction resulted in legal difficulties. Nonetheless, he continued to record and perform during the 1970s and '80s, demonstrating an increased interest in country music.

Hariprasad Chaurasia
(1938–present, Indian)
The son of a wrestler, Hariprasad Chaurasia began his training as a singer as a 15-year old in Uttar Pradesh, India. Under the tutelage of Pandit Bholanath, he began playing the flute and secured a position as a composer and performer with All India Radio in 1957. During the 1960s, he continued to study, achieving virtuoso proficiency through his innovative use of breathing techniques. He collaborated with the string musicians Shivkumar Sharma and Brijbhushan Kabra to record *Call of the Valley* in 1967. Telling the story of a day in the life of a shepherd through the use of traditional ragas (melodic modes), the album became popular with audiences beyond India. An enthusiastic experimenter, Chaurasia has worked with many Western musicians and has taught at the Rotterdam Music Conservatory, educating students in Hindustani music. He was awarded the Padma Vibhushan, the second highest honor in Indian civilian life, in 2000.

The Chemical Brothers
(active 1991–present, English)
Ed Simons and Tom Rowlands began their musical careers as DJs in the nightclubs of Manchester, under the name The Dust Brothers. They played an eclectic variety of music styles, including hip-hop and house, and their

THE CHEMICAL BROTHERS

early singles were influential in the development of big beat. Changing their name to The Chemical Brothers, they released their first album, *Exit Planet Dust*, in 1995, collaborating with pop vocalists, including Beth Orton. The album reached number nine in the UK charts, but its success was eclipsed by their following album, *Dig Your Own Hole*. Supported by the single "Setting Sun," which featured the vocals of Oasis songwriter Noel Gallagher, it topped the UK charts and achieved significant sales in the US, prompting extensive tours of North America by the group. The Chemical Brothers moved towards a commercial form of house music in 1999, achieving critical acclaim with their third album, *Surrender*. Expanding their repertoire further during the 2000s, they released their first soundtrack for the film *Hanna* in 2010. They are one of the few dance acts to headline major music festivals, including Glastonbury.

Leslie Cheung

(1956–2003, Hong Kong)

Born in Hong Kong, China, Leslie Cheung studied in England. On his return to his native country he pursued simultaneous careers as a singer and an actor and released his first successful single, "Wind Continues to Blow" in 1982. His fame increased throughout the decade as he established himself as a dominant figure in Cantonese music. In 1986 Cheung gained critical acclaim and pan-Asian stardom for his performance in the John Woo film, *A Better Tomorrow*. He retired from music in 1989 at the age of 33, performing 33 farewell concerts at the 12,500-seater Hong Kong Coliseum. During the early 1990s, Cheung concentrated on his film work, but he returned to music in 1995 and went on to release successful albums. He gave sold-out concerts around the world until his death in 2003.

The Chieftains

(active 1962–present, Irish)

Formed in 1962 by the accordionist and piper Paddy Moloney, The Chieftains spent the 1960s and early '70s operating as a semi-professional touring band in Ireland and England. A predominantly instrumental group, their fame spread to the United States during the early 1970s, and their reputation was bolstered significantly by their contribution to the soundtrack of Stanley Kubrick's film, *Barry Lyndon*, released in 1975. During the late 1970s and early '80s, they were a prolific studio band, releasing an album a year to positive commercial response. They have subsequently attempted to expand their sound, incorporating a range of influences, including flamenco, frequently collaborating with international stars, such as Van Morrison. The band are widely credited with having popularized Irish folk music around the world. In 1983, they became the first Western band to perform on the Great Wall of China.

FREDERIC CHOPIN

Frederic Chopin

(1810–1849, Polish)

Having studied at the Warsaw Conservatory, Chopin emigrated from Poland after the Russian capture of the city in 1831. He moved to Paris, making his home and name in the then piano capital of the world. During his time there, he preferred private performances in the salons of the French capital's nobility to the strain and artistic compromises of courting the general public, and developed a lucrative career teaching ladies of aristocratic birth. In 1836, the Hungarian virtuoso pianist and composer Franz Liszt introduced him to George Sand, a novelist who had outraged Parisian society by refusing to conform to society's expectations of how a woman should behave. A nine-year relationship followed, during which Chopin wrote the majority of his most important works, starting with *The Preludes*. Partially written during a stay in Majorca, these 24 pieces for solo piano are perhaps the most innovative of all his works and inspired many later composers, including Claude Debussy and Sergei Rachmaninoff. A significant composer in the history of the piano, Chopin was particularly drawn to dance forms. The waltz is evident in many of his works and through the use of the mazurka and the polonaise he made references to his Polish identity—this technique is evident in the third movement of his Piano Concerto No. 2 in F Minor. During the 1840s, Chopin's health began to fail and he separated from Sands in 1847. Following the end of his marriage, his health deteriorated rapidly and he wrote almost no new music. In 1841, he made an extended visit to England and Scotland and finished by giving his last-ever concert in London. He died the following year in Paris, and 3,000 people attended his funeral.

Eric Clapton

(1945–present, English)

Eric Clapton learned to play the blues guitar as a teenager growing up in England. He found early success with the blues-influenced band The Yardbirds in 1965, before leaving for a brief spell in John Mayall and the Bluesbreakers in 1966. In the same year, he formed the group Cream with two other established musicians—the virtuoso drummer Ginger Baker and bassist Jack Bruce. Together for slightly more than two years, the band established Clapton's reputation as a guitar virtuoso. After a brief spell in the bands Blind Faith and Delaney and Bonnie and Friends, he began a solo career with the eponymous album *Eric Clapton* in 1970, although drug addiction resulted in lengthy gaps between tours and albums. However, he was prolific during the second half of the 1970s, releasing five best-selling albums (studio and live) and by the early 1980s he had achieved mainstream pop-star status. Clapton suffered a personal tragedy in the early 1990s with the death of his son, but he continued to work, receiving critical acclaim for his return to a more blues-driven sound. He has continued to explore the genre, interpreting the songs of the great blues guitarist Robert Johnson and duetting with B. B. King.

The Clash

(active 1976–1986, English)

Formed in London in 1976, The Clash played their first gig as a support act for the innovative punk band the Sex Pistols. Led by singer-songwriter Joe Strummer, they achieved critical and commercial success in the UK with their self-titled debut in 1977. They consolidated their reputation as a leading punk group in the UK, before the release of their third album, *London Calling*, established them as a significant act in both the UK and the United States. Although they were typically categorized as a punk band, their music demonstrated a range of influences, including rock 'n' roll and reggae. *London Calling* signified the height of the group's critical credibility, but they achieved their greatest commercial success in the UK and the United States with the release of their 1982 album *Combat Rock*, containing the song "Rock the Casbah," which became a mainstream hit. However, the group began to fall apart around this time, with the departure of drummer Topper Headon and lead guitarist Mick Jones, from 1982–1983. The Clash split up in 1986, although all members of the band continued to work in music.

THE CLASH

Reverend James Cleveland
(1931–1991, American)
A boy soprano in the choir at his Baptist church in Chicago, James Cleveland turned his focus toward the piano when his voice broke. He joined a trio called the Gospelaires in 1950, working as a composer and arranger. This exposure earned him a job as a composer for the well-known pianist Roberta Martin and he joined the gospel group the Caravans in the mid-50s, playing piano and writing new settings for traditional hymns and spiritual songs. In 1959, he branched out as a fully fledged solo artist, and the success of his version of "The Love of God" took him beyond the confines of the gospel community. During the 1960s, he enjoyed nationwide renown, touring across the United States with The James Cleveland Singers and releasing the hugely popular *Peace Be Still* album, which sold close to one million copies. Through The Gospel Music Workshop of America, he taught his style of gospel music to a younger generation of musicians and this initiative ensured that his legacy persisted beyond his death in 1991.

Jimmy Cliff
(1948–present, Jamaican)
Jimmy Cliff began writing songs while he was an elementary school student. He released his first hit single, "Hurricane Hattie," at the age of 14 and several subsequent singles were also successful. Cliff established himself as an international star in 1968 with his debut album, *Hard Road to Travel*, and the single "Waterfall" won the International Song Festival prize. His follow-up album, *Wonderful World, Beautiful People*, capitalized on this international success and in 1972, he launched an acting career in the film *The Harder They Come*, contributing a number of songs to the soundtrack. Although Cliff's star was eclipsed during the late 1970s by Bob Marley, he achieved some success in the United States during the mid-1980s and has continued to record and perform. In 2003, he was honored with the Order of Merit by the Jamaican government.

Coldplay
(active 1998–present, English)
Formed in 1998 by four students at University College London, Coldplay found immediate success with their debut album, *Parachutes*. Founded on the rock songwriting and distinctive singing style of Chris Martin, they continued their rise to prominence with *Rush of Blood to the Head* in 2003, and their fame was increased by Martin's marriage to American film actress Gwyneth Paltrow in the same year. Moving away from low-key indie rock toward a more electronic and anthemic sound, Coldplay became mainstream stars with their 2005 album, *X&Y*, which sold more than thirteen million copies around the world. One of the most commercially successful and prominent rock bands of the 2000s, they have collaborated with rapper Jay-Z and producer Brian Eno and continue to perform sold-out concerts around the world.

COLDPLAY

John Coltrane
(1926–1967, American)
After having spent a year serving in the Navy, John Coltrane took up the formal study of jazz music in 1946. In the late 1940s and early 1950s he worked as a saxophonist for well-known bandleaders, including the trumpeter Dizzy Gillespie. During this period he became addicted to heroin, though this did not prevent him from becoming a crucial member of the Miles Davis Quintet for the recording of landmark albums such as *Cookin'* and *Relaxin'*. The quintet disbanded in 1957 and Coltrane released *Blue Train*, receiving his first critical acclaim as a bandleader. In 1959, after joining Miles Davis, Coltrane worked on Davis' landmark jazz album *A Kind of Blue*. He then embarked on a successful solo career, coming to the attention of the wider musical community as a bandleader with *Giant Steps* (1960), and recording a critical and commercial hit with the 1961 album, *My Favourite Things*. An innovator, Coltrane began to experiment with free jazz and Indian music during the early 1960s, and his music was increasingly concerned with spiritual matters. This focus is best demonstrated by the album *A Love Supreme*—a powerful expression of Coltrane's faith, which went on to become his best-selling work. He died suddenly of liver cancer at the age of 40.

Aaron Copland
(1900–1990, American)
Born in New York into a prosperous family, Aaron Copland spent his teenage years studying music privately, searching libraries for new scores, and taking an interest in jazz. He lived in Paris for three years from 1921 onward, learning from his teacher Nadia Boulanger, and his early compositions on his return to the United States earned him a reputation as an iconoclastic modernist. In 1925, he completed his first major work, *Symphony for Organ and Orchestra*, and earned a living as teacher and writer. During the 1930s he wrote workers' choruses and in 1938, his ballet *Billy the Kid* premiered; it was the first of three ballets that established him as the popular voice of American classical music. In 1945, *Appalachian Spring* won the Pulitzer Prize and in the same decade he wrote an article on proletarian music that led to him being targeted by Senator McCarthy's House Committee on Un-American Activities. However, in 1954 he was elected to the American Academy of Arts and Letters and in 1958 he made his debut as a conductor with the New York Philharmonic, launching a 20-year career. In his later years, he was a friend and adviser to aspiring young composers such as Leonard Bernstein. He ceased composing in 1975, 15 years before his death.

Elvis Costello
(1954–present, English)
The son of a professional musician, Elvis Costello experienced minor success in a pub rock band during the mid-1970s before attracting attention with his 1977 debut album, *My Aim is True*. A year after its release, he recruited a backing band, The Attractions, and in 1979, he achieved commercial and critical success in both the UK and the United States with his third album, *Armed Forces*. During the early 1980s he expanded his stylistic range as a songwriter, leaving behind his early guitar-based punk sound to experiment with a range of styles, including country (*Almost Blue*) and orchestral pop (*Imperial Bedroom*). Costello's changing sound resulted in a split with Attractions in 1986 and during the late 1980s he broadened his stylistic palette further, even branching into classical music.

Celia Cruz
(1925–2003, Cuban)
Born in Havana in 1925, Celia Cruz began to sing in the cabaret clubs of her native city as a teenager and made her first recordings in Venezuela in 1948. In 1950, she became the lead singer of the popular orchestra La Sonora Matancera, and it was with them that she became famous in Cuba, singing a range of Latin American dance styles. Moving to the United States in 1960 after the Cuban Revolution, she left La Sonora Matancera in 1965 and began work as a solo performer. She achieved international fame in 1974 through her collaboration with the Dominican bandleader Johnny Pacheco and his band, the Fania All-Stars. A Grammy Award winner, Celia Cruz is one of the most commercially successful salsa performers in the history of Latin American music.

CELIA CRUZ

The Cure
(active 1976–present, English)
Formed in 1976 by school friends Robert Smith, Michael Dempsey, and Laurence Tollington, The Cure secured a record deal in 1978 on the strength of a demo tape, and released their first album, *Three Imaginary Boys*, in 1979. Smith's experience of playing with the goth-influenced Siouxie and the Banshees encouraged him to move away from the band's punk esthetic toward a darker, more ambitious sound, culminating in the release of *Pornography* in 1983. This music, and Smith's striking appearance,

are now regarded as significant contributions to the development of goth rock. The band's music changed frequently and dramatically during the mid-to-late-1980s, but the general trend was toward a more pop-based sound, resulting in increased commercial success. Their 1985 album *The Head on the Door* contained the international hit singles "In Between Days" and "Close to Me," and they continued their move toward the mainstream during the 1990s. Despite their commercial success, the band members' personal relationships had become strained and by 1988 Smith was the only original member of the group remaining.

Daft Punk
(active 1993–2021, French)

Former members of a Parisian punk band called Darling, Guy-Manuel de Homem-Christo and Thomas Bangalter formed a house music duo, called Daft Punk, in 1993. Their early singles—"The New Wave," "Da Funk," and "Musique"—received attention from the dance music community and prompted offers from several interested record labels. Their debut album, *Homework*, a combination of disco, house, and electro, was influential in shaping the sound of dance music during the late 1990s and early 2000s and went on to sell more than two million copies worldwide. Despite their fame, the duo cultivated an image of mystery, appearing in robot masks during their live shows. Their 2001 album, *Discovery*, met with a mixed critical reception but gave rise to several popular singles, including "One More Time" and "Digital Love." One of the few dance music acts to have achieved significant mainstream success, Daft Punk have produced a soundtrack for the film *Tron: Legacy* and composed music for the catwalk shows of the fashion house Yves Saint Laurent.

Miles Davis
(1926–1991, American)

Born in St. Louis, the son of a music teacher, Miles Davis began to learn the trumpet at the age of 13 and moved to New York in 1944 to study at the Juilliard School of Music. He left a year later, embarking on a career as a jazz musician, and by the late 1940s he was recording as the leader of a band. By the early 1950s, Davis was struggling with a heroin addiction. However, he remained a prolific figure in the recording studio, releasing several albums between 1955 and 1959, all of which demonstrated his creative chemistry with his band, featuring John Coltrane on the saxophone and Cannonball Adderley on the piano. Perhaps his most fruitful creative partnership was with Gil Evans, the arranger with whom he collaborated on three albums: *Miles Ahead*, *Porgy and Bess*, and *Sketches of Spain*. Davis's early recording period culminated with *Kind of Blue* (1959), which went on to sell five million copies worldwide. He continued to record throughout the 1960s, making albums such as *Live at Carnegie Hall*, which were critical and commercial successes. An innovator and experimenter, during the late 1960s he became one of the first performers to combine jazz with rock, a project which resulted in the *Bitches Brew* album of 1970. Working and recording throughout the 1970s and 1980s, Davis continued to experiment with new sounds and techniques until his death from pneumonia at age 65.

MILES DAVIS

> "**You** have to **play a long time** to be **able** to play like **yourself.**"
>
> MILES DAVIS, TRUMPETER AND COMPOSER

De La Soul
(active 1987–present, American)

Formed by three New York high school students in 1987, De La Soul achieved significant critical acclaim for their debut album, *3 Feet High and Rising*. Supported by the commercially successful single, "Me Myself and I," it established them as the leaders of an alternative rap movement which also included groups such as The Jungle Brothers and A Tribe Called Quest. This movement was defined by playful, witty rapping and jazz- and funk-influenced music production. Although their debut album was commercially and critically popular, De La Soul encountered legal difficulties over their use of music sampled from other artists, resulting in a four-year delay in the release of their second album, *De La Soul is Dead*. Less playful than their previous work, it signaled a decline in their commercial popularity which continued throughout the 1990s. However, many subsequent hip-hop artists have been influenced by their music and *3 Feet High and Rising* was recognized as a work of significant cultural importance by the United States' National Recording Registry in the year 2010.

Claude Debussy
(1862–1918, French)

Claude Debussy was born in the town of Saint-Germain-en-Laye in northern France, to a shopkeeper father and a seamstress mother. He began studying the piano at the age of seven and overcame his family's lack of affinity for music, entering the prestigious Paris Conservatoire at the age of 10. Although he was awarded the Grand Prix de Rome for composition in 1884, his earliest published works met with little success. Largely self-taught, Debussy traveled across Europe, absorbing the Oriental cultures that were becoming increasingly popular in the West, an influence that Debussy would eventually express in *Estampes* (1903). From 1892, his music started to attract wider attention and his *Prèlude a l'aprés midi d'une Faune* (1894) was a definitive moment in his emergence as a unique voice. However, another decade was to pass until the significance of Debussy's groundbreaking ideas were fully recognized. Written during this period, the opera *Pelléas et Melisande* (1902) rejected Italian conventions and pushed the genre beyond the influence of Richard Wagner, employing an abstract quality that seemed shockingly new at the time. Debussy was an outspoken music critic, writing under the pseudonym Monsieur Croche (Mr. Quaver). In 1903, he had an affair with the singer Emma Bardac (whom he eventually married), distancing many of his friends who remained loyal to his wife. Debussy completed a series of sonatas in 1917 and died of cancer a few months prior to the end of World War I in 1918.

CLAUDE DEBUSSY

Desmond Dekker
(1941–2006, Jamaican)

Desmond Dekker signed a record deal while working as a welder in Kingston, Jamaica, in 1961. However, it was not until 1963 that he began to release a steady flow of hits. His fourth single, "King of Ska," made him a star on his native island and he continued to develop and popularize the emerging genre after which the track was named. In 1967, his single "007 (Shanty Town)" became a hit in the UK and Dekker's performances in England established him as a star in the country. The single "Israelites" was successful in both the UK and the United States, making Dekker one of the first Jamaican artists to achieve mainstream success in the latter. He moved to the UK in 1969 and continued his success there with "You Can Get it if You Really Want," written by Jimmy Cliff, and benefited from the 2 Tone movement, popularized by new, ska-influenced bands like The Specials and Madness. Dekker died at the age of 64, having done much to popularize Jamaican music beyond the island.

Frederick Delius

(1862–1934, English)

Born in Yorkshire in the north of England, Frederick Delius lived in a musical household and developed a love of music at a very young age. His father, Julius Delius, hoped his son would work in the family wool business, but when it became obvious that this was unlikely, he sent him to Florida to run an orange grove. However, in 1886, he submitted to his son's wishes and Delius went to Germany to study at the Leipzig Conservatory. In 1897, he moved to Grez-sur-Loing near Paris, France, and married the German painter Jelka Rosen in 1903. Throughout the 1900s, he produced a procession of outstanding orchestral works, including tone poems, such as "In a Summer Garden" (1908), which evoked a strong sense of atmosphere and place. During the 1920s, however, Delius began to display symptoms of syphilis and by 1928 he was blind and paralyzed, making it necessary for him to dictate his final works through Eric Fenby, his amanuensis.

Manu Dibango

(1933–2020, Cameroonian)

Having first studied music at church, Manu Dibango worked as a saxophone and vibraphone player in Europe and Africa during the 1950s. He became a member of the seminal Congolese rumba group, African Jazz, in 1960 and 12 years later he recorded an international hit with the song "Soul Makossa." He went on to become a prominent and prolific figure in African music in the late 1970s.

MANU DIBANGO

Bo Diddley

(1928–2008, American)

Bo Diddley's first serious experience of music came as trombonist and violinist in the orchestra at his Baptist church. However, while working as a carpenter and mechanic, he watched a performance by John Lee Hooker, which deepened his interest in the guitar. By the early 1950s, he was playing blues music at clubs in Chicago, and he released his successful first single, "Bo Diddley," in 1955. Diddley continued to record throughout the 1950s, and although he only enjoyed moderate commercial success, he was a hugely influential figure in rhythm and blues and in the development of rock 'n' roll. Respected by his peers, his music was covered by many of the biggest bands of the 1960s, including the Rolling Stones and The Animals. This exposure cemented his popularity as a live performer, and he later toured with the English punk band, The Clash.

Fats Domino

(1928–2017, American)

Born in New Orleans, Fats Domino released his first hit, "The Fat Man," at the age of 22. The song, one of the earliest contributions to the genre that came to be known as rock 'n' roll, went on to sell over one million copies. Five years later, his music typified the rhythm and blues sound, but he achieved an enormous mainstream pop hit with the song "Ain't That a Shame." Domino capitalized on this success throughout the rest of the decade and into the early 1960s. His most notable recording of this time was "Blueberry Hill" (1956), which sold more than five million copies around the world between 1956 and 1957. Domino's recording career faded during the 1960s, although he continued to perform live during the 1970s. A lifelong resident of New Orleans, his home was badly damaged by Hurricane Katrina in 2005 and he returned to live performance in 2007 for a fund-raising show.

The Doors

(active 1965–1973, American)

The Doors were formed in Los Angeles in 1965, when singer Jim Morrison and drummer John Densmore joined up with three brothers, Rick, Ray, and Jim Manzarek. Taking their name from the title of Aldous Huxley's *The Doors of Perception*, they performed as a house band at bars in Los Angeles, before releasing their self-titled debut album in 1967. The single, "Light My Fire," sold over one million copies in the United States. Their second album, *Strange Days*, was only moderately successful, but their third, *Waiting for the Sun*, topped the Billboard charts. The Doors became notorious for their live performances, and Morrison was arrested for public indecency after a 1969 show in Miami, L.A. The band's sixth studio album, *L.A. Woman*, was released in 1971 to public acclaim and following its recording, Morrison moved to Paris. He died of a drug overdose a few months later. The band broke up in 1973.

THE DOORS

John Dowland

(1563–1626, English)

Believed to have been born in London or Dublin, John Dowland went to Paris in 1580 as an assistant to the English ambassador to the French court. Returning to England in 1594, he failed to secure a significant position as lutenist at the court of Elizabeth I, possibly because his Catholicism conflicted with the Protestantism of the time. As a result, he left England to work in Germany and his *First Book of Songs* was published in 1597. It was a best-seller, cementing his reputation as one of the most important lute musicians and composers of his time. In 1598, he accepted a position as a musician at the Danish court and published his most important instrumental work, *Lachrimae*, during his tenure there. He was released from his position in Denmark in 1606 and he finally secured a job as a lutenist at the court of James I in 1612.

Dr. Dre

(1965–present, American)

Starting as a DJ in Los Angeles with the group World Class Wreckin' Cru, Dr. Dre first rose to prominence with the rappers Ice Cube and Eazy-E in the group N.W.A. The explicit lyrics and antiestablishment attitude of their debut album, *Straight Outta Compton*, was highly influential in the development of hardcore and gangster rap. Although the group continued to work for two years after the departure of Ice Cube, their popularity declined and Dr. Dre embarked on a career as a solo artist in 1992. *The Chronic*, featuring the rapper Snoop Doggy Dogg, was the first album to be released under his own name and it made him a mainstream star. Supported by best-selling singles such as "Nuthin' but a 'G' Thang," the album established a template that many subsequent rap groups would follow. Collaborating with high-profile rappers such as Tupac Shakur for the rest of the 1990s, Dr. Dre won major commercial success for a second time in 1999 with the album *2001*. He has been instrumental in the development of modern rap artists such as Eminem and 50 Cent.

John Dunstable

(*c.*1390–1453, English)

Believed to have been born in Dunstable, Bedfordshire, John Dunstable is thought to have traveled to France in 1422 in the service of John of Lancaster, the brother of Henry V. A property owner, he entered the service of the Duke of Gloucester in 1438, while enjoying a reputation as the leading English composer of the period. Attribution and dating of his works is difficult, but he was a prime exponent of the mellifluous new English style, and his influence in Europe was enormous.

Antonín Dvořák

(1841–1904, Czech)

As a young man, Antonín Dvořák showed promise at the viola, and after studying at the Prague Organ School from 1857, he took a position with the Bohemian Provisional Theatre

Orchestra in 1862. At this time, his style of composition was increasingly influenced by nationalist music and he received recognition in 1873 with the premier of *Cantata Hymnus* (more usually known as his patriotic cantata, *The Heirs of the White Mountain*). The composer Johannes Brahms was on the Ministry of Education panel that awarded Dvořák a stipend for composition in 1875; two years later, he won the stipend again and Brahms was sufficiently impressed with his work to recommend Dvořák to his publisher. Thanks to this connection and artistic patronage, Dvořák's name

ANTONÍN DVOŘÁK

became known across Europe over the next decade, and he gained a strong following in England, where he conducted a series of concerts. He wrote Symphony No. 7, one of the finest examples of symphonic composition, during this time. In 1892, Dvořák accepted the role of Director of the National Conservatory of Music in New York and produced Symphony No. 9, "From the New World" the following year. He returned to Prague in 1901 and remained there until his death.

Bob Dylan

(1941–present, American)

Born in Minnesota, Bob Dylan learned guitar and harmonica while he was at school. In 1959, he began to perform as a folk singer while studying art at the University of Minnesota. Dropping out of school and relocating to New York in 1961, he released his first album of original songs, *The Freewheelin' Bob Dylan*, in 1963, which gained a significant public profile thanks to a cover of "Blowin' in the Wind" by the folk trio, Peter, Paul, and Mary. By 1965, he had moved away from pure acoustic folk music toward an electric sound, alienating many of his fans in the folk community. Despite this, his albums were significant commercial hits; *Highway 61 Revisited* (1965) reached the top 10 of the US charts, while *Blonde on Blonde* sold over 10 million copies worldwide. After the end of his marriage in the late 1960s, Dylan experimented with country music and returned to commercial and critical acclaim with 1975's *Blood on the Tracks*, a recorded prompted by the breakdown of his marriage. He converted to Christianity in the late 1970s, and released albums of religious music, which were poorly received. During the 1980s, he spent much of his time working on his live act. In 2006, he released the well-received album *Modern Times* and continues to tour, playing around 100 gigs a year.

The Eagles

(active 1971–1980; 1994–present, American)

Formed in Los Angeles in 1971, the Eagles consisted of drummer and singer Don Henley, guitarist and singer Glenn Frey, guitarist Bernie Leadon, and bassist Randy Meisner. The group found instant success with their debut album, a country-rock recording called *Eagles* in 1972. The album produced three hit singles, although their 1973 follow-up album, *Desperado*, was less successful. They transitioned to a harder rock sound in 1974, with *On the Border*. Its success was eclipsed in 1975 with the release of *One of These Nights*, which turned them into international stars. Despite the departure of Leadon, The Eagles continued their upward commercial trajectory with the album *Hotel California*, released in 1976. A massive hit, the album contained the single "Hotel California," the song for which they are best known. After the release of *The Long Run* in 1979, The Eagles disbanded in 1980. However, they reunited in 1994 and have continued to record and perform together sporadically. Following Frey's death in 2016, his son Deacon joined the band and started touring with them in 2017.

Edward Elgar

(1857–1934, English)

Edward Elgar was born in a village outside Worcester, England. He left school in 1872 to work as an organist, piano teacher, conductor, and violinist, traveling around the countryside to visit his piano pupils. In 1889, he married one of these pupils, Caroline Alice Roberts, and his overture, *Froissart*, was performed at the Three Choirs Festival in Worcester the following year. During this decade, he built up a solid reputation through his choral works but it was his "Enigma Variations" of 1899 that truly cemented his national reputation as a composer. Following this success, his works were hugely anticipated, but *The Dream of Gerontius*, an oratorio of 1900, while recognized as having great musical qualities, had a poor initial performance. It first gained acclaim in Germany before being reintroduced in Britain. Elgar often cast himself as an outsider due to his lack of academic training, his social status as the son of a shopkeeper, and his deep Roman Catholic faith in a Protestant society. He was knighted in 1904 and he composed his last major work, the Cello Concerto, in 1919.

> "...there is **music** in the **air...** and you simply **take as much** as you **require.**"
>
> EDWARD ELGAR, COMPOSER, "LETTERS OF A LIFETIME"

Farid el-Atrache

(1910–1974, Egyptian)

Born in Syria, Farid el-Atrache moved to Egypt with his family when he was a child, to escape the French occupation of their country. Inspired by his mother, a singer and *oud* player, el-Atrache studied music at a conservatory as a young man and worked for a composer. He became a professional musician in the 1930s, singing and playing the *oud* on Egyptian radio stations. He often worked with his sister, a singer and actress known as Asmahan, until she died in a car crash in 1944. El-Atrache was a respected composer who wrote for himself and others, however, he was best known for his virtuosity as an instrumentalist, reviving the practice of the improvized solo during live performances. On his death in 1974, he was regarded as the most prominent *oud* player in the Arab world and is often described as "King of the *'Oud*."

THE EAGLES

DUKE ELLINGTON

Duke Ellington

(1899–1974, American)
Born in Washington, D.C., to pianist parents, Duke Ellington began studying the instrument at the age of seven. As a young adult, he financed his musical endeavors by working as a soda jerk, a freelance sign painter, and a messenger and in 1917 he formed a group that played at parties and dances. In 1918, he married Edna Thompson, who gave birth to their only son a year later. Ellington relocated to New York in 1923 and became an established bandleader by 1927. During the 1930s he toured Europe and recorded many of his most famous compositions, including hits such as "Mood Indigo," "It Don't Mean a Thing," and "In a Sentimental Mood." Ellington continued this trend of success into the 1940s, staging annual concerts at Carnegie Hall from 1943–1948 and stretching himself as a composer with pieces like the jazz symphony *Black, Brown, and Beige*—his longest work. By 1950, however, musical trends were moving away from big bands and Ellington fell out of favor. His time out of the spotlight was brief, though, and he returned to prominence with a landmark appearance at the Newport Jazz Festival in 1956. Constantly testing his range as a composer, he wrote an acclaimed score for the film *Anatomy of a Murder* in 1959 and continued to work with other prominent jazz musicians. Ellington died one month after his 75th birthday and over 12,000 people attended his funeral in New York. He was posthumously awarded the Pulitzer Prize in 1999.

Eminem

(1972–present, American)
Eminem developed his distinctive rapping style as a teenager by participating in competitive "battle rap" performances in Detroit. Having failed to find success with rap groups, he released his first work as a solo artist in 1996, but it was not well received. However, in 1997, success in the prestigious Rap Olympics competition resulted in the acclaimed *The Slim Shady LP* two years later. This record brought commercial success along with controversy, provoked by the violence of its lyrics. However, he capitalized on its popularity with *The Marshall Mathers LP*, which became a landmark album both in hip-hop and pop, superseding Britney Spears's *Baby One More Time* as the fastest-selling solo album in the history of the United States. Despite his controversial lyrics, Eminem increased his mainstream appeal with the rap-ballad "Stan" and in 2002 he began his acting career in *8 Mile*, a rap film loosely based on his life. After 2003's *Encore*, he took a six-year break from music, returning to public attention in 2009 with the albums *Relapse:Refill*.

Brian Eno

(1948–present, English)
Having studied at art college, Brian Eno joined the glam rock band Roxy Music in 1971. He initially worked as a studio engineer and producer, before playing the synthesizer at the band's live performances. He left the band in 1973, rejecting rock stardom to work with more experimental sounds and genres. His solo albums from 1973–1977, including *Here Come the Warm Jets*, displayed his enthusiasm for the electronic aspects of pop and by the late 1970s he had started to release his influential Ambient series. He also collaborated with several high-profile artists at this time, including David Bowie on the acclaimed "Berlin Trilogy." An art theorist, as well as a musician, Eno is well known for his "Oblique Strategies" cards, a set of suggestions which can be selected at random to overcome creative block.

Fisk Jubilee Singers

(active 1871–present, American)
Consisting of African-American students from Fisk University, the Jubilee Singers were originally formed by university authorities as part of a fundraising initiative. Performing a range of styles of spiritual music, their tours of the United States and Europe were phenomenally popular and financially lucrative. The profits from their concerts were used to construct a new building at Fisk University. The Jubilee Singers continue to be part of the musical life of the institution.

Ella Fitzgerald

(1917–1996, American)
Ella Fitzgerald had a difficult upbringing, which included spells in orphanages and periods of homelessness. However, in 1935 she gained her first regular job in music as the singer with Chick Webb's swing band and received critical acclaim for her recordings during the late 1930s. On Webb's death in 1939 she became the leader of the band, recording hundreds of swing songs with them. She embarked on an instantly popular solo career in 1942, adapting her sound to respond to the growing popularity of bebop. As part of this effort, she developed her skills as an influential scat singer, using abstract sounds, rather than lyrics, to improvise over instrumental passages of music. During the 1950s, Fitzgerald released several albums featuring her interpretations of the work of major jazz and popular songwriters, including Duke Ellington and Cole Porter. These recordings increased her mainstream appeal, and during the 1960s she branched out into other genres beyond jazz, including country music. She continued to perform throughout the 1970s and '80s and recorded her last album in 1991. Her last public performance was in 1993.

> "The **only** thing **better** than singing is **more singing.**"
>
> ELLA FITZGERALD, SINGER

Fleetwood Mac

(active 1967–present, British-American)
Fleetwood Mac was formed by Peter Green, Mick Fleetwood, and John McVie, former members of the British blues band John Mayall and the Bluesbreakers. In 1968, they found success in Britain with the release of their debut album, *Peter Green's Fleetwood Mac*. However, Green left the band in 1970 because of mental health issues provoked by his use of hallucinogenic drugs and was replaced by John McVie's wife. Fleetwood Mac struggled to maintain their musical identity without Green's songwriting skills and in 1975, with a drastically changed lineup featuring Stevie Nicks and Lindsey Buckingham, they released *Fleetwood Mac*, an album which featured a more mainstream sound. They built on its commercial success with the release of *Rumours* in 1977, which topped the Billboard charts for 31 consecutive weeks. Although they continued to record during the 1980s, several members began to pursue solo projects. The band has continued to record and perform sporadically.

FLEETWOOD MAC

Aretha Franklin

(1942–2018, American)

The daughter of a Baptist minister from Detroit, Aretha Franklin began her career by singing spiritual music, first in her father's church and then as a gospel recording artist at the age of 14. She turned to pop and soul at the age of 18, and by the late 1960s she was a mainstream star, releasing hit singles such as "Respect" and "Chain of Fools." Her trajectory of success continued during the early 1970s and the three albums she released between 1970–1972—*Spirit in the Dark, Young, Gifted and Black,* and *Amazing Grace*—are regarded as her best works. The latter was a return to gospel music, and became the biggest selling gospel album ever released. During the 1980s, Franklin moved away from soul towards mainstream pop and rock, collaborating with George Michael and the Eurythmics. Dubbed "The Queen of Soul," she continues to record and is believed to have sold over 75 million records worldwide.

Ichiro Fujiyama

(1911–1993, Japanese)

Born in Tokyo, Ichiro Fujiyama studied classical music, including Western theories of composition, at the Tokyo Music School. Trained as a classical baritone singer, Fujiyama first achieved fame as a performer of ryukoka (Japanese popular music). He released his debut single in 1931, and achieved a hit in the same year with "Sake wa Namida ka Tameiki ka," which sold around one million copies. In 1933, he graduated from music school and continued his recording career, mixing compositions by contemporary Japanese songwriters such as Shinpei Nakayama with Japanese-language versions of popular Western songs. At the end of World War II, he was taken prisoner in Indonesia, but on his return to Japan he continued to release successful records. However, in 1954 he retired from pop music and drew on his classical education to forge a career as a conductor and composer. He was given a People's Honor Award in 1992 by the Prime Minister of Japan.

Serge Gainsbourg

(1928–1991, French)

Having worked as a bar pianist in Paris, Serge Gainsbourg's early career as a recording artist combined albums released under his own name with songs written for more popular artists, such as Petula Clark and Juliette Greco. In 1965, his composition won the Eurovision song contest for Luxembourg, and by the end of the 1960s he was involved in a creative and romantic partnership with Brigitte Bardot. During this period, his work made a definitive leap from traditional French chanson to more inventive, experimental rock and pop. A provocateur, he produced the controversial and sexually explicit "Je T'Aime... Moi Non Plus" in 1969, before moving on to the 1971 concept album, *Histoire de Melody Nelson*. He experimented with different genres throughout the 1970s, composing music that incorporated funk, rock 'n' roll, and reggae. During the 1980s, alcoholism caused his behavior to become erratic: his relationship with Jane Birkin ended and he often appeared drunk in public. Gainsbourg died of a heart attack in 1991, and his funeral drew thousands of people onto the streets of Paris.

MARVIN GAYE

Marvin Gaye

(1939–1984, American)

The son of a Pentecostal minister, Marvin Gaye developed his musical talent in the church choir, later taking up the piano and drums. After a brief stint in the US Air Force, he joined a local doo wop group, the Rainbows, and went on to work as a backing singer for a rhythm and blues singer called Harvey Fuqua. Working as a session musician for Motown Records in 1961, Gaye married Anna Gordy, the sister of the label's founder, Berry Gordy, and he launched his solo career shortly after. By 1965, he was an established chart artist, releasing successful albums and singles on his own and as part of a duo with Mary Wells. He continued to enjoy success in the duet format with Tammi Terrell in the late 1960s, before defining the Motown sound with his phenomenally popular single, "I Heard it Through the Grapevine," in 1968. Around the same time, Gaye went through a number of personal problems, including the death of Terrell in 1970 from a brain tumor, and the end of his marriage. He released the critically acclaimed album, *What's Going On*, in 1971 and built on its success two years later with *Let's Get it On*, which stayed on the Billboard charts for two years. By the mid-1970s Gaye was at the height of his appeal as a live performer, but by the late 1970s he had fallen out with the Motown label and was experiencing financial difficulties. He also struggled with drug dependency. In 1982, his single "Sexual Healing" was a commercial hit and, despite his continuing drug problems, he completed a nationwide tour of the United States. He was shot dead by his father after an argument in 1984 and his funeral in Los Angeles attracted thousands of mourners.

George Gershwin

(1898–1937, American)

George Gershwin's parents were Russian Jews who emigrated to the United States in the 1890s. He studied piano seriously from 1910 and soon mastered the works of important composers like Chopin, Liszt, and Debussy. In 1914 he abandoned classical music in favor of Tin Pan Alley, dropping out of high school to work for Jerome Remick and Co. Three of his songs were accepted by Broadway shows in 1918, and the following year his first full Broadway musical, *La La Lucille,* opened. In 1920 he had his first hit song with "Swanee," recorded by Al Jolson. Over the next four years he wrote five Broadway reviews, two London musicals, and three Broadway ones. Out of these, *Lady Be Good* was the first of many to feature lyrics by his brother, Ira. His jazz-influenced classical work, *Rhapsody in Blue,* premiered in 1924, and he followed its success with other "classical" pieces, including Concerto in F. He traveled to Europe in 1928, meeting fellow composers Sergey Prokofiev, Maurice Ravel, and Alban Berg. Throughout the 1930s he divided his time between concert tours as a pianist and composing musicals, such as *Girl Crazy*, and the opera *Porgy and Bess*. Gershwin died at the height of his fame in 1937.

João Gilberto

(1931–2019, Brazilian)

Born in Bahia on the northeastern coast of Brazil, João Gilberto began playing the guitar at the age of 14. He was recruited as the lead singer of a Rio-based vocal group, Garotos da Lua in 1950. The project was not successful and he left the group after a year, embarking on an unproductive period spanning much of the 1950s. A move to the coastal city of Porto Alegre changed his fortunes and he became a popular live act. In 1959, he released an acclaimed album, *Chega de Saudade,* featuring several compositions by Antônio Carlos Jobim. This album did much to define the sound of bossa nova ("new style"). Gilberto left Brazil for the United States after its release, capitalizing on his success with the subsequent album *Getz/Gilberto*, a collaboration with the saxophonist Stan Getz, which turned bossa nova into a worldwide phenomenon. Gilberto moved to the US in the mid-1960s, following the coup in Brazil. He returned to the country in 1981 and worked with a new generation of Brazilian musicians. In Brazil, he is known as "O Mito" (The Legend).

JOAO GILBERTO

Philip Glass

(1937–present, American)
A student at the Juilliard School of Music in New York during the late 1950s, Philip Glass moved to Paris in 1964 to study with Nadia Boulanger. Heavily influenced by German composer Karlheinz Stockhausen, Glass's early work, such as *Music in 12 Parts*, was minimalist in style. In 1966, he met Indian sitar player Ravi Shankar and this encouraged him to develop a hypnotic, repetitive style that was well suited to the rhythmic saxophone-and-keyboard sound of the Philip Glass Ensemble. During the late 1970s and 1980s, Glass regularly worked in music theater, producing operas such as *Satyagraha* (1980) and *Akhnaten* (1984). He has continued to work in this medium and has also written scores for films, such as the soundtrack for Stephen Daldry's *The Hours*, in 2002.

The Golden Gate Quartet

(active 1934–1998, American)
Formed by four students in Norfolk, Virginia, in 1934, the Golden Gate Jubilee singers began by performing barbershop-style arrangements of hymns and sacred music on television and radio. Displaying an innovative approach to gospel music driven by two of their members, Willie Johnson and William Langford, their reputation grew and in 1937 they began to record and release music, and an appearance at Carnegie Hall in New York the following year helped them to achieve nationwide fame. Langford left the group in 1939 but they signed with Columbia Records in 1940, changing their name to The Golden Gate Quartet in the process. By far the most popular gospel group in America at the time, they had their own nationwide radio show and performed at the White House on several occasions. Developments in gospel music in the late 1940s resulted in their diminishing fame but the Quartet revived their career in 1955 with a hugely successful tour of Europe. In 1998 they were inducted into The Vocal Group Hall of Fame.

Goldie

(1965–present, English)
As a teenager in England during the 1980s, Goldie's first involvement with music came as a breakdancer. Having moved to London in the late 1980s, he developed an interest in rave culture and high-tempo breakbeat music, immersing himself in the technical aspects of music production and engineering. He released his first single in 1992 and became a star of the nascent drum and bass genre with the single "Terminator," notable for its innovative use of production techniques and its brooding atmospherics. He founded a record label, Metalheadz, which released music by major exponents of drum 'n' bass and jungle. He went on to achieve mainstream success and critical acclaim with the release of his 1995 album, *Timeless*. An ambitious piece of work, it featured a 21-minute symphonic piece. His second album, *Saturnz Return*, was even more epic in scope, featuring tracks that were over an hour long, and collaborations with famous pop musicians, such as David Bowie.

Benny Goodman

(1909–1986, American)
Born in Chicago, Benny Goodman took up the clarinet at the age of 10. He quickly proved his talent, making his first professional appearance in 1921, aged 12, and was a fully fledged working and recording musician with the prestigious Ben Pollack Orchestra by the age of 16. In 1926, his father, David, was killed in a traffic accident, and it was to be a lifelong regret for Goodman that his father did not live to see his success. After periods in New York and Los Angeles, both as a session player and a bandleader, Goodman experienced a solid but unspectacular career until 1935. In July of that year his band's recording of a Fletcher Henderson arrangement, "King Porter Stomp," gained positive reviews. The relationship with Henderson, coupled with increased exposure to a younger audience through their appearances on the NBC radio show *Let's Dance*, gave the band's live performances a huge boost, and they often played to a rapturous reception. Their tenure at Palomar Ballroom in Los Angeles is cited as a catalytic moment in the development of swing music, and Goodman became popularly known as the "King of Swing." In 1938, his band performed at Carnegie Hall in New York and achieved 14 top ten hits. A virtuoso clarinetist as well as a bandleader, Goodman continued to perform well into the 1980s, venturing beyond swing music into classical and bebop. A member of the Jazz Hall of Fame, Goodman died in 1986.

> "It takes the **black keys** and the **white keys** both, to make **perfect harmony.**"
>
> BENNY GOODMAN, BANDLEADER, ON HIS RACIALLY INTEGRATED BAND

BENNY GOODMAN

Kancherla Gopanna

(*c.*1620–1988, Indian)
Born in the modern-day state of Andhra Pradesh, on the southeastern coast of India, Kancherla Gopanna (popularly known as "Bhakta Ramadasu") was a revenue collector for Sultan Abul Hassan Tana Shah and a devotee of the god Rama. In the history of Hinduism, he is famous for overseeing the restoration of the Bhadrachalam Temple in Andhra Pradesh, a significant temple for devotees of Rama. He is one of the most influential figures in Carnatic music, famous for his contribution to the tradition of the *vaggeyakaras*, in which the role of the lyricist and composer are combined. Kancherla Goppana is credited with the composition of nearly 300 songs, the devotional lyrics of which are known in South Indian classical music as *Ramadaasu Keertanalu*.

Edvard Grieg

(1843–1907, Norwegian)
After studying in Leipzig, Germany, Edvard Grieg moved to Copenhagen in 1863 to develop his career as a pianist. It was there that he met the young Norwegian composer Rikard Nordraak, who emphasized to him the need for a distinctive Norwegian music. On his return to Norway, he began studying traditional folk songs, and elements of this gradually pervaded his own romantic musical language. His *Piano Concerto in A minor* premiered to great success in Copenhagen in 1869. A master of miniature pieces, Grieg wrote short pieces as incidental music for Henrik Ibsen's play *Peer Gynt* in 1876. In 1880 he became conductor of the Harmonien Orchestra in Bergen, Norway. In 1903, Grieg recorded some of his piano music in Paris. He died four years later after a long illness.

EDVARD GRIEG

Grandmaster Flash

(1958–present, American)
Born in Barbados, Grandmaster Flash began his career as a DJ in New York, first at local parties and then on the disco scene. An innovator with a deep knowledge of musical equipment thanks to his training in electronics, he developed a reputation for his unorthodox and groundbreaking DJing techniques. During the mid-1970s he began to work with rappers and by the late 1970s he was performing in the group Grandmaster Flash and the Furious Five, the "five" consisting of rappers Melle Mel, Cowboy, Kid Creole, Mr. Ness, and Rahiem. Known for their energetic live performances, they released their first single "Superrappin'" in 1979 and in 1980 they achieved their first chart hit. In 1981 they released "The Adventures of Grandmaster Flash on the Wheels of Steel," a demonstration of Flash's DJ skills. One of the earliest hip-hop singles to deal with social issues, "The Message," released in 1982, was a critical rather than commercial success, but is now regarded as one of the defining releases in the development of the genre.

GUNS N' ROSES

Grateful Dead

(active 1965–1995, American)

Formed in California in 1965, the Grateful Dead were originally known as the Warlocks, before settling on their eventual name at the end of 1965. Founded on the songwriting of Jerry Garcia, they established their reputation as a live act, eventually succeeding in translating their sound to record in 1970, with the albums *Workingman's Dead* and *American Beauty*. They continued to tour for the majority of the 1970s, despite the death of one of their founding members, Ron "Pigpen" McKernan. Garcia's health fluctuated during the 1980s, making the Grateful Dead only an occasional presence on tour and in the studio. He died in 1995 but the band have continued to tour, playing to large audiences of "Deadheads," the name by which their fans are widely known. Despite their reputation as a live act, the Grateful Dead have sold 35 million albums and their music remains a cornerstone of the psychedelic rock genre.

Guns N' Roses

(1985–present, American)

Formed in Los Angeles in 1985, Guns N' Roses—consisting of singer and songwriter Axl Rose, lead guitarist Slash, rhythm guitarist Izzy Stradlin, bassist Duff McKagan, and drummer Steven Adler—developed their hard rock sound through gigs in the Hollywood area of the city. Just one year after the band formed, they signed a lucrative record deal and in 1987 they released their debut album, *Appetite for Destruction*. After an initially lukewarm reception, the single "Sweet Child o' Mine" became a number one hit on the pop chart, earning the band significant mainstream exposure. The album's hard rock was more melodic than many other examples of the genre, resulting in widespread popularity, and *Appetite for Destruction* became the best-selling debut album in the history of the US pop charts. Despite tempestuous personal relationships and the departure of Adler, Guns N' Roses continued their commercial success into the early 1990s with the albums *Use Your Illusion I* and *II*, which were released on the same day and charted at numbers one and two respectively, an unprecedented achievement in US musical history. From 1994 onward, the band's productivity declined and Slash left the band in 1996. Guns N' Roses continue to perform and record sporadically, but Axl Rose is the only remaining member of the original lineup.

Sexteto Habanero

(active 1920–*c.*1940, Cuban)

Originally a trio performing folk music from western Cuba, the band expanded to become a sextet in 1918. Some of the earliest performers of Afro-Spanish son music, in 1920 they took the name Sexteto Habanero. By the mid-1920s, they were established as the premier performers of son, winning the Concurso de Sones competition for the years 1925 and 1926. Sexteto Habanero were a huge success until the late 1930s, but by the end of that decade, musical trends had changed and Sextetos were out of fashion. The bandleader Gerardo Martinéz formed a new group, Conjunto Tipico Habanero, responding to the enthusiasm for conjunto, a style of music that originated in southern Texas, and is defined by the prominence of the button organ.

George Frideric Handel

(1685–1759, German/English)

Handel initially began studying law before turning his attention to a career in music. After a brief period at university, he moved to Hamburg and took up an orchestral position at the opera house, where he composed his first opera, entitled *Almira*. From Hamburg he traveled to Italy in 1706, and then to Hanover, where he took up the position of Kappellmeister at the electoral court. The post allowed for extensive travel and so he went to London, where Italian opera was gaining in popularity. His opera *Rinaldo*, premiered in 1711, was a great success—his dramatic works were the focus of much of his career and the vehicle through which he made his name. Although Handel returned briefly to Hanover, he received permission to travel again to London on condition he return within a reasonable time. However, in 1714, his employer the elector of Hanover succeeded to the English throne as George I and Handel entered the service of the Royal Court. Early in his tenure, in 1717, he wrote *Water Music*, an orchestral piece that juxtaposes traditional minuets with English country dances. Over the next decade, Handel experienced mixed fortunes as he competed with the Italian opera and as opera itself gained and lost the interest of the public. However, his oratorios and other choral works achieved more success, none more than *Messiah*, a 1741 response to the Lord Lieutenant of Ireland's request to help raise money for three Dublin charities through musical performances. The result—a collaboration between Handel and librettist Charles Jennens—was a critical success in both Dublin and London and remains a perennial favorite today. During the last decade of his life, Handel's health deteriorated and in the 1760s his sight began to fail irreparably. He continued to compose, arrange earlier works, and supervise productions until his death.

GEORGE FRIDERIC HANDEL

W. C. Handy

(1873–1958, American)

William Christopher Handy was born in Alabama in the southeastern United States. His father was a pastor in a local church and as a young man Handy received lessons in the organ and the cornet. A gifted school student, he moved to Birmingham, Alabama, in 1893, to take up a teaching position, but soon secured a job at a factory paying higher wages. Up to 1903, Handy divided his time between teaching—principally at the Huntsville Normal School, where he acted as band director from 1900–1902—and working as a cornet player on national tours with Mahara's Minstrels. His career began to take off in 1909 when he published his first song "Mr. Crump," which was republished (with revised lyrics) three years later under the title of "Memphis Blues," referencing the genre with which he is now inextricably associated. The 1910s were a fertile creative period for Handy, and he set up his own publishing company to release his compositions "The Saint Louis Blues," "Yellow Dog Blues," and "Beale Street Blues." In 1918, he moved his business and band to New York where, despite his failing eyesight, he continued to collate, publish, and write about blues and folk songs. Handy died of bronchial pneumonia in 1958 and over 25,000 people attended his funeral in Harlem. In the same year, a movie of his life was released, titled *St. Louis Blues*, with popular American singer and pianist Nat King Cole portraying Handy on screen.

P. J. Harvey

(1969–present, English)

Polly Harvey learned the saxophone and guitar while at school in Dorset and began her professional career in music as the leader of the P. J. Harvey Trio. Having achieved critical acclaim for the two albums she released with the band, she found mainstream success as a solo artist with the 1995 album *To Bring You Love*. A shift in musical style toward a more ambitious and expansive sound, the album was a defining record in the alternative rock movement of the 1990s, and the single "Down by the Water" became a minor hit in the United States. Although her follow-up album, the more experimental *Is This Desire?*, received a mixed critical reception, she returned to a more rock-oriented style, and critical acclaim, with the album *Stories from the City, Stories from the Sea*, which won the prestigious Mercury Prize in the UK in 2001. Harvey continued to record and perform throughout the 2000s, and her work included compositions for the theater. She won the Mercury Prize for a second time in 2011 for her album, *Let England Shake*.

Franz Joseph Haydn

(1732–1809, Austrian)

As a boy in Vienna, Franz Joseph Haydn received elementary musical training as a member of the choir at St. Stephen's Cathedral. When his voice broke, he earned a meager living performing in ensembles and giving music lessons to children and continued his studies by reading musical treatises. Later in his career, he claimed that this period of self-education was one of the sources of his originality as a composer. In 1753, he started work as an accompanist to the singer Nicola Porpora, who helped him hone his compositional skills. During this time, he made many important contacts and became Count Morzin's music director in 1759. On the strength of his Symphony No. 1, Haydn was appointed Vice kapellmeister at the court of the Esterházys—one of the richest and most influential Hungarian families—and by 1766, he had taken full responsibility for their music. He composed new instrumental works for the twice-weekly concerts, as well as for festivities, church, and theatre. When Prince Nikolaus died in 1790, Haydn's music had already been published all over Europe. The impresario J. P. Salomon invited Haydn to present new works in England. During his two extended stays Haydn amassed a fortune and was awarded a doctorate from Oxford University. He was recalled to the

FRANZ JOSEPH HAYDN

Royal Court in 1795, following the accession of Prince Nikolaus's grandson, and remained active as a composer in Vienna until 1803. His body of work includes practically every popular genre of his time, from folk song to opera, but it is through his innovations in instrumental music that he had the greatest influence. Often referred to as the "father of the symphony," Haydn's 106 works in the genre, such as the "London" symphonies, pioneered the evolution of the genre.

Jimi Hendrix

(1942–1970, American)

Jimi Hendrix taught himself to play the guitar as a young man growing up in Seattle during the late 1950s. He spent some time in the army, before turning his attention to a career in music in the early 1960s, working as a session musician and sideman for established performers such as Little Richard, before setting out as a solo artist in New York in the mid-60s. However, it was in England, as the leader of The Jimi Hendrix Experience, that he became a star. The psychedelic rock of his 1967 debut album, *Are You Experienced*, cemented his reputation in the United States and he confirmed his status as an international star with his two subsequent albums, *Axis: Bold as Love* and *Electric Ladyland*. Hendrix broke up The Experience in 1969 and gave a headline performance at the Woodstock Festival in the same year. He worked in the recording studio throughout 1970 but died of drug-related asphyxia in September 1970, without releasing another album.

"**Music** doesn't **lie.** If there is something to be **changed...** then it can only **happen** through music."

JIMI HENDRIX, SONGWRITER, SINGER, AND GUITARIST

Billie Holiday

(1915–1959, American)

Billie Holiday suffered a traumatic childhood; she was raped as a young girl and became a prostitute in her early teens. However, by the early 1930s she was an established singer in the clubs of New York and she recorded her first hit, "Riffin' the Scotch" in 1933, which sold 5,000 copies on its release. In the late 1930s, she sang with Count Basie and Artie Shaw, but in 1939 she launched herself as a solo act, performing at the Café Society Club. It was here that she gave her debut performance of "Strange Fruit," an anti-lynching song that became the biggest record of her career, significantly increasing her public profile. Holiday was a songwriter as well as a performer, often basing her compositions on incidents from her life—"God Bless the Child," was prompted by an argument she had with her mother. Her personal life was difficult—she was a heroin addict and became involved in a series of exploitative and abusive relationships with men—and her career declined. In 1947, she was arrested for possession of drugs, but staged a comeback during the early 1950s, touring Europe and selling out two concerts at Carnegie Hall in New York, in 1956. However, Holiday's health began to fail and in July 1959 she died as a result of complications caused by cirrhosis of the liver.

John Lee Hooker

(1917–2001, American)

Born into a religious family in Mississippi, Hooker's earliest exposure to music was through sacred songs. In 1922 his mother married a blues musician, William Moore, who provided him with an early grounding in both the genre and the guitar. In 1943, after several years in Memphis, he moved to Detroit, where he worked for Ford Motors and played at a blues club in the city. In the same year he made his first recording "Boogie Chillen'," which captured the sound of his live performances and became a commercial hit. However, as a consequence of his restrictive and commercially unrewarding contract with his record label, Modern Records, Hooker was forced to make several records for other labels under a variety of pseudonyms, including Texas Slim and Birmingham Sam and His Magic Guitar. He continued to enjoy success during the 1960s but his popularity declined during the 1970s and '80s until the release of his album, *The Healer*, which included collaborations with Carlos Santana. Hooker had recorded over 100 albums by the time he was 83.

Whitney Houston

(1963–2012, American)

The daughter of gospel singer Cissy Houston, Whitney Houston began to work as a session singer and backing vocalist while she was still a teenager. In 1985 she released a debut solo album which produced three successful singles and became the best-selling debut ever by a female singer. Her follow-up album, *Whitney*, was even more successful on its release, giving rise to four number one singles, including "I Wanna Dance With Somebody." Houston launched a career in film during the early 1990s, acting opposite Kevin Costner in *The Bodyguard* and recorded a cover of Dolly Parton's "I Will Always Love You" for the soundtrack, which was an enormous hit, topping the US chart for 14 weeks and becoming one of the best-selling singles of all time. However, during the late 1990s, she experienced personal crises, including difficulties with drugs and a

WHITNEY HOUSTON

tumultuous marriage with the singer Bobby Brown. At the time of her sudden death in 2012, Houston was one of the biggest-selling singers of all time.

Howlin' Wolf

(1910–1976, American)

Born in a farming community in Mississippi, Howlin' Wolf was a relative latecomer to music, developing an interest in blues at the age of 18 after a meeting with the popular Delta bluesman, Charley Patton. Patton taught Wolf to play the guitar and Wolf gave solo performances around the southern states of the United States during the 1930s. After a spell in the army in the early 1940s, he returned to farming, performing music in his spare time. Due to exposure on a Memphis-based radio station, he began a recording career and released a handful of successful singles during the 1950s, including "How Many More Years" and "Smokestack Lightning." He also assembled a Chicago-based electric blues band. Having fully developed his distinctive roaring vocal style, he formed a partnership with the songwriter Willie Dixon in 1960, creating the critically acclaimed album *Howlin' Wolf*. He influenced many young rock musicians, such as Led Zeppelin and The Doors, and several of these acts released cover versions of his music, exposing him to a larger, and younger, audience, before his death in 1976.

Pedro Infante

(1917–1957, Mexican)

The son of an amateur musician, Pedro Infante was enthusiastic about music from a young age and studied a variety of instruments, including the guitar, during his teenage years. Raised in Guamúchil, northern Mexico, Infante led a string orchestra which worked at local night clubs, and also performed with the well-established Orquesta Estrella de Culiacan. In 1939, Infante and his wife, María Luisa León, moved to Mexico City and he released his first record, "El Soldado Raso" in 1943. He went on to record approximately 350 songs, principally in the mariachi and ranchera genres—many of these became national favorites, earning Infante the title "King of Bolero." In the early 1940s, his career as a film actor gathered momentum and he became famous throughout South and Central America for his portrayals of *charros* (Mexican horsemen). His private life was complicated—he fathered children through several extramarital affairs—but his popularity was unaffected. An enthusiastic amateur pilot, Infante's death in a plane crash in 1957 resulted in many tributes, including the erection of several statues across Mexico.

Camarón de la Isla

(1950–1992, Spanish)

Camarón de la Isla was born in a gypsy family in Cadiz, Spain. The premature death of his father left his family impoverished and at the age of eight he began to work as a busker (one who entertains in public places for money) to earn a living. Isla won a flamenco singing contest when he was 16 and released his debut album in 1969, collaborating with the virtuoso guitarist Paco de Lucía. It was a landmark recording in the history of flamenco and the duo continued to record and perform together until 1977. During the 1980s, de la Isla incorporated electric instruments into his music and fused flamenco with other genres, including jazz and rock; this work was central in establishing the genre of *nuevo flamenco* ("new flamenco"). He died of lung cancer at the age of 42 and thousands of people attended his funeral.

CAMARÓN DE LA ISLA

Charles Ives

(1874–1954, American)

Hailing from Connecticut in the northeastern United States, Charles Ives was the son of a provincial bandmaster with an adventurous taste in music. George Ives encouraged his children to sing a hymn in one key while he accompanied them in another, a musical influence that left an indelible mark on his son. Ives was a precocious child and by the age of 14 he had become the youngest salaried organist in Connecticut and composed dozens of works. He studied music for four years at Yale University but in 1898 he took a job as an actuary. Ten years later, he married Harmony Twichell after a long courtship. In 1907, Ives set up his own insurance business with Julian Myrick and made it one of the most respected firms in New York. At the same time, he composed works such as "Three Places in New England," a complex orchestral piece that encompasses many of the hallmarks that established Ives as a founder of modernism. In 1921, he bought a farm and invited poor families to stay there. One of these families allowed him to adopt their daughter, whom he named Edith Osborne Ives. A heart attack in 1918 encouraged him to put his manuscripts in order and declining health forced him to give up composing in 1926. Ives retired from business a few years later and was awarded the Pulitzer Prize in 1947.

Michael Jackson

(1958–2009, American)

Born into a showbusiness family, Michael Jackson made his professional debut as a performer with his brothers in the Jackson Five at the age of six. During the 1960s and early '70s, the group combined pop music with rhythm and blues and disco to create several hugely successful singles, including "I Want You Back" in 1969. Already a star, Jackson established himself as an adult solo artist in 1979 with the release of his fifth album, *Off the Wall*, and became a global phenomenon with the release of *Thriller* in 1982. Produced by Quincy Jones, it gave rise to seven singles, including "Billie Jean," and was the best-selling album in the world in 1983. Jackson added to his ubiquitous presence by fully exploiting the burgeoning popularity of music videos and earned a reputation for spectacular live shows. Although he only released one more album during the 1980s—*Bad* (1987)—his fame was undiminished and he was the subject of constant rumor and speculation in the popular press throughout the world. Jackson's infrequent musical releases were overshadowed by controversy and scandal during the 1990s and 2000s. He died in 2009 from a heart attack induced by an overdose of prescription drugs while preparing for a series of comeback concerts.

Jay-Z

(1969–present, American)

As a fledgling rapper in Brooklyn, New York, during the early 1990s, Jay-Z released his debut album, *Reasonable Doubt*, through his own label, Roc-a-Fella Records in 1996. A moderate success at the time, it paved the way for his breakthrough with the albums *Vol. 2: Hard Knock Life* and *Vol. 3: Life and Times of S. Carter*. Released between 1998–1999, they established Jay-Z as a significant force in American music and produced mainstream pop hits such as "Hard Knock Life" and "Big Pimpin'." He reached his creative peak during the early 2000s with the release of the *The Blueprint* and *The Blueprint 2*, both of which sold over two million copies in the United States alone. Reconciling hardcore rap with mainstream appeal, they sparked verbal feuds with several other rappers that only added to the fame of those involved. With the release of the multimillion-selling *The Black Album*, Jay-Z announced his retirement from the music industry, although he maintained a prominent public profile through his commercial activities. He married the pop sensation Beyoncé Knowles and returned to music in 2006 with the album *Kingdom Come*. He continues to create and is saluted as one of the most successful and influential rappers of our time.

MICHAEL JACKSON

Antônio Carlos Jobim
(1927–1994, Brazilian)
Born into a middle-class family in Rio de Janeiro, Jobim's early musical inclinations were encouraged by his stepfather, who bought him his first piano. In his early 20s he worked as a pianist in bars and nightclubs and in 1956 he collaborated with poet Vinícius de Moraes to create music for a play entitled *Orfeu de Conceicão*. This collaboration was fruitful for both men and they worked together again in 1959 to create a score for a film, *Black Orpheus*. Later, Moraes would write lyrics for some of Jobim's most successful songs. During the early 1960s, Jobim's compositions, mainly performed by saxophonist Stan Getz and singer João Gilberto, were triggers for a worldwide bossa nova craze. Although this popularity had peaked by the late 1960s, he continued to compose throughout the 1970s, mainly working on scores for television programs and films. The world music boom during the late 1980s increased appetite for Jobim's music and he staged several successful tours before his death in 1994.

ANTONIO CARLOS JOBIM

Elton John
(1947–present, English)
Having studied at the Royal Academy of Music in London as a teenager, Elton John began to collaborate with lyricist Bernie Taupin in 1967, writing songs for established acts, the singer Lulu being just one. In 1970, his second album, supported by the single "Your Song," achieved moderate success, and by 1973 he was a popular artist in the United States, thanks to his 1972 number one album *Honky Chateau* and registering a significant hit with "Crocodile Rock." He cemented his growing reputation with the album *Goodbye Yellow Brick Broad* (1973), which produced several of his most popular songs, including "Bennie and the Jets." He enjoyed huge popularity until 1976, when it

ELTON JOHN

began to decline, partly as a result of diminished productivity and partly because he had come out as bisexual in an interview, and not all of his audience reacted well to this. John took a break from performing, and pledged to only record one album per year. He returned to live performance during the 1980s, and his concerts were more successful than his records. However, John experienced difficulties in his private life, struggling with alcoholism and drug addiction and ending his marriage after three years when he was no longer able to deny his homosexuality. During the 1990s and 2000s, he continued to write and perform, collaborating with several contemporary pop artists and writing songs for films and musicals. Since then, John has announced his final tour, dubbed Farewell Yellow Brick Road, and been the subject of the 2019 biopic *Rocketman*.

Robert Johnson
(*c.*1911–1938, American)
Born in Hazelhurst, Mississippi, Robert Johnson learned the harmonica as a child, but showed no promise with the guitar. He married in 1929, but his wife died in childbirth shortly after their wedding and he became a traveling blues musician. By the time he returned to his home in Robinsonville a few years later, he was a virtuoso guitarist, a transformation that sparked rumors of a pact with the Devil, creating the legend for which he is now best known. During the 1930s, he worked continuously, traveling the cities of the Mississippi Delta, performing in restaurants, barbershops, and even on street corners. In 1936, he released *Terrapin Blues*, a moderately successful record. Later that year, he was poisoned, and eventually succumbed to pneumonia. In subsequent years, Johnson's virtuoso skill as a guitarist, his emotional power as a singer and composer, and the myth of the Faustian pact, combined to make him one of the most famous musicians in the history of the genre.

Scott Joplin
(1867–1917, American)
As a young man growing up in Texas, Scott Joplin taught himself the piano on an instrument in a house in which his mother worked as a cleaner. From the ages 11 to 16, he received lessons from Julius Weiss, a German-born music professor who educated him in classical music, opera, and folk music. After a stint during the late 1880s working a traveling musician, Joplin established himself during the 1890s and some of his compositions were published. However, he continued to supplement his income by teaching piano and enrolled himself as a student of composition at a college in Sedalia, Missouri. His career was transformed with the release of "Maple Leaf Rag." Published in 1899, the initial print run was slow to sell but its popularity grew with time and later sales provided Joplin with a steady income for many years. The 1900s were eventful for Joplin: he moved to St. Louis, fathered a daughter who died only a few months after her birth, and separated from his wife. He married for a second time, only for his new wife to die from complications from a cold just 10 weeks after their wedding. During this time he also wrote many of his most popular rags, earning the nickname "King of ragtime writers." After marrying for a third time in 1909, Joplin moved to New York in 1911 and spent the years before his death focusing on opera, without much success. In January 1917, Joplin— suffering from syphilis —was admitted to an institution in Manhattan, where he died a few months later.

Enrique Jorrín
(1926–1987, Cuban)
Born in Havana, Enrique Jorrín began to learn the violin at the age of 12 and later studied at Havana's Municipal Conservatory. Securing a position as a violinist at the National Institute of Music, he developed an interest in the dance music of the island during the 1940s, and he joined Antonio Arcana y sus Maravillas, a famous dance group. These experiences culminated in Jorrín's tenure with the successful dance band, Orquesta América. He is credited with creating the genre of cha-cha-cha with compositions such as "La Enganadora." He was a prolific recording artist from the mid-1960s onward, and he started a new dance band in the 1970s. His music is still performed by Latin American dance bands today.

Kassav
(1979–present, Guadeloupean/French)
Pierre-Edouard Décimus and Jacob F. Desvarieux, two established musicians with a desire to fuse traditional Caribbean music with modern electronic production techniques, formed Kassav in Paris in the late 1970s. Building a reputation as a live act throughout the city, they established themselves as innovators of a new genre of music, known as "zouk," and were a prolific studio and live band during the early 1980s. They achieved international success in 1985 with the album *Yélélé* and capitalized on their success by touring throughout the world, earning a reputation for their energetic live performances. Hugely influential and prolific, Kassav have released 20 studio albums and members of the group have also released numerous solo albums. Founding member Jacob Desvarieux died in 2021.

Oottukkadu Venkata Kavi
(*c.*1700–1760, Indian)
Venkata Kavi was born in the town of Mannagurdi in South India, the eldest of five children. Later, his family moved to the village Oottukkadu, after which he is now known. Venkata Kavi is credited with the creation of over 500 compositions in a variety of languages, including Sanskrit. As a composer, his work is notable for its complex and innovative use of ragas, the melodic modes on which Carnatic music is based, and an innovative use of rhythmic variations. His compositions are diverse, from *varnams* (relatively long songs for a single singer) to group songs, and even an opera describing the birth and childhood of the Hindu deity Krishna. Veneration of Krishna is the focus of many of Venkata Kavi's songs and is drawn on as evidence for the folk story that his musical knowledge and talent was the result of divine inspiration.

Khaled
(1960–present, Algerian)
Born in Algeria, Khaled studied the accordion at school and embarked on a career in music while he was

still a teenager, under the name Cheb Khaled. An innovator in the genre of raï, he blended Western music and instrumentation, including synthesizers and drum machines, with traditional Arabic music. He moved to France at the age of 26 and released his debut record three years later. He rose to prominence in his adopted country with the album *Khaled* and its accompanying single "Didi," which became the first Arabic song to reach the French singles chart, remaining there for 50 weeks. It also achieved popularity in many Arabic-speaking countries and even some parts of Asia. Nicknamed "the king of raï," Khaled is one of the most famous performers in the genre.

Amjad Ali Khan

(1945-present, Indian)

Born in 1945, the son of a court musician in Gwalior in northern India, Amjad Ali Khan studied the *sarod* (pictured below) with his father. He made his first public appearance at age 12 and studied music formally at Delhi until 1963. From the mid-1960s onward he performed throughout the world, developing his technique and his inventive use of Carnatic melodic modes. In 2001, he was awarded the Padma Vibhushan, India's second-highest civilian honor.

Vilayat Khan

(1928–2004, Indian)

Born in present-day Bangladesh, Vilayat Khan was the son of famous sitar player, Enayat Khan. After his father's death in 1938, he received musical training from other members of his family, including his mother and his uncle. He began to establish a reputation as a sitar virtuoso during the 1940s, and during the 1950s, he sought to develop a sound that resembled the human voice. Although he reinterpreted many established classical ragas (melodic modes), he also devised new ones. Based in Kolkata for most of his life, he toured India and the world for 50 years, showcasing his predominantly classical repertoire.

AMJAD ALI KHAN

Angelique Kidjo

(1960–present, Beninoise)

The daughter of an actress, Angelique Kidjo began to perform with her mother's theater group at the age of six. She achieved a hit in Benin while still a teenager, which resulted in a successful tour of West Africa. Political unrest in Benin led to her moving to Paris in the early 1980s, where she studied at the prestigious jazz school, CIM. This influence was reflected i n her first international album, *Parakou*. During the 1990s she continued to experiment with fusions of Western pop and African rhythms and instrumentation. This style reached its critical and commercial peak with the 1995 album, *Fifa*, which was recorded in Benin and featured a contribution from the Mexican-born American guitarist Carlos Santana. In 2002, Kidjo became a United Nations Goodwill Ambassador and continues to be a prominent spokesperson on social and political issues.

> **"The Blues?** It's the **mother** of **American** music. That's what it is—**the source."**
>
> B. B. KING, SINGER, SONGWRITER, AND GUITARIST

B. B. King

(1925–2015, American)

Raised by his grandmother in the Mississippi Delta, B. B. King worked as a sharecropper after he left school. He improved his guitar-playing skills by studying with his cousin, Bukka White, and built an audience by performing on local radio stations. In 1949, King started to record and release his music and he achieved his first significant hit in 1951 with "Three O'clock Blues." This set a pattern for the rest of the decade—King frequently occupied the charts with his interpretations of classic blues songs such as "Every Day I Have the Blues" and "Sweet Little Angel." He continued to record and perform throughout the 1960s, and in 1969, he garnered attention from mainstream pop audiences, touring with The Rolling Stones, who were admirers of his work, and winning a Grammy Award for his interpretation of "The Thrill is Gone." King's popularity has persisted throughout his career, and he continues to record and perform. Over a 64-year-long career, he is credited with giving approximately 15,000 performances.

The KLF

(active 1987–1992, British)

Formed in 1987 by musician Bill Drummond and artist and musician Jimmy Cauty, The KLF began their career by making high-concept sample-based music with a strong hip-hop and house influence. In 1989, they released the critically acclaimed *Chill Out* album, an influential release in the development of ambient and chill out music. Between 1990 and 1991 they returned to house music, releasing a series of internationally popular singles, including "What Time is Love" and "Last Train to Trance Central," which did much to turn dance music into an established form of chart music. Experiencing unprecedented levels of popularity for a dance music group, they sold more singles in 1991 than any other act in the world. Withdrawing from music in 1992, at the height of their commercial success, they turned their attention to high-profile stunts and art projects, deleting their back catalog of music and burning £1 million ($1.5 million) on the Scottish island of Jura.

BEYONCÉ KNOWLES

Beyoncé Knowles

(1981–present, American)

An enthusiastic singer and dancer as a child in Houston, Texas, Beyoncé Knowles joined the contemporary R&B group Destiny's Child at the age of 12. Between 1997 and 2001, they became one of the biggest selling all-female acts in history, before separating to allow the members to pursue solo careers. Released in 2003, Knowles's first solo album, *Dangerously in Love*, produced four hit singles, including "Crazy in Love." In 2008, she received six Grammy Award for her third solo record, *I Am... Sasha Fierce*, winning acclaim as both a songwriter and as a singer. One of the most commercially successful singers of modern times, Knowles is believed to have sold 118 million records worldwide as a solo performer and 60 million worldwide as a member of Destiny's Child. She has appeared in several films as an actress and received a Golden Globe nomination in 2006 for her performance in *Dreamgirls*. By the end of 2021, she held 28 Grammys, more than any other female artist.

Frankie Knuckles

(1955–2014, American)

As a student in New York during the late 1970s, Frankie Knuckles worked as a DJ in nightclubs around the city, playing an eclectic selection of soul, disco, and rhythm and blues. He moved to Chicago in 1977, becoming a regular DJ at the Warehouse club, where he developed his ability to blend one track into another, creating a seamless sequence of music that allowed audiences to dance without interruption. To make it easier to effect a transition between songs, he often relied on heavily rhythmic tracks, doing much to popularize the beat-based sound that came to be known as house music. During the early 1980s, Knuckles began to make his own music, recording songs that set the course for house, such as "You Got the Love." Returning to New York in the late 1980s, he went on to produce remixes for major pop artists, such as Michael Jackson and Diana Ross.

Kraftwerk

(active 1970–present, German)

The founding members of Kraftwerk, Florian Schneider and Ralf Hütter, met at the Dusseldorf Conservatory, where they were both studying classical music. During the early 1970s they started experimenting with electronic music equipment, including drum machines and synthesizers. Recruiting additional members, Karl Bartos and Wolfgang Flür, they developed a cold, clinical aesthetic, and their third album, *Ralf und Florian*, garnered critical attention. They became popular around the world in 1974 with the release of their fourth album, *Autobahn*, and enjoyed success as both experimental and commercial artists throughout the 1970s. They continued to record, and in 2012, a traveling exhibition visited venues including the Museum of Modern Art in New York. An album of the live recordings from the event was released in 2017 as *3-D: The Catalogue* and won a Grammy award for best dance/electronic album.

Umm Kulthum

(*c.*1904–1975, Egyptian)

Born in a rural village, Umm Kulthum's musical talent was encouraged by her father, an imam at the local mosque. In her late teens she met the composer and *'ud* player Zakarriya Ahmad, who encouraged her to relocate to Cairo to further her musical career. Kulthum moved to Cairo permanently in 1923. Lacking a formal musical education, she trained herself, studying literature as well as music, with the poet Ahmad Rami. By 1928 she was famous in

UMM KULTHUM

Cairo and in 1932 she was sufficiently well known to tour the Middle East. In 1934, she sang on the first broadcast of the state radio station, and the medium did much to elevate her status as a performer; her concerts were often broadcast live. During the 1940s and '50s Kulthum moved away from purely popular music, regularly singing settings of poems written in classical Arabic. Vocally, she was a virtuoso, famed for her aptitude with the improvisatory techniques used in classical Arabic singing. Her work was admired by Arabic and Western musicians and when she died, mourners lined the streets of Cairo for her funeral procession.

Fela Kuti

(1938–1997, Nigerian)

Having moved to London from Nigeria in 1958 to study medicine, Fela Kuti instead enrolled at the Trinity College of Music and formed his first band, Koola Lobitos. On his return to Nigeria in 1963, he worked as a musician and a radio producer, but it was in Ghana in 1967 that he began to develop the music that would become known as afrobeat. Influenced by the ideology of the Black Panthers during a trip to the United States in 1969, his work from 1970 onward was overtly political. During that decade he became a star in West Africa, but suffered violence and oppression at the hands of the government. During one such attack, Kuti's mother, Kalakuta, suffered fatal injuries. He continued his involvement with politics during the 1980s, and his imprisonment in 1984 on charges of currency smuggling resulted in a concerted campaign for his release. Although Kuti's musical output dwindled during the 1980s, more than one million people are reported to have attended his funeral in 1997. His son, Femi Kuti, has also become a famous musician.

Lady Gaga

(1986–present, American)

Influenced by New York cabaret and performance artists, Lady Gaga dropped out of her studies as an art student to pursue a career in music. Having worked in rock duos and bands, she first found paid work in the music industry by writing songs for other performers, including Britney Spears. However, she achieved international renown as a solo performer with the dance-pop crossover albums *The Fame* and *The Fame Monster*, both of which produced worldwide best-selling singles, including "Bad Romance" and "Poker Face." Famous for her spectacular live performances, her Monster Ball Tour of 2010 became one of the most profitable tours in music history, featuring eye-catching stage sets and theatrical effects. She is also famous for her use of elaborate clothing.

Lead Belly

(1888–1949, American)

Born Huddie William Leadbitter (or Ledbetter), the son of farmers, Lead Belly's musical career began as a teenager in Shreveport, Louisiana, singing and playing the guitar at local dances and, later, in the city's red-light district. He married in 1908, fathering two children, and spent several years traveling around in pursuit of work, both as a musician and a laborer. In 1915, he was convicted of carrying a gun and sentenced to work for 30 days on a chain gang, but he escaped and for two years he worked and performed under the name Walter Boyd. In 1918, he was imprisoned for stabbing one of his relatives in a fight and was released from prison in 1925. In 1930, he was imprisoned again, this time for attempted homicide. During his time in jail, Lead Belly's music was recorded by folk musician and archivist Alan Lomax, and he worked for Lomax after his release in 1934. During the 1940s, he recorded and performed regularly, establishing himself in the folk, rather than the blues, community. He served out another spell in prison and after his death in 1949, many of his songs became popular standards; "Goodnight, Irene," for example, was a successful release for several artists, including Frank Sinatra.

Led Zeppelin

(active 1968–1980, English)

Despite being formed in London in 1968 by guitarist Jimmy Page, singer Robert Plant, bassist John Paul Jones, and drummer John Bonham, Led Zeppelin made their reputation in the United States. Supported by a heavy touring schedule, their first

LED ZEPPELIN

two albums—*Led Zeppelin I* and *Led Zeppelin II*—were chart successes and their driving blues-influenced hard rock music is now credited with paving the way for the genre of heavy metal. During the early 1970s, they expanded their sound to include folk music, an influence that gave rise to "Stairway to Heaven," one of their most popular songs, taken from the album *Led Zeppelin IV*. They continued to develop during the mid-1970s, adding funk influences and synthesizers to their sound. This period culminated with the release of the album *Physical Graffiti* in 1975, which is widely regarded as Led Zeppelin's critical and commercial peak. Although the band retained their popularity during the late 1970s—the 76,229 attendance for a show in Michigan in 1977 set a new world record—the members experienced tumultuous personal lives and they broke up after the sudden death of drummer John Bonham in 1980.

Yao Lee

(1922–2019, Chinese)

Born in Shanghai, Yao Lee's first exposure as a singer came at the age of 13, when she began to appear on the radio. She signed with Pathé Records at the age of 14 and released her first single in the same year. Her career flourished during the late 1930s, during which time she usually sang popular standards, such as "Wishing You Happiness and Prosperity." In 1940, she released "Rose, Rose, I Love You," which was to become the defining song of her career. Famous for her high voice and soft delivery, Yao Lee often worked with her brother, Yao Min, a prominent writer of early Chinese pop music. She married in 1947 and stopped her stage work to spend time with her family. In 1950, following the Communist Party's coming into power, she left China for Hong Kong. Yao Lee continued to record and perform during the 1950s, changing her singing style to reflect the growing influence of Western music in Hong Kong. She stopped singing in 1967, after the death of her brother but continued to work in music, taking a position at the record label, EMI Hong Kong. One of the "Seven Great Singing Stars" of China, Yao Lee is credited with over 400 recordings.

Magnus Lindberg

(1958–present, Finnish)

Magnus Lindberg studied at the Sibelius Academy in Helsinki under notable composers Einojuhani Rautavaara and Paavo Heininen. He began to experiment with electronics and in 1977, he co-founded the modernist group "Korvat auki" (Ears Open Society). In 1981, he moved to Paris to study further. Four years later he composed his first successful orchestral work, *Kraft*. A composer with a high international profile, Lindberg directed the Meltdown arts festival in 1996 in London. In 1997, he composed *Related Rocks*, a musical piece inspired by geology and written for two percussionists, two pianos, and electronics, including the sampled recordings made during the demolition of a grand piano. He was the composer in residence for the New York Philharmonic from 2009–2012.

FRANZ LISZT

Franz Liszt

(1811–1886, Hungarian)

Born in a village in northwestern Hungary, Franz Liszt's earliest musical education came from his father, a musician who had played the cello in an orchestra conducted by Austrian composer Joseph Haydn. The family moved to Paris in 1823 and by age 12, Liszt had already performed throughout Europe. Ill health and religious contemplation during his late teens caused Liszt to withdraw from public life. In 1831, inspired by Italian virtuoso violinist Niccolo Paganini, he returned to the piano, dazzling audiences with the unprecedented complexity of his music and earning fame across Europe. In 1835, Liszt shocked Parisian society by eloping with the already married Countess Marie d'Agoult. The couple lived in Switzerland and Italy, and had three children, before eventually separating. Liszt returned to performing in 1838 and established the template of the modern concert pianist by performing from memory and inventing the solo recital. He toured for eight years, but by 1847 he wished to settle down and marry his new lover, Princess Carolyne Sayn-Wittgenstein. He became Kapellmeister at the court of Weimar, where he wrote or revised most of his most important works, including, *Faust-Symphonie* and the *Piano Concerto No.1*, a piece designed to make the most of Liszt's incendiary piano playing. He also invented the genre of the symphonic poem, with compositions such as *Prometheus* and *Orpheus*, both based on Greek myths. When the Vatican blocked the annulment of Princess Carolyne's first marriage, and following the deaths of two of his children, Liszt sought solace in the Catholic Church, becoming an abbé (a low-ranking clergyman). He continued to compose and teach until his death of pneumonia in Beuyreuth, Germany, at the age of 74.

Little Richard

(1932–2020, American)

Born Richard Wayne Penniman into a religious family in Georgia, Little Richard's first involvement with music came through church gospel choirs. He left home at the age of 16, and worked as a nightclub performer. This exposure resulted in his first rhythm and blues recordings in the early 1950s. In 1951, he achieved a local hit with the song "Every Hour" but it was the release of "Tutti Frutti" in 1955 that propelled Richard to stardom, a position he maintained with the release of "Long Tall Sally" in 1956. His suggestive, raucous rock 'n' roll music was the key to much of his success, but his live performances were equally important in developing a devoted following. A showman, his performances involved dramatic lighting and flamboyant piano playing, designed to compliment the energy of his music. In 1957, he suddenly left the music industry to study theology and, although he returned with spiritual music in 1959 and secular music in 1964, his popularity had diminished.

"**God** gives us **the ability,** but **rock 'n' roll** was created by **men.**"

LITTLE RICHARD, SINGER AND SONGWRITER

Andrew Lloyd Webber

(1948–present, English)

The son of classical musicians, Andrew Lloyd Webber began to write music as a child, before studying at the Royal College of Music in 1965. Working with lyricist Tim Rice, he found success with the rock-influenced musical *Jesus Christ Superstar* in 1971, first as a record and then as a West End show. The pair achieved further success in 1976 with the concept album *Evita*, and the song "Don't Cry for me Argentina" became one of Lloyd Webber's most famous compositions. *Evita* became a musical two years later. He found more success with *Cats*, based on the poems of T. S. Eliot, which ran in London for 21 years. He pursued a more classically influenced direction during the 1980s and produced *The Phantom of the Opera* in 1986. Webber's success continued in the 2000s, and included television talent shows to find cast members for revivals of his shows. With a live production of *Jesus Christ Superstar* earning him an Emmy Award as its co-producer, he became one of few artists to have received the top awards in film (Oscar), music (Grammy), theater (Tony), and television (Emmy).

ANDREW LLOYD WEBBER

Lord Shorty
(1941–2000, Trinidadian)
Born in Trinidad, Lord Shorty rose to fame as a star of the calypso genre during the 1960s. However, he began to experiment during the early 1970s, fusing calypso music with East Indian influences. His song "Indrani" (1973), is now regarded as a fundamental release in the development of soca music. In the 1980s, he converted to Rastafarianism, changing his name to Ras Shorty I, and experimented with spiritual music. It was a style that he developed with his band Love Circle, which featured many of his children.

Paco de Lucía
(1947–2014, Spanish)
The son of a flamenco guitarist, Paco de Lucía began to learn the guitar at the age of five. A child prodigy, he had won a prestigious flamenco contest and appeared on the radio by the time he was a teenager. He began his recording career at the age of 12, and released three albums of traditional flamenco guitar music with the guitarist Ricardo Modrego from 1964–1965. He launched a solo recording career in 1967, which was accompanied by well-received performances around Europe. In 1968, he started to collaborate with the well-known flamenco singer Camarón de la Isla and the two went on to make 10 critically acclaimed albums together. Driven by a desire to expand the range of his music and to push the boundaries of the flamenco genre, de Lucía formed a sextet in 1981. He played with them for the majority of the 1980s and experimented with other styles, including jazz. De Lucía's innovative approach is acknowledged as crucial to the development of *nuevo flamengo* ("new flamenco").

Jean-Baptiste Lully
(1632–1687, French)
The son of an Italian miller, Jean-Baptiste Lully entered the court of Louis XIV as a page and tutor at the age of 13 and became a court ballet dancer in 1652. Shortly after, he was promoted to court composer and eventually appointed Superintendent of the King's Chamber Music. His responsibilities included direction of the King's prestigious string ensemble, the "24 Violins du Roi." In 1670, Lully wrote the comedy ballet *Le Bourgeois Gentilhomme,* and he established the Académie Royale de Musique for the performance of opera in 1672. Many of Lully's later works were written for this genre, including *Armide,* a lyric tragedy based on an epic poem by Torquato Tasso, which premiered in 1686. Lully stabbed himself in the toe with a cane while conducting in 1687; gangrene set in as a result of the injury and he died soon after.

JEAN-BAPTISTE LULLY

Lynyrd Skynyrd
(1964–1977, American)
Lynyrd Skynyrd was founded in Florida by three high school students—Ronnie van Zant, Allen Collins, and Gary Rossington. They developed their southern rock sound throughout the late 1960s and early '70s. The band rose to prominence in 1973 with the song "Free Bird," from their debut album, before a support slot on The Who's Quadrophenia tour of the United States expanded their fan base further. As a result, their next album, *Second Helping,* was a commercial success, supported by the single "Sweet Home Alabama," which would go on to become one of their most popular songs. Lynyrd Skynyrd's success continued with their third album, *Nuthin' Fancy,* but their fourth proved less popular. Three days after the release of their fifth album, lead singer van Zant, guitarist Steve Gaines, and his sister Cassie, a backing vocalist, were killed in a plane crash. The remaining members of Lynyrd Skynyrd decided to disband, although they reunited in 1987, and have continued to tour and record since then, with a changing lineup.

Madonna
(1958–present, American)
Having trained as a ballet dancer in New York during the late 1970s, Madonna played in several bands during the early 1980s before releasing her first solo single in 1982. She built up a following on the dance scene and established herself as a mainstream pop artist with a sequence of successful dance-pop singles, including "Lucky Star." She embarked on a parallel career as an actress in films, which increased her fame further, and her provocative image and live shows, coupled with her celebrity lifestyle—she married actor Sean Penn in 1985—turned her into an international superstar. Nonetheless, she continued to develop as a recording artist, achieving commercial success and critical acclaim with her two subsequent stand-alone albums of the 1980s, *True Blue* and *Like a Prayer*. Her music was less innovative during the early 1990s but she returned to credibility and acclaim with *Ray of Light*, an electronica-influenced collaboration with the dance music producer William Orbit. Continuing with this trend, Madonna's 13th and 14th albums updated her style for the 21st century with collaborations with rap artists such as Kanye West and Swae Lee. The best-selling female rock artist of the 20th century, Madonna is also acknowledged to be a shrewd businesswoman, and is reported to have a net worth of around $850 million.

Lata Mangeshkar
(1929–present, Indian)
As a child, Lata Mangeshkar developed her ability as a singer under the guidance of her father, a theatrical impresario and classical singer. She began her career as a playback artist, recording songs to be lip-synched by actors in films. By 1945, she was studying classical music, while continuing to work as a playback singer. She registered a significant hit with *Aayega Aanewaala,* from the film *Mahal* in 1949. During the 1950s and '60s, Mangeshkar was a prolific contributor to film scores, and continued to register popular hits, while simultaneously expanding her repertoire to include *bhajans* (devotional songs). She composed the music for several films under the pseudonym Anand Ghan and also recorded non-film songs, experimenting with a range of genres and styles. During the 1980s, she recorded an album of *ghazals* with the prominent songwriter Jagjit Singh. Mangeshkar recorded 30,000 songs in 39 years, and her contribution to Indian music was acknowledged in 2001 when she was honored with the Bharat Ratna, the country's highest civilian honor.

LATA MANGESHKAR

Bob Marley
(1945–1981, Jamaican)
Bob Marley recorded his first two singles while he was still a teenager in Kingston, Jamaica, but they were not successful. By 1963 he was part of The Wailers, along with Bunny Wailer (Neville Livingston) and Peter Tosh, and together they recorded over a 100 songs. In 1966 Marley married Rita Anderson and took up the Rastafarian faith. The band became widely known in 1973 with their album *Catch a Fire,* but Livingstone and Tosh left the group shortly after. Marley recruited a backing group, the I-Threes, featuring his wife, and this lineup propelled him to international superstardom. He played successful shows around the world to racially mixed audiences, cementing reggae's newfound status as chart-friendly pop music. Marley left Jamaica in 1977 after an assassination attempt and his albums, *Exodus* and *Kaya,* were hugely successful. However, in 1980, at the height of his fame, he collapsed while jogging in New York. He died of cancer the following year, at the age of 36.

> "One **good thing** about **music,** when it **hits you,** you feel **no pain."**
>
> BOB MARLEY, SINGER AND SONGWRITER

Massive Attack
(active 1987–present, English)
Massive Attack emerged during the mid-1990s from the Wild Bunch hip-hop collective, which was based in Bristol, England. They won critical acclaim with their 1991 debut album, ***Blue Lines,*** which mixed slow hip-hop beats and samples of funk and reggae songs with soul vocals and restrained rapping, and was fundamental in establishing the trip-hop genre. They achieved critical acclaim with their third album, ***Mezzanine,*** in 1998. During the 2000s, members of the group produced film soundtracks and two more Massive Attack albums. While they only achieved moderate commercial success, they are hailed as innovators who established a blueprint for much of dance music of the 1990s. In 2020, they released ***Eutopia,*** an album featuring three tracks, each recorded in a different quarantined city during the Covid-19 pandemic.

YUMI MATSUTOYA

Yumi Matsutoya
(1954–present, Japanese)
Yumi Matsutoya began working as a session musician at the age of 14 and released her first album in 1973. She achieved her first significant commercial success three years later with *The 14th Moon,* and had three albums in the top 10 of the Japanese charts in 1976. These contained several songs which are considered to be early classics of the J-pop genre. In the same year, she married her arranger and producer, Masataka Matsutoya. From the mid-1980s onward, she continued to record and develop her live act, earning a reputation for spectacular shows, with commercial endorsements and advertising campaigns adding to her visibility.

Curtis Mayfield
(1942–1999, American)
Curtis Mayfield dropped out of high school in the late 1950s to pursue a career in music. He found early success with the gospel and soul group, The Impressions, achieving a number one pop hit with the single "For Your Precious Love" in 1958. Mayfield replaced Jerry Butler as lead singer of the group, and also assumed responsibility for some songwriting, resulting in the 1961 pop hit, "Gypsy Woman." During the mid-1960s his work became increasingly socially and politically aware, as demonstrated by The Impressions' chart singles "Keep on Pushing," "People Get Ready," and "We're a Winner." Mayfield left The Impressions in 1970 to pursue a career as a solo artist, expanding the breadth and ambition of the soul genre with his debut album, *Curtis*. In 1972, he combined his politically conscious lyrics with a harder-edged funk sound on the soundtrack to the film *Super Fly*. Although he was paralyzed in an on-stage accident in 1990, he created a final album, *New World Order*, before his death in 1999.

Felix Mendelssohn
(1809–1847, German)
Born in the then-independent city-state of Hamburg (present day Germany) to a wealthy and cultured family, Felix Mendelssohn was privately educated at great expense. His musical training was so comprehensive that he was able to hire orchestras to test his early compositions. He displayed talent not only as a violinist, pianist, organist, composer, and conductor, but also in fine art and poetry—in his teens, he became a protégé of Goethe. His style of composition crystallized at an early age and is illustrated by his overture to *A Midsummer Night's Dream*. Written in 1826, it follows well-established forms, a style that contrasted with the often-radical work of his Romantic contemporaries. Mendelssohn had complete knowledge of music history, and he conducted the second ever performance of Bach's *St. Matthew Passion*, resulting in a 19th-century Bach revival. He spent three years traveling and giving concerts, making 10 lengthy visits to England and Scotland. He returned to conducting posts in Düsseldorf and then Leipzig, where he conducted the Gewandhaus orchestra and established the now universal concept of programing both historical and modern works. Following the death of his sister Fanny, also a gifted pianist and composer, Mendelssohn suffered a series of strokes and died at the age of 38.

Metallica
(active 1981–present, American)
Formed in Los Angeles in 1981 by drummer Lars Ulrich and singer James Hetfield, Metallica initially also featured guitarist Dave Mustaine and bassist Ron McGovney. However, McGovney was replaced by Cliff Burton, and Mustaine by Kirk Hammett, shortly before the recording of the band's 1983 debut album, *Kill 'Em All*. This album established Metallica as significant figures on the underground heavy metal scene. However, it was not until the release of their third album, *Master of Puppets*, that Metallica grew into a dominant force within the genre, attracting critical acclaim and developing a more mainstream audience. Despite the death of Cliff Burton in 1986, the group continued to capitalize on their success, achieving full-blown mainstream recognition with their self-titled album of 1991, which reduced the more technically complex aspects of their music in favor of a more conventional and accessible style of songwriting. The album has now sold more than 15–16 million albums worldwide. Although Metallica's critical reputation diminished during the 1990s, they continued to produce commercially successful music. In 2000 they were involved in a controversial legal dispute with the Internet file-sharing company Napster.

MIGHTY SPARROW

Mighty Sparrow
(1935–present, Grenadian)
Beginning his musical career as head choirboy at St. Patrick's Catholic Church in Trinidad, Mighty Sparrow created a steel band at the age of 14. He won two prestigious calypso competitions in 1956 with his composition "Jean and Dinah," which would go on to become one of his most popular songs. Famed for his witty lyrics, Sparrow enjoyed some success in England during the 1950s. He returned to Trinidad and went on to win both the renowned Calypso Monarch contest and the Carnival Road March eight times during the 1960s. A versatile songwriter, he made the transition into soca during the 1970s and '80s, becoming a prominent artist in the genre. He continues to tour and perform despite recurring illness and in 2020 released a live album recorded the previous year.

Charles Mingus
(1922–1979, American)
As a child growing up in Los Angeles, Mingus learned the trombone and cello and turned his attention to jazz music when it became clear that racial prejudice and a lack of formal training would make it difficult for him to pursue a career as a classical musician. A prodigy, as both a bass player and composer, Mingus had established himself as a professional jazz musician by the early 1940s. He toured with some of the giants of the genre, including Louis Armstrong, although his fiery personality sometimes made him difficult to work with. Mingus founded a record label in 1952 and released *Pithecanthropus Erectus* in 1956, the first of a series of albums, including *The Clown* and *Ah Um*, which established him as a visionary composer and a virtuoso double bassist. Continually testing and expanding his range as a writer, he recorded *The Black Saint and the Sinner Lady*—a ballet written for a big band—in 1963. After a difficult period during the late 1960s, Mingus reestablished himself as a unique creative voice with his 1971 autobiography, *Beneath the Underdog*. A Guggenheim Fellowship in composition also allayed his financial worries. However, as the 1970s wore on, he began to display the symptoms of Lou Gehrig's disease—a degenerative illness—and in the years leading up to his death, he was confined to a wheelchair.

Kylie Minogue
(1968–present, Australian)
Having shot into the limelight as an actress in the Australian soap opera *Neighbours*, Kylie Minogue became a successful singer in Australia and the UK with the release of her first single, "The Loco-Motion," in 1987. Her debut album, *Kylie*, produced with British songwriters and producers Stock, Aitken, and Waterman, was particularly successful in Australia and the UK and she continued to be popular throughout the 1980s. As her record sales declined during the early 1990s, she broke away from Stock, Aitken, and Waterman, and her collaboration with the alternative rock singer Nick Cave brought her credibility. Minogue returned to fame in 2000 with her album *Light Years*, which successfully exploited the popularity vogue for dance-based pop music with a disco-influenced sound, exemplified by the hit single "Spinning Around." She cemented her position as a chartbusting pop star with *Fever*, which brought her fame in the United States—something which had previously evaded her. After a hiatus to undergo treatment for cancer, she returned in 2006. Her subsequent albums have continued to feature disco and electro-pop elements but have also incorporated ideas from country music, notably with her 2018 album, *Golden*.

KYLIE MINOGUE

Ibn Misjah
(d.715, Persian)
Born in Mecca, Saudi Arabia, the Persian musician Ibn Misjah was the first significant musician of the Ummayad caliphate, an Islamic state ruled by the Ummayad family from *c.*661–750. A singer and lute player, Misjah traveled around Syria and Persia, developing his knowledge of Byzantine and Persian music. A musical theorist as well as a practitioner, Ibn Misjah made a significant contribution to the understanding and use of melody and rhythm in Islamic classical music. Although none of his compositions exist today, he is regarded as an influential figure in the development and systemization of this genre.

Thelonious Monk
(1917–1982, American)
Growing up in New York, Thelonious Monk took up the piano at the age of five or six. After a stint as a church organist, he found work as a jazz musician from 1940 onward, recording with the saxophonist Coleman Hawkins in 1944. He recorded solo sessions in the late 1940s and early 1950s, but his eccentric behavior and unorthodox style of playing often made it hard for him to find work. However, a residency at the Five Spot Club in New York, and the release of the critically acclaimed album *Brilliant Corners* in 1957, established his reputation as a virtuoso pianist and composer. He toured and recorded throughout the remainder of the 1950s and 1960s, and many of his original compositions, such as "Round Midnight," became standards of the jazz repertoire. Monk's health declined during the 1970s and the last six years of his life were spent in relative seclusion.

Bill Monroe
(1911–1996, American)
As a child in Kentucky, Bill Monroe learned to play the mandolin, before going on to play in his uncle's band. During the 1930s he played in a country group, first with both of his brothers, Birch and Charlie, and then as a duo with Charlie. In 1938, the duo split after a minor hit single and Monroe formed a new band, The Bluegrass Boys and, with it, a new genre. His band appeared on nationwide radio on a weekly basis and emerged as one of the most popular groups in the United States in 1946, performing successful shows and recording hit singles. Although the original lineup of The Bluegrass Boys broke up in 1948, Monroe continued with the band, further developing the bluegrass genre. He released his first album in 1958 and the folk revival of the 1960s led to a resurgence in his popularity. He was awarded a Grammy for lifetime achievement in 1993.

Claudio Monteverdi
(1567–1643, Italian)
Monteverdi began his musical career at a young age, publishing his first book of madrigals at the age of 15. After a stint as a lowly court musician for the Duke of Mantua, during which time he met his wife Claudia Cattaneo, Monteverdi returned to his hometown of Cremona. *L'Orfeo*, written in 1607, established him as a pivotal figure in the development of opera. Based on the classical Greek myth of Orpheus, it was the first fully realized example of this new genre. In 1613, Monteverdi took up the prestigious post of maestro di cappella at St. Mark's Basilica in Venice and the focus of his writing shifted toward sacred, choral music. In addition to his duties, he undertook outside commissions, including several from his old employer, the Duke of Mantua, and wrote music for the annual Venetian carnival, most notably the stage work *Il Combattimento de Tancredi e Clorinda* of 1624. Monteverdi enjoyed a quiet middle age until 1630, when a plague and a war in Mantua rocked Venice; he subsequently joined the priesthood. His final years were spent revising his early works and completing his treatise on *seconda prattica* or *stile moderno*, advocating a freer use of dissonance and counterpoint. These writings, and Monteverdi's madrigals, sacred music, and operas in the *seconda prattica* style, make him the most influential composer of his time.

Carlos Montoya
(1903–1993, Spanish)
The son of a Romany family from Madrid and the nephew of Ramón Montoya, a famous flamenco guitarist, Carlos Montoya was working as a café musician by the age of 14. He toured Europe, North America, and Asia during the 1920s and '30s, earning recognition for his skill as a flamenco guitarist. Living in New York during World War II, he toured America, presenting a show in which he experimented with a number of musical styles, including jazz and blues. During this period he recorded for several labels and by the late 1940s, he was touring with a full orchestra, becoming one of the first guitarists to do so. Montoya died of heart failure at the age of 89, having established flamenco as a musical form in its own right, rather than simply as an accompaniment to dance.

Ennio Morricone
(1928–2020, Italian)
The son of a jazz trumpeter, Ennio Morricone began to experiment with composition at the age of six. He entered the conservatory of the National Academy of Saint Cecilia in Rome at the age of 12, studying trumpet, composition, and choral music. After World War II, Morricone worked as a jazz trumpeter and he began to compose music for film and television during the late 1950s; he wrote his first film score in 1959 for *Morte Di Un Amico*, directed by Franco Rossi. However, he made his name with his compositions for Westerns, creating memorable scores for movies including *A Fistful of Dollars* and *The Good, the Bad and the Ugly*, which often make prominent use of the acoustic guitar. Morricone received an Honorary Academy Award in 2007 for his work as a composer of film scores. His music continues to be sampled and referenced by a variety of modern musicians, such as the rapper Jay-Z.

ENNIO MORRICONE

Jelly Roll Morton
(1890–1941, American)
Born in New Orleans, Louisiana, Jelly Roll Morton took up the piano at the age of 10. At 12, he started earning a living by playing at a brothel in the city's Storyville district, which led to him having to move out of his grandmother's house. From 1904 onward, Morton worked as a touring musician and wrote his own music. His compositions from this time include "Jelly Roll Blues" and "King Porter Stomp," both of which are now regarded as fundamental to the development of early jazz music. Morton moved to Chicago in 1922, and his stint in the city until 1928 coincided with the peak of his musical career. He made several recordings with his band, the Red Hot Peppers, for Victor, the largest record company in the country at the time, and these are regarded as highlights of his career, as well as definitive performances in the evolution of the genre. In 1928, Morton married a showgirl, Mabel Bertrand, and moved to New York, the center of jazz in the United States. However, his career began to drift and, despite some recording sessions, the last years of his career were spent playing the piano in bars. He died in Los Angeles at 50.

Wolfgang Amadeus Mozart

(1756–1791, Austrian)

The son of a gifted musician, Mozart's first musical experiences involved hearing his child prodigy sister, Nannerl, at her harpsichord lessons. When Mozart's own accomplishments surpassed those of his sister, their father gave up his career to showcase his children's ability before the royalty and musical cognoscenti of Europe. Despite extensive tours, Mozart managed to keep working on his studies and compositions but, by 1772, he had only been able to secure a lowly position as a court musician. Dissatisfied at the court of Salzburg but unable to obtain a better position, he left to become one of the first freelance music professionals. Arriving in Vienna in 1781, he married Constanze Weber and started to give concerts, publish music, and receive commissions, particularly for operas, such as the acclaimed *Die Entführung aus dem Serali* of 1782. Over the next 10 years, he consolidated his reputation with more than 200 works across an impressive range of styles and genres, including sonatas, symphonies, and piano trios. The highlights from this period are the complex piano concertos of 1785–1786—a genre he is credited with elevating to new levels of sophistication—and three hugely successful operas, *The Marriage of Figaro* (1786), *Don Giovanni* (1787), and *Cosi fan tutte* (1790), all written with the Italian poet, Lorenzo da Ponte. These works confirmed Mozart's fame, but he continued to struggle financially, giving piano lessons, taking in boarders, and borrowing money to maintain his lifestyle. He died in 1791, probably from rheumatic fever, and was buried in a mass grave according to Viennese custom.

Anita Mui

(1963–2003, Hong Kong)

Born in poverty in Hong Kong, Anita Mui began working as a singer at the age of four to earn a living. She developed her distinctive low-pitch singing style after experiencing problems with her vocal chords as a teenager. In 1982, she beat 3,000 other contestants to win a major singing competition, and she released her first album the following year. Her career thrived throughout the 1980s, with award and best-selling albums and singles establishing her as a groundbreaking female Cantopop artist. She also developed a reputation as a spectacular live performer, famous for her elaborate costumes and wild dance moves. In 1987, she staged a series of 28 consecutive concerts at the 12,500-seater Hong Kong Coliseum. Her fame was not restricted to Asia and her international presence was enhanced by her film career, particularly through her appearance in *Rumble in the Bronx* with Jackie Chan. One month before she died of cancer in 2003, Mui performed eight successful farewell concerts in Hong Kong, appearing on stage with a lineup of famous Cantopop singers.

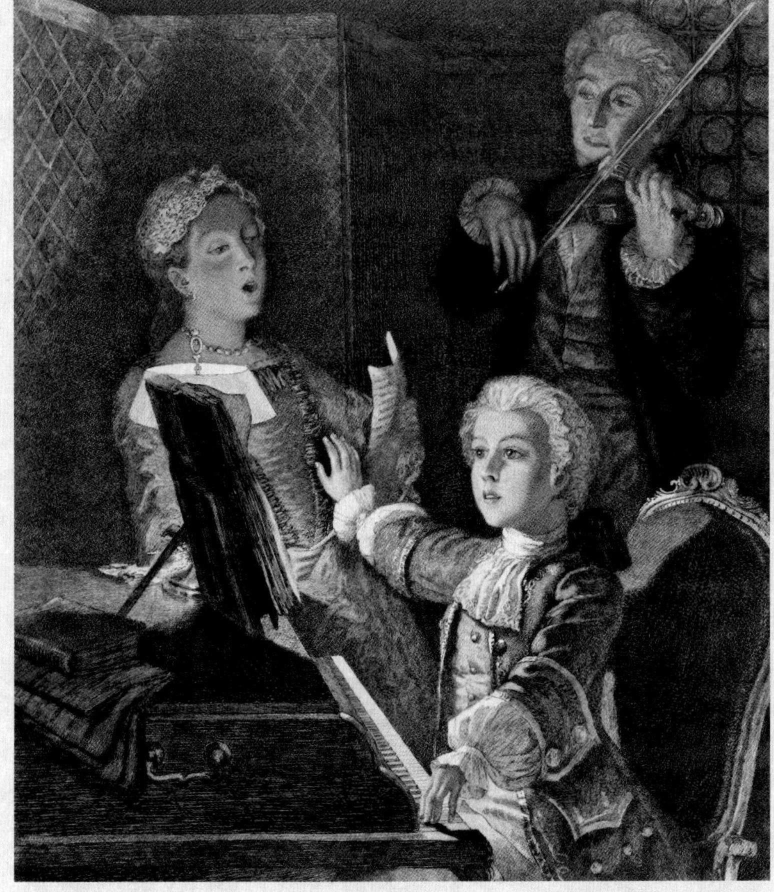

WOLFGANG AMADEUS MOZART

Modest Mussorgsky

(1839–1881, Russian)

Despite being a prodigy at the piano, Modest Mussorgsky joined the army in 1852, but resigned his commission in 1858. After taking up a job in the civil service, he began to work on a symphony and an opera but these came to nothing. In 1861, he was forced to work on his family estate following the emancipation of serfs in Russia and he suffered his first serious alcoholic episode in 1865. Committed to composing music that resonated with the Russian people, Mussorgsky wrote *St. John's Night on the Bare Mountain* in 1867 and composed the song cycle *The Nursery* in 1872. Two years later, he produced two of the works for which he would become best known: the opera *Boris Godunov*, with its innovative and realistic use of Russian speech patterns, and *Pictures at an Exhibition*, a solo piano work written as a tribute to his close friend, the artist Viktor Hartmann, who died in 1873. Debilitated by alcoholism, Mussorgsky's productivity declined during the 1870s, and he died in 1881.

Youssou N'Dour

(1959–present, Senagalese)

Taught to sing by his mother as a child in Dakar, Youssou N'Dour formed his own band, Super e'Toile de Dakar, at the age of 21. During the early 1980s, the group moved away from playing a predominantly Latin American style of music toward a unique and distinctively African sound, pioneering the genre of mbalax in the process. Garnering international attention, N'Dour performed in Europe and North America during the mid-1980s and the attention resulted in collaborations with mainstream pop musicians, including Peter Gabriel. N'Dour released his first international album, *The Lion*, as a solo artist in 1989, garnering commercial and critical success. He continued to maintain a high profile throughout the 1990s, releasing hit singles and composing an opera of African music for performance at the prestigious Paris Opera. A prominent figure in Senegal's public life, N'Dour was appointed Minister of Culture and Tourism in 2012.

WILLIE NELSON

Willie Nelson

(1933–present, American)

Willie Nelson studied the guitar when he was growing up in Texas during the Great Depression and had written some of his first songs by the age of seven. A member of several bands during his high school years, he worked as a radio disk jockey during the 1950s while developing his skills as a songwriter. In 1960, he secured a publishing deal—making his compositions available to other artists—and a position as bassist in the touring band of the country singer Ray Price. Several of his compositions became hits for other country artists, including Patsy Cline, who achieved a number two hit with "Crazy" in 1962. Nelson had a succession of minor hits as a solo artist throughout the 1960s. In 1972, he retired from country music only to return a year later. His 1975 concept album, *The Red Headed Stranger*, became a significant commercial success. His popularity as a recording artist continued throughout the 1970s and early 1980s, and the end of this period included a spell in The Highwaymen, a country "supergroup" also featuring Johnny Cash.

> "I was **influenced** a lot by those around me—there was a lot of **singing... in the cotton fields.**"
>
> WILLIE NELSON, SINGER AND SONGWRITER

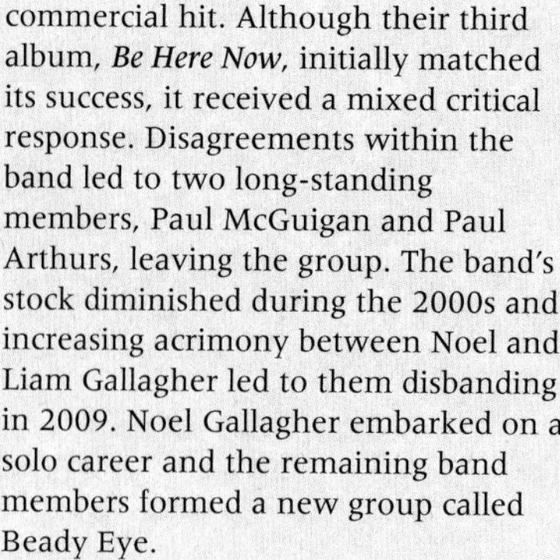

Nine Inch Nails

(1965–present, American)

Active classical music student, Trent Reznor studied the piano, tenor saxophone, and tuba in Pennsylvania, before becoming a music engineer in the late 1980s. He began to record under the name Nine Inch Nails in 1988, making music in the subgenre of industrial rock and his 1989 debut album, *Pretty Hate Machine*, slowly gathered momentum, eventually spending 113 weeks on the US album chart. Reznor's profile was enhanced further by touring with more mainstream rock acts and his second album, *The Downward Spiral*, continued his trend of commercial success. He composed film soundtracks and worked as a producer for other alternative rock artists in the late 1990s and, despite being an alternative musician, he was a popular figure, appearing in *Time* magazine's list of most influential people in 1997. Reznor continued to release successful records from 2000 onward, experimenting with different formats and methods of music distribution, including digital memory sticks, which were hidden at concert venues for fans to discover.

Nirvana

(active 1987–1994, American)

Formed by singer and guitarist Kurt Cobain and bassist Krist Novoselic, Nirvana built up a fan base through touring and support from college radio stations. Although the band's early music was influenced by punk and heavy metal, a transition to a more melodic sound on their second album, *Nevermind*, resulted in enormous mainstream popularity from 1991 onward, significantly exceeding the expectations of the band and their management. Supported by the hit single "Smells Like Teen Spirit," the album continued to sell 400,000 copies a week three months after its release and did much to establish grunge music, and alternative rock in general, as a commercial force. Nirvana's third album, *In Utero*, was released in 1993 to critical acclaim. Tragedy struck in 1994 when Kurt Cobain committed suicide. Nirvana disbanded immediately, although Krist Novoselic and drummer Dave Grohl both continued to produce music under different guises.

NIRVANA

K. P. H. Notoprojo

(1909–2007, Indonesian)

Born in Java, Notoprojo began to study gamelan at the age of five under the tutelage of his father, the leader of the gamelan orchestra at the Paku Alaman palace. He played with many of Indonesia's well-known gamelan groups and worked as gamelan director at a number of radio stations in the 1940s. He taught at various universities abroad during the 1950s, returning to Indonesia in 1962 to take over the leadership of the palace gamelan from his father, developing and refining the Pura Pakualaman style with which they were associated. Instrumental in spreading the music of Javanese gamelan around the world, he taught at the California Institute of the Arts from 1971 to 1992, and returned to Indonesia after his retirement. He is credited with over 250 compositions, ranging from the accessible to the experimental, many of which are staples of the gamelan repertoire.

Oasis

(active 1992–2009, English)

Formed around the songwriting and guitar-playing of Noel Gallagher, and the vocals of his brother, Liam Gallagher, Oasis was born in Manchester in the north of England in 1992. The band released their debut album, *Definitely Maybe*, in 1994 and, supported by the rock ballad, "Live Forever," it became the fastest selling debut album in Britain, establishing the band as a defining act of the Britpop genre. Although the two brothers had a fractious relationship, their success as a mainstream act was boosted by the release of *(What's the Story) Morning Glory?* in 1995. An expansion of their melodic, Beatles-influenced sound, it was a worldwide commercial hit. Although their third album, *Be Here Now*, initially matched its success, it received a mixed critical response. Disagreements within the band led to two long-standing members, Paul McGuigan and Paul Arthurs, leaving the group. The band's stock diminished during the 2000s and increasing acrimony between Noel and Liam Gallagher led to them disbanding in 2009. Noel Gallagher embarked on a solo career and the remaining band members formed a new group called Beady Eye.

Bulat Okudzhava

(1924–1997, Russian)

Born in Moscow, Bulat Okudzhava was 13 when his father was executed on suspicion of being a German spy and his mother was sentenced to 18 years in a prison camp. A soldier during World War II, he studied at Tblisi State University at the end of the conflict and on his graduation he sought work, first as a teacher and then in the publishing industry. He began to write folk songs during the 1950s. Despite being untrained, he had a talent for writing lyrics and melodies, and his compositions spread throughout the USSR via unofficial recordings. During the 1980s, he won acclaim as a poet and novelist, perhaps eclipsing the importance of his work as a songwriter. Nonetheless, he wrote over 200 songs during his lifetime and is regarded as one of the founders of the Russian folk genre of "author song."

Niccolò Paganini

(1782–1840, Italian)

As a child, Niccolo Paganini's violin playing was rigorously nurtured by his father, who forced him to practice intensively, even depriving him of food and water when he faltered. He made his first public appearance in 1793 and moved to Parma in Italy the following year to study violin and composition. Paganini returned to Genoa in 1796 and in 1805 he took up a position as an orchestra leader in Lucca. Paganini was a traveling virtuoso by 1809, and went on to make a triumphant debut in Milan with a series of concerts in 1813. At this time, he wrote his variations of Süssmayr's ballet score, *Le Streghe*, which showcased his astounding violin technique. Despite this success, he toured Italy sporadically and only launched his international career at the age of 46, mesmerizing audiences across Europe and amassing great wealth. He settled in Parma in 1834 and his health began to deteriorate. A critical illness led to the loss of his voice and he died six years later.

Giovanni Pierluigi da Palestrina

(1525–1594, Italian)

Born in the town of Palestrina, Italy, Giovanni Pierluigi da Palestrina is believed to have begun his career as organist and choirmaster in 1544 in his native city. His reputation grew and he gained his first Roman post in 1551 as a choirmaster at the Capella Giulia, a subsidiary of the Sistine Chapel. Palestrina's brief spell at the Chapel ended with his dismissal, ostensibly because he was married. This rejection affected his health but he went on to recover and enjoy the patronage of the wealthy Cardinal Ippolito Il d'Este from 1567–1571. It was during this period that some of his finest mass settings were published, including *Missa Brevis* and *Missa "L'Homme Armé,"* which demonstrate why his sacred music is widely regarded as a pinnacle of contrapuntal style. After this period of patronage, Palestrina spent the rest of his musical career back at the Capella Giulia and married Virginia Dormoli, a fur merchant, after the death of his first wife. Having helped her business flourish, he was wealthy enough to publish 16 collections of his own works. Although the majority of his music was produced for use in religious worship, he also composed over 100 madrigals, both secular and sacred.

GIOVANNI PALESTRINA

Charlie Parker

(1920–1955, American)

Born in Kansas City, Charlie Parker began learning the baritone saxophone during high school, and played the alto saxophone in his school band at the age of 13. Shortly after, he dropped out of school to concentrate on his music and had begun to work as a professional touring musician by 1938. Working with the trumpeter Dizzy Gillespie and saxophonist Ben Webster, Parker was an influential figure in the development of bebop in early-to-mid-1940s New York. The recordings Parker made at the Savoy Club during this period are milestones of the genre, showcasing his technical skill, speed, and imaginative brilliance as an improviser. A heroin addict since early adulthood, Parker's unpredictable behavior began to impact on his career, although the successful *Charlie Parker with Strings* album of 1950 led to further demand for live performances. He married for the third time in 1948, but he began living with Chan Richardson in 1950, and had two children with her. He died in New York in 1955 from a combination of ulcers, cirrhosis of the liver, and a heart attack.

Arvo Pärt
(1935–present, Estonian)

As a child, Arvo Pärt attended evening music school and his early compositional experimentation was encouraged by necessity—only the lowest and highest notes on the piano at his home worked properly. After having survived a serious illness, he entered the Tallinn Conservatory. By the time he graduated, he was working for Estonian radio, and writing film and television scores. An experimental composer, he wrote *Nekrolog* for an orchestra in 1960; it was the first piece of Estonian 12-tone music and earned the authorities' disapproval. In 1962, he started to write "collage" pieces mixing various styles, and joined the Russian Orthodox Church in the early 1970s. These influences culminated in *Credo*, an orchestral piece that was vilified by the authorities for its use of a religious text. He moved to Germany in 1980.

Dolly Parton
(1946–present, American)

Dolly Parton began her music career as a child in Tennessee, releasing a debut album at the age of 14. It was not a success and Parton returned to school. In Nashville, she found work as a songwriter for other performers while struggling to raise her profile as a performer. She secured a television spot alongside the established country star Porter Wagoner in 1967 and her initial success as a performer came in a duo with him. It was not until the early 1970s that Parton began to be recognized as a solo recording artist, but her 1974 number one "Jolene" established her as a bona fide solo star and a first-class songwriter. She built on this success during the 1970s with singles like "I Will Always Love You." In 1980, she began a film career. Parton has continued to test herself as a songwriter and performer, winning a Grammy Award in 2001 and collaborating with younger artists such as Emmylou Harris. In 2018, Parton combined her career paths by writing and performing the music for the Netflix hit *Dumplin'*.

DOLLY PARTON

Luciano Pavarotti
(1935–2007, Italian)

Having performed as a chorister as a young man in his hometown of Modena, Italy, Luciano Pavarotti began to study music formally from the age of 19, and began his professional career as a tenor opera singer in 1961. He developed his reputation during the early 1960s with performances in Europe, Australia, and the United States, and won acclaim for his portrayal of the role of Tonio in Donizetti's *La Fille du Régiment* in 1966. His 1972 reprisal of the role at the Metropolitan Opera in New York brought him international fame and he was featured on the cover of *Time* magazine in 1979. Pavarotti continued to perform, reaching the height of his fame in the early 1990s; his performance of the aria *Nessun Dorma* from Puccini's *Turandot*, became his signature song and his concerts as part of The Three Tenors, with Plácido Domingo and José Carreras, gave rise to a best-selling album. He performed until shortly before his death in 2007.

"**Music making** is the most **joyful** activity...the most perfect expression of any emotion."

LUCIANO PAVAROTTI, OPERA TENOR

Pet Shop Boys
(active 1981–present, English)

Formed in London by Neil Tennant, a former music journalist, and Chris Lowe, a keyboardist, the Pet Shop Boys released three commercially unsuccessful electronic pop singles—"West End Girls," "One More Chance," and "Opportunities ("Let's Make Lots of Money")—between 1984 and 1985. Re-released in 1986, "West End Girls" became a number one single in nine different countries. The band's ensuing debut album, *Please*, reached the top 10 in the UK. Their success continued into the early 1990s—their 1988 album, *Introspective*, experimented with extended song structures and gave rise to the hit singles "Left to My Own Devices" and "Domino Dancing." From 2000 onward, the duo expanded their range as composers, collaborating with the playwright Jonathan Harvey to produce a West End musical in 2001, and releasing a soundtrack for the 1925 Russian silent film *Battleship Potemkin* in 2005. Having sold more than 100 million records during their career, the Pet Shop Boys are recognized by Guinness World Records as the most successful British duo of all time. They are still performing and recording new material, including their 2020 album, *Hotspot*.

PET SHOP BOYS

Oscar Peterson
(1925–2007, Canadian)
Oscar Peterson started taking both trumpet and piano lessons with his father at the age of five. After tuberculosis stopped him from playing the trumpet, he focused on the piano, winning a talent contest at 14 and earning a weekly spot on a Montreal radio station. Peterson began to record during the 1940s and had a hit in 1950 with his interpretation of "Tenderly." From 1953–1958, the Oscar Peterson trio—featuring the bassist Ray Brown and the guitarist Herb Ellis—developed a reputation for their exciting and sophisticated interplay; they are now regarded as one of the greatest trios in the history of jazz. After the trio broke up, Peterson applied his piano skills to a variety of compositions, including duets, quartets, trios, and also to big bands. His first piano solos, recorded in 1968, won him critical acclaim. Peterson was unable to play for two years after suffering from a stroke in 1993 but he returned to music and continued to work for another ten years. He died in Ontario, Canada, at the age of 82, having been made a Companion of the Order of Canada, one of the highest honors in Canadian civilian life.

Edith Piaf
(1915–1963, French)
After a tumultuous childhood, Edith Gassion began performing at the age of 14, participating in acrobatic street performances across France with her father. She began a career as a solo street singer in Paris at 16. A year later, she had a daughter, Marcelle, who died of meningitis at the age of two. In 1935, Gassion began singing at a club near the Champs-Élysées where she honed her vocals, earning the nickname "The Little Sparrow" for her frail appearance and nervous demeanor. She released two records in the same year, but was mired in controversy after being accused and subsequently acquitted of being involved in the murder of a nightclub owner. It was at this time that she changed her name to Edith Piaf and began to perform songs that reflected her early experiences of life on the streets. By 1946, her signature songs, such as "La Vie en Rose," and her highly emotional performance style had made her the most popular entertainer in France and she won international acclaim between the mid-1950s and early 1960s when she gave a series of lauded performances at the Paris Olympia music hall. Piaf died of liver cancer in 1963 and tens of thousands of people took to the streets of Paris during her funeral.

PINK FLOYD

Ástor Piazzolla
(1921–1992, Argentinean)
A prodigal student of classical piano and the bandoneon, Piazzolla joined the prominent tango orchestra of Anibal Troilo in 1939, working as an arranger, bandoneonist, and pianist. During the early 1940s, he embarked on a period of concerted classical study, expanding his work as a composer. He won an award for the *Buenos Aires Symphony* in the early 1950s and traveled to Paris in 1954 to undertake further studies of European classical music. During this times, Piazzolla was encouraged to apply his studies to tango and, on his return to Buenos Aires in 1960, his compositions revolutionized the genre, earning condemnation from traditionalists and praise from the wider music community. In 1967, he wrote *María de Buenos Aires,* a tango opera, but continued to struggle to find a sympathetic audience in Argentina. However, the *nuevo tango* style was accepted by the mid-1980s, winning over tango and classical audiences.

Pink Floyd
(active 1965–1995, English)
Syd Barrett, Roger Waters, Nick Mason, and Richard Wright formed a band in London in 1965, initially known as the Pink Floyd Sound. With Barrett as front man, Pink Floyd signed to EMI records in 1967 and released their debut album, *Piper at the Gates of Dawn.* However, Barrett's drug use led to erratic behavior and he left the group in 1968 and was replaced by David Gilmour. Between 1969 and 1971, the band released three albums, before achieving international stardom with their 1973 release, *The Dark Side of the Moon.* A predominantly instrumental album, it spent more than 950 weeks on the Billboard charts. They consolidated their success with subsequent albums of the 1970s, including *Wish You Were Here (*1975) and *The Wall* (1979), which included the number one single, "Another Brick in the Wall." Waters left Pink Floyd in 1987, although the band continued to perform in a number of permutations.

Cole Porter
(1891–1964, American)
Cole Porter had learned violin and piano, and begun to compose his own music, before the age of 10. He wrote hundreds of piano-based songs while studying at Yale, and had his first song performed on Broadway in 1915. Moving to Paris in 1917, Porter achieved limited success as a composer during the early 1920s, despite experimenting with a number of genres, including comic songs, ballet music, and symphonic pieces. However, in 1928 he had a hit with the Broadway musical *Paris,* which contained some of the songs for which he would be best known, including "Let's Do It" and "Let's Misbehave." Porter maintained his position as a major popular composer during the 1930s with the musicals *Anything Goes* and *Jubilee,* among others. He also wrote the scores for several films, including *Born to Dance, Rosalie,* and *In the Still of the Night.* After a horse-riding accident in 1937 left him paralyzed and in severe pain, Porter struggled with his work during the early 1940s, but managed to return to both critical acclaim and mainstream popularity with the popular 1948 musical, *Kiss Me, Kate,* which became the most commercially successful show of his career. However, Porter's creative output dwindled during the 1950s, and he died of kidney failure in 1964 at the age of 73.

Dámaso Pérez Prado
(1916–1989, Cuban)
Born on Cuba's northern coast, Dámaso Pérez Prado learned classical piano as a child, and went on to find work as a pianist and organ player in clubs and cinemas. Learning his craft as a pianist and arranger for well-established groups, Pérez moved to Mexico in 1948. There he founded his own orchestra, working with a number of prominent collaborators, including the singer Benny Moré. Having experimented with a range of musical styles, including big band jazz and bebop, he focused his attention on the Afro-Cuban rhythms of mambo, a nascent genre that he worked hard to develop and popularize. From 1950 onward, he released several successful singles, including *Que Rico el Mambo,* and elevated his profile further by starring in films. Mambo grew in popularity during the 1950s, and Pérez became a star in Central, South, and North America. In 1955, he recorded "Cherry Pink and Apple Blossom White," which spent several weeks at number one on the US pop chart. Although he was known as the King of Mambo, Prado worked in different genres, even composing tone poems such as *The Exotic Suite of the Americas.* Mambo's popularity declined toward the end of the 1950s, along with Prado's commercial success, but he continued to record and play, performing before a full house at the Hollywood Palladium in 1987, two years before his death.

PEREZ PRADO

Elvis Presley
(1935–1977, American)
Born into a poor family in Tupelo, Mississippi, Presley took up the guitar in around 1950, although he never learned to read music. In 1954, he was picked up as part of a trio by Sun

Records, and they released rock 'n' roll singles that were successful in the Memphis area. In 1955, he transferred to the RCA label and began to record the music that would turn him into a pop phenomenon, including "Heartbreak Hotel" and "Hound Dog." In the same year, assisted by his manager, Colonel Tom Parker, Elvis launched his film career with *Love Me Tender.* Despite being drafted into the army in 1958, Presley's music continued to be released, and his star status stayed intact up to 1960, when he returned to civilian life. Although he maintained a high public profile during the 1960s, Presley released little notable music until late in the decade —his *Elvis in Memphis* album was well received and the single "Suspicious Minds" became a nationwide hit in 1969. In the same year, he performed a series of very popular live shows in Las Vegas, showcasing the excitement, intensity, and energy that his early popularity was built on. He continued to record and perform during the 1970s, but his personal problems, including a broken marriage and a dependency on prescription drugs, began to take their toll. He died in his home in Memphis at the age of 42.

"Some people tap their feet, some snap their fingers, and **some sway** back and forth. I just sorta do 'em all together..."

ELVIS PRESLEY, SINGER

Prince

(1958–2016, American)

The son of professional musicians, Prince wrote his first song as a seven-year old boy growing up in Minnesota. Having worked with his cousin's band, 94 East, he struggled to generate interest in his early demo recordings and it was not until his second album, the self-titled *Prince,* that he began to garner attention. However, his *Dirty Mind* album of 1980 crystallized his fusion of funk, soul, and pop music, and it started a run of commercial and critically acclaimed releases, culminating with *Purple Rain* in 1984; a soundtrack to a film of the same name, it was the most accessible record of his career and went on to sell over 20 million copies around the world. A virtuoso musician capable of playing several instruments, Prince also established himself as a flamboyant live performer. In 1987, he disbanded his backing band, The Revolution, and released *Sign "O" the Times,* which was a critical success. During the early 1990s, a contractual dispute with Warner Bros. records resulted in Prince changing his name to an unpronounceable symbol and releasing five albums between 1996 and 1998 in an effort to quickly fulfill his contractual obligations. He reverted to the name Prince in 2000 and continued to perform and record until his death following an accidental overdose in 2016.

PRINCE

Sergey Prokofiev

(1891–1953, Russian)

As a child with a musically inclined mother, Prokofiev had already composed two operas by his eleventh birthday. From 1905, he studied at the St. Petersburg Conservatory, where he became known as a rebellious composer of brashly modernist music. In 1918, after the upheavals of the Bolshevik Revolution, Prokofiev left Russia for a period of 18 years. Residing in the United States, he scored an instant hit as a pianist, and received a commission for *The Love for Three Oranges,* the only one among his operas to win international fame in his lifetime. In 1921, his ballet *Chout* became a great success in Paris, and he resettled the following year, first in Bavaria and then Paris. The 1920s brought two new successes with the Ballets Russes: *Le Pas d'Acier* (*The Steel Step*) and *The Prodigal Son.* In between composing, Prokofiev undertook many successful tours as a pianist to the United States, Europe, and the Soviet Union. In 1936, he returned to the Soviet Union, which was in the grip of Stalinist terror, and the authorities criticized him for "formalist tendencies" in the late 1940s. He died of a brain hemorrhage on the same day as Stalin.

Public Enemy

(active 1982–present, American)

The brainchild of Chuck D, a New York graphic design student, Public Enemy released their debut album, *Yo! Bum Rush the Show*—a combination of hip-hop beats and politically engaged rapping—in 1987. They achieved critical and commercial success with their second album, *It Takes a Nation of Millions to Hold Us Back,* which employed abrasive sounds and high-tempo rhythms to recreate the energy of their popular live shows. The album also refined the interaction of the group's two principal rappers, with Flavor Flav acting as an enthusiastic and humorous foil to Chuck D's political message of African American empowerment. This dynamic was developed on "Fight the Power," the theme tune for Spike Lee's 1989 film *Do the Right Thing.* Public Enemy began the 1990s with the release of their third album, *Fear of a Black Planet,* which was another critical and commercial success. Frequently mired in controversy during their most prolific and creative period, they were inducted into the United States Rock 'n' Roll Hall of Fame in 2013.

Giacomo Puccini

(1858–1924, Italian)

Giacomo Puccini was born in Lucca, in Tuscany, Italy, into the fifth generation of a family of church musicians. His father died when Puccini was only five, but the position of organist was kept open for him. However, a performance of Verdi's *Aïda,* which he saw in Pisa in 1876, convinced him that opera was his true vocation. He took up the position of church organist at 19 and left to study at the Milan Conservatory in 1880. When the publisher Sonzogno launched a competition for one-act operas, Puccini entered *Le Villi,* which failed to win. Sonzogno's rival, Giulio Ricordi, commissioned another opera from Puccini. Entitled *Edgar,* its premiere in 1889 was a failure but *Manon Lescaut,* a subsequent commission from Ricordi, enjoyed great success in Turin in 1893. From then on, Puccini devoted himself to writing opera. In 1891, he bought an estate on a lake near Lucca, where he lived with his married companion, Elvira Bonturi. Their relationship was a tempestuous one—in 1909, a servant killed herself after Elvira accused her of having an affair with Puccini. Puccini's great operas written around the turn of the century—*La Boheme* (1896), *Tosca* (1900), and *Madame Butterfly* (1904)—are some of the final expressions of Romantic lyricism. In 1924, Puccini was diagnosed with throat cancer and died during treatment in Brussels. His masterpiece, *Turandot,* was left incomplete, but he had already begun to explore the music of the 20th century in the finished sections.

GIACOMO PUCCINI

QUEEN

Tito Puente

(1923–2000, American)

Growing up in Spanish Harlem, Tito Puente studied at the Juilliard School of Music in New York and the New York School of Music, learning composition and arrangement, and expanding the range of instruments he could play to include percussion, piano, and saxophone. A virtuoso on the timbales, Puente started a group called the Piccadilly Boys in 1947 and began to make mambo recordings as the genre grew popular. As a bandleader during the 1950s, he popularized Latin music in North America and Europe, becoming synonymous with both mambo and cha-cha-cha, and was the only non-Cuban to perform at a celebration of Cuban music on the island in 1952. He built on his success during the 1960s, expanding his repertoire to include pop music and the nascent genre of bossa nova. In later years, the Latin fusion music he produced came to be known by the generic name of "salsa," although this was a label that Puente rejected. Famed for his appetite for hard work, Puente continued to tour and record into his 70s, appearing at the closing ceremony of the Olympic Games in Atlanta in 1996.

> "If there is **no dance,** there is **no music.**"
>
> TITO PUENTE, PERCUSSIONIST AND BANDLEADER

Queen

(active 1970–present, English)

Formed in London in 1970, Queen originally consisted of the singer Freddie Mercury, the guitarist Brian May, the bass guitarist John Deacon, and the drummer Roger Taylor. Initially a progressive rock and heavy metal band, Queen received critical acclaim for their debut album, *Queen*, released in 1973, and their second album, *Queen II*, found chart success in the UK, despite featuring unusual song structures and complex guitar parts; it was also a minor hit in the United States. With their next two albums, *Sheer Heart Attack* and *A Night at the Opera*, released in 1974 and 1975 respectively, they cemented their reputation as one of the most popular heavy rock bands in the world. The single "Bohemian Rhapsody" consisted of several sections of wildly varying styles, from ballad to hard rock, and crystallized the combination of catchy hook-driven songwriting and experimentation on which their popularity was founded. The video they made for this single, more than any, other inaugurated the modern music video. "Bohemian Rhapsody" occupied the number one position in the UK chart for nine weeks and went on to become the third best-selling single in the history of the chart. In 2019, it became the first pre-1990s music video to hit one billion views on YouTube. Two years later, it became the first British song to achieve RIAA Diamond status. Famed for their flamboyant live shows, in 1985, Queen's performance at Live Aid, one of the most watched concerts and the most successful charity concerts ever, revitalized their career. That year, they played two outdoor concerts in Rio de Janeiro, Brazil, to audiences of over 300,000. Mercury died in 1991, and although the band has released very little music since then, they have continued to perform live, using guest singers such as Adam Lambert.

Sergey Rachmaninoff

(1873–1943, Russian)

Sergey Rachmaninoff's education was disrupted by the separation of his parents during his childhood at St. Petersburg. He was sent to study at the Moscow Conservatory where he boarded with his piano teacher, practicing all day, and graduated with the highest marks for his composition and playing. His career had a promising start: his opera, *Aleko*, was successfully premiered in 1893, and he enjoyed the revered Russian composer Tchaikovsky's support. However, a calamitous performance of his Symphony No. 1 drew savage reviews; he was unable to compose for three years and turned to conducting, with increasing success, until a hypnotist doctor and musician, Nikolai Dahl, persuaded him to compose again. The Piano Concerto No. 2 was among the works he steadily produced as his reputation as a composer and performer grew. By his 40s, he had toured the United States, Russia, and Europe, but he lost his estates during the Russian Revolution and had to flee to Scandinavia. He spent the last 25 years of his life in the United States and Europe, composing, touring, and recording, until he died of cancer at the age of 69.

Radiohead

(active 1989–present, English)

Formed by Thom Yorke, Ed O'Brien, Jonny Greenwood, and Phil Selway while they were at school in Oxford, Radiohead's early singles were not commercially successful. The release of their album *Pablo Honey* in 1993 resulted in a hit with the single "Creep," leading to increased exposure in both the UK and the United States. Critical acclaim followed with the release of their second album, *The Bends*, though more prominent Britpop bands, such as Oasis, overshadowed them in commercial terms. Radiohead moved further away from conventional guitar pop with the release of their third album, *Ok Computer*; despite producing successful chart singles, including "Karma Police," the record employed unconventional song structures and

RADIOHEAD

ambient sounds. This experimentation continued throughout the 2000s, with excursions into jazz and electronica. Radiohead also experimented with different methods of distributing their music, including a "pay-what-you-want" model of downloading the 2007 album, *In Rainbows*. In the spirit of innovation and variety, both Yorke and Greenwood have produced music in their own right, the latter working as composer-in-residence for the BBC Symphony Orchestra and having his symphonic work *Horror Vacui* performed at the 2019 BBC Prom.

The Ramones

(active 1974–1996, American)

Founded by Jeffry Hyman, John Cummings, and Douglas Colvin—all band members would shortly adopt pseudonyms ending with the name "Ramone"—the Ramones made their first public appearance in New York in 1974. Founded on the writing skills of bassist Dee Dee Ramone, they caught the public's attention through eye-catching live performances of their brutally simple and short songs. The band quickly earned a reputation as pioneers in the punk genre and released their self-titled debut album in 1976, to critical acclaim. The record was not a commercial success but a highly publicized tour of England raised their profile and the group's third album, released in 1977, sold more copies. During the early 1980s, they underwent several changes in personnel and moved away from raw punk toward a more mainstream sound. Commercial success in the United States continued to evade them, although they continued to tour, racking up a total of 2,263 performances before they disbanded in 1996.

Maurice Ravel

(1875–1937, French)

Maurice Ravel was born in a Basque town near Biarritz in France, less than 12 miles from the Spanish border, although his family moved to Paris just three months after his birth. In 1889, he entered the Paris Conservatoire as a piano student and won the first prize in the institution's piano competition in 1891. In 1898, he began to study composition with French composer, organist, and pianist, Gabriel Fauré, and had his first works published in the same year. Alongside Debussy, Ravel established a French style that broke away from the conservative strictures of Romanticism. This style is sometimes referred to as Impressionism, although it was a label Debussy rejected. Ravel received a commission from Serge Diaghilev for his legendary Ballets Russes in 1909. The result, *Daphnis et Chloé*, provoked a lukewarm response at its première, but it went on to be hailed not only as one of Ravel's masterpieces, but also a high point for the golden age of ballet. Ravel was a perfectionist and he produced only a moderately sized body of work, covering chamber music, compositions for piano, and orchestral and stage works, before his death in Paris, at the age of 62.

MAURICE RAVEL

Lou Rawls

(*c.*1933–2006, American)

Having sung in the gospel choir at his church in Chicago while a teenager, Lou Rawls performed with several gospel groups during the early 1950s. After a brief stint in the army, he returned to music, working with the Pilgrim Travelers and touring with the singer Sam Cooke. In 1958, Cooke and Rawls were involved in a major car crash—Rawls was seriously injured and was unable to perform again until 1959. He sang secular music during the 1960s and became a major star with the release of the album *Soulin'*, in 1966, which gracefully combined his smooth vocal style with soul influences. The single from the album, "Love is a Hurtin' Thing," won him loyal fans. Although his popularity declined during the early 1970s, he returned to prominence in 1976 with the album *All Things in Time*, which showcased a more upbeat sound. Rawls continued to work as an actor and entertainer throughout the 1980s and '90s.

Red Hot Chili Peppers

(active 1983–present, American)

Founded by four high school friends in Los Angeles in 1983, the Red Hot Chili Peppers built their reputation through live appearances—in which the band frequently performed seminaked—and exposure on college radio stations. Although they struggled to capture the energy of their live performances on their first two albums, they achieved some recognition with *The Uplift Mofo Party Plan* in 1987. When one of the founders, Hillel Slovak, died of a drug overdose a year later, the band was reconfigured: the existing members Anthony Kiedis (vocals) and Flea (bass) were joined by the drummer Chad Smith and the guitarist John Frusciante. This lineup achieved recognition with *Mother's Milk* in 1989 and propelled themselves into the mainstream with *Blood Sugar Sex Magik*, an album that added anthemic songwriting to their fusion of funk and rock. The group struggled with drug addiction during the 1990s but the group enjoyed its biggest success in 1999 with the album *Californication*—which sold 15 million copies. Frusciante left in 2009, and the band has since produced several albums and toured extensively.

Otis Redding

(1941–1967, American)

Otis Redding began his career as a teenaged rock 'n' roll and rhythm and blues singer in his home state of Georgia. In 1962, he released his first single as a solo performer, while working as a member of The Pinetoppers. Entitled "These Arms of Mine," its success provided a platform for his debut album, *Pain in My Heart*, which was a moderate hit in 1964. From then on, Redding concentrated on soul music, as demonstrated by his 1965 release, *Otis Blue: Otis Redding Sings Soul*. A critical success, it also gained him exposure to a mainstream audience and this trend continued with his 1966 album, *Complete & Unbelievable*, which featured one of his most popular songs, "Try a Little Tenderness." Redding died in a plane crash in 1967 and the single, "(Sittin' On) The Dock of the Bay," released in 1968, became his biggest hit, topping the US chart and selling four million copies around the world.

Lou Reed

(1942–2013, American)

As a young man growing up in New York, Lou Reed taught himself to play the guitar by listening to the radio. During the mid-1960s, he established himself as the leader of The Velvet Underground, an art band who collaborated with Andy Warhol. Their debut album, *The Velvet and Underground and Nico*, which was not a commercial success, is now regarded as one of the most influential albums in rock music. Although two subsequent albums, *The Velvet Underground* (1969) and *Loaded* (1970), were more popular, Reed left the band in 1970. His second solo album, *Transformer*, released in 1972 and coproduced by David Bowie and Mick Ronson, became an international hit. It featured two of his most popular works, "Walk on the Wild Side" and "Perfect Day." Reed continued to experiment during the 1970s, releasing some of his most challenging music, including *Berlin* (1973) and *Metal Machine Music* (1975), an album of electronic noise. He was reunited with the Velvet Underground during the early 1990s.

OTIS REDDING

Steve Reich
(1936–present, American)
Having studied composition with the composers Luciano Berio and Darius Milhaud in California during the early 1960s, Steve Reich began to experiment with 12-tone composition, before developing an interest in the way identical tape loops moved out of synchronization. This resulted in his first loop-phase piece, *Come Out* (1966), which manipulated recordings of the voice of Daniel Hamm, a victim of police brutality. He began to apply these phasing effects to conventional instruments to create ingenious and unusual sounds, as in 1967's *Violin Phase*. A pioneer of minimalism, Reich had established his method of making music from repeating slowly changing patterns by the mid-1970s. During the 1980s, he returned to speech recordings and continued this practice into the 1990s and 2000s. He also experimented with multimedia projects such as *The Cave*, a 1993 work about Judaism and Islam created with his wife, the video artist Beryl Korot.

R.E.M.
(active 1980–2011, American)
Formed by four students of the University of Georgia—singer Michael Stipe, guitarist Peter Buck, bassist Mick Mills, and drummer Bill Berry—R.E.M. developed their alternative rock sound by performing throughout the southern United States during 1981. They released their first single, the critically acclaimed "Radio Free Europe," in 1981 and followed it with their first album, the minor chart success *Murmur*, in 1983. Building up a loyal, grassroots fan base through years of touring and regular exposure on college radio stations throughout the United States, R.E.M.'s fifth album, *Document*, became a commercial hit in 1987, supported by the best-selling single, "The One I Love." After extensive tours of America and Europe, and a break to allow members of the band to pursue other projects, they earned significant mainstream success with their introspective alternative rock albums of the early 1990s, *Out of Time* and *Automatic for the People*. The former spent over 100 weeks on the US and UK album charts, despite the band's refusal to support the record with live performances. They returned to a more rock-driven sound with their 1994 album, *Monster*, which was another significant critical and commercial success. Bill Berry left R.E.M. in 1997 and the band continued to perform as a trio before disbanding in 2011.

Django Reinhardt
(1910–1953, French)
Raised in Romany encampments near Paris in a family of Romany descent, Django Reinhardt's first instrument was the violin. He took up the guitar at the age of 12 and, despite having no formal training, found work as a musician by the time he was 13. In 1928, Reinhardt and his wife, Florine Mayer, were caught in a fire in the caravan where they lived, and Reinhardt sustained burns that limited the use of the third and fourth fingers of his left hand. As a result, he relearned the guitar and discovered a new way to play, developing virtuoso proficiency. His career took off in 1934 with the formation of the Quintette du Hot Club de France, a jazz string band that also featured the violinist Stephane Grappelli. They rose to international prominence, and Reinhardt also played with other notable jazz musicians, including Louis Armstrong. Based in Paris during World War II, he separated from his wife and remarried. Despite being of Romany origin, he escaped persecution from the Nazis and during the 1940s he experimented with other forms of music, including classical. After World War II, he worked in the United States and Europe and died in France from a brain hemorrhage in 1953.

DJANGO REINHARDT

Buddy Rich
(1917–1987, American)
Buddy Rich began his career in music when he was 18 months old, working in a vaudeville show under the stage name "Traps, the Drum Wonder." He played in a number of jazz and big bands during the late 1930s and early 1940s, including those led by Artie Shaw and Tommy Dorsey, establishing a reputation as a phenomenon and virtuoso who combined speed with technique, leading to his billing as "the world's greatest drummer." After World War II, Rich formed his own band and during the 1950s he collaborated with several high profile jazz musicians, including Charlie Parker and Lester Young. A perfectionist with a notoriously explosive temper, Rich continued to perform until the end of his life.

Terry Riley
(1935–present, American)
In the early 1960s, Riley co-founded the San Francisco Tape Music Center, where he created highly innovative pieces using montage and tape-echo techniques, sometimes collaborating with the underground composer La Monte Young. After studying composition at the University of California, he traveled around Europe and the United States, playing the piano in bars and absorbing the influence of jazz improvisers such as John Coltrane and Charles Mingus. In 1964, he wrote *In C*, a celebration of the chord C major and a defining work of minimalism, but a 1970 meeting with the Kirana vocal master Pandit Pran Nath inspired him to introduce Indian classical music influences into his compositions. He began to teach at the Chishti Sabri School of Indian classical music in New Delhi in 1993.

Roaring Lion
(1908–1999, Trinidadian)
Born Rafael de Leon in the hills of northern Trinidad, Roaring Lion spent some of his childhood in orphanages before being adopted by a Muslim Indian family in the city of San Fernando. He was interested in words from an early age—he practiced poetry as well as music—and put this interest into practice in his early calypso work. He recorded some pieces in his late teens, winning a calypso competition during the 1920s. He rose to prominence in the 1930s with a series of high-profile, self-penned singles, including "Mary Ann," "Netty Netty," and his most famous composition, "Ugly Woman." Some of these songs were recorded in New York and Roaring Lion's work was a major factor in making the genre of calypso music internationally popular. An innovator, he was renowned for his articulate, witty lyrics and creative approach to melody. Although his popularity peaked in the 1930s and '40s, he continued to record into the 1990s, retaining his unique vocal style but using modern electronic backings. One of the few early calypso artists to read and write music, Roaring Lion was also a historian and theorist of the genre and the author of a book expounding the idea that calypso music was of French origin. He died in Trinidad in 1999.

R.E.M

Tabu Ley Rochereau

(1940–2013, Congolese)

Having begun composing and performing in high school, Tabu Ley Rochereau rose to prominence with the band African Jazz between 1960 and 1963. In the same year he formed his own band, African Fiesta National, which propelled him to superstar status in Africa. During the late 1960s, he sold over one million records and worked with some of the finest musicians on the continent, including Papa Wemba. In 1970, his band expanded to become the Orchestre Afrisa International—they achieved hits throughout Africa and were instrumental in transforming the Congolese rumba sound into soukou. During the mid-1980s, his collaborations with his wife, the singer M'bilia Bel, brought further success. He became involved with Congolese politics during the late 1990s and 2000s, and was appointed vice-governor of the country's capital city, Kinshasa.

Rodgers and Hammerstein

(active 1943–1959, American)

Prior to their partnership, composer Richard Rodgers and librettist Oscar Hammerstein II had both enjoyed successful careers in musical theater. In combination with Lorenz Hart, Rodgers had written the music for several successful Broadway shows, while Hammerstein had worked with the renowned composer Jerome Kern to produce the landmark musical *Show Boat*. The duo produced their first collaboration, *Oklahoma*, in 1943, pioneering the idea that music and song should be fully integrated into a musical's plot. *Oklahoma* centered on the romance between Curly, a cowboy, and Laurey, a young farm girl, and was a commercial phenomenon, running for 2,212 performances over a period of five years. The pair continued to enjoy success in the 1940s, first with *Carousel*—one of the earliest musicals to have a tragic plot—and then with *South Pacific*, which ran to packed houses for over five years and won its authors the Pulitzer Prize for Drama. In the 1950s, their major works included the hit musicals *The King and I* and *The Sound of Music*. Hammerstein died of cancer a year after *The Sound of Music* premiered on Broadway in 1959, but his partner Rodgers continued to compose until shortly before his death in 1979 at the age of 77. While extraordinary for their time, their musicals no longer chime with contemporary outlooks, and it is not unusual for modern productions to change or cut some of the more problematic lines.

ÁMALIA RODRIGUES

Amália Rodrigues

(1920–1999, Portuguese)

Raised by her grandmother in Lisbon, Rodrigues was forced to earn a living as a child by working as a seamstress and street vendor. During her teens, she performed as a tango dancer and made her first professional appearance as a fado singer in 1939. Her partnership in the early 1940s with the composer Frederico Valéro resulted in some of her best work, in which her vocals were set against an orchestral backdrop. Rodrigues quickly became Portugal's most famous singer and staged a series of successful concerts in Rio de Janeiro, Brazil, in 1945. She began to record in earnest during the 1950s, interpreting the work of some of Portugal's greatest poets. Although fado's popularity diminished during the 1960s, Rodrigues' fame was maintained, in part due to her career as a film actress. She continued to perform into her 70s and her funeral was a significant state occasion, attended by thousands of mourners.

> "We **can't define** fado. Fado is a **mystery.**"
>
> AMÁLIA RODRIGUES, SINGER

Arsenio Rodríguez

(1911–1971, Cuban)

Born in the western Cuban province of Mantazas, Arsenio Rodríguez was blinded at the age of seven by a kick to the head from a horse. Throughout his childhood he experimented with different instruments, including guitar and percussion, and by his early 20s he was an established musician, working with the Sexteto Boston and the Septeto Bellamar. He developed his skills as a composer during this stint, and made his first recording in 1939 with the Orquesta Casino de la Playa. In the early 1940s, as leader of his own band, he revolutionized Cuban son music, emphasizing the rhythm section by adding a conga drum and making the trumpet more dominant. He recorded some of his most famous pieces during this decade, including the bolero *La Vida es un Sueno* ("Life is a Dream")—inspired by a failed effort to restore his sight. Rodríguez moved to New York during the 1950s, where he continued to experiment, and innovate, creating a brand of Afro-Cuban fusion music, which he called "quindembo." Due to his unorthodox use of contrapuntal techniques, he is often credited with laying the foundations for the mambo style of music that became popular in the 1950s. Rodríguez continued to record until he died of pneumonia in 1970.

The Rolling Stones

(active 1962–present, English)

The definitive early incarnation of the Rolling Stones—Mick Jagger, Keith Richards, Brian Jones, Charlie Watts, and Billy Wyman—came together in London in 1963 and registered a minor hit in June of that year with a cover of Chuck Berry's rock 'n' roll single, "Come On." In 1964, their version of Buddy Holly's "Not Fade Away" gained an international audience and after the release of their debut album, they staged a popular tour of the United States and began to record original material. One of these original songs, "(I Can't Get No) Satisfaction," heralded a sequence of commercially successful singles, including "Get Off My Cloud." Jagger, Richards, and Jones were all arrested for drug possession in 1967, earning the band a reputation for rebelliousness. After experimentation with a psychedelic aesthetic on *Their Satanic Majesties Request* in 1967, the Stones returned to their blues-driven sound in 1968, with the release of *Beggar's Banquet*. Despite the band's success, Brian Jones left the Stones, and he died in 1969. Tragedy followed the Stones to the US when Hells Angels hired for security killed a man at their show at Altamont Speedway, California. The band released several landmark albums during the 1970s, including *Exile on Main Street* (1971), recorded while they were living as tax exiles in France. Their recorded output declined in popularity during the 1980s, but they continue to give sold-out performances to audiences around the world. Their drummer, Charlie Watts, died in 2021.

Gioachino Rossini

(1792–1868, Italian)

Born a few months after the great Mozart's death, Gioachino Rossini was the son of Pesaro's town horn player and his wife, a singer. He entered the Bologna Conservatory in 1806 and by the time he was 21, he had written 10 operas, including *Tancredi* and *L'italiani in Algeri*. Around 1814–1815, he was engaged as music director for the two opera houses in Naples and went on to write for theaters in Milan, Venice, and Rome. In 1824, he moved to Paris where he wrote five more operas, culminating in 1829 with *William Tell*, one of his best-known works. After its production, Rossini stopped writing operas and only composed occasionally for the remaining 38 years of his life. He died of pneumonia at the age of 76.

GIOACHINO ROSSINI

RUN-D.M.C.

Run-D.M.C.
(active 1982–2002, American)
Joey Simmons and Darryl McDaniels formed their rap duo, Run-D.M.C., in New York in 1982. Taking the stage names Run and D.M.C. respectively, they recruited the DJ Jam Master Jay to assist with production and released their first single in 1983. Their innovative sound, a combination of sparse beats and intelligent lyrics, resulted in critical acclaim for their eponymous debut album. Commercially astute and musically inventive, Run-D.M.C. began to experiment with a fusion of rap and rock, resulting in popular success for their third album, *Raising Hell*. Released in 1986, it was supported by the single "Walk this Way," which featured members of the hard rock band Aerosmith. The commercial success of these records resulted in massive sales and television exposure, turning Run-D.M.C. into hip-hop's first popstars and cementing the nascent genre's status as chart-friendly music.

Pepe Sanchéz
(1856–1918, Cuban)
Pepe Sanchéz was born in Santiago de Cuba, the second largest city in Cuba. Trained as a tailor, he had no formal education in music and practiced several other professions during his life, including those of cloth manufacturer and owner of a copper mine. Nonetheless, he is regarded as the originator of the Cuban tradition of the *trovadores*—a singer, guitarist, and sometimes songwriter, who performs poetic songs. He is also acknowledged as the father of the bolero but, because he was unable to write musical notation, many of these boleros have been lost, although some are still performed. Sanchez earned an impressive reputation thanks to his range of musical achievements.

Oumou Sangaré
(1968–present, Malian)
Oumou Sangaré began to sing as a child growing up in Bamoko, the capital of Mali. She became a professional musician at the age of 16 with the percussion group Djoliba and released her debut album, *Moussoulou*, in 1989, which made her a superstar in West Africa. The success of her work was partly credited to her socially engaged lyrics, which often comment on the role of women in a traditional society. Known as "The Songbird of Wassoulou," she makes use of traditional instruments of the Wassoulou area, such as the calabash. She continued to record throughout the 1990s and 2000s and performed live with several other prominent African artists, including Femi Kuti. Sangaré has taken the social concerns expressed in her songs into the wider world in her work as an ambassador for the United Nations.

OUMOU SANGARE

Carlos Santana
(1947–present, Mexican-American)
Born in Mexico, Carlos Santana learned violin and guitar as a child, and began his music career in earnest in San Francisco in the mid-1960s. The virtuoso guitarist formed the Santana Blues Band (later renamed Santana) in 1966 with the bassist David Brown and keyboardist Gregg Rolie. They developed their sound—a fusion of blues, rock, and Latin American music—through live performances in San Francisco and the group made a well-received appearance at the Woodstock Festival in 1969, attracting international attention. They built on this success with their debut album, *Santana*, which reached number four on the US album chart. The band's subsequent albums, *Abraxas* and *Santana III*, were also significant commercial successes, and displayed a more overt jazz influence. Although Santana separated from Brown and Rolie after the release of *Santana III*, he continued to record under the name Santana and his 1972 album, *Caravanserai*, showcased his continued interest in jazz and avant-garde music. During the late 1970s, Santana released several commercially successful Latin- and blues-rock albums with the Santana band, while simultaneously pursuing a more eclectic and experimental solo career. Although his mainstream appeal flagged during the 1980s, he returned to commercial prominence in 1999 with the award-winning album, *Supernatural*.

Alfred Schnittke
(1934–1998, Russian)
Growing up in the Soviet Union as the son of German-Jewish parents, Alfred Schnittke entered the Moscow Conservatory in 1953. Heavily influenced by Dmitri Shostakovich, he fell foul of Soviet hostility toward experimentation in 1958 when the Union of Composers condemned his oratorio, *Nagasaki*. In 1962, he began a career as a freelance composer and experimented with creating tension in music throughout the 1960s by combining several styles within the same piece—he called this technique "polystylism." In 1974, he completed Symphony No. 1, a piece which begins with the players arriving on stage one by one and improvising chaotically until the conductor signals for silence. It was condemned by the Union of Composers and when Schnittke abstained from a Union's vote in 1980,

he was banned from leaving the Soviet Union. He suffered from ill health during the mid- to late 1980s and moved to Hamburg, Germany in 1991. The collapse of the Soviet Union in the same year allowed a wider audience to hear his work.

Arnold Schoenberg

(1874–1951, Austrian)

Born in Vienna, Arnold Schoenberg began composing as a child. He married Mathilde, the sister of his contemporary Alexander Zemlinsky in 1901. In 1906, he composed the radically dissonant Chamber Symphony No. 1. He continued with an experimental approach with the atonal piano work *Three Pieces*, written in 1909. His epic cantata, *Gurrelieder*, was produced in 1911. Schoenberg is credited with the "invention" and dissemination of serial composition, which was the lifeblood of 20th-century music for more than half a century. It was taken up by composers from Stravinsky to Britten and influenced Boulez and Stockhausen. In 1933 Schoenberg rejoined the Jewish faith and left Europe for America, eventually settling in Los Angeles, where he took a teaching post at the University of California. He lived in California for the rest of his life.

FRANZ SCHUBERT

Franz Schubert

(1797–1828, Austrian)

Born into a musical family in Vienna, Franz Schubert demonstrated a precocious talent for the violin and piano. By the age of 10 he was studying harmony and the following year he became a chorister at the Court Chapel in Vienna, where he studied composition with Antonio Salieri, who had also taught the famous composer Ludwig van Beethoven. When Schubert left in 1813, he was already an accomplished composer, having written numerous works, including a symphony, and even started an opera. Following his father's wishes, he became a school teacher, but he continued to compose and eventually felt confident enough to give up teaching. Schubert struggled for recognition, and he suffered from syphilis from 1822. Despite these problems on the personal front, he was always a prolific composer. His impressive output includes 70 chamber music works, 21 piano sonatas, and 60 works for piano duet. By 1825, Schubert had been published and was becoming known in Vienna. In 1827, he composed the first part of the *Winterreise*, a song cycle, and it was for his contribution to the German art song, or *Lied*, that he won initial recognition. He gave his only public concert in 1828, but by the end of the year his health had deteriorated markedly, and he died on November 19. In the same year, the German composer Robert Schumann visited Schubert's brother and discovered the No. 9 Symphony. Schumann sent it to Felix Mendelssohn, who premiered it the following year.

> "I try to **decorate my imagination** as **much** as I can."
>
> FRANZ SCHUBERT, COMPOSER

Robert Schumann

(1810–1856, German)

Robert Schumann was born in the Kingdom of Saxony (present-day Germany) and although he received no thorough formal education in music and literature, he was obsessed by both, possibly influenced by his bookseller father. Persuaded by his mother to pursue a career in law, he moved to Leipzig to study. In 1830, he decided to become a musician after hearing Paganini play. He gave up his studies and moved into the home of the piano teacher, Friedrich Wieck, whose 11-year old daughter, Clara, was already a piano prodigy. Forced to give up his ambitions for a career as a concert pianist owing to a hand injury, he concentrated on composition. Over the next 10 years, he published several piano masterpieces, such as the *Fantasy in C* of 1837, dedicated to Franz Liszt. He edited a new music journal, which brought the music of Frederick Chopin and Johannes Brahms to the attention of the public. In spite of the gap in their ages, Clara and Schumann fell in love, exchanging their first kiss in 1835. The following year, Clara's father banned their liaison, and Schumann was forced to break off relations with her. However, the couple took Friedrich Wieck to court, and were eventually married in 1840. Throughout his career, Schumann had claimed the song was an inferior medium to instrumental music, but in 1840 he started to work in the genre. He had written more than 150 pieces before the year was over, including the masterful *Dichterliebe* cycle. Schumann and Clara had a large family (seven children survived). Unfortunately, Schumann, whose family had a history of mental illness, had begun to suffer from severe depression by 1844. He tried to kill himself by jumping into the Rhine River in 1854 and he died in an asylum in 1856.

Alexander Scriabin

(Russian, 1872–1915)

A precocious child born into an aristocratic family in Moscow, Alexander Scriabin studied piano from an early age, and even experimented with building his own instruments. After a period of study at the Moscow Conservatory, he launched into a career as a concert pianist. An injury to his right hand put a temporary halt to his performing career but gave him more time to compose. In 1896, his first orchestral score, *Piano Concerto*, was well received by audiences and earned him some fame. In 1897, Scriabin married and a year later he took up the post of Professor of Piano at the Moscow Conservatory. In 1904, he moved to Switzerland, separated from his wife, and married again. He continued to compose and wrote Piano Sonata No. 5 in 1907, which was a landmark in his rejection of the Romantic legacy. This innovative approach made him a highly influential figure. Composed around the same time, *The Poem of Ecstasy*, an orchestral piece, reflects his interest in the esoteric philosophy of theosophy. Scriabin died from septicemia in Moscow at the age of 43.

ALEXANDER SCRIABIN

Peter Sculthorpe

(1929–2014, Australian)

Peter Sculthorpe wrote music under the bedsheets by flashlight as a boy, after being rebuked by his piano teacher for composing rather than practicing, and he was only 16 when he began studying music at the University of Melbourne. In 1955, his "Piano Sonatina" was selected to represent Australia at the International Society for Contemporary Music Festival in Germany and in 1958 he won a scholarship to study in England. On returning to Australia in 1961, he composed *Irkanda 1*, a moving tribute to his father and a farewell to Europe. From that time onward, he explored the unique sound world of Australia, reflecting the continent's landscape through his work. For example, *Earthcry* (1986) uses the suggestion of Aboriginal chant to lament abuse of the environment by modern civilization. Although Sculthorpe incorporated elements from Japanese and Balinese music into his work, reasoning that Australian art should link to the wider Pacific Rim culture, he most regularly employed sounds native to Australia, as in *Requiem* (2004), a substantial work that makes use of didgeridoos.

Sex Pistols
(active 1975–1978, English)
Formed in 1975, the Sex Pistols were initially comprised of the singer Johnny Rotten, the guitarist Steve Jones, the bassist Glenn Matlock, and the drummer Paul Cook. Overseen by Malcolm McLaren, a former art student, the band built up a following through their iconoclastic attitude and confrontational live shows. Their notoriety was confirmed by adverse reaction to their first single, "Anarchy in the UK," and a pre-watershed television appearance in which they swore. Matlock left the band in 1977 and was replaced by Sid Vicious, a friend of Johnny Rotten, who was initially unable to play the bass. Later in the year, they released their second single, the anti-establishment "God Save the Queen," to coincide with Queen Elizabeth's silver jubilee celebrations. The song was a commercial success, despite being met by widespread condemnation. They released their only album at the end of 1977 and embarked on a brief tour of the United States in early 1978. During this time, schisms emerged between Rotten and the rest of the band and the group broke up. Johnny Rotten went on to form the critically acclaimed post-punk band, Public Image Ltd., and Sid Vicious died of a heroin overdose in 1979.

Ravi Shankar
(1920–2012, Indian)
Born in Varanasi, India, Shankar expressed an early interest in dance, attaching himself to his brother's Company of Hindu Dance and Music. However, in 1938 he traveled to Maihar to study music with Allauddin Khan. From 1944–1948, he performed in venues around India and launched his career as a recording artist in 1948. Shankar left his job as music director for All India Radio in 1956 to become an international performer, visiting the United States and Europe and educating audiences in Indian Carnatic music. By the late 1960s, Shankar's popularity with pop stars such as George Harrison of The Beatles had boosted his fame, and he spent much of the 1970s and '80s performing to international audiences and occupying a teaching post in California, where he lived until his death at the age of 92.

"Pop changes week to week, month to month. But **great music is like literature."**

RAVI SHANKAR, COMPOSER AND SITAR PLAYER

DMITRI SHOSTAKOVITCH

Dmitri Shostakovitch
(1906–1975, Russian)
Born in St. Petersburg, Shostakovich began to learn the piano with his mother at age nine, displaying signs of talent from an early age. He entered the St. Petersburg Conservatory two years after the Bolshevik Revolution of 1917, and enjoyed his first major success at the age of 25, with his Symphony No. 1. He spent much of the 1920s and '30s writing film and theatre scores and in 1932 he married Nina Varzar, a physics student, although he would go on to have several affairs. A victim of the Soviet state's repressive attitude toward art, his 1936 opera was condemned in the state newspaper, *Pravda*. From then on, he was obliged to write state-sanctioned optimistic pieces alongside his more personal work, such as Symphony No. 10, an ambiguous piece written in 1953, the year of Stalin's death. After Varzar's death in 1957, he remarried twice, but during the 1960s his health began to decline. In 1962, he premiered Symphony No. 13: a description of a massacre of Jews in Russia in 1943, it is typical of the bare and hollow style of his later work. After a heart attack in 1966, he spent much of the remainder of his life in the hospital, although he went to England in 1972 to meet his friend, the composer Benjamin Britten.

Jean Sibelius
(1865–1957, Finnish)
Born into a Swedish-speaking family in Finland, Jean Sibelius went to Helsinki to study law, but soon abandoned this to study music full-time at The Helsinki Music Institute. After two years in Berlin and Vienna, he returned to Finland in 1891, taking a position at the Institute. Success came almost instantaneously with the symphonic poem *Kullervo*, a statement of nationalism at a time when Finland was under Russia's control. Although Sibelius was immediately popular with the Finnish cultural establishment, it was not until his Symphony No. 1 in 1899 that he began to achieve international recognition. In 1904, unable to concentrate on composition in Helsinki, he built a house in the country and lived there for the rest of his life. While there, he composed the significant symphonies, Symphony No. 6 and Symphony No. 7.

Flor Silvestre
(1929–2020, Mexican)
Born in the state of Gunanajato in the center of Mexico, Flor Silvestre moved with her family to Mexico City at the age of 13. It was there she began her career as a singer, performing classic songs from the ranchera repertoire. Her profile was boosted by radio stations, firstly XFO, where she rose to prominence, and then XEW, where she won a talent contest that secured her an opportunity to tour Mexico and Central and South America. At the age of 21, she built on her profile as a singer to begin a career as a film actress, which further increased her popularity. She married for the first time in her 20s and had three children, but the defining relationship of her life was with the hugely successful Mexican actor and singer, Antonio Aguilar. Their two sons, Antonio Aguilar Jr. and Pepe Aguilar, are both successful singers in their own right.

Simon and Garfunkel
(active 1957–1970, American)
Childhood friends from New York, Paul Simon and Art Garfunkel enjoyed minor commercial success during the mid-1950s as a pop duo called Tom and Jerry. Although they separated during the late 1950s to go to college, they re-formed in 1963 as a folk duo, releasing the initially unsuccessful album, *Wednesday Morning, 3 A.M.* After a short hiatus, during which time Paul Simon pursued a solo career, Simon and Garfunkel re-formed as a result of enthusiasm for a reworked version of "The Sound of Silence" from their *Wednesday Morning* album. Developing their folk-rock sound, they reached a large audience with their 1966 album *Parsley, Sage, Rosemary, and Thyme,* and their single "Mrs. Robinson," from the soundtrack for the movie *The Graduate,* was a huge commercial hit. They capitalized on this success with the release of *Bridge Over Troubled Water* in 1970, which contained four hit singles and won several Grammy Award. The duo stopped recording together after 1970, with the exception of the 1975 single "My Little Town," although they continue to stage occasional concerts.

SIMON AND GARFUNKEL

FRANK SINATRA

Frank Sinatra
(1915–1998, American)
A native of New Jersey, Sinatra began his singing career with a vocal group called The Hoboken Four, but it was his time working as a vocalist for the bandleader Tommy Dorsey that catapulted him into the public eye. During that two-year period, from 1940–1942, he achieved his first significant hit, "I'll Never Smile Again," which topped the charts for 12 consecutive weeks. However, Sinatra's relationship with Dorsey soured, and he released several records as a solo artist in 1943. In the same year, he began a film career that enhanced his burgeoning fame, but his popularity dwindled in the late 1940s. In 1953, he won an Oscar for Best Supporting Actor in *From Here to Eternity* and a prolific and popular phase of recording followed, beginning with the critically acclaimed album, *In the Wee Small Hours* (1955). Famed for his skill as a singer of ballads, Sinatra also included swing music into his repertoire during this period. His success continued until his premature retirement in 1970. He returned to performing in 1973, continuing to work until he suffered a heart attack in 1997.

Noble Sissle
(1889–1975, American)
Having joined the army in 1918, Noble Sissle played the violin and drums with an acclaimed regimental jazz band, led by Lieutenant James Reese Europe. He continued working with Europe's band after the end of World War I and assumed control of the group with his friend, the pianist and composer Eubie Blake, after Europe's murder in 1919. Sissle and Blake achieved fame in 1921, when they became the first African Americans to write a hit Broadway musical, *Shuffle Along*. Sissle enjoyed success as a bandleader during the 1930s and '40s, touring Europe and working with acclaimed musicians, including the singer Lena Horne and the clarinetist Sidney Bechet. Sissle became a radio DJ in 1954 and continued to promote African-American music until his death in 1975.

Sly and the Family Stone
(active 1967–1975, American)
Involved with professional music as a teenager, Sly Stone studied music during the early 1960s before becoming a DJ and record producer. In 1967, he founded Sly and the Family Stone and their debut album, *A Whole New Thing*, received positive critical reactions, despite being largely ignored by the public. However, their 1968 album *Dance to the Music*, a fusion of pop, rock, and soul, achieved commercial success and *Stand!*, released in 1969, turned them into pop stars. Accessible and innovative, fusing psychedelic rock with funk and pop, the record eventually sold more than three million copies. The band's performance at the Woodstock Festival in the same year established their reputation as a great live act. However, Stone's drug abuse and disaffection with American politics led to friction within the group. Several members left after the release of *There's A Riot Goin' On* in 1970, an album that was definitive in shaping the sound of funk during the 1970s.

Patti Smith
(1946–present, American)
Starting her musical career as a street performer in Paris in 1969, Patti Smith established a reputation as a writer and spoken word artist in New York during the early 1970s, occasionally setting her words to the music of guitarist Lenny Kaye. They began to record their material in 1974, and in 1975 Smith released her debut album, the critically acclaimed *Horses*. Buoyed by the success of punk, she was a popular live performer in Europe and the United States, and she released three other albums during the late 1970s, with *Easter* (1978) achieving the greatest commercial success. After her marriage to a fellow musician in 1980, Smith became a less frequent performer, but her influential early work has earned her the nickname "Godmother of Punk." Her memoir, titled *Just Kids*, won the National Book Award in 2010.

PATTI SMITH

The Smiths
(active 1982–1987 English)
Formed in Manchester in 1982 by the singer Steven Morrissey and the guitarist Johnny Marr, The Smiths also consisted of the bassist Andy Rourke and the drummer Mike Joyce. Their earliest singles, such as "This Charming Man" and "What Difference Does It Make," established the blueprint for their sound, defined by Marr's jangling, melodic guitar riffs and the literate lyrics and distinctive crooning singing style of Morrissey. Having developed a fervently enthusiastic fan base through their singles and live performances, The Smiths released their debut album, *The Smiths*, in 1984 and it reached number two in the UK charts. Despite receiving less critical acclaim, their second album, *Meat Is Murder*, charted at number one in the UK, and their third album, *The Queen Is Dead*, earned them growing support in the United States. They disbanded in 1987 and *Strangeways, Here We Come*, released after their breakup, became their most commercially successful record in the UK.

Southern All Stars
(active 1975–present, Japanese)
Led by the singer and guitarist Keisuke Kuwata, the Tokyo-based pop-rock band Southern All Stars first came to the attention of the public in 1978 with two novelty singles, supported by entertaining live shows. They established themselves as serious artists in 1979 with a ballad, *Itoshi no Ellie*, and released five number-one charting studio albums between 1980 and 1985. In 1982, Kuwata married the band's singer and keyboardist, Yuko Hara. Southern All Stars released their critically acclaimed album *Kamakura* in 1985, and Hara and Kuwata had a child together in the same year. The group returned from a three-year break in 1988, and continued to enjoy success throughout the 1990s and 2000s. They have sold over 47 million records in Japan and are regarded by many people as the most important J-pop band of all time.

Britney Spears
(1981–present, American)
A child television star, Britney Spears achieved instant international fame at the age of 16 with the release of her first album, *Baby One More Time*, which produced several successful singles and earned her the title, "Princess of Pop." Having begun a trend for young female solo performers, Spears released her second album, *Oops!... I Did It Again*, which reached number one in 13 countries. She moved toward a more dance-based adult sound with her fourth album, *In the Zone*, and worked with several famous dance and R&B producers, including Moby and R. Kelly. Although her personal life was the subject of constant media attention throughout the 2000s, she sustained her commercial popularity, releasing several albums—including the critically acclaimed *Glory* (2016)—staging international tours, and enjoying a four-year residency at Planet Hollywood, Las Vegas (2013–2017). Spears is credited with having sold more than 100 million albums around the world.

Bruce Springsteen

(1949–present, American)

Bruce Springsteen launched himself as a solo artist in 1973. Although his first two albums garnered some critical acclaim, 1975's *Born to Run* captured a mainstream audience for his ambitious, melodic rock music. Despite legal battles and a changing musical landscape, he maintained his position as a commercial success during the late 1970s. He experimented with haunting acoustic ballads and crowd-pleasing pop-rock during the early 1980s, before releasing *Born in the USA* in 1984. The album secured Springsteen's position as a giant of mainstream rock, selling 15 million copies, producing seven singles, including "Dancing in the Dark," and launching a two-year tour of large venues. Springsteen continued to challenge his audience during the late 1980s and '90s, turning away from his popular pop-rock sound and releasing several intimate, folk-influenced albums, including *The Ghost of Tom Joad* (1995). From 2000 onward, he actively involved himself with social and political issues, releasing *The Rising*, a 2002 album reflecting on the September 11 attacks of 2001, and supporting Barack Obama's US presidential campaigns of 2008 and 2012. In 2016, Obama awarded Springsteen the Presidential Medal of Freedom.

BRUCE SPRINGSTEEN

Sting

(1951–present, English)

Born Gordon Sumner, Sting began his music career by playing in jazz bands while working as a teacher in the northeast of England. He moved to London in 1977 and formed the band The Police with Stewart Copeland and Henri Padovani. Although they were influenced by punk bands, their music displayed a greater tendency toward catchy, well-produced pop songs with a pronounced reggae influence, often manifested in Sting's bass lines and vocals. With their second album, *Reggatta de Blanc*, and the singles "Walking on the Moon" and "Message In a Bottle," The Police achieved popularity throughout Europe in 1979, and their success spread to America in the early 1980s. Their fifth album, *Synchronicity*, released in 1983, reached number one on both the UK and US charts. The Police disbanded in 1987 and Sting released *Nothing Like the Sun*, an album that displayed the jazz influences of his earliest work in music. In 1993, he moved back toward conventional rock and pop with *Ten Summoner's Tales*, and in 2006, he released an album of John Dowland lute songs to critical acclaim. In 2007 The Police reformed to perform a series of successful concerts. In addition to continuing his music, Sting is known for his ecological activism.

Karlheinz Stockhausen

(1928–2007, German)

As an adolescent growing up in Germany during the 1930s and '40s, Stockhausen's life was dominated by war; his father was declared missing in action in 1945 and his mother is believed to have been a victim of the Nazi's euthanasia policy. In postwar Cologne, Stockhausen funded his music studies by playing in piano bars and accompanying a stage magician. He moved to Paris in 1952 where he studied with the composer Olivier Messiaen and became involved in the birth of electronic music, producing seminal works such as *Gesang der Jünglinge* (1956). He taught at the prestigious Darmstadt school during the late 1950s, and during the 1960s he formed his own ensemble and embarked on several world tours. Always experimenting as a composer, in 1968 he produced *Stimmung*, a 70-minute work for six singers based on a single chord. Toward the end of his life, he focused on completing a cycle of seven operas titled *Licht*—the 29-hour cycle took decades to complete. The first to be written, *Donnerstag*, was staged in Milan in 1981; the last, *Sonntag*, was completed in 2003, and premiered in Cologne in 2011, four years after his death. Alhough they are markedly different in character, all seven operas are linked by three key melodies.

Johan Strauss Sr.

(1804–1849, Austrian)

Of humble origins, Johan Strauss Sr. learned to play the violin in his teens while apprenticed to a bookbinder, spending the evenings performing traditional dances in local taverns. Inspired by Carl Maria von Weber's 1819 piece *Invitation to the Dance*, he expanded the Viennese waltz into a chain of dances framed by an introduction and coda and formed his own orchestra to present these works in 1825. A six-year contract to play at the prestigious Sperl Dance Hall consolidated his fame and he was soon in demand at ballrooms across Europe. During this period, he composed many successful waltzes, including the *Loreley Rheinklänge* of 1844. In 1846 Strauss was appointed the first ever Royal and Imperial Hofballmusicdirektor and two years later he composed the stirring *Radetzky March*, a celebration of an Austrian military victory of Italian revolutionaries.

Richard Strauss

(1864–1949, German)

Born in Munich, Strauss was the son of a horn player in the court orchestra. He began composing at the age of six and received private lessons in music theory and orchestration, but he did not attend a conservatory. In 1885, Strauss became assistant conductor to Hans von Bülow in Meiningen, during which time he developed a deep knowledge of the symphony orchestra. He married the soprano Pauline de Ahna, a general's daughter, in 1894 and she inspired many of his songs. His tone poems of the 1890s established his reputation as an original and unusual composer. The successful Strauss built himself a large villa at Garmish, Germany in 1908. He was the conductor of the Berlin Royal Opera from 1898–1918, and during this period he wrote the hugely successful opera, *Salome*. After a stint as Joint Director of the Vienna Opera, Strauss was given the position of Director of the Reichsmusikkamer by the Nazi party, although he lost the post two years later because of his collaboration with the Jewish librettist Stefan Zweig. Strauss spent much of World War II in Vienna, then returned to Garmish. He died in 1949, but not before completing *Four Last Songs*, settings of four poems, three written by Hermann Hesse and one by Joseph von Eichendorff.

RICHARD STRAUSS

Igor Stravinsky

(1882–1971, Russian)

Stravinsky was born near St. Petersburg, where his father was principal bass singer with the Imperial Opera at the Mariinky Theatre. As a consequence, he grew up around famous musicians, writers, and artists; Borodin, Dostoyevsky, and his future teacher, Rimsky-Korsakov, were all family friends. As a young man, Stravinsky did not display exceptional musical talent and in 1902 he began to study law at St. Petersburg University, learning music with Rimsky-Korsakov in his spare time. Musical success came in 1910 when Serge Diaghilev, director of Ballets Russes, commissioned *The Firebird*. The ballet's Paris première was very successful and also launched the career of another Diaghilev protégé, the dancer Vaslav Nijinsky. As a result, Stravinsky joined Europe's artistic elite, including Picasso, Gide, and Cocteau, many of whom he collaborated with in further ballets. *The Rite of Spring* received its premiere in 1913, displaying an entirely original kind of music that could not be written in a constant time signature. Stravinsky's midcareer period was increasingly influenced by European "Classical" heritage, such as the ballet *Apollon Musagete*, which had its US première in 1928. Stravinsky adopted French citizenship in 1937, but escaped World War II by leaving Europe for America in 1939, after the deaths of his wife and eldest daughter. In the final phase of his career, he adopted unusual compositional techniques, as demonstrated by works such as *Agon* (1954–1957) and *The Flood* (1962). Stravinsky died at the age of 88 and was buried on the island of San Michele in the Venetian lagoon, close to the tomb of Diaghilev.

Arthur Sullivan

(1842–1900, English)

The son of an Irish bandmaster, Arthur Sullivan joined the Chapel Royal as a chorister in 1854 and around the same time he published his first composition. After studying in London at the Royal Academy of Music and then at the Leipzig Conservatory, he wrote cantatas and symphonies before writing his first comic operetta, *Cox and Box*. In 1871 he met the playwright, W. S. Gilbert, and their collaboration produced many notable operettas, including *HMS Pinafore* in 1878 and *The Pirates of Penzance* a year later. Sullivan was knighted in 1883 and he produced his only opera, *Ivanhoe*, in 1891. His famous partnership with Gilbert ended in 1896 and he died four years later.

Donna Summer

(1948–2012, American)

Growing up in a religious family in Boston, Donna Summer's first experience as a singer came as a member of a church gospel choir. During the early-to-mid-1960s she sang with several bands, including the rock group Crow, but her first professional job as a performer was in musical theater. She moved to Germany in the late 1960s to appear in a production of the psychedelic musical *Hair* and married a German citizen, Helmut Sommer. In 1974, Summer collaborated with the Italian producer Giorgio Moroder for her first album, *Lady of the Night*, and the following year they worked together again on "Love to Love You Baby," a huge hit that made her a star in Europe and America. She strengthened her connection to disco in 1977 with the release of the single "I Feel Love," which brought her mainstream popularity and was hugely influential in the development of electronic dance music. Her success continued into the late 1970s, and in 1979 she became the first woman to have three US number one singles in the same year.

THE SUPREMES

The Supremes

(active 1959–1977, American)

The trio of Diana Ross, Florence Ballard, and Mary Wilson, were originally part of a quartet (with Barbara Martin), known as The Primettes, formed as a sister group to the Detroit-based male vocal group The Primes. Their early years, with Ross and Ballard sharing lead vocals, were unsuccessful. Martin left the group in 1961 and The Supreme's registered their first minor hit in 1963, with Ross assuming sole responsibility for lead vocals. Between 1964 and 1965 they made five consecutive number one hits, including "Baby Love" and "Stop! In the Name of Love." The most commercially successful of all the artists on Berry Gordy's Motown label, their 1966 album, *The Supremes A' Go-Go*, displaced The Beatles at the top of the Billboard charts. Despite continued success, Ballard left in 1967 and the group's name was changed to Diana Ross and the Supremes, reflecting Berry Gordy's feelings about Ross's superior public appeal. Ross's stardom eventually led to her leaving the group in 1970 to pursue a solo career. Alhough The Supremes continued until 1977, they were unable to re-create the success of the 1960s.

> "**Music** fills the **infinite** between **two souls**."
>
> RABINDRANATH TAGORE, COMPOSER

Rabindranath Tagore

(1861–1941, Indian)

Born in Kolkata to an aristocratic family, Tagore was exposed to a huge variety of arts and culture, including performances of Bengali and Western classical music. Although he had no interest in formal education, his father wanted him to become a lawyer, and he briefly studied at University College London, though he was more interested in being exposed to English culture, through performances of Shakespeare and folk music. In 1880, Tagore returned to India and in 1883 he married Mrinalini Devi, with whom he went on to have five children. A polymath, Tagore was a prolific author—producing works in several genres, most notably the short story —and a composer. He is credited with the composition of over 2,000 songs. Known as Rabindrasangeet ("Tagore songs"), their structures vary: some follow the well-established ragas of Indian classical music while others are new, drawing on Tagore's knowledge of music from around the world. In 1915, Tagore was knighted but he renounced the honor in 1919 after a massacre of Indians by the British Army. At the age of 60, he took up drawing and painting and his works were exhibited in venues around Europe. Posthumously, two of Tagore's songs became national anthems, making him the only composer to have written anthems for two different countries (India and Bangladesh).

Rachid Taha

(1958–2018, Algerian)

Born in Algeria in 1958, Taha moved to Lyon in France with his parents in 1968. As a teenager in the mid-1970s, he worked as a DJ in the city, playing a variety of musical styles. In 1980, he formed a band called Carte de Sejour, inspired by the attitude and musical experimentation of the British punk group, The Clash. Taha's band released two albums and in 1986, he achieved notoriety with an ironic and anti-establishment cover of a classic sentimental pop song, "Douce France" ("Sweet France"), which was banned from French radio. He launched his solo career in 1989, and during the 1990s his work demonstrated a greater Arabic influence. His greatest critical and commercial success came in 1998 with *Diwan*, an album of raï music, which foregrounded the sound of the traditional Arabic guitarlike instrument, the *'ud*.

RACHID TAHA

ALAN TAM

Seo Taiji

(1972–present, South Korean)

As a teenager growing up in Seoul, Seo Taiji performed with several amateur bands before dropping out of school at the age of 17 to begin a career in music. A year later he formed Seo Taiji and Boys and their first album, a dance-pop crossover, was a huge commercial success, introducing a new sound and aesthetic to South Korea and occupying the number one spot in the charts for 17 weeks, a record at the time. Between 1994 and 1996 the band built up a huge following in South Korea and East Asia as whole, while making a transition from pop music to heavy metal and rap. Although this was a popular move with fans, Taiji was frequently criticized by the Korean Media Ratings Board for producing music that was judged to be inappropriate for his teenage audience. After the group disbanded in 1996, Taiji returned to music and achieved acclaim and popularity throughout the 2000s. Nicknamed the "President of Culture" because of his prominent position in South Korean music, he wrote *The Great Seotaiji Symphony* in 2008, an orchestral reworking of his music to be performed by the Royal Philharmonic Orchestra of London.

Alan Tam

(1950–present, Hong Kong)

Alan Tam began his musical career in 1969 as a vocalist with the Hong Kong band The Wynners. As they rose to fame during the 1970s their style evolved, moving from covers of Western pop songs to original songs written in Cantonese. These recordings were central to the development of the Cantopop genre. Tam built on this success as a solo artist during the early 1980s, achieving fame and phenomenal record sales with his albums and singles of modern ballads. By the end of the decade his prestige was so significant that he began to mentor other artists, resulting in the nickname "Principal."

Ebo Taylor

(1936–present, Ghanaian)

Ebo Taylor rose to prominence in Ghanaian music during the 1950s with two highlife bands, the Stargazers and the Broadway Dance Band. In 1962, he formed the Black Star Highlife band and moved to London, where he collaborated with other UK-based African musicians. Back in Ghana during the 1970s, he developed his sound, combining highlife music with other genres, including afrobeat. Taylor continues to perform and record, and interest in his music from modern hip-hop artists has produced a late flowering of creativity, resulting in several acclaimed albums.

Pyotr Ilyich Tchaikovsky

(1840–1893, Russian)

Pyotr Tchaikovsky was born into a large middle-class family in the provincial town of Votkinsk, in present-day Udmurtia, Russia. After studying law in St. Petersburg, he became a civil servant, studying music privately and displaying only average ability. He left his job to concentrate on music at St. Petersburg Conservatory and during five years under the tutelage of Russian musician Anton Rubinstein he progressed rapidly. He moved to Moscow in 1865 to teach at the newly established Moscow Conservatory and enjoyed celebrity in artistic circles. At the age of 37, Tchaikovsky, a homosexual, entered into a platonic marriage of convenience with an infatuated student, Antonina Milyukova. This situation had a damaging effect on his emotional state and his ability to compose, and the couple separated after two months. In 1875, Tchaikovsky's Piano Concerto No. 1 received its première; its unorthodox mix of Ukranian folk themes, French song, and grand opening tune had caused an argument between Tchaikovsky and his chosen performer, the pianist Nikolai Rubinstein, but the performance was a success. From 1876 onward, Tchaikovsky corresponded with Nadezhda von Meck, a wealthy widow and lover of his music, who became his financial supporter (although they never met, by mutual agreement). By his early 50s, he was ill and depressed. In 1893 he died of cholera. Tchaikovsky composed across a range of genres and styles, including choral settings, symphonies, concertos, and chamber music. However, he is probably best known for his contribution to ballet music. Despite an unsuccessful première in 1877, *Swan Lake* was revised two years after Tchaikovsky's death. This later version is the basis of the ballet we know today.

Georg Philipp Telemann

(1681–1767, German)

Georg Telemann's career in music began with several Church and court positions in Poland and Germany: he took up the role as director of the Leipzig Orchestra in 1704, then moved to the New Church in Leipzig in *c.*1704, before assuming the role of Konzertmeistet in Eisenach, where he formed a friendship with J.S. Bach. In 1721, he was appointed music director and cantor at Hamburg, a prestigious post that he held until his death. Telemann was one of the most prolific composers of the Baroque period and his instrumental works include many orchestral suites, concertos, quartets, trios, and compositions for keyboard. His cantatas and larger church works number over 1,000 and he also wrote 50 operas, including the comedy *Der geduldige Socrates* (*The Patient Socrates*), of 1721. Telemann was an innovator and he was attracted to the forms and styles of French and Italian music that had recently become fashionable. This influence was reflected by his suites and overtures in the French style, concertos and sonatas in the Italian style, and the elements of Polish folk song he incorporated into his work. During his lifetime he was the best-known composer in Germany, supplying demand for his work with a seemingly never-ending stream of compositions. Today, Telemann is chiefly known for his solo and trio sonatas, best exemplified by his magnum opus, *Musique de Table*, a set of works published in three separate anthologies, each containing an orchestral suite, trio, quartet, concerto for solo instruments, and a single-movement piece titled "Conclusion." Another of Telemann's innovations was the German periodical *Der getreue Music-Meister*, which provided amateur musicians with instrumental and vocal pieces for domestic music-making.

Tinariwen

(active 1979–present, Malian)

A Malian Tuareg group formed in Libya, Tinariwen began their musical career by fusing African music, particularly traditional Tuareg melodies and rhythm, with western instrumentation such as steel-string acoustic guitars. The group returned to Mali in 1989 and, after the Tuareg rebellion against the government in 1990, they began to record and perform throughout the Sahara region. Addressing political and social issues through their work,

TINARIWEN

they released their first music outside northern Africa in 2001. Subsequent releases include *Tassili*, winner of a Grammy Award for Best World Music Album (2011), and *Amadjar* (2019).

Ali Farka Touré

(1939–2006, Malian)

Having taught himself several Malian instruments as a teenager, Ali Farka Touré secured a government job as a regional musical director during the 1960s, accompanying, training, and rehearsing troupes of dancers and singers. In 1968, he began to play the six-string acoustic guitar, fusing traditional African music with American blues. He developed his proficiency and unique style while working as an engineer and orchestra member at National Radio Mali and began to release music during the late 1970s. During the late 1980s, the burgeoning interest in world music helped him rise to international prominence and his tours of Europe and North America during the 1990s added to his fame. Touré is often cited as one of the greatest guitarists in the history of the instrument.

Mark-Anthony Turnage

(1960–present, English)

Shortly after his graduation from the Royal College of Music, London, Mark-Anthony Turnage won the Guinness Prize in 1981 for his composition *Night Dances*. In 1988 he was commissioned to write an opera for the Munich Biennale and the result, *Greek*, written along with the playwright Steven Berkoff, was an international success. In 1989, Sir Simon Rattle invited Turnage to become composer-in-association with the City of Birmingham Symphony Orchestra, resulting in the abrasive piece, *Three Screaming Popes*. A jazz music enthusiast, Turnage collaborated with the musician John Schofield in 1996 to produce *Blood on the Floor*, a piece for an ensemble and jazz trio that combines composed music with jazz improvisation. A commercially successful composer, Turnage wrote *Anna Nicole*, a controversial opera about the former model and television personality, in 2011.

U2

(active 1976–present, Irish)

Formed in Dublin while the members were still teenagers, U2 spent six years developing their sound before they won a talent show in 1978. The demo they recorded as part of their prize helped them to secure a record deal and they released their first album, *Boy*, in 1980. Establishing their large-scale, atmospheric rock sound, founded on Bono's strong vocals and The Edge's echoing guitar, their album *War* (1983) gave rise to the major tour that established them as a popular band worldwide. Frequently raising political and social issues, U2 gave powerful live performances until the release of *The Joshua Tree* in 1987, which was a critical and commercial success and became their first number one album in the United States. During the 1990s, they experimented with a range of styles, including industrial and dance, and continued to win acclaim for their ambitious live performances. In 2014, U2 released *Songs of Innocence and Experience*, free on iTunes, to 500 million people. The gesture marked the largest album release ever.

U2

> "The **truth** is when that singer is **saying** something... it affects you right down **within you.**"
>
> BONO, SINGER AND SONGWRITER

Caetano Veloso

(1942–present, Brazilian)

Born in the province of Bahia, Brazil, Caetano Veloso was influenced by the bossa nova music of Joao Gilberto. He moved to Rio de Janeiro in 1965, winning a songwriting competition and signing a record deal shortly afterward. During the late 1960s, Veloso was a founding member of the Tropicalia movement, combining rock with more traditional Brazilian music and writing lyrics that were highly critical of the country's military dictatorship. As a result of government persecution, Veloso moved to London in 1968, returning to Brazil in 1972 to cement his status as one of the country's leading artists. During the 1970s and '80s he stretched himself as a songwriter, combining traditional Brazilian rhythms and sounds with the song structures of pop music. Today, Veloso is acknowledged as an influential figure in music throughout the world.

Giuseppe Verdi

(1813–1901, Italian)

Giuseppe Verdi was born in the village of La Roncole near Parma in Italy, in 1813. His first music teacher was a church organist and Verdi was able to study music at The Milan Conservatory thanks to the patronage of a local grocer. Initially unable to enter The Conservatory because of his inadequate piano technique, he studied privately for two years, then returned to Busseto and married his patron's daughter. In 1839 Verdi's opera, *Oberto*, was performed at the prestigious La Scala, in Milan, but he was afflicted by tragedy when his wife died in 1840. Grief-stricken, he was close to giving up on composing when he was commissioned to write *Nabucco*. The opera's theme of national independence resulted in its great chorus, "Hebrew Slaves," becoming an anthem for the movement for Italian unification. After years of composing one opera every year, Verdi achieved financial independence by the late 1840s. He bought a farm in Sant'Agata in the Emilia-Romagna region of northern Italy and settled down with the singer Giuseppina Streppini, whom he eventually married. During the 1850s, he cemented his reputation as a giant of opera, with the dramatically skillful and musically subtle works of *Rigoletto* (1851) and *La Traviata* (1853). After independence was declared in 1860, Verdi was elected to the first Italian parliament. Verdi continued writing into his old age, composing *Aïda* for the opening of a new opera house in Cairo in 1871, and expanding the power and expression of his vocal writing in *Otello* (1887). Verdi died aged 88 and his body was interred at the Casa di Riposo per Musicisti, a rest home for retired musicians he had established in Milan.

GIUSEPPE VERDI

HEITOR VILLA-LOBOS

Heitor Villa-Lobos
(1887–1959, Brazilian)

Born to a middle-class family in Rio de Janeiro, Heitor Villa-Lobos's early youth was marked by a period of political and social upheaval in Brazil, including the abolition of slavery and the collapse of Brazil's empire. At the outset of his career, Villa-Lobos had very little formal training; he worked as a café musician and toured northeast Brazil to collect folk music. In 1923, he moved to Paris to study, as the beneficiary of a government grant. As a consequence of his background, Villa-Lobos had a diverse set of influences, which are reflected in the eclectic nature of his output. While in Paris, he completed the *Chôros* series; scored for different instrumental ensembles, these are Villa-Lobos's interpretation of the "chorinho," a Brazilian style of music that blends European melodies with Afro–Brazilian rhythms. In 1930, he returned to Brazil and became director of music education for a new nationalist government, incorporating his knowledge of the country's folk music into his reforms. In 1945, he completed his *Bachianas Brasileiras* series, a thorough attempt to fuse Bach's contrapuntal techniques with the spirit of the native music of Brazil. An important composer, educator, and passionate advocate of Brazilian music, Villa-Lobos was awarded a civic funeral in the then capital, Rio de Janeiro, on his death in 1959.

Antonio Vivaldi
(1678–1741, Italian)

Born in Venice, the son of a violinist, Antonio Vivaldi himself worked as a violinist while training to be a priest. In 1703, he obtained a post at Pio Ospedale della Pieta, an institution for abandoned girls where, under his tutelage, his students earned international recognition for their musical prowess. He rapidly made a name for himself as a composer, and publications of his music were widely praised and emulated. In 1713, the governors of the Ospedale commissioned several sacred pieces from him and, later in his career, they requested two concertos a month. It was as a composer of concertos that Vivaldi harnessed his skill as a violinist and orchestrator, writing challenging roles for solo instruments and ensembles. The most famous of Vivaldi's concertos are *Le Quattro Staggioni* (*The Four Seasons*), published in 1725. Each concerto is based around the theme of a season, and was accompanied by an illustrative sonnet printed in the principal violin's partbook. These concertos remained popular long after Vivaldi's death and today they are some of the most frequently recorded and performed works of the classical canon. Vivaldi developed an association with singer Anna Giraud, who appeared in many of his operas and, in 1737, during a public contracts dispute, rumors about their relationship, combined with his refusal to say Mass (due to a bout of asthma), led to him being barred from the city of Ferrara. After some of his operas fared badly, he fell out of favor with the public. On a trip to Vienna, he became ill and died, and was buried in a pauper's grave. Vivaldi is currently credited with over 800 works, including sacred solo and choral pieces, operas, and more than 500 concertos.

ANTONIO VIVALDI

Richard Wagner
(1813–1883, German)

Born in Leipzig, Richard Wagner was educated in Dresden and at the Thomasschule, Leipzig, studying literature and music intensively. He was appointed choral conductor at Würzburg in 1833 and then secured conducting posts at Lauchstädt and Magdeburg. He married actress Minna Planer, but his extravagance and infidelities placed a strain on their relationship. After working in Riga, he went to Paris, where he struggled financially, then returned to Dresden in 1842, eventually becoming court opera conductor. In Dresden he studied German epic poetry, which was to provide him with subjects for the rest of his life's work. Wagner's opera *Tannhäuser*, based on a poem by Ludwig Tieck, was written shortly after his return to Dresden. During a period of exile in Switzerland he wrote several essays, including the important "Opera and Drama" and the anti-Semitic tract "Jewishness in Music." In 1859, he completed the epic music drama of love and death, *Tristan und Isolde*. The turning point in his fortunes came when King Ludwig II of Bavaria invited him to Munich and allowed *Tristan und Isolde* to be staged, conducted by Hans vön Bulow. Wagner fell in love with von Bülow's wife, Cosima, and fathered two children with her before the death of his wife Minna allowed them to marry. In 1871, he moved to Bayreuth, Germany, and was instrumental in the building of a new opera house, Festspielhaus, where his masterpiece, *The Ring Cycle*, was first performed. A complete opera festival in itself, the full cycle takes place over three days and a preliminary evening. Wagner completed his final opera, the Arthurian *Parsifal*, in 1882, and died in Venice in 1883.

Muddy Waters
(1913–1983, American)

As a child growing up in Mississippi, McKinley Morganfield acquired the nickname "Muddy" from his grandmother, Della, and it remained with him for the rest of his life. He started his musical life as a student of the harmonica, but by the age of 17 he was playing the guitar at local parties. In 1932, Waters married but the relationship ended when he had a child with another woman. Over the next 10 years, he became a prominent musician in Mississippi, performing live and recording some songs for folk musician and archivist Alan Lomax. In 1943, he moved to Chicago, initially supporting his music by working as a truck driver, and in 1947 his song "I Can't Be Satisfied" made him famous within the Chicago blues genre. Forming a fruitful creative partnership with the harmonica player Little Walter, Waters was the most prominent electric blues performer of the 1950s, releasing a series of successful singles, including "Rollin' and Tumblin'" and "Mannish Boy." However, his career stagnated during the 1960s—a tour of England was poorly received by audiences unused to his loud electric sound. He revived his career with an impressive performance at a 1976 farewell gig for the roots-rock group The Band, following it up with the critically acclaimed album, *Hard Again*. In 1982 Waters played with Eric Clapton, on whom he had been a significant influence. His health declined rapidly and he died of heart failure the following year.

Judith Weir
(1954–present, Scottish)

As a student, Judith Weir studied with the British composer John Tavener and with Robin Holloway. Interested in Chinese and Indian traditions of classical music, one of her earliest successful works was *The Consolations of Scholarship*, a 1985 piece written for ensemble and soprano, based on a Chinese drama of the Yuan period. She has taught music at universities in Britain and the United States while forging a career as a composer of accessible works with broad appeal, working with children and amateurs to build wider musical communities. She also collaborated with Indian

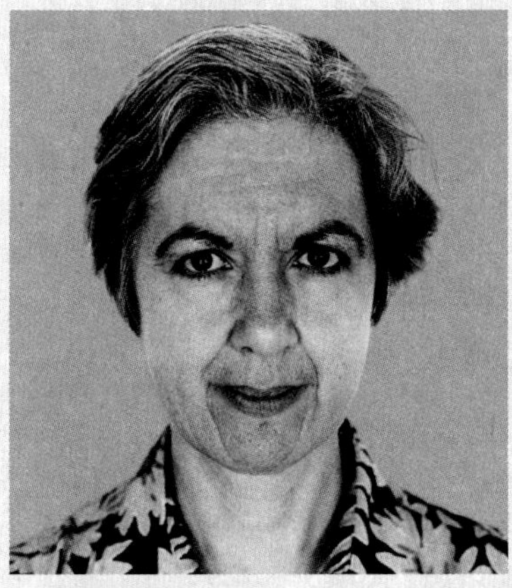
JUDITH WEIR

storyteller Vayu Naidu to create *Future Perfect*, a blend of music and narrative. In 2014, Weir became the UK's first female Master of the Queen's Music.

The Who
(active 1964–present, English)
The definitive lineup of The Who—Pete Townshend, Roger Daltrey, Keith Moon, and John Entwistle—came together in 1964, inspired by a shared love of rhythm and blues. Founded on Pete Townshend's songwriting, the band elevated themselves above other London groups with their combustible stage act, involving the destruction of their instruments. They became a significant recording act in the UK in 1965 with the release of their debut song, "My Generation," and throughout the rest of the 1960s Townshend broadened his palette as a songwriter, culminating with the 1968 rock opera, *Tommy*. Songs from the project constituted a large part of their performance at the Woodstock Festival in the same year. The Who's international fame as a live act grew during the 1970s, and they became the first rock band to perform at New York City's Metropolitan Opera House. Their second rock opera, *Quadrophenia*, was a hit in the UK and the United States on its release in 1973. Their successful run continued until Keith Moon's death from a prescription drug overdose in 1978.

THE WHO

Stevie Wonder
(1950–present, American)
Blind from shortly after birth, Stevie Wonder's first experience of music came as a child member of a church choir in Detroit. A gifted musician, he was able to play several instruments by the age of 10, including the piano. He released his first full album with Motown Records at the age of 12 and had a hit single the following year. During the 1960s, Wonder worked to improve as a songwriter, and his singles from that time, including "My Cherie Amour" and "Signed, Sealed, Delivered," established him as a commercially successful pop-soul crossover artist. He also worked on other chart records, including the Smokey Robinson and the Miracles' hit, "Tears of a Clown." Beginning with the album *Music from my Mind*, from 1972 onward Wonder cemented his reputation as a powerful and creative singer and songwriter. *Talking Book* featured the hit funk single "Superstition," while *Innervisions* produced the single "Living for the City," demonstrating his strength as a political songwriter. His critical reputation peaked with *Songs in the Key of Life* (1976), a double album featuring an ambitious combination of funk, rhythm and blues, soul, and pop. During the 1980s, Wonder enjoyed huge commercial success. He has won more Grammy Award than any other male solo artist.

Yellow Magic Orchestra
(active 1978–1993, Japanese)
Formed by the fledgling keyboardist and music student Ryuichi Sakomoto, the Tokyo-based electronic group Yellow Magic Orchestra also featured drummer Yukihiro Takashi, and bassist Haruomi Hosono, a founder member of the successful Japanese rock group Happy End. Influenced by the innovative German electronic group Kraftwerk, the band released their first album in 1978 and its moderate success encouraged them to perform live and write a second album. Released in 1979, *Solid State Survivor* was an international hit, helped by English lyrics and the single "Behind the Mask," which would later be covered by Michael Jackson. The album went on to sell over two million copies worldwide and turned them into the most popular group in Japan. Prolific pioneers of electronic music, the group disbanded in 1983 having produced eight studio albums. Ryuichi Sakomoto went on to have a solo career as an innovative and prestigious composer.

> "**Music** is the only **religion** that delivers the **goods.**"
>
> FRANK ZAPPA, SONGWRITER AND GUITARIST

Zhou Xuan
(*c.*1918–1957, Chinese)
Born into a poor family in the city of Changzhou in the east of China, Zhou Xiahong was adopted at the age of three by a couple from Shanghai. Displaying talent as a singer from an early age, she enrolled in a musical company at 13 and experienced success in singing competitions. By the mid-1930s, Zhou Xuan—now nicknamed "The Golden Voice"—was China's most famous singer, helped in part by her concurrent career as an actress in successful films. Her repertoire consisted of popular Chinese standards and songs taken from her films. Despite her professional success, Zhou Xuan's personal life was unhappy; all of her romantic relationships failed and during the early 1950s she suffered a series of breakdowns. She died of encephalitis in Shanghai at the age of 39.

Frank Zappa
(1940–1993, American)
As a young man in California with an eclectic taste in music, Frank Zappa played the drums in a rhythm and blues band, before shifting his attention to guitar playing and writing music for films during the early 1960s. In 1965, Zappa joined the rhythm and blues band, the Soul Giants, as a guitarist and in the same year he became chief songwriter and leader of the band. The following year the Soul Giants secured a record deal and changed their name to The Mothers of Invention in the process. Their first album, *Freak Out!*, was released in 1966; a double-LP, it combined conventional rock 'n' roll with more ambitious avant-garde and classically influenced sounds, and occasionally surreal lyrics. After their second album, *Absolutely Free*, The Mothers of Invention moved to New York, where they developed their skills as a live band through regular performances at the Garrick Theatre. In 1968, The Mothers of Invention released the critically acclaimed album, *We're Only in it for the Money*; it was not a major commercial success, and Zappa disbanded the group in 1969. In the same year, he released the well-received solo album, *Hot Rats*, before forming a new version of the band in 1970. In 1971, Zappa sustained serious injuries after being pushed off the stage by a fan, but he returned to music in 1973 and enjoyed the greatest commercial success of his career with the solo album, *Apostrophe* (1974). He continued to work throughout the 1970s and '80s, displaying an increased interest in producing electronic classical music until his death in 1993.

Ziryab
(*c.*789–857, Persian)
Ziryab is believed to have been born in Baghdad at the end of the 8th century during the time of the Abbasid caliphate (750–1258). His musical career began in the city of his birth, where he was a student of the influential teacher and musician, Ishaq al-Mawsili. However, it was after his arrival in Islamic Iberia (an Islamic caliphate located in present-day Spain and Portugal) in 813 that he made a lasting contribution to Arabic music. A virtuoso singer, he developed new methods of vocal training and is credited as the father of Andalusian music, a style of music that is still played across Europe and North Africa. Ziryab is also credited with developing the guitarlike *'ud*, an important traditional instrument in Arabic music.

Instruments

This section contains an overview of musical instruments played in cultures around the world, from the steelpan percussion instruments of the Caribbean to the Western classical violin. A variety of systems are used to classify instruments: the material from which the instrument is constructed, its function, and the primary source of its sound.

Strings

String instruments are those in which sound is generated through the vibration of strings. Although some string instruments use electronic amplification to increase volume, the majority of them are acoustic, and tend to feature a hollow resonating chamber. They are usually plucked, played with a plectrum, or bowed.

Acoustic guitar

The standard acoustic guitar is a hollow-bodied wooden instrument strung with steel or nylon strings. When the strings are sounded, through picking or strumming with the fingers or a plectrum, their vibrations are transmitted to the body of the guitar via the saddle and bridge, creating an amplifying effect. A Renaissance development of medieval stringed instruments, the acoustic guitar is pivotal in rock, blues, folk, and country music.

BANJO

Bağlama

A long-necked, guitarlike instrument, the *bağlama* has a pear-shaped body. Bağlamas vary in size but typically have seven strings, which are separated into two groups of two, and one group of three. These can be played with the fingers or plucked with a cherry-bark plectrum. A traditional instrument, the first written use of the word *"bağlama"* dates back to the 18th century. It is an important instrument in Turkish folk music and is still played widely today.

Balalaika

A three-stringed guitarlike instrument with a triangular body, the balalaika is a traditional instrument in Russian folk music. Although the balalaika began to be used in Russia during the 17th century, its modern incarnation was developed and patented by the violinist Vasily Vasilievich Andreyev during the 1880s. It varies in size and pitch, from the contrabass balalaika (the largest and lowest), to the prima balalaika (the smallest and highest).

Banjo

First developed in the 17th century by enslaved West Africans, and probably derived from African instruments such as the kora, the banjo is a long-necked guitarlike instrument, typically fitted with four to nine strings. The body of a banjo consists of a circular frame with parchment stretched over it, creating a drumlike effect. When a string is plucked or picked, it vibrates on the skin of the drum, creating a loud twangy sound. The banjo was played in minstrel shows during the late 19th century and found its place in jazz bands of the 20th century as well as in folk, country, and bluegrass.

Bass guitar

A four-stringed guitar that is tuned one octave lower than the four lowest strings of an acoustic guitar, the bass guitar has a solid body wired for electric amplification. First developed during the 1930s, its popularity grew along with the development of rock music during the 1960s. It eventually replaced the double bass as the most popular bass instrument for rock and pop groups. It is also a prominent instrument in reggae, funk, and jazz.

Biwa

Played in Japan from the 7th century onward, the *biwa* is a pear-shaped lutelike instrument with a short neck and four or five silk strings, depending on style and size. From the point of its development, the *biwa* was used to provide musical backing to storytelling and as an accompaniment to religious rites. Its popularity declined during the late 19th and early 20th century as enthusiasm for Western music increased. However, the *biwa* has been reincorporated into the work of Japanese composers from the 1960s onward.

Bouzouki

Introduced to Greece in the 1900s by Turkish immigrants, the bouzouki is a deep-bodied, lutelike instrument, usually fitted with six strings separated into three pairs (known as a three-course) and, after World War II, fitted with eight strings (known as a four-course). A staple instrument in Greek folk music, a variant of the bouzouki is also used in Irish folk music. It is not finger-picked but played with a plectrum and produces a clean, metallic sound.

Cello

Developed during the 16th century, the cello is a violin-like instrument with four strings, tuned one octave lower than the viola. Second only in size to the double bass in a symphony orchestra, the large, hollow body of the cello produces a deep, resonant sound and is used as both a solo instrument and as part of a larger ensemble. The cello's popularity grew during the 1700s, and it became a staple instrument in the classical repertoire, replacing many other large bowed instruments. It is also occasionally used in jazz and soul recordings.

Charango

A lutelike instrument slightly more than 24 inches in length, the *charango* is a folk instrument used in South America, primarily in the Andean countries such as Ecuador and Bolivia. It is usually fitted with 10 strings grouped into five pairs. The bodies of traditional *charangos* of the 18th and 19th century were made from the shells of armadillos. Now they are usually made from wood.

CHARANGO

Cittern

A round-bodied, lutelike instrument, the cittern is one of the few stringed instruments from the Renaissance to use steel rather than animal gut strings. Unlike the lute, it has a flat back rather than a rounded one, and usually has eight strings separated into four courses (pairs). It was a popular and widely used instrument between the 16th and 18th centuries.

Classical guitar

The design of the classical guitar is basically the same as the acoustic guitar, but it has a smaller body and wider finger board. It uses synthetic strings, rather than the steel strings of the acoustic guitar, resulting in a mellower sound. The classical guitar is played with the fingers, not a plectrum, and is a staple instrument of the Western classical repertoire.

Cuatro

The name *"cuatro"* refers to the number four in Spanish, historically the number of strings on this small guitarlike instrument. Today, the *cuatro* is a plucked, 10-string (5 course) instrument that comes in a variety of shapes. It accompanies singing ensembles and religious music festivals across Latin America and the Caribbean but especially in Puerto Rico, where it is celebrated as a "national instrument."

Đàn bau
A box zither, with a flexible stem and consisting of a single string positioned over a soundboard, the acoustic *dàn bau* has historically been used in the folk music of Northern Vietnam and Southwest China. However, electrically amplified *dàn bau's* are now a feature of rock music throughout Asia.

Double bass
Measuring approximately 5 ft 10 in, the double bass is the largest and lowest-pitched bowed string instrument in a symphony orchestra. Similar in shape to the violin and the viola, its large hollow body produces its low sound. The four strings—today, made of aluminum-covered steel or nylon-core—can be played with a French or German bow or plucked with the fingers. A staple instrument of classical music, including symphony orchestras and chamber ensembles, the double bass is also regularly used in jazz, blues, and rock 'n' roll.

Dulcimer
Although "dulcimer" is used to describe two different instruments—the hammered dulcimer and the plucked dulcimer—the two differ considerably in form, sound, evolution, and manner of playing. Both have strings stretched across a neckless sound box, making them zithers in certain classification schemes. The plucked dulcimer relies on the fretting of strings to produce many pitches with one or few strings. Guitars, banjos, and fiddles work in this way. The alternative is to have one string or course of strings tuned to each desired pitch, as in the harp, piano, psaltery, and hammered dulcimer. The dulcimer is believed to have originated in the Near East around 900 CE, and probably arrived in Europe during the 16th century. The hammered dulcimer remained popular in the Renaissance and throughout the 19th century. However, except for the newly invented cimbalom, with its sustaining pedal similar to a piano's, the dulcimer disappeared during the first half of the 20th century possibly due to competition from the piano.

Dutār
The *dutār* is a fretted lute with a long, tapering neck, a pear-shaped soundtable, and two or more strings. A traditional folk instrument, it is used in the Middle East and Asia. Methods of playing involve strumming, plucking, or a combination of the two.

Ektārā
Predominantly used in the folk music of southern Asia, the *ektārā* consists of one—or occasionally two—strings positioned over a hollow spherical head, usually made from wood or a dried pumpkin gourd measuring more than 3 ft 3 in long. The string is supported by a split neck, which is pinched together to loosen the string and lower its pitch. The pitch of the instrument is determined by its size, from the largest (bass) to the smallest (soprano).

Electric guitar
The solid-bodied electric guitar uses a device known as an electromagnetic pickup to convert the vibrations of the strings into an electrical signal that is transmitted through an amplifier, then broadcast through a speaker. After its invention in 1931 it became popular with jazz and blues musicians, before achieving prominence in pop and rock music in the second half of the 20th century. More than six decades after bursting onto the American music scene, the electric guitar is featured in all types of music, from country to funk and contemporary classical music.

Erhu
The *erhu* is a Chinese bowed instrument with two strings positioned closely together on a long, narrow neck. The finger is placed on the string to change the pitch of the note but, unlike other fretted instruments, the string is not fully pressed against the neck. Traditionally, the *erhu* was used as an ensemble instrument in opera but during the 20th century it grew in prevalence as a solo classical instrument.

FIDDLE

Fiddle
Developed in Europe during the 11th century, the fiddle is a bowed string instrument that is usually synonymous with the violin. However, it can be used for other stringed instruments. The word "fiddle" tends to be applied to violin-like instruments when they are used in a folk, rather than a classical, context.

Flamenco guitar
The flamenco guitar is similar in design to the classical guitar but has a lighter build, resulting in a more resonant sound. The instrument is held in a vertical position and is played with the fingers rather than a plectrum. A capo—a bar that clamps across the strings—is frequently used to raise the pitch and provide a sharper, clearer sound.

Gayageum
The *gayageum* is a 12-string, zitherlike instrument predominantly used in Korea. The strings are positioned over a wooden fretboard and supported by bridges, which can be moved up and down the neck to adjust the tuning. The strings are plucked with the right hand and fretted with the fingers of the left. The *gayageum* is used in ensembles and as a solo instrument.

Harp
Originating in Mesopotamia in the present-day Middle East, the modern Western harp has 47 strings, spanning six and a half octaves, arranged across a roughly triangular, wooden frame. The harp is usually positioned between the harpist's legs and rested against their right shoulder. The longest side of its frame, known as the column, contains rods connected to seven foot pedals at the base of the column. When pressed, these vary the pitch of the notes. Variations of the harp are found in nearly all the music cultures of the world and are typically used in classical music, often in a solo setting.

HARP

Hurdy-gurdy
The hurdy-gurdy is a short, stringed instrument that shows up in history during the 13th century and became popular with the masses during the 17th century. In the 18th century the French aristocracy favored the instrument and it was included in works by Mozart and Haydn. Sound is produced by using a handle to turn a wheel that rubs against three central melody strings. The music produced by these melody strings can be varied through the use of a small keyboard positioned next to them. The instrument is also usually fitted with drone strings that supply an accompaniment to the melody.

Kayagŭm
The *kayagŭm* is a 12-string zitherlike instrument predominantly used in Korea. It is held in the lap with the lower end pointing away from the body, to the left. The top end rests on the right knee. There are two sizes, with the larger used for court and aristocratic musicians and the smaller for folk and virtuoso music. The strings are plucked with the thicker part of the three fingers and thumb of the right hand, as well as the finger nails, which are flicked along the strings outwardly. Two or three fingers of the left hand, are used to press down on the fretted strings slightly to the left of the bridges.

Kemençe
Kemençe are bowed folk instruments popular in the Eastern Mediterranean. They are fitted with three strings and vary in shape and form. By holding the instrument vertically with the left hand and playing with the right, the player is free to dance.

Kithara
The kithara was an Ancient Greek and Roman instrument used to accompany epics, hymns, and other songs. From the 6th century, it was predominantly used by professional musicians in solos or to accompany singers. More sophisticated than the lyre, it consisted of a large wooden sounding box situated beneath a set of seven strings strung vertically from a crossbar. The strings were picked with a plectrum while unused strings were dampened with the free hand.

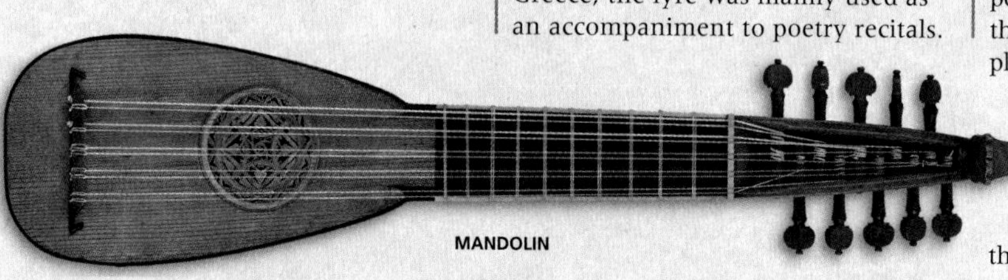
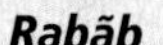
MANDOLIN

Kokyû
The only traditional Japanese string instrument played with a bow, the *kokyû* consists of an unfretted long neck and a smaller resonator. It is similar to the *shamisen*, a long-necked lute that is plucked with a large plectrum. The *kokyû* is usually played during puppet theater or narrative song as a trio with the *shamisen* and koto, a Japanese zither.

Kora
A member of the harp family, the kora is a traditional folk instrument of western Africa. It is typically made from a gourd, cut in half and fixed to a long, hardwood neck. Its 21 strings run from the top of the neck to the bottom of the gourd, and are supported by a bridge positioned in the middle of the gourd. Both hands are used to pluck the strings of the instrument. The kora is usually played by a griot, or storyteller, to provide a musical accompaniment to a story.

Lute
A staple of the secular music of the Renaissance, the lute has a short neck and a pear-shaped body, usually made from hardwood. Medieval lutes usually featured four or five courses of strings, and this number increased through the Renaissance and Baroque eras, when typical lutes were fitted with 13 courses (pairs) of strings. Early lutes were played with a quill, limiting the tone to a single note or a strummed chord. As music developed, strings were plucked with the fingertips, allowing several notes to be played at once. Although the lute was used as a solo instrument and an accompaniment, its popularity declined during the Baroque era. It was rarely used after 1800.

Lyre
A prominent instrument of Ancient Greece, the classical lyre consists of a hollow body made from turtle shell, attached to a frame consisting of two vertical arms and a crossbar. The four to ten strings were played with a plectrum, while the fingers of the non-picking hand were used to dampen the unused strings. In Ancient Greece, the lyre was mainly used as an accompaniment to poetry recitals.

Mandolin
The mandolin consists of a round or droplet-shaped hollow body, featuring a sound hole, a flat or deep back, and a fretted neck. The modern form of the mandolin, with eight strings split into four courses, was developed in Naples, Italy, in the late 18th century. It regularly features in the Baroque and classical repertoire of European music and is also used in the classical and popular music of Australasia, Asia, and South America. It is also prominent in the genres of folk, country, and bluegrass.

Phorminx
Similar in design to the lyre and the kithara, the phorminx is an Ancient Greek instrument consisting of two to seven strings strung from a crossbar between two supporting arms, and positioned over a crescent-shaped wooden sound box, which features two eyelike holes. It was mainly used to accompany recitals of epic poetry and was replaced in popularity by the lyre and the kithara.

Pipa
The *pipa* is a Chinese lutelike instrument with a pear-shaped hollow body and short neck, both of which are fretted. It is fitted with four strings, originally silk, but usually made of nylon, which are plucked with one hand and fretted with the other. Developed more than 1,000 years ago, the *pipa* was most popular between the 6th and 10th centuries, and today, is also used as a solo instrument.

Psaltery
Typically shaped like a trapezoid or rectangle, the psaltery consists of a set of strings stretched over a soundboard. The open strings are plucked with the fingers. It was developed from the *qanum*, a zither from the Middle East that reached Europe in the 11th century. The psaltery was popular in Europe during the Middle Ages, and is still played in Eastern Europe.

Rabāb
The *rabāb* is a two-string lute with a small body and a thin, unfretted neck. A long, wooden or ivory spike pierces the neck and supports the strings at the top while making a foot at the bottom. The strings are played with a curved horsehair bow. Developed in Spain more than 2,000 years ago, it proliferated in North Africa, the Middle East, and the Far East during the Middle Ages. The limited range of the instrument led to it being gradually abandoned in favor of the violin and the lute.

Ravanahatha
Used in the traditional music of Western India, the *ravanahatha* is a fiddle fitted with two strings, one made of steel, the other of bunched horsehair. At its base is a bowl made of coconut shell. The *ravanahatha* enjoyed its greatest popularity with court musicians during the Middle Ages but has recently been revived in Sri Lanka.

Rebec
The rebec is a bowed instrument carved from a single piece of wood with a round or droplet-shaped body tapering into a short neck, topped by a head with tuning pegs. It has two or three strings, which are sounded with a bow. A European version of the Arabic *rabāb*, it was popular during the Middle Ages and early Renaissance but was replaced by the viola during the late Renaissance.

Saz
The term *saz* describes a family of long-necked, deep-bodied lutes, the most common of which is the *bağlama*. It is used in Ottoman classical music and the folk music of the Middle East.

Sitar
The sitar consists of a spherical body, topped by a long neck and a head. It features two sets of strings—principal and sympathetic—supported by two bridges. Seven strings (four melody and three drones) make up a top layer that is actively played, while an additional 12–20 sympathetic strings positioned underneath the fretboard resonate when the top strings are picked. The current incarnation of the sitar was developed in India during the 18th century and is still played today. Although it is mainly a solo classical instrument, it has also featured in Indian and Western pop music.

SITAR

Tamburā
A classical and folk instrument of India, the *tamburā* is a four-stringed lute instrument. It is held vertically and used as a drone. It ranges in size from 2–5 ft long and its strings are plucked in regular patterns.

Tanbūr
The *tanbūr* refers to a diverse group of long-necked lutes, picked string instruments popular in many countries of Central and southern Asia.

Tar
The modern design of the *tar* was developed in Persia during the 18th century. It consists of a long neck,

six strings, sixteen frets per octave spaced at varying intervals, and a body made from two wooden bowls shaped like a figure eight. In addition to the six main strings, there is a bass string positioned outside the fretboard and two support strings situated beneath this bass string. The *tar* is used in the classical music of the Middle East.

Theorbo

Developed in Italy during the 16th century, the theorbo is an adaptation of the bass lute with a deep body, three sound holes, and two sets of strings. The first short set is tuned by pegs on the sides of the fretboard, and gives a higher range, and the second longer set is tuned by pegs at the top of the fretboard, providing the deeper, more powerful bass sound that other lutes of the period could not accommodate. The theorbo could be up to 7 ft long and was used in chamber and orchestral pieces in Europe.

'Ud

A cornerstone of traditional Arabic music, the *'ud* is similar in design, construction and sound to the lute, and has a deep body with a short and fretless neck. The number of strings on an *'ud* varies by type and region. There are typically 10–12 strings, separated into five or six courses. Occasionally, there is a drone string, which provides a continuous backing to the sounds created by the melodic strings. It is used as an accompaniment to secular and religious music, and is a prominent instrument in the musical cultures of Asia, the Middle East, and Africa. It was pivotal to the classical music developed in Islamic Iberia between the 8th and 15th century.

Ukulele

The ukulele is a small guitar developed in Hawaii during the 19th century from the Portuguese *cavaquinho*. It has four strings that are plucked or strummed, while the pitch of the notes is changed by fretting the strings at the neck. Different sizes relate to different pitches, from the smallest (soprano) to the largest (baritone). The ukulele is mainly used in folk, jazz, and pop music.

Veena

The *veena* is an ancient stringed instrument of India. It has a large round body made from a gourd and a long, wide, hollow neck topped by a dragon head. The neck includes 24 metal frets and a resonator at the rear. Four metal strings produce the melody while three drone strings run alongside the neck. Used in Indian classical music, it is believed to have given rise to the sitar in the 18th century.

Viol

The term "viol" is used to describe a family of bowed string instruments popular during the Renaissance and Baroque periods. While viols have a similar shape to the violin, they are larger and played between the legs like the cello. Viols have six strings, flat blacks, and flat, fretted necks. They were primarily used in European orchestral ensembles.

Viola

The second highest member of the violin family, the viola is slightly larger than the violin and has a deeper sound. Its construction is similar to that of the violin, with four strings, "f" sound holes, an unfretted neck, and a slightly rounded back. Traditionally playing an important role in chamber and orchestral music, in the 20th century, its solo repertoire considerably expanded.

Violin

The violin is the highest pitched and smallest member of the violin family. Its proportions were developed during the 16th century and underwent modification during the late 18th century. The modern bow was developed in the 19th century. The violin consists of an hourglass-shaped hollow body with a pair of "f" sound holes, and an unfretted neck, topped with a scroll. It is fitted with four strings which can be bowed or plucked. It is a central instrument of classical music and is also used in Indian classical music, folk music, and pop and jazz.

'UD

ACCORDIAN

Zheng

A traditional Chinese zither, the *zheng* consists of 18–23 strings mounted on a soundboard, supported by movable bridges. The strings are plucked or picked with one hand and fretted with the other to change the note.

Zither

The zither is a class of stringed instruments with no neck, where the strings run the length of the body, which acts as the resonator. The classes are divided on the basis of shape, construction, and playing technique, and include the trough zither, stick zither, tube zither, long zither, and board or box zither such as the Appalachian dulcimer and psaltery. Most popular in Central and Eastern Europe and East Asia, the zither is predominantly a folk instrument.

Woodwind

Most woodwind instruments feature a mouthpiece fitted with a single or double cane reed. When air is blown into them, the vibration of the reed creates sound. Flutes and piccolos are not fitted with reeds, but are still classed as woodwind instruments.

Accordion

The box-shaped accordion has a set of keys, or buttons, and a bellows. The player contracts and expands the bellows to push wind across brass strips located inside the instrument. The keys or buttons are pressed to determine which strips the air passes over, thus sounding different notes. Developed in 19th-century Europe, it is mainly a folk instrument and is now also played in North and South America.

Arghūl

A single-reed instrument, the *arghūl* features two pipes made of cane, one long and one short. The short pipe usually features six finger holes that are used to create melodies, while the longer pipe acts as a drone. Developed more than 2,000 years ago in Egypt, it is now played across the Arab world.

Atenteben

The recorder-like *atenteben* is made of bamboo, with seven finger holes—six on top and one underneath—and a mouthpiece with a slit through which air is blown. Developed in Ghana, it is used as a folk and classical instrument.

Aulos
The term *aulos* refers to a family of single- and double-piped flutelike instruments featuring a double-reeded mouthpiece. The most important wind instrument of Ancient Greece, the *aulos* is believed to have produced a high-pitched sound and was traditionally associated with professional musicians.

Bagpipes
Bagpipes consist of a windbag and a set of pipes. The bag is positioned under the arm and the player pumps the bag to force air across the double-reeds of the pipes. The number of pipes in a set varies and includes a melody pipe with multiple drone pipes, which produce a sustained accompanying note or notes. Prevalent in Europe from the Middle Ages onward, where they are often referred to as musettes, bagpipes are also popular in the folk music of the Middle East, although they are probably most closely associated with Scotland.

BASSOON

Bandoneon
The *bandoneon* consists of a bellows positioned between two sets of buttons. The bellows are pumped to drive air through the instrument while the buttons control the chords that are produced. A staple of Argentinean tango ensembles from the early 20th century, the *bandoneon* is also popular as a folk instrument in Eastern Europe.

Bassoon
The bassoon evolved from Renaissance instruments, though its modern form—and that of its cousin the contrabassoon—is the result of 18th- and 19th- century improvements. Its long narrow body is made of wood and has five main finger holes and additional finger pads on the sides. It features a horizontally protruding hooked mouthpiece equipped with a double reed, in which two pieces of reed vibrate against each other when air is blown across them. The bassoon and contrabassoon—which usually plays music an octave lower—are prominent members of the concert orchestra.

Bawu
The *bawu* is a horizontally played flutelike instrument fitted with a single reed. It has a long cylindrical body made of a bamboo tube that is closed off at one end. The tube typically features six finger holes. With its pure sound, the *bawu* is a popular traditional solo and ensemble instrument in southern China.

Calliope
The calliope consists of large whistles tuned to different notes that are sounded with steam or compressed air. The choice and length of note sounded can be controlled through a keyboard or a mechanical operation. The instrument enjoyed its greatest popularity during the 19th century and was mainly used on riverboats, due to the availability of steam.

Chalumeau
A recorder-like instrument, the *chalumeau* consists of a short, cylindrical wooden body with seven finger holes on the front and one finger hole on the back. It is played vertically by blowing through a mouthpiece fitted with a single reed. Developed during the Middle Ages, it was popular in Europe in the 17th century, although it was later superseded by the clarinet.

Clarinet
The clarinet is a cylindrical tube, usually made of wood or plastic, with a bell-shaped end. It features numerous finger holes on both its back and front, and is played through a single-reed mouthpiece. Clarinets range in size and pitch from the piccolo (smallest and highest) to the contrabass (largest and lowest). The modern clarinet grew in popularity during the 18th century and is now a staple of the European concert orchestra. It is also used in jazz music and in the klezmer music of Jewish eastern European origin.

Concertina
Similar to the accordion, but hexagonal in shape, the concertina features a bellows positioned between two sets of button keyboards, one for each hand, that determine the melody. Developed in Germany and England during the 19th century, the concertina was a popular dance instrument. It is now a feature of European folk music.

Crumhorn
A curved horn, the crumhorn consists of wooden body shaped like the letter "J" and dotted with finger holes. It features a double reed enclosed inside a cap with a slot to blow into to produce sound. The pitch of the note is altered by opening or closing the finger holes. The crumhorn was a popular instrument during the Renaissance but fell out of favor during the Baroque period.

CRUMHORN

Didgeridoo
Consisting of a long tubular body usually made from hardwood, the didgeridoo has two open ends, one of which is treated with wax to create a mouthpiece. The player sounds the instrument by blowing into the mouthpiece using circular breathing, a technique in which air is drawn in through the nose while simultaneously being expelled from the mouth. By blowing into it and singing at the same time, the didgeridoo can combine a variety of rhythms, pitches, and timbres. It was one of three original instruments of northern Australian Aboriginal people as much as 1,500 years ago. Used as a secular and spiritual instrument, it is still played today.

Duct flute
The term duct flute applies to flutetype instruments that consist of a simple tube. These include the fipple flute, whistle flute, recorder, penny whistle, or slide whistle. Their pitch is produced by air moving through a narrow channel (duct), then strikes a sharp edge of a hole causing the air to split and vibrate. The upper end of the channel is blocked by a fipple (a plug or block) that forces the air through the duct. Finger holes change the length of vibration and thus change the pitch.

English horn
Similar to an oboe, the English horn has a wooden tubular body with a bulb-shaped end and a mouthpiece fitted with a double-reed. It was developed during the early 18th century in what is now Poland. It grew in popularity in the 19th century in the orchestral repertoire.

Fife
A fife is a wooden, narrow, flutelike instrument that is played horizontally. The player creates sound by blowing across the embouchure hole (mouthpiece) and changes the notes by using the fingers to block the six sound holes. Used in the Middle Ages as a dance accompaniment, the fife is now a staple of European and North American military marching bands.

Flageolet
There are two types of flageolet: the French, which consists of a tubelike body with four front finger holes on the front and two thumb holes on the back, and the English, which has six, sometimes seven finger holes on the front, and one thumb hole on the back. The player blows into the mouthpiece to create sound and varies the note by covering the finger holes. The flageolet was developed during the 16th century and was popular in England with amateur musicians. It was played in France until the 19th century.

Flute
The flute is made of a cylindrical tube typically featuring 16 finger pads, one closed end, and one open end. It is held horizontally and is played by blowing across the embouchure hole (mouthpiece). The notes are altered by pressing on the pads. The current incarnation of the flute was developed

"I do not consider myself as having **mastered the flute,** but I **get a real kick out** of **trying.**"

JAMES GALWAY, FLAUTIST

during the Baroque period and is a now a staple of concert and chamber orchestras. Variations of the flute are used around the world in folk music, Latin American dance music, and jazz.

Guan
Consisting of a short, cylindrical tube made of hardwood, the *guan* traditionally features seven finger holes on the front and one on the back. Its mouthpiece is fitted with a double reed. Over 1,000 years old, the *guan* began as a court instrument but is now a staple of Chinese folk music, also called *guanzi*.

Harmonica
The harmonica, or "mouth organ," is a handheld instrument consisting of reeds enclosed between two cover plates. The player blows directly into the air chambers forcing air over the reeds. Air is directed towards different reeds and keys to create notes of different pitch. The harmonica was developed in Europe during the 19th century and is used mainly in blues, folk, and country music.

Harmonium
The harmonium is a small reed organ in which the player generates sound by pumping foot pedals. It was intended for use in homes and small churches as a compact replacement for a full-sized organ. Popular in Europe, America, and the Indian subcontinent during the 19th century, manufacture ceased in the 1950s. Although the harmonium is played in Western classical and pop music, it was mainly used for religious music earlier. Today, a smaller harmonium, used in India since around 1875, is featured widely in Indian classical and nonclassical music.

PANPIPES

Melodica
The melodica consists of a small portable keyboard fitted with a mouthpiece. The player blows air through the mouthpiece over a reed, and the keyboard is used to create an organlike effect. The modern melodica was developed during the 1950s and has predominantly been used in dub and reggae music.

Nay
The *nāy* is a flutelike instrument consisting of a hollow tube, typically made of reed or cane, and featuring six finger holes on the front and one thumb hole on the rear. Estimated to be 4,000–5,000 years old, it is a staple of the traditional music of the Middle East, as a solo or orchestral instrument, or an accompaniment to storytelling.

Nose flute
Typically consisting of a single piece of bamboo with three or four finger holes, the nose flute is a popular instrument in Polynesia, Africa, China, and India. The player positions the top end of the flute by their nostril and breathes into it. Techniques of playing vary based on region: in the Philippines, for example, the free nostril is plugged to increase the power of the breath coming from the active nostril.

Oboe
The oboe is a wooden tube featuring metal keys, a flared bell, and a protruding double reed. Developed during the 17th century, its clear and bright sound makes it an effective instrument in the concert orchestra. Despite being a predominantly classical instrument, the oboe is occasionally used in jazz music.

Panpipes
The pan flute, or panpipes, are a hand-held rack of pipes, usually made from bamboo or cane, and gradually increasing in length; the longer the pipe, the lower the pitch. The pipes are stopped at one end and the player blows across the open end to create a melody. Panpipes are a popular instrument in the traditional music of East Asia, Eastern Europe, and the Andean region of South America.

Piccolo
A half-sized flute, the piccolo sounds an octave higher than the normal flute. Apart from its size, it is similar in construction to the concert flute, though the body of the instrument can be made from resin, wood, brass, or a variety of other materials, while the western concert flute is traditionally made from metal or wood. Invented in the late 1700s, it is used in classical music.

Rackett
The soft sounding rackett is a double reed cylindrical instrument produced in four sizes and pitches: Descant (highest), Tenor-alt, Bass, and Great bass (lowest). During the Renaissance period, a pirouette or cap partially encased the reed, but in the Baroque era, the pirouette was replaced by a bocal that allowed the double reed to be fully exposed.

Recorder
The recorder is one of the most widely used duct flutes. It consists of a tube, usually made of wood or plastic, with seven finger holes on the front of the instrument and a thumb hole on the back. The recorder was popular as a classical instrument during the Middle Ages and Baroque era but was usurped in popularity by the clarinet and flute. Today it is popular in musical education.

Regal
The regal is a small, portable organ made up of a keyboard and two bellows. The bellows are used to pump air over the brass reeds of the instrument, which are positioned next to resonators. Typically, regals were operated by two people—one to play the keyboard and the other to pump the bellows. Popular during the Renaissance, the regal was used both as an ensemble and as a solo instrument.

Saxophone
The saxophone is a woodwind instrument with a brass body, a mouthpiece fitted with a single reed, and between 20 and 23 tone holes that are pressed to effect changes in pitch. The earliest saxophones came in seven sizes in two parallel groups, one for the orchestral and another for the band, or military, group. The pitches and sizes range from the sopranissimo (highest) to the subcontrabass (lowest). Invented by Adolphe Sax in the 19th century, the saxophone gained popularity as a marching band instrument, but is now best known as a staple of jazz. It is also featured in classical orchestras and in funk, soul, pop, rock, and Afrobeat repertoires.

Shawm
The shawm, a woodwind instrument, predecessor to the oboe, and popular during the Renaissance and Middle Ages, consisted of a single tube of wood with a flared end. It came in seven sizes and featured a double-reed. The shawm was a popular instrument in military bands and as a dance accompaniment.

Shehnai
The *shehnai* is an oboelike instrument consisting of a wooden, tubelike body with a metal flare bell at the lower end. It uses a quadruple reed and typically features between six and nine finger holes. The *shehnai* is played in religious and secular music in India, Pakistan, and Iran.

Tárogató
The *tárogató* has a wooden conical-shaped body and a single-reed mouthpiece. Similar in design to the clarinet, it was heavily revised and developed during the late 19th century and is a prominent instrument in the folk music of Hungary.

Zhaleika
The *zhaleika* is a wooden-bodied pipe with a single reed. It is fitted with a cow horn at the end, which produces extra resonance. A staple of Russian folk music, it is used as both a solo and ensemble instrument, as well as an accompaniment for song and dance.

TAROGATO

Brass

Brass instruments are wind instruments in which sound is produced through a combination of air and the vibration of the player's lips on the mouthpiece. Many of these instruments are fitted with valves, which are used to control the pitch of the note played. Although many brass instruments are made of brass, not all instruments constructed from brass are classified as brass instruments; saxophones, for example, are categorized as woodwind instruments.

Alto horn

Resembling a small, upright tuba, the alto horn is a three-valved brass instrument with a large bell flare, which is pointed forward when it is played. The alto horn was a staple feature of European and American brass bands of the first half of the 19th century. In concert bands, it was replaced by the French horn and the euphonium during the second half of the 20th century.

BUGLE

Bugle

The bugle is a brass horn that typically features no valves, unlike the trumpet or the cornet. The player creates different notes by changing the shape of their mouth against the mouthpiece. Popular in Europe from the late 18th century, the bugle is predominantly a military instrument.

Cornet

Similar to the trumpet, but more mellow in sound, the cornet has a more compact shape and a smaller mouthpiece. It evolved from the horn during the 19th century and became a fixture of the symphony orchestra before eventually being replaced by the trumpet. It was used in jazz bands in the early 20th century, but is now primarily a feature of brass band music around the world.

Euphonium

The euphonium is a miniature member of the tuba family, featuring a conical bore, flared bell, and four valves for controlling pitch. The instrument is usually held from the bottom with the bell facing upward. Developed during the 19th century, it is a staple of military bands.

Flügelhorn

Similar to a trumpet, the pitch of a flügelhorn is controlled through three valves. Developed during the 19th century, it is widely used in jazz and brass band music.

Mellophone

The mellophone is a hornlike, three-valved brass instrument with a large bell flare that points forward when the instrument is played. The mellophone is a staple feature of marching bands and, from the 1950s onward, has been used as a concert instrument.

Organ

The organ drives pressurized air through multiple pipes of different pitch and timbre to create a rich sound that can be sustained indefinitely while a key is being pressed. The player operates the organ through the use of a keyboard and a pedalboard operated with the feet. Fixed-position pipe organs became more common in churches during the Renaissance and Baroque period and much of the music composed for the instrument is religious, although organs do appear in many concert halls.

Sackbut

The English term sackbut, meaning literally "push-pull," was the Renaissance and Baroque equivalent of the trombone. It is a brass instrument that uses a slide to effect changes in pitch. During both periods the sackbut was used in a large repertoire of pieces, including sacred music, chamber music, and also as an accompaniment to courtly dancing.

Sarrusophone

The sarrusophone is a double-reeded instrument with a brass body. It was developed during the 1850s as a louder alternative to the oboe and the bassoon. It comes in eight sizes and pitches, from the smallest and highest (sopranino) to the largest and lowest (contrabass). The sarrusophone is rarely used today and although it occasionally featured in the classical repertoire, it was mainly used in wind bands.

Trombone

This brass instrument uses a slide mechanism to extend its length, thus changing the pitch of musical notes. Trombones come in a range of pitches, from the piccolo (highest) to the contrabass (lowest); the most commonly encountered version of this instrument is the tenor and bass. Trombonelike instruments were used in Europe from the 15th century onwards and were prominent features of the concert orchestra during the Baroque and Classical eras. It is also a staple of brass bands, jazz, and Latin American and Caribbean music.

Trumpet

The trumpet is a brass instrument, featuring three valves that can be used to alter the pitch of notes when pressed. Trumpets come in a range of keys and sizes, although the most commonly used trumpet is the B flat. Trumpetlike instruments have existed around the world for more than 3,000 years and the instrument was a feature of the classical repertoire during the Middle Ages, Renaissance, and Baroque eras. However, the trumpet is now most closely associated with jazz and Latin American music.

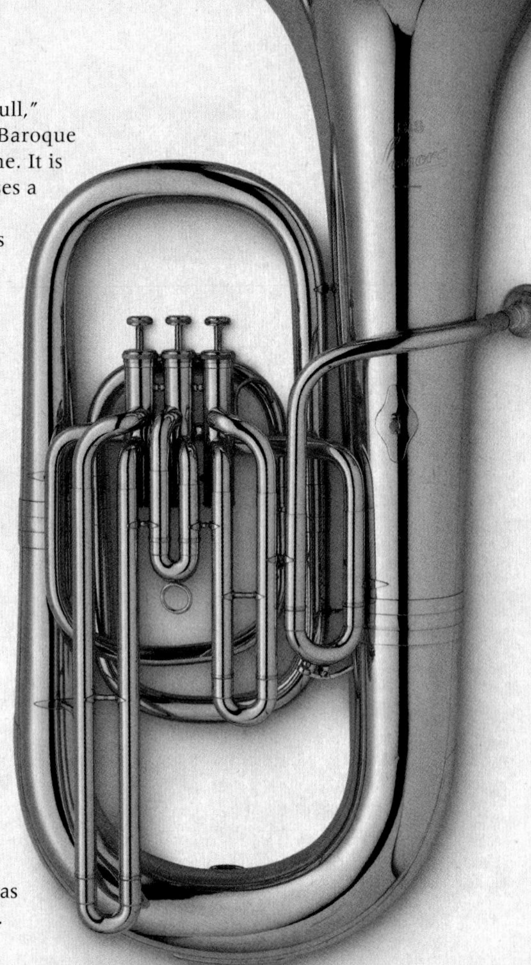

TUBA

Tuba

The tuba is a large, brass instrument that has three to five valves to alter the pitch of its notes. It comes in a variety of pitches, from the subcontrabass tuba to the tenor. It can be played in the lap or cradled under the arm. It was developed during the mid-19th century, and is now a staple instrument in concert orchestras and brass bands. The tuba is also a popular jazz instrument.

"Men have died for **this music.** You **can't get more serious** than that."

JOHN BIRKS "DIZZY" GILLESPIE
JAZZ TRUMPETER & COMPOSER

Percussion and Keyboards

Percussion instruments are sounded by being struck with the hand or with a stick. Although the percussion family is traditionally associated with instruments such as the drums, keyboard instruments are technically members of the percussion family.

Idiophones

Idiophones are percussion instruments in which sound is created through the vibration of the body of the instrument.

Castanets
A pair of castanets consist of two shallow, shell-shaped pieces of wood, which are linked by a cord and looped around the thumb. The castanets are clicked together to create percussive rhythms. Associated with the music of Spain, particularly the flamenco genre, castanets have also been used in opera, and African and Ottoman dance music.

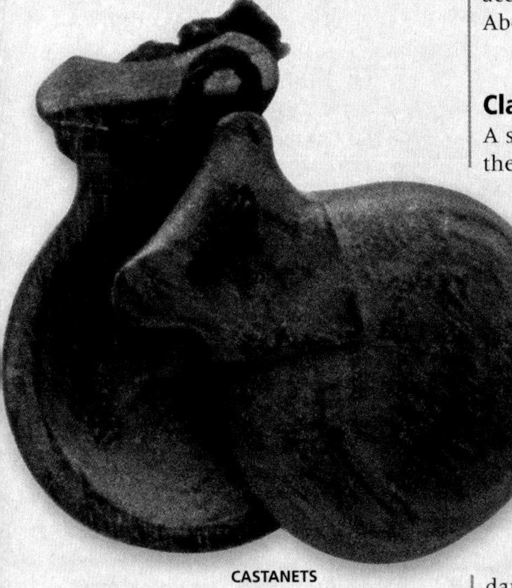
CASTANETS

Balafon
Cousin to the xylophone, the *balafon* usually has up to 21 tuned keys, either mounted above gourd resonators or positioned on a flat surface. The keys are struck with padded sticks. Developed in West Africa, it is best known as a traditional solo and ensemble instrument. It enjoyed a resurgence in popularity in West African pop during the 1980s.

Cajon
The *cajon* consists of a box, usually made from thick wood, with a thin piece of plywood attached to it. The player sits on top of the box and strikes this piece of plywood, known as the head, generally using the palms of their hands. The volume produced by the instrument is increased by a sound hole cut into the wood on the opposite side to the head. The *cajon* was developed by Afro-Peruvian enslaved people and today is used widely in all types of music.

Chimes
Chimes, also known as tubular bells, consist of a set of metal tubes hung from a frame. Each tube, or bell, is of a different length, resulting in a set of tubes that produce different notes when struck with a padded hammer. Chimes are used within classical music, pop, and occasionally in religious compositions.

Clapsticks
Indigenous to the Aboriginal tribes of Australia, clapsticks, or *bimli* (a Yolngu Aboriginal name), are short, thick wooden sticks used to accompany the didgeridoo. They are held in separate hands by the player and clashed together to create a rhythmic accompaniment, often to an Aboriginal vocal chant.

Clavichord
A small stringed keyboard instrument, the clavichord was invented during the 14th century. The sound of a clavichord is generated by iron or brass strings, which are struck by small metal blades when a key is pressed. Its comparatively quiet sound meant that it was generally used as an instrument for practice rather than performance.

Cowbell
Frequently used in Latin American dance music, clapperless cowbells are bells made from metal that are struck with a stick or, in West Africa, clashed together. Although they are most commonly used as a rhythmic accompaniment in South and Central American dance music, the cowbell is also occasionally used in pop music. The clapper cowbell is sometimes used in orchestral pieces.

Cymbals
Cymbals are thin metal disks used in musical cultures throughout the world. In the ancient world, they were tuned to a specific note but in modern music they are used for their percussive quality. In popular music they are typically a part of the drum kit, either in the form of a crash or ride cymbal, or a hi-hat. In an orchestra, hand-held clash cymbals are used—these are played by bringing two cymbals together to create a crashing sound.

Gamelan
The term "gamelan" refers to an Indonesian musical ensemble composed mainly of percussion instruments. It also refers to the instruments used by these ensembles. These include drums, gongs, and metallophones. Every individual element of the gamelan is tuned to the other instruments in the orchestra.

Gankogui
The *gankogui* consists of two connected bells—a large, low-pitched bell at the bottom of the instrument, and a small higher-pitched bell at the top. The bells are struck in varying patterns to create a rhythmic effect, providing a reference point for other instruments. It is mainly used by the Ewe people in Ghana, Togo, and Benin, though it is known throughout West Africa.

Glockenspiel
The glockenspiel consists of a set of metal bars arranged by size and pitch, from the longest (lowest) to the shortest (highest). The keys are struck with mallets with a plastic, metal, or hard rubber head. Its range of pitch allows for melodic and percussive effects. Taking its modern form in the 17th century, the glockenspiel is popular throughout the world. It is often used in the Western classical orchestra.

Gong
Although gongs vary in shape and design, they are united by the presence of a metallic disk that is sounded with a mallet. The suspended gong—hung from a frame—is the most widely used. It consists either of a flat, metallic disk, or one with a raised center, called a boss. These gongs produce different sounds; a flat surface results in multiple notes, while the boss gong provides a tuned note. Gongs are a staple of the Indonesian gamelan.

GONG

Handbell

A small hand-held bell fitted with a flexible leather wrist strap, a handbell is usually played in ensembles, known as "handbell choirs," with each bell tuned to a different note of a scale. The size of handbell choirs ranges from 25 to 97 bells. They are generally used to play church music.

Hang

Developed in Switzerland in 2000 by Felix Rohner and Sabina Schärer, the Hang is constructed from two hollow steel hemispheres joined together. The top has a center raised note with seven or eight indentations or "tone fields" around it. The lower half is plain with a center hole; when struck on the rim, it creates a note. The Hang is typically rested in the player's lap and sounded with the palms and fingers.

Harpsichord

Prominent in Europe during the Renaissance and Baroque periods, the harpsichord is a keyboard-based instrument. It is often set in a large wooden casing similar in shape to today's grand piano, though with a narrower and longer rear. Harpsichords generally have two keyboards, tuned to different octaves, so as to accommodate a wider range of notes. Many classical pieces are written for harpsichord solos but during the 19th century, the instrument's popularity was eclipsed by the piano.

MARACAS

HARPSICHORD

Maraca

The maraca is a hand-held percussion instrument made up of a gourd shell, or a wooden or plastic oval, filled with seeds or dried beans, and attached to a handle. The maracas are usually played in pairs and sound is generated by shaking the instrument, causing the beans or seeds to rattle inside the shell. The maracas are a regular feature of Latin American music but are also used in pop and rock music.

Marimba

The marimba consists of wooden bars covering between 4 and 5.5 octaves. These bars are fitted above resonator tubes that are usually made from aluminum. Originally from Africa, marimbas are a prominent percussion instrument in Latin American music but also frequently appear in jazz and classical music.

Mbira

The mbira is the most important instrument in sub-Saharan Africa. Depending on the region, the mbira, as it is called in Zimbabwe, has many different names and designs. Generally it consists of 5 to 33 wooden or metals keys, divided into two layers. The fingers of both hands are used to play the instrument by stroking the keys. Small brittle objects, such as bottle caps or shells, may be positioned on the soundboard, creating a buzzing sound.

Piano

One of the most popular instruments in the world, the recognizably modern form of the piano began to emerge in the late 17th century, designed by the Italian Bartolomeo Cristofori. Building on medieval keyboard instruments—such as the clavichord—the smoother action of the piano allowed for subtler, more nuanced forms of playing. Its louder volume made it a suitable instrument for public performance. This early form of the piano was known as the fortepiano. There are two main types of modern piano which evolved during the 19th century—the grand, in which the strings are arranged in a horizontal frame, and the upright, in which the strings are arranged in a vertical frame. Although the piano is a staple instrument of the classical repertoire in Europe, much of the 18th- and early-19th-century music performed on it today was written for the fortepiano. It is now popular in many genres of music, including jazz, blues, pop, and rock 'n' roll.

Steelpan (steel drum)

The steelpan is a large percussion instrument, traditionally made from the top of a large steel barrel or oil drum. The base and sides of the steelpan are struck with rubber-tipped mallets to produce notes of different pitch and tone. Developed in Trinidad and Tobago, the steelpan is played throughout the Caribbean and is a feature of calypso and soca music, as well as Latin American music and jazz.

Tambourine

The tambourine has a circular frame, usually made of wood or plastic, inset with small cymbals known as "jingles" or "zils." One face of the frame is covered with a drumskin. The tambourine is played by shaking the frame or striking the

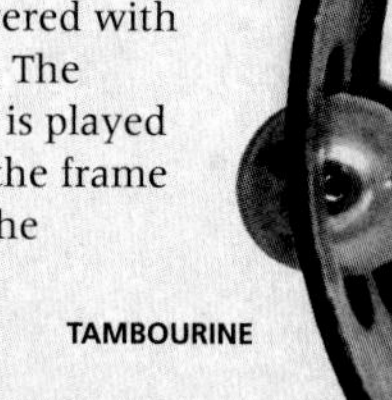

TAMBOURINE

drumskin with the hand or a stick. The instrument is a feature of Greek, Italian, Middle Eastern, and American folk music. It is also used in Western classical music, pop, and rock.

Triangle

The triangle is a hand-held instrument made of a metal bar bent into the shape of a near-complete triangle. The player strikes it with a metal hammer. Inspired by its use in Turkish military bands, the instrument has featured in the Western classical orchestra since the 18th century and is still used today. It also features in the folk and pop of Europe and South America.

Vibraphone

The vibraphone consists of a set of aluminum bars tuned to different notes—typically spanning a three-octave range—positioned over a corresponding resonator tube. The resonators each have valves at their upper end, controlled by a motor. Pedals similar to those on a piano are used to dampen the sound, if the pedal is not used, or lengthen the sound, if depressed. Similar in appearance to a xylophone, the vibraphone is played by striking the metal bars with padded-headed mallets. Developed during the 1920s, it is predominantly used in jazz.

Wood block

The wood block is made from a single piece of wood, with a section of wood removed to increase resonance. The wood block is struck to produce a percussive sound. Designs vary around the world, from the rectangular wood block of the Western classical orchestra to the hollowed log drums of East Asia.

Xylophone

Xylophones vary in size and can cover between 2.5 and 4 octaves. They consist of differently pitched wooden bars, with an equal size resonator beneath, which are struck with plastic or rubber-tipped mallets. Xylophone-like instruments are used around the world, including Africa and Southeast Asia, where they are called *marimba*. In the West, they are mostly used in classical and jazz music.

Membranophones

The majority of membranophones are drums, in which sound is produced from the vibration of a stretched skin, or membrane. An instrument within this category that does not require a stretched skin is the kazoo, a voice-operated mirliton.

Ashiko

Developed by the Yoruba people of Nigeria, the *ashiko* is a tapered cone-shaped drum with a wooden base, a goat-skin hide that is slapped with the palms of the hand, and tuning ropes. It can produce a range of tones and pitches and is used in all of sub-Saharan Africa.

Bass drum

The bass drum is large and cylindrical, and usually fitted with a drumskin on both faces. Methods of playing and mounting vary, depending on its function; marching bands, for example, employ a portable bass drum carried on straps around the neck, orchestral bass drums are mounted on a stand and beaten with drum sticks, while the bass drum in a rock drum kit is operated with a foot pedal. The instrument was developed in the Middle East and is now a feature of many genres of music around the world.

Bodrhán

The *bodrhán* has a circular frame with one face covered with a drumskin and the other left open. The most common method of playing the instrument involves the use of a double-headed stick, known as a beater. The non-striking hand is positioned at the open side of the drum and can be used to dampen the sound or change the pitch of the drum by applying pressure to different areas of the skin. The *bodrhán* is a popular instrument in traditional Irish and Scottish music.

Bongo

The bongo consists of two connected drums, one slightly larger in diameter, both featuring a hollow, wooden body and one playable end covered with a drumskin. They are usually struck with the palms of the hands, although they can also be played with drum sticks. The instrument can be placed between the knees or mounted on a stand. Of Afro-Cuban origin, the bongos are a dominant feature of son, rumba, and many other Latin American genres. The instrument is also used in jazz and funk.

BONGO

Candombe

An upright barrel-shaped drum, the *candombe* comes in bass, tenor, and alto pitch variations. The drum's body is made of wood and the skin at the top end of the instrument is played with sticks or with hands. The *candombe* drum is used as an accompaniment to the spiritual *candombe* dancing of Argentina and Uruguay.

Chenda

The *chenda* consists of a cylindrical, wooden body with two playable covered ends. It is a portable drum that is normally hung from the player's neck with a strap. The ends of the drum occupy different pitches—one end is covered with several layers of skin to create a deeper sound. Usually played with a stick, the *chenda* is used in Hindu ceremonies, as well as in dance and ritual ensembles in the southwestern state of Kerala in India.

Conga

Developed in Cuba, the conga is a narrow, upright barrel-shaped drum with one playable skin-covered end. It is played with the hands, and depending on where and how it is struck, the instrument can produce a variety of tones. Conga drums grew in popularity through their use in Cuban genres such as rumba, but they are now also popular in Latin America and the Caribbean, regularly featuring in salsa and reggae music.

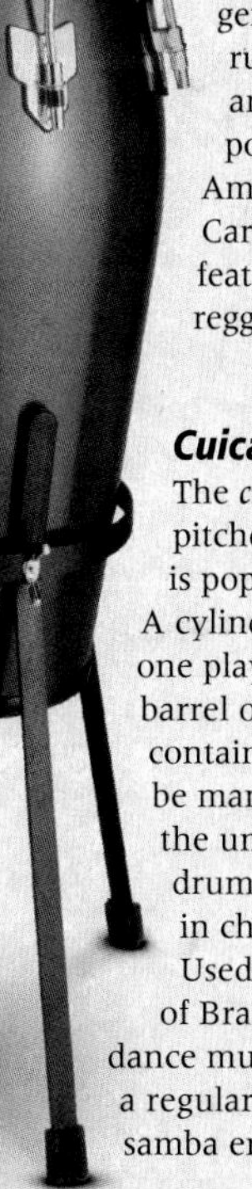

CONGA

Cuica

The *cuica* is a high-pitched drum that is popular in Brazil. A cylindrical drum with one playable end, the barrel of the drum contains a stick that can be manipulated against the underside of the drum skin resulting in changes in pitch. Used in a variety of Brazilian folk and dance music genres, it is a regular feature of samba ensembles.

Daff
The *daff* is a portable round, square, or octagonal drum, with one or two playable skin-covered faces. The frame is usually inset with metal ringlets or, in some cases, small cymbals. It was developed in Iran before the 7th century and was used in Iranian religious ceremonies and classical music. It continues to be an important instrument in the Middle East, usually as an accompaniment to a stringed instrument, such as an *'ud*.

Darabukkah
The *darabukkah* is an Islamic goblet-shaped drum with a single head. The body can be made of wood, clay, or various metals. The *darabukkah* is the heart of an ensemble, providing the rhythmic base. It is predominantly used in folk music of the Middle East, as well as during wedding celebrations.

Davul
The *davul* is a portable double-headed bass drum with a cylindrical, hardwood body. The ends of the drum are covered with different thicknesses of skin, resulting in variations of pitch. These differences are accentuated by the use of a heavy drum stick on the thick-skinned end and a light switch on the thin-skinned end. The *davul* is a common feature of folk music in the Middle East and Eastern Europe.

Dhol
A portable and double-headed, barrel-shaped drum, the *dhol* is created from a wooden body and has heads that can be adjusted to different pitches. The *dhol* is hung from the player's neck with a strap and played with sticks of varying thickness, which correspond to the deeper and thicker, as well as, higher and thinner heads of the drum. It was developed during the 15th century and is used as a folk and religious instrument throughout the Indian subcontinent.

Djembe
The djembe has a wooden, goblet-shaped body with a single playable head. A loud instrument with a variety of tones, the djembe is played with the hands. It has been popular throughout West Africa since the 13th century and is used in a range of musical styles.

Drum kit
Developed in its modern form during the early 20th century, the drum kit is a collection of percussion instruments and is a staple set in a range of Western music genres, including pop, rock, blues, jazz, soul, and funk. The drum kit includes a range of cymbals, such as the hi-hat, and drums, including the bass drum. Some of these are played with sticks while others are operated with foot pedals.

Dunun
Dunun is a term used to describe a family of double-headed cylindrical drums that are popular in West Africa. From largest to small, they are the *dundunba*, *sangban*, and *kenkeni*. They are played horizontally, either on a stand or hung from the player. *Dununs* are usually played in an ensemble, creating melodic variations between the instruments.

Mridangam
The *mridangam* of southern India is a double-headed barrel-shaped drum which is used to accompany dancing. The right drum is the female voice and includes a "black eye" in the center of the drumhead, while the left, is male with a plain drumhead. The player sits crossed-legged with the drum on its side and plays with the hands.

Snare drum
A vertical double-headed cylindrical drum, the snare drum features an unplayed head fitted with snares that make a rattling sound when the drum is struck. It is played with sticks or, if a softer sound is required, with brushes. Its distinctive sound was developed during the 18th century. Today it is used in marching bands and, most frequently, in the rock or pop music drum kit.

Surdo
The *surdo* is a double-headed bass drum with a body typically made of plastic or steel. Its top head is played with a large, padded drumstick, while the bottom head of the drum is not played. Despite its large size, the *surdo* is a portable instrument and is hung from a shoulder strap or belt worn by the player. It is an important instrument in the samba music of Brazil.

DRUM KIT

TABLA

Tabla
The tabla consists of two portable and unconnected, upright single-headed drums. These vary in size, with the larger drum supplying a deeper pitch. It is played with a variety of strokes, using the fingers and palms of both hands. It is a central instrument in Hindustani classical music and is a feature of religious music in the Indian subcontinent.

Tabor
The tabor consists of a wooden cylindrical frame covered with two skins and fitted with a catgut snare. Hung from the left shoulder, the instrument is sounded by striking the snare with a stick. It is often paired with a duct flute with three holes. The player plays the pipe with his left hand and the tabor with his right. The pair were played in Western Europe between the 13th and 19th centuries.

Tambora
Similar to West African drums in both rhythm and technique, the *tambora* is prominent in the Dominican Republic. It is a two-headed drum made of a hollowed tree trunk. The left end is played with the hand and the right with a stick. It is used for fast upbeat music such as merengue, the cumbia music of Colombia, and gaita style of Venezuela.

Taogu
The *taogu* is a small double-sided, hand-held, pole-mounted drum with two wooden beads at the end of strings, which are attached to either side of the drum. Holding the pole between both hands and rubbing them back and forth make the drum whirl and the beads hit either side of the drum. The *taogu* is played in Chinese folk music as well as Confucian rituals.

> "I haven't loved any other instrument as I have **loved the tabla** and the tabla is my life..."
>
> USTAD ALLAH RAKHA QURESHI
> TABLA PLAYER

Timpani
Timpani, or kettledrums, have a large, bowl-shaped body with a single head stretching over a hoop, which is held in place by a metal ring with screws. The screws allow the skin's tension to vary, producing a definite pitch. Typically made of copper, the drums are mounted on a stand and played with drumsticks fitted with a large, padded head usually made of tightly wrapped felt. Timpani were first used in an orchestral setting in Europe during the 15th century and are now a staple of the classical orchestra.

Tombak
The *tombak* is a hand drum comprising of a single head stretched over a goblet-shaped wooden body. Played with the hands, it is regarded as the primary percussion instrument of Persia (modern-day Iran). Although its early use was restricted to accompaniment, the *tombak* is now an established solo instrument.

Tom-tom
A cylindrical drum, the tom-tom consists of a shell body with one playable head and is not fitted with a snare (rattles). Developed in Asia, the tom-tom is now a staple feature of the Western rock and pop drum kit.

Electronic

Electronic instruments describe any instrument in which sound is produced electronically. The range of electronic instruments is large, from synthesizers to more esoteric instruments such as the theremin.

Drum machine
The drum machine is an electronic instrument used to replicate the sound of a drum kit. The first commercial drum machine was produced in 1959 and they were increasingly used in popular music during the 1960s and '70s. As the drum machine became more sophisticated, its popularity also increased, and it was a staple of music production from the 1980s onward due to its use in dance genres.

Electronic keyboard
The electronic keyboard features a plastic keyboard that can be used to play a variety of synthesized instruments and prerecorded sound effects. Its modern form developed from early electronic instruments, such as the Hammond organ. It is mainly used in pop and electronic music.

Ondes Martenot
The ondes Martenot is an electronic keyboard that uses vacuum tubes to produce a distinctive wavering sound. Developed during the 1920s by the French musician and cellist Maurice Martenot, it is used in classical and pop music and has also featured in many film and television scores.

Sampler
The sampler is used to electronically record and play samples of sounds and instruments. It typically features effects such as filtering or modulation that can be used to alter the original sound. Although samplers were used during the 1960s and '70s, the development of digital sampling made the process more cost-effective and they grew in popularity with dance-music producers during the 1980s. They are frequently used in pop music and occasionally feature in classical works.

Sequencer
Sequencers are used to record and edit music. Originally produced in analogue form between the 1940s and '60s, sequencers have developed into digital and software-based forms. The sequencer is now used in the recording and editing of most forms of music.

Synthesizer
The synthesizer is designed to replicate the sound of numerous instruments and is typically played through a keyboard. The modern form of the synthesizer was developed during the 1950s, and grew in popularity with rock and pop musicians during the '60s. It became established as a staple instrument during the '70s and '80s with the rise of electronic pop, hip-hop, and dance.

Theremin
The theremin is an electronic instrument consisting of an amplifier and two antennae—a looped antenna that controls volume and an upright antenna that controls pitch. To play the instrument, the player moves the hands around the antennae without actually touching them, producing a wavering electronic noise. Developed in Russia during the 1920s, the theremin is used in classical and pop music and also in film scores.

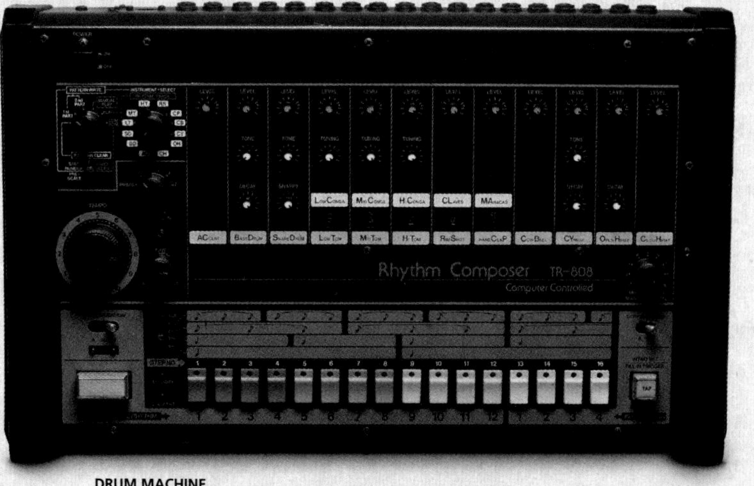

DRUM MACHINE

Index

Page numbers in **bold** indicate main entries

D

E

K

L

M

N

S

T

U

V

W

X

Y

Z

Acknowledgments

Dorling Kindersley would like to thank the following for their contributions:

National Portrait Gallery, Catalogue of American Portraits: Linda Thrift, E. Warren Perry, Jr., Eden Stone for allowing us to photograph their collections:

National Music Museum Inc. of the University of South Dakota.
Special thanks to Dr. Cleveland Johnson, Dr. Margaret Banks, Rodger Kelly, Anthony Jones, Dr. Deborah Check Reeves, Dennis Acrea, Arian Sheets, Matt Zeller, Hannah McLaren Boyd, Micky Rasmussen; Bate Collection, Faculty of Music, University of Oxford.
Special thanks to Andrew Lamb; Royal Academy of Music. Special thanks to Angela Doane, Ian Brearey, Barbara Meyer; Southbank Centre Enterprises Ltd. Special thanks to Shauna Wilson, Sophie Ransby.

For editorial and design assistance: Lili Bryant, Sanjay Chauhan, Amy Child, Steve Crozier, Susmita Dey, Suhita Dharamjit, Phil Fitzgerald, Dharini Ganesh, Alison Gardner, Clare Joyce, Anita Kakar, Himani Khatreja, Rakesh Khundongbam, Amit Malhotra, Rupa Rao, Anna Reinbold, Upasana Sharma, Pallavi Singh, Priyaneet Singh, Sharon Spencer, Ina Stradins, Jacqui Swan, Duncan Turner, Francis Wong, Michael Yeowell. For his Kylie Collection: Joe Luff

Picture Credits

The publisher would like to thank the following for their kind permission to reproduce their photographs:

(Key: a-above; b-below/bottom; c-center; f-far; l-left; r-right; t-top)

1 Dorling Kindersley: Southbank Enterprises (br). **2–3 Photo SCALA, Florence. 4 Corbis:** Werner Forman (tc). **Dorling Kindersley/The National Music Museum Inc** (crb). **Getty Images:** A. DAGLI ORTI / De Agostini (bc); Donald Nausbaum (cb). **4–5 Dorling Kindersley:** (cb); The Bate Collection (bc). **5 The Bridgeman Art Library:** Giraudon (br). **Corbis:** Fred de Noyelle/Godong (tc). **Dorling Kindersley:** The Royal Academy of Music (cr). **6 Dorling Kindersley:** The Bate Collection (c). **Getty Images:** John Kobal Foundation (br); Universal History Archive (bl). **7 Getty Images:** Phil Dent / Redferns (br); Michael Ochs Archives (bl). **8–9 Getty Images:** Michael Ochs Archives. **10–11 Dorling Kindersley/The National Music Museum Inc. 12 Corbis:** Gianni Dagli Orti (cb). **Dorling Kindersley:** Geoff Dann (bl); Philip Dowell (cra, cl); Dave King (cr). **Getty Images:** De Agostini (br); Werner Forman / Universal Images Group (cla). **13 Corbis:** Alfredo Dagli Orti / The Art Archive (cl). **Dorling Kindersley:** Kate Clow, Terry Richardson, Dominic Whiting (bl); Dave King (cr). **Getty Images:** The Bridgeman Art Library (br); A. DAGLI ORTI / De Agostini (ca). **14 Alamy Stock Photo:** Images & Stories (b). **15 Dorling Kindersley:** Dave King (bl). **Getty Images:** Werner Forman / Universal Images Group (tl). **Rex Features:** Michael Runkel / Robert Harding (br). **16 Getty Images:** De Agostini (bl). **17 akg-images:** R. & S. Michaud (br). **Dorling Kindersley:** Geoff Brightling (clb). **Getty Images:** De Agostini (ca). **18–19 akg-images:** (b). **18 Corbis:** Gianni Dagli Orti (cla); Alfredo Dagli Orti / The Art Archive (cra). **19 Ancient Art & Architecture Collection:** Archaeological Museum of Delphi (tl). **TopFoto.co.uk:** Charles Walker (cr). **20 Corbis:** Ruggero Vanni (ca). **Dorling Kindersley:** Kate Clow, Terry Richardson, Dominic Whiting (b). **21 Corbis:** Robbie Jack (tl). **Getty Images:** Hulton Archive (bc). **22 Corbis:** Werner Forman (cla). **Dorling Kindersley:** Andy Crawford / Pitt Rivers Museum, University of Oxford (cr); Philip Dowell (ftl, tl, tc); The National Music Museum(tr, ftr); Geoff Dann (c, clb, cb); Clive Streeter (crb); The Bate Collection (bl); Peter Hayman / The Trustees of the British Museum (br). **23 Dorling Kindersley:** Geoff Brightling (tr); Alan Hills / The Trustees of the British Museum (bl); Dave King (tc); Dave Rudkin / Birmingham Museum And Art Gallery (l/ cl). **Getty Images:** G. DAGLI ORTI / De Agostini (ca, cl). **24–25 Getty Images:** A. DAGLI ORTI / De Agostini (b). **24 Getty Images:** Werner Forman / Universal Images Group (cl). **25 Dorling Kindersley:** Christi Graham and Nick Nicholls / The Trustees of the British Museum (c). **Getty Images:** The Bridgeman Art Library (tc). **26–27 Getty Images:** The Bridgeman Art Library. **28 Alamy Stock Photo:** Domenico Tondini (br). **Dorling Kindersley:** Demetrio Carrasco (cra); The National Music Museum (c). **Getty Images:** The British Library / Robana (cla); DeAgostini (bl). **29 Dorling Kindersley:** Geoff Dann (cra); Laurence Pordes / By permission of The British Library (br). **Dreamstime.com:** Shchipkova Elena (bc). **Getty Images:** The British Library / Robana (clb); DeAgostini (cr). **30 Dorling Kindersley:** Tony Souter (bc, clb). **Getty Images:** DeAgostini (cra). **31 Getty Images:** The British Library / Robana (l). **32 Country Life Picture Library:** (tr). **Getty Images:** DeAgostini (bl); Universal History Archive (c). **33 Getty Images:** DeAgostini (l). **34 Dorling Kindersley:** Geoff Dann / Tony Barton Collection (tl, c, br); Philip Dowell (ftl); The Bate Collection (tc, tr); Geoff Dann (cr). **35 Dorling Kindersley:** Andy Crawford (ftl); Geoff Dann / Tony Barton Collection (tl, tc, clb, br); The Bate Collection (ftr); Geoff Dann (bl). **Lebrecht Music and Arts:** (tr). **36 Dorling Kindersley:** Laurence Pordes / By permission of The British Library (t). **37 Alamy Stock Photo:** Domenico Tondini (br). **Corbis:** Stefano Bianchetti (tr). **Dorling Kindersley:** Laurence Pordes / By permission of The British Library (tc). **Getty Images:** The British Library / Robana (bl). **38 Getty Images:** De Agostini (cla). **38–39 Dorling Kindersley:** Geoff Dann (b). **39 Alamy Stock Photo:** Loop Images Ltd (br); Photos 12 (tl). **40 Getty Images:** The British Library/ Robana. **41 Dorling Kindersley:** Idris Ahmed (bl); The National Music Museum (c). **Getty Images:** ACK GUEZ / AFP (crb). **42 Dorling Kindersley:** Geoff Dann (br); The National Music Museum (bc, cra, cb, bl, tr); The Bate Collection (l). **43 Alamy Stock Photo:** AA World Travel Library (ca). **Dorling Kindersley:** Philip Dowell (tr); The National Music Museum (fcr, tl, tc, bc, cr); Dave King (bl, c, bl). **44 Alamy Stock Photo:** The Art Archive (tl). **Getty Images:** Werner Forman / Universal Images Group (b). **45 Corbis:** Lawrence Manning (tl). **Dorling Kindersley:** Demetrio Carrasco (br); Geoff Dann (cl). **46–47 Dreamstime.com:** Shchipkova Elena (bc). **46 Getty Images:** DeAgostini (cla). **47 akg-images:** (cl). **Corbis:** Bettmann (br). **SuperStock:** Newberry Library (tr). **48–49 Dorling Kindersley/ The National Music Museum Inc. 50 Corbis:** The Gallery Collection (br). **Dorling Kindersley/The National Music Museum Inc** (cr). **Getty Images:** De Agostini (c); Murat Taner (cl). **51 Corbis:** The Gallery Collection (cr). **Dorling Kindersley:** The Bate Collection (cl); The National Music Museum (bc). **Getty Images:** The British Library / Robana (crb, c). **52 Dorling Kindersley:** Geoff Dann / Tony Barton Collection (cl). **SuperStock:** Fine Art Images (bc). **53 Corbis:** The Gallery Collection (bc). **54 Getty Images:** De Agostini. **55 Corbis:** Ken Welsh / Design Pics (cla). **Dorling Kindersley:** Dave King (cr). **Getty Images:** The British Library / Robana (br). **56 Corbis:** The Gallery Collection (t). **Dorling Kindersley:** By permission of The British Library (bl). **57 Dorling Kindersley:** Geoff Dann (l). **Lebrecht Music and Arts:** (bc). **58 The Bridgeman Art Library:** Private Collection / Archives Charmet (b). **Dorling Kindersley:** Nigel Hicks (cla). **Getty Images:** The British Library / Robana (tr). **59 Corbis:** David Lees (tc). **Dorling Kindersley:** John Heseltine (bc). **Lebrecht Music and Arts:** R Booth (cra). **60 akg-images:** (r). **61 The Bridgeman Art Library:** Private Collection (cr). **Lebrecht Music and Arts:** leemage (bl); Graham Salter (tc). **62 Photo SCALA, Florence. 63 Alamy Stock Photo:** Pictorial Press (cra). **Getty Images:** The British Library / Robana (c); JME International / Redferns (br). **64–65 Dorling Kindersley/The National Music Museum Inc. 64 The Bridgeman Art Library:** British Library Board. All Rights Reserved (ca). **Dorling Kindersley:** Geoff Dann (cla); The National Music Museum (cr, bl); The Bate Collection (tl). **Getty Images:** De Agostini (tr). **65 Dorling Kindersley:** The Royal Academy of Music (tc, tr, cra). **SuperStock:** Newberry Library (tl). **66 Dorling Kindersley:** Christine Webb (ca). **Lebrecht Music and Arts:** (br). **67 Getty Images:** The British Library /Robana (l). **68 Dorling Kindersley:** Geoff Dann (bl); The National Music Museum (bc); The Bate Collection (ftr, clb, tc, cb, fbl, c, tr). **69 Dorling Kindersley:** The Royal Academy of Music (tl, cl); The National Music Museum (br, bc, bl, cr). **70 akg-images:** Album / Oronoz (t). **71 Corbis:** Charles Caratini / Sygma (tc). **Dorling Kindersley/The National Music Museum Inc** (bl). **Mary Evans Picture Library:** Iberfoto (cr). **72–73 Getty Images:** Mondadori Portfolio / Contributor / Hulton Fine Art Collection (b). **72 akg-images:** Russian Look (cl).**73 Photoshot:** World Illustrated (br). **Photo SCALA, Florence:** (tl). **74–75 Dorling Kindersley/The National Music Museum Inc. 76 Dorling Kindersley/ The National Music Museum Inc** (cr, bl, cl). **Getty Images:** Filippo Lauri (crb). **77 Corbis:** Stefano Bianchetti (c). **Dorling Kindersley:** The Bate Collection (bl); James Tye (crb). **Getty Images:** DeAgostini (bc); Patrick Landmann (ca); RDImages / Epics (cl); Universal History Archive (cb/a). **78 Dorling Kindersley:** Dave King (cl); The National Music Museum(br). **Getty Images:** DeAgostini (ca). **79 Dorling Kindersley:** The Bate Collection (l).**80 akg-images:** Erich Lessing. **81 Alamy Stock Photo:** MORANDI Bruno / hemis.fr (br); Lebrecht Music and Arts Photo Library (bl). **Getty Images:** Murat Taner (cra). **82–83 The Bridgeman Art Library:** Leeds Museums and Art Galleries (Temple Newsam House) UK (b). **82 The Bridgeman Art Library:** Musée des Beaux-Arts, Orleans, France/ Giraudon (ca). **83 Getty Images:** DeAgostini (tl). Lebrecht Music and Arts: (cr). **84 akg-images:** (cl). **Dorling Kindersley/ The National Music Museum Inc** (ca). **Getty Images:** Filippo Lauri (bl). **85 Photo SCALA, Florence:** White Images (t). **86 Dorling Kindersley:** The Royal Academy of Music (br); The National Music Museum(bc, crb); The Bate Collection (clb). **Getty Images:** De Agostini (bl). **86–87 Dorling Kindersley:** The Royal Academy of Music (t). **87 Alamy Stock Photo:**epa european pressphoto agency b.v. (crb). **Corbis:** Bettmann (bc). **Dorling Kindersley:** The Royal Academy of Music (tr, ca); Stephen Oliver (bl). **Getty Images:** De Agostini (cb); Image Source (br). **88 Dorling Kindersley:** Anna Mockford (l). 89 **Dorling Kindersley:** The National Music Museum(bc, cl). **Getty Images:** Patrick Landmann (tc). **Lebrecht Music and Arts:** Celene Rosen (crb). **90 Dorling Kindersley:** Dave King (crb); Gary Ombler (cra); The National Music Museum(tc, tl, br); The Bate Collection (tr, cr). **90–91 Dorling Kindersley:** The National Music Museum (t). **91 Dorling Kindersley:** Dave King (ca, c); The National Music Museum (tc, bl); The Royal Academy of Music (cb); The Bate Collection (br). **Getty Images:** DeAgostini (bc). **92–93 Corbis:** Stefano Bianchetti. **93 Corbis:** Arne Hodalic (bc, cr). **Getty Images:** DeAgostini Picture Library / Scala, Florence (tc). **94 Alamy Stock Photo:** The Picture Art Collection (t). **The Bridgeman Art Library:** 2011 Her Majesty Queen Elizabeth II (b). **95 Dorling Kindersley: 96 akg-images:** Stefan Diller (bl). **Corbis:** Arno Burgi / dpa (fcl). **Dorling Kindersley/The National Music Museum Inc** (cl, cra, crb, r). **Getty Images:** De Agostini (clb). **Lebrecht Music and Arts:** (br, fbr). The Bate Collection (t). **Getty Images:** Johan Closterman (cr); Peter Willi (c). **97 Getty Images:** Don Paulsen/Michael Ochs Archives (br). **Alamy Stock Photo:** Everett Collection Historical (bc). **Dorling Kindersley/The National Music Museum Inc** (c). **98 akg-images:** IAM (clb). **Alamy Stock Photo:** The Art Archive (bc). **99 Alamy Stock Photo:** The Art Archive (br). **Getty Images:** The British Library /Robana (l). **100 Corbis:** Alfredo DagliOrti / The Art Archive (l). **Getty Images:** DEA PICTURE LIBRARY / De Agostini(cr). **101 Corbis:** Richard Klune (tc). **Dorling Kindersley:** James Tye (br). **Getty Images:** DEA PICTURE LIBRARY/ De Agostini (bl). **102 Dorling Kindersley:** Dave King (bc). **102–103 Lebrecht Music and Arts:** Leemage (c). **103 Getty Images:** DeAgostini (tr). **104 The Bridgeman Art Library:** Victoria & Albert Museum, London, UK (t). **Dorling Kindersley:** Geoff Dann (cr); The National Music Museum (cl, cra). **Photo SCALA, Florence:** The Metropolitan Museum of Art / Art Resource (br). **105 Dorling Kindersley:** The Bate Collection (tr, bl); The National Music Museum (cra, cr, br, l). **106 The Bridgeman Art Library:** © Wallace Collection, London, UK (t). **107 Getty Images:** De Agostini (tc). **Lebrecht Music and Arts:** (br). **108 Getty Images:** RDImages / Epics (c); Universal History Archive (r). **109 The Bridgeman Art Library:** Private Collection (bc, cr); The Foundling Museum, London, UK (ca). **Getty images:** DEA/A. DAGLI ORTI / De Agostini (tl). **110 Dorling Kindersley:** Dave King (cl); Gary Ombler / Durham University Oriental Museum (tr). **Getty Images:** DeAgostini (cr). **111 Corbis:** Michael S. Yamashita (bc). **Getty Images:** HerveBruhat / Gamma-Rapho (cra); QuimLlenas / Cover (tl). **112–113 Dorling Kindersley/The National Music Museum Inc. 114 Corbis:** Alfredo Dagli Orti / The Art Archive (cr). **Dorling Kindersley/The National Music Museum Inc** (cl). **Getty Images:** DeAgostini (cb, bl, br). **115 Corbis:** ML Sinibaldi (ca). **Dorling Kindersley:** The Bate Collection (bl). **Getty Images:** Imagno (c); Universal History Archive (br). **SuperStock:** DeAgostini (cla). **116 Corbis:** Alfredo Dagli Orti / The Art Archive (cl). **Dorling Kindersley/The National Music Museum Inc** (r). **117 akg-images:** (tr). **Dorling Kindersley:** Andy Crawford / Calcografia Nacional, Madrid (bc). **118 Getty Images:** DeAgostini (t, bc). **119 Dorling Kindersley:** The Bate Collection (cr). **119 Alamy Stock Photo:** The Picture Art Collection (t). **120 Alamy Stock Photo:** INTERFOTO (b). **121 Dorling Kindersley:** The Royal Academy of Music (br). **Getty Images:** DeAgostini (tc). **122 Dorling Kindersley:** Philip Dowell (tr, cr); The Bate Collection (tl, bl, cl, clb). **122–123 Dorling Kindersley:** Philip Dowell (cb). **122-123 Dorling Kindersley:** The Bate Collection (b). **123 Dorling Kindersley:** Geoff Dann (bl, tl); The Bate Collection (r, l, c, cl, ca). **124 Getty Images:** DeAgostini (t). **Lebrecht Music and Arts:** (bl). **125 Lebrecht Music and Arts:** (tl). **126 akg-images:** Erich Lessing (cr). **Getty Images:** Imagno (l). **127 The Bridgeman Art Library:** Kunsthistorisches Museum,Vienna, Austria (b). **Corbis:** Perry Mastrovito / Design Pics (cr). **Getty Images:** DeAgostini (tl). **128 Corbis:** Alfredo Dagli Orti / The Art Archive (b). **Dorling Kindersley:** Philip Dowell (tl). **129 Dorling Kindersley:** The Bate Collection (tl). **Getty Images:** DeAgostini(bc). **Lebrecht Music and Arts:** (tr). **130 Rough Guides:** Demetrio Carrasco(ca). The Stapleton Collection: (bc). **131 Getty Images:** Universal History Archive (tc). **SuperStock:** DeAgostini (b). **132 Getty Images:** Buyenlarge (c); A. DAGLI ORTI / De Agostini (bc). **133 akg-images:** Erich Lessing (t). **Alamy Stock Photo:** The Art Archive (br). **134–135 Getty Images:** Imagno (b). **134 Getty Images:** Imagno (c). **135 Getty Images:** Buyenlarge (cr). **Lebrecht Music and Arts:** (ca). **136 Alamy Stock Photo:** GL Archive (r). **Corbis:** Stiftung Mozart / John Van Hasselt (bl). **137 Alamy Stock Photo:** Mary Evans Picture Library (tr). **Corbis:** Katy Raddatz / San Francisco Chronicle (bc). **138 Getty Images:** Hiroyuki Ito (t). **139 Dorling Kindersley/The National Music Museum Inc** (bl). **Getty Images:** DeAgostini (cr). **140 Dorling Kindersley:** The Royal Academy of Music (tr, cr, crb); The National Music Museum (bl, bc); The Bate Collection (clb). **Lebrecht Music and Arts:** (br). **141 Corbis:** Stefano Bianchetti (bl). **Dorling Kindersley:**The Royal Academy of Music (t). **Getty Images:** Education Images/ Universal Images Group (br). **Getty Images:** DeAgostini (bc). **142 Getty Images:** Universal History Archive (r). **143 Dorling Kindersley:** Jiri Kopriva (cra). **Getty Images:** The British Library / Robana (tl); Imagno (bc). **TopFoto.co.uk:** The Granger Collection (c). **144 Corbis:** ML Sinibaldi (t). **145 Alamy Stock Photo:** INTERFOTO (tl). **Corbis:** Alfredo DagliOrti / The Art Archive (bl). **Photo SCALA, Florence:** The Metropolitan Museum of Art / Art Resource (r). **146–147 Dorling Kindersley**/The National Music Museum Inc.**148 Dorling Kindersley:** Dover Publications (cl); Dave King (cr); Steve Gorton (bl). **Getty Images:** A. DAGLI ORTI / De Agostini (ca, cb); Universal History Archive (br). **149 Corbis:** Bettmann (bl). **Dorling Kindersley/The National Music Museum Inc** (ca). **Collection of the Smithsonian National Museum of African American History and Culture:** (crb); Imagno (cr); Ilya Efimovich Repin (cl). **150 Alamy Images:** The Art Archive (ca, cl). **The Bridgeman Art Library:** Museum of Fine Arts, Boston, Massachusetts, USA/ Leslie Lindsey Mason Collection (bc). **Getty Images:** Universal History Archive (br). **151 Alamy Images:** INTERFOTO (bl). **Photo SCALA, Florence:** BPK, Bildagentur für Kunst, Kultur und Geschichte, Berlin (t). **152 Getty Images:** DEA / A. DAGLI ORTI / De Agostini (bc, cra). **Lebrecht Music and Arts:** (tl). **153 The Bridgeman Art Library:** Christie's Images (l). **Corbis:** Hulton-Deutsch Collection (br). **154 Getty Images:** Imagno (l). **155 Dorling Kindersley:** Peter Wilson (br). **Getty Images:** Kean Collection (ca); Imagno (tl, bl). **156 Corbis:** Rune Hellestad (bl). **Photo SCALA, Florence:** Opera del Duomo of Orvieto (tr). **157 The Bridgeman Art Library:** Private Collection / Archives Charmet (l). **Corbis:** Bettmann (cra). **158-159 Corbis:** Fine Art Photographic Library (t). **159 Alamy Stock Photo:** PRISMA ARCHIVO (c). **Dorling Kindersley:** Dave King (br). **160 Corbis:** Bettmann (ca); Alfredo Dagli Orti / The Art Archive (cl). **Getty Images:** VittorioZunino Celotto (bl). **161 Alamy Stock Photo:** Pictorial Press Ltd (l). **162 Getty Images:** Imagno (clb). **Lebrecht Music and Arts:** (tr). **163 Alamy Stock Photo:** Juergen Schonnop (tr). **Lebrecht Music and Arts:** (crb, bl). **164 Dorling Kindersley:** Linda Whitwam (cra). **Lebrecht Music and Arts:** Costa Leemage (bl). **165 The Bridgeman Art Library:** Private Collection / Courtesy of Swann Auction Galleries (tc). **Corbis:** adoc-photos (bl). **Getty Images:** Mick Hutson / Redferns (crb). **166 Corbis:** FRIEDEL GIERTH / epa (cla). **Lebrecht Music and Arts:** culture-images (b). **167 Corbis:** Hulton-Deutsch (cr). **Library of Congress, Washington, D.C.:** LC-USZ62-650923b12657r (tc). **Photo SCALA, Florence:** BPK, Bildagentur fuer Kunst, Kultur und Geschichte,Berlin (br). **168 Alamy Stock Photo:** Science History Images (r). **SuperStock:** DeAgostini (l). **169 akg-images:** Bildarchiv Monheim (bl). **Alamy Stock Photo:** Lebrecht Music & Arts (cr); imageBROKER (br). **Irving S. Gilmore Music Library, Yale University Library** (t). **170 Alamy Stock Photo:** Science History Images (br). **Dorling Kindersley:** Geoff Dann (bl). **Getty Images:** Transcendental Graphics (t). **171 Corbis:** Historical Picture Archive (t). **Dorling Kindersley:** Dave King / Museum of the Moving Image (bc). **172 Getty Images:** Kean Collection (l). **TopFoto.co.uk:** ullsteinbild (cr). **173 akg-images:** (bl); Erich Lessing (tc). **Getty Images:** Universal History Archive (tl, br). **174 Alamy Stock Photo:** TheProtected Art Archive (cl). **Dorling Kindersley:** Peter Wilson (br). **175 Getty Images:** A. DAGLI ORTI / De Agostini. **176 Alamy Stock Photo:** Lebrecht Music & Arts (tl). **Dorling Kindersley:** Nigel Hicks (tc). **Library of Congress, Washington, D.C.:** LC-USZ62-122324 (cl). **177 Lebrecht Music and Arts:** Tristram Kenton (r). **Photo SCALA, Florence:** DeAgostini Picture Library (l). **178–179 The Bridgeman Art Library:** Isabella Stewart Gardner Museum, Boston, MA, USA (b). **178 Corbis:** (tr). **179 Corbis:** mColita (tr). **Getty Images:** Philip Ryalls /Redferns (br). **180 Getty Images:** Hippolyte Delaroche (bl); Ilya Efimovich Repin (t). **181 The Bridgeman Art Library:** Tretyakov Gallery, Moscow, Russia (tl). **Dorling Kindersley:** DaveKing (bl). **Rough Guides:** Jonathan Smith (br). **182 Corbis:** Bojan Brecelj (l).**183 akg-images:** Vsevolod M. Arsenyev (tl). **Corbis:** Bojan Brecelj (ca). **Getty Images:** Ian Gavan (bl). **184 The Bridgeman Art Library:** Ateneum ArtMuseum, Finnish National Gallery, Helsinki, Finland (ca). **Corbis:** Bettmann (br). **Dorling Kindersley:** Dave King (bl). **185 Corbis:** Paul Panayiotou / Paul Panayiotou (cr). **Dorling Kindersley:** Dave King (l). **186 Dorling Kindersley:** Dover Publications (r). **187 Getty Images:** DeAgostini (ca); Time & Life Pictures (cr). **TopFoto:** Sputnik (br). **188 Dorling Kindersley/The National Music Museum Inc** (cl); The Bate Collection (bl). **Getty Images:** Pierre Petit / Hulton Archive (br). **189 Dorling Kindersley/ The National Music Museum Inc** (t). **190 Corbis:** Michael Nicholson (cra). **Dorling Kindersley:** The Bate Collection (tl, ca); The NationalMusic Museum (tr). **190–191 Dorling Kindersley/The National Music Museum Inc** (c). **191 Dorling Kindersley:** The Bate Collection (tl); The National Music Museum (clb, cra, crb, bl). **Getty Images:** Time Life Pictures/ Mansell/Time Life Pictures (br). **Lebrecht Music and Arts:** Nigel Luckhurst (tr). **Library of Congress, Washington, D.C.:** LOC-LC-GLB23-0400 (cr). **192-193 Photoshot:** Lu Peng / Xinhua/ Boston Symphony Orchestra (t). **192 Lebrecht Music and Arts:** (br). **193 Dorling Kindersley:** Geoff Dann (cra). **Getty Images:** Imagno (bc). **194–195 Alamy Stock Photo:** The Art Archive (b). **194 Lebrecht Music and Arts:** (bl). **195 Alamy Stock Photo:** Hemis (tl). **Getty Images:** Buyenlarge (tr). **196 Alamy Stock Photo:** Lebrecht Music and Arts Photo Library (cl). **Getty Images:** De Agostini (cb). **197 Corbis:** Robbie Jack (b). **Dorling Kindersley:** Dave King/ Science Museum, London (tr). **Getty Images:** Romano Cagnoni (cl). **198 Dorling Kindersley:** (t); Colin Sinclair (bc). **199 Alamy Stock Photo:** charistoone-travel (br). **Corbis:** Bettmann (cra). **Dorling Kindersley/The National Music Museum Inc** (tc). **200 Alamy Stock Photo:** The Art Archive (cla). **Dorling Kindersley/The National Music Museum Inc** (cra). **200–201 Dorling Kindersley/The National Music Museum Inc** (b). **201 Getty Images:** Tim Graham (tr). **Library Of Congress,Washington, D.C.:** National Photo Company Collection (Library of Congress) (tl). **202 Dorling Kindersley:** Geoff Dann (t, cla, bl); Steve Gorton (cr); Philip Dowell (cra); The Bate Collection (crb, clb, br, ca, bc, cl). **203 Dorling Kindersley:** Geoff Dann (tc); The National Music Museum (l); The Bate Collection (cr, tr, c). **204–205 The Bridgeman Art Library:** Musee du Vieux Montmartre, Paris/Archives Charmet (b). **205 Corbis:** Leonard de Selva (c). **Getty Images:** G. DAGLI ORTI/ De Agostini (bc); Imagno (tl). **206–207 Corbis:** Nation Wong. **208 Dorling Kindersley:** Dave King (c, crb); The National Music Museum (clb); Sloans & Kenyon / Judith Miller (bc). **Getty Images:** De Agostini (cl); Imagno (bl). **209 Corbis:** Bettmann (cl); Lebrecht Music & Arts (c); (cb, bl). **Dorling Kindersley:** Dave King (br). **Getty Images:** Hulton Archive (cr). **210 Alamy Stock Photo:** The Art Archive (clb). Lebrecht Music and Arts: (ca). **211 Alamy Stock Photo:** The Art Archive (l). **Corbis:** Lebrecht Music & Arts (cra). **Getty Images:** A. DAGLI ORTI / De Agostini (br). **212 The Art Archive:** Bibliothèque Nationale Paris / Eileen Tweedy (cr). **Getty Images:** Imagno (l). **213 akg-images:** (cr). **Corbis:** Hulton-Deutsch Collection (tl); Robbie Jack (bl). **214 Corbis:** Bettmann (crb). **Dorling Kindersley/The National Music Museum Inc** (c); Karl Shone (bl). **215 Bridgeman Art Library:** Sputnik (b). **Miriam Matthew photograph collection, Special Collections, Charles E. Young Research Library, UCLA:** (t). **216–217 Dorling Kindersley/The National Music Museum Inc** (c). **216 akg-images:** (cb, br); North Wind Picture Archives (clb). **Dorling Kindersley:** Geoff Dann (bl); Philip Dowell (c); The National Music Museum (bc). **217 Dorling Kindersley/The National Music Museum Inc** (tl, cra, cb, ca); The Bate Collection (bl, br);Gary Ombler (c, cl). **Getty Images:** Gamma-Rapho (crb). **218–219 4Corners:**Massimo Ripani / SIME (b). **218 Lebrecht Music and Arts:** Archivo Manuel deFalla (tr). **219 Corbis:** Bettmann (ca). **Getty Images:** Beatriz Schiller / TimeLife Pictures (tr). **220–221 Corbis:** Ted Soqui (b). **220 Corbis:** Bettmann (clb). **221 Corbis:** Rafa Salafranca / epa (br). **Dorling Kindersley/ The National Music Museum Inc** (tc). **Getty Images:** Cristian Lazzari (tl); Michael Tran/FilmMagic (cra). **222 Lebrecht Music and Arts:** (ca); culture-images (bl). **RexFeatures:** CSU Archives / Everett Collection (crb). **223 Getty Images:** DeAgostini (l, tr). **224 Alamy Stock Photo:** North Wind Picture Archives (bl). **Library of Congress, Washington, D.C.:** Omaha Powwow

Project collection (AFC 1986 / 038) (bc). **225 Special Collections, University of Arkansas Libraries, Fayetteville** (t). **Corbis:** Jerry Cooke (b). **227 Corbis:** Bettmann (br). **Getty Images:** Hulton Archive (c); Michael Ochs Archives (cl). **228 Alamy Stock Photo:** Pictorial Press Ltd (ca). **Dorling Kindersley:** The Bate Collection (br). **Getty Images:** Frank Driggs Collection (bl). **229 Corbis:** (tl). **230 Dorling Kindersley:** Jon Spaull (bl). **Getty Images:** CBS Photo Archive (br). **Johns Hopkins University:** The Lester S. Levy Collection of Sheet Music (c). **231 Dorling Kindersley/The National Music Museum Inc** (tl, tc, cl, c). **Getty Images:** Jim McCrary / Redferns (crb). **232 Getty Images:** PHOTRI / De Agostini (bl). **Lebrecht Music and Arts:** (r). **233 Corbis:** Hulton-Deutsch Collection (tc). **Getty-Images:** GAB Archive / Redferns (bc). **Lebrecht Music and Arts:** Photofest- (crb). **234 Corbis:** Bettmann (ca). **Getty Images:** Timepix / Time Life Pictures (bl).- **234–235 Getty Images:** Frank Driggs Collection (b). **235 Dorling Kindersley:** Dave King (tl). **236–237 Getty Images:** Michael Ochs Archives (c). **236 Getty Images:** Bob Willoughby / Redferns (bl). **237 Getty Images:** John D. Kisch / Separate Cinema Archive (tc, bc). **Roland Smithies / luped.com:** (cr). **238 akg-images:** De Agostini (tl). **Dorling Kindersley:** The Bate Collection (ca, tr). **Lebrecht Music and Arts:**-(cra); Chris Stock (tc). **238–239 Dorling Kindersley:** The Bate Collection (t, c). **239 The Bridgeman Art Library:** Private Collection (cra). **Dorling Kindersley:** The Bate Collection (tl); The National Music Museum (cla, bl, br, clb, crb). **Getty Images:** Michael Ochs Archives (tr). **240 Getty Images:** JP Jazz Archive/ Contributor/Redferns. **241 Alamy Stock Photo:** Brent T. Madison (tr). **Corbis:** Eudora Welty (bl). **Dorling Kindersley:** Jon Spaull (br). **242 Getty Images:** George Karger/Contributor/The Chronicle Collection. **Dorling Kindersley:** Dave King (br). **243 Corbis:** Bettmann (cla, br). **Dorling Kindersley:** Geoff Dann (tc). **244–245 Dorling Kindersley/The National Music Museum Inc** (t). **244 Dorling Kindersley:** The Bate-Collection (clb, cb, br). **Getty Images:** The Bridgeman Art Library (bl); Bridgeman Art Library (bc). **245 Alamy Stock Photo:**GL Archive (clb); J Hayward (fbr). **Dorling Kindersley:** Geoff Dann (bl, bc); The National Music Museum (br, cl). **246 Dorling Kindersley:** Dave King (tr, cl). **247 Dorling Kindersley:** Dave King (bc). **Getty Images:** William Gottlieb / Redferns (tc, crb). **248 Rex Features:** Everett Collection (l). **249 Alamy Stock Photo:** EyeBrowz (bl). **Dorling Kindersley:** Dave King (tl). **Getty Images:** Frank Driggs Collection (c). **Rex Features:** Moviestore Collection (br). **250 Dorling Kindersley:** Ranald MacKechnie / Ashmolean Museum, Oxford (bl). **Getty Images:** Hulton Archive (ca). **251 akg-images:** (t). **Getty Images:** Andrew Lepley / Redferns (br). **252–253 Dorling Kindersley:** Geoff Dann (c). **Latin Percussion / lpmusic.com:** (b). **252 Dorling Kindersley:** Geoff Dann (fbr); The National Music Museum (cla). **Getty Images:** Gavin Roberts / Rhythm Magazine (tl). **Latin Percussion / lpmusic.com:** (fbl, bl, bc). **253 Dorling Kindersley:** Geoff Dann (cr); The National Music Museum (br, bl, tl, ftr, bc); Dave King (ftl); Philip Dowell (cb, tr). **Dreamstime.com:** Mark Fairey (l). **Latin Percussion / lpmusic.com:** (ca, cla). **254 The Bridgeman Art Library:** Private Collection / DaTo Images (tr). **255 akg-images:** Erik Bohr (cr). **Alamy Stock Photo:** Peter Horree (tc). **Corbis:** Bettmann (tl). **Dorling Kindersley:** Sloans & Kenyon / Judith Miller (bl). **256 Getty Images:** Michael Ochs Archives (t). **257 Alamy Stock Photo:** INTERFOTO (bl). **Getty Images:** G.D.Hackett / Hulton Archive (tc); Lake County Museum (cr). **Rex Features:** Courtesy Everett Collection (br). **258 Alamy Stock Photo:** Caro (c). **The Art Archive:** Culver Pictures (clb). **Corbis:** Bettmann (tl). **Dorling Kindersley:** Dave King / Science Museum, London (ca). **Getty Images:** SSPL (ftr). **259 Alamy Stock Photo:** National Music Museum Inc (tl, tc, cl, c). **Getty Images:** Jim McCrary / Redferns (crb). **232 Getty Images:** PHOTRI / De Agostini (bl). **Lebrecht Music and Arts:** (r). **233 Corbis:** Hulton-Deutsch Collection (tc). **Getty Images:** GAB Archive / Redferns (bc). Lebrecht Music and Arts: Photofest (crb). **234 Corbis:** Bettmann (ca). **GettyImages:** Timepix / Time Life Pictures (bl). **234–235 Getty Images:** Frank DriggsCollection (b). **235 Dorling Kindersley:** Dave King (tl). **236–237 Getty Images:** Michael Ochs Archives (c). **236 Getty Images:** Bob Willoughby / Redferns (bl). **237 Getty Images:** John D. Kisch / Separate Cinema Archive (tc, bc). **Roland Smithies / luped.com:** (cr). **238 akg-images:** De Agostini (tl). **Dorling Kindersley:** The Bate Collection (ca, tr). **Lebrecht Music and Arts:** (cra); Chris Stock (tc). **238–239 Dorling Kindersley:** The Bate Collection (t, c). **239 The Bridgeman Art Library:** Private Collection (cra). **Dorling Kindersley:** The Bate Collection (tl); The National Music Museum (cla, bl, br, clb, crb). **Getty Images:** Michael Ochs Archives (tr). **240 Corbis:** Eudora Welty (t). **241 Alamy Stock Photo:** Brent T. Madison (tr). **Dorling Kindersley:** Jon Spaull (crb). **Getty Images:** MPI (bl). **242 Corbis:** Bettmann (t). **Dorling Kindersley:** Dave King (br). **243 Corbis:** Bettmann (cla, br). **Dorling Kindersley:** Geoff Dann (tc). **244–245 Dorling Kindersley / The National Music Museum Inc** (t). **244 Dorling Kindersley:** The Bate Collection (clb, cb, br). **Getty Images:** The Bridgeman Art Library (bl); Bridgeman Art Library (bc). **245 Alamy Stock Photo:** GL Archive (clb); J Hayward (fbr). **Dorling Kindersley:** Geoff Dann (bl, bc); **The National Music Museum** (br, cl). **246 Dorling Kindersley:** Dave King (tr, cl). **247 Dorling Kindersley:** Dave King (bc). **Getty Images:** William Gottlieb / Redferns (tc, crb). **248 Rex Features:** Everett Collection (l). **249 Alamy Stock Photo:** EyeBrowz (bl). **Dorling Kindersley:** Dave King (tl).**Getty Images:** Frank Driggs Collection (c). **Rex Features:** Moviestore Collection (br). **250 Dorling Kindersley:** Ranald MacKechnie / Ashmolean Museum, Oxford(bl). **Getty Images:** Hulton Archive (ca). **251 akg-images:** (t). **Getty Images:** Andrew Lepley / Redferns (br). **252–253 Dorling Kindersley:** Geoff Dann (c). **Latin Percussion / lpmusic.com:** (b). **252 Dorling Kindersley:** Geoff Dann (fbr); The National Music Museum (cla). **Getty Images:** Gavin Roberts / RhythmMagazine (tl). **Latin Percussion / lpmusic.com:** (fbl, bl, bc). **253 Dorling Kindersley:** Geoff Dann (cr); The National Music Museum (br, bl, tl, ftr, bc); Dave King (ftl); Philip Dowell (cb, tr). **Dreamstime.com:** Mark Fairey (l). **Latin Percussion / lpmusic.com:** (ca, cla). **254 The Bridgeman Art Library:** Private Collection / DaTo Images (tr). **255 akg-images:** Erik Bohr (cr). **Alamy Stock Photo:** Peter Horree (tc). **Corbis:** Bettmann (tl). **Dorling Kindersley:** Sloans & Kenyon / Judith Miller (bl). **256 Getty Images:** Michael Ochs Archives (t). **257 Alamy Stock Photo:** INTERFOTO (bl). **Getty Images:** G.D. Hackett / Hulton Archive (tc); Lake County Museum (cr). **Rex Features:** Courtesy Everett Collection (br). **258 Alamy Stock Photo:** Caro (c). **The Art Archive:** Culver Pictures (clb). **Corbis:** Bettmann(tl). **Dorling Kindersley:** Dave King / Science Museum, London (ca). **Getty Images:** SSPL (ftr). **259 Alamy Stock Photo:** Adem Demir (tl); Kevin Wheal (ftl). **Dorling Kindersley:** Paul Wilkinson (ftr). **Getty Images:** The Bridgeman Art Library (br). **260–261 Dorling Kindersley:** Dave King (c). **260 Corbis:** The Jim Heimann Collection (bl). **261 Alamy Stock Photo:** Everett Collection Historical (tc). **Dorling Kindersley:** Dave Rudkin (cr). **Getty Images:** Gilles Petard / Redferns (br). **262–263 Dorling Kindersley / The National Music Museum Inc. 264 Dorling Kindersley / The National Music Museum Inc** (cl, c). **Getty Images:** Hulton Archive (bl); Michael Ochs Archives (ca); Elliot Landy / Redferns (crb); Graham Wiltshire /Redferns (br). **265 Getty Images:** Jack Vartoogian (bc). **Dorling Kindersley:** Dave King (c). **Getty Images:** Phil Dent / Redferns (cr); Kevin Mazur / WireImage (ca); Michael Ochs Archives (cl); Andrew Putler / Redferns (clb); Theo Wargo / Staff / Wireimage (br). **266 Getty Images:** Fred Ramage / Keystone Features (clb). **Lebrecht Music and Arts:** (t). **267 Alamy Stock Photo:** Pierre BRYE (bl). **Corbis:** Jacques Haillot / Apis/ Sygma (br). **Lebrecht Music and Arts:** T. Martinot (tc). **268 Getty Images:** Apic (c); Buyenlarge (bl). **269 Corbis:** Alain Dejean / Sygma (tr). **Getty Images:** Apic (tl); Gjon Mili / Time Life Pictures (b). **270 Corbis:** Hans-Peter Merten / Robert Harding World Imagery (t). **Lebrecht Music and Arts:** (br). **271 akg-images:** (c). **Corbis:** Murat Taner (br). **Getty Images:** Erich Auerbach (tr). **272 Getty Images:** Yale Joel / Time Life Pictures (br). **273 Dorling Kindersley:** Geoff Dann (c). **Getty Images:** William Gottlieb / Redferns (tr); Philip Ryalls / Redferns (br). **274 Getty Images:** Antonello (bl). **275 Dorling Kindersley:** Alex Robinson (l). **Getty Images:** Lionel FLUSIN / Gamma-Rapho (br); MichaelOchs Archives (cr). **276 Getty Images:** Frank Driggs Collection (t); Odile Noel / Redferns (bl). **277 Corbis:** Diego Goldberg / Sygma (br). **Dorling Kindersley:** Geoff Dann (tc). **Getty Images:** Michael Ochs Archives (clb). **278 Corbis:** Reuters (r). **University of Miami Libraries: Cuban Photograph Collection, Cuban Heritage Collection, University of Miami Libraries, Coral Gables, Florida** (cl). **279 Rex Features:** Moviestore Collection (cb); Sony Pics / Everett (tl). **SuperStock:** Alvaro Leiva / age fotostock (cr). **280 Getty Images:** Alex Bender / Picture Post (b); Imagno (cla). **281 Getty Images:** Jack Vartoogian (tr); Gerti Deutsch / Hulton Archive (tl); Timothy A. Clary / Contributor/AFP (br). **282 Alamy Stock Photo:** Pictorial Press Ltd (ca). **Corbis:** Bettmann (bl). **Getty Images:** Michael Ochs Archives (crb). **283 Corbis:** Herbert Pfarrhofer / APA (crb). **Dorling Kindersley/The National Music Museum Inc** (tl). **284 Alamy Stock Photo:** Theo Moye (bl). **The Art Archive:** Victoria and Albert Museum London (l). **285 Alamy Stock Photo:** Universal Images Group / DeAgostini (bl). **Getty Images:** Tim Graham / Evening Standard (br); Gordon Parks / Time Life Pictures (tl). **Lebrecht Music and Arts:** (c). **286–287 Dorling Kindersley / The National Music Museum Inc.** (b). **286 Dorling Kindersley:** Nick Harris (br); The National Music Museum (clb, cla, c, tr). **Getty Images:** Universal History Archive / UIG (ftl). **Lebrecht Music and Arts:** Museum of Fine Arts, Boston (ca). **Photo SCALA, Florence:** BPK, Bildagenturfuer Kunst, Kultur und Geschichte, Berlin (tl). **287 Dorling Kindersley:** Nick Harris (ca); The Royal Academy of Music (tl). **Getty Images:** Nigel Osbourne / Redferns (tc); Andrew Putler/ Redferns (tr). **288 Alamy Stock Photo:** United Archives GmbH (b). **289 Alamy Stock Photo:** EyeBrowz (tl). **Dorling Kindersley:** Clive Streeter / Science Museum, London (bl). **Getty Images:** Michael Ochs Archives (cra); Virginia Sherwood / NBC NewsWire (br). **290 Alamy Stock Photo:** Everett Collection Historical (bl). **Corbis:** Hulton-Deutsch Collection (t). **291 Dorling Kindersley:** (tl). **291 Getty Images: Bachrach/Contributor** (bl). **Rex Features:** Solent News (cr). **292 Getty Images:** John Kobal Foundation (cl); Silver Screen Collection / Hulton Archive (r). **293 Corbis:** Alan Pappe (br). **Getty Images:** Frank Driggs Collection / Archive Photos (bl); GAB Archive / Redferns (cra); MGM Studios / Hulton Archive (tl). **294 Corbis:** Terry Cryer (t). **Getty Images:** Hulton-Deutsch Collection / CORBIS (bl); The Estate of David Gahr / Contributor (br). **295 Alamy Stock Photo:** Troy Harvey / ZUMA Wire / Alamy Live News (cr). **Getty Images:** Jamie McCarthy / Staff (b); Joel Richardson/The Washington Post / Contributor (tc). **296 Dorling Kindersley:** Geoff Dann (c); Dave King / Museum of the Moving Image (bl). **296–297 Corbis:** Paul Almasy (b). **297 Getty Images:** Paul Kennedy (tl); Philip Ryalls / Redferns (tr). **298 Dorling Kindersley:** Southbank Enterprises (br, cr, tr, cra, cl, c, cla, tl, ca). **299 Dorling Kindersley:** Southbank Enterprises (br, cl, tl, tr, ca,cla, cra). **300 Alamy Stock Photo:** Photo Resource Hawaii (cla). **Corbis:** Richard A. Cooke (b). **TopFoto.co.uk:** The Granger Collection (cra). **301 Dorling Kindersley:** Geoff Dann (bc). **Getty Images:** GAB Archive / Redferns (tr); Michael Ochs Archives (tl). **Mountain Apple Company Hawaii /** izhawaii.com: (bl). **302 Dorling Kindersley:** Tim Daly (bl); Philip Dowell (cl). **303 Corbis:** Andrew Fox (tr). **Dorling Kindersley:** Dave King (l). **304 Dorling Kindersley:** Linda Whitwam (t). **Getty Images:** Hulton Archive (bl). **305 Dorling Kindersley:** Linda Whitwam(crb). **Getty Images:** Lipnitzki / Roger Viollet (bl). **Lebrecht Music and Arts:** Museum of Fine Arts, Boston (c). **306 Getty Images:** Gilles Petard / Redferns (tl); Transcendental Graphics (bc). **307 Getty Images:** John Cohen (tl); David Redfern / Redferns (br); GAB Archive / Redferns (cr). **308–309 Dorling Kindersley/The National Music Museum Inc** (t). **308 Dorling Kindersley/The National Music Museum Inc.** (crb, bc, clb, br, bl, fbl). **Getty Images:** RB / Redferns (c). **309 Dorling Kindersley/The National Music Museum Inc.** (cla, cb/a, bl, c, cr, cl/a, cl/b, cb/b). **Getty Images:** Michael Ochs

Archives (fbr); Jan Persson / Redferns (clb, bc). **310 Getty Images:** Gilles Petard / Redferns (t). **Shutterstock.com:** 20th Century Fox / Kobal (b). **311 Getty Images:** LMPC / Contributor (l) ;David Redfern / Redferns (br). **312 Corbis:** Bettmann (b); Michael Ochs Archives (bc). **Dorling Kindersley:** Andy Crawford (cla). **Getty Images:** Joby Sessions / Total Guitar Magazine (cr). **313 Getty Images:** Mike Coppola (br); David Redfern / Redferns (tc). **314 Dorling Kindersley:** Steve Gorton / The Jukebox Showroom, RS Leisure (br). **Getty Images:** Michael Ochs Archives (bl, c). **315 Alamy Stock Photo:** Marc Tielemans (bc). **Getty Images:** Michael Ochs Archives (t). **316 Corbis:** Sunset Boulevard (r); Michael Ochs Archives (clb). **317 Getty Images:** Hulton Archive (tc); Gary Null / NBC / NBCU Photo Bank (bc). **Rex Features:** BEHAR ANTHONY / SIPA (cra); Everett Collection (crb). **318 Corbis:** Walter McBride / Retna Ltd. (bl). **Getty Images:** Ray Avery (cr). **Roland Smithies / luped.com:** (crb). **319 Dorling Kindersley:** (br). **Getty Images:** Michael Ochs Archives (tr); PoPsie Randolph / Michael Ochs Archives (bl). **320 Getty Images:** Gilles Petard / Redferns (tr); Popperfoto (b). **321 Getty Images:** ABC (bl); Gilles Petard / Redferns (tc); Michael Ochs Archives (crb). **322 Corbis:** Minneapolis StarTribune / ZUMA Press (bc). **Dorling Kindersley/The National Music Museum Inc.** (tr). **322 Corbis:** Bettmann (t); Minneapolis Star Tribune/ ZUMA Press (b). **323 Getty Images:** Jan Persson / Contributor (b); Jim Britt / Contributor / Michael Ochs Archives (tc). **324 Getty Images:** Michael Ochs Archives (t, bl). **325 Dorling Kindersley/ The National Music Museum Inc.** (cr). **Getty Images:** Keystone (tc); Michael Ochs Archives (bl). **326 Getty Images:** Paris Match (t). **327 Alamy Stock Photo:** CBW (crb). **Dorling Kindersley:** Nick Harris (cl). **Getty Images:** Jeremy Fletcher / Redferns (tr); GAB Archive / Redferns (bl). **328 Alamy Stock Photo:** CBW (bl). **Getty Images:** Chris Morphet / Redferns (cl); Hulton Archive (tr); Redferns (cr); Simon Lees / Guitarist Magazine (br). **329 Alamy Stock Photo:** EyeBrowz (tr). **Corbis:** Neal Preston (b). **Getty Images:** Geoff Dann / Redferns (tl). **330 Dorling Kindersley:** Nick Harris (bl, cb, br). **Getty Images:** JP Jazz Archive / Redferns (bc); Michael Ochs Archives (crb). **330–331 Dorling Kindersley/The National Music Museum Inc** (t). **331 Dorling Kindersley:** Nick Harris (clb, cb). **Getty Images:** Simon Lees / Total Guitar Magazine (bl); Joby Sessions/ Guitarist Magazine (cr); David Redfern / Redferns (crb). **332–333 Alamy Stock Photo:** BNA Photographic (b). **332 Getty Images:** Tony Russell / Staff / Redferns (t). **333 Getty Images:** Sumy Sadurni / Contributor / AFP (cr). **Photoshot:** UPPA (tc). **Rex Features:** ITV (br). **334 Dorling Kindersley:** Geoff Dann (cla, bl). **335 Getty Images:** Tom Kopi. **336 Dorling Kindersley:** Andy Crawford / British Film Institute (cra). **336–337 Corbis:** Bob King (b). **337 Getty Images:** Gijsbert Hanekroot / Redferns (tc); Nigel Osbourne / Redferns (cr). **Rex Features:** Dick Wallis (br). **338 Dorling Kindersley:** Duncan Turner/ Anna Hall (bl, bc). **Photo Duffy © Duffy Archive:** (l). **Roland Smithies / luped.com:** Masayoshi Sukita (cr). **339 Alamy Stock Photo:** Pictorial Press Ltd (cr). **Getty Images:** Jorgen Angel / Redferns (tc). **340 Corbis:** Christie's Images (br). **Getty Images:** Tony Russell / Redferns (cl). **341 Alamy Stock Photo:** Pictorial Press Ltd. (cr). **Dorling Kindersley:** Geoff Dann (bc). Amit Pasricha / Avinash Pasricha: (tc). **342 Alamy Stock Photo:** Dinodia Photos (cr). **Dorling Kindersley:** Deepak Aggarwal (tc, tr, ftr, cr); Geoff Dann (ftl, clb); Dave King (tl); The National Music Museum (bl). **Getty Images:** PhotosIndia. com (cl). **343 Dorling Kindersley:** Geoff Dann (cr, ftl); The National Music Museum (cl, ftr, cra, tl, tc, c, b); Dave King (tr). **344 Dorling Kindersley:** Nick Harris (cla). **344–345 Getty Images:** Elliot Landy / Redferns (b). **345 Getty Images:** GAB Archive / Redferns (tl); Timothy Norris / Contributor (cr). **346 Dorling Kindersley:** Nick Harris (cra). **Getty Images:** GAB Archive / Redferns (crb). **Rex Features:** Everett Collection (cl). **SuperStock:** (bl). **347 Getty Images:** Kevin Mazur / WireImage (br); Andrew Putler/ Redferns (l). **348 Dorling Kindersley:** Nick Harris (r). **Getty Images:** FilmMagic (bc); Michael Ochs Archives (cl). **349 Getty Images:** Graham Wiltshire / Redferns (t). **350 Dorling Kindersley:** Wallis and Wallis / Judith Miller (cl). **Getty Images:** Olle Lindeborg / AFP (bl). **351 Alamy Stock Photo:** CBW (c). **Getty Images:** Tom Hill / WireImage (cra). **Rex Features:** Gill Allen (l); FremantleMedia Ltd (br). **352 Alamy Stock Photo:** Freddie Jones (cra); ZUMA Press, Inc. (br). **Getty Images:** ABC Photo Archives / ABC (bl). **353 Alamy Stock Photo:** CBW (tc); Pictorial Press Ltd (cra). **354 Corbis:** James Andanson / Sygma (br). **Photoshot:** © Bill Bernstein / Retna Pictures (c). **Rex Features:** Everett Collection (tr). **355 Getty Images:** Waring Abbott (l). Vintage Gear America: (crb). **356 Getty Images:** David Corio / Michael Ochs Archives (br); Michael Ochs Archives (ca); Richard McCaffrey / Michael Ochs Archive (tl); GAB Archive / Redferns (cr). **357 Getty Images:** Richard E. Aaron / Redferns (bc); Michael Ochs Archives (tl). **Rough Guides:** Nelson Hancock (cr). **358 Alamy Stock Photo:** DWD-Media (c). **Getty Images:** Kevin Mazur/WireImage (br). **Rex Features:** Marks (bl). **359 Corbis:** Santiago Bueno / Sygma (br). **Getty Images:** Morena Brengola / Redferns (cr); Nigel Osbourne / Redferns (tl). **360 Alamy Stock Photo:** David Grossman (tc); Lebrecht Music and Arts Photo Library (cla). **Corbis:** Hulton-Deutsch Collection (br). **Getty Images:** Blank Archives (bl). **361 Getty Images:** Theo Wargo / Staff. **362 Alamy Stock Photo:** Aflo Co. Ltd. (cra). **Dorling Kindersley:** Geoff Dann (ca). **Getty Images:** Buyenlarge (clb); KAZUHIRO NOGI / AFP (bc). **363 Getty Images:** Charley Gallay (br); YOSHIKAZU TSUNO / AFP (tl). **364 © Crammed Discs:** Vincent Kenis (t). **Bridgeman Art Library:** Alinari (b). **365 Alamy Stock Photo:** Aviv Small / ZUMA Press (br); Martin Lindsay (tr); PA Images (bl). **Global Groove / www. globalgroovers.com:** (tl). **366 Alamy Stock Photo:** Irene Abdou (bl). **Mary Evans Picture Library:** Africa Media Online (cl). **367 Alamy Stock Photo:** Records (cr). **Getty Images:** Michael Putland / Contributor/ Hulton (t); Michael Ochs Archives / Stringer (b). **368 Getty Images:** Lisa Haun / Michael Ochs Archives (bl); Michael Ochs Archives (cl). Vintage Gear America: (br). **369 Getty Images:** Prince Williams / Contributor / Wireimage (tl); Theo Wargo / Staff / Wireimage (b); Kevin Mazur / WireImage (cr). **370 Getty Images:** Lisa Haun / Michael Ochs Archives (bl); Michael Ochs Archives (cl). **Vintage Gear America:** (br). **371 Getty Images:** KMazur / WireImage (tl); Kevin Mazur / WireImage (cr); William B. Plowman (bc). **372 Getty Images:** Des Willie / Contributor / Redferns (t); Phil Dent / Redferns (b). **373 Alamy Stock Photo:** Joe Bird (cl). **Getty Images:** Luca Sola / Contributor / AFP (br). **Rex Features:** Jonathan Hordle (t). **374 Corbis:** Imaginechina (bc). **Getty Images:** DeAgostini (cla); Han Myung-Gu / WireImage (cra). **375 Alamy Stock Photo:** Aflo Co. Ltd. (b). **Getty Images:** Photo12.com: DR (tl). **376 Alamy Stock Photo:** ilpo musto (bl). **Roland Smithies / luped.com:** (t). **Getty Images:** Theo Wargo (br). **377 Alamy Stock Photo:** Everett Collection Inc (cr); Sam Kovak (bl). **386 Dorling Kindersley / The National Music Museum Inc. 388 Getty Images:** De Agostini (br); Prisma / UIG (c). **389 Dorling Kindersley:** The Bate Collection (br). **391 Corbis:** Ira Nowinski (bc). **Getty Images:** Mondadori Portfolio (tl). **392 Corbis:** Bettmann (bc). **393 Dorling Kindersley / The National Music Museum, Inc** (cr). **Getty Images:** Archivio Cameraphoto Epoche (tl). **394 Getty Images:** CBS Photo Archive (c); Frank Driggs Collection (br). **395 Corbis:** Richard Booth / Lebrecht Music & Arts (tr). **Getty Images:** Michael Ochs Archives (c). **396 Getty Images:** Frank Driggs Collection (cr); Michael Ochs Archives (bl). **397 Corbis:** Henry Diltz (cr); Hulton-Deutsch Collection (tl). **398 Corbis:** Neal Preston (clb). **Getty Images:** Ron Howard / Redferns (tr). **399 Corbis:** Bettmann (cla). **Getty Images:** Keystone-France / Gamma-Keystone (br). **400 Getty Images:** CatherineMcGann (cl); Fin Costello / Redferns (b). **401 Getty Images:** Al Pereira / Michael Ochs Archives (br); Jason Merritt / FilmMagic (tl). **402 Corbis:** Underwood & Underwood (tr). **Getty Images:** Ross Gilmore / Redferns (bc). **403 Corbis:** Holger Leue (tr). **Dorling Kindersley / The National Music Museum Inc.** (bl). **404 Corbis:** Luc Gnago / Reuters (tr). **405 Getty Images:** Kaushik Roy / IndiaToday Group (bl); Orlando / Three Lions (tr). **406 Corbis:** adoc-photos (cl); BrunoMorandi / Hemis (br). **Getty Images:** Judith Burrows (tr). **407 Corbis:** Christophe Boisvieux (tl). **Getty Images:** Thomas Bregardis / AFP (br). **408 Corbis:** Bradley Smith (br); Hulton-Deutsch Collection (cl). **409 Corbis:** Bettmann (tc). **Getty Images:** De Agostini (br). **410 Corbis:** Bettmann (cr). **Getty Images:** Michael Ochs Archives (bl). **411 Corbis:** Alfredo Dagli Orti / The Art Archive (tr); Raminder Pal Singh / EPA (bc). **412 Corbis:** Bettmann (tr); Michael Nicholson (cl). **413 Corbis:** Hulton-Deutsch Collection (tc); Neal Preston (bl). **414 Alamy Stock Photo:** Pictorial Press Ltd (tl). **Corbis:** Hulton-Deutsch Collection (crb). **415 Corbis:** Tim Mosenfelder (tc). **Getty Images:** Michael Ochs Archives (br). **416 Alamy Stock Photo:** ZUMA Press, Inc. (br). **Getty Images:** GAB Archive / Redferns (tc). **417 Corbis:** adoc-photos (c); Roger Ressmeyer (br). **418 Corbis:** Manuel Zambrana (cr); Pool / Retna Ltd. (tc). **419 Corbis:** Hulton-Deutsch Collection (bc); Mosaic Images (tc). **420 Corbis:** Bettmann (tl); Jeremy Bembaron / Sygma (bl). **421 Corbis:** Bettmann (cl); Roger Ressmeyer (br). **422 Corbis:** Bettmann (br); Miroslav Zajíc (tl). **423 Getty Images:** EbetRoberts / Redferns (tc); Tom Copi / Michael Ochs Archives (br). **424 Corbis:** Bettmann (cr, bc). **425 Corbis:** Sunset Boulevard (tl); (bc). **426 Corbis:** AlfredoDagli Orti / The Art Archive (tc). **Getty Images:** Rob Verhorst / Redferns (br). **427 Getty Images:** Dave Hogan / Hulton Archive (br); Quim Llenas / Cover (c). **428 Corbis:** Tobias Hase / dpa (tc). **Getty Images:** GAB Archive / Redferns (cl). **429 Corbis:** Robbie Jack (bl). **Getty Images:** WireImage (cr). **430 Getty Images:** AFP (tc); Michael Ochs Archives (br). **431 Getty Images:** John Downing(br); Redferns (tc). **432 Getty Images:** De Agostini (tc); Sebastian D'souza / AFP(bc). **433 Getty Images:** Jun Sato / WireImage (cl); Michael Ochs Archives(tr). **434 Corbis:** Dirk Waem / epa (cl); Rune Hellestad (tr). **435 Corbis:** Bettmann (tr, bl). **436 Corbis:** Chris Cuffaro / The Hell Gate (bl); LebrechtMusic & Arts (cr). **437 Corbis:** Bettmann (tc, br). **438 Corbis:** Bettmann (crb). **Getty Images:** Michael Ochs Archives (tc). **439 Corbis:** Bettmann (cr). **Getty Images:** Michael Ochs Archives (bl). **440 Corbis:** Hulton-Deutsch Collection (tl); Jay Blakesberg / Retna Ltd. (br). **441 Getty Images:** Lipnitzki / RogerViollet (tc); Michael Ochs Archives (br). **442 Corbis:** Lynn Goldsmith (bl). **Getty Images:** Michael Ochs Archives (tc). **443 Corbis:** Joao Paulo Trindade / epa(tc);. **444 Corbis:** Bettmann (tl); Lindsay Hebberd (bc). **445 Corbis:** Bettmann (tr,bl). **446 Corbis:** Chris Kleponis / epa (br). **Getty Images:** Tony Vaccaro / Hulton Archive (c). **447 Corbis:** Bettmann. **Getty Images:** Jeff Kravitz/ FilmMagic (cb). **448 Corbis:** Brooks Kraft / Sygma (cl); E.O. Hoppe (tr). **449 Corbis:** Stephane Masson/ Kipa (br). **Getty Images:** CBS (tl). **450 Corbis:** Laurent Gillieron/epa (br); photomall / Xinhua Press (tl). **451 Corbis:** Hulton-Deutsch Collection (br); Martyn Goddard (tr). **452 Corbis:** (bc); Bettmann (tl). **453 Getty Images:** Michael Ochs Archives (bl). **Lebrecht Music and Arts:** Kate Mount (tl). **454 Dorling Kindersley / The National Music Museum, Inc.** (cl). **455 Dorling Kindersley / The National Music Museum, Inc.** (br). **456 Dorling Kindersley / The National MusicMuseum, Inc.** (cl). **457 Dorling Kindersley:** The Bate Collection. **PunchStock:** Stockbyte (tr). **458 Dorling Kindersley:** The Bate Collection (bl). **459 Dorling Kindersley / The National Music Museum, Inc.** (r). **460 Dorling Kindersley:** The Bate Collection (cl). **462 Dorling Kindersley / The National Music Museum, Inc.** (tr); (bl). **463 Dorling Kindersley / The National Music Museum, Inc.** (tr).**Front Endpapers: Dorling Kindersley / The National Music Museum, Inc. Back Endpapers Getty Images:** Joby Sessions / Guitarist Magazine

Cover images: *Front:* **123RF. com:** bragapictures cb/ (Violin), cl/ (French horn), miswanto fcra/ (Piano); **Dreamstime.com:** Togrul Babayev tc/ (Accordion), Klavapuk cra, Hafiza Samsuddin tc, fbr, tl/ (Vinyl record), cla/ (Bongo), Svitlana Varfolomieieva (All remaining illustrations); *Spine:* **Dreamstime. com:** Svitlana Varfolomieieva

All other images © Dorling Kindersley
For further information,
see www.dkimages.com.

AUG 0 8 2022